News You Can Use	Ask the Expert	Money Psychol	
Chapter 8: Automobile and Housing Decisions	How Can a Hybrid Help Your Budget?	The Car Buyer's Art	Strategies for Female Car Buyers It's Hard to Sell the Losers	Calculating an Affordable Home Price Comparing Mortgages
Chapter 9: Property and Liability Insurance Planning	Many Insurers Washed Up After Florida Hurricanes Do Dogs Really Get Two Bites? Shopping for Auto Insurance Can Save You Money	How Can I Save Money on Homeowner's Insurance?	Risk, What Risk?	Calculating Expected Losses
Chapter 10: Analyzing Jobs and Employee Benefits: Health, Disability, and Retirement Plans	Winning by Losing: Insurance Incentives for Weight Loss Recent Legal Changes That Affect Your Health Coverage	How Much Is Needed to Fund Retiree Health Costs?	Why Do Employees Like Company Stock?	Deductibles and Coinsurance Comparing Jobs and Benefits
Chapter 11: Fundamental Concepts in Investing	Can a Security Wiggle? The Benefit of Perfect Foresight	How to Avoid Five Common Pitfalls in Investing	Demographic Differences in Stated Risk Aversion Beyond Greed and Fear	Developing Your Investment Goals How Does Dollar Cost Averaging Work?
Chapter 12: Investing in Stocks	Google IPO Scam What Event Studies Tell Us About Insider Trading How the Dow Jones Average Began What Happens When a Stock Is Dropped from an Index?	Avoiding Irrational Exuberance	Which Household Decision Makers Use Financial Advisors?	
Chapter 13: Investing in Bonds and Preferred Stocks	Investing in Your Favorite Rock Star	Here's an Investment TIP		Calculating After-Tax Yields on Different Types of Bonds Estimating Bond Risk Premiums
Chapter 14: Mutual Funds, Investment Real Estate, and Other Investment Alternatives	Mutual Fund Scandals Prompt SEC to Act	How Do I Get Started Investing in Real Estate?	What Does It Cost to Feel Good?	Calculating Returns on Investment for Income Properties
Chapter 15: Saving for Distant Goals: Retirement and Education Funding	Why Do Women Have Lower Retirement Income Than Men? How Anna Swanson Got Her Money's Worth	Top Tips for Retirement Saving	Why Don't People Plan Better for Retirement?	Estimating Total Retirement Wealth Needed
Chapter 16: Life Insurance and Long-Term Care Planning	Live Long and Prosper The Ethics of Viatical Settlements	Tax Considerations in Long-Term Care	What's the Risk of an Airplane Crash?	
Chapter 17: Estate Planning	The Bird Lives On Life or Something Like it: The Case of Terry Schiavo	Choosing a Pension Beneficiary		

eGrade Plus

www.wiley.com/college/bajtelsmit

Based on the Activities You Do Every Day

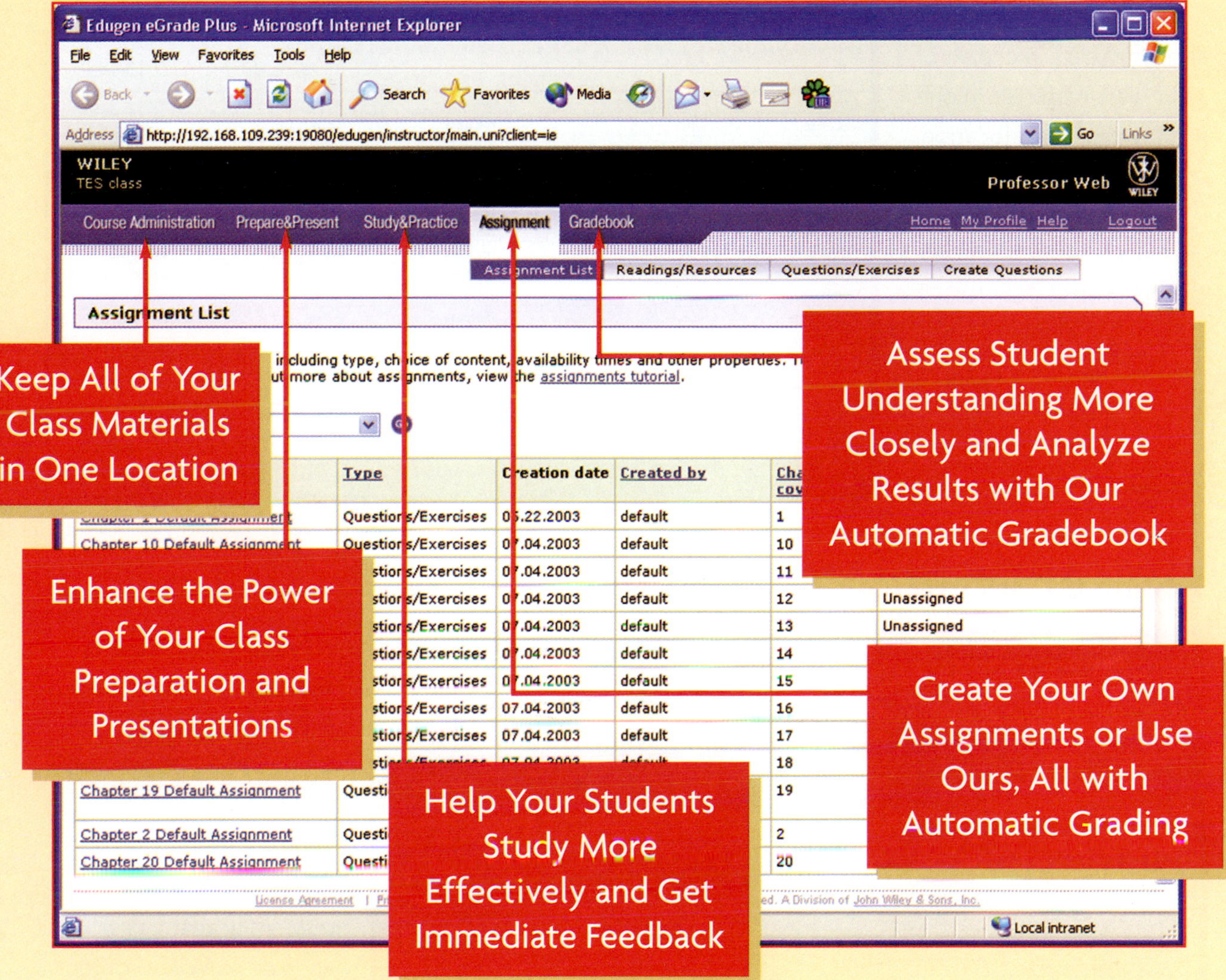

All the content and tools you need, all in one location, in an easy-to-use browser format. Choose the resources you need, or rely on the arrangement supplied by us.

Now, many of Wiley's textbooks are available with eGrade Plus, a powerful online tool that provides a completely integrated suite of teaching and learning resources in one easy-to-use website. eGrade Plus integrates Wiley's world-renowned content with media, including a multimedia version of the text, PowerPoint slides, and more. Upon adoption of eGrade Plus, you can begin to customize your course with the resources shown here.

See for yourself!

Go to www.wiley.com/college/egradeplus for an online demonstration of this powerful new software.

Keep All of Your Class Materials in One Location

Course Administration tools allow you to manage your class and integrate your eGrade Plus resources with most Course Management Systems, allowing you to keep all of your class materials in one location.

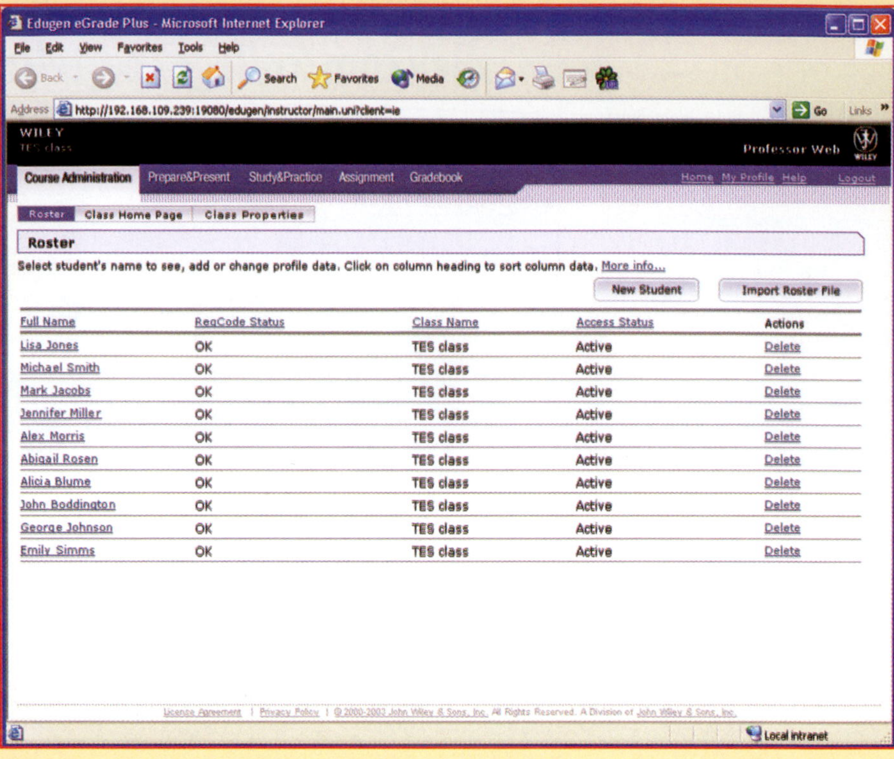

Enhance the Power of Your Class Preparation and Presentations

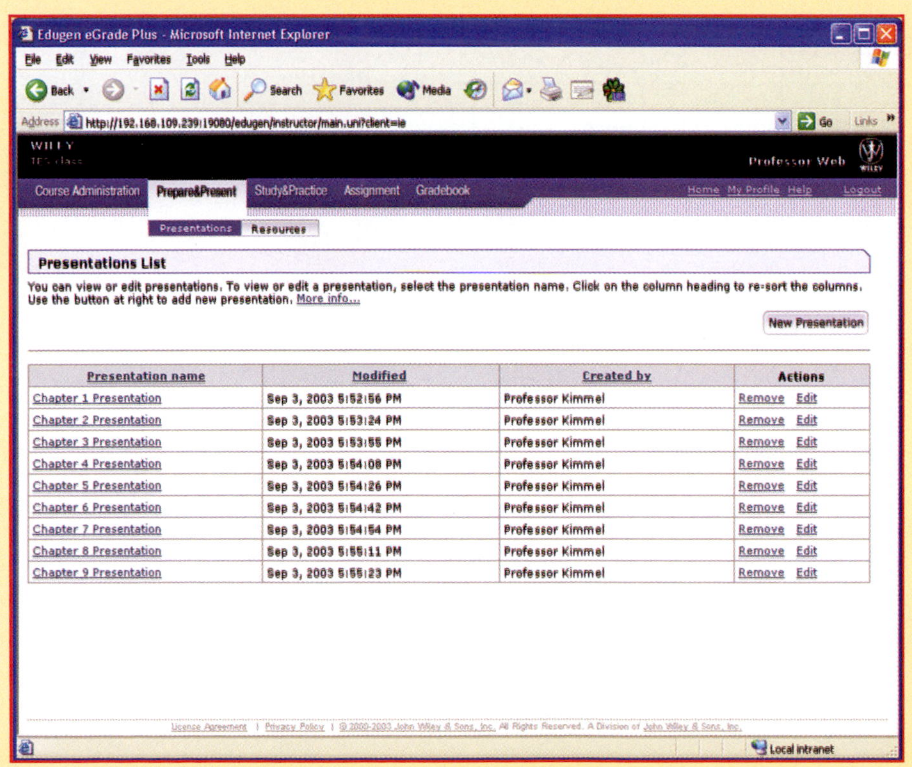

A **Prepare and Present tool** contains all of the Wiley-provided resources, such as **PowerPoint slides** and **Instructor's Resource Guide,** making your preparation time more efficient. You may easily adapt, customize, and add to Wiley content to meet the needs of your course.

Create Your Own Assignments or Use Ours, All with Automatic Grading

An **Assignment** area allows you to create **student homework** and **quizzes** by using **Wiley-provided question banks,** or by writing your own. You may also assign readings, activities and other work you want your students to complete. One of the most powerful features of eGrade Plus is that student assignments will be automatically graded and recorded in your gradebook. This will not only save you time but will provide your students with immediate feedback on their work.

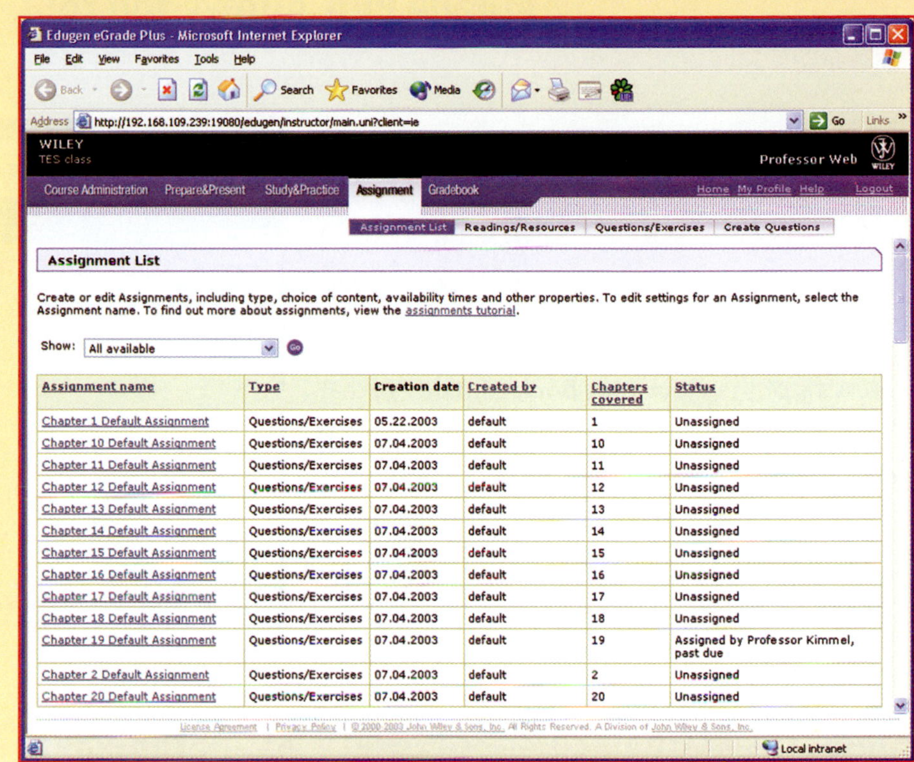

Assignment name	Type	Creation date	Created by	Chapters covered	Status
Chapter 1 Default Assignment	Questions/Exercises	05.22.2003	default	1	Unassigned
Chapter 10 Default Assignment	Questions/Exercises	07.04.2003	default	10	Unassigned
Chapter 11 Default Assignment	Questions/Exercises	07.04.2003	default	11	Unassigned
Chapter 12 Default Assignment	Questions/Exercises	07.04.2003	default	12	Unassigned
Chapter 13 Default Assignment	Questions/Exercises	07.04.2003	default	13	Unassigned
Chapter 14 Default Assignment	Questions/Exercises	07.04.2003	default	14	Unassigned
Chapter 15 Default Assignment	Questions/Exercises	07.04.2003	default	15	Unassigned
Chapter 16 Default Assignment	Questions/Exercises	07.04.2003	default	16	Unassigned
Chapter 17 Default Assignment	Questions/Exercises	07.04.2003	default	17	Unassigned
Chapter 18 Default Assignment	Questions/Exercises	07.04.2003	default	18	Unassigned
Chapter 19 Default Assignment	Questions/Exercises	07.04.2003	default	19	Assigned by Professor Kimmel, past due
Chapter 2 Default Assignment	Questions/Exercises	07.04.2003	default	2	Unassigned
Chapter 20 Default Assignment	Questions/Exercises	07.04.2003	default	20	Unassigned

Assess Student Understanding More Closely

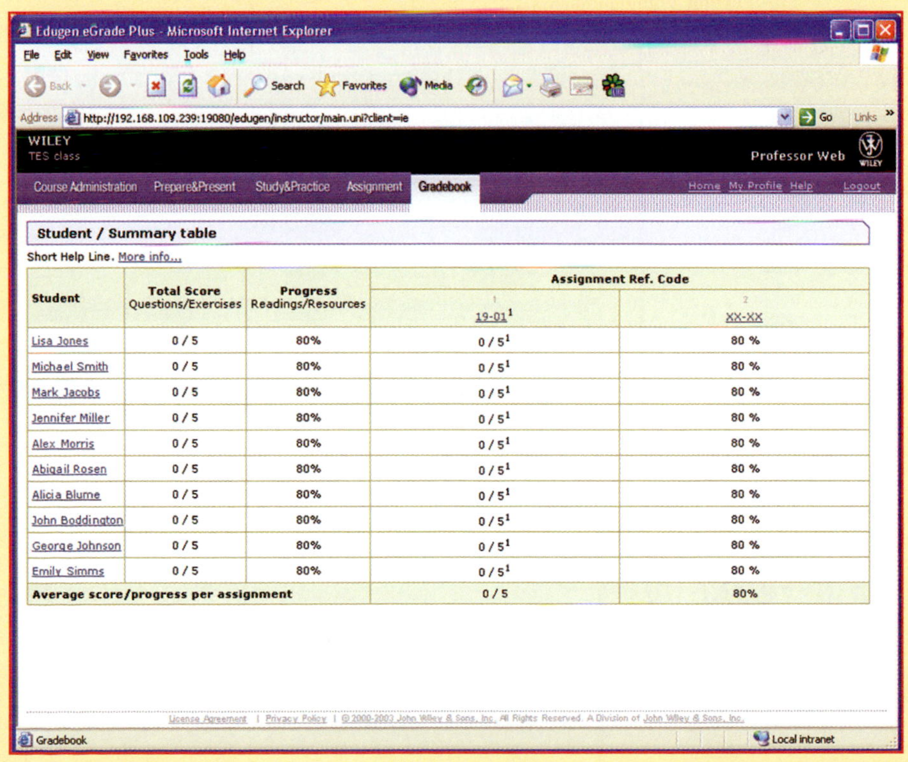

Student	Total Score Questions/Exercises	Progress Readings/Resources	Assignment Ref. Code 1 19-01[1]	2 XX-XX
Lisa Jones	0 / 5	80%	0 / 5[1]	80 %
Michael Smith	0 / 5	80%	0 / 5[1]	80 %
Mark Jacobs	0 / 5	80%	0 / 5[1]	80 %
Jennifer Miller	0 / 5	80%	0 / 5[1]	80 %
Alex Morris	0 / 5	80%	0 / 5[1]	80 %
Abigail Rosen	0 / 5	80%	0 / 5[1]	80 %
Alicia Blume	0 / 5	80%	0 / 5[1]	80 %
John Boddington	0 / 5	80%	0 / 5[1]	80 %
George Johnson	0 / 5	80%	0 / 5[1]	80 %
Emily Simms	0 / 5	80%	0 / 5[1]	80 %
Average score/progress per assignment			0 / 5	80%

An **Instructor's Gradebook** will keep track of your students' progress and allow you to analyze individual and overall class results to determine their progress and level of understanding

Students,

eGrade Plus Allows You to:

Study More Effectively

Get Immediate Feedback When You Practice on Your Own

eGrade Plus problems link directly to relevant sections of the **electronic book content**, so that you can review the text while you study and complete homework online. Additional resources include **student quizzes, financial planner** and other problem-solving resources.

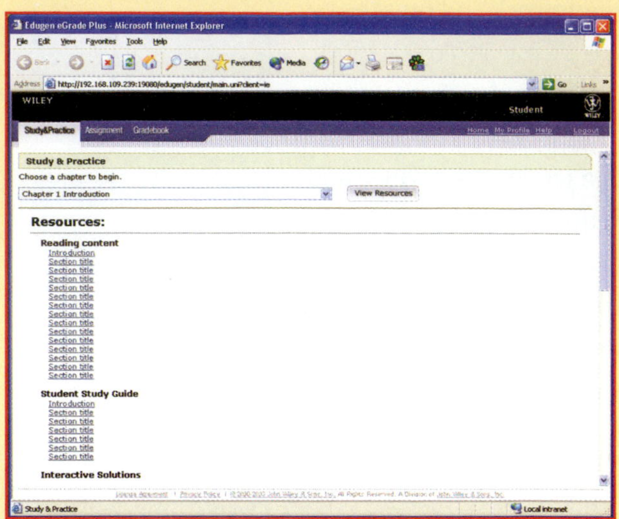

Complete Assignments / Get Help with Problem Solving

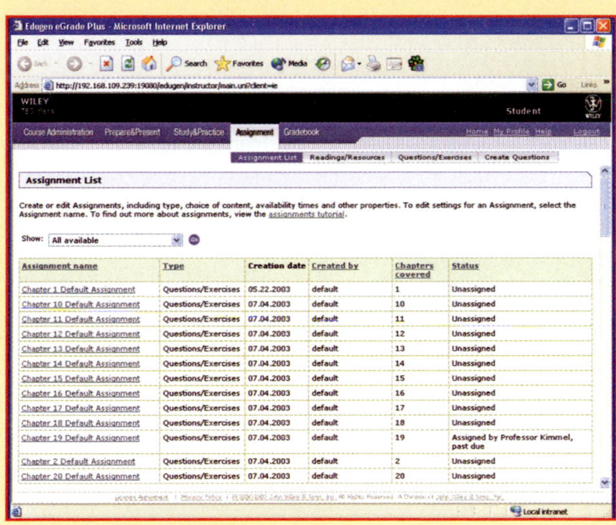

An **"Assignment"** area keeps all your assigned work in one location, making it easy for you to stay on task. In addition, many homework problems contain a **link** to the relevant section of the **electronic book**, providing you with a text explanation to help you conquer problem-solving obstacles as they arise.

Keep Track of How You're Doing

A **Personal Gradebook** allows you to view your results from past assignments at any time.

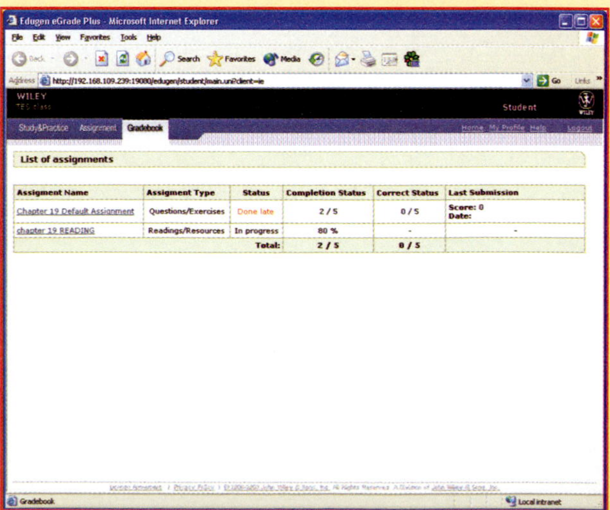

PERSONAL FINANCE

Skills for Life

Vickie Bajtelsmit
Colorado State University

John Wiley & Sons, Inc.

ASSOCIATE PUBLISHER	Judith R. Joseph
SENIOR DEVELOPMENT EDITOR	Marian D. Provenzano
MARKETING MANAGER	Heather King
SENIOR PRODUCTION EDITOR	William A. Murray
DESIGN DIRECTOR	Harry Nolan
PROJECT EDITOR	Cindy Rhoads
FREELANCE EDITOR	Beverly Peavler
MEDIA EDITOR	Allison Morris
SENIOR ILLUSTRATION EDITOR	Anna Melhorn
SENIOR PHOTO EDITORS	Sara Wight/Lisa Gee
EDITORIAL ASSISTANTS	Masha Maizel/Brigeth Rivera
COVER DESIGN	Howard Grossman
COVER PHOTO	Randy Wells/Corbis Images

This book was set in 10/12 Adobe Garamond by GGS Book Services, Atlantic Highlands and printed and bound by VonHoffman Press, Inc. The cover was printed by VonHoffman Press, Inc.

This book is printed on acid free paper. ∞

Copyright © 2006 John Wiley & Sons, Inc. All rights reserved. No part of this publication may be reproduced, stored in a retrieval system, or transmitted in any form or by any means, electronic, mechanical, photocopying, recording, scanning or otherwise, except as permitted under Sections 107 or 108 of the 1976 United States Copyright Act, without either the prior written permission of the Publisher, or authorization through payment of the appropriate per-copy fee to the Copyright Clearance Center, Inc., 222 Rosewood Drive, Danvers, MA 01923, (978)750-8400, fax (978)646-8600. Requests to the Publisher for permission should be addressed to the Permissions Department, John Wiley & Sons, Inc., 111 River Street, Hoboken, NJ 07030-5774, (201)748-6011, fax (201)748-6008.

To order books or for customer service please call 1-800-CALL WILEY (225-5945).

ISBN 0-471-47151-8

Printed in the United States of America.

10 9 8 7 6 5 4 3 2 1

To the three most important people in my life—my husband Rich and our sons Kristopher and Kyle.

About the Author

Vickie L. Bajtelsmit, J.D., Ph.D., received her Ph.D. from the Wharton School of Business at the University of Pennsylvania and is currently a professor of finance and real estate at Colorado State University and First Community Bank Faculty Fellow. She has been teaching at the college level for 21 years, and has taught most courses in the finance curriculum. While at CSU, she has received two teaching awards in the College of Business: Professor of the Year in 2000 and the Pinnacle Professor Award in 2003 (for contributions in teaching, research, and service). Professor Bajtelsmit is the author of more than 30 articles, books, and book chapters, including *The Busy Woman's Guide to Financial Freedom* (AMACOM, 2001). Her research has focused on personal finance issues related to retirement, real estate, investments, and insurance. She has been actively involved in the leadership of the Academy of Financial Services and the American Risk and Insurance Association and helped to develop the model curriculum for CFP- Board certification.

PREFACE

PEOPLE

People who are familiar with my professional work know that I have spent the majority of my career writing and speaking on topics related to personal financial planning, primarily in the areas of insurance, benefits, and retirement planning. Although I've taught many different courses in my 22 years as a college professor, I know that I've made the greatest impact on the lives of my personal finance students. Unlike many college-level courses, students can usually see the immediate relevance of personal finance to their lives, and this motivates them to acquire the skills and tools necessary for lifelong personal financial success. My students undoubtedly have also been influenced by my personal enthusiasm for the subject matter and my experience with many aspects of personal financial planning. *Personal Finance: Skills for Life* is therefore a natural melding of my passion for personal finance in my dual roles as researcher and teacher.

As any experienced teacher can tell you, selecting the right textbook for a course can make a huge difference in educational outcomes. It's critical that students be engaged in the subject matter, and this objective requires a text that both supports and supplements the classroom experience. My goal in writing *Personal Finance: Skills for Life* is to provide a textbook that not only has better coverage than its competitors but, more important, is better designed to enhance the students' learning experience. Students who have used early drafts of this text have given high marks to the clear and easy-to-read style of writing, the relevance of examples to their lives, and the many interesting features and learning tools.

Personal Finance: Skills for Life is written for a one-semester introductory undergraduate course in personal finance or personal financial planning offered at two- and four-year colleges, and is also appropriate for similar courses offered in continuing education or certificate programs. Since these courses have no prerequisites at most schools and are taken by a diverse group of students, the presentation assumes only high-school level math skills at the outset of the course. Although more advanced financial concepts are introduced throughout the text, the concepts are explained at a level that should be understandable to students of any background. The text provides a foundation in the basic principles of financial planning and an introduction to more advanced personal financial-planning topics, with an emphasis on decision making and the development of life skills.

The complexity of personal financial planning continues to escalate. New tools, products, services, institutions, and delivery mechanisms are continually being developed. For this reason, a comprehensive understanding of personal finance is more important as a life skill than ever before. If you develop a financial plan earlier in life, you are more likely to be financially successful later in life and to avoid some of the more common personal finance mistakes. It's important to note, however, that the essential life skill is not the ability to quote the facts and figures, but rather a foundation in the basic principles of financial planning and their application coupled with well-developed decision-making skills. A person's circumstances will change over the life cycle, and he or she will therefore need to draw on this foundation knowledge to adapt financial plans to meet future needs.

Goals of the Book

1. Develop financial skills for life

A major objective of this text is to provide students with the tools and skills needed to make sound financial decisions throughout their lives. Each chapter contains several features that are designed to help students acquire lifelong skills. In addition to many detailed examples and cases throughout the text, the *Go Figure!* boxes provide step-by-step methods for solving financial math problems. A unique end-of-chapter section, *Developing Personal Financial Skills for Life*, is designed to help students develop their financial skills and build their own financial plan.

2. Develop decision-making skills

Personal Finance: Skills for Life emphasizes critical thinking and decision making in several ways. It introduces strategies for effective decision making in the introductory chapter and applies these strategies to different types of financial problems throughout the text. *Learning by Doing* exercises after each subsection of material require students to apply the chapter content to make "mini-decisions." This feature helps them master basic concepts before proceeding to more advanced material and increases their comfort level with making financial decisions. End-of-chapter problems and cases include conceptual, skills-building, and application problems.

3. Provide relevant real-world applications

The book provides students with a sense of the importance and applicability of the subject matter. Each chapter begins with a *Myth or Fact?* quiz, highlighting certain personal finance misconceptions related to the chapter content. Students can check for the correct answers in *Fact* boxes that appear throughout the chapter. The text also emphasizes real-world application by including interesting and relevant examples within the text and highlighting newsworthy, real-world stories in *News You Can Use* boxes. Helpful hints and checklists from professionals appear in *Ask the Expert* boxes, and applicable psychology and academic research results, which help students recognize their own psychological biases, are highlighted in *Money Psychology* boxes. Each chapter includes references to Internet resources throughout.

4. Apply the planning process as a unifying theme

Each chapter begins with a section that discusses how the chapter content fits within the integrated financial planning process. This theme is consistently explored throughout the text. Continuing case examples require students to consider simultaneous elements of a financial plan for representative households and, for some topics, changing elements of the financial plan over a family's life cycle. Students are encouraged to apply the financial planning process concepts to the development of their own comprehensive personal financial plan.

Organization and Content of the Book

A central theme of this text is that personal financial planning can be seen as a lifelong process that includes certain logical steps. Accordingly, this text is organized to correspond with the order in which a person should build his or her personal financial plan, separately considering foundation elements, short-term planning to secure basic needs, long-term planning to meet household wealth goals, and planning designed to protect income and assets for one's heirs.

Part I. The Foundations of Personal Financial Planning (Chapters 1–4)

This section is a "tools" section that introduces students to the fundamentals underlying all of personal financial planning, including a basic understanding of the personal financial planning process, financial math calculations, personal financial statements and budgets, goal-setting, and federal income taxation. This organization is somewhat unique, but I have found that early mastery of these fundamental concepts is essential to successful understanding of nearly everything that follows.

Part II. Securing Basic Household Needs (Chapters 5–10)

Once an individual has evaluated his or her current finances and set particular goals for the future, the next step is to establish a plan for achieving these goals. Since households need to secure their basic needs for liquidity, housing, and insurance first, the second section of the text considers these short-term decisions. A unique element of this text is the inclusion of a *specific chapter on employee benefit planning*. Choosing among employee benefit options, most importantly, health insurance and retirement savings vehicles, is often a college student's first important financial decision. Given the costs involved and the complexity of compensation schemes today, this is an essential element of personal financial planning and is deserving of chapter-level coverage, as opposed to its piecemeal treatment in competing texts.

Another unique feature of this text is the separation of the property and liability insurance chapter from the life insurance chapter, which appears in the last section of the text. This corresponds to the timing of these decisions. Although most students have already had to make auto insurance decisions and many also have homeowner's or renter's coverage, life insurance and long-term care insurance are generally less important at this stage. In addition, the explanation of life insurance policies makes more sense after students have already been introduced to alternative savings and investment vehicles.

Part III. Building Household Wealth (Chapters 11–15)

The third section of the book is related to long-term investment decisions and developing a plan to meet long-term goals such as retirement and college funding. Coverage of retirement and college funding in the same chapter is somewhat unique, but makes sense in that the planning process and mathematical calculations for each are so similar. Students will already be familiar with the retirement plan types and investment vehicles that they can use to achieve their objectives, so this chapter is devoted to estimating needs and developing a savings plan to meet those needs.

Part IV. Protecting Household Wealth (Chapters 16–17)

The last section of the text relates to protecting household wealth for yourself and your heirs through life insurance, planning for long-term care needs, and estate planning.

FEATURES OF THIS BOOK

The pedagogical features are designed to engage students in the learning process and provide them with the knowledge and skills they need to make personal financial decisions throughout their lives.

Myth or Fact?

Each chapter begins with a short quiz that asks the student to read several statements and decide whether each is a *myth* or a *fact*. The questions are designed to engage student interest in the chapter material and to highlight certain commonly held misconceptions about personal finance. The student is then encouraged to check his or her answers by looking for *Fact* boxes throughout the chapter, which include the answer as well as other interesting information related to the topic. ■

Myth or Fact?

Consider each of the following statements and decide whether it is a *myth* or a *fact*. Look for the answers in the *Fact* boxes in the chapter.

	MYTH	FACT
1. The only negative outcome from having a bad credit record is that it makes it more difficult to get additional credit.	☐	☐
2. The average household owes money on several credit cards and has trouble making payments.	☐	☐
3. Credit cards originated in the ... and Visa were first introduced ...		
4. It makes sense to always pay ... due on your credit card in or... you owe.		
5. With improved computer enc... of people who have their ide...		

Fact #2

The average U.S. household has eight credit cards and owes more than $8,000 on them. About 50 percent report having difficulty making their minimum payments. The total amount of consumer credit outstanding in the United States increased 372 percent in the last 20 years, from $445 billion in 1983 to $2.1 trillion in 2003.

Applying the Planning Process

Every chapter begins with a unifying graphic and discussion of how the chapter content fits within the integrated financial planning process. This theme is consistently carried throughout the text. This helps the student see the big picture and to internalize this process so that it becomes second nature. ■

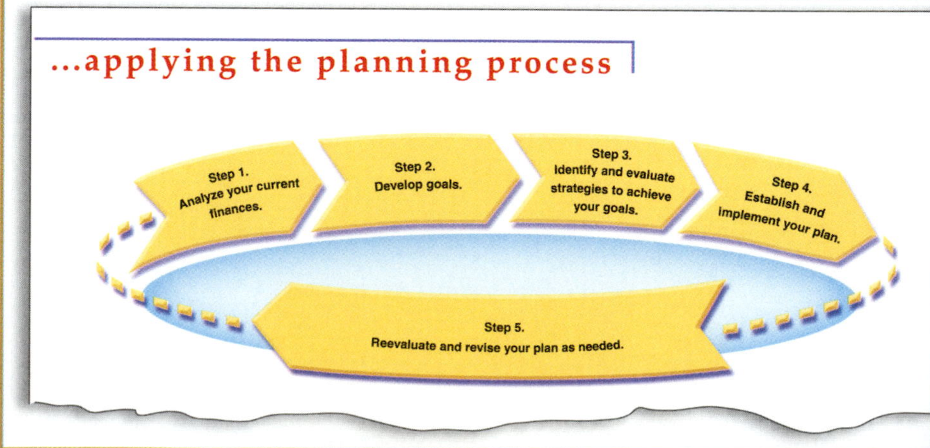

Learning by Doing

This feature appears several times in a chapter, at the end of a section of material. Unlike the more usual section concept review questions, these exercises require students to *apply* what they have learned to a short decision-making problem, thereby encouraging active learning. ■

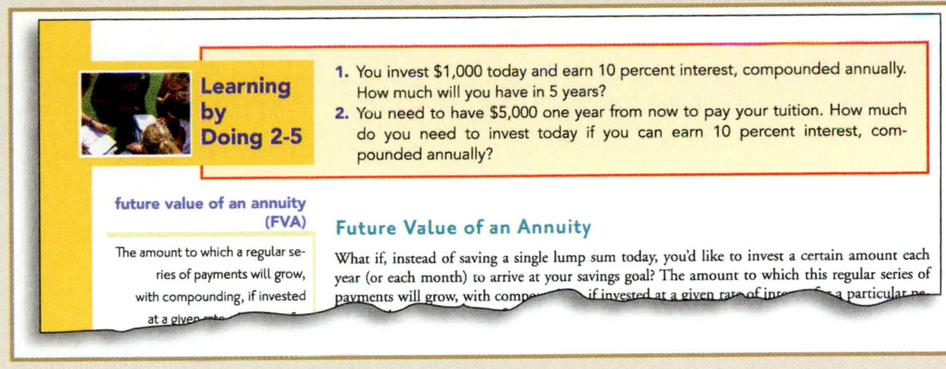

Learning by Doing 2-5

1. You invest $1,000 today and earn 10 percent interest, compounded annually. How much will you have in 5 years?
2. You need to have $5,000 one year from now to pay your tuition. How much do you need to invest today if you can earn 10 percent interest, compounded annually?

future value of an annuity (FVA)

The amount to which a regular series of payments will grow, with compounding, if invested at a given rate

Future Value of an Annuity

What if, instead of saving a single lump sum today, you'd like to invest a certain amount each year (or each month) to arrive at your savings goal? The amount to which this regular series of payments will grow, with comp... if invested at a given rate of inte... a particular ne...

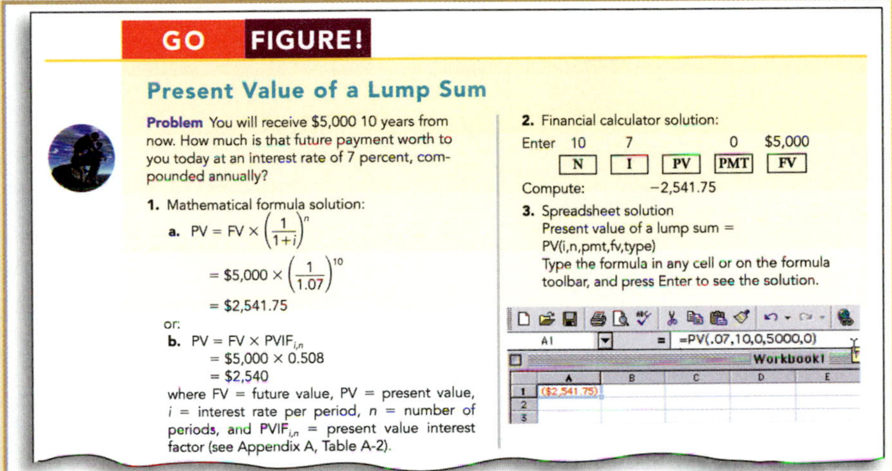

GO FIGURE!

Present Value of a Lump Sum

Problem You will receive $5,000 10 years from now. How much is that future payment worth to you today at an interest rate of 7 percent, compounded annually?

1. Mathematical formula solution:

   a. $PV = FV \times \left(\frac{1}{1+i}\right)^n$

   $= \$5,000 \times \left(\frac{1}{1.07}\right)^{10}$

   $= \$2,541.75$

   or:

   b. $PV = FV \times PVIF_{i,n}$

   $= \$5,000 \times 0.508$

   $= \$2,540$

   where FV = future value, PV = present value, i = interest rate per period, n = number of periods, and $PVIF_{i,n}$ = present value interest factor (see Appendix A, Table A-2).

2. Financial calculator solution:

Enter	10	7		0	$5,000
	N	I	PV	PMT	FV
Compute:			−2,541.75		

3. Spreadsheet solution

   Present value of a lump sum = PV(i,n,pmt,fv,type)

   Type the formula in any cell or on the formula toolbar, and press Enter to see the solution.

Go Figure!

Most professors indicate that their greatest challenge is that students have difficulty with the math required for personal finance. This box feature provides step-by-step directions for financial math calculations applied to specific personal finance problems. These examples are easy references for students to follow when doing homework involving financial math. ■

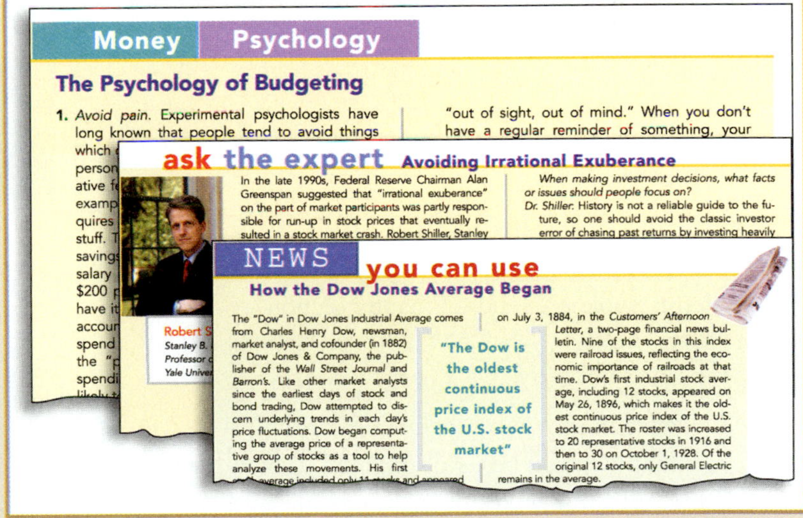

Money Psychology

The Psychology of Budgeting

1. *Avoid pain.* Experimental psychologists have long known that people tend to avoid things ...

"out of sight, out of mind." When you don't have a regular reminder of something, your

ask the expert **Avoiding Irrational Exuberance**

In the late 1990s, Federal Reserve Chairman Alan Greenspan suggested that "irrational exuberance" on the part of market participants was partly responsible for run-up in stock prices that eventually resulted in a stock market crash. Robert Shiller, Stanley

When making investment decisions, what facts or issues should people focus on?

Dr. Shiller: History is not a reliable guide to the future, so one should avoid the classic investor error of chasing past returns by investing heavily

NEWS you can use

How the Dow Jones Average Began

The "Dow" in Dow Jones Industrial Average comes from Charles Henry Dow, newsman, market analyst, and cofounder (in 1882) of Dow Jones & Company, the publisher of the *Wall Street Journal* and *Barron's*. Like other market analysts since the earliest days of stock and bond trading, Dow attempted to discern underlying trends in each day's price fluctuations. Dow began computing the average price of a representative group of stocks as a tool to help analyze these movements. His first

"The Dow is the oldest continuous price index of the U.S. stock market"

on July 3, 1884, in the *Customers' Afternoon Letter*, a two-page financial news bulletin. Nine of the stocks in this index were railroad issues, reflecting the economic importance of railroads at that time. Dow's first industrial stock average, including 12 stocks, appeared on May 26, 1896, which makes it the oldest continuous price index of the U.S. stock market. The roster was increased to 20 representative stocks in 1916 and then to 30 on October 1, 1928. Of the original 12 stocks, only General Electric remains in the average.

News You Can Use, Ask the Expert, and Money Psychology

In addition to numerous examples and real-world facts contained in exhibits and text, each chapter includes one or more *News You Can Use, Ask the Expert,* or *Money Psychology* boxes. These features serve to emphasize the applicability of the chapter content to the real world and also make the text more interesting to read. *Ask the Expert* boxes summarize an interview with an expert on a topic related to the chapter. *News You Can Use* boxes summarize current events or research applicable to the chapter content. *Money Psychology* boxes highlight the latest research results in behavioral psychology as they apply to personal financial planning. ■

Extensive Internet Emphasis

The Internet is a valuable resource for personal financial planning, providing access to detailed historical data, planning tools, and useful educational materials. *Personal Finance: Skills for Life* incorporates the Internet in several ways. To point students toward the most useful Web resources, margin references to specific sites and content are provided throughout the text. An end-of-chapter section *Using Web Resources for Financial Planning* includes exercises designed to connect students with the wealth of online information and planning tools that are available and to encourage students to obtain and apply this information to making personal finance decisions. ■

Using Web Resources for Financial Planning

1. **Create a Budget.** Check out the budget maker at *www.money.cnn.com.* Input your own income and expenses, and calculate your net cash flow.
2. **How Does Your Spending Affect Your Finances?** Go to the Budget Analyzer at the Finance Center at www.financenter.com/products/calculators/budget/. If you enter your actual budget expenditure and the amount you would like to reduce it to, the analyzer will tell you how much this change will affect your future wealth. For example, suppose that you plan to save $50 per month by cutting out your afternoon lattés. What impact will that budget change have on

the Harris Interactive website at *www.harrisinteractive.com* to find the results of two recent Harris polls related to job satisfaction. You can search by subject or simply by the specific poll number. Which occupations have the most prestige (Harris Poll #57, October 1, 2003)? What three factors have the most impact on job satisfaction (Harris Poll #74, December 20, 2000)?

5. **Job Descriptions and Salaries.** Two excellent websites for career planning and job searching are *www.monster.com* and *www.jobweb.com.* Identify three career areas that you are considering. What is the average sta… …your geographic area for each? What

End-of-Chapter Mini Cases and Comprehensive Continuing Cases

Students are encouraged to apply chapter content and to develop their decision-making skills in several ways. In addition to the *Learning by Doing* and *Go Figure!* features discussed, *continuing case* examples appear throughout the text, *mini-case problems* are included in the end-of-chapter material, and a *comprehensive case* at the end of each of the four parts of the book provides the opportunity for integration and review. Applying concepts to real-life problems makes the material more "real" for students. The more practice they get with making personal financial decisions, the better their own decisions will be. End-of-chapter and end-of-part cases can be used as homework exercises or projects. ■

Developing Personal Financial Skills for Life

Unique to this book is an end-of-chapter section designed to help develop financial skills and build a personal financial plan. The section has two parts: *Learning About Yourself,* which includes personal assessments that help you better understand your money attitudes and style of financial decision making, and *Developing Your Skills,* exercises that apply the chapter content to your own financial situation, with the goal of developing a comprehensive personal financial plan by the end of the course. ■

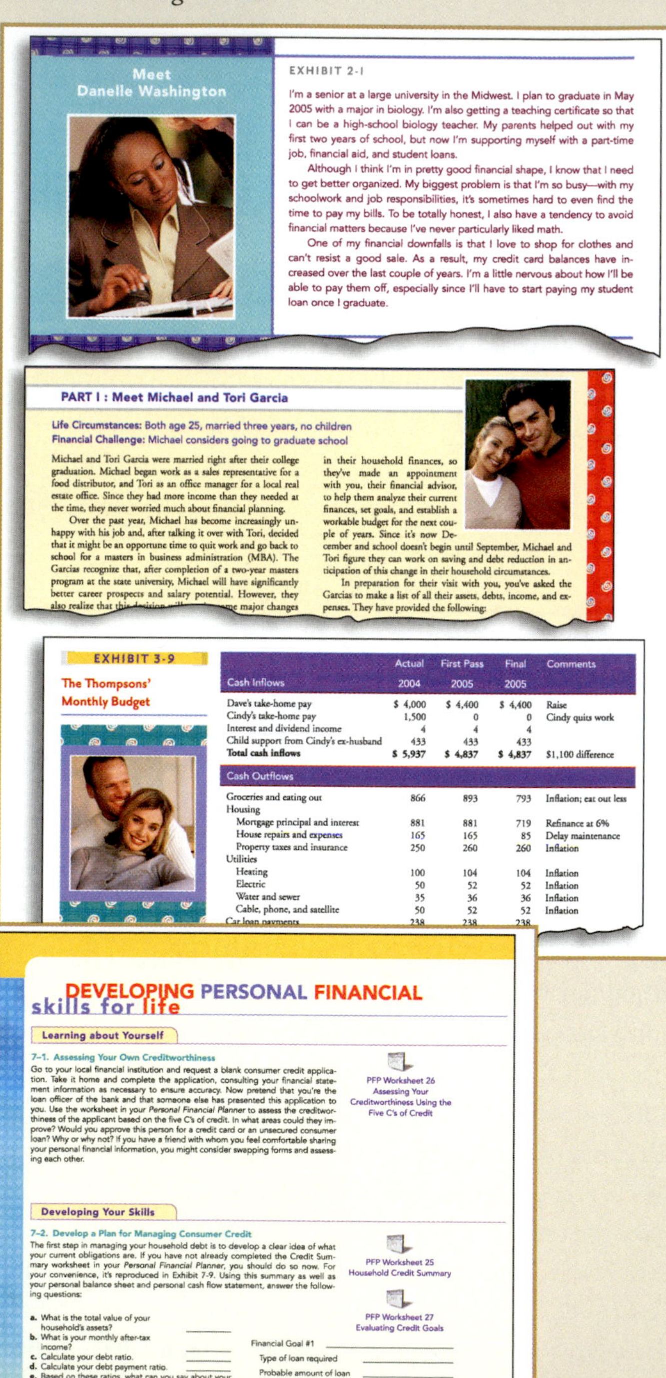

Meet Danelle Washington

EXHIBIT 2-1

I'm a senior at a large university in the Midwest. I plan to graduate in May 2005 with a major in biology. I'm also getting a teaching certificate so that I can be a high-school biology teacher. My parents helped out with my first two years of school, but now I'm supporting myself with a part-time job, financial aid, and student loans.

Although I think I'm in pretty good financial shape, I know that I need to get better organized. My biggest problem is that I'm so busy—with my schoolwork and job responsibilities, it's sometimes hard to even find the time to pay my bills. To be totally honest, I also have a tendency to avoid financial matters because I've never particularly liked math.

One of my financial downfalls is that I love to shop for clothes and can't resist a good sale. As a result, my credit card balances have increased over the last couple of years. I'm a little nervous about how I'll be able to pay them off, especially since I'll have to start paying my student loan once I graduate.

PART I : Meet Michael and Tori Garcia

Life Circumstances: Both age 25, married three years, no children
Financial Challenge: Michael considers going to graduate school

Michael and Tori Garcia were married right after their college graduation. Michael began work as a sales representative for a food distributor, and Tori as an office manager for a local real estate office. Since they had more income than they needed at the time, they never worried much about financial planning.

Over the past year, Michael has become increasingly unhappy with his job and, after talking it over with Tori, decided that it might be an opportune time to quit work and go back to school for a masters in business administration (MBA). The Garcias recognize that, after completion of a two-year masters program at the state university, Michael will have significantly better career prospects and salary potential. However, they also realize that this decision … some major changes in their household finances, so they've made an appointment with you, their financial advisor, to help them analyze their current finances, set goals, and establish a workable budget for the next couple of years. Since it's now December and school doesn't begin until September, Michael and Tori figure they can work on saving and debt reduction in anticipation of this change in their household circumstances.

In preparation for their visit with you, you've asked the Garcias to make a list of all their assets, debts, income, and expenses. They have provided the following:

EXHIBIT 3-9

The Thompsons' Monthly Budget

Cash Inflows	Actual 2004	First Pass 2005	Final 2005	Comments
Dave's take-home pay	$ 4,000	$ 4,400	$ 4,400	Raise
Cindy's take-home pay	1,500	0	0	Cindy quits work
Interest and dividend income	4	4	4	
Child support from Cindy's ex-husband	433	433	433	
Total cash inflows	**$ 5,937**	**$ 4,837**	**$ 4,837**	$1,100 difference
Cash Outflows				
Groceries and eating out	866	893	793	Inflation; eat out less
Housing				
Mortgage principal and interest	881	881	719	Refinance at 6%
House repairs and expenses	165	165	85	Delay maintenance
Property taxes and insurance	250	260	260	Inflation
Utilities				
Heating	100	104	104	Inflation
Electric	50	52	52	Inflation
Water and sewer	35	36	36	Inflation
Cable, phone, and satellite	50	52	52	Inflation
Car loan payments	238	238	238	

DEVELOPING PERSONAL FINANCIAL skills for life

Learning about Yourself

7-1. Assessing Your Own Creditworthiness

Go to your local financial institution and request a blank consumer credit application. Take it home and complete the application, consulting your financial statement information as necessary to ensure accuracy. Now pretend that you're the loan officer of the bank and that someone else has presented this application to you. Use the worksheet in your *Personal Financial Planner* to assess the creditworthiness of the applicant based on the five C's of credit. In what areas could they improve? Would you approve this person for a credit card or an unsecured consumer loan? Why or why not? If you have a friend with whom you feel comfortable sharing your personal financial information, you might consider swapping forms and assessing each other.

PFP Worksheet 26 Assessing Your Creditworthiness Using the Five C's of Credit

Developing Your Skills

7-2. Develop a Plan for Managing Consumer Credit

The first step in managing your household debt is to develop a clear idea of what your current obligations are. If you have not already completed the Credit Summary worksheet in your *Personal Financial Planner,* you should do so now. For your convenience, it's reproduced in Exhibit 7-9. Using this summary as well as your personal balance sheet and personal cash flow statement, answer the following questions:

PFP Worksheet 25 Household Credit Summary

PFP Worksheet 27 Evaluating Credit Goals

a. What is the total value of your household's assets? ______
b. What is your monthly after-tax income? ______
c. Calculate your debt ratio. ______
d. Calculate your debt payment ratio. ______
e. Based on these ratios, what can you say about your current use of credit?
f. Revisit the goals that you set for yourself in Chapter 3. If you plan to take on any new consumer debt in …

Financial Goal #1 ______
Type of loan required ______
Probable amount of loan ______
Impact on financial ratios ______
Financial Goal #2 ______
Type of loan required ______

PEDAGOGY THAT HELPS STUDENTS

The pedagogical features of this book are specifically designed to enhance the learning process for all types of learners. Students can take a *Learning Styles Quiz* (p. xxxiii) to help them identify how they learn best—visually, aurally, through reading and writing, kinesthetically, or through a combination of these styles. They will find tips on in-class and at-home learning strategies and they can identify the text features that would be most useful to them based on their learning style. These features include within-chapter elements, end-of-chapter material, and end-of-book material.

CHAPTER PEDAGOGY

The personalized writing style, attractive design, and well-organized presentation make the text easy to read and comprehend. Practical and interesting examples throughout each chapter help to improve retention of information. Several features direct students to core concepts and terminology.

Before Studying This Chapter

The beginning of each chapter includes a list of specific topics from previous chapters that should be reviewed in preparation for moving on to the new material presented in the chapter. This feature enhances the learning process by encouraging review and also emphasizes the integrated nature of personal financial planning decisions. ■

The Navigator

The Navigator is a learning system designed to guide you through each chapter and help you succeed in learning the material. After assessing your learning style to determine the most effective method of study, you can use the checklist at the beginning of the chapter to guide you through the study process. ■

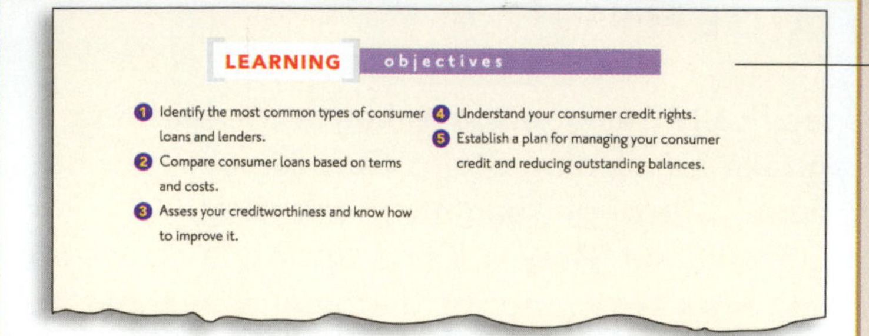

LEARNING objectives

1. Identify the most common types of consumer loans and lenders.
2. Compare consumer loans based on terms and costs.
3. Assess your creditworthiness and know how to improve it.
4. Understand your consumer credit rights.
5. Establish a plan for managing your consumer credit and reducing outstanding balances.

Learning Objectives

At the beginning of each chapter, a set of *Learning Objectives* for the chapter is identified. These objectives, which correspond to the organization of the chapter, reappear in the margins at the point where the related topic is discussed. ■

Chapter Preview

Every chapter begins with an organizational chart that provides a visual roadmap for the chapter content. This helps identify the structure of the chapter and can also be a useful study aid. ■

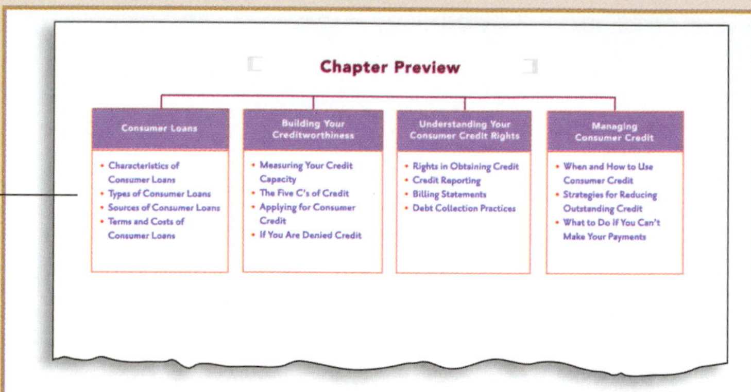

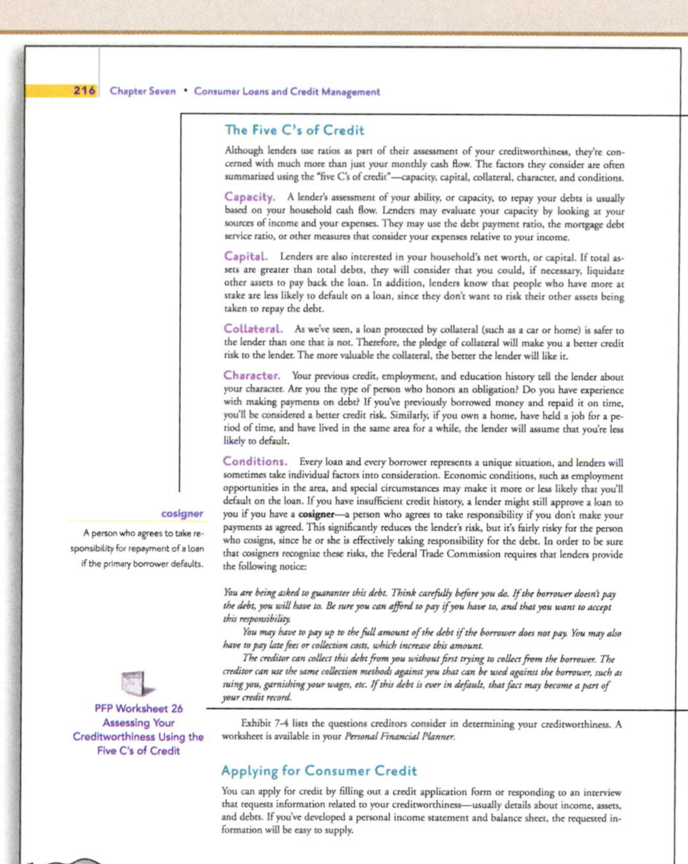

216 Chapter Seven • Consumer Loans and Credit Management

The Five C's of Credit

Although lenders use ratios as part of their assessment of your creditworthiness, they're concerned with much more than just your monthly cash flow. The factors they consider are often summarized using the "five C's of credit"—capacity, capital, collateral, character, and conditions.

Capacity. A lender's assessment of your ability, or capacity, to repay your debts is usually based on your household cash flow. Lenders may evaluate your capacity by looking at your sources of income and your expenses. They may use the debt payment ratio, the mortgage debt service ratio, or other measures that consider your expenses relative to your income.

Capital. Lenders are also interested in your household's net worth, or capital. If total assets are greater than total debts, they will consider that you could, if necessary, liquidate other assets to pay back the loan. In addition, lenders know that people who have more at stake are less likely to default on a loan, since they don't want to risk their other assets being taken to repay the debt.

Collateral. As we've seen, a loan protected by collateral (such as a car or home) is safer to the lender than one that is not. Therefore, the pledge of collateral will make you a better credit risk to the lender. The more valuable the collateral, the better the lender will like it.

Character. Your previous credit, employment, and education history tell the lender about your character. Are you the type of person who honors an obligation? Do you have experience with making payments on debt? If you've previously borrowed money and repaid it on time, you'll be considered a better credit risk. Similarly, if you own a home, have held a job for a period of time, and have lived in the same area for a while, the lender will assume that you're less likely to default.

Conditions. Every loan and every borrower represents a unique situation, and lenders will sometimes take individual factors into consideration. Economic conditions, such as employment opportunities in the area, and special circumstances may make it more or less likely that you'll default on the loan. If you have insufficient credit history, a lender might still approve a loan to you if you have a **cosigner**—a person who agrees to take responsibility if you don't make your payments as agreed. This significantly reduces the lender's risk, but it's fairly risky for the person who cosigns, since he or she is effectively taking responsibility for the debt. In order to be sure that cosigners recognize these risks, the Federal Trade Commission requires that lenders provide the following notice:

cosigner A person who agrees to take responsibility for repayment of a loan if the primary borrower defaults.

You are being asked to guarantee this debt. Think carefully before you do. If the borrower doesn't pay the debt, you will have to. Be sure you can afford to pay if you have to, and that you want to accept this responsibility.

You may have to pay up to the full amount of the debt if the borrower does not pay. You may also have to pay late fees or collection costs, which increase this amount.

The creditor can collect this debt from you without first trying to collect from the borrower. The creditor can use the same collection methods against you that can be used against the borrower, such as suing you, garnishing your wages, etc. If this debt is ever in default, that fact may become a part of your credit record.

PFP Worksheet 26 Assessing Your Creditworthiness Using the Five C's of Credit

Exhibit 7-4 lists the questions creditors consider in determining your creditworthiness. A worksheet is available in your *Personal Financial Planner.*

Applying for Consumer Credit

You can apply for credit by filling out a credit application form or responding to an interview that requests information related to your creditworthiness—usually details about income, assets, and debts. If you've developed a personal income statement and balance sheet, the requested information will be easy to supply.

Marginal Definitions

Key terms and concepts are highlighted in boldface when they are first explained in the text and are defined in the margin next to their discussion in the text. All key terms appear in the end-of-book Glossary. ■

Personal Financial Planner

The application of the *Personal Financial Planner* workbook is highlighted throughout the text with margin references to the appropriate worksheets. ■

END-OF-CHAPTER PEDAGOGY

The end-of-chapter material, written entirely by the author, is designed to enhance student learning through repetition and reinforcement of key concepts and extensive hands-on practice.

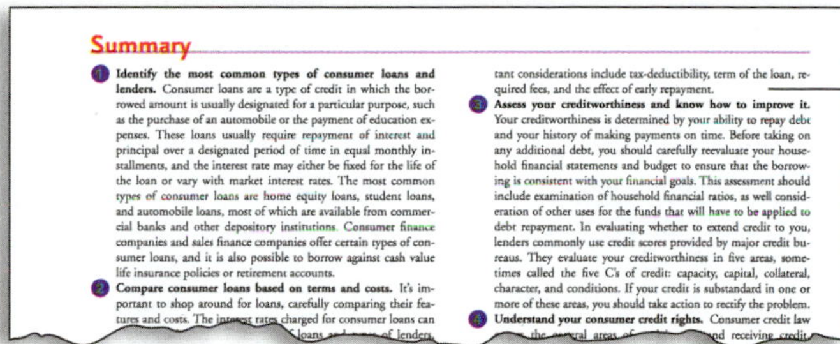

Summary

1. **Identify the most common types of consumer loans and lenders.** Consumer loans are a type of credit in which the borrowed amount is usually designated for a particular purpose, such as the purchase of an automobile or the payment of education expenses. These loans usually require repayment of interest and principal over a designated period of time in equal monthly installments, and the interest rate may either be fixed for the life of the loan or vary with market interest rates. The most common types of consumer loans are home equity loans, student loans, and automobile loans, most of which are available from commercial banks and other depository institutions. Consumer finance companies and sales finance companies offer certain types of consumer loans, and it is also possible to borrow against cash value life insurance policies or retirement accounts.
2. **Compare consumer loans based on terms and costs.** It's important to shop around for loans, carefully comparing their features and costs. The interest rates charged for consumer loans can [illegible] loans and types of lenders. [illegible] tant considerations include tax-deductibility, term of the loan, required fees, and the effect of early repayment.
3. **Assess your creditworthiness and know how to improve it.** Your creditworthiness is determined by your ability to repay debt and your history of making payments on time. Before taking on any additional debt, you should carefully reevaluate your household financial statements and budget to ensure that the borrowing is consistent with your financial goals. This assessment should include examination of household financial ratios, as well consideration of other uses for the funds that will have to be applied to debt repayment. In evaluating whether to extend credit to you, lenders commonly use credit scores provided by major credit bureaus. They evaluate your creditworthiness in five areas, sometimes called the five C's of credit: capacity, capital, collateral, character, and conditions. If your credit is substandard in one or more of these areas, you should take action to rectify the problem.
4. **Understand your consumer credit rights.** Consumer credit law [illegible] the general areas of [illegible] and receiving credit,

Summary

At the end of each chapter, the *Summary* section reviews the main concepts presented in the chapter with reference to the specific *Learning Objectives*. It provides students with another opportunity to review what they have learned as well as to see how the key topics within the chapter fit together. ■

Key Terms and Key Calculations

Key terms are listed at the end of each chapter with page references. Financial math calculations introduced in the chapter are summarized at the end of the chapter for easy review and study. ■

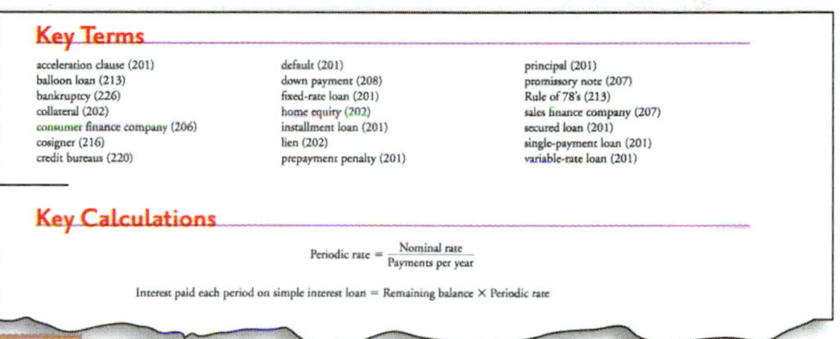

Key Terms

acceleration clause (201)
balloon loan (213)
bankruptcy (226)
collateral (202)
consumer finance company (206)
cosigner (216)
credit bureaus (220)
default (201)
down payment (208)
fixed-rate loan (201)
home equity (202)
installment loan (201)
lien (202)
prepayment penalty (201)
principal (201)
promissory note (207)
Rule of 78's (213)
sales finance company (207)
secured loan (201)
single-payment loan (201)
variable-rate loan (201)

Key Calculations

$$\text{Periodic rate} = \frac{\text{Nominal rate}}{\text{Payments per year}}$$

Interest paid each period on simple interest loan = Remaining balance × Periodic rate

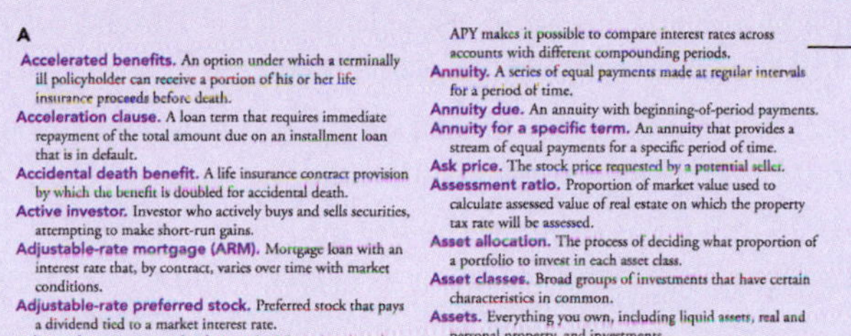

A

Accelerated benefits. An option under which a terminally ill policyholder can receive a portion of his or her life insurance proceeds before death.
Acceleration clause. A loan term that requires immediate repayment of the total amount due on an installment loan that is in default.
Accidental death benefit. A life insurance contract provision by which the benefit is doubled for accidental death.
Active investor. Investor who actively buys and sells securities, attempting to make short-run gains.
Adjustable-rate mortgage (ARM). Mortgage loan with an interest rate that, by contract, varies over time with market conditions.
Adjustable-rate preferred stock. Preferred stock that pays a dividend tied to a market interest rate.
Adjusted expense method. A method for estim[illegible]
APY makes it possible to compare interest rates across accounts with different compounding periods.
Annuity. A series of equal payments made at regular intervals for a period of time.
Annuity due. An annuity with beginning-of-period payments.
Annuity for a specific term. An annuity that provides a stream of equal payments for a specific period of time.
Ask price. The stock price requested by a potential seller.
Assessment ratio. Proportion of market value used to calculate assessed value of real estate on which the property tax rate will be assessed.
Asset allocation. The process of deciding what proportion of a portfolio to invest in each asset class.
Asset classes. Broad groups of investments that have certain characteristics in common.
Assets. Everything you own, including liquid assets, real and personal property, and investments.

Glossary

All key terms are also gathered in a complete, cumulative glossary at the end of the text. ■

End-of-Chapter Questions and Problems and End-of-Part Exercises

The end-of-chapter exercises are designed to develop personal finance knowledge, skills, and abilities. *Concept Review Questions* are designed for review of chapter concepts and recognition of key terms. The *Application Problems* consider personal finance decisions independently and provide students with reference to the type of problem solving required. Once concepts and skills are mastered, the student is ready to apply this knowledge to solving realistic personal finance problems in the *Building Financial Planning Skills Through Case Applications* section. At the end of each of the four parts of the book, a comprehensive continuing case, in which we visit the same family over time, encourages the integration of course concepts and recognition of changing financial needs over the life cycle. ■

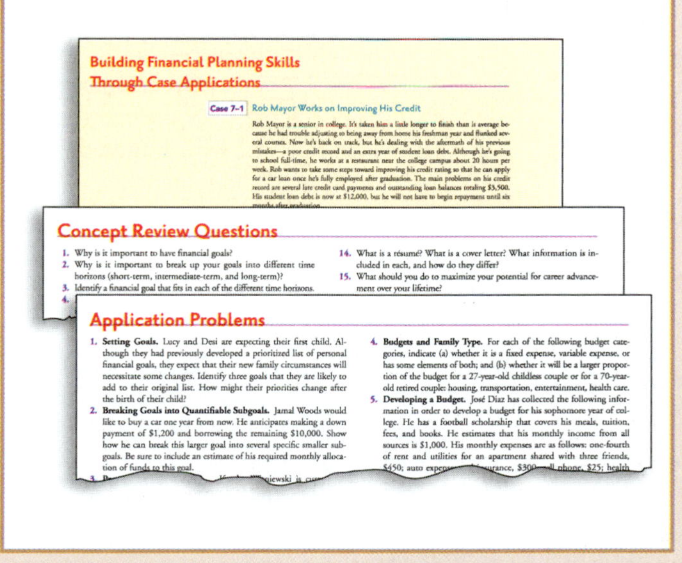

Building Financial Planning Skills Through Case Applications

Case 7-1 Rob Mayor Works on Improving His Credit

Rob Mayor is a senior in college. It's taken him a little longer to finish than is average because he had trouble adjusting to being away from home his freshman year and flunked several courses. Now he's back on track, but he's dealing with the aftermath of his previous mistakes—a poor credit record and an extra year of student loan debt. Although he's going to school full-time, he works at a restaurant near the college campus about 20 hours per week. Rob wants to take some steps toward improving his credit rating so that he can apply for a car loan once he's fully employed after graduation. The main problems on his credit record are several late credit card payments and outstanding loan balances totaling $3,500. His student loan debt is now at $12,000, but he will not have to begin repayment until six months after graduation.

Concept Review Questions

1. Why is it important to have financial goals?
2. Why is it important to break up your goals into different time horizons (short-term, intermediate-term, and long-term)?
3. Identify a financial goal that fits in each of the different time horizons.
4. [illegible]

14. What is a résumé? What is a cover letter? What information is included in each, and how do they differ?
15. What should you do to maximize your potential for career advancement over your lifetime?

Application Problems

1. **Setting Goals.** Lucy and Desi are expecting their first child. Although they had previously developed a prioritized list of personal financial goals, they expect that their new family circumstances will necessitate some changes. Identify three goals that they are likely to add to their original list. How might their priorities change after the birth of their child?
2. **Breaking Goals into Quantifiable Subgoals.** Jamal Woods would like to buy a car one year from now. He anticipates making a down payment of $1,200 and borrowing the remaining $10,000. Show how he can break this larger goal into several specific smaller subgoals. Be sure to include an estimate of his required monthly allocation of funds to this goal.
3. [illegible]
4. **Budgets and Family Type.** For each of the following budget categories, indicate (a) whether it is a fixed expense, variable expense, or has some elements of both; and (b) whether it will be a larger proportion of the budget for a 27-year-old childless couple or for a 70-year-old retired couple: housing, transportation, entertainment, health care.
5. **Developing a Budget.** José Diaz has collected the following information in order to develop a budget for his sophomore year of college. He has a football scholarship that covers his meals, tuition, fees, and books. He estimates that his monthly income from all sources is $1,000. His monthly expenses are as follows: one-fourth of rent and utilities for an apartment shared with three friends, $450; auto expen[illegible]insurance, $300; cell phone, $25; health

Instructor and Student Resources

Personal Finance: Skills for Life is accompanied by a host of ancillary materials designed to be a comprehensive teaching and learning package. Driven by the same basic beliefs as the textbook, these supplements provide a consistent and well-integrated learning system.

Instructor Resources

1. **Instructor's Resource Guide** (prepared by Karen Eilers Lahey, University of Akron) includes the following for each chapter:
   - Chapter outline
   - Learning objectives
   - Teaching suggestions
   - Concept review questions and answers
   - Solutions to end-of-chapter problems and cases
   - Additional websites
   - Additional Web assignments
   - One to three mini-cases with discussion questions
   - Additional problems and solutions
   - Additional Excel worksheet problems with solutions
2. **Test Bank** (prepared by Cheryl McGaughey, Angelo State University) contains approximately 1,000 to 1,500 questions in total, consisting of multiple choice, true/false, and three to four mini-cases with questions requiring short answers per each chapter. Also included is an answer key, arranged by chapter, at the end of the Test Bank, which provides the correct answer and a page and section reference where related material can be found within the textbook along with a rating of level of difficulty.
3. **Computerized Test Bank** is for use on a PC running Windows. It contains content from the Test Bank provided within a test-generating program that allows instructors to customize their exams.
4. **PowerPoint** presentation materials, prepared by the author, are provided for each chapter and include lecture outlines based on the key concepts and topics covered within each chapter.
5. **Video Lecture Launchers** provide a compilation of brief video clips that are tied to topics throughout the text. These videos offer an excellent starting point for lectures and discussion.
6. **HP Calculator** Using Hewlett-Packard's free PC emulator software, instructors can turn their PC into a working calculator. The emulator software gives you a mouse-controlled, onscreen replica of a completely functional HP calculator.
7. **Business Extra Select Online Courseware System**
   (http://coursepacks.xanedu.com/businessselect/index.html) Wiley has recently launched this program which provides an instructor with millions of content resources from an extensive database of cases, journals, periodicals, newspapers, and supplemental readings. This courseware system lends itself extremely well to the integration of real-world content within **Personal Finance** to enable instructors to convey the relevance of the course content to their students. A link is available from this text's website to a sample course pack created specifically for this text. Instructors also have the option to bundle or customize this text with hundreds of best-selling Wiley titles and supplements. Wiley will even clear and add copyrighted material!
8. **Companion Website**: The text's website at www.wiley.com/college/bajtelsmit contains a myriad of resources and links to aid both learning and teaching.

Student Resources

1. **Personal Financial Planner (PFP)** is packaged **FREE** with each new copy of the text. Prepared by the author, the Personal Financial Planner contains 55 worksheets that make it easy to apply the skills taught in the course. Throughout the textbook, there are margin icon references to the relevant worksheets in the Planner.
2. **Interactive Personal Financial Planner Worksheets** An electronic version of the Planner is available and contains all the worksheets in an interactive format to help students analyze a variety of scenarios, make decisions, and develop a comprehensive financial plan.
3. **Practice Quizzes** (prepared by Joan K. Moss, University of Georgia) enable students to assess their comprehension of the key concepts and ideas within each chapter by responding to multiple-choice questions correlated to each chapter.

Online Teaching and Learning

eGrade Plus Helping Teachers Teach and Students Learn
www.wiley.com/college/bajtelsmit

Personal Financial: Skills for Life is available with eGrade Plus, a powerful online tool that provides instructors and students with an integrated suite of teaching and learning resources in one easy-to-use website. eGrade Plus is organized around the essential activities you and your students perform in class:

For Instructors

- **Prepare and Present.** Create class presentations using a wealth of Wiley-provided resources—such as an online version of the textbook and PowerPoint slides—making your preparation time more efficient. You may easily adapt, customize, and add to this content to meet the needs of your course.
- **Create Assignments.** Automate the assigning and grading of homework or quizzes by using question banks prepared by Holly Hunts, Montana State University, or by writing your own. Student results will be automatically graded and recorded in your gradebook. eGrade Plus can link homework problems to the relevant section of the online text, providing students with context-sensitive help.
- **Track Student Progress.** Keep track of your students' progress via an instructor's gradebook, which allows you to analyze individual and overall class results to determine their progress and level of understanding.
- **Administer Your Course.** eGrade Plus can easily be integrated with another course management system, gradebook, or other resources you are using in your class, providing you with the flexibility to build your course, your way.

For Students

Wiley's eGrade Plus provides immediate feedback on student assignments and a wealth of support materials. This powerful study tool will help your students develop their conceptual understanding of the class material and increase their ability to solve problems.

- **A "Study and Practice"** area links directly to text content, allowing students to review the text while they study and complete homework assignments.
- **An "Assignment"** area keeps all the work you want your students to complete in one location, making it easy for them to stay "on task." Students will have access to a variety of interactive problem-solving tools, as well as other resources for building their confidence and understanding. In addition, many homework problems contain a link to the relevant section of the multimedia book, providing students with context-sensitive help that allows them to conquer problem-solving obstacles as they arise.
- **A Personal Gradebook** for each student will allow students to view their results from past assignments at any time.

Please view our online demo at *www.wiley.com/college/egradeplus.* Here you will find additional information about the features and benefits of eGrade Plus, how to request a "test drive" of eGrade Plus for this title, and how to adopt it for class use.

Acknowledgments

Special Thanks

I would like to personally thank and acknowledge the efforts of many extraordinary people who have helped in the development of *Personal Finance: Skills for Life.* I cannot say enough good things about the incredible team of talented professionals I have worked with at John Wiley & Sons. They have made the job of a first-time textbook author so much easier and I know I could not have done it without them. While I'm sure there are even more people who have worked behind the scenes, my heartfelt thanks go to: Susan Elbe, *Publisher*, who has supported this project from the beginning; Leslie Kraham, *Development Editor*, who initially convinced me to write the book; Judith Joseph, *Associate Publisher*, for her superb and professional management of the entire project; Marian Provenzano, *Senior Development Editor*, for her creativity and attention to detail which added so much to the final product; Beverly Peavler, *Freelance Editor*, for her careful reading of many drafts, her invaluable advice throughout the writing process, and for compiling the permissions; Heather King, *Marketing Manager*, for her enthusiastic and creative marketing ideas; Cindy Rhoads, *Project Editor*, for developing an excellent supplements package; Harry Nolan, *Design Director*, for creating the most attractive book design I've ever seen; William Murray, *Senior Production Editor*, for keeping to our incredibly ambitious production schedule; Allison Morris, *Media Editor*, for developing the excellent Web materials; Anna Melhorn, *Senior Illustration Editor*, for the book's unique art program; Sara Wight and Lisa Gee, *Senior Photo Editors*, for finding the perfect photographs; and Brigeth Rivera and Masha Maizel, *Editorial Assistants*, for their many contributions to the finished product.

I am delighted that several excellent teachers agreed to write supplements for the text. I cannot think of anyone more qualified to write the Instructor's Resource Guide than my long-time friend and colleague Karen Lahey, University of Akron. Cheryl McCaughey, Angelo State University, has written a large and comprehensive Test Bank and Holly Hunts, Montana State University, has provided an excellent set of Web quizzes to complement the text. Additional quizzes have been written by Joan Koonce Moss, University of Georgia.

I owe a special debt of gratitude to John Ellis, retired professor of finance at Colorado State University, who tirelessly read through the entire manuscript, solved all the text and end-of-chapter problems and cases, and created many of the graphs that appear throughout the text. John's attention to detail is unparalleled. I would also like to thank Joan Koonce Moss, University of Georgia; David L. Jones, Johnson County Community College; and Andrew Light, Liberty University, for carefully reading all the chapters for accuracy. Due to the efforts of these four colleagues, I am confident that this text is as error-free as any first edition text has ever been.

An important component of the development process for *Personal Finance: Skills for Life* is the many helpful comments and suggestions I received from colleagues who teach personal finance courses around the country. The willingness of these teachers to review and critique the book at various stages in the process was instrumental to the quality and completeness of the final product. I would like to personally acknowledge the contributions made by the following individuals:

Reviewers

Timothy Alzheimer, Montana State University
Clifford Barnes, Bethune Cookman College
Michael Barry, Boston College
Jerry Basford, University of Utah
Jami Jarnigan Beavers, University of Central Oklahoma
Charles A. Blaylock, Lamar University
Howard Bohnen, St. Cloud State University
Karin Bonding, University of Virginia
Jack Bucco, Austin Community College
Barry Bunn, Valencia Community College
Craig Bythewood, Florida Southern College
Steven Chambers, Johnson County Community College
Robert Chapman, Oral Roberts University
Raju Chenna, Kentucky Wesleyan College
Christopher Coyne, Saint Joseph's University
Thomas D'Arrigo, CUNY Bronx Community College and SUNY Nassau Community College
Nandita Das, Bloomsburg University of Pennsylvania
Joseph Dubanowitz, Montclair State University
Caroline Fulmer, University of Alabama
Tom Gausman, Minnesota State Community and Technical College
Michael Gordinier, Washington University
Joseph Greene, Augusta State University
Donald Hardwick, Lexington Community College
Ling He, University of Central Arkansas
Steven Huntley, Florida Community College
Holly Hunts, Montana State University
Samira Hussein, Johnson County Community College
Charlotte Jacobsen, Montgomery College
David Jones, Johnson County Community College
Jeanette Karjala, Winona State University
Jim Keys, Florida International University
Katherine Kocher, University of Central Oklahoma
Karen Lahey, University of Akron
John Lasik, Central Washington University
David Leapard, Eastern Michigan University
Andrew Light, Liberty University
Ruth Lytton, Virginia Tech
Abbas Mamoozadeh, Slippery Rock University
Ken Mark, Kansas City Kansas Community College
Allen Martin, California State University
Lee McClain, Western Washington University
Mike McGay, Wilmington College
Norman McElvany, Johnson Sate College
Noel McKeon, Florida Community College
Judith Mills, University of Hawaii, Manoa
Mitch Mokhtari, University of Maryland
Joan Koonce Moss, University of Georgia
David Payne, Ohio University
James Pettijohn, Southwest Missouri State University
Armand Picou, University of Central Arkansas
Padmaja Pillutla, Western Illinois University
Wei Rowe, University of Nebraska
Julia Sampson, Malone College
Elizabeth Scull, University of South Carolina
Tulin Sener, SUNY New Paltz
Joseph Simon, Casper College
Andrew Solocha, University of Toledo
Suresh Srivastava, University of Alaska
Rachel Lea Templer, College of the Canyons
Andrew F. Thompson, University of Northern Iowa
Shafi Ullah, Broward Community College
Dick Verrone, University of North Carolina
Mike Weeks, University of Missouri
Debra Wood, Kansas State University
Carol Wysocki, Columbia Basin College

Focus Group Participants

Kenneth Bigel, Touro University
Patricia Clark, Simmons College
Thomas Coe, Quinnipiac University
Bruce Costa, University of Montana
Halil Kiymaz, University of Houston
Tom Krueger, University of Wisconsin
Karen Lahey, University of Akron
John Manley, Iona College
Barbara S. Poole, Roger Williams University
Antonio Rodriguez, Texas A&M International University
Tarek S. Zaher, Indiana State University

Brief Contents

Contents

Part II SECURING BASIC HOUSEHOLD NEEDS

Learning Styles Quiz

How Do I Learn Best?

This questionnaire aims to find out something about your preferences for the way you work with information. You will have a preferred learning style, and one part of that learning style is your preference for the intake and the output of ideas and information.

Circle the letter of the answer that best explains your preference. Circle more than one if a single answer does not match your perception. Leave blank any question that does not apply. You will notice that some answers are out of alphabetical sequence.

1. You are about to give directions to a person who is standing with you. She is staying in a hotel in town and wants to visit your house. She has a rental car. Would you
   - **a.** draw a map on paper?
   - **b.** tell her the directions?
   - **c.** write down the directions (without a map)?
   - **d.** pick her up at the hotel in your car?

2. You are not sure whether a word should be spelled "dependent" or "dependant." Do you
   - **c.** look it up in the dictionary?
   - **a.** imagine the word in your mind and choose a spelling by the way it looks?
   - **b.** sound it out in your mind?
   - **d.** write both versions down on paper and choose one?

3. You have just received a copy of your itinerary for an around the world trip. This is of interest to a friend. Would you
   - **b.** call her immediately and tell her about it?
   - **c.** send her a copy of the printed itinerary?
   - **a.** show her a copy of a printed itinerary?
   - **d.** share what you plan to do at each place you visit?

4. You are going to cook something as a special treat for your family. Do you
   - **d.** cook something familiar without the need for instructions?
   - **a.** thumb through a cookbook looking for ideas from the pictures?
   - **c.** refer to a specific cookbook where there is a good recipe?

5. You have been assigned to instruct a group of tourists about wildlife reserves or parks. Would you
   - **d.** drive them to a wildlife reserve or park?
   - **a.** show them slides and pictures?
   - **c.** give them pamphlets or a book on wildlife reserves or parks?
   - **b.** deliver a talk on wildlife reserves or parks?

6. You are about to purchase a new CD player. Other than price, what would most influence your decision?
   - **b.** The salesperson telling you what you want to know.
   - **c.** Reading the details about it.
   - **d.** Playing with the controls and listening to it.
   - **a.** Its fashionable and upscale appearance.

7. Recall a time in your life when you learned how to do something like playing a new board game. Try to avoid choosing a very physical skill, for example, riding a bike. How did you learn best? By
   - **a.** visual clues: pictures, diagrams, charts?
   - **c.** written instructions?
   - **b.** listening to someone explain it?
   - **d.** doing it or trying it?

8. You have an eye problem. Would you prefer that the doctor
   - **b.** tell you what is wrong?
   - **a.** show you a diagram of what is wrong?
   - **d.** use a model to show what is wrong?

9. You are about to learn to use a new program on a computer. Would you
   - **d.** sit down at the keyboard and begin to experiment with the program's features?
   - **c.** read the manual that comes with the program?
   - **b.** call a friend and ask questions about it?

10. You are staying in a hotel and you have rented a car. You would like to visit friends whose address/location you do not know. Would you like them to:
    - **a.** draw you a map on paper?
    - **b.** tell you the directions?
    - **c.** write down the directions (without a map)?
    - **d.** pick you up at the hotel in their car?

11 Apart from price, what would most influence your decision to buy a particular book?

d. You have used a copy before.

b. A friend talking about it.

c. Quickly reading parts of it.

a. The appealing way it looks.

12 A new movie has arrived in town. What would most influence your decision to go (or not go)?

b. You heard a radio review about it.

c. You read a review of it.

a. You saw a preview of it.

13 Do you prefer a lecturer or teacher who likes to use

c. a textbook, handouts, readings?

a. flow diagrams, charts, graphs?

d. field trips, labs, practical sessions?

b. discussion, guest speakers?

Count your choices

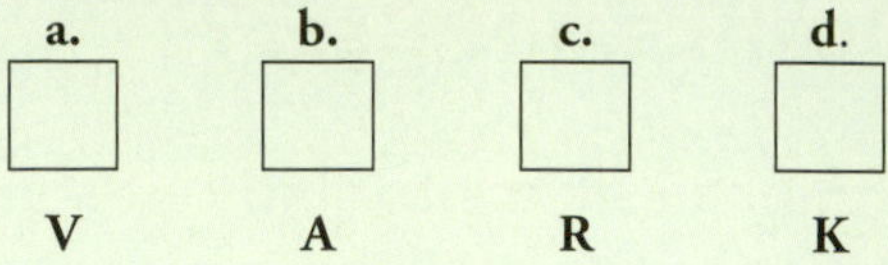

Now match the letter or letters you have recorded most to the same letter or letters in the Learning Styles Chart. You may have more than one learning style preference—many people do. Next to each letter in the chart are suggestions that will refer you to different learning aids throughout this text.

© Copyright Version 2.0 (2000) held by Neil D. Fleming, Christchurch, New Zealand and Charles C. Bonwell, Green Mountain Falls, COLORADO 80819 (719) 684-9261. This material may be used for faculty or student development if attribution is given. It may not be publsihed in either paper or electronic form without consent of the authors. There is a VARK website at www.vark-learn.com.

Learning Styles Chart

Visual

INTAKE: TO TAKE IN THE INFORMATION	TO MAKE A STUDY PACKAGE	TEXT FEATURES THAT MAY HELP YOU THE MOST	OUTPUT: TO DO WELL ON EXAMS
• Pay close attention to charts, drawings, and handouts your instructor uses. • Underline. • Use different colors. • Use symbols, flow charts, graphs, different arrangements on the page, white space.	Convert your lecture notes into "page pictures." To do this: • Use the "Intake" strategies. • Reconstruct images in different ways. • Redraw pages from memory. • Replace words with symbols and initials. • Look at your pages.	The Navigator Applying the Planning Process The Myth or Fact statements The Chapter Preview Infographics/illustrations/photos Words in bold Concept Review Questions Application Problems Using Web Resources for Financial Planning	• Recall your "page pictures." • Draw diagrams when appropriate. • Practice turning your visuals back into words.

Aural

INTAKE: TO TAKE IN THE INFORMATION	TO MAKE A STUDY PACKAGE	TEXT FEATURES THAT MAY HELP YOU THE MOST	OUTPUT: TO DO WELL ON EXAMS
• Attend lectures and tutorials. • Discuss topics with students and instructors. • Explain new ideas to other people. • Use a tape recorder. • Leave spaces in your lecture notes for later recall. • Describe overheads, pictures, and visuals to somebody who was not in class.	You may take poor notes because you prefer to listen. Therefore: • Expand your notes by talking with others and with information from your textbook. • Tape record summarized notes and listen. • Read summarized notes out loud. • Explain your notes to another "aural" person.	The Navigator Applying the Planning Process Infographics/illustrations Summary of Learning Objectives Glossary Concept Review Questions Application Problems Building Financial Planning Skills Through Case Applications Developing Personal Financial Skills for Life	• Talk with the instructor. • Spend time in quiet places recalling the ideas presented in class. • Practice writing answers to old exam questions. • Say your answers out loud.

Reading/Writing

INTAKE: TO TAKE IN THE INFORMATION	TO MAKE A STUDY PACKAGE	TEXT FEATURES THAT MAY HELP YOU THE MOST	OUTPUT: TO DO WELL ON EXAMS
• Use lists and headings. • Use dictionaries, glossaries, and definitions. • Read handouts, textbooks, and supplementary library readings. • Use lecture notes.	• Write out words again and again. • Reread notes silently. • Rewrite ideas and principles into other words. • Turn charts, diagrams, and other illustrations into statements.	The Navigator Before studying this chapter, you should review. . . Applying the Planning Process Learning Objectives Marginal definitions Summary of Learning Objectives Glossary Concept Review Questions Application Problems	• Write exam answers. • Practice with multiple-choice questions. • Write paragraphs, beginnings and endings. • Write your lists in outline form. • Arrange your words into hierarchies and points.

Kinesthetic

INTAKE: TO TAKE IN THE INFORMATION	TO MAKE A STUDY PACKAGE	TEXT FEATURES THAT MAY HELP YOU THE MOST	OUTPUT: TO DO WELL ON EXAMS
• Use all your senses. • Go to labs, take field trips. • Listen to real-life examples. • Pay attention to applications. • Use hands-on approaches. • Use trial-and-error methods.	You may take poor notes because topics do not seem concrete or relevant. Therefore: • Put examples in your summaries. • Use case studies and applications to help with principles and abstract concepts. • Talk about your notes with another "kinesthetic" person. • Use pictures and photographs that illustrate an idea.	The Navigator Applying the Planning Process The Myth or Fact statements Learning by Doing examples News You Can Use Go Figure! Ask the Expert Money Psychology Application Problems Using Web Resources for Financial Planning Building Financial Planning Skills Through Case Applications Developing Personal Financial Skills for Life	• Write practice answers. • Role-play the exam situation.

THE NAVIGATOR

- ☐ Review Before Studying this Chapter list.
- ☐ Scan Learning Objectives.
- ☐ Take Myth or Fact quiz and find the answers throughout the chapter.
- ☐ Read chapter text and answer Learning by Doing exercises.
- ☐ Review Key Terms and Key Calculations.
- ☐ Do end-of-chapter exercises.
- ☐ Take review quiz on the text website.
- ☐ Solve end-of-chapter cases.

BEFORE studying this chapter, you should review

- Your learning style, as determined in the Learning Styles exercise in the text preface.

The Financial Planning Process

CHAPTER 1

Myth or Fact?

Consider each of the following statements and decide whether it is a *myth* or a *fact*. Look for the answers in the *Fact* boxes in the chapter.

	MYTH	FACT
1. A large proportion of American adults are financially illiterate.	☐	☐
2. Your personal values and attitudes are an important determinant of your money style, and can sometimes negatively impact your personal finances.	☐	☐
3. A dollar today is worth more than a dollar tomorrow.	☐	☐
4. Financial websites are mostly trying to sell you something, so you shouldn't trust any educational materials they provide.	☐	☐
5. In order to become a financial planner, you must have at least an undergraduate degree with a major in finance or economics.	☐	☐

LEARNING objectives

1. Recognize the importance of studying personal financial planning.
2. Describe the five steps in the personal financial planning process.
3. Identify the factors that influence personal financial planning decisions.
4. Understand how the elements of a comprehensive financial plan fit together.
5. Consider opportunity costs and marginal effects in making personal finance decisions.
6. Understand when and how to select qualified financial planning professionals.

...applying the planning process

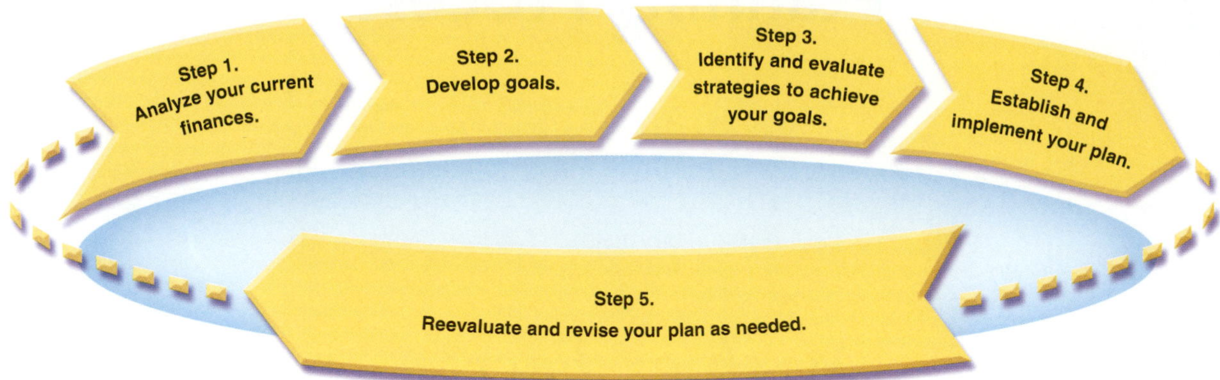

How much do you already know about personal finance? The *Myth or Fact?* feature that opens this and other chapters is designed to illustrate common misconceptions about personal finance. If you know all the answers, you are in better shape than most people—survey results show a fairly low level of financial literacy in the United States.

As you read this text, you'll learn about the financial planning process and how it can help you make better decisions in the future. As illustrated in the diagram above, the financial planning process is made up of five steps. To make effective financial planning decisions, you must: (1) analyze your current finances, (2) develop specific goals, (3) identify and evaluate possible strategies for meeting your goals, (4) establish and implement your plan, and (5) reevaluate and revise your plan as needed. Since this process is fundamental to all aspects of financial planning, we will be revisiting it at the beginning of every chapter and applying it to that chapter's specific subject matter. By the time you get to the end of this course, thinking in terms of the financial planning process will be second nature to you. You'll also know more about your own financial habits and attitudes.

In this chapter, we begin the quest for financial literacy by looking at some important background material. First, we consider why it's important to study financial planning. We then discuss the planning process, the factors that influence it, and the elements of a comprehensive financial plan. Next, we cover strategies for making effective financial decisions. Finally, we discuss when and how to use the services of financial planning professionals.

Chapter Preview

Why Study Personal Financial Planning?	Personal Financial Planning: The Five Steps	Factors That Influence Personal Financial Planning	Elements of a Comprehensive Financial Plan	Making Effective Decisions	Selecting Qualified Financial Planning Professionals
• Benefits of Planning • Why People Avoid Planning • Problems with Avoiding Planning	• Analyze Current Finances • Develop Goals • Determine Strategies • Implement Strategies • Reevaluate and Revise	• Life Cycle Stage • Values and Attitudes • Life Situation • General Economic Conditions	• Establishing Foundation • Meeting Basic Needs • Building Wealth • Protecting Wealth	• Reasonable Assumptions • Marginal Reasoning • Opportunity Costs • Sensitivity Analysis	• Factors to Consider • Costs • When and How to Hire a Planner

Why Study Personal Financial Planning?

LEARNING objective

1 Recognize the importance of studying personal financial planning.

Personal financial planning will help you make better decisions about money, but its effect on your life will go much further than that. Because almost every aspect of life has a financial component, the benefits of good financial management extend into many areas.

What Are the Benefits of Personal Financial Planning?

As a college student, you probably have already faced some financial challenges. For example, maybe you've asked yourself one of the following questions:

- Should I take out a student loan to pay for college expenses?
- How can I get out from under my credit card debt?
- Can I afford to replace my car's transmission?
- Where should I go to buy my auto insurance?

Or perhaps you've had to deal with more complex decisions:

- Is graduate school a good investment?
- How much should I contribute to my 401(k) retirement plan?
- Should I start a savings plan to fund my child's college education?
- How do I decide among the employee benefit options that my employer offers?

These questions are all related to **personal finance**—a specialized area of study that focuses on individual and household financial decisions, such as budgeting, saving, spending, insurance, and investments. Understanding these topics will help you in many ways. You'll make better decisions when you buy an auto, shop for a home mortgage, choose a career, and save for retirement. You may also be able to pay less in taxes and interest.

personal finance
The study of individual and household financial decisions.

Personal financial planning is the process of developing and implementing an integrated, comprehensive plan designed to meet financial goals, to improve financial well being, and to prepare for financial emergencies. In this course, you'll learn the elements of personal financial planning and how to prepare your own financial plan. Unlike many classes you'll take in college, this course will help you to gain knowledge, skills, and abilities that have immediate application to your own life situation. Furthermore, these benefits will continue throughout your life. In short, mastering the subject matter in this course will provide you with the knowledge and skills you need to achieve personal financial success.

personal financial planning
Developing and implementing an integrated, comprehensive plan to meet financial goals and prepare for financial emergencies.

The primary goal of personal financial planning is to develop and achieve financial goals, such as buying a first home or a bigger home, making a major consumer purchase, supporting a growing family, or preparing financially for retirement. But people who have their finances in order gain important social and psychological benefits as well. Generally, they feel less stressed and experience improved relationships with friends, family, and coworkers. As many couples know, financial difficulties are a major contributor to marital problems. Most people also find that the self-sufficiency that eventually results from good financial planning improves their self-esteem.

Why Do People Avoid Financial Planning?

Surveys indicate that most people recognize the need to manage their finances, but most admit that they're not doing an adequate job of it. Why is this the case? Some of the most common reasons offered by people who avoid financial planning are:

- They don't believe their math and finance skills are adequate.
- They fear failure.
- They expect someone else to take care of it.

- They aren't interested.
- They don't know whom to trust.
- They believe they're too busy.
- They are overwhelmed with the quantity of information and don't know where to start.

If you've used some of these excuses yourself, rest assured that you're not alone. You might be able to relate to the all-too-familiar case of David Keller. While a college freshman, David fell victim to the multitude of credit card offers that abound on campuses across the United States. Although his parents were paying his basic expenses, David used his credit cards for extras such as concert tickets, occasional pizzas, movie tickets, and CDs. Since David wasn't employed, the credit card balances mounted, and he began to have trouble meeting his minimum payments. With late charges and over-limit fees, his situation quickly got out of control. David was too embarrassed to tell his parents, even when he started getting stomachaches from the stress. Fortunately, on the advice of a friend, David signed up for a personal finance course at the beginning of his sophomore year. By establishing a budget and taking a part-time job to pay down his credit card debt, David was able to get out from under.

What Problems Are Associated with Poor Financial Planning?

What happens to people who don't manage their finances well or at all? David's example in the preceding discussion illustrates just of few of the many unfortunate outcomes—stress, worry, embarrassment, and difficulty in meeting current obligations. Individuals experiencing the financial distress that often comes with poor financial planning are unable to handle financial emergencies or unexpected job loss. They are often the victims of "get rich quick" scams. Their children may be unintended victims, since high-quality educational opportunities and extracurricular activities may not be affordable without advance planning. Many people suffer from anxiety or depression related to their finances and may, as a result, have difficulty maintaining personal relationships. Spouses who lack an understanding of household finances often find themselves in serious trouble upon divorce or widowhood. And adult children who mismanage their finances may end up living with their parents well into their 20s and 30s. For all these reasons, mastering the financial planning process is well worth your investment of time and effort.

Fact #1

When it comes to their personal finances, most people know what they should do, but a lot of them don't do it, according to a 2003 survey commissioned by Bankrate.com. The average grade on the financial literacy quiz was only 67 out of 100. The older participants tended to have the highest scores, and those who flunked were, on average, younger and lower-income than the rest of the group.

The Five Steps in the Personal Financial Planning Process

LEARNING objective

2 Describe the five steps in the personal financial planning process.

We first introduced the five-step personal financial planning process at the beginning of the chapter, and now we'll examine each step in more detail. It's important as you read about the steps to recognize the circular flow of the planning process. Although you'll use the process to develop a personal financial plan as you work your way through this book, your plan won't ever be a finished product—you'll need to reevaluate and revise it continually as your life circumstances change. The process of personal financial planning is a life-long activity.

Step 1: Analyze Your Current Financial Position

At the end of the month, many people struggle to meet their expenses. "Where did all the money go?" is a common lament. Before you can move forward with your financial plan, you need to determine where you are starting from—where your money is coming from and where it is going. Analyzing your current financial position requires that you collect and organize all your financial information, create personal financial statements, and quantitatively evaluate your current financial position to establish a baseline against which you can measure improvement in the future. This step may involve hard work for those who are "organizationally challenged." Nevertheless, careful record keeping is vital to good financial planning, because it enables you to track actual expenditures and identify small financial problems before they turn into big ones. In Chapter 2, you'll learn more about how to analyze your current finances.

Step 2: Develop Short-Term and Long-Term Financial Goals

Everyone has a personal conception of "success." Have you thought about where you want to be five years from now? Ten years from now? For some, success may be defined in money terms; for others, in levels of personal satisfaction. However you define success, the second step in the personal financial planning process requires that you identify and prioritize specific goals and objectives. You will begin to develop your short-term and long-term personal financial goals in Chapter 3.

The process of setting goals should involve some introspective assessment of *why* you have the goals you do. For example, are your objectives focused on your own needs or the needs of others? Are your objectives related to pressures from family or peers?

Keep in mind, too, that short-term and long-term goals change over time and may be influenced by changes in economic circumstances. Consider an example. In early 2002, Jack Naughton was a partner at Arthur Anderson, a large public accounting firm. The Naughton family lived very comfortably on Jack's six-figure salary. His partnership interest, their largest investment, seemed secure. They had recently stretched their finances a little to buy a larger house in a better neighborhood, but they planned to increase their retirement account contributions and to begin a college savings plan for their baby daughter in the near future. Then came the Enron scandal, massive layoffs, and the eventual bankruptcy of Jack's employer. The Naughtons' goals had to change drastically. Instead of retirement and college savings, their new goals were to pay their bills and find a new job for Jack.

Step 3: Identify and Evaluate Alternative Strategies for Achieving Your Goals

Although every person's goals and objectives are unique to that person's circumstances, the strategies for achieving them are more similar. In general, in order to have more money available to meet current or future goals, you either have to reduce spending or increase earnings. Step 3 in the personal financial planning process requires that you identify alternative strategies for achieving goals and compare the costs and benefits of each.

As an example, let's revisit the Naughton family a few months after his layoff. Jack has found a new job but has taken a significant pay cut, and his earnings no longer cover the family's expenses. To achieve the goal of meeting expenses, the Naughtons could use one or more of the following strategies:

- Mrs. Naughton could get a job.
- They could sell the house or possibly refinance it at a lower interest rate to reduce their monthly mortgage payments.
- They could sell other assets.
- They could dip into savings.
- They could borrow money.

Each of these strategies has costs and benefits that must be carefully identified and evaluated. As you learn more about each aspect of personal finance in future chapters, you'll be identifying and evaluating strategies for achieving goals related to that area of your plan.

Relocating for a new job will require that you reevaluate your financial plan.

Step 4: Implement a Plan for Achieving Your Goals

Using the information developed in Step 3, you are now prepared to decide on the best strategies for achieving your goals so that you can implement your plan. How do you make such decisions? How do you know which strategies are the best ones for achieving your goals? As you proceed through this course, you'll acquire fundamental knowledge and master analytical tools that will help you to make effective personal financial planning decisions. The result will be a personal financial plan that meets your basic household needs, builds wealth over time, and protects your income and assets.

Step 5: Regularly Reevaluate and Revise Your Plan as Necessary

Many changes will occur over the course of your life. Not only will changes in your personal circumstances (graduation, a new job, marriage, children) affect your financial planning objectives and strategies, but economic conditions may necessitate revision of the plan as well. An effective financial plan must be adaptable to changing circumstances. Thus, Step 5 takes you continually back to Steps 1 through 4.

Learning by Doing 1-1

Consider each of the following activities, and identify which of the five steps in the financial planning process it pertains to:

1. In your senior year of college, you have two job offers and need to decide which one to take.
2. You and your husband find out that you are expecting your first child.
3. You take out a home equity loan at a low rate of interest in order to pay off your high-interest credit cards and reduce your monthly payments.

Factors That Influence Personal Financial Planning

LEARNING objective

3 Identify the factors that influence personal financial planning decisions.

As you build your financial plan, you'll need to consider many factors that influence your spending and saving behavior. Some are unique to you, such as where you are in your life cycle, your family makeup, your values, and your attitudes. Others, such as inflation and interest rates, affect everyone to some extent. Both types of factors can be expected to change over time, so your plan will need to continually adapt to new circumstances.

Changing Needs over the Life Cycle

Your household will go through several phases over your life cycle, and your financial situation will change as well. Exhibit 1-1 illustrates how a person's income and wealth might change over the life cycle. There are many different types of family situations, and this exhibit is not intended to imply that everyone's situation is the same; rather, it is meant to illustrate the significant differences in planning needs over the life cycle.

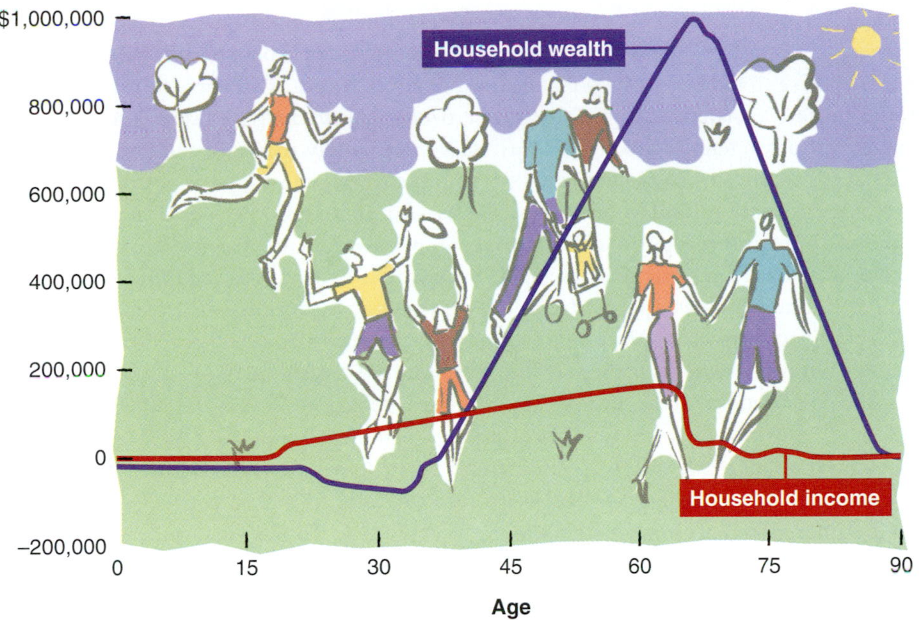

EXHIBIT 1-1

Household Income and Wealth Over the Life Cycle

In general, your income level through your early 20s will be lower than it will be later, and your wealth may even be negative—that is, you may have more debts than assets at this point in your life. That's because you're currently making investments in your education that have not yet paid off.

Marriage, career development, the purchase of a home, and investments in your children's education will likely occur from your late 20s through your 40s. During this time, your household will focus on setting goals, establishing savings, and protecting the family from unexpected negative events, such as premature death or job loss due to illness or disability. This is also the beginning of the wealth accumulation phase, which continues through your 50s to early 60s.

As retirement approaches, most people in their 50s and 60s pay closer attention to meeting retirement income and health needs and preserving wealth for their heirs. The earlier you plan for these needs, the better off you will be once you get to that stage in the life cycle. During your retirement period, on average beginning at age 65, you will *decumulate*, or spend, your accumulated wealth. Your goals during retirement may include maintaining an active lifestyle, including travel and leisure activities, and having sufficient income throughout your retirement period.

Many people want to maintain an active lifestyle in retirement.

Values and Attitudes

People have different money styles—different values and attitudes regarding money and its use. Your money style generally is the result of both learned behaviors and inherent tendencies. For example, if you were raised in a household where money was tight and consumer purchases were made with careful deliberation, you might carry the money skills learned from your parents' example into your adult life. Whether your parents were spendthrifts or tightwads, however, your own genetic makeup will also impact your personal money style. Individuals who are impulsive by nature often have difficulty controlling their spending, just as those with a tendency to orderliness are more likely to have their finances in order as well. Thus, both "nature and nurture" help to form your values and attitudes toward money. In fact, it is not uncommon to find that siblings raised in the same households have very different money styles.

Values are fundamental beliefs about what is important in life. What do you think is most important: family, friends, things, education, religious faith, financial success, fame, health, self-sufficiency? The weight you place on each will influence the goals that you set and the strategies

values

Fundamental beliefs about what is important in life.

attitudes

Opinions and psychological differences between people.

risk

Uncertainty with regard to potential loss.

that you develop to achieve your goals. **Attitudes** are opinions and psychological differences between people that affect their decisions. Are you an optimist or a pessimist? Conservative or liberal? Do you like to have everything planned out in advance or just go with the flow? Of particular importance to financial planning is your attitude toward **risk**, or uncertainty—are you a risk-taker, or do you tend to avoid risk? We'll look more closely at risk attitudes in later chapters.

What if you already know that you have a problem with money? Is it possible to overcome your biological makeup and your learned values and attitudes? Of course, it is! To do this, though, you must first recognize what your values and attitudes are, particularly where they may run counter to achieving your goals. Remember David Keller from the beginning of the chapter? David's credit card problems in college didn't come about by accident—he learned bad money habits from his parents. He grew up in a home where money was no object. As a child, his parents bought him toys whenever they set foot in a store. As a teen, he didn't need a part-time job like most of his friends, and he always had the latest video games and CDs. When he went away to college, he didn't really know *how* to control his spending. If you are a "spender," like David, you may need to approach your budget differently than someone who is naturally inclined to be more conservative in spending. Similarly, if you are a natural risk-taker, you will approach investing quite differently than someone who tends to avoid risk. To help you understand your own inclinations, we've included a money attitudes assessment in the *Developing Personal Financial Skills for Life* section at the end of this chapter.

Fact #2

Values and attitudes play an important role in how you deal with money. Spontaneous and generous people may have more difficulty controlling spending than those who are more analytical. People who are natural "planners" are more inclined to set goals and follow through on their strategies for achieving them.

Life Situation

Family makeup and demographic characteristics—such as age, marital status, income, and wealth—significantly affect financial planning. Households with children, for example, tend to have higher expenses and therefore less ability to save during their child-rearing years. In fact, a recent study suggests that it costs more than $250,000 to raise a child to age 18. In addition, children's college expenses can take a big bite out of family savings. Double-income couples, particularly those with no children, tend to be better off financially than singles. Those without children are also more able to focus on career goals and therefore can more quickly move up the employment ladder. However, the financial and social support provided by children to their parents in old age may eventually offset the increased earlier costs.

Perhaps most important, education plays a critical role in financial success. College-educated people, particularly those with specialized skills (such as business, education, or engineering), tend to receive higher starting salaries and larger wage increases over their careers. White-collar employers are also more likely to offer retirement plans and fringe benefit packages, as discussed in Chapter 10.

Demographic factors such as gender, age, income, and education have often been linked to risk attitudes. In the *Money Psychology* box "Socioeconomic Differences in Risk Attitudes," we summarize the results of this research within the context of personal financial decision making. As you might expect, risk-takers are more likely to be male, childless, educated, and high-income. Throughout this book, the *Money Psychology* boxes will highlight research relating to behavioral and psychological factors that influence people's money decisions—an area of increased interest over the last decade.

General Economic Conditions

A fundamental truth about the economy is that it is very unpredictable. Even the experts cannot say with certainty what the future may hold. Nevertheless, some factors in the economy have a known influence on personal finances, and it's important for you to recognize these factors and incorporate them in your financial planning decisions. Throughout this course, you'll be developing a knowledge base related to many economic factors that affect financial planning. Some factors that are highly likely to affect your future are inflation, interest rates, employment conditions, political unrest, and global issues.

MONEY PSYCHOLOGY

Socioeconomic Differences in Risk Attitudes

Although there are many factors that might influence whether a person is more or less inclined to be a risk-taker, there have been many recent studies that attempt to quantify these differences. Finance and economics academics tend to focus on investment risk-taking, but researchers in psychology and sociology have taken a broader approach, looking at many dimensions of risk-taking, including risky decisions with respect to physical safety (seat-belt usage) or health (smoking). This diverse body of literature is by no means entirely consistent, but some relatively consistent trends have emerged. The table below summarizes the demographic and socioeconomic characteristics that have been found to be associated with greater risk-taking.

Characteristic	More Inclined to Take Risk	Less Inclined to Take Risk
Gender	Male	Female
Marital status	Single	Married
Age	Young	Old
Family type	No kids	One or more kids
Wealth	Wealthy	Poor
Employment	White-collar job	Blue-collar job
Income	High-income	Low-income
Education	College-educated	High school

Inflation. Everyone has at one time or another heard an older person say, "When I was a kid, it was a lot less expensive to. . . ." Such statements describe the effects of **inflation**, the change in general price levels over time. Occasionally, we have a negative inflation rate—that is, the prices of goods and services actually decline over a given period. Generally, however, inflation refers to an increase in prices. As prices of goods and services go up, the spending power of your money goes down—a dollar will not purchase as much as it previously did.

inflation

Change in the prices of goods and services over time.

Inflation affects nearly every aspect of your finances. Your grocery bills are probably higher this year than they were last year. You're likely paying more for gasoline than in the past. Your monthly rent will probably go up next year, too. As prices of goods get higher over time, you can only maintain your standard of living if your income after taxes also rises by the same amount. For your standard of living to improve, your income must rise at a rate *faster* than the inflation rate. Inflation affects your investments as well. If the costs of goods rise at a rate of 4 percent, but your savings account is only paying you 3 percent, then you are actually losing spending power.

Fact #3

A dollar today is usually worth more than a dollar tomorrow. Inflation implies that prices keep rising, so if you keep your money in a piggy bank, it won't buy as much in the future as it would today.

For the overall U.S. market, inflation is measured by the change in the **consumer price index (CPI)**, reported monthly by the Bureau of Labor Statistics. The CPI tracks prices of a representative basket of more than 400 goods and services used by urban households, including food, housing, consumer goods, gasoline, and clothing. Exhibit 1-2 illustrates the changing costs of various goods and services over the last 25 years. Whereas the price of a college education has tripled since 1980, that of gasoline has increased only 78 percent over the same period. Just for fun, we've also included the price of a new Ford Mustang. When they were first produced in 1966, the base sticker price was just $2,372 as compared to $18,775 in 2004.

consumer price index (CPI)

A measure of the price of a representative basket of household goods and services in the U.S. market.

Depending on various factors, you may experience a larger or smaller change in expenses than the price changes indicated by the CPI. For example, some areas of the country have higher rates of inflation than average, primarily because of higher fuel and housing costs. Housing in

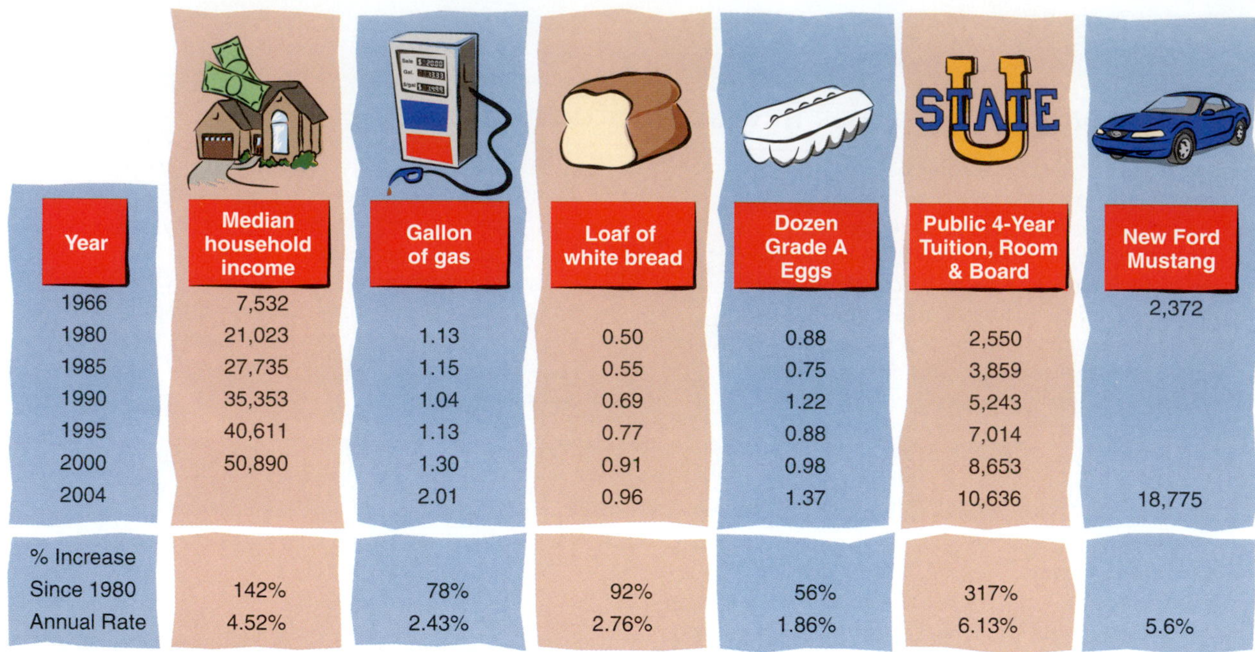

Year	Median household income	Gallon of gas	Loaf of white bread	Dozen Grade A Eggs	Public 4-Year Tuition, Room & Board	New Ford Mustang
1966	7,532					2,372
1980	21,023	1.13	0.50	0.88	2,550	
1985	27,735	1.15	0.55	0.75	3,859	
1990	35,353	1.04	0.69	1.22	5,243	
1995	40,611	1.13	0.77	0.88	7,014	
2000	50,890	1.30	0.91	0.98	8,653	
2004		2.01	0.96	1.37	10,636	18,775
% Increase Since 1980	142%	78%	92%	56%	317%	
Annual Rate	4.52%	2.43%	2.76%	1.86%	6.13%	5.6%

EXHIBIT 1-2 Changes in Income and Prices over Time

Sources: U.S. Census Bureau, *Statistical Abstract of the United States, 2003;* U.S. Department of Education, National Center for Education Statistics, *Digest of Education Statistics, 2003;* United States Bureau of Labor Statistics available at www.bls.gov.

areas of the country that are in high demand can be extremely costly. According to Chamber of Commerce reports for each city, in 2003 the median resale price of a home in St. Louis, Missouri, was only $104,900, whereas the median resale price in San Francisco, California, was $571,000.

You will also have different demands for goods and services at different stages in the life cycle. For example, health-care costs, which have risen at a much faster rate than other elements of the CPI, are a bigger component of a retiree's expenses—12.6 percent of total household expenses, compared with only 2.5 percent for those under age 25 and 4 percent for households aged 35 to 44. Housing costs, in contrast, have less importance for retirees, since many retirees have paid off their home mortgages. Furthermore, inflation can be particularly problematic for people on fixed incomes. If your retirement income doesn't increase over time, but your expenses do, your standard of living will gradually decline.

The price of a new Ford Mustang is now more than seven times its original 1966 sticker price of $2,372.

GO FIGURE!

Calculation of Percentage Change

Problem Your salary in 2003 was \$24,000, and in 2004, it increased to \$25,000. Your new salary for 2005 is \$27,500.

1. What was the percentage increase in your salary from 2004 to 2005?
2. What was the annual percentage increase in your salary from 2003 to 2005?

Solution
You will often find it useful to be able to measure how much something has increased in percent terms. Here are two ways to calculate such changes.

1. To calculate total increase over a period:

$$\text{Percentage change} = \frac{\text{New value} - \text{Old value}}{\text{Old value}}$$

$$\text{OR} = \frac{\text{New value}}{\text{Old value}} - 1$$

So for the first problem, the percentage increase in your salary is:

$$\text{Percentage change}_{2004 \text{ to } 2005} = \frac{27{,}500 - 25{,}000}{25{,}000}$$

$$= \frac{2{,}500}{25{,}000} = 0.1 \quad \text{or} \quad 10\%$$

Your salary increased 10% from 2004 to 2005.

2. To calculate annual percentage change over a longer time period:
   a. Calculate the percentage change over the entire period by either method above.
   b. Then calculate the annual percentage change as follows:

$$\text{Annual percentage change} = (1 + \text{Percentage change})^{1/N} - 1$$

where N = Number of years

Your salary in 2003 was \$24,000. Your salary in 2005 is \$27,500. By using the method above, the percentage change from 2003 to 2005 is calculated as

$$\text{Percentage change}_{2003 \text{ to } 2005} = \frac{\$27{,}500 - \$23{,}000}{\$23{,}000}$$

$$= 0.1458 \quad \text{or} \quad 14.58\%$$

Next, you can calculate the annual change as

$$\text{Annual percentage change}_{2003 \text{ to } 2005} = (1 + 0.1458)^{1/2} - 1 = 1.0704 - 1$$

$$= 0.0704 \quad \text{or} \quad 7.04\%$$

Note that, as an approximation, you can take individual annual changes and average them, but for longer time periods, this will be very time-consuming and will not be as accurate.
(*Note*: Most calculators will allow you to raise a number to any power using a key labeled y^x. Enter the number you want to raise to the power (e.g. 1.1458 in this case) push the y^x button, and then enter the power (e.g. 1/2, or 0.5).

The CPI on January 2004 was 185.2, which represented an increase from the January 2003 CPI of 182.2. To find the percentage increase, we divide the change in the CPI by the value it started from; this provides a measure of inflation over the period:

$$\text{Inflation in prices of goods and services, 2003–2004} = \frac{CPI_{2004} - CPI_{2003}}{CPI_{2003}}$$

$$= \frac{185.2 - 182.2}{182.2}$$

$$= 0.016 = 1.6\%$$

To learn more about the CPI, visit the website of the Bureau of Labor Statistics at www.bls.gov. In additional to including general educational material and articles, this governmental site includes a rich set of data covering a wide variety of statistics collected by government agencies over time—interest rates, average wages for various occupations, household spending patterns, and more.

In general, you can use the method outlined in the *Go Figure!* box "Calculation of Percentage Change" to calculate percentage increases (or decreases) for any variable, if you know the beginning and ending values. This is useful not only for the inflation calculation here but also for calculating percentage increases in your salary and investments over time.

Although inflation has averaged 4.8 percent per year since 1970, the annual rates of inflation have ranged from 1.2 to 13.3 percent. Over that same period, the minimum wage rate increased from \$1.60 to its current rate of \$5.15, the equivalent of only 3.6 percent per year. Similarly, the average wage for production workers in private industry has increased 4.3 percent. These statistics illustrate an important economic reality—wages don't always keep up with prices—and this is particularly true during periods of high inflation. For example, in 1979, when inflation hit a high of 13.3 percent, production workers' average wages that year increased only 8.5 percent. Since 8.5 percent probably seemed like a good raise at the time, it's likely that the average worker didn't realize that his or her standard of living had actually declined.

interest rate

Cost of borrowed money or return on invested money.

Interest Rates. An **interest rate** is a cost of money. Interest is usually expressed as a percentage of the amount lent or borrowed. When you borrow money, the interest rate is a cost to you. When you invest money, it is a measure of your earnings, or return, on that investment. Interest rates can also be thought of as a cost of consumption. How much additional money will you need to get in the future to be willing to *not* spend a certain amount today on consumption? For example, if your roommate asks you to lend him $1,000 and promises to pay you back exactly one year from now, how much will you require that he pay you at that time? If you have to take the money out of a savings account that pays you 4 percent interest per year, you'll probably want him to pay you at least the $1,000 plus 4 percent interest. But what if lending him the money means that you will have to forego that trip to Mexico over spring break? How much additional money in the future will it take to convince you to give up spending the money now on the trip?

Like the prices of goods and services, interest rates are driven by supply and demand. When there is a lot of demand for borrowing, but not a lot of money available to borrow, interest rates go up. In recessions, when businesses do not need or want to invest in growth, the demand for borrowing is lower, and rates may go down.

Federal Reserve Bank

The central bank in the United States, which controls the money supply.

federal funds rate

The rate that banks charge each other for short-term loans.

The **Federal Reserve Bank**—the central bank that controls the money supply in the United States—sometimes takes actions to increase or decrease the supply of money in the economy in order to manipulate the rate of interest on short-term, low-risk borrowed funds. For example, from 2000 to 2003, the Federal Reserve several times took action to lower the **federal funds rate**, the rate that banks charge each other for short-term loans, in an attempt to stimulate the sluggish economy. By reducing the rate from 6.5 to 1 .0 percent gradually over that time period, the Federal Reserve actions reduced short-term borrowing rates, which in turn resulted in lower commercial loan and mortgage loan rates. These actions helped to pull the country out of the recession. In June 2004, the Fed reversed this trend and began to increase rates.

In addition to actions by the Federal Reserve, inflation and other economic conditions cause interest rates to go up and down over time, as you can see in Exhibit 1-3. Since these factors in-

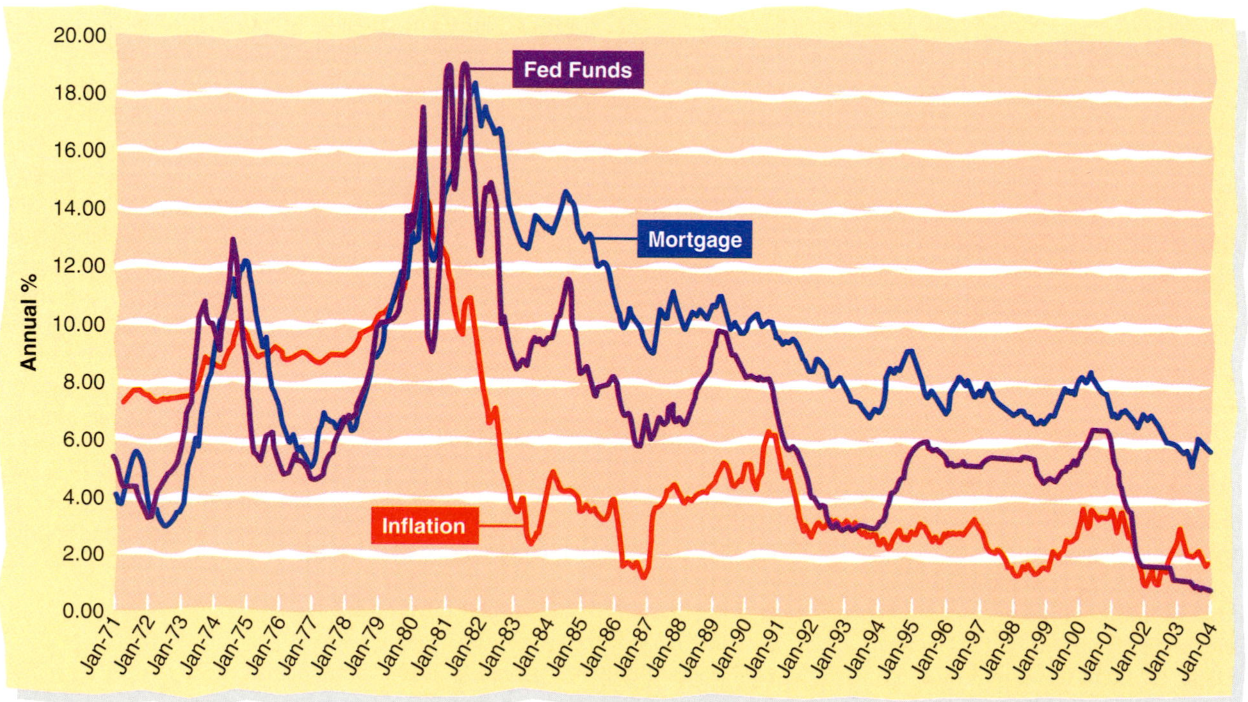

EXHIBIT 1-3 Inflation, Federal Funds, and Mortgage Rates, 1971 to 2004

fluence all types of borrowing, the interest rates on different types of borrowing tend to track each other closely. You can see that the 1982 recession was a high point for inflation as well as short-term borrowing rates and long-term home mortgage rates. Conversely, as the federal funds rate was lowered in 2003, average mortgage rates fell to a 40-year low, bottoming out at 5.23 percent in May 2003.

Although the ups and downs in interest rates tend to track each other, there are always differences among interest rates on various types of loans at any given time. These differences are primarily due to differences in risk. For example, what is the chance that payments will not be made on time or that the loan will not be repaid? The higher the chances, the riskier the loan and the higher the rate that will be charged by lenders. If the borrower does not pay the loan as agreed, does the lender have any way of recouping the loan? If not, the loan is riskier than it would otherwise be. Consumer loans are riskier in that the borrower is an individual rather than a financial institution and might be unable to pay if his or her financial situation changes in the future. However, car loans have much lower rates than credit cards, since the bank normally has the right to take back the car in the event of nonpayment. It's important to remember that the riskier the investment or loan, the higher the interest rate will be, since the lender or investor must be compensated for the risk of not being repaid. Since risk is so fundamental to personal financial decisions, we consider it in greater detail in later chapters.

You can visit the Federal Reserve System's website at www.federalreserve.gov. Each of the Fed's regional offices sponsors its own website, which includes valuable educational information for consumers. For example, check the site of the Federal Reserve Bank of San Francisco at www.frbsf.org and that of the Federal Reserve Bank of St. Louis at www.stlouisfed.org.

The Economic Cycle and Employment Conditions. Your personal finances will also be affected by cyclical business and employment conditions. Historically, the U.S. economy has experienced a pattern of ups and downs, commonly referred to as the **economic cycle**, or business cycle. A low point in the cycle is called a **recession** (or, in the extreme, a depression), and is characterized by reduced business investment and high unemployment rates. Economic **expansion** periods are characterized by increased business investment and employment opportunities. In times of growth and low unemployment, salaries tend to rise more quickly, and there are better opportunities for advancement. During the technology boom of the 1990s, for example, even undistinguished computer sciences majors had multiple job offers at graduation and were constantly bombarded by headhunters trying to entice them to different jobs for better pay and benefits. A few years later, new graduates in these fields were happy to get any job at all. Widespread layoffs at technology firms meant that they were competing in the job market with individuals who had many more years of experience.

economic cycle

A pattern of ups and downs in the level of economic activity.

recession

A phase in the economic cycle characterized by reduced business investment and increasing unemployment.

expansion

A phase in the economic cycle characterized by increased business investment and increasing employment opportunities.

Your future will be less sensitive to changes in employment conditions if you choose an area of study that is likely to have continuing strong demand over time. You can also minimize the risk of layoff by keeping your skills up-to-date. We return to this topic and other issues related to career planning in Chapter 3.

Political Unrest and Global Issues. It should be obvious that political and global factors can affect your personal finances. For some time following September 11, 2001, the looming threat of terrorism had a negative impact on the U.S. economy. The stock market, which had already seen substantial declines from its high of the previous year, continued to plummet, losing more than 20 percent of its value from September 2001 to September 2002; unemployment increased rapidly; and governmental spending on homeland security cut into state budgets.

How have these factors affected your personal finances? Here are some examples:

- You may have benefited from lower interest rates on student loans and car loans that resulted from the Federal Reserve's interest rate reductions. The resulting economic growth will cause rates to go up in the future.
- Your university tuition is likely higher this year than last, and such increases can be expected into the indefinite future as a result of state budget deficits that are cutting into state support for higher education.
- In some areas of the country, it may still be difficult to find employment.
- During the Iraq war and occupation, members of the National Guard who were called into service faced unexpected financial burdens, such as the need to make arrangements for child care.

The lesson from this brief review of general economic conditions is clear. Because no one can predict what the future may hold, it is extremely important to have a financial plan that is adaptable to changing circumstances. In addition, you should attempt to keep up on changing economic conditions—reading the paper regularly or subscribing to a news or financial magazine—so that you can take appropriate actions when necessary.

Learning by Doing 1-2

1. Your employer has just given you a 4 percent annual raise. Explain why the following information might be important:
   a. The average raise in the United States for your profession was 3 percent.
   b. Inflation averaged 5 percent.
2. Your school just announced a tuition increase of 10 percent for next year. Tuition represents 25 percent of your $16,000 total college costs this year. If you expect your remaining costs to increase by only 5 percent, what is the expected percentage increase in your total college costs for next year?

Elements of a Comprehensive Financial Plan

LEARNING objective

4 Understand how the elements of a comprehensive financial plan fit together.

In this course, you will begin the process of building a comprehensive, integrated financial plan. Critical to the success of this plan is that you approach its creation in a logical order. The "steps to success" in Exhibit 1-4 illustrates the elements of a comprehensive financial plan. The material presented in this book parallels the steps as follows:

- Foundation. Acquire necessary tools and skills—Chapters 1 to 4.
- Securing basic needs. Short-term planning for security and liquidity—Chapters 5 to 10.
- Wealth building. Long-term planning to meet future needs—Chapters 11 to 15.
- Wealth protection. Insurance and estate planning to protect income and assets—Chapters 16 to 17.

Your first step to success in your personal finances will be to establish the necessary foundations, including an understanding of the personal financial planning process, the necessary tools, and the tax effects of your financial decisions. The second step will be to secure your basic needs. This step will include meeting your consumption and housing needs, setting aside funds for financial emergencies, protecting your assets with insurance, establishing a career path, and making educated employee benefit decisions. Once basic needs have been secured, you can begin to think about wealth building to meet future needs, such as retirement and college funding. With financial security comes the need to protect your wealth. The final step therefore includes the protective elements of life insurance, long-term care insurance, and estate planning.

Learning by Doing 1-3

Identify where you think each of the following fits in a comprehensive financial plan (Foundation, Securing Basic Needs, Wealth Building, or Wealth Protection):

1. Career development
2. Checking and savings accounts
3. Stock investing
4. Retirement plan
5. Life insurance

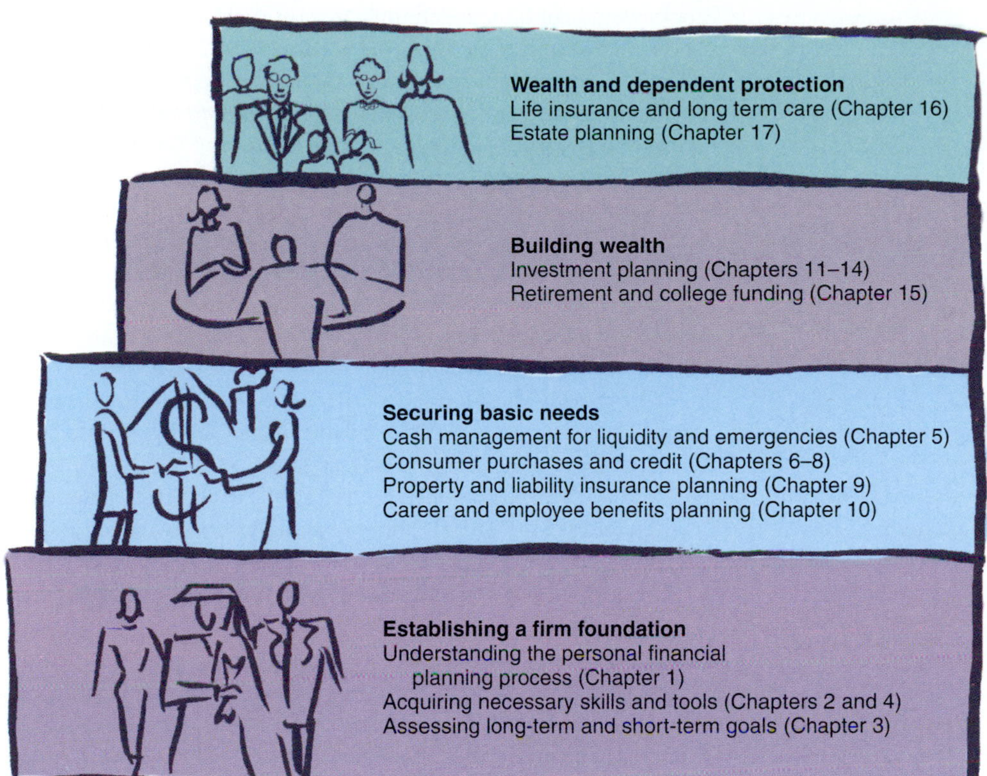

EXHIBIT 1-4

Components of a Comprehensive Financial Plan

Making Effective Decisions

LEARNING objective

5 Consider opportunity costs and marginal effects in making personal finance decisions.

As you work on your financial plan, you'll be making many important decisions. Once you've identified your goals, you'll need to make decisions about consumption, savings, and investment alternatives. These decisions will more effectively help you achieve your goals if you use these decision-making strategies:

- Base your decisions on reasonable assumptions.
- Apply marginal reasoning.
- Consider opportunity costs.
- Use sensitivity analysis.

Let's look at each of these strategies in more detail.

Make Reasonable Assumptions

Most financial decisions require you to forecast, or predict, future events and economic circumstances: What will your needs be 5 or 10 or even 20 years from now? What will your family circumstances require from you financially? When will you retire? How long will you live? Which investments will perform better over time? What will the rate of inflation be in the future? What rate of return will you earn on your investments? What kinds of risks will you face?

Life is, of course, unpredictable. But even if you don't know an outcome for certain, you can still use the information available to you to come up with a reasonable assumption. This is a critical component of successful decision making.

One of the biggest mistakes people make in their finances is that they are too optimistic in their assumptions. During the 1990s, for example, the stock market enjoyed a long period of strong growth. Investors who had never experienced a market downturn actually thought that

Fact #4

The Internet is a good source of information for financial planning decisions. In addition to the multitude of information provided on federal government and agency websites, many for-profit companies include educational material on their websites in order to attract a wider audience for their products.

stocks would continue indefinitely to earn such high rates of return. Unreasonably optimistic investors eventually lost a large percentage of their investment portfolios when the market declined.

Consider an example: Karen and Luke Amato were planning to retire in 2001, when both would reach the age of 65. They had invested all their retirement funds in the stock market over the 1990s, accumulating a total portfolio of about $1.5 million by the time the market reached its peak, an amount they thought would be more than adequate to meet their expected retirement needs. Unfortunately, one year later they had to reconsider their plans, as the value of their retirement nest egg had fallen by more than a third, to less than $1 million. Although the Amatos might have limited their losses by moving their money to safer investments earlier, they, like many other investors, had unrealistically clung to the hope that the stock market would recover. In fact, they were lucky—some investors experienced much larger losses. If they had applied more realistic assumptions based on a longer-term history of stock market returns, the Amatos and others might have avoided such extreme losses and been able to retire as they had planned.

Apply Marginal Reasoning

marginal reasoning

Analysis that considers the increased benefit which would result from a particular decision.

In choosing among potential strategies to achieve your financial goals, it is important to apply **marginal reasoning**. The term "marginal" refers to the *change* in outcome, or the *additional* benefit, that will result from the decision you make. For example, suppose you and your spouse share a car and you're considering buying a second car. In applying marginal analysis, you will consider only the additional benefits that the second car brings and not the general benefits of having a car in the first place. Similarly, if you're choosing between two possible cars, you'll consider how much extra benefit you would get from the more expensive of the two and balance that against the extra cost.

Consider Opportunity Costs

opportunity cost

What you have to give up in order to take a particular action.

sensitivity analysis

Estimation of the change in outcome that results from a change in assumptions.

Every financial decision you make has an **opportunity cost**—a measure of what you have to give up in order to take a particular action. The opportunity cost often is measured in dollars but may also include less quantifiable costs, like your time and effort. For example, suppose you're faced with the decision of whether to take money from savings for your college education or to work while attending school to earn the money. If you choose to take money from savings, you'll be giving up what you could have earned on that investment—this is your opportunity cost. But if you otherwise would have to work 30 hours per week while you attend school, the lost investment earnings might be small relative to the personal costs you would incur—less time and energy to apply to your studies and extracurricular activities. Evaluating opportunity costs carefully results in better decisions.

What kind of decision maker are you?

Use Sensitivity Analysis

Suppose you are deciding on the purchase of a new home. Although the loan payment will be a bit of a stretch for you the first year, you anticipate that you will get a good raise next year, which will make the payment affordable. But what if this assumption is wrong—what if you do *not* get the raise or, even worse, are laid off from your job? **Sensitivity analysis** asks the question "What effect would it have on my personal finances if my assumptions turn out to be wrong?" By considering how the outcome changes with changes in other uncertain variables, you can reduce the risk that your plan will have an adverse impact on your finances.

Psychology research has shown that people exhibit different decision-making styles, many of which result in less than optimal outcomes. Several of these are discussed in the *Money Psychology* box "Decision-Making Styles." Even if you are naturally inclined to make decisions in a different way, you can still learn to apply the strategies and tools discussed in this section and throughout the chapter in order to make more effective decisions.

MONEY PSYCHOLOGY

Decision-Making Styles

Your style of decision making can have a big impact on the way that you approach your finances and also on the likelihood of your getting into financial trouble. Psychologists often classify people on a continuum based on how they approach and solve problems. Some people have a natural inclination to think through decisions carefully before they take action, whereas others have a tendency to make snap decisions without careful consideration of their alternatives or the consequences of their decision. There are also people who simply avoid making decisions as much as possible. Consider each of the following and decide which best describes your style of decision making:

1. Rational decision makers. People who use a systematic approach to making decisions. They will weigh the pros and cons, often making careful lists for comparison.
2. Intuitive decision makers. People who go with their "gut" feeling in making a decision. This type of spontaneous approach is often justified by them if their instincts in the past have turned out to be correct.
3. External decision makers. People who rely on talking over a situation with others. They tend to collect opinions from several people and go with the consensus viewpoint. They may have trouble making independent decisions.
4. Agonizers. People who intentionally delay making decisions, often spending excessive amounts of time thinking over their alternatives, even for relatively inconsequential decisions.
5. Avoiders. People who are *not* decision makers and try to avoid making decisions whenever possible. They may pass the decision to others or they may simply ignore it, hoping it will go away.

Although no perfect method of decision making exists for everyone, there are advantages and disadvantage to certain types. If you're an avoider or if you're overly spontaneous in making financial decisions you may:

- Have trouble sticking to a budget
- Be in too much debt
- Pay too much for major purchases
- Incur personal costs from taking too many wrong turns in life

If you're an overly "rational" decision maker or an agonizer, you may also have negative consequences, such as:

- Missed opportunities because you take too long to make a decision
- Reduced investment returns
- Missed career advancement opportunities
- Increased personal costs due to time and effort spent on decision making.

To take an online decision-making style assessment, go to www.acu.edu/campusoffices/careercounseling/CareerAssessments/decision.html.

Learning by Doing 1-4

You're choosing whether to go to graduate school at State University, an in-state college, or Private University, an out-of-state college. These schools are similar in size and ranking. The tuition at State is $5,000 per year, and the tuition at Private is $25,000 per year. Other expenses at both schools are comparable.

1. Explain how you would consider opportunity costs in making this decision.
2. Explain how marginal reasoning can be applied to this decision.

Selecting Qualified Financial Planning Professionals

LEARNING objective

6 Understand when and how to select qualified financial planning professionals.

Although a course in personal financial planning will provide you with the basic tools and knowledge to handle your own finances, you will by no means be an expert at the end of the semester. Many areas of personal finance, such as tax and estate planning, are fairly specialized and have complex rules that tend to change over time.

As your life and finances become more complicated, you may need to get some professional help with financial matters. If so, you have many choices. Lawyers, accountants, insurance agents, and stockbrokers can all assist with aspects of your plan that are within their realms of expertise. Alternatively, rather than obtaining piecemeal help for a single issue at a time, you may want to consider hiring a professional financial planner who has a broad education in all areas of financial planning. This type of professional can help you to develop your plan from the outset and to implement strategies to achieve your financial goals. Since virtually anyone can claim to be a financial planner, you'll need to carefully evaluate the educational credentials and certifications of any professional you are considering hiring.

What Are the Factors to Consider in Choosing a Planner?

In choosing a professional to help you with your personal finances, you should consider the following factors:

- Education
- Certification(s)
- Experience
- Reputation

Planners may come from a number of different educational backgrounds, but a solid knowledge of law, finance, insurance, and tax accounting will ensure that they can handle all the components of your plan. This education may come from specific degree programs, or be gained through experience or specialized study programs leading to certifications.

A number of different organizations provide certifications attesting to the knowledge base of a professional planner. Certification requirements and contact information for several accrediting organizations are provided in Exhibit 1-5. The best-known and most rigorous certification is the Certified Financial Planner (CFP™) designation. Planners who have a CFP™ mark after their names have passed a 10-hour, two-day exam covering all the topic areas considered necessary in the practice of financial planning, and they have at least three years' work experience in the field. In addition, to maintain their designation, they must adhere to a rigorous code of ethics, summarized in the *News You Can Use* box "CFP-Board Code of Ethics and Professional Responsibility," and fulfill continuing education requirements.

Fact #5

You don't have to have a business degree—or even a college degree—to be a financial planner. Many financial services firms say they prefer to recruit liberal arts majors, since they find that these students have, on average, better communications skills. If you're hiring a planner, however, you may find that those with finance degrees will have greater depth of knowledge about financial products.

The Chartered Financial Consultant (ChFC) designation is given to individuals who have completed a program of study offered by the American College in Bryn Mawr, Pennsylvania. Although there is no certification examination requirement, a person with a ChFC has completed a series of at least eight courses covering all the fundamental financial planning areas. A person who already has a CFP™ can obtain the ChFC upon completion of three additional courses. The American College also offers specialized certifications in life insurance (CLU), property and casualty insurance (CPCU), and health insurance (RHU).

The Association for Financial Counseling and Planning Education (AFCPE) offers the Accredited Financial Counselor (AFC) designation for individuals who pass required examinations and adhere to their code of professional ethics.

Tax specialists may have a Certified Public Accountant (CPA) designation, which is obtained by passing a national comprehensive accounting examination after completion of a four-year degree program or masters program in accounting. The AICPA, the certifying organization for CPAs, also offers a special designation, Personal Financial Specialist (PFS), for accountants specializing in financial planning. Lawyers all have a J.D. degree, but may also obtain an additional degree (L.L.M.) with a tax or estate planning specialization. In addition to optional professional designations, any professional who sells financial products, such as a stockbroker or insurance agent, will be required to pass examinations required by federal and/or state law.

Exhibit 1-5 gives website addresses and contact information for organizations that provide certification and education for financial planners.

Sponsoring Organization	Designation	Requirements: Course Work	Work Experience	Compulsory Exam	Ethics Code	Continuing Education	Contact Information
CFP™ Board of Standards and Practices	Certified Financial Planner, CFP™	Yes	Yes	Yes	Yes	Yes	www.cfp-board.org
American College	Chartered Financial Consultant, ChFC	Yes	No	No		No	www.amercoll.edu
American Institute of Certified Public Accountants	Certified Public Accountant, CPA	Yes	Yes	Yes	Yes	Yes	www.aicpa.org
	Certified Financial Analyst, CFA	Yes	Yes	Yes	Yes	Yes	
	Accredited Estate Planner (AEP)		Yes		Yes		
National Endowment for Financial Education and the Investment Company Institute	Mutual Fund Chartered Counselor (MFCC)	Yes		Yes	Yes		www.nefe.org
Association for Financial Counseling and Planning Education	Accredited Financial Counselor (AFC)	Yes		Yes	Yes	Yes	www.afcpe.org
AICPA Personal Financial Planning Division	Accredited Personal Financial Planning Specialist (CPA-APFS)	Yes	Yes	Yes	Yes	Yes	www.aicpa.org
Financial Planning Association	Membership organization (CFPs)	No	No	No	Yes	No	www.fpa.org
National Association of Personal Financial Advisors	Membership organization (fee-only planners)	No	No	No	Yes	No	www.napfa.org
International Association of Registered Planners	Registered Financial Planner (RFP)	Yes		Yes	Yes	Yes	www.iarfc.org

EXHIBIT 1-5 Financial Planning Organizations and Certifications

How Are Planners Paid?

With so many different types of professionals calling themselves financial planners, it should come as no surprise that there is some variation in the ways in which planners are paid. The two basic compensation arrangements are commissions and fees, but several combinations are possible:

- Fee only. The planner charges based on services provided. This may be a set fee for a particular service (such as $150 to write a will), an hourly fee for services rendered ($50–$200 per hour), or an annual fee that is a percentage (typically 1%) of the client's assets being managed.
- Commission only. The planner receives no payment for helping you develop your financial plan, but receives a commission when you buy a financial product, such as a mutual fund or insurance. Although this may be the cheapest way to get a professional to help you with your financial plan, you must take into account the planner's inherent conflict of interest before acting on his or her product recommendations. Because the planner will have an incentive to sell you high-commission products, you will need to comparison shop before buying anything.
- Fee plus commission. The planner charges a fee for developing your financial plan and also receives commissions on any financial products sold to you. The fee for the plan may be lower than that charged in a fee-only arrangement.

NEWS you can use

CFP-Board Code of Ethics and Professional Responsibility

If you're concerned about the integrity of financial advisors, consider hiring a Certified Financial Planner™. This group of professionals subscribes to a rigorous Code of Ethics and Professional Responsibility, and a member can lose the CFP™ designation for violating any of the following requirements:

- Integrity. Financial planners must be trustworthy.
- Objectivity. Financial planners must be intellectually honest and impartial.
- Competence. Financial planners must maintain the necessary knowledge and skill to give appropriate advice to clients, or seek outside help when necessary.
- Fairness. Financial planners must disclose conflicts of interest and treat others without regard to personal bias or desire.
- Confidentiality. Financial planners must not disclose client information to others unless required to by a court of law.
- Professionalism. Financial planners should always conduct their activities in a way that enhances and maintains the profession's public image.
- Diligence. Financial planners shall render services in a reasonably prompt and thorough manner.

A CFP™ must be intellectually honest and impartial.

Source: Adapted from the website of the Financial Planners Standards Council, www.cfp-ca.org/public/public_codeofethicssynopsis.asp. Published by Financial Planners Standards Council (FPSC), 2003, used by permission. The Financial Planners Standards Council controls CFP™ licensing in Canada.

- Fee offset by commission. The planner charges a fee for services as in a fee-only arrangement, but will offset some of the fee for commissions earned on products. This reduces the conflict of interest inherent in the commission-only arrangement, since the planner does not make extra money by selling you the financial products.

When Do You Need a Financial Planner?

Not everyone needs—or can afford—the services of a professional financial planner. If you earn less than $50,000 a year, have little wealth, and have relatively uncomplicated taxes, you probably don't need to hire a professional. As with other financial decisions, you should consider the marginal benefits of paying for financial advice, as well as the opportunity costs. For wealthier people, if the advice given by the planner results in marginal increases in investment earnings or reductions in taxes, these gains may offset the planner's fees. For others, the benefit may be largely psychological, since hiring a professional reduces the time and effort required to stay informed about financial matters such as investments, taxes, and insurance. People who find that they like managing their own finances may decide that they need to consult professionals only for special needs, such as drawing up legal documents or filing taxes.

Even if you hire a planner, you'll still have to be involved in the planning process to develop goals and decide among various strategies to achieve them. The planning process followed by financial planners is much the same as the personal financial planning process that you will use in this course. Tips for selecting a financial planner appear in the *Ask the Expert* box "How to Select a Financial Planner."

Learning by Doing 1-5

1. You have a friend who just graduated from college with a liberal arts major. He has a new job as a financial planner at a local brokerage firm. You are thinking of hiring a professional to help with your financial planning needs. Would your friend be a good choice? Why or why not?

ask the expert How to Select a Financial Planner

The Financial Planners Standards Council suggests the following ten tips to help you find the right planner:

1. Know what you want. Determine your general financial goals and specific needs.
2. Be prepared. Read the newspapers and finance publications to maximize your familiarity with financial planning strategies and terminology.
3. Talk to others. Get referrals from advisors you trust, from colleagues and friends.
4. Look for competence. Many degrees and designations are held by individuals working in financial planning and investment services. Choose a professional such as a Certified Financial Planner licensee who has met high skill standards and abides by a code of ethics.
5. Interview more than one planner. Ask all planners to outline their education, experience, and specialties, the size and duration of their practices, how often they communicate with clients, and whether assistants handle client matters. Make sure you feel comfortable discussing your finances with the individual you select.
6. Check the planner's background. Depending on the planner's background, call his or her professional associations to check on a complaint record and to see if the planner is in good standing with his or her certifying organization.
7. Ask for references. Find out if the financial planner works with any other professionals such as accountants, insurance agents, or legal advisors. Request references from these individuals as well.
8. Know what to expect. Ask for a registration or disclosure document detailing method of compensation, conflicts of interest, business affiliations, and personal qualifications.
9. Get it in writing. Request a written advisory contract or engagement letter to document the nature and scope of services the planner will provide. You should also understand how the planner will be compensated.
10. Reassess the relationship regularly. Financial planning relationships are quite often long-term. Review your relationship on a regular basis, making sure your planner understands your needs as they change and develop over time.

Source: Adapted from the website of the Financial Planners Standards Council, www.cfp-ca.org/public/public_choosingaplanner.asp. Published by Financial Planners Standards Council (FPSC), 2003, used by permission. The FPSC controls CFP™ Licensing in Canada.

Summary

1 Recognize the importance of studying personal finance. Personal finance is the study of individual and household financial decisions, and includes such topics as budgeting, saving, tax planning, financing major purchases, buying insurance, and investing to achieve long-term goals. The primary purpose of studying personal financial planning is to help you develop and achieve your financial goals in these and other areas. Many people avoid financial matters because they lack the necessary skills or are overwhelmed by the process and, as a result, may experience negative financial outcomes and psychological distress.

2 Describe the five steps in the personal financial planning process. The personal financial planning process includes five steps: (1) Analyze your current finances; (2) develop specific goals; (3) identify and evaluate possible strategies for meeting your goals; (4) establish and implement your plan; and (5) reevaluate and revise your plan as needed.

3 Identify the factors that influence personal financial planning decisions. Personal financial planning decisions are affected by family circumstances, changing needs over the life cycle, values and attitudes, and general economic conditions such as inflation, interest rates, employment, political unrest, and global factors.

4 Understand how the elements of a comprehensive financial plan fit together. A comprehensive financial plan can be seen as steps to success: (1) Establish a firm foundation by acquiring the necessary tools (understanding the process, analytical tools, and taxes) and establishing goals; (2) secure basic needs (consumption and housing, liquidity, property and liability insurance, employee benefits, and career development); (3) build wealth through saving and investment; (4) protect your wealth and dependents by planning for death and incapacity.

5 Consider opportunity costs and marginal effects in making personal finance decisions. In comparing multiple alternatives for achieving the same goal, you should always consider the opportunities that might be lost under each alternative, whether in time, effort, or money. Using marginal reasoning, you should weigh the additional benefit to be received from one possible alternative action compared with another. Your decisions will also benefit by the application of sensitivity analysis, in which you evaluate what would happen if your initial assumptions are incorrect.

6 Understand when and how to select qualified financial planning professionals. Although you don't necessarily need to seek professional help for your personal financial planning, if you do decide to hire a financial planning professional, you should first carefully evaluate the person's educational credentials, certifications, reputation, and fee structure.

Key Terms

attitudes (8)
consumer price index (CPI) (9)
economic cycle (13)
expansion (13)
federal funds rate (12)
Federal Reserve Bank (12)
inflation (9)
interest rate (12)
marginal reasoning (16)
opportunity cost (16)
personal finance (3)
personal financial planning (3)
recession (13)
risk (8)
sensitivity analysis (16)
values (7)

Key Calculations

$$\text{Percentage change} = \frac{\text{New value} - \text{Old value}}{\text{Old value}}$$

$$\text{OR} = \frac{\text{New value}}{\text{Old value}} - 1$$

$$\text{Annual percentage change} = (1 + \text{Percentage change})^{1/N} - 1$$

where N = Number of years

Concept Review Questions

1. What is financial literacy, and why do you think that the general level of financial literacy in the United States is so low?
2. Explain why people often avoid financial planning even when they know it's important to their future.
3. Name three benefits that you're likely to gain by having a better understanding of personal finance.
4. Define *personal financial planning*, and give three examples of personal financial planning decisions.
5. Describe the five steps in the personal financial planning process.
6. Give an example of a personal financial goal that you have today that will probably change in the future. Explain.
7. What are the potential costs of failing to manage your finances appropriately?
8. Explain how your financial planning needs are likely to change over your life cycle.
9. How does your attitude toward risk affect your financial decisions?
10. Where does a person's money style come from?
11. Why do banks pay interest rates on bank savings accounts that are so much lower than the rates you can earn on other types of investments?
12. What is inflation, and how can it affect your personal finances?
13. Why might inflation affect you differently at different points in your life cycle? Give an example.
14. Why does the Federal Reserve Bank take actions to increase or decrease interest rates?
15. Give an example of how general economic conditions can have an adverse impact on your personal finances.
16. Why is it important to establish a foundation and take care of basic needs before beginning to invest?
17. For each component of a comprehensive financial plan, identify a decision that must be made.
18. Explain what is meant by marginal analysis and give an example.
19. Give an example of an opportunity cost.
20. What factors should you consider in selecting a financial planning professional?
21. What are the advantages of using a fee-only planner compared with a commission-based planner?

Application Problems

1. ***Personal Financial Planning Process.*** Allen has just graduated from college and is considering the purchase of a new or used car. Describe how Allen can use the personal financial planning process in making this purchase.
2. ***Inflation.*** If your expenses total $20,000 in 2005 and you expect inflation to be 3 percent, how much more will you have to spend to buy the same goods and services in 2006, assuming that all your expenses increase at the same rate as inflation?
3. ***Inflation.*** The January 2004 CPI was 185.2. If the January 2005 CPI was 190.8, what was the inflation rate for 2004? Optional: Look up the CPI for January 2005 and calculate the actual inflation rate for that year.
4. ***Percentage Change.*** Your starting salary in 2005 is $30,000. If you receive a raise of $5,000 for 2006, what is your percentage change in salary?
5. ***Annual Percentage Change.*** You purchase a house in 2000 for $100,000. In 2005, the house is worth $250,000. What was the annual increase in value?
6. ***Federal Reserve.*** Under what circumstances might the Federal Reserve take action to increase short-term interest rates?
7. ***Interest Rates and Risk.*** Put the following investments in order from highest to lowest interest rate:
   a. Credit card held by a person who frequently makes late payments
   b. Car loan to a person with perfect credit
   c. Student loan
   d. Bank savings account

   Explain why you put them in that order.
8. ***Changing Life Circumstances.*** Identify three areas of your personal financial plan that you expect will change when you graduate from college. For each area, give a specific example.

9. ***Opportunity Cost.*** Janelle has asked her friend Danny to drive her to the airport, which is a 60-mile round trip, so that she can save the $20 cost of the shuttle bus. Danny will have to miss his personal finance class in order to take her there. If Janelle is willing to pay Danny for this service, how much should he charge? What are his opportunity costs in addition to the cost of gas?

10. ***Life Cycle Effects.*** For each of the following stages in the life cycle, identify two areas of financial planning that will be particularly important.
    - **a.** Single college student
    - **b.** Young married couple with two children under the age of 5
    - **c.** Double-income couple with children in college
    - **d.** Recently retired couple

Using Web Resources for Financial Planning

1. ***General Web Resources.*** Throughout this course, we will be visiting many excellent websites for financial planning. To get your feet wet by navigating through some of the most comprehensive sites, go to each of the following websites and find the information requested:
    - **a.** *www.money.cnn.com:* Use the saving calculator to figure out how much savings you will have 20 years from now if you invest $50 per month.
    - **b.** *www.kiplinger.com:* Click on "Tools" and use the calculator to find out how much you should set aside for emergencies.
    - **c.** *finance.yahoo.com:* What is the current value of one of the three major U.S. stock market indexes (S&P 500, NASDAQ, and Dow), and how much has it changed in the past year?
    - **d.** *www.fool.com:* What tips does Motley Fool suggest to help you reduce your tax bill this year?
    - **e.** *www.aarp.org:* How can you determine your credit score?
2. ***Inflation.*** To see if your grandfather was exaggerating when he told you that milkshakes were only 50 cents when he was a boy, check out the inflation calculator at *www.woodrow.mpls.frb.fed.us.* Try the following exercises:
    - **a.** If your parent earned $20,000 per year in 1983, what would that be worth in today's dollars?
    - **b.** If a movie ticket cost 25 cents in 1970, what should it cost in today's dollars?
    - **c.** The original Volkswagen Beetle sold for $2,000 in 1970 and the new Beetle costs $20,000 today. Has the price increased more or less than inflation?
    - **d.** What was the average inflation rate in the1980s? the 1990s?
3. ***Financial Planning Careers.*** Go to the website for the Certified Financial Planning Board at *www.cfp-board.org* and click on "Learn About Financial Planning." After reading the information there, consider whether financial planning might be a career interest for you.
4. ***Keeping Tabs on Economic Conditions.*** There are many excellent sources for economic data, including several of the financial websites listed in item 1. In some cases, it's best to get your information directly from a government-sponsored website. Go to each of the following sites and find the information requested:
    - **a.** How have prices changed in your state over the past year? Go to *www.bls.gov* for CPI data from the Bureau of Labor Statistics. To calculate how much prices have changed nationally, click on the "Inflation Calculator" and follow the directions. At this site, you can also look up the current level of unemployment in your state.
    - **b.** A comprehensive source for links to all kinds of federal statistics can be found at *www.fedstats.gov.* Click on "Topic Links A–Z" and browse for whatever you are interested in. Find the latest interest rates at *www.federalreserve.gov.* and tax information at *www.irs.gov/individuals.*
5. ***Just for Fun.*** In case you're already getting tired of financial planning, take a break with fun and games at *www.ihatefinancialplanning.com/games.* Try out "Name That Term," a financial vocabulary game, or "Weight in Gold" to measure your true worth.

Learning by Doing Solutions

LBD 1-1: 1. Step 3: You have identified two alternatives for achieving career goals and must evaluate which job will best help you meet your goals; 2. Step 5: You will have to reevaluate your financial plan in light of your growing family. This will require that you go back to Steps 1-4; 3. Step 4: You are implementing a plan for reducing credit card debt.

LBD 1-2: 1. A raise that is greater than the average represents an improvement in your position relative to peers in your profession; 2. You actually have less purchasing power than you did in the previous year despite the fact that you got a raise.

LBD 1-3: 1. Foundation; 2. Securing Basic Needs; 3. Wealth Building; 4. Wealth Building; 5. Wealth Protection.

LBD 1-4: 1. The opportunity cost of attending the more expensive graduate school is the earnings you could make on the additional $20,000 per year or the additional cost of borrowing the money; 2. Marginal analysis requires that you consider the additional benefit you would get from going out of state compared to in state and consider whether that benefit is worth the additional cost of $20,000 per year. Some additional benefits might be location, access to employment, different programs offered at the schools, difference in student body make-up, scholarship availability.

LBD 1-5: 1. Pro: He's your friend so you may feel comfortable talking with him. Con: He lacks experience, certification, and training. His liberal arts degree probably included very few areas of study that are relevant to financial planning. You may not be comfortable revealing your personal financial information to a friend.

Building Financial Planning Skills Through Case Application

Case 1-1 And Then There Were Three—A Baby Changes Everything

Kenny and Ellen were married during their senior year in college. They planned and saved $3,000 for a honeymoon trip to Europe after graduation. They both have offers for jobs that begin in July. Two months before graduation, they discover that Ellen is pregnant.

a. Should they change their honeymoon plans?

b. Explain why they should reevaluate this decision based on the change in their life circumstances.

Case 1-2 Living on the Edge—What Happens If the Car Breaks Down?

Miranda is a single mother of two, struggling to make ends meet. Her salary of $40,000, after taxes and child-care expenses, doesn't go very far. Miranda is a careful budgeter, and she has been setting aside $40 per month for Christmas presents for her kids. By October, she is proud to have $400 in her savings account. And then disaster strikes. Her car breaks down, and the mechanic tells her the cost of fixing it will be $350.

a. What are Miranda's options?

b. What are some ways that Miranda might lessen the impact of financial emergencies in the future?

Case 1-3 Costs and Benefits of Graduate School

Sanjay is currently employed as an engineer at a major technology firm and earns $50,000. He thinks that an MBA degree will increase his chances of being promoted to a management position. He is trying to decide whether to enroll in a part-time evening program that will take two years or in a one-year full-time MBA program.

a. Identify the factors that Sanjay should consider in making this decision.

b. What are the opportunity costs of each alternative?

c. Does he need any additional information to make an effective decision? If so, what?

d. How can marginal reasoning be applied to this analysis?

DEVELOPING PERSONAL FINANCIAL skills for life

As you work through this text, the exercises in the Developing Personal Financial Skills for Life section at the end of each chapter will give you the opportunity to apply the chapter's content to developing your own personal financial plan. In addition, many chapters will include brief, informal assessments that will help you to learn more about yourself and your financial habits and attitudes. In most cases, worksheets for the exercises are also included in the *Personal Financial Planner*.

Learning About Yourself

1-1. Assessing Your Values and Attitudes Toward Money

For each of the following statements, write the number that shows the extent to which the statement accurately describes your views (5 = strongly agree; 4 = agree; 3 = undecided; 2 = disagree; 1 = strongly disagree):

_____ **1.** I would be a lot happier if I had more money.

_____ **2.** I usually buy things after they are marked down, and it bothers me when I discover an item I just purchased on sale for less somewhere else.

_____ **3.** I love it when I get a small windfall of money, like a tax refund or birthday gift, so I can spend it on something I usually don't have the money for.

_____ **4.** Whenever possible, I use coupons at the grocery store, and I always look through ads to find the best deals on the items I buy regularly.

_____ **5.** If I see something that I want to buy and I have the money at the time, I usually go ahead and buy it rather than waiting to get it as a birthday or Christmas present.

_____ **6.** Whenever I make a major purchase, I always feel guilty that I didn't save the money instead.

_____ **7.** It would be worth it to me to pay a little more for brand-name clothing since the right clothes are important to how people perceive me at work and school.

_____ **8.** I argue or complain about the cost of things.

_____ **9.** I like to buy nice things for other people during the holidays, even if it means I exceed my budget a bit—my friends and family are worth it.

_____ **10.** I worry about my finances.

Scoring

This assessment tells you the degree to which money is a controlling factor in your life. The odd-numbered questions relate to the degree to which you are focused on what money can buy. The even-numbered questions relate to the degree that money adds stress and worry to your life.

Total your scores for each group of questions:

Total for odds: #1, #3, #5, #7, #9 _______________

Total for evens: #2, #4, #6, #8, #10 _______________

Overall total _______________

Your total for the odd-numbered questions may range from 5 to 25. If you are on the low end of this scale, money and the things it can buy are less important to you. If your score is between 20 and 25, you have a tendency to value material things and you have difficulty delaying the gratification you get from spending money. Your total for the even-numbered questions may also range from 5 to 25. If your total is 20 to 25, money and financial matters are significant sources of stress for you. If your total score is between 40 and 50, money is a controlling factor in your life and you have some unhealthy spending habits that will make it more difficult for you to achieve your financial goals.

Developing Your Skills

1-2. Talking About Money with Your Family

For most families, money is a difficult issue to talk about. As you go through the life cycle, there will be many situations that will require frank and positive communication. Try the following exercise with one or more members of your family (spouse, child, parent, grandparent). Each of you should answer the questions individually and then compare answers. This questionnaire is included in your *Personal Financial Planner* (PFP) so that you can make copies for each person.

PFP Worksheet 2
Talk About Money
with Your Family

1. If you received $2,000 tax-free, what would you do with it?

$______ for ____________________________
$______ for ____________________________
$______ for ____________________________
$______ for ____________________________
$______ for ____________________________

2. If you had to make a major cut in your spending, what would you cut first?

____

3. Rank the following activities from 1 to 7, with 1 being the activity you would enjoy doing the most and 7 being the activity you would enjoy the least:

______ Family activities at home
______ Going out to eat
______ Exercising or outdoor recreation
______ Spending time with friends
______ Some quiet time by myself
______ Participating in my hobby
______ Shopping

4. Indicate whether you agree (A) or disagree (D) with each of the following statements:
   _____ I spend too much money.
   _____ Other members of my family spend too much money.
   _____ Equality in family decision making is important to me.
   _____ I feel good about the way financial decisions are made in my family.
   _____ I believe in enjoying today and not worrying about tomorrow.
   _____ I always wish I had more money than I do.
5. I'd like to see our family spend less money on_______________ and see more money applied to _______________________.
6. What money problem is the most frequent cause of argument in your family? ___________________
   ____
7. What is the most sensible financial thing you have done in your family? ___________________
   ____
8. What is the most foolish financial thing you have done in your family? ___________________
   ____
9. Do you know the dollar amounts that should go in the following blanks?
   Family take-home income is $____________ per month.
   Family monthly rent or mortgage payment is $__________ per month.
   Our family spends $_____________ on food each month.
10. Buying on credit is ______________________.
   ____

1-3. Money Attitudes and Family

Ask several of your family members to use Exercise 1-1 above to assess their own money attitudes and values. Do you see similarities among your family members? Differences? Discuss possible reasons for any similarities or differences. The assessment instrument is included in your *Personal Financial Planner* so that you can make copies.

PFP Worksheet 3
Money Attitude Comparisons

1-4. Practice Interviewing a Financial Planner

Use the Financial Planner Interview Checklist provided in the *Personal Financial Planner* to do a mock interview with a friend.

PFP Worksheet 4
Checklist for Interviewing a Financial Planner

Directions: Make a copy of this worksheet for each prospective planner and use it as an outline for your initial interview.

Name of Planner: ______________________________________

Company: ______________________________________

Address: ______________________________________

Phone: ____________________ Fax: ____________________

1. How long have you been offering financial planning advice to clients?
   - ☐ Less than one year
   - ☐ One to four years
   - ☐ Five to ten years
   - ☐ More than ten years
2. How many clients do you currently have?
   - ☐ Less than 10
   - ☐ 10 to 39
   - ☐ 40 to 79
   - ☐ 80+
3. Briefly describe your work history

4. What educational background qualifies you to be a financial planner?
   - ☐ Certificate
   - ☐ Undergraduate degree
   - ☐ Advanced degree
   - ☐ Other _______________

5. What financial planning certifications do you have?
   - ☐ Certified Financial Planner™
   - ☐ Certified Public Accountant
   - ☐ Chartered Financial Consultant
   - ☐ Attorney
   - ☐ Other
6. What licenses do you hold?

7. Are you or your firm a licensed or registered investment advisor in this state?

8. In which areas do you have experience and do you specialize in one or more of these areas?
   - ☐ Retirement planning
   - ☐ Investment planning
   - ☐ Tax planning
   - ☐ Estate planning
   - ☐ Insurance planning
   - ☐ Integrated planning
9. What services do you offer?

10. What is your approach to financial planning?

11. How are you paid for your services?
    - ☐ Fee
    - ☐ Commission
    - ☐ Salary
    - ☐ Other
12. What do you typically charge?
    Hourly rate ____________
    ____% of assets under management
    ____% commission on stocks and bonds
    ____% commission on mutual funds
    Flat fee ____________
    ____% commission on annuities
    ____% commission on insurance
13. Do you have a business affiliation with any company whose products or services you are recommending? If so, explain.

14. Do you provide a written client engagement agreement? If not, why?

THE NAVIGATOR

- ☐ Review Before Studying this Chapter list.
- ☐ Scan Learning Objectives.
- ☐ Take Myth or Fact quiz and find the answers throughout the chapter.
- ☐ Read chapter and answer Learning by Doing exercises.
- ☐ Review Key Terms and Key Calculations.
- ☐ Do end-of-chapter exercises.
- ☐ Take review quiz on the text website.
- ☐ Solve end-of-chapter cases.

[BEFORE] studying this chapter, you should review

- The financial planning process (Chapter 1).

Financial Planning Tools:
Personal Financial Statements and the Time Value of Money

CHAPTER 2

Myth or Fact?

Consider each of the following statements and decide whether it is a *myth* or a *fact*. Look for the answers in the *Fact* boxes in the chapter.

	MYTH	FACT
1. You should keep your tax returns and supporting documentation for at least ten years.	☐	☐
2. Most families don't track their household expenditures very carefully.	☐	☐
3. People whose incomes are in the top 5 percent are happier than other people.	☐	☐
4. It's always bad to be in debt.	☐	☐
5. Financial math is so complex that you need a business degree to understand it.	☐	☐

LEARNING objectives

1. Develop a system for organizing and maintaining your financial records.
2. Calculate your net worth using a personal balance sheet.
3. Summarize your current inflows and outflows of cash using a personal cash flow statement.
4. Use personal financial ratios to evaluate your current financial position.
5. Understand and apply the basic principles of the time value of money.

...applying the planning process

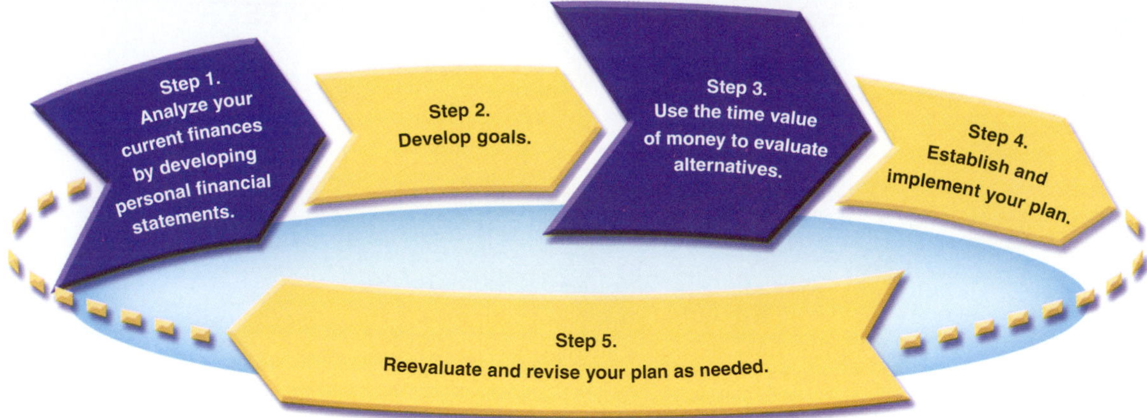

As you learned in Chapter 1, the first step in the personal financial planning process is to evaluate your current finances. For many people, this step is a stumbling block that prevents them from getting started on their financial plan because they don't have the necessary skills to perform the evaluation.

Some of you may wonder why you can't skip the materials in the first few chapters of the text and get right to the fun stuff—how to invest your money. A simple and all-too-common example of the pitfalls of skipping the evaluation step in planning is illustrated by Jack, a college student. Jack never found time to budget or plan. In order to jump-start his financial future, in September 1999, Jack took his $5,000 student loan and invested it in stocks, earning 10 percent on his investments by the end of the academic year. Since he didn't want to sell any of his stocks to pay expenses, he used his credit card to pay for tuition, books, and food; and his credit card balance gradually climbed to $5,000. A few late payments, and the interest rate went up to 22.9 percent. In May 2000, Jack was proud to announce that he had turned his $5,000 investment into $5,500, but he conveniently forgot about his $5,000 credit card balance, which had accrued more than $700 in interest and fees over that same period. If Jack had evaluated his cash flows and developed a budget, he might have been able to find a way to invest in the stock market (although on a much smaller scale) and avoid building up so much debt. He would also have better understood that his focus should be on building his net worth, not just his stock account balance.

This chapter describes many of the tools you will need to establish a strong foundation for financial planning. You'll learn how to evaluate your current financial condition by developing personal financial statements and using financial ratios. The chapter also introduces a key concept in financial planning—the time value of money. In later chapters, you will apply all these tools to achieving your spending, saving, and investing goals.

Chapter Preview

Collecting and Organizing Your Financial Information

- Why Do You Need to Save Bills and Documents?
- How Long Should You Save Documents?
- Where Should You Keep Documents?

Summarizing Your Current Financial Condition

- Preparing a Personal Balance Sheet
- Preparing a Personal Cash Flow Statement

Using Financial Ratios to Evaluate Your Financial Standing

- Measuring Liquidity
- Measuring Debt Usage
- Measuring Savings

Understanding the Time Value of Money

- Calculation Methods
- Timelines
- Future Value of a Lump Sum
- Present Value of a Lump Sum
- Future Value of an Annuity
- Present Value of an Annuity
- Computing Payments for Loans
- Non-annual Compounding

Collecting and Organizing Your Financial Information

LEARNING objective

1 Develop a system for organizing and maintaining your financial records.

PFP Worksheet 5 Organizing Your Financial Records

Although some people simply love to file and organize, most of us do not. The older you get, though, the more "stuff" you will accumulate, and it won't take long for that small pile of paperwork to grow to fill several file cabinets. The earlier you can develop a system for organizing your financial records, the easier it will be to maintain order as your life becomes more complex. Your *Personal Financial Planner* includes a worksheet to help you get started organizing your records.

Why Do You Need to Save Bills and Documents?

The first rule of organization is that there should be a particular purpose for everything you save and file. Although this list is not exhaustive, some possible reasons for keeping particular documents include the following:

- Paying bills
- Tracking your budget
- Preparing for tax reports
- Making investment decisions
- Making insurance or warranty claims
- Ensuring prompt access to essential records

Fact #1

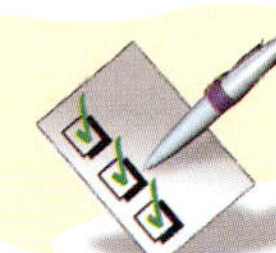

It's generally recommended that you keep tax records for 7 years, not 10. This is because, assuming you didn't intentionally attempt to defraud the government, any legal action against you for additional taxes owed must be brought within 6 years of the date you filed your original return.

How Long Should You Save Documents?

Of course, you need not keep all your documents forever. How long you should save each item depends on what you will use it for. Documents that are necessary for bill paying and budgeting have only short-term usefulness. Receipts for ATM withdrawals and deposits and for cash or credit purchases thus need only be saved until you receive a statement verifying that your account was correctly charged. Bills for utilities, telephone, car expenses, and other irregular expenses that are not tax deductible should be kept for a full year so that you can accurately report the costs in your budget and personal cash flow statements. Any documents that support tax deductions should be filed with your tax records. Although most Internal Revenue Service (IRS) audits occur within three years of the filing of the return, they can also occur later, so it's generally recommended that you keep tax records for seven years to be safe. The IRS audits about 1 out of every 174 returns, and most audits occur in the first year following filing. Audits in later years are usually the result of irregularities discovered in auditing earlier returns.

A neatly organized file cabinet makes it easier to find necessary financial information.

Where Should You Keep Documents?

You can keep your personal financial documents anywhere, as long as you can easily access them when necessary. A system of file folders kept in a file cabinet or box is effective for most people. Although computer filing is also a possibility, it is still the case that most bills exist on paper, so even if you can use your computer for some filing purposes, you'll still need to store paper copies as well.

Important personal documents and valuables, particularly those that are difficult to replace—passports, birth and marriage certificates, social security cards, stock certificates, wills, and deeds—should be in a safe deposit box or fireproof lockbox. A **safe deposit box** is a secure private storage area (usually a small locking drawer) maintained at a remote location, often at a financial institution's place of business. A **lockbox**, which is a fireproof keyed safe kept in your home, is not as secure as a safe deposit box, since it's usually moveable and may be the first thing thieves look for when they break into a house. The primary purpose of a lockbox is to prevent loss or damage to the documents in the event of a fire.

safe deposit box
A secure private storage area maintained at a remote location, often a financial institution's place of business.

lockbox
A fireproof safe that may be kept in the home.

personal financial statements

Reports that summarize personal financial information.

If you use your home computer for managing your finances, you should be sure to regularly back up the information on a disk and to store that disk in a separate location, such as a friend's house, your place of employment, or a safe deposit box. In the event of theft, fire, electrical outage, or water damage, you need to ensure that your electronic records will be safe. The best way to do this is to back up your records immediately whenever you make any major changes to the files, as when you pay bills or revise your budget.

Learning by Doing 2-1

Identify the purpose for saving each of the following documents, if any, and the length of time you should save it:

1. Paid bill for your annual subscription to *Cosmopolitan*
2. Your checking account statement
3. Your student loan statement
4. Your cell phone bill
5. Your credit card statement showing a zero balance
6. Your tax return for 2003

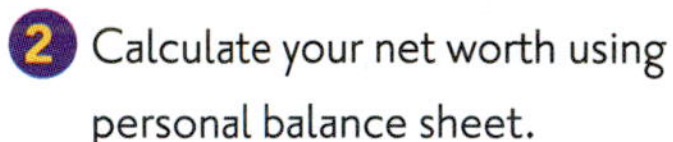

LEARNING objective

2 Calculate your net worth using a personal balance sheet.

personal balance sheet

A financial statement that details the value of what you own and what you owe to others to arrive at an estimate of your net worth at a given point in time.

net worth

The amount of wealth you would have left after paying all your outstanding debts.

assets

Everything you own, including liquid assets, real and personal property, and investments.

debts

Everything you owe to others, including unpaid bills, credit card balances, car loans, student loans, and mortgages.

liquid assets

Cash and near-cash assets that can be easily converted to cash without loss of value.

Summarizing Your Current Financial Condition

Once you've collected and organized your financial information, you can use it to begin evaluating your financial condition. **Personal financial statements** summarize your financial information in a way that makes it easy to see where you stand and to plan for where you want to be in the future. Just as companies make regular reports on their financial status to their shareholders, you are making a financial report to yourself. Others might request this information from you as well—financial companies considering your application for a loan, organizations evaluating your qualifications for a scholarship, or financial advisors helping you with your personal financial plan, for example.

In this section, you'll learn how to develop a personal balance sheet to estimate your financial net worth and a personal cash flow statement to evaluate your cash inflows and outflows. As we walk through the steps, we'll illustrate them by using Danelle Washington, who is introduced in Exhibit 2-1, as an example.

Preparing a Personal Balance Sheet

How much are you worth today? In other words, how wealthy are you? This calculation is a good starting point for financial planning. A **personal balance sheet** is a financial statement that details the value of everything you own and subtracts what you owe to others to arrive at your **net worth**, as illustrated graphically in Exhibit 2-2. The things you own are **assets**, and amounts you owe are **debts**, or liabilities. Assets include liquid assets (such as cash), personal property, real estate, and investments. Debts include both short-term obligations, such as unpaid bills and credit card debt, and long-term debts, such as student loans, car loans, and home mortgages.

Organization of the Personal Balance Sheet. To prepare a personal balance sheet, start by making a list of everything you own, beginning with the most **liquid assets**—cash and near-cash assets that can easily be converted to cash without loss of value—and ending with the least liquid. Checking and savings accounts are examples of liquid assets, whereas your automobile and home are not liquid, since it would take time to sell them and you would incur

Meet Danelle Washington

EXHIBIT 2-1

I'm a senior at a large university in the Midwest. I plan to graduate in May 2005 with a major in biology. I'm also getting a teaching certificate so that I can be a high-school biology teacher. My parents helped out with my first two years of school, but now I'm supporting myself with a part-time job, financial aid, and student loans.

Although I think I'm in pretty good financial shape, I know that I need to get better organized. My biggest problem is that I'm so busy—with my schoolwork and job responsibilities, it's sometimes hard to even find the time to pay my bills. To be totally honest, I also have a tendency to avoid financial matters because I've never particularly liked math.

One of my financial downfalls is that I love to shop for clothes and can't resist a good sale. As a result, my credit card balances have increased over the last couple of years. I'm a little nervous about how I'll be able to pay them off, especially since I'll have to start paying my student loan once I graduate.

transaction costs such as advertising and commissions. If you needed cash in a hurry, you would probably also have to discount the price to make a quick sale.

The next step in constructing your personal balance sheet is to make a list of your debts. As with your assets, start with short-term debts, such as currently unpaid bills, and end with long-term debts, such as your student loans and home mortgage.

Exhibit 2-3 shows you how to itemize assets and debts using those of Danelle Washington as an example. A blank copy of this worksheet is provided in the *Personal Financial Planner.*

PFP Worksheet 6
Personal Balance Sheet

EXHIBIT 2-2

Net Worth

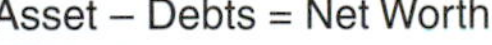

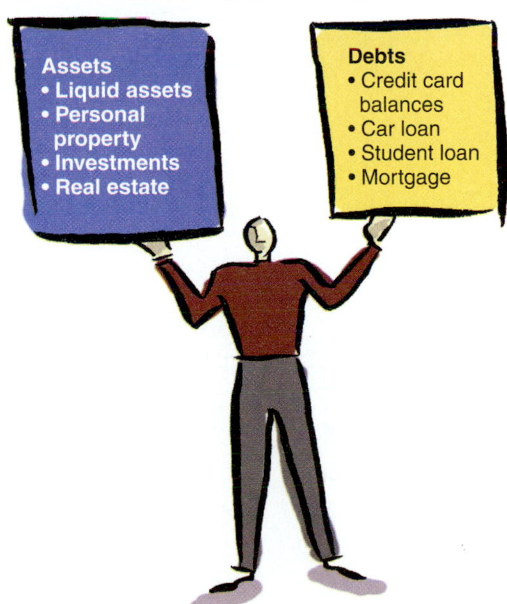

EXHIBIT 2-3

Danelle Washington's Personal Balance Sheet, December 31, 2004

Assets		
Checking accounts	$ 500	
Savings accounts	1,000	
Money market accounts		
Cash value of life insurance		
Total Liquid Assets		$ 1,500
Home furnishings	1,200	
Jewelry/art collectibles	500	
Clothing/personal assets	3,000	
Market value of automobiles	5,000	
Total Personal Property		$ 9,700
Market value of investments (stocks, bonds, mutual funds)		
Employer-sponsored retirement plan		
Individual Retirement Accounts (IRAs)		
Other retirement savings		
College savings plan		
Other savings or investments		
Total Investment Assets		
Market value of home		
Market value of investment real estate		
Total Real Property		
TOTAL ASSETS		$11,200

Debts		
Rent or mortgage payment	$ 500	
Utilities and other bills	130	
Credit card minimum payments	150	
Total Current Bills		$ 780
Credit card balances		
1. Master Card	4,200	
2. JCPenney	1,000	
Personal Loans		
Car loans	3,000	
Alimony/child support owed		
Taxes owed (above withholding)		
Total Short-Term Debts		$ 8,200
Student loans	18,000	
Home mortgage balance		
Home equity loan		
Other real estate loans		
Other investment loans and liabilities		
Total Long-Term Debt		$18,000
TOTAL DEBTS		$26,980
Net Worth = Assets − Debts		**−$15,780**

List the values of your liquid assets (Chapter 5), household goods, and automobiles (Chapter 8).

List the market value of assets, investments, and real property (Chapters 8, 11–15).

List your short-term and long-term debts (Chapter 6–8).

Calculate your net worth by subtracting total debts from total assets.

NEWS you can use

Your Car May Reduce Your Net Worth

Since January 2002, automobile dealers have competed vigorously for customers by offering below-market interest rates on car loans and by financing loans over longer time periods, as much as 72 months. It isn't unusual to see advertisements offering 0 percent interest on new cars. Prices have been reduced to such a low level that dealers are pricing vehicles close to their actual cost. This sounds great, right? Well, it is—unless you need to sell or trade a used car.

The unusually low prices on new cars have caused used car prices to drop at much faster rates than they did in the past. After all, a used car has to cost less than a new car, or no one would buy a used car. *Consumer Reports* reported that the average two-year depreciation from 2001 to 2003 was 45 percent, a slight increase from the 2000 to 2002 depreciation rate of 43 percent. Based on this level of depreciation, if you purchased a new car for $15,000 two years ago, it's worth about $8,250 today. However, if you financed the whole $15,000 for six years at 6 percent interest, you still owe $10,585! Looks like you'll be keeping that car for a little while longer.

New car values fall 45% in the first 2 years.

Source: *Consumer Reports 2003 Cars*, April 2003; *Consumer Reports New Car Preview 2004*, January 2004.

Valuing Your Assets and Debts. How do you go about assigning a dollar value to each asset and debt? Your most recent bank financial statements will give you the value of your checking and savings accounts. For other assets, try to estimate the **market value**, the price you could sell it for today. The market value is not the same as what the asset cost when you bought it. For example, if you just bought a new car, you won't be able to sell it now for what you paid for it. Similarly, the market value of your stereo system is much lower than what you paid for the system, even if it's practically new. In contrast, you may own some assets that have much higher market values than what you paid for them. A first-edition comic that you paid $1 for 10 years ago may be worth $100 today; and normally, real estate increases in value over time, so your home will probably have a higher market value now than when you purchased it.

market value

The price that something can be sold for today.

For some of your assets, such as your car, there may be a corresponding debt. If so, enter the market value of your vehicle on the asset side of your balance sheet and the loan balance on the debt side. Notice that Danelle has entered $5,000 as the value of her car and $3,000 as the remaining balance on her car loan. If you lease a car, your payment obligations are a debt, but you don't own the car, so you shouldn't include it as an asset. You can estimate the market value of your car using a current automotive *Blue Book*, available at most bookstores and libraries, or by consulting one of several Internet resources. In some cases, as explained in the *News You Can Use* box, "Your Car May Reduce Your Net Worth," your car's value may actually be less than what you still owe in car payments.

A good Internet source for new and used car values is www.edmunds.com.

Although real property, including homes and other real estate, is not very liquid, it may be your largest investment. Real estate values are determined by the values of comparable properties in the area, so if you just enter what you paid for the property on your balance sheet, you will be understating your actual wealth. If you don't know of a recent sale of a similar property, you can consult a real estate professional to help you determine the value of your home or other real estate investment. In general, real estate values increase over time, so you'll need to update this information regularly. Since Danelle is renting an apartment with some friends from school, she doesn't own any assets in this category.

An insurance policy is counted as an asset only if it's a policy that accumulates cash value over time. If you cancel an insurance policy that has a **cash surrender value**, the insurer will return that amount of money to you. Since this is an available source of cash to you, you should count it as an asset. Homeowner's, auto, and health insurance (discussed in Chapters 9 and 10) don't accumulate cash value, but some types of disability and life insurance policies (discussed in Chapters 10 and 16, respectively) may have cash value. This value is determined by the contract

cash surrender value

The amount the insurer will pay to the policy owner if a cash-value insurance policy is canceled.

NEWS you can use

The Balance Sheet Impact of Divorce

Despite the common media portrayal of the man who is left with nothing after his ex-wife takes the house, the car, the kids, and half his income in the divorce settlement, recent studies have shown that divorce more commonly has a negative financial impact on women. Clearly, attorneys' fees in contested divorces impact both spouses, but women often choose to give up rights to important financial assets such as employer-sponsored retirement plans and individual retirement accounts (IRAs) in return for keeping the family home and the car, both of which are likely to be financed with debt and therefore have little net value. When the wife is focused on custody issues, family assets might be held for psychological blackmail—"If you don't agree to my demands, I'll take the kids away from you!" As reprehensible as it may sound to use your children as a bargaining chip, this is, in fact, a strategy commonly recommended by divorce attorneys.

Given that women on average also have lower earnings than their husbands, the loss of financial wealth in divorce can cause significant negative financial consequences for women. According to the Consumer Federation of America, households headed by women have, on average, one-half the income, one-third the wealth, and shorter planning horizons than other households. Divorced women are more likely to be living below the poverty level than other women their age. The long-term effects are even more significant, as divorced women find themselves inadequately prepared for retirement. Many experts believe that the solution to these problems lies in education—women need to take responsibility for their own finances, and they need to be better informed about the financial value of joint household resources. They should also take advantage of recent changes in the law allowing larger annual contributions to be made to retirement accounts each year.

"Divorced women are more likely to be living below the poverty level . . .".

terms and is generally much smaller than the face value of the policy. In some cases, insurance policies also allow you to borrow against the cash value. If you have borrowed from one or more of your polices, include the amount owed as a debt on your personal balance sheet. Danelle doesn't have any cash-value insurance.

Calculating Your Net Worth. Once you've entered all the required information on your personal balance sheet, you can calculate your net worth using the following equation:

$$\text{Net worth} = \text{Total assets} - \text{Total debts}$$

Notice in Exhibit 2-3 that Danelle's net worth is *negative* $15,780. What does this mean? If Danelle sold all her assets and used the money to repay her debts, she would *still* owe $15,780. In contrast, if your net worth is *positive*, it represents how much you would have left over after you've paid everything. Your net worth is therefore a measure of your wealth. There is no "magic number" representing the ideal amount of net worth, since this depends on an individual's life cycle stage and personal goals. However, in general, the larger your net worth, the better off you are.

What if you have negative net worth like Danelle? If you're like most students, you're in the accumulation phase of your life cycle. You're developing skills and abilities that will lead to greater income and wealth in the future. You may have student loans and car loans but little in the way of financial investments. This situation is not overly troubling at such an early stage of life. However, if it continues indefinitely, it will eventually result in **insolvency**—the inability to pay your debts as they come due—and possibly bankruptcy, which is explained in Chapter 7. It's not uncommon for an individual's net worth to decline due to an unexpected change in life circumstances, such as an extended illness, death of a spouse, or divorce, as discussed in the *News You Can Use* box, "The Balance Sheet Impact of Divorce." One of the purposes of developing and evaluating personal financial statements is to identify ways to improve your situation so that you can be better prepared for these types of problems. As you proceed through the financial planning process, you should keep this in mind and conscientiously attempt to reduce debt and increase assets over time.

insolvency
The inability to pay debts as they come due.

Learning by Doing 2-2

1. Identify whether each of the following is an asset (A) or a debt (D):
   a. Car loan
   b. Unpaid bill
   c. Jewelry
   d. Artwork
   e. Mortgage
   f. Checking account
   g. Student loan
   h. House
2. You have estimated your total assets to be $10,000 and your total debts to be $11,000. What is your net worth?

Preparing a Personal Cash Flow Statement

LEARNING objective

3 Summarize your current inflows and outflows of cash using a personal cash flow statement.

Your net worth is highly related to your spending and saving behavior. If you consistently spend more than you earn, you'll end up financing this extra consumption through borrowing. In contrast, if you're a regular saver, you'll accumulate more in assets over time. On average, Americans spend more than they earn and have very low savings rates. Not surprisingly, average household debt continues to rise over time. This problem has been exacerbated over the last few years as increasing home values and low mortgage rates have encouraged many homeowners to access home equity lines of credit to pay for vacations and other noninvestment expenses. When this happens, total debt goes up, and net worth declines, as we will see when we look at credit in more detail in Chapters 6 and 7.

A **personal cash flow statement** is a financial statement used to evaluate the relationship between your income and expenditures. Whereas your personal balance sheet is like a snapshot of your finances at a certain point in time, your personal cash flow statement shows inflows and outflows of cash over a period of time, often one month or one year. In this financial report, you carefully itemize the amounts of money that come into your household from various sources as well as all the money that goes out over the same period of time.

personal cash flow statement

A summary of income and expenditures over a period of time, such as a month or a year.

You can utilize a worksheet such as the one in Exhibit 2-4 to record your cash inflows and outflows, using Danelle Washington's personal cash flow statement for 2004 as an example. A blank copy of this worksheet is provided in the *Personal Financial Planner.* Alternatively, you may want to use the worksheets provided with a personal finance software package, such as *Microsoft Money* or *Quicken.*

PFP Worksheet 7 Personal Cash Flow Statement

When Should Cash Flows Be Recorded?

The cash flow statement is prepared on a "cash basis," which means that cash flows are recorded when they are received or paid. Thus, if you receive a bill on January 5 but don't pay it until February 1, you will record it as an expense in February, not in January. If certain amounts are deposited directly to or withdrawn directly from your checking account, such as paycheck deposits or car payments, you should record them when they occur.

Identifying Your Cash Inflows.

For the purpose of creating a personal cash flow statement, you should include as cash inflows all amounts of money you receive during the period of time in question. Obviously, you need to include any income you earn from a job—wages, salaries, tips, and commission. But your other sources of income may include one or more of the following:

- Scholarships
- Cash allowances or gifts from your parents or others
- Proceeds from the sale of your assets
- Alimony or child support
- Government benefits such as welfare, unemployment, or social security
- Investment earnings (income from dividends and interest)
- Gambling winnings

EXHIBIT 2-4

Danelle Washington's Personal Cash Flow Statement, 2004

Cash Inflows

	Monthly	January 1 to December 31, 2004
Salary/wage income (gross)	$792	9,500
Interest/dividend income		
Other income (self employment)		
Rental income (after expenses)		
Cash from sale or assets		
Student loans	500	6,000
Scholarships	108	1,300
Other income		
Gifts	17	200
Total Cash Inflows	$1,417	$17,000

Cash Outflows

	Monthly	January 1 to December 31, 2004
Income and payroll taxes	$71	$852
Groceries	171	2,052
Housing		
Mortgage or rent	300	3,600
Property tax & insurance		
Maintenance/repairs		
Utilities		
Heating	40	480
Electric	25	300
Water and sewer		
Cable/phone/satellite	15	180
Car loan payments	113	1,356
Car maintenance/gas	80	960
Credit card payments	125	1,500
Other loan payments		
Other taxes		
Insurance		
Life		
Health	42	504
Auto	67	804
Disability		
Other insurance		
Clothing	25	300
Gifts	30	360
Other consumables (TV's, etc.)		
Child-care expenses		
Sports-related expenses	13	156
Health club dues		
Uninsured medical expenses	17	204
Education	333	3,996
Vacations/travel	25	300
Entertainment	84	1,008
Alimony/child support		
Charitable contributions		
Required pension contributions		
Magazine subscriptions/books		
Other payments/expenses		
Total Cash Outflows	$ 1,576	$ 18,912

	Monthly	Annual
Net Cash Flow = Cash Inflows − Cash Outflows =	**−$159**	**−$1,912**

Notice that Danelle records her annual **gross income**—that is, income before taxes and expenses—and records the taxes she paid during the year as a cash outflow. Last year, she earned $9,500 from a part-time job and received a $1,300 scholarship and gifts of $200. She also took out a student loan in the amount of $6,000. Her total cash inflows are therefore $17,000 for the year.

gross income

Income before taxes and expenses.

Detailing Your Expenditures. Whereas income is generally easy to identify and calculate, expenditures are more difficult to track accurately. You can probably easily determine the big **fixed expenses**—items that are the same from month to month, such as rent and car loan payments. But few people do a good job of keeping track of their **variable expenses**, such as grocery bills and gas money, even though these can be a big portion of their total cash outflows. You can see that on Danelle's personal cash flow statement, $2,052 for groceries was one of her largest annual expenditures, exceeded only by her rent at $3,600 and her college expenses at $3,996.

fixed expenses

Expenses that are a constant dollar amount each period.

variable expenses

Expenses that vary in amount from period to period.

Small daily expenditures, such as money for the parking meter or for candy bars from a snack machine, are especially easy to overlook, but often these expenditures can make the difference between achieving your financial goals and not achieving them. Even if you just buy a latté at the coffee shop every weekday afternoon on the way home from school or work, the seemingly small cost of $3 per day adds up to $780 in a year—enough to take a nice vacation or to add to your investment portfolio.

If you spend money primarily by writing checks and using a debit card, it's a little easier to track your cash outflows, since your bank statement and check register will be useful sources of information. Alternatively, you can track your expenditures on a daily basis in a spending log in which you record all your cash outflows for a month or longer. Your *Personal Financial Planner* includes a spending log worksheet you can use for this purpose. At the end of the time period you have chosen, you can then total up the amounts entered in your spending log to put into your personal cash flow statement. You'll need to do this for at least a month to be sure that you've included even the irregular cash outflows.

Fact #2

According to a survey by Bankrate.com, many households do not regularly track their household expenditures even though they know that they should. The most common excuse given was insufficient time.

Be careful not to alter your normal spending behavior temporarily simply because you're recording everything. Suppose, for example, that you never realized how much money you spent on lattés until you began keeping your spending log. Even if you plan to reduce your latté spending in the future, you need to incorporate this expense in your log so that you can more realistically evaluate your *current* finances. If you quit your latté habit during your spending log period and decided to allocate the $780 per year to a savings program, what would happen if you "fell off the wagon" and returned to your prior spending behavior? At this stage, it's better to be brutally honest with yourself and record all of your spending, regardless of whether you plan to make changes in the future.

PFP Worksheet 8
Spending Log

Calculating and Evaluating Net Cash Flow. Once you've entered and totaled your cash inflows and outflows on the personal cash flow statement, you can calculate your net cash flow. Danelle calculates hers as follows:

$$\text{Net cash flow} = \text{Total cash inflows} - \text{Total cash outflows}$$
$$= \$17{,}000 - \$18{,}912 = -\$1{,}912$$

Based on Danelle's personal cash flow statement, which shows a *negative* net cash flow, she has been spending more than her income during the past year. How did this happen? Looking back at her personal balance sheet can give us some clues. Danelle has credit card debt totaling $5,200 and total student loan debt of $18,000. Since the personal balance sheet is cumulative, this amount represents debt she has accumulated over time, not just in the past year. For example, we know that she received $6,000 from a student loan this year, which

NEWS you can use

How Do You Compare to the Average U.S. Household?

How do your finances compare to other similar households? According to a federally sponsored survey, the average U.S. household includes 2.5 people and less than one of them is a child under the age of 18. The average family earns $49,430 before taxes, has annual expenditures of $42,557, owns their own home, and has two cars. The right-hand portion of the table shows the budget amounts for families by income quintile (lowest 20 percent by income to highest 20 percent by income). It's interesting to note that lower-income households, on average, spend more then they earn. As average income rises for the groups, average expenditures in each category increase as well.

"Lower-income households, on average, spend more then they earn."

Household Characteristic	All Households	By Income Group Lowest	2	3	4	Highest
Number in household	2.5	1.7	2.2	2.5	2.8	3.2
Number of children under 18	0.7	0.4	0.5	0.6	0.8	0.9
Number of vehicles owned	2.0	1.0	1.5	2.0	2.5	2.9
Percent homeowners	66%	42%	56%	65%	77%	89%
Income before taxes	$49,430	$8,316	$21,162	$36,989	$59,177	$121,367
Annual expenditures	42,557	19,061	27,140	36,881	50,432	79,199
Housing expenditures	13,491	6,633	9,119	11,728	15,331	24,552
Food at home	3,234	2,154	4,152	5,053	6,556	9,108
Eating out	2,383	1,048	1,466	1,992	2,925	4,594
Clothing	1,873	953	1,167	1,512	2,118	3,643
Transportation	8,001	3,278	5,021	7,487	10,389	13,781
Charitable contributions	1,362	457	868	1,106	1,563	2,851

Source: U.S. Bureau of Labor Statistics, Consumer Expenditure Survey 2001–2002. Available at www.bls.gov.

means she must already have had $12,000 in student loan debt at the beginning of the year. In addition to taking on more student loan debt, Danelle spent $1,912 more than she earned last year, so these expenditures must have been made using credit cards. The increased debt resulted in a decline in her net worth. As you can see, Danelle's income and spending habits have had a big effect on her overall financial picture.

We might be tempted to explain Danelle's financial position by pointing to her low income. However, an interesting economic truth is that those who have more tend to spend more. If you're struggling to make it on a student's budget, you likely eat Ramen noodles at least once a week and make do with your current wardrobe. If you're a movie star earning millions of dollars each year, you probably have more than one extravagant home, entertain lavishly, and buy only designer clothes. Everything is relative. By the same token, just because you have high income doesn't mean that your finances are in good shape. There are numerous examples of seemingly well-off people who have had to declare bankruptcy. To see how you compare to others, consider the financial information reported for average households in the *News You Can Use* box, "How Do You Compare to the Average U.S. Household?," taken from a national federally sponsored survey.

Fact #3

A 2002 *Town and Country* magazine survey seems to support the idea that money and happiness go together. Compared with those earning less, people who earned $100,000 per year or more were generally more content with their lot in life, were more likely to have a happy marriage, and more likely to have one or more children. National household financial statistics also show that this group has a higher percentage of homeownership and retirement savings, and has proportionately less debt than those in lower-income groups.

Learning by Doing 2-3

Masako would like to buy a new car. She currently has after-tax monthly income of $2,000. Her monthly expenses are as follows:

- Car insurance $100
- Rent $900
- Groceries $300
- Entertainment $200
- Utilities $200
- Credit card payment $100
- Other $100

1. What is Masako's net cash flow?
2. Can she afford to buy a car? Why or why not?

Using Financial Ratios to Evaluate Your Financial Standing

LEARNING objective

4 Use personal financial ratios to evaluate your current financial position.

Financial ratios provide another important tool for evaluating your financial condition. You can calculate your financial ratios from the information you've collected on your personal financial statements, compare your ratios to recommended targets, and track your ratios over time as a measure of your progress toward achieving your financial goals. In this section, we examine ratios designed to measure three aspects of your finances: liquidity, debt management, and adequacy of savings. The individual ratios and their calculations are explained below using Danelle Washington's financial information, and the methodology is summarized in the *Go Figure!* box, "Evaluating Personal Financial Statements and Calculating Financial Ratios" with a different illustration.

Measuring Liquidity

liquidity ratio

Financial ratio that measures ability to pay household expenses out of liquid assets in the absence of regular income.

If you experience a total loss of income—for example, if you're temporarily disabled or laid off—you may need to meet your expenses without having the regular income that you normally rely on for this purpose. The **liquidity ratio** tells you how many months you could pay your monthly expenses from your liquid assets. This ratio is calculated as follows:

$$\text{Liquidity ratio} = \frac{\text{Liquid assets}}{\text{Monthly expenses}}$$

For example, look again at Danelle Washington's personal balance sheet in Exhibit 2-3. Danelle has liquid assets equal to $1,500, the total value of her checking and savings accounts. Her annual expenses, from the cash flow statement in Exhibit 2-4, are $18,912, and her monthly expenses total $1,576. Thus, Danelle's liquidity ratio (rounded to one decimal place) is

$$\text{Liquidity ratio} = \frac{\$1{,}500}{\$1{,}576} = 1.0$$

This means that Danelle could meet her expenses for only one month without her regular income sources. Financial planners often recommend that you have liquid assets sufficient to cover your expenses for three to six months, so liquidity is a concern for Danelle, particularly at the end of the school year, when she has depleted her student loan and scholarship funds. A low liquidity ratio, however, does not necessarily imply that she needs to increase her allocation of funds to liquid assets. She may have other sources of funds that can be tapped in an emergency, such as family loans or credit cards.

GO FIGURE!

Evaluating Personal Financial Statements and Calculating Financial Ratios

You have summarized your household financial data as follows:

Gross monthly income	$7,000
After-tax monthly income	$5,000
Monthly total expenses	$4,500
Monthly debt payments	$1,400
Mortgage, property taxes, homeowners' insurance	$1,200
Monthly savings	$500
Liquid assets	$10,000
Total assets	$150,000
Total debts	$180,000

Problem Evaluate your household finances.

Solution

1. Calculate your net worth and net cash flow:

Net worth = Total assets − Total Debts
= $150,000 − $180,000
= −$30,000

Net cash flow = Cash inflows − Cash outflows
= $5,000 − 4,500
= $500

Although your net worth is negative, you have substantial net cash flow which you are currently applying to savings.

2. Calculate your personal financial ratios:

$$\text{Liquidity ratio} = \frac{\text{Liquid assets}}{\text{Monthly expenses}} = \frac{\$10{,}000}{\$4{,}500} = 2.2 \text{ months}$$

$$\text{Debt ratio} = \frac{\text{Total debts}}{\text{Total assets}} = \frac{\$180{,}000}{\$150{,}000} = 1.2 \quad \text{or} \quad 120\%$$

$$\text{Debt payment ratio} = \frac{\text{Total monthly debt payments}}{\text{After-tax monthly income}} = \frac{\$1{,}400}{\$5{,}000} = 0.28 \quad \text{or} \quad 28\%$$

$$\text{Mortgage debt service ratio} = \frac{\text{Monthly mortgage debt service}}{\text{Gross monthly income}} = \frac{\text{Principal + Interest + Taxes + Insurance}}{\text{Gross monthly income}} = \frac{\$1{,}200}{\$7{,}000} = 0.17 \quad \text{or} \quad .17\%$$

$$\text{Savings ratio} = \frac{\text{Monthly savings}}{\text{After-tax income}} = \frac{\$500}{\$5{,}000} = 0.1 \quad \text{or} \quad 10\%$$

You have sufficient liquid assets to cover more than two months of expenses. Although you have sufficient income to make your required monthly debt payments, your household has too much debt relative to assets.

Measuring Debt Usage

Everywhere we turn, it seems there's someone inviting us to borrow money to buy something today instead of waiting until we've saved enough to pay cash. Small wonder that one of the biggest financial problems facing American households is that they have too much debt. If your money style is to spend impulsively or if you tend to avoid financial matters altogether, you may already understand the problems associated with monthly payments on credit cards. Although debt is not inherently bad, payments made to lenders include interest charges and fees—funds that could be better used to build your financial wealth. You will learn more about these matters in later chapters. For now, you can use your personal financial statements to assess your debt management.

Fact #4

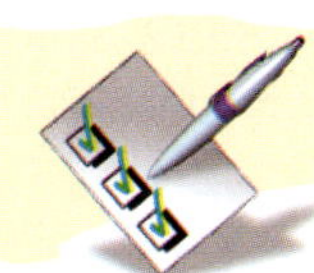

Although debt can cause a number of problems, it isn't inherently bad. In general, the easy availability of borrowing at low rates of interest has increased the average standard of living and fueled the economy. For example, most families today own their own home and two or more cars as a result of household borrowing.

Financial institutions such as banks and mortgage companies use a variety of debt ratios when they evaluate you for mortgage or car loans. The three ratios we discuss in this section—the debt ratio, the debt payment ratio, and the mortgage debt service ratio—are the ones most commonly used by financial institutions in their mortgage lending process.

Debt Ratio. The **debt ratio** measures the percent of your total assets that you've financed with debt. It is calculated as

$$\text{Debt ratio} = \frac{\text{Total debt}}{\text{Total assets}}$$

As your credit card balances increase, so will your debt ratio, since credit card purchases are usually for consumer goods that add little if any value to your assets. For example, suppose you use a credit card to pay for dinner and a movie for you and your significant other. This will cause your debts to increase by, say, $50, but your assets won't increase at all. Therefore, your debt ratio goes up. The debt ratio will generally decline as you get older, since your financial assets and home equity will increase in value.

debt ratio

Total debt divided by total assets.

Debt Payment Ratio and Mortgage Debt Service Ratio. Both the debt payment ratio and the mortgage debt service ratio measure your ability to pay your financial obligations. In determining your creditworthiness, lenders commonly compare these or similar ratios to maximum values. For example, a mortgage lender might require that your total debt payments be no more than 35 percent of your gross income or that your total mortgage-related expenses be no more than 25 percent of your gross income.

The **debt payment ratio** estimates the percentage of your *after-tax income* that goes to paying required monthly minimum debt payments of all types, including mortgage loans, student loans, car loans, and credit card payments. The debt payment ratio is calculated as follows:

$$\text{Debt payment ratio} = \frac{\text{Total monthly debt payments}}{\text{After-tax monthly income}}$$

debt payment ratio

Financial ratio that measures percentage of disposable income required to make debt payments.

Note that we use after-tax income in the denominator of the equation, since the purpose is to assess ability to pay.

As you can see in Exhibit 2-4, Danelle's monthly after-tax income is $1,346 (calculated as monthly gross income of $1,417 less $71 in income and payroll taxes). Her monthly debt payments total $238 per month ($125 for credit cards plus $113 for her car loan). Using this information, we can calculate Danelle's debt payment ratio as follows:

$$\text{Debt payment ratio} = \frac{\$238}{\$1{,}346} = 0.177 \quad \text{or} \quad 17.7\%$$

Bank lenders commonly require that total debt payments not exceed 33 percent to 38 percent of *gross income*, which implies that the debt payment ratio (based on *after-tax* income) could be even higher. By that measure, Danelle's 17.7 percent debt payment ratio is not very high, but she will have to begin paying her student loan a few months after graduation, so this ratio is likely to rise in the future. In addition, this ratio tends to understate her actual financial obligations since it doesn't include her required monthly rent payments.

Most individuals find that their housing costs, either rent or mortgage payments, are their largest monthly expenditure. The total monthly cost of a mortgage, including the principal and interest paid to the lender, property taxes paid to the local municipality, and homeowners insurance, is called the **mortgage debt service**. Mortgage lenders commonly require that borrowers make a single monthly payment to cover all these expenses. The **mortgage debt service ratio**, which measures the percentage of your gross income that you pay out in mortgage debt service alone, is calculated as follows:

$$\text{Mortgage debt service ratio} = \frac{\text{Principal} + \text{Interest} + \text{Taxes} + \text{Insurance}}{\text{Gross monthly income}}$$

Since Danelle doesn't have a mortgage, this ratio is not relevant to her situation.

mortgage debt service

Total dollar amount of monthly mortgage principal, interest, property taxes, and homeowners insurance.

mortgage debt service ratio

Percentage of gross income used for mortgage debt service.

Measuring Savings

You can assess how well you're implementing your savings goals by tracking the savings ratio over time. The **savings ratio** measures the percentage of your after-tax income that is being allocated to savings:

$$\text{Savings ratio} = \frac{\text{Monthly savings}}{\text{After-tax monthly income}}$$

savings ratio

Financial ratio that measures the percentage of after-tax income going to savings.

Since the amount you have available for savings is what's left over from your income after you've paid all your expenses and taxes, it's quite possible to have negative savings. This will happen whenever your cash outflows exceed your cash inflows. In that case, your savings ratio will be negative as well. Danelle Washington's savings ratio is

$$\text{Savings ratio} = \frac{-\$159}{\$1,346} = -11.8\%$$

Since a negative savings ratio implies that, rather than saving, Danelle is accumulating more debt, this financial situation cannot continue for long. As she begins to develop her personal financial goals, she will probably want to include goals related to improving some of the financial ratios introduced in this section. Financial advisors commonly recommend that households target at least a 10 percent savings ratio and that they attempt to increase this ratio over time.

Learning by Doing 2-4

The Sandell family reports the following financial information:

• Checking and savings account	$3,000
• Monthly after-tax income	$2,500
• Total monthly expenses	$2,000
• Monthly savings	$500
• Total debt	$10,000
• Total assets	$40,000

1. Calculate the Sandell's liquidity ratio.
2. Calculate the Sandell's debt ratio.
3. Calculate the Sandell's savings ratio.

Understanding the Time Value of Money

LEARNING objective

5 Understand and apply the basic principles of the time value of money.

time value of money

The principle that money received today is worth more than money to be received in the future because of the power of compounding.

compounding

The process by which interest is paid on both the original investment and interest already earned.

Personal financial planning is all about making choices. How will you spend your money? Where will you invest your savings? How will you finance a major purchase? For every financial choice you must make, there is inevitably a tradeoff. For example, if you want to send your children to college, you'll have to spend less on other things so that you can save for this important goal.

In evaluating and comparing various alternatives for achieving financial goals, we will often make use of an important personal financial planning tool called the **time value of money**. The basic idea is simple: Money received today is worth more than money to be received in the future because you can invest it to earn compound interest. **Compounding** occurs when you earn interest on your investment balance and then leave the interest in the account so that you earn future interest on the original balance plus the accumulated interest earnings. The time value of money is also the reason you shouldn't keep your savings in a piggy bank or under your mattress at home. Aside from the risk of fire or theft, money that is *not* invested in interest-earning or growth assets will actually lose purchasing power over time because of the eroding effects of inflation.

To illustrate the concept of compounding, suppose you're offered an investment opportunity on which you will earn 10 percent interest per year, payable at the end of the year. If you keep $10,000 in the account for one year, you will receive 10 percent of $10,000, or $1,000, in interest at the end of the year. Now suppose you leave both the original amount and the earned interest, totaling $11,000, in the account. At the end of the next year, you will receive interest on the full $11,000. Thus, your interest earnings at the end of year 2 will be 10 percent of $11,000, or $1,100; at the end of year 3, you will earn $1,210 (10 percent of $12,100); and so on. The longer you leave your money in the account, the greater the dollar interest earnings each year will be. As illustrated in Exhibit 2-5, your money will also grow faster if you can earn a higher rate of interest on the invested amounts.

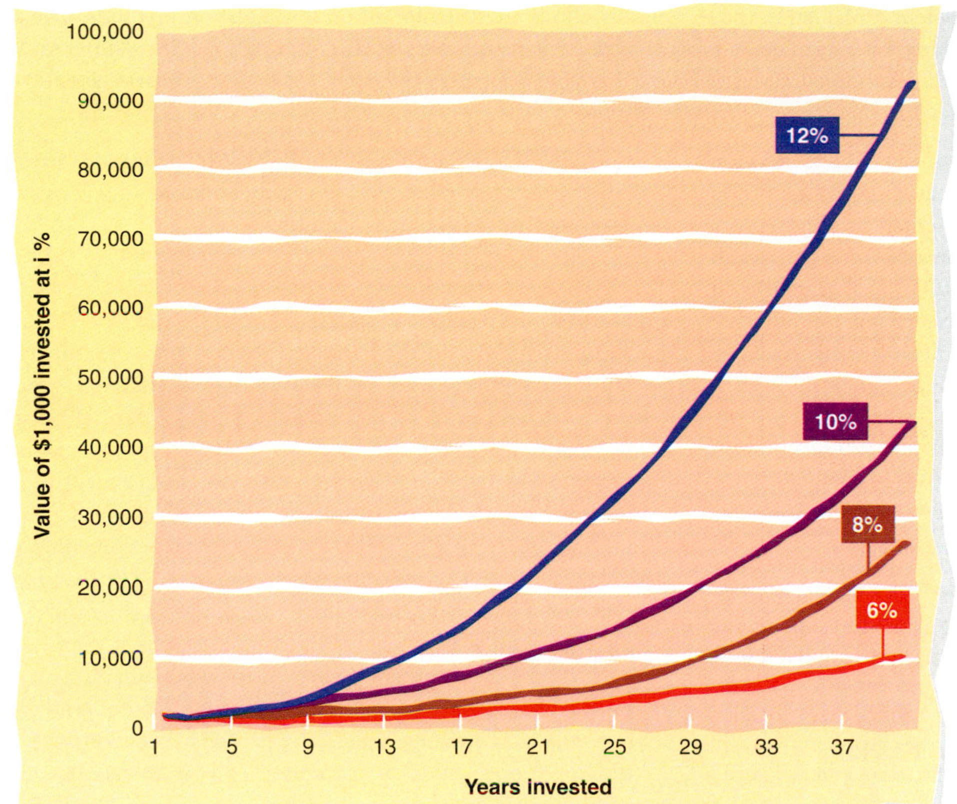

EXHIBIT 2-5

The Power of Compounding

All financial calculations are based on this simple concept, although the problems can become more complicated when interest is compounded more frequently (monthly or daily) or when you add to your account balance on a regular basis. Once you've mastered time value of money calculations, you can use them to answer important personal finance questions such as:

- How much will my car loan payment be?
- How much do I need to save today to reach a particular savings goal?
- How much will my investment grow over time?
- How can I compare dollar amounts in different time periods?

Fact #5

The National Council of Teachers of Mathematics recognizes that math anxiety is a very real and widespread national problem with long-term consequences. For example, early experiences of pain and frustration with mathematics may cause people to avoid personal financial tasks as well. Here's the good news—financial math uses only basic math functions and can therefore be mastered with a little practice.

The purpose of this section is to familiarize you with the basic time value of money calculations used in this text—calculations of present value and future value. In addition to presenting three different methods for solving these problems (mathematical formulas, financial calculators, and electronic spreadsheets), the discussion provides examples of the most common applications of time value of money concepts to personal finance. Since nearly all financial decisions involve cash inflows and outflows over time, it is absolutely essential to your personal financial plan that you master these concepts. For this reason, we'll revisit these concepts and apply them to your financial decisions throughout the text.

Calculation Methods

You can perform the calculations in this section using three different methods. Although your instructor may have a preference for one over the others, all three should yield the same answer to a particular question, subject to small differences due to rounding errors. For each type of problem explained in the section, directions are given for all three calculation methods. The upcoming *Go Figure!* boxes provide a convenient summary of this information with a different numerical example for you to follow. For your reference, these methodology summaries are also included in the *Personal Financial Planner.*

Method 1: Mathematical Formulas. The solution to any financial problem can be arrived at through the use of mathematical formulas that will be presented in this section. When using formulas, be certain to express all interest rates in decimal format (e.g., 5% is expressed as 0.05). This can be a bit confusing, since the financial calculator solutions require that you enter information in integer form (simply 5 rather than 5% or 0.05). As you get more practice, you'll be less likely to confuse the inputs for the various methods.

Mathematical calculations can sometimes produce rounding and other errors. Although you should check with your instructor about his or her preferences for rounding, it's generally recommended that you round only after completely solving an equation. A convenient shortcut is to use the time value of money tables located in Appendix A. As you will see later in this section, these tables precalculate portions of the mathematical formula to make the calculation simpler. These tables are by necessity abbreviated to include only whole-number interest rates, however, and so cannot be used to solve all possible problems. For example, if the problem you are solving involves an interest rate of $2\frac{1}{4}$ percent, you will need to use a different method.

Method 2: Financial Calculators. The quickest and easiest way to solve financial problems is with a hand-held financial calculator. You can purchase these calculators in various places—university bookstores, electronics stores, and discount department stores, for example. In general, financial calculators have five buttons representing the inputs necessary for time value calculations: number of periods (*N*); periodic interest rate (*I*); present value (*PV*); payment (*PMT*); and future value (*FV*). These buttons correspond to the definitions used in mathematical formulas and are usually arranged in a consistent order regardless of the manufacturer:

Examples of appropriate calculators include the Texas Instruments BAII Plus and the Hewlett Packard 10B. The calculator examples in this chapter are presented in a relatively generic form so that you can easily apply them to any financial calculator; however, in some cases, we may include a specific example using the TI BAII Plus. Although there are more expensive calculators that include additional features you might have use for in the future, it is probably better to buy a cheaper one now and wait until you really need the other. Not only will there likely be advances in quality and reductions in price in the future, the trend is toward greater reliance on computers rather than calculators. If you have a programmable scientific calculator, you can program the equations or purchase a download that will allow your calculator to solve financial equations. Your *Personal Financial Planner* includes a summary of how to use the most common types of financial calculators.

Method 3: Financial Spreadsheet Programs. Electronic spreadsheet programs, such as Microsoft Excel, include built-in formulas for solving financial problems. If you have easy access to a personal computer, you may find that this method will be the best one for you. However, for this class, it's unlikely that you will have access to a computer during exams, so you'll still need to be able to solve problems with one of the other methods as well.

Using Timelines to Clarify the Timing of Cash Flows

You will probably find time value of money problems easier to visualize if you take the time to draw a timeline that shows each of the cash flows for the problem you are attempting to solve. A timeline is simply a graphical representation of time going from today (time 0) to some future date in appropriate increments. In the timelines shown for each type of problem, *PV* stands for *present value*, the value of the cash flow today, and *FV* stands for *future value*, the value of the cash flow at a particular time in the future. If the problem you are solving involves a series of equal payments, they are labeled *PMT.* Before attempting to solve a problem, you should get in the habit of drawing a timeline representing the cash flows. This will help determine which type of calculation is necessary to solve the problem.

future value (FV)

The value a given amount will grow to in the future if invested today at a given rate of interest.

Future Value of a Lump Sum

If you invest a sum of money today at a certain rate of interest, how much will it be worth at some point in the future? The **future value (FV)** of a lump sum is its value at a particular time in the future if invested today at a given rate of interest. For example, suppose that you have $1,000 invested in an account that earns 5 percent interest per year, compounded annually. *Annual compounding* means that the interest on the balance is calculated once per year. How much will you have at the end of one year? at the end of two years? We'll solve this problem using each of the three calculation methods, which are summarized in the *Go Figure!* box, "Future Value of a Lump Sum." The timeline for the problem is shown below:

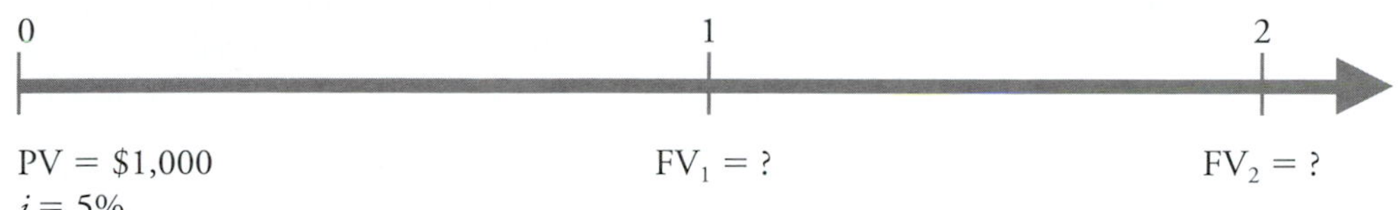

PV = \$1,000 $\quad$ FV_1 = ? $\quad$ FV_2 = ?
$i = 5\%$

Method 1: Mathematical Formula Solution. The future value (FV) of a lump sum is the present value (PV), or the amount invested today, plus the compound interest earned on the present value for the period. In this case, we're looking for the value in one year and in two years. We know that the present value is \$1,000 and the interest rate is 5 percent. Thus, we can easily see that after one year, we'll have the original \$1,000 plus \$50 in interest (\$1,000 × 0.05 = \$50), for a total of \$1,050. Notice that this is the same as multiplying the original \$1,000 times 1 plus the interest rate, since \$1,000 × 1.05 = \$1,050.

Now suppose you leave the \$1,050 in your account for another year. At the end of the second year, you'll have the \$1,050 from year one plus \$52.50 in interest for the second year (\$1,050 x 0.05 = \$52.50), for a total of \$1,102.50. This is the same as multiplying the original \$1,000 times 1.05^2 since \$1,000 × 1.1025 = \$1,102.50. We can therefore generalize the equation for future value as follows:

$$FV = PV \times (1 + i)^n$$

where

FV = Future value

PV = Present value, or the amount invested today

i = interest rate for one period

n = Number of periods

To solve the two-year problem above, we need only substitute the appropriate values and solve for the future value FV:

$$\begin{aligned} FV &= PV \times (1 + i)^n \\ &= \$1{,}000 \times (1 + 0.05)^2 \\ &= \$1{,}102.50 \end{aligned}$$

Alternatively, we can solve this problem by using Table A-1 in Appendix A at the back of this book. The term $(1 + i)^n$ in the future value equation is called the *future value interest factor*, and the table provides values for future value interest factors for various interest rates and periods, saving us the need to calculate the values. The future value interest factor $FVIF_{i,n}$ can thus take the place of $(1 + i)^n$ in the future value equation, which can be restated as

$$FV = PV \times FVIF_{i,n}$$

To use this equation, we first determine the future value interest factor for 2 years and 5 percent interest. By looking across the columns in Table A-1 to i = 5 percent and down the rows to n = 2, we find that this value is 1.103. Since the amount invested is \$1,000, we then multiply this present value by the future value interest factor to find the future value:

$$FV = \$1{,}000 \times 1.103 = \$1{,}103$$

This answer is slightly different from the \$1,102.50 solution using the full mathematical formula because the future value interest factors in Exhibit A-1 are rounded to three decimals.

Method 2: Financial Calculator Solution. To solve a time value problem using a financial calculator, you need to enter the values that you know and solve for the one that you don't know. For most financial calculators, you key in the value of a variable and then push the appropriate button to enter it in the memory of the calculator. Thus, to use a financial calculator to solve for the future value when you know the present value, the interest rate, and the number of periods, you can use the following keystokes:

1. Key in 2 and then press N.
2. Key in 5 and then press I.
3. Key in −1,000 and then press PV.
4. Key in 0 and then press PMT.
5. Press CPT (on the TIBAII Plus) and then FV.

The order of entry of the variables doesn't matter as long as you've entered all the necessary information before you attempt to compute the solution. If the problem doesn't include a value corresponding to one of the keys—as in the case of our sample problem, where there is no payment (PMT)—we enter zero for that variable. (Note that if you've cleared the memory correctly before starting a new problem, each variable will have been reset to zero, so you actually don't have to separately enter the 0. Check your calculator manual for the proper way to clear memory; on the TI BAII Plus, as an example, you'll hit [2nd] [CLR TVM].)

You may also wonder why we entered the present value as a negative number above. For financial calculators and spreadsheets, you must enter cash *inflows* as positive numbers and cash *outflows* as negative numbers, using the +/− key to change the sign before entering the value. Since, in this problem, you are investing the original $1,000, it is a cash outflow to you, and so it is entered as a negative value.

Method 3: Spreadsheet Solution. Microsoft Excel and other spreadsheets come with built-in formulas for many different purposes. When using Excel, you can see a list of these built-in formulas by clicking the function key (*fx*) on the toolbar at the top of the page. A box will open; click Financial in the list on the left-hand side of the box, and a lengthy list of abbreviations for financial formulas will appear at the right. You can click on one of these abbreviations and then click OK at the lower right, and Excel will help you build the formula using your variables. You can also click the Help button at the lower left for an explanation of each variable, as well as an example.

The general future value equation in Microsoft Excel is

= FV(rate,nper,pmt,pv,type)

To solve a future value problem, set your cursor on any cell in a spreadsheet and type the equation, entering values for each of the variable names above in the order given, separated by commas, and a zero for any variable that isn't applicable to the problem. As you can probably guess, the variables employed in Excel correspond directly to those we used in the mathematical formula and financial calculator methods:

- rate = the periodic interest rate i (in decimal format)
- nper = the number of periods n
- pv = the present value PV
- pmt = the dollar amount of a regular periodic payment of money
- "type" refers to when payments and compounding will occur (for beginning-of-period timing, enter 1; for end-of-period timing, enter 0)

To solve our two-year investment problem using the spreadsheet method, we type the following into a cell:

= FV(.05,2,-1000,0,0)

and then hit Enter on the computer keyboard. The solution, $1,102.50, should immediately appear in the cell. Excel templates for solving this and other time value problems are available on the text website. The *Go Figure!* box, "Future Value of a Lump Sum," summarizes the calculations discussed in this section.

GO FIGURE!

Future Value of a Lump Sum

Problem You invest $2,500 today. How much will it be worth in 5 years if your account earns 8 percent per year, compounded annually?

1. Mathematical formula solution:

a. $FV = PV \times (1 + i)^n$
$= \$2{,}500 \times (1.08)^5$
$= \$3{,}673.32$

or

b. $FV = PV \times FVIF_{i,n}$
$= \$2{,}500 \times 1.469$
$= \$3{,}672.50$

where FV = future value, PV = present value, i = interest rate per period, n = number of periods, and $FVIF_{i,n}$ = future value interest factor (see Appendix A, Table A-1).

2. Financial calculator solution:

Enter	5	8	−2,500	0	
	N	I	PV	PMT	FV
Compute					3,673.32

3. Spreadsheet solution:
Future value of a lump sum formula
= FV(i,n,pmt,−pv,type)
Type the formula in any cell or on the formula toolbar and press Enter to see the solution.

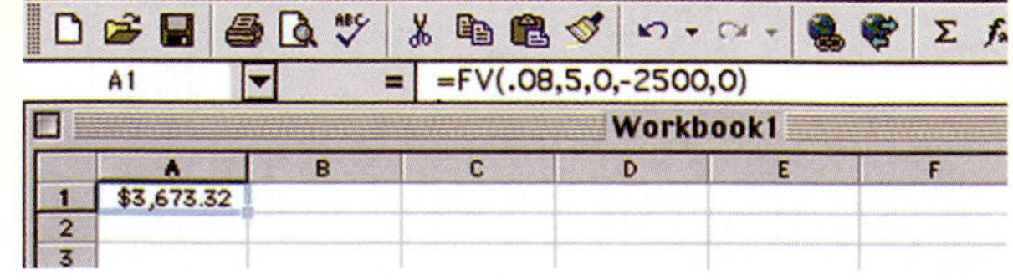

Present Value of a Lump Sum

In personal financial planning, we often set goals for the future and then attempt to take steps to achieve those goals. Therefore, a common type of problem is one in which we need to determine how much to invest today in **present value (PV)** in order to have a desired amount in the future. Another use of present value is to determine how much an amount to be received in the future is worth to you today. Since a present value will always be less than its future value, we often use the word **discounting** to describe the process of calculating present value.

present value (PV)

The amount of money that would have to be invested today to grow to a given future value over a specified period at a specified interest rate.

discounting

The process of calculating the present value of a lump sum or a series of payments to be received in the future.

Suppose, for example, that you want to buy a $10,000 car four years from now. You would like to set aside enough money today so that, if you earn 5 percent interest over the four years, you'll have exactly $10,000 to buy the car at the end of the fourth year. We'll use each of the three methods, to solve this problem. Your timeline for this problem should look like this:

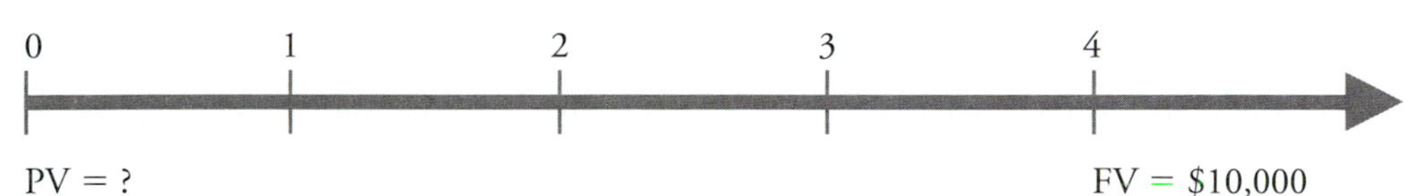

PV = ?   FV = $10,000
i = 5%

Method 1: Mathematical Formula Solution. We already know that FV = PV × $(1 + i)^n$. We can simply turn that equation around—dividing each side by $(1 + i)^n$—to arrive at the formula for present value. The result is

$$PV = FV \times \left(\frac{1}{1+i}\right)^n$$

where, as before,

FV = Future value
PV = Present value
i = Interest rate for one period
n = Number of periods

We can enter the values from our example to find the solution:

$$\begin{aligned} PV &= \$10{,}000 \times \left(\frac{1}{1.05}\right)^4 \\ &= \$10{,}000 \times (0.9524)^4 \\ &= \$10{,}000 \times 0.8227 \\ &= \$8{,}227 \end{aligned}$$

Based on this calculation, if you deposit $8,227 in an account earning 5 percent per year, compounded annually, and leave it there with all accumulated interest for four years, you'll have $10,000 in the account at the end of the four years.

The term $[1/(1 + i)]^n$ is known as the *present value interest factor*, or $PVIF_{i,n}$, and is precalculated in Appendix A, Exhibit A-2, for many possible values of i and n. Thus, as we did earlier for the future value calculations, we can substitute the present value interest factor for the second term of the present value equation as follows:

$$PV = FV \times PVIF_{i,n}$$

For this problem, we look across the columns to the one labeled 5 percent and then down the rows to 4; the value from the table is 0.823. Substituting this value into the equation above, we calculate:

$$PV = \$10{,}000 \times 0.823 = \$8{,}230$$

As before, we find that the answer we get using the table is slightly less precise than the one we calculated with the full mathematical formula, due to rounding.

Method 2: Financial Calculator Solution. To solve present value problems with a financial calculator, we enter the values that we know, enter zero for those that don't apply, and compute the result. After clearing your previous work, use the following keystrokes to solve for the present value of a lump sum:

1. Key in 4 and then press N.
2. Key in 5 and then press I.
3. Key in 10,000 and then press FV.
4. Press CPT and then press PV.

Regardless of the order in which you enter the variables, the answer will be −8,227. Note that this is a negative number, since it represents a cash outflow to you, as explained earlier.

Method 3: Spreadsheet Solution. The Excel formula for present value is

= PV(rate,nper,pmt,fv,type)

As with the future value Excel formula, we set our cursor on an empty cell in the spreadsheet and type in the equation, entering the appropriate values for the variables in the order indicated. For this problem, the equation is

= PV(.05,4,0,10000,0)

The solution that appears in the cell, rounded to the nearest dollar, is −$8,227, which corresponds to the answers we found by using the mathematical formula and the financial calculator. Like the minus sign in the financial calculator solution, the answer will appear as a negative number, since the present value represents a cash outflow to you. The *Go Figure!* box, "Present Value of a Lump Sum," summarizes the calculations discussed in this section using a different example.

Learning by Doing 2-5

1. You invest $1,000 today and earn 10 percent interest, compounded annually. How much will you have in 5 years?
2. You need to have $5,000 one year from now to pay your tuition. How much do you need to invest today if you can earn 10 percent interest, compounded annually?

future value of an annuity (FVA)

The amount to which a regular series of payments will grow, with compounding, if invested at a given rate of interest for a particular period of time.

annuity

A series of equal payments made at regular intervals for a period of time.

Future Value of an Annuity

What if, instead of saving a single lump sum today, you'd like to invest a certain amount each year (or each month) to arrive at your savings goal? The amount to which this regular series of payments will grow, with compounding, if invested at a given rate of interest for a particular period of time, is called the **future value of an annuity**, or **FVA**. An **annuity** is a series of payments of equal dollar amounts made at regular intervals for a period of time. Examples of annuities include fixed mortgages and car payments. An **ordinary annuity** is one in which each payment occurs at the *end* of the period, such as your weekly paycheck. An **annuity due** is one in which each payment occurs at the *beginning* of the period, such as your rent payment.

GO FIGURE!

Present Value of a Lump Sum

Problem You will receive $5,000 10 years from now. How much is that future payment worth to you today at an interest rate of 7 percent, compounded annually?

1. Mathematical formula solution:

   a. $PV = FV \times \left(\frac{1}{1+i}\right)^n$

   $= \$5{,}000 \times \left(\frac{1}{1.07}\right)^{10}$

   $= \$2{,}541.75$

   or:

   b. $PV = FV \times PVIF_{i,n}$

   $= \$5{,}000 \times 0.508$

   $= \$2{,}540$

   where FV = future value, PV = present value, i = interest rate per period, n = number of periods, and $PVIF_{i,n}$ = present value interest factor (see Appendix A, Table A-2).

2. Financial calculator solution:

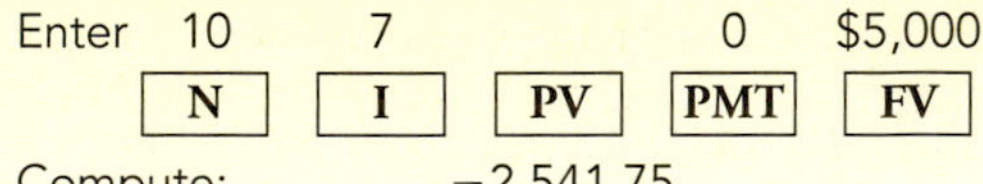

Enter	10	7		0	$5,000
	N	I	PV	PMT	FV
Compute:			−2,541.75		

3. Spreadsheet solution

   Present value of a lump sum = PV(i,n,pmt,fv,type)

   Type the formula in any cell or on the formula toolbar, and press Enter to see the solution.

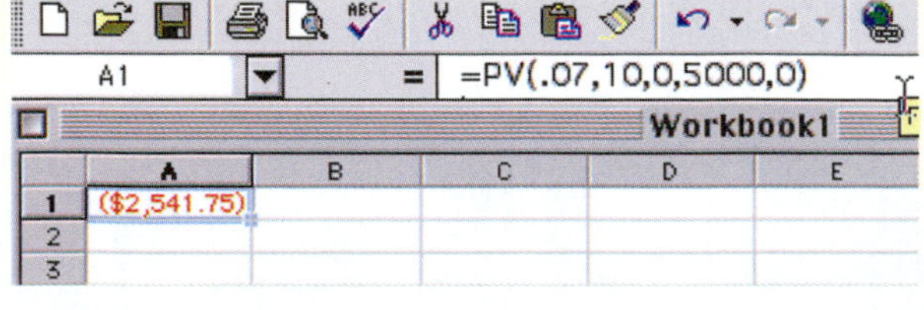

Calculating the future value of an annuity is the equivalent of calculating the future value for each of the payments as lump sums and then adding them together. Finding the solution in this way, though, can be fairly tedious for longer investment periods. Consider a simple example: You plan to make two payments of $100, one invested one year from now and one invested two years from now, and you expect your investment to earn 5 percent per year, compounded annually. Because each payment is made at the end of the year, this is an ordinary annuity. If you reinvest all your interest earnings, how much will the total be worth at the end of two years? First, we draw the timeline for the problem:

ordinary annuity

An annuity with end-of-period payments.

annuity due

An annuity with beginning-of-period payments.

0	1	2
	PMT_1 = $100	PMT_2 = $100
$i = 5\%$		FV = ?

At the end of the two-year period, the first $100 payment, PMT_1, will have been in the account for only one year so it will have grown to $100 \times (1.05) = \$105$. The second $100 payment, PMT_2, will be invested at the end of year two and therefore will not have earned any interest yet. So it's still worth only $100 at the end of the second year. Altogether, you'll have $205. Now, what if you paid $100 at the end of each year *for three years*? At the end of the third year, you'd have

$$\underbrace{[100 \times (1.05)^2]}_{PMT_1} + \underbrace{[100 \times (1.05)]}_{PMT_2} + \underbrace{100}_{PMT_3} = \$315.25$$

But what if you wanted to invest $100 per year each year all the way to retirement? You can see what a chore it would be to calculate this value with separate lump sums. Fortunately, there's a single formula that combines all the compounding calculations. The *Go Figure!* box, "Future Value of an Annuity," summarizes the mathematical formula, financial calculator, and spreadsheet methods for solving future value of annuity problems.

How much will *her* wedding cost fifteen years from now?

GO FIGURE!

Future Value of an Annuity

Problem

You plan to make end-of-year payments of $5,000 every year for 40 years into a retirement account earning 12 percent interest. How much will you have accumulated by the time you retire?

1. Mathematical formula solution:

a. $FVA = PMT \times \dfrac{(1+i)^n - 1}{i}$

$= \$5{,}000 \times \dfrac{(1.12)^{40} - 1}{0.12}$

$= \$5{,}000 \times 767.091$

$= \$3{,}835{,}457$

or

b. $FVA = PMT \times FVIFA_{i,n}$

$= \$5{,}000 \times 767.091$

$= \$3{,}835{,}455$

where *FVA* = future value of an ordinary annuity, *PMT* = payment per period, *i* = interest rate per period, *n* = number of periods; and $FVIFA_{i,n}$ = future value interest factor of an annuity (see Appendix A, Table A-3).

2. Financial calculator solution:

Enter	40	12	0	5000	
	N	I	PV	PMT	FV
Compute:					−$3,835,457

3. Spreadsheet solution:
   Future value of an annuity = FV(i,n,pmt,pv,type)
   Type the formula in any cell or on the formula toolbar, and press Enter to see the solution.

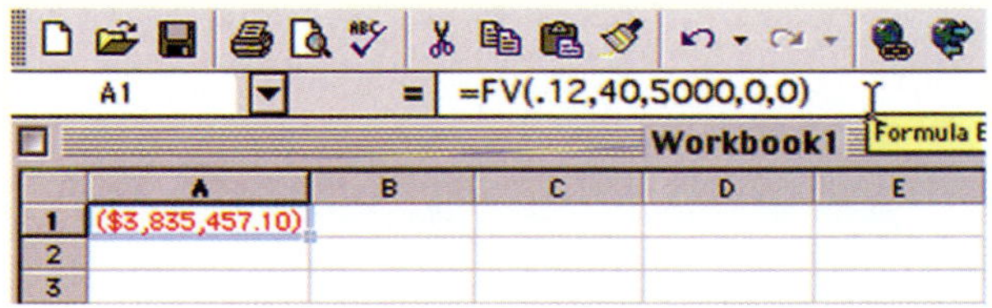

Method 1: Mathematical Formula Solution. We can calculate the future value of an ordinary annuity FVA mathematically with the following formula:

$$FVA = PMT \times \frac{(1 + i)^n - 1}{i}$$

where

$$\begin{aligned} FVA &= \text{Future value of an ordinary annuity} \\ PMT &= \text{Payment per period} \\ i &= \text{Interest rate for one period} \\ n &= \text{Number of periods} \end{aligned}$$

Let's use the equation to solve the three-period problem presented earlier. Since we know that PMT = \$100, $i = 0.05$, and $n = 3$, we can substitute these values into the equation and solve for FVA:

$$\begin{aligned} FVA &= \$100 \times \frac{(1.05)^3 - 1}{0.05} \\ &= \$100 \times \frac{0.157625}{0.05} \\ &= \$100 \times 3.1525 \\ &= \$315.25 \end{aligned}$$

The second part of this equation, $[(1 + i)^n - 1]/i$, is called the *future value interest factor of an annuity*, or $FVIFA_{i,n}$. Exhibit A-3 in Appendix A provides values of $FVIFA_{i,n}$ for various interest rates and periods. If we look across the columns to $i = 5$ percent and then down the row to $n = 3$, we find that the appropriate value is 3.153. Using this value, we can calculate:

$$\begin{aligned} FVA &= PMT \times FVIFA_{i,n} \\ &= \$100 \times 3.153 \\ &= \$315.30 \end{aligned}$$

As in the calculations of present value and future value, the table solution is slightly less precise due to rounding.

Method 2: Financial Calculator Solution. The calculator button for annuity payments is PMT. As before, you'll enter the values you know and solve for the one you don't know. After clearing your previous work, use the following keystrokes to solve for the future value of an annuity:

1. Key in −\$100 and then press PMT.
2. Key in 3 and then press N.
3. Key in 5 and then press I.
4. Press CPT and then press FV.

The answer should be \$315.25, regardless of the order in which you enter the variables.

So far we've been working with an ordinary annuity, in which payments are made at the end of each period. Now suppose that you make an investment contribution at the *beginning* of each year instead of at the end—an annuity due. Compare the annuity due timeline below with the timeline presented earlier for an ordinary annuity. Note that making beginning-of-period payments means that you gain an extra year of interest compounding for each payment.

You can use your financial calculator to solve for the future value of an annuity due by adjusting your calculator setting. For the TI BAII Plus calculator, the keystrokes for toggling between end-of-period END and beginning-of-period BGN settings are [2nd] [BGN] [2nd] [SET]. The END setting is the default, so an indicator BGN will appear in the LCD display if you are set for beginning-of-period payments. After you switch to the BGN setting, you can use the same keystrokes you used above to solve the ordinary annuity problem. The result is \$331.01, a little more than the \$315.25 future value that resulted for the ordinary annuity. The difference is the extra interest received, a factor of $(1 + i)$; that is, \$331.01 = \$315.25 × 1.05.

Method 3: Spreadsheet Solution. The Microsoft Excel formula for the future value of an annuity is the same as that for the future value of a lump sum:

=FV(rate,nper,pmt,pv,type)

The difference is that we input a value for pmt instead of for pv. So for this problem, we calculate the future value of an annuity by typing the following formula into a cell on the spreadsheet:

=FV(.05,3,-100,0,0)

When you press ENTER on your keyboard, the solution that appears in the cell will be the same as the calculator solution: \$315.25. To solve for the future value of an annuity due, enter the *type* as 1 instead of 0:

=FV(.05,3,-100,0,1)

The result should be \$331.01, again the same as the calculator solution.

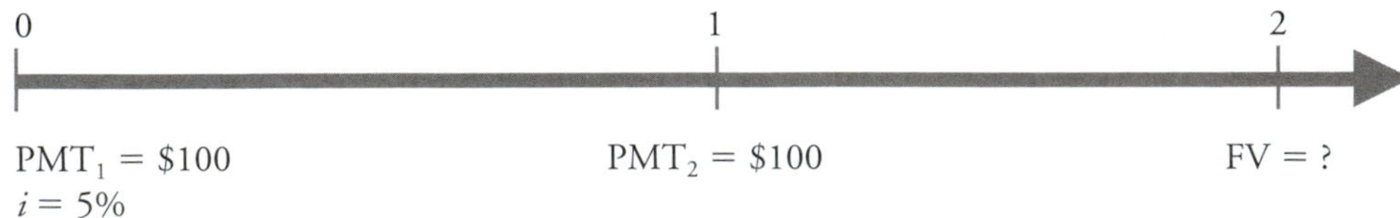

Present Value of an Annuity

The primary personal finance application of the FVA calculation just discussed is to determine the future accumulated value of a series of steady payments made to an investment account. Conversely, the **present value of an annuity (PVA)** is the amount you would have to set aside today to be able to withdraw a particular amount of money each period for a given number of periods. This original amount will be less than the total of the payments because the account will continue to earn interest each period on the gradually declining balance. Thus, if you want to take $10,000 per year from an account for 10 years, you don't need to deposit $100,000 today; you need to deposit a smaller amount that, together with compound interest, will be sufficient to allow you to withdraw the $10,000 per year, leaving you with a zero balance by the end of the tenth year. To calculate the amount you would need to deposit, we use the present value of an annuity calculation presented in this section.

present value of an annuity

The lump sum amount that must be deposited today to provide for equal periodic payments for a given number of periods in the future.

Annuities are a way of providing a stable cash flow for a period of time. For this reason, financial investments that provide annuity payments are popular with retirees. We also commonly pay back loans by making a series of equal payments to the lender, often on a monthly basis, as in the case of a typical 30-year level-payment mortgage or a 5-year level-payment car loan.

As an example, suppose you're considering the purchase of an annuity contract in which your bank promises to pay you $2,000 at the end of every year for the next three years. Note that this is an ordinary annuity, since the payments are made at the end of each year. The timeline for this annuity is presented below:

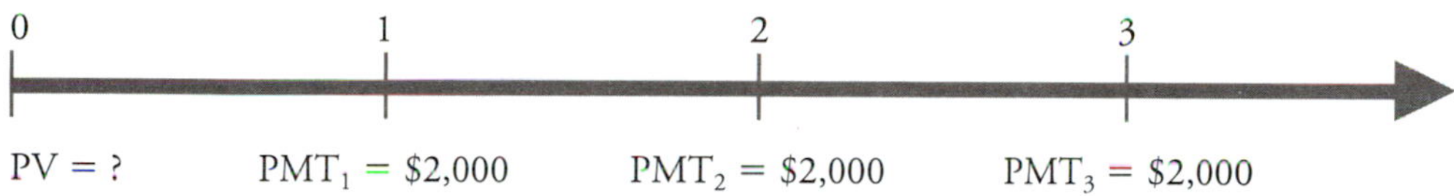

How much will you have to pay the bank today for this annuity? The answer depends on the rate of interest that the bank is able to earn. Let's assume that the interest rate is 10 percent. Since an annuity is just a series of lump sum payments, we can calculate the present value of each one separately and add them up. Recall that the formula for the present value of a lump sum is $PV = FV \times [1/(1 + i)]^n$. Since the amounts to be received in the future are the three payments PMT_1, PMT_2, and PMT_3, these can be substituted in that equation with the appropriate number of periods to find the present value of each individual payment. The present value of the series of payments, rounded to the nearest dollar, will therefore be

$$\begin{aligned} PVA &= \left[PMT \times \left(\frac{1}{1+i}\right)^3\right] + \left[PMT \times \left(\frac{1}{1+i}\right)^2\right] + \left[PMT \times \left(\frac{1}{1+i}\right)^1\right] \\ &= \left[\$2{,}000 \times \left(\frac{1}{1.1}\right)^3\right] + \$2{,}000 \times \left(\frac{1}{1.1}\right)^2\right] + \$2{,}000 \times \left(\frac{1}{1.1}\right)^1\right] \\ &= (\$2.000 \times 0.7513) + (\$2{,}000 \times 0.8265) + (\$2{,}000 \times 0.9091) \\ &= \$1{,}503 + \$1{,}653 + \$1{,}818 \\ &= \$4{,}974 \end{aligned}$$

This means that if your bank takes the $4,974 and invests it to earn 10 percent interest per year, it can pay you $2,000 at the end of each year and have enough to get to the end. To see that this is so, consider the bank's account balances over this three-year period:

Year	Beginning Balance	Interest	Payment	Ending Balance
1	$4,974.00	+$497.40	−$2,000	$3,471.40
2	3,471.40	+347.14	−2,000	1,818.54
3	1,818.54	+$181.85	−$2,000	0.39

The few cents that are left at the end are the result of rounding the payment to the nearest dollar. An important point to remember is that the present value of a series of payments will always be less than the sum of those payments. The difference is the interest earned on the gradually declining balance.

As problems get more complex, with longer time periods, it becomes less efficient to calculate the present value for each payment separately. Again, a mathematical formula is available to combine the calculations. The formula solution, financial calculator solution, and spreadsheet solutions are summarized in the *Go Figure!* box "Present Value of an Annuity."

Method 1: Mathematical Formula Solution. Given the complexity of solving for the present value of a series of payments, it shouldn't be surprising that the mathematical formula for the present value of an annuity is a bit complicated:

$$PVA = PMT \times \frac{\left[1 - \left(\frac{1}{1+i}\right)^n\right]}{i}$$

where

PVA = Present value of an ordinary annuity
PMT = Payment per period
i = Interest rate for one period
n = Number of periods

In our example, we can solve for the present value of the three $2,000 payments as follows:

$$\begin{aligned} PVA &= \$2{,}000 \times \frac{\left[1 - \left(\frac{1}{1.1}\right)^3\right]}{0.1} \\ &= \$2{,}000 \times \frac{[1 - 0.7513]}{0.1} \\ &= \$2{,}000 \times 2.4869 \\ &= \$4{,}973.70 \end{aligned}$$

The second term in the PVA equation is called the *present value interest factor of an annuity*, or $PVIFA_{i,n}$, so we can also write the PVA equation as

$$PVA = PMT \times PVIFA_{i,n}$$

GO FIGURE!

Present Value of an Annuity

Problem You want to be able to draw out $20,000 at the end of each year for the next 15 years to fund your estimated retirement needs. If your investment account earns 6 percent per year and you will have zero left at the end, how much do you need to have in your account when you retire?

1. Mathematical formula solution

a. $$PVA = PMT \times \frac{1 - \left(\frac{1}{1+i}\right)^n}{i}$$

$$\begin{aligned} &= \$20{,}000 \times \frac{1 - \left(\frac{1}{1.06}\right)^{15}}{0.06} \\ &= \$20{,}000 \times 9.71225 \\ &= \$194{,}245 \end{aligned}$$

or

b. $$\begin{aligned} PVA &= PMT \times PVIFA_{i,n} \\ &= \$20{,}000 \times 9.712 \\ &= \$194{,}240 \end{aligned}$$

where PVA = present value of an ordinary annuity, PMT = payment, i = interest rate per period, n = number of periods, and $PVIFA_{i,n}$ = present value interest factor of an annuity (see Appendix A, Table A-4).

2. Financial calculator solution:

Enter	15	6		20,000	0
	N	I	PV	PMT	FV

Compute: −$194,245

3. Spreadsheet solution:
Present value of an annuity = PV(i,n,pmt,fv,type)
Type the formula in any cell or on the formula toolbar, and press Enter to see the solution.

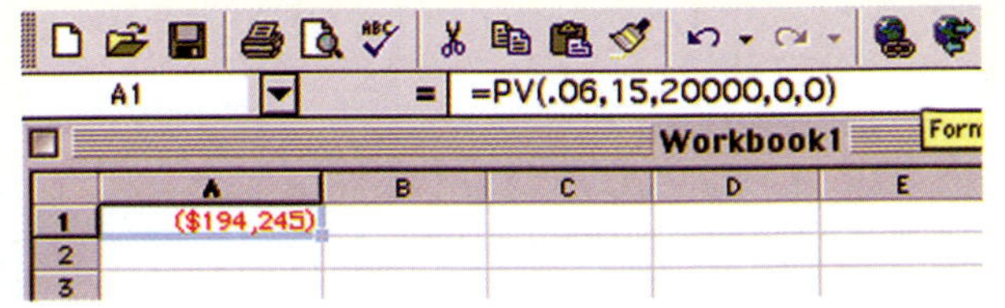

Exhibit A-4 in Appendix A gives precalculated $PVIFA_{i,n}$ values for various interest rates and periods. We find in Exhibit A-4 that the value for a 10 percent interest rate and three periods is 2.487. Substituting this value into the equation, we solve the problem as follows:

$$\begin{aligned} PVA &= \$2,000 \times 2.487 \\ &= \$4,974 \end{aligned}$$

Once again, the answer differs slightly from the previous one because of rounding.

Method 2: Financial Calculator Solution. To solve for the present value of an annuity using a financial calculator, we again enter the information we know, enter zero for terms that don't apply, and solve for what we don't know—the present value.

1. Key in $2,000 and then press PMT.
2. Key in 10 and then press I.
3. Key in 3 and then press N.
4. Press CPT and the press PV.

The answer should be the same as that we arrived at with the formula: $4,973.70, except that it will be presented as a negative number, since it represents a cash outflow to you. If you get a different answer, don't forget to check your calculator settings to be sure you're set for end-of-period payments rather than beginning-of-period payments, as discussed in the previous section.

Method 3: Spreadsheet Solution. The Microsoft Excel formula for the present value of an annuity is the same as that for the present value of a lump sum:

=PV(rate,nper,pmt,fv,type)

The difference is that we input a value for pmt instead of for fv. For this problem, we type the equation into a cell on the spreadsheet as follows:

=PV(.1,3,2000,0,0)

The solution that appears will be a negative number, −$4,973.70, since the spreadsheet shows cash outflows as a negative.

Learning by Doing 2-6

1. You would like to begin saving for a down payment on a home. If you want to buy the home five years from now, and you will make annual end-of-year payments into your savings, how much will you have for your down payment if you save $500 per year and earn 10 percent on your investment, compounded annually?
2. You've just won a $10 million lottery, and the payout is 1/25 of the jackpot ($400,000) payable at the end of each year for 25 years.
   a. What is the present value of the annuity if annual interest on the balance is 8 percent?
   b. What is the present value of the annuity if annual interest on the balance is 10 percent?
   c. What does this say about the benefits of taking the cash value option of 40 percent of the jackpot ($4,000,000 in this case) in lieu of the annuity?

Computing Payments for Loans Using Time Value Principles

Now that we've covered the four types of time value calculations, we can tackle a practical personal financial planning problem. As mentioned earlier, loan payments represent one of the most common types of annuities. **Amortization** is the technical word for the process of paying interest on a declining loan balance in addition to repaying some of the face value of the loan with each payment. The payments on an amortized loan are calculated so that by the time you make your last payment, you've paid off the total loan balance as well. Sound familiar? It should, because the process is the same as the one just described in the discussion of calculating the present value of an annuity. Instead of solving for the present value, though, we need to solve for the payment.

The time value of money can be used to calculate car loan payments.

Let's consider an example similar to the one used to illustrate the present value of an annuity. There, we found that it would cost you $4,973.70 to purchase an investment that would pay you $2,000 per year for three years if the bank earned 10 percent on its funds. Now, suppose instead that you want to buy a used car and your bank is willing to lend you $4,973.70 at

amortization

The process of calculating equal payments on a loan that include principal repayment and interest on the declining balance.

10 percent interest for three years (a bit steep by today's standards, but maybe you're a risky customer). How much would your payments be per year? You already know that the answer is $2,000 per year, but let's see how we could arrive at that answer using time value of money calculations. The following diagram illustrates the timeline:

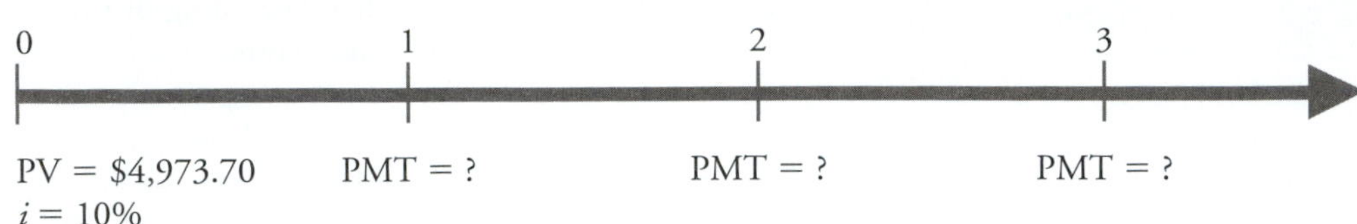

PV = $4,973.70 PMT = ? PMT = ? PMT = ?
i = 10%

Method 1: Mathematical Formula Solution. We already know the equation for the present value of an annuity:

$$PVA = PMT \times \frac{\left[1 - \left(\frac{1}{1+i}\right)^n\right]}{i}$$

With a little algebra, we can solve for PMT and simplify to get:

$$PMT = PVA \times \frac{i}{\left[1 - \left(\frac{1}{1+i}\right)^n\right]}$$

That equation looks a bit intimidating. We also know, however, that $PVA = PMT \times PVIFA_{i,n}$. It follows, then, that

$$PMT = \frac{PVA}{PVIFA_{i,n}}$$

Substituting the present value ($4,973.70) and the present value interest factor for 10 percent and 3 periods from Exhibit A-4 (2.487), we can calculate the payment:

$$PMT = \frac{\$4{,}973.70}{2.487}$$

$$= \$2{,}000 \quad \text{(rounded to the nearest dollar)}$$

Method 2: Financial Calculator Solution. It is particularly easy to solve for loan payments with a financial calculator. The keystrokes in this case are as follows:

1. Key in 4,973.70 and then press PV.
2. Key in 3 and then press N.
3. Key in 10 and then press I.
4. Press CPT and then press PMT.

The answer, rounded to the nearest dollar, should be −$2,000. Once again, it's a negative number because car loan payments are cash outflows to you.

Method 3: Spreadsheet Solution. Calculating payments in Excel requires an equation different from those we used previously. (If you're ever unsure of the correct equation to use to solve a particular problem in Excel, click the f_X key and browse the formulas as described earlier.) The equation used to solve for a payment is called PMT, conveniently the same abbreviation we've been using. The formula is as follows:

=PMT(rate,nper,pv,fv,type)

As always, we key in the appropriate values and then hit the Enter key. Note that for all amortized loan payment problems, the future value is always zero, since you will have fully paid off the loan by the end:

=PMT(.1,3,4973.70,0,0)

The answer $2,000 should appear in the cell as a negative value.

What If Payments Are Not Annual?

We've so far assumed that interest is compounded annually. On most loans today, however, payments are made on a monthly basis, and interest is compounded monthly. If you review the definitions above, you'll notice that we've consistently expressed interest and payments as *per period* amounts. Therefore, all you need to do to solve a problem for monthly payments is to convert your interest to a monthly rate (divide i by 12) and enter the number of months as n. You can use any of the three methods of calculation for solving problems with nonannual payments, although the financial calculator and the spreadsheet methods are considerably simpler. To illustrate, let's use the same example as before and determine how much you would have to pay per month for the three-year car loan of $4,973.70.

Method 1: Mathematical Formula Solution. First, calculate the interest per period and the number of periods:

$$i = \frac{10\%}{12}$$
$$= 0.8333 \text{ percent} \quad \text{or} \quad 0.008333$$
$$n = 3 \times 12 = 36$$

Using the mathematical formula to solve for the payment, we calculate as follows:

$$\text{PMT} = \text{PVA} \times \frac{i}{\left[1 - \left(\frac{1}{1+i}\right)^n\right]}$$
$$= \$4973.70 \times \left[\frac{0.008333}{1 - \left(\frac{1}{1.008333}\right)^{36}}\right]$$
$$= \$160.49$$

To get as exact an answer as possible, try to avoid rounding until you reach the final solution to the problem. As in the other mathematical calculation methods, we can sometimes use a table to simplify the math. However, because of the infinite number of monthly i and n combinations that are possible, the limited choices offered in tables will not always correspond to the facts of the problem you are solving. Exhibit A-5 in the Appendix provides precalculated payment amounts per $1,000 borrowed for a range of interest rates and periods.

Method 2: Financial Calculator Solution. To solve this problem using a financial calculator, use the following keystrokes:

1. Key in 10/12 = and then press I.
2. Key in 3 × 12 = and then press N.
3. Key in 4973.70 and then press PV.
4. Press CPT and then press PMT to get the solution: −160.49.

Although you could simply enter the value for the interest rate (0.8333), as well as the number of periods (36), you will avoid rounding errors on future problems if you use the method above.

Method 3: Spreadsheet Solution. To solve the problem using a spreadsheet, simply enter the periodic interest rate and the number of periods in the same formula as above:

=PMT(rate,nper,pv,fv,type)

In this case, we would enter the following values:

=PMT(.0083333,36,4973.70,0,0)

to arrive at the solution, $160.49, which should appear as a negative number, since it represents a cash outflow to you.

Learning by Doing 2-7

1. Suppose you obtain a mortgage in the amount of $50,000 to buy a condo. If rates are currently at 6 percent and you'll take a 30-year loan with fixed payments, how much will your mortgage payment be under the following scenarios:
   a. You will make annual end-of-year payments.
   b. You will make regular payments at the end of each month.

Summary

1 **Develop a system for organizing and maintaining your financial records.** Evaluating and tracking your personal finances are activities that require you to have access to accurate financial information for planning, budgeting, and tax filing. You need to safeguard important documents and develop an effective system of organization.

2 **Calculate your net worth using a personal balance sheet.** Your personal balance sheet is a financial statement that lists the market values of everything you own (assets) and all the amounts you owe to others (debts or liabilities) at a particular point in time. Based on this information, you can calculate your net worth, which is the total value of your assets minus the total value of your debts.

3 **Summarize your current inflows and outflows of cash using a personal cash flow statement.** A personal cash flow statement details inflows and outflows of cash over a period of time, often one month or one year. You can use this financial statement to calculate net cash flow for the period by subtracting cash outflows from cash inflows.

4 **Use personal financial ratios to evaluate your current financial position.** Financial ratios allow you to evaluate your current financial position based on your personal balance sheet and cash flow statement data. By comparing your ratios over time, you can track your progress toward achieving your financial goals. The most common ratios measure liquidity, debt management, and savings adequacy.

5 **Understand and apply the basic principles of the time value of money.** The time value of money is an important concept in personal finance. The underlying principle of all time value

calculations is that a dollar today is worth more than a dollar in the future. The four basic types of time value calculations are future value of a lump sum, present value of a lump sum, future value of an annuity, and present value of an annuity. Present value calculations help you better understand the amounts you need today to meet future obligations. Future value calculations are useful for calculating the amount to which your current savings will grow.

Key Terms

amortization (56)
annuity (50)
annuity due (51)
assets (32)
cash surrender value (35)
compounding (44)
debt payment ratio (43)
debt ratio (43)
debts (32)
discounting (49)
fixed expenses (39)
future value (46)
future value of an annuity (50)
gross income (39)
insolvency (36)
liquid assets (32)
liquidity ratio (41)
lockbox (31)
market value (35)
mortgage debt service (43)
mortgage debt service ratio (43)
net worth (32)
ordinary annuity (51)
personal balance sheet (32)
personal cash flow statement (37)
present value (49)
present value of an annuity (53)
safe deposit box (31)
savings ratio (43)
time value of money (44)
variable expenses (39)

Key Calculations

$$\text{Net worth} = \text{Total assets} - \text{Total debts}$$

$$\text{Net cash flow} = \text{Cash inflows} - \text{Cash outflows}$$

$$\text{Liquidity ratio} = \frac{\text{Liquid assets}}{\text{Monthly expenses}}$$

$$\text{Debt ratio} = \frac{\text{Total debt}}{\text{Total assets}}$$

$$\text{Debt payment ratio} = \frac{\text{Total monthly debt payment}}{\text{After-tax monthly income}}$$

$$\text{Mortgage debt service ratio} = \frac{\text{Principal} + \text{interest} + \text{taxes} + \text{insurance}}{\text{Gross monthly income}}$$

$$\text{Savings ratio} = \frac{\text{Monthly savings}}{\text{After-tax monthly income}}$$

Future value of a lump sum:

$$FV = PV \times (1+i)^n = PV \times FVIF_{i,n}$$

Present value of a lump sum:

$$PV = FV \times \left(\frac{1}{1+i}\right)^n = FV \times PVIF_{i,n}$$

Future value of an annuity:

$$FVA = PMT \times \frac{(1+i)^n - 1}{i} = PMT \times FVIFA_{i,n}$$

Present value of an annuity:

$$PVA = PMT \times \frac{1 - \left(\frac{1}{1+i}\right)^n}{i} = PMT \times PVIFA_{i,n}$$

Payments on an amortized loan:

$$PMT = PVA \times \frac{i}{\left[1 - \left(\frac{1}{1+i}\right)^n\right]} = \frac{PVA}{PVIFA_{i,n}}$$

Concept Review Questions

1. Why is it important to have a system for organizing your financial records?
2. How long should you save copies of your regular bills? What is the purpose of saving them?
3. What types of documents should be kept for more than one year?
4. What options do you have for safeguarding your important records and documents? Explain which types of records each option is appropriate for.
5. What are personal financial statements, and why are they important for personal financial planning?
6. What types of information are reported on your personal balance sheet? List the primary categories of assets and the primary categories of debts.
7. What is net worth, and how is it calculated? Give an example.
8. Under what circumstances will net worth be negative?
9. When you are constructing a personal balance sheet, what is the most appropriate measure of the value of your assets? Why?
10. Explain the difference between short-term and long-term liabilities. Give an example of each.
11. What is a personal cash flow statement, and why is it important to personal financial planning?

12. Differentiate between fixed and variable expenses, and give an example of each.
13. How is net cash flow calculated? Under what circumstances is net cash flow negative?
14. What are the three aspects of your finances measured by personal financial ratios?
15. How is the liquidity ratio calculated, and what does it measure?
16. How is the debt ratio calculated, and what does it measure?
17. How is the debt payment ratio calculated, and what does it measure?
18. How is the mortgage debt service ratio calculated and what does it measure?
19. How is the savings ratio calculated, and what does it measure?
20. What is compound interest?
21. Give an example that illustrates the importance of the time value of money.
22. For each of the following types of problems, identify which time value of money calculation must be used to solve the problem (*PV, FV, PVA, FVA*):
    a. You plan to invest a certain amount of money at the end of each month for 5 years. How much will your investment be worth at the end of the 5 years?
    b. You expect to receive a sum of money 10 years from now. How much is it worth today?
    c. How much is a single lump sum invested today going to be worth 10 years from now?
    d. You can afford to make monthly payments of a certain amount for 3 years. How much can you borrow today?

Application Problems

1. **Keeping Records.** Identify the purpose for saving each of the following documents, if any, and how long you should save it:
    a. Your Visa bill
    b. Your apartment rent receipt
    c. Your bank checking account statement
    d. Your tax return
    e. Your college tuition, fees, and housing bill
2. **Personal Balance Sheet.** Identify whether each of the following is an asset, a debt, or neither:
    a. Credit card balance
    b. Weekly employment earnings
    c. Car
    d. Rent paid to landlord
    e. Checking account
3. **Evaluating the Personal Balance Sheet.** Use the following personal balance sheet to answer the questions below:

Assets		Debts	
Bank accounts	$3,000	Current bills	$1,500
Car	$5,000	Student loan	$10,000
Personal assets	$2,000	Car loan	$3,000

    a. Calculate net worth.
    b. Calculate total liquid assets.
    c. Calculate the debt ratio.
    d. Assuming that monthly expenses total $1,200, calculate the liquidity ratio.
4. **Valuing Assets and Debts.** Holly is putting together her financial statements for year-end 2004. She isn't sure how to classify some of her financial data. Which of these transactions are assets, liabilities, income, or expenses, if any?
    a. She borrowed $1,000 from her parents this year, but will not begin to pay it back until she graduates from college in 2006.
    b. She is due a 2004 tax refund of $360, but has not yet received it.
    c. She receives income of $200 per month from a trust fund.
    d. She rents an apartment for $800 per month in her name, but her roommate pays $400 per month to her. Her roommate has not yet paid her for the December rent.
5. **Net Cash Flow.** Lucin earns $30,000 per year. She pays 30 percent of her gross income in federal, state, and social security taxes. She has fixed expenses of $750 per month and variable expenses that average $900 per month. What is her net cash flow for the year?
6. **Personal Financial Ratios.** Use the following balance sheet and cash flow statement information to answer the questions that follow:
    Liquid assets: $5,000
    Total assets: $180,000
    Current bills: $1,500
    Short-term debt: $4,500
    Long-term debt: $160,000
    Monthly gross income: $10,000
    Monthly after-tax income: $7,000
    Monthly mortgage payment (principal, interest, taxes, and insurance): $1,300
    Monthly nonmortgage debt payments: $450
    Total monthly expenses (not including taxes or current savings): $6,200
    Current monthly savings: $700
    a. Calculate the liquidity ratio.
    b. Calculate the debt ratio.
    c. Calculate the mortgage debt service ratio.
    d. Calculate the debt payment ratio.
    e. Calculate the savings ratio.
    f. Calculate net worth.
    g. Calculate net cash flow.
7. **Present Value of a Lump Sum.** Calculate the present value of the following future values, using one or more of the methods presented in this chapter:
    a. $200,000 to be received 30 years from today, discounted at 12 percent
    b. $200,000 to be received 30 years from today, discounted at 10 percent
    State in words the effect that the discount rate has on the present value of a lump sum to be received in the future.
8. **Present Value of a Lump Sum.** Calculate the present value of the following future values, using one or more of the methods presented in this chapter:
    a. $50,000 to be received 10 years from today, discounted at 8 percent
    b. $50,000 to be received 5 years from today, discounted at 8 percent
    State in words the effect that the time until receipt of a lump sum has on its present value.
9. **Future Value of a Lump Sum.** Calculate the future value of the following present values, using one or more of the methods presented in this chapter:

a. $5,000 invested today at a 4 percent rate and held for 10 years
b. $5,000 invested today at a 6 percent rate and held for 10 years

State in words the effect that the interest rate has on the future value of a lump sum invested today.

10. **Future Value of a Lump Sum.** Calculate the future value of the following present values, using one or more of the methods presented in this chapter:
a. $2,500 invested today at a 3 percent rate and held for 6 years
b. $2,500 invested today at a 3 percent rate and held for 8 years

State in words the effect that the length of the investment period has on the future value of a lump sum invested today.

11. **Present Value of an Annuity.** Calculate the present value of the following payment streams, using one or more of the methods presented in this chapter:
a. $1,000 at the end of each year for 10 years, assuming a 5 percent discount rate
b. $1,000 at the end of each year for 10 years, assuming a 10 percent discount rate

State in words the effect that the discount rate, or interest rate, has on the present value of an annuity.

12. **Future Value of an Annuity.** Calculate the future value of the following investments, using one or more of the methods presented in this chapter:
a. $2,000 invested at the end of each year for 6 years at 8 percent interest
b. $2,000 invested at the end of each year for 6 years at 12 percent interest

State in words the effect that the interest rate has on the future value of an annuity.

13. **Annual Versus Nonannual Compounding.** Miguel would like to save money to pay for his daughter's college expenses. He estimates that he will need to accumulate $40,000 over the next 10 years.
a. How much will he need to invest at the end of each year for 10 years to achieve his savings goal if he can earn 10 percent per year on the investment?
b. If Miguel would prefer to make monthly investment contributions, how much would he need to invest at the end of each *month* for 10 years in order to meet his savings goal?

14. **Time Value of Money.** You just won a $20 million lottery. You can choose between receiving: (a) $8 million today or (b) $800,000 per year for 25 years.
a. Which time value of money calculation should you use to decide between these two alternatives?
b. Assuming you think you can earn 8 percent per year on your investments, compounded annually, which of these alternatives is preferable?

15. **Time Value of Money.** Jerry wants to buy a new car. He has $2,000 for a down payment, and he estimates that he can afford to make a loan payment of up to $300 per month. Current car loan rates are at 6 percent for 36-month loans.
a. How much can Jerry borrow for a loan payment of $300?
b. What is the maximum total cost that Jerry can afford, including taxes and dealer charges?
c. How much difference will it make if the dealer offers 0 percent financing?

Using Web Resources for Financial Planning

1. **How Do You Compare with Others?** To see how your cash flows compare to others, go to *www.money.cnn.com* and select "Money 101" under "Financial Tools." Enter your monthly cash flows and then evaluate how you compare to others with similar income.

2. **What Are Your Collectibles Worth?** Do you have a collection of baseball cards, action figures, or Grateful Dead memorabilia? If you're wondering how to value these assets, one of the best sources of information on value is eBay. A quick search on *www.ebay.com* will tell you what others are paying for items similar to yours. Just for fun, find out what the going price is for a mint-condition *Amazing Spiderman* comic book #122, in which the Green Goblin dies in a battle with Spiderman.

3. **Payment Calculations on the Web.** If you don't own a financial calculator, many financial websites include calculators for your use. Although most are designed for a particular purpose, such as estimating mortgage payments, you can use them to solve any similar type of time value problem. A payment calculator, for example, can be used to calculate amortized loan payments of any type. Try the following:
a. To find the car loan payment calculator at *finance.yahoo.com,* click on "Loans," then "Auto," then "Calculator." Use the calculator to estimate how much your monthly car payment will be if you borrow $10,000 at 4.9 percent for 6 years.
b. Find the mortgage payment calculator, also at *finance.yahoo.com* (click on "Loans," then "Mortgage," then "Calculator"), and calculate how much your monthly mortgage payment will be if you borrow $100,000 at 5.8 percent for 30 years.
c. Try doing the car payment problem on the mortgage calculator to see if you get the same answer.

4. **Investment Accumulation Calculations on the Web.** You can estimate how much your current investment or series of investments will grow over a given period using the calculator at *www.money.cnn.com.* To get there, click on "Financial Tools," then "Calculators," then "Retirement Planner." Try the following exercises:
a. If you invest $200 per month for 10 years, how much will you have at the end of the 10-year period?
b. You currently have $8,000 in your savings account, which earns 3 percent interest. How much will you have in the account in 5 years with compound interest?

Learning by Doing Solutions

LBD 2-1: 1. pay bills, 1 month; 2. verify deposits and withdrawals, track budget, prepare taxes, 1 year or more; 3. tracking your budget, 1 year or more; 4. paying bills, tracking budget, 1 year; 5. paying bills, 1 year; 6. taxes and records, 7 years

LBD 2-2: 1a. D; 1b. D; 1c. A; 1d. A; 1e. D; 1f. A; 1g. D; 1h. A; 2. − $1,000

LBD 2-3: 1. Net cash flow = $2,000 − $1,900 = $100 per month; 2. Unless Masako can reduce some of her other expenses, she cannot afford to buy the car since she only has $100 left per month after her other expenses.

LBD 2-4: 1. Liquidity Ratio = $3,000/$2,000 = 1.5; 2. Debt Ratio = $10,000/$40,000 = 25%; 3. Savings Ratio = $500/$2,500 = 20%.

LBD 2-5: 1. Future Value = $1,610.51; 2. Present Value = $4,545.45

LBD 2-6: 1. Future Value of an Annuity = $3,052.55; 2a. Present Value of an Annuity = $4,269,910; 2b. $3,630,816; 2c. If you have the opportunity to invest your money at high rates of return, the annuity is worth less in present value than the $4 million cash.

LBD 2-7: 1a. $3,632.45 per year; 1b. $299.78 per month.

Building Financial Planning Skills Through Case Applications

Case 2-1 Homer and Marge Evaluate Their Personal Finances

As their daughter Lisa starts high school, Homer and Marge decide that it is time to take stock of their family finances to see how they will be able to pay for Lisa's education. They have constructed the following personal balance sheet and cash flow statements:

Assets		Debts	
Bank accounts	$3,000	Current bills	$1,200
Car	5,000	Credit cards	10,000
Cash value life insurance			
Personal assets	20,000	Car loan	8,000
Homer's retirement account	50,000		
Marge's IRA	9,000		
Other investments	0		
Market value of home	150,000	Mortgage	100,000
Total Assets	$237,000	Total Debts	$119,200

Cash Inflows		Cash Outflows	
Homer's gross income	$5,400	Income/payroll taxes	$2,000
Interest income	500	Groceries	600
		Mortgage payment	750
		Property taxes	190
		Homeowners insurance	60
		Utilities	150
		Car loan payment	240
		Car expenses	125
		Auto insurance	60
		Credit card payments	215
		Clothing/gifts	170
		Entertainment	235
		Vacations	300
		Retirement funds	400
		Church donations	80
		Other expenses	160
Total Cash Inflow	$5,900	Total Cash Outflow	$5,735

a. Describe how Marge and Homer probably determined the value of their car and home.
b. Calculate net worth and net cash flow for Homer and Marge.
c. After calculating their net cash flow, Marge is surprised to find that they should have a little money left over every month. She has usually found that they are down to their last dollar by the end of the month. "D'oh!" says Homer, "I forgot to count my tab at Moe's." If they have itemized all their other expenses accurately, how much is Homer spending each month on beer at Moe's? How should they revise their cash flow statement to reflect this expenditure? Will this change their net worth or net cash flow?
d. Evaluate Homer and Marge's financial status with respect to liquidity, debt, and savings using personal financial ratios.
e. Based on their current financial situation, do you think that Homer and Marge are prepared to send Lisa to college in four years? Do you have any suggestions for improving their personal finances?

Case 2-2 Can Kristopher Stephens Afford to Purchase a Car?

Kristopher Stephens is a 19-year-old college student. His parents pay his college tuition, buy his books, and cover his room and board expenses, but they expect him to earn enough to cover all the incidental expenses involved in going to school. He estimates that these cost him about $60 per week for the 40 weeks that he isn't home for the summer. He nets $2,600 after taxes from his summer job, and he has a part-time job at the university from which he earns $50 per week after taxes. Kristopher would like to buy a used car that costs $5,000. He estimates that he can obtain a car loan at 6 percent interest for three years. He expects to make a down payment of $500.

a. What is Kristopher's annual net cash flow?
b. What will the monthly payment on his car loan be under the terms identified above? How much will he pay each year?
c. Are there any additional car expenses that Kristopher should take into account?
d. Can he afford to buy the car? Why or why not?

Case 2-3 The Veronas Begin Saving for the Future

Melody and Charles Verona have been married for less than one year and currently live in a one-bedroom apartment. They would like a bigger place to live and, with two incomes, they think they could afford to pay a mortgage on a small home or condominium. Unfortunately, they don't have enough for a down payment yet, so they want to begin saving for this purpose. Over the last few months, Melody has been dismayed to find that they always seem to be a little short on cash at the end of the month. She decides to sit down with Charles to look more carefully at their spending habits and begin making a plan that will enable them to buy a house. The Veronas have collected the following financial information in preparation for evaluating their current finances and determining how much to save.

Cash Inflows	Gross Income	After-tax income
Melody	$22,000	$18,000
Charles	28,000	22,400

Cash Outflows	Monthly	Annual
Groceries	$400	
Eating out	200	
Rent	950	
Credit card payments	200	
Telephone	50	
Utilities	150	
Car loan payments	360	
Car expenses and fuel	160	
Clothing	100	
Entertainment	150	
Health club membership	60	
Travel and vacations	100	

a. Assuming that the cash flows above are accurate and complete, calculate the Veronas net cash monthly cash flow.

b. If the Veronas allocate their net cash flow to savings each month and they can earn 4 percent after taxes, how much will they have in the account after 2 years?

c. What is a possible explanation for why the Veronas are having cash flow problems each month? What would you suggest they do to identify the reasons for this problem?

d. Based on the information above, are there any categories of expenditures that the Veronas may have neglected to include on the list?

e. Calculate the couple's debt payment ratio. What does this say about their ability to manage additional debt?

f. Assuming that Melody and Charles receive 4 percent raises each year for the next two years and that tax rates remain the same, what will be the total of their after-tax income at that time?

g. If the Veronas use their accumulated savings to purchase a home two years from now and their mortgage debt service is $1,000 per month, what will their mortgage debt service ratio be (assuming after-tax income as calculated in part f)?

DEVELOPING PERSONAL FINANCIAL skills for life

Learning about Yourself

2-1 Assessing Your Personality Type

Getting personal financial data in order is generally easier for some personality types than for others. Psychology tells us that some people tend to be more detail-oriented and predisposed to organization than others. Use this exercise to get an idea of how your personality type may influence your personal finances.

For each of the following, choose the answer that best fits your approach to handling the given situation:

______ **1.** When my friends and I are discussing what movie to go see:
- **a.** I always check out the latest movie reviews before deciding.
- **b.** I go along with what everyone else wants to do.
- **c.** I prefer to decide at the last minute based on what I feel like at that time.

______ **2.** When I am involved in a team project at work or school:
- **a.** I'm the person everyone knows they can rely on to help keep the group on track.
- **b.** I always consult with my teammates before making any major decisions for the part of the project I am working on.
- **c.** I tend to leave my part of the work to the last minute, but I usually always get it done.

______ **3.** In managing the time I spend on my various activities:
- **a.** I always plan my weeks in advance so that I am sure to be able to get everything done.
- **b.** I like to receive regular reminders of when things are due.
- **c.** There never seems to be enough time in every day to get things done.

______ **4.** I would prefer a job:
- **a.** Where my employer's expectations are clearly stated and where I am rewarded based on how well I meet those expectations.
- **b.** Where I do not have too much independent responsibility and my employer gives me fairly detailed instructions so that I know I am doing the job correctly.
- **c.** Where I can be more independent and there isn't too much structure to the work day.

______ **5.** When I make a major purchase:
- **a.** I always carefully investigate my alternatives and compare them based on price and quality.
- **b.** I ask for advice from my coworkers, friends, or family.
- **c.** I like to just go to the store and buy it without spending too much time agonizing over the decision.

______ **6.** My approach to studying for exams is:
- **a.** I reread the assigned material and review my class notes carefully, often making a review sheet to study from.
- **b.** I get together with my study group to review the course material and be sure that I am on the right track.
- **c.** I start studying the night before the exam, and I usually focus my studying on the most important concepts we studied since I may not have read everything that was assigned.

______ **7.** When I am doing research for a paper or project:
- **a.** I use as many resources as possible and then organize my notes carefully before I begin to write the paper.
- **b.** I ask the teacher's advice on what I should write about and where I should start looking for information.
- **c.** I have good intentions, but sometimes get started a little bit late on the project.

______ **8.** Other people consider me to be:
- **a.** A natural leader
- **b.** A person who tends to go with the majority
- **c.** A free spirit

______ **9.** My bedroom is:
- **a.** Always neat and organized
- **b.** Cleaned up whenever anyone is coming to visit
- **c.** Often messy.

______ **10.** If I had to decide how to invest $1,000:
- **a.** I would read a book on investing and then follow the steps outlined in the book.
- **b.** I would ask for advice from a friend, coworker, or family member who knows more about investing than I do.
- **c.** I would invest in whatever seems right at the time.

Scoring

Score this assessment as follows: a = 3; b = 2; c = 1. Mark where your score falls on the following continuum:

10	20	30
Impulsive	Dependent	Rational

If your score is 10 to 15, you have a tendency to make impulsive decisions. You will need to work harder at curbing your tendencies toward spontaneity in your finances. A score from 15 to 25 implies that you are inclined to depend on others to help you make decisions. You will be more inclined to seek the services of a financial advisor. A score from 25 to 30 says that you are a rational decision maker and have natural inclinations to make decisions in a way that is very consistent with the financial planning process.

Developing Your Skills

2-2 Organizing Your Personal and Financial Data

The first step in the personal financial planning process is to evaluate your current finances. To do this, you will need to have all your records in order. You can use the worksheet in your *Personal Financial Planner* to help you think through what documents you need and decide where to keep them.

PFP Worksheet 5
Organizing Your Personal and Financial Records

2-3 Creating Personal Financial Statements

Once you have all your information collected, you can summarize it in personal financial statements.

1. Use the worksheets in your *Personal Financial Planner* to create these statements. If necessary, you should use a spending log to track your expenditures for a period of time to help you estimate your cash outflows more accurately.
2. Calculate your net worth.
3. Calculate your net cash flow.

PFP Worksheet 8
Spending Log

2-4 Evaluating Your Personal Finances

Evaluate your liquidity, debt management, and savings adequacy using the personal financial ratios presented in this chapter. You can use the worksheet in your *Personal Financial Planner* to calculate and track these ratios over time.

PFP Worksheet 9
Personal Financial Ratios

2-5 Identifying Which Time Value of Money Calculation to Use

Although some of you might find it tempting to think that you can do personal finance without doing any math, the truth is that you cannot. Consider the following list of actions and check those that represent things you expect to do at some point in your life. For each of the actions, identify which time value of money principle(s) could be used to help you select your best options (*present value, future value, present value of annuity, future value of annuity*). Explain.

Action	Type of TVM Calculation
☐ Borrow money to buy a car	__________________
☐ Borrow money to buy a home	__________________
☐ Pay off a credit card	__________________
☐ Pay back a student loan	__________________
☐ Save for retirement	__________________
☐ Save for your child's college education	__________________

2-6. Applying the Time Value of Money

Use time value of money principles to fill in the following blanks:

1. I would like to buy a new car. If I finance the full purchase price of $__________ for __________ years at __________% interest, my monthly payment will be $__________.
2. I would like to save $__________ per month. If I stick to this savings plan and I can earn __________ percent interest after taxes, compounded monthly, I will be able to accumulate __________ by the end of five years.
3. I estimate that I will need to accumulate $1.5 million by the time I retire. Since I have _____ years until retirement, this means that if I can earn 8% interest on my invested funds, I would need to invest $_________ per year from now until retirement.
4. I currently owe $__________ in credit card debt which has an average annual interest rate of ______%. If I make a payment of $__________ per month, I will be able to pay back all of this money within ______ months.

THE NAVIGATOR

- ☐ Review Before Studying this Chapter list.
- ☐ Scan Learning Objectives.
- ☐ Take Myth or Fact quiz and find the answers throughout the chapter.
- ☐ Read chapter and answer Learning by Doing exercises.
- ☐ Review Key Terms and Key Calculations.
- ☐ Do end-of-chapter exercises.
- ☐ Take review quiz on the text website.
- ☐ Solve end-of-chapter cases.

BEFORE studying this chapter, you should review

- Personal financial statements (Chapter 2).
- Time value of money principles (Chapter 2).

Goal Setting, Career Planning, and Budgeting

CHAPTER 3

Myth or Fact?

Consider each of the following statements and decide whether it is a *myth* or a *fact*. Look for the answers in the *Fact* boxes in the chapter.

	MYTH	FACT
1. Retirement is the most important financial goal for most American families.	☐	☐
2. My standard of living will undoubtedly improve as I get older.	☐	☐
3. Most employers are looking for people with good communication skills, but new college graduates often fall short in this area.	☐	☐
4. Since the purpose of an initial interview is just to give you information about the company, it's a waste of time to research the company before the interview.	☐	☐
5. The most common reason for a person to work a second job is because they enjoy it.	☐	☐

LEARNING objectives

1. Identify your short-term and long-term personal financial goals.
2. Evaluate your skills, abilities, and interests to establish a career plan.
3. Develop and implement a household budget.
4. Monitor and control your expenses through a system of regular evaluation.
5. Understand how money attitudes affect budgeting.

...applying the planning process

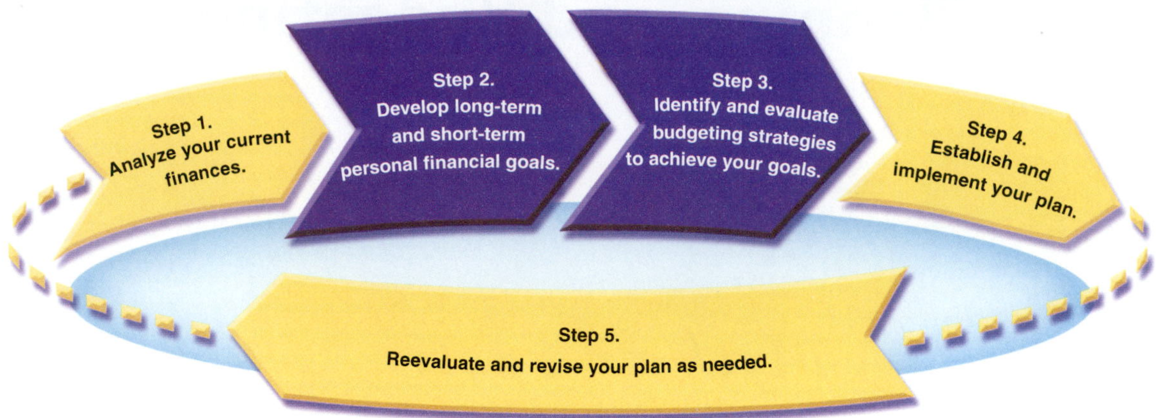

Once you've organized your records and evaluated your financial health as described in Chapter 2, you'll have completed the first step in the personal financial planning process. This chapter takes you through the second step, in which you'll develop a set of long-term and short-term personal financial goals. In addition to setting goals related to specific financial outcomes (such as buying a house or paying for college), you'll learn how your career plan and your household budget can help you to achieve your objectives.

Although you might not immediately see the connection among all these topics, they are integrally related. Your career choice will have a large impact on your future employment earnings, which in turn will provide you with the cash flow necessary to spend and save. Your household budget plays an important role in the process too, since it's the roadmap that will keep you from veering off the path to financial success. Achieving your personal financial goals in the future therefore depends on the career and budgeting decisions you make along the way.

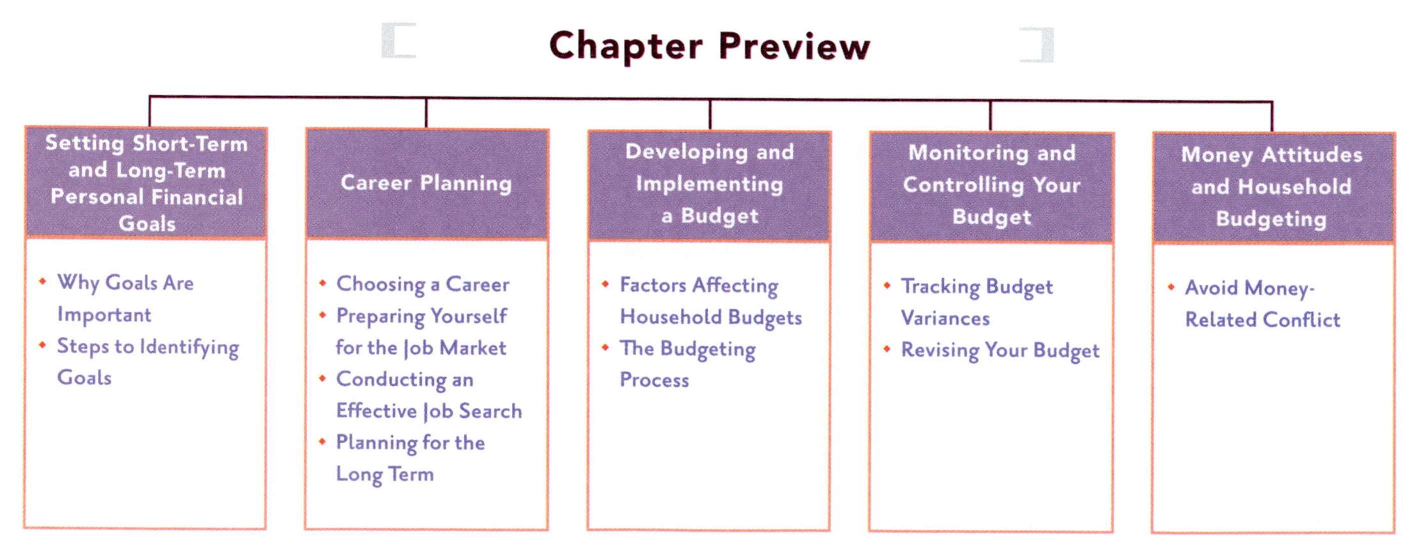

Setting Short-Term and Long-Term Personal Financial Goals

LEARNING objective

1 Identify your short-term and long-term personal financial goals.

Have you ever noticed how a whole day can go by and you don't get anything accomplished? When you were a child, that was the best kind of summer day—nothing to do and no one to answer to. But now that you're an adult, and particularly if you're a student as well, you have many obligations—homework, house cleaning, yard work, and grocery shopping, to name a few. You have a million things you *should* do, but sometimes, you don't seem to get any of them done. In many cases, the reason that nothing gets done is because you didn't *plan* for anything to get done.

Why Goals Are Important

For most people, the key to successfully accomplishing a set of tasks is to establish a set of specific objectives or goals and persistently plug away at achieving them. Have you ever looked at what some people can accomplish on a regular basis, and wondered if they somehow have more than twenty-four hours in a day? This is just proof of the old saying: "The more you do, the more you *can* do." Unfortunately, the opposite is also true—if you *don't* do much, you won't get much done. The reason these statements are both true is that people who are very busy have no choice but to be organized in using their time and setting their objectives. And as they succeed in their short-term endeavors, they find themselves motivated to do even more.

Those of you who are athletes will perhaps appreciate the importance of goals better than anyone. Whether you're a runner, a body builder, or a member of a sports team, you know that success in athletics requires setting goals and making a plan to achieve those goals: Running a little further each day. Bench-pressing a few more pounds. Increasing speed, endurance, and accuracy in your chosen sport. Small successes each day add up to large successes in the long run.

Achieving financial success requires a similar approach. Without some specific goals, it's very easy to go nowhere fast. But if you have a prioritized list of specific goals with measurable outcomes and a plan for how to achieve them, you'll be able to make progress toward financial success.

Taking it step by step, consistent effort will allow you to reach your goals.

Steps to Identifying Goals

Although goals are an essential component of everyone's personal financial plan, there is no magic formula for identifying and prioritizing your goals. No one can make your goals for you, since they are unique to you and your household. However, most people's lists will have certain features in common. Areas that should probably be addressed on your list include:

- Consumer spending and borrowing
- Career advancement
- Education for yourself, your spouse, and your children
- Home purchase and maintenance
- Managing risk
- Retirement planning
- Vacations and recreation
- Charitable giving
- Estate planning

To be effective, your goals should be realistic and within your control. If your income is relatively low right now and you have barely enough money to meet your current expenses, it doesn't make sense to set a goal that would require you to save $500 a month. Your goals should also

EXHIBIT 3-1

Cindy and Dave Thompson are both 34 years old. They have a son Kyle, age 14, from Cindy's previous marriage, and they are expecting a baby in the near future. Although both of them currently work outside the home, they are considering visiting a financial planner to determine if it is feasible for Cindy to quit work after the baby is born. They feel that their two children will both benefit from having a stay-at-home mom, and they will avoid costly child-care expenses.

Dave's job as a computer systems analyst seems secure, but he knows he will need to continue to keep his skills current in such a rapidly changing field. So far, with the luxury of two incomes, the Thompsons haven't worried much about their personal finances.

be stated in precise and measurable terms so that it will be possible for you to track your progress. Instead of just deciding to "save money each month," you should target a specific dollar amount of money and have it automatically deposited to a designated savings account. Each month, as you get your bank statements, you'll be able to track your progress.

You can follow the steps described below to make your own prioritized list of personal financial goals. As we go through the steps, we'll see how the Thompson family, introduced in Exhibit 3-1, approaches this step in the financial planning process.

1. Make a wish list. The first step in establishing a set of goals is to make a "wish list." Generally, your goals will fall into three categories based on the timing of the outcomes as illustrated in Exhibit 3-2. *Short-term goals* are those that can reasonably be accomplished within the next year, such as buying a car or taking a vacation. *Intermediate-term goals*, like paying off debt or saving for a down payment on a home, are those that will take up to five years to accomplish. Finally, you will probably have several *long-term goals* that will take much longer, perhaps a lifetime, to achieve—retirement funding, for example.

Fact #1

According to the 2001 Survey of Consumer Finances, only 32.1 percent of U.S. households in 2001 reported retirement as their most important reason for saving. Many families cited liquidity (31.2%), education (10.9%), and purchases (9.5%) as their goals.

EXHIBIT 3-2

Setting Goals with Different Time Horizons

Your list of goals will also differ depending on your stage in the life cycle and your family makeup. Your age, income, marital status, employment, and values will all influence your financial objectives. For example, a young couple's primary goal may be to buy their first home, whereas families with children may be more focused on building a college fund. Retired couples may dream of a cruise to the Bahamas or setting up a trust for their grandchildren. Whatever your goals, the important thing at this stage is to get them all down on paper.

Be sure to make your goals concrete and specific. To the extent possible, you should state them in positive terms with projected dates and estimated dollar costs. To give you some ideas, Exhibit 3-3 suggests several goals in each category with rough estimates of the cost. In some cases, you may not be able to put a precise dollar amount on a goal. In other cases, achieving the goals may simply involve an investment of your time and effort, as in the case of organizing your finances and creating a household budget. As you move through the material in this book, you'll learn more about how to estimate the costs of attaining certain financial objectives, but a rough measure will be sufficient for now.

2. Prioritize. Once you have a wish list, you need to prioritize the list so you can focus on the goals that are most important to you and your family. Unless you were very conservative in making your initial list, it's not likely that you'll be able to achieve *all* the goals on your wish list—at least not in the near future—so deciding which ones have the highest priority is an important step in the goal-setting process. There will be inevitable tradeoffs. If you have children, for example, the extra costs you bear as a result may mean that you won't be able to take an annual vacation to Europe, and you'll probably have to forgo the Porsche sports car. Your decision to go to graduate school will temporarily cut into your retirement savings and may delay your purchase of a larger home.

If you have trouble prioritizing your goal list, try using the Goal Prioritizor tool at www.money.cnn.com/pf/101.

3. Break big goals into smaller steps. By breaking your bigger goals into smaller, more manageable steps, you'll more quickly see progress toward your goals. And the more often you see rewards from your endeavors, the more motivated you'll be to stick with your plan. For example, suppose you want to buy your first home two years from now. After considering the prices of smaller homes in your area, you've determined that you need at least $10,000 for a down payment. You're also concerned that you might not be able to qualify for a mortgage if you don't reduce your credit card debt (currently $3,000). Thus, two subgoals are associated with your primary goal of buying a home: saving for the down payment and reducing your credit card debt. These subgoals, along with the steps necessary to achieve each of them, are listed in Exhibit 3-4.

As you can see in the exhibit, the steps toward achieving your subgoals include calculating the additional amount you'll save each month and the amount you'll pay each month to the credit card company. How do you estimate these amounts? This is where you can apply the time value of money tools from Chapter 2. Since both of these problems involve solving for equal payments of money over time, we know that they are annuity problems.

EXHIBIT 3-3 Developing Goals with Different Time Horizons

Short-term (<1 year) Goal	Cost $	Intermediate-term (1–5 years) Goal	Cost $	Long-term (5+ years) Goal	Cost $
Vacation	1,000	Pay off credit cards	200/month	Comfortable retirement	3,000,000
Increase life insurance	500	Down payment on new car	3,000	Send kids to college	50,000
Eat out once per week	50/week	New roof for home	3,000	Remodel the house	30,000
Organize finances	–	Graduate school	5,000/year	Provide for surviving spouse	?
Emergency fund	40/week	Hire housekeeper	50/week	Buy vacation home	50,000
Create budget	–	Down payment on home	20,000	Leave inheritance for kids	?
Make a will	150	Learn about investing	–		
Work on career plan	–				

EXHIBIT 3-4

Breaking Larger Goals into Subgoals

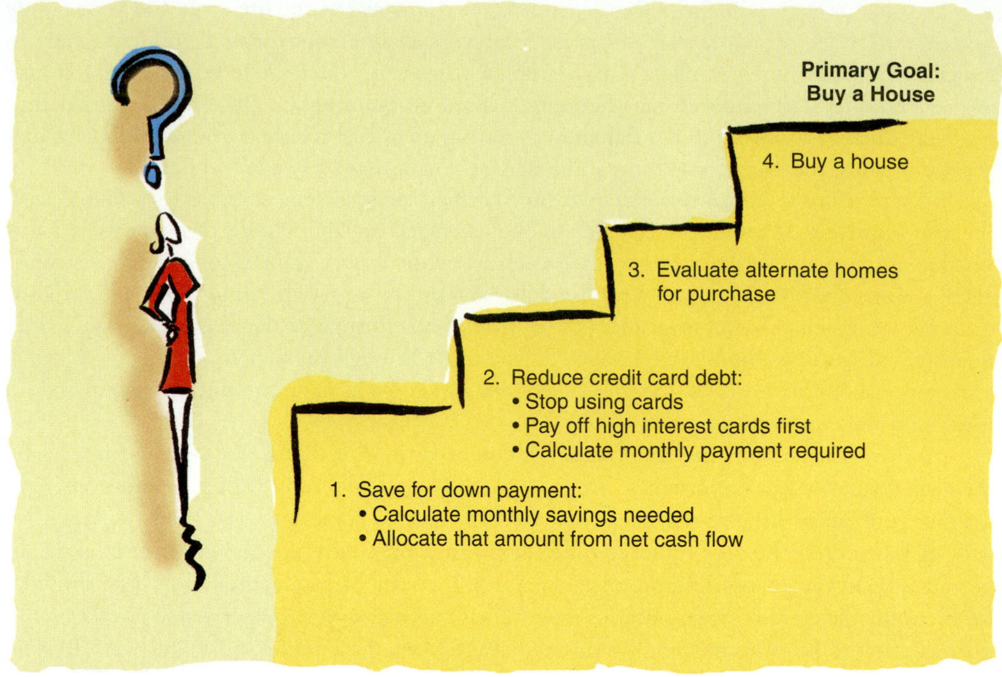

Let's solve the savings problem first: You need to have \$10,000 saved up at the end of two years. So \$10,000 is the future value of an annuity, you have 24 months to save, and let's say that you can earn 6 percent on your investment, or 0.5 percent per month. You can use any of the three methods for solving this problem, of course, but we'll use the financial calculator method here: Enter $FV = \$10{,}000$; $N = 24$; $I = 6/12 = 0.5$; and compute the $PMT = \$393.21$.

EXHIBIT 3-5

Payment Necessary to Pay Off Specific Debt Amounts

Months to Pay	Interest Rate (%)	Monthly Payments Necessary to Pay Off Debt in the Amount of			
		$1,000	$2,500	$5,000	$10,000
12	12	89	222	444	888
	15	90	226	451	903
	18	92	229	458	917
	21	93	233	466	931
24	12	47	118	235	471
	15	48	121	242	485
	18	50	125	250	499
	21	51	128	257	514
36	12	33	83	166	332
	15	35	87	173	347
	18	36	90	181	362
	21	38	94	188	377
48	12	26	66	132	263
	15	28	70	139	278
	18	29	73	147	294
	21	31	77	155	310
60	12	22	56	111	222
	15	24	59	119	238
	18	25	63	127	254
	21	27	68	135	271
72	12	20	49	98	196
	15	21	53	106	211
	18	23	57	114	228
	21	25	61	123	245

In the case of the debt repayment problem, you know that the present value of the annuity is \$3,000 (because it's the amount you owe today), the number of periods in which you want to pay it off is 24 months, and the interest is whatever your credit card company charges—let's say 18 percent, or 1.5 percent per month. Therefore, to calculate how much you'll need to pay each month on your credit cards to reduce your balance to zero—if we assume that you stop using the cards—you can solve for the payment using your financial calculator as follows: Enter $PV =$ \$3,000; $N = 24$; $I = 18/12 = 1.5$; and then compute the $PMT = -\$149.77$.

Since debt reduction is a relatively common goal, Exhibit 3-5 is included to make it easier for you to roughly estimate the monthly payments necessary to reduce an existing debt to zero within a particular time period at various interest rates. As you proceed through this course, you will of course have to be more precise, but at this point, a rough estimate will give you a quick measure of the monthly cost.

Exhibit 3-6 is the prioritized wish list developed by the Thompson family. They've identified goals in all areas of their finances, but because of their family circumstances, their highest priority is for Cindy to quit work and stay home with their new baby for a few years. Later in this chapter, we consider more carefully how the Thompsons can develop and implement a budget that will help them to achieve this goal.

4. Reevaluate regularly. Your personal financial plan must be flexible to accommodate changes that you will face in the future. As your life progresses, your priorities will change, as will your strategies for achieving your goals. Thus, your list should be viewed as a work in progress. You will need to revisit your goals regularly, at least every one or two years for major goals and more often for subgoals. Of course, you should also reevaluate whenever your family

EXHIBIT 3-6

The Thompsons' Prioritized List of Goals

Short-Term Goals

Goal 1. Establish a household budget.
a. Create a personal cash flow statement.
b. Create a personal balance sheet.
c. Estimate future income and expenses.

Goal 2. Reduce credit card debt.
a. Calculate how much we need to pay.
b. Stop using credit cards.
c. Cut some of our other expenses and apply the money to the credit card debt.

Goal 3. Cindy quits work in 6 months.
a. Cut down on current expenses.
b. Save money over the next 6 months.

Long-Term Goals

Goal 1. Increase retirement savings.
a. Learn about tax rules for retirement saving.
b. Start an IRA for Cindy.
c. Determine how much we both need to be saving.

Goal 2. Send both kids to college.
a. Learn about college funding options.
b. Start a college fund for Kyle.
c. Start a college fund for the baby.

experiences a significant change in circumstances. If Cindy Thompson is able to quit her job, the family will certainly need to revisit their objectives as the new baby nears school age. They may also need to reconsider this decision as they face the costs of sending their older son Kyle to college.

Learning by Doing 3-1

1. Assume that you're a 20-year-old college student. For each of the following categories, identify one short-term and one long-term financial goal that you should include on your list: a. education; b. home; c. retirement; d. vacation/recreation.
2. Assume that you are now 45 years old. Are the goals you identified above still applicable? Will your priorities be the same?
3. Dan has decided that one of his short-term goals is to reduce his credit card debt. He currently has a $2,000 balance on a MasterCard and $3,000 on a Visa. How can he break this goal into a number of small, concrete steps?

LEARNING objective

2 Evaluate your skills, abilities, and interests to establish a career plan.

human capital

The present value of your future earnings, based on skills, abilities, and education.

Career Planning

Career decisions throughout your life will not only influence your choice of goals, but also will affect the probability of your achieving them. For this reason, any discussion of financial planning must include a discussion of career planning. The time and effort you invest in your career will affect your earnings level and your future advancement opportunities. As we discussed in Chapter 1, you need to achieve steady growth in wages, in excess of the rate of inflation, if you want to improve your standard of living over time. This will result in greater job satisfaction and increase the likelihood that you'll be able to achieve your financial goals.

Fact #2

Although most people assume that their standard of living will improve as they get older, this is not always the case. If wages do not keep up with inflation, as is often the case with minimum-wage, unskilled jobs, your standard of living will actually decline.

The present value of your future earnings is sometimes referred to as your **human capital**. (In some contexts, human capital might also be used to refer to the sum total of all workers' productive capacity.) If you don't invest in your human capital by keeping your skills and abilities current, you may find that your income will stagnate as your skills and knowledge decline in value or become obsolete. For example, consider the case of Ben, who took a job at age 18 as a waiter at a high-class restaurant. In 1990, Ben earned $30,000 in wages and tips, enough that he decided he didn't need to go to college. It is now 15 years later, and Ben is making $45,000 in wages and tips. Although it may seem that Ben's circumstances have improved, since his disposable income is 50 percent higher than before, this is an illusion created by inflation. Since the prices of goods over that same time period have increased by approximately the same amount, Ben is actually no better off financially than he was in 1990, and he has little opportunity for advancement. Ben's example illustrates how important a career plan is to your long-term financial opportunities. If Ben had gone to school part-time and studied restaurant management, he might have been able to use his experience and education to increase his earnings potential.

How much do you think a college education is worth? The *Go Figure!* box, "The Present Value of Your Education," uses time value of money principles to estimate the present value of the increased income potential realized from higher education based on average salary differences reported by a national survey in 2003. For example, the average college graduate in liberal arts at that time earned $8,543 more per year than a high-school graduate. The present value of this "education premium" over a 45-year working career is $177,011, discounting the future earnings at a rate of 4 percent. (Think of it as $8,543 annuity you will be paid each year for 45 years.) Since this method of calculating the value of education assumes that the wage differential stays

GO FIGURE!

The Present Value of Your Education

Problem: Manny graduated from high school in 2003 and earns $21,000 as an office clerk. He is thinking about going to college to earn a degree. How much would a business degree be worth to him if he expects to be able to earn $15,000 more per year for 45 years after he graduates.

Highest Level of Education	2003 Starting Salary	Present Value of Amount in Excess of High-School Graduate[a]	Present Value of Amount in Excess of Liberal Arts Graduate[a]	Present Value of Amount in Excess of Undergraduate Business
High-school graduate	$21,000	—	—	—
College graduate				
B.A. Liberal Arts	$29,543	$177,011	—	—
B.S. Business	$36,515	$321,471	$144,460	—
B.S. Chemical Engineering	$52,169	$645,823	$468,812	$324,352
Post-graduate				
Business (M.B.A.)	$75,000	$1,118,882	$941,871	$797,411
Pharmacy	$83,642	$1,297,945	$1,120,933	$976,473
Law (J.D.)	$97,830	$1,591,921	$1,414,909	$1,270,449
Medicine (M.D.), General	$125,000	$2,154,884	$1,977,873	$1,833,413

[a]Discounted at 4% for inflation and assumes salary differential is maintained for 45-year working career.

Solution: Manny can estimate the present value of his increased earning potential over his career as the present value of an annuity. For example, if he gets a B.S. in business and earns $15,000 more per year, he will probably continue to earn at least this much extra per year (compared with a high-school graduate) for 45 years. To solve this problem, use any of the methods explained in Chapter 2 for calculating the present value of an annuity. For example, you can solve this problem using the mathematical equation, substituting for PMT = $15,000, the annual increase in Manny's earnings; $i = 0.04$, the interest rate for one period, in this case the estimate of future inflation; and $n = 45$, the number of periods Manny will earn his education premium, as follows:

$$PV = \$15{,}000 \times \frac{\left[1-\left(\frac{1}{1.04}\right)^{45}\right]}{0.04}$$

$$= \$15{,}000 \times \frac{1-0.1712}{0.04}$$

$$= \$15{,}000 \times \frac{0.8288}{0.04} = \$310{,}801$$

If you are using a financial calculator, you can enter the values for *I*, *N*, and *PMT* and then compute the *PV*. The answer should be $310,801, as above. For various reasons, the actual benefit is likely to be higher than this amount, and Manny needs to subtract the estimated costs of his attending college.

Sources: National Association of Colleges and Employers, *Spring 2003 Salary Survey* (for college graduate salaries); Internet Legal Resource Guide (for first-year lawyer salaries) at www.ilrg.com/employment/salaries; Physician Search.com (for physician and pharmacist salaries) at www.physiciansearch.com.

constant over your career, the present value of your education will be greater if it makes it possible for you to realize greater-than-average increases in income over time—for example, if high-school graduates average 3 percent wage growth and you average 5 percent wage growth, the education premium will become gradually larger over time. In general, average wage increases have historically been higher and rates of unemployment have been lower for educated workers.

To arrive at a more precise estimate, you should also offset the calculated present value by the cost of the education itself and the income you give up while going to school. This ensures that you are fairly comparing the two career strategies, including both costs and benefits.

Suppose, for example, that you graduate with a bachelor's degree in liberal arts and have a job opportunity that will pay you $29,543 per year. Instead, you decide to go to graduate school to get an MBA, which costs $15,000 per year for two years. Based on the table in the *Go Figure!* box, the present value of the extra income from this advanced degree as compared to a liberal arts undergraduate degree is $941,871. The cost you incur to obtain that extra income is $89,086—two years of lost earnings (2 × $29,543 = $59,086) and the price of the education (2 × $15,000 = $30,000). Although this seems like a lot, your net benefit from this investment in your human capital is $852,785. Even taking the costs into consideration, we see that the investment in a graduate-school education would be well worth the cost based on these assumptions!

Choosing a Career

Your choice of career is perhaps the most important life decision you will make. The choice will play a vital role in not only your financial future but also your personal satisfaction and growth. As with other decisions, you should apply good decision-making skills to the process. The process should include the following steps:

- Assess your natural abilities and interests.
- Identify alternatives that fit your interests.
- Evaluate the costs, benefits, and risks of each alternative.
- Select the most appropriate career path for you, given your strengths and constraints.
- Make a plan to acquire the necessary training, education, skills, and certifications.

Assess Your Abilities and Interests. Studies show that people who are working in careers that support their intrinsic interests are happier and more successful. If, for example, Amanda enjoys charitable work and volunteering, she would probably find satisfaction in a career with a nonprofit that fits her ideals and values. What if you're a closet musician, but you know that you can't make a career of it? You might consider other alternatives in the music business—as a concert promoter or an entertainment lawyer, for example. The point is that you will be most satisfied with your career if you're doing what you love.

The Career Services office at your college or university likely has one or more standardized tests that can help you to identify career options which fit your interests and abilities. The most popular assessment tools used by career advisors include the Myers–Briggs Type Indicator, the Strong Interest Inventory, and the Keirsey Character and Temperament Sort. If you don't want to consult a specialist to administer these tests to you, online versions are available at certain websites for a fee.

Even without the results of a career aptitude or personality test, however, you no doubt already know a good deal about your own interests, strengths, and weaknesses. Furthermore, the evidence suggests that motivation and attitude—setting clear goals and working toward them with passion—are also important ingredients in a successful career. Even if a test reveals that you would make a terrific salesperson, if your heart's desire is to be an elementary-school teacher, then that's what you should work toward.

At www.web.tickle.com/tests/rightjob/, you can take a free quiz that helps you identify job characteristics which fit your personality.

As a starting point to evaluating your interests, answer the following questions:

- What activities do you enjoy most?
- When you're doing what you want, what are you doing?
- What do you like to do in your leisure time?
- What are your hobbies?
- Are you a "people person"?
- What courses have you enjoyed the most in college?
- What projects or assignments did you enjoy the most in college?

After you have answered these questions, you may see a pattern that will help you link your activities, hobbies, or interests to possible careers.

Identify Alternatives That Fit Your Interests. Once you've identified your abilities and interests, your next step is to identify a set of suitable career paths to consider. These should take into account not only your aptitudes and interests, but also any particular preferences you have with respect to work environment.

Begin by making a list of characteristics your ideal job would have. Consider the day-to-day routine as well as the work environment. Would you like working at a desk all day, or would that be stifling? Are you a "people person," or do you prefer to work by yourself? Do you want a job that offers the possibility of advancement? Which is more important: the money or the job attributes? Is long-term job security an important factor in your decision? Do you need to feel like you've made a difference?

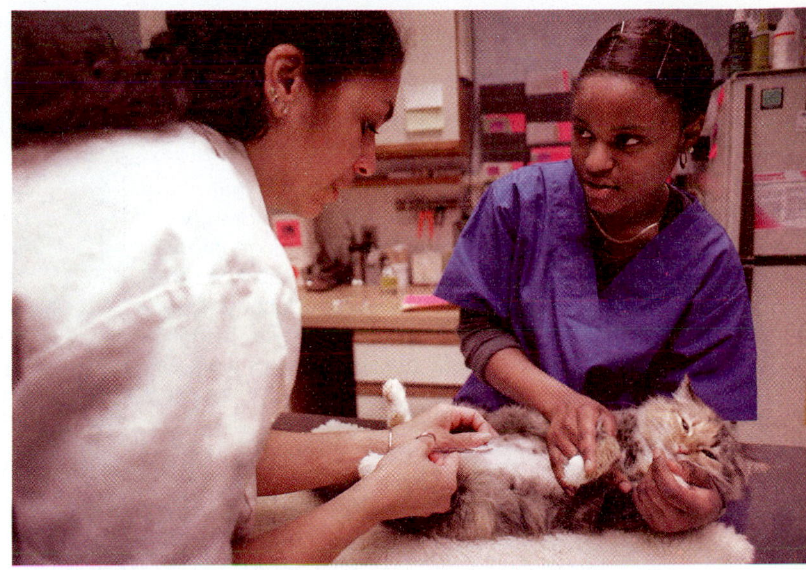

People tend to be happier in careers with organizations that fit their values and ideals.

You may have to do a little research to determine how your unique interests might fit with particular careers. In many cases, the general perception of what a particular job entails is different from reality. A classic example is the legal field. Television shows depicting lawyers in nice suits arguing interesting cases every week make the job seem exciting and glamorous. What you don't see on TV is that most lawyers never set foot inside a courtroom, instead spending long hours reading, writing, and talking on the telephone.

A common lament among college students is that they really don't have a good feel for what their options are. What types of jobs are out there? What are the usual job responsibilities? How much potential is there for advancement? Who are the major employers? These questions and more can be answered with a little research. Although the most obvious place to look for job descriptions is in your college Career Services office, most libraries and bookstores have large career and job search sections. Perhaps the most convenient source of information is the Internet.

America's Career Infonet at www.acinet.org, is a government-sponsored website that offers useful career information, updated job outlook information, and an extensive library of downloadable articles and videos. Two other popular job search and career websites are www.monster.com and www.wetfeet.com.

Making the right decision up front can save you time and money, but a wrong turn is not the end of the world. Most people change jobs several times during their working lives, and about one-third actually switch careers. This happens for many reasons. In times of economic recession, widespread layoffs may force workers to reconsider their career paths. Perhaps your original career choice was made without careful consideration or under pressure from parents or peers. Maybe your interests have changed or the career itself has changed. For example, medical malpractice liability has become such a large and expensive problem that many doctors are leaving the profession or changing their area of specialization.

Evaluate the Costs, Benefits, and Risks. As with all financial decisions, there are costs and benefits. Good decision making requires that you weigh the benefits—salary, advancement, prestige, personal growth, and satisfaction—against the costs and risks. Although the time and money you invest in education and skill development are the most obvious costs, you should also consider the impact your career will have on your family and the risks associated with future trends in employment. If your career choice is made without sufficient thought, for example, without consideration of how well it matches your personality and interests, one of the costs might be your own job dissatisfaction and the impact on your quality of life.

Today, having children does not preclude the possibility of having a career as well, but it may limit your choices or slow down your career progress. Families with two working parents are very common. Although women are still more likely to be the primary caregivers in these families, family issues affect both working parents to some extent. It's important to note that some careers are more conducive to the demands of parenthood than others—more flexible hours, fewer hours per week—so it's advisable that you consider your plans for children in making your career decisions. The *News You Can Use* box, "Family Considerations in Career Choice," lists some family issues you should think about.

NEWS you can use

Family Considerations in Career Choice

Current household statistics suggest that more parents, even those with preschool children, work outside the home than in any previous generation. Single parents work out of necessity, but even two-parent families consider the second income essential to maintaining their desired lifestyle. Evidence suggests that balancing the demands of work and family is often challenging and stressful, and it is more difficult to do in some types of employment than in others. Therefore, if you plan to have children someday, you should consider the following issues before choosing a career:

1. What hours will you typically have to work? Many professional jobs require you to be in the office from 10 to 12 hours a day. Some may require you to work weekends or evening hours.
2. How much vacation time will you have? Children are usually in school for only 6 to 7 hours a day; they also have many vacation days, as well as $2\frac{1}{2}$ months off in the summer.
3. Can you leave work unexpectedly if your child becomes sick? Most schools and day-care providers will not keep a child who is sick. At least one parent needs to have a job flexible enough to accommodate a child's sudden illness. Some companies provide special facilities for their employees' sick children.
4. Is the pay enough to cover child-care costs? Full-time child-care costs differ across the country but tend to range from $150 to $250 per week per child. Before- and after-school care can cost $50 to $150 per week per child.
5. Will you have time for your child's homework and extracurricular activities? From second or third grade on, most children have one to two hours of homework per night. Someone has to have the energy to make dinner and help with homework.
6. Will your family responsibilities take away from your advancement potential at work? Despite the trend toward dual-career families, it is still unfortunately the case in the corporate world that those employees who put their families first tend to be overlooked when it comes to promotion and advancement. This attitude can differ substantially from company to company, so it pays to research which companies are considered "family friendly."

"Balancing the demands of work and family can be challenging and stressful."

Research Employment Trends. Many trends occurring today are expected to change the employment landscape of the future. If you choose a career in a high-demand occupation, you'll probably have higher income potential and more opportunities for advancement in the future. In contrast, if you choose a career that has too many job seekers and not enough jobs, or one where the demand for employees is likely to decline over time, you risk future job uncertainty, declining pay scales, and obsolescence. Exhibit 3-7 shows the expected increase in the number of jobs in various sectors over the next decade, based on the U.S. Department of Labor's Occupational Outlook Survey.

Read the latest government Occupational Outlook Survey at www.bls.gov.

Even in a high-demand field, you must be prepared for change and invest in continuing education to keep your skills up-to-date. Twenty years ago, when personal computers first came onto the scene, many older workers resisted learning to use them. Some insisted they could type faster on their old typewriters. Others said they could do calculations faster in their heads. We know where those workers are today—unemployed. As new tools and techniques become available—and we *know* they will—a good strategy is to volunteer as the first person in your workplace to learn to use them.

In addition to the inevitable changes in technology that will occur over your working career, other trends that might affect you include the following:

- *Aging of the population.* Families are having fewer children, and people are living longer, healthier lives. That means increasing demand for goods and services targeted to the older population. Financial services, medical and rehabilitative services, recreation, and travel are all areas that may see increased demand.

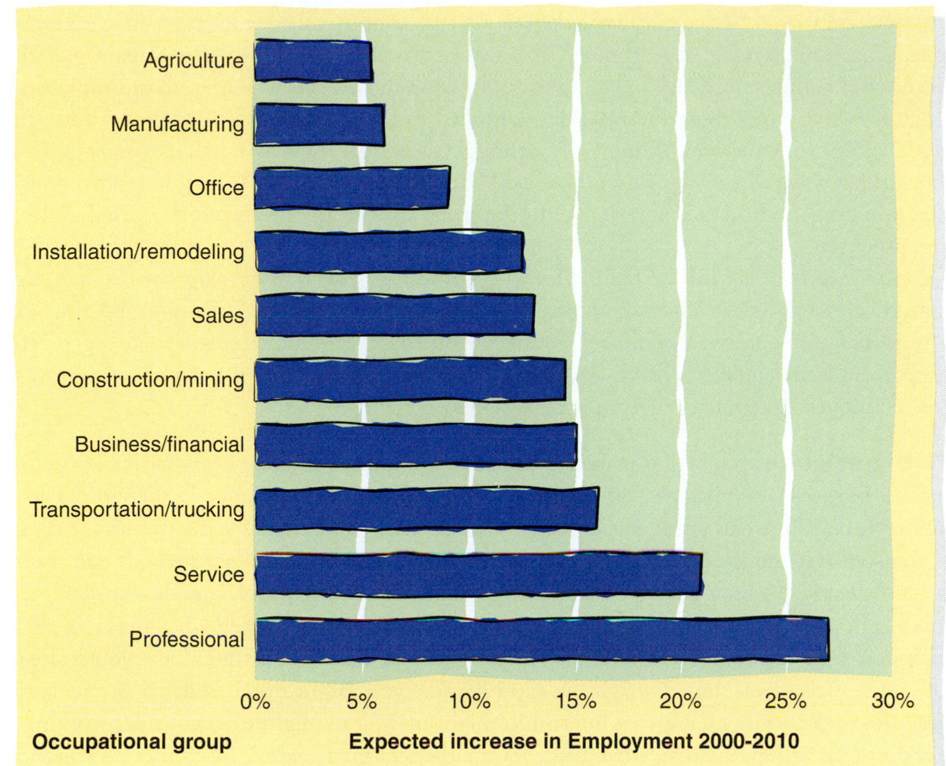

EXHIBIT 3-7

Occupational groups expected to experience the largest increases from 2000 to 2010

Source: U.S. Bureau of Labor Statistics, "Tomorrow's Jobs," *Occupational Outlook Handbook*, 2003, available at http://www.bls.gov/gov/oco/0c02003.htm.

- *Increasing importance of the service sector.* Government estimates of employment trends suggest that there will be increased employment opportunities in companies which provide financial, insurance, health-care, education, food, travel, recreation, maintenance, and other services to the growing population. Higher productivity in the manufacturing sector means that it takes fewer workers to produce goods, so even though we are buying more goods, the percentage of total employment in this sector is declining.
- *Continued globalization.* Most companies now buy and sell goods in multiple countries. Workers of tomorrow will therefore be more valuable if they are fluent in a second language and are willing to travel for their job. Furthermore, even in the United States, the population is increasingly diverse, so we can expect changes in consumer demand for goods as a result. A downside to globalization is that many companies, in an effort to take advantage of cheaper labor, have moved their manufacturing operations overseas. In the past, this trend has primarily affected low-skilled jobs, but more recently, it has extended to skilled occupations, such as computer programming.
- *Concentration of the population.* The population of the United States is increasingly concentrated in coastal regions and near transportation centers. To keep costs low, jobs are likely to be in these areas as well.

The aging of the population implies increased demand for goods and services by retirees.

Preparing Yourself for the Job Market

Picking a career is only the first step. You must next prepare yourself for the job market by acquiring the necessary skills and experience, developing contacts, and executing an effective job search.

As an intern, you can gain valuable work experience and improve your skills.

Acquire Skills. We've already looked at the value of a college education for your career. The fact that you attend college, though, does not necessarily mean that you're actually acquiring the skills and abilities necessary to be successful in your chosen career. Rather than simply sitting back and passively absorbing information, you need to take a proactive role in your education. In your coursework, instead of doing only enough to get by, learn as much as you can, do the extra reading, solve the challenging problems. When a class involves working in teams, don't be the team member who lets someone else do the work. You'll only be cheating yourself and your future potential.

Many careers today require familiarity with computers and well-developed written and oral communication skills, which may or may not be required in your curriculum. Take an extra course in computer software, public speaking, or business. Join an extracurricular organization that provides leadership opportunities. You'll not only improve your skills—you'll also show potential employers that you're a person with initiative.

Get Experience. The job market today is very competitive—for every available position, there are numerous applicants with similar backgrounds. Job experience is therefore a must. Whether you acquire this experience through summer jobs or internships, the important thing is that you seek out employment experiences that are relevant to your chosen career. If you want to be a biology teacher, get a job in a lab or volunteer in a school. If you're a pre-law student, clerk in a law office or courthouse. Although *any* job experience is better than no experience at all, the typical part-time restaurant and retail job is not going to help you as much as a job related to your career goals—you should weigh the extra income you might make from an alternative job against the opportunities a targeted internship might offer. You might even consider working for free if doing so will give you an edge in the job market. In many cases, firms end up hiring from their pool of part-time workers and interns. Exit interviews of college graduates indicate that those students with internship experience receive more job offers and are more likely to find employment upon graduation.

Getting an internship is actually easier than you might think. Most firms are very interested in hiring interns—not only do the firms get motivated workers at relatively low pay, but they have an excellent opportunity to judge whether those workers would fit in well as permanent employees. You can apply for an internship in the same way you would apply for any other job. However, many students find internships through networking, as described in the next section.

networking

The process of developing contacts with people who might be helpful in your career.

informational interview

An interview requested by a job seeker for the purpose of learning more about a potential career or job.

Network. The process of developing contacts with people who might be helpful in your career is called **networking**. To some people—those who are more social and have outgoing personalities—this comes naturally; to others, it requires conscious effort. You should consider friends, relatives, neighbors, coworkers, and fellow members of organizations such as churches and volunteer groups to be potential business contacts. When you begin your job search, or even when you're still considering your career path, make a list of people you know, where they work, and what they do. These people can provide valuable information and advice, not necessarily just about specific job openings but about career choices, industry salaries, corporate culture, and advancement opportunities. If you approach them for an **informational interview**, asking for *information only*, you will find that most people are more than happy to talk about themselves and their jobs. In many cases, they'll even be willing to share their own networking contacts with you. Career office surveys have found that more students find jobs through informal networks than any other job search strategy.

Conducting an Effective Job Search

Once you've acquired the necessary credentials and skills, your next step is to execute an effective job search. Don't underestimate the time that this will require—you'll get out of the process what you put into it. College career counselors usually recommend that you plan to allocate about 10 hours a week, almost as much time as you would spend on a three-credit semester course.

Use Available Resources. Numerous resources are available for job hunters. If you know the geographical area you want to live in, you can subscribe to the local newspaper and regularly check the classified ads. Major city newspapers such as the *New York Times*, the *Los Angeles Times*, and the *Washington Post* are also good resources. Your school or city may sponsor job fairs where prospective employers collect résumés and provide information about their firms. In addition, there are local and national websites designed to connect employers with job seekers. Although search engines make it easy to find job postings that fit your requirements, these sites receive so many applications (400,000 posted on www.monster.com at any given time) that your résumé will probably be screened, at least initially, by a computer rather than a person. The larger websites, such as those identified in the *Ask the Expert* box, "Which Are the Best Internet Job Sites?" include other useful information, such as job descriptions, average salaries, and required credentials for particular careers, so you may want to visit them even if you have no intention of applying for a job over the Internet.

Perfect Your Résumé and Cover Letter. A **résumé** is a summary of your education and experience and should be carefully written to present you in the best possible light. Since prospective employers must look at many such résumés, make sure that you cover all the necessary information concisely; a résumé for a recent college graduate generally should be no more than one page long. The résumé should be attractively formatted and free of grammatical errors and inconsistencies.

résumé

A written summary of a person's education, experience, and other qualifications.

There are many ways to organize the information in a résumé. At a minimum, you should include the following information:

- *Contact information.* Your name, address, telephone number, and e-mail address.
- *Education and certifications.* Where and when you went to school (omit high school), the degree you received, and your major(s) and minor(s). Your GPA is optional, but most employers consider its omission to be an indication that it was low, so you may as well include it. You might also consider including, with an appropriate description, the GPA you received in your major courses alone, if it is higher than your overall GPA.
- *Experience.* When and for whom you have worked in the past and your major job responsibilities. Along with paid employment, this part of the résumé can include experience in student organizations, work-study programs, and volunteer activities.

In addition to this required information, you might also consider providing the following optional information:

ask the expert — Which Are the Best Internet Job Sites?

Ron and Caryl Krannich
Authors of America's Top Internet Sites, 2nd ed.

In the second edition of their book *America's Top Internet Sites*, Ron and Caryl Krannich have identified the most popular general-interest career and employment websites, based on the number of unique visitors each month:

- www.ajb.org (America's Job Bank, the only one on this list that is government-sponsored and maintained by tax dollars instead of advertising revenue)
- www.monster.com
- www.flipdog.com
- www.directemployers.com
- http://hotjobs.yahoo.com
- www.careerbuilder.com
- www.4work.com
- www.nationjob.com
- www.employment911.com
- www.careerjournal.com

In general, the sites are primarily aimed at providing the services required by their employer sponsors. Nevertheless, prospective job candidates will find that each site has a wealth of helpful information for job searches. Literally millions of employers and job seekers post their information at these sites.

Although the sites listed above are the biggest, perhaps the best website for college students is www.jobweb.com. This site is based on the cumulative information resources of many university and college career centers and also has links to hundreds of other useful sites.

Source: Ron and Caryl Krannich, *America's Top Internet Job Sites*, 2nd edition. Manassas Park, Va.: Impact Publications, 2004.

Fact #3

If you want to separate yourself from the competition, you should develop your communication, interpersonal, and teamwork skills. The skill category that received the highest ranking in a recent employer survey conducted by the National Association of Colleges and Employers (NACE) was communication, followed closely by honesty or integrity. Ironically, when asked what skills and qualities new college graduates are most likely to lack, survey participants cited communication skills.

- *Career objectives.* A simple statement of your objectives as they apply to the position you are seeking.
- *Summary of skills and abilities.* A trend in résumé writing today is to organize the résumé around skills rather than previous jobs. This can work particularly well for a student who has little paid work experience but has marketable skills to showcase—for example, skills related to computers, communication, leadership, or teamwork. Merely listing a skill isn't enough—you should provide a statement that shows where it came from. For example, you might say, "Excellent leadership skills gained while serving as president of my sorority."
- *Honors, awards, and extracurricular activities.* In this area, list only those items that provide some relevant information about your potential as an employee. For example, you should definitely include your Eagle Scout Award, since potential employers view that as a sign of early maturity and leadership potential. Your listing in a *Who's Who Directory* is not worthy of mention.

cover letter

A letter of introduction sent with a résumé to prospective employers.

A **cover letter** is a letter of introduction, no more than one page in length, sent with a résumé to prospective employers. Although the letter should not repeat all the information contained in the résumé, you can use it to highlight particular accomplishments or abilities. The cover letter is also your opportunity to demonstrate your enthusiasm for employment with the organization to which you're applying and to make use of your networking contacts. As with the résumé, you need to pay close attention to grammar and punctuation. It's a good idea to ask two or more people to error-check both documents before you send them to any prospective employers. A professional career counselor offers several suggestions for résumés, cover letters, and interviews in the *Ask the Expert* box, "Job Search Tips."

ask the expert Job Search Tips

Bill Shuster
Career Center Liaison
Colorado State University

Bill Shuster has reviewed countless résumés in his role as career counselor at a major university, and he's seen plenty of bloopers and blunders along the way. Drawing on his many years of experience in helping students search for jobs and decide on careers, he offers the following tips to college students:

Résumé Tips

- Don't focus so much on the content of the résumé that you forget the obvious—students often forget to include basic information, such as their phone number or home address.
- Don't just list your degree and major. List or demonstrate the skills you have gained from your major.
- Don't assume that unrelated previous employment is unimportant. Show how the skills are transferable. For example, don't just say, "waited tables"—talk about how you built customer loyalty, developed your customer service skills, and mediated problems.
- Always check carefully for typographical errors.

Cover Letter Tips

- Avoid hedge phrases such as: "I hope," "I feel," "I think." Be assertive.
- Don't just repeat your résumé. A cover letter has to show in a conversational way what you can do for an employer, utilizing active examples to demonstrate your abilities. "I have strong leadership experience gained from serving in several officer positions in my fraternity."
- Make sure that your e-mails are written as professionally as your résumé and cover letter.

Interview Tips

- Research the company! Know what the firm does, what it is good at, and how this relates to your skills.
- If you are excited about the opportunity, tell the interviewer. Don't give him or her the impression that you don't care.
- Utilize your college Career Center. Participate in practice interviews. Find out the most frequently asked questions and prepare some possible answers in advance.

Career Tips

- Always start first with you and your interests (hobbies, classes you like, best projects, best work experiences).
- Integrate your interests with your values and education. Then match yourself up against the market.
- Keep in mind that you have 45 years to work, so why not enjoy it!

Applications, Follow-up, and Interviews. Having identified your target employment opportunities, you can now mail your polished résumé and cover letters to prospective employers. In general, it's a good idea to follow up on all your applications, either in person or with a phone call. If you're asked to come in for an interview, be sure to dress appropriately and to do your homework beforehand, familiarizing yourself with the company and the job requirements.

Although there are many sources of information on how to interview, nothing substitutes for experience. Your first interview will never be your best interview, so it's a good idea to get a little practice before you go for your dream job. If your school offers mock interviews, you should take advantage of the opportunity. Not only will you get over the jitters after a few rounds, but you'll also become familiar with some of the more common interview questions.

Fact #4

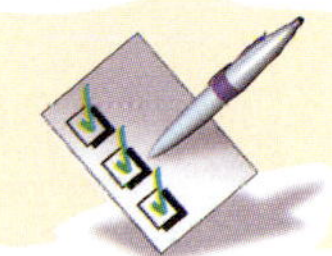

You should never go to a job interview unprepared. An interviewer will expect you, at a minimum, to be familiar with the firm and the job description. They will be most impressed with job candidates who have researched the company and who ask specific questions that indicate thoughtful preparation for the interview.

For sample interview questions and interview tips, visit www.interview.com and www.job-interview.net, as well as www.interview.monster.com.

Planning for the Long Term

As with other areas of financial planning, your career plan should incorporate both short-term goals, such as getting a job, and long-term goals. Long-term goals might include furthering your education, moving up into a management-level position, changing careers later in life, or starting your own business. Whatever they might be, identifying your goals and having a plan for how and when you will achieve them will increase your likelihood of success.

Learning by Doing 3-2

1. How does your chosen career fit with your natural abilities and interests?
2. What are some of the costs and risks associated with your current career path?

Developing and Implementing a Budget

LEARNING objective

3 Develop and implement a household budget.

In this chapter, we began with the process of developing personal financial goals. Career planning necessarily is part of that process since, without future income, it would be difficult if not impossible to achieve your other financial goals. Once you have a plan for earning income, the next step is to plan how to spend and save that income.

In the last chapter, you created a personal balance sheet and a personal cash flow statement in order to evaluate how well you've managed your money *in the past.* A **budget** is a plan for spending your money *in the future* so that you can achieve your financial goals. The budgeting process, whereby you plan for future income and expenditures and track your actual cash flows over time, is critical to implementation of your financial plan.

budget

A plan for spending and saving.

Factors Affecting Household Budgets

Many factors affect each household's budget and how the household allocates resources to various categories of expenditures. Family size and makeup, age and education of household members, sources and amount of income, and money attitudes all have an impact on budget decisions. Exhibit 3-8 shows the differences in allocations across several categories of expenditures for families in different life-cycle stages. If you're a full-time student, it's likely that your allocation of funds to educational expenses are high, but you are not yet allocating funds to savings. Families

EXHIBIT 3-8

Average household budget allocations at different ages

Source: U.S. Bureau of Labor Statistics, *Consumer Expenditure Survey 2001–2002*, available at http://www.bls.gov.

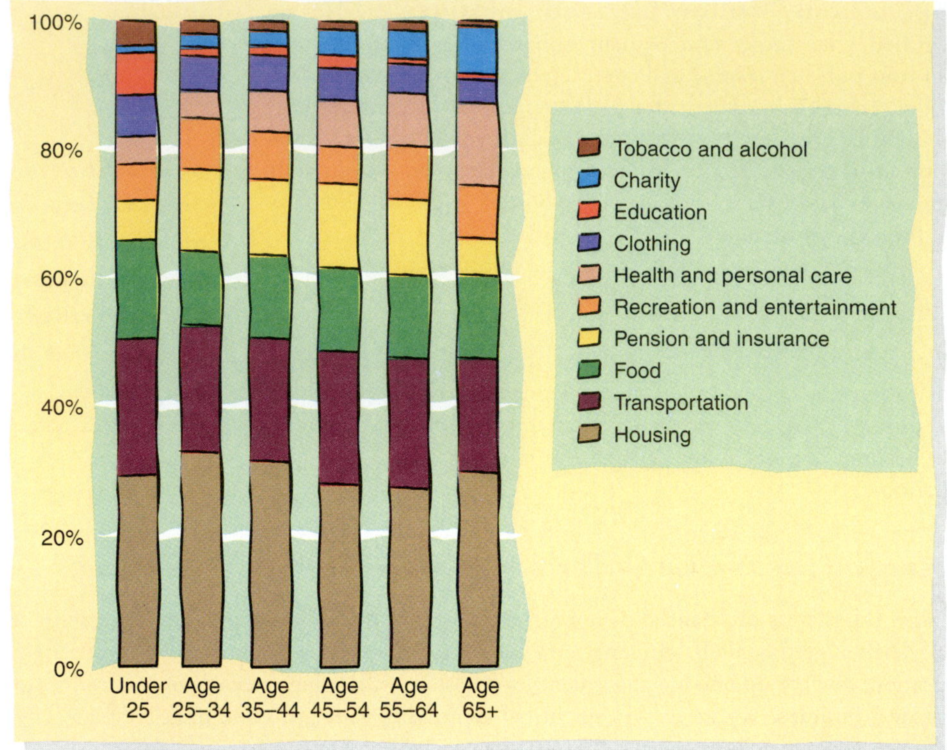

with young children spend more on housing and child care, whereas retirees have relatively greater health-care expenditures. Even within each category, however, you will find wide variation across households.

The Budgeting Process

The budgeting process includes four steps—forecasting, implementing, monitoring, and evaluating. If you haven't already organized your financial data, as explained in Chapter 2, then you need to do so before proceeding with the budgeting process. In this section, we discuss the first two steps and illustrate them by using the Thompson family, introduced at the beginning of this chapter, as an example. Later, we'll turn to the third and fourth steps, which involve monitoring and evaluating the budget.

Forecasting Future Income and Expenditures. Since your budget is a plan for future spending, you'll need to forecast your future income and expenditures in setting up the budget. Before you begin, you'll need to answer several questions.

First, what time period will your budget cover? Although an annual budget can help with the big picture, most families find it necessary to budget on a monthly basis to coincide with payment obligations.

Second, how will you keep your records? You need to make decisions at the outset regarding the record-keeping format that you'll employ. You can use your personal cash flow statement as a starting point, but you may want to condense or expand on the categories of income and expenses used in that financial statement to develop a budget system that works for you. The process of recording day-to-day expenditures can be tedious but is absolutely necessary, so make it simple enough to ensure that you'll persist in doing it on a regular basis. You can use the budget worksheets provided in your *Personal Financial Planner* for record keeping. Alternatively, you can purchase a home budget ledger at a business supply store or use one of the budget calculators available on the Internet. If you're comfortable with computers and have more than just a few expense items per month, you may find it worthwhile to purchase a software package such as *Microsoft Money* or *Quicken* to help with the budgeting process.

PFP Worksheet 12
Budget Forecast

After determining the period the budget will cover and how records will be kept, you'll be ready to tackle the key forecasting question: How will your income and expenses change over time? In preparing your forecasting estimates, the best approach is to make two passes. In the first pass, go through each income or expense item on your financial statements and estimate its value for the coming year based on past spending patterns and your reasonable expectations of the future. At this stage, don't add any expenditures for your new financial goals. The net cash flow under this scenario will tell you how much you have available (or how much you will have to cut) to apply to these objectives.

The starting point of your forecast is to estimate changes in your future income. Salary changes will be easy if you already know what your raise will be—as in the case that your employer has announced raises or you have a union-negotiated salary scale. Tips and bonuses are not as easy to estimate, but you should make a best (conservative) guess and plan to revise this part of your budget as you obtain new information.

Next, estimate your expenses. Fixed expenses are, by definition, going to be the same next year as they are currently. If the principal and interest on your fixed-rate home mortgage totaled $750 per month last year, it will be $750 per month next year, unless you refinance. However, your property taxes and homeowners' insurance payments will probably increase. Variable expenses may be more difficult to estimate. One approach is to take current variable expenses and increase them by the expected rate of inflation in your area. For example, if your homeowners' insurance premium was $600 last year and you anticipate 4 percent inflation, your premium for the coming year can be estimated as $600 × (1.04) = $624. Note that this is the calculation for the future value of a lump sum for one period at 4 percent interest.

Simple downloadable budget tools for students are available from the National Counsel for Financial Education at www.ncfe.org/college_students.cfm and from American Express at www.americanexpress.com. Download a more comprehensive budget planner at www.practicalmoneyskills.com. (Click on "Calculators.")

Reconciling Your Budget and Applying Funds to Your Goals. Once you've estimated all the line items in the first pass, you can calculate your estimated net cash flow—total cash inflows less total cash outflows. If this value is *negative*, you must determine how you're going to increase your income or reduce your expenditures to reconcile your budget. **Reconciling a budget** is the process of adjusting income and spending so that your expenses do not exceed your income. Variable expenses can be changed most easily in the short run but even fixed expenses can be reduced in the long run. You can increase your income by asking for a raise, changing jobs, or taking a second part-time job. If your net cash flow in the first pass is *positive*, you can use the second pass to determine where you will apply the extra funds—to increases in your savings or spending consistent with your prioritized financial objectives.

reconciling a budget

Adjusting income, expenses, and saving so that you don't spend more than you earn.

After determining your net cash flow, you'll adjust your budget, in a second pass, to reflect anticipated changes in spending and saving. Most important, you should now include in your budget the estimated costs of your new financial goals. If these costs exceed the extra cash flow that you estimated in the first pass, your reconciliation will require you to make decisions to reduce your expenses, increase your income, or adjust your financial goals to be more realistic, given your financial constraints.

An Example: The Thompson Family Budget

To observe the budgeting process in action, take a careful look at Exhibit 3-9, which shows Cindy and Dave Thompson's income and expenditures from the current year and their forecasts for next year. This year, Cindy and Dave have $9,300 in net positive cash flow ($775 per month times 12 months = $9,300). They've been saving this money to build an emergency fund—a store of liquid assets that can be used to pay expenses in the event of an unexpected cash shortfall. But recall that the Thompsons are hoping that Cindy will be able to quit work after their child is born. To determine the feasibility of this option, their first-pass forecast is an estimate of their income and expenses assuming that Cindy becomes a full-time homemaker. Unfortunately, the first pass at the 2005 budget shows that, without Cindy's income, the family will not be able to meet their expenses without a change in spending behavior. Even with Dave's anticipated 10 percent raise in January, they'll be $433 short per month, more than $5,000 per year. And keep in mind that this pass still doesn't incorporate any of the family's other financial objectives identified in Exhibit 3-6. Clearly, the estimated shortfall calls for some changes.

EXHIBIT 3-9

The Thompsons' Monthly Budget

Cash Inflows	Actual 2004	First Pass 2005	Final 2005	Comments
Dave's take-home pay	$ 4,000	$ 4,400	$ 4,400	Raise
Cindy's take-home pay	1,500	0	0	Cindy quits work
Interest and dividend income	4	4	4	
Child support from Cindy's ex-husband	433	433	433	
Total cash inflows	**$ 5,937**	**$ 4,837**	**$ 4,837**	$1,100 difference
Cash Outflows				
Groceries and eating out	866	893	793	Inflation; eat out less
Housing				
Mortgage principal and interest	881	881	719	Refinance at 6%
House repairs and expenses	165	165	85	Delay maintenance
Property taxes and insurance	250	260	260	Inflation
Utilities				
Heating	100	104	104	Inflation
Electric	50	52	52	Inflation
Water and sewer	35	36	36	Inflation
Cable, phone, and satellite	50	52	52	Inflation
Car loan payments	238	238	238	
Car maintenance and gas	265	276	250	Cindy drives less
Credit card payments	120	120	0	Pay off balance
Insurance				
Life	12	13	25	Insure Cindy
Health	150	200	200	
Auto	100	110	110	
Disability			50	For Dave
Clothing	100	104	60	
Gifts	180	187	90	Careful shopping
Other consumables (TV, etc.)	150	156	125	
Child-care expenses	225	95	95	
Sports-related expenses	15	17	17	
Health club dues	35	35	35	
Uninsured medical expenses	45	90	90	Baby costs
Education and training expenses	50	50	50	Dave's continuing ed
College fund			200	Kyle
Vacations	500	520	260	Cheaper vacation
Entertainment	170	177	83	Cut back
Charitable contributions	100	104	104	
Nonemployer retirement contributions	250	275	525	IRA for Cindy
Magazine subscriptions and books	10	10	10	
Other expenses	50	50	50	
Total cash outflows	**$ 5,162**	**$ 5,270**	**$ 4,768**	
NET PERSONAL CASHFLOW = Cash inflows − Cash outflows	$ 775	$ (433)	$ 69	

For most variable expenses in the first pass, Cindy and Dave simply assumed an increase of 4 percent for inflation. Now they carefully go through and cut down some of their estimates for discretionary expenses, such as housing maintenance (no more cleaning service), eating out (twice a month instead of weekly), entertainment, and vacations. They also estimate that they can save some money by refinancing their home, since market rates have fallen to 6 percent and their current mortgage interest rate is 8 percent. In addition, the Thompsons decide that they will use the next few months, before Cindy quits work, to pay off their credit card debt. By doing so, they will save $120 per month in credit card payments.

After making these changes, Cindy and Dave are able not only to meet their expenses but also to apply some funds to their objectives of starting a college fund for their older son ($200 per month), increasing their retirement savings ($250 per month for Cindy's retirement), and building an emergency reserve fund with their remaining positive net annual cash flow of $69 per month. They also decide to buy a life insurance policy for Cindy ($12 per month) and to purchase disability insurance for Dave ($50 per month), since the family will now be so dependent on his income.

As you can see from the preceding discussion, careful consideration of your family's pattern of expenditures can help you identify ways to reallocate funds to achieve your financial objectives. Now the challenge will be for the Thompsons to stick to their plan—reducing their credit card debt and their expenditures in certain budget categories.

Fact #5

More than $8\frac{1}{2}$ million workers held a second job in 2000, and most did so to achieve financial objectives—to meet regular household expenses (30.9%), to pay off debts (10.5%), to save for the future (8.7%), or to buy something special (7.9%). Relatively few did so because they enjoyed the second job (14.5%), although the percentage was higher for those over age 55.

Learning by Doing 3-3

1. Erikka estimates that her take-home pay for the coming year will be $1,000 per month. She expects total monthly expenses as follows: housing and utilities, $500; food, $200; auto, gas, and insurance, $220; credit card payment, $60. The balance on her credit card is $3,000, and she currently pays 18 percent interest on this balance. Erikka would like to reduce her credit card debt. Set up a budget that will help her achieve this goal.

2. You have estimated your budget for next year. Based on your first pass, your net cash flow is negative. What are your choices for reconciling your budget?

Monitoring and Controlling Your Budget

LEARNING objective

4 Monitor and control your expenses through a system of regular evaluation.

Planning to reduce your expenditures is one thing—implementing the plan may be more difficult, since old spending habits are sometimes hard to break. To make sure that your actions are consistent with your plan, you should regularly review your actual spending. You can best accomplish this by creating a monthly spending plan and tracking your actual spending to see how much it varies from your projections. If necessary, you can revise your budget as a result of what you learn.

Tracking Budget Variances

There are two main reasons for tracking budget variances:

- To identify small cash leakages as soon as possible so that you can change your behavior before you have a major budget shortfall.
- To ensure that large irregular cash expenses do not cause financial hardship. Income often comes in regular, predictable amounts, whereas some expenses, such as car and home repairs, tuition bills, or tax payments, may come in chunks and must be budgeted for in advance.

To track your expenses, as the Thompsons have done in Exhibit 3-10, you can use the worksheet in your *Personal Financial Planner*. The Thompsons' actual monthly expenditures for January through March 2005 show that, in January, they had to pay their health club dues of $400 for the year. And since they had not yet met their annual health insurance deductible, their uninsured medical expenses were larger than budgeted. Fortunately, their income is sufficient to

PFP Worksheet 13
Tracking Your Budget

EXHIBIT 3-10

The Thompsons' Track Their Budget

	Budgeted Monthly	Actual					
		January	Variance	February	Variance	March	Variance
CASH INFLOWS	$ 4,837	$ 4,837	$ —	$ 4,837	$ —	$ 4,837	$ —
CASH OUTFLOWS							
Groceries and eating out	$ 793	$ 900	$(107)	$ 800	$ (7)	$ 750	$ 43
Housing							
Mortgage debt service	979	979	0	979	0	979	0
House repairs and expenses	85	0	85	0	85	300	(215)
Utilities							
Heating	104	150	(46)	145	(41)	130	(26)
Electric	52	45	7	50	2	35	17
Water and sewer	36	36	0	36	0	36	0
Cable, phone, and satellite	52	52	0	52	0	52	0
Car loan payments	238	238	0	238	0	238	0
Car maintenance and gas	250	150	100	230	20	200	50
Credit card payments	0	0	0	0	0	0	0
Insurance							
Life	25	25	0	25	0	25	0
Health	200	200	0	200	0	200	0
Auto	110	110	0	110	0	110	0
Disability	50	50	0	50	0	50	0
Clothing	60	0	60	75	(15)	50	10
Gifts	90	50	40	0	90	0	90
Other consumables (TVs, etc.)	125	0	125	0	125	0	125
Child-care expenses	95	75	20	75	20	75	20
Sports-related expenses	17	50	(33)	0	17	0	17
Health club dues	35	400	(365)	0	35	0	35
Uninsured medical expenses	90	200	(110)	30	60	30	60
Education and training	50	0	50	0	50	0	50
College fund	200	200	0	200	0	200	0
Vacations	260	0	260	0	260	0	260
Entertainment	83	50	33	40	43	100	(17)
Charitable contributions	104	104	0	104	0	104	0
Nonemployer retirement fund	525	525	0	525	0	525	0
Magazines and books	10	0	10	0	10	30	(20)
Other expenses	50	55	(5)	45	5	35	15
Total Cash Outflows	**$ 4,768**	**$ 4,644**	**$ 124**	**$4,009**	**$ 759**	**$4,254**	**$ 514**
NET PERSONAL CASH FLOW	$ 69	$ 193		$ 828		$ 583	
Cumulative variance			$ 124		$ 883		$1,397

cover these expenses, but many households are not so lucky and must plan in advance to cover large irregular expenses. You can deal with this problem in various ways:

- Build a fund for this purpose (over the course of the previous months). If, for example, you pay your health club dues every January, the very next month you could begin to set aside the money for the following year's dues so that, by the following January, you would have the funds and it wouldn't be a big hit to your budget for that month.
- Use emergency funds (and replace them in later months).
- Obtain a short-term loan (but be sure to include financing costs in your budget).

Revising Your Budget

A common reason for exceeding your budget is that you're failing to control your discretionary spending in certain areas (most commonly entertainment-related). In this case, you should take the time to review your financial goals, evaluate your progress toward meeting them, and carefully weigh the benefits and costs of the purchases that are interfering with your plan. You might consider trying some budgeting tricks from behavioral psychology, described in the *Money Psychology* box, "The Psychology of Budgeting," to help you stick to your budget.

After tracking your budget for several months, you might find that your expenditures are higher than you estimated. This can happen for various reasons. On the one hand, you may have been too conservative in estimating certain expenses; or perhaps you had a large unplanned expenditure, such as new brakes for your car that diverted funds you had allocated to another purpose. In either case, you need to go back to the original budget and revise it so that, going forward, you will be able to meet your expenses. Some advice for dealing with "budget busters" is offered in the *News You Can Use* box, "Tips for Surviving the Seven 'Budget Busters.'"

Money Psychology

The Psychology of Budgeting

1. *Avoid pain.* Experimental psychologists have long known that people tend to avoid things which cause pain or regret. Unfortunately, many personal finance tasks are associated with negative feelings—paying bills and filing taxes, for example. Even saving is painful since it often requires you to reduce your spending on "fun" stuff. To apply this behavioral principle to your savings plan, make a plan to save from *future* salary increases. For example, when you get a $200 per month raise, immediately arrange to have it automatically deposited to your savings account. Since you never had the money to spend in the first place, you won't feel the "pain" of having to cut back on spending and your savings plan is more likely to succeed.
2. *Reward yourself for successes.* Just as individuals try to avoid pain, they also like to repeat activities that cause them to feel good. To apply this to your personal finances, you should develop a way to savor your budgeting successes. Perhaps you could tape a chart to the refrigerator that shows the growth in your savings account. Or, if you prefer more overt rewards for your hard work, you might plan to have a special dinner out with your spouse whenever you reach a personal financial milestone. But don't forget to include the cost of the "reward" in your budget!
3. *Pay yourself first.* The principle of paying yourself first, which was introduced in Chapter 1, is based on the well-known psychological bias "out of sight, out of mind." When you don't have a regular reminder of something, your mind tends to get "fooled" into thinking it isn't there. This behavioral principle is easily applied to your personal finances. If you have amounts withdrawn automatically from your paycheck and applied to your personal financial objectives at the beginning of a pay period—debt repayment or retirement contributions, for example—you are more inclined to spend as if you had less to start with.
4. *Use mental accounting.* "Mental accounting" is a term used by psychologists to describe a process by which people consider money differently, depending on where it comes from and where it goes to. For example, many people look at end-of-year bonuses or tax refunds as funds that are outside their regular budget and can therefore be spent more frivolously. Although this example shows how mental accounting might not always be beneficial from a financial planning perspective, since all your income *should* be included in your budget, this psychology principle can sometimes be helpful in budgeting. For example, if you are having trouble sticking to a budget, you could make the budget more concrete by cashing your paycheck each pay period and putting the cash into individual envelopes that correspond to your budget categories. When an envelope is empty, then you can't spend any more in that category until the next pay period.

NEWS you can use

Tips for Surviving the Seven "Budget Busters"

Although most budget advice focuses on controlling your discretionary expenditures, credit and bankruptcy experts warn that the biggest problems arise from fixed expenses over which you have less control. When the major breadwinner is laid off from his or her job, for example, the family's previously reasonable budgeted expenses suddenly can seem extravagant. Fixed expenses related to housing, tuition, and automobiles are often most troublesome. Consider the following suggestions for dealing with these problems:

"Twenty percent of bankruptcies are triggered by medical bills."

Budget Busters	Budget Solutions
1. *Too much house.* Expensive houses usually come with expensive utilities, maintenance, taxes, and insurance.	Downsize. Keep your basic housing expenses to no more than 25 percent of your pretax income.
2. *Too many children.* Face it—kids are expensive—about an extra $10,000 per year, per child. Married couples with children are more than twice as likely to file for bankruptcy.	Live more frugally. Parents must accept the reality that they can't spend the way they did when they were childless.
3. *Too much tuition.* Preschool costs, private schools for K-12, and college costs take a huge bite out of some household budgets.	Never borrow to pay for precollege education. Consider less expensive options for college, including community colleges and in-state universities. Make your child pay for some of it.
4. *Too much car.* If you have large payments and/or owe more than a car's worth, you could be in for trouble.	Don't trade a car before it's paid for. Don't take long-term car loans.
5. *Too many marital troubles.* If you and your spouse separate or divorce, you will be supporting two households instead of one, on the same joint income.	Go to counseling before splitting. If divorce is inevitable, close joint accounts and refinance mortgages to avoid getting tangled in your ex-spouse's bankruptcy.
6. *Too little health insurance.* Accident or illness can be financially disastrous, especially if you are one of the many people with no health insurance. Twenty percent of bankruptcies are triggered by medical bills.	Budget to be able to afford some health insurance. Consider a high deductible plan to protect against catastrophes.
7. *Too little emergency cash.* Many families live paycheck to paycheck. A lost job, car breakdown, or unexpectedly large bill can easily cause a financial crisis.	Start an emergency fund now using automatic transfer from your paycheck to a liquid savings account. Deposit any windfalls or refunds.

Source: Liz Pullman Weston, "How to Survive 7 Budget Busters," available at http://moneycentral.msn.com/content/savinganddebt/learntobudget/P58710.asp.

Learning by Doing 3-4

Sanjay has just completed an annual budget for his family. He has determined that his family has a very small positive net cash flow for the year. Explain to Sanjay why he should also evaluate his budget on a monthly basis and track his budget variances.

Money Attitudes and Household Budgeting

LEARNING objective

5 Understand how money attitudes affect budgeting.

Our consideration of budgeting would be incomplete without some discussion of the relationship between budgeting and money attitudes. Individual differences in money attitudes and spending behavior are a major cause of conflict in relationships, not only for families who are struggling to meet a minimum standard of living, but also in affluent households. If you are a saver and your spouse is a spender, you are bound to have problems developing and sticking to a household budget.

Consider the following common scenario: Robert and Jamie are newlyweds in their 20s. Both are employed, although Robert's monthly take-home pay is substantially more than Jamie's. When they sit down to pay their bills together for the first time, Robert suggests that they just split everything down the middle. Jamie isn't sure this is fair but is uncomfortable saying so. After paying her share, Jamie doesn't have enough left over each month to pay her regular monthly out-of-pocket expenses and has to ask Robert for money each week. She feels even more uncomfortable and finds herself resenting Robert's regular purchases of CDs, sporting goods, and other personal items. In the end, because she is hesitant to speak up, Jamie's unhappiness builds until it begins to affect other aspects of their relationship.

How could this problem have been avoided? First and foremost, this example illustrates the importance of frank discussion about money with your significant other, preferably before you marry or move in together. Robert and Jamie made a quick decision to split expenses down the middle without a careful look at their actual cash outflows. If they had developed a budget, it would have been obvious that Jamie should not be responsible for half of the household expenses on her income.

In general, you can usually avoid future problems by setting ground rules at the beginning that are agreeable to both of you. These should not be established without careful consideration of the consequences. Some issues that you should resolve up front include the following:

- How will you manage the finances in the household, pay regular bills, and make investment decisions? These responsibilities may be managed jointly or split up.
- Will each person retain individual control over some of the money? Although the simplest arrangement for a family is to pool everything, many families do not do this. Indeed, most experts agree that each person should have control over some discretionary funds. In the extreme, you might decide to maintain totally separate accounts and split all expenses evenly or in proportion to income, a solution that would have worked better for Robert and Jamie.
- Which household discretionary expenditures require joint agreement? Some families only jointly decide on very large purchases such as new furniture or cars, and others set a dollar limit on discretionary purchases. For example, you might decide that if something costs more than $100, you can't buy it without consulting one another.
- What are your individual attitudes about spending and borrowing? If one person hates to be in debt and the other would rather finance a higher lifestyle with credit cards, conflict is inevitable unless you have resolved these issues before intermingling your finances.

- What are your individual attitudes about planning and saving for the future? If you and your spouse have vastly different financial goals, then you may disagree about how to allocate net cash flow.
- What are your attitudes toward gift giving? Families differ in their gift-giving traditions, and this can be a cause for conflict. If your future wife's family always gives extravagant gifts for Christmas and birthdays and you think it's a waste of money, this will be a cause for conflict every year if you don't deal with it up front.
- Who pays for the debt that precedes the marriage? Even if you buy into the "yours, mine, and ours" philosophy of marriage, if one partner brings a lot of debt to the marriage, it may not be fair to expect the other to pay for it. In numerous cases, a starry-eyed newlywed has paid off her or his new spouse's debts only to have the spouse leave the marriage shortly thereafter—with no debt. Having a plan for resolving past financial difficulties will reduce this problem.
- How will you pay for expenses associated with children from previous marriages? Although you may receive child support from another parent, additional costs for children living in your home are inevitable. Depending on the circumstances of the divorce, the parents may be tempted to compete for the child's affections by spending money on him or her. Whether the new stepparent should have any obligation to contribute to the child's upkeep is an individual decision but one that should be resolved prior to the marriage (and should never be discussed in front of the child). In discussing this issue, don't forget about college funding costs.
- Should you have a prenuptial agreement? With the prevalence of divorce, individuals who bring substantial assets to a marriage may want to consider a **prenuptial agreement**, which is a written contract in advance of the marriage that specifies how the assets will be distributed in the event of a divorce. It is also possible to make a postnuptial agreement at a later date to accomplish the same end. Although it may seem very unromantic to anticipate divorce when you aren't even married yet, the process of discussing the prenuptial may actually force you to talk about your money attitudes and important financial issues in advance of the marriage.

prenuptial agreement

A written contract in advance of a marriage that specifies how the assets will be distributed in the event of a divorce.

Learning by Doing 3-5

Clark, age 45, and Lois, age 40, are engaged to be married. Both of them have been married previously, and both have well-paying jobs. Under what circumstances would you advise them to have a prenuptial agreement?

Summary

1. **Identify your short-term and long-term personal financial goals.** The second step in the personal financial planning process is to make a prioritized list of realistic personal financial goals. Whenever possible, these goals should be broken down into smaller subgoals, including a specific timeframe, estimated costs, and itemized steps to be taken. You should regularly reevaluate your goals and your progress toward achieving them.
2. **Evaluate your skills, abilities, and interests to establish a career plan.** Your choice of career has a significant impact on your ability to achieve your other financial goals; thus, career planning is an essential component of your financial plan. You should research potential career paths that match your natural abilities and interests, acquire the necessary training, education, skills, and certifications, and execute an effective job search.
3. **Develop and implement a household budget.** A budget is a plan for spending and saving to achieve your household financial goals. The first step in the budgeting process is to forecast your future income and expenses. Since the objective is to ensure that you spend no more than you earn, cash shortfalls are reconciled by reducing future variable expenses. Positive net cash flow is allocated to saving or spending to meet particular financial goals.
4. **Monitor and control your expenses through a system of regular evaluation.** You should monitor your actual income and expenditures over time to see whether they vary substantially from budgeted amounts. If necessary, you can make changes to your budget or to your actual spending behavior.
5. **Describe how money attitudes affect budgeting.** People differ in their attitudes toward spending and saving. Since this can be a major cause of stress in relationships, it is important for household members to talk about money issues and establish mutually agreeable ground rules.

Key Terms

budget (83)
cover letter (82)
human capital (74)
informational interview (80)
networking (80)
prenuptial agreement (92)
reconciling a budget (85)
résumé (81)

Concept Review Questions

1. Why is it important to have financial goals?
2. Why is it important to break up your goals into different time horizons (short-term, intermediate-term, and long-term)?
3. Identify a financial goal that fits in each of the different time horizons.
4. List the nine categories of financial planning goals. For each one, identify one goal that you might include on your goal wish list.
5. Identify the characteristics of effective goals.
6. Why is it helpful to break larger goals into smaller, concrete steps?
7. Why is career planning so fundamental to financial planning?
8. What is human capital, and how can you invest in it?
9. What are the steps you should take in deciding on a career?
10. If you plan to have children, how might that impact your career plan?
11. What employment and demographic trends are likely to affect your career opportunities in the future?
12. Why is work experience so important to obtaining a good job?
13. Other than working in an actual job, what opportunities do you have to obtain work-related experience?
14. What is a résumé? What is a cover letter? What information is included in each, and how do they differ?
15. What should you do to maximize your potential for career advancement over your lifetime?
16. What is networking, and why is it important to your career plan?
17. Identify the steps you should take to conduct an effective job search.
18. What is a budget, and what is its purpose?
19. How does the budget differ from the personal cash flow statement?
20. What are the four steps in the budgeting process, and what activities should you undertake in each?
21. How do you reconcile a budget?
22. How can a budget help you identify cash leakages?
23. Why is it important to analyze budget variances at the end of each month?
24. Which household financial issues should be resolved prior to marriage?
25. Under what circumstances might a prenuptial agreement be advisable?

Application Problems

1. **Setting Goals.** Lucy and Desi are expecting their first child. Although they had previously developed a prioritized list of personal financial goals, they expect that their new family circumstances will necessitate some changes. Identify three goals that they are likely to add to their original list. How might their priorities change after the birth of their child?
2. **Breaking Goals into Quantifiable Subgoals.** Jamal Woods would like to buy a car one year from now. He anticipates making a down payment of $1,200 and borrowing the remaining $10,000. Show how he can break this larger goal into several specific smaller subgoals. Be sure to include an estimate of his required monthly allocation of funds to this goal.
3. **Present Value of Education.** Kendra Wisniewski is currently a middle-level manager earning $60,000 per year. She is thinking about quitting work to go back to school for a law degree. She expects her total expenses during the three years of law school to be $35,000 per year. Assuming that she will earn $80,000 as a lawyer, what is the present value of obtaining this additional education assuming 4 percent inflation and a 45 year working career?
4. **Budgets and Family Type.** For each of the following budget categories, indicate (a) whether it is a fixed expense, variable expense, or has some elements of both; and (b) whether it will be a larger proportion of the budget for a 27-year-old childless couple or for a 70-year-old retired couple: housing, transportation, entertainment, health care.
5. **Developing a Budget.** José Diaz has collected the following information in order to develop a budget for his sophomore year of college. He has a football scholarship that covers his meals, tuition, fees, and books. He estimates that his monthly income from all sources is $1,000. His monthly expenses are as follows: one-fourth of rent and utilities for an apartment shared with three friends, $450; auto expenses and insurance, $300; cell phone, $25; health insurance, $50; entertainment, $150. Develop a budget based on his current expenditures, and calculate his net monthly cash flow.
6. **Determining Budget Variances.** José has developed his budget, but when he tracks his actual income and expenses, he finds that he is always out of money. Use his actual expenses for the months of September and October to calculate his budget variances. What areas of his budget does he need to work on?

Item	Budgeted	September Actual	Budget Variance	October Actual	Budget Variance
Housing	$450	$450		$470	
Auto	300	280		320	
Cell phone	25	50		25	
Health insurance	50	50		50	
Entertainment	150	220		175	

7. **Effect of Inflation.** Suppose that you have developed a budget for 2005 assuming that the costs of your variable expenditures on goods and services will increase by 2.5 percent from their 2004 levels. Your total variable expenditures in 2004 were $1,000 per month. How much will they be in 2005, assuming no other changes? If it turns out that inflation is actually 4 percent in 2005, how much budget variance will this cause?

Using Web Resources for Financial Planning

1. **Create a Budget.** Check out the budget maker at *www.money.cnn.com.* Input your own income and expenses, and calculate your net cash flow.
2. **How Does Your Spending Affect Your Finances?** Go to the Budget Analyzer at the Finance Center at www.financenter.com/products/calculators/budget/. If you enter your actual budget expenditure and the amount you would like to reduce it to, the analyzer will tell you how much this change will affect your future wealth. For example, suppose that you plan to save $50 per month by cutting out your afternoon lattés. What impact will that budget change have on your wealth?
3. **Where Are the Jobs?** Check out *www.collegegrad.com* to find out which large employers are hiring. Click on "Top Entry Level Employers" to see the projected number of new hires for the year. For example, in March 2004, Enterprise Rent-A-Car, Disney, and GEICO Direct topped the list, with each expected to hire 6,000 new entry-level employees.
4. **Which Jobs Are Best?** Although having a job is better than not having one, most people look for more out of their careers. Go to the Harris Interactive website at *www.harrisinteractive.com* to find the results of two recent Harris polls related to job satisfaction. You can search by subject or simply by the specific poll number. Which occupations have the most prestige (Harris Poll #57, October 1, 2003)? What three factors have the most impact on job satisfaction (Harris Poll #74, December 20, 2000)?
5. **Job Descriptions and Salaries.** Two excellent websites for career planning and job searching are *www.monster.com* and *www.jobweb.com.* Identify three career areas that you are considering. What is the average starting salary in your geographic area for each? What benefits are usually provided by the employer?
6. **Research Money Management Software.** As your finances get more complicated, you may find it helpful to use a money management software package for paying bills, budgeting, and tracking investments. Use a search engine to identify three alternatives you might consider purchasing for this purpose. Research price, features, and customer satisfaction, and summarize your findings in a table. Which package do you think will best meet your needs?

Learning by Doing Solutions

LBD 3-1: 1a. ST: graduate from college; LT: go to graduate school. b. ST: find a larger/cheaper apartment; LT: buy a condo. c. ST: start a retirement savings account; LT: accumulate enough wealth to retire comfortably; d. ST: join a health club; LT: take a backpacking trip to Europe; 2. Undoubtedly, the goals will change, particularly if your family circumstances have changed.; 3. A possible set of subgoals could be: Stop using the credit cards. Calculate the amount to pay toward debt reduction each month. Apply this amount to the card with the highest interest rate until it's paid off, then to the next.

LBD 3-2: Answers will vary.

LBD 3-3: Her net cash flow without the credit card payment is $1,000 − $920 = $80. If she applies this amount to her credit card balance each month, she can pay off the debt in a little more than two years. PV = 3,000; I = 18/12; PMT = 80; solve for N = 56 months. 2. Reduce discretionary expenditures; increase income; take action to reduce fixed expenditures such as downsizing a car or house, getting a roommate, refinancing to obtain a lower interest rate.

LBD 3-4: Although his income is constant, his expenses may occur in chunks. Tracking the monthly variances will allow him to quickly identify small problem areas before they become bigger ones.

LBD 3-5: A prenuptial may be advisable if either brings a lot of wealth or a lot of debt to the marriage, or if either has children from a previous marriage.

Building Financial Planning Skills Through Case Applications

Case 3-1 Katie Stewart Confronts Her Spending Habits

Katie Stewart is a legal secretary at a major law firm in New York City, where she has worked for the last two years since graduating from Brookdale Community College. It's too expensive to live in the city on her $24,000 salary, so Katie commutes from New Jersey at a cost of $50 per week. Katie is worried about her personal finances. In the two years she has worked in New York, she has spent more than she has earned, primarily to buy clothes for work. A few lunch-hour shopping sprees with coworkers have resulted in impulse purchases on credit cards, and Katie now has $4,500 in credit card debt. Katie is considering a legal secretary position with a small firm in New Jersey that will pay $3,000 less than her current job.

a. Explain why Katie's first step should be to develop a budget.
b. What alternatives does Katie have for reducing her credit card debt.
c. If her credit card interest rate is 14 percent, and she wants to pay her credit card debt off over four years, what payment will she need to make each month?
d. What factors should Katie consider in deciding on the alternative job? How will the New Jersey job affect her finances?

Case 3-2 Ron Harrington Faces a Layoff

Ron Harrington works for a large technology company as a software engineer and currently earns $120,000 per year. He and his wife Nancy live in a five-bedroom suburban home with their three children ages 10 to 17. Although Nancy has a business marketing degree, she has not worked outside the home since their last child was born. Ron's employer recently announced plans to lay off a substantial number of employees over the course of the following year as a cost-cutting measure, and Ron is worried that he might lose his job in the next three to six months. Although the company has not explicitly said anything about severance pay, the rumor is that laid-off workers will receive only one month's pay after they are fired. Ron will also be eligible for unemployment compensation for several months, but he is concerned that this amount will be insufficient to cover their household expenses, and he knows it will take a long time to find a comparable job. He estimates that he will have to take a lower-level job at a salary significantly lower than what he now makes. Ron and Nancy currently live comfortably on Ron's income, they have no credit card or student loan debt, and they have about $50,000 in home equity. They recently bought their current home, and it was financed with a $180,000 mortgage.

a. Explain why the Harringtons need to develop a budget.
b. What financial steps should Ron and Nancy be taking to prepare for the possible layoff?
c. What career steps should Ron take now to prepare for the coming layoff?
d. Nancy is considering returning to her prior career in the event that Ron loses his job. What are the pros and cons of this strategy? What should Nancy be doing now to prepare for that possibility?

DEVELOPING PERSONAL FINANCIAL skills for life

Learning about Yourself

3-1. What Is Your Goal Orientation?

You will be more likely to achieve financial success if you better understand yourself and your motivations. Use the following exercise to evaluate your goal orientation.

PFP Worksheet 14: Goal Orientation Assessment

For each of these statements, write the number that shows the extent to which the statement accurately describes your views (5 = strongly agree; 4 = agree; 3 = undecided; 2 = disagree; 1 = strongly disagree).

_____ **1.** Buying things for myself makes me feel guilty.

_____ **2.** The happiness of my family is more important to me than my career satisfaction.

_____ **3.** Parents are not obligated to leave an inheritance for their children.

_____ **4.** Parents should pay for their children's college education.

______ **5.** I regularly do volunteer work.
______ **6.** Before I spend any of my paycheck on extras, I make sure that I have paid my regular bills.
______ **7.** If I had children, I would want to buy a home in a nice neighborhood near a school.
______ **8.** I would not consider a career that required too much travel away from home.
______ **9.** My favorite type of vacation is to stay at home with my family.
______ **10.** Every year, I donate clothes, books, or food to a charity.

Scoring:
Total your score for all questions: ________.

Interpretation:
A score of 10 to 30 may indicate that you have a greater focus on yourself than others. Your goals might include those that provide more immediate benefit to yourself, such as vacations and consumer goods. A score of 40 to 50 may indicate that your goals are focused on others' needs rather than your own. You should watch out for your tendency to underallocate resources to your future needs, such as retirement and health care.

3-2. How Important Is Your Career Relative to Other Goals?

The following statements are about the importance of career relative to other goals. For each of these statements, write the number that shows the extent to which the statement accurately describes your views (5 = strongly agree; 4 = agree; 3 = undecided; 2 = disagree; 1 = strongly disagree).

______ **1.** Being successful in my career is more important than finding the right person to marry.
______ **2.** Being successful in my career is more important than having a lot of money.
______ **3.** Being successful in my career is more important than having good friends.
______ **4.** When I am developing my career, it is more important for me to spend time at work than to spend time with my family.
______ **5.** Getting ahead in my career is more important than having time to enjoy my own interests and hobbies.
______ **6.** Spending time in my line of work is just as important as spending time in community and service organizations.
______ **7.** I prefer a job that keeps me so busy that I don't have time for anything else.
______ **8.** I would like to have a career that requires a lot of travel away from home.
______ **9.** I am willing to make many sacrifices to get ahead in my career.
______ **10.** A job with a high income is more important to me than a job that will allow me to help others.

Scoring:
Total your score for all questions: ________.

Interpretation:
High scores (35–50) indicate that a successful career is important to you. Low scores (10–25) indicate that other factors in your life are more important than your career.

Developing Your Skills

3-3. Informational Interviews

What if you don't know what you want to be when you grow up? As discussed in the chapter, a great way to explore your possibilities is to conduct informational interviews with people in different careers. Identify five people who are in professions that interest you. Ask them the following questions and summarize your findings in your *Personal Financial Planner*.

PFP Worksheet 15
Informational Interview

1. How did you decide on this career and this employer?
2. What did you study in college or graduate school that prepared you for this career?
3. What does a typical workday look like?
4. What is a typical starting salary and benefits package?
5. What do you like best about your job?
6. What do you like least about your job?
7. What is your greatest challenge?
8. Tell me about the career and salary advancement potential in this career.
9. What is your best advice to someone who is thinking about this as a career alternative?
10. Do you have any good sources of information about this career that you could share with me?

3-4. Comparing Career Alternatives

Using as many resources as possible, including informational interviews, Internet resources, and library materials, investigate two or more career alternatives. Summarize and record the results of your research.

3-5. Preparing a Résumé and Cover Letter

a. Begin the process of creating your résumé by collecting the necessary personal and employment information, and recording it in your *Personal Financial Planner*. Use the worksheet to help you organize the information and then write a rough draft of a résumé that includes everything a potential employer will need and is no more than one page in length. You can organize your résumé in the format provided in the *Personal Financial Planner* or develop your own. Most word processing software includes one or more templates for résumés or you can develop one of your own. After you have completed your rough draft, ask two people to critique it for you and make any necessary corrections.

b. Identify a potential employment opportunity or internship that you would like to apply for. Draft a cover letter that would be appropriate for this application. You can use the template provided in *Personal Financial Planner* or write one yourself. After you have completed your rough draft, ask two people to critique it for you and make any necessary corrections.

PFP Worksheet 16
Personal and Employment Data

PFP Worksheet 17
Cover Letter Template

3-6. Developing and Prioritizing Your Goals

Follow the steps discussed in this chapter to develop and prioritize your personal finance goals. Start by creating a wish list, prioritize your list, and break the big goals into smaller goals. Record your results in the *Personal Financial Planner*.

PFP Worksheet 10
Prioritizing Goals

PFP Worksheet 11
Personal Financial Goals with Subgoals

3-7. Sticking to a Budget

Use the personal financial statements you developed in Chapter 2 to prepare a budget for the coming year. Be sure to estimate increases in each category due to raises, inflation, expected changes in household circumstances, changes in housing arrangements, and geographic location, as needed. You can use worksheets in the *Personal Financial Planner* to develop your budget and to track your budget variances over the course of this semester. Evaluate your adherence to your budget and revise your estimates in each category as necessary.

a. In what categories did you have the largest budget variances? Why?
b. Are there expenses that you could easily trim from your budget?
c. If you have any consumer debt, evaluate how much difference it would make if you could reduce the interest rate that you pay.
d. Reconsider the goals that you developed in the previous exercise in light of your budget.

PFP Worksheet 12
Budget Forecast

PFP Worksheet 13
Tracking Your Budget

THE NAVIGATOR

- ☐ Review Before Studying this Chapter list.
- ☐ Scan Learning Objectives.
- ☐ Take Myth or Fact quiz and find the answers throughout the chapter.
- ☐ Read chapter and answer Learning by Doing exercises.
- ☐ Review Key Terms and Key Calculations.
- ☐ Do end-of-chapter exercises.
- ☐ Take review quiz on the text website.
- ☐ Solve end-of-chapter cases.

BEFORE studying this chapter, you should review

- Marginal analysis (Chapter 1).
- Personal financial statements (Chapter 2).

Income Tax Planning

CHAPTER 4

Myth or Fact?

Consider each of the following statements and decide whether it is a *myth* or a *fact*. Look for the answers in the *Fact* boxes in the chapter.

	MYTH	FACT
1. Current federal income tax rates are relatively low compared to historical rates.	☐	☐
2. Even if your parents are paying for college, they can only claim you as a dependent on their income taxes until you're 21.	☐	☐
3. I can get my tax refund more quickly if I file my tax return electronically.	☐	☐
4. I can save a lot on my taxes by donating my old junk car to charity.	☐	☐
5. Tax evasion is a crime punishable by jail time.	☐	☐

LEARNING objectives

1. Understand the major features of the federal income tax system.
2. Know when and how to file your taxes.
3. Calculate taxable income and determine your tax liability.
4. Establish strategies to legally minimize the taxes you pay.
5. Understand how the tax system is enforced, and be aware of recent trends in the system.

...applying the planning process

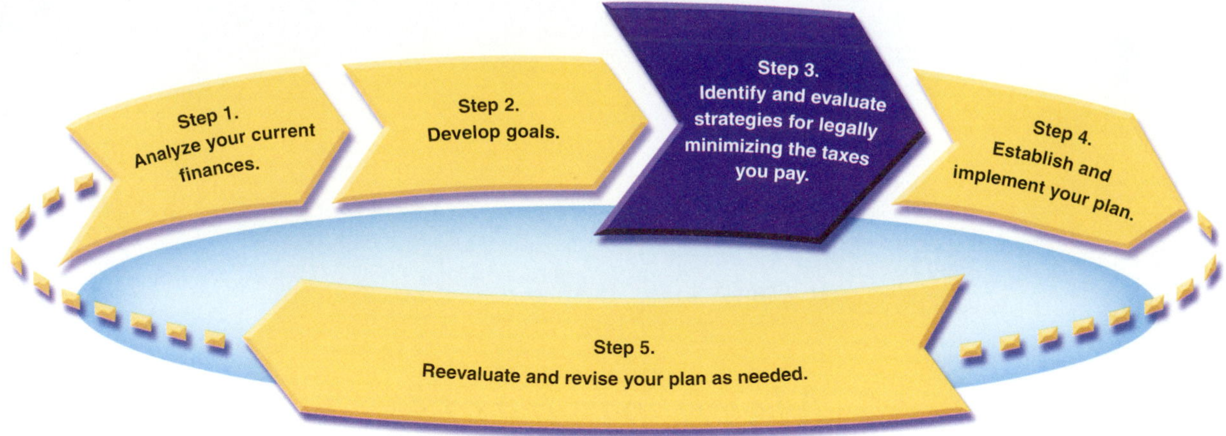

More than 200 years ago, Ben Franklin is reported to have said, "In this life, nothing is certain but death and taxes." Today, these words continue to ring true, perhaps because it isn't unusual to see half of your hard-earned income going toward the payment of various taxes. Since tax payments—federal, state, and local income taxes, Social Security and Medicare payroll taxes, sales taxes, property taxes, sin taxes, and luxury taxes—can take such a big bite out of your budget, your strategies for legally minimizing the taxes you pay are critical to the success of your financial plan. Thus, it's important to take into account the tax implications of your potential financial decisions and to be proactive in developing a plan to minimize tax payments. As you learn more about federal income taxes in this chapter, you'll discover that there are many ways to legally reduce your tax burden by taking advantage of tax incentives designed to encourage you to own a home, save for retirement, and invest in higher education, among others.

To provide a context for our discussion of tax planning, we first explain the main features of the federal income tax system and the requirements for filing, calculating, and paying taxes. The better your understanding of the rules, the easier it is to use them to your advantage. After identifying the most common tax planning strategies, we conclude with a discussion of how tax laws are enforced and recent trends in tax law.

Chapter Preview

The Federal Income Tax System	Filling Requirements	Calculating Taxable Income and Taxes Owed	Paying Taxes	Tax Planning Strategies	Enforcement of the Tax System and Recent Trends
• History of U.S. Income Taxation • Progressive Nature of the U.S. Tax System • Marginal Tax Rates • The Internal Revenue Service	• Who Must File a Federal Income Tax Return? • When and Where to File • IRS Forms	• Reporting Income • Standard Versus Itemized Deductions • Exemptions • Final Calculation of Taxes Owed • Applying Available Credits • Alternative Minimum Tax	• Withholding • Estimated Tax • Additional Taxes on the Self-Employed • Payments and Refunds	• Tax Evasion versus Tax Avoidance • Strategies for Minimizing Taxes	• Enforcement of Tax Laws • Complexity of the Tax System • Would a Flat Tax Be Better?

The Federal Income Tax System

LEARNING objective

1 Understand the major features of the federal income tax system.

There's no question about it—the U.S. federal income tax system is very complicated. The statutes and regulations describing our country's tax laws fill literally thousands of pages, and it is estimated that, on average, taxpayers spend more than ten hours per year filling out the required forms. Rather than allowing yourself to be overwhelmed by the complexity, one of your personal financial goals should be to learn more about the tax system so that you can keep adequate records and thereby reduce what you owe each year. After all, your income tax obligation is one of your household's largest cash outflows each year and the government estimates that you work more than four months out of the year just to pay your federal income taxes.

In this section, we provide an overview of income taxation in this country and its main features. We also discuss the responsibilities of the Internal Revenue Service, the government agency that administers U.S. tax law.

A Brief History of U.S. Income Taxation

In our country's relatively short history, the federal tax system has changed dramatically, both in philosophy and in practice. In its infancy, our country had no income tax at all. As you can see from Exhibit 4-1, it wasn't until the 16th amendment to the U.S. Constitution was passed in 1913 that Congress was allowed to impose a tax on income. This change was necessary to pay national security expenses associated with World War I. Since that time, tax rates have increased or decreased as economic and political circumstances dictated. Today, federal income taxes are used to finance many worthwhile government activities, including the national defense, education, social programs, drug safety, transportation, and road maintenance.

There are many self-help resources for tax preparation.

The Progressive Nature of the U.S. Tax System

Although there have been many changes in the tax law over our country's history, the United States has always maintained a **progressive tax,** one that imposes higher tax rates on taxpayers with higher incomes. Since a progressive tax is based on taxpayer's ability to pay, lower-income families do not bear a large tax burden in this country. In fact, some people in the United States pay no federal income tax at all. If you earned less than $7,800 in 2003 ($15,600 if married and filing jointly), you didn't even need to file a tax return. As a result, high-income taxpayers account for the lion's share of all income tax revenues collected and the poorest don't pay any taxes at all.

progressive tax

A tax that requires higher-income taxpayers to pay proportionately more in taxes, through either higher tax rates or other rules.

In contrast to a progressive tax, a **regressive tax** places a disproportionate burden on those taxpayers with lower incomes. Anytime the same tax rate is levied on all taxpayers—as in the case of payroll, consumption, and sales taxes, for instance—the tax is regressive. In other words, it takes a bigger bite out of low-income families' disposable incomes. Although rich people spend more on food, clothing, and other consumer purchases than poor people, the *proportion* of their income going to these categories is still lower, so the tax affects them less. The tax that finances Social Security and Medicare, the federal systems for retirement income and retiree health care, is a classic example of a regressive tax. If you look at your pay stub, you'll probably see an amount withheld for **FICA** (Federal Insurance Contributions Act), which is the tax paid to help finance Social Security and Medicare. The FICA tax is regressive not only because everyone pays the same rate, but also because there is a maximum income on which the Social Security portion of the tax (6.2%) is imposed; earnings over the maximum (which was $87,900 in 2004) are subject only to the 1.45 percent Medicare portion of the tax.

regressive tax

A tax that places a disproportionate financial burden on low-income taxpayers.

FICA tax

A payroll tax levied on earned income by the U.S. government to fund Social Security and Medicare.

EXHIBIT 4-1

History of the U.S. Federal Income Tax System

Date of Law	Major Effect
1789	Constitution gave Congress the power to impose taxes to pay federal debts and to provide for the common defense and general welfare of the United States.
1861–1862	Revenue Act of 1861 imposed the first tax on personal income to pay for the Civil War (3% on all income over $800 per year). Amended in 1862 to look more like modern system with graduated tax rates withheld by employers (3% on income to $10,000, 5% on higher incomes, standard deduction of $600 plus itemized deductions).
1872–1912	Income tax was abolished in 1872. Post-war federal revenue from excise taxes. Flat tax enacted in 1894 but was held unconstitutional by the Supreme Court.
1913	16th amendment to the Constitution allowed income taxes not proportional to state population. Congress passed new graduated tax that ranged from a minimum of 1% to 7% (for income greater than $500,000). Form 1040 introduced.
1916–1918	To pay for World War I, Congress changed definition of income to include illegal income such as gambling winnings and increased tax rates to range from minimum 6% to maximum 77% (applicable to income over $1.5 million). Estate tax enacted.
1932–1936	Facing budget deficits of the Depression, Congress increased tax rates to range from minimum 4% to maximum 79%.
1940–1941	To pay for World War II, Congress reduced exemptions and increased tax rates to range from minimum 23% to maximum 94% (on income over $1 million).
1953	The Internal Revenue Service was created.
1959–1967	Computers used to automate handling of returns and screen for audits.
1981	Economic Recovery Act of 1981 (Reagan tax cut) reduced individual tax brackets by 25% (making top rate 50%) and indexed for inflation. Introduced accelerated depreciation for business investment and Individual Retirement Account deductions.
1986	Tax Reform Act of 1986 reduced number of brackets, reduced maximum tax rate to 28%; personal exemptions and standard deductions were increased and indexed to inflation. Alternative Minimum Tax enacted.
1990–1993	Tax rates increased—new maximum tax rate 39.6%.
1994–1997	Various laws to reduce tax burden (medical savings accounts, education savings accounts, Roth IRA), culminating in the Taxpayer Relief Act of 1997 that added a $500 per child refundable tax credit
2001	Economic Growth and Tax Relief and Reconciliation Act of 2001 lowered marginal tax rates (maximum rate 35%), increased child tax credit to $600, increased dependent child tax credit, added savings incentives, repealed estate tax.
2003	Jobs and Growth Tax Relief Reconciliation Act of 2003 increased child tax credit to $1,000, phased out the marriage penalty, tax rates reduced to 10% to 35%, reduced tax on capital gains and dividends to either 5% (for low brackets) or 15%.

Source: U.S. Department of the Treasury.

Marginal Tax Rates

marginal tax rate

Tax rate imposed on the taxpayer's next dollar of income.

taxable income

The amount of income that is subject to taxes under the law.

The U.S. income tax system maintains its progressive nature through a combination of increasing marginal tax rates, exemptions, credits, and deductions. These features of the tax system imply that not all your income is taxable and your taxable income is not all taxed at the same rate. The calculation of taxable income will be explained later in the chapter, so we limit our discussion here to the importance of increasing marginal tax rates in the U.S. system. A **marginal tax rate** is the rate that applies to your *next* dollar of income. Our current tax rules assess taxes on **taxable income**—the amount of income that is subject to taxes under the law—according to a table of marginal tax rates. A portion of the table applicable for the 2003 tax year is shown in Exhibit 4-2.

EXHIBIT 4-2 Marginal Tax Rates, 2003

Schedule X. Tax Rate Schedule for Single Filers
If your taxable income is

Over	But not more than	You will owe	Taxable income over
$0	$7,000	10% of	$0
$7,000	$28,400	$700 + 15% of	$7,000
$28,400	$68,800	$3,910 + 25% of	$28,400
$68,800	$143,500	$14,010 + 28% of	$68,800
$143,500	$311,950	$34,926 + 33% of	$143,500
$311,950	+	$90,515 + 35% of	$311,950

Schedule Y-1. Tax Rate Schedule for Married Filing Jointly
If your taxable income is

Over	But not more than	You will owe	Taxable income over
$0	$14,000	10% of	$0
$14,000	$56,800	$1,400 + 15% of	$14,000
$56,800	$114,650	$7,820 + 25% of	$56,800
$114,650	$174,700	$22,283 + 28% of	$114,650
$174,700	$311,950	$39,097 + 33% of	$174,700
$311,950	+	$84,389 + 35% of	$311,950

The Tax Rate Schedules. Tax rate schedules tell you how much income tax you'll pay for particular ranges of income. There are separate schedules for different household types. Exhibit 4-2 shows two of these schedules—Schedule X, for single taxpayers, and Schedule Y-1, for married taxpayers filing jointly. Each schedule includes lists of income ranges and rates.

A **tax bracket** is the range of taxable income to which a particular marginal tax rate applies. Taxpayers sometimes use this term to describe the highest bracket that applies to their income. Thus, a single filer who, in 2003, told you that she was "in the 25 percent bracket," meant that her taxable income was between $28,400 and $68,800.

As you can see, you pay lower tax rates on your first dollars of income and higher rates on later dollars of income. For example, Schedule X indicates that the tax rate on the first $7,000 of taxable income is only 10 percent. Thus, if you were a single filer with taxable income of $7,000 or less, you would be in the lowest tax bracket and pay only 10 percent of your taxable income in taxes. The 10 percent bracket was first implemented in 2001 as part of the Economic Growth and Tax Relief Reconciliation Act of 2001. Prior to that time, the lowest bracket was 15 percent. That law originally had been designed to phase in the lower marginal brackets through 2006, but tax legislation passed in 2003 accelerated the rate reductions to be effective for the 2003 tax year.

Fact #1

Marginal tax rates today are low by historical standards. Not only is the bottom bracket lower than it's been in decades, but the current top marginal tax rate, which applies to any income in excess of $311,950 in 2003, is only 35 percent. Compare that to the top bracket at the end of World War II, which was 94 percent on income over $1 million. Not much incentive to be a millionaire if the government took 94 cents out of every additional dollar you earned!

tax bracket
The range of income to which a particular marginal tax rate applies.

It's important to understand that, unless your taxable income falls in the lowest tax bracket, the same marginal tax rate does not apply to your entire taxable income. As an example, let's suppose that you're a single filer and your taxable income is $65,000. Although this income puts you in the 25 percent tax bracket, the first $7,000 will be taxed at 10 percent, the income between $7,000 and $28,400 will be taxed at 15 percent, and the remainder will be taxed at 25 percent, for a total of $13,060 in taxes owed.

$$\begin{aligned}\text{Taxes owed} &= [0.10 \times \$7{,}000] + [0.15 \times (\$28{,}400 - \$7{,}000)] \\ &\quad + [0.25 \times (\$65{,}000 - \$28{,}400)] \\ &= \$700 + \$3{,}210 + \$9{,}150 \\ &= \$13{,}060\end{aligned}$$

Now what happens if you earn another $1,000? Since having taxable income of $66,000 wouldn't push you into a new tax bracket, the calculation of your taxes will be exactly the same as above, except that you'll apply the 25 percent rate to an additional $1,000—resulting in an additional $250 in federal income taxes (25% of $1,000).

average tax rate
The proportion of a taxpayer's total taxable income that goes to paying taxes.

Marginal Versus Average Tax Rates. Since you can't do much about what tax bracket you fall in, much of tax planning is aimed at minimizing your **average tax rate**, for a given level of income, or the proportion of total taxable income paid in taxes. Your average tax rate is calculated as

$$\text{Average tax rate} = \frac{\text{Taxes paid}}{\text{Taxable income}}$$

Note that for some purposes, it may be useful to consider the proportion of your *total income* paid in taxes. You may also see this ratio referred to as your average tax rate on occasion. Because of the progressive, or increasing, tax rate schedule, your average tax rate will always be less than your marginal tax rate. As an example, let's return to the previous scenario involving taxable income of $65,000 and taxes of $13,060. Although the marginal tax rate is 25 percent (your highest bracket), the average tax rate is only 20 percent:

$$\text{Average tax rate} = \frac{\$13{,}060}{\$65{,}000} = 0.20 \quad \text{or} \quad 20 \text{ percent}$$

Exhibit 4-3 shows the proportion of taxable income paid in taxes and average tax rates for taxpayers at various income levels.

Inflation Indexing of Tax Brackets. Although federal income tax rates can only be changed by Congress, the levels of income that trigger each successive increase in tax rate are automatically increased each year for inflation. This feature of the tax system has been in place since 1981—a year of double-digit inflation, as mentioned in Chapter 1. If you look at the current year's tax rate schedules, you'll see that the income levels for each bracket are higher than the 2003 levels shown in Exhibit 4-2. The fact that certain aspects of our tax law are indexed for inflation is an important protection for taxpayers in lower tax brackets. The government doesn't want households to have an extra tax burden unless they're actually experiencing a higher level of purchasing power.

To see how important inflation indexing is, consider an example. Suppose you're a single filer with a taxable income of $28,400 in 2003—the top of the 15 percent bracket. In 2004,

EXHIBIT 4-3

Taxes Paid, After-Tax Income, and Average Tax Rates for Selected Taxable Income Levels

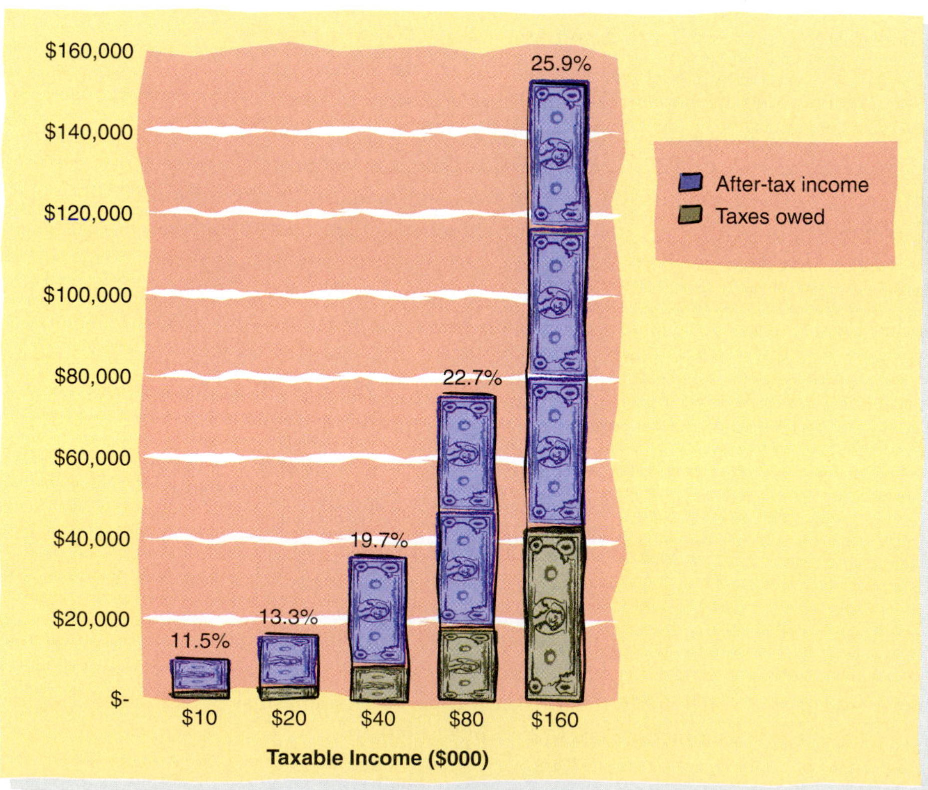

you receive a raise equal to the inflation rate, which we'll say is 4 percent—that is, your raise is $1,136, or 4 percent of $28,400. Although your income is now higher, you have not increased your purchasing power, since your income has risen at the same rate as the cost of goods. If the tax brackets *were not* inflation-indexed, your $1,136 raise would put you into the next tax bracket, subjecting your additional income to a 25 percent rate. The net effect would be that you'd have *less* purchasing power than you had in 2003. Thankfully, many aspects of recent tax reforms are designed to minimize the negative effects of this so-called bracket creep.

Considering the Marginal Tax Effect in Making Financial Decisions. As noted earlier and discussed in later sections of this chapter, the tax laws include many rules that can reduce your taxable income. For example, contributions to certain employer-provided retirement plans can be subtracted from your gross income before you calculate your tax. When deciding whether to take advantage of these opportunities for tax-advantaged saving, you should always consider the **marginal tax effect**—the reduction in taxes owed as a result of a financial decision. As we discussed in Chapter 1, effective decision making requires that you always evaluate your alternatives based on the *change* in your financial circumstances that will result from the decision.

marginal tax effect

The change in taxes owed as a result of a financial decision.

In estimating the marginal tax effect, you should apply a tax rate that includes all types of taxes that the income would otherwise be subject to—most commonly, federal income tax, state income tax, Social Security and Medicare tax. Some people also pay a small local tax on income. For example, suppose Jeremiah has a taxable income of $40,000 (25% federal tax bracket) and lives in a state with a 5 percent state income tax. His next dollar of taxable income will be subject to 25 percent + 5 percent + 7.65 percent Social Security and Medicare tax, for a total of 37.65 percent paid in taxes. Suppose Jeremiah has the opportunity to work overtime for his employer and expects to earn an additional $2,000. How much better off will he be if he decides to do so? Since his additional earnings will be subject to the 37.65 percent marginal tax rate, he will net only $2,000 × (1 − 0.3765) = $1,247 after taxes.

Although this chapter covers only the basics of the tax system, in future chapters, there will be many more specific examples where tax rules will make certain financial decisions more attractive than others. In each case, it will always be important to focus on the marginal tax effects in making these decisions.

The Internal Revenue Service

The **Internal Revenue Service (IRS)** is the government agency responsible for collecting federal income taxes according to the rules laid out by Congress. Since there are sometimes ambiguities in the laws as written, the IRS also writes regulations and makes rulings that interpret the laws, often giving specific taxpayer examples for clarification. When there are disputes about how to interpret and apply these laws and regulations fairly, the federal tax court sometimes hears cases and makes rulings. The **Internal Revenue Code**, a compilation of all tax laws passed by Congress, along with the IRS regulations and tax court judicial decisions, make up the totality of tax laws in the United States.

Internal Revenue Service (IRS)

The U.S. government agency responsible for collecting federal income taxes and enforcing tax laws and regulations.

Internal Revenue Code

A compilation of all statutes, regulations, and court decisions relating to U.S. income tax.

Although the IRS is often seen in a negative light—after all, nobody likes to pay taxes—it performs a truly amazing function every year. It processes 130 million individual income tax returns each year, collects more than $1.7 trillion in taxes, and issues more than $200 billion in refunds, most within a few short months. In recent years, Congress has provided funding to further automate the process, a trend that causes some taxpayers concern as they envision a futuristic government with electronic access to their most intimate financial information. More likely, though, honest taxpayers will benefit from further automation, and dishonest ones will be more easily forced to pay their fair share.

The IRS also offers many free services to taxpayers, most of which are described and accessible at its website, www.irs.gov. Informational publications on most tax topics are available for download or by mail. The comprehensive tax preparation reference *IRS Publication 17, Your Federal Income Tax* is a must-have for individuals who prepare their own taxes. And if you get

The IRS provides a wealth of tax information at www.irs.gov. Students should read IRS Publication 970: Tax Benefits for Education.

stuck, you can call the IRS information service Teletax (1-800-829-4477) to hear prerecorded phone messages on selected tax topics (although the line might be busy if you've waited until the last minute to do your taxes).

Learning by Doing 4-1

In 2003, Susan has taxable income of $30,000. She is single.

1. What is Susan's marginal tax rate?
2. Use Exhibit 4-2 to calculate how much Susan owes in federal income taxes.
3. What proportion of taxable income does Susan owe in taxes?
4. Susan has been offered the opportunity to work overtime for her employer in December for $30 per hour. Assuming she works an additional 100 hours this year, what proportion of her overtime income will she pay out in federal income taxes? (*Hint*: You already know her marginal tax rate.)

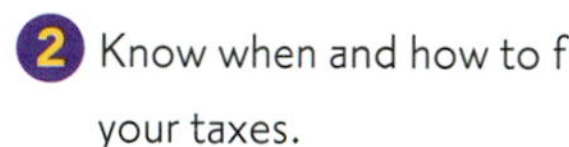

LEARNING objective

2 Know when and how to file your taxes.

Filing Requirements

Filing a tax return involves reporting income to the IRS on official tax forms and paying any outstanding taxes owed. In this section, we explain the requirements for filing—who must file a tax return, when to file, which forms to use, and how to file them.

Who Must File a Federal Income Tax Return?

Whether you must file a federal income tax return depends primarily on your filing status, income, and age. These rules are described below.

Filing Status. Your **filing status** identifies your household type. Since your filing status may change over time, every year you must identify yourself as one of the following, based on your status as of the last day of the year:

- *Single.* Unmarried or legally separated from your spouse.
- *Married filing jointly.* Married couple filing a single tax return, even if only one spouse had income.
- *Married filing separately.* Each spouse files an individual tax return, reporting his or her own income and allowed deductions from income.
- *Head of household.* Single person who lives with and pays more than half of the support for a **dependent** child or relative.
- *Qualifying widow(er) with dependent child.* Person whose spouse died within two years of the tax year and who lives with and pays more than half of the support for a dependent child.

Income. Your taxable income is a major determinant of whether you must file a tax return and will, of course, also determine the amount of taxes you pay, as discussed earlier. The IRS defines your **adjusted gross income** as the total of your **earned income** (including salaries, wages, tips, bonuses, and commissions) plus **unearned income** (interest, dividends, capital gains, rents, royalties, and net business income) minus certain allowed adjustments which are described later in the chapter.

You are allowed to subtract certain amounts from your adjusted gross income to arrive at your taxable income. The most important of these are called exemptions and deductions. You are allowed a personal **exemption** of $3,050 (in 2003, indexed for inflation) for each qualifying person in your household, including yourself and each dependent, although this allowance is phased

filing status Household type for tax filing purposes.

dependent Member of a household who receives at least half of his or her support from the head of the household.

adjusted gross income (AGI) Earned income and unearned income minus certain allowed adjustments to income.

earned income Income from salaries, wages, tips, bonuses, commissions, and other sources.

unearned income Income from investments, interest, dividends, capital gains, net business income, rents, and royalties.

exemption Dollar amount per household member that is subtracted from adjusted gross income in calculating taxable income.

out for very high-income households. In addition, you are allowed a **standard deduction** to cover certain qualifying expenses on which you are not required to pay taxes. The standard deduction for single taxpayers in 2003 was $4,750, whereas married couples filing jointly were allowed to deduct $9,500, and heads of household could deduct $7,000. Standard deductions are higher for people who are age 65 or older and for people who are blind. The allowed deductions are indexed for inflation so the amount you can deduct will increase each year. Although the standard deduction for married couples was historically less than twice that for singles, resulting in a "marriage penalty," as explained in the *News You Can Use* box, "The IRS Divorces the Marriage Penalty!", the Jobs and Growth Tax Relief and Reconciliation Act of 2003 removed this long-standing inequity from the tax law.

standard deduction

Dollar amount based on filing status that is subtracted from adjusted gross income in calculating taxable income.

If your annual expenses in certain allowed categories exceed, in total, the standard deduction for your filing status, you should use **itemized deductions** instead of the standard deduction in calculating your taxable income. Itemizing deductions involves filing an additional form on which you detail all allowed deductions, in accordance with the rules and limitations for each category. Whereas the standard deduction is available without proof of expenses, you must keep supporting documentation for all itemized deductions. The specific allowed expenses are discussed in detail later in the chapter.

itemized deductions

An alternative to the standard deduction in which the taxpayer reports and deducts actual expenses in certain allowed categories to arrive at taxable income.

If your earned income is no more than the total of your exemptions and standard or itemized deductions, then your taxable income is zero, and you need not file a tax return. For a single taxpayer, this means that you could have earned up to $3,050 + $4,750 = $7,800 in 2003 without having to file a return. Married couples filing jointly had to file if they earned more than $6,100 + $9,500 = $15,600. Of course, if you made less than these amounts but had taxes withheld from your pay, you would still need to file a return in order to get a refund of the taxes you paid.

Fact #2

If you are a full-time student, your parents can claim you as a dependent on their taxes as long as you are under age 24. Otherwise, if your gross income is greater than the amount of the personal exemption ($3,050 in 2003), your parents can't claim you as a dependent unless you're under age 19.

In addition to exemptions and deductions, you can also use a **tax credit** to reduce the taxes you owe. Tax credits, unlike exemptions and deductions, do not represent adjustments to your income. Rather, they are subtracted directly from the taxes you owe. You'll learn more about the specific application of all these tax rules later in this chapter.

tax credit

A reduction applied directly to taxes owed rather than to income subject to taxes.

Age. Age also affects your obligation to file and pay taxes. For example, the larger standard deduction for individuals age 65 or older means that they can earn more income without being subject to tax. In certain circumstances, dependent children up to age 24 do not have to file. However, even if your parents claim you as a dependent on their tax returns, you still need to file a return if any of the following apply:

- Your earned income was more than $4,750 (based on 2003 tax law).
- Your unearned income (such as earnings on investment accounts) was more than $750.
- Your gross income was more than the larger of:
    - $750, or
    - your earned income (up to $4,500) plus $250.

In addition, you should file if you want to get a refund of taxes withheld from your income or if you qualify for a tax credit.

When and Where to File

There are very specific rules as to when and where you must file your taxes. Failure to meet these requirements is a violation of the tax law and may subject you to interest and penalties. It may also take longer for you to receive any refund to which you are entitled.

Filing Deadlines. Tax returns must be postmarked by midnight on April 15 of the year following the tax year. So for income you earn in 2005, you must file your return by April 15, 2006. If April 15 falls on a day that the post office is closed, the due date is extended by

NEWS you can use

The IRS Divorces the Marriage Penalty!

Sally Feller and Christopher Reynolds, a middle-aged, childless couple in their 50s, shared a household for 25 years, owned a home together, and had a committed relationship. Despite their long relationship, they were not married. Why not? It's not because they were products of the 1960s and didn't believe in marriage. In fact, their decision was entirely a financial one—they stayed single because of income taxes!

For years, there was a "marriage penalty" inherent in the federal income tax system that resulted in higher total taxes on married couples than on single couples with the same total income. The standard deduction for married couples was less than twice that of single people. So if Sally and Christopher both filed as singles, they would jointly be entitled to a larger deduction from income.

["they stayed single because of income taxes"]

While it is doubtful that the marriage penalty resulted in many couples avoiding the altar over the years, Sally and Christopher understood the rules well enough to decide that the extra money in their pocket was worth their staying single. Fortunately, wedding plans are now in the works—the 2003 Jobs and Growth Tax Relief Reconciliation Act of 2003 removed the marriage penalty, increasing the standard deduction for married couples to be exactly twice the deduction allowed for single filers.

one day. If you need more time, you can extend the deadline by four months, to August 15, by filing Form 4868, Application for Automatic Extension, on or before the April 15 deadline. If four months is still not enough time, you can file another form to get an additional extension to October 15. About 9 million taxpayers request extensions each year. Although it might seem like a good way to avoid doing your taxes, extensions do *not* extend the deadline for paying the actual taxes you owe, so you still have to include a check for any estimated amount you owe or be subject to penalties and interest. If you discover that you made a mistake on a prior year's taxes, you are allowed to file an amended return using Form 1040X for up to three years after the original tax year. The IRS receives about 4 million amended returns each year.

Fact #3

More than 40 percent of all individual federal tax returns are now submitted electronically, and the IRS projects that this percentage will increase to 60 percent by 2009. One of the advantages of e-filing is that you can get a refund quicker—three weeks instead of six, on average.

Where to Send Your Return. The IRS operates several service centers where tax returns are processed. When you get your tax forms in the mail each year, they include a preprinted address label that directs your return to the appropriate service center. Even if you file your taxes electronically, the IRS will still send you the preprinted label in the mail. You can also find out where to mail your return by checking your zip code on the IRS website at www.irs.gov.

IRS e-file
A system allowing electronic filing of federal tax returns.

Many taxpayers choose to file their taxes electronically, either online, through their tax accountant, or by telephone. The **IRS e-file** uses online automation to replace many of the manual steps needed to process paper returns, resulting in faster processing with fewer errors (less than 1% of all electronic tax returns included errors in 2002). Most professional tax preparation services and software packages offer, and even encourage, electronic filing, but you can also do so on your own. Although using e-file supposedly does not increase your chances of being audited, it does allow the IRS to better track the information contained in your forms—with paper forms, the IRS only inputs certain data items from each return into their database.

If you have a very simple return, as is the case for many dependent students, you can even file electronically by telephone, entering the information using your telephone keypad. A TeleFile package is automatically sent to any taxpayer who filed a Form 1040EZ in the previous tax year.

EXHIBIT 4-4

Which Income Tax Form Should You File?

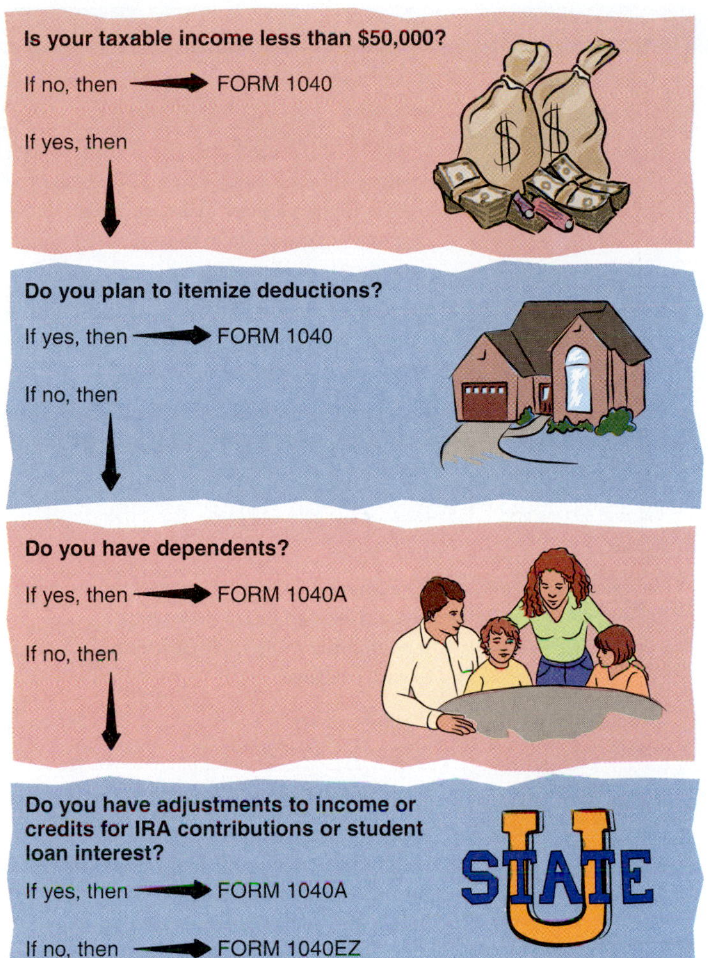

IRS Forms

You have a choice of three primary tax forms: Form 1040, known as the long form, and two short forms, Form 1040EZ and Form 1040A. Which form to use depends on your filing status, your income (type and amount), and the deductions and credits you can claim. Exhibit 4-4 will help you to determine which tax form is best for you. Even if you qualify to use either of the short forms (1040EZ or 1040A), you can always use the standard 1040 long form instead.

Depending on your income, deductions, and credits, you may need to include a number of additional forms along with your 1040. Although there are literally hundreds of forms, the most commonly used ones are identified and described in Exhibit 4-5.

Your tax forms may be filled out by hand, typed, or electronically completed. You can also pay a professional tax preparer to complete your tax return for you, although you'll still need to collect the documentation necessary for him or her to complete the forms. Tax software packages such as TurboTax and TaxCut can often make it easier to complete your return and identify the appropriate forms to file. These programs walk you through the entry of information by asking specific questions to which you must respond, and then use this information to fill in the appropriate forms for you. Once you've used one of these programs, in future tax years, it will remember information you included in previous years, which makes it less likely you'll forget potential deductions or credits. It can also help you avoid making some of the common filing errors that are identified by the Internal Revenue Service in the *Ask the Expert* box, "The IRS Identifies the Most Common Filing Errors."

EXHIBIT 4-5

Additional Forms You May Need to File

Form	Name	When You Can Use It
1040X	Amended Return	• If you made a mistake on any of the previous three years' tax forms.
Schedule A	Itemized Deductions	• If your total itemized deductions for medical expenses, mortgage interest paid, state and local taxes paid, charitable contributions, casualty losses, and other deductible expenses are greater than the applicable standard deduction.
Schedule B	Interest and Dividend Income	• If you have interest and dividend income greater than $1,500. • If you received tax exempt interest.
Schedule C/ Schedule C-EZ	Profit or Loss from Business or Profession	• If you have income and expenses from self-employment.
Schedule D	Capital Gains and Losses	• If you have gains or losses from the sale of investments.
Schedule E	Supplemental Income	• If you have income and expenses from a rental property. • If you have income from royalties. • If you have income from partnerships, S-corporations, estates, or trusts.
Schedule EIC	Earned Income Credit	• If you work and are low-income. Higher credit for taxpayers with children.
Schedule R	Credit for Elderly or Disabled	• If you are eligible for the elderly or disabled tax credit.
Schedule SE	Social Security Self-Employment Tax	• If you have self-employment income on which you owe Social Security payroll taxes.
2119	Sale of Your Home	• If you sell your primary residence during the tax year.
3903	Moving Expenses	• If you are eligible to adjust your income for job-related moving expenses incurred during the year.
4562	Depreciation and Amortization	• If you report depreciation or amortization expense for your rental property or business.
4684	Casualties and Thefts	• If you claim a deduction for uninsured personal casualty or theft loss.
4868	Application for Automatic Extension	• If you want to extend the due date for filing your tax return. You still must pay any taxes owed by the usual due date.
8283	Noncash Charitable Contributions	• If you make a noncash charitable contribution in excess of $500.
8606	Nondeductible IRA Contributions	• If you make contributions to a nondeductible IRA.
8615	Computation of Tax for Children Under Age 14	• If your child has income from interest, dividends, or capital gains in excess of $1,500 during the tax year.
8829	Expenses for Business Use of Your Home	• If you claim a home office deduction on your Schedule C.

ask the expert The Most Common Filing Errors

Internal Revenue Service
Washington, DC

No one has ever argued that filing taxes is easy. Even people with advanced degrees make mistakes on their tax returns. But these mistakes can cost you money. Your refund might be delayed. Or, worse yet, you might have to pay additional taxes, interest, and penalties. According to the IRS, the most common mistakes are just that—mistakes, and mostly stupid mistakes at that:

- Making math errors. This is the number one mistake, both addition and subtraction. Don't forget to clearly indicate negative numbers, preferably with parentheses.
- Incorrect or missing social security numbers for members of your household.
- Incorrect tax entered from the tables.
- Withholding and estimated tax payments entered on the wrong line.
- Computation errors in figuring the child and dependent care credit and the earned income credit. Also, missing or incorrect identification numbers for child-care providers.

Although somewhat less common than those above, the IRS also sees the following mistakes:

- Not signing and dating your return. No signature, no refund!
- Forgetting to report interest and dividend income. The IRS gets independent verification from your financial institution.
- Not including all the required forms, especially those indicating taxes withheld (W-2 and 1099).
- Making out the check incorrectly (wrong amount, failure to sign). If your tax payment doesn't get to the IRS by the filing deadline because there is no signature, you will be subject to penalties and interest.
- Putting insufficient postage on the envelope. The post office will return the envelope to you and you could miss your filing deadline.
- Giving the incorrect address for refunds. The IRS has refund checks totalling $80 million that came back as undeliverable.
- Checking more than one filing status. You can't be married and single at the same time.

Source: "Topic 303" at www.irs.gov.

Learning by Doing 4-2

1. Cassandra is 19 years old. Her parents claim her as a dependent on their tax form. Her earned income this year was $10,000, and she had $250 in taxable interest income from a bank savings account.
   a. Does Cassandra need to file a tax return?
   b. If so, which form should she use?

Calculating Taxable Income and Taxes Owed

LEARNING objective

3 Calculate taxable income and determine your tax liability.

Although many people whine and moan about filling out their tax forms as April 15 approaches each year, individuals who have their finances in order generally find that completing tax forms is a fairly painless exercise. The steps involved in calculating how much tax you owe are illustrated in Exhibit 4-6. In this section, we review key terminology and rules and then apply this knowledge to the completion of the most important federal income tax forms, using Cindy and Dave Thompson's tax return as an illustration.

Reporting Income

As indicated in Exhibit 4-6, the first step in doing your taxes is to calculate your income. The calculation of income for tax purposes requires that you report most types of income and then make certain allowed adjustments to that income.

EXHIBIT 4-6

Steps in Calculating Federal Income Taxes Owed

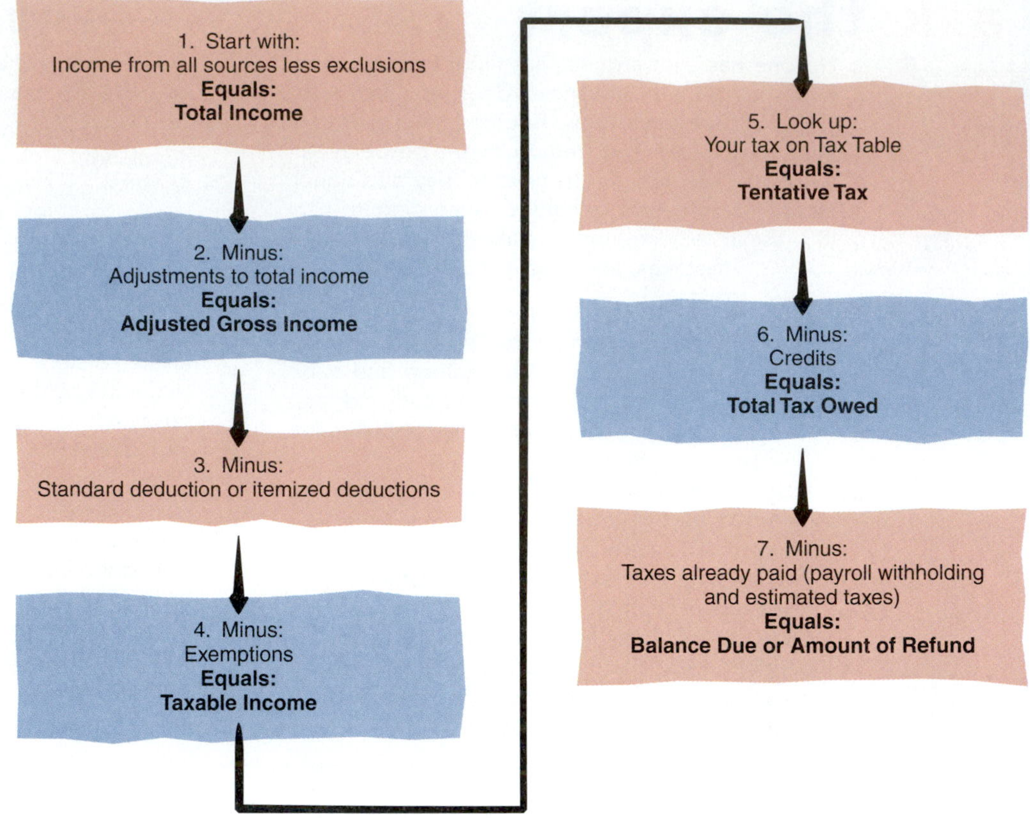

gross income
Income from all sources, including earned income, investment income, alimony, unemployment compensation, and retirement benefits.

total income
Gross income less certain exclusions allowed by the IRS.

Total Income. **Gross income** is your income from all sources. However, some categories of income are excluded to arrive at **total income** on your tax forms, an amount that can be thought of as gross *taxable* income—income from all sources less allowed exclusions. Exhibit 4-7 details what is included and what is excluded in reporting total income. For example, you don't have to report scholarships used for tuition and course-related expenses or child support payments received from an ex-spouse. You do, however, have to report scholarships and grants applied to room and board expenses.

As you can see in Exhibit 4-8, Cindy and Dave Thompson reported their combined $88,000 salaries and $48 in taxable interest income to arrive at a total income of $88,048. For most people, the largest source of total income is earned income from employment—salaries, hourly wages, bonuses, tips, and commissions—all of which is included in gross taxable income. Other sources of gross taxable income include business income, investment income, alimony, unemployment compensation, and retirement benefits. Unearned income may include interest and dividends from investments, net business income, rents, and royalties you received during the year, annuity and pension income, awards for scientific and charitable achievement, gambling and lottery winnings, and scholarships spent on room and board.

Employers and financial institutions are required to report the amounts that they pay to you each year, and you will generally receive an informational copy of this report in January following the tax year (Form W-2 for employment income and Form 1099 for other types of income), but you are also required to report other income, such as cash tips you receive as a waitress, even if these amounts do not appear on your W-2. Your taxable income, as reported on the W-2, will exclude any payments made on your behalf for tax-qualified health insurance and retirement plans—in other words, those amounts get taken off the top of your income and are not subject to tax.

In addition to reporting profits from businesses, you may sometimes be able to subtract losses by entering a negative number in the business income category. However, the tax laws limit the deduction of losses to situations in which you actively participate in the management of

EXHIBIT 4-7

What Is and What Is Not Included in Gross Taxable Income

Included	
Alimony	Investment gains/losses
Business or partnership income	Moving expense reimbursement (if deducted)
Commissions, fees	Pension income
Dividends	Property rental income/loss
Employer-paid disability income	Royalties
Gambling winnings and prizes	Unemployment compensation
Hobby income	Wages, salaries, tips, bonuses
Interest	

Not Included (limitations apply to those categories with *)	
Annuities*	Long-term care benefits
Child support	Military cost-of-living allowance
Disability payments*	Qualified fringe benefits paid by employer*
Gifts	Required travel expenses paid by employer*
Inheritance	Scholarships and fellowships*
Insurance claim payments	State and local bond interest
Jury awards	Welfare
Life insurance proceeds	Workers compensation payments
Long-term capital gain on sale of primary residence*	

the business. If you do not participate in management, there are limits on the losses you can deduct.

Gross income also includes any **capital gain,** or increase in value, of taxable investments that you sold during the year. For example, if you sold a rental property during the year for $100,000 and you had only paid $80,000 for it, you will owe tax on the $20,000 capital gain (less some allowed expenses for the sale). Note that even though you may have received the whole $100,000 in cash flow that year, you only report the gain for tax purposes. If you hold an investment longer than one year, the gain on sale is subject to a special lower tax rate—5 percent for taxpayers in the 10 and 15 percent tax brackets and 15 percent for those in higher tax brackets. These rates, under a new tax law, also apply to certain dividend income.

capital gain

Profit on the sale of an investment; subject to a lower tax rate if the investment has been held for more than one year.

As mentioned previously, a special capital gain rule applies for profits made on the sale of your primary residence, defined as the place that you lived for two of the last five years before the sale. You can exclude up to $250,000 of the gain on the sale of your home ($500,000 for married couples) from your total income.

Adjusted Gross Income. The tax rules allow certain expenses to be subtracted from total income to arrive at adjusted gross income (AGI). Although in some cases these adjustments are subject to income limitations, it's important to be aware of them, since they represent significant tax breaks for some families. In addition, if you qualify for one of these adjustments, you can benefit from it even if you don't itemize deductions. Some of these adjustments include the following:

- For teachers of kindergarten through grade 12, unreimbursed expenses up to $250
- Deductible individual retirement account contributions up to $4,000
- Interest paid on student loans during the year
- Tuition and fees for higher education up to $3,000

Without itemizing deductions, you can also make adjustments for one-half of the Social Security taxes paid on business income and for moving expenses, if required for a new job. To see if you qualify for these or other adjustments to total income, you should consult the applicable IRS publication. The amount you have left after making all these adjustments is your adjusted gross income. For the Thompsons, this amount is the same as their gross income—$88,048—since they didn't qualify for any of the adjustments to total income.

You're required to report tip income on your tax return.

EXHIBIT 4-8

The Thompsons' 1040

Form **1040** Department of the Treasury — Internal Revenue Service
U.S. Individual Income Tax Return (99) IRS Use Only — Do not write or staple in this space.

For the year Jan 1 - Dec 31, 2004, or other tax year beginning , ending , 20 OMB No. 1545-0074

Label (See instructions.)
Use the IRS label. Otherwise, please print or type.

Your first name	MI	Last name	Your social security number
David	J.	Thompson	000-00-0000
If a joint return, spouse's first name	MI	Last name	Spouse's social security number
Cynthia	M.	Thompson	000-00-0000

Home address (number and street). If you have a P.O. box, see instructions. Apartment no.
34 Main St.

City, town or post office. If you have a foreign address, see instructions. State ZIP code
Any town NJ 12345

▲ **Important!** ▲ You **must** enter your social security number(s) above.

Presidential Election Campaign (See instructions.)
▶ **Note:** Checking 'Yes' will not change your tax or reduce your refund.
Do you, or your spouse if filing a joint return, want $3 to go to this fund? ▶ You ☐ Yes ☑ No Spouse ☐ Yes ☑ No

Filing Status
Check only one box.
1 ☐ Single
2 ☑ Married filing jointly (even if only one had income)
3 ☐ Married filing separately. Enter spouse's SSN above & full name here . . ▶
4 ☐ Head of household (with qualifying person). (See instructions.) If the qualifying person is a child but not your dependent, enter this child's name here . ▶
5 ☐ Qualifying widow(er) with dependent child. (See instructions.)

Exemptions
6a ☑ **Yourself.** If your parent (or someone else) can claim you as a dependent on his or her tax return, **do not** check box 6a
b ☑ **Spouse**
No. of boxes checked on 6a and 6b: 2

c **Dependents:**

(1) First name	Last name	(2) Dependent's social security number	(3) Dependent's relationship to you	(4) ✓ if qualifying child for child tax credit (see instrs)
Kyle	Larson	000-00-0000	step-son	☑
				☐
				☐
				☐
				☐

If more than five dependents, see instructions.

No. of children on 6c who: • lived with you: 1
• did not live with you due to divorce or separation (see instrs):
Dependents on 6c not entered above:
d Total number of exemptions claimed — Add numbers on lines above ▶ 3

Income
Attach Forms W-2 and W-2G here. Also attach Form(s) 1099-R if tax was withheld.
If you did not get a W-2, see instructions.
Enclose, but do not attach, any payment. Also, please use Form 1040-V.

Line	Description		Amount
7	Wages, salaries, tips, etc. Attach Form(s) W-2	7	$88,000
8a	**Taxable** interest. Attach Schedule B if required	8a	$48
b	**Tax-exempt** interest. **Do not** include on line 8a — 8b		
9a	Ordinary dividends. Attach Schedule B if required	9a	
b	Qualified dividends (see instructions) — 9b		
10	Taxable refunds, credits, or offsets of state and local income taxes (see instructions)	10	
11	Alimony received	11	
12	Business income or (loss). Attach Schedule C or C-EZ	12	
13a	Capital gain or (loss). Att Sch D if reqd. If not reqd, ck here ▶ ☐	13a	
b	If box on 13a is checked, enter post-May 5 capital gain distributions — 13b		
14	Other gains or (losses). Attach Form 4797	14	
15a	IRA distributions — 15a — b Taxable amount (see instrs)	15b	
16a	Pensions and annuities — 16a — b Taxable amount (see instrs)	16b	
17	Rental real estate, royalties, partnerships, S corporations, trusts, etc. Attach Schedule E	17	
18	Farm income or (loss). Attach Schedule F	18	
19	Unemployment compensation	19	
20a	Social security benefits — 20a — b Taxable amount (see instrs)	20b	
21	Other income	21	
22	Add the amounts in the far right column for lines 7 through 21. This is your **total income** ▶	22	$88,048

Adjusted Gross Income

Line	Description		Amount
23	Educator expenses (see instructions) — 23		
24	IRA deduction (see instructions) — 24		
25	Student loan interest deduction (see instructions) — 25		
26	Tuition and fees deduction (see instructions) — 26		
27	Moving expenses. Attach Form 3903 — 27		
28	One-half of self-employment tax. Attach Schedule SE — 28		
29	Self-employed health insurance deduction (see instrs) — 29		
30	Self-employed SEP, SIMPLE, and qualified plans — 30		
31	Penalty on early withdrawal of savings — 31		
32a	Alimony paid b Recipient's SSN ▶ — 32a		
33	Add lines 23 through 32a	33	0
34	Subtract line 33 from line 22. This is your **adjusted gross income** ▶	34	$88,048

BAA For Disclosure, Privacy Act, and Paperwork Reduction Act Notice, see instructions. FDIA0112 Form **1040**

Standard Versus Itemized Deductions

As already noted, the tax law allows you to deduct certain expenses from your income to arrive at the taxable amount: You can either claim a specified standard deduction or itemize your deductions. In this section, we examine the deductible amounts more closely.

The amount of the standard deduction increases annually with inflation and depends on your filing status. For tax year 2003, the allowed standard deduction amounts were as follows:

- Single $4,750
- Married filing jointly $9,500
- Married filing separately $4,950
- Head of household $7,000
- Qualified widower $9,500

Form 1040 Page 2

Tax and Credits

Line	Description		Amount
35	Amount from line 34 (adjusted gross income)		35 \$88,048
36a	Check if: ☐ You were born before January 2, 1939, ☐ Blind. ☐ Spouse was born before January 2, 1939, ☐ Blind. Total boxes checked ► 36a ☐		
b	If you are married filing separately and your spouse itemizes deductions, or you were a dual-status alien, see instructions and check here ► 36b ☐		
37	Itemized deductions (from Schedule A) or your standard deduction (see left margin)		37 \$17,808
38	Subtract line 37 from line 35		38 \$70,240
39	If line 35 is \$104,625 or less, multiply \$3,050 by the total number of exemptions claimed on line 6d. If line 35 is over \$104,625, see the worksheet in the instructions		39 \$9,150
40	Taxable income. Subtract line 39 from line 38. If line 39 is more than line 38, enter -0-		40 \$61,090
41	Tax (see instrs). Check if any tax is from a ☐ Form(s) 8814 b ☐ Form 4972		41 \$8,889
42	Alternative minimum tax (see instructions). Attach Form 6251		42
43	Add lines 41 and 42 ►		43 \$8,889
44	Foreign tax credit. Attach Form 1116 if required	44	
45	Credit for child and dependent care expenses. Attach Form 2441	45	
46	Credit for the elderly or the disabled. Attach Schedule R	46	
47	Education credits. Attach Form 8863	47	
48	Retirement savings contributions credit. Attach Form 8880	48	
49	Child tax credit (see instructions)	49 \$600	
50	Adoption credit. Attach Form 8839	50	
51	Credits from: a ☐ Form 8396 b ☐ Form 8859	51	
52	Other credits. Check applicable box(es): a ☐ Form 3800 b ☐ Form 8801 c ☐ Specify	52	
53	Add lines 44 through 52. These are your total credits		53 \$600
54	Subtract line 53 from line 43. If line 53 is more than line 43, enter -0- ►		54 \$8,289

Standard Deduction for –
- People who checked any box on line 36a or 36b or who can be claimed as a dependent, see instructions.
- All others: Single or Married filing separately, \$4,750
- Married filing jointly or Qualifying widow(er), \$9,500
- Head of household, \$7,000

Other Taxes

Line	Description		Amount
55	Self-employment tax. Attach Schedule SE		55
56	Social security and Medicare tax on tip income not reported to employer. Attach Form 4137		56
57	Tax on qualified plans, including IRAs, and other tax-favored accounts. Attach Form 5329 if required		57
58	Advance earned income credit payments from Form(s) W-2		58
59	Household employment taxes. Attach Schedule H		59
60	Add lines 54-59. This is your total tax ►		60 \$8,289

Payments

If you have a qualifying child, attach Schedule EIC.

Line	Description		Amount
61	Federal income tax withheld from Forms W-2 and 1099	61 \$14,300	
62	2003 estimated tax payments and amount applied from 2002 return	62	
63	Earned income credit (EIC) No	63	
64	Excess social security and tier 1 RRTA tax withheld (see instructions)	64	
65	Additional child tax credit. Attach Form 8812	65	
66	Amount paid with request for extension to file (see instructions)	66	
67	Other pmts from: a ☐ Form 2439 b ☐ Form 4136 c ☐ Form 8885	67	
68	Add lines 61 through 67. These are your total payments ►		68 \$14,300

Refund

Direct deposit? See instructions and fill in 70b, 70c, and 70d.

Line	Description		Amount
69	If line 68 is more than line 60, subtract line 60 from line 68. This is the amount you overpaid		69 \$6,011
70a	Amount of line 69 you want refunded to you ►		70a \$6,011
► b	Routing number ► c Type: ☐ Checking ☐ Savings		
► d	Account number		
71	Amount of line 69 you want applied to your 2004 estimated tax ►	71	

Amount You Owe

Line	Description		Amount
72	Amount you owe. Subtract line 68 from line 60. For details on how to pay, see instructions ►		72
73	Estimated tax penalty (see instructions)	73	

Third Party Designee

Do you want to allow another person to discuss this return with the IRS (see instructions)? ☐ Yes. Complete the following. ☒ No

Designee's name ► Phone no. ► Personal identification number (PIN) ►

Sign Here

Joint return? See instructions. Keep a copy for your records.

Under penalties of perjury, I declare that I have examined this return and accompanying schedules and statements, and to the best of my knowledge and belief, they are true, correct, and complete. Declaration of preparer (other than taxpayer) is based on all information of which preparer has any knowledge.

Your signature	Date	Your occupation	Daytime phone number
David J. Thompson	4/15/04	Computer Systems Analyst	(123) 555-1000
Spouse's signature. If a joint return, both must sign.	**Date**	**Spouse's occupation**	
Cynthia M. Thompson	4/15/04	Office Manager	

Paid Preparer's Use Only

Preparer's signature ► Date Check if self-employed ☐ Preparer's SSN or PTIN

Firm's name (or yours if self-employed), address, and ZIP code ► Self-Prepared EIN Phone no.

Form 1040

FDIA0112

If your deductible expenses are greater than the standard deduction, it makes sense to report itemized deductions on the allowed form, Schedule A, provided that you keep careful records. Although you don't have to provide supporting documentation to the IRS when you file your tax return, you must be able to produce proof of the actual expense if the IRS requests it. For example, if you've made charitable contributions during the year, you should have a statement or receipt that acknowledges your donation. In contrast, if you take the standard deduction, you won't have to keep this type of record. If you do decide to itemize, you must file the long form 1040 instead of the 1040A or 1040EZ.

The categories for itemized deductions include medical and dental expenses, taxes you paid, some types of interest you paid, gifts to charity, casualty and theft losses, job expenses, and most other miscellaneous deductions. The average deductions in certain categories for various income levels, as reported by the IRS for tax returns in 2000, are shown in Exhibit 4-9. The table also gives the percentage of itemizers in each income group. As you can see, the percentage of people

EXHIBIT 4-9

Average Deductions for Different Income Levels

	Adjusted Gross Income					
Itemized Deduction Category	0 – $15,000	$15,000 – $30,000	$30,000 – $50,000	$50,000 – $100,000	$100,000 – $200,000	$200,00 and higher
Percent who itemize	3.76%	15.02%	37.53%	68.86%	89.59%	92.72%
Medical expenses	$6,908	$5,340	$4,707	$6,156	$12,122	$34,436
Taxes paid	$1.987	$2,175	$3,026	$4,899	$9,283	$38,200
Interest paid	$6,312	$6,024	$6,422	$7,828	$11,161	$22,598
Student loan interest	$494	$600	$661	$495	$0	$0
Charitable contributions	$1,299	$1,684	$1,895	$2,349	$3,761	$19,559
Moving expenses	$1,658	$1,536	$1,953	$2,550	$2,565	$5,714
Medical savings accounts	$907	$1,562	$1,535	$2,116	$2,285	$2,334
IRA deductions	$1,746	$1,946	$2,021	$2,163	$2,548	$3,338
Keough, SEP deductions	$2,641	$2,899	$3,865	$5,253	$9,965	$18,563
Alimony paid	$9,357	$6,729	$5,952	$8,156	$12,098	$32,838

Source: Internal Revenue Service "2000 Statistics of Income Bulletin."

who itemize deductions increases with income. This makes sense when you consider that people with greater income are likely to have greater expenses, most notably for mortgage interest and taxes, so the amount of their actual expenses is more likely to exceed the standard deduction. We discuss each category of itemized deductions in more detail below. For an illustration, you can refer to the Thompsons' Schedule A, which is reproduced as Exhibit 4-10.

Medical and Dental Expenses. You can deduct out-of-pocket medical and dental expenditures for medical insurance premiums, medical services (doctor, dentist, optometrist, nurses, hospitals), prescription drugs, eyeglasses, hearing aids, travel for medical purposes, special schooling for disabled children, nursing homes, alternative medicine (chiropractors, acupuncture), and other medical expenses as long as the sum of these expenses adds up to *more than 7.5 percent of your adjusted gross income.* IRS Publication 502 includes a long list of legally deductible expenses. If your expenses are paid by your health insurer or employer, you can't deduct them for tax purposes—you can deduct only nonreimbursed expenses. To determine your deduction, you first total your medical and dental expenses and then subtract 7.5 percent of your AGI. The remainder is your deduction. Thus, Cindy and Dave Thompson, who had an AGI equal to $88,048, would only have been able to deduct medical and dental expenses to the extent that they exceeded $6,604 (7.5% of $88,048). This means that the first $6,604 would not be deductible at all, so it would take a fairly large uninsured illness or injury to get them over this limit. However, for individuals who do not have health insurance fully paid for by their employer, it is possible that the annual premiums for family coverage (say, $650 per month for 12 months, or $7,800 per year) will exceed this floor.

Taxes You Paid. You're allowed to deduct state and local income taxes you paid during the tax year, real estate property taxes paid on your primary residence, and personal property taxes

SCHEDULE A (Form 1040)

Department of the Treasury Internal Revenue Service (99)

Itemized Deductions

► Attach to Form 1040.
► See Instructions for Schedule A (Form 1040).

OMB No. 1545-0074

07

Name(s) shown on Form 1040: David J. Thompson / Cynthia M. Thompson

Your social security number: 000-00-0000

Section	Line	Description	Line no.	Amount	Line no.	Amount
Medical and Dental Expenses		Caution. Do not include expenses reimbursed or paid by others.				
	1	Medical and dental expenses (see instructions)	1			
	2	Enter amount from Form 1040, line 35 2				
	3	Multiply line 2 by 7.5% (.075)	3			
	4	Subtract line 3 from line 1. If line 3 is more than line 1, enter -0-			4	
Taxes You Paid (See instructions.)	5	State and local income taxes	5	$4,000		
	6	Real estate taxes (see instructions)	6	$2,400		
	7	Personal property taxes	7			
	8	Other taxes. List type and amount ►	8			
	9	Add lines 5 through 8			9	$6,400
Interest You Paid (See instructions.)	10	Home mtg interest and points reported to you on Form 1098	10	$9,958		
	11	Home mortgage interest not reported to you on Form 1098. If paid to the person from whom you bought the home, see instructions and show that person's name, identifying number, and address ►	11			
Note. Personal interest is not deductible.	12	Points not reported to you on Form 1098. See instrs for spcl rules	12			
	13	Investment interest. Attach Form 4952 if required. (See instrs.)	13			
	14	Add lines 10 through 13			14	$9,958
Gifts to Charity	15	Gifts by cash or check. If you made any gift of $250 or more, see instructions	15	$1,200		
If you made a gift and got a benefit for it, see instructions.	16	Other than by cash or check. If any gift of $250 or more, see instructions. You **must** attach Form 8283 if over $500	16	$250		
	17	Carryover from prior year	17			
	18	Add lines 15 through 17			18	$1,450
Casualty and Theft Losses	19	Casualty or theft loss(es). Attach Form 4684. (See instructions.)			19	
Job Expenses and Most Other Miscellaneous Deductions	20	Unreimbursed employee expenses — job travel, union dues, job education, etc. Attach Form 2106 or 2106-EZ if required. (See instructions.) ►	20	$500		
	21	Tax preparation fees	21			
(See instructions.)	22	Other expenses — investment, safe deposit box, etc. List type and amount ►	22			
	23	Add lines 20 through 22	23	$500		
	24	Enter amount from Form 1040, line 35 ..... 24 $88,048				
	25	Multiply line 24 by 2% (.02)	25	$1,761		
	26	Subtract line 25 from line 23. If line 25 is more than line 23, enter -0-			26	$0
Other Miscellaneous Deductions	27	Other — from list in the instructions. List type and amount ►			27	
Total Itemized Deductions	28	Is Form 1040, line 35, over $139,500 (over $69,750 if MFS)? ☑ **No.** Your deduction is not limited. Add the amounts in the far right column for lines 4 through 27. Also, enter this amount on Form 1040, line 37. ☐ **Yes.** Your deduction may be limited. See instructions for the amount to enter.			28	$17,808

BAA For Paperwork Reduction Act Notice, see Form 1040 instructions. FDIA0301 Schedule A (Form 1040)

EXHIBIT 4-10

Continuing Case: The Thompsons' Schedule A

(imposed in some states on cars and other personal property). If you take a deduction for state income taxes, you may have to make an adjustment to your income in a later year for tax refunds that you might receive from the state. Cindy and Dave paid state income taxes of $4,000 (reported on their W-2's) and $2,400 in property taxes on their home (reported to them by their mortgage lender).

Interest You Paid. Perhaps the most beneficial of all tax deductions is the mortgage interest deduction. You can deduct interest paid on your mortgage and home equity loans as well as certain charges paid by borrowers to obtain their home mortgage, sometimes called points or loan origination fees. In some cases, however, you won't be able to deduct the full amount of points in the year paid, but rather will be required to spread them out over the life of the loan. The Thompsons report mortgage interest for the year in the amount of $9,958. Interest paid on credit cards, personal loans, and car loans is not deductible.

Gifts to Charity. The tax laws allow you to deduct contributions made to charitable organizations. There are separate lines on which to report cash donations and noncash donations. Cindy and Dave report their regular cash contribution to their church in the amount of $1,200 for the year. You can also take a deduction for any noncash contributions you made during the year—for example, food you've donated to the local food bank or a bag of used clothing given to a local charitable organization. Cindy took several bags of clothes and toys to the Goodwill drop-off and received receipts for her donations totalling $250. You can deduct only the current market value of the items you have donated, however. If you're unsure of how much to deduct, consider what the item would sell for at a flea market, or, for a fee, you can get a list of fair market values for commonly donated items from www.taxsave.com. People who are actively involved in volunteer organizations can also deduct expenses incurred in their volunteer work, including mileage expenses. For example, if you took a group of Boy Scouts on a camping trip during the summer and incurred expenses for minivan rental, gasoline, and food, you can deduct your costs.

Fact #4

For a charitable donation to be deductible, it must be made to a legitimate organization and the donated item must be appropriately valued. One of the IRS "hot buttons" is charitable deductions taken for donations of junk vehicles. Many of the supposedly charitable organizations that solicit this type of contribution are not legitimate non-profits, and they encourage donors to claim that their old "clunker" is actually worth more than it is.

Casualty and Theft Losses. Suppose your car, which was worth $3,000, was stolen during the year, and you did not have theft insurance on it. For such an unreimbursed loss, the tax law allows you to deduct the amount of the loss that exceeds 10 percent of your AGI, less $100. For example, if your AGI is $25,000, and you suffer an uninsured theft loss of $3,000, the amount that exceeds 10 percent of your AGI is $\$3{,}000 - (0.1 \times \$25{,}000) = \$500$. From this, you subtract $100 to calculate your deduction of $400.

Job Expenses and Miscellaneous Deductions. Many people incur expenses that are required for their employment but are not reimbursed by their employer—union dues, licenses and fees, books and software for use in their profession, professional liability insurance, tools and supplies, job hunting costs, and travel costs, for example. Ordinary and necessary job-related expenses are deductible to the extent that they exceed 2 percent of your AGI. Up to the 2 percent limit, you must pay the expenses yourself, but you can deduct any amount over the limit. Dave Thompson incurred expenses for books and software used in his profession in the amount of $500. However, once he does the calculation, he realizes that this will not meet the 2 percent limit—his job-related expenses would have to be over $1,761 (2% of $88,048) for him to get a deduction in this category.

Other Miscellaneous Deductions. Several special rules apply to the miscellaneous deductions category. Gambling losses up to the amount of reported gambling income can be deducted without regard to the 2 percent limitation. Handicapped workers are also allowed to deduct all their job-related expenses.

Totaling Your Itemized Deductions. After calculating all your itemized deductions, you should total them and compare the amount to the standard deduction to which you would be entitled. Cindy and Dave Thompson have total itemized deductions of $17,808, which is substantially greater than their allowed standard deduction of $9,500. Therefore, by itemizing, they'll save several thousand dollars in taxes. Note that although it's obviously a good idea to claim all deductions to which you are entitled, unusually large deductions in a given year might subject your return to greater scrutiny by the IRS.

Exemptions

The last step in calculating your taxable income is to subtract the appropriate amount for your exemptions. Recall that an exemption is an amount of money that you're allowed to subtract for each qualifying person in your household. This will usually mean one exemption each for yourself, your spouse, and each of your dependents. Since Cindy and Dave report themselves and Cindy's son Kyle, they get to take three exemptions. In the case of divorce, the divorce decree will usually spell out who gets to take the exemption for each child. Although Kyle's biological dad is paying child support to Cindy, he has agreed to allow her to take the exemption. At $3,050 per person in 2003, the exemptions further reduce the Thompson's income by $9,150.

The allowed exemption amount increases annually with inflation and is phased out for taxpayers with income over $139,500 ($209,250 for joint filers). Each person can only be claimed as an exemption on one tax form per year. So if you're being claimed as a dependent on your parents' taxes, you can't take an exemption on your own tax form. Note that the marginal benefit to your family will be higher if the exemption is claimed by the taxpayer in the highest tax bracket—and this is likely to be your parents rather than you.

Learning by Doing 4-3

1. June's 85-year-old father has lived with her family for all of tax year 2004. June is receiving a stipend of $15,000 per year from her father's estate for taking care of him. Can she claim him as a dependent for 2004?
2. Rashid has a total income of $21,000 in 2003 and tuition expenses of $1,000, resulting in an adjusted gross income of $20,000. He can claim an exemption for himself in the amount of $3,050, and he incurred the following expenses during the year: medical expenses, $500; property taxes, $1,500; mortgage interest, $5,000; state income taxes, $500. If the standard deduction for a single filer in 2003 is $4,750, should he itemize deductions? Why or why not?

Final Calculation of Taxes Owed

Subtracting deductions and exemptions from adjusted gross income gives you taxable income. You'll use this amount to calculate the taxes you owe. From our earlier discussion of marginal tax rates, you know that different rates apply to different layers of income. Exhibit 4-11 shows how each layer of income is taxed. In financial planning, we always consider the effects on the last layer of income.

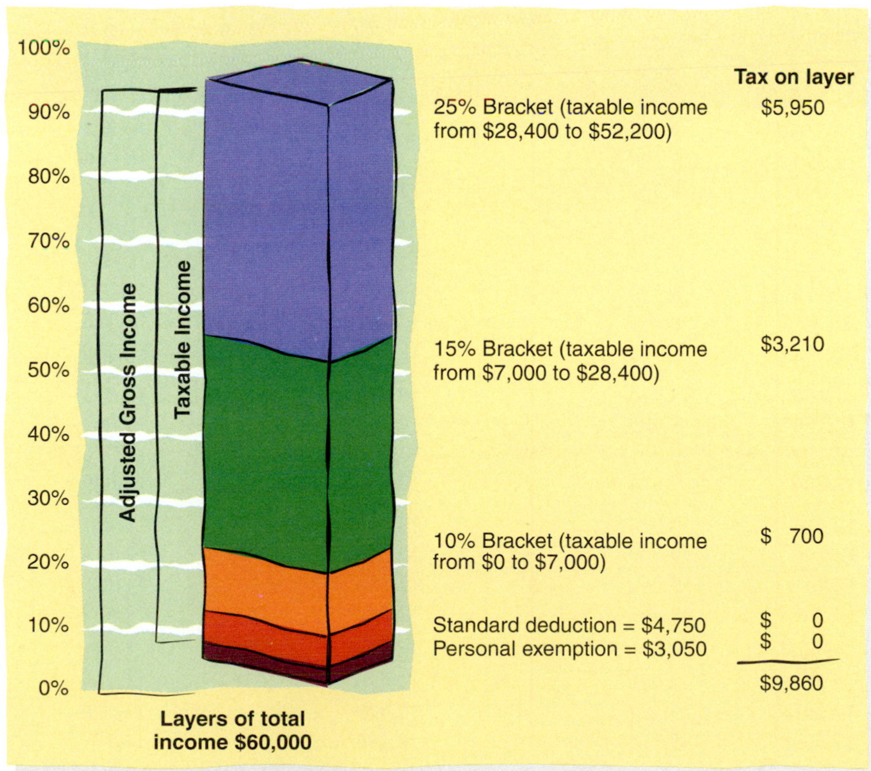

EXHIBIT 4-11

The Taxation of Your Income by Layer

According to Cindy and Dave Thompson's calculations, their taxable income is $61,090. They can find the appropriate tax amount easily by using the tax table provided in the income tax instruction booklet that came with their tax forms. Although we previously illustrated the increasing marginal tax rates by explaining how each layer of income was taxed, individual taxpayers are not expected to do that type of calculation themselves. Instead, the IRS has precalculated the tax for many different ranges of taxable income. So all you have to know is your taxable income, and you can look up the tax amount that you must pay.

The *Go Figure* box, "Using the Tax Table and Tax Rate Schedules," shows you how to use the applicable portion of the tax table to determine the Thompsons' tax obligation. Cindy and Dave look down the column to find their income level and then across the row to their filing status. The tax amount is $8,889—but this amount may be further reduced if the Thompsons qualify for any tax credits. Recall that a tax credit is an amount that you can subtract directly from your taxes owed.

GO FIGURE!

Using the Tax Table and Tax Rate Schedules

Problem: The Thompsons have completed their 1040 and calculated their taxable income, which is $61,090. How much tax do they owe?

Solution: Referring to the applicable segment of the tax table, they look down the column to find their income level, which falls between $61,050 and $61,100. Looking across to the column entitled Married Filing Jointly, they determine that their tax is $8,889.

Segment of the 2003 Tax Table

If line 41 (taxable income) is . . .		And you are . . .			
At least	But less than	Single	Married filing jointly	Married filing separately	Head of a household
		Your tax is. . .			
61,000					
61,000	61,050	12,066	8,876	12,177	10,951
61,050	61,100	12,079	8,889	12,191	10,964
61,100	61,150	12,091	8,901	12,205	10,976
61,150	61,200	12,104	8,914	12,219	10,989
61,200	61,250	12,116	8,926	12,233	11,001
61,250	61,300	12,129	8,939	12,247	11,014
61,300	61,350	12,141	8,951	12,261	11,026
61,350	61,400	12,154	8,964	12,275	11,039
61,400	61,450	12,166	8,976	12,289	11,051
61,450	61,500	12,179	8,989	12,303	11,064
61,500	61,550	12,191	9,001	12,317	11,076
61,550	61,600	12,204	9,014	12,331	11,089
61,600	61,650	12,216	9,026	12,345	11,101
61,650	61,700	12,229	9,039	12,359	11,114
61,700	61,750	12,241	9,051	12,373	11,126
61,750	61,800	12,254	9,064	12,387	11,139
61,800	61,850	12,266	9,076	12,401	11,151
61,850	61,900	12,279	9,089	12,415	11,164
61,900	61,950	12,291	9,101	12,429	11,176
61,950	62,000	12,304	9,114	12,443	11,189

Once you've determined your tentative tax, you're almost done. The final two steps are determining eligibility for tax credits, which may result in a reduction in taxes owed, and the calculation of the alternative minimum tax (AMT), which may result in an increase in the taxes you owe if it applies to you. These two steps are discussed below.

Applying Available Credits

As mentioned earlier, tax credits directly reduce the taxes you owe. The currently available credits, summarized in Exhibit 4-12, include credits for foreign taxes paid, child and dependent care expenses, elderly and disabled status, education expenses, retirement contributions, dependent children, and adoption. You generally must follow specific guidelines to determine whether you qualify for each credit and how much it will reduce your tax. Several of the available credits are particularly helpful for working parents and contribute to the progressive nature of the tax system. In addition to a flat credit per child under the age of 17, you can take a tax credit for a portion of the costs of child care incurred while you are at work. For lower-income families in which both parents are employed, the earned income credit can significantly reduce taxes paid. Some college students may qualify for this tax credit as well. The Hope Scholarship Credit and the Lifetime Learning Credit, both discussed in more detail in Chapter 15, are important credits for college students (and parents of college students) to be aware of. Although many of the credits are fairly straightforward, some have specific income limitations or are phased out for higher-income families, so you may have to use an IRS worksheet to determine your eligibility and the amount of your credit. All the credits except for the child tax credit require that you file a special form (referenced on the appropriate line of Forms 1040 and 1040A) to claim the credit.

The Thompsons know that they are eligible for the child tax credit. A change in the 2003 tax law increased that credit to $1,000 per child under the age of 17, but some of that credit was

EXHIBIT 4-12

Summary of Most Commonly Applied Tax Credits, 2003

Credit	Purpose	Amount of Credit
Foreign Tax Credit	Prevent double taxation	Taxes paid to another country.
Child and Dependent Care Expenses	Cover the costs of child care necessary to allow you to work	If AGI <$43,000, 20–35% of actual expenses (up to $3,000 for one child, $6,000 for two or more); for greater AGI, maximum credit is $600 for one child, $1,200 for two or more.
Credit for Elderly and Disabled	Help cover additional expenses associated with working while disabled	15% of a base amount of income. Credit up to $1,125.
Child Tax Credit	Reduce tax burden on working parents	$1,000 per child.
Earned Income Credit	Help working poor	For AGI < $34,692 (married filing jointly), AGI < $11,230 for childless single. Maximum credit $4,240 for family of four, $382 if no children. Single college students may qualify.
Hope Scholarship Credit	Encourage higher education	100% of first $1,500 of college expenses for first two years for each qualifying student. Credit phased out for AGI $41,000–$51,000 single or $83,000–$103,000 joint.
Lifetime Learning Credit	Encourage higher education	20% of first $10,000, maximum $1,000 per family per year. Credit phased out for AGI $41,000–$51,000 single or $83,000–$103,000 joint.
Retirement Savers Tax Credit	Encourage investment in IRAs and employer retirement plans	Singles with AGI <$25,000 and couples with AGI < $50,000, credit equals 10%–50% (scaled by income) of contributions up to $1,000 singles, $2,000 couples.
Adoption Credit	Encourage adoption	Up to $10,160 for adoption of an eligible child.

rebated to taxpayers during the 2003 tax year, so Cindy and Dave can only claim $600 on their 2003 taxes. This reduction brings their total taxes owed down to $8,289. Since they have actually paid more than that in withholding taxes ($14,300) during the year, the Thompsons will be receiving a refund of $6,011.

Alternative Minimum Tax

alternative minimum tax

Federal income tax calculations designed to ensure that people who receive certain tax breaks pay their fair share of taxes.

Some taxpayers end up owing more in taxes than the calculation above would indicate because of the **alternative minimum tax (AMT).** This tax was originally designed to make sure that high-income people couldn't take advantage of too many special tax rules to avoid paying their fair share of taxes, but in recent years, it has impacted many middle-income taxpayers as well.

The AMT works this way: You are supposed to recalculate your taxes under a different set of rules in which many of the current deductions, exemptions, and special tax breaks do not apply. If the tax calculated in that way is larger than the one calculated in the normal way described above, then you must pay the AMT. Whether you should take the time to do this depends on whether your tax situation includes many of the AMT "triggers." Some of the triggers for AMT liability in a given year include: a large number of exemptions claimed; exercise of incentive stock options; long-term capital gains; and large itemized deductions, particularly for medical expenses or second home mortgage interest. If any of these apply to you, you should follow the IRS directions for calculation of the AMT to see whether it applies to your circumstances. And don't be surprised if it does—more than 2.7 million taxpayers were subject to it for tax year 2003, and the AMT is estimated to reach more than 35 million within the next decade. Thankfully, the Thompsons don't have to pay the AMT.

The IRS automatically calculates the AMT based on your submitted tax form, so if you neglect to do so and therefore underpay your taxes, you may end up paying additional interest and penalties. (Tax preparation software and tax professionals will automatically calculate the AMT for you.)

Paying Taxes

Taxes are supposed to be paid on your income as you receive it. However, our tax system is complex enough that it isn't always easy to determine exactly how much you will be obligated to pay until you actually prepare your return. It is therefore your obligation to make an estimate of this amount and to be sure that you have paid enough to cover it.

Withholding

payroll withholding

Money regularly withheld from employees' pay by employers for payment of the employees' taxes.

For earned income from employment, the payment of estimated taxes is usually accomplished through **payroll withholding,** whereby the employer takes money out of your income and sends it to the government. The amount of taxes withheld is determined by a calculation based on expected income and estimated number of exemptions as indicated on your W-4 form, the Employee's Withholding Allowance Certificate. You complete a W-4 form whenever you begin a new job. The lower the number of exemptions claimed, the larger the amount withheld from your pay. Alternatively, if you don't expect to owe any taxes for the tax year—if you have fairly low income, as discussed previously—you can indicate on the form that you are tax exempt so that no taxes will be withheld. The majority of taxpayers have more withheld than they will owe in taxes and are eventually entitled to a tax refund (without interest) when they file their taxes. Even if an appropriate number of exemptions is claimed on the W-4, you may still end up paying too much in withholding, because the amount withheld is calculated assuming you'll take the standard deduction. Since the Thompsons had a lot of itemized deductions, the IRS estimate, based on their reported three exemptions, resulted in tax overpayment.

Estimated Tax

If you are self-employed or have investment income that hasn't been subject to withholding, you must still pay your taxes *in advance of* the April 15 due date. The law requires that you pay the tax in quarterly estimated tax installments during the tax year (on April 15, June 15, September

15, and January 15). If you underpay, you'll be subject to penalties. To avoid underpayment penalties, make sure that the total of your withholding plus estimated tax payments is at least as much as 100 percent of your prior year's tax owed.

Additional Taxes on the Self-Employed

If you're self-employed, you'll probably owe additional taxes beyond the federal income tax. Self-employed individuals report total business revenues and certain deductible expenses on a Schedule C. The difference between their revenues and expenses is taxable and therefore must be reported as business income (or loss) on their 1040 form. Since no income tax or Social Security/Medicare payroll tax has been withheld from this income, business owners are supposed to make quarterly estimated tax payments throughout the year, as discussed above.

Individuals who report self-employment income are also required to file a Schedule SE (for self-employment) with their federal tax forms. This is a worksheet to determine the amount of Social Security and Medicare payroll taxes owed on any business income. Whereas wage and salary workers split the 15.3 percent tax with their employer (each paying 7.65%), self-employed people are their own employers and thus must pay both portions of the tax. The combined effect of federal and state income taxes plus the Social Security and Medicare tax is a hefty bite out of business income, sometimes more than 50 percent for those in the highest marginal income tax bracket.

Payments and Refunds

If your total withholding and estimated taxes paid during the year are less than the amount of taxes you owe for the year, you must include a check for the remainder with your submitted tax form. If you've paid too much in withholding, you're entitled to a tax refund. In some cases, you may receive a refund even when you didn't have sufficient income to require any payment of taxes. This occurs because Congress has made certain tax credits refundable—you can get them even if you have no taxes owed to credit them against. The most important refundable tax credit is the additional child tax credit, which allows some households to receive the credit even if they owed no tax.

It makes sense to plan so as to minimize the amount of refund you'll receive, since overpaying taxes is essentially like giving the government a zero-interest loan. Some taxpayers, however, like to overpay their taxes. Even though this strategy doesn't make good financial sense, several explanations for why so many people do this are discussed in the *Money Psychology* box, "Saving Refunds."

Money Psychology

Saving Refunds

You check the mail every day, hoping that today will be the day. And then, finally, it arrives—an official-looking envelope from the U.S. Department of the Treasury—and it feels as if you won the lottery. About 75 percent of taxpayers get tax refunds each year, and many people look at the refund check as a windfall—perhaps enforced saving or a summer vacation fund. Since the government is not paying you interest on this "loan," overpaying taxes is not a good personal finance strategy—if you receive the money earlier, you can earn interest by investing it. So why do so many people overpay their taxes and delay getting refunds? Behavioral psychology provides two good explanations:

1. *People like to avoid pain and savor joy.* Having your taxes subtracted from your income before you even see the money is not very painful, whereas a big payment to Uncle Sam would hurt. The tax refund feels like a windfall.
2. *Mental accounting.* If you had a little more income each month instead of over-withholding, you might feel that it should be applied to your budgeted goals, such as payment of credit cards. Getting it back all in one check allows you to put it in a different mental account labeled "fun money."

Sources: John R. Nofsinger, *Investment Madness*, Upper Saddle River, NJ: Prentice Hall (2001), p. 150; Benjamin Ayers, Steven Kachelmeister, and John Robinson, "Why Do People Give Interest-Free Loans to the Government? An Experimental Study of Interim Tax Payments," *Journal of the American Taxation Association* 21, no. 2 (1999): 55–74.

Tax Planning Strategies

LEARNING objective

4 Establish strategies to legally minimize the taxes you pay.

Understanding the fundamentals of income taxation is important to financial planning because it enables you to anticipate the tax consequences of your other financial decisions. Applying the financial planning process requires that you evaluate different strategies for achieving your objectives. In some cases, the tax laws will make one strategy clearly preferable to another—for example, one investment alternative may offer tax benefits, while another doesn't. In addition, your tax knowledge will allow you to better evaluate whether you need to consult a tax professional and to prepare the necessary information for your financial planner. If your taxes are simple, you should be able to handle them yourself, using concepts and examples from this chapter. If your situation is more complex, you might benefit from a tax specialist's more detailed knowledge of the law.

In later chapters, you'll be learning more about how taxes impact your financial decisions so that you can better develop strategies for minimizing taxes. Here, we consider several general strategies that are useful for most individual tax plans.

Fact #5

Tax evasion is a crime and can, in some cases, result in imprisonment. When a crime boss is successful in avoiding prosecution for his murder and mayhem activities, federal officials sometimes choose to prosecute him for tax evasion instead because it's easier to prove. In 1930, for example, gangster Al Capone was sentenced to eleven years in prison for his failure to pay taxes for four years.

Tax Evasion Versus Tax Avoidance

Effective personal financial management requires that you attempt to minimize unnecessary cash outflows—and that includes any taxes which you pay unnecessarily. Of course, you must pay taxes that you legally owe. **Tax evasion**—the deliberate failure to pay taxes that are legally owed—is against the law. Examples of tax evasion include failure to report tip income or earnings received "under the table." Since waiters and waitresses usually earn more in tips than they earn in wages, the IRS regularly audits these jobs to estimate average tips and requires that employers withhold sufficient taxes from the employees' wage income, in some cases leaving them with very little in their paychecks. However, it is generally the case that restaurant workers receive more in tips than what is reported by their employers in these audits, thus resulting in under-withholding.

tax evasion
Deliberate nonpayment of taxes legally owed.

Working "under the table" means working for someone who pays you in cash and doesn't withhold taxes. This is also illegal. It is suspected that many farm and agricultural workers and their employers, particularly in areas near the U.S. borders, illegally evade taxes in this way. Since these workers are often transient, it is difficult for the government to catch them.

Although tax evasion is illegal and can have serious consequences, there is nothing illegal about **tax avoidance.** When you use your knowledge of the tax rules to make financial decisions that reduce the taxes you owe, you are ensuring that you do not pay more taxes than you are legally obligated to pay. The money you save in taxes can be applied to achieving your other financial goals. Although we will cover these issues in more depth in later chapters, consider the example of tax-deductible versus nondeductible investment contributions. A tax-deductible investment allows you to put the money into the investment without paying taxes on it first. In other words, $1,000 of income results in $1,000 invested. If you invest instead in something that does not carry that tax benefit, then you will pay taxes on the $1,000 in income first, leaving you with substantially less to actually invest. For example, if your marginal federal income tax rate is 25 percent and your state tax is 5 percent, you will only have $700 left to invest after taxes.

tax avoidance
Strategic use of knowledge of tax rules to avoid overpayment of taxes.

Strategies for Minimizing Taxes

Tax avoidance requires thoughtful planning. In general, tax planning is the ongoing process of using the provisions of the tax law to reduce your taxes or defer them to later years. As you begin to work toward achieving long-term financial goals, you'll need to consider not just the current year's taxes, but future years as well. Since there are frequent changes to the tax law, you should try to stay informed about new rules that might benefit your tax situation.

Tax planning strategies are those that are intended to:

- Reduce taxable income.
- Defer taxable income.
- Receive income that is subject to lower tax rates.
- Increase deductions and exemptions from income.
- Maximize tax credits.

We look at each of these strategies in the remainder of this section.

Reduce Taxable Income. There are several strategies for reducing taxable income without reducing gross income. Many employers offer the opportunity to make pretax contributions to employee benefit and retirement plans. These will be discussed more fully in Chapter 10, but the basic concept is that the law allows you to use your pretax income to buy your benefits. Federal, state, and local income taxes as well as Social Security payroll taxes are then calculated based on the income left after these expenditures have been made. You save whatever tax you would have paid on that income, and your employer saves its portion of the Social Security tax.

You can reduce your day care costs by paying with pretax dollars from a flexible spending account.

Let's consider an example to see how this can benefit you. Suppose you work for an employer that offers you the opportunity to purchase your health insurance with pretax dollars at a cost of \$300 per month. Your friend Jonah, who earns the same salary at a competing firm, has no health insurance through his employer so must pay for it out of pocket, again for \$300 per month. How much better off are you than your friend if you are both subject to a marginal tax rate of 30 percent? Your taxable income will now be lower by the \$300 amount, so you'll be able to avoid paying \$90 per month in taxes (\$300 × 0.30), or \$1,080 per year. Jonah must pay taxes on his full earnings. In effect, the tax deductibility allows you to get a \$1,080 discount on the cost of the health insurance (equal to your tax savings), money that you can apply to one of your financial goals.

Many larger employers also allow employees to take advantage of a **flexible spending account,** a reimbursement account for qualified medical and child-care expenses. Each pay period, the employer subtracts a certain amount from your paycheck and deposits it in your flexible spending account. The amount deposited is not part of your taxable income. You can then obtain reimbursement from the account as you incur qualified expenses, such as the money you pay to your child-care provider. Effectively, this allows you to pay for your child care with pretax dollars, substantially reducing the out-of-pocket cost to you because you save the amount in taxes you would have paid on that income. If your marginal tax rate is 20 percent (15% federal plus 5% state tax) and you normally pay \$5,000 per year for child care, you would save about \$1,000 in taxes (\$5,000 × 0.2) for the year by using one of these accounts. If you had instead taken the \$5,000 in taxable earnings and paid taxes on it, you would have only had \$4,000 left after taxes [\$5,000 × (1 − 0.2) = \$4,000]—not enough to pay for your child-care expenses.

flexible spending account

An account maintained by an employer in which the pretax earnings of an employee are set aside and can be used for reimbursement of qualified medical and child-care expenses.

For taxpayers in high tax brackets, it may be beneficial to consider investing in real estate properties that will produce a tax loss after expenses. As you'll see in Chapter 14, investment real estate owners are allowed some deductions that aren't actually out-of-pocket expenses. As a result, it's not unusual for a profitable investment property to produce a tax loss that can be applied against other income to reduce taxes.

Defer Taxable Income. As noted, employer retirement plans may allow you to make investment contributions on a pretax basis and therefore avoid current income taxes on that income. But in addition to reducing current taxable income, these plans also allow you to defer paying taxes on the investment earnings in the plan. If you earn \$1,000 in investment income in a taxable account—such as interest on your bank savings account—you'll owe income taxes on these earnings in the year received, the actual amount being a function of your marginal tax rate (including state and federal income tax). In a tax-deferred account, you won't pay tax on the income until you withdraw it, which may be many years in the future. At that point, you may be in a lower marginal tax bracket. But even if you're not, you will benefit from the time value of money—it's always better to pay a given amount in the future than it is to pay the amount today. As you know, a dollar today is worth more than a dollar in the future.

If you aren't fortunate enough to have a retirement plan option at your current place of employment, tax rules allow you to set up an individual retirement account (IRA). Currently, there

traditional IRA

Individual retirement account that allows the holder to subtract current contributions from taxable income and to defer income tax until withdrawal at retirement.

Roth IRA

Individual retirement account to which contributions are made with after-tax dollars, but investment earnings and withdrawals at retirement are tax-free.

are two types of IRAs, which are defined here but will be considered in greater detail in a later chapter. A **traditional IRA** allows you to subtract your annual contribution to the account from income and to defer the payment of taxes until withdrawal. Note that this type of IRA has a tax effect similar to that of employment-based retirement plans. In contrast, the **Roth IRA** does not allow you to take a current deduction, so you must make the contribution with after-tax dollars. However, assuming you use the funds for retirement or other allowed purposes, you *never* have to pay tax on the money again—the account, including all accumulated investment earnings, can grow tax-free, and you can take the money out at retirement without paying any taxes on it.

Another way to defer taxable income is to postpone receiving the income until a future tax year. For example, suppose a family friend hired you to build a deck for him in the fall of 2004. You know that your 2004 income is relatively high because you worked the whole year. Since you'll be attending college in 2005, you expect to be in a lower tax bracket that year. If you can delay the receipt of payment for your deck-building services until 2005—for example, by waiting to bill your friend—you won't have to pay the tax until the following year, and you'll reduce the overall tax owed (since you'll be in a lower tax bracket). Certain professions—small businesses and consulting practices, for example—can more easily take advantage of this type of tax strategy.

Receive Income That Is Subject to Lower Tax Rates. Capital gains and certain dividends from long-term investments are taxed at a lower rate than ordinary income, as discussed earlier. For this reason, an important tax strategy is to avoid investments that pay you current income (interest or dividends) in favor of those that provide returns in the form of increased value. Since a capital gain is not reported on your taxes until you sell the asset, you can accumulate substantial wealth without incurring any current tax. When you do realize a gain on a qualifying investment, you'll pay at a lower tax rate, in most cases 15 percent. Your home has an even greater advantage in this respect, since most capital gains from the sale of your primary residence are tax-free.

Families can achieve lower taxes overall by shifting some income to household members who are in lower tax brackets. For example, you can give taxable investment accounts to your children. You are allowed to make gifts of up to $11,000 each per year tax-free to as many people as you want without the receiver having to declare it as income. Children can earn up to $750 in investment income per year without paying any tax. If the child is under age 14, the next $750 in unearned income is taxed at the child's marginal tax rate (10 percent) and unearned income above $1,500 is taxed at the parent's marginal tax rate (under a rule commonly referred to as the "kiddie tax"). Children age 14 and over pay their own tax rate on all income over $750. So, if you have $11,000 in a taxable savings account earning 4 percent per year, or $440, you can avoid the taxes you would normally have to pay on the interest earnings by gifting the account to your child who can receive the interest without any taxes being owed.

Increase Deductions and Exemptions from Income. In order to maximize your tax deductions, it is important to plan ahead for the record keeping and timing of expenditures. Careful record keeping will help to ensure that you are reporting all deductible expenses. When you have a choice as to when to incur an expense, you should consider how the timing will affect your taxes. To see that lots of people apply this rule to their finances, you need only go to an office supply or computer store on New Year's Eve. The store will probably be packed because December 31 is the last day to make purchases that can be deducted for the tax year. It's a good idea to roughly estimate your expected tax liability before that time. Any deductible expenditures you make will have a much lower effective cost to you, since you would otherwise be paying some of that money in taxes.

Another example of strategic end-of-year expenditures involves the timing of uninsured medical procedures. Let's say that in tax year 2004, you've already incurred sufficient medical costs (greater than 7.5% of the AGI) to qualify for the medical expense deduction. Any additional uninsured medical expenses—including out-of-pocket premiums, deductibles and co-pays, doctor visits, surgery, vision care, and prescriptions—can all be itemized in 2004, reducing the effective cost to you by the amount of your marginal tax bracket. If, for example, you need a new pair of glasses, this is the time to get them.

Charitable contributions are another way to increase your deductions. Be sure to keep track of all the times you've taken a bag of used clothing to Goodwill or donated food to a food drive. Although it's always a good idea to get receipts, they're only required by the IRS for large contributions of cash or goods. In high tax years, consider making an end-of-year contribution to your favorite charity. If you donate a total of $400, it could save you $100 to $200 in taxes, depending on your tax bracket, substantially reducing the effective cost of making the contribution.

Don't forget the tax-sheltering value of your home. In addition to the capital gain advantage described in the previous section, mortgage interest and property taxes are both deductible, so your home is an incredible tax shelter. You might also consider using home equity loans as an alternative to other types of financing. Not only do they usually have a lower interest rate than consumer loans, but the interest on up to $100,000 in home equity loans ($50,000 for married filing separately) is tax-deductible, reducing the effective cost even more.

How many exemptions can this family claim?

To see how home ownership can produce tax benefits, consider the difference between two taxpayers, each in the 25 percent marginal tax bracket. Assume that the first one is a renter and the second is a homeowner. Both have identical annual housing expenditures of $12,000 per year. The renter cannot deduct any of this; the homeowner, however, can deduct all the mortgage interest and property taxes. Let's say this amount is $10,000. Since this is greater than the standard deduction, the homeowner's income is effectively reduced by $10,000, a tax savings of 25 percent of $10,000 = $2,500. That's like cash in the pocket! The effective housing cost to the homeowner is $12,000 − $2,500 = $9,500 compared with the renter's $12,000 cost. Plus, the home can increase in value tax-free.

Exemptions are another type of deduction from your income. Although no one would advise that you have more children for tax reasons, it is not unusual for expectant parents to schedule a Caesarean section for December 31 (subject to the approval of their physician, of course) rather than waiting for a January 1 due date. One day makes a big difference in your taxes—an extra $3,050 exemption.

Maximize Tax Credits. Many people are eligible for various tax credits but don't claim them. This generally happens when they either don't know about the credits or haven't kept adequate records to claim them. Your tax planning strategies should therefore include a careful review of available credits and evaluation of your eligibility for each.

Learning by Doing 4-4

For each of the following taxpayer characteristics, identify potential strategies for minimizing taxes that you would recommend they investigate:

1. Real estate investor in a high tax bracket.
2. Working parents with preschoolers.
3. College student who is independent of parents.

Enforcement of the Tax System and Recent Trends

LEARNING objective

5 Understand how the tax system is enforced, and be aware of recent trends in the system.

What happens if you don't pay your taxes or if you underreport income or exaggerate deductions? These actions are illegal under federal law and, at a minimum, you will be subject to interest and penalties on your underpayments. In the extreme, you can actually go to jail for tax evasion. Unfortunately, the threat of these adverse consequences isn't enough to deter some people. In fact, surveys have shown that most people think it's okay to cheat on their taxes a little. That kind of attitude, while perhaps not surprising, hurts everyone—we all pay higher tax rates to cover the lost revenue from tax cheats and the additional enforcement costs. In this section, we explain the enforcement process used by the IRS.

Enforcement of Tax Laws

audit

Process by which the IRS more carefully examines particular tax returns for errors and omissions.

The IRS employs several levels of scrutiny to investigate tax returns for errors and intentional omissions. A tax **audit** can range from a simple electronic screening of returns for errors all the way up to the dreaded visit from the "men in black." Although there have always been stories in the paper about people who claim to have avoided paying taxes for years, today's high-tech environment makes it fairly easy for the IRS to track down most tax cheats. All earned income, investment income, and interest expenses are independently reported to the government, so errors and omissions in reporting these items are usually caught within a few months of filing a return. You'll simply get a bill for the underpayment plus any applicable penalties.

In addition to automatically correcting errors, the IRS randomly selects returns for more careful scrutiny. In some cases, your return might be selected for evaluation in a truly random process; in others, your audit may have been triggered by screening programs designed to identify suspect returns based on key characteristics of income and deductions that have been correlated with tax fraud in the past. Although the odds of being audited are still relatively low—less than 1 percent of all returns are audited—you can significantly reduce your chances of being audited by filling out your tax forms correctly and being sure to completely report income from all sources. The *News You Can Use* box, "What Are the Odds of Getting Audited?", provides some recent audit statistics and suggestions for reducing the likelihood of being audited.

If you are audited, you may be asked to provide documentation for specific deductions. In rare cases, you may even have to appear at a local IRS office. Alternatively, an IRS agent may come to your home to investigate, most commonly to verify small business and home office deductions.

Complexity of the Tax System

Many people have argued that the current tax system is unfair, in part because it's so complex that the average person can't understand his or her rights and obligations. The Internal Revenue Code and IRS Regulations are literally thousands of pages long, and they seem to undergo a major overhaul with every new presidential administration. Although the complexity of the tax system may seem daunting, much of it can actually be beneficial to you—the special rules offer opportunities to reduce the taxes you pay. If you fail to take advantage of every available opportunity for tax savings, you're throwing money away.

NEWS you can use

What Are the Odds of Getting Audited?

For the average taxpayer, the likelihood of getting audited has never been lower. According to the most recent Treasury Department tables, the IRS examines less than 1 percent of all individual returns, down from about 5 percent in the mid-1960s. Budget cuts and staff reductions, as well as a greater emphasis on customer service at the IRS, have reduced the number of tax returns subject to audits. In 2002, only 1 in 174 returns were audited, a lower rate than the previous year. Since the IRS is concentrating its audit attention on high-income taxpayers (resulting in collection of $32.6 billion in previously unpaid taxes in 2002), the rate for filers with less than $100,000 income has decreased. This doesn't imply that there's a zero chance of getting audited if you're low-income, however. In fact, the actual *number* of low-income audits has increased slightly over time—but it's still pretty low.

The IRS is currently focusing on key areas of noncompliance with the tax laws, which may reduce the odds of audits for other violations in the near term.

"In 2002, only 1 in 174 returns were audited."

If you want to reduce the odds of being audited, consider the following list of audit "triggers" identified in the *Ernst and Young Tax Guide 2004:*

- Reported income that doesn't agree with your W2 and 1099 Forms
- Married taxpayers filing separately who file inconsistent tax returns
- Taxpayers who should have paid the alternative minimum tax
- Receipt of substantial cash income (doctors, lawyers, retail businesses, waiters)
- Large deductions relative to income, particularly charitable deductions and employee business expenses
- Schedule C business income greater than $100,000 and large business deductions relative to income
- Complex investment or business transactions without clear explanations
- Earned income tax credit claimed

Source: *Ernst and Young Tax Guide 2004*, New York: John Wiley & Sons (2004).

Would a Flat Tax Be Better?

Periodically, politicians and taxpayer lobby groups put forward proposals for simplifying federal income taxes. One reform idea that gained support in the 1990s, after presidential hopeful Steve Forbes campaigned heavily on this platform, was to change the system so that all taxpayers would pay a **flat tax,** such as 10 percent, on every dollar of income. The simplicity of this type of tax would mean that all tax collection could be handled at the employer level, much as is currently done for Social Security payroll taxes and withholding—no tax returns to file or process and no refunds to mail.

flat tax

A single tax rate imposed on every dollar of income for every taxpayer.

Although a flat tax would certainly be simple and save the government and the taxpayers much of the time and money currently spent on completing and processing tax returns, it's not as perfect as its proponents would argue. The primary disadvantage is that it would necessarily be less progressive than the current system, since low-income and high-income people would all pay the same rate. Proponents argue that the government could still set a minimum income on which the tax would apply (through an exemption or deduction), so that low-income citizens would not pay taxes. Doing that, however, would reduce the system's simplicity, since taxpayers would have to file returns to get the exemption.

Additional problems would further reduce the simplicity of a flat tax system and add costs similar to those in the current system. How would you report unearned income from small businesses, rentals, and investments, for example? If these forms of income were not taxed, the system would be even more regressive, since low-income workers are primarily wage earners. A flat tax would also reduce the ability of Congress to use tax policy to help special groups (such as families with children) or influence consumer behavior (with special incentives for retirement saving or higher education).

Learning by Doing 4-5

1. Which of the following might increase your chances of being audited?
   - You file a Schedule C to report business income.
   - You are a waiter.
   - You claim a deduction for a home office.
   - You donate your old car to a charity and take a large charitable deduction.
2. Identify three advantages and three disadvantages of our current system of taxation compared with a flat tax system.

Summary

1. **Understand the major features of the federal income tax system.** The federal income tax system is a progressive tax system, which means that high-income taxpayers are subject to higher marginal tax rates than low-income taxpayers. The current system incorporates marginal tax rates that range from 10 percent to 35 percent. Exemptions and deductions are applied to reduce taxable income.
2. **Know when and how to file your taxes.** Federal income tax returns are due by April 15 of the year following the tax year. You may file an extension to extend the deadline but must still pay the taxes you owe by April 15. Your income and allowed deductions must be reported on official tax forms, and you may file your return either on paper or electronically. If you have wage or salary income, your employer will withhold money from your earned income for payment to the IRS.
3. **Calculate taxable income and determine your tax liability.** Taxes are calculated on your taxable income. Taxable income is your total income from all sources less allowed exclusions, adjustments, exemptions, and deductions. You may take a standard deduction based on your filing status, or you may choose to itemize your deductions by filing a form that reports your expenses in allowed categories. After calculating the tentative tax owed based on taxable income, you may be able to reduce the amount owed by claiming certain tax credits.
4. **Establish strategies to legally minimize the taxes you pay.** Although you should never illegally evade paying taxes, good financial planning requires that you attempt to legally minimize the amount you pay wherever possible. You can do this by reducing your current taxable income, deferring taxable income to future years, maximizing deductions, receiving capital gains income, which is subject to a lower marginal tax rate, and taking advantage of allowed tax credits. In all cases, tax planning should include careful record keeping to allow verification of deductions and credits claimed.
5. **Understand how the tax system is enforced, and be aware of recent trends in the system.** The IRS is charged with administering the U.S. tax system and ensuring that all taxpayers pay the amount of tax that they legally owe. The IRS regularly audits individual tax returns to ensure compliance with the tax law. Audits can range from simple corrections of math errors to more involved examinations and investigations. You can reduce your risk of audit by carefully reporting income from all sources.

Key Terms

adjusted gross income (AGI) (106)
alternative minimum tax (AMT) (122)
audit (127)
average tax rate (103)
capital gain (113)
dependent (106)
earned income (106)
exemption (106)
FICA tax (101)
filing status (106)
flat tax (129)
flexible spending account (125)
gross income (112)
Internal Revenue Code (105)
Internal Revenue Service (IRS) (105)
IRS e-file (108)
itemized deductions (107)
marginal tax rate (102)
marginal tax effect (105)
payroll withholding (122)
progressive tax (101)
regressive tax (101)
Roth IRA (126)
standard deduction (107)
tax avoidance (124)
tax bracket (103)
tax credit (107)
tax evasion (124)
taxable income (102)
total income (112)
traditional IRA (126)
unearned income (106)

Key Calculation

$$\text{Average tax rate on taxable income} = \frac{\text{Taxes paid}}{\text{Taxable income}}$$

Concept Review Questions

1. Explain why tax planning is important to your financial decisions.
2. In what ways does our current federal income tax system attempt to more equitably distribute the tax burden among taxpayers?
3. What is the difference between a progressive tax and a regressive tax? Which type of tax is our federal income tax? Which type is the Social Security payroll tax?
4. What impact did recent tax legislation have on tax rates?
5. What is the difference between your marginal tax rate and your average tax rate? In making financial decisions, which is more important to consider?
6. What is a tax bracket? Why is it important to inflation-index tax brackets?
7. What are the responsibilities of the Internal Revenue Service?
8. What are the five allowed filing status categories for federal income taxes?
9. What are the factors that determine whether you must file a tax return?
10. Under what circumstances are you allowed to file a 1040EZ or a 1040A?
11. Under what circumstances should you file a tax return even when you're not required to?
12. What is included in adjusted gross income?
13. What is the difference between earned income and investment income?
14. Under what circumstances does a person qualify as a dependent for tax purposes?
15. What determines the number of personal exemptions you can claim on your taxes?
16. What is the difference between the standard deduction and itemized deductions? Under what circumstances should you itemize deductions? What form must you use?
17. What is the deadline for filing your taxes? If you cannot complete your forms by that time, what are your options?
18. What is e-filing, and what are its advantages?
19. Identify the major steps to calculating how much tax you owe.
20. What is a capital gain, and why is this type of income preferable to earned income, from a tax standpoint?
21. What are the major categories of itemized deductions? Are there any limitations on expenses you may deduct in each of these categories?
22. If you incur necessary expenses for your job that are not reimbursed by your employer, under what circumstances can you deduct them in calculating your taxes?
23. Identify the major types of tax credits. How are tax credits different from deductions?
24. What is the alternative minimum tax?
25. What are the two primary ways to pay taxes in advance?
26. If you are self-employed, what tax form must you file? What additional taxes will you have to pay with your federal income tax return?
27. What is the difference between tax evasion and tax avoidance? Give an example of each.
28. Name five categories of tax planning strategies. Give an example of each.
29. How can a flexible spending account help reduce your out-of-pocket medical expenses and child-care costs?
30. Why is it beneficial to defer income to later tax years?
31. What are the tax advantages in saving for retirement by investing in an IRA? Does it matter which type of IRA you have?
32. In what ways is your home a tax shelter?
33. Why does the IRS audit returns? How does it select tax returns to be audited?
34. Identify several audit triggers.
35. How would a flat tax system differ from the current tax system? In what ways would a flat tax be preferable? In what ways would it be less desirable?

Application Problems

1. **Taxable Income.** You and your wife have an adjusted gross income of $25,000. In 2003, you can claim two personal exemptions and the standard deduction for married couples filing jointly. What is your taxable income?

2. **Marginal Versus Average Taxes.** You are single and have an adjusted gross income of $35,000 and taxable income of $24,000.
   a. What is your marginal tax rate?
   b. How much tax will you owe, assuming you don't qualify for any tax credits?
   c. What is the average tax rate you paid on your taxable income? on your adjusted gross income?
3. **Tax Effects.** You are in the 25 percent marginal tax bracket. What is it worth to you to have:
   a. an additional itemized deduction of $200
   b. an additional tax credit of $200
4. **Capital Gains.** Jack Spratt has an investment that gives him $1,000 per year in interest income. His friend Peter Pumpkineater has been telling Jack that he should invest in something that provides him with capital gains instead of interest. This year, for example, Peter sold some shares of a mutual fund (which he had held for more than one year) for a $1,000 profit. Assuming that Jack and Peter are both in the top marginal tax bracket (35%), how much difference did the type of income they received from these two investments make to the taxes owed on the income?
5. **Marginal Benefit of Deductions.** Assume that you are in the top marginal tax bracket (35%) and you normally itemize deductions. If you make an end-of-year contribution to your church in the amount of $1,000, what is the effective cost of that gift to you, taking into consideration the tax savings it will generate?
6. **Medical Expenses.** Tamika tore a knee ligament in 2004 and had to undergo arthroscopic surgery. Her total medical expenses were $8,000, but her health insurance covered all but $2,400. If her adjusted gross income is $20,000, how much of this out-of pocket cost can she deduct on her taxes if she itemizes her deductions?
7. **Taxable Income.** Carly Simmons's adjusted gross income is $45,000. She has the following expenses:
   - Medical expenses $4,500
   - Mortgage interest $7,500
   - Property taxes $1,800
   - State income tax $1,000
   - Charitable gifts $500

   a. Should Carly take the standard deduction or itemize her deductions?
   b. Calculate Carly's taxable income.

Using Web Resources for Financial Planning

1. ***Obtaining Forms from the IRS.*** It's the evening of April 15, and you are desperately trying to fill out your tax forms so you can mail them by the deadline. Then, disaster strikes—maybe you realize you made a calculation error, or maybe you simply don't have a copy of the form you need to take a certain credit or deduction. In the old days, you either erased or whited out your errors, but now there's an easier solution. You can simply go to the IRS website, *www.irs.gov*, and download fresh copies of the forms you need. If you aren't sure how to fill one out, the complete directions for each form are also available there. To see how easy this is, go to the IRS website and download Form 8863 for Education Credits as well as the directions for that form, if any. Will you qualify for a credit this year?
2. ***Tax Tips for Different Stages in the Life Cycle.*** Tax strategies may differ as you go through your life cycle. To get some tax tips for your current life stage, go to *www.bankrate.com/brm/green/taxes/*. Which of the life stages listed there best fits your situation? Identify three suggestions that might be helpful to you within the next five years.
3. ***Calculating Withholding.*** How much should you have withheld from your paycheck? Go to the IRS website and use the withholding calculator there to find out: *www.irs.gov/individuals.*
4. ***Sources of Tax Advice.*** Go to each of the following websites and find the top two recommendations for this year's tax filers:
   a. Motley Fool: *www. fool.com/taxes*
   b. H & R Block: *www.hrblock.com/taxes*

Learning by Doing Solutions

LBD 4-1: 1. 25 percent; 2. $4,310; 3. 14.4 percent; 4. 25 percent.

LBD 4-2: 1a. Yes; 1b. She can file a 1040EZ.

LBD 4-3: 1. She must have paid more than 50 percent of his support for the year, so it's doubtful she can claim an exemption.; 2. Yes. His itemized deductions, not including the medical expense that doesn't meet the 7.5 percent minimum, total $7,000, which is greater than the standard deduction.

LBD 4-4: 1. Defer income to future year, accelerate expenditures at end of tax year; 2. Make use of flexible spending plan if available at employer; use child tax credit, see if eligible for earned income tax credit; 3. Take Hope Scholarship Credit or Lifetime Learning Credit or tuition deduction and consider whether itemized deductions will be greater than standard deduction.

LBD 4-5: 1. All these are possible audit triggers.; 2. Advantages: progressive, can be used to encourage desirable saving and investment behavior, can be used to defray the cost of certain expenditures such as medical and education costs. Disadvantages: complexity, cost to the government of enforcement and regulation, lost time to taxpayers.

Building Financial Planning Skills Through Case Applications

Case 4-1 Yenni Oey Figures Her Taxes

Yenni Oey, a single woman with no children, graduated from college with a degree in psychology in May 2003. She had been working part-time during school at the local J.C. Penney department store and was offered a job as assistant manager after graduation, beginning in June 2003. It is now February 2004 and she is getting ready to file her taxes. This is the first year that she has been independent from her parents.

Yenni has collected the following information to use in preparing her return:

- Her W-2 form from J.C. Penney. The form shows that she had wages of $22,300 for 2003. It also shows $1,200 federal income taxes withheld, $600 state tax withheld, and FICA (Social Security) tax of $1,850.
- Rent $4,200
- Student loan interest $50
- Groceries $2,500
- Dress clothes for work $1,000
- Health insurance premiums $2,000
- Unreimbursed medical expenses $500
- Church offerings $250
- Donation to Salvation Army $150
- Graduation gifts received $1,000
- Credit card interest payments $900
- 2002 state tax refund $150

a. Should Yenni itemize deductions? Why or why not?
b. Calculate Yenni's taxable income.
c. Is Yenni entitled to any tax credits? If so, which one(s)?
d. What is Yenni's marginal tax bracket?
e. Would it be beneficial for Yenni to put money in an IRA at this time? Explain.
f. Calculate how much Yenni owes in taxes or how much she should receive as a refund. Based on this calculation, should Yenni change her payroll withholding for 2004?

Case 4-2 Christine and Rich Schaeffer Prepare to File Their Taxes

Christine Schaeffer and her husband Rich have four children, ages 4 to 10. Chris works as a marketing executive for a cosmetics firm, and Rich is a stay-at-home dad. Their combined salaries in 2003 total $65,000. They have collected the following information to use in tax preparation:

- Unreimbursed medical expenses $2,500
- Mortgage interest $10,500
- Property taxes $2,300
- State income tax withheld $2,750
- Traditional IRA contributions $4,000
- Gambling winnings $600
- Chris's student loan interest $100
- Chris's unreimbursed job expenses $2,300
- Federal income tax withheld $5,750

a. Calculate the Schaeffers' taxable income for 2003, assuming that their filing status is married filing jointly.
b. Use the tax rate schedule (Exhibit 4-2) to calculate the tax they owe or the amount they should be refunded.
c. Are the Schaeffers eligible to take any tax credits? Explain.

Case 4-3 Carlos Santiago Determines His Estimated Tax Payments

Carlos Santiago is a self-employed home remodeling contractor. He is trying to figure out how much he should send the IRS in estimated tax payments for 2004. In 2003, he had net business income of $25,000 and taxable income of $17,200, and he paid $2,234 in federal income taxes. Carlos has added an employee to his business so that he can do more jobs during the year, and as a result he expects that his net business income will increase substantially in 2004. Based on his projections, he expects to have the following:

- Total business income $95,000
- Total materials costs $30,000
- Employee wages and taxes $15,000
- Taxes and insurance for employee $1,700
- Advertising $2,000
- Other business expenses $3,000

a. Assuming that Carlos has no other sources of income, what is his estimated net business income. Don't forget that he can deduct his business expenses from his total business revenues to arrive at his net business income.
b. As a self-employed person, Carlos must also pay FICA (Social Security payroll) taxes on his own income. He estimates that this will be 15.3 percent of his net business income.

He can subtract half of this amount from his business income to arrive at adjusted gross income. What is his adjusted gross income after making this adjustment to income?

c. If Carlos is single and takes the standard deduction, what is his estimated taxable income?

d. Using the facts above, estimate the approximate total taxes that Carlos will owe for 2004.

e. What is the minimum amount of estimated tax per quarter that Carlos must pay to avoid an IRS penalty for underpayment?

LIFELONG PLANNING CASE

INTRODUCTION

At the end of each of the four parts of this text, you'll have the opportunity to apply the material you've learned to a Lifelong Planning Case, in which you'll meet with a family at different points in their lives (ages 25, 30, 35, and 40) and help them to resolve or deal with particular financial challenges. This continuing case may be assigned by your instructor as a required comprehensive semester project, or it may be used as an opportunity for review of key concepts. In each case, you'll act as the financial advisor and make recommendations based on your knowledge of personal financial planning.

PART I : Meet Michael and Tori Garcia

Life Circumstances: Both age 25, married three years, no children

Financial Challenge: Michael considers going to graduate school

Michael and Tori Garcia were married right after their college graduation. Michael began work as a sales representative for a food distributor, and Tori as an office manager for a local real estate office. Since they had more income than they needed at the time, they never worried much about financial planning.

Over the past year, Michael has become increasingly unhappy with his job and, after talking it over with Tori, decided that it might be an opportune time to quit work and go back to school for a masters in business administration (MBA). The Garcias recognize that, after completion of a two-year masters program at the state university, Michael will have significantly better career prospects and salary potential. However, they also realize that this decision will require some major changes in their household finances, so they've made an appointment with you, their financial advisor, to help them analyze their current finances, set goals, and establish a workable budget for the next couple of years. Since it's now December and school doesn't begin until September, Michael and Tori figure they can work on saving and debt reduction in anticipation of this change in their household circumstances.

In preparation for their visit with you, you've asked the Garcias to make a list of all their assets, debts, income, and expenses. They have provided the following:

Assets		Debts	
Checking account	$1,400	Car loan (Michael)	$7,000
Savings account	6,200	Car loan (Tori)	10,000
Home furnishings	15,000	Student loan (Michael)	7,500
Clothing/personal assets	5,000	Student loan (Tori)	6,000
Mutual fund (stocks)	7,500	VISA balance	3,500
Michael's car	6,500	MasterCard balance	4,200
Tori's car	$12,200	Dillard's credit card	1,200
		Sears credit card	750
		Current bills due	$1,400

Income (Monthly)			
Tori's gross income	$4,000	Interest	10
Michael's gross income	3,000	Dividends	50

Expenses (Monthly)			
Rent	$1,000	Groceries	$600
Utilities (electric, gas, cable)	200	Eating out	600
Credit card minimums	150	Gasoline	240
Student loan (Michael)	90	Uninsured medical	50
Student loan (Tori)	80	Vacations	700
Income tax (federal) withholding	1,050	Clothing	250
Income tax (state) withholding	350	Gifts	100
Social Security payroll tax	535	Telephone/cell phones	120
Health club dues	40	Entertainment	200
Tori's 401(k) retirement plan	160	Automobile insurance	200
Health insurance (withheld from Tori's pay)	$220	Car loan payment (Michael)	180
		Car lease payment (Tori)	$220

1. Use the Garcias' financial information to create a balance sheet and cash flow statement. You can use the balance sheet and cash flow statement worksheets in the *Personal Financial Planner* for this or develop your own. Calculate their net worth and net cash flow.
2. Evaluate the Garcias' liquidity, debt management, and savings using personal financial ratios. What do you conclude about their current situation?
3. At this stage in their lives, what categories of short-term and long-term goals would be appropriate for the Garcias to consider? Explain to them how to break up a larger goal into subgoals using Michael's graduate school goal as an example.
4. Michael has been notified by the state university that he will qualify for a graduate student assistantship that will pay his tuition costs and provide him with $100 per week in income in return for working ten hours per week for a professor.
   a. Based on current patterns of spending, can they afford to have Michael quit work to get his MBA?
   b. Identify some expenditures that could be modified to help the Garcias develop a workable budget for the period of time that Michael is in school.
   c. Over the eight months between now and when Michael expects to start graduate school, what savings and debt reduction strategies would you recommend to the Garcias?
   d. The Garcias currently file taxes jointly and take the standard marital deduction. Are there any ways that the Garcias could save money on their taxes? What tax planning strategies would you recommend for the future?

PFP Worksheet 6
Personal Balance Sheet

Margin PFP Worksheet 7
Personal Cash Flow Statement

DEVELOPING PERSONAL FINANCIAL skills for life

Learning about Yourself

4-1. Refund Psychology

Which would you prefer—paying $100 less in taxes per month or receiving a $1,200 tax refund next year? Talk to at least three of your friends or relatives and ask them this question as well. See if the responses you get are consistent with the explanations offered for tax overpayment in the *Money Psychology* box in this chapter.

Learning about Yourself

4-2. Attitudes Toward Different Types of Cheating

For each of the following, indicate how often you have ever taken the action or would consider doing so in the future (1 = never; 2 = once or twice; 3 = several times):

1. Stealing a candy bar from a convenience store.
2. Switching a price tag in order to buy an item at a cheaper price.
3. Returning an item at a different store than the one you bought it at in order to get a bigger refund.
4. Copying someone else's homework.
5. Changing your answers on an exam after looking at someone else's.

6. Submitting a report or paper that you didn't write yourself.
7. Plagiarizing a portion of someone else's written work.
8. Understating your income to the IRS.
9. Overstating your deductions to the IRS.

Do you have a different attitude toward questions 8 and 9 than you do about the others? Ask several of your friends to answer these questions to see if tax cheating is generally thought of differently than other types of cheating.

Developing Your Skills

4-3. Taking Taxes into Consideration in Deciding Where to Live

Not all states are created equal when it comes to income taxes. Some have relatively high income and sales tax rates, and others have no taxes at all. In some locations, you may have to pay both state income tax and a local income tax. To find out how "taxing" your own state is and how it compares to others, go to www.tax-admin.org, a website sponsored by the Federation of Tax Administrators.

1. Find the state with the lowest income tax rate and the one with the lowest sales tax rate. (In case of a tie, pick one in each category.)
2. Calculate how much you would save per year if you moved from your current state to each of those states. For comparison purposes, assume your annual taxable income is $20,000 and your total purchases subject to sales tax are $10,000.

4-4. Tax Preparation Checklist

Use the checklist at www.taxes.yahoo.com to see if you have all the information necessary to estimate your taxes for next year. Are there any items on this list that you should have started thinking about before you began working on your taxes? How will that impact your tax planning for next year?

4-5. Estimate Your Taxes Owed

Consider your own tax situation for the coming year. Use the worksheet in your *Personal Financial Planner* to prepare your tax information and estimate your taxes owed.

PFP Worksheet 18
Federal Income Tax Estimator

1. What is your filing status?
2. What types of income and in what amounts will you have to declare?
3. Are you entitled to any adjustments to income?
4. Which tax form should you file and why?
5. Do you have sufficient itemized deductions to file a Schedule A? In either case, how much will your deductions be?
6. How many exemptions are you entitled to?
7. Calculate your estimated adjusted gross income and estimated taxable income.
8. Go to the IRS website to find the applicable tax tables and estimate the tax you will owe.
9. Do you anticipate being able to claim any tax credits?
10. If you will actually owe taxes for the year, what could you do now to reduce the amount you owe?

4-6. Evaluate Tax Planning Software

Someday, you may decide that it will be beneficial to purchase tax planning software. In preparation for this, search the Web for tax planning software alternatives. Determine which three are most popular. Enter the information you find on the worksheet provided in your *Personal Financial Planner* to compare the most important features, including, at a minimum, the price and ease of use. Ask friends and family if they use one of the programs and what their experience has been.

PFP Worksheet 19
Comparison of Tax Planning Software

THE NAVIGATOR

- ☐ Review Before Studying this Chapter list.
- ☐ Scan Learning Objectives.
- ☐ Take Myth or Fact quiz and find the answers throughout the chapter.
- ☐ Read chapter and answer Learning by Doing exercises.
- ☐ Review Key Terms and Key Calculations.
- ☐ Do end-of-chapter exercises.
- ☐ Take review quiz on the text website.
- ☐ Solve end-of-chapter cases.

BEFORE studying this chapter, you should review

- The elements of an integrated, comprehensive financial plan (Chapter 1).
- The importance of opportunity costs in financial decision making (Chapter 1).
- Marginal tax rates (Chapter 4).

Cash Management and Financial Institutions

CHAPTER 5

Myth or Fact?

Consider each of the following statements and decide whether it is a *myth* or a *fact*. Look for the answers in the *Fact* boxes in the chapter.

	MYTH	FACT
1. The best way to regularly track my checking account balance is to get a report from an ATM machine.	☐	☐
2. A savings account is a safe place to put my money because it's FDIC insured.	☐	☐
3. Most people aren't eligible to join a credit union.	☐	☐
4. It's always better to have a checking account that pays interest than one that doesn't.	☐	☐
5. You can't buy auto insurance from a bank.	☐	☐

LEARNING objectives

1. Apply the objectives of cash management to assessing your need for cash management products and services.
2. Explain the rules of effective cash management and why it is important to regularly balance your checkbook.
3. Understand the differences among providers of cash management products and services.
4. Identify cash management products and services that are important to your financial plan.
5. Compare cash management account options based on liquidity, safety, costs, and after-tax annual percentage yield (APY).
6. Select appropriate tools for dealing with cash management errors.

...applying the planning process

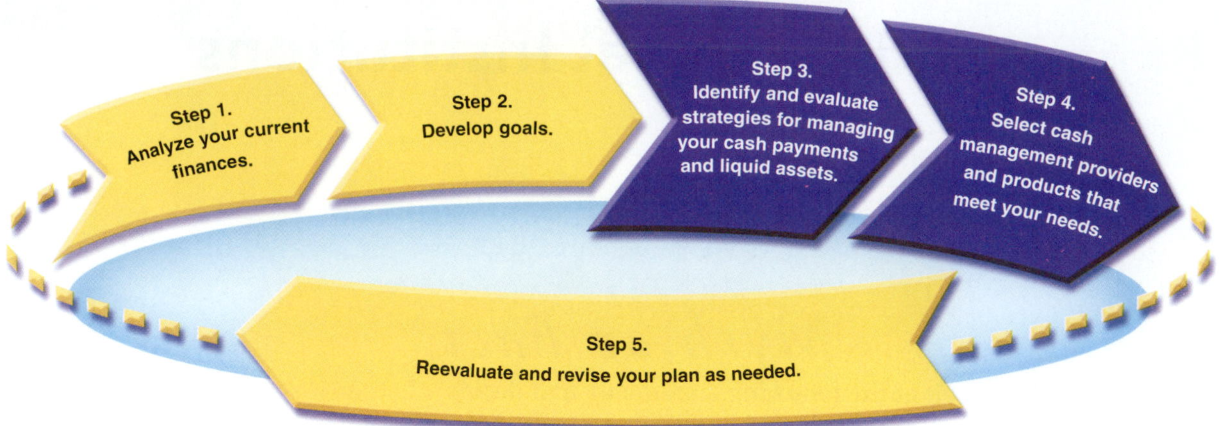

Everyone manages cash. In fact, your very first exposure to personal financial management was probably related to cash management. Perhaps you received a small allowance when you were a child and had to decide how to spend or save the money. You may have even had a savings account at your local bank where you were encouraged to "save for college" or another long-term goal. You didn't know it at the time, but you were on your way to developing many of the money habits that you use regularly today.

As you know, having access to cash to meet transaction needs and emergencies is an essential component of your financial plan. We now look more closely at these objectives and introduce methods you can use to manage your cash effectively. As with other components of your plan, it's important to begin by identifying alternative strategies for cash management. Once you have evaluated which ones best meet your needs, you can then take steps to implement your plan.

A central part of your cash management strategies will involve choosing cash management services—checking accounts, savings accounts, and so forth. Because there are so many providers of cash management services to choose from, each offering a multitude of products, it's easy to become a little overwhelmed. This chapter will help you to identify the types of companies and products that are available and the methods you can use to evaluate these cash management alternatives. We begin by identifying the objectives of cash management and the rules to follow in managing cash.

Chapter Preview

The Objectives of Cash Management	Rules of Effective Cash Management	Providers of Cash Management Services	Cash Management Products and Services	Resolving Cash Management Problems
• Managing Monthly Transactions • Preparing for Emergencies • Making Temporary Investments • How Much Should You Hold in Cash?	• Balance Your Checkbook Every Month • Pay Your Bills on Time • Pay Yourself First • Evaluate Alternative Accounts and Providers	• Depository Institutions • Nondepository Institutions • Evaluating Financial Institutions	• Checking Accounts • Short-term Savings Accounts • Savings Alternatives • Other Cash Management Products and Services • Evaluating Cash Management Account Choices	• If You Bounce a Check... • If You Receive a Bad Check... • If You Discover Fraudulent Activity on Your Account... • If You Want to Stop Payment on a Check... • If You Need Money in a Hurry . . .

The Objectives of Cash Management

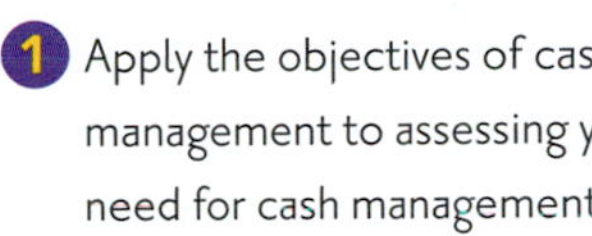

1 Apply the objectives of cash management to assessing your need for cash management products and services.

cash management

Management of cash payments and liquid investments.

Many people are guilty of occasionally, or not so occasionally, neglecting to balance their checkbook or making a bill payment after the due date. Keeping track of your cash and paying your bills are both important, although not necessarily enjoyable, tasks associated with **cash management**, a foundation component of your financial plan. Cash management includes all your decisions related to cash payments and short-term liquid investments. As discussed in Chapter 2, liquid investments are those that can easily be converted to cash without loss of value, such as a checking or savings account. Although you can of course leave money in these accounts for longer periods, they are not generally the best choice for long-term savings, so we can also think of cash management as decisions related to investments of one year or less in duration.

When you hold cash, whether it's in your pocket or in a bank checking or savings account, you incur certain costs. For one, you give up the opportunity to invest those dollars in a way that will earn you a higher rate of return. In fact, you may even *pay* for the privilege of holding money in certain types of accounts. Most people hold some of their money in a checking account. In some cases, this account might pay a small amount of interest, but in most cases, it will not. The lost interest is an important consideration: For example, if you carry an average balance of $1,000 in your checking account for a year, and you could instead have invested it to earn 10 percent interest, you've given up about $100 in interest (10% of $1,000).

An additional cost of holding cash is psychological—if you have money sitting in your checking account, you can spend it very easily. It would be a shame if all your hard work in developing your budget went to waste because you couldn't resist the temptation of writing a check for an expensive item you hadn't planned to buy. In contrast, if you keep your cash in an account that's not as easily accessible, such as a savings account, you'll be more likely to stick to your plan.

Cash accounts, then, pay less interest and increase the risk of overspending. Why are we willing to incur these costs? There are three general reasons for holding cash:

- Managing transaction needs
- Preparing for cash emergencies
- Making a temporary investment

All these purposes are related to managing liquidity. Money held in less liquid investments, such as bonds, stocks, and real estate, provides a better investment return than money held in checking and saving accounts but it's also more difficult to access on short notice. Next, we look in more detail at each of the reasons for holding cash.

Managing Monthly Transactions

Everyone has bills. Rent, food, utilities, car payments, and other expenses must be paid as they come due. To pay your bills easily, you need to have sufficient cash in a transaction account. A transaction account, commonly called a checking account, is an account that allows you to regularly make deposits, write checks, withdraw funds, or make electronic payments in a timely fashion and at minimal cost.

Many people find it convenient to deposit their paycheck each month into a checking account and then to pay their bills from that account. As already noted, there's a cost to using this banking service in the form of lost interest earnings. So why not have your paycheck deposited in a savings account instead? Although it's usually fairly easy to make transfers between accounts, the time and effort required to make multiple transfers each month as bills come due would probably outweigh the minimal interest that could be earned. Since the money is coming in and then promptly going out, the actual amount of time that it will earn interest is likely to be relatively short, and the interest you earn may not be enough to justify the time spent shifting money between accounts. However, if your paycheck is normally *greater* than the total monthly payments you make from the account, then it makes sense to carefully estimate your transaction needs and to have the extra amount automatically transferred to an interest-earning account each month.

Preparing for Cash Emergencies

cash reserve
Liquid assets held to meet emergency cash needs.

Life is full of unpredictable events. Maybe the car needs a new $2,000 transmission. Or your son breaks his arm playing football and you have to pay $400 in doctors' bills. More serious emergencies might involve the loss of a job or temporary disability. In order to meet your emergency cash needs, it's important to manage your financial assets so that you can access cash when needed. For most households, this should include a **cash reserve**—an accumulation of liquid assets that you can turn to in the event of an emergency. In your grandparents' day, a family might have had a few hundred dollars hidden in the bottom of a cookie jar or under a mattress for this purpose. Today, there are many other options for emergency cash flow needs. In addition to traditional checking and savings accounts, you can arrange for credit cards and home equity lines of credit that can be accessed in the event of an emergency but that otherwise incur no interest. In the next chapter, you'll see that you should avoid using credit cards as much as possible because of their high interest costs. However, it's worth noting here that they can be a source of short-term liquidity as long as you anticipate having the funds to repay the borrowed amounts in the future.

Do you have a large enough cash reserve to fix the car?

Making a Temporary Investment

The third reason you might hold cash is in anticipation of a near-term need for the funds. Perhaps you're saving for a vacation or a new car. Maybe you're planning to apply the funds to the purchase of a new home. Or you may have sold some other assets recently and haven't yet decided how to reinvest the funds. During the recent ups and downs in the stock market, many investors used cash accounts to temporarily store funds as they bought and sold stocks.

How Much Should You Hold in Cash?

There's considerable debate among financial experts on how much money a typical household should hold in cash. Very conservative advice suggests that you should have enough liquid assets to cover five to eight months of regular expenses. Others suggest that two months is more than enough and recommend investing the rest for higher returns. For an average household with expenses of $2,000 per month, these rules of thumb would imply that from $4,000 to $16,000 should be held in cash or liquid assets. Even if we split the difference between the two positions and hold $10,000 in liquid assets, the risk of cash shortfall in the event of a big shock to household income will be greatly reduced. But the cost can also be significant.

Just how much would it cost you to be so "safe"? Suppose, for example, that you keep $4,000 in a checking account earning 0 percent interest and $6,000 in a short-term savings account earning 2 percent interest per year. Let's assume also that your alternative to holding cash would be an investment you expect to earn 8 percent per year. The opportunity cost of holding this much in cash is the average annual amount in cash multiplied by the difference between the interest you could earn on an alternative investment and the interest you earn on the cash account. In this case, the annual lost interest earnings are substantial—$680 per year, or ($4,000 × 0.08) + ($6,000 × 0.06). The lost interest earnings may, however, be more than made up for by the reduction in risk. As you will learn in a later chapter, investments that provide higher potential earnings also expose you to the risk of losing some of your money. Since the purpose of holding cash is to meet short-term needs, you may not be willing or able to take that risk.

As part of your personal financial plan, you should assess your cash needs for transactions and emergencies, taking into consideration alternative sources you can tap into in the event of an emergency. Exhibit 5-1, which is also available in the *Personal Financial Planner*, provides a sample worksheet you can use for this purpose. If you have a high risk of job loss, you might consider holding a conservatively large amount in cash. In contrast, if you have a secure job and alternative sources of funds for emergencies, then you might hold only enough to meet your transaction requirements.

PFP Worksheet 20
Cash Needs Analysis

EXHIBIT 5-1

Cash Needs Analysis Worksheet

Steps

1. What are your cash management needs?
2. How are you currently meeting those needs?
3. What alternatives should you consider and what services do you still need?

Step 1: Cash Management Needs

a. My liquid assets are sufficient to cover ____ times my monthly expenses.
b. Based on my current balance sheet and cash flow statement, my liquidity ratio is ____.
c. My short-term cash management goals include:

____
____
____

Step 2: Current Strategies / Step 3: Other Alternatives

Type of Service	Financial Institution(s)	Interest	Type of Service Needed
Transaction Needs	____	____	____
Regular or interest-earning checking, debit cards, money orders	____	____	____
Savings Accounts			
Regular savings, CDs, money market accounts, money market mutual funds, U.S. savings bonds	____	____	____
Borrowing			
Credit cards, overdraft protection, car and personal loans, home mortgages	____	____	____
Other Services			
Special checks, online banking, electronic payments, investment and financial services	____	____	____

Learning by Doing 5-1

1. Hanna is a college student who is working to pay for her own education. She has no savings and usually has no money left at the end of each pay period. She recently received an inheritance of $5,000. Explain to Hanna why it might be a good idea for her to set aside some of that money in a cash account rather than use all of it for a down payment on a car.

Rules of Effective Cash Management

LEARNING objective

2 Explain the rules of effective cash management and why it is important to regularly balance your checkbook.

We've seen that most people need to hold cash for transaction needs, cash emergencies, and temporary investments. Cash management is thus an important part of your financial plan. Effective cash management will minimize the risk of bank charges for overdrafts and extra interest or penalties on overdue payments. Keeping careful track of cash flow is also necessary for budgeting expenditures so that you can achieve financial goals. In this section, we consider four rules that, if followed, will result in better cash management outcomes:

1. Keep track of your cash by balancing your checkbook every month.
2. Develop a system to ensure that you pay your bills on time.
3. Stick to your financial plan by paying yourself first.
4. Use sound criteria to evaluate financial institutions and select products or services.

Balance Your Checkbook Every Month

Regularly balancing your checkbook is important for several reasons. With the use of checks, debit cards, and automated teller machines (ATMs), it's very easy to lose track of how much you spend every month, particularly in a household where more than one person is using the same account for transactions. If you don't balance your checkbook regularly, you're more likely to exceed your budget or, worse yet, bounce checks.

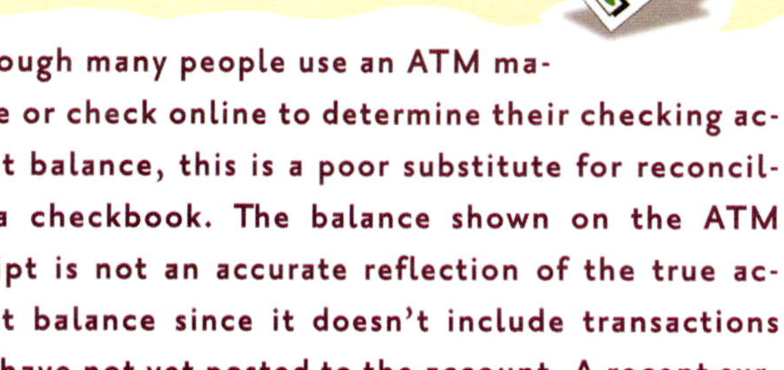

Although many people use an ATM machine or check online to determine their checking account balance, this is a poor substitute for reconciling a checkbook. The balance shown on the ATM receipt is not an accurate reflection of the true account balance since it doesn't include transactions that have not yet posted to the account. A recent survey showed that even though most people know that balancing their checkbook is important, a large proportion fail to do so on a regular basis.

Balancing your checkbook can be a daunting bookkeeping task if you write lots of checks each month and particularly if you aren't careful about entering other withdrawals and deposits over the course of the month. But the benefits to your personal finances far outweigh the costs.

The *Go Figure!* box, "How to Reconcile a Checkbook with a Bank Statement," provides a worksheet that outlines the process for balancing a checkbook and an example to illustrate the steps that you should take each month. A blank copy of this worksheet is provided in your *Personal Financial Planner*. The objective is to reconcile the balance reported by the bank on the statement—in Danny's case, \$217.60—with the \$246.79 balance recorded in the checkbook register. To do this, you need to first adjust the bank balance for any additional checks and deposits that aren't reflected on the statement. Then you need to adjust your checkbook register to reflect checks and deposit transactions that aren't yet recorded, as well as any bank charges or interest. If there's still a discrepancy between the checkbook balance and the bank statement balance after making these adjustments, then you should:

PFP Worksheet 21
Reconciling a Checkbook

- Go over the withdrawals and deposits again to be sure you haven't missed any.
- Check your addition and subtraction again.

With computerized account records, it is highly unlikely that a bank statement will contain a mathematical error. There is, however, the possibility of errors in automatic withdrawals or ATM transactions. In rare cases, you may even find that someone has fraudulently accessed your account. It's important that you discover any such problems promptly, because delay in discovering and reporting an incident of abuse or error makes it more difficult to get the problem corrected. The last section in this chapter discusses this and several other cash management problems and offers some methods for dealing with them.

Pay Your Bills on Time

Timely payment of bills will not only reduce your costs, but also minimize the risk that your credit rating will be adversely affected. As will be discussed in more detail in the next chapter, a history of late payments will make you a less attractive credit risk to financial institutions. As a result, you may not be able to qualify for loans, you may have to pay higher rates of interest, and you may have increased insurance premiums. By paying your bills on time, you'll also avoid getting annoying phone calls from your creditors.

GO FIGURE!

How to Reconcile a Checkbook with a Bank Statement

Problem: Danny just received his bank statement, dated February 11, 2005. The statement gives his checking account balance as $217.60. Based on his checkbook register, Danny thinks that the balance should be $246.79. Use the worksheet below to help him balance his checkbook. The applicable segment of his checkbook register is reproduced below:

Check #	Date	Description	Debit	Credit	Balance
					452.37
450	1/16/2005	Safeway	62.49		389.88
451	1/20/2005	Einstein's Bagels	8.47		381.41
452	1/21/2005	Best Buy	26.78		354.63
453	1/27/2005	Safeway	75.26		279.37
	1/30/2005	Deposit-Paycheck		134.75	414.12
454	1/30/2005	Ticketmaster	54.00		360.12
456	2/5/2005	Safeway	52.60		307.52
457	2/12/2005	Safeway	47.89		259.63
458	2/16/2005	Subway	12.84		246.79

Solution: After the bank statement is adjusted for two checks (#457 and #458) written since the closing date of the statement, the bank balance is $156.87. Danny has not made any new deposits in the last week. He adjusts his checkbook register by subtracting an ATM withdrawal in the amount of $60 and the associated $1.50 fee, both of which he had neglected to enter in his checkbook register. This gives an adjusted checkbook register of $185.29. Since that amount is not the same as the adjusted bank statement, Danny looks more carefully at the recorded checks on his statement and finds that he has neglected to enter check #455 in the amount of $28.42. He recalls that this probably occurred because he took a check out of his checkbook rather than carrying it on the day he played intramural football with his friends.

Part 1: Adjusting the Bank Statement

	Amount ($)	
1. Enter balance on current bank statement.	217.60	
2. Add total new deposits. (Include all deposits made that do not appear on bank statement.)	0	
3. Subtract total outstanding checks. (Include all checks written that do not appear on bank statement.)	60.73	(Check #457, #458)
Adjusted bank balance	156.87	

Part 2: Adjusting Your Check Register

	Amount ($)	
1. Enter balance from your check register.	246.79	
2. Add automatic and ATM deposit not yet recorded.	0	
3. Subtract automatic and ATM withdrawals not yet recorded.	60.00	(Forgot to enter.)
4. Subtract bank charges. (Monthly fees, minimum balance fees, ATM fees)	1.50	
5. Add interest earned.	0	
Adjusted checkbook register	185.29	(Doesn't match adjusted bank balance!)

Part 3: Reconcile Bank Statement and Check Register

The adjusted bank balance and the adjusted checkbook register should be equal. If not, then one or more of the following is true:

a. You made a math error.
b. You didn't balance your checkbook last month.
c. You neglected to enter one or more transactions.
d. Your bank made an error. — 28.42 (Forgot to enter.)

156.87

Pay Yourself First

The single most common advice given by financial planners to their clients is "Pay yourself first." What this means is that you should set aside the money necessary for achieving personal goals *before* you do anything else. If you wait until the end of the month to see how much is left to put into savings, inevitably there will be none left. If, instead, you treat savings as a primary expenditure and take it off the top before paying any other expenses, you are more likely to stick to your financial plan and avoid casual erosion of your cash flow.

There are many convenient ways to pay yourself first. Most banks and financial institutions offer the option of automatic funds transfer by which you arrange with your bank to have a certain amount of money automatically transferred from your checking to your savings or investment account as soon as your paycheck is deposited each pay period. Another useful tool is automatic bill paying, which can be done in various ways. Not only can you arrange directly with your creditor or service provider for automatic payments each month, but you can also consider taking advantage of online bill-paying services that will electronically pay all your regular bills each month. This can be particularly helpful for busy individuals who have trouble paying bills on time.

How much should you pay yourself first? In Chapter 3, you learned how to forecast your income and expenses to determine how much you have left over each month. This is the amount that you should set aside at the beginning of the month or apply to meeting your financial goals.

Evaluate Alternative Accounts and Providers

Effective cash management requires that you carefully evaluate your alternatives and select the services and service providers that best meet your needs. You have many providers and services to choose from, and they vary widely in a number of ways: interest paid on similar accounts; fees charged for particular services; safety; and customer service. In the remaining sections of this chapter, we'll look more closely at the types of financial institutions you can choose from and the variety of cash management products and services they offer.

Learning by Doing 5-2

1. For each of the rules of cash management discussed in this section, identify a potential cost that you could incur by not following the rule.
2. Under what circumstances might it be worthwhile to pay a monthly fee for a bill-paying service?

Providers of Cash Management Services

LEARNING objective

3 Understand the differences among providers of cash management products and services.

At one time, cash management services could be obtained only at certain types of financial institutions. Today, however, many different types of financial institutions provide such services. This is the result of legislation introduced over the last two decades to foster competition among these institutions. The good news *and* the bad news is that you now have many choices for your cash management services. It's good news because competition often results in higher interest paid on accounts and lower interest charged on loans. It's bad news because having more choices means that it will take more time and effort to investigate your alternatives thoroughly.

The various types of financial institutions are identified and distinguished by their general characteristics, which are discussed below, but it's important to recognize that these differences are, for the most part, small and they are becoming less important over time. In general, financial institutions are classified according to where they primarily get their funds, or money to invest, and what they primarily invest in. Some institutions—such as commercial banks, savings institutions, and credit unions—get their funds from customer deposits; they are called **depository institutions**. Others—such as insurance companies, mortgage companies, and finance companies—get funds from other sources; they are called nondepository institutions.

depository institutions

Financial institutions that obtain funds from customer deposits.

Depository Institutions

As just noted, depository institutions include commercial banks, several types of savings institutions, and credit unions. All these types of firms are similar in two major ways:

- Their primary source of funds comes from customer deposits.
- Their primary source of income is interest earned on loans.

Commercial Banks. Often simply called a "bank," a **commercial bank** is a depository institution that gets its funds from checking and savings account deposits and uses the money to provide a wide array of financial services, including business and personal loans, mortgages, and credit cards. Personal accounts held in commercial banks are insured for up to $100,000 per depositor by the **Federal Deposit Insurance Corporation (FDIC)**, a government-sponsored insurance agency. A common misconception is that this insurance covers *accounts* up to $100,000, but in fact, the guarantee is for $100,000 per *depositor* in a single institution. Therefore, a good rule of thumb is to keep no more than $100,000 at any institution or to keep it in two different names (e.g., your name and your spouse's name).

commercial bank

A depository institution offering a wide variety of cash management services to business and individual customers.

Federal Deposit Insurance Corporation (FDIC)

A government-sponsored agency that insures customer accounts in banks and savings institutions.

Fact #2

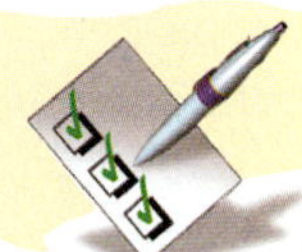

Although most checking, savings, and CD accounts in depository institutions are insured by the FDIC or a comparable federal agency, and thus are very safe places to put your money, checking and savings accounts offered by mutual funds, brokerage firms, and insurance companies are not insured. So, even if an uninsured account pays a little higher interest, it might not be worth the risk.

Savings Institutions. There are a number of types of savings institutions, including **savings and loan associations (S&Ls)**, thrift institutions, and savings banks. All these were originally designed to give individuals access to banking services that had previously only been available (through commercial banks) to business customers. For this reason, savings institutions were at first limited to offering savings accounts and making home and personal loans to individuals. More recently, however, savings institutions have been able to offer a more competitive selection of checking and savings accounts; they can even offer credit cards, business loans, and financial planning services. However, they still are primarily home mortgage lenders. In fact, S&Ls are required to use at least 70 percent of their money to make home mortgage loans, as opposed to other types of loans. As with commercial banks, accounts in these institutions are insured for up to $100,000 per depositor.

Although the various types of savings institutions are likely to offer similar products and services, one distinction among them is their form of ownership. A **mutual savings institution** is one that is owned by its depositors. A **stock-held savings institution** is owned by stockholders. If you have an account in a mutual savings institution, even though the rates of return will be competitive, the earnings you receive on your investments will be called "dividends" rather than "interest." If the mutual is very profitable in a given year, you'll receive a higher dividend that year, since the dividend is the way the company passes on the profits to its owner-depositors.

savings and loan association (S&L)

A depository institution that receives funds primarily from household deposits and uses most of its funds to make home mortgage loans.

mutual savings institution

A savings institution owned by its depositors.

stock-held savings institution

A savings institution owned by stockholders.

Credit Unions. A **credit union** is a special form of mutual depository institution. It gets its funds from checking and savings deposits and makes loans to its depositors, who are also the owners of the institution. An important distinction between credit unions and other depository institutions is that credit unions have non-profit status and often make use of a partially volunteer labor force, allowing them a low-cost advantage over other institutions. Their reduced costs of operation often mean that credit unions can offer lower loan rates and higher interest on deposits than other institutions. Depositors in credit unions are insured for up to $100,000 by the National Credit Union Association, which operates the National Credit Union Share Insurance Fund (NCUSIF). The *Ask the Expert* box "Credit Unions! A Good Choice for Students" offers some good advice for students.

Credit unions were originally designed to give individuals access to personal credit, which was not widely available at commercial banks and savings institutions. At that time, credit union members were supposed to have a common bond, such as a religious or employment affiliation.

credit union

A nonprofit depository institution owned by its depositors.

If you'd like to locate a credit union near you, the Credit Union National Association website at www.cuna.org includes a list of its members and where they are located.

ask the expert Credit Unions! A Good Choice for Students

Dr. John Olienyk, Chairman of the Board
Norlarco Credit Union

The following is a summary of an interview with Dr. John Olienyk, Chairman of the Board of the Norlarco Credit Union. Olienyk is also a frequent speaker at national credit union organization meetings.

What is the common bond among Norlarco members?
To become a member of the Norlarco Credit Union, you must work for one of several employers in the area or live or work in one of several local communities. In other words, just about anyone in the area can qualify.

Has Norlarco been able to compete effectively with larger financial institutions?
Yes. Through continued commitment to the local community and by offering competitive rates and services, Norlarco has managed to grow substantially over the last twenty years. In fact, it's now one of the largest financial institutions in Northern Colorado. We're not alone in this either—in the last twenty years, the number of credit union members in the U.S. has nearly doubled to more than 80 million with $500 billion in total savings.

Should students consider using a credit union instead of a bank or S&L?
Yes, students who are looking for a financial institution to meet their transaction and savings needs while they go to school should seriously consider a local credit union. There are usually several to choose from in any metropolitan area. In our case, we actually try to attract students by offering them special low-cost checking and savings account options, such as our RAM e-style checking that has no minimum balance or fees as long as students only access their accounts electronically. We also offer competitive rates on savings accounts, credit cards, and auto loans.

Fact #3

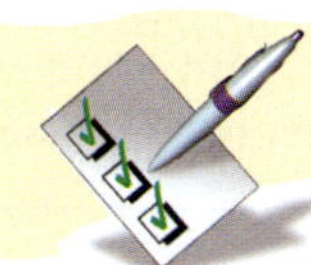

Many credit unions are not very restrictive on membership. This is great news since credit unions can often beat the rates offered by other financial institutions because they pass on their profits to their owner-customers. This means that the rates paid on savings will be higher and the rates charged on auto loans will be lower.

For example, the federal government has a credit union for government employees and their families. Similarly, most states have a credit union for public employees. The common bond requirement, particularly for smaller employers or organizations, necessarily limited the size of these institutions and the variety of services they were able to provide. Today, however, the common bond requirement is defined fairly loosely. For example, some credit unions limit membership to people who live in a particular town or area. As a result, credit unions can now be just as large as competing banks and offer a similar selection of products and services, including credit cards and mortgage loans.

Web-Only Financial Institutions. A relatively new phenomenon in financial institutions is the increasing number of Web-only financial institutions. These are financial institutions that have no physical location but offer a menu of cash management accounts, loans, and investments. Presumably, web-only firms might have a cost advantage over traditional depository institutions, but consumers seeking higher interest and lower loan rates are cautioned to check out an institution's credentials before sending money to it. At the FDIC website, you can find out whether the bank is legitimate and whether it is insured.

For more information about online banking, you can visit one of several government regulator websites: www.fdic.gov (FDIC); www.occ.treas.gov (Office of the Comptroller of the Currency); and www.ots.treas.gov (Office of Thrift Supervision). If you have visited a bank website that appears to be fraudulent, you can report it at the FDIC website.

Nondepository Institutions

Nondepository institutions include mutual fund companies, life insurance companies, brokerage firms, and other financial services firms. Although such institutions have always offered loans in competition with banks, savings institutions, and credit unions, only more recently have they begun to provide cash management services. Nondepository institutions now compete with other types of institutions for their primary customers by offering a full range of products and services. For the consumer, this means more choices and potentially lower prices. Notably, however, none of the accounts offered by these firms are federally insured.

Mutual Fund Companies. A **mutual fund** is an investment company that sells shares to investors and then invests the pool of funds in a selection of financial securities. Some mutual fund companies have low-risk mutual fund investment account options that also allow limited check writing. As noted, these accounts are not federally insured. Mutual funds will be discussed in much more detail in Chapter 14.

mutual fund

A nondepository financial institution that sells shares to investors and then invests the money in financial assets.

Life Insurance Companies. A **life insurance company** sells products, called life insurance policies, intended to provide financial security for dependents in the event of the death of the policy owner. Its primary source of funds is therefore the payments made to purchase the policies, usually called the policy premiums. These companies invest the collected premiums in stocks, bonds, and other financial assets. Many life insurance products include savings and investment features and thus can be considered an alternative to other savings accounts. In addition, life insurers are active lenders in the home mortgage market.

life insurance company

A nondepository financial institution that obtains funds from premiums paid for life insurance, invests in stocks and bonds, and makes mortgage loans.

Brokerage Firms. A **brokerage firm** is a company that facilitates investors' purchases of stocks, bonds, and other investments. An investor generally keeps money in an account with a brokerage firm and authorizes an employee of the firm, called a broker, to take money out of the account to pay for new purchases for the investor and to deposit money received from sales of the investor's securities. The brokerage firm usually makes its money by charging a commission for each purchase and sale. Today, more banks are competing for the brokerage business; in turn, traditional brokerage firms are offering a variety of cash management services and products.

brokerage firm

A nondepository financial institution that helps its customers to buy and sell financial securities.

Financial Services Firms. Recently, many financial institutions that had previously fit into one category or another have been trying to redefine themselves as multiservice financial institutions in an attempt to provide one-stop shopping for their customers and to take advantage of their existing market penetration. For example, State Farm Insurance, previously a large insurance company, has added mutual funds and cash management products to its offerings. Other examples of this trend include Merrill Lynch, formerly a brokerage firm and investment bank, and Citigroup, formerly a commercial bank. All these firms offer a fairly complete menu of checking and savings accounts, insurance products, consumer and mortgage loans, and mutual fund investments.

Evaluating Financial Institutions

With so many different financial institutions to choose from, how should you decide which to use? This decision should be based on how each financial service provider rates based on the "Four P's":

- Products
- Price
- People
- Place

Products. The ideal financial institution will provide you with all the products you need to manage your cash effectively. These products include not only checking and savings accounts but also many others, which you'll read about later in this chapter. In choosing among financial service providers, it's a good idea to begin with a list of the products and services you'd like to have. You'll want to find out which institutions offer the greatest number of products and services you want, and you'll also want to compare the products and services qualitatively. For example, a savings account offered by a federally insured depository institution is obviously less risky than one offered by an uninsured financial institution. A bank near your workplace may at first seem like a good choice, but you might find that the bank is so understaffed over the lunch hour that you would have to wait on line for thirty minutes just to get to a teller. As with most decisions, you may not come up with a clear-cut answer—you'll have to weigh a variety of pluses and minuses for each financial institution.

Price. Price includes both the interest you earn on liquid asset accounts and the fees you pay for cash management services. Whereas many financial institutions offer similar selections of products, the pricing of these products may vary dramatically.

Interest rates on demand savings accounts—that is, accounts that allow you to withdraw your funds at any time "on demand"—are usually much lower than those for other types of saving. For example, the average rate on demand savings was only 1.13 percent in March 2004, whereas rates on five-year certificates of deposit, which require that you leave your money on deposit for the full five years, at that time were averaging 3.52 percent.

Financial institutions also differ substantially in the fees they charge for various services. For example, some require that you maintain a minimum balance in your checking account, and others don't. It's fairly common for accounts to be subject to a monthly fee if the balance drops below a stated minimum, which might be $100 or $1,000. Bounced check fees can range from $10 to $50.

People. The level of customer service, although somewhat less important today than it once was because of the widespread use of electronic transactions, should still be an important factor in your decision. If you need to transact business in person, you should consider whether the main office and drive-up tellers are open during times that are convenient to your schedule. Are the lines long? When you call with questions, do you get to speak to a knowledgeable person? Are your phone calls returned promptly and courteously?

In some instances, you may be choosing between smaller locally owned institutions that focus on relationship banking and larger multistate institutions that offer more services. This decision should be made based on your unique needs and preferences. You may be willing to live with a smaller selection of products in return for the more personal touch offered by a local institution. If there are substantial differences in costs, of course, these should also be weighed.

Place. Finally, consider the location of the institution. Where are the ATMs located? Where is the main office? In deciding between a nearby institution and one that is farther away but offers a slightly better interest rate or lower costs, remember to consider whether the cost advantage will outweigh the inconvenience of traveling the greater distance when you need to visit the institution in person.

You can choose the best cash management provider for you by applying the decision-making tools from Chapter 1. After deciding what features you consider most beneficial, collect information from several financial institutions and see how they stack up against one another. Keep in mind that although you're by no means limited to using only one financial institution for all your banking needs, it is sometimes more cost-effective to do so. Not only do you save time through one-stop shopping, but you may be entitled, as a depositor, to receive better consumer and home loan rates.

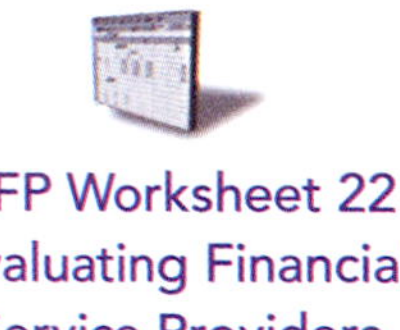

PFP Worksheet 22 Evaluating Financial Service Providers

An easy way to summarize the information you gather about each financial institution is to create a comparison worksheet such as the one shown in Exhibit 5-2, which compares three hypothetical financial institutions in a decision grid format. A blank sample of this worksheet is included in your *Personal Financial Planner.* In completing your worksheet, compare the features and services that are most important to you.

Learning by Doing 5-3

1. Zelda has just moved to a new state and needs to open a checking account. Which types of financial institutions would you recommend that she call for information?
2. Luis, a student at a large public university, opened his checking account at the largest bank in town because it offered free checking to students. He is planning to buy a car and will need a car loan. Explain to him why he might be able to get a lower interest rate at the university credit union. What other factors should he consider?

EXHIBIT 5-2

Evaluating Financial Service Providers

Directions:

Set up a grid for evaluating important features of financial institutions. Comparisons can be based on desired features, as in the product comparison below; specific numerical comparisons, as in the price comparison; or subjectively assigned grades for more qualitative features, such as customer service. A blank version of this worksheet appears in your *Personal Financial Planner.*

PRODUCTS: Does the financial institution offer the selection of products you need? Do the products have the features you need?
PRICE: Are the financial products competitively priced?
PEOPLE: Does the financial institution provide the desired level of customer service?
PLACE: Is the financial institution located conveniently for your needs?

	Financial Institution #1	Financial Institution #2	Financial Institution #3
PRODUCTS			
Free checking	√	√	
Unlimited checks	√	√	
Online account review	√	√	√
Bill-paying service		√	√
Debit card	√	√	√
Overdraft protection	√	√	√
IRAs		√	√
Home equity loans		√	√
PRICE			
Checking account fees	0	0	$5/month
Checking account interest	0	0	1.5 percent
Fee for using other ATM	$1.50	$1.00	$2.50
Savings account interest	1.5%	1.25%	1.75%
PEOPLE			
Prompt/courteous service	A−	A+	B+
Knowledgeable staff	B+	A	A−
PLACE			
Convenient	√	√−	√
Sufficient free ATMs	10	5	15
Online presence	√	√	√

Cash Management Products and Services

LEARNING objective

4 Identify cash management products and services that are important to your financial plan.

Financial institutions provide cash management services that include checking and savings accounts, loans, and asset management services. Each of these services may play an important role in your financial plan, so you need to understand the options that are available to you, as well as the costs and benefits of various features.

Checking Accounts

As noted earlier in this chapter, one of the reasons for holding cash is to manage transaction needs. These needs will probably be best met with a checking account. Checking accounts allow you to make deposits and pay bills easily. Before opening an account, you should find out the following about any checking account you are considering:

- Will you earn interest on your balance? If so, at what rate?
- Will you be required to keep a minimum balance in the account? If so, how much is it, and what is the penalty for going below that minimum?

- Is there a monthly fee? If so, how much?
- Can you access the account with a debit card (a card that enables you to withdraw money electronically from your account, as described later in the chapter)?
- Does the account offer overdraft protection?
- Are there any other fees?

demand deposits

Deposit accounts, such as checking accounts, from which money can be withdrawn with little or no notice to the financial institution.

All checking accounts are **demand deposits** in that you have the right to "demand" withdrawal of your deposited funds with little or no notice to the financial institution. For the purposes of cash management, the most important distinction between types of checking accounts is whether or not they pay interest. Exhibit 5-3 summarizes the advantages and disadvantages of different types of checking accounts.

regular checking account

Checking account that does not pay interest and requires the payment of a monthly service charge unless a minimum balance is maintained in the account.

Regular Checking Accounts. Although your particular bank or savings institution may call it something different, such as "basic checking," the key feature of a **regular checking account** is that it pays no interest. In some cases, a bank may advertise these accounts as "free checking," since the bank will waive the monthly service charge if you keep a minimum balance in the account—anywhere from $100 to $1,000, or more, depending on the institution. Not all regular checking accounts require a minimum balance, however. These accounts usually also limit the number of checks you can write each month and are unlikely to offer additional services, such as debit cards, without assessing an additional fee.

Many financial institutions offer "no frills" free checking accounts. These are often a good choice for students.

Because of the generally low account balances and the high cost of processing transactions and maintaining records, financial institutions make very little money on regular checking accounts. Instead, institutions rely on this type of account to entice people to use other services they offer—services on which they can make more profit. In university towns, financial institutions often compete actively for student accounts, offering regular checking options with low minimum balance requirements and no monthly service charges. If available, such accounts may be good choices for students who do not need accounts that provide more "bells and whistles."

Interest-Earning Checking Accounts. We've seen that regular checking accounts offer minimal services. As an alternative, you may want to consider whether a checking account that pays interest and includes other features, such as debit cards and unlimited check writing, might better meet your needs. Such accounts usually have higher minimum balance requirements than regular checking accounts. If your balance falls below the minimum, your interest rate on the account will be reduced or, in some cases, eliminated, and you may have to pay a fee—typically $3 to $7 per month. A checking account that pays interest is technically called a **negotiated order of withdrawal (NOW) account**, but few banks and savings institutions use this terminology. Your bank may call it "Gold Plus Checking" or "First Checking" or some other name that sounds attractive.

negotiated order of withdrawal (NOW) account

A type of checking account that pays interest.

In addition to paying interest, NOW accounts may include other services that you would otherwise have to pay for. For example, most financial institutions no longer include copies of written checks with monthly checking account statements sent to customers, but this service may be available with NOW accounts.

If you plan to hold cash reserves in a checking account and will therefore be able to meet the minimum balance requirement, an interest-earning checking account is certainly a better choice than a regular checking account. However, since these accounts generally pay lower interest than savings account alternatives, you should consider the opportunity costs involved in keeping your cash reserves in checking rather than transferring them to a higher-interest savings alternative. Recall that the opportunity cost of a particular action is what you have to give up to take that action. The *Go Figure!* box, "Estimating Opportunity Costs for Cash Management Options," walks you through this decision process.

Savings Accounts

Whereas checking accounts vary in whether they pay interest, all savings accounts pay interest. The rate of interest depends on the type of account. Savings accounts can be classified as either demand deposit accounts or time deposit accounts.

EXHIBIT 5-3

Advantages and Disadvantages of Checking Alternatives

Type of Account	Advantages	Disadvantages
Regular checking	• Highly liquid. • If offered by bank or savings institution, insured by FDIC. • No monthly fee if minimum monthly balance maintained.	• No interest paid on balances. • May limit number of checks that may be written per month. • May impose higher fees for various services, including stop payments, fund transfer, certified checks, debit cards.
Interest-earning checking	• Interest paid on balance. • Highly liquid. • May include other services, such as debit cards, certified checks, fund transfer. • If offered by bank or savings institution, insured by FDIC. • No monthly fee if minimum monthly balance maintained.	• Interest may be reduced or eliminated if account drops below minimum balance. • May require minimum balance.
Money market account	• Pays higher interest than other checking alternatives. • Highly liquid • If offered by bank or savings institution, insured by FDIC.	• Limited to a small number of checks per month. • Higher minimum balance than other checking alternatives. • Usually does not include any other banking services.

Demand Deposits. Like a checking account, a demand deposit savings account allows you to withdraw your money at any time. This feature makes these accounts more liquid than those that require you to leave your money deposited for a period of time. Since demand deposits are easily converted to cash, they are less risky to you; because they're less risky, they pay a lower rate of interest on balances. Recall from Chapter 1 that the riskier the investment or loan, the higher the interest rate. You can see this important investment principle clearly illustrated in Exhibit 5-4, which summarizes your savings account alternatives, including interest rates paid on each at a given point in time.

Time Deposits. Whereas demand deposits can be withdrawn at any time, a **time deposit account** requires that you keep the money in the account for a minimum period of time and may require a waiting period before you can withdraw funds. When you deposit your money in a financial institution and agree to leave it there for a set period of time, the institution can more easily use the money to make profitable long-term investments so it can pay you a higher rate of interest. Generally, the longer the time restriction, the higher the interest rate paid on the account. Since a time deposit is less liquid than other cash management account alternatives, it does expose you to greater risk. You may not be able to withdraw your money in a hurry, or there may be a cost to doing so. However, the higher rates paid on these accounts make them preferable when the money in the account is earmarked to meet a particular financial goal—perhaps a house down payment—and you are fairly certain you won't need to use the money sooner. The power of compound interest will work to help your savings grow faster.

Fact #4

It's not always better to have an interest-earning checking account. You need to compare the account's restrictions and fees to its non-interest-earning alternative before making that decision. Many interest-earning checking accounts have monthly service charges or other fees that more than offset the interest if your account balances are relatively low.

time deposit account

A savings account from which the depositor may not withdraw money, without penalty, until after a certain amount of time has passed.

GO FIGURE!

Estimating Opportunity Costs for Cash Management Options

Problem: Miranda Tafoya has been keeping her cash reserves in an interest-earning checking account earning 2 percent per year. She has to keep a minimum balance of $1,000 in the account to earn this rate of interest and avoid the monthly service charge, but she actually keeps about $5,000 in her account on average. She writes very few checks each month. Miranda is considering whether it would be better to switch to a regular checking account (that requires a $100 minimum balance and a $3 per month service charge) for her limited transaction needs, and a savings account (that pays 4 percent interest) for her cash reserves.

Solution: In estimating the opportunity cost Miranda incurs by leaving her cash reserves in the interest-earning checking account, we must consider the lost interest on her average balance—she is earning only 2 percent instead of the 4 percent she could earn in the savings account—and the differences in costs—the $3 monthly fee for the regular checking is $36 per year, whereas she currently pays no monthly fee for her checking. Her current situation and her other account options are summarized below:

		Miranda's Other Alternatives	
Miranda's Current Account		Regular Checking	Savings
Annual interest	2.0%	0	4.0%
Minimum balance	$1,000	$100	$100
Annual fees	0	$3 × 12 = $36	0
Average balance	$5,000	$1,000	$4,000
Annual interest	$100	$0	$160

If Miranda switches to a regular checking account for her transactions needs, she will incur the additional cost of $36 per year, and she will lose the $100 interest that she is currently earning on her interest-earning checking. However, she will gain $160 in annual interest paid on the new savings account. Her net gain from switching would thus be $160 − $100 − $36 = $24 per year. This amount is the opportunity cost associated with her current choice of cash management account. It isn't substantial and may be offset by other features of her current checking account.

Savings Alternatives

We've seen that savings accounts can be classified as demand or time deposits. Over the last decade or so, the variety of short-term savings options in both categories has increased markedly. To select the type that will best meet your needs, you'll need to understand the different types of accounts and their unique features. In this section, we consider regular savings accounts, certificates of deposit, money market mutual funds, money market accounts, and savings bonds.

Regular Savings Accounts. Regular savings accounts were once called *passbook accounts*, since the account holder actually had a little book in which the financial institution would enter deposit and withdrawal information. Although these types of accounts still exist today, account records are now kept electronically, and your bank will send you periodic statements, either monthly or quarterly, showing deposits, withdrawals, fees, and interest. In hopes of saving mailing and printing costs, financial institutions are developing online access tools that may eventually replace the mailed statements which are currently sent to customers.

You may find it convenient to have a regular savings account in the same institution as your checking account. Generally, that makes it easy to move money between your savings and checking accounts. In some cases, you can arrange for automatic transfer of funds from one to the other in the event that you would otherwise bounce a check.

EXHIBIT 5-4

Advantages and Disadvantages of Savings Account Alternatives

Type of Savings	Advantages	Disadvantages	Average Rate, March 2004
Regular savings	• Low minimum balance. • Highly liquid. • Insured by FDIC.	• Low rate of interest. • Federal, state, and local income tax owed on interest.	1.13%
Certificates of deposit	• If offered by depository institution, insured by FDIC. • Guarantees the rate of interest for the period. • Higher rates of interest than regular savings; increasing with maturity.	• Requires minimum balance. • Subject to reduced rate and/or penalty for early withdrawal. • Federal, state, and local income tax owed on interest.	6-month 1.31% 12-month 1.72% 5-year 3.52%
Money market mutual funds	• Higher rates of interest than regular savings; rate changes with market. • Usually allows limited check-writing.	• Not FDIC insured. • Federal, state, and local income tax owed on interest. • Requires minimum balance.	1.78%
Money market accounts	• If offered by depository institution, insured by FDIC. • Higher rates of interest than regular savings; rate changes with market.	• Requires minimum balance. • Federal, state, and local income tax owed on interest.	1.36%–2.04%
U.S. Series EE savings bonds	• Low minimum investment. • Higher rates of interest than regular savings; rate changes with market. • Government guaranteed. Exempt from state and local income tax. • Federal income tax on interest can be deferred by purchasing U.S. Series HH bonds.	• Cannot be redeemed in first six months. • Lower interest paid if redeemed in less than five years. • Federal income tax may be owed on interest at redemption unless used for qualified educational expenses.	2.6%
U.S. Series I savings bonds	• Same advantages as Series EE above. • Pays inflation plus the stated rate.	• May be lower interest than other types of accounts if inflation is low.	1.1% fixed + 1.08% inflation

Source: Rate information obtained from www.bankrate.com.

certificate of deposit (CD)

An account that pays a fixed rate of interest on funds left on deposit for a stated period of time.

maturity date

For a CD, the date on which the depositor can withdraw the invested amount and receive the stated interest.

Certificates of Deposit. As mentioned earlier, you'll get the highest interest rates on savings by putting money in time deposit accounts. A **certificate of deposit (CD)** is a savings account that pays a stated rate of interest if you agree to leave your money on deposit for a certain period of time. The end of that period is called the **maturity date** of the CD. Rates are higher for CDs of longer duration and for larger deposit amounts. For example, in Exhibit 5-4, you can see that a five-year CD can earn twice as much interest as a one-year CD (3.5% as compared to 1.72% in March 2004). At any given point in time, the actual difference in these rates might be smaller or larger than it was at that time, but it definitely pays to shop around. Even the rates paid on CDs with similar maturities can vary widely. CDs offered by depository institutions are very safe, since they are federally insured, but CDs are not highly liquid, since you may not be able to access funds immediately when you need them.

If you need access to your funds before the end of the CD term, you generally can do so, but you'll incur a penalty in the form of a sharply reduced interest rate, usually equivalent to a demand deposit rate. If you cash out a CD within a short time of when you made the deposit, you may even pay a penalty fee in addition to the reduction in interest. Let's say that you have $10,000 in a five-year CD which is paying 4 percent annual interest when demand deposits are only paying 1.5 percent. If you get into a financial pinch and need this money, how much will you lose by "breaking the CD" prior to maturity? The penalty for early withdrawal is usually a forfeit of some or all the interest. The CD's interest of $400 per year is substantially greater than the $150 per year for the regular savings alternative. Therefore, you could lose a significant amount of interest if you have to withdraw the funds early. Clearly, it makes sense to manage your money so as to minimize the likelihood that this kind of thing will happen. One way to do so is to separate your investments into several smaller CDs which mature at different times, a strategy sometimes called "laddering." Instead of putting $10,000 in a CD that matures in five years, for example, you might put $5,000 in the 5-year CD, $3,000 in a 2-year CD, $1,000 in a 12-month CD, and $1,000 in a 6-month CD. Although you will earn lower rates on the shorter-term CDs, the opportunity cost may be outweighed by the reduced risk of incurring an early withdrawal penalty should you need the funds prior to maturity.

To find out where to get the best CD rates, check www.bankrate.com.

When CDs mature, your financial institution will usually automatically roll over the funds into a comparable account unless you file the necessary paperwork to change your investment plan. For example, if you have your money in a one-year CD, the institution will roll it into another one-year CD at maturity. Although this makes things simpler for you, it can cause problems as well. Consider what happened to Joseph Gianetti, a retiree with three adult children. As part of his estate planning, he decided to give a tax-free gift of $11,000 to each of his children in 2004 and was planning to take it from a $35,000 five-year CD that was maturing at the end of the year. Unfortunately, when he went to his bank in December to withdraw the funds, he discovered that the CD had actually matured in October. Joseph had apparently overlooked the notice sent to him by his bank. Since he had not responded, the bank had rolled it into another five-year CD; Joseph had to pay a penalty to cash in the CD. The moral of this story is that you should keep careful track of maturity dates and be sure to read any documentation sent to you by your bank.

In addition to offering CDs with different maturity dates, your financial institution may offer special types of CDs, including the following:

- *Indexed CDs.* The interest paid on the CD will depend on the performance of an investment category, such as the stock market, the bond market, or international currencies. If you own a stock-indexed CD, for example, you'll earn higher rates of interest when the prices of stocks are rising, but you may earn zero interest or even lose some of your investment if the stock market goes down.
- *Rising-rate CDs.* The interest paid on the CD increases at stated intervals. For example, you might be promised 3 percent for the first year, 4 percent for the second year, and 5 percent for the third year.
- *Callable CDs.* In return for giving your financial institution the right to *call*, or cancel (and pay you back), your CD at some point in the future, you'll earn a higher rate of interest today. So, for example, if noncallable ten-year CDs are currently paying 4 percent, you might be able to find a callable ten-year CD that will pay 5.5 percent. If market rates go down, however, you can expect that your CD will be called.

The FDIC provides tips on investing in CDs at www.fdic.gov/deposit/deposits/certificate. Current rates on CDs of various maturities are available at www.bankrate.com.

Obviously, with so many alternatives to consider, you need to make sure you fully understand the terms of your CD *before* you invest. The Federal Deposit Insurance Corporation website at www.fdic.gov offers several tips for investors to consider in deciding what CD features make sense for them.

Money Market Mutual Funds. Mutual funds, as noted earlier, are financial companies that pool investors' funds and use the money to purchase a wide variety of financial assets. Most of these investment companies now offer one or more money market mutual funds with characteristics that make them alternatives to other liquid savings accounts (e.g., limited check writing privileges). A **money market mutual fund** is a fund that invests in short-term, low-risk financial assets, such as short-term debt securities issued by the federal government, federal agencies, and large public corporations. These types of investments are generally referred to as *money market securities*, which is why the funds are called money market mutual funds. When you buy shares of a money market mutual fund, the interest you earn will depend on the interest that the mutual fund is earning on its portfolio of investments. Generally, this will be 1 to 2 percentage points higher than what you can earn on a regular savings account. But, as you should now understand, these higher returns come with greater risk. Although money market mutual funds may be sold by your financial institution and may look similar to other bank products, they are not federally insured, nor is the interest rate guaranteed. If interest rates go down, you'll earn less than you originally expected on the account; if the mutual fund goes belly-up, you could lose everything you put in.

money market mutual fund

A mutual fund that holds a portfolio of short-term, low-risk securities issued by the federal government, its agencies, and large corporations and pays investors a rate of return that fluctuates with the interest earned on the portfolio.

Money Market Accounts. A **money market account** looks similar to a money market mutual fund in that it pays interest that fluctuates with market rates on money market securities. Again, the rate is generally higher than that on regular savings accounts—in March 2004, when the average rate paid on regular savings accounts was 1.13 percent, money market accounts were averaging 1.36 percent to 2.04 percent, depending on the size of the account. Like money market mutual funds, money market accounts usually allow some check writing privileges. Although at one time you'd have been limited to writing three to five checks per month, today you can sometimes get unlimited check writing. On the negative side, you must usually keep a fairly high minimum balance in a money market account, so, as with interest-earning checking accounts, you need to consider the opportunity cost of holding more in the account than you would otherwise. Finally, it's important to note that money market accounts offered by depository institutions are usually federally insured, whereas those offered by insurance companies and brokerage firms are not.

money market account

A savings account which pays interest that fluctuates with market rates on money market securities.

Government Savings Bonds. Individual savers should also consider **U.S. savings bonds** for short-term, low-risk investing. These bonds are exempt from state and local income taxes and pay interest that fluctuates with changes in market interest rates. We discuss the features of Series EE bonds, Series HH, and Series I bonds below.

U.S. savings bonds

Bonds issued by the U.S. Treasury that pay interest that fluctuates with current Treasury security rates and are exempt from state and local taxes.

Series EE bonds. Series EE bonds, renamed "Patriot Bonds" after September 11, 2001, are bonds issued by the U.S. Treasury that can be bought at most depository institutions. Investors pay 50 percent of the face value, which may be as little as $50 or as much as $10,000, and can redeem the bonds later for the original price plus interest earned over the holding period. So, for example, to purchase a Series EE bond with a $50 face value, you'd pay $25. These bonds are called **discount bonds** because the purchase price is less than the face value of the bond.

Your bond will be redeemable for the full $50 face value when it has accumulated $25 in interest. The maturity date is uncertain—it depends on the interest rate. Once you know the interest rate, you can figure out how much time it will take for your bond investment to double in value by applying the **Rule of 72**. Take the number 72 and divide by the interest rate. The result is an approximation for the number of years to double your money. You can use this rule of thumb with any investment.

discount bonds

Bonds that sell for less than their face value.

Rule of 72

Method of calculating the time for a sum of money to double by dividing 72 by the rate of interest earned on the funds.

Interest on EE bonds accrues semiannually on May 1 and November 1 of each year, but is not paid to investors until they redeem the bonds. The interest, in addition to being exempt from state and local income taxation, is not subject to federal income tax until the bond is cashed in, which can be many years in the future. For lower- and middle-income families, the interest income is exempt if it is used to pay for qualified higher education expenses.

The rate of interest you earn on Series EE bonds is linked to rates on short-term federal Treasury securities and also depends on how long you hold the bonds; you earn a better rate if you hold them for five years or more. Since these bonds are very low risk, the interest paid is comparable to that for other types of cash accounts with similar maturities. If you live in an area with high state and local tax rates, though, the tax advantages may make this saving alternative preferable to taxable cash accounts offered by financial institutions.

Series HH Bonds. If you have a Series EE bond that has accumulated enough interest to be redeemed at its face value and you'd like to receive regular interest income from your savings without having to pay federal income tax on the whole amount, you can use your Series EE bonds to buy Series HH bonds. This is the only way to purchase Series HH bonds. These bonds pay interest to the holder semiannually, and this interest income is subject to federal income tax but exempt from state and local income tax.

To see how this works, suppose that you've accumulated a total of $100,000 in fully matured U.S. Series EE savings bonds. You're nearing retirement and would like to get some income from these bonds, but don't want to pay federal income taxes right now on the full $50,000 in interest you've earned on the bonds since you purchased them. You can use the $100,000 to buy $100,000 in Series HH bonds. If those bonds are currently paying 5 percent interest, you'll receive $5,000 this year in two semiannual installments and will have to pay tax on that interest. You will not, however, have to pay tax on the accumulated interest of $50,000.

Series I Bonds. In 1998, the U.S. Treasury began offering Series I savings bonds. These bonds are similar to EE bonds in their tax features but are designed to provide protection from inflation. The semiannual interest rate is fixed when you purchase the bond, but the face value on which the interest is calculated adjusts semiannually with the CPI index. Suppose, for example, that you have a Series I bond with a face value of $1,000 that promises to pay an annual rate of 1.5 percent more than the current rate of inflation. The bond will accrue $7.50 in interest the first 6 months (half of the annual interest rate of 1.5% on the face value of $1,000). Now suppose the CPI index goes up 3 percent during that same time. The face value of your bond will increase by 3 percent, to $1,030. Over the next six months, you'll earn half of 1.5 percent on the new face value of $1,030. In fact, you'll always earn 1.5 percent more than the inflation rate—even if the inflation rate returned to double digits, as in 1980. Although individuals can buy up to $30,000 in I-Series bonds each year, sales have been slow because inflation has been relatively low in the last decade.

The Savings Bond Calculator at www.publicdebt.treas.gov will tell you how much your Series EE and Series I bonds are currently worth. The website also has a Savings Bond Wizard to help you manage your savings bond inventory.

An Example: The Thompsons

Consider how Cindy and Dave Thompson, whom we met in Chapter 3, could use U.S. savings bonds to save for their new baby's college education. Suppose they buy $10,000 in Series EE bonds in 2004 for the discounted price of $5,000. If the average rate of interest paid on these bonds is 5 percent, they will mature (be worth the face value of $10,000) in approximately 14 years. We can determine this by using the Rule of 72, as explained earlier—dividing 72 by the interest rate, 5, for a result of 14.4.

If the Thompsons use the bond proceeds to pay for their child's college expenses, the entire $5,000 in interest will be tax-free, assuming their income doesn't exceed the limits in place at the time they redeem the bond. Compare that outcome to a regular savings account at a bank, and you'll see why buying U.S. savings bonds can be a good strategy. The rate on savings accounts is usually lower, *and* the interest earned is taxable annually.

The calculation used to estimate the value of currently owned savings bonds is explained in the *Go Figure!* box, "Estimating the Value of U.S. Savings Bonds." You can also obtain a table of savings bond redemption values (Form PD 3600) from your local financial institution or from the Savings Bond Marketing Office, 800 K Street, NW, Washington, DC 20226. To find out the current rate on savings bonds, you can call (800) 487-2663. The www.publicdebt.treas.gov website also includes several useful tools for savings bond investors.

Learning by Doing 5-4

1. For each of the following pairs, indicate which will probably pay a higher rate of interest:
   a. Regular checking account or NOW account
   b. Demand savings account or CD
2. For each of the following pairs, indicate which is more liquid:
   a. Demand deposit or time deposit
   b. One-year CD or five-year CD

GO FIGURE!

Estimating the Value of U.S. Savings Bonds

Problem: Ivana has a Series EE bond in her safe deposit box that was issued in November 1997 and given to her as a wedding gift. The bond has a face value of $100. It is now November 2003 (six years later). How much is Ivana's bond currently worth? When will it mature?

Solution: Ivana has several alternatives for determining the value of her bond:

1. She can go to a financial institution and ask them to look up the redemption value of her bond.
2. She can go to www.publicdebt.treas.gov and use the Savings Bond Calculator there to calculate how much her bond is worth.
3. She can roughly measure the value based on the five-year Treasury note. Series EE bonds issued on or after May 1997, and held at least five years, pay holders 90 percent of the yield on five-year Treasuries, calculated semiannually in May and November. To estimate this rate, calculate 90 percent of the current annual yield on five-year Treasury notes (reported at a number of financial websites, including finance.yahoo.com). In this example, Ivana finds that the November 2003 yield on the five-year Treasury is 3.35 percent, so she calculates: 0.9 × 3.35 percent = 3.02 percent.

Assuming that the 3 percent (rounded) annual rate applies to the full six years she has owned the bond, Ivana can solve this problem using the mathematical formula, financial calculator, or spreadsheet method for calculating future value. The original purchase price of the bond (50% of the face value) is the present value (PV) and she needs to solve for the future value (FV), assuming that the bond is held for twelve six-month compounding periods (n) and earns $\frac{3\%}{2}$, the semiannual interest rate (i). Inputting these values into the future value formula from Chapter 2, she gets

$$
\begin{aligned}
FV &= PV \times (1 + i)^n \\
&= 50 \times \left(1 + \frac{3\%}{2}\right)^{12} \\
&= 50 \times (1.015)^{12} \\
&= 59.78
\end{aligned}
$$

This is only a rough measure because, in fact, interest is accrued every six months based on interest rates applicable for that period. Since rates declined over the time that Ivana held her bond, she has actually earned about 4 percent on average over the six years.

Ivana can estimate how long it will take for her bond to mature by using the Rule of 72. If she averages 4 percent annual interest it will take $\frac{72}{4} = 18$ years from the original issuance for the bond to mature at which time it will be worth the face value of $100.

Other Cash Management Products and Services

In addition to checking and savings accounts, financial institutions offer a wide variety of other cash management services, including electronic banking services and specialized checks, as described below. Your bank or savings institution may also offer credit cards, car loans, home mortgages, financial planning and investment management services, and insurance; these products and services are discussed in later chapters.

Electronic Banking Services. Banking services today are much different from those available a decade ago because of the increase in electronic transactions and services, which include debit cards, automated teller machines, and automated bill paying and other fund transfers.

Fact #5

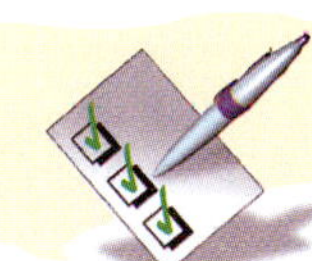

Recent financial deregulation has made it possible for financial institutions to offer products that were previously only available through specialized firms. For example, banks can now sell some insurance products, such as auto and homeowner's, and insurers can offer cash management and investment accounts.

Debit Cards. Many checking accounts allow you to use a **debit card**, a plastic card encoded with account information that enables you to withdraw funds electronically to pay for purchases. You need only swipe the card through the retailer's point-of-sale (POS) terminal and enter your personal identification number (PIN) to authorize the withdrawal. Not all retailers have the equipment necessary for you to pay electronically in this way, but it's expected that the use of debit cards will continue to increase over time. Even now, some retailers (such as Old Navy)

debit card

A plastic card that effects immediate electronic withdrawal of funds from a bank account.

You can find ATM machines in many unusual locations. There are even mobile ATMs.

don't take paper checks at all, instead converting check transactions to electronic withdrawals from your checking account. Retailers benefit from accepting electronic payments because transaction costs, as well as the risk of bounced checks, are reduced. Consumers like the freedom from carrying cash and the ease of making transactions. Of course, the simplicity of paying with a debit card also means that you may be more likely to overspend. You should therefore be sure to record debit transactions as they occur so that your financial records will be up-to-date.

It's important to note that using a debit card is identical to writing a check—the only real difference is that the debit, or withdrawal, occurs at the moment you use the card. Although debit cards look almost identical to credit cards, which will be discussed in the next chapter, they're quite different in that when you use a debit card, you're paying with your own money rather than borrowing money from the financial institution.

Given the ease with which unauthorized users could gain access to your account if they have your PIN, you should never keep the number in written form in your wallet or purse. It is also advisable to select a PIN number that is something you can easily remember but that will not be too easy for a thief to guess. Don't use numbers a thief will be likely to try, such as 1234 or 1111. And since many debit cards can be used to make online or phone transactions without entering a PIN, you should guard your card carefully as well.

automated teller machines (ATMs)

Computer terminals used to complete certain financial transactions, including obtaining account balances, making deposits and withdrawals.

Automated Teller Machines. **Automated teller machines (ATMs)** are regularly used by bank customers to check account balances, deposit checks, and withdraw cash using their ATM or debit cards. These "cash machines" have reduced the demand for in-person transactions made through tellers, thus allowing financial institutions to cut their overhead costs—an important issue in today's highly competitive financial services marketplace. ATMs offer the convenience of 24-hour-a-day access, and they can be found at hundreds of locations—outside financial institutions, in shopping malls, in airports, at university student centers, and in high-traffic retail establishments, such as gas stations and convenience stores.

An important thing to remember is that ATM transactions are only free when you use a terminal owned by your financial institution. If you withdraw money at a terminal owned by another bank, you'll have to pay a fee—anywhere from \$1.50 to \$4.00—and your own institution may charge you \$1.00 to \$2.00 as well. These small dollar amounts may not seem like much, but they can easily add up to more than the annual interest on your account!

Other Electronic Banking Services. Most financial institutions now accept automatic deposits of paychecks and will allow you to authorize automatic electronic withdrawals for regular payments of everything from loan payments to monthly fees at retailers like Hollywood Video. A natural extension of this trend in electronic transactions is that many people now make all their regular bill payments electronically, either through their financial institution or a private service. Several ways to pay bills electronically are discussed in the *News You Can Use* box, "Click On and Pay Up: Paying Bills Online." In deciding whether this is a good way to manage your own payments, you need to weigh the monthly costs, if any, against the convenience. An additional advantage of making payments this way is that many of the services allow you to download financial information to financial management and tax planning software packages, making it easier to balance your checkbook and prepare your taxes.

Private electronic bill-paying services include www.paymybills.com and www.checkfree.com

Some financial institutions also offer special asset management accounts (AMAs) that automatically transfer your account balances among different accounts and investments to get you the highest rate of return on your funds, but these accounts may require higher minimum balances than are optimal for your financial plan.

Specialized Checks. Financial institutions also provide various kinds of specialized checks, including the following:

- *Traveler's checks.* Traveler's checks are checks issued in specific denominations (\$10, \$20, \$50, and \$100) by large financial institutions and accepted worldwide. The typical fee for issuance is 1 percent. You sign the checks when you receive them and then sign them again when you use them to pay for something, thus verifying to the payee that you are the owner of the

NEWS you can use

Click on and Pay Up: Paying Bills Online

In today's busy world, it's easy to be late paying the piper. Maybe you get so much junk mail that the bills get lost in the stack. Or perhaps you're juggling a family, a job, and school, and the last thing you want to do with your free time is pay bills. Did you forget to buy stamps, *again*?

Take Sarah Corsova, for example. She travels frequently on business and used to come home to a waiting stack of bills. She was often late making payments, incurring late penalties and additional interest. She also spent a lot of time worrying about her bills. That was before a friend suggested she try an online bill-paying service. Now, with the click of a mouse, she can pay her insurance premiums, credit card bills, and utility bills, even when she's away from home on travel. No more stamps. No more piles of bills to face when she returns from a trip.

"More than 25 million Americans now pay their bills online."

More than 25 million Americans now pay their bills online, and that number is expected to double in the next few years, according to Gartner Research, a technology-based research company in Stamford, Connecticut. If you're interested in setting up a bill-paying system, you should first investigate your options. In general, you have three ways to go.

First, you can arrange separately with each of the businesses you normally make payments to during the month to have your payments automatically withdrawn from your bank account. There's usually no charge for this type of arrangement; in fact, some companies will actually give you a discount for making automatic payments. American Family Insurance, for example, waives its normal fee for making monthly instead of semiannual payments on auto insurance if the customer agrees to electronic withdrawals. In some cases, you may have to go to the company's website or call a designated phone number to make the payment each month, but this still eliminates the step of writing checks and mailing the payment.

A second option is to continue to receive the bills but to authorize a bill-paying company to send out the payments. You first have to set up an account that includes the names, addresses, and account numbers for all your payees. Then, each month as your bills come in, you go online and fill in the amount to be automatically sent.

The third and simplest option is to sign up with a service that will actually receive your bills and pay them for you. The company notifies you when a bill comes in and, subject to your approval, makes the electronic payment. No more paper bills. Most large banks offer a bill-paying service to their customers, often with a free trial period, after which the service is available for a small fee, commonly $5 to $7 per month. Examples include www.wellsfargo.com and www.citibank.com. In addition, several specialty companies, such as www.checkfree.com, www.paymybills.com, and www.ezpayusa.com, offer these services.

check. The primary advantages for travelers are that, if traveler's checks are lost or stolen, you can't lose any money and, even in a foreign country, their replacement is guaranteed.

- *Certified checks.* A certified check is a personal check drawn on your own account and guaranteed by the financial institution in which you have the account. Since the institution certifies (guarantees) that the funds are actually available and places a freeze on those funds, these checks are accepted as cash for many official transactions, such as when you are paying off a car loan or making a down payment on a new home. Fees for this service range from $2 to $10.
- *Cashier's checks.* A cashier's check is used similarly to a certified check, to make payments where the payee wants to be sure the funds are available. But instead of being drawn on your own account, the check is drawn on the account of the financial institution itself and made out to the party you specify. The person ordering the check pays the financial institution the amount of the check plus a fee from $2 to $10.
- *Money order.* A money order is a legal request for a company to pay a particular sum of money to a person or business that you designate. In effect, a money order is like a check drawn on the account of a business. If you don't have your own checking account, you can purchase money orders to pay your bills or other obligations. They're sold by financial institutions, by the U.S. Post Office, and by businesses such as 7-11, for a small fee.

Evaluating Cash Management Account Choices

LEARNING objective

5 Compare cash management account options based on liquidity, safety, costs, and after-tax annual percentage yield (APY).

As you can see, there are many different products and services you can use for cash management. How do you decide which are most appropriate for your needs? What are the most important factors to consider in choosing your cash management accounts? Recall that the basic purposes of cash management are to meet transaction needs, to develop a cash reserve for emergencies, and to have a safe place to park money in anticipation of the planned need for cash. Since all these needs require that the account have minimal risk and be easy to access, your primary concerns in evaluating account choices should be liquidity and safety. Once you've narrowed your choices to the accounts that meet this initial screen, you can make your final decision based on differences in costs and after-tax interest earnings.

Liquidity. Can you withdraw money from the account without incurring fees or losing any of your original investment? In evaluating your account options, pay careful attention to features that limit the account's liquidity, such as minimum balance requirements, limitations on withdrawals, and number of transactions or checks allowed each month.

Safety. Investment options differ in their level of risk, as do the institutions offering these options. Does the cash management account expose you to any risk of default by the financial institution? Is there any risk of losing your money? Is the interest rate paid on the account guaranteed, or does it fluctuate with market conditions?

Since cash management accounts are earmarked as a component of your finances that you can't afford to risk, you should consider limiting your choices to insured deposits and federally guaranteed investments. Although FDIC-insured accounts are obviously less risky than uninsured accounts, the failure of your financial institution will still impose some costs on you, however. During the 1980s, numerous savings and loans failed, and many insured depositors were unable to access their funds for several months, although they were eventually repaid by the government insurance program.

An often overlooked risk of supposedly safe investments is inflation. The *News You Can Use* box, "Inflation: The Hidden Risk of 'Safe Accounts'," explains how inflation can increase the risk of holding cash.

Costs and After-Tax Interest. When you're deciding between savings alternatives, you'll inevitably have to make tradeoffs. Generally, the safer the investment and the institution, the lower the rate of interest paid on investments. Accounts that are more liquid will usually pay lower rates of interest and may have higher costs, such as monthly service charges, fees, and

NEWS you can use

Inflation: The Hidden Risk of "Safe Accounts"

Suppose you're planning to buy a new mountain bike one year from now. The cost of the bike is $1,000 today, so you set aside $1,000 in your FDIC-insured savings account at Safety First Bank, which pays 2 percent annual interest. At the end of the year, you'll have $1,020. But what if inflation this year turns out to be 4 percent? The cost of the bike, if we assume that it only goes up by the *average* increase in the cost of goods, will have risen to $1,040. The spending power of your $1,000 will actually have declined over the one-year period, since it would have been enough to buy the bike at the beginning of the period but it's not enough at the end of the year. Investors in "safe" accounts like this one have practically zero risk of losing the nominal value of their invested money, but they still risk losing purchasing power through the eroding effects of inflation. Although interest rates on bank savings accounts are quick to go down when market rates fall, institutions do not usually increase the rates they pay nearly as quickly when inflation and market interest rates rise.

"Investors in safe accounts still risk losing purchasing power."

penalties. It's not uncommon for an account advertised as "free" to include many hidden costs that are very profitable to the lender, such as fees for check printing, overdrafts, stop payments, and debit cards.

In comparing the annualized interest that you can earn on each type of account, you may find that the accounts have different rules for when they credit you with interest. Recall from Chapter 2 that the frequency with which interest is calculated and added to your account is called compounding. The more often the interest compounds—daily instead of monthly, for example—the more you get the advantage of interest paid on interest. The difficulty in comparing accounts is that the stated, or nominal, interest rate is not directly comparable between accounts with different rates of compounding. The interest earnings on the account may also be eroded by fees, so that the actual annual rate of return on your invested funds may be lower than the nominal quoted rate of return.

Fortunately for consumers of financial services, the Truth in Savings law requires that financial institutions report the **annual percentage yield (APY)** on all interest-earning accounts, in addition to the nominal rate. This measure adjusts for different compounding periods and any interestlike fees to make it possible to compare "apples with apples." However, fees for specific services (debit cards, checks, and the like) aren't factored into this calculation, so you'll still need to consider those in your evaluation of account options. Although you can use the method shown in the *Go Figure!* box, "Calculating Annual Percentage Yield," to calculate the APY yourself, in most cases this won't be necessary, since you can simply compare your savings account alternatives based on the APY stated in the materials provided by each financial institution.

annual percentage yield (APY)

The amount of interest paid each year, given as a percentage of the investment; the APY makes it possible to compare interest rates across accounts with different compounding periods.

GO FIGURE!

Calculating Annual Percentage Yield

Problem: You're comparing two savings account options in which to place your $10,000 emergency fund. These accounts pay the same 5.0 percent nominal rate, but they compound the interest at different intervals, as follows:

Account 1: quoted rate 5.0 percent, compounded daily
Account 2: quoted rate 5.0 percent, compounded quarterly

Assuming there are no other fees to be considered, what is the APY of each account?

Solution: Given a nominal interest rate and the frequency of compounding, you can calculate APY using the following formula:

$$\text{Annual percentage yield (APY)} = \left[1 + \left(\frac{\text{nominal yield}}{m}\right)^m\right] - 1$$

where m is the number of compounding periods per year (in this example, 365 for daily compounding and 4 for quarterly compounding) and the nominal yield is the advertised rate on the account (5.0% for each account).

Using this formula, we calculate:

$$\text{APY}_{\text{Account 1}} = \left[1 + \left(\frac{0.05}{365}\right)\right]^{365} - 1$$
$$= (1.000137)^{365} - 1$$
$$= 0.05127 \quad \text{or} \quad 5.127\%$$

$$\text{APY}_{\text{Account 2}} = \left[1 + \left(\frac{0.05}{4}\right)\right]^{4} - 1$$
$$= (1.0125)^{4} - 1$$
$$= 0.05095 \quad \text{or} \quad 5.095\%$$

As you can see, the first account will pay a little more in annualized interest than the second account because interest is compounded more frequently (daily as opposed to quarterly).

You can also use your financial calculator to calculate APY. Most calculators have a specific function to convert an annual nominal rate to an annualized yield. To calculate the APY for Account 2 above on the TI BAII Plus calculator, use the following key strokes:

1. Press 2nd and then press I Conv (which appears over the 2).
2. Key in the nominal rate 5 and then press ENTER.
3. Press ↑.
4. Key in the number of compounding periods per year 4 and then press ENTER.
5. Press ↑ and then press CPT to calculate the effective annual rate.

The solution should appear in the LCD display as: EFF = 5.0945.

After finding the APY for each account, don't forget to take into consideration any tax effects, since the taxability of interest makes a big difference in your net earnings from the investment. Since rates of return on liquid savings accounts are already low, the additional costs of federal, state, and local income taxes can erode your yield to very low levels. If your APY on a regular savings account is 2 percent, for example, and your marginal tax rate is 40 percent, your after-tax yield will be only $2 \times (1 - 0.4) = 1.2$ percent after you pay the taxes on your interest earnings. In addition to being important in your selection of what to invest in, taxes should be a factor in your calculation of the opportunity cost of regular checking accounts.

To best meet your overall cash management needs, you may want to consider having multiple accounts that vary in liquidity, cost, and interest in order to maximize your overall return. Most people have a transaction account for regular bill paying and a highly liquid savings account for short-term emergency needs. In addition, as they build their emergency fund to a desirable level, they may attempt to increase their interest earnings by spreading their funds among higher-yield savings options, such as U.S. savings bonds and CDs with varying maturities. This makes sense because, in most financial emergencies, you won't need the entire amount immediately. For example, if you lose your job, you'll only need to cover one month of expenses at a time.

Learning by Doing 5-5

1. Use the Rule of 72 to determine how long it will take for a $100 EE savings bond that you received as a wedding gift to mature if the average interest paid over the time you hold the bond is 4.25 percent?
2. Which savings account will have a greater APY: one that pays 2 percent interest compounded monthly or one that pays 2 percent interest compounded daily?
3. Suppose you're considering investing $1,000 in either a five-year CD paying 5 percent compounded semiannually or a Series EE bond with an average interest of 5 percent. Your tax rate (in state and federal income taxes) is 30 percent. What factors should you consider in deciding between the two investment options?

Resolving Cash Management Problems

LEARNING objective

6 Select appropriate tools for dealing with cash management errors.

Most people at some point in their lives have unexpected cash management problems. Such problems can result from your own cash management mistakes, as in the case of a bounced check or a seriously overdue bill. Or they can be someone else's fault—you deposit a check in your account, but the person who wrote it didn't have the funds to cover it. Worse yet, you may have your checkbook or debit card stolen. In this section, we consider how to deal with some of these problems.

If You Bounce a Check . . .

overdraft protection
An arrangement by which a financial institution places funds in a depositor's checking account to cover overdrafts.

The best way to avoid bouncing checks is to keep careful track of your cash flows. If the unexpected occurs, you can avoid hefty overdraft charges, often assessed by both your financial institution and the party to whom you wrote the bad check, by arranging in advance with your financial institution for **overdraft protection** on your account. This can be managed with an automatic transfer from a different account or through automatic credit in the amount of the overdraft. Credit of this type will be very similar to a credit card loan and may have a relatively high rate of interest, so you need to pay it off promptly.

If you do bounce a check, this information will be reported to one or more check approval companies (such as Tele-check and Checkrite). These companies provide two valuable services to participating businesses. First, they take care of the hassle of collecting the amount of your bounced check (usually requiring cash or a certified check) and assessing any penalties. Second, they keep an electronic record of individuals who have bounced checks at *any* participating business. Thus, if you bounce a check at the grocery store, your checks will be refused at *all* establishments using the same check approval service the grocery store uses until you've paid the amount due plus any fees (often $20 to $30). To maintain your ability to use your checking account, you should be sure to resolve the overdraft as quickly as possible.

An additional cost of bouncing a check is that your depository institution will also assess a penalty, usually ranging from $20 to $30. Thus, your $50 bounced check to the local grocery store could end up costing you an additional $40 to $60 after you've paid the penalties to the store and your financial institution.

If You Receive a Bad Check . . .

If you deposit a check from someone else and it bounces, your own institution will often charge you a fee, even though you were not at fault. This fee is comparable to a bounced check fee ($20 to $30). If, as a result of the bad check, you end up bouncing checks of your own, you'll pay penalties on those as well. Although you can try to get the wrongdoer to pay you back, you're unlikely to be successful. Therefore, the best way to avoid the problem is to take checks only from reliable sources and not to write checks against funds that have not yet been credited to your account.

If You Discover Fraudulent Activity on Your Account . . .

Suppose you are reconciling your bank statement and see a record of an electronic payment made to an Internet retailer, but it's for a transaction you never made. The risk of unauthorized use of cash management accounts has increased substantially with the increasing popularity of electronic transactions. If this happens to you—and unfortunately it's becoming a commonplace occurrence—you must act promptly to correct this "mistake." By law, a contact phone number for the company or person who received the payment from your account must be provided on your bank statement, so you can simply call and ask the company to reverse the charges. Although these charges sometimes are the result of legitimate errors, as when someone has inputted an account number incorrectly, more commonly the charge to your account is part of a larger scam in which a company requests electronic payments from numerous accounts, counting on enough careless consumers to not check their statements carefully. When you call to contest the payment, the person who answers will likely say that you or another member of your family requested the service, or whatever you're being charged for, over the phone or on the Internet.

Legally, your financial institution is not supposed to make payments without your authorization. Obviously, a signed check is one form of authorization. The use of your PIN number is another. As more transactions are being made electronically without these verification procedures, it is increasingly difficult for a financial institution to be the gatekeeper to your account. Thus, the primary responsibility lies with you, the owner of the account, to safeguard the account number and access.

If You Want to Stop Payment on a Check . . .

In some cases, you may want to keep a person or business from cashing a check that you have given them. For example, you might have paid a contractor to do some work on your house but realized soon after he left that he hadn't actually finished the job you paid him for. In this circumstance, you can request that your financial institution issue a **stop payment order** on the check for a fee of between $10 and $25. Although this request can be made over the phone, you should follow up in writing to protect your rights in the event that the check slips through. Stop orders can be extended beyond their usual two-week period for an additional fee.

stop payment order

An order by which a financial institution promises not to honor a check that a depositor has written.

Western Union office in Monrovia, Liberia.

If You Need Money in a Hurry . . .

wire transfer

Electronic transmittal of cash from an account in another location; requires payment of a fee.

Nearly every college student has had the experience of calling home for money, particularly late in the semester when the money earned at a summer job is all gone. In most cases, this can be handled by mailing a check. Suppose, though, that you're in a serious financial bind and need the money in a hurry. In that case, you may need to arrange for a **wire transfer** of funds. For a fee, your parents' bank will agree to electronically transfer funds to your account at another institution, usually in 24 hours or less. A quicker but more expensive alternative is the cash-delivery service offered by Western Union, Money-gram, and American Express, which all have branches around the world and promise quick delivery of cash. If you're in Mexico on spring break and have your wallet stolen at the beach, you may consider using one of these companies' services.

Summary

1 **Apply the objectives of cash management to assessing your need for cash management products and services.** Cash management includes all your decisions related to cash payments and short-term liquid investments. People hold cash for three general reasons: to manage transaction needs, to prepare for cash emergencies, and to make temporary investments.

2 **Explain the rules of effective cash management and why it is important to regularly balance your checkbook.** Following several rules will result in better cash management outcomes: (1) Keep track of your cash by balancing your checkbook every month. (2) Develop a system to ensure that you pay your bills on time. (3) Stick to your financial plan by paying yourself first. This means you should allocate funds to your financial goals at the beginning of the month rather than waiting to see how much is left at the end. (4) Use sound criteria to evaluate financial institutions and select cash management products and services.

3 **Understand the differences among providers of cash management products and services.** Cash management services are offered by many financial institutions. Some, called depository institutions, obtain the funds they invest from customer deposits; these institutions include commercial banks, savings institutions, and credit unions. Others, called nondepository institutions, get their investment funds from other sources; these institutions include insurance companies, mutual funds, and brokerage firms. Financial institutions can also be distinguished by whether they are organized as mutual companies, which are owned by customers, or stock companies, which are owned by outside stockholders. Recent deregulation has made it possible for most types of financial institutions to offer a diverse menu of financial products and services. In deciding among different financial institutions, you should consider whether they have what you need (product), whether they are competitive in costs imposed and interest rates paid (price), whether they provide high-quality customer service (people), and how convenient their locations are (place).

4 **Identify cash management products and services that are important to your financial plan.** The cash management services offered by particular financial institutions include checking and savings accounts, as well as electronic banking. Regular checking accounts pay no interest on the account balance; NOW accounts (which go by various names) do pay interest, although the rates are fairly low. Accounts also differ in monthly service charges, minimum balances required, and fees for additional services. Savings accounts generally differ in their liquidity and risk, with higher rates of interest paid on riskier accounts and those with more restric-

tions on withdrawals. The most common types of savings vehicles include regular savings accounts, CDs, U.S. savings bonds, money market mutual funds, and money market accounts.

5 Compare cash management account options based on liquidity, safety, costs, and after-tax annual percentage yield (APY). Since the primary purpose of cash management accounts is to provide a liquid source of funds to meet cash emergencies, liquidity and safety are of utmost importance in selecting a cash management account. When evaluating comparably safe account alternatives, you should consider the differences in costs, such as monthly fees and penalties for early withdrawal, and the taxability of the interest earned. Annual percentage yield (APY) makes it possible to compare interest rates across accounts with different compounding periods.

6 Select appropriate tools for dealing with cash management errors. Cash management problems can result from your own errors, as in the case of overdrafts and late payments, or they can be due to the carelessness or intentional actions of others. In either case, you'll probably incur some costs, so it's important to resolve these problems as quickly as possible.

Key Terms

annual percentage yield (APY) (161)
automated teller machines (ATMs) (158)
brokerage firm (147)
cash management (139)
cash reserve (140)
certificate of deposit (CD) (153)
commercial bank (145)
credit union (145)
debit card (157)
demand deposits (150)
depository institution (144)
discount bonds (155)
Federal Deposit Insurance Corporation (FDIC) (145)
life insurance company (147)
maturity date (153)
money market account (155)
money market mutual fund (155)
mutual fund (147)
mutual savings institution (145)
negotiated order of withdrawal (NOW) account (150)
overdraft protection (162)
regular checking account (150)
Rule of 72 (155)
savings and loan association (S&L) (145)
stock-held savings institution (145)
stop payment order (163)
time deposit account (151)
U.S. savings bonds (155)
wire transfer (164)

Key Calculations

$$\text{Annual percentage yield (APY)} = \left(1 + \frac{\text{nominal yield}}{m}\right)^m - 1$$

where nominal yield = annual quoted interest rate on the account
m = number of compounding periods per year

After-tax yield = APY × (1 − marginal tax rate percent)

Concept Review Questions

1. What are the primary reasons people need to hold cash?
2. What costs do you incur when you hold cash instead of investing in riskier assets?
3. What is a transaction account, and what are the primary financial activities for which you need it?
4. What is the difference between using a debit card and writing a check as a means of payment?
5. How much do experts recommend that a typical household hold in cash? Why doesn't everyone agree on how much?
6. What are the rules of effective cash management?
7. What does it mean to "reconcile your checkbook"? If you don't do this regularly, what are the potential negative outcomes?
8. Why do so many financial advisors recommend that you "pay yourself first"?
9. What is the difference between a depository institution and a nondepository institution? Give three examples of each.
10. Why are cash management accounts in depository institutions usually considered less risky than those in other institutions?
11. What are the limits on FDIC insurance protection?
12. What are the primary differences between credit unions and other depository institutions? Why might these differences enable credit unions to offer higher interest rates on deposits and lower rates on loans?
13. What are the four key factors you should use in evaluating providers of financial services? Give an example of each.
14. What is the difference between a demand deposit and a time deposit?
15. Explain the similarities and differences between regular checking accounts and NOW accounts. Is it always better to have an interest-earning checking account?
16. What are the primary savings options for individuals interested in maintaining liquidity?
17. When a bank offers several certificates of deposit (CDs) with different maturities, which will have a higher APY, a five-year CD or a one-year CD? Why?
18. How is a money market mutual fund different from a money market account?
19. How is a money market account different from a NOW account?
20. What are the three types of U.S. savings bonds discussed in this chapter? What are their primary advantages over other liquid savings alternatives?
21. What is a traveler's check, and when might you need to use one?
22. What is the difference between a certified check and a cashier's check?
23. What does an online bill-paying service do? What are the advantages and disadvantages of using this type of service?
24. In evaluating your cash management options, what should your primary considerations be? What other criteria should you use?
25. What is annual percentage yield, and why is it important to compare interest-earning accounts using this measure?
26. How does your marginal tax rate affect your decision regarding cash management accounts?

Application Problems

1. ***Opportunity Cost*** First National Bank requires a minimum balance of $1,000 on its interest-earning checking accounts. Account holders are paid 2.0 percent on the average balance if the balance stays above the minimum all month. If you normally have an average balance of $2,500, what is the opportunity cost of keeping the money in a First National checking account instead of a savings account that pays 3.5 percent?
2. ***Emergency Fund*** Pam Johannsen earns $25,000 and takes home $1,200 per month after taxes. She has total monthly expenses of $1,100. How much of an emergency fund should she have? What factors should she consider in deciding how much would be necessary?
3. ***After-tax Yield*** You have $10,000 invested in a five-year CD that promises 5 percent APR. It will mature four years from now. If you withdraw money from the CD prior to maturity, the interest rate drops to 3 percent.
   a. If your marginal tax rate is 25 percent, what is your after-tax yield on this investment assuming you leave the money in the account to maturity?
   b. What risks are you exposed to by holding this much cash in a CD? What are your alternatives?
4. ***After-tax Yield*** As part of his cash management plan, José Ramirez invested money in a five-year CD paying 4 percent interest. His marginal tax rate is 20 percent. Assume that two years after the purchase of the CD, the economy enters a boom period, and the prices of goods and services rise at an annual rate of 5 percent.
   a. What is José's after-tax yield?
   b. Explain inflation risk to José and why he is effectively losing money on this investment.
5. ***Establishing an Emergency Fund*** You have estimated that you need $6,000 in liquid assets. You currently have only $1,000, which is invested in a savings account earning 3 percent nominal interest, compounded monthly. Your current budget leaves $300 per month to apply to this goal. If you plan to add this money to your savings at the end of every month, how much will you have after one year? (*Hint:* Use the future value of an annuity formula with monthly payments and a monthly interest rate.)
6. ***Rule of 72*** You currently have $6,000 invested in a taxable savings account with an APR of 7 percent. Your marginal tax rate is 20 percent. If you leave the money in the account with all the interest, how long will it take for you to have $12,000? (*Hint:* Calculate your after-tax yield, and then use the Rule of 72 to estimate the time until it doubles in value.)
7. ***Comparing Account Alternatives*** You live in a college town and notice that a local financial institution is advertising "free checking" to students. After calling the bank, you find that the $10 per month service charge is waived as long as the account balance stays above $200 during the month; in addition, the number of checks is limited to 20 per month. Is this really a "free account"? Why or why not?

Using Web Resources for Financial Planning

1. ***Comparing Rates.*** Search for the latest interest rates paid on savings accounts, checking accounts, money market accounts, and CDs. Check *www.bankrate.com* and *www.banx.com* for information on several types of accounts. In addition, check local financial institution websites for rates offered in your area. Make a table that shows the best rates for each type of account and where you can get those rates. Be sure to look for any restrictions and fees.
2. ***Anticipate Interest Rate Changes.*** The Federal Reserve Bank Open Market Committee (FMOC) meets every six weeks to consider making changes to the target federal funds rate. Since this rate is considered a base rate in the economy, other rates will react accordingly. Search the Web for the following information:
   a. When is the next FMOC meeting?
   (Check *www.federalreserve.gov* for this information.)
   b. What is the Fed expected to do to interest rates at its next meeting? You can find this information at any major financial website, such as *kiplinger.com*, *money.cnn.com*, or *www.fool.com*.
3. ***Investigate Your Online Bill-Pay Options.*** Search the Web for companies that offer bill-paying services. Make a table that compares their features, including security, fees, and interfaces with financial planning software.
4. ***How Secure Is Your Financial Institution's Website?*** It's important to learn how to safeguard your banking information and personal data. Look at your bank's website for information about its security practices, or contact the bank directly and ask for this information. Some banks, as an added convenience to their customers, offer online links to merchants, retail stores, travel agents, and other nonfinancial sites. You should note that these products and services are not insured by the FDIC, and your bank probably does not guarantee the products and services. Furthermore, the security provided for your financial information on the bank's website does not extend to these links.
5. ***How Can Savings Bonds Help You Reach Your Financial Goals?*** Go to *publicdebt.treas.gov* and find the page for calculators. Use the Savings Bond Calculator to see how savings bonds can help you reach your financial goals. Find out how to set up a regular savings plan using the Savings Planner. Determine the difference between the after-tax returns for U.S. savings bonds and alternative savings plans by using the Tax Advantages Calculator.

Learning by Doing Solutions

LBD 5-1: 1. Hanna needs to consider whether any of the objectives of cash management apply to her. For example, since she usually runs out of money each month, she may be risking bank overdraft charges. She is also at risk for emergencies such as temporary illness or loss of job.

LBD 5-2: 1. Balance checkbook: overdraft charges, overspending: pay bills on time: later charges, bad credit rating; pay yourself first: reduced saving, overspending; evaluate accounts and providers: higher costs, lower earnings; 2. If the monthly fee is less than the cost in time and effort and the late fees you would otherwise incur.

LBD 5-3: 1. Any type of depository institution; 2. Because credit unions are nonprofits, they can offer loans at lower prices, but Luis will have to open an account there, since loans are only made to members. He should consider all four P's: product, price, people, and place. Does the institution offer the products he wants, competitive interest rates, good service and a convenient location?

LBD 5-4: 1a. NOW; 1b. CD; 2a. demand deposit; 2b. one-year CD.

LBD 5-5: 1. Approximation: 72/4.25 = 16.9 years; 2. Daily compounding; 3. Assuming you can exclude all the interest from taxation, you'll save about 0.3 × 0.05 × $1,000 = $15 per year in taxes by investing in the Series EE bond. You should also consider how much you would lose in each case if you needed to access the money before the five years are up.

Building Financial Planning Skills Through Case Applications

Case 5-1 Erica Whitman Gets into Cash Flow Trouble

Erica Whitman, a college junior, normally prides herself on keeping control of her finances. But the fall semester of 2004 was a disaster. She contracted the West Nile virus and was very sick for months. It was an effort just to keep up with her classes, let alone balance her checkbook. Since she had to quit her part-time job, she knew her checking account balance was getting a little low, but she didn't quite realize how low until she got a bank notice indicating that she had bounced several checks.

a. Assuming that each retailer (but not the electric company) charges her a penalty of $20 and her bank charges $25 for each bounced check, how much will this cash management mistake cost her in total?

b. How much does she need to deposit in the account to have enough to make good on all her bills plus pay her penalties? The returned checks are as follows:

Written to:	$	Purpose
Valley Electric Authority	40.32	Electric bill
Safeway	64.28	Groceries
Hot Wok Café	8.54	Take-out Chinese
Papa John's	13.68	Pizza
Current account balance	−119.40	

c. Since her current account balance is not the same as the total of her bounced checks, this means that Erica had at least some funds in her account when these checks came in. Assuming that the bounced check fees were already subtracted to arrive at the amount shown and she has no other bank charges, how much did she have in her account to start with?

d. What advice would you offer to Erica that will help her avoid this problem in the future?

Case 5-2 Weighing Liquidity Needs Against Higher Returns on Savings

Phil and Kendra Gonzalez graduated from college in May 2003 and were married the following December. They both work for the same high-tech company as software designers, and their combined take-home pay is $5,200 per month. With monthly expenses that average only $3,000, they've been able to accumulate $14,000 over the last year in a joint savings account that currently pays 3 percent interest. They also generally keep a little more than their $500 minimum balance in a checking account that pays no interest. If their checking account drops below the $500 minimum in any given month, the bank assesses a monthly fee of $10. This happens to them about once every three months. At present, Phil and Kendra have no investment accounts other than their savings account and their employment-based retirement funds. Phil is trying to talk Kendra into putting $5,000 of their savings into a higher-interest CD and another $5,000 into a stock mutual fund. He has found an online bank that is offering 6 percent interest on five-year CDs, and he has been investigating several stock funds that have had good returns over the last year. Kendra is not so sure. To investigate their options, she calls their current bank and asks about cash management account alternatives that might provide them with better interest earnings. The bank officer suggests that they consider moving their checking to an interest-earning account that pays 2 percent per year and carries a $1,000 minimum balance. He suggests spreading their investments into several CDs with increasing maturities. The five-year CD at this institution pays 5.75 percent.

a. How much do you think the Gonzalezes should hold in liquid accounts? Explain your reasoning.

b. What are the risks of putting the money in CDs or in stocks instead of keeping it in regular savings? Would Kendra and Phil be exposed to any unusual liquidity risk?

c. Based on your analysis of their needs and options, what course of action would you recommend to the Gonzalezes? What additional information do they need to consider in making their decision?

Case 5-3 Felicia Kobayashi Seeks a New Bank

Felicia Kobayashi has been using the same financial institution since she moved to Springfield in 1992. Since that time, there's been a lot of consolidation in the banking community, and her formerly local bank has been bought up by a national conglomerate. After the resulting layoffs in the small branch office where she usually conducts business, Felicia began to notice that it took much longer to make deposits and withdrawals, whether at the drive-through teller or inside the branch. As a result, she's considering switching her business to a different financial institution. She currently maintains a regular checking account for paying bills and has a savings account with $15,000 in it. Based on what you've learned in this chapter, outline a plan for Felicia to use in choosing a new bank and deciding among alternative account choices.

DEVELOPING PERSONAL FINANCIAL skills for life

Learning about Yourself

5-1. Are You a Procrastinator?

For each of the following statements, write the number that shows the extent to which you agree (5 = strongly agree; 4 = agree; 3 = undecided; 2 = disagree; 1 = strongly disagree).

_____ **1.** I tend to have trouble finishing jobs, even when they're important.

_____ **2.** I'm always on time for appointments.

_____ **3.** I put off starting on things that I don't like to do.

_____ **4.** Whenever I make a plan of action, I follow it.

_____ **5.** I like to take shortcuts when I'm doing something boring.

_____ **6.** When I have to work with others on a project, everyone knows they can rely on me to get the job done.

_____ **7.** If I have a deadline for a project, I usually wait until the last minute to start.

_____ **8.** When I'm done with my work, I always check it over.

_____ **9.** I tend to be good at wasting time.

_____ **10.** I always try to finish projects before they're due.

Scoring:

Add up your total for the even-numbered statements (2, 4, 6, etc.) and your total for the odd-numbered statements (1, 3, 5 etc.). Subtract the even total from the odd total. The larger the difference, the greater the likelihood that you tend to procrastinate. You'll be more likely to put off paying bills and balancing your checkbook. You may have previously bounced checks. Procrastinators need to develop methods to overcome their natural tendencies, such as setting up automatic bill-paying services and keeping a larger minimum balance. If your total score is zero or less, then you're probably a person who tends to be organized and takes responsibility for finishing tasks. In your personal finances, you'll be less likely to violate the rules of effective cash management.

Develop Your Skills

5-2. Evaluate Your Cash Management Needs and Implement Your Plan

1. Using the personal financial statements you developed in Chapter 2, evaluate your cash needs. Do you have enough to meet emergency needs? Use the worksheet in your *Personal Financial Planner* to summarize your cash needs and to record your work for the rest of this exercise.
2. Make a list of any factors that might increase your liquidity risk for the coming year.
3. What are your current sources, if any, of cash to meet these emergency needs?
4. Identify your cash management goals. Assuming that increased liquidity is one of your personal financial goals, break down this goal into at least two subgoals and identify the steps you must take to accomplish them.
5. Summarize information on the financial institutions you currently use to meet your cash management needs.
6. Identify any additional cash management products or services that you may need within the next five years.
7. Identify three alternative financial institutions to investigate. Collect information on each and summarize the information in your *Personal Financial Planner*.
8. Based on your analysis using the four P's (product, price, people, and place), decide on your strategies for cash management.

PFP Worksheet 20
Cash Needs Analysis

PFP Worksheet 22
Evaluating Financial
Service Providers

BEFORE studying this chapter, you should review

- Household financial ratios (Chapter 2).
- Present value of a monthly annuity (Chapter 2).
- Annual percentage yield (Chapter 5).

THE NAVIGATOR

- ☐ Review Before Studying this Chapter list.
- ☐ Scan Learning Objectives.
- ☐ Take Myth or Fact quiz and find the answers throughout the chapter.
- ☐ Read chapter and answer Learning by Doing exercises.
- ☐ Review Key Terms and Key Calculations.
- ☐ Do end-of-chapter exercises.
- ☐ Take review quiz on the text website.
- ☐ Solve end-of-chapter cases.

Purchasing Strategies and Credit Cards

CHAPTER 6

Myth or Fact?

Consider each of the following statements and decide whether it is a *myth* or a *fact*. Look for the answers in the *Fact* boxes in the chapter.

	MYTH	FACT
1. The only negative outcome from having a bad credit record is that it makes it more difficult to get additional credit.	☐	☐
2. The average household owes money on several credit cards and has trouble making payments.	☐	☐
3. Credit cards originated in the 1970s when MasterCard and Visa were first introduced.	☐	☐
4. It makes sense to always pay the minimum payment amount due on your credit card in order to reduce the amount that you owe.	☐	☐
5. With improved computer encryption technology, the number of people who have their identity stolen every year is declining.	☐	☐

LEARNING objectives

1. Apply the personal financial planning process to making consumer purchase decisions.
2. Identify the advantages and disadvantages of using consumer credit to make purchases.
3. Understand the various types of consumer credit.
4. Evaluate credit card alternatives, including terms and costs.
5. Recognize the hazards of credit card use, including the risk of identity theft.

...applying the planning process

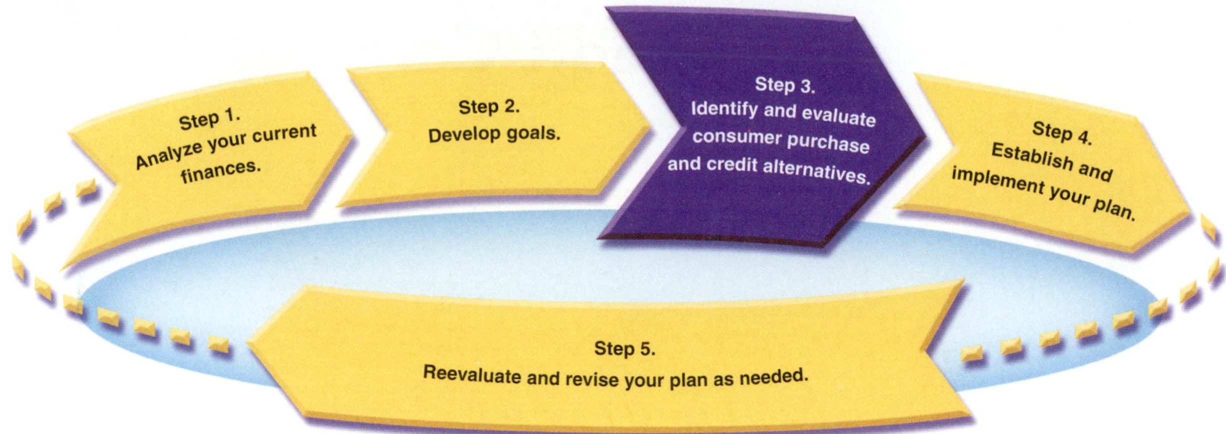

The most recent consumer finance statistics show that U.S. households on average spend more than they earn each year. Americans are buying restaurant meals, cars, consumer electronics, clothes, and vacations in record quantities, and they're commonly financing these purchases by taking on more debt—borrowing through both loans and credit cards. Since excessive spending and high debt payments make it more difficult to achieve financial goals, managing these two problems is a critical component of personal financial planning. Recent survey evidence reported on www.cardweb.com indicates that this principle is fairly well understood—eight out of ten consumers interviewed at the end of 2003 indicated that debt reduction was one of their New Year's resolutions for 2004. Seven out of ten said they planned to limit credit card usage. But, despite good intentions, it's not easy to stick to the plan—in general, around a fourth of such resolutions last only two weeks, and about half are scrapped after three months.

How can you ensure that your financial plan won't be undermined by excessive spending and borrowing? In this chapter, you'll learn how to avoid the debt trap by limiting your consumer purchases to those that are consistent with your financial plan and by reducing your reliance on consumer debt. We start by examining how to make better decisions by applying the planning process to making consumer purchases—carefully researching alternatives and using sound evaluation criteria. We also consider the advantages and disadvantages of consumer credit, types of credit, credit card terms and costs, and the risk of identity theft. Chapter 7 continues the discussion of consumer credit by describing the sources and types of consumer loans, which are an alternative to credit card borrowing. In Chapter 7, you'll also learn about consumer credit rights and general management of your credit.

Chapter Preview

Consumer Purchases and Your Financial Plan

- Is the Purchase Consistent with Your Prioritized Goals?
- Can You Afford It?
- Cash or Credit?
- Making the Consumer Purchase Decision

The Advantages and Disadvantages of Consumer Credit

- Advantages of Consumer Credit
- Disadvantages of Consumer Credit
- Consumer Credit and the Economy

Types of Consumer Credit

- Closed-end credit
- Open-end Credit

Credit Cards

- What Are Credit Cards?
- History of Credit Cards
- Types of "Plastic"
- Common Contract Terms
- Finance Charges
- Choosing Cards Based on APR

The Advantages and Disadvantages of Credit Card Use

- Advantages of Credit Cards
- Disadvantages of Credit Cards

Consumer Purchases and Your Financial Plan

LEARNING objective

1 Apply the personal financial planning process to making consumer purchase decisions.

Whether or not you're aware of it, when you decide to buy something today, you're also deciding *not* to spend the money on something else and *not* to save or invest the money. Unfortunately, it has never been tougher to refrain from excess spending. Most people are bombarded daily with media ads intended to make them overcome their carefully developed financial plans and buy more "stuff." If you don't have the money right now, no problem—there are plenty of credit cards, "zero interest financing," and "no payments until next year." It's easy to see why so many U.S. families are in financial trouble—it's simply much easier to spend than it is to stick to a budget. And it's also easy to see why retailers would prefer that you forget your budget and buy their products—their companies' financial health depends on it.

In order for you to stick to your financial plan, your purchase and credit decisions should be directly related to the financial goals you developed in Chapter 2. Purchases that are for **necessities**—things you need in order to live, such as food, clothing, and shelter—must have priority over those that are **luxuries**, things you want but can live without—the desirable "extras" like a new car, a home theater system, or a trip to Mexico over spring break. All spending decisions have a ripple effect on your financial plan—money spent on one thing means less money to spend on another or to save for the future. Using credit to buy something now only delays the inevitable cash outflow and entails the additional cost of interest on the borrowed funds.

necessities

Things needed for basic living, such as food, clothing, and shelter.

luxuries

Things that you want but can live without.

The next time you're thinking about buying something, try applying the decision process outlined in Exhibit 6-1. First, ask yourself whether it fits with your financial plan. Answering this question should include an evaluation of whether it will help you to achieve any of your goals and whether you can afford to make the purchase at the current time. If you decide to make the purchase, you may also want to consider whether to pay cash or to borrow the funds for the purchase.

Is the Purchase Consistent with Your Prioritized Goals?

Since every purchase decision influences your ability to achieve your short-term and long-term goals, you should not make major purchases without careful reference to the priorities that you identified when you set these goals. Before making any purchase, particularly a large one, ask yourself whether the item you are considering purchasing is consistent with your financial plan. If it isn't, then ask yourself whether you need to reevaluate your prioritized goals to include it.

The purchase of a car may not have been on your original list of goals, for example, but if your 1985 Chevy Blazer has just "died" and you need transportation to get to and from school or work, then you probably need to add a car to your list. However, despite all the new car ads in the paper, you do not *need* a new car—you need transportation, and a used car is also an alternative. You might ultimately decide that the current deals on new cars and the reduced cost of repairs and maintenance make it worthwhile to buy a new car. Nevertheless, you should initially approach the question with a wider set of alternatives. If you do decide to add the purchase of a new car to your list of financial goals, you'll need to consider how it will affect your ability to achieve your other goals—in other words, you'll need to reevaluate your priorities and your allocation of funds to each. If you've been contributing $300 per month to a savings account for your daughter's college education and the new car will cost you an additional $300 in loan costs and insurance, then you must consider whether this is a tradeoff you're prepared to make.

Buying a car is a major purchase decision, but large purchases aren't the only ones to be considered. In fact, when people analyze their excess spending, they often find that the little stuff is to blame—clothes, books, food, and other less expensive consumer items seem inconsequential alone but can add up to thousands of dollars each year. Although you may not have included specific goals related to such purchases, you probably did include goals related to increased saving or a reduction in household debt. Always keep in mind that every dollar spent on consumer goods is one less dollar spent on these goals.

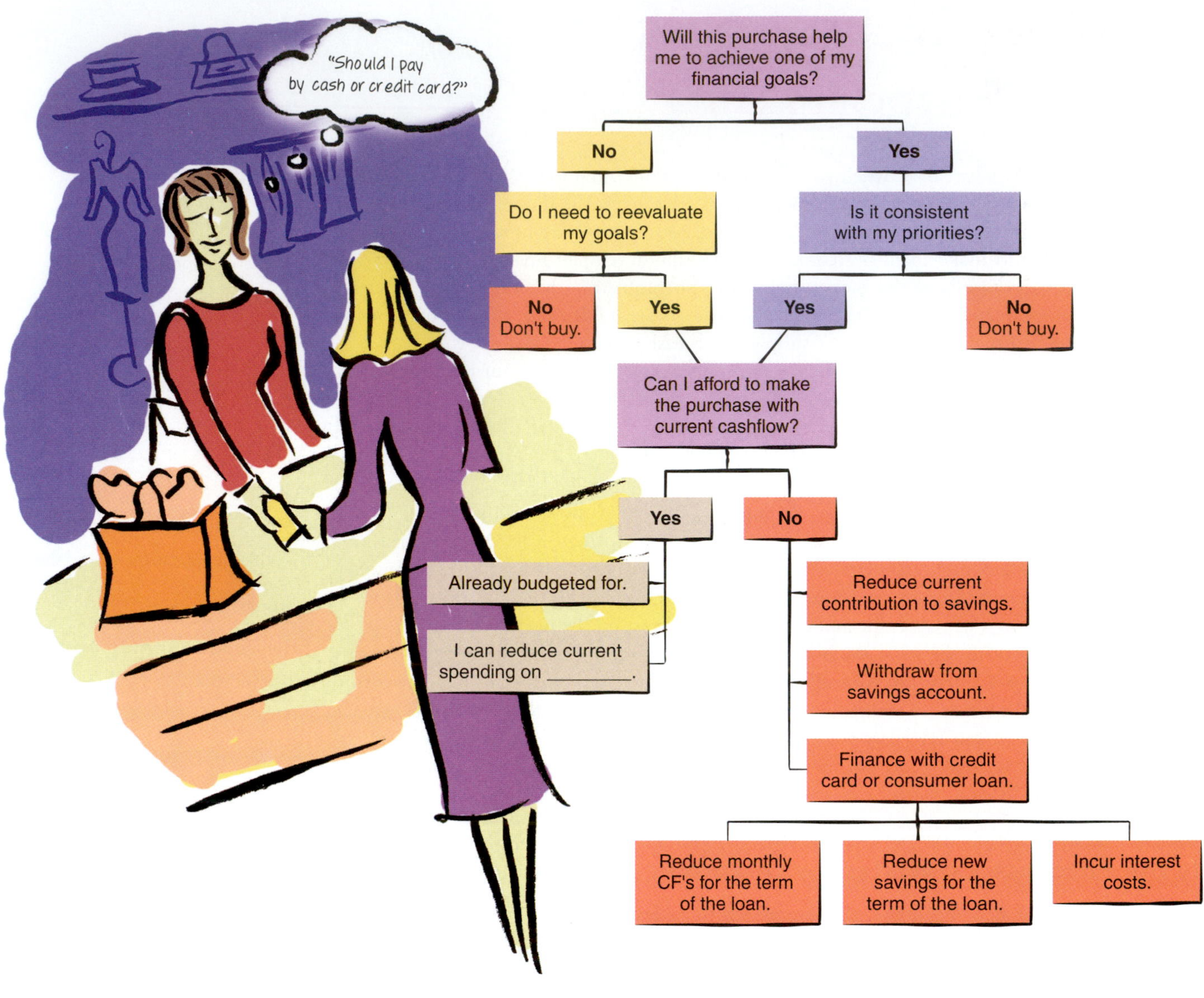

EXHIBIT 6-1 Decision Process for Making Consumer Purchases

In addition to sales pressure from retailers, many people also have psychological reasons for making unnecessary purchases. The *Money Psychology* box, "Why Do You Shop?" suggests that some people may shop for recreation, to offset depression, or for other reasons that are inconsistent with sound financial planning. Although these bad financial habits are often deeply rooted and thus difficult to overcome, recognizing them is certainly a step in the right direction.

Can You Afford It?

Related to the question of how a purchase fits with your goals is the more practical question of whether you have sufficient funds to pay for it. As illustrated in Exhibit 6-1, if you don't have the cash, you can't make the purchase without either reducing your current contributions to savings, withdrawing money from accumulated savings, or borrowing money to make the purchase. Each of these three alternatives will adversely affect your progress toward achieving financial goals.

Money Psychology

Why Do You Shop?

In principle, you should shop only when you need to buy something—food, clothing, a birthday present for your mother, or whatever. But, in part because of product advertising intended to make you want things you don't need, "shopping" has taken on new meaning. In fact, people shop for so many reasons that there is actually a discipline of study called "consumer psychology." Experts in this field, who specialize in tracking the latest shopping trends and identifying ways of attracting shoppers to particular products, are in high demand.

Do you shop for the wrong reasons? Ask yourself the following questions:

- Is shopping a preferred leisure activity for me?
- Do I shop when I'm unhappy in an attempt to make myself feel better?
- Am I an impulsive shopper, unable to resist certain purchases?
- Do I buy some consumer goods to "keep up with the Joneses"?
- Do I ever spend money to "get even" with my spouse or partner?
- Do I buy toys or candy for my children as bribes for good behavior?

If you've answered "yes" to one or more of these questions, you might want to consider strategies to modify your behavior so that your financial plan will not be negatively affected by your shopping behavior.

In Chapter 2, you created a personal balance sheet and personal cash flow statement to evaluate your current financial situation. Based on these financial statements, you developed a budget in Chapter 3 in which you allocated your excess monthly cash flow to specific goals. If the purchase you're considering is consistent with your spending plan, and your other expenditures during the month have been as well, then you know that you can afford to make a cash purchase at this time. For small cash purchases, such as dinner out at a nice restaurant or a new pair of jeans, you may decide to deviate from your budget in a given month, spending more in one budget category and less in another. However, if the purchase will require you to reduce your contribution to savings or will cause your cash outflows to exceed your cash inflows for the month, this decision requires a higher level of deliberation.

Cash or Credit?

Any time you receive cash, goods, or services now and arrange to pay for them later, you are buying on **credit**. If you use credit for personal needs other than home purchases, you're using **consumer credit**. You can borrow from a friend or family member, a firm with which you do business, or a financial institution (such as a bank, credit union, or insurance company). The most common types of consumer credit are credit card accounts, automobile loans, home equity loans, and student loans. In each case, the lender is letting you have the use of the money now and is expecting you to repay it with interest, often over a specified time period.

credit

Arrangement to receive cash, goods, or services now and pay later.

consumer credit

Credit used for personal needs other than home purchases.

Before you decide to borrow funds to make a purchase, whether through a credit card or a consumer loan, be careful to evaluate the short-term and long-term effects on your monthly cash flow. The future payments, including the original purchase price and interest charges, will reduce your net monthly cash flow and thus your ability to make contributions to savings. Interest charges will increase the total cost of the product you are purchasing. Therefore, in deciding whether to pay cash, take money from savings, or borrow the funds to make a purchase, be sure to consider the tradeoffs between the cost of borrowing and the lost earnings on savings.

Many types of consumer credit—most credit cards, for example—require that you pay interest rates that are much higher than what you can earn on your savings. If you have to pay 18 percent interest on your credit card and you're only earning 5 percent on a savings account, you'll be better off taking the money from savings rather than borrowing the funds for the purchase. Sometimes, though, consumer loan rates are *lower* than the rate you're earning on your invested dollars, making it preferable to borrow. For example, suppose you plan to purchase a car for $10,000. You have sufficient savings to make this purchase and are earning 5 percent per year interest on your savings account. If the car dealer is offering 3 percent interest on a car loan, you may be better off taking out the loan, making payments from the savings account, and earning the 2 percent difference. The advisability of this strategy will depend on the terms of the loan (discussed in detail in Chapter 7) and any restrictions on your savings withdrawals.

Making the Consumer Purchase Decision

Suppose you've determined that a particular purchase is consistent with your financial plan and that you can afford to make the purchase. The next step is to apply the tools of financial decision making, as presented in Chapter 1. As with other types of financial decisions, you should always identify and evaluate your alternatives before making the actual purchase. This implies that you should avoid making impulse or spur-of-the-moment purchases. Obviously, the more expensive the item, the more important it is to take the time to consider all your options.

Identify Your Alternatives. The first step in making the purchase decision is identifying what your alternatives are. Although doing your own research may be necessary in some circumstances, your time is valuable. You can often save yourself significant time and effort by making use of knowledge that has been developed by others. For example, *Consumer Reports*, a monthly magazine available in most libraries, provides information about a wide variety of household products and services, including comparison of features, reliability, and independent testing results. For most types of products, the Internet is another good source of information, even if you don't feel comfortable making your actual purchase on the Internet. Some search engines will even identify the vendor with the lowest price for a given name-brand item.

Comparison shop with www.consumerreports.org and www.pricescan.com; find ratings for online retailers at shop.bizrate.com and www.ratingwonders.com.

In identifying your alternatives, don't overlook the possibility of buying a used product. It makes sense to consider buying some products—sports gear and CDs, for example—in "gently used" condition. Traditional sources for used goods include garage sales, newspaper ads, pawnshops, and flea markets. However, the cost savings may not justify the time and effort you'll have to invest in searching all these sources. And if you live in a rural area, you may not have easy access to these markets at all. Fortunately, you do have access to a large marketplace for buying and selling used products through the Internet. Online auctions have been in place for several years and attract huge numbers of buyers and sellers each day. For example, ebay.com, the most popular Internet auction site, boasts millions of items for sale and facilitates billions of transactions per year. If you're interested in buying on eBay, consider the suggestions of a professional online seller in the *Ask the Expert* box, "Tips for Buying on eBay."

Browse eBay's many product offerings at www.ebay.com.

ask the expert — Tips for Buying on eBay

Pat Prill
eBay Seller,
Owner, Mom 'n Me

For many years, music teacher Pat Prill owned and operated Mom 'n Me, a side business selling used items at local flea markets. After retiring in the late 1990s, Pat decided to expand the business by selling her merchandise on the Internet. She has significantly increased her annual business income as a result. Based on her extensive experience as an eBay seller, Pat offers the following tips for individuals interested in making Internet auction purchases:

1. Read the directions provided in the eBay Buyers Guide.
2. Be sure to read everything about an item before you bid on it.
3. Find out the shipping charge before you bid. Sellers often try to make extra money by charging unreasonable shipping fees.
4. E-mail the seller with any questions you have. There is nothing more disappointing than receiving an item and finding that it's the wrong color, size, or has a defect.
5. Check the "Seller's Feedback" provided on the eBay site. This will tell you positive and negative information about the seller reported by previous customers.
6. Don't make an impulse bid. Check completed items and other sellers who are listing the same item to see if you're getting a fair price.
7. Send payment in a timely manner and inform the seller that payment has been sent.
8. Leave positive feedback for the seller (if you're satisfied) and ask that the seller leave positive feedback about you as well.

GO FIGURE!

Evaluating Purchase Alternatives

Problem: Guy Dimotto has decided to buy a new 17-inch flat panel display monitor for his computer. Based on *Consumer Reports* ratings, he narrowed his choices down to three monitors, for which he has the following information. Identify the trade-offs that he must consider in deciding between these alternatives. Is there anything more that he should investigate before making his decision?

Feature	Monitor 1	Monitor 2	Monitor 3
Price	$400	$450	$500
Where to buy	Store in city 1 hour away	Local store	Local store
Warranty	1 year parts and labor	3 years parts and labor	4 years parts and labor
Consumer rating	Very good	Very good	Excellent
Compatible with other equipment	Yes	Yes	Yes

Solution: Guy is primarily trading price and quality. He must consider whether the lower price of Monitor 1 outweighs the higher consumer rating, location convenience, and longer warranty period offered by the more expensive montiors. Deciding between Monitors 2 and 3 will require balancing the $50 price difference against the better rating and warranty.

Evaluate Your Alternatives. Once you've identified your alternatives, you can evaluate the pros and cons of each. This step requires that you weigh various product characteristics in light of your requirements. A good approach is to set up a table that summarizes the key features of each alternative. If you decide that certain features are absolutely necessary, you can eliminate alternatives that don't meet these criteria before going on with your comparison. The *Go Figure* box, "Evaluating Purchase Alternatives," outlines this decision process applied to the purchase of a flat-panel display monitor for a computer. Depending on what you are buying and what your requirements are, your table categories may be different from those shown in the example. But for most purchase decisions, you'll probably include the price and the specific product attributes of interest (size, quality, manufacturer), along with any quality ratings you can find. In some cases, you may also consider availability, recommendations of friends, purchase location, personal inspection at a local store, and whether a warranty is offered.

A **warranty** is a promise or guaranty made by the manufacturer or seller. Unless a product is sold "as is," it automatically comes with implied warranties that it is suitable for sale and will work as intended. In addition to the implied warranties, a product may also have an express, or written, warranty. An express warranty may be fairly limited—for example, promising to pay for replacement parts but not labor—or it may provide more extensive protection or complete replacement of the product.

warranty

A promise or guaranty made by the manufacturer or seller of a product, which may include repair or replacement of defective or damaged merchandise.

Although most warranties come from manufacturers of products, retailers may sometimes offer to sell you an extended warranty, or service contract, on certain products, such as automobiles and consumer electronics. In general, these contracts tend to be very profitable for the companies that sell them, so you should read the terms carefully. It's generally not a good idea to buy insurance to cover small costs that you could easily cover out of current cash flow.

Implement Your Purchase Decision. The last step in the purchase decision is to actually buy the product. Although many people skip the other steps and move right to the purchase, application of good decision-making skills will result in purchases that better meet your needs and better fit with your financial plan. If you've decided to use credit to make the purchase, you need to carefully consider your alternative sources of borrowing.

Learning by Doing 6-1

You've just moved into an apartment, and you've determined that you need to purchase a sofa for your living room. You plan to pay for it with cash saved for this purpose.

1. Describe the process you should apply to your sofa purchase.
2. Identify alternative sources for buying your sofa.
3. If you were to set up a table to compare your purchase alternatives, what features would you include in the table?

The Advantages and Disadvantages of Consumer Credit

LEARNING objective

2 Identify the advantages and disadvantages of using consumer credit to make purchases.

Although too much debt can obviously have an adverse impact on your household finances, credit is not inherently bad, and it may play an important role in your financial plan. In this section, we outline the advantages and disadvantages of consumer credit in general. Some of the specific problems associated with using high-interest credit cards will be discussed later in the chapter.

Advantages of Consumer Credit

Consumer credit allows you to spread the cost of more expensive purchases over time. It may offer a convenient and safe alternative to carrying cash and also provides a source of emergency cash.

Buy Now, Pay Later. Most people strive to improve their standard of living over time. The ability to purchase large-ticket items on credit—with borrowed funds—can sometimes make this dream a reality sooner. Being able to buy more expensive items now and pay for them over time makes it possible to fit purchases into your budget. You don't have to save up the entire purchase price of a car, for example, before buying one. Instead, you can essentially enjoy the use of the product *while* you are paying for it. This type of arrangement is advantageous as long as (1) you can afford the payments without sacrificing other worthy financial goals, and (2) the product you purchase lasts at least as long as the time period over which you make payments.

Convenience and Safety. Instead of carrying large amounts of cash, you can simply carry a credit card. It's convenient, and although a card can be stolen, it's not as easy as cash for a thief to use. If you pay off your balance every month before the due date, you can take advantage of free credit offered by the card issuer and still have the convenience and safety of not carrying cash. It's important to note, however, that debit cards offer similar advantages.

Source of Emergency Cash. Credit lines can be a source of funds to meet emergency needs, as discussed in Chapter 5. As always, though, in deciding whether to use credit in this way, it's important to consider whether you'll be able to repay the debt in accordance with the credit terms and how the payments will affect your household cash flow.

Retail establishments commonly indicate the credit cards they will accept by putting stickers on their doors.

Disadvantages of Consumer Credit

The primary reasons for limiting your use of credit include the impact on your household financial health, the costs associated with borrowing, the potential for overspending, and the impact on your insurance premiums.

Financial Statement Impact. The more you borrow, relative to your total wealth, the worse your liquidity and debt ratios will look. This means that you may limit your financial flexibility if you take on too much credit. You may also expose your household to too much risk, since you're committing your family to greater fixed expenses; if you or your spouse were laid off, you might not be able to meet these expenses. In addition, if you're planning to buy a home, high levels of consumer debt may make it more difficult for you to qualify for a mortgage.

Increased Costs. When you use consumer credit as a means of spreading the cost of a purchase over time, you nearly always pay more for your purchase in the long run because of the financing costs of the loan. Credit is never free. Lenders charge interest for the use of their funds and commonly also charge additional fees and penalties, as will be discussed in more detail later. Even when retailers offer zero-interest financing, you can be sure that they're making money on fees or, alternatively, that you could get a better deal on the price if you didn't take the cheap financing.

Risk of Overspending. The availability of consumer credit increases the risk that you will overspend. Without credit cards, if you don't have enough cash in your pocket or your checking account, you can't make the purchase. If you have a credit card, though, not only can you make the purchase but you also can more easily find a good reason to do so. Instead of buying one sweater at that great sale price, why not buy one in each of the three colors? Why make yourself choose between those two CDs, when you can buy both? Retailers even use advertising to reinforce the painlessness of making credit purchases. Next to the full price, you might see: "Only $25 per month if you take advantage of in-store credit."

Fact #1

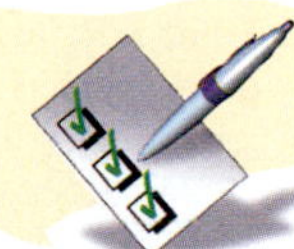

Bad credit can hurt much more than your ability to get a loan. Prospective landlords and employers commonly check your credit before doing business with you. Most insurers now use credit information in pricing auto and homeowners insurance policies—this means that late payments on credit cards or large outstanding credit balances can now cause your premiums to increase or your policy to be canceled.

Higher Insurance Premiums. For the last several years, insurance companies have been using consumer credit history as a factor in pricing individual auto and homeowner's insurance policies. Thus, if you have a lot of outstanding debt or a history of making late credit card payments, you may be paying a higher insurance premium than others with better credit.

Consumer Credit and the Economy

In addition to offering certain advantages to consumers, credit benefits the U.S. economy as a whole. When consumers spend more, businesses profit, employment increases, and the economic outlook improves. The construction industry has benefited from recent low mortgage rates, which have also allowed more people to become homeowners and thus benefit from growing home equity. Even in the recent recession, consumer spending remained relatively strong, a fact generally attributed to the low interest rates that prevailed during that period.

Despite these benefits, many experts believe that the level of household debt in the United States, relative to income and wealth, may be cause for concern. As a result of easy credit and changing attitudes about debt, the average household is relying more on borrowed funds than in the past. In 2003, for example, Americans added $30 billion to total revolving credit.

Fact #2

The average U.S. household has eight credit cards and owes more than $8,000 on them. About 50 percent report having difficulty making their minimum payments. The total amount of consumer credit outstanding in the United States increased 372 percent in the last 20 years, from $445 billion in 1983 to $2.1 trillion in 2003.

Increasing levels of household debt have adversely affected personal balance sheets, particularly in conjunction with the decline in household wealth caused by the stock market decline in recent years. Exhibit 6-2 shows aggregate U.S. household debt relative to aggregate household wealth and income over time. The trend is clear—the ratio of debt to assets has increased more than 30 percent over the last two decades, from 13.8 percent to 18.1 percent. Americans have been taking on more debt relative to total wealth. Interestingly, the home mortgage share of total debt has remained relatively stable over time—around 75 percent—so this implies that households have increased their use of all kinds of debt. Of greater concern, though, is the even greater change in household debt relative to aggregate disposable income—the increase from 72 percent to 104 percent represents nearly a 50 percent increase in only 17 years. Households generally are able to achieve a higher standard of living in the short run by borrowing to finance current consumption, but in the long run, the bills must be paid. Since incomes are rising more slowly than debt, household budgets are likely to feel the strain in the near future.

For statistics related to credit card use, go to www.cardweb.com.

EXHIBIT 6-2

Household Debt in the United States

Source: Ratios calculated using aggregate household assets and debts reported by the Federal Reserve, "Balance Sheet of Households" (2003), available at www.federalreserve.gov. Total debt includes outstanding home mortgages, home equity loans, and consumer credit. Total assets include real estate, consumer goods, and financial assets.

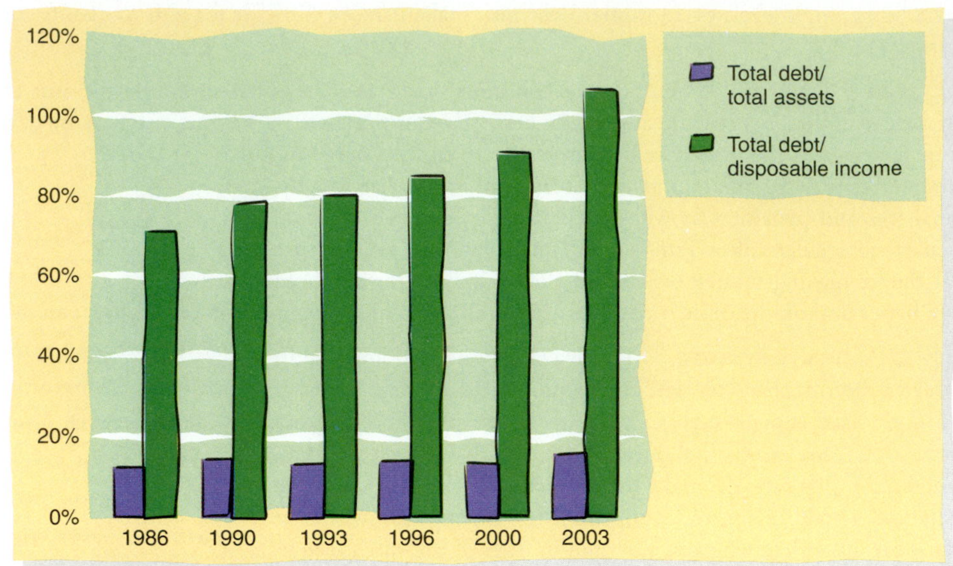

Learning by Doing 6-2

Penny has just found out from her dentist that she needs to have her wisdom teeth removed. Since she has been experiencing some jaw complications, she can't delay this expenditure, and she doesn't have dental insurance.

1. What are Penny's options?
2. Explain the advantages and disadvantages of using credit to pay for this expense.

Types of Consumer Credit

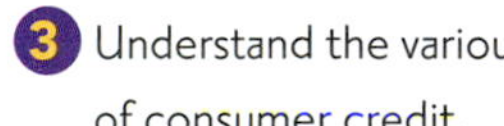

LEARNING objective

3 Understand the various types of consumer credit.

We've already seen that generally, when you buy something, you must either use current cash flow, take money from savings, or borrow the money and repay it later. Most people who choose to borrow for their consumer purchases use some type of consumer credit. Consumer credit is usually placed in different categories based on the type of contractual arrangement. The two general types of credit arrangements are closed-end and open-end credit.

closed-end credit Loans for a specific purpose paid back in a specified period of time, usually with monthly payments.

open-end credit or revolving credit Preapproved continuous loan that can cover many purchases and usually requires monthly partial payments.

credit limit or credit line Preapproved maximum amount of borrowing for open-end credit account.

Closed-end Credit

Closed-end credit is credit that a lender approves for a specific purpose (such as the purchase of a television or a car). It must be paid back with interest either in a single payment or according to an installment agreement, with equal payments per period ending at a specific time. This type of credit is often called a consumer loan. The types of consumer loans and their unique characteristics are discussed in Chapter 7.

Open-end Credit

In contrast to closed-end credit, **open-end credit**, also called **revolving credit**, is generally not earmarked for a particular purchase, and the payment period is not specified in advance. Instead, the lender preapproves an amount of credit, called a **credit limit** or **credit line**, in advance of any purchase. You can then use this credit as you wish until you've reached your credit limit. Credit cards—such as Visa and MasterCard, discussed in greater detail later in this chapter—are familiar examples of this type of credit. Personal loans, home equity lines of credit, and other delayed payment arrangements offered by retail and government service providers (such as your utility company) are also open-end credit arrangements. Examples of each of the two major types of credit arrangements are provided in Exhibit 6-3.

CLOSED-END CREDIT	
Type	Examples of Issuers
Mortgages	Depository institutions, insurance companies
Car loans	Depository institutions, auto manufacturers, such as General Motors and Ford
Student loans	Depository institutions
Installment contracts	Consumer finance companies

OPEN-END CREDIT	
Type	Examples of Issuers
Credit cards	
Bank cards	Depository institutions (seviced by MasterCard, Visa)
Retail cards	Sears, Foley's Home Depot, Target, JCPenny's
Travel and entertainment cards	American Express, Diner's Club
Overdraft protection	Depository institutions
Home equity line of credit	Depository institutions

EXHIBIT 6-3

Types of Credit

Credit Cards

LEARNING objective

4 Evaluate credit card alternatives, including terms and costs.

Credit cards, as just mentioned, are a familiar type of open-end credit. Since credit cards are so widely used, most people have some familiarity with them. However, credit cards come in several different types and include many features that are less commonly understood. In this section, we look at the various types of cards and their contract terms and conditions.

What Are Credit Cards?

The term **credit card** is used to cover a variety of types of cards. In general, a credit card is a plastic card printed with an account number and identifying the holder as a person who has entered into a revolving credit agreement with a lender. Some credit cards, in addition to allowing the holder to make consumer purchases, permit the holder to borrow cash in a transaction called a **cash advance**. You can get a cash advance at a participating financial institution, from an automated teller machine (ATM), or by writing a **convenience check**, a check supplied by the lender to make cash advances easier.

credit card

A plastic card printed with an account number and identifying the holder as a participant in a revolving credit agreement with a lender.

cash advance

A cash loan from credit card account.

convenience check

A check supplied by a credit card lender for the purpose of making a cash advance.

The History of Credit Cards

The idea of using credit cards to make purchases originated around 1950, with a card offered by Diners Club to wealthy individuals who didn't want to carry cash to pay for restaurant meals. Although cards initially were available only to the rich, the concept expanded to include middle-income households when BankAmericard was introduced in 1958; within a decade, more than 1 million BankAmericards were in use. By 1970, credit card debt hit $7 billion. Today, more in-store purchases are made with credit and debit cards than with cash, as shown in Exhibit 6-4.

Types of "Plastic"

Various types of credit cards differ somewhat in their features. Here, we review the differences among bank credit cards, retail credit cards, and travel and entertainment cards. We also compare these cards to debit and smart cards, which are similar to credit cards in some ways but offer users access to their checking or savings accounts rather than borrowed funds.

Fact #3

Credit cards have been around for half a century. The first credit cards were Diners Club and American Express cards, issued to wealthy New Yorkers for the purpose of paying for restaurant meals. Credit cards as we know them first appeared in 1958, when 60,000 BankAmericards were mailed to nearly every household in Fresno, California. Within two years, these households had racked up $59 million in debt—$350 million in today's dollars.

EXHIBIT 6-4

Cards Versus Cash: In-store Purchases by Payment Type

Source: Chart reprinted with permission from *Fortune*, February 23, 2004, p. 132. (c) 2004 Time Inc. All rights reserved. Data from Dove Consulting.

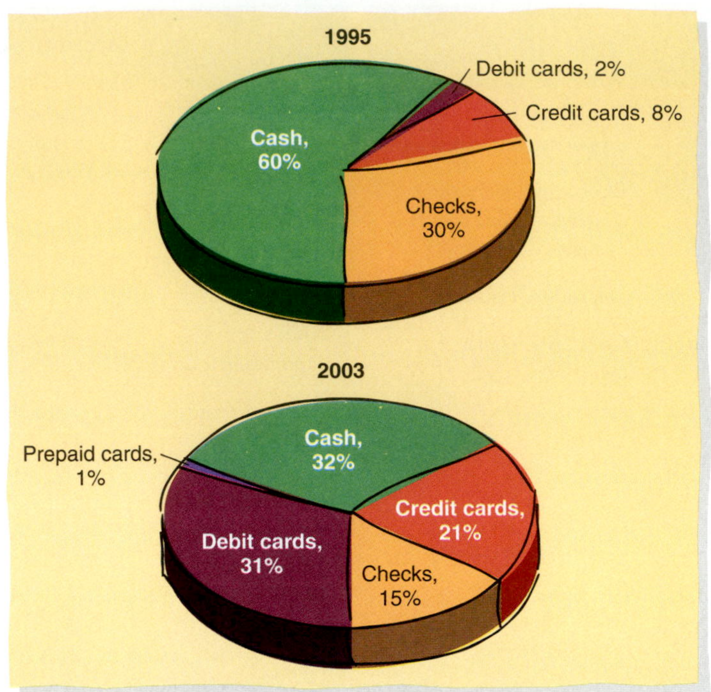

bank credit card

Credit card issued by a depository institution.

Bank Credit Cards. A **bank credit card** allows the holder to make purchases anywhere the card is accepted. Although these cards carry a brand name from a particular service provider (usually Visa, MasterCard, Discover, or Optima), the lender is usually a depository institution, such as a bank or credit union. Nearly all financial institutions offer credit cards today, and they pay transaction fees to the service providers for managing payments to retailers and billing of account holders.

It is now fairly common for nonfinancial companies to offer these types of cards in collaboration with a financial institution to encourage spending on their products. An example is the United Mileage Plus Visa card, which gives the holder miles in the United Airline frequent flier program for all purchases made with the card. Such credit cards may also offer points for each dollar charged, redeemable at specific retailers or tradable for airline miles. Even alumni associations and other affinity groups (charitable organizations, political groups, fraternities, and sororities) can issue credit cards this way. Typically, the group will get a small percentage of the finance charge paid to the financial institution that issues the card and services the account.

Some businesses don't accept credit cards; others take some cards but not others—for example, a business may accept Visa and MasterCard but not American Express. This is because the retailer incurs a cost for accepting credit purchases, usually ranging from 1.5 to 5 percent of the purchase, with the highest fees charged by American Express and Discover. At the beginning of the 1990s, only 5 percent of supermarkets accepted credit cards, since their slim profit margins on food items made it unprofitable to pay such high fees. Similarly, fast food retailers like McDonald's were historically "cash only." More recently however, large chains have been able to negotiate better fees with card issuers. Wal-Mart actually sued Visa and MasterCard in 1996 for charging excessive fees. In response to consequent fee reductions, about 90 percent of supermarkets now accept debit and credit cards, and fast-food retailers are quickly following suit.

retail credit card

Credit card that can only be used at the sponsoring retailer's outlets.

Retail Credit Cards. Some businesses offer a **retail credit card** that can only be used at their own outlets. Retailers ranging from Home Depot to Neiman Marcus offer such cards. On average, every U.S. household has at least one retail credit card.

Issuing their own cards offers several advantages to retailers. The cards may encourage greater spending at the retailer's stores. In addition, they can be quite profitable because of their high rates of interest and annual fees. The cards also offer a marketing opportunity, since cardholder mailing lists can be used to advertise special sales and discounts. It is fairly common to see a "10 percent off your first purchase" offer used to entice new borrowers.

Travel and Entertainment Cards. Some types of cards are designed primarily to allow business customers to delay payment of certain travel and entertainment expenses to coincide with their company's reimbursement system. These **travel and entertainment (T&E) cards** are thus a type of credit card, but they generally require that outstanding balances be paid in full each month. Diners Club and American Express are the best known of these cards, but financial institutions such as Citibank may also issue them through contracts with specific large employers. Since holders who pay their accounts according to the terms of the agreement will never incur any interest charges, these types of accounts tend to carry significant annual fees and penalties in order to make them profitable to the issuers.

travel and entertainment (T&E) card

Credit card that requires payment of the full balance each billing cycle.

Debit Cards. As discussed in Chapter 5, a debit card allows you to subtract the cost of your purchase from your checking or savings account electronically. Although these cards are a convenient substitute for paying cash and writing checks, they are not a means of borrowing—if you don't have enough money in your account, the transaction will be denied, and you may be required to pay a penalty fee. Some debit card issuers do offer overdraft protection, which allows you to spend more than your account balance, essentially borrowing the funds from the bank. The terms of such arrangements are similar to credit card terms.

Smart Cards and New Technology. Although credit cards are a fixture in our modern culture, new technologies could soon make them seem outdated. Already in use, with potentially unlimited applications, is the **smart card**, a card embedded with a computer chip that can store substantially more information than the magnetic strip on a traditional credit card. Unlike debit and ATM cards, smart cards actually store **electronic cash**. These funds have already been withdrawn from a bank account and are essentially "on deposit" in the card until used. Many universities have found smart cards to be a convenient way for students to access a variety of services on campus, from dining halls to copy machines. Prepaid cards such as Best Buy or Starbucks gift cards operate on the same principle and are increasing in popularity. Six out of ten people received a gift card during the 2003 holiday season.

smart card

Card that stores identification and electronic cash in a computer chip.

electronic cash

Money in digitized format.

Similar in concept to gift cards are "digital wallets" offered at Internet sites such as www.americanexpress.com for the storage of electronic cash. To use a digital wallet, you pay money in advance into an account and then use those funds to make electronic purchases over the Internet. This gives you greater security in making online purchases since you only need to worry about the security system in place at the site of the digital wallet as opposed to that of the individual retailer.

Many experts believe that smart cards will eventually replace the multitude of other cards and identification that we currently carry. The storage capacity of the chips used on these cards will allow issuers to include additional security features and could permit consumers to record a great deal of information—driver's license, credit cards, checking and savings accounts, health club memberships—in one place. And this may not be the limit. Major cell-phone companies are working on methods to allow users to pay remotely using cell phones, and MasterCard and Visa are testing chips that could be worn on clothing or embedded under the skin. All this may sound like science fiction, but don't be surprised if it becomes a reality in the near future!

Retail stores often give incentives to entice buyers into opening a new credit account.

Common Credit Card Contract Terms

Credit card agreements are legal contracts subject to numerous terms and conditions. You effectively agree to these terms and conditions when you apply for the card. We next look at key credit card features that you should be familiar with.

Annual Fees. Some credit cards charge you an annual fee for the privilege of being a cardholder. Although competition has caused many lenders to eliminate these fees altogether, some cards charge as much as $300 per year. If possible, you shouldn't hold cards that impose annual fees unless the cards offer other financial benefits that offset this cost. For example, suppose you have a card with a $1,000 balance, on which you pay 10 percent annual interest, or $100 per year. If you pay a $50 annual fee in addition to your interest charges, your total costs for the account are actually $150. The annual fee therefore increases your annual cost to 15 percent of your balance (150/1,000 = 15%). Compensating features might include insurance, rebates, discounts, frequent flier miles, or other services provided to cardholders. The value of these additional perks, however usually doesn't come close to compensating for the cost of the annual fee.

annual percentage rate (APR) Standardized annual cost of credit, including all mandatory fees paid by the borrower, expressed as a percentage rate.

Annual Percentage Rate (APR). The most important feature of your credit card is the interest rate charged on borrowed funds. Recall that in Chapter 5, we compared rates of interest on investments using annual percentage yield (APY). In the same way, we can compare the costs of borrowing using the **annual percentage rate (APR)**. Although the Truth in Lending Act (a corollary to the Truth in Savings Act mentioned in Chapter 5) requires lenders to report the APR on all types of loans and credit arrangements, credit card advertising normally emphasizes the nominal rate, which is generally lower than the APR. Therefore, you need to look carefully to be sure you're comparing different types of consumer financing based on the APR. APR takes into account all the finance charges associated with the account, even if these are not technically called "interest"—annual fees and charges for credit reports, for example. The APR is calculated as follows:

$$\text{Annual percentage rate (APR)} = \frac{\text{Total annual finance charges} + \text{Annual fee}}{\text{Average loan balance over the year}}$$

teaser rate Short-term below-market interest rate intended to encourage new customers to apply for a credit card.

Finance charges can vary tremendously across different types of credit and may even be negotiable with particular lenders, so it pays to shop around. The average rate in 2003 across all types of credit card accounts was 16.44 percent. Many issuers offer a below-market **teaser rate** to attract new customers and to encourage current credit card holders to transfer balances from cards offered by companies charging higher rates. Although this might seem like it makes financial sense, the difficulty lies in the details. The cards may also carry high annual fees and commonly have clauses that allow the rate to increase substantially if you make payments late, exceed your credit limit, or experience a change in credit status.

As an example, one card issuer recently advertised an attractive 6.9 percent rate. Unfortunately, the low rate applied for only six months and did not apply to cash advances. Some other important conditions were buried in the "fine print." At the end of the teaser period, the rate reverted to the issuer's "normal" rate of 18.9 percent. If any payments were late during the six-month low-rate period, the rate would immediately increase to 18.9 percent for the first offense and to 22.9 percent for the second late payment.

In another case, an Illinois doctor was surprised to find that the interest rate on his MasterCard went from 6.2 percent to 16.99 percent in one month. When he checked with his financial institution, he was told that the change was due to a "change in his credit status." This surprised him, since he had always paid his bills on time and stayed within his credit limit. It turned out that the change the lender was referring to was the fact that the doctor had obtained a new home mortgage.

transaction date The date on which you make a credit card purchase.

billing date The last day of a billing cycle; credit card transactions made after that date appear on the next month's bill.

Credit Limit. When you have a credit card account, the credit limit, or credit line, is the maximum amount you are allowed to borrow under the terms of your credit card agreement. Lenders usually start new cardholders with relatively low limits, such as $300, and then increase them with responsible card usage. Some people have credit limits of $50,000 or more, although the average is closer to $5,000 per card.

due date The date by which payment must be received by the lender if the holder is to avoid late penalties and, in some cases, interest on new transactions.

Transaction, Billing, and Due Dates. Credit card statements are issued once per month. The date you use your credit card to make a purchase is called the **transaction date**. The lender will close off reporting of transactions on a predetermined **billing date**, say, the 20th of the month, and any new charges you make after that date will appear on the next bill. Federal law requires that the bill be mailed to you at least 14 days before the **due date**, which is the date on which partial or full payment on the account is due. This date will usually be 20 to 25 days from the billing date. If you find it more convenient to have your payments due on a different date—for example, to coincide with your paydays—you can request a change in your billing cycle from the lender. Many credit cards do not calculate interest on new charges (other than cash advances) until the due date; this period of time is therefore called the **grace period**. When you make payments, the lender will credit you as they are received. If you return purchases, these credits will appear on the next month's statement as a reduction in the total amount owed.

grace period

The time before interest begins to accrue on new transactions.

As an example of how these dates might affect you, suppose that your billing date is March 20, you make a $100 credit purchase on March 21, and you receive your bill on March 24 with a due date of April 15. Your March bill will not include the March 21 transaction; it will appear on the April bill the following month, with a due date of May 15. Most cards will charge interest on new transactions beginning on the due date, so in this case, you could avoid all interest on the $100 by paying the bill by May 15. If you did that, you would have had the benefit of the credit for nearly two months without owing any interest. With some cards and with all cash advances, as we'll see later in the chapter, interest begins to accrue from the transaction date, so you need to carefully read your agreement to find out the terms of your card.

Fact #4

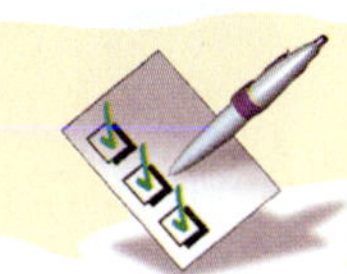

Making only minimum payments on your credit card will not do much to reduce your outstanding credit. It's usually only a little bit more than the finance charge for the month. If you have credit card debt of $1,000 at 16 percent interest, make no additional charges, and pay the minimum payment of $15 per month, it will take almost 14 years to repay the debt!

Minimum Payment. Under the terms of most credit card agreements, you must make a **minimum payment** each month to be in good credit standing. This amount is calculated according to the terms of your agreement with the lender, but it will usually be the greater of $15 or a specific percentage of the outstanding balance. The minimum payment will always be at least as great as the amount of interest due on the account for the period, but it won't be much more. Making only the minimum payment each month will therefore make very little dent in your overall debt.

minimum payment

Minimum amount that must be paid by the due date to maintain good credit standing and avoid late payment penalties.

Penalties and Fees. Credit card issuers generally assess penalties for paying late, exceeding the credit limit, and bouncing a check. A payment received after the due date is subject to a **late payment penalty**, which can range from $10 to $50. Although most credit card issuers charge the same fee to everyone who pays late, some have graduated fee schedules based on the payment amount that is past due. Cardholders in the MBNA "Gold Option Program," for example, pay only $15 if their past due payment is less than $100, $39 if it is between $100 and $1,000, and $49 if it is greater than $1,000.

late payment penalty

Penalty fee charged to an account for making a payment after the due date.

If you make charges on your card that cause your balance to exceed your credit limit, the lender will assess an **overlimit charge**, which can be as much as $50. Since both making a late payment and going over your credit limit are violations of the terms of your loan, these actions may affect your ability to get future credit.

overlimit charge

Penalty fee charged to an account for exceeding the credit limit.

Fees for cash advances and for ATM usage are also relatively common. For example, some issuers charge as much as $70 per transaction for balance transfers, and many assess a $12 to $20 fee for making payments over the phone. Note that it might still be worth incurring that fee if you would otherwise be making your payment late and consequently paying a higher late payment penalty. Fees and penalties, although specified in the terms of your original agreement, are subject to change with written notification to cardholders.

Calculation of Finance Charges on Open-End Credit

One of the big disadvantages of credit cards and other open-end credit accounts is the high rate of interest commonly charged by issuers. In fact, credit cards generate more than $50 billion in finance charges each year for credit card lenders. When you're considering this type of financing or comparing different credit card offers, you should understand how finance charges are calculated and what factors will increase your monthly costs.

The **finance charge** is the dollar amount of interest charged by the lender in a particular billing cycle. It is calculated as follows:

finance charge

The dollar amount of periodic interest charged by the lender on a credit account.

$$\text{Finance charge} = \text{Periodic rate} \times \text{Account balance owed}$$

GO FIGURE!

Calculation of Credit Card Finance Charges

Problem: Calculate the account balance owed and the monthly finance charge for the August 30 billing date using each of the five methods. The following information applies to each example:

- Billing cycle ends on 30th of the month
- Periodic rate = 18%/12 months = 1.5%/month
- Beginning balance July 31 = $1,000
- New billing cycle transactions
  - August 1 New charge, $500
  - August 15 Payment received by lender, $1,000

Solution

1. **Average Daily Balance Without a Grace Period (including new charges).** The following are the daily balances owed under this method:

Dates	Days out of Billing Cycle	Amount Owed ($)
July 31	1/31	1,000
August 1–August 14	14/31	1,500
August 15–August 30	16/31	500

The average daily balance is therefore (1/31) × 1,000 + (14/31) × 1,500 + (16/31) × 500 = $967.74. The monthly finance charge is 1.5% × $967.74 = $14.52.

2. **Average Daily Balance with a Grace Period (not including new charges).** The following are the daily balances owed under this method:

Dates	Days out of Billing Cycle	Amount Owed ($)
July 31–August 14	15/31	1,000
August 15–August 30	16/31	0

The average daily balance is (15/31) × 1,000 + (16/31) × 0 = $483.87, and the finance charge is 1.5% × $483.87 = $7.26.

3. **Two Cycle Method.** For this method, we must average both the current billing cycle (31 days) and the previous billing cycle (30 days). The daily balances are as follows:

Dates	Days out of Billing Cycle	Amount Owed ($)
July 1–July 31	31/61	1,000
August 1–August 14	14/61	1,500
August 15–August 30	16/61	500

The average daily balance using this method is (31/61) × 1,000 + (14/61) × 1,500 + (16/61) × 500 = $983.61, and the monthly finance charge is 1.5% × $983.61 = $14.75.

4. **Previous Balance Method.** This method calculates interest on the balance at the close of the last cycle, without subtracting payments made during the current cycle. Since the balance at the end of the previous cycle (July 30) was $1,000, the finance charge will be 1.5% × 1,000 = $15.

5. **Adjusted Balance Method.** This method calculates interest on the balance at the close of the last cycle, less any payments made during the current cycle. Since the balance at the end of the previous cycle (July 30) was $1,000, and a payment of $1,000 was made during the current cycle, there's no finance charge for this billing cycle.

periodic rate
The nominal rate divided by the number of billing periods per year.

In this calculation, the periodic rate is equal to the nominal, or stated, rate of interest divided by the number of billing periods per year, usually 12. For example, if your nominal rate is 18 percent, then your **periodic rate** is 18/12 = 1.5 percent per month. The periodic rate must be disclosed by the lender and will be specifically identified on your monthly bill.

The first term in the equation above, the periodic rate, is a known value, but the second term, the account balance owed, presents more of a problem because issuers use different methods for calculating this amount. These methods are discussed below and the mathematical calculations are explained in the *Go Figure!* box, "Calculation of Credit Card Finance Charges."

average daily balance
The average of the balances owed on each day of the billing cycle.

Average Daily Balance Method Without a Grace Period.

The most common method for calculating the account balance owed is based on the **average daily balance** without a grace period—that is, including any new purchases. In this method, the lender calculates the balance owed on each day of the billing period, adding any new charges made and subtracting any payments received during the period. The lender adds these daily balances together, determines the average, and uses this value to calculate the finance charge for the period.

Consider the hypothetical example described in the *Go Figure!* box. You begin the billing cycle on July 31 with a balance of $1,000; you make a new charge of $500 on August 1, the second day of the billing cycle; and you make a payment of $1,000 on August 15. If the lender uses the average daily balance method without a grace period for new purchases, your daily balances will be

July 31 (1 day out of 31)	$1,000
August 1 to August 14 (14 days out of 31)	$1,500
August 15 to August 31 (16 days out of 31)	$500

This results in an average daily balance of $967.74. Thus, with a periodic rate of 1.5 percent, your finance charge for the period will be $0.015 \times 967.74 = \$14.52$.

Average Daily Balance with a Grace Period. When a credit card issuer uses this method, the finance charge is applied to the average daily balance, including payments received but excluding new purchases. This method provides the cardholder with what is essentially "free credit" from the date of purchase until the beginning of the next billing cycle, since no finance charge is assessed on charges made during the current billing cycle. Applying this method to the earlier example, we find that excluding the new purchase from the calculation of average daily balance results in a finance charge of only $7.26, about half as much as when the average daily balance without a grace period is used.

Two-Cycle Average Daily Balance. The two-cycle average daily balance method, which has become more popular in recent years, is used by some issuers any time the balance has not been paid in full. With this method, the finance charge is applied to the average daily balance for the previous *two* billing cycles, including payments received and new purchases. If your average daily balance in the previous cycle was less than that of the current cycle, this method will result in a lower total finance charge. However, for cardholders who make irregular large purchases or those who are gradually paying off account balances over several months, this method can result in greater finance charges.

Previous Balance. If a lender uses the previous balance method, the finance charge is assessed on the balance owed at the close of the *last* billing cycle, without consideration of payments made during the current billing cycle. If you made a large payment during the current billing cycle, you end up paying interest on credit you have already paid back.

Adjusted Balance. The finance charge under the adjusted balance method is applied to the balance owed at the close of the last billing cycle less a credit for payments made during the current billing cycle, which makes this method preferable to the previous balance method.

Choosing Cards Based on APR

Although lenders are required to provide an explanation of how finance charges are determined, the complexity of these calculations makes it easy for lenders to disguise differences between credit cards. Most people simply consider the nominal rate in making comparisons, and few read the fine print on the back of their billing statement. Low-rate cards, and those that offer other perks, often employ one of the less favorable methods for calculating interest so that the lender will be able to make up for the lower rate in other ways. For example, the Discover Card, which advertises that it will "pay you cash" for each purchase—1 to 2 cents per dollar charged is added back to your account—uses the two-cycle method for calculating finance charges. If you used your card to make a large purchase in the previous month in order to get the 2 cent rebate, you would likely find that, unless you paid the balance fairly quickly after the purchase, your finance charges on those borrowed funds for the month of purchase and the month after would exceed the rebated amount.

There are two important rules to remember in comparing credit card terms. First, always compare the rates based on APR rather than the nominal, or stated, rate. Second, read your credit agreement carefully to determine how finance charges are calculated. In general, the best deals will be on cards that calculate the finance charge using either the average daily balance with a grace period or the adjusted balance method, since these methods give you access to short-term free borrowing. If your credit card balances are gradually increasing, your highest monthly finance charge will come from the average daily balance without a grace period. Since your personal financial plan probably includes a debt reduction goal, it is important to note that consumers who are gradually reducing their outstanding credit card debt should avoid cards that use the previous balance method or the two-cycle method, since both place more weight on your previous balance, which will always be greater than your current balance as you continue to pay off the debt. A comparison worksheet is included in your *Personal Financial Planner.*

PFP Worksheet 23
Comparing Credit Cards

Learning by Doing 6-3

You've just received a credit card solicitation in the mail that offers you a 4 percent APR. Your current card, which has an outstanding balance of $5,000, has an APR of 14 percent.

1. What factors should you consider in making the decision to transfer your balance?
2. How much interest will you save the first month by switching cards, assuming you make no additional charges and both cards calculate interest based on the average daily balance?

The Advantages and Disadvantages of Credit Card Use

LEARNING objective

5 Recognize the hazards of credit card use, including the risk of identity theft.

Earlier in this chapter, we noted that using consumer credit involves both advantages and disadvantages, both for individuals and for the economy. Although credit cards offer these same advantages, as well as some others discussed in this section, the high costs of interest and fees tend to outweigh the benefits of this form of borrowing, from the perspective of personal financial planning. In this section, we look at the additional advantages and disadvantages of credit card use. Exhibit 6-5 compares the costs and benefits of consumer credit in general, which includes consumer loans of various types, with the costs and benefits of credit cards. Debit cards offer many of the same advantages without the disadvantages of borrowing.

Advantages of Credit Cards

Like other forms of consumer credit, credit cards provide the opportunity to delay payment for purchases, the convenience and safety of not carrying cash, and a source of emergency funds. In addition, they may offer the following positive features.

Method of Identification. Although most people use their driver's license for their primary means of identification, a credit card is a secondary method for verifying your identity. Some cards are now being imprinted with photos to make them more useful as an identification tool, as well as to reduce the risk of fraudulent card use.

Means of Record Keeping for Business Expenses. Credit cards provide a convenient way to organize business-related and tax-deductible expenses. Using a specific credit card for all reimbursable business expenses makes it easier to submit requests for payment to your employer. Similarly, if you have tax-deductible business expenses that need to be kept separate from household expenses, a credit card may offer an easy method of record keeping. American Express even provides an end-of-year summary that separates total annual expenditures into various categories, such as restaurants, hotels, and airfare.

ADVANTAGES OF CONSUMER CREDIT	All Consumer Credit	Credit Cards Only
Buy now, pay later	√	√
Convenient and safe alternative to cash	√	√
Source of emergency cash	√	√
Helps fuel the economy	√	√
Method of identification		√
Record keeping for business expenses		√
Ability to make remote purchases		√
Easier to return merchandise		√
Free credit		√
Required to reserve rental cars, hotels		√
May include other perks		√

DISADVANTAGES OF CONSUMER CREDIT	All Consumer Credit	Credit Cards Only
Financial statement impact	√	√
Increases cost of consumer purchases	√	√
Risk of overspending	√	√
Higher insurance premiums	√	√
High cost of interest and fees		√
Annoying marketing tactics		√
Loss of privacy		√
Risk of fraud and identity theft		√
Interest not tax-deductible		√

EXHIBIT 6-5

Advantages and Disadvantages of Consumer Credit and Credit Cards

Ability to Make Remote Purchases. Credit cards enable you to pay for purchases remotely—by phone or over the Internet. With the increasing popularity of electronic payments, it's practically impossible to get by without having a credit card for this purpose. In fact, most airlines, car rental companies, and hotels will not accept reservations from you unless you have one. Many people worry about the safety of making purchases over the Internet, but transaction verification—a new feature offered by both MasterCard ("Shop Safe") and Visa ("Verified by Visa")—reduces the risk. To use transaction verification, you must register a password, similar to a PIN number for your ATM card, on the card issuer's website and then use the number every time you shop online.

See www.visa.com and www.mastercard.com to find out more about their transaction verification services.

Easier to Return Merchandise. Some retailers will allow you to return merchandise without showing a receipt if you paid by credit card, since the record of a credit card purchase can be pulled up at a cash register terminal. If you received faulty merchandise and are having difficulty in getting satisfaction from the seller, some credit card issuers promise they'll credit your account with the purchase price and deal with the seller directly on your behalf.

Free Credit. Some credit cards—those that calculate finance charges without including new charges during the billing cycle—allow you the opportunity to borrow without paying for the privilege. Of course, you must repay the borrowed funds by the end of the grace period to avoid the finance charge.

Other Advantages. Credit card issuers may offer additional benefits to their cardholders, including travel insurance (if you are injured on a trip you paid for using the card), rebates (cash back for purchases made, often 1 or 2 cents per dollar of merchandise paid for with the card), frequent flier miles, and discounts on specific merchandise. In some cases, these additional features may require the payment of a one-time or monthly fee. In addition, cards that have these features may charge a higher rate of interest than those that do not.

Disadvantages of Credit Cards

Like other forms of consumer credit, credit card debt can have a negative effect on your household financial statements and may cause you to overspend. Without a doubt, the interest and fees on credit cards can significantly increase the cost of goods and services purchased. In addition to those disadvantages, credit card ownership and usage can increase the amount of junk mail you receive, expose you to the risk of loss of privacy, and increase the chances of your identity being stolen.

Most Expensive Way to Borrow. The rates of interest paid by credit card users are higher than those paid by most other types of borrowers. They generally also are higher than the rates earned on most investments. In addition, they're relatively insensitive to market interest rate movements, so as rates fall on auto loans and savings accounts, double-digit credit card rates continue. Furthermore, since interest paid on credit card balances is not tax-deductible, you bear the full cost of these charges. In contrast, as you'll read in Chapter 7, the interest on certain types of consumer loans—namely, home equity loans and some student loans—is tax-deductible, which further increases the difference in cost between credit cards and these types of financing. If you take out a home equity loan to pay off your credit card debt, you'll likely be able to borrow at a much lower rate and the tax savings from deductible interest payments will make your actual costs even lower. For example, suppose your marginal tax bracket is 25 percent and you have $5,000 in credit card debt on which you're paying 15 percent interest, or $750 a year. If you take out a home equity loan at 6 percent interest, your annual interest costs will be only $300, and since the interest is deductible, your effective after-tax interest cost will be $\$300 \times (1 - 0.25) = \$225$. If you apply the annual $525 ($= \$750 - \$225$) savings to debt reduction, the net benefit will be even greater.

Negative Effects of Credit Card Marketing. Financial institutions spend a lot of money attempting to entice you to add more cards to your wallet. This means more unsolicited mail, e-mail, and telephone calls. It also means more gimmicky attempts to get your attention, such as cards emblazoned with photos of famous people or your alma mater. Unfortunately, the latest target group is young teenagers. Some believe that this presents ethical issues similar those raised in lawsuits against cigarette manufacturers. These critics say that issuers hope to get kids to develop the "credit habit" early and grow into adults who like to use credit cards as well. This marketing strategy seems to be on target. A survey by the American Savings Education Council found that 7 percent of high-school students and 55 percent of college students have at least one major credit card, and about one-third of teens fail to pay their bills in full each month. Here's another scary fact from the Consumer Credit Counseling Service—within the first year of being a credit card holder, one in five college freshmen owes more than $10,000.

Credit card marketing also has a significant negative impact on the environment. Although recent evidence suggests direct mail credit card solicitations are on the decline, the U.S. mail service still carries millions of pieces of mail related to preapproved credit cards every day. Think of the number of trees that it takes to produce that much paper, as well as the space all the trash takes up in landfills!

Loss of Privacy. Another disadvantage of credit cards is reduced privacy of financial information—your credit card provider may sell your credit and financial information to other companies who wish to solicit you for magazine and product sales. The federal government and some states have passed legislation that specifically prohibits telephone calls to the phone numbers on "no-call lists," and evidence suggests that the lists have significantly reduced unwanted calls. Telemarketing is still big business, though, and marketers are challenging the no-call laws.

You can request removal from certain junk mail and telemarketing lists by contacting the following companies, although the method isn't foolproof:

- Acxiom: 877-774-2094
- Donnelley Marketing: 888-633-4402
- Opt Out for Equifax, Experian, Trans Union, and Innovus: 888-567-8688

To be added to the federal no-call list, log on to www.donotcall.gov. Many states have their own lists as well. Finally, some individuals have reduced the number of calls they receive by putting on their answering machines a message requesting removal from any telemarketer's list.

Go to www.ftc.gov/bcp/conline/edcams/donotcall, a website maintained by the Federal Trade Commission, to sign up for the federal no-call list. You can also call 888-382-1222 to register the phone you are calling from as a "do not call" number.

Fraud and Identity Theft. Here's an increasingly common occurrence. You receive your credit card billing statement and see one or more charges that you know you didn't make—a sign that someone has stolen your credit card information. Or you check your credit bureau report after a credit denial and see a loan listed that you never applied for—a sign that someone has applied for a loan masquerading as you. Both scenarios are commonly referred to as identity theft.

Fraudulent credit card charges often involve online or telephone orders, since it's easier to use someone else's identity in a venue where no additional identification, such as a driver's license with a picture, is required. The negative outcomes, of course, can be severe: Your credit may be damaged, and it takes time and effort to correct the fraudulent charges. And it's not just credit card information that is at stake.

It takes very little information to steal your identity. With your Social Security number, name, and address, a thief can apply for credit cards, cell phones, loans, bank accounts, apartments, and utility accounts. For this reason, most universities no longer use Social Security numbers for student and faculty IDs. To use your credit card, a thief only needs your credit card number and expiration date. With a little more information, he or she can open up accounts in your name. The popular online job search engine www.monster.com warns its customers that thieves may pose as legitimate employers in an effort to obtain personal information.

Fact #5

Bankrate.com estimates that more than 500,000 consumers are robbed by identity thieves every year, and that number is on the increase. Talk show hostess Oprah Winfrey, CNN founder Ted Turner, pro golfer Tiger Woods, and director Steven Spielberg have all had their identities stolen.

You might even be the victim of someone you know. The Federal Trade Commission says that about 6 percent of the cases reported to the agency involve family members. In some cases, parents who have botched their own finances are using their children's identities to open credit card accounts. Exhibit 6-6 offers some valuable suggestions for avoiding identity theft.

Most card issuers now use sophisticated software to track card usage patterns and look for suspicious card activity. If your lender thinks you've been the victim of fraud, it will temporarily put a hold on the card, disallowing any credit purchases until the issue has been resolved. Although you certainly benefit from these antifraud mechanisms when they result in the early detection of fraudulent card usage, it is also possible that your own behavior could trigger the antifraud system. This might happen, for example, if you use your card at the same retailer more than once on the same day (since that could be an indication that a store employee stole your number when you used the card to make a purchase) or if you use a card that has been inactive for a period of time.

EXHIBIT 6-6 How to Avoid Identity Theft

- Don't give out your Social Security number, and don't print it on your checks.
- Check your credit report regularly.
- Shred old bank and credit statements before throwing them away.
- Notify credit bureaus to remove your name from marketing lists.
- Add your name to no-call lists.
- Do not carry extra credit cards and IDs.
- Keep a copy of your drivers license (both sides) and credit card numbers, expiration dates, and contact phone numbers in a secure location in case your wallet or purse is stolen.
- Mail bill payments at the post office or a locked mailbox.
- Examine the charges on your credit card statements before paying.
- Cancel unused credit card accounts.
- Never give your credit card number or personal information over the phone unless you have made the call and trust the business on the other end.
- Never give your credit card number or personal information over the Internet unless you have made the contact and the site has a high level of security.

My name is Wanda Nicholas and I never use my credit card. (Identity theft victim)

My name is Wanda Nichols and I just used my credit card to buy a new sound system for my car. (Identity thief)

If you're a victim of credit card fraud or theft, your maximum liability for charges made without your authorization is $50, provided that you report your loss promptly. If you report a lost card before any charges can be made with it, you will have no liability at all. In most cases, Visa and MasterCard will credit your account for any unauthorized charges without charging you the fee. Since identity thieves are rarely caught and prosecuted for their crimes, fraud losses are absorbed by credit card lenders—to the tune of several billion dollars a year—which is partly why credit card interest rates are so high.

Summary

1 **Apply the personal financial planning process to making consumer purchase decisions.** Most personal financial goals are related to current and future household expenditures. Whether you are buying necessities, such as food and shelter, or luxury items, such as new cars or vacations, you should carefully consider whether the purchases are consistent with your prioritized goals and your budget. Before making a purchase, identify your alternatives and carefully evaluate each alternative to determine which best meets your consumer needs.

2 **Identify the advantages and disadvantages of using consumer credit to make purchases.** Consumer credit allows you to spread the cost of more expensive purchases over time. It is often a convenient and safe alternative to carrying cash and may be a source of liquidity in an emergency. The existence of consumer credit also benefits the economy as a whole, since it results in increased consumer spending. The disadvantages of consumer credit include the negative impact on household financial statements, the additional costs of interest and fees, and the increased risk of overspending. People with too much debt or a history of late payments also may pay more for auto and homeowner's insurance.

3 **Understand the different types of consumer credit.** The two major types of consumer credit are closed-end credit and open-end credit. With closed-end credit, the lender approves a loan amount for a specific purpose, such as the purchase of a car. Repayment is usually made in equal monthly installments for a specified period of time. Open-end credit arrangements, such as credit cards, are those in which the lender preapproves the borrower for a maximum credit limit but does not specify the purpose of the credit. The borrower can use the credit as he or she chooses until the limit is reached.

4 **Evaluate credit card alternatives, including terms and costs.** The various types of credit cards include bank credit cards, retail credit cards, and travel and entertainment cards. These cards commonly carry high rates of interest and may require the payment of an annual fee. Other costs include penalties for making payments late and exceeding the credit limit. The finance charge assessed on unpaid balances differs depending on the method used by the lender to calculate the account balance.

5 **Recognize the hazards of credit card use, including the risk of identity theft.** In addition to the general advantages of credit, credit cards sometimes provide free credit, serve as identification, enable holders to pay for purchases remotely, and offer a convenient way to organize reimbursable or tax-deductible expenses. Outweighing these advantages, however, are high costs, loss of privacy, and increased risk of identity theft.

Key Terms

annual percentage rate (APR) (184)
average daily balance (186)
bank credit card (182)
billing date (184)
cash advance (181)
closed-end credit (180)
consumer credit (175)
convenience check (181)
credit (175)
credit card (181)
credit limit (180)
due date (184)
electronic cash (183)
finance charge (185)
grace period (185)
late payment penalties (185)
luxuries (173)
minimum payment (185)
necessities (173)
open-end credit (180)
overlimit charge (185)
periodic rate (186)
retail credit card (182)
smart card (183)
teaser rate (184)
transaction date (184)
travel and entertainment (T&E) card (183)
warranty (177)

Key Calculations

$$\text{Annual percentage rate (APR)} = \frac{\text{Total annual finance charges} + \text{Annual fee}}{\text{Average loan balance over the year}}$$

$$\text{Periodic rate} = \frac{\text{Nominal rate}}{\text{Number of billing periods per year}}$$

$$\text{Finance charge} = \text{Periodic rate} \times \text{Account balance owed}$$

Concept Review Questions

1. Describe the decision process for making consumer purchases.
2. In deciding between consumer purchase alternatives, what types of factors will commonly need to be compared?
3. What is a limited warranty? Is it always advisable to purchase extended warranties when they are available?
4. Explain the advantages and disadvantages of consumer credit for individuals.
5. Why is the availability of consumer credit good for the economy?
6. How is open-end credit different from closed-end credit? Give an example of each.
7. What is a cash advance, and how is it treated differently than a new purchase by credit card lenders?
8. Briefly discuss the history of credit cards in the United States.
9. Identify the three basic types of credit cards, their similarities, and their differences.
10. What is a debit card? What is a smart card? Are these types of credit cards? Why or why not?
11. How is electronic cash used to make Internet purchases?
12. What is annual percentage rate (APR)? How is it different from and similar to annual percentage yield (APY), discussed in the previous chapter?
13. Define each of the following credit card terms or features: (a) annual fee, (b) teaser rate, (c) credit limit, (d) transaction date, (e) billing date, (f) due date, (g) average daily balance, (h) grace period, (i) minimum payment, (j) late payment penalty, and (k) overlimit charge.
14. How is the monthly finance charge determined for a credit card?
15. What are the methods that credit card lenders use to compute the account balance on which the periodic rate is charged? Which one(s) will result in the lowest finance charge if you regularly pay off your balance every month? Which one(s) will result in the highest finance charge if you carry a balance forward every month? Explain.
16. In addition to the general advantages and disadvantages of consumer credit identified in question 4 above, what are the additional costs and benefits of credit cards?
17. How can credit cards be used to help with business record keeping?
18. Why is it sometimes said that credit cards give you "free" credit? Under what circumstances does this occur?
19. Explain how credit cards increase your risk of identity theft. What are some methods you can use to minimize this risk?
20. Identify the basic rules for wise use of credit cards.
21. How can you estimate the monthly payment necessary to reduce your outstanding credit card debt? Why is it insufficient to simply make the monthly minimum payments required by your lender?

Application Problems

1. ***Consumer Purchase Decisions.*** You are shopping at Wal-Mart for some toiletries when you notice that the store is offering a fabulous deal on a 32-inch television set with a built-in DVD player—only $350. You have a smaller television already, but you don't have a DVD player. You could write a check to pay for the TV, since you have enough money in your checking account; or you could put it on your MasterCard. Apply the decision-making process shown in Exhibit 6-1 to help you decide whether to buy the television.
2. ***Annual Percentage Rate.*** The total annual finance charges on your credit card account are $200. You also pay an annual fee of $50. If your average outstanding balance during the year is $1,000, what is the annual percentage rate?

3. ***Calculating Finance Charges.*** Your credit card lender charges an annual rate of 15 percent on the average daily balance without a grace period. Your balance on March 10, the end of the last billing cycle, was $5,000. The following transactions were posted to your account during the billing cycle:

3/15	New credit purchase	$500
3/20	Payment received	$750
4/1	New credit purchase	$1,000

The last day of the monthly billing cycle is April 10.
   a. Calculate the finance charge.
   b. How much difference would it make if your lender gave a grace period for new purchases?
4. ***Cost of Credit.*** Mary and Joe Belinksy went out to dinner for Valentine's Day and paid for the meal using a credit card, which has an APR of 20 percent. If they make only minimum payments each month, and therefore do not repay the $100 cost of the dinner for a full year, how much did the dinner actually cost them? What if they carry forward a balance for five years?
5. ***Effect of Bad Credit.*** Perry's insurance agent recently notified him that his auto insurance premium is going to increase because his credit report shows so many late payments in the last six months. In addition, the agent noted that Perry had applied for several new credit cards during that time period. While hanging out with his friends, Perry complains that this treatment is totally unfair and argues that there is no possible relationship between his bad credit and his risk of having auto accidents or damaging his vehicle. Do you agree with Perry's reasoning? Can you think of any reasonable explanation for the insurer's use of credit information in setting its premium rates?
6. ***Cost of Credit.*** It's not uncommon to see gas stations offering lower prices to consumers who pay by cash or check than to those who pay with credit. Explain why this practice makes sense from a business standpoint.
7. ***Opportunity Cost of Credit.*** If the average household in the United States carries $8,000 in credit card debt on two cards, the average annual rate is 16 percent, and the average annual fee is $30 per card, how much is each household paying in total interest and fees per year? If a household could instead contribute this amount of money each year to a retirement savings account that earned an average of 6 percent per year, compounded annually, how much money would they have in the account when they retired 40 years from now?
8. ***Identity Theft.*** Carrie Chandler opens her June credit card bill and sees that her balance is a bit higher than she thought. When she more carefully examines the bill, she sees that there was a $75 payment to "Shoppers Cooperative" and she knows that she did not authorize this charge. Looking back at her May bill, which she unfortunately didn't look at very carefully the previous month, she sees that there was a $75 payment to the same company that month as well. Explain the steps that Carrie should take to resolve this problem. How much might she be responsible for paying?

Using Web Resources for Financial Planning

1. ***Comparing Credit Cards.*** Several websites can help you to shop for credit card offers that meet your needs. Go to *www.quicken.com* and click on Bills and Banking to find advice on credit card features that are right for you. Once you've decided on the features you want, try the "Credit Card Search" function under "Play Your Cards Right."
2. ***Credit Card Statistics.*** Go to *www.cardweb.com.* Click on "Card News" for the results of recent studies. What is the average credit card debt per household? How much credit card debt do college students carry on average?
3. ***What Are the Top 10 Purchase Mistakes?*** The Consumer Literacy Consortium recently released a list of the top consumer purchase mistakes as a part of its ongoing campaign to reduce wasteful consumer spending. Although you can order the full report at no cost by sending a self-addressed stamped envelope to Ten Mistakes: CFA, 1424 16th Street NW, Suite 604, Washington DC 20036, a summary of the report is provided at *www.moneymanagement.org/Education/onlinearticles/* . Are you guilty of making any of the top 10 consumer purchase mistakes? What can you do to correct your mistakes?
4. ***See How Your Spending Compares with That of Others.*** Go to *www.debtadvice.org* and click on "Personal Plans and Solutions." This page includes a budget calculator that you can use to see how your spending in certain categories, as a percentage of your total budget, compares with the spending of others.
   a. Do you spend proportionately more than average in a particular budget category? Why do you think this is the case?
   b. How do you measure up in savings as a percentage of your budget?

Learning by Doing Solutions

LBD 6-1: 1. Identify your alternatives, evaluate the pros and cons of each, and implement your purchase.; 2. Department stores, new and used furniture stores, garage sales, classified ads in newspapers.; 3. Price, quality, condition, additional costs of cleaning used sofa, search time.

LBD 6-2: 1. Have the surgery and pay in cash or credit, delay having the surgery, sell assets to generate cash to pay for the surgery.; 2. Paying with credit allows her to maintain liquidity and meet her other cash outflows. If she uses credit, her debt ratio will go up, and her monthly net cash flow will decline as she makes payments on the loan.

LBD 6-3: 1. You should consider other terms and conditions such as when the new rate expires and what it will revert to after the teaser period, annual fees, penalties, and differential rates for cash advances and purchases. You should also consider whether a higher rate applies to balance transfers and cash advances.; 2. Old card: 14%/12 × $5,000 = $58.33; new card: 4%/12 × $5,000 = $16.67; difference $58.33 − $16.67 = $41.66 per month.

Building Financial Planning Skills Through Case Applications

Case 6-1 Ray Martinez Buys a New Microwave

One morning, Ray Martinez wakes up to find that his microwave no longer works. Since Ray isn't much of a cook and he can't live without a microwave to warm his morning breakfast roll, he heads to Dunkin' Donuts for a cup of coffee and a sweet roll while he contemplates his options for replacing the appliance. Although he's tempted to buy a simple model from the local discount store and be done with it, Ray knows that there are many possible features to consider and that prices can vary from store to store, so he wants to do a little research before making the purchase. Outline the steps that Ray should take. Create a table that Ray could use to compare microwave features.

Case 6-2 Cash Versus Credit

It's almost Christmas time, and you still need to buy presents for eleven relatives. Although you plan to work over the semester break to earn some extra money, your current cash resources are low—you have only $250 in your checking account, and you still need to pay your half of the phone bill ($50) before you leave for home. However, you do have a Target card (current balance $1,000), and the lender recently sent you a notice that your credit limit had been increased by $500 to $1,500. Discuss the pros and cons of using your Target credit card for your holiday purchases. What other options do you have?

Case 6-3 Impact of Credit Card Debt on Household Financial Ratios

Lana and Zack Worzala were married in June 2004. A year has passed, and they're thinking about buying a home. They've saved $10,000 to put toward the down payment, but they're wondering if they should pay off some of their consumer debt instead. Their combined gross monthly income is $5,000, and their after-tax monthly income is $4,000. They have the following debts:

	Balance Owed ($)	Rate (%)	Monthly Minimum Payment ($)	Number of Payments Left
Zack's car loan	2,000	6	340	6
Lana's Visa	1,300	18	35	
Zack's MasterCard	4,200	21	110	
Lana's student loan	3,370	5	37	114
Zack's student loan	10,600	6	122	114

a. Calculate the Worzalas' debt payment ratio, based on their current situation.

b. Assume mortgage lenders require that monthly mortgage debt service for a home (including mortgage principal and interest, property taxes, and insurance) not exceed 28 percent of gross monthly income. Given Zack and Lana's gross income, what is the maximum mortgage debt service that would be allowed by a lender?

c. If mortgage lenders require that total debt payments not exceed 36 percent of after-tax disposable income, will Zach and Lana have any trouble meeting this requirement?

d. Zach and Lana estimate that, given the prices of homes in the area and the costs of property taxes and insurance, the minimum mortgage debt service they would have to pay is $1,000 per month. If that is the case, will they be able to get a loan with their current debt obligations? Should they consider applying some of their savings to debt repayment? What other alternatives should they consider?

DEVELOPING PERSONAL FINANCIAL skills for life

Learning about Yourself

6-1. Assessing Your Preferences

PFP Worksheet 24
Assessing Your Preferences

For each of the following statements, write the number that shows the extent to which the statement accurately describes your views (5 = strongly agree; 4 = agree; 3 = undecided; 2 = disagree; 1 = strongly disagree).

_____ **1.** I consider how things might be in the future and try to influence those things with my day-to-day behavior.

_____ **2.** I only act to satisfy my immediate concerns, figuring that the future will take care of itself.

_____ **3.** I often engage in a particular behavior in order to achieve outcomes that may not result for many years.

_____ **4.** My behavior is more influenced by things that will happen in the near future (a matter of weeks or days) than it is by things that will happen a long time in the future.

_____ **5.** I am willing to sacrifice my immediate happiness or well-being in order to achieve future outcomes.

_____ **6.** I generally ignore warnings about possible future problems because I think the problems will be resolved before they reach crisis level.

_____ **7.** I think it's important to take warnings about negative outcomes seriously even if the negative outcome will not occur for many years.

_____ **8.** Even when I know I should be spending my time studying or working on projects that are due later in the semester, I am usually willing to go out and do something fun with my friends instead.

_____ **9.** I think it's more important to focus on actions that have important future consequences than on actions with less important immediate consequences.

_____ **10.** I prefer to spend my money on things that I can enjoy right now, rather than saving for a long time to get something else in the future.

Scoring:
This is an assessment of your tendency toward either immediate gratification or long-term planning, an aspect of your personality that can affect your spending behavior as well as your willingness to incur consumer debt. Add up your total for the even-numbered statements (2, 4, 6, etc.) and your total for the odd-numbered statements (1, 3, 5, etc.). If your total for the odd-numbered statements is greater than your total for the even-numbered statements, then you tend to be more forward-looking, able to consider the future consequences of your actions. You are less likely to spend impulsively and to use credit cards for immediate gratification. If your score for the odd-numbered statements is greater, then the opposite is true—you are inclined to do things today without considering the long-term consequences. Of course, you may find that you exhibit a balance between these two extremes.

Source: Adapted from Lawrence J. Belcher, "Behavior and Attitudes Toward Credit and Bankruptcy: Evidence from College Student Surveys," Working Paper, Stetson University (2003). Used by permission of the author.

6-2. Are You in Debt Danger?

Barbara O'Neill, CFP™, Ph.D., offers the following list of "debt danger signals" in her recent book *Saving on a Shoestring: How to Cut Expenses, Reduce Debt, and Stash More Cash*. She suggests that, if 10 or more apply to your household, you are in financial trouble. If 5 or more apply, you are *headed for* trouble. Check any of the following that describe things you have done within the last two years:

_____ **1.** Used credit for items that you previously purchased with cash.

_____ **2.** Obtained a debt consolidation loan to pay existing debt.

_____ **3.** Charged more in a month than you made in payments.

_____ **4.** Paid only the minimum required payment.

_____ **5.** Juggled rent or mortgage and other large bills to pay debts.

_____ **6.** Rotated bills: Paid half of your bills one month and half the next.

_____ **7.** Used checking account overdraft to pay bills.

_____ **8.** Used credit card advances to pay living expenses.

_____ **9.** Wrote postdated checks.

_____ **10.** Took out a new loan before an old one was repaid.

______ **11.** Was overdrawn at the bank more than two times.
______ **12.** Borrowed from friends or relatives.
______ **13.** Used savings to pay bills that you previously paid by cash or check.
______ **14.** Had to work overtime or take a second job to make ends meet.
______ **15.** Borrowed against life insurance without repayment.
______ **16.** Was at or near maximum credit limits.
______ **17.** Was often late paying bills.
______ **18.** Increased the percentage of take-home pay spent on consumer debt.
______ **19.** Had late penalties assessed on outstanding debt.
______ **20.** Received calls or overdue notices from creditors.
______ **21.** Received threats of repossession or legal action.
______ **22.** Negative information was added to credit report.
______ **23.** Was denied credit due to negative remarks in a credit report.
______ **24.** Hid credit card statements and bills from others.
______ **25.** Worried about money and financial distress.
______ **26.** Had more than seven or eight creditors.
______ **27.** Owed more than 20 percent of your take-home pay to creditors.
______ **28.** Committed all of a secondary earner's income to debt.
______ **29.** Total credit balance rarely decreased.
______ **30.** Was dishonest with spouse or partner about spending.

Source: Barbara O'Neill, *Saving on a Shoestring: How to Cut Expenses, Reduce Debt, and Stash More Cash*, Dearborn Financial Publishing (1999). Used by permission of the publisher.

Developing Your Skills

6-3. Evaluate Your Consumer Credit Usage

Create a record of your current credit information in your *Personal Financial Planner*. For each of your obligations, record the lender, the account number, the current balance owed, and the monthly payment. Keep this information up-to-date over time so that you can track your usage of consumer credit. Based on this summary of your current credit usage, reevaluate your financial goals, if necessary.

PFP Worksheet 25
Household Credit Summary

6-4. Evaluate Your Credit Cards Based on Terms and Costs

Using your most recent statements, evaluate the credit cards you currently hold, if any. Use the comparison worksheet provided in your *Personal Financial Planner.*

PFP Worksheet 23
Credit Card Comparison

a. Make a table that compares their features, including annual fee, APR, method of finance charge calculation, and penalty fees.
b. If you carry a balance forward on one or more cards, make a plan for paying off your cards, starting with the one with the highest costs and least desirable features.
c. Consider transferring your balances to a lower-rate card and canceling the high-rate card.

6-5. Credit Cards and the Life Cycle

Interview friends and members of your family who are in different life cycle stages. Ask them about their attitudes toward credit card usage, how many credit cards they have, the average APR on their accounts, whether they pay their balances in full each month, and whether they are working to reduce outstanding household debt. Are there any significant differences between younger and older people's attitudes about credit cards? Between men and women's attitudes? If so, what are some possible explanations?

THE NAVIGATOR

- ☐ Review Before Studying this Chapter list.
- ☐ Scan Learning Objectives.
- ☐ Take Myth or Fact quiz and find the answers throughout the chapter.
- ☐ Read chapter and answer Learning by Doing exercises.
- ☐ Review Key Terms and Key Calculations.
- ☐ Do end-of-chapter exercises.
- ☐ Take review quiz on the text website.
- ☐ Solve end-of-chapter cases.

BEFORE studying this chapter, you should review

- Household financial ratios (Chapter 2).
- Time value of money (Chapter 2).
- Types of depository institutions (Chapter 5).
- Advantages and disadvantages of consumer credit (Chapter 6).

CHAPTER 7

Consumer Loans and Credit Management

Myth or Fact?

Consider each of the following statements and decide whether it is a *myth* or a *fact*. Look for the answers in the *Fact* boxes in the chapter.

	MYTH	FACT
1. If you are late making your car loan payments, the lender can take the car away from you.	☐	☐
2. Most college students graduate with significant student loan debt.	☐	☐
3. Consumer loans are always less costly than credit card debt.	☐	☐
4. Mistakes on credit reports are fairly uncommon.	☐	☐
5. If you can't afford your current consumer credit payments, you can make an arrangement with your creditors for lower payments.	☐	☐

LEARNING objectives

1. Identify the most common types of consumer loans and lenders.
2. Compare consumer loans based on terms and costs.
3. Assess your creditworthiness and know how to improve it.
4. Understand your consumer credit rights.
5. Establish a plan for managing your consumer credit and reducing outstanding balances.

...applying the planning process

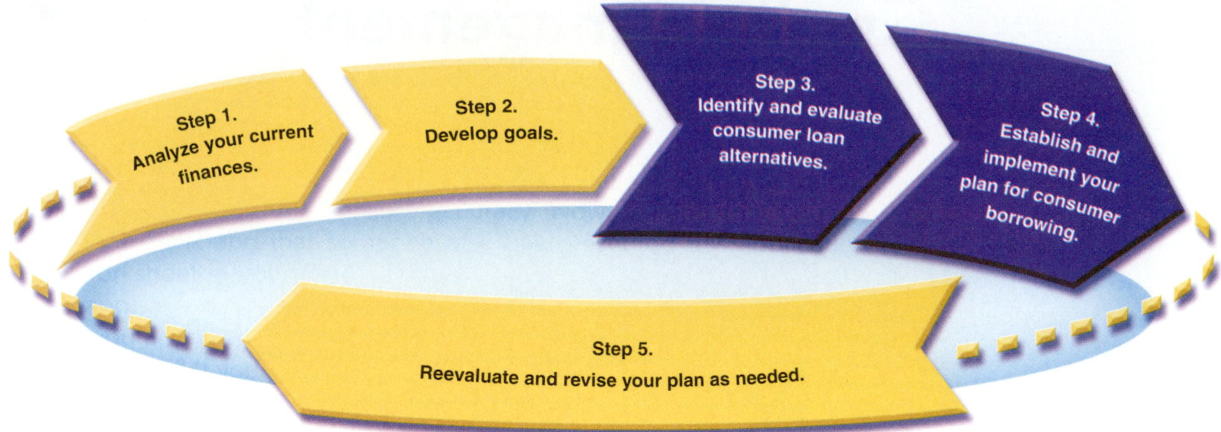

In Chapter 6, we introduced the role of consumer credit in your financial plan, with particular emphasis on open-end credit. In this chapter, we continue that discussion by looking at closed-end credit alternatives, which include various types of consumer loans such as automobile loans, student loans, and home equity loans. Your financial plan will undoubtedly benefit from wise use of consumer credit over your lifetime, but you'll need to select the least expensive financing alternatives to best meet your household's borrowing needs. In making consumer credit decisions as part of your personal financial plan, you should evaluate your choices for consumer borrowing based on the terms and costs of these loans. This chapter identifies potential lenders and explains the characteristics of each type of loan, including in-depth discussions of the most common types—home equity loans, student loans, and automobile loans.

Before deciding to increase your household's total indebtedness, whether using credit cards or consumer loans, it's important that you revisit your household budget to evaluate whether the additional debt will adversely affect your ability to achieve your other financial goals. As you know, debt payments reduce your net cash flow, and increased consumer debt can decrease your net worth. It's also important to understand the methods that creditors use for evaluating your creditworthiness so that you can maintain a good credit rating throughout your life. This chapter explains these methods, details your consumer credit rights, and provides some guidelines for managing consumer credit accounts, reducing outstanding debt, and dealing with credit problems.

Chapter Preview

Consumer Loans	Building Your Creditworthiness	Understanding Your Consumer Credit Rights	Managing Consumer Credit
• Characteristics of Consumer Loans • Types of Consumer Loans • Sources of Consumer Loans • Terms and Costs of Consumer Loans	• Measuring Your Credit Capacity • The Five C's of Credit • Applying for Consumer Credit • If You Are Denied Credit	• Rights in Obtaining Credit • Credit Reporting • Billing Statements • Debt Collection Practices	• When and How to Use Consumer Credit • Strategies for Reducing Outstanding Credit • What to Do If You Can't Make Your Payments

Consumer Loans

As the preceding chapter pointed out, consumer loans are an alternative to credit card borrowing. Most financial institutions offer several types of consumer loans, and many of these loans are available at lower rates of interest than credit cards. In deciding what type of consumer credit is best for you, you should consider the costs and benefits associated with each of your sources of borrowing. Typically, any contract terms that reduce the risk of your defaulting on the loan will result in a lower interest rate charged by the lender.

Characteristics of Consumer Loans

Consumer loans vary in the interest rates charged, payment arrangements, and collateral required for the loan. In this section, you'll read about your options with respect to each of these characteristics.

Interest Rates. Interest rates on consumer loans can be either fixed or variable. With a **fixed-rate loan**, the same interest rate applies throughout the life of the loan. With a **variable-rate loan**, the periodic rate fluctuates along with a pre-determined measure, such as the prime rate or the Treasury bill rate. For example, suppose you took out a loan in February 2004, when the prime rate was 4 percent, and agreed to pay the prime rate plus two percentage points in interest. The interest rate on your loan would have started out at 6 percent. In periods when interest rates are rising, especially when they rise rapidly, a variable-rate loan can subject you to unexpected increases in required payments. However, variable-rate loans generally carry lower initial interest rates than fixed-rate loans, since the lender isn't facing the risk of having the interest rate fall behind market rates on comparable loans. Therefore, if the introductory rate is low enough, or if you don't expect to borrow the money for a long period of time, you might find it worthwhile to take a variable-rate loan despite the risk of increased payments.

Certain types of loans are more likely than others to have fixed rates. For example, it's relatively common for rates on automobile loans to be fixed, whereas rates on home equity loans can be either fixed or variable. The interest rates on credit cards, discussed in Chapter 6, can be either fixed or variable under the terms of the contract. In practice, though, revolving credit agreements are more often classified as variable-rate since the issuer generally retains the right to change the rate at any time in the future.

Payment Arrangements. Loan agreements may be single-payment or, more commonly, installment arrangements. A **single-payment loan** requires that the balance be paid in full at some point in the future, including the **principal**—the original borrowed amount—and the interest owed on the borrowed funds. For example, many tax preparation firms offer to lend their customers money on the condition that it be repaid in full when the customers receive their income tax refunds.

An **installment loan** allows the borrower to repay over time, usually in monthly installments that include both principal and interest. An installment loan is said to be in **default** whenever a required payment is overdue. Loan agreements specify the consequences of defaulting, which may include late fees or even cancellation of the loan. Some loans include an **acceleration clause** that makes the entire balance due and payable in the event that the borrower falls behind in payments. A **prepayment penalty**—a fee charged for early repayment—can apply to certain loans.

Secured and Unsecured Loans. A **secured loan** gives the lender the right to take certain assets or property in the event that the loan is not repaid according to its terms. The

LEARNING objective

Identify the most common types of consumer loans and lenders.

fixed-rate loan
Loan for which the rate of interest remains the same throughout the term of the loan.

variable-rate loan
Loan for which the rate of interest varies periodically with a changing market rate, such as the prime rate.

single-payment loan
A loan that requires the repayment of interest and principal in a single payment at a specified date in the future.

principal
The original amount borrowed or invested.

installment loan
A loan that requires repayment in equal periodic installments which include both interest and principal.

default
Failure to meet the terms of a loan agreement, as when payments are not made in a timely fashion.

acceleration clause
A loan term that requires immediate repayment of the total amount due on an installment loan that is in default.

prepayment penalty
A fee charged to the borrower when a loan balance is repaid before the end of the loan term.

secured loan
A loan that includes a pledge of collateral.

collateral

Valuable assets or real property that can be taken by the lender in the event of a loan default.

pledged property—which can be any valuable asset, such as an automobile, home, or business property—is called the **collateral** for the loan. Obviously, the right to take the collateral reduces the potential cost of default to the lender; thus, lenders usually charge lower rates of interest on secured loans than on unsecured loans.

Compare, for example, the average rates on credit cards, which are unsecured, with the rates on automobile loans, which give the lender rights to your car if you don't pay the loan. The difference at any given point in time is quite large, often 10 percentage points or more. If you don't make your credit card payments, the lender has few options for recovering your bad debt, but if you don't make your car payments, the lender can *repossess*, or take back, the car, sell it, and keep the proceeds. Some loan agreements even include a *deficiency judgment clause*, which gives lenders the right to bill you for the difference between what was owed and the value of the repossessed collateral. So if your car didn't sell for a high enough price to pay back the loan, the lender has a right to seek financial compensation from you for the difference.

Metropolitan Asset Recovery Solutions tows a vehicle during repossessions.

When real property is used as collateral, as in the case of a home mortgage, the lender will record a **lien** against the property at the county courthouse, putting the public on notice of its potential right to the property. This ensures that, if you sell the home, the loan will be repaid before you can take any of the proceeds from the sale.

Types of Consumer Loans

Fact #1

If you don't make your car loan payments, car lenders will hire a "repo" firm to take your car back, usually by towing it from wherever it's parked. The car will then be sold at a wholesale auction to pay back your loan. About 1 out of every 1,000 car loans ends up in repossession, and the average net loss after an auction proceeding is more than $6,000.

Although you can obtain a consumer loan for almost any consumer purchase, subject to your creditworthiness, certain very common consumer loans are designed to be used for specified purposes. Examples include home equity loans, car loans, and student loans.

lien

Public notice of a right to real property.

home equity

The market value of a home minus the remaining mortgage balance.

Home Equity Loans. A home is the most valuable asset most households possess. As your property value increases and your mortgage is repaid over time, you will gradually build up **home equity**, defined as the difference between the market value of your home and the remaining balance on your mortgage loan (discussed in more detail in Chapter 8). A home equity loan allows you to borrow against this valuable asset. Like your primary mortgage loan, the home equity loan is secured by your home. The lender's right to the home is secondary to that of the primary mortgage lender, however, so these loans are also referred to as second mortgages. In the event of default, the first mortgage must be repaid from the proceeds of the sale of the home before the second mortgage lender gets anything.

Depending on the lender, you may be able to borrow as much as 100 percent of your home equity, although most lenders limit your total mortgage debt to 80 to 90 percent of the market value of your home. For example, suppose you own a home worth $150,000 and your mortgage balance is $100,000. Your home equity is $150,000 − $100,000 = $50,000. If you're approved for a home equity loan in the amount of $20,000, your total debt on the home will be $120,000, which amounts to 80 percent of the market value. The *Go Figure!* box, "How Much Can You Borrow with a Home Equity Loan?" shows how to estimate the amount you can borrow, given the ratio requirements of your lender and your current mortgage balance.

Home equity loans are usually installment loans payable over 5 to 15 years in equal monthly payments. They are often established as lines of credit that you can access as needed. Generally, home equity loan proceeds can be used for any purpose.

An important feature of home equity loans is the fact that the interest is tax-deductible up to a maximum of $100,000. The tax benefits, particularly for households in higher tax brackets, can make this type of borrowing significantly less costly than other credit choices. If your marginal tax rate is 30 percent (including federal and state taxes) and the interest rate on your home equity loan is 6 percent, you are effectively paying only 70 percent of that

GO FIGURE!

How Much Can You Borrow with a Home Equity Loan?

Home equity lenders commonly have maximum loan-to-value ratios of between 75 and 90 percent. This means that they will not allow your total debt on the home, including the first mortgage and the home equity loan, to exceed that percentage of the current market value of the home.

Problem: Barbara and Matt Montoya own a home with a current market value of $180,000. When they bought their home five years ago, the value was $140,000, and they financed the purchase by taking a first mortgage for $112,000, with payments of $745 per month. Their current mortgage loan balance is $105,000. They would like to make some home improvements and want to know how much they could borrow using a home equity line of credit. The lenders in their area allow an 80 percent loan-to-value ratio. Use the worksheet to determine the Montoyas' maximum home equity credit line. If you own a home, you can use this worksheet to calculate your own maximum as well.

Solution:

	The Montoyas' Home	Your Home
1. Market value	$180.000	______
2. Lender's maximum loan-to-value ratio	0.8	______
3. Maximum total debt (Line 1 × Line 2)	$144,000	______
4. Current mortgage balance	105,000	______
5. Home equity credit limit (Line 3 − Line 4)	$ 39,000	______

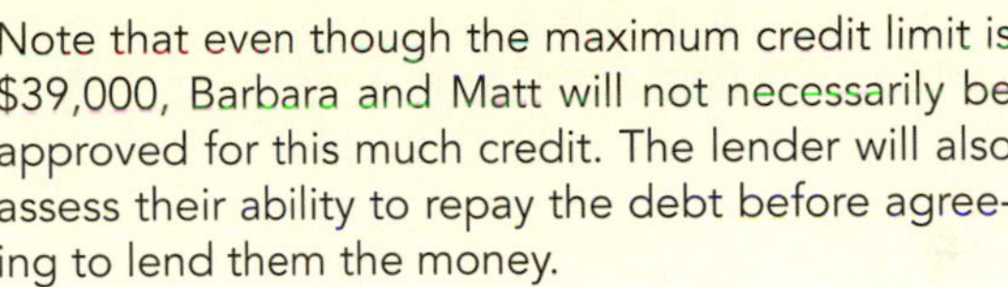

Note that even though the maximum credit limit is $39,000, Barbara and Matt will not necessarily be approved for this much credit. The lender will also assess their ability to repay the debt before agreeing to lend them the money.

amount in interest after your tax deduction, or 4.2 percent. To see how this works, suppose that you have 6 percent interest on a $20,000 home equity loan over the year for a total of $1,200. If you can deduct this interest on your taxes, your taxable income will be lower by $1,200—let's say $45,000 instead of $46,200. If we assume a marginal tax rate of 30 percent, the amount of tax you *would have paid* on that additional income is 30 percent of $1,200, or $360. Since you now do not have to pay that tax, the actual cost of the loan is the $1,200 in interest less the $360 in tax savings, for a net marginal cost of $840, or 4.2 percent of the loan amount.

Recently, some lenders have begun offering loans that combine the characteristics of low-risk secured loans with those of high-risk unsecured credit, as explained in the *News You Can Use* box, "130 Percent Mortgages." These types of loans, although they're called home equity loans, are more similar to credit cards and carry much higher rates of interest than typical secured loans.

Car Loans. A car loan is a secured loan made specifically for the purpose of buying a car. Lenders typically limit the amount of the loan to some percentage of the current market value of the car being purchased, and they require that the borrower pledge the car as security for the loan. In addition, the borrower must list the lender as an insured party on his or her auto collision insurance, which will be discussed in more detail in Chapter 9. Because of the relatively short economic life of a car, car loan maturities are typically from two to six years.

Both new car prices and rates on car loans have been unusually low in the last few years due to competition among auto dealers and generally low market interest rates. As a result, consumers have taken on significant car loan debt and monthly payments. It's worth noting, though, that getting a below-market interest rate from an auto dealer doesn't necessarily mean you've come out ahead. As discussed in Chapter 8, dealers generally make up the difference in higher prices and fees.

The average automobile loan rate in late February 2004 was 5.25 percent for a 48-month loan, according to www.bankrate.com. In contrast, home equity loan rates at that

In order to attract new car buyers, dealers sometimes offer below-market rates of interest on loans—even 0.0%.

NEWS you can use

130 Percent Mortgages

Some lenders have come up with a new idea for getting people to part with their home equity. Advertisements such as "Borrow 130 Percent of Your Home's Value" have appeared in newspapers all across the country. What's the deal? How can lenders afford to make loans that are greater than the value of the collateral?

Suppose, for example, you own a home worth $100,000 and you have an $80,000 mortgage. This type of lender might be willing to give you a $50,000 home equity line of credit, bringing your total debt to $130,000 and resulting in a loan-to-value ratio of 130 percent. If you were to default on this loan, your lenders will take the home and sell it to repay the loans. But since the home value is *less* than the total of the two loans, they will come up short and you will be held personally responsible for the difference between the sale price of the home and the total debt on the property. Since your first mortgage lender has the right to be paid first, the home equity lender is taking substantial risk. Therefore, it should come as no surprise that these loans often carry high rates of interest to compensate the lender for the risk it is taking. The rates are generally comparable to unsecured consumer loans and revolving credit accounts. It's like getting a home equity loan and a credit card in one, but you risk your house in the process.

"it's like getting a home equity loan and credit card in one"

same time averaged 6.5 percent. Since home equity loan interest is tax-deductible and car loan interest is not, the after-tax cost of home equity loans was actually very comparable to that of auto loans, although the difference depends on your marginal tax rate.

Fact #2

On average, students graduating in 2000 had about $17,000 in student loans debt, according to a survey by the National Center for Education Statistics. Medical students often graduate with more than $50,000 owed.

Student Loans. A student loan is a loan made for the purpose of paying educational expenses. In Chapter 15, we discuss financial strategies for college expenditures, primarily focusing on advance funding of these costs. However, many people use borrowed funds to cover some or all of the costs of higher education. Understandably, as the costs of both public and private higher education continue to rise at a faster rate than inflation, student loan debt is also on the increase.

Since your education is an investment you hope will pay off later in the form of increased income, borrowing for this purpose may make good financial sense. Nevertheless, as with other types of debt, it's much easier to get in debt than it is to get out. Consider how much it costs a typical student to repay a $17,000 student loan. If we assume that it's repaid over the average 10-year period offered by lenders, at an interest rate of 5 percent, payments will be about $180 per month, a significant burden for most new college graduates living on entry-level salaries. (Later in this chapter, we review how to calculate your expected loan payments and your repayment options.)

Rates on student loans tend to be more favorable than those on other forms of borrowing and in some cases are subsidized by the federal government. For this reason, it is generally better to borrow money for your education through student loan programs than it is to use other forms of consumer financing to pay for college. About two-thirds of all student financial aid comes from federal programs, including the loans discussed in this section and the grant programs discussed in Chapter 15. To be eligible for a federal student loan, you must:

- Be a U.S. citizen with a high-school diploma or the equivalent.
- Be taking courses to fulfill requirements for a degree or certificate.
- Meet satisfactory progress standards set by your school.

- Certify that you will use the funds only for educational purposes.
- Certify that you are not in default on any other federal student loan.
- Comply with Selective Service registration, if you're a male aged 18 through 25.

The Student Guide, a free Department of Education publication, tells you about federal student aid programs and how to apply for them. You can request a copy from Federal Student Aid Information Center, P.O. Box 84, Washington, D.C. 20044-0084 or by calling 1-800-433-3243.

You can download a free copy of *The Student Guide* at http://studentaid.ed.gov/students/publications/.

Student loans are available through campus-based aid programs or directly from local financial institutions. Exhibit 7-1 summarizes the most important features of the four major student loan programs: subsidized Stafford loans, unsubsidized Stafford loans, PLUS loans, and federal Perkins loans. A federal Perkins loan is a low-interest (5%) loan for undergraduate and graduate students with demonstrated financial need. The lender is the educational institution, but the U.S. Department of Education contributes some of the funds used to make the loans. The Department of Education also administers the Federal Family Education Loan (FFEL) Program and the William D. Ford Federal Direct Loan (Direct Loan) Program. Loans made through these programs directly to students are called Stafford loans, and those made to parents of dependent

EXHIBIT 7-1 **Student Loan Types and Characteristics**

Source: U.S. Department of Education.

	Subsidized Stafford Loan	Unsubsidized Stafford Loan	PLUS Loan	Federal Perkins Loan
Annual limits for dependent (independent) students	Undergraduate: Yr 1: $2,625 Yr 2: $3,500 Yrs 3,4: $5,500 Graduate: $8,500	Undergraduate: Yr 1: $2,625 ($6,625) Yr 2: $3,500 ($7,500) Yrs 3,4: $5,500 ($10,500) Graduate: $18,500	Cost of attendance not covered by other financial aid.	Undergraduate: $4,000 Graduate: $6,000
Total maximum for dependent (independent) students	Undergraduate: $23,000 Graduate: $65,500	Undergraduate: $23,000 ($46,000) Graduate: $138,500	Cost of attendance not covered by other financial aid.	Undergraduate: $20,000 Graduate: $40,000
Disbursement	Direct loans from federal government go to school; loans from private lenders go to students.	Direct loans from federal government go to school; loans from private lenders go to students.	Direct loans from federal government go to school; loans from private lenders go to students.	School disburses the funds to students.
Repayment begins	6 months after graduation	6 months after graduation	2 months after disbursement	9 months after graduation
Maximum schedule for payment	Several choices; 25 years if total loan > $30,000	Several choices; 25 years if total loan > $30,000	Several choices; 25 years if total loan > $30,000	10 years
Other terms	Department of Education pays interest while student is in school and during deferrals.	Borrower pays interest during the life of the loan.	Available to parents of dependent undergraduate students.	Lender is the school and federal government. Not all schools participate.
Interest rates	Adjusted annually Maximum: 8.25% 7/1/02–6/30/03: 4.06%	Adjusted annually Maximum: 8.25% 7/1/02–6/30/03: 4.06%	Adjusted annually Maximum: 9% 7/1/02–6/30/03: 4,86%	5%

undergraduates are called PLUS loans. Loans made to students can be either subsidized or unsubsidized. Subsidized loans are awarded on the basis of need and do not require the payment of interest or repayment of principal until six months after graduation. Unsubsidized loans accrue interest from the time they are awarded, although you can sometimes defer the payment until after graduation.

You can get the FAFSA at www.studentaid.ed.gov. To better understand how the EFC is calculated, download the "EFC Formula Worksheets and Tables" at www.ifap.ed.gov.

To qualify for subsidized student loans, you must demonstrate financial need by filling out the Free Application for Student Aid (FAFSA). Based on the financial information provided on this form, the federal government calculates an "Expected Family Contribution (EFC)" amount that is compared to your expected costs to determine any shortfall, which tells them how much you will need from other sources (grants, loans, work-study, or scholarships).

In addition to their other benefits, student loans generally allow borrowers to defer loan payments under certain circumstances. Loan payments can be temporarily deferred for up to three years for economic hardship, postsecondary study (at least half-time), unemployment, or service in the military or the Peace Corps. Perkins loans have the added advantage of being forgiven in whole or part if the borrower dies or is disabled, or if the borrower takes permanent employment in certain professions (such as math and science teachers in inner-city schools, special education teachers, law enforcement, and nursing).

Learning by Doing 7-1

1. You're considering an unsecured loan at 7 percent interest from your local home improvement store for the purchase of new kitchen cabinets. Alternatively, you could take out a home equity loan at a rate of 8.5 percent. Assume that your marginal tax rate is 25 percent. What are the advantages and disadvantages of these different courses of action?

A home equity loan can be used to finance home improvements such as a kitchen remodel, which will increase the value of your home.

Sources of Consumer Loans

Most financial institutions offer one or more types of consumer loans. Exhibit 7-2 summarizes the loan types offered by various lenders.

Depository Institutions. Recall from Chapter 5 that depository institutions, such as banks, savings and loans, and credit unions, are financial institutions that obtain funds from deposits into checking and savings accounts. These institutions offer the widest variety of consumer loans and, on average, the most favorable interest rates. They can offer lower rates because they pay relatively low rates of return to their depositors, from whom they obtain the funds they lend out. In return for lower rates, however, they tend to be a bit picky about the risk characteristics of those to whom they lend. Thus, if you have very little experience with borrowing or have made payments late in the past, these lenders may not be willing to do business with you. They are also likely to require that borrowers have funds on deposit at their institutions, such as in regular checking or savings accounts. Despite these restrictions, nearly half of all consumer lending is done through commercial banks.

consumer finance company
A nondepository institution that makes loans to riskier consumers.

Consumer and Sales Finance Companies. Consumers who cannot borrow from depository institutions, either because of poor credit or insufficient credit history, might consider borrowing from a **consumer finance company**. These firms do not take deposits; instead, they obtain their funds from their investors and from short-term borrowing. Because generally these companies make riskier loans and pay more for the funds they lend out than do depository institutions, they tend to charge higher rates of interest to consumers. Their advantages include access and speed, with approvals often taking 24 hours or less. Many consumer finance companies specialize in debt consolidation loans and offer credit-counseling services, but they may require home equity as collateral for such loans. You're likely to find several consumer finance companies in any town. In addition, if you do an Internet search on "installment loans," you'll find hun-

EXHIBIT 7-2 Sources for Various Types of Consumer Credit

Types of Consumer Credit Products	Depository Institutions	Consumer and Sales Finance Companies	Brokerage Firms	Cash-value Life Insurance Policies	Retirement Plans	Pawn Shops
First mortgage	✘					
Home equity loan	✘				✘	
Car loan	✘	✘				
Credit card	✘	✘				
Debit card	✘					
Student loan	✘					
Unsecured personal loan	✘	✘				
Secured personal loan	✘	✘	✘	✘	✘	✘

dreds of lenders to choose from and may be able to complete an application through the mail or online. While many of these firms are perfectly legitimate businesses, some are not, so you should never do business with an unfamiliar financial institution before checking on its status with appropriate authorities.

A **sales finance company** makes consumer loans to buyers of products offered through its parent company, usually a large retailer. For example, most of the major automakers have their own finance companies, as do large department stores such as JC Penney and Sears. These companies usually require that the item being purchased be pledged as collateral for the loan. The rates charged by sales finance companies are likely to be lower than those charged by consumer finance companies.

sales finance company

A nondepository institution that makes consumer loans to buyers of products offered through its parent company.

Other Sources of Consumer Loans. You can also obtain short-term consumer loans through investment accounts at brokerage firms (discussed in Chapter 12), cash-value life insurance policies (discussed in Chapter 16), and retirement plans (discussed in Chapter 15). Since these accounts are primarily designed for distant savings goals, however, borrowing from them may jeopardize your ability to achieve other financial goals. For example, if you borrow against a life insurance policy and then die before you've repaid the loan, the proceeds of your life insurance policy will be reduced by the amount of the outstanding loan. If you borrow from a retirement account, your investment returns will be earned on a smaller principal balance, and you may owe income taxes on the amount you withdraw.

Certain types of businesses, known as pawnshops, regularly provide short-term loans to people who don't have other less costly options. The pawnshop makes the loan in return for holding something of value as collateral, such as jewelry, electronics equipment, or a musical instrument. The maximum loan amount is usually a percentage of the resale value of the item being held, often 50 percent or less, and the pawnshop has the right to sell your valuable if you don't repay the loan within the allowed period of time.

LEARNING objective

Compare consumer loans based on terms and costs.

Terms and Costs of Consumer Loans

Like other financial contracts, consumer loans include a variety of features and terms. In choosing between different loans, you must therefore evaluate the characteristics of each type of loan and select the one that best meets your needs. All the important loan terms are spelled out in the **promissory note**, the legal document that represents your promise to repay the loan amount. Several of the most common terms and clauses are described below.

promissory note

Legal contract that specifies the terms and conditions of the borrower's agreement to repay a sum of money.

down payment

The amount of the purchase price that a buyer pays in cash.

Down Payment. When you take out a loan to buy a consumer good, the lender may require that you pay a portion of the purchase price in cash, called the **down payment**. Suppose, for example, that you buy a new car for a total price of $14,000 and borrow $10,000 in the form of a car loan from your local bank. The amount you pay out of your own funds—$4,000—is your down payment. For some types of loans, such as car loans, lenders may offer better financing terms if you make a larger down payment and borrow a smaller proportion of the total cost.

Loan Term. The feature that differentiates closed-end credit from open-end credit is that closed-end credit requires repayment over a specified period of time. In the case of a single-payment loan, the contract will specify the date by which the loan must be paid in full. For an installment loan, the contract will specify the monthly payment amount and the term of the loan—the amount of time the loan will cover. For example, a lender may offer 36-month, 48-month, and 60-month terms for its car loans. The date on which the last payment is due is called the maturity date.

Monthly Payments and Finance Charges. The term of the loan affects both your monthly payments and the rate of interest you pay. The longer the term, all else being equal, the smaller your monthly payments. In addition, lenders usually charge higher rates of interest on loans with longer terms.

You can use time value of money principles to determine the effect of loan term on your payments. Exhibit A-5 in Appendix A shows you how much your payment will be per $1,000 borrowed for different annual interest rates and terms. Consulting that table, you simply multiply the value in the table by the amount you wish to borrow divided by 1,000. For example, if you're borrowing $5,000, multiply the value by 5 (5,000/1,000 = 5). At an 8 percent rate, your payments on a 24-month, $5,000 loan will be $226.14 per month (45.227 × 5 = $226.14), whereas your payments on a 48-month loan will be $122.07 per month (24.413 × 5 = $122.07).

Longer terms reduce your monthly payments but produce higher total payments because you'll be paying more interest on a longer-term loan. In the example above, 24 payments of $226.14 total $5,427.36. Since the original amount borrowed was $5,000, you'll pay $427.36 in interest on the loan. If instead you take the 48-month loan, you'll pay a total of $122.07 × 48 = $5,859.36. That's $859.36 in total interest, more than twice as much as in the 24-month example.

Learning by Doing 7-2

1. You're shopping for a $10,000 car loan. For each of the following pairs of loans, indicate which maturity and interest combination will result in a *lower* monthly payment:
   - **a.** 36-month loan at 6 percent versus 48-month loan at 6 percent
   - **b.** 48-month loan at 6.5 percent versus 48 month loan at 6 percent
2. For each of the pairs of loans in the previous question, indicate which will result in lower *total* payments?

Collateral. As mentioned previously, loans may be secured or unsecured. The promissory note for a secured loan will include a description of the collateral pledged for the loan and specify the conditions under which the lender can take possession of the collateral. Auto lenders usually hold the title to the car until you repay the loan in full, and home equity lenders usually hold a legal interest in any real property being used as collateral. If you don't repay the loan, these lenders have the right to take the property from you.

Finance Charges. As with revolving credit accounts, there are different methods for calculating interest on consumer loans. Most common are the simple interest method, add-on interest method, and bank discount interest method. Since lenders use different methods to compute finance charges, the nominal, or quoted, rate is not directly comparable across loans. For this reason, you should always use the APR to compare the annualized costs. Recall that the APR is the total annual finance charges divided by the average loan balance over the year—and that lenders are required by the Truth in Lending Act to state the APR on the loan agreement and in any advertising materials.

To illustrate each type of interest calculation, let's consider an example in which you borrow $2,000 for one year at 12 percent interest and pay it back in equal monthly installments.

Fact #3

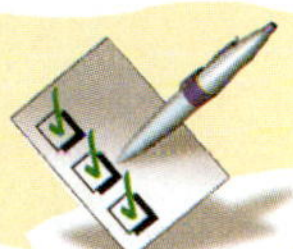

The average APRs on home equity loans, car loans, and student loans are usually much lower than those charged on credit cards. Rates on unsecured consumer loans offered by consumer finance companies are likely to be more comparable to credit card rates. At the end of 2003, according to Federal Reserve statistics, the average rate offered by commercial banks on 48-month car loans was 7.34 percent and new car loans from automobile finance companies averaged 3.14 percent. At the same time, these institutions charged an average of 12.24 percent for 24-month personal loans and 13.13 percent on credit cards.

Simple Interest. Most depository institutions use the simple interest method to determine finance charges on consumer loans. Here, the amount of interest you pay in any given period is determined by the outstanding balance on the loan. If there are no interestlike fees associated with a simple interest loan, the quoted rate is also equal to the APR. Unlike credit cards, consumer loans usually don't require the payment of an annual fee, so the annual interest charges are the only finance charges. As you make payments and your balance declines, so does the dollar amount of interest you pay each period.

The actual amount of interest owed in each payment period for a simple interest loan is calculated as follows:

$$\begin{aligned}\text{Interest} &= \text{Remaining balance of loan} \times \text{Periodic rate}\\ &= \text{Remaining balance of loan} \times \frac{\text{Nominal rate}}{\text{Payments per year}}\end{aligned}$$

The periodic rate in our example is equal to 1 percent (12%/12 = 1%). Thus, the amount of interest you'll pay in the first month when the balance of the loan is still $2,000 is

$$\begin{aligned}\text{Interest} &= \$2{,}000 \times 0.01\\ &= \$20\end{aligned}$$

Each payment includes both principal and interest. As you make payments, the remaining balance goes down, and so does the interest you pay. The total payment, however, remains the same so you'll be repaying more principal with each payment.

You can calculate the total monthly payment using any of the methods introduced in Chapter 2: mathematical formula, financial calculator, or electronic spreadsheet. Since you're calculating equal monthly payments, this is an annuity problem. You know the periodic interest rate, the present value (the amount of the loan), the number of payments (months to pay), and the future value (zero, since you'll have completely paid back the loan by the end). You need to solve for the payment amount. To find the solution using a financial calculator, for example, enter $PV = 2{,}000$, $N = 12$; and $I = 1$ and then solve for *PMT*. You should get an answer of $177.70. This will appear as a negative value since it's an outflow to you.

We know that the interest portion for the first payment is $20.00. For the first payment, then, the difference of $157.70 will be applied to reduce the principal balance owed to $1,842.30 ($2,000 − $157.70 = $1,842.30). This amount will be used to calculate the interest paid in the second month, with the difference again applied to repaying the principal of the loan.

Exhibit 7-3 provides a complete table of payments for this 12-month installment loan. Note that although the payment stays constant over the life of the loan, the portion allocated to interest declines and the portion that repays principal increases. Summing the interest column, we

EXHIBIT 7-3

Sample Amortization Schedule for a Simple Interest Loan (original principal = $2,000; nominal interest = 12%; and term = 12 months)

Month	Beginning Balance	Monthly Payment	Monthly Interest	Principal Repayment
1	$2,000.00	$177.70	$20.00	$157.70
2	1842.30	177.70	18.42	159.28
3	1683.02	177.70	16.83	160.87
4	1522.15	177.70	15.22	162.48
5	1359.67	177.70	13.60	164.10
6	1195.57	177.70	11.96	165.74
7	1029.83	177.70	10.30	167.40
8	862.43	177.70	8.62	169.08
9	693.35	177.70	6.93	170.77
10	522.58	177.70	5.23	172.47
11	350.11	177.70	3.50	174.20
12	$175.91	$177.67	$1.76	$175.94
Average balance $1,103.08				
Total payments		$2,132.40		
Total finance charge			$132.37	
Total principal Repaid				$2,000.00

Note: Last payment is slightly smaller because of rounding.

find that the total finance charges for the year are $132.37. Since the average monthly balance owed on the loan is $1,103.08, we can calculate the APR as follows:

$$\text{APR} = \frac{\text{Total annual finance charges}}{\text{Average loan balance over the year}}$$

$$= \frac{\$132.37}{\$1,103.08}$$

$$= 0.12 \quad \text{or} \quad 12.0\%$$

Note that the APR is equal to the nominal rate.

Add-on Interest. When the add-on interest method is used, the interest is added to the amount borrowed before the payments are calculated; the total is then divided by the number of payments to determine the payment amount. The equation is as follows:

$$\text{Payment} = \frac{\text{Amount of loan} + (\text{Amount of loan} \times \text{Nominal rate} \times \text{Number of years})}{\text{Number of payments}}$$

Thus, returning to our example, we see that the monthly payments calculated using the add-on interest method would be

$$\text{Payment} = \frac{\$2,000 + (\$2,000 \times 0.12 \times 1)}{12}$$

$$= \frac{\$2,240}{12}$$

$$= \$186.67$$

By comparison, payments under the simple interest method were $177.70—a substantial difference. In the simple interest case, the amount of interest you pay is always proportional to the amount of your outstanding loan balance. But with add-on interest, you're paying the nominal rate on the original balance even after you've repaid most of the loan.

Add-on interest will always result in a higher APR than simple interest because you'll always be paying interest on more funds than you actually have available to use. Recall that we normally calculate APR as the total annual finance charge divided by the average monthly balance. Precise calculation of the APR for an add-on interest loan is a little tricky because the changing allocation of your payment dollars to interest and principal makes it more difficult to measure the average loan balance. Although a more precise method for estimating the APR is described in the *Go Figure!* box, "N-Ratio Method of Calculating APR for Add-On Interest Loans," you can roughly estimate the APR for an add-on interest loan much more simply with the following formula:

$$\text{APR approximation for add-on interest loan} = \frac{\text{Total annual finance charges}}{\text{Original loan amount} \times 0.5}$$

The denominator (Original loan amount × 0.5) is an approximation of the average loan balance, based on the idea that, since you're paying back the principal evenly over time, the average balance owed will be about half of the original amount borrowed. In our example, the total finance charge is 12 percent of \$2,000, or \$240, and the original loan amount is \$2,000, yielding an APR approximation of 24 percent:

$$\text{APR approximation for add-on interest loan} = \frac{\$240}{\$2{,}000 \times 0.5}$$
$$= 0.24 \quad \text{or} \quad 24 \text{ percent.}$$

The N-ratio method described in the *Go Figure!* box yields an APR of 21.45 percent for our example—slightly lower than that obtained using the approximation method.

Discount Interest. Like the add-on interest method, the discount interest method results in relatively expensive financing. With this method, which is more commonly used for single-payment loans, the lender subtracts the interest due from the principal amount before the borrower gets the money. Then, at the maturity date, the entire principal amount is due. Since you're paying the interest up front on the entire principal amount, but you'll receive only that amount less the interest, you'll again end up paying interest on funds that are not available to you.

GO FIGURE!

N-Ratio Method of Calculating APR for Add-On Interest Loans

Problem: Calculate the APR for a \$2,000, 12 percent nominal rate, monthly payment one-year loan and three-year loan.

Solution: The method used for calculating APR for an add-on interest loan is called the N-ratio method, and the formula is as follows:

$$\text{APR} = \frac{m \times (95\,N + 9) \times F}{12\,N \times (N + 1) \times (4\,P + F)}$$

where

m = Number of payments per year
N = Number of total loan payments
F = Total finance charges (interest and mandatory fees)
P = Amount borrowed (principal)

Applying the formula to the one-year loan, we calculate:

$$\text{APR} = \frac{12 \times [(95 \times 12) + 9] \times 240}{(12 \times 12) \times (12 + 1) \times [(4 \times 2{,}000) + 240]}$$
$$= \frac{12 \times 1{,}149 \times 240}{144 \times 13 \times 8{,}240}$$
$$= 0.02145 \quad \text{or} \quad 21.45\%$$

The three-year loan solution is

$$\text{APR} = \frac{12 \times [(95 \times 36) + 9] \times 720}{(12 \times 36) \times (36 + 1) \times [(4 \times 2{,}000) + 720]}$$
$$= \frac{12 \times 3{,}429 \times 720}{432 \times 37 \times 8{,}720}$$
$$= 0.02126 \quad \text{or} \quad 21.26\%$$

Not surprisingly, the discount method results in a higher APR than the simple interest method. Suppose in our example that you were repaying the $2,000 in a single payment instead of installments. Under the discount method, you'd receive $2,000 − $240 = $1,760 at the beginning of the loan, and repay the full $2,000 at the end of the year. Applying the APR formula to this scenario, we find that the APR is 13.6 percent:

$$\begin{aligned} \text{APR} &= \frac{\text{Total annual finance charges}}{\text{Average loan balance over the year}} \\ &= \frac{\$240}{\$1{,}760} \\ &= 0.136 \quad \text{or} \quad 13.6 \text{ percent} \end{aligned}$$

Note that the denominator in the equation is the amount of money that you actually have available to use, not the original borrowed amount. Since you don't repay any of the money until the end of the year with a single-payment loan, the average loan balance is constant throughout the period.

When the discount interest method is used for an installment loan rather than a single-payment loan, the APR is even higher. To approximate it, we use the same estimation method described for the add-on method. Here, your balance is $1,760 at the beginning of the loan. This amount will gradually be paid back over the life of the loan so that, on average, your balance is half the original amount. Thus, the approximate APR = $240/($1,760 × 0.5) = 27.3 percent.

Credit Insurance. Occasionally, lenders suggest that you purchase credit life insurance or credit disability insurance when you get your loan. This type of insurance pays back the loan balance in full if you die or become disabled before the loan maturity date. Although such protection might seem like a good idea, this type of insurance is generally overpriced relative to other life and disability insurance. As a result, it's very profitable to lenders, so don't be surprised if your lender exerts a little pressure. If the insurance is a condition of loan approval, it will add to your costs and should be factored into the APR calculation when comparing loan alternatives.

Default and Recourse. Promissory notes usually specify the lender's rights in the event of default. Most loans specify that the lender can collect the debt from you and recoup any collection costs if you fail to live up to the terms of the agreement. Even if the agreement involves collateral, it may not be enough to cover what you owe, especially since lenders usually sell repossessed assets at wholesale rather than retail prices. If, for example, your car was worth $7,000 and the remaining balance on your defaulted loan was $8,000, the lender would have the right to seek a judgment against you for the remaining $1,000 and any collection costs. The terms of your loan might even allow the lender to have payments on the $1,000 automatically subtracted from your wages until the debt is paid in full.

Learning by Doing 7-3

1. Which of the methods of interest calculation for installment loans requires that you pay interest on funds which you do not actually have available to use?
2. Which of the methods of interest calculation for installment loans results in the highest APR, assuming that the nominal rates on the loans are the same?

Early Repayment of Installment Loans. Suppose you want to pay off your installment loan balance before the maturity date. If you have a simple interest loan, the amount you need to pay will be easy to determine. In fact, lenders will usually provide customers with the payoff amount over the phone based on the loan's amortization schedule. Since you may want to pay off a loan at a time that falls between monthly payment dates, the lender will calculate the amount owed as of the last payment date and apply a daily rate (APR/365) to the additional days. If you have a simple interest loan, you can use the amortization function on your financial calculator or spreadsheet to calculate the remaining balance at any point in time, as explained in the *Go Figure!* box, "Calculating Simple Interest Loan Payoffs."

GO FIGURE!

Calculating Simple Interest Loan Payoffs

Problem: Geoffrey Spinelli bought a car on January 15, 2002, and financed it with a 60-month, simple interest car loan from his bank. His original loan balance was $15,000, and the annual rate is 8 percent. On January 15, 2005, Geoffrey makes a loan payment, and because he is thinking about trading in his vehicle for a new car, he wants to know what his remaining loan balance is after making 36 monthly payments.

Solution: Most financial calculators include a built-in amortization table function that will allow you to find the balance owed after a given number of payments have been made. The directions below are for the Texas Instruments BAII Plus calculator.

1. Calculate the monthly payment amount using the time value functions on the calculator.

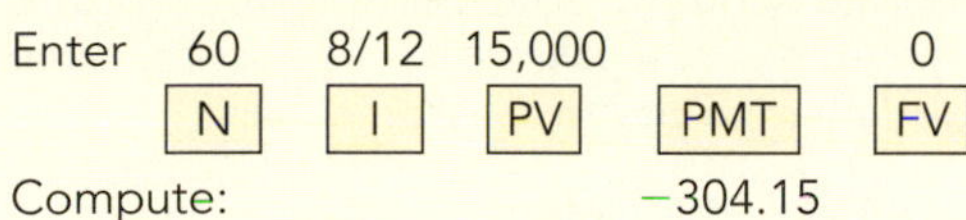

Enter	60	8/12	15,000		0
	N	I	PV	PMT	FV
Compute:				−304.15	

2. Without clearing the information from item 1 above, push [2nd] [Amort]. This will access the amortization table for the loan problem you entered in item 1. To calculate the balance owed, you will use the down arrow key [↓] to scroll through the variables and enter the number of payments you have already made as follows:
   a. The first screen will say P1 = 1. Do not change this. Push the down arrow key [↓].
   b. The next item on the menu is P2. You should enter the number of payments you have made. For this problem, key in 36 and push ENTER. Then push the down arrow key [↓].
   c. The value that appears will be the balance owed on Geoffrey's loan after he has made 36 payments: BAL = $6,725.

Although it's not required for this problem, you can also use the amortization function to determine how much principal and interest Geoffrey has paid over the three years he has had this loan. After the balance is calculated, you can press the down arrow key again to find PRN, the total principal repaid between months 1 and 36 (P1 and P2), and once more to find the total interest (INT) paid in those 36 months. For this problem, PRN = $8,275 and INT = $2,674. Note that if you only wanted to know your principal and interest amounts for the 36th month, you could enter P1 = 36 and P2 = 36.

In the case of add-on loans, it's more difficult to estimate the balance owed for early repayment. Since an add-on loan spreads the interest cost evenly over the term of the loan, but the balance still declines over time, the amount of interest you have paid to date is actually less than what the lender is legally entitled to. Therefore, the balance must be adjusted upward to reflect the amount of interest you still owe the lender for the period you've had the loan. Although the actual calculation of outstanding balance for an add-on loan is fairly complicated, the **Rule of 78's**, also known as the *sum of the years' digits method*, will help you figure the dollar value of the finance charges you'll avoid by paying the loan off early. From this, you can calculate the amount necessary to repay the loan. The *Go Figure* box, "Using the Rule of 78's to Calculate Payoffs for Add-On Loans," shows the process for this calculation.

Rule of 78's

A mathematical formula used to calculate the amount of interest remaining to be paid on an add-on installment loan.

Balloon Payments. A **balloon loan** is a special type of installment loan involving a final "balloon" payment that is substantially larger than the other installment payments. Although a balloon payment is not technically an early repayment of the loan, since it is required by the terms of the contract, we include the discussion in this section because the amount you owe at the end is usually calculated like an early repayment. For example, the payments on a simple interest balloon loan could be calculated using a 10-year amortization term, but require that the loan balance be paid in full at the end of three years. The balloon payment at the end is the same as what you would have owed if you had a 10-year simple interest loan and wanted to pay it off at the end of three years.

balloon loan

A loan for which the regular installment payments are calculated using a longer amortization period, but a single large payment is required after a shorter period of time to repay the balance in full.

Balloon loans are useful if you need the funds for only a short period of time but don't want to be burdened with a large monthly payment in the interim. Lenders like to issue this type of loan when interest rates are rising, since they prefer not to be locked into longer-term loans at low interest rates in that situation.

GO FIGURE!

Using the Rule of 78's to Calculate Payoffs for Add-On Loans

Problem: Kelly borrowed $2,000 at 12 percent for 24 months. If her loan was an add-on loan, how much does she still owe with four months remaining on the loan. Her monthly payment amount is $103.33 (= $2,480/24)

Solution: Follow these steps to calculate the early payoff amount for an add-on installment loan:

1. **Number each month.** Assign each month of the loan a number, with the numbers in descending order, with the first month being the highest number. For Kelly's two-year loan, the months would be numbered from 24 down to 1.
2. **Sum all the months' digits.** Add up all the numbers (24 + 23 + 22 + . . .) or apply the following formula:

$$\text{Sum of digits} = \frac{N}{2} \times (N + 1)$$

where N = total number of loan months:

$$\text{Sum of digits} = \frac{24}{2} \times (24 + 1) = 12 \times 25 = 300$$

3. **Sum the digits for months remaining on the loan.** Now add up only the numbers of the months remaining on the loan. Since Kelly has four months to go on her 24-month loan, add 4 + 3 + 2 + 1 = 10.
4. **Calculate the proportion of finance charges avoided by early payment.** Divide the total from Step 3 by the total from Step 2 to obtain the proportion of total finance charges that can be avoided by paying off the loan early. In Kelly's case, where she is avoiding four months' worth of finance charges:

$$\text{Percent of finance charge avoided} = \frac{\text{Sum of remaining digits}}{\text{Sum of all digits}} = \frac{10}{300} = 0.033 \quad \text{or} \quad 3.33\%$$

5. **Calculate the dollar finance charges avoided by early payment.** Multiply the percentage from Step 4 by the total dollar finance charge on the loan to arrive at the finance charges to be avoided by early payment of the loan. In this example, the original finance charge was 0.12 × $2,000 × 2 = $480, and the finance charges to be avoided are 0.033 × $480 = $15.84.
6. **Calculate the payoff for the loan.** Subtract the results of Step 5 from the total amount due for the remaining payments. This is the amount you need to pay to satisfy the loan.

Total of remaining payments	= Number of payments × Payment amount
	= 4 × 103.33
	= 413.32
Minus finance charges avoided	= 15.84
Total payoff amount	= $397.49

Note that even though Kelly has been paying a total finance charge of $480/24 = $20 per month, she will only save a total of $15.98, or approximately $4 per month, by repaying the loan early. As mentioned, add-on loans are extremely costly in APR terms. Early repayment doesn't change this fact, since the law credits the lender with a proportionate amount of the total finance charge.

Building Your Creditworthiness

LEARNING objective

3 Assess your creditworthiness and know how to improve it.

We've now examined the basics of both open-end and closed-end credit. But how much outstanding credit is financially feasible for your family? Will a lender be willing to lend it to you? These questions are related to your creditworthiness—whether you can afford to make payments on a loan and whether you will be responsible about making payments on time. Although lenders commonly do their own evaluation before making loans, good financial planning requires that you be aware of your own financial situation and make responsible decisions about credit. The starting point is to develop personal financial statements and a household budget, as has been discussed in previous chapters. By understanding your financial situation, you may better assess how much debt you can afford to take on. You'll also be better able to identify areas of your finances that need to be addressed before you apply for a loan.

Measuring Your Credit Capacity

In Chapter 2, we identified several ratios that are useful in evaluating how debt usage affects your financial health—specifically, the debt payment ratio, the mortgage debt service ratio, and the debt ratio. Recall that the debt payment ratio measures your ability to make required payments by dividing total monthly debt payments (including credit card payments, consumer loan payments, and home mortgage loan payments) by monthly disposable income, or after-tax income. The mortgage debt service ratio specifically looks at your payments that are related to home ownership—mortgage principal and interest, property taxes, and homeowners insurance—relative to gross monthly household income. Your household's reliance on debt financing is measured by the debt ratio, the total of your outstanding loan balances divided by your total assets. In addition to their usefulness in assessing your *current* financial health, these ratios may be used to evaluate whether your finances can handle an *increased* level of debt.

Lenders commonly use ratio guidelines to assess your creditworthiness as well. But it's important to keep in mind that meeting a lender's guidelines does not automatically mean that your level of debt is acceptable from a financial planning perspective. For one thing, you need to think about the alternative uses you have for those funds. For another, you need to consider whether you may generally spend more on other budget categories than the average household and therefore have less available to apply to debt repayment.

Suppose, for example, that according to your lender's guideline, your total monthly debt payments could equal as much as 35 percent of your gross monthly income. This is the equivalent of an even greater payment ratio, since the payment ratio uses disposable income, or take-home pay, in the denominator. If your gross income is \$2,000 per month, the lender's 35 percent maximum would mean you could have total debt payments of $\$2,000 \times 0.35 = \$700$. But if your take-home pay is only \$1,600, you'll be paying out 44 percent of it in debt payments ($\$700/\$1,600 = 0.44$), many times greater than the 10 to 20 percent maximum recommended by financial experts. Why the difference? The reason that lenders allow such high ratios is that they're concerned only with your ability to make payments, not with your ability to achieve your other financial goals. But the dollars spent on repayment of debt are dollars that are not being allocated to savings and investment. Thus, in weighing the advisability of taking on more debt, even when you can afford the payments, you should take into consideration the impact this decision will have on other aspects of your financial plan.

Consider just one example of the effect that additional debt can have on your financial plan. Suppose you're currently saving \$300 per month, in an account earning 5 percent interest, so that you can attend graduate school six years from now. You decide to buy a car and take out a six-year loan with payments of \$150 per month. This decision means that you will have to reduce your monthly graduate-school savings contributions by that same amount. At the end of the six years, your graduate-school account will be \$12,565 smaller than it would have been if you had continued with your original savings plan (the future value of six years of \$150 monthly payments).

Learning by Doing 7-4

Ellen's gross monthly income is \$2,500. Her take-home pay is 80 percent of her gross income. She currently pays \$75 per month for credit cards and \$310 per month for a car loan.

1. What is Ellen's debt payment ratio?
2. Ellen is considering the purchase of a \$1,500 living room set, and the store has offered financing with \$50 per month payments. If she takes on this loan, what will be her new debt payment ratio?
3. Assuming that she has already comparison shopped for the living room set, what other factors should she consider before making this credit decision?

The Five C's of Credit

Although lenders use ratios as part of their assessment of your creditworthiness, they're concerned with much more than just your monthly cash flow. The factors they consider are often summarized using the "five C's of credit"—capacity, capital, collateral, character, and conditions.

Capacity. A lender's assessment of your ability, or capacity, to repay your debts is usually based on your household cash flow. Lenders may evaluate your capacity by looking at your sources of income and your expenses. They may use the debt payment ratio, the mortgage debt service ratio, or other measures that consider your expenses relative to your income.

Capital. Lenders are also interested in your household's net worth, or capital. If total assets are greater than total debts, they will consider that you could, if necessary, liquidate other assets to pay back the loan. In addition, lenders know that people who have more at stake are less likely to default on a loan, since they don't want to risk their other assets being taken to repay the debt.

Collateral. As we've seen, a loan protected by collateral (such as a car or home) is safer to the lender than one that is not. Therefore, the pledge of collateral will make you a better credit risk to the lender. The more valuable the collateral, the better the lender will like it.

Character. Your previous credit, employment, and education history tell the lender about your character. Are you the type of person who honors an obligation? Do you have experience with making payments on debt? If you've previously borrowed money and repaid it on time, you'll be considered a better credit risk. Similarly, if you own a home, have held a job for a period of time, and have lived in the same area for a while, the lender will assume that you're less likely to default.

Conditions. Every loan and every borrower represents a unique situation, and lenders will sometimes take individual factors into consideration. Economic conditions, such as employment opportunities in the area, and special circumstances may make it more or less likely that you'll default on the loan. If you have insufficient credit history, a lender might still approve a loan to you if you have a **cosigner**—a person who agrees to take responsibility if you don't make your payments as agreed. This significantly reduces the lender's risk, but it's fairly risky for the person who cosigns, since he or she is effectively taking responsibility for the debt. In order to be sure that cosigners recognize these risks, the Federal Trade Commission requires that lenders provide the following notice:

cosigner

A person who agrees to take responsibility for repayment of a loan if the primary borrower defaults.

You are being asked to guarantee this debt. Think carefully before you do. If the borrower doesn't pay the debt, you will have to. Be sure you can afford to pay if you have to, and that you want to accept this responsibility.

You may have to pay up to the full amount of the debt if the borrower does not pay. You may also have to pay late fees or collection costs, which increase this amount.

The creditor can collect this debt from you without first trying to collect from the borrower. The creditor can use the same collection methods against you that can be used against the borrower, such as suing you, garnishing your wages, etc. If this debt is ever in default, that fact may become a part of your credit record.

PFP Worksheet 26
Assessing Your Creditworthiness Using the Five C's of Credit

Exhibit 7-4 lists the questions creditors consider in determining your creditworthiness. A worksheet is available in your *Personal Financial Planner.*

Applying for Consumer Credit

You can apply for credit by filling out a credit application form or responding to an interview that requests information related to your creditworthiness—usually details about income, assets, and debts. If you've developed a personal income statement and balance sheet, the requested information will be easy to supply.

EXHIBIT 7-4 **Assessing Your Creditworthiness Using the Five C's of Credit**

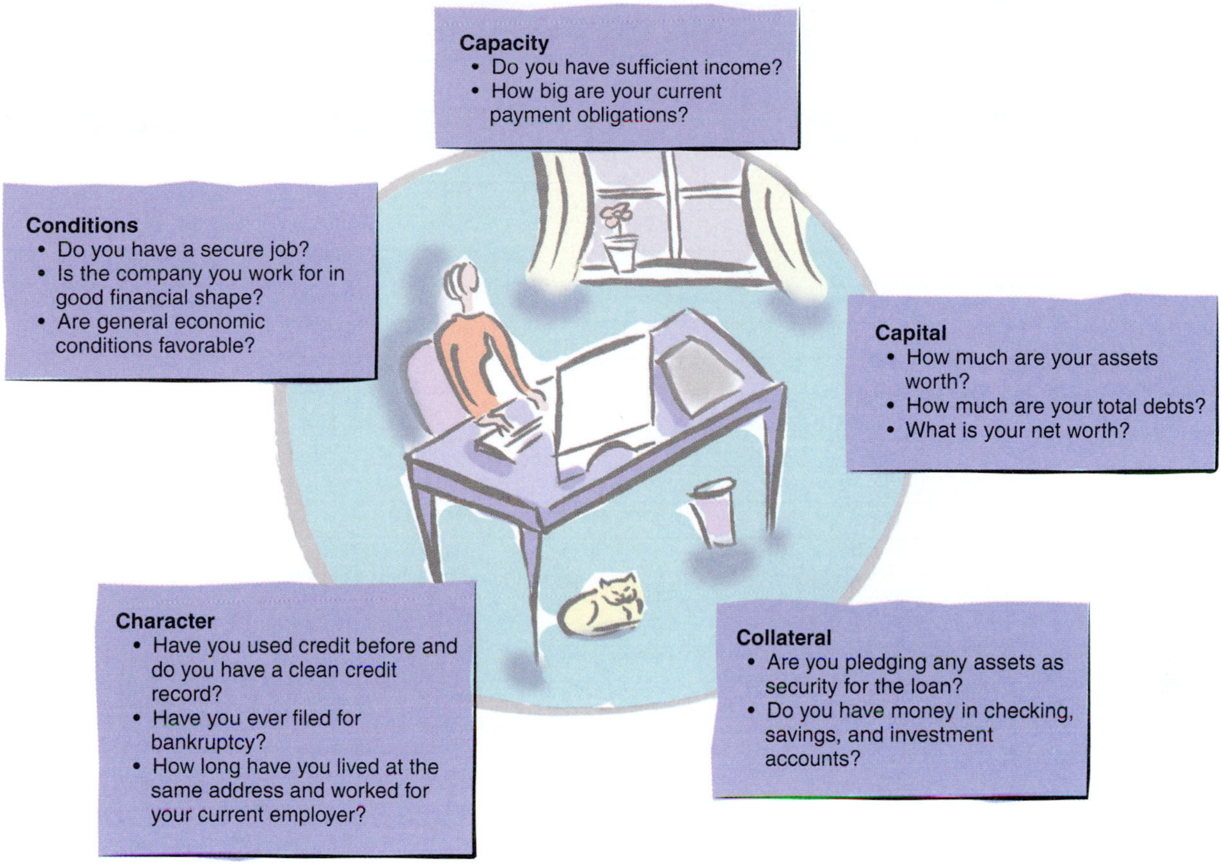

Capacity
- Do you have sufficient income?
- How big are your current payment obligations?

Conditions
- Do you have a secure job?
- Is the company you work for in good financial shape?
- Are general economic conditions favorable?

Capital
- How much are your assets worth?
- How much are your total debts?
- What is your net worth?

Character
- Have you used credit before and do you have a clean credit record?
- Have you ever filed for bankruptcy?
- How long have you lived at the same address and worked for your current employer?

Collateral
- Are you pledging any assets as security for the loan?
- Do you have money in checking, savings, and investment accounts?

In some cases, it may seem that lenders are not carefully evaluating the creditworthiness of applicants. For example, college students are often inundated with credit card offers that ask for little more than their name, address, and signature. Although students may not seem to be the best credit risks, the rates are generally high, and lenders know that parents often step in to pay their children's debts. When credit offers are received over the telephone or through the mail, it's possible the lender has already prescreened your income and credit using credit bureau information, as will be discussed in the next section. In other cases, the lender will check your credit after receiving the signed application.

On university campuses, students are commonly offered a free T-shirt or an entry in a prize drawing in return for filling out an application. Credit card lenders even offer student organizations the opportunity to use credit card applications as fundraisers—for example, an organization might be paid a $5 fee for each completed application it obtains. Even though you might be tempted to take the T-shirt and cancel the card later, it's a better idea to simply say no. It will be a lot harder to do so when your brand new credit card arrives with a $1,000 credit line. And if you don't cancel your card quickly enough, your application acceptance may obligate you to pay an annual fee.

Applications for consumer loans usually are more involved than those for credit cards. Since depository institutions prefer to make loans to the best credit risks, they ask for more detailed information on your income and assets, often using a form such as the one shown in Exhibit 7-5. In an attempt to streamline the application process and speed up approval, consumer lenders sometimes have online application forms or will take your information over the phone. Again, the more organized your finances, the simpler these forms will be to complete.

EXHIBIT 7-5 Sample Consumer Loan Application

Credit Application

Branch

In addition to this request for credit, may we provide you with an application for a credit card? ☐ YES ☐ NO

Purpose: (Disclosure Required) ☐ Line of Credit Secured by Residential Real Estate (5b). ☐ Variable Rate Installment Loan Secured by Principal Residence (19b) ☐ Other

Amount Requested	Terms Requested

APPLICANT INFORMATION		CO-APPLICANT INFORMATION	
Applicant Name (First, Middle Initial, Last, Suffix)		Applicant Name (First, Middle Initial, Last, Suffix)	
By completing the e-mail address field, you authorize us to communicate with you using electronic mail.			
E-mail Address (Optional)			
Business Name (Business Loans Only)			
Address		Address	
Address		Address	
City, State, ZIP		City, State, ZIP	
County	Length of Residence Years Months	County	Length of Residence Years Months
Phone	Social Security Number	Phone	Social Security Number
Birth Date	Number of Dependents	Birth Date	Number of Dependents
Previous Address (*if less than two years*)		Previous Address (*if less than two years*)	
City, State, ZIP		City, State, ZIP	
Length of Residence Years Months		Length of Residence Years Months	
Employer		Employer	
Occupation		Occupation	
Phone	Length Employed Years Months	Phone	Length Employed Years Months
Previous Employer (*if less than two years*)		Previous Employer (*if less than two years*)	
Occupation		Occupation	
Phone	Length Employed Years Months	Phone	Length Employed Years Months
Gross Salary	Weekly (W) / Bi-Weekly (B) / Monthly (M) / Annual (A)	Gross Salary	Weekly (W) / Bi-Weekly (B) / Monthly (M) / Annual (A)
Alimony, child support or separate maintenance need not be revealed if you do not wish to have it considered as a basis for repaying this obligation. Alimony, child support or separate maintenance received under: ( ) COURT ORDER (C) ( ) WRITTEN AGREEMENT (W) ( ) ORAL AGREEMENT (O)		Alimony, child support or separate maintenance need not be revealed if you do not wish to have it considered as a basis for repaying this obligation. Alimony, child support or separate maintenance received under:	
Other Income W / B / M / A	Source	Other Income W / B / M / A	Source
Name of Nearest Relative Not Living With You		Please charge the monthly payment for this obligation to my ( ) checking) ( ) savings account with your bank. ( ) YES ( ) NO ACCOUNT NUMBER ______________	
Address			
Phone	Relationship		

CHECKING / SAVINGS ACCOUNTS

Bank Name	Account Number	Account Type
Bank Name	Account Number	Account Type

CREDIT EXPERIENCE / OBLIGATIONS

(i.e., include all existing payments such as credit cards, department stores, bank or finance co. loans and other obligations such as alimony, child support or separate maintenance, guarantees or co-maker on loans.)

Creditor	Account Number	Balance	Monthly Payment	Payoff (Y/N)
( ) Mortgage ( ) Rent ( ) Other				
Second Mortgage/ Home Equity				
If Real Estate Owned: Date of Purchase	Purchase Price	Credit Market Value		
Auto Year of Auto Make				

Everything I have stated in this application is correct to the best of my knowledge. I understand you will retain this application whether or not it is approved. You are authorized to check my credit and employment history and to answer questions about your credit experience with me. If I am applying for a line of credit, I agree to be bound by the terms and conditions of the line of credit agreement and disclosure statement which you will send to me. If I am applying for a line of credit or loan secured by real estate, my signature below acknowledges receipt of the disclosure statement and brochure for the type of line or loan secured by real estate specified above. OH Residents Only: The Ohio laws against discrimination require that all creditors make credit equally available to all creditworthy customers, and that credit agencies maintain separate credit histories on each individual upon request. The Ohio civil rights commission administers compliance with this law. NY Residents Only: A consumer credit report may be requested in connecting with this application or in connection with updates, renewals or extensions of any credit granted as a result of this application. Upon my request, I will be informed whether or not a consumer credit report was requested, and if so, the name and address of the agency that furnished such report.

We intend to apply for joint credit. ____________ Initials of Applicant ____________ Initials of Co-Applicant

Applicant's Signature	Date	Co-Applicant's Signature	Date

If You Are Denied Credit

If you apply for a credit card or a consumer loan and are denied, you have the right to know why. Most lenders will send you a form letter that specifies the reason for the denial. The most common reasons are:

- Adverse information in your credit report
- Insufficient income relative to expenses
- Insufficient collateral
- Insufficient job history
- Insufficient residency at current address

Notice that each of these is related to one or more of the five C's of credit.

If you're denied on the basis of accurate information, such as a poor record of making credit payments on time, there's little you can do to immediately change the outcome. Your only real option is to apply for credit with another lender. The lenders that are most likely to overlook your past credit problems will also be the ones that charge the highest rates of interest. It might, in that case, be worthwhile to reconsider your financial situation and take steps to correct the problems noted by the lender before making additional applications. For example, if your credit record reflects late payments made within the last 12 months, you should resolve to pay your existing obligations on time so that you can show a 12-month history of on-time payments in the future. If you haven't worked at your current job for a long enough period of time, consider reapplying after the requisite time period has passed. If your current monthly payments are too large relative to your income, consider applying additional funds to debt reduction before seeking additional consumer financing.

Understanding Your Consumer Credit Rights

4 Understand your consumer credit rights.

Because financial transactions are complex and many consumers don't understand them very well, Congress has passed a number of laws to protect consumers in credit transactions, including the Truth in Lending Acts of 1968, 1971, and 1982; the Equal Credit Opportunity Acts of 1975 and 1977; the Fair Credit Billing Act of 1975; the Fair Debt Collection Practices Act of 1978; and the Fair Credit Reporting Reform Act of 1996, which revised the Fair Credit Reporting Act of 1971. Combined, these laws address consumers' rights to obtain credit, to receive full information about the cost of credit, to have their credit information fairly and accurately reported, to be billed accurately, and to have their debts collected according to acceptable standards. In this section, we consider consumer rights in several important areas.

Rights in Obtaining Credit

In seeking credit, you have the right to full information, and you are protected from discrimination.

Full and Accurate Information. Perhaps the most important consumer credit right is the requirement that creditors provide you with full and truthful information, written in plain English, including the true cost of consumer credit as measured by APR. This information enables you to make better decisions when choosing among potential lenders and reduces the likelihood that you'll be taken advantage of by unscrupulous lenders.

Freedom from Discrimination. Under the Equal Credit Opportunity Act, lenders can't discriminate against you based on certain protected characteristics—race, sex, marital status, religion, age, national origin, or receipt of public benefits. However, it's not against the law to deny credit based on income and credit history.

Special Concerns for Women. Historically, it was common for women to be denied credit. Female homemakers who didn't work outside the home were often unable to qualify for consumer loans or credit cards in their own names because of their lack of income. Even married women with careers outside the home were considered to be too big a risk, since lenders worried that they might be forced to quit their jobs in the future due to pregnancy. Upon divorce or the death of a spouse, many women found themselves without access to credit at all.

Today, lenders can't consider either marital status or gender in making their credit decisions. For that reason and because of the wide availability of credit cards, it's much easier for women to obtain credit and establish a credit history. It's important for a woman to develop a credit history in her own name—if she only has a history of joint credit with her spouse, and she later divorces or is widowed, a lender could deny her credit based on an insufficient credit history. However, if she has had credit in her own name, the Equal Credit Opportunity Act prohibits lenders from requiring her to reapply when her marital status changes.

Credit Reporting

As we've seen, lenders evaluate your creditworthiness in part by checking your outstanding debt obligations and your history of making payments. This information is reported by your creditors and compiled by companies called **credit bureaus**. The names and contact information for the largest credit bureaus—Equifax, Experian, and Trans Union—are provided in Exhibit 7-6.

credit bureaus

Companies that collect credit information on individuals and provide reports to interested lenders.

Your consumer credit rights under the Fair Credit Reporting Act of 1971 include the right to know what is contained in your credit report, to have information reported fairly and accurately, and to dispute items on the report that you disagree with. To ensure that your credit report is correct, you need to take responsibility for regularly checking it for any errors.

What Information Is Included in Your Credit Report? Many consumers are surprised to find that their credit report contains a lot more than just information on credit accounts. Typically, your report will include previous, current, and future credit history; specific information about average balances, late payments, and overlimit charges; employment and income history; and home mortgage amounts and payments. Credit reports also include a list of every request for your credit report in the last two years. When you apply for new loans, credit cards, or insurance, the financial institution will nearly always check your credit with one or more of the major credit bureaus. If there have been too many recent requests for your credit report, lenders may be concerned that you're applying for a lot of other loans, an indication of potential future credit problems.

EXHIBIT 7-6

Contact Information for Major Credit Bureaus

Credit Bureau	E-mail and Telephone	Mailing Address
Equifax Credit Information Services	www.econsumer.equifax.com 800-685-1111 (to get report) 800-685-5000 (to dispute report) 888-766-0008 (to report fraud)	Equifax Credit Information Services P.O. Box 740241 Atlanta, GA 30374-0241
Experian	www.experian.com 888-397-3742	Experian P.O. Box 949 Allen, TX 75013-0949
Trans Union	www.transunion.com 800-916-8800	Trans Union P.O. Box 2000 Chester, PA 19022-2000

Your Credit Score. Based on the information in their files, credit bureaus classify individuals according to their credit risk, commonly using a credit scoring system such as the FICO system developed by Fair, Isaac and Company, Inc. This system and others use statistical models to calculate your probability of repayment. Although each system weights factors differently, the FICO system scores each person from 300 to 850 based on payment history (35%), debt (30%), length of credit history (15%), variety of debt sources (10%), and recent credit activity (10%). A score of 700 to 800 is considered good.

If your credit score is too low, you can use one or more of these methods to raise it:

- Correct outdated and incorrect information in your credit report.
- Consistently make timely payments.
- Reduce your total debt.
- Develop a longer credit history.
- Include a mix of types of credit, not just credit cards.
- Close accounts that you haven't used recently.

Correcting Errors on Credit Reports. Until the Fair Credit Reporting Act (FCRA) was passed in 1971, consumers often complained of incorrect or outdated information in their credit reports, but they had no recourse against lenders or credit bureaus. Today, you have the right to view your credit report (for free if you've recently been turned down for credit because of information in the report), and a credit reporting agency must notify you whenever new negative information is added to your file. Negative credit information must be removed from your file after 7 years, with the exception of bankruptcies, which remain on record for 10 years.

If there is incorrect information in the file, you can notify the credit bureau, and it will investigate and make corrections, if warranted. Under the Consumer Credit Reporting Reform Act of 1997, the burden of proof for accuracy of credit information is placed on creditors rather than consumers. Lenders must certify that disputed information has been accurately reported. Even if the negative information in your file is correct, you still have the right to add an explanatory statement of your own. For example, if you're notified that your credit card issuer reported late payments during a specific period of time, you can request that a note be included on your report explaining any extenuating circumstances, such as unemployment or illness.

Despite the extensive regulation of credit reporting, it is estimated that a large percentage of all reports contain some inaccurate, misleading, or outdated information and that it isn't always easy to get this misinformation corrected. If you have a common name, such as John Smith, you might find that your credit report includes negative information about a different John Smith's credit. When you divorce, you should be sure to notify credit bureaus so that your individual credit will not be affected by the possibly poor credit habits of your ex-spouse.

Fact #4

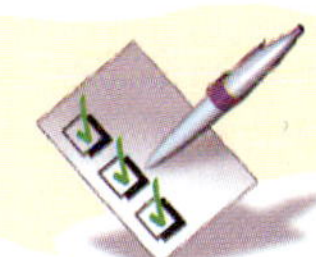

Your credit report is likely to include at least one error. The Federal Trade Commission reports that 20 percent of all complaints it receives involve credit bureaus. Common errors include the failure to remove outdated information and the inclusion of credit information for another person with the same name.

Billing Statements

Another component of consumer credit legislation relates to the billing statements provided by lenders. Lenders are required to provide you with full information related to all charges made to the account, and they must clearly explain any finance charges and how they are calculated.

If you find an error on a bill, specific rules identify your right to contest the bill. Within 60 days of the billing error, you should:

- Send a written notice to the credit card issuer, including copies of verifying documents, explaining why you believe the item to be incorrect. Under the Fair Credit Billing Act (FCBA), the company must immediately credit your account by that amount, pending resolution of the dispute.

- Withhold payment for the disputed item. The issuer cannot charge you interest or penalties on this amount while it is in dispute.
- Check your credit bureau file to see whether a notice has been sent relating to this item or your nonpayment.

Debt Collection Practices

When borrowers fall behind on their payments, lenders attempt to collect past-due amounts by employing a variety of strategies, including past-due notices in the mail and telephone calls. If you're extremely delinquent, your creditor might employ the services of a debt collection agency. The Fair Debt Collection Practices Act of 1978 gives you the right to be treated fairly and civilly by debt collectors. It specifically prohibits actions that would be considered abusive or deceptive and establishes acceptable procedures for debt collection.

Managing Consumer Credit

LEARNING objective

5 Establish a plan for managing your consumer credit and reducing outstanding balances.

Controlling the use of consumer credit is, for many consumers, the most difficult aspect of their financial plan. No one can do it for you, and there isn't a one-size-fits-all answer to the question "How much debt is too much?" In fact, your own use of credit will likely change over the life cycle, as discussed in the *News You Can Use* box, "Retiring in the Red." In this section, we consider how and when it makes sense for you to use credit, how you can reduce outstanding debt, and what to do if you can't make your payments.

NEWS you can use

Retiring in the Red

Picture this: Grandma and Grandpa are getting by on Social Security and a small pension from Grandpa's former employer—it's just enough to pay their necessary expenses. Grandpa gets sick and requires medication that costs several hundred dollars per month, an expense that isn't covered by their health insurance. Rather than take a chance with his health, Grandma responds to a couple of credit card offers she previously received in the mail and soon has a $10,000 credit line. Before they know it, the couple has several high-interest credit card balances.

A study conducted by Dēmos, a nonpartisan think tank, suggests that problems like this are on the rise for the over-65 population. Based on an analysis of the Federal Reserve's survey of consumer finances in 1992 and 2001, Dēmos found that seniors are, on average, less likely to borrow than other age groups. Only one in three older Americans reported credit card debt in 2001, compared with 55 percent of all households, similar to the 1992 percentages. The problem, however, is that those who *are* borrowing are borrowing a lot more than in the past. The average credit card balance for people over 65 went from $2,138 in 1992 to $4,041 in 2001, an increase of 89 percent. Seniors age 65 to 69 saw the largest increase, from $1,842 to $5,844. The study also reports a striking increase in the percentage of older households spending more than 40 percent of their income on debt payments, putting them in significant "debt hardship."

> "credit problems are on the rise for the over-65s"

Why are these seniors "in the red"? The authors of the study suggest that many older Americans are struggling with rapidly increasing medical costs and prescription drug costs, eroded pension income, and reduced investment returns resulting from economic conditions. Retirement savings have been siphoned off to pay for college and other family expenses. What is the result of so much debt? The number of elderly who have declared bankruptcy in the last decade has increased at a higher rate than for any other age group.

Note: You can read the full results of the Dēmos study in Tamara Draut and Heather C. McGhee, "Retiring in the Red," Borrowing to Make Ends Meet Briefing Paper #1, February 2004; available at the Dēmos website at www.demos-usa.org.

ask the expert — Signs of Consumer Credit Trouble

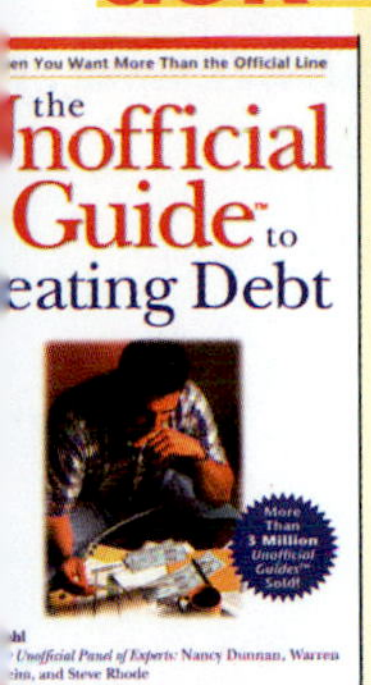

Greg Pahl
Author, The Unofficial Guide to Beating Debt

Greg Pahl, in his book *The Unofficial Guide to Beating Debt*, offers many sensible solutions for reducing outstanding debt and keeping out of consumer credit trouble. According to Pahl, if you answer "yes" to many or most of the following questions, you definitely have a problem with credit and should seriously consider getting help:

- Are you spending increasing amounts of your income to pay your bills?
- Are you paying bills late or juggling your bills because you don't have enough money to cover them?
- Are you at or over the limit on your credit account?
- Are you making only minimum payments on your bills?
- Are you paying your bills with money that was supposed to go for something else?
- Are you using credit cards to pay for normal living expenses?
- Are you using your savings to pay your bills?
- Are you paying off one loan with another one?
- Have you had any credit cards cancelled due to poor payment history?
- Are you getting letters or phone calls from creditors regarding overdue payments?
- Are you repeatedly overdrawn at the bank?
- Do you worry a lot about money?
- Do you and your spouse argue about money problems?
- Are you embarrassed to tell others about your financial situation?

Source: Greg Pahl, *The Unofficial Guide to Beating Debt*, Hoboken, N.J.: John Wiley & Sons (2001), pp. 166–169.

When and How to Use Consumer Credit

In Chapter 6, we suggested that an important advantage of consumer credit is to spread the cost of a purchase over time, allowing you to use the purchased item while making payments that you can easily budget for. Another good use of credit is to make investments that will earn a return in the future, such as investments in education or real estate. Unfortunately, though, most consumer credit is used to finance assets that actually decline in value over time.

When is the use of credit appropriate? Here are some guidelines to consider:

1. Don't borrow money to pay for items you can't afford to buy with cash, unless you have a specific plan for repaying the debt.
2. If possible, pay your credit card balance in full by the due date in order to avoid finance charges.
3. Keep track of monthly expenditures to ensure that your net monthly cash flow is on target.
4. Limit yourself to a small number of credit cards.
5. Avoid high-interest consumer credit.
6. Avoid consumer credit with annual fees.
7. Don't use consumer credit to pay for regular expenditures unless you're doing so in order to take advantage of free frequent flier miles and discounts and you plan to pay the balance in full each month.

Consider the signs of credit trouble offered by a consumer credit expert in the *Ask the Expert* box. If any of these apply to you, you need to develop a plan for reducing your debt. If your list of financial goals doesn't already include debt reduction, revisit it to include this objective as a short-term or intermediate-term financial goal.

Reducing Outstanding Credit

No matter what kinds of consumer credit you currently have, it makes sense to regularly evaluate your credit usage and, if necessary, take action to reduce your outstanding debt. It's always harder to pay back borrowed funds than it is to build up the debt in the first place, so the earlier you get things under control, the easier it will be. To help you approximate the impact of debt reduction on your budget, the monthly payments necessary to reduce specific amounts of total indebtedness are shown in Exhibit 7-7. For example, if you currently owe $10,000 at 18 percent, you'll need to pay almost $293.75 per month for 48 months to reduce that debt to zero. (This is an application of the time value of money—the loan balance owed is the present value of a series of payments, given the number of months and the interest rate.)

You can also use the Card Calculator at www.cardweb.com or the calculator available through the Debt Help Center at www.debtsmart.com to determine the payments necessary to reduce a debt.

EXHIBIT 7-7

Monthly Payments Necessary to Achieve Debt Reduction Goals

		Amount of Total Indebtedness					
Months	APR %	$1,000	$2,500	$5,000	$7,500	$10,000	$15,000
12	15	90.26	225.65	451.29	676.94	902.58	1,353.87
	18	91.68	229.20	458.40	687.60	916.80	1,375.20
	21	93.11	232.78	465.57	698.35	931.14	1,396.71
24	15	48.49	121.22	242.43	363.63	484.87	727.30
	18	49.92	124.81	249.62	374.43	499.24	748.86
	21	51.39	128.46	256.93	385.39	513.86	770.78
36	15	34.67	86.66	173.33	259.99	346.65	519.98
	18	36.15	90.38	180.76	271.14	361.52	542.29
	21	37.68	94.19	188.38	282.56	376.75	565.13
48	15	27.83	69.58	139.15	208.73	278.31	417.46
	18	29.37	73.44	146.87	220.31	293.75	440.62
	21	30.97	77.41	154.83	232.24	309.66	464.49
60	15	23.79	59.47	118.95	178.42	237.90	356.85
	18	25.39	63.48	126.97	190.45	253.93	380.90
	21	27.05	67.63	135.27	202.90	270.53	405.80
72	15	21.15	52.86	105.73	158.59	211.45	317.18
	18	22.81	57.02	114.04	171.06	228.08	342.12
	21	24.54	61.34	122.68	184.02	245.36	368.04

Meeting Payment Obligations

Although debt reduction is the ideal outcome, some people get into so much debt that they have trouble meeting even the minimum payments out of their current cash flow. Under these circumstances, it will be necessary to take some intermediate steps first to reduce monthly cash outflows or increase monthly cash inflows. Consumer credit counselors suggest the following options for people who are having payment troubles:

1. **Obtain a debt consolidation loan at a lower interest rate**. A debt consolidation loan is a loan earmarked for repayment of higher-interest debt. For example, if your credit card interest rate is 18 percent on your $10,000 balance, and you could get a home equity loan from your local financial institution at 6 percent, you could repay the loan in four years with a monthly payment of $234.85, a savings of almost $60 per month. In many cases, consolidating several individual credit card balances can save you even more because, if you cancel the credit cards, you eliminate all the fees as well. If you decide to consolidate your debts to reduce your payments, though, you *absolutely must* refrain from running up your credit cards again. If you couldn't afford the payments before, you certainly won't be able to make payments on both the new loan *and* new credit card debt. Another factor to consider is the term of the loan. Obviously, your monthly payment will be lower if you stretch out the payment schedule, but that will mean additional interest charges, and it will take you that much longer to get your finances back on track. For those reasons, it's best to take the shortest loan that you can reasonably afford to pay.

2. **Take a second job specifically earmarked to pay down the debt**. Although working two jobs may not sound like fun, it's often the fastest way to reduce your outstanding credit card debt. If you can work an extra 20 hours per week, at $6 per hour after taxes, you'll be able to get rid of your $10,000 debt in less than two years. Of course, if you also make additional payments from your regular household cash flow, if you earn more at your second job, or if you and your spouse both work toward this goal, it will take less time.

3. **Develop a zero-based budget**. Zero-based budgeting is a strategy often recommended by financial planners. To construct a zero-based budget, you start with absolute necessities and debt payments and then add expenditures until you run out of cash. Thus, fun money for entertainment, eating out, and clothes shopping would all have lower priority than payments to reduce your debt.

4. **Live with your parents or other family members to cut your expenses**. The latest government statistics show that more than 25 percent of adult children move back in with their parents at some time during their 20s. Although this arrangement may not be ideal, particularly for parents

who were previously enjoying their "empty-nester" status, it can be quite helpful as a means of reducing the debt load that many college students accrue during their years of education. Starting salaries for college grads are often insufficient to pay a student loan, car loan, credit card bills, and still put food on the table. Adult children who are considering this option should keep in mind that it is quite reasonable for parents to then require their payment of a portion of household expenses.

5. Sell assets. Many families who get into consumer credit trouble have done so to finance a higher standard of living. If you can't afford to maintain that standard of living, then an obvious solution is to downsize. Perhaps this will mean selling an expensive car and buying a cheaper one or even downsizing your home. If you have other marketable valuables, such as musical instruments, collectibles, or consumer electronics, these could also be contributed to the debt repayment cause. It only makes sense to do so, however, if you will not need to replace the item in the future at a much higher cost.

An Example: Danelle Washington

In Chapter 2, you met Danelle Washington, a college senior supporting herself on a part-time job and student loans. Danelle has accumulated a lot of consumer debt during her college years, and she's starting to worry about the burden it will place on her finances once she graduates. So far, she's been very responsible about making payments on her two credit cards and her car loan, so she has a good credit rating. You can review Danelle's full financial statements in Exhibits 2-4 and 2-5, and a quick summary of her finances appears in Exhibit 7-8.

Danelle has calculated that her monthly student loan payments will be around \$200 per month for 10 years, beginning six months after graduation. Her current monthly debt payments for her car loan and credit cards total \$238, so the additional \$200 will give her total payments of \$438. Danelle wants to work on reducing her current debt so that, when her student loan payments begin, she'll be in better shape to meet those obligations.

When Danelle evaluated her finances, as described in Chapter 2, she found that she was spending beyond her income, which is part of the reason her credit card debt is so high. She knows she'll have to make some changes in her budget if she wants to balance it and, at the same time, work on her debt reduction goal. Let's consider whether Danelle can apply any of the suggestions discussed in the previous section:

- *Debt consolidation.* Danelle's car loan carries a rate of 8 percent, which isn't too bad, but the rate on both of her credit cards is 18 percent. She has checked with her bank and found that she can get a \$5,200 three-year loan at 8 percent interest. The payments on this loan will be about \$163, a little more than the total minimum payments on her credit cards (\$125), but a larger portion of the monthly payments will be going toward repaying the principal. With this loan and her car loan, her total debt payments will be \$276 per month, which is \$38 more than it was before the new loan. In conjunction with this decision, Danelle plans to avoid the risk of running up her credit again by canceling her JC Penney and MasterCard credit accounts. She has a debit card that can be used for things like travel expenses, so she doesn't really need the cards.

EXHIBIT 7-8

Danelle Washington's Credit Information

Monthly after-tax employment income	\$730	
MasterCard		
Minimum payment	100	
Balance outstanding	4,200	
JC Penney		
Minimum payment	25	
Balance outstanding	1,000	
Car loan		
Monthly payment	113	
Balance outstanding	3,000	
Student loan		
Monthly payment	0	(to 6 months from graduation)
Balance outstanding	\$18,000	

- *Take a second job.* So far, Danelle has only been working part-time in order to focus on her schoolwork. Her course load isn't too bad this semester, so she estimates that she can work 10 more hours per week, which will net an additional $80 per week. If she applies all this extra income to the debt consolidation, it will also help her net cash flow.
- *Zero-based budget.* After carefully evaluating her necessary expenditures, Danelle thinks she can cut her other expenses by about $50 per month.
- *Live with family.* Danelle's family does not live nearby, so this isn't an option.
- *Sell assets.* Danelle doesn't have anything that she can sell to raise money so this isn't an option.

Avoiding Bankruptcy

We've looked at some strategies for getting your debt under control before you get into serious credit trouble. But what if it's too late for that—what if you've already gotten so far behind on your payment obligations that you can't see any way to resolve your financial problems. Probably the most common strategy taken by people experiencing this kind of financial distress is avoidance—throwing the past due notices in a pile and refusing to answer the phone. This is *not* a good approach, and it increases the risk that your creditors will take more serious steps to collect the debt. Instead, you should contact your creditors directly and seek out consumer credit counseling. As a last resort, you might consider declaring bankruptcy. These options are discussed below.

Fact #5

Most creditors are willing to accept reduced payments temporarily (for two to three months) if notified of special circumstances, such as short-term unemployment or illness. Debtors can make these arrangements themselves or seek the help of professional debt counselors.

Contact Your Creditors Directly. When you know that you can't pay your debts as agreed, you should immediately contact your creditors and let them know. Consumers are often surprised to find out that, although accumulated interest and late fees will still accrue, their creditors are often willing to make alternative payment arrangements. Creditors much prefer to get something rather than nothing. If your budget crunch is temporary, as in the case of a short period of unemployment, this type of arrangement may help you get through it without becoming seriously delinquent.

Consumer Credit Counseling. In addition to making arrangements with your creditors on your own, individuals with serious financial problems should consider getting professional consumer credit counseling. There are many reputable sources of free help, so you should generally avoid organizations that charge for this service. Some organizations that advertise credit counseling services prey on desperate people, making a profit by charging high fees to those who can least afford them, or providing consolidation loans at unreasonably high rates of interest.

Consumer credit counseling information, budgeting calculators, and contacts for local branches are available on the web at www. nfcc.org (National Foundation for Consumer Credit), www. consumercredit.com (American Consumer Credit Counseling, Inc., and www.profina.org (Profina).

Large employers may offer financial counseling through their human resources departments, or you may be able to get free counseling through your financial institution, a county extension office, or an employee union. The National Foundation for Consumer Credit (NFCC), an organization sponsored by large creditor firms, offers free consumer credit counseling through local nonprofit branches called Consumer Credit Counseling Services (CCCS). In addition to providing educational materials on many financial matters, the counselors at these offices help millions of consumers each year to develop realistic budgets, plan for debt reduction, and negotiate with creditors.

Bankruptcy as a Last Resort. Some people get so deeply in debt that repayment isn't really an option. In this situation, it's sometimes necessary to declare bankruptcy as a last resort. **Bankruptcy** is the legal right, specified under the U.S. Bankruptcy Act of 1978, to ask a court of law to relieve you of certain debts and obligations. If bankruptcy is granted, your creditors will divide up your assets in a fair and equitable process overseen by a trustee, and you'll be relieved of any further obligations to these creditors, with some exceptions.

bankruptcy

The legal right under the U.S. Bankruptcy Act of 1978 to be relieved of certain debts and obligations by a court of law.

According to the American Bankruptcy Institute, more than 2 million *personal bankruptcies*—those filed by individuals rather than businesses—were filed in 2003, a record number. This number has in fact been increasing at an average of 20 percent per year since the early 1990s. What accounts for the rise in personal bankruptcies? When the economy slows, as it did at the beginning of the twenty-first century, layoffs and reductions in earnings are common, and families with too much debt and too little liquidity can't survive even brief periods of lost income.

You might be surprised at how common bankruptcy is among young people who, at least theoretically, haven't had much time to accumulate debt. Although baby boomers still account for the largest share of bankruptcies, about 120,000 people under age 25 declare bankruptcy each year, and that number is on the rise. Most people who declare bankruptcy have low incomes, earning less than $20,000 per year, but bankruptcy isn't limited to the poor. Even some celebrities—Kim Basinger and Burt Reynolds, for example—have declared bankruptcy in the past.

To learn more about bankruptcy and to find the latest bankruptcy statistics, go to www.bankruptcy.org

Despite the growing popularity of bankruptcy, it is an extreme measure that should be your *last* alternative to resolving credit management difficulties. A bankruptcy will appear on your credit record for ten years and may affect your ability to obtain a home mortgage or other credit in the future. This long-lasting impact may outweigh the benefits of debt reduction accomplished through the bankruptcy proceedings. In addition, before considering bankruptcy, you should consider the costs associated with taking this legal action—court costs, attorney's fees, and trustee's fees can add up to more than $1,000.

Bankruptcies take several forms, each named for the relevant section of the U.S. Bankruptcy Code, the federal statute governing bankruptcy. Here, we'll look at two major forms of personal bankruptcy: Chapter 7 and Chapter 13. In either case, the debtor files an application for bankruptcy with the appropriate court, which may either accept the application or deny it.

Chapter 7 Bankruptcy. A *Chapter 7 bankruptcy* requires the liquidation, or sale, of most of your assets. Under current law, debtors are allowed to keep a small amount of home equity, Social Security and unemployment insurance payments, a vehicle, household goods, trade tools, and books. The proceeds of the sale of your remaining assets are used to pay creditors to the extent possible, and most of your financial obligations are then cleared. However, certain obligations—alimony and child support, student loans, and debts that were not disclosed in court—are unaffected by a Chapter 7 bankruptcy, and you must still pay them. In addition, debtors are not allowed to repay certain preferred creditors (such as family members) in anticipation of the bankruptcy.

Chapter 13 Bankruptcy. A *Chapter 13 bankruptcy* is actually a method of protecting you from creditors' claims while you develop and implement a plan to repay your debts. The plan, which must be approved by the court, generally includes new payment arrangements with your creditors for reduced balances and payments. In a Chapter 13 bankruptcy, the debtor generally can keep all of his or her assets. If the repayment plan fails, though, the debtor may eventually end up losing the assets in a Chapter 7 liquidation.

Summary

1. **Identify the most common types of consumer loans and lenders.** Consumer loans are a type of credit in which the borrowed amount is usually designated for a particular purpose, such as the purchase of an automobile or the payment of education expenses. These loans usually require repayment of interest and principal over a designated period of time in equal monthly installments, and the interest rate may either be fixed for the life of the loan or vary with market interest rates. The most common types of consumer loans are home equity loans, student loans, and automobile loans, most of which are available from commercial banks and other depository institutions. Consumer finance companies and sales finance companies offer certain types of consumer loans, and it is also possible to borrow against cash value life insurance policies or retirement accounts.

2. **Compare consumer loans based on terms and costs.** It's important to shop around for loans, carefully comparing their features and costs. The interest rates charged for consumer loans can vary dramatically between types of loans and types of lenders. Furthermore, lenders use different methods of interest calculation, so you should always compare loans based on the APR. Secured loans generally cost less but expose you to the risk of the loss of the asset pledged as collateral for the loan. Other important considerations include tax-deductibility, term of the loan, required fees, and the effect of early repayment.

3. **Assess your creditworthiness and know how to improve it.** Your creditworthiness is determined by your ability to repay debt and your history of making payments on time. Before taking on any additional debt, you should carefully reevaluate your household financial statements and budget to ensure that the borrowing is consistent with your financial goals. This assessment should include examination of household financial ratios, as well consideration of other uses for the funds that will have to be applied to debt repayment. In evaluating whether to extend credit to you, lenders commonly use credit scores provided by major credit bureaus. They evaluate your creditworthiness in five areas, sometimes called the five C's of credit: capacity, capital, collateral, character, and conditions. If your credit is substandard in one or more of these areas, you should take action to rectify the problem.

4. **Understand your consumer credit rights.** Consumer credit law covers the general areas of applying for and receiving credit, billing, reporting, and collection practices. Important rights include the right to freedom from discrimination, the right to full information about consumer credit terms and costs, the right to have credit information reported truthfully, the right to contest

incorrect information in credit reports, and the right to be treated civilly by debt collectors.

5 **Establish a plan for managing your consumer credit and reducing outstanding balances.** Before incurring consumer credit, you should have a plan for how you will repay it, and you should be sure to make payments as required by your credit agreement. If used wisely, paying off balances every month, and refraining from charging items that don't fit within your monthly budget, credit cards can be beneficial. Your financial planning process should include regular evaluation of your household's debt usage and cash flow to ensure that consumer credit does not limit your ability to achieve other financial goals. You should develop and apply strategies to reduce outstanding credit balances and make regular payments so that you can avoid more serious financial difficulties that might lead to personal bankruptcy.

Key Terms

acceleration clause (201)
balloon loan (213)
bankruptcy (226)
collateral (202)
consumer finance company (206)
cosigner (216)
credit bureaus (220)
default (201)
down payment (208)
fixed-rate loan (201)
home equity (202)
installment loan (201)
lien (202)
prepayment penalty (201)
principal (201)
promissory note (207)
Rule of 78's (213)
sales finance company (207)
secured loan (201)
single-payment loan (201)
variable-rate loan (201)

Key Calculations

$$\text{Periodic rate} = \frac{\text{Nominal rate}}{\text{Payments per year}}$$

$$\text{Interest paid each period on simple interest loan} = \text{Remaining balance} \times \text{Periodic rate}$$

$$\text{APR} = \frac{\text{Total annual finance charges}}{\text{Average loan balance over the year}}$$

$$\text{Add-on interest payment} = \frac{\text{Amount of loan} + (\text{Loan amount} \times \text{Nominal rate} \times \text{Number of years})}{\text{Number of payments}}$$

$$\text{APR approximation for add-on interest loan} = \frac{\text{Total annual finances charges}}{\text{Original loan amount} \times 0.5}$$

$$\text{N-ratio method for add-on interest APR} = \frac{m \times (95\,N + 9) \times F}{12\,N \times (N + 1) \times (4\,P + F)}$$

where

m = Number of payments per year
N = Number of total loan payments
F = Total finance charges
P = Amount borrowed

Concept Review Questions

1. What is the difference between a fixed-rate loan and a variable-rate loan? Explain the advantages and disadvantages of each.
2. What is the difference between a single-payment loan and an installment loan? How do they differ from revolving credit?
3. Explain the differences between secured and unsecured loans. What types of consumer loans are usually secured loans, and why do lenders require collateral for these loans?
4. Explain why the rates charged on secured loans are usually lower than those for unsecured personal loans.
5. Under what conditions can a lender repossess your car? Would it ever be a good idea to voluntarily turn over your car to a lender to get out of the debt?
6. What are the most common types of consumer loans?
7. What types of financial institutions act as consumer lenders? Which are likely to impose the highest costs on borrowers?
8. How does a lender determine the maximum amount of a home equity loan?
9. Why are rates on student loans lower than rates on most other types of consumer loans?
10. What are the usual limitations placed on the use of student loan proceeds?
11. Distinguish between simple interest, add-on interest, and discount interest loans. Which type generally results in the lowest APR, given the same nominal rate of interest?

12. What is the relationship between the maturity of a loan and the monthly payment?
13. Explain why lenders often charge lower rates of interest on loans with shorter maturities.
14. If you default on a loan, what options does the lender have for collecting the debt?
15. What is a cosigner, and why might you need to have one to qualify for a loan?
16. How can you measure your credit capacity? If a lender assesses your credit capacity and determines that it will make a loan to you, does that necessarily imply that you can afford the loan? Why or why not?
17. What are the "five C's of credit"? Give an example of each.
18. What is a credit bureau, and what kinds of information do credit bureaus collect?
19. If you discover an error on your credit report, what should you do to correct it?
20. If you discover a fraudulent or incorrect charge on a billing statement, what should you do to correct it?
21. Identify three common consumer credit mistakes. Explain why each one is inconsistent with financial planning principles.
22. Identify the basic rules for using consumer credit.
23. How can you estimate the monthly payment necessary to reduce your outstanding consumer credit balances? Why is it insufficient to simply make the monthly minimum payments required by your lender?
24. How can a debt consolidation loan help you to reduce your outstanding credit obligations?
25. List and explain four strategies often recommended by consumer credit counselors for individuals who are having trouble meeting their payment obligations and/or reducing outstanding credit balances.
26. Under what circumstances would you recommend that someone consult a consumer credit counselor?
27. Under what circumstances might it be advisable to declare bankruptcy? What impact will the bankruptcy have on your personal finances?
28. What is the difference between a Chapter 7 bankruptcy and a Chapter 13 bankruptcy?

Application Problems

1. ***Payment Ratios.*** You have after-tax monthly income of $1,200, and your monthly debt payments total $300. What is your debt payment ratio? Is that ratio acceptable? Why or why not?
2. ***Opportunity Costs.*** You currently have $10,000 in a savings account at your local financial institution earning 5 percent interest. Your outstanding consumer credit totals $3,000 and costs you 15 percent interest per year. Your monthly debt payment is $60. Should you take the money from your savings to repay the debt? Why or why not?
3. ***Payments Necessary to Achieve Debt Reduction Goals.*** For each of the following amounts of debt and annual nominal interest rates, use Exhibit 7-7 to estimate the payment necessary to reduce the debt to zero by the end of the time specified, assuming simple interest.
   - **a.** $1,000 debt, 15 percent interest, 2 years
   - **b.** $5,000 debt, 15 percent interest, 5 years
   - **c.** $10,000 debt, 18 percent interest, 6 years
   - **d.** $15,000 debt, 21 percent interest, 6 years
4. ***Payments for Loans.*** For each of the following simple interest loans and terms, calculate the monthly payment for a $10,000 car loan. Use a financial calculator, a spreadsheet, or Exhibit A-5.
   - **a.** 3 years, 6 percent
   - **b.** 4 years, 6.5 percent
   - **c.** 5 years, 7 percent
   - **d.** 6 years, 7.5 percent
5. ***Finance Charges.*** Calculate the APRs for each of the following $1,000, 2-year loans:
   - **a.** 10 percent simple interest single-payment loan
   - **b.** 10 percent simple interest installment loan
   - **c.** 10 percent add-on installment loan
   - **d.** 10 percent discount single-payment loan
6. ***Finance Charge.*** For each of the following $3,000, 3-year loans, calculate the APR and the total interest paid over the life of the loan.
   - **a.** 8 percent simple interest single payment loan
   - **b.** 8 percent simple interest installment loan
   - **c.** 6 percent add-on installment loan
   - **d.** 7 percent discount single payment loan
7. ***Decision Factors in Loan Choice.*** Al and Janet Fernandez have two alternatives for financing their son Joel's college costs—an unsubsidized student loan with a variable rate that is currently at 6 percent or a fixed-rate home equity loan at 7 percent. Assume that both loans will have 10-year terms for repayment. What factors should they consider in deciding between these two alternatives?
8. ***Loan Payoff for Simple Interest Loan.*** Assume that Danny's original car loan amount was $13,000. If the loan is a 6 percent simple interest, 48-month loan, what is the remaining balance on his loan after two years (24 months)? (*Hint:* Construct an amortization table or use the amortization function on your financial calculator.)
9. ***APR and Loan Payoff for Add-on Loans.*** Redo application problem 8, assuming that the original loan was an add-on loan.
   - **a.** What is the monthly payment?
   - **b.** What is the APR?
   - **c.** What is the loan payoff after two years?
   - **d.** Why are the loan payoffs so different?
10. ***Consumer Credit Rights.*** Which of the following are illegal?
    - **a.** Bill collector raises his voice and threatens to tell your employer that you are a "deadbeat" in a phone call related to a late payment.
    - **b.** You are denied a credit card because you have never borrowed any money before.
    - **c.** Your credit report contains information that relates to a person that has the same name as you.
    - **d.** A credit card company sends you a notice that the periodic rate on your account is going to be double the original rate you were offered.
11. ***Improving Creditworthiness.*** Your younger sister is 18 years old and just starting college. At present, she has no credit history. What are some strategies you can suggest to help her build a credit history? How can you help her avoid getting into trouble with credit while she is a student?
12. ***Home Equity Loan Amounts.*** Your home is currently valued at $120,000. You have a first mortgage in the amount of $80,000. If your lender applies a 90 percent loan-to-value ratio for approving home equity lines of credit, what is the maximum amount you can borrow, assuming you meet all other lender requirements?

Using Web Resources for Financial Planning

1. ***Shopping for Consumer Loans.*** Several websites can help you shop for consumer loans that meet your requirements. For example, you can go to *www.lendingtree.com* and click on the type of loan you're interested in. After answering several questions, you can enter your request and receive up to four loan offers in less than 24 hours. If you just want to get an idea of current rates without actually disclosing any personal financial information or contacting any lenders, *www.bankrate.com* reports national average debt costs based on their regular lender survey.
2. ***Find the Best Rates on Auto Loans.*** You can find out about auto loan rates at *http://loan.yahoo.com* without making an actual application. Click on "Auto Loans," and provide the requested information on amount of loan, term of loan, type of car, and self-assessment of your credit rating. The website will provide you with an estimate of the applicable interest rate.
3. ***Advice for Reducing Debt.*** The *www.finance-center.com* website includes a multitude of information for financial planning. Click on "Articles" to find "Give Your Credit a Check-up" and "Becoming Debt Free." What advice does the latter article offer regarding the advisability of refinancing your mortgage to pay off high-interest credit? To see whether it makes sense to borrow from your retirement account to pay off debt, go to *www.smartmoney.com/debt/* and click on "Should you borrow from your 401k?"
4. ***Consumer Credit Counseling.*** What types of consumer credit assistance can be found on the Internet? If you do an Internet search for "Consumer Credit Counseling," it will probably yield thousands of hits. Be aware, though, that many so-called consumer credit counseling companies make a profit by charging consumers for their services or by making debt consolidation loans. Instead, look for counseling services sponsored by the National Foundation for Credit Counseling, a nonprofit dedicated to providing assistance to people with credit trouble. Go to *www.debtadvice.org* and find out what free information is available. Does the foundation charge for any of its services? If so, which ones, and how much?
5. ***Find Out More about Bankruptcy.*** To find out more about personal bankruptcy, visit *www.bankruptcy.org*. There, you can find bankruptcy statistics, learn about alternatives to bankruptcy, and determine whether you are exposed to greater risk than average.

Learning by Doing Solutions

LBD 7–1: 1. The home equity loan is tax-deductible, whereas the store loan is not. To compare them, you must therefore consider the after-tax cost. If you itemize deductions on your federal income taxes, the after-tax cost on the home equity loan is 8.5 percent × (1 − 0.25) = 6.38 percent. You probably will be able to pay the home equity loan over a longer period of time, which will reduce your monthly payments but will also increase the total interest you pay over time. The disadvantage of the home equity loan is that it ties up home equity you may need in the future since you cannot borrow against it again until the first loan is repaid.

LBD 7–2: 1a. 48 month loan; 1b. 6 percent loan; 2a. 36 month loan; 2b. 6 percent loan.

LBD 7–3: 1. discount interest and add-on interest; 2. discount interest.

LBD 7–4: 1. $(75 + 310)/(0.8 \times 2{,}500) = 19.25\%$; 2. $(385 + 50)/2{,}000 = 21.75\%$; 3. She should evaluate her household budget, consider the impact of debt repayment on her financial plan, and shop around for better financing terms.

Building Financial Planning Skills Through Case Applications

Case 7–1 Rob Mayor Works on Improving His Credit

Rob Mayor is a senior in college. It's taken him a little longer to finish than is average because he had trouble adjusting to being away from home his freshman year and flunked several courses. Now he's back on track, but he's dealing with the aftermath of his previous mistakes—a poor credit record and an extra year of student loan debt. Although he's going to school full-time, he works at a restaurant near the college campus about 20 hours per week. Rob wants to take some steps toward improving his credit rating so that he can apply for a car loan once he's fully employed after graduation. The main problems on his credit record are several late credit card payments and outstanding loan balances totaling $3,500. His student loan debt is now at $12,000, but he will not have to begin repayment until six months after graduation.

a. Recommend several things that Rob can do to improve his credit rating.

b. Should Rob work on reducing his outstanding credit card debt? How can he do this?

Case 7–2 Assessing the Impact of Debt on the Payment Ratio

Brenda Gallagher's after-tax monthly income is $1,500, but she will shortly be changing jobs and expects to net $2,000 per month after taxes. She currently has two credit cards with balances totaling $2,000. The minimum payments on these cards total $75 per month. She also has a student loan payment of $240 per month. Since her new job is farther from where she lives, Brenda is considering buying a car and estimates that she will need to borrow $10,000 to finance the purchase.

a. What is Brenda's debt payment ratio now (without the future car loan payments or the new job)?

b. If Brenda can get a car loan at a 6 percent simple interest rate for six years, how much will her monthly car loan payment be?

c. What would Brenda's new debt payment ratio be if she starts the new job and buys the car as planned?

d. Why might it be advisable for Brenda to try to repay her credit card debt before she takes on a car loan? What are some strategies she might consider for accomplishing this objective?

Case 7–3 Recognizing the Early Warning Signs of Credit Trouble

You're out shopping with your friend Andrea and find some wonderful bargains on last season's clothing. You're standing next to Andrea in the check-out line when both her credit cards are denied. She laughs it off and rummages around in her purse for her checkbook, saying that she probably just made a late payment. You're not so sure. You recall other instances in which her card has been turned down, and you know that she's always spending more on clothes than her income would seem to justify. When you ask Andrea about her credit, she confesses that she has gotten in over her head. In fact, she recently applied for a new credit card, figuring that she'd be able to make overdue payments on her other cards using cash advances from the new one.

a. Does Andrea exhibit any of the warning signs of credit trouble? Explain.

b. If Andrea asks for your advice, where would you suggest she go for more information? Would you suggest that she seek professional help? If so, where would you recommend she go?

c. What are some strategies that Andrea might employ to dig herself out of this debt trap?

Case 7–4 Dealing with Financial Problems

Jack and Allison Randall are middle-income baby boomers. Jack works as an engineer for a well-established company, and Allison works part-time so that they can afford to send their two children to a private elementary school. Although they have a combined pre-tax income of $120,000 and after-tax income of $90,000, the Randall's budget has been a little tight ever since they decided to buy a larger home two years ago. As a result, they are not currently making contributions to savings other than those required by Jack's employer for his retirement account. Allison estimates that their debt ratio is about 90 percent and their debt payment ratio is 35 percent.

One day, Allison is surprised to come across a bill for a credit card she didn't know they had. According to the statement, the card is maxed out to the full credit limit of $10,000, and the minimum monthly payment is $200. When Allison confronts her husband, he confesses to her that he has a small gambling problem and has been too embarrassed to tell her about it. In addition to the amount he owes on the account she discovered, he owes an additional $5,000 on another. Jack tells his wife that he's been looking into the possibility of a debt consolidation loan.

a. What risks do Jack and Allison face as a result of their high level of debt payments? If they have little in savings, what options would they have in the event that Jack lost his job?

b. Why is it important that the Randalls confront the cause of their credit problems and not simply deal with the symptoms? Where would you suggest they go for help?

c. What might be some problems associated with applying for and being approved for the debt consolidation loan?

d. What are some other strategies that this family should consider for dealing with their debt problems?

DEVELOPING PERSONAL FINANCIAL skills for life

Learning about Yourself

7–1. Assessing Your Own Creditworthiness

Go to your local financial institution and request a blank consumer credit application. Take it home and complete the application, consulting your financial statement information as necessary to ensure accuracy. Now pretend that you're the loan officer of the bank and that someone else has presented this application to you. Use the worksheet in your *Personal Financial Planner* to assess the creditworthiness of the applicant based on the five C's of credit. In what areas could they improve? Would you approve this person for a credit card or an unsecured consumer loan? Why or why not? If you have a friend with whom you feel comfortable sharing your personal financial information, you might consider swapping forms and assessing each other.

PFP Worksheet 26
Assessing Your Creditworthiness Using the Five C's of Credit

Developing Your Skills

7–2. Develop a Plan for Managing Consumer Credit

The first step in managing your household debt is to develop a clear idea of what your current obligations are. If you have not already completed the Credit Summary worksheet in your *Personal Financial Planner*, you should do so now. For your convenience, it's reproduced in Exhibit 7-9. Using this summary as well as your personal balance sheet and personal cash flow statement, answer the following questions:

PFP Worksheet 25
Household Credit Summary

PFP Worksheet 27
Evaluating Credit Goals

a. What is the total value of your household's assets? ____________

b. What is your monthly after-tax income? ____________

c. Calculate your debt ratio. ____________

d. Calculate your debt payment ratio. ____________

e. Based on these ratios, what can you say about your current use of credit?

f. Revisit the goals that you set for yourself in Chapter 3. If you plan to take on any new consumer debt in the next five years, summarize your plans below, or in your *Personal Financial Planner*, and estimate the impact that those plans will have on your debt and payment ratios.

Financial Goal #1 ______________________________

Type of loan required ____________________

Probable amount of loan ____________________

Impact on financial ratios ____________________

Financial Goal #2 ______________________________

Type of loan required ____________________

Probable amount of loan ____________________

Impact on financial ratios ____________________

Type of Debt	Interest Rate (APR)	Annual Fees	Minimum Payment	Most Recent Finance Charge	Balance Still Owed
Credit cards	______	______	______	______	______
	______	______	______	______	______
	______	______	______	______	______
	______	______	______	______	______
Student loans	______	______	______	______	______
	______	______	______	______	______
	______	______	______	______	______
Auto loans	______	______	______	______	______
	______	______	______	______	______
	______	______	______	______	______
Other consumer loans	______	______	______	______	______
	______	______	______	______	______
	______	______	______	______	______
Home equity loans	______	______	______	______	______
	______	______	______	______	______
	______	______	______	______	______
Mortgage loans	______	______	______	______	______
	______	______	______	______	______
	______	______	______	______	______

EXHIBIT 7-9

Household Credit Summary

7–3. Evaluate Your Credit Report

Obtain a copy of your credit report from www.transunion.com or www.creditbase.com. Carefully check it for errors and report any discrepancies to all of the major credit bureaus. If you don't have a perfect credit record or if you have a limited credit history, identify three steps you can take to improve it.

7–4. Calculate Payments to Reduce Debt

If you currently have any outstanding consumer debt and one of your financial goals is to pay it off, use the worksheet in your *Personal Financial Planner* to calculate the necessary monthly payments to do so.

PFP Worksheet 28 Calculating Payments to Reduce Debt

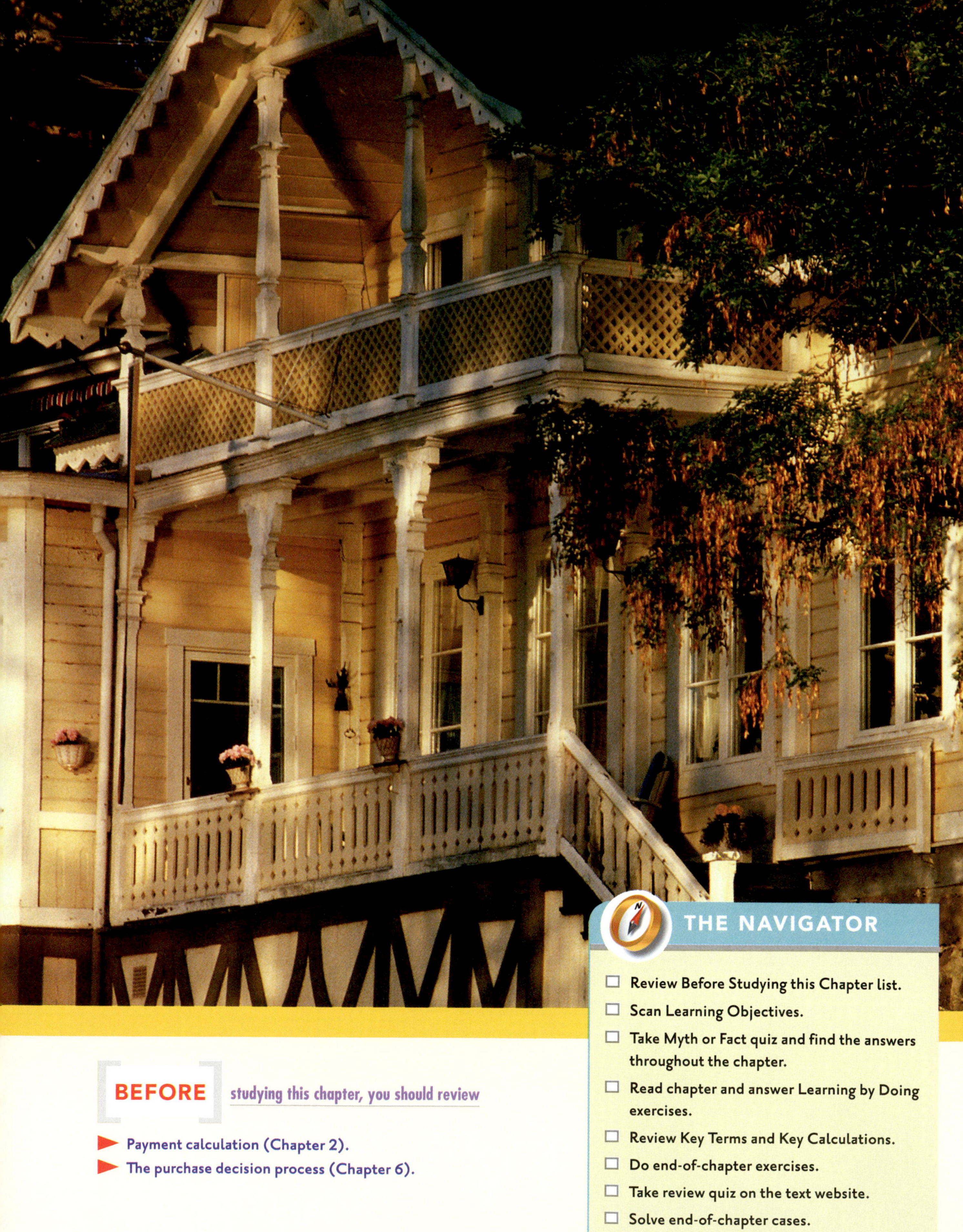

THE NAVIGATOR

- ☐ Review Before Studying this Chapter list.
- ☐ Scan Learning Objectives.
- ☐ Take Myth or Fact quiz and find the answers throughout the chapter.
- ☐ Read chapter and answer Learning by Doing exercises.
- ☐ Review Key Terms and Key Calculations.
- ☐ Do end-of-chapter exercises.
- ☐ Take review quiz on the text website.
- ☐ Solve end-of-chapter cases.

BEFORE studying this chapter, you should review

- Payment calculation (Chapter 2).
- The purchase decision process (Chapter 6).

Automobile and Housing Decisions

CHAPTER

8

Myth or Fact?

Consider each of the following statements and decide whether it is a *myth* or a *fact*. Look for the answers in the *Fact* boxes in the chapter.

	MYTH	FACT
1. If you're in a car crash, it's always safer to be in a big car, like an SUV or a minivan, rather than a small car, like the Volkswagon Beetle.	☐	☐
2. If anything goes wrong with my new car, the manufacturer's warranty will cover the costs of fixing it.	☐	☐
3. My landlord has to return my security deposit at the end of my lease but doesn't have to pay me interest on it.	☐	☐
4. The percentage of people who are getting their home mortgages from Internet-only banks is increasing rapidly.	☐	☐
5. Whenever mortgage rates go down by one percentage point or more, it pays to refinance.	☐	☐

LEARNING objectives

1. Evaluate your automobile needs and determine what you can afford.
2. Decide between automobile financing alternatives.
3. Be an informed automobile consumer.
4. Evaluate your housing needs and determine what you can afford.
5. Select a home that meets your needs and negotiate an acceptable price.
6. Choose between financing options and know how to apply for and qualify for a mortgage.

...applying the planning process

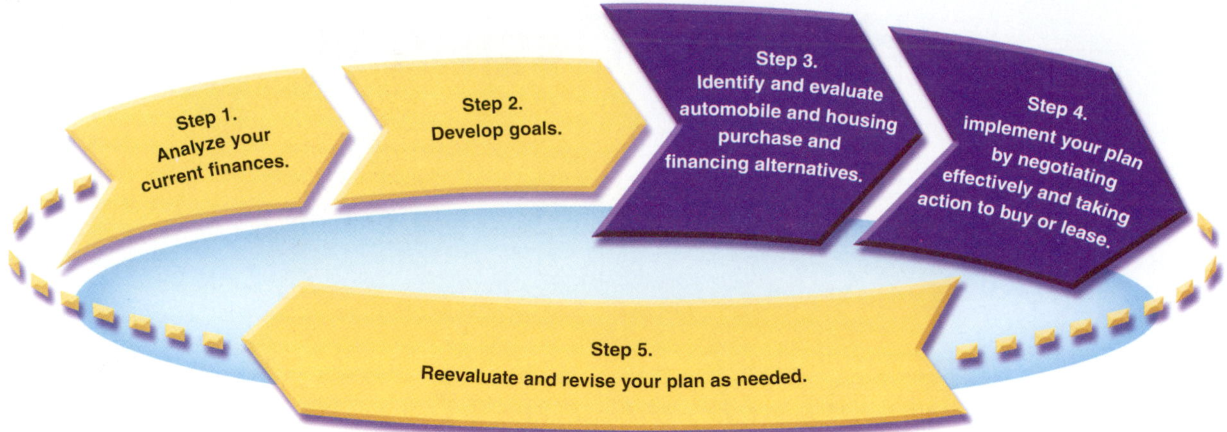

For most families, automobiles and homes make up a significant portion of household net worth. It's also the case that the auto and home loans that finance these purchases represent the lion's share of household debt. For these reasons, your decisions relating to the purchase or lease of automobiles and housing are extremely important components of your financial plan.

As you learned in Chapter 6, the decision-making process for purchase decisions involves determining your needs, evaluating your financial ability to make the purchase, researching and evaluating your alternatives, and implementing your decision. In this chapter, we apply this process to automobiles and housing. Even though you've already walked through the process of making consumer purchases, it's worthwhile to spend a little more time on auto and housing decisions, which can be significantly more complex. They deserve more attention for several reasons, including the larger impact on your budget; the wide selection from which to choose (including both new and used); the hidden costs associated with ownership; the negotiability of prices; and the greater variety of financing alternatives. In this chapter, we first apply the purchase process to auto decisions, identifying needs, assessing costs, determining affordability, and evaluating financing alternatives. We then apply a similar process to the housing decision. In both auto and housing decisions, you'll usually have the choice whether to lease or buy. We'll therefore explore the advantages and disadvantages of your financing choices in some detail.

Chapter Preview

The Automobile Decision

LEARNING objective

1 Evaluate your automobile needs and determine what you can afford.

You'd be surprised how many people buy new cars on impulse. They stop in at a dealership "just to look" at the new models, and two hours later they drive away with a new car and a big monthly payment. How can a person spend less time on a major financial decision like this than they'd spend buying a new television set? The answer is complex but is related to both the nature of the car sales experience and the nature of human beings. Fortunately, you have the power to control both of these elements by applying good purchasing skills and avoiding situations where you might be influenced to make poorly thought out decisions. Exhibit 8–1 shows the process that should be applied to making auto and housing decisions. In this section, we discuss how to evaluate your automobile needs and how to determine what kind of automobile you can afford.

Do You Need a Car?

For all purchase decisions, the first question is whether you actually *need* to buy the item. Since needs have higher priority in your goal setting, this will change the way you approach the problem. It's probably true that, in suburban and rural areas, having *one* car is a necessity, but families can usually get by with fewer cars than they have. In urban areas, vehicles are even less necessary, since mass transportation routes generally allow access to work, shopping, and recreation locations. Nevertheless, 88 percent of all households in the United States own at least one vehicle, and the average household owns two. For most auto purchase decisions, then, and particularly for those related to second and third family vehicles, the answer to the first question is "I really don't *need* it."

When a new vehicle is not a necessity, the purchase decision should be analyzed against other luxury and convenience expenditures. If the car purchase will reduce or slow your ability to achieve more important goals, you might want to give serious consideration to alternative methods of meeting your transportation needs—car pooling, using mass transit, bicycling, walking, or renting a car for weekends and holidays, for example. At $19.99 to $29.99 per day and no maintenance obligations, occasional renting is a practical and often overlooked alternative to owning a car, particularly for urban consumers.

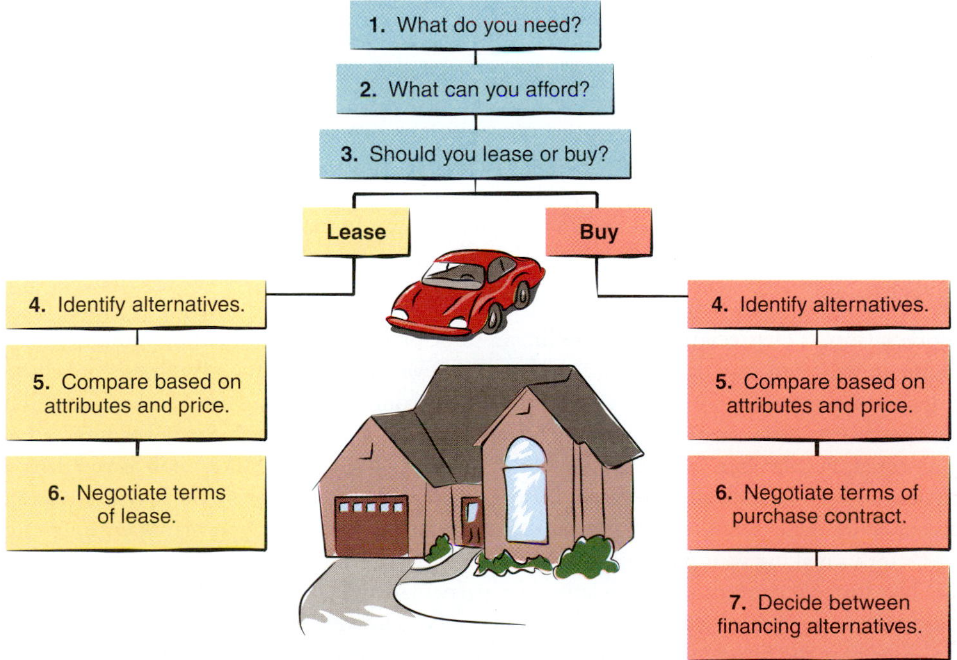

EXHIBIT 8-1

The Auto and Housing Decision Process

Does the Purchase Fit into Your Budget?

Even if you need something, you may not be able to afford it. Therefore, the next step in the process is to evaluate your ability to meet your auto purchase goal in light of your household budget. To illustrate this decision, we revisit the Thompson family, who are considering the purchase of an additional vehicle.

An Example: The Thompsons. As you may recall, the Thompsons are currently allocating their net family cash flow to meet several household goals, including the purchase of insurance and investments targeted for retirement and college expenses. The family currently has two vehicles. They purchased Dave's pickup fairly recently and are paying $237.61 per month (with more than three years remaining on the loan). Cindy's older minivan is fully paid for.

Kyle, Cindy Thompson's teenage son from her first marriage, will soon get his learner's permit, and so the family is considering the purchase of a vehicle for his use. In assessing their needs, Cindy and Dave are particularly concerned with safety and want to purchase a vehicle with dual front airbags. The Thompsons realize that the purchase of an additional vehicle will require that they reduce some of their other fixed or discretionary expenditures. After carefully considering their budget, they estimate that they can put $2,000 from their savings toward a down payment on a car and $300 per month toward a loan or lease payment by reducing expenditures on food, entertainment, and vacations. They must next determine the car price this monthly allocation will allow them to buy or lease.

Recognizing the Total Costs of Automobile Ownership

Many people make the mistake of estimating the cost of automobile ownership based on their auto lease or loan payment. Many other costs should enter into the decision process as well, however, since nonfinancing costs can amount to thousands of additional dollars per year.

PFP Worksheet 29 Automobile Costs Log Sheet

For better financial planning, it's a good idea to keep a record of all your auto-related expenses, at least until you have a good estimate of your average monthly outflows. Many people keep a log book in their car and regularly record mileage, gasoline, and maintenance expenditures. If some or all of your auto expenses are tax-deductible for business, you'll need a written record to justify the deduction in the event of an IRS audit, so this type of log is absolutely necessary. A sample log that you can use for this purpose is included in your *Personal Financial Planner.*

The costs of car ownership can be separated into two categories: fixed expenses—those that stay the same regardless of how much you use your car or how well you take care of it—and variable operation expenses—those that increase with your car usage. Let's look more closely at each category.

Fixed Expenses of Automobile Ownership. Fixed expenses include finance charges, depreciation, auto insurance, licensing, registration, and taxes.

Finance Charges. Whether you borrow money to buy a car or take the money from an investment or savings account, you incur an opportunity cost. You're *paying the interest* to one financial institution or you're *not getting the earnings on investment* from another financial institution. Either way, it's a fixed cost that you should take into account in making a car purchase or lease decision. The amount of this cost will vary depending on market rates and the purchase price of the vehicle.

depreciation

The decline in value of an asset over time due to wear and tear, obsolescence, and competitive factors.

Depreciation. **Depreciation** is the decline in value of an asset over time. Automobiles depreciate due to wear and tear, obsolescence, and competitive factors. Although businesses are allowed to deduct depreciation of business assets from their income, individuals are not, so the declining value of your vehicle over time implies that your net worth will also decline over time, all else being equal. People often joke about the loss in new car value that occurs as soon as you drive off the dealer's lot, but it's really not funny. Within the first two years, a new car may lose 40 to 60 percent of its value. Since not all vehicles depreciate at the same rate, you may want to consider this factor in making your purchase decision.

The historic patterns of depreciation for particular makes and models are accessible from many sources and are even a factor in the ratings of various vehicles. However, past history is no guarantee that the future will be the same. Values of used cars in 2002 and 2003, for example, declined much more quickly than they had historically, because of unusually stiff competition from the new car market. Stagnant new car pricing and low auto financing rates led to sharply reduced used car prices.

To find out more about the value of new and used cars, you can consult *The Kelley Blue Book*, at www.kbb.com or *Edmunds*, at www.edmunds.com

Incremental Auto Insurance Cost. If you already have auto insurance, then the relevant insurance cost to consider is not the total premium but, rather, the incremental increase in premium that results from the purchase of a new car. In the case of the Thompson family, Kyle will presumably need to be covered by his parents' insurance policy regardless of whether they have two cars or three. However, the premium increase for a third driver in a household with two cars is much lower than it is for a household with three cars, since the insurer will rate the new driver in the latter case as a "primary" driver rather than an "occasional" driver. Another insurance-related factor to consider in making auto purchase decisions is that some makes and models of cars require the payment of higher insurance premiums than others. You can generally ask your insurance agent for an estimate of the incremental cost increase in premiums that will result from adding a car and/or a driver to your policy. Automobile insurance is discussed in more detail in Chapter 9.

Other Fixed Costs. Other fixed costs include car registration, licenses, and taxes. Some states charge a fixed price per vehicle for registration. Others use a sliding scale, with more expensive vehicles being more expensive to register. All sales of motor vehicles are subject to sales tax, and a few states impose personal property taxes, usually calculated annually based on a percentage of all personal property owned.

Variable Operating Expenses. Variable expenses, as noted, depend on how much you use your vehicle. The more you use a vehicle, the more you'll spend on gas and maintenance. The more miles you drive, the more often you'll need to change the vehicle's oil and repair or replace parts such as belts, brakes, and tires. Additional variable expenses for those who commute could include parking and tolls.

Your total operating costs will depend primarily on miles driven and the age of the car but may also be related to the conditions under which you drive. New vehicles generally require less maintenance than older vehicles. Furthermore, larger vehicles can have much higher variable operating expenses, not only due to higher gasoline costs, but also because replacement parts and maintenance tend to be more expensive.

It's important to remember that regular maintenance of your vehicle can reduce your overall costs. Cars that are well maintained tend to depreciate less than those that are not—they will have higher resale value and higher trade-in value. And as with wellness care for your personal health, regular tune-ups can put off or avert more expensive repairs.

Evaluating Affordability in Light of Total Costs. You can compare the costs of different vehicles by considering the total annual cost or the cost per mile. Since a portion of the total cost is fixed, the cost per mile decreases with mileage driven as the fixed costs are spread over a larger number of miles. However, from a budgetary point of view, the total dollar cost is probably the more relevant number to consider.

Exhibit 8–2 illustrates this type of comparison for the Thompsons' case. Since they are initially assessing affordability so that they can narrow their vehicle search, they focus here on the increased costs without including financing. They include a range of values for each category because

EXHIBIT 8-2

The Thompsons Estimate the Monthly and Annual Budget Impact of an Additional Vehicle (not including depreciation)

	Monthly	Annual
Fixed Costs		
Insurance	\$40–\$60	\$480–\$720[a]
License and registration		\$100–\$350[a]
Variable Costs		
Gasoline, oil	\$60–\$120	\$720–\$1,440[a]
Maintenance	\$20–\$100	\$240–\$1,200[a]
Total Costs	\$120–\$280	\$1,540–\$3,710

[a]Depends on vehicle choice.

some of the costs depend on their choice of vehicle. For example, they'll have lower maintenance costs on a new vehicle but higher registration costs. In all cases, they assume that the vehicle will be a larger SUV or truck that will provide the safety features they're interested in. Although they include an estimate of increased insurance and gas costs, this will not be a major factor in their purchase decision, since they plan to require that Kyle pay the regular operating expenses and insurance himself. Based on this assessment and their $300 per month budgeted expense, the Thompsons estimate that they can apply from $200 to $280 toward the financing or lease costs of an additional vehicle.

Learning by Doing 8-1

1. Joel looks up the value of his four-year-old vehicle and finds that the average resale value is $6,000. He paid $13,000 for the vehicle new.
   a. How much has it depreciated over the four years he has owned it, in percentage terms?
   b. Explain to him why it might have been a better idea to buy a one-year old car instead of a new car.

Evaluating Vehicle Choices

The most widely used source for vehicle ratings is *Consumer Reports*, www.consumerreports.com, which regularly evaluates new car models each year. Auto Site, www.autosite.com, also includes extensive information on new cars, including reviews and insurance premium information.

The purchase of an automobile is a multidimensional decision. If cost were not a factor, you could purchase a new car with every option available. Most people, however, are not independently wealthy and therefore must make their purchase decisions based on predefined priorities.

What are the key vehicle features that will meet your needs? Although price is usually a major factor, most people enter into the car-buying process with other objectives in mind as well, whether safety and reliability as in the Thompsons' case, sufficient size for a growing family, or ruggedness for an avid off-roader. This section identifies some of the objectives that might be important in the auto purchase decision and identifies some of the tradeoffs you should consider. Whatever your needs, there are many sources of information on vehicles, their features, and their costs.

sticker price
The manufacturer's suggested retail price (MSRP) for a new vehicle, including manufacturer-installed accessories and options.

dealer's invoice price
The price that a dealer pays to purchase a new vehicle from the manufacturer.

Price. Manufacturers provide a printed form for new cars that identifies the manufacturer's suggested retail price (MSRP) for the car with its accessories and options. This is usually referred to as the **sticker price**, but some dealers use this term to refer to a different sticker they have placed on the car that gives the total price as the MSRP *plus* additional charges for delivery, detailing, and other dealer-provided services which add to their profit on the car. The **dealer's invoice price** is the price that the dealer paid to purchase the vehicle from the manufacturer and is an important piece of information to have in the negotiation process discussed later in this chapter. In some cases, automobile dealers advertise that they'll sell vehicles for a set amount—say, $200—over their invoice price. In essence, they're implying that this is the limit of the profit they'll make on the sale. Although this may be true, in many cases, the "invoice" they're using is actually the dealer's invoice plus all the dealer-installed options on which they'll also earn some profit.

Used cars are sold by used car dealers and private owners. An asking price may be advertised in the newspaper, on the Internet, or on the vehicle itself. Both sticker prices for new vehicles and asking prices for used vehicles are negotiable, so the actual price that you end up paying will depend on the motivation of the seller and the local market for the vehicle.

The price range that you can consider is directly related to your household budget and financial goals. If you know how much you have available for up-front costs and how much you can allocate to your total automobile costs each month, you can use time value of money calculations to get a rough estimate of the price range you can afford. Although you may need to revise this estimate later as you get more information about costs, it doesn't make sense to waste your time looking at vehicles that are outside the range you can consider, so you should at least establish a ballpark price range.

We can use the Thompsons' case as an illustration. Recall that they can allocate $200 to $280 per month to financing costs, after taking into consideration expected maintenance costs on the vehicle and assuming that their son will cover operating expenses. To be conservative, let's

estimate the total loan value they can afford assuming a $250 monthly payment. Note that, since they'll be making equal monthly payments for a set period of time and we're interested in the loan value *today*, this is a *present value of an annuity* problem. Suppose their bank has quoted them a 6 percent rate on a 48-month car loan. We can calculate a hypothetical loan value by using any of the methods described in Chapter 2 for this type of problem. To solve the problem using a financial calculator, we enter $PMT = \$250$, $N = 48$, and $I = 6/12 = 0.5$ and solve for PV; the result is $10,645.

You can find MPG estimates, as well as other information on specific models, at auto manufacturer websites: www.chrysler.com, www.ford.com, www.gm.com, www.honda.com, and www.toyota.com.

At this point, we might consider how much difference it would make if they took a longer-term loan or made a smaller or larger payment. To do this, we simply change our assumptions and recalculate to arrive at different estimates for the loan value. For example, let's use the financial calculator again to find the value if the loan were for six years instead of four, assuming the same annual rate. We enter: $PMT = \$250$, $N = 72$, and $I = 0.5$ and solve for PV; the result is $15,085.

After coming up with a range of feasible loan values, we need to do one more thing to arrive at an affordable purchase price: We add the amount of any money that can be applied to the price to reduce the loan amount. Since the Thompsons have $2,000 to allocate to a down payment, they estimate that they can buy a car in the range of $12,000 to $17,000 (the loan values as estimated above plus the down payment amount).

New Versus Used. Based on your price range, you may find that you can't consider the new car market. If a used vehicle is an option, you may find that there are many attractive alternatives, through both private sale and dealerships. As we've seen, the market values of used cars have declined substantially in the last several years, so you may be able to get a low-mileage car that is one or two years old at a fraction of the cost of a new car. You do take a risk buying a used vehicle that may have hidden defects, but you can minimize that risk by taking the car to a mechanic for a systems check-up prior to finalizing your purchase. In addition, dealerships usually offer a 30-day warranty. If you're buying from a private party, be sure to ask the seller why the car is being sold and what kind of maintenance has been done over the vehicle's life. Although there's no guarantee that you'll get an honest answer, you might learn something useful so it's worth asking.

PFP Worksheet 30
Automobile Options Checklist

Equipment. Depending on make and model, vehicles can differ substantially in standard equipment, options, and accessories. Based on your needs, create a list of options that you require and a list of options that you'd like to have but don't absolutely need. A sample checklist for this purpose is included in your *Personal Financial Planner*. If you're buying a used car, you may not be able to be as picky, but it's still a good idea to think about the features that are most important to you. As you consider different vehicles, keep track of which ones satisfy your requirements.

Size and Fuel Efficiency. The gasoline shortages of the mid-1970s resulted in the first real push for American auto manufacturers to produce more fuel-efficient vehicles. Since that time, gasoline prices have risen at less than half the rate of inflation, and consumers have turned a blind eye to the risk of spiraling oil prices. Nevertheless, all new car dealers are required by federal law to report the estimated mileage per gallon (MPG) for city and highway driving. *Consumer Reports* also provides independent, and often lower, MPG results based on its own driving tests.

Obviously, the larger and heavier the car, the less fuel-efficient it will be, and the greater the costs of operation will be. If you drive a lot, this may be a significant expense. For example, if Kyle has a car at his disposal and consequently drives 10,000 miles per year (about half the average for a male teenaged driver), the additional gasoline costs to the family at $2.00 per gallon could range from about $500 per year for a fairly fuel-efficient car (40 MPG) to $2,000 for a gas guzzler (10 MPG). To estimate your annual gasoline costs, divide the number of miles you drive by the miles per gallon you think your vehicle will get on average to find the

The 2004 Toyota Prius gas/electric hybrid boasts an EPA rating of 60mpg for city driving.

NEWS you can use

How Can a Hybrid Help Your Budget?

Several manufacturers are experimenting with automobiles that are partially or fully powered by electricity. Original "electric" models had limited range because they relied completely on batteries, which kept their charge for only 50 miles or so. New versions, though, use a combination of gas and electricity, which is why they're called "hybrids." Honda and Toyota have produced moderately priced versions that are quite popular with consumers, and other automakers are quickly moving in the same direction.

"it won't take long to recoup the additional cost of buying a hybrid"

Although current hybrids cost about $3,000 more than similarly equipped traditionally powered cars, these vehicles could make a significant impact on your household budget. The IRS currently allows a $2,000 deduction to help defray the cost, and you'll also save a lot on gas. If, for example, you're currently driving a car that gets 20 miles per gallon and you buy a Toyota Prius, which boasts 60 MPG for city driving, it won't take long to recoup the additional cost of buying the hybrid. If you drive 15,000 miles per year, you currently use 750 gallons (15,000/20). At 60 MPG, you'll use only 250 gallons, for a savings of 500 gallons, or $1,000 each year (at $2.00 per gallon).

Fact #1

Although big cars can easily crush little cars in a collision, that doesn't necessarily mean people are safer in SUVs. You can view the results of front and side crash tests for various makes and models of vehicles at www.nhtsa.dot.gov, the website for the National Highway Traffic Safety Administration. Surprisingly good performers are the new Volkswagon Beetles which, although small, have been specifically redesigned to protect the driver and front passenger from collision injuries.

number of gallons of gas the vehicle will consume per year. Then multiply the gallons per year by the average price per gallon to get the annual fuel cost. Keep in mind that this dollar cost could rise rapidly in the face of sudden oil price changes. In Europe, where the price of gasoline is two to three times that in the United States, consumers prefer to buy small, fuel-efficient cars and to use alternative modes of transportation, such as the gasoline-electric hybrids discussed in the *News You Can Use* box, "How Can a Hybrid Help Your Budget?"

Safety. The odds of having a minor accident, or fender-bender, in any given year are fairly high, and increase with the number of miles you drive each year. In addition, past statistics suggest that there will be at least 40,000 auto accident fatalities per year. Given these statistics, safety should be a factor in any automobile purchase. Safety harnesses and air bags are required in all new cars, and auto manufacturers are continuously working to develop new ways to keep drivers safer.

Small car manufacturers are particularly active in safety research, since they know they could lose market share if buyers become wary of the risks of competing for road space with cars the size of the Ford Expedition. For example, Honda Motor Co., a Japan-based maker of small and mid-sized vehicles, is testing new technology that will actually sense when your car is getting too close to the one in front of you. If, for example, you've fallen asleep at the wheel and you don't respond to the initial warning buzzer, the car's brakes will automatically activate, and your seatbelt will tug several times to wake you up. Although not yet approved for sale in the United States, Honda's Inspire sedan is being marketed in Japan with these features.

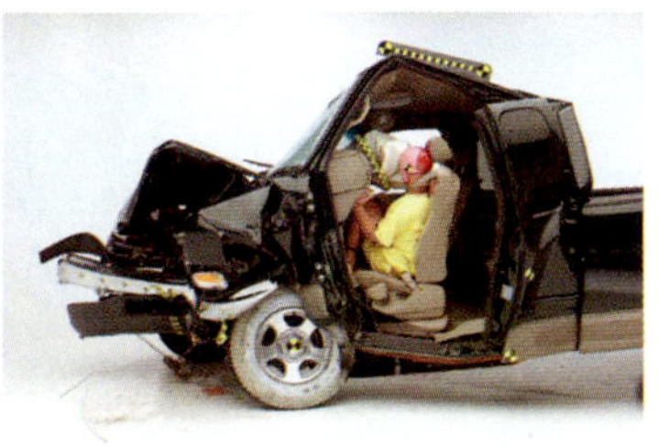

The Insurance Institute for Highway Safety regularly conducts front and side impact crash tests on new vehicles.

Reliability. Buying a new car doesn't guarantee that you'll have zero expenses for maintenance and repairs in the first several years. Some makes and models are notorious for their lack of reliability. *Consumer Reports* and other auto information providers usually report information on reliability based on customer surveys. For example, despite its great popularity in the SUV category, the Ford Explorer has generally received relatively low reliability marks. In contrast, the competing Toyota Highlander is reported to have very low repair and maintenance costs.

Warranties. Most new vehicles and late-model used vehicles sold at dealerships come with both express and implied warranties. A warranty is a legal promise made by the seller, in this case with respect to the qualities of the vehicle being sold. An **express warranty** is a promise made by the seller orally or in writing. Even without an express warranty, there is an **implied warranty** that a purchased vehicle is suitable for its intended use—unless it was explicitly sold "as is," which means that the seller makes no warranties at all.

Express warranties may include a promise to repair certain types of defects within a period of time after the sale. If the seller promises to fix any problems or, in the event that a problem isn't fixable within a reasonable amount of time, replace the vehicle, the warranty is a full warranty. Auto dealerships and manufacturers usually offer a **limited warranty**, however, and it is labeled as such. These warranties are likely to cover parts and labor for certain types of repairs for some number of years or miles driven, whichever comes first. After your warranty has expired, most manufacturers still cover the costs of repairs that result from defects in workmanship or design if you complain loud enough.

In addition to their regular warranties, most manufacturers and dealers offer the opportunity to purchase an **extended warranty** or service contract. This either extends the amount of time that your car is covered by the original limited warranty or adds services or coverage to your existing warranty. You should read the fine print on such a warranty carefully, because many extended warranties exclude coverage for the problems you're most likely to experience. It is also generally the case that the warranty contract price is greater than the expected costs of covered repairs.

Comfort and Style. In addition to the more practical features discussed in this section, most buyers are interested in qualitative features, such as comfort, smoothness of ride, color, and attractiveness. When you research your alternatives, be sure to test-drive the vehicle under normal driving conditions so that you can judge these features. Several auto manufacturers (GM, Chrysler, and Ford, so far) are experimenting in some markets with allowing potential qualified buyers to take cars for overnight test drives. And no, you don't have to take the car salesman with you. Presumably, sellers hope that, by spending more time with the car, you'll get attached to that "new car smell."

Fact #2

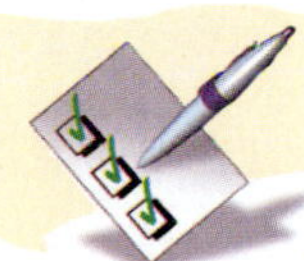

All new car manufacturers offer some type of "bumper-to-bumper" warranty, at a minimum for the first three years or 36,000 miles, whichever comes first. Some, such as BMW, are more generous (four years or 50,000 miles). This type of warranty covers the costs of most problems you might experience with your vehicle, except for routine maintenance and accident damage. Powertrain problems are usually covered for a longer period of time, ranging from five to ten years, depending on the manufacturer.

express warranty
Written or oral promise by seller.

implied warranty
Legal obligation that the product for sale be suitable for intended use.

limited warranty
Less than a full promise to repair or replace, often covering parts and labor for specifically identified types of problems.

extended warranty
Service contract agreement that, for a set price, extends an original warranty or adds services or coverage.

Automobile Financing Alternatives

LEARNING objective

2 Decide between automobile financing alternatives.

You have many choices for financing the purchase of an automobile. In Chapter 7, we identified the primary sources for consumer loans and explained the usual terms of such agreements. An alternative to buying is leasing, which is similar in many ways to financing the purchase with a loan. In this section, we address the lease-versus-buy decision and explain the key features of automobile leases.

The Lease-Versus-Buy Decision

In deciding whether to lease or buy, you can use the worksheet in Exhibit 8–3, which is also available in your *Personal Financial Planner*. Generally, the up-front and monthly costs of buying are higher than the costs of leasing. This tends to make leases attractive to consumers who don't have enough money for a down payment or those who want to limit their monthly expenses. However, the difference may be made up at the end of the lease term. After two years, a buyer may have equity in the vehicle—the buyer may owe less on the loan than the car is worth—but a person who leases will have nothing but the use of the vehicle.

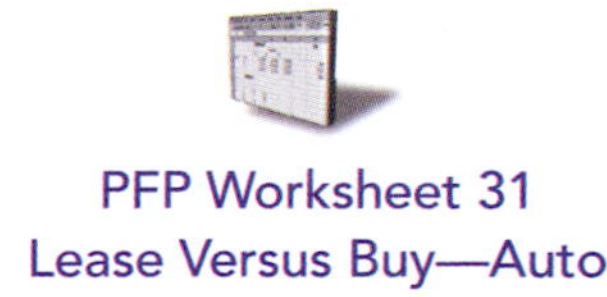

PFP Worksheet 31
Lease Versus Buy—Auto

EXHIBIT 8-3

Lease Versus Buy Worksheet—Auto

Cost of Leasing		Cost of Buying	
Capitalized cost reduction and security deposit	____	Down payment	____
Foregone interest on capitalized cost reduction and security deposit	____	Foregone interest on down payment	____
Total lease payments = monthly payment x ____ months	____	Total loan payments = monthly payment x ____ months	____
Expected end-of-lease charges	____		
Less: Return of security deposit	____	Less: Expected end-of-loan value	____
Total: Cost of Leasing	____	Total: Cost of Buying	____

What Is a Lease?

lessor

An owner of an asset, commonly a vehicle or real property, who charges money for the use of that asset for a period of time.

lessee

A person who pays money for the privilege of using someone else's vehicle or real property for a period of time

A lease is essentially a rental agreement between the owner of the car, the **lessor**, and you, the **lessee**, in which you agree to pay money for the right to *use* the vehicle for the period of your contract. The newspapers are full of ads touting low monthly payments for new cars. Usually, these are lease as opposed to loan payments. Why are leases so much cheaper? The reason is that the lessor can afford to charge a lower monthly payment during the lease term because it retains the ownership of the vehicle and can make additional money on the vehicle by selling it at the end. If you bought the vehicle instead of leasing, *you* would be the one who could benefit from selling the car. Leases are increasingly popular, with about a third of all new cars being leased rather than purchased, primarily because of the attractively low monthly payments and the ability to turn in your car for a new one every two or three years.

The cost of a lease is determined by the difference between the initial value of the car and the resale value at the end of the lease—or, in other words, how much the car will depreciate in value over the two- or three-year term of the lease. If the car is worth $29,000 today and is expected to be worth $15,000 in two years, then your lease payments must compensate the lessor for the $14,000 depreciation plus finance charges.

closed-end lease

Lease in which the lessor bears the risk that the value of the car at the end of the term is less than originally estimated.

open-end lease

Lease in which the lessee is responsible for the additional depreciation at the end of the lease term if the value of the car is less than originally estimated.

Closed-end and Open-end Leases. Leases are either closed-end or open-end. In a **closed-end lease**, the lessor takes the risk that the resale value of the car will be less than what was originally assumed. This type of lease is also sometimes called a *walk-away lease* because you can return the car in good condition and simply walk away from any further responsibilities. In the example above, if you didn't exceed the mileage limitation on the lease but the resale value at the end of the two years turned out to be only $13,000 instead of the assumed $15,000, the $2,000 additional depreciation cost would be borne by the lessor. However, if you exceeded the mileage limitations or if your car had too much wear and tear, you'd still be subject to a surcharge, as discussed below. A disadvantage of closed-end leases is that you are committed to the full term of the lease and may be subject to a large penalty for canceling prematurely. Most auto leases are closed-end leases.

An **open-end lease**, which is not very common, requires you to bear the risk of greater than expected depreciation. The contract makes you responsible for any difference between the actual and estimated depreciation. However, the amount you may be charged is limited by the Consumer Leasing Act to three times the monthly lease payment.

Important Lease Terminology

As with any financial contract, if you don't understand your rights and obligations under a lease agreement, you may be taken advantage of by the other party. Under the Federal Consumer Leasing Act, lessors are required to tell you all the relevant information about your lease on a disclosure form, such as the one shown in Exhibit 8–4, but the form itself can be confusing. This section summarizes the most important terminology and common contractual clauses for automobile lease agreements.

- *Gross capitalized cost.* The value of the vehicle is called the gross capitalized cost. You should negotiate this price before discussing leasing—statistics show that negotiated prices for leased vehicles are, on average, about 4 percent higher than prices for a purchased vehicle.
- *Up-front fees.* You may be required to pay some up-front or acquisition fees, which cover the cost of obtaining your credit report and processing your application. In some cases, these fees may be included in the capitalized cost of the vehicle.
- *Capitalized cost reduction.* If you make a down payment, benefit from a rebate, or trade in another vehicle, the gross capitalized cost will be reduced by this amount.
- *Residual value.* The residual value is the expected depreciated value of the vehicle at the end of the lease term.
- *Rent charge.* The rent charge is the total dollar finance charges for the term of the lease. Since this is added to the expected depreciation of the vehicle to determine the payment, leases are like add-on interest loans which were discussed in Chapter 7.
- *Lease term.* The number of months in the lease is called the lease term.
- *Excess wear and mileage limits.* Automobile lessors commonly charge a penalty for excessive wear and use of a vehicle. This penalty can be assessed for physical damage to the vehicle (not usually defined clearly in the contract) and for mileage in excess of that specified in the contract, commonly 12,000 to 15,000 miles per year. Charges can range from 10 cents to 30 cents per mile. If your contract specified 12,000 miles per year and you drove 30,000 miles during your two-year lease, you would therefore be subject to a charge of at least $600 (6,000 extra miles times 10 cents per mile) when you return the vehicle.
- *Purchase option.* Most leases allow you to purchase your leased vehicle at the end of the lease term. The amount you'll be required to pay will be specified in the lease contract and may include a purchase option fee. This amount is often the same as the residual value used for calculation of the depreciation amount.
- *Early termination.* If you decide to terminate the contract early, you may be assessed a penalty for early termination, in addition to owing the balance on the lease. This penalty may also be imposed if the car is stolen or destroyed in an accident, although auto insurance may cover some or all of the loss.
- *Disposition fee.* The lessor may charge a disposition fee to be paid at the end of the lease if you choose not to purchase the vehicle.

Learning by Doing 8-2

1. All else equal, will the following changes to an automobile lease contract increase or decrease your lease payment?
   a. Increased gross capitalized cost
   b. Increased residual value
   c. Increased lease term
   d. Increased finance charge
   e. Increased mileage limitation

EXHIBIT 8-4 **Copy of Federal Consumer Leasing Disclosure Form**

Federal Consumer Leasing Act Disclosures

Lessor(s) ____________ Lessee(s) ____________

Amount Due at Lease Signing or Delivery	Monthly Payments	Other Charges (not part of your monthly payment)	Total of Payments (The amount you will have paid by the end of the lease)
(itemized below)* $ ________	Your first monthly payment of $________ is due on ______________, followed by ______ payments of $ ________ due on the ________ of each month. The total of your monthly payments is $ ________.	Disposition fee (if you do not purchase the vehicle) $________ ____________ ________ Total $ ________	$____________

*** Itemization of Amount Due at Lease Signing or Delivery**

Amount Due at Lease Signing or Delivery:		How the Amount Due at Lease Signing or Delivery will be paid:	
Capitalized cost reduction	$ ________	Net trade-in allowance	$ ________
First monthly payment	________	Rebates and noncash credits	________
Refundable security deposit	________	Amount to be paid in cash	________
Title fees	________	____________	________
Registration fees	________		
____________	________		
Total	$ ________	Total	$ ________

Your monthly payment is determined as shown below:

Gross capitalized cost. The agreed upon value of the vehicle ($__________) and any items you pay over the lease term (such as service contracts, insurance, and any outstanding prior credit or lease balance) .... $________

If you want an itemization of this amount please check this box. ☐

Capitalized cost reduction. The amount of any net trade-in allowance, rebate, noncash credit, or cash you pay that reduces the gross capitalized cost .... − ________

Adjusted capitalized cost. The amount used in calculating your base monthly payment .... = ________

Residual value. The value of the vehicle at the end of the lease used in calculating your base monthly payment .... − ________

Depreciation and any amortized amounts. The amount charged for the vehicle's decline in the value through normal use and for other items paid over the lease term .... = ________

Rent charge. The amount charged in addition to the depreciation and any amortized amounts .... + ________

Total of base monthly payments. The depreciation and any amortized amounts plus the rent charge .... = ________

Lease payments. The number of payments in your lease .... ÷ ________

Base monthly payment .... = ________

Monthly sales/use tax .... + ________

____________ .... + ________

Total monthly payment .... = $ ________

Early Termination. You may have to pay a substantial charge if you end this lease early. The charge may be up to several thousand dollars. The actual charge will depend on when the lease is terminated. The earlier you end the lease, the greater this charge is likely to be.

Excessive Wear and Use. You may be charged for excessive wear based on our standards for normal use [and for mileage in excess of ________ miles per year at the rate of ________ per mile.]

Purchase Option at End of Lease Term. [You have an option to purchase the vehicle at the end of the lease term for $ ________ [and a purchase option fee of $ __________].] [You do not have an option to purchase the vehicle at the end of the lease term.]

Other Important Terms. See your lease documents for additional information on early termination, purchase options and maintenance responsibilities, warranties, late and default charges, insurance, and any security interest, if applicable.

Getting the Most for Your Money

LEARNING objective

 Be an informed automobile consumer.

Whether you lease or buy, it's important to negotiate the best possible terms. A lower price will reduce the amount to be financed in the case of a purchase and the depreciation charge in the case of a lease. Very few people pay the price originally asked by the seller, and those who do are paying too much. You should go into any negotiation process with as much information about the vehicle's value as possible so that you can negotiate effectively. Although it's a mistake to focus on price alone, since a number of other factors can make your car more or less expensive—needed repairs, fuel efficiency, and finance charges, for example—the negotiated price still makes the most difference. In this section, we provide some background on the components of dealer profit and how dealers use them to make auto buyers erroneously think they are "getting a deal." Lastly, we suggest some strategies for dealing with a defective car.

Understanding Auto Dealer Profit

You can negotiate most effectively on new car prices if you understand how dealers make their profit. The main sources of dealer profit are:

- The difference between what dealers pay for the car (dealer's invoice price) and what they sell it for
- Profit on dealer-installed options, dealer delivery and preparation, and undercoating (a generally overpriced rust-proofing process)
- Manufacturer incentives, such as rebates, allowances, and discounts
- Extended warranties and service contracts
- Finance charges and application fees
- Profit to be made on traded vehicle

When car sales are slow, dealers often offer fairly good prices with minimal mark-ups to attract customers, but they make up this difference in other charges, which may vary widely from seller to seller. For example, the delivery and preparation charge, which covers the dealer's cost of getting the car to the lot and cleaning it up before putting it on the lot, can add as much as $1,000 to the originally contracted price. And you often don't see this until you're signing the final paperwork.

In light of the dealer's different profit sources, you can see that the uninformed consumer could easily be fooled into thinking that he or she got a good deal on a car by paying only $100 over the dealer's invoice when the dealer is making several thousand dollars on other aspects of the deal. Trade-in values are usually significantly lower than resale values. Financing is quite profitable as well, particularly if borrowers fail to compare loans based on APR. In the *Ask the Expert* box, a

ask the expert — The Car Buyers Art

Darrell Parrish
Author, The Car Buyer's Art

Darrell Parrish, an author and former car salesman gives advice in his books for beating the car salesman at his own game. The following suggestions are based on ideas from Parrish's books *The Car Buyer's Art* and *Used Cars: How to Buy One*.

In the shopping phase:

- Visit several dealerships and always get the youngest salesperson to help you. A less experienced salesperson won't be as good at the "trickery."
- Don't negotiate or go into a salesperson's office. You're only shopping.
- Test-drive only the cars you are seriously considering.
- Write down car details and any "offers" made by salespersons on the back of their business cards. These can be used in negotiation later and encourages competition among dealerships for your business.

In the negotiation phase:

- Know what your bottom line is and don't make that offer first.
- Understand the car salesperson's objectives and the dealer's profit sources.
- Always act like you are willing to walk away, even when you have almost closed the deal.
- Plan to spend three hours.

Sources: Based on information in Darrell Parrish, *The Car Buyer's Art* (1998) and *Used Cars: How to Buy One* (1998), available from Book Express, P.O. Box 1249, Bellflower, CA 90706. You can download free chapters on car buying and leasing at Darrell Parrish's website at www.3carbooks.com, or search on the keywords "Darrell Parrish."

Money Psychology

Strategies for Female Car Buyers

Undercover buyer tests have consistently shown that women don't fare well in the automobile marketplace. They tend to get less attention from salespeople, and they don't negotiate as effectively. Some tips for women (or men) who want to use principles of psychology to more effectively negotiate a car sale or lease agreement:

- **Bring along a male relative or friend**. Although this strategy might sound sexist, it can serve two purposes. First, it might prevent the salesperson from trying to dazzle you with meaningless car jargon. And second, it's easier to make the salesperson worry that you might walk away from the deal. ("I don't know about this one, Dad—I really liked that car at the Ford dealership better. . . .")
- **Bring along a poorly behaved or tired child**. Although this will be a trying experience for you as well, salespeople are much more motivated to close a deal quickly when faced with a screaming child who is pulling papers off the desk and throwing them on the floor.
- **Make sure the salesperson knows that you've done your homework**. Since the primary problem is that car salespeople tend to underestimate female buyers, you should make it clear that you are a well-informed consumer. A simple way to do this is to bring along an Internet printout that gives the dealer invoice and other information on the vehicle.

car sales expert gives some tips on how to get the best deal on a new car. Some special issues for women are discussed in the *Money Psychology* box, "Strategies for Female Car Buyers."

Making Consumer Complaints

Although no one likes to think about what can go wrong, you may find that the car you've purchased doesn't live up to your expectations. Most of your problems with a new car should be covered by the manufacturer's warranty. If you don't get satisfaction at the service department, your complaints will have to move up the ladder to the service manager or owner. The next level of complaint is the manufacturer, where you'll need to contact someone in the Consumer Affairs Department. If this fails, you can contact your state consumer protection office. All complaints should be made in writing, and you should provide adequate documentation of each attempt you've made to get the defect fixed. In some cases, when a vehicle is clearly defective and repairs don't help, state **lemon laws** may require that the dealer reimburse you for repair expenses or refund the price you paid for the vehicle. Since these laws vary, check your state's lemon law for requirements.

lemon laws

State laws that protect consumers against chronically defective vehicles.

The Housing Decision

LEARNING objective

4 Evaluate your housing needs and determine what you can afford.

As with other financial decisions, your choice of housing must be made after careful consideration of your needs and your budgetary constraints. We will follow the same decision process here as we did with the automobile decision, beginning with needs analysis and affordability before considering the lease-versus-buy decision in more detail.

Housing Needs Analysis

Housing is generally the largest budget expenditure, accounting for one-third or more of all household spending. Not surprisingly, housing expenditures increase with income, but the proportion of a household budget that is spent on housing is relatively consistent across income brackets. Although celebrity couples might spend several million dollars to buy and furnish a home, the amount they spend is usually in line with their income. When you make $50 million per year, you can buy a mansion, too!

Changing Housing Needs over the Life Cycle

Over your life cycle and with changing life circumstances, your housing needs will change. As a young single adult, you might rent a small apartment or share living quarters with friends. Married couples tend to prefer to live on their own, and families with children often need more space, including a yard and proximity to schools. This usually means they must consider more expensive options, renting or buying single-family housing. Consistent with this logic, federal government statistics show that average housing expenditures are greatest for people during the child-rearing years, ages 35 to 44, averaging $16,452 per year. Postretirement-age households experience reduced housing expenditures—either due to downsizing or reduced costs as mortgages are paid off.

In 2000, 19-year-old Britney Spears built this 3 million dollar mansion as a gift for her parents.

Housing as a Component of Your Financial Plan

Spending more on housing necessarily involves a tradeoff—the more you spend on any one thing, the less you have available to meet your other budgetary needs or to apply to achieving your financial goals. Since you have a wide variety of choices to meet your housing needs, it's up to you to make this decision in light of your other priorities. For example, if reducing your credit card debt is a high priority for you, it would make sense to rent a smaller apartment and live with a roommate until you have achieved that goal. It's also fairly common for new college graduates to live with their parents for a few months to a year after graduation so that they can pay off debt and increase savings before going out on their own.

The next step is to consult your budget to determine what you can afford to spend on housing. Generally, this calculation will be made some time in advance of the actual change in your situation. You may be anticipating the end of your current lease agreement, your college graduation, a job relocation, an increase in salary, or a change in family circumstances. Therefore, you need to estimate your budget assuming the new cash inflows and cash outflows. As you learned in Chapter 3, you should do your best to estimate your income and expenses accurately. If you're currently allocating funds to other financial goals, you should keep those in your budget so that you can better see how the housing decision might affect your other financial priorities.

The Rent-Versus-Buy Decision

The decision whether to rent or buy housing depends on your preferences, your budget, and your creditworthiness. Although it usually costs more to buy than to rent equivalent space, homeowners generally experience long-term financial advantages from the growing value of their home and the tax deductibility of interest and property taxes. You should consider the advantages and disadvantages of each alternative, as discussed below.

The Advantages of Renting

The advantages of renting include lower costs, increased mobility, and reduced responsibility.

Lower Monthly Payments. Rent is usually less expensive than monthly costs for a comparable-sized house. As a tenant, you don't generally pay property taxes or homeowner's insurance, and you avoid expenses for maintenance and repairs, since that's the responsibility of your landlord. In most cases, you don't have to provide appliances, such as a refrigerator or washer/dryer, and depending on your lease agreement, your landlord may pay some or all of your utilities. These cost differences can add up to a lot of money that you can apply to other components of your financial plan.

Mobility. If you're not yet settled in a job and permanent family situation, renting provides you with the ability to move on short notice. Leases are commonly made for one year, but many landlords will agree to reduce the term if they're given sufficient notice to find a replacement tenant. At worst, you might lose your security deposit. In comparison, it usually takes at least several months to find a buyer for a house.

Less Responsibility. Renters of apartments usually have no responsibility for maintenance of lawns and gardens, clearing of snow, or exterior cleaning and painting. However, if you rent a home, your lease is likely to include some of these responsibilities. As a renter, you also have less legal liability for injuries that occur on the property.

The Disadvantages of Renting

The disadvantages of renting can also be substantial, as discussed below.

Increasing Costs over Time. Rent usually increases with the rate of inflation over time, whereas mortgage payments are often fixed for the life of the loan.

No Investment Value. Paying rent doesn't contribute to your wealth, since you don't benefit from the increase in value of the property over time. In contrast, homeowners benefit from the growth in their housing investment and can even borrow against their home equity to meet their financial objectives.

No Tax Deduction. Rent is not tax-deductible, which makes it more expensive than a mortgage payment of the same amount, after taxes. The interest paid on a mortgage as well as the property taxes are tax-deductible. The extent to which this is a disadvantage to renting is directly related to your unique tax situation. If you're in a low tax bracket and do not itemize deductions, then this will not be a factor in your decision. For most people, however, the annual expenses of home ownership exceed the standard deduction and so provide tax advantages over renting.

Restrictions on Use of the Property. Lease contracts often restrict how you can use your property—how many people can live with you, whether you can have pets, and how much noise will be tolerated, as well as your ability to upgrade and decorate according to your tastes. Although some subdivisions and most condominium complexes place restrictions on homeowners, these restrictions are generally limited to such matters as exterior color, fencing, and landscaping.

Uncertainty. There are no guarantees that you'll be able to continue renting the property after the end of the lease term.

PFP Worksheet 32
Lease Versus Buy—Housing

You should decide between renting and buying by weighing the relative costs and benefits, both financial and personal. You can use the worksheet provided in Exhibit 8–5 and in your *Personal Financial Planner* to help you compare the financial costs. Note that in the short term, renting tends to have the cost advantage, but over time, the tax and investment benefits of home ownership make owning more attractive than renting.

security deposit

Dollar amount required at the beginning of a lease to cover the costs of any damage to the property over the lease term.

Legal Issues for Tenants

If you choose to rent, you will generally sign a lease with your landlord. The lease outlines the responsibilities and rights of the landlord and the tenant. It specifies the amount of rent and security deposit, the length of the lease (usually six months or one year), penalties for late payment, procedures to be taken in case of nonpayment, and lease termination. A **security deposit** is an extra amount of money paid up front, out of which the landlord will deduct the cost of any damage (not normal wear and tear) to the property over the term of the lease. Security deposits are commonly one month's rent, but college students sometimes are required to pay more.

By law, leases don't have to be in writing unless they're for a period of more than a year, but it's a good idea to have a written lease to guard against misunderstandings at a later date. Some leases specify exactly what the penalty will be for certain types of damage. For example, if you leave the unit at the end of the lease term without cleaning the oven, you might have $75 subtracted from your security deposit. These itemized lists are helpful to tenants in that they spell out what must be done to obtain repayment of their entire security deposit.

Even with a written lease, you can attempt to negotiate the terms if you find some of them unacceptable. For example, your lease might say that the landlord can cancel the lease with 30 days notice to you,

Fact #3

The law in most states requires that a landlord hold your security deposit in a separate account and return it to you within 30 days of the end of your lease, less any deductions for damage that you have caused to the property. In most states, the landlord must also credit you with interest earned on your funds minus up to one percentage point of interest for the expense of managing the money. When savings interest rates are low, this will result in little or no interest being paid to the lessee.

EXHIBIT 8-5

Lease Versus Buy—Housing

- Apartment rent: $500 per month
- Home price: $80,000
- Down payment to purchase home: $4,000
- Total closing costs: $3,000
- Mortgage rate (fixed, 30-year, no points): 6%
- Marginal tax bracket: 25%
- Interest on savings: 4%

	Costs	
Cost of Renting	**1 year**	**5 year**
Annual rent (= monthly rent × 12)	$6,000	$30,000
Renters' insurance (= $150/year)	150	750
After-tax interest lost on security deposit (= 2 months rent @ 3%/year)	30	150
Total Cost of Renting	$6,180	$30,900
Cost of Buying		
Mortgage payments (= monthly principal and interest × 12)	$5,468	$27,340
Property tax	1,200	6,000
Homeowner's insurance	600	3,000
Private mortgage insurance (if <20% down = $\frac{1}{2}$% of mortgage/year)	380	1,900
Repair and maintenance expenses	500	2,500
Down payment	4,000	4,000
Closing costs	3,000	3,000
Lost after-tax interest on down payment and closing costs @ 3%/year)	210	1,050
Subtotal: Costs	*15,358*	*48,790*
Less: Savings from repaying principal	933	5,279
Less: Appreciation of home (@ 3%/year)	2,400	12,742
Less: Tax savings from interest deduction	1,134	5,515
Less: Tax savings from property tax deduction	300	1,500
Less: Tax savings from points deduction	0	0
Subtotal: Savings	*4,767*	*25,036*
Total cost of buying (= Costs − Savings)	$10,591	$23,754

but you might try to have that changed to 60 days to give yourself enough time to find a new apartment. You should also carefully inspect the premises before signing the lease. You don't want to be held responsible for a cigarette burn in the carpet if it was there before you moved in.

All states have laws that govern landlord–tenant relations. If you don't pay your rent in a timely fashion, the landlord has the right to take legal action against you for nonpayment but generally cannot evict you without a court hearing. Any rental unit, regardless of how inexpensive, must meet minimum standards of habitability, which include running hot and cold water, heat, electricity, and safe access. If you have requested in writing that your landlord make certain repairs, but your request has been ignored, you have the right to make the repair yourself and deduct the cost from your next month's rent.

Learning by Doing 8-3

1. Consider each of the following households. Which are more likely to prefer to rent a home rather than buy one, and why?
   a. Full-time student who plans to relocate after graduation
   b. Married parents of two young children, with stable employment, in high tax bracket
   c. Single low-income adult

Calculating How Much House You Can Afford

If, after evaluating your housing needs, you decide that you'd like to buy a home, the next step is to identify an affordable price range. To do that, follow these steps:

1. Estimate the monthly amount you can allocate to total housing costs consistent with your budget and financial goals.
2. Estimate the nonfinancing costs of home ownership and subtract them from your total budgeted amount.
3. Estimate the amount you can borrow with that level of payment.
4. Add other sources of funds and subtract closing costs to calculate the house price you can afford.

Each of these steps is explained in more detail below.

The Costs of Home Ownership

To calculate how much you can allocate to the mortgage, take the total amount of monthly cash flow that you have available for housing expenses and subtract any additional costs of home ownership not related to the mortgage itself. In comparing the costs of renting and buying, it's easy to make the mistake of assuming that the mortgage payment is the total monthly financial cost of buying. However, in addition to the financing costs, you'll also pay local property taxes, homeowner's insurance, and repairs and maintenance on the property. For condominiums and some residential developments, you may have to pay an association fee to cover the maintenance of common areas. All these costs can vary substantially in different areas of the country and for different properties, but will likely constitute 20 to 25 percent of your total housing cost.

Principal and Interest. Your mortgage payment will usually include a level payment for the amortized loan, although other options are discussed in a later section. This payment will include tax-deductible interest on the balance of the mortgage as well as some repayment of principal.

property tax rate

Local tax assessed on real estate proportional to value.

assessment ratio

Proportion of market value used to calculate assessed value of real estate on which the property tax rate will be assessed.

Property Taxes. Most local jurisdictions pay for community services such as roads, schools, fire, and police protection by levying a tax on real property. Property taxes are usually calculated by multiplying a **property tax rate**, often called the *mil rate*, times the assessed value of the property in thousands—a property assessed at $90,000 would pay the tax rate times 90, for example, whereas a property assessed at $150,000 would pay the tax rate times 150. The more expensive the house, the more you pay in property taxes.

The assessed value of your property is determined by a government official usually called the tax assessor. Periodically, the assessor estimates market values for every property in the town or city and then multiplies each by the applicable **assessment ratio**, a fraction less than 1, to determine the assessed value. You can call the local taxing authority to determine the applicable tax rate and assessment ratio in your jurisdiction. Depending on the changing values of properties in the area and demands on local services due to growth, tax rates may go up or down over time.

As an example, suppose you find out from your local taxing authority that the applicable tax rate is 20.319 mils and the assessment ratio is 60 percent. If the home you're thinking about buying has a market value of $160,000, you can estimate the property tax by first calculating the assessed value and then applying the property tax rate to that value, as follows:

$$\begin{aligned}\text{Assessed value} &= \text{Market value} \times \text{Assessment ratio}\\ &= \$160{,}000 \times 60\%\\ &= \$96{,}000\end{aligned}$$

$$\begin{aligned}\text{Property tax} &= \frac{\text{Assessed value}}{1{,}000} \times \text{Tax rate}\\ &= \frac{\$96{,}000}{1{,}000} \times 20.319\\ &= \$1{,}950\end{aligned}$$

Based on this calculation, your estimated annual property tax is therefore $1,950.

Although home buyers can use the previous owner's property taxes as an estimate, this may understate their property tax liability if the town has not recently reassessed. When a property is sold, most jurisdictions will use the new sales price to reestimate the market value in the calculation of property taxes. When prices are rising rapidly, this can result in large increases in taxes for the new owners relative to what the previous owners paid.

Homeowner's Insurance. All lenders require that borrowers carry homeowner's insurance on their property. You'll learn more about homeowner's insurance in Chapter 9. At this point, simply remember to include an estimate in your calculation of monthly costs. This type of insurance can range from $200 per year and up, and the cost increases with the value of the property. A real estate broker can generally give you an estimate of insurance costs in your area, or you can contact a local insurance agent.

Repairs and Maintenance. Buying a home may result in significant additional costs for repairs and maintenance, from lawn maintenance to repair of major systems such as plumbing and electricity. The older the house you buy, the more you can expect to spend.

Association Dues. Condominiums and some residential properties require that homeowners pay dues to a homeowners' association. These pay for the maintenance of common areas, such as gardens and sidewalks, and in some cases more expensive items, such as a neighborhood swimming pool. Consequently, such fees can range from $100 to several thousand dollars per year. Although your mortgage costs are fixed by contract, association dues are usually determined by a volunteer board made up of a few homeowners. If the neighborhood pool needs to be resurfaced, homeowners can even be hit with a one-time special fee to cover the costs.

Offsetting Tax Benefits. Although home ownership can cost quite a bit more than renting, the tax savings from deductibility of mortgage interest and property taxes provide an offsetting benefit. In addition, subject to some limitations, your home can appreciate in value without triggering any capital gains or tax liability upon sale.

Estimating What You Can Allocate to the Monthly Mortgage Payment

The worksheet provided in the *Go Figure!* box "Calculating an Affordable Home Price" (also available in your *Personal Financial Planner*) walks you through the steps to determine the mortgage that will fit your budget. As an example, let's assume that, based on your budget, you know that the maximum you have available to apply to housing is $1,000 per month. From this, you must subtract the additional costs of home ownership as identified above. You estimate that property taxes will be $150 per month, homeowner's insurance $30 per month, and repairs and maintenance $60 per month. You don't expect to pay any association dues. The amount you have available to pay the principal and interest on a mortgage is therefore $1,000 − $150 − $30 − $60 = $760.

PFP Worksheet 33
Calculating Affordable Home Price

Estimating Principal and Interest Payments

Once you know the amount of money you can allocate to the mortgage, you can use time value of money principles to estimate the amount you can borrow. Like the auto loan amount calculation discussed earlier, this is a present value of an annuity problem. You can use a financial calculator, spreadsheet, or formula to calculate the present value of an annuity, but remember that the appropriate interest rate is the *monthly rate*, which is equal to the annual rate divided by 12. If you're unsure of what mortgage rates might apply, you can call your local lender or check on the Internet.

For the latest mortgage rates, go to www.bankrate.com.

Suppose your local lender is currently quoting a rate of 6 percent for a 30-year (360-month) fixed-rate mortgage. The *Go Figure!* box demonstrates how to find the amount you can borrow given this rate using a table in Appendix A so that you don't need a financial calculator. Note that you can't use the PFIVA table in the appendix, Exhibit A–4, to solve the problem, since the

GO FIGURE!

Calculating an Affordable Home Price

Problem: You have $1,000 per month to allocate to housing costs. You estimate the following monthly costs for housing: property taxes, $150; homeowner's insurance, $30 per year; and repairs and maintenance, $60. You have $10,000 available for a down payment and expect closing costs for your loan to total $3,000. What is the maximum you can afford to pay for a home?

Solution: Use the following worksheet to solve the problem:

Step 1.	Monthly amount you can allocate to total housing costs:	**$1,000**
Step 2.	a. Expected cost of property taxes	150
	b. Expected cost of homeowner's insurance	30
	c. Expected cost of repairs and maintenance	60
	d. Expected cost of association dues	0
	Total nonfinancing housing costs (= a + b + c + d)	**240**
	Total available for financing costs (principal and interest) = Step 1 − Step 2	**$760**
Step 3.	a. Mortgage factor$_{i,n}$ (Exhibit A–6, 6%, 360 months)	166.8
	b. × Total available for financing costs (from Step 2)	760
	c. Maximum affordable mortgage amount (= 3a × 3b)	**$126,768**
Step 4.	a. Down payment available	10,000
	b. Gifts from parents or others	0
	c. Expected closing costs	3,000
	d. Maximum house you can afford (= 3b + 4a + 4b − 4c)	**$139,768**

table assumes *annual* payments, whereas mortgage payments are monthly. To calculate present values for *monthly* payments, you need a special table set up with monthly payments and monthly interest rates. Recall that we previously used Exhibit A–5 to solve for monthly payments, given a present value and interest rate. Similarly, Exhibit A–6 provides mortgage factors that you can use to solve for the present value or mortgage amount, given a series of equal monthly payments at a given interest rate i for a period of months n. To use this table, simply multiply the payment times the mortgage factor to get the maximum affordable mortgage amount:

$$\begin{aligned}\text{Maximum mortgage amount} &= \text{Affordable payment} \times \text{Mortgage factor}_{i,n}\\ &= \$760 \times 166.80\\ &= \$126{,}768\end{aligned}$$

Using a financial calculator for the problem above, you can calculate the mortgage amount that you are able to finance with a $760 monthly payment by entering N = number of months = 360, I = monthly interest rate = 6/12 = 0.5, and PMT = affordable mortgage payment = $760 and then solving for the present value, PV = $126,761, the maximum mortgage amount. This is slightly different from the answer we found using the table because of the rounding of the mortgage factors in the table.

How much difference would it make if you could find a lender offering a slightly lower rate? Suppose, for example, that you could get your loan at 5.5 percent. If you look carefully at Exhibit A–6, you can see that as the interest rate gets smaller, the multiplier becomes larger, implying that you can afford a larger mortgage. At 5.5 percent, the affordable mortgage amount would be $760 × 176.12 = $133,851, about $7,000 more. In the early 1980s, when mortgage rates reached all-time highs of slightly more than 18 percent, a payment of $760 would only have paid for a 30-year mortgage of approximately $50,000.

Understand Limits Set by Lenders

Just because you think you can afford a loan of a particular amount doesn't mean that a lender will be willing to lend you that much. Likewise, a lender may be willing to lend you more than you can realistically afford. Lenders commonly use two ratios to evaluate your ability to pay your loan: the debt payment ratio and the mortgage debt service ratio. Recall from Chapter 2 that we previously defined these personal financial ratios as

$$\text{Mortgage debt service ratio} = \frac{\text{Monthly mortgage debt service (PITI)}}{\text{Gross monthly income}}$$

$$\text{Debt payment ratio} = \frac{\text{Total monthly debt payments}}{\text{After-tax monthly income}}$$

$$= \frac{\text{PITI + Nonmortgage debt payments}}{\text{After-tax monthly income}}$$

where PITI is the monthly payment for mortgage principal, interest, property taxes, and homeowner's insurance in both equations. For simplicity, lenders commonly use gross monthly income rather than after-tax monthly income as the denominator for both ratios and adjust their minimums accordingly.

Although the minimums can vary substantially from lender to lender, a common requirement is that the mortgage debt service ratio be no more than 31 percent. In the example above, if your gross monthly income is $3,400, would you qualify for a loan requiring a $760 payment? Based on your estimates, property taxes will total $150 per month and insurance will cost $30, so your total mortgage debt service for this loan would be $940. Thus, your mortgage debt service ratio is

$$\text{Mortgage debt service ratio} = \frac{\$940}{\$3{,}400} = 0.276 \quad \text{or} \quad 27.6\%$$

Since this is lower than the 31 percent maximum, you'd be okay with this ratio.

The maximum debt payment ratio, calculated as a percent of gross rather than after-tax income, is commonly 41 percent, but can range from 33 percent to much more, depending on loan and lender. If your other debt payments include a $300 car loan payment and $125 in minimum payments on credit cards, will you be able to meet the 41 percent maximum in this example? The lender would calculate the following:

$$\text{Debt payment ratio} = \frac{\$940 + \$300 + 125}{\$3{,}400} = 0.401 \quad \text{or} \quad 40.1\%$$

With your current debt payments, you also meet the 41 percent maximum.

If either ratio had been too high, you'd have needed either to take a slightly lower mortgage or to reduce your other debt payments (e.g., by paying off your credit cards). Alternatively, in completing your estimation of an affordable home price, you could adjust your maximum affordable mortgage amount to reflect the maximum you can qualify for. Exhibit 8–6 will help you to get a quick idea of the amount of monthly PITI you could qualify for, given your other debt payments and gross monthly income. Select the column that represents your current monthly debt payments (on car loans and leases, student loans, and credit accounts). Look down the column to

EXHIBIT 8-6

Minimum Gross Monthly Income to Qualify for Mortgage Payment (PITI)

Monthly, Principal Interest, Taxes, and Insurance ($)	Other Monthly Debt Payments ($)						
	100	200	300	400	500	600	700
500	1,613	1,707	1,951	2,195	2,439	2,683	2,927
600	1,935	1,951	2,195	2,439	2,683	2,927	3,171
700	2,258	2,258	2,439	2,683	2,927	3,171	3,415
800	2,581	2,581	2,683	2,927	3,171	3,415	3,659
900	2,903	2,903	2,927	3,171	3,415	3,659	3,902
1,000	3,226	3,226	3,226	3,415	3,659	3,902	4,146
1,200	3,871	3,871	3,871	3,902	4,146	4,390	4,634
1,400	4,516	4,516	4,516	4,516	4,634	4,878	5,122
1,600	5,161	5,161	5,161	5,161	5,161	5,366	5,610

The calculations here assume that the lender requires:

- Mortgage debt service ≤31% of gross monthly income.
- Total debt payments ≤41% of gross monthly income

find the value closest to your monthly gross income. The far left column will tell you the maximum amount of PITI you can qualify for, assuming that the lender limits your PITI to 31 percent of gross income and your total debt payments to no more than 41 percent of gross income.

At www.financenter.com, click on "Calculators for Public Use" to find a Web-based calculator to estimate the type of house you can afford, given your available funds and income.

Maximum Affordable House after Including Other Sources of Funds

The last step in the process of identifying an affordable home price is to take into consideration any other funds you can apply to the purchase and any other expenses you will incur. The total purchase price plus any other costs will be paid for with the mortgage loan proceeds combined with the cash that you plan to apply to the purchase, usually called the down payment.

mortgage insurance premium (MIP)

Insurance charged to a mortgage borrower to protect the lender against the risk of borrower default.

Down Payment Amount. The amount of your down payment is affected by the minimums imposed by lenders, your available cash, and the opportunity cost of using cash for this purpose. First-time home buyers can often obtain mortgages with only 5 percent down, but you should consider trying to make a 20 percent down payment, if possible. If your loan-to-value ratio is less than 80 percent, lenders charge you a **mortgage insurance premium** (MIP) that adds 0.25 to 0.5 percent to your annual interest costs. This insurance is paid by you but benefits only the lender, who is insured against the possibility that you will default on your loan terms.

Even if you can't—or choose not to—make a 20 percent down payment, you'll eventually be able to stop paying the MIP—by law, lenders can't charge for MIP once you've paid down your balance to 80 percent of your home's *original purchase price* (which will take about 10 years on a typical 30-year mortgage originally financed with 5 percent down). Furthermore, if the market value of your home appreciates sufficiently, you can notify your lender to remove the insurance. For example, suppose you buy a $100,000 home and borrow $95,000. If your home appreciates to $120,000 after a couple of years, you can notify the lender to remove the MIP, since 95/120 = 79 percent, which is less than the 80 percent loan-to-value minimum.

Unless you receive a gift exclusively earmarked for helping you to buy a house, any cash you apply to the purchase of a home necessarily reduces your savings. Thus, you need to consider the opportunity cost of using it for this purpose. If you didn't use the money for a down payment—for example, if instead you borrowed more or bought a cheaper house—what would you do with the cash? If the alternative is to invest the money and earn 8 percent when mortgage rates are 6 percent, you would effectively lose 2 percent in interest over the life of your mortgage by using the money for a down payment. For this reason, people tend to maximize their loan amounts when mortgage rates are low relative to investment returns. In contrast, if your investments are earning less than your mortgage financing costs—as in the case where your money is held in bank checking or savings accounts—you're better off applying the money to reducing the amount you need to borrow.

Although it's generally not recommended that you divert retirement funds to nonretirement purposes, new rules do allow first-time home buyers to withdraw funds from individual retirement accounts without incurring penalties if the funds are to be used to purchase a home. These accounts will be discussed more fully in a later chapter.

closing costs

Transaction costs paid at the closing of a home purchase.

closing

Meeting at which participants sign the required paperwork to finalize a home purchase and mortgage agreement.

Expected Closing Costs. Some of your cash will go to paying various costs associated with the real estate transaction—often called **closing costs**, because the meeting where you sign all the required paperwork to finalize your purchase is called the **closing**. These costs, which we consider in more detail later in the chapter, can vary widely and be a substantial drain on your available cash. Your realtor and lender will give you a better idea of what to expect, given the price range you're considering and the other common costs paid by the buyer at closing. In the earlier *Go Figure!* example, for instance, the down payment amount was $10,000 and the closing costs were estimated to be $3,000.

LEARNING objective

5 Select a home that meets your needs and negotiate an acceptable price.

Buying a Home

Once you have a price range in mind, you can begin looking for a home that will meet your needs. In this section, we look at the factors that affect real estate value, the selection of professionals who can help you with this process, and some suggestions for the negotiation of contract terms.

The Determinants of Real Estate Market Value

Although your home purchase decision will no doubt be made based on many factors, including affordability and personal preference, you shouldn't forget that your home is also an investment. As such, you should be sure to consider each alternative property's potential for appreciation in value.

In the real estate business, it a common joke to ask, "What are the three determinants of real estate value?" The answer, as everyone knows, is (1) location, (2) location, and (3) location. Although of course this isn't entirely true, it's true enough that the joke never goes away. A beautiful mansion with all the amenities will still be worth practically nothing if it's located next to a smelly landfill. And a run-down little bungalow on the beachfront in Florida may still be worth a million dollars. A home in a good location will appreciate more quickly and you'll have an easier time reselling it later.

Location includes many related factors—the town, the values of surrounding properties and their use (commercial vs. residential), proximity to (and quality of) schools and transportation, and zoning laws. If you have a house that backs up to a large vacant lot which is zoned for commercial use, you might find that a few years down the road, you will have WalMart in your backyard.

Other factors that influence the value of homes include the type of structure (single- or multi-family), age, characteristics of the structure and land (condition, size, number of rooms/baths, square footage, acreage, landscaping, outbuilding), curb appeal (attractiveness from the street), and asking price relative to value. Perhaps most important, real estate values are determined by what a reasonable buyer is willing to pay for the property, and this is highly dependent on market conditions and mortgage rates at a given time.

Real Estate Brokers

A **real estate broker** or agent is a licensed professional who helps match up buyers and sellers. Since it's likely that you'll buy or sell a home only a few times in your life, having an experienced broker to guide you through the process will make it easier. Brokers' familiarity with the properties for sale in the area and available financing terms and lenders, as well as the negotiation process, can be invaluable to you, and their fee is paid by the seller. When you sell, a broker can also help you price your home more realistically, since psychological factors sometimes cause you to be unrealistic about your home's value, as discussed in the *Money Psychology* box, "It's Hard to Sell the Losers." Although you're not legally required to use a broker, many homes are advertised and shown exclusively through real estate brokers, so you won't have the same selection if you don't use one. Similarly, if you're selling a home, you'll be exposed to a larger number of qualified buyers if you go through a broker.

real estate broker

Professional who helps home owners find buyers for their homes and assists in the purchase transaction, in return for a fee.

Money Psychology

It's Hard to Sell the Losers

Real estate markets, like stock and bond markets, experience bull (up) and bear (down) markets. Homes may appreciate rapidly in value over a short period, but they can also decline in value. Observation of sellers' pricing behavior in the housing market provides support for a behavioral psychology principle called "loss aversion." According to this principle, people experience greater pain when selling at a price that is less than what they paid than they do when selling at a price that is less than some earlier value but that is still greater than what they paid.

As an illustration, consider two homeowners with identical homes in the same neighborhood. Kris bought his home in 1990 for $120,000 and saw the value increase to $200,000 by 2000. Melody bought hers in 2000 for $200,000. In 2004, both homes are worth $180,000. Even though both Kris and Melody have experienced the same loss since 2000, Melody will have a harder time accepting its current lower value and will be more likely to set an unrealistically high asking price. One study showed that sellers facing a loss relative to their original purchase price tended to list their homes at prices that were 25 percent to 35 percent over market value. This initial overpricing means the house takes longer to sell, and the price will eventually have to be lowered anyway.

Note: For more information about loss aversion, see John Nofsinger, *The Psychology of Investing* (Upper Saddle River, N.J.: Prentice-Hall, 2002).

Choosing a Broker. How do you select a broker? As when you're selecting any other professional, you should choose among brokers by evaluating their qualifications and professionalism. What if you go out to look at some houses with a particular broker but decide you don't like her? You're not legally obligated to continue to work with her, but the rule in the industry is that the first broker to show you a particular property is the one who will get the commission. So it pays to do a little homework first and make sure you're working with a professional you feel will best serve your needs.

In your first meeting with a broker, in addition to assessing whether you feel comfortable working with the person, consider asking the following questions:

- How long have you been selling real estate? An experienced agent who is very familiar with the area will be better able to assist you with finding a home and arranging financing.
- Is real estate your primary profession? You don't want a broker who is doing this as a second job. Not only will you get lower-quality service, but this may be an indication that the person can't make a living selling real estate.
- What is your sales track record, and what is the average price of the homes you have sold? This tells you how successful the agent is and whether he or she is familiar with homes in your price range.
- Do you have references from former buyers or sellers you have worked with? Follow up to find out about service, dependability, personality, and handling of paperwork.
- How big is the office you work out of? Larger offices may have more in-house listings. When the market is "hot," the best properties may all be sold before they are even advertised.

commission

Percentage of sales price paid to broker(s) who assist in the sale of a home.

How a Broker Is Paid. Brokers are paid on a **commission** basis by the seller; the commission is a percentage of the negotiated sale price of the house, commonly 6 to 7 percent. Let's say that you buy a house for $100,000 and that two agents are involved in the sale—Pete and Sandra. Pete is the broker who originally contracted with the seller of the house you're buying. Pete is called the *listing broker* and, in a standard listing contract, he is entitled to one-half of the full commission, to be split between himself and the supervising broker in his office. So if the full commission is 6 percent, Pete's commission will be 1.5 percent of the sales price, and his boss will get 1.5 percent as well. Sandra is the broker who originally showed you the house and helped you negotiate the sales price. She is called a *cooperating broker* and is entitled to the other half of the 6 percent, to be shared with her office. Since the sales price is $100,000, the listing broker, the cooperating broker, and each of their managing offices will get $1,500, all paid for by the seller out of the money received from the sale of the home.

agent

A person who is acting on behalf of another through a contractual agreement.

principal

A person who has delegated responsibility to an agent and to whom the agent has a duty.

Your Legal Relationship with a Broker. A real estate broker is an **agent**, which means that he or she has a legal duty to act in the best interests of the **principal** for whom the broker works. Although studies show that most buyers believe that their brokers are acting as their agents—after all, the brokers are taking them to look at houses and then shepherding them through the negotiation and transaction—this is not actually the case. The seller is the one who pays the broker the commission and is therefore the one to whom the broker has a primary legal duty. The relationship between the broker and the buyer is therefore a bit ambiguous, since the broker has an obvious conflict of interest. The objective of the seller is to get the highest price possible for the house, and the objective of the buyer is to pay the lowest amount possible. The broker obviously cannot act in the best interests of both parties. Some states have acted to create a "dual agency" rule under which the broker has legal duties (such as confidentiality and professionalism) to both buyer and seller, but this doesn't really remove the conflict inherent in the negotiation process. A good rule of thumb is to never reveal information to your broker (such as the highest price you're willing to pay) that you don't want relayed to the seller.

buyer broker

A real estate broker who works exclusively for the buyer and owes no legal duty to the seller.

A relatively new development in the real estate brokerage business is the **buyer broker**, a real estate agent who works exclusively for the buyer and has no legal duty to the seller. These agents will help buyers find suitable homes, negotiate the price, and facilitate the transaction without any of the conflicts of interest inherent in the usual real estate broker relationships. This sounds like a good thing; the problem is that these brokers still need to be paid. Since the listing broker's contract is with the seller, a buyer who wants this type of service may have to pay for it separately, with fees ranging from hourly rates to 3.5 percent of the sales price. In some states, a buyer broker may be able to share the seller commission as a cooperating broker.

Negotiating the Contract

Once you find a home that you want to buy, you must initiate the negotiation process. Although your broker may be helpful in this process, you should keep in mind that he or she will get paid about the same amount regardless of the price you negotiate. A $1,000 difference in the price, while significant to you, translates to only a $15 difference in commission. Therefore, you should use your own judgment on whether the "price is right."

Since you already know the price that the seller is asking, you will probably make an offer that is less than this amount. The asking price for a home is usually higher than what it will eventually sell for, since sellers assume that buyers will want to negotiate. Offers commonly focus on price, but may also include other conditions and features as discussed in this section. The seller may counter your suggested price with a new price somewhere between the original price and your offer. If the offer is accepted, a contract will be drawn up and you will be required to make an initial "good faith deposit" that will be applied to your down payment at the closing, and you will then begin to look for mortgage financing.

Although price is obviously the most important term of the contract, other factors may also affect the final purchase agreement, such as which appliances will be included, what costs the seller will pay at closing, when the closing will occur, and what circumstances will allow you to get out of the agreement.

Price. As discussed previously, many factors will influence the value of a home and hence the price you're willing to pay for it. Your broker may be able to offer some advice on this aspect of the negotiation, but you could also consult an appraiser or investigate government records yourself for recent sales prices in the area. In some cases, where the demand for housing is greater than the supply of available units, there will be little or no room for negotiation, and buyers will have to make full-price offers with no conditions to be sure that they get the house they want. At other times, when the market it slow, a house may have been on the market for many months, so the seller may be highly motivated to negotiate.

Conditions. Most purchase offers for houses are made contingent on the buyer's ability to obtain mortgage financing at favorable rates. Your agreement will usually give you 15 to 30 days to find financing. A buyer may also make an offer contingent on selling another home. Although this is clearly in the buyer's best interest, a seller is not generally willing to wait very long.

Other Terms. There are many other items you might want to negotiate. If you don't specify what is included with the house, certain conventions will apply. Although furniture and personal property of the seller are obviously not included (and must be removed from the premises prior to sale), most appliances (except the washer/dryer and sometimes the refrigerator) are included. Light fixtures, window treatments, wall-to-wall carpeting, and landscaping stay with the house unless otherwise agreed. If you inspect the home before closing and find that the seller has removed the dining room chandelier without prior agreement, you can request compensation for that item at the closing.

Mortgage Financing

LEARNING objective

 Choose between financing options and know how to apply for and qualify for a mortgage.

Needless to say, very few people pay for a home purchase in cash. Instead, they finance the purchase by borrowing. In this section, we explore your home financing options.

What Is a Mortgage?

A **mortgage** is a long-term amortized loan that is secured by real property. As you learned in earlier chapters, a secured loan carries a lower interest rate than an unsecured loan because the lender has less at risk. If you don't make your mortgage payments as promised, the lender has the right to foreclose—to take your home in satisfaction of the debt.

mortgage

A long-term amortized loan that is secured by real property.

Mortgages are made by many different types of financial institutions, including depository institutions, such as commercial banks and savings and loans, and nondepository institutions, such as insurance companies. There are also mortgage brokers who, for a fee, shop around and arrange appropriate financing for buyers.

Like other amortized loans, mortgages usually have level payments that include interest and some principal repayment. At the end of the mortgage term, you will have completely paid back the original loan with interest. During the early years of the mortgage, when the balance you owe is high, most of your payment will go toward paying interest. As you gradually pay back the loan, your payment will stay the same, but the interest charge will be a smaller proportion of the total payment, since the balance on which the interest is computed is lower.

The Mortgage Market

primary mortgage market

Market in which lenders originate mortgage loans with borrowers.

secondary mortgage market

Market in which lenders sell mortgages after initial origination.

You'll obtain your mortgage from a lender in the **primary mortgage market**. After originating your mortgage, your lender will most likely sell the loan to another financial institution in the **secondary mortgage market**. This allows your lender to recoup the cash and lend it out again. The lender makes money from the fees you and other borrowers pay for the loan application, origination of the loan, and servicing of the loan (collecting and processing payments).

Secondary mortgage market institutions raise money to buy the loans by selling mortgage-backed securities to investors, investments that are backed by the thousands of mortgages they have in their loan portfolios. The buyers of mortgage-backed securities receive a proportionate share of the interest and principal repayments made by you and other borrowers. Understanding a little about the secondary mortgage market is important because the buyers of loans in that market, such as the Federal Home Loan Mortgage Corporation (commonly called FreddieMac) and the Federal National Mortgage Association (commonly called FannieMae), impose loan-to-value and other ratio restrictions that mortgage lenders must apply to mortgages they make.

Types of Mortgages

Many types of mortgages can be found in the marketplace today, but all fall into a few general categories that differ in the contractual terms related to interest rates, term to maturity, and type of payment.

conventional mortgage

A fixed-rate, fixed term, fixed payment mortgage loan.

Conventional Mortgages. A **conventional mortgage** is a fixed-rate, fixed-term, fixed-payment loan. Rates vary with market conditions and borrower qualifications but, once contracted for, are fixed for the life of the loan, which is commonly 15, 20, 25, or 30 years. Payments are fixed as well and made monthly. For example, a \$100,000 30-year conventional mortgage at 6 percent interest will have fixed payments of \$599.55 per month for 360 months. As mentioned, a portion of the monthly payment will go toward paying interest on the balance owed, and the remainder will be applied to repayment of principal. In the first month, for example, your interest will amount to 0.5 percent (6% divided by 12 months) of the mortgage amount of \$100,000, or \$500. The remaining \$99.55 will go toward paying back part of the principal. In the next month, you'll owe 0.5 percent interest of the new balance, \$99,900.45 (\$100,000 − \$99.55), or \$499.50. Since the monthly payment is fixed and the interest portion is declining over time (as you gradually reduce your loan amount through the repayment of principal), you'll be applying more to the principal with each payment.

Insured Mortgages. To help certain home buyers qualify for mortgages, the Veterans Administration (VA) and the Federal Housing Authority (FHA) offer insurance for conventional loans under certain circumstances. These agencies do not actually provide the mortgage financing money—they simply guarantee to pay lenders (usually banks and savings institutions) the promised interest and principal if the borrower defaults. This guarantee makes lenders more willing to provide favorable financing terms to buyers with higher loan-to-value ratios and less income. Minimum down payments range from 3 to 5 percent, and these loans commonly require the payment of points, which are discussed below.

adjustable-rate mortgage (ARM)

Mortgage loan with an interest rate that, by contract, varies over time with market conditions.

Adjustable-Rate Mortgages (ARMs). An **adjustable-rate mortgage (ARM)** has an interest rate that changes over time with market conditions. Since the lender is less exposed to the risk that mortgage rates in the market will rise to exceed the rate being paid by the borrower, the initial rates on ARMS are generally from one to three percentage points lower than those on conventional mortgages. Changes in the rate over time are governed by the terms of the mortgage contract. Most commonly, the rate will adjust based on changes in a defined index or market rate, such as the 10 year Treasury bond rate or the prime rate, every one or two years. The amount that the rate can change is limited by **interest rate caps**, which apply to both the change per year and the total change over the life of the loan. You might, for example, have an ARM with an initial rate of 4 percent, an annual rate cap of 1 percent, and a lifetime rate cap of 5 percent. The most you will ever pay on that loan is 9 percent per year (the original rate plus the lifetime rate cap), and you will never see a larger increase than one percentage point per year. However, the payment might grow to be more than you can afford. If you borrow $100,000, your payment at 4 percent is only $477 per month, but if rates rise steadily over the next five years, the payment could increase to more than $700 by year 5.

interest rate caps

Caps on annual and lifetime increases in an ARM interest rate.

Some ARMs also have a payment cap, which limits the amount that your payment can change over the life of the loan. Although this will protect you from payment increases that you can't afford, a payment limit that is less than the amount of interest you owe for the period will result in **negative amortization**—that is, the unpaid interest will be added to the balance owed on the loan. This may mean that, at the end of the loan term, you will still owe some additional principal to the lender.

negative amortization

Addition to loan balance that occurs when the monthly payment is insufficient to cover the monthly interest cost.

Many variations on ARMs have been developed over the last several years. In addition to variations in interest rate caps and payment caps, you can find ARMs that are convertible to fixed-rate loans at some point in the future, ARMs that are fixed for several years at the outset of the loan, and ARMS that adjust only once during the life of the loan, usually at around year 7. In all these cases, the innovations have been designed to help reduce lender risk and to help borrowers qualify for loans and afford the payments.

Balloon Mortgages.

As noted in Chapter 7, a balloon is a loan for which the final payment is much larger than the earlier, regular payments. The payments are calculated based on a long amortization schedule, as in conventional fixed-rate mortgages, but the payments don't continue for the full length of the schedule. Instead, the entire balance is due at a specified point, usually 5 to 10 years after the mortgage begins. This type of loan was popular during the mid-1980s, when interest rates were very high and lenders expected that borrowers would be refinancing as rates fell.

Graduated Payment Mortgage.

Another innovation in the mortgage market is the **graduated payment mortgage**, which carries a fixed rate of interest but allows payments to be lower in the early years and increase over the life of the loan. Since the costs are shifted to later years, you may be able to qualify for a larger loan balance with this type of loan. However, this type of arrangement will produce negative amortization in the early years of the loan. As in the case of the payment caps on certain ARMs, discussed above, this implies that your mortgage balance will actually increase. If you think that home values will rise proportionately and that you'll have the income necessary to support the higher future payments, a graduated payment mortgage might be an appropriate choice for you.

graduated payment mortgage

Mortgage that allows for gradually increasing payments over the life of the loan, resulting in negative amortization during the early years.

A similar arrangement called a **lender buy-down mortgage** allows borrowers to have lower early-year costs but doesn't result in negative amortization. In this type of loan, the rate changes on a set schedule to produce gradual increases in the payment. Higher rates in the later years of the mortgage offset the slightly reduced rates in the early years.

lender buy-down mortgage

Mortgage that imposes a schedule of increasing interest rates over the life of the loan, resulting in gradually increasing payments.

Growing Equity Mortgage.

Payments on a **growing equity mortgage** also increase over time, but the added amounts are applied to the principal so that the loan balance can be paid off more quickly. A common form of this type of loan is the **bi-weekly mortgage**, sometimes call the 26-pay mortgage. Here, you make payments every two weeks in an amount equal to half the amount you would have paid per month on your conventional fixed-rate, fixed-payment loan. Since there are 52 weeks in the year, you'll make the equivalent of an extra monthly payment over the course of each year, and this amount is applied to principal. Of course, you can generally accomplish this result on your own by making extra principal payments throughout the life of the loan.

growing equity mortgage

A mortgage whose payments increase over time, with the increase applied to reduce the balance owed on the loan.

bi-weekly mortgage

An arrangement in which mortgage payments are made every two weeks in an amount equal to half the required monthly payment, resulting in an extra month's payment over the course of a year.

shared appreciation mortgage

Mortgage that gives a lender the right to a proportion of the increase in the value of the home in return for a lower rate of interest.

reverse annuity mortgage

An arrangement in which the homeowner sells equity in a home in return for a stream of income but retains the use of the home.

Shared Appreciation Mortgage. In a **shared appreciation mortgage**, the buyer agrees to share the increase in value of the home with the lender when the home is sold. In return for this promise, the lender charges a much lower rate of interest, often one-third or more lower than the going rate on conventional loans.

Reverse Annuity Mortgage. If you have a great deal of equity in your home and would like to apply the cash to something else, you may be able to access this cash through a **reverse annuity mortgage**, also known as a home equity conversion mortgage. A financial company will take the equity in your home and convert it to a tax-free stream of payments, either for life (which will generally result in a lower amount per year) or for a certain term. Older homeowners who need cash but don't want to sell their homes can use this as a method of financing their living expenses in retirement.

Factors Affecting Mortgage Payments

With what you already know about the valuation of annuities, you can probably guess at the factors that will affect mortgage payments. The most important ones are discussed below.

Term. All else being equal, the longer the term of the loan, the smaller the mortgage payment. Most lenders now offer both 15- and 30-year mortgages. The payment for a 15-year mortgage will generally be 30 to 40 percent greater than that for a 30-year mortgage. Most lenders will give you a lower interest rate for the 15-year mortgage.

Interest Rate. The higher the annual percentage rate charged on a mortgage, the larger the mortgage payment. Take a look at the payment table in Appendix A (Exhibit A–5) to see this. At 6 percent per year, the monthly payment factor is 5.996 for every $1,000 of the mortgage loan. At 7 percent, the factor is 6.653 for every $1,000, almost 11 percent more than the 6 percent factor. Similarly, the 8 percent payment factor of 7.338 is 10.3 percent higher than the 7 percent factor. In general, for every percentage-point increase in the rate, you will pay about 10 percent more per month in your mortgage payment. Although the increase is not proportional, this is still a good rule of thumb to use for a rough estimate.

discount points

Interest paid up front to a lender in return for a reduction in annual rate on a mortgage.

Points. Lenders often let you pay **discount points** to reduce your loan interest rate. A point is 1 percent of the loan amount, so for a $70,000 mortgage, one point is equal to $700. The points required for a specific rate reduction vary over time with competition and market conditions. In deciding whether to pay points in return for a lower rate or to take a higher rate and pay no points, you need to evaluate the up-front cost against the present value of future reduced interest payments. The *Go Figure!* box, "Comparing Mortgages," describes this calculation in more detail.

Economic Factors. Mortgage rates vary widely over time with different economic conditions. In the last 25 years, the average annual mortgage rate has ranged from less than 5 percent to more than 18 percent. More recently, rates have been attractively low, allowing homebuyers to afford more expensive homes and homeowners to refinance their original mortgage loans to free up cash for other purposes. Most economic forecasters predict that mortgage rates will return to the 7 to 8 percent range in the future.

Location. Although the mortgage market is increasingly national in scope, rates may still be lower in some areas of the country than in others. For this reason, you shouldn't limit your search for a lender to local companies. Although you might get a little more personal service locally, remember that the local lender is going to sell your loan anyway, so it's probably more important to get the best deal you can.

Your Default Risk. Your mortgage payment is also affected by the risk that you represent to the lender. If your ratios are too high or if you have a less-than-perfect credit history, you'll end up paying higher interest and having fewer loan options. As you learned in Chapter 7, lenders use credit bureau reports to consider your creditworthiness. If you have a poor credit history—prior loan defaults, late payments, or too much debt—you won't be eligible for favorable mortgage terms.

GO FIGURE!

Comparing Mortgages

Problem: You are deciding between a $70,000 15-year mortgage at 6 percent and a 30-year mortgage at 6.5 percent. In either case, you have the opportunity to buy down the rate by 0.5% with the payment of one point up front. What should you do?

Solution: In considering your mortgage choices, you should evaluate the difference in payments, your opportunity costs, and the total interest costs over the time you will own the home. You can construct a comparison chart like the one below in Excel or by using the amortization spreadsheet template on the text website.

1. *Term of loan.* The total of all payments on a 30-year loan will be about 50 percent greater than the total payments on the 15-year loan in this example, and you'll pay about $2\frac{1}{2}$ times as much in interest over the life of the loan. Balance that against the additional cash flow you'll have for the first 15 years of the longer loan—money that you can apply to other uses, such as a retirement savings plan. The opportunity cost is the amount you could earn on those dollars. If you can earn more than the interest cost of the mortgage, it would make financial sense to invest the money instead.
2. *Paying points.* One point for a $70,000 mortgage is $700 up front. For the 30-year mortgage, the difference in total payments is $5,309 − $5,036 = $273 per year, so it will take approximately $700/273 = 2.6 years to recoup that cost. If you expect to keep the home that long and have sufficient cash to do so, then it may be worthwhile to pay the extra amount up front.

	15-Year Mortgage		30-Year Mortgage	
	6%, No Points	5.50%, 1 Point	6.50%, No Points	6%, 1 Point
Mortgage payment				
Monthly	$590.70	$571.96	$442.45	$419.69
Annual	$7,088.40	$6,863.52	$5,309.40	$5,036.28
Total	$106,326.00	$102,952.80	$159,282.00	$151,088.40
Interest paid				
1 year	$4,119.23	$3,772.86	$4,526.96	$4,176.62
5 years	$18,648.36	$17,019.80	$22,074.54	$20,319.17
15 years	$36,326.00	$32,952.80	$60,431.97	$55,277.56
30 years	N/A	N/A	$89,282.00	$81,088.40
Remaining balance				
1 year	$67,030.83	$66,609.36	$69,217.72	$69,140.39
5 years	$53,206.37	$52,702.30	$65,614.72	$65,138.05
15 years	$0.00	$0.00	$50,957.82	$49,904.36
30 years	N/A	N/A	0	0

The Property. Lenders also evaluate the property that you're purchasing. Based on an independent appraisal, they try to ensure that the loan-to-value ratio is low enough to meet their requirements. Appraisers assign a value to your home most often based on recent sales prices of comparable homes in your area.

Learning by Doing 8-4

1. All else being equal, which of the following are likely to increase the price of the house you can afford to buy?
   a. Increasing mortgage rates
   b. Longer mortgage term
   c. Higher gross income
   d. Better credit history
   e. Fixed-rate mortgage rather than adjustable

good faith estimate

An estimate of loan costs provided by the lender to the borrower.

The Mortgage Application

After finalizing a purchase contract and shopping around to evaluate your mortgage options, you need to select a lender and make a formal loan application. You can use the four P's from Chapter 5 (price, product, people, and place) to help you evaluate potential lenders. Although you may be most concerned with the rates a lender offers, the lenders with the lowest rates may also be slower at processing loans. If your loan will be sold in the secondary market, the location of the lender is not very important.

Once you have applied for the loan, the lender by law must provide you with a **good faith estimate** of the costs associated with the transaction, including the APR, all fees, and all costs you will incur in closing the loan. The application can usually be processed within a few days but may take longer during very busy times (as when rates have recently fallen and many homeowners are refinancing).

Mortgage rates may change, favorably or unfavorably for you, between the time you apply for a loan and the time you complete the transaction. If rates are rising, you may want to get a **lock-in** from your lender, which guarantees you a particular rate even if rates rise before your closing date. Some lenders will lock in within 30 or 45 days of closing at no charge, but others may require that you pay a point or a portion of a point for a lock-in. What if rates fall? With most lock-in agreements, you won't be entitled to have your rate reduced when rates fall before the closing.

Fact #4

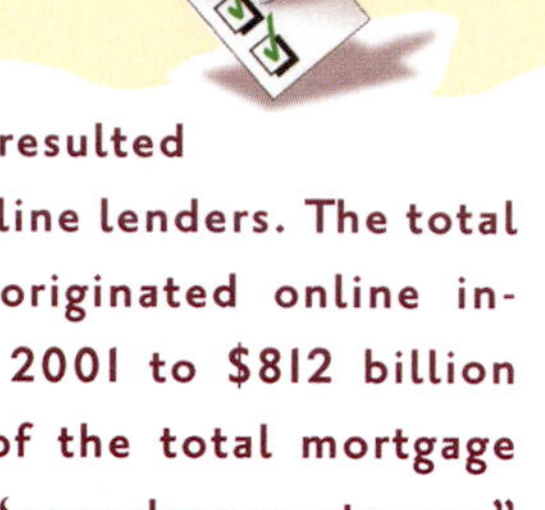

The growth of the Internet has resulted in greater competition from online lenders. The total dollar amount of mortgages originated online increased from $266 billion in 2001 to $812 billion 2003, more than one-fourth of the total mortgage market. Uniform standards for "paperless mortgages" were put in place in 2003, and federal law now allows electronic signatures, so it is expected that these numbers will continue to increase.

lock-in

Agreement with a lender that guarantees a particular mortgage interest rate at closing.

refinancing

Obtaining a new mortgage to pay off a previous, usually higher-rate mortgage.

Refinancing Your Mortgage

Although the preceding discussion has focused on getting a mortgage to buy a home, there are many circumstances when you may want to consider obtaining a new mortgage to pay off your old mortgage, a process called **refinancing**. Suppose you bought a home and financed it with a 7 percent mortgage. Mortgage rates have now fallen to 6 percent. If you refinance by taking out a new mortgage, you'll be able to reduce your mortgage payment. Although it might seem like a simple problem—exchanging the old rate for the new rate and the higher payment for a lower payment—the many costs associated with refinancing might outweigh the benefits of refinancing. You should make this decision by comparing the refinancing costs with the present value of the reduction in after-tax mortgage interest costs, taking into account the probable amount of time you'll own the home. As a result of large rate reductions in the last several years, it is estimated that about half of all existing mortgages have been refinanced.

Reasons to Refinance. What are some good reasons for refinancing? First and foremost, if you'll save money by doing so, then it makes financial sense to refinance. A second reason to refinance is to access your home equity. Although you can do this with a second mortgage, it's often cheaper to do so by refinancing your first mortgage for a larger amount. Again, you need to evaluate both choices to see which one is better for you.

Another good reason to refinance is to reduce the term of your mortgage. If you have 25 years to go on your current mortgage and the lower rate will allow you to reduce the term to 15 years for a similar monthly payment, this might be a good financial move.

Costs of Refinancing. Since a refinance is a completely new mortgage, you will incur most of the same mortgage-related finance charges. You may get a little break on the cost of an appraisal if the lender asks the same appraiser to do an update appraisal. Title insurance companies will charge a slightly reduced rate relative to the original rate to transfer the insurance to the new loan. In addition, some loans carry a prepayment penalty, which means that you will have to pay a fee if you cancel the loan prior to the end of its original term.

When to Refinance. You can get a rough estimate of whether a rate change is sufficient to make refinancing worthwhile by using the following calculation:

1. Estimate the change in monthly payment.
2. Estimate the closing costs for refinancing the loan.

3. Divide the nonescrow closing costs by the payment savings to determine the number of months it will take to recoup the closing costs.

Although you know your current payment, you'll need to know how much you're financing with the new loan to estimate the new payment. If you've been making mortgage payments for several years, you'll have paid off some of the original mortgage, so you can refinance a smaller amount. In some cases, lenders may allow you to add the closing costs to the loan balance so that you don't have to bring any cash to the closing. This may seem attractive but is not necessarily a good idea, since it means you'll be paying interest on these costs for years to come.

Fact #5

You will often hear rules of thumb like "if rates fall 1.5 percentage points, then you should refinance," but this is not necessarily the case. The advisability of refinancing depends on whether the present value of the reduction in future payments will be greater than your costs to refinance. The amount of reduction in rate that will make it worthwhile depends on whether you keep the home long enough to recoup the costs.

To estimate the mortgage payoff amount, you can use the same method described in Chapter 7 in the *Go Figure!* box, "Calculating Simple Interest Loan Payoffs." You can also use the amortization schedule on the text website. This calculation can be helpful if you're thinking about selling your home and need to know what the mortgage payoff will be. Exhibit 8–7 reproduces a portion of a monthly amortization schedule for the 7 percent mortgage above. At the beginning of the twentieth month of the loan repayment schedule, you owe a balance of $68,850 and you expect closing costs to total $2,000. If you don't finance the closing costs, the monthly payment on your new 30-year mortgage at the 6 percent rate will be $412.79, which will save you $53 per month. The present value of saving $53 per month for 360 months, if we assume you could earn 6 percent per year on the invested funds, is $8,840, which more than offsets your expected $2,000 closing costs. (Enter $N = 360$, $I = 6/12 = 0.5$, and $PMT = 53$; solve for $PV = \$8{,}840$). This analysis however, assumes you will stay in the home for 30 years. If this isn't the case, you should substitute the expected number of months. As mentioned earlier, you can roughly estimate whether refinancing is worthwhile by dividing the closing costs by the monthly savings to find the number of months it will take to recoup the cost. This estimate gives us $2,000/$53, or 38 months, a conservative estimate since it doesn't incorporate potential investment earnings on the funds. So if you plan to remain in the home for more than three years, the new loan makes financial sense.

EXHIBIT 8-7

Partial Amortization Schedule, 30-year 7% loan for $70,000

Month	Beginning Balance	Monthly Payment	Monthly Interest	Principal Repaid	Total Cumulative Interest	Total Principal Repaid
1	$70,000.00	$465.71	$408.33	$57.38	$408.33	$57.38
2	$69,942.62	$465.71	$408.00	$57.71	$816.33	$115.09
3	$69,884.91	$465.71	$407.66	$58.05	$1,233.99	$173.14
4	$69,826.86	$465.71	$407.32	$58.39	$1,631.32	$231.53
5	$69,768.47	$456.71	$406.98	$58.73	$2,038.30	$290.26
6	$69,709.74	$465.71	$406.64	$59.07	$2,444.94	$349.33
7	$69,650.67	$465.71	$406.30	$59.42	$2,581.24	$408.75
8	$69,591.25	$465.71	$405.95	$59.76	$3,257.18	$468.51
9	$69,531.49	$465.71	$405.60	$60.11	$3,662.79	$528.62
10	$69.471.38	$465.71	$405.25	$60.46	$4,068.03	$589.08
11	$69,410.92	$465.71	$404.90	$60.81	$4,472.93	$649.90
12	$69,350.10	$465.71	$404.54	$61.17	$4,877.47	$711.07
13	$69,288.93	$465.71	$404.19	$61.53	$5,281.66	$772.59
14	$69,227.41	$465.71	$402.83	$61.89	$5,685.49	$834.48
15	$69,165.52	$465.71	$403.47	$62.25	$6,088.95	$869.72
16	$69,103.28	$465.71	$403.10	$62.61	$6,492.05	$959.33
17	$69,040.67	$465.71	$402.74	$62.97	$6,894.79	$1,022.31
18	$68,977.69	$465.71	$402.37	$63.34	$7,297.16	$1,085.65
19	$68,914.35	$465.71	$402.00	$63.71	$7,699.16	$1,149.36
20	$68,850.64	$465.71	$401.63	$64.08	$8,100.79	$1,213.44
*	*	*	*	*	*	*
*	*	*	*	*	*	*
*	*	*	*	*	*	*

At www.mortgagecalc.com, you can generate an amortization schedule for a mortgage loan by entering the interest rate and time period.

If you finance the closing costs, adding the $2,000 to the borrowed amount, the new mortgage amount will be $70,850. At the 6 percent rate, your new payment will be $424.78, which will still save you $41 per month. In addition to consideration of the reduced monthly payments, your analysis should take into account the added years if you have refinanced a shorter loan with a new 30-year loan, any prepayment penalties on your previous mortgage, and uncertainty associated with how long you'll stay in the home.

Completing the Real Estate Transaction

Your home purchase and mortgage financing will be finalized at the real estate closing or settlement. In this section, we outline what happens at this meeting and the costs you can expect to pay.

At a real estate closing, there are numerous documents to sign.

The Closing

The date of the closing is set by the mutual agreement of the buyer, seller, and lender. Prior to that date, your lender will give you a detailed accounting of the mortgage-related costs and you will also receive an accounting of the other purchase-related funds that will be collected and disbursed at the closing, such as property tax and insurance escrows discussed in the following section. Most important, you will be told the specific amount of funds (usually in the form of a certified check) that you must bring to the closing. Before coming to the closing—usually earlier on the same day—you'll have an opportunity to inspect the property to be certain that the former owners have removed all of their belongings and that it's in the agreed upon condition. Any problems you find can then be negotiated at the closing. The location of the closing is also agreed upon in advance and is usually at the office of a title insurer, real estate broker, or lawyer who is involved in the transaction.

At the actual closing, which will usually take no more than an hour, you, the seller, and the lender or the lender's legal representative will sign all the necessary legal documents to transfer property ownership to you, record the transaction, and finalize the mortgage. Although this can vary from state to state, in most cases, a title insurance agent collects and disburses the funds and ensures that all the closing costs are paid to the appropriate parties and governmental units.

Closing Costs

A number of expenses must be paid by you and the seller at the closing. These closing or settlement costs are identified in Exhibit 8–8 but are difficult to quantify, since every purchase and financing transaction is unique. Some of the more important costs related to your mortgage, tax and insurance escrows, and title insurance are discussed below.

Mortgage Costs. Your good faith estimate from the lender will identify the mortgage-related costs fairly accurately. In addition, you'll bring the remainder of the down payment to the closing. With your down payment, the total cost of the mortgage, including applications fee, credit report, points, loan origination fee, and interest to the end of the month, can easily add up to a large dollar amount.

escrow account

A reserve account held by the mortgage lender in which it collects a monthly prepayment of property taxes and insurance and then pays these bills as they come due.

Escrows. Lenders commonly agree to take responsibility for making sure your property tax and homeowner's insurance payments are made in a timely fashion. To make this possible, you will include money for taxes and insurance in each monthly mortgage payment. The lender will collect some amount in advance at the closing to hold in an **escrow account**, and will then use the funds in the account, together with additions from your monthly payments, to pay your taxes and insurance premiums as they come due. Although two months' payment of each is usually collected at closing, your lender may require as many as six months' payment in advance, depending on when the tax and insurance bills are due. If your property taxes and homeowner's insurance total $1,200 per year, your monthly mortgage payment will be $1,200/12 = $100 more than your principal and interest

EXHIBIT 8-8

Closing Costs

Total closing costs will range from 2 to 6% of the mortgage amount.

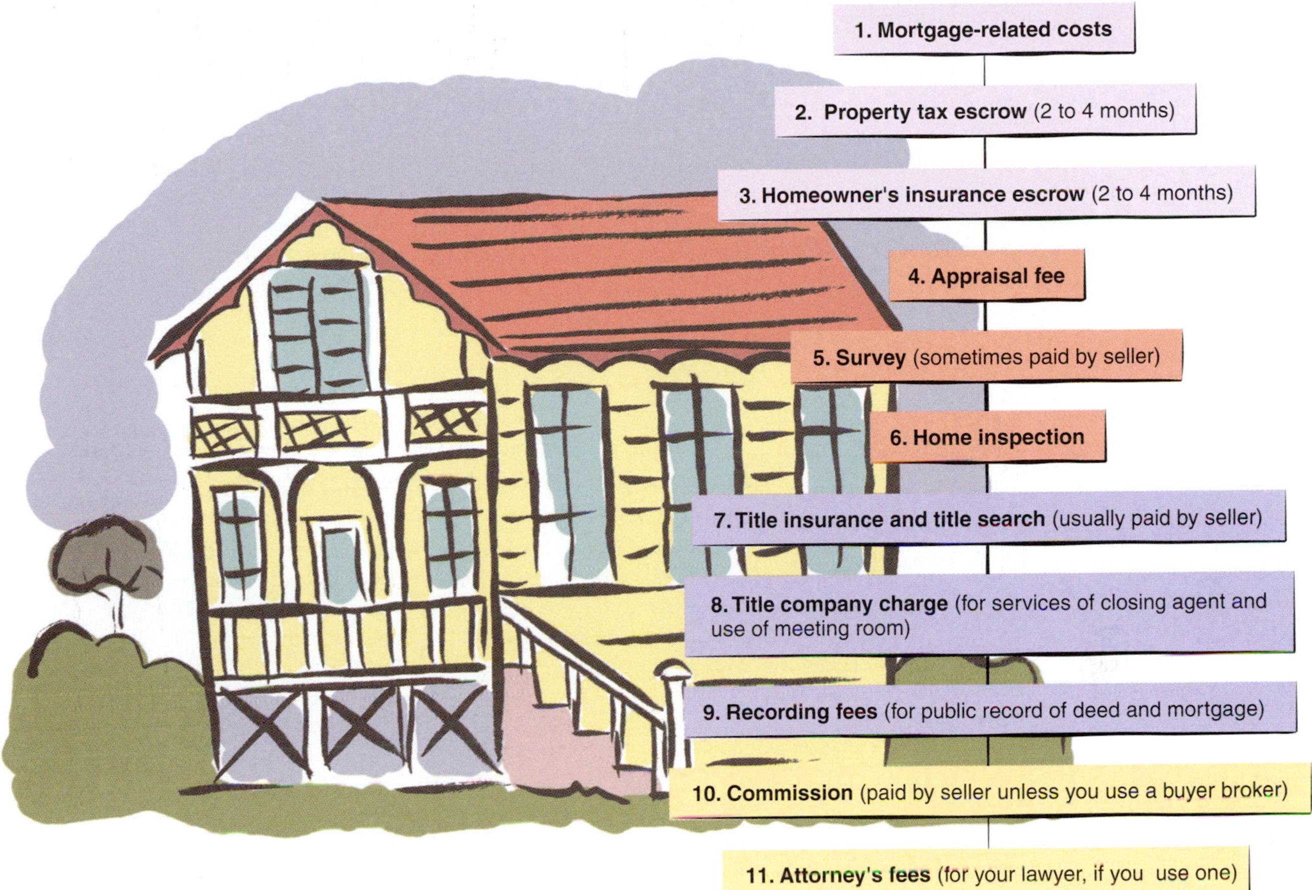

alone, but you will have to pay $200 to $600 at the closing to establish the escrow account. In the future, if these bills go up, your lender will adjust your payment amount to reflect the change.

Title Insurance. The seller has promised to give you ownership of the property you're buying. But what if the seller doesn't actually own it? The purpose of title insurance is to verify the seller's legal ownership of the property and to ensure that there aren't any other claims on the property that might interfere with the buyer's future ownership. The title insurance company researches this information and identifies any potential problems so that they can be cleared up prior to the closing. After you purchase the property, the title company protects you and the lender from any financial losses resulting from problems with the title to the property. Rates for title insurance vary but are based on the value of the home.

Summary

1 **Evaluate your automobile needs and determine what you can afford.** Before purchasing a car, you should carefully consider your needs and the impact of the purchase or lease on your financial plan. This requires that you revisit your budget and that you recognize the total costs of automobile ownership, which can be significantly more than just the monthly loan or lease payment. Your choice of vehicle should be based on an analysis of alternatives, using predefined criteria.

2 **Decide between automobile financing alternatives.** There are many choices for automobile financing. In deciding whether to lease or buy and borrow, you should carefully analyze the terms of alternative contracts to determine which is financially more attractive, given your expected usage of the vehicle and financing costs.

3 **Be an informed automobile consumer.** Whether you lease or buy a vehicle, it's important to negotiate the best possible terms. A lower price will reduce the amount to be financed in the case of a purchase

and the depreciation charge in the case of a lease. To negotiate effectively, you should understand the components of dealer profit and know the vehicle's market value. In the event that your car turns out to be defective, there are certain state laws that might protect you.

4 **Evaluate your housing needs and determine what you can afford.** Housing needs change over the life cycle and with changes in life circumstances. Housing decisions should be made in light of the household budget and prioritized financial goals. Before deciding whether to rent or buy, you should carefully evaluate the advantages and disadvantages of each. If you decide to buy a home, you should determine the price range in advance by considering your budget allocation to housing costs and taking into account the nonfinancing costs associated with home ownership.

5 **Select a home that meets your needs and negotiate an acceptable price.** In the process of finding a home to buy and negotiating a purchase price, you may find it beneficial to use the services of a real estate broker. The market value of the home will primarily be determined by its attributes—where it is located, its size, and its characteristics—and the values of similar properties in the area.

6 **Choose between financing options and know how to apply for and qualify for a mortgage.** Most home purchases are financed with a long-term mortgage loan, which can be either fixed-rate or variable-rate. There are many sources of mortgage financing, so it pays to shop around for the best terms and rates. When mortgage rates drop significantly, it may be financially worthwhile to refinance your mortgage.

Key Terms

adjustable-rate mortgage (ARM) (260)
agent (258)
assessment ratio (252)
bi-weekly mortgage (261)
buyer broker (258)
closed-end lease (244)
closing (256)
closing costs (256)
commission (258)
conventional mortgage (260)
dealer's invoice price (240)
depreciation (238)
discount points (262)
escrow account (266)
express warranty (243)
extended warranty (243)
good faith estimate (264)
graduated payment mortgage (261)
growing equity mortgage (261)
implied warranty (243)
interest rate caps (261)
lender buy-down mortgage (261)
lemon law (248)
lessee (244)
lessor (244)
limited warranty (243)
lock-in (264)
mortgage (259)
mortgage insurance premium (MIP) (256)
negative amortization (261)
open-end lease (244)
sticker price (240)
primary mortgage market (260)
principal (258)
property tax rate (252)
real estate broker (257)
refinancing (264)
reverse annuity mortgage (262)
secondary mortgage market (260)
security deposit (250)
shared appreciation mortgage (262)

Key Calculations

$$\text{Assessed value} = \text{Market value} \times \text{Assessment ratio}$$

$$\text{Property tax} = \frac{\text{Assessed value}}{1{,}000} \times \text{Property tax rate}$$

Concept Review Questions

1. Explain the process that should be followed in making auto and housing decisions.
2. Why is it important to evaluate your budget before making an auto or housing decision?
3. In addition to financing costs, what other costs do you incur when you buy or lease a car? Which of these costs are fixed, and which are variable? Why does that matter?
4. How do you take depreciation into account in the selection of a vehicle?
5. What are the key factors to consider in deciding whether to buy or lease a vehicle?
6. Explain the difference between sticker price and dealer's invoice price. Why is it important to know the dealer's invoice price when buying a new car?
7. How do warranties differ for new and used cars?
8. Where can you get information on the fuel efficiency and safety of various vehicles? Why are these features important?
9. What is the difference between a full warranty and a limited warranty? What type of warranty typically comes with a new car?
10. What is an extended warranty? What factors should you consider in deciding whether to buy one for your vehicle?
11. What is an automobile lease, and how does it differ from an automobile loan?
12. What is the difference between a closed-end lease and an open-end lease? Which one places more risk on the lessee?
13. Explain the following lease terminology:
    - **a.** gross capitalized cost
    - **b.** capitalized cost reduction
    - **c.** residual value
    - **d.** rent charge
    - **e.** mileage limit
    - **f.** purchase option
    - **g.** disposition fee

14. Why is it important to negotiate the price of a car even when you are leasing instead of buying?
15. Why are loan payments higher than lease payments on the same vehicle?
16. At the end of a lease, what rights related to the vehicle do you have?
17. If you tend to put more wear and tear on your vehicle than average, why might it be better to buy a car than to lease it?
18. What are the sources of automobile dealer profit? Why is it important to understand what they are?
19. Why do car salespeople like you to focus on the monthly payment amount rather than on other terms of the purchase or lease?
20. What is a lemon law and how does it protect automobile buyers?
21. Explain how housing needs may change over the life cycle.
22. What are the tax advantages of home ownership?
23. What factors should be taken into account in deciding whether to rent or buy a home?
24. In an apartment lease agreement, what is a security deposit, and what is it used for?
25. Describe the potential consequences of the following:
    a. failing to make your rent payment
    b. failing to pay your mortgage payments
26. Explain how to estimate the maximum home price you can afford.
27. In addition to mortgage principal and interest costs, what other costs of home ownership should you take into account in estimating the total monthly impact of home ownership on your budget?
28. What is property tax, and how is it calculated?
29. What ratios do lenders commonly use to determine how large a loan you can qualify for? Why are they interested in these ratios?
30. Under what circumstances will you be required to pay private mortgage insurance (PMI)?
31. What is a real estate closing? What costs are you likely to have to pay at the closing?
32. What are the three most important determinants of real estate value?
33. What are real estate brokers? To whom do they owe their primary duty?
34. How are real estate brokers usually paid?
35. Explain the difference between a conventional mortgage and an adjustable-rate mortgage. Why are the rates on ARMs usually lower than those on conventional loans?
36. When rates are low and expected to increase in the future, is it better to take an ARM or a conventional mortgage? Explain.
37. What is negative amortization, and to what types of loans does it commonly apply?
38. What method should you use to decide whether to refinance an existing mortgage?

Application Problems

1. ***Total Costs of Automobile Ownership.*** Given the following information, calculate the total costs of automobile ownership, including finance costs, and the per mile cost for the first year of ownership, assuming you pay $14,000 for the car:
   Loan amount $12,000, 48 months, 8 percent APR
   Incremental mileage driven: 5,000 per year
   Average cost of gasoline: $1.70 per gallon
   Miles per gallon: 22
   First-year depreciation: $3,000
   Incremental insurance cost: $200
   Registration and license: $250
   Sales tax: 4 percent of sales price
   Regular oil changes: $120
2. ***Costs of Automobiles.*** Assume you own a car that gets 20 miles per gallon on average. If you typically drive 16,000 miles per year and the price of gasoline goes up from $1.65 per gallon to $1.95 per gallon, what is your additional cost per year?
3. ***Finance Charges.*** Assume that you are considering the purchase of a used car for $6,000. You have been offered the following terms by your lender: 48-month loan at 6 percent APR or 36-month loan at 5 percent APR.
    a. Calculate the monthly payment under each of those alternatives.
    b. Which of these loans will result in greater total interest charges?
    c. What factors should you consider in deciding between these two alternatives?
4. ***Car Loan Payments and Balance Owed.*** You bought a car three years ago for $20,000 and financed $16,000 at 6 percent simple interest for 60 months. You are now thinking about trading in your vehicle for a new one and would like to know how much you still owe on the loan.
    a. What is your monthly payment?
    b. Assuming that you have made 36 payments so far, what is the balance remaining on your loan? (You can solve this with a financial calculator or construct an amortization table.)
5. ***Auto Lease Versus Buy Decisions.*** Based on what you know about leases, under what conditions would a lease make the most sense?
6. ***Mileage Penalties.*** Your lease includes a mileage penalty of 25 cents per mile in excess of 12,000 miles per year. At the end of your three-year lease, your mileage is 40,000. How much will you owe to the lessor for the extra mileage?
7. ***Rent Versus Buy.*** Maria is comparing two housing alternatives. She can rent an apartment for $800 per month, or $9,600 per year. The security deposit is $1,200 ($1\frac{1}{2}$ months rent). Renter's insurance is $140 per year. Alternatively, she can buy a condominium and will incur the following costs: annual mortgage payments, $7,200 (of which $5,966 is interest); property tax, $1,300; insurance and maintenance, $500; down payment and closing costs, $5,000; annual increase in value, $4,000. She earns 2 percent on her savings account after tax, and her marginal tax rate is 25 percent. Based on her first-year costs, which alternative will have a lower cost? What would you recommend to Maria and why?
8. ***Mortgage Payments.*** Calculate the mortgage payments for each of the following conventional mortgages, assuming a loan amount of $75,000:
    a. 30-year loan at 8 percent
    b. 15-year loan at 8 percent
    c. 15-year loan at 6 percent
9. ***Adjustable-Rate Mortgages.*** Suppose that you're deciding between a conventional 30-year mortgage loan at 6 percent and an adjustable-rate mortgage at a lower rate. The mortgage amount is $100,000.
    a. Calculate the mortgage payment and balance owed at the end of the second year for the conventional loan.
    b. Assuming that interest rates will increase sufficiently to cause it to hit the annual cap, calculate first- and second-year monthly payments for an ARM with an initial rate of 4 percent, an annual interest rate increase cap of one percentage point, and a lifetime cap of five percentage points. (The balance at the end of the first year is $98,239.)
    c. What is the maximum annual interest rate you could end up paying on the ARM?

Using Web Resources for Financial Planning

1. ***What's Your Car Worth?*** Go to the Kelly Blue Book website, *www.kbb.com*, to find the current value of your car or other vehicle. If you don't own a car, look up one owned by your parents or a friend. Why is the reported trade-in value different from the resale value? Consider how much your particular make and model depreciates over time by looking up the value for older models of the same vehicle. For example, if your current vehicle is a 1999 model, look up the value of the 1995 to 1998 models to see how much less they are now worth. This will give you an estimate of how much you can expect your vehicle to depreciate over the next few years.
2. ***See If Your Vehicle Has Had Any Recalls.*** In addition to reporting the results of its regular crash tests, the National Highway Traffic Safety Administration has an online database that lists all recalls. Although these occasionally will require vehicle replacement, more commonly they call for installation of a defective part. Look up your vehicle on the NHTSA website at *www.nhtsa.dot.gov* to see if any recalls are listed for your vehicle. If there are, check into the process for getting the required repair.
3. ***Learn More about Buying or Financing a Car.*** If you are a new car buyer, what is the first step you should take? Go to *www.carbuyingtips.com* and click on "Buying New Cars" to learn more about the car-buying process. For more information on auto financing, go to *www.eloan.com* and click on "Auto and Motorcycle Purchase."
4. ***How Long to Recoup Discount Points?*** Go to the Bank Rate Monitor website at *www.bankrate.com* and find the national average mortgage rates for a conventional 30-year mortgage loan with no points and a conventional 30-year mortgage loan with one point. Then go to the Money Advisor's website at *www.interest.com* and click on "Mortgage Calculators" to find out how long it will take to recoup the cost of that point. Assume that your loan in both cases is for $120,000.
5. ***Effect of Making Extra Payments on My Loan.*** If you currently have a car or home loan, you can find out how quickly it might be paid off by making extra payments each month at *www.compareloans.com*. Click on "Specialized Mortgage Calculators" and then select one of the term-shortening headings.

Learning by Doing Solutions

LBD 8–1: 1a. The car depreciated $7,000/$13,000, or 54 percent over the four years. b. Since the first-year decline in value is usually the largest, he would have been able to get an almost new car for 20 to 30 percent less in price.

LBD 8–2: 1a. Increase; b. Decrease; c. Decrease; d. Increase; e. Increase

LBD 8–3: 1a. Rent. Cost, mobility, less responsibility. b. Buy. Desire stable environment for children, tax benefits. c. Rent. Cost, less tax benefit from owning.

LBD 8–4: Longer mortgage term, higher gross income, and better credit history.

Building Financial Planning Skills Through Case Applications

Case 8–1 Rami and Sara Sayed Decide Whether to Rent or Buy

Rami and Sara Sayed are young married professionals who have been renting a two-bedroom apartment in a major metropolitan area for the last two years. Their landlord has recently informed them that he will be increasing their rent to $1,500 per month for the coming year. Although they think that this amount is still an affordable housing expense, Rami and Sara are seriously thinking about buying a home instead of continuing to rent. They have collected the following information to use in making their decision:

Combined gross income:	$6,000 per month
After-tax income:	$5,000 per month
Car loan payments:	$550 per month
Credit card payments:	$150 per month
Student loan payments:	$230 per month
Available down payment:	$20,000
Expected closing costs:	$3,000
30-year fixed-rate mortgage:	6 percent, 0 points
Estimated property tax:	$1,800 per year
Estimated homeowner's insurance:	$600 per year
Estimated maintenance costs:	$150 per month
Additional utilities:	$60 per month

a. Assuming that the Sayeds do not want to spend more than $1,500 per month on total housing expenses, use their financial information to calculate the price of a home they can afford to buy. You can use the worksheet in your *Personal Financial Planner.*
b. If their mortgage lender requires a debt payment ratio of no more than 41 percent and a mortgage debt service rate of no more than 28 percent (both as a percentage of gross income), will the Sayeds be able to qualify for the mortgage amount necessary to buy a home at the price you estimated in part a?
c. Assume that the Sayeds buy a home in January and that they are in the 25 percent marginal tax bracket. Approximately how much will they save in taxes the first year by being able to deduct their mortgage interest and property tax? Don't forget that previously they were entitled to take the standard deduction for married persons filing jointly ($9,500).
d. Based on your analysis, would you advise the Sayeds to buy a home? What other factors should they consider?

PFP Worksheet 33 Calculating Affordable Home Price

Case 8–2 Carrie and Brad Crenshaw Consider Refinancing Costs

Carrie and Brad Crenshaw are refinancing their home to take advantage of falling mortgage rates. Their current rate is 7.5 percent for a 30-year conventional mortgage originated four years ago in the amount of $130,000. They are deciding between the following two options for refinancing: For a $250 fee, their current lender (Bank A) is willing to reduce their rate to 6 percent on a new 30-year conventional mortgage with no points as long as they don't increase the amount of their loan. Their only closing costs will be an updated appraisal and title insurance certificate, for a total of $500. The Crenshaws' second option is to get a conventional loan with Bank B, which is offering 5 percent with one point. This lender's application fee is $250, and appraisal and credit report fees total $300. Bank B will allow them to finance the remaining balance on their loan plus an additional $15,000, and some of this can be used to pay their closing costs so that they will have no up-front costs.

a. Calculate the balance owed on the Crenshaws' current mortgage.
b. Calculate the monthly payment for a new 6 percent loan from Bank A. How long will it take the Crenshaws to recoup the financing costs?
c. Calculate the monthly payment for a new loan from Bank B, assuming they borrow the extra $15,000.
d. Discuss the pros and cons of each of the Crenshaws' options.
e. Explain to the Crenshaws why they might want to consider a shorter-term mortgage rather than refinancing for another 30 years.

Case 8–3 Is an ARM Worth the Risk?

Jonas was reading the paper and saw an ad for a 30-year mortgage at 1.5 percent. The ad promised very quick processing and minimal closing costs. Jonas currently owns his home, which he originally financed 10 years ago with an 8 percent, 30-year conventional mortgage. As rates have fallen, he has refinanced twice, most recently in the amount of $80,000, two years ago, with a 30-year conventional mortgage at 5 percent. Assume that the lowest quoted rate today on 30-year conventional loans is 4.5 percent.

a. Explain why it is likely that the advertised rate is for an adjustable-rate mortgage.
b. How can lenders afford to offer rates as low as 1.5 percent? Would you expect that the interest rate caps and annual caps will also be low? Why or why not?
c. Assume that Jonas calls the lender and finds that the 1.5 percent is a teaser rate for the first year. The lender also charges two points. After the first year, the loan rate will be calculated by adding two percentage points to a particular index (which would make it 4% at present). The annual interest rate increase cap after the first adjustment is 1 percent per year, and the lifetime interest rate increase cap is 7 percent. If the index goes up to 3 percent next year, what is the maximum rate that this loan could carry in the future?
d. Assuming that Jonas's current loan balance is $77,579, what would his first-year monthly payments be? How much will he save per month?
e. How long would it take him to recoup his mortgage financing costs?
f. Discuss the factors that Jonas should consider in deciding whether to take advantage of the 1.5 percent ARM.
g. Explain how Jonas should evaluate the advisability of refinancing with this loan.

Case 8–4 Annette Decides Whether to Lease or Buy

Annette Thoreson is a single mother of two. Her children are getting bigger, and she wants to replace her old car with a new minivan. In addition to extra room for camping gear and carpools, Annette is looking for safety features, such as dual front airbags and antilock brakes. She has decided that the best choice is a Dodge Caravan, for which she has negotiated a purchase price of $16,000. She has $3,000 to put toward the purchase and has prearranged for a car loan with her bank at 7 percent simple interest for 48 months. At the last minute, the car dealership's financing people have been pressuring her to consider leasing the van for two years at $199 per month. The lease terms are as follows: capitalized cost reduction, $2,000; security deposit, two lease payments; mileage limit, 12,000 miles per year; overmileage penalty, $0.20 per mile; purchase option, $12,000.

a. What would Annette's monthly loan payment be if she borrows the money from her bank?

b. Compare the total costs of leasing versus buying in this example, assuming that Annette's opportunity cost after taxes is 2 percent. Which is the lower-cost option, assuming that Annette will want to keep the minivan at the end of the lease term? You can use the worksheet in your *Personal Financial Planner* to help with this calculation.

c. What does the auto dealership have to gain by encouraging her to lease instead of buy the minivan?

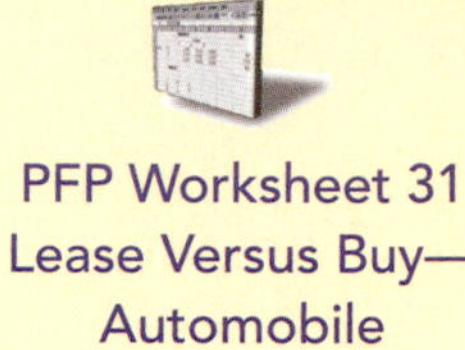

PFP Worksheet 31 Lease Versus Buy—Automobile

DEVELOPING PERSONAL FINANCIAL skills for life

Learning about Yourself

8–1. Assessing Your Assertiveness

The following statements pertain to your assertiveness. For each of the following statements, write the number that shows the extent to which the statement accurately describes you (5 = strongly agree; 4 = agree; 3 = undecided; 2 = disagree; 1 = strongly disagree).

_____ **1.** When I'm angry with someone, I find it difficult to express my negative feelings to him or her.

_____ **2.** I am very sociable and find it easy to meet new people and make small talk in group situations.

_____ **3.** I don't like to ask people to do favors for me.

_____ **4.** If I were in a rush at the grocery store and only had a few items, I would ask the person in front of me to let me check out first.

_____ **5.** I rarely criticize others.

_____ **6.** I contribute frequently to class discussion and ask the teacher questions if I don't understand something.

_____ **7.** Even when someone makes what I consider to be an unreasonable request of me, I have difficulty saying no.

_____ **8.** If I were doing a group project for school and one member of the team wasn't doing his or her share of the work, I would confront that person about it or request that the teacher remove the person from my team.

_____ **9.** Even when I would rather spend my leisure time with my friends doing something else, I usually let the others decide what to do.

_____ **10.** If I am served food at a restaurant that isn't cooked to my satisfaction, I always bring it to the waiter's attention.

Scoring:

Total your points for the even and odd statements separately.

1. Total for evens (2, 4, 6, 8, 10) ________
2. Total for odds (1, 3, 5, 7, 9) ________

If your total for the even statements is greater than that for the odds, then you are probably relatively assertive; if your total for the odd statements is greater, then you are probably relatively unassertive. Very assertive people (those with scores of 20–25 for the evens and 5–10 for the odds) will fare better in situations that require them to speak their mind and to object to unreasonable or pushy behavior by others. Unassertive people (those with scores of 20–25 on the odds and low scores on the evens) are more likely to let others take advantage of them and may have more difficulty in negotiating favorable sales contracts for both autos and homes. You should note that being assertive in this context is not the same as being aggressive, a personality characteristic that most people find less socially appropriate. You can learn to be more assertive by taking little steps in that direction—forcing yourself first to make eye contact with others, then practicing small talk, until it becomes easier to be assertive in other contexts. Until then, however, it's probably a good idea to let someone else do your negotiating for major purchases.

Developing Your Skills

8–2. Search for Your Dream Car

Do you have a dream car? Use the worksheet in your *Personal Financial Planner* to identify all the options you would like it to have. Go to www.edmunds.com to find out how much that car would cost with all your desired extras. Check out Edmunds' comparison tests to see whether your choice does better than its competition.

PFP Worksheet 30 Automobile Options Checklist

8–3. Assess Your Housing Needs

Carefully evaluate your current and future housing needs by answering the following questions:

a. What proportion of your budget do you currently allocate to total housing costs?
b. Does your current housing choice adequately meet your needs?
c. Do you need to consider making any changes in the near future? How will your housing needs change in the next five years?
d. If you expect your income to rise over that time period, how will that change your budgeted allocation to housing? How will that affect the tax benefits of home ownership?

8–4. Search for Housing

Pick an area of the United States in which you would like to live and search for available housing on the website for the National Association of Realtors at www.realtor.com. Find out the price range for the size and location of the home you are interested in. How does it compare with housing in your immediate area?

THE NAVIGATOR

- ☐ Review Before Studying this Chapter list.
- ☐ Scan Learning Objectives.
- ☐ Take Myth or Fact quiz and find the answers throughout the chapter.
- ☐ Read chapter and answer Learning by Doing exercises.
- ☐ Review Key Terms and Key Calculations.
- ☐ Do end-of-chapter exercises.
- ☐ Take review quiz on the text website.
- ☐ Solve end-of-chapter cases.

BEFORE studying this chapter, you should review

- Elements of an integrated, comprehensive financial plan (Chapter 1).
- Credit scoring (Chapter 7).

Property and Liability Insurance Planning

CHAPTER 9

Myth or Fact?

Consider each of the following statements and decide whether it is a *myth* or a *fact*. Look for the answers in the *Fact* boxes in the chapter.

	MYTH	FACT
1. If there's a fire in my apartment complex, my losses will be covered by my landlord's insurance policy.	☐	☐
2. I can't be held financially responsible for the drowning death of a child in my pool if I can prove that the child climbed over my tall fence without my knowledge or permission.	☐	☐
3. My insurer can't raise my homeowner's insurance premium to compensate for losses on other people's policies, even if the company had a bad year and paid out more in claims for wildfire or hurricane losses than it collected in premiums.	☐	☐
4. Young men pay higher auto insurance rates than young women because they're more inclined to be reckless drivers.	☐	☐
5. Airbags can reduce the risk of serious head injury and death in head-on collisions, but this benefit doesn't outweigh the large number of deaths that are actually caused by airbags.	☐	☐

LEARNING Objectives

1. Apply the risk management process to developing an insurance plan.
2. Understand how insurance works.
3. Identify your homeowner's or renter's property and liability risk exposures.
4. Know how to select the right homeowner's or renter's insurance for you.
5. Identify your automobile insurance coverage requirements, options, and costs.

...applying the planning process

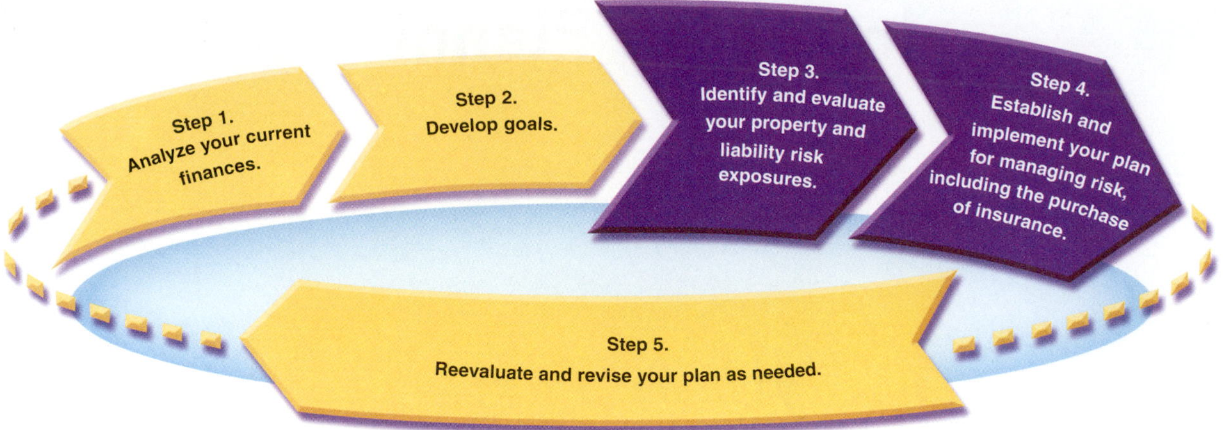

As we've seen, an integrated, comprehensive financial plan requires that you acquire the necessary tools and skills, secure basic household needs, build wealth to meet household goals, and take action to protect your assets and dependents. In all of these areas, you'll be exposed to various risks, and you must take these risks into account in making decisions. In Chapter 8, for example, we considered the fatality risks associated with various makes and models of cars and the payment risk you would incur with an adjustable-rate mortgage.

In order to appropriately take risk into account in making financial planning decisions, it's necessary to recognize your risk exposures, be able to measure and evaluate them, and have a plan for managing them. In this chapter, we introduce the risk management process. As you read this chapter, you'll find that the steps in the risk management process are similar to the steps in any decision-making context: identifying the problem, evaluating alternative solutions, and developing and implementing a plan. The similarity is not accidental—it's because personal financial planning is all about risk management. So far, we've covered liquidity risk management and credit risk management, but in future chapters, we'll consider many other risks as well—the risk of not having enough money to retire, the risk of not being able to afford medical care when you need it, and the risk of dying without adequate resources for your surviving dependents, among others. In this chapter, you'll learn about the importance of risk management in your financial plan, how to identify your property and liability insurance needs, and what to look for in homeowner's and automobile insurance.

Chapter Preview

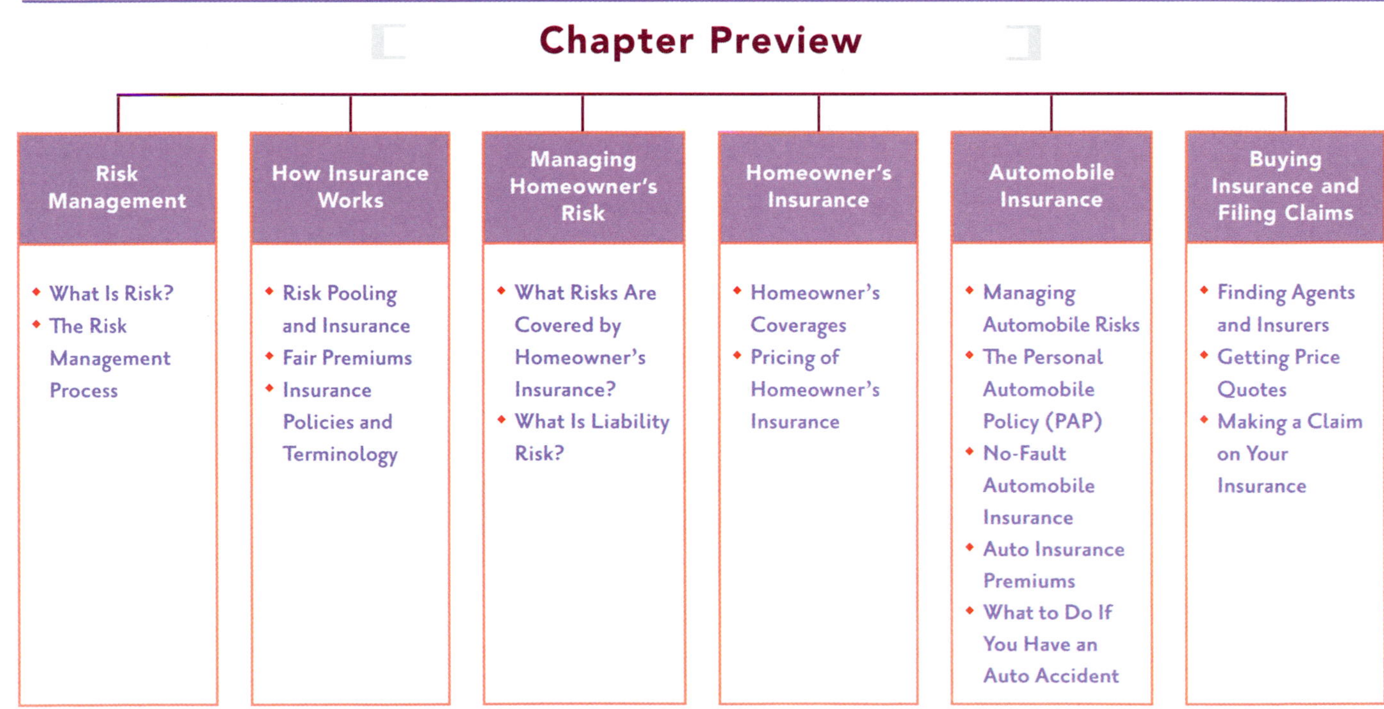

Risk Management

Modern life is full of risks. In some cases, you can control your exposure to these risks by the choices you make. For example, you may choose not to smoke cigarettes, or you may choose to avoid risky sports. Other risks, though, are beyond your control. At some point in the future, your house might be hit by lightning, or you might be the victim of a drunk driver. As many people learned in the stock market downturn of the early twenty-first century, you are also exposed to the risk of financial loss through your investments. In this section, we more precisely define what we mean by risk, introduce the risk management process, and identify the most commonly applied risk management methods.

LEARNING Objective

 Apply the risk management process to developing an insurance plan

What Is Risk?

Risk is, in its most general sense, simply another word for uncertainty. From a financial planning perspective, the common factor in all risks is the uncertainty of what will happen to you or your property in the future. A distinction is often made between a **pure risk**—risk that only produces bad outcomes (car accident or fire)—and **speculative risk**—risk that involves the possibility of either loss or gain (gambling or investment). Since pure risks happen at random, insurance is often available to help spread the risk across the population, as will be explained later. In contrast, risks associated with investments often happen to large groups of investors at the same time, so it isn't possible to spread that risk with insurance.

pure risk

Exposure to risk of loss.

speculative risk

Exposure to risk of loss or gain.

Although your financial plan will necessarily involve both pure and speculative risks, investment risk will be covered in later chapters. We focus our attention in this chapter on developing a plan for managing certain pure risk exposures—those that result from property ownership. In particular, we focus on auto and homeowner (or renter) risks. In later chapters, these concepts will be applied to other pure risks as well, including health, disability, and mortality risk.

The Risk Management Process

The risk management process is a series of steps that will help you to organize your decision making with respect to risk exposures and their management. Exhibit 9-1 summarizes the key steps in the process and gives some examples in the context of auto and property risks.

1. Identify your risk exposures.

The first step to managing a risk is to recognize that it exists. Although it may seem that most risks are obvious, some of the biggest ones are not. In general, people are not very good at recognizing and evaluating their own risk exposures. They often fail to recognize unfamiliar risk exposures and tend to overestimate others. Certain known psychological biases, discussed in the *Money Psychology* box, "Risk, What Risk?," cause people to underestimate personal risk exposures, even when they are well informed about the risk to the general population.

Some risks are overlooked because they rarely occur. This is illustrated by the hundreds of households and businesses that suffered losses in a major flood a few years ago in Fort Collins, Colorado. Residents were more accustomed to drought conditions than rain, so few had flood insurance. An unusually heavy rain, combined with the blockage of a runoff stream, resulted in a flood that caused damage to thousands of homes and apartments, as well as 25 buildings on the Colorado State University campus.

In contrast, you may tend to overestimate certain risks because extensive media attention leads you to believe they occur more frequently than they actually do. This explains why so many people buy airline accident insurance policies at airport kiosks, despite the fact that plane crashes are extremely rare events.

In assessing your own risk of loss, a good strategy is to use a checklist, such as the one in Exhibit 9-2 (also available in your *Personal Financial Planner*). For the most part, the risk of loss of property is fairly easy to recognize—after all, if you own something, there's a risk of loss or

PFP Worksheet 35 Property Loss Exposure Checklist

EXHIBIT 9-1

Steps in the Risk Management Process

	Auto Example	Home Example
1. Identify your risk exposures.	• Injury to self • Injury to others • Injury to car	• Fire damage • Theft of property • Injury to visitors
2. Evaluate your potential losses: a. Estimate the probability the loss will occur. b. Estimate your dollar cost if it does occur.	Collision risk: a. You estimate there's a 50% chance you'll have a small fender bender. b. Minimum cost $500, maximum cost $3,000 (value of your car).	Theft risk: a. You estimate there's a 5% chance your home will be broken into. b. Jewelry $2,000, electronics $800, damage from the breaking and entering $500.
3. Choose the appropriate risk management tool: a. Avoid the risk. b. Retain the risk. c. Reduce the risk. d. Transfer the risk.	High-frequency, low-severity risk, so you should retain the risk. Your car is not worth very much, so collision insurance is probably not cost-effective.	Low-frequency, moderate-severity risk, so you should take action to reduce the risk, retaining smaller losses and insuring against larger losses.
4. Implement the risk management plan.	Budget to be able to cover the cost of the loss, if it occurs.	Lock doors and windows, keep jewelry in safe location, budget for homeowner's insurance with jewelry coverage.
5. Reevaluate your plan regularly.	Reconsider insurance if you buy a new, more expensive car.	Add to insurance coverage as the value of your assets increases.

liability risk
The risk that you will be held financially responsible for losses to another person or that person's property.

frequency of loss
The probability that a loss will occur.

severity of loss
The dollar value of a loss.

damage. However, it's more difficult for the average person to identify **liability risk**—the risk of being held responsible for losses to another person's self or property—since this requires at least a basic understanding of legal rules.

2. Evaluate your potential losses. Once you've identified your potential losses, you need to evaluate them. When you evaluate losses, you estimate both the **frequency of loss,** the likelihood or probability that a loss will occur, and the **severity of loss,** the dollar value of the

Money Psychology

Risk, What Risk?

Studies of behavioral psychology have documented several psychological biases that make it difficult for individuals to accurately identify and evaluate their own risks. One particularly pervasive tendency is that, even when informed of the probability of loss, people believe that their *own* risk of loss is lower than that of the population at large. "It won't happen to me" is a particularly powerful attitude in young people.

A good illustration of this psychological bias can be seen in seatbelt usage patterns. States began to mandate seatbelt usage in the mid-1980s, and all new cars have been equipped with them for decades. The importance of buckling up has been widely discussed in the media and is even taught to young school children. Despite a general understanding of auto risks, teenagers' actions imply that they underestimate their own risks of accident and injury. "Safety Belts and Teens 2003," available on the National Highway Traffic Safety Administration website, at www.nhtsa.dot.gov, reports that almost half of high-school students fail to wear a seatbelt regularly, even when riding with adults who are belted. Motor vehicle crashes are the leading cause of death for 15 to 20 year olds in the United States, a group that has a fatality rate (per mile driven) that is four times the rate for older drivers. Although there are obviously multiple reasons for higher teen accident rates, including inexperience, speeding, and substance abuse, the link between seatbelt usage and fatalities is fairly clear—about two-thirds of teenagers who die in auto accidents are not wearing seatbelts.

EXHIBIT 9-2 **Property Risk Exposure Checklist**

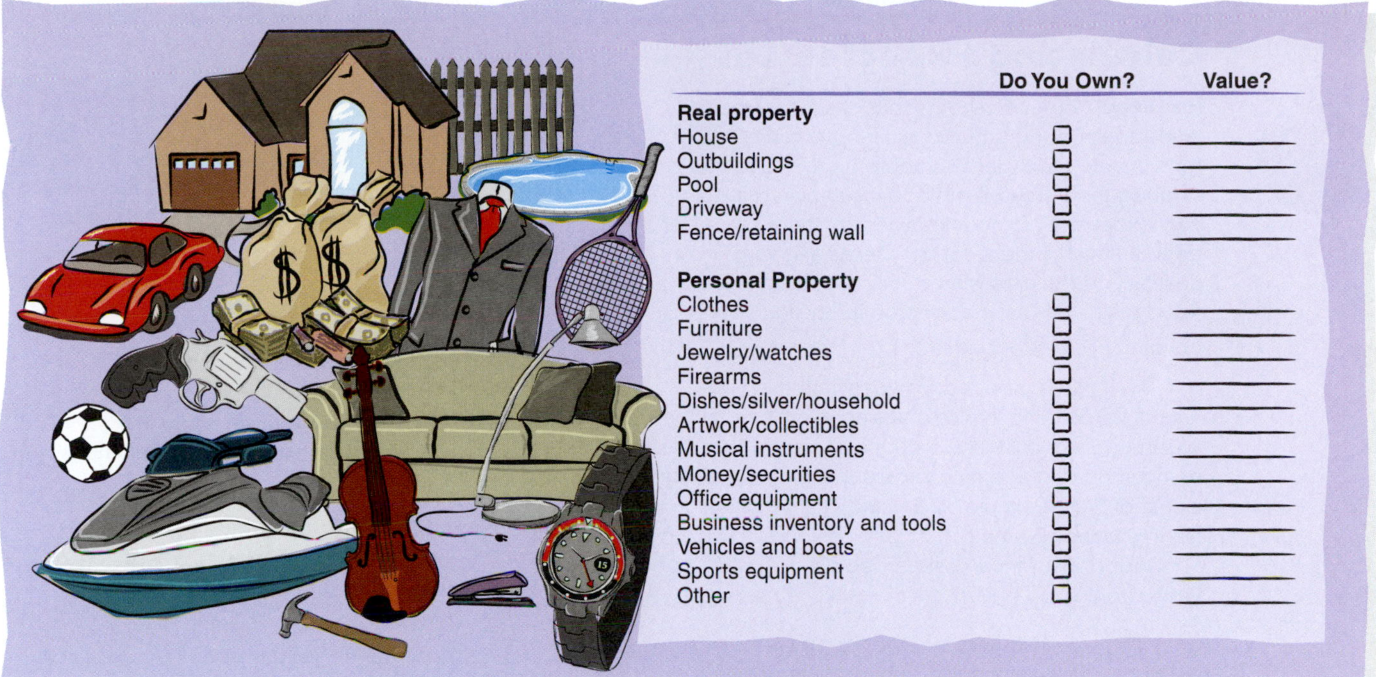

	Do You Own?	Value?
Real property		
House	☐	______
Outbuildings	☐	______
Pool	☐	______
Driveway	☐	______
Fence/retaining wall	☐	______
Personal Property		
Clothes	☐	______
Furniture	☐	______
Jewelry/watches	☐	______
Firearms	☐	______
Dishes/silver/household	☐	______
Artwork/collectibles	☐	______
Musical instruments	☐	______
Money/securities	☐	______
Office equipment	☐	______
Business inventory and tools	☐	______
Vehicles and boats	☐	______
Sports equipment	☐	______
Other	☐	______

loss if it does occur. Although it obviously won't be possible for you to precisely estimate the probability of loss, this step requires that you assess the *relative* likelihood the loss will occur within a particular period of time (highly likely, not very likely, hardly ever happens) as well as the relative severity of the loss (enough to bankrupt you, a significant amount relative to your resources, a budgetable amount). The choice of risk management tools and the expense you are willing to incur to manage each risk should depend on the combination of frequency and severity of loss. For example, certain types of losses occur with great frequency (your pen gets stolen), but the severity of such a loss is so small that you won't spend too much time worrying about that risk. In contrast, the theft of your laptop might cause you a financial hardship and interfere with your studies, so it's a risk that you'd want to address in your risk management plan.

Mathematically, we can estimate your expected, or average, loss by multiplying the expected frequency times the expected severity. For example, let's say you estimate that you have a 25% chance of having a car accident within the next year (and therefore a 75% chance of having no accident) and that the average cost of an accident is \$2,000. We can calculate the expected cost of the loss to your vehicle as follows:

$$\begin{aligned}\text{Expected loss} &= \text{Expected frequency} \times \text{Expected severity}\\ &= 0.25 \times \$2{,}000\\ &= \$500\end{aligned}$$

In this example, the expected, or average, cost of the accident is given as a single value, but in fact, the actual severity of loss can take on many values, and they don't all have equal likelihood of occurring. In the case of auto accidents, for example, you have a much greater likelihood of experiencing a small fender-bender than of being in a major crash in which your car is totaled and you are seriously injured. The *Go Figure!* box, "Calculating Expected Loss," explains the calculation of expected value when you have a distribution of possible outcomes that are not all equally likely. Although you will generally not do such an involved calculation in estimating your expected losses, the important thing to keep in mind is that you need to consider not only the potential loss amounts but also the probability associated with each.

Calculating Expected Losses

Problem: You own a home that has a basement-level family room outfitted as an entertainment center with a lot of expensive equipment. You're considering the purchase of flood insurance, but it's very expensive. To your knowledge, there has never been a flood in the area, but there's a stream nearby and the area is therefore in a designated flood plain. The estimated probability that your building will be flooded in the next year is $\frac{1}{100}$, or 0.01. If you're flooded, you estimate that you have a 25 percent chance of losing everything in the basement, at a cost of $20,000; a 25 percent chance of incurring damage only to carpet and furniture, at a cost of $4,000; and a 50 percent chance of just having to replace the carpet, at a cost of $2,000.

If flood insurance costs an additional $150 per year, should you buy it?

Solution: In deciding whether to buy the insurance, you should consider your expected loss relative to the cost of the insurance:

$$\text{Expected loss} = \text{Expected frequency} \times \text{Expected severity}$$

An expected value is similar to an average value for an uncertain variable. When the probabilities of each outcome are not all the same, you need to weight each outcome by its respective likelihood of occurring. For this problem, the expected frequency, which is just the likelihood that there will be a flood in the next year, is given in the problem as $\frac{1}{100}$, or 0.01. To calculate the expected severity, we need to calculate the weighted average of the different possible losses. To do this, you can use the following general equation for the expected value:

$$\text{Expected value} = (p_1 \times V_1) + (p_2 \times V_2) + (p_3 \times V_3) + \ldots + (p_n \times V_n)$$

where

$$p_n = \text{Probability of value n}$$
$$p_1 + p_2 + \ldots p_n = 1$$
$$V_n = \text{Value } n$$
$$n = \text{Number of possible values}$$

$$\begin{aligned}\text{Expected severity} &= (0.25 \times \$20{,}000) + (0.25 \times \$4{,}000) + (0.5 \times \$2{,}000) \\ &= \$5{,}000 + \$1{,}000 + \$1{,}000 \\ &= \$7{,}000\end{aligned}$$

Putting both pieces together, we now can calculate the expected loss as

$$\begin{aligned}\text{Expected loss} &= \text{Expected frequency} \times \text{Expected severity} \\ &= 0.01 \times \$7{,}000 \\ &= \$70\end{aligned}$$

Although the $150 premium is more than double your expected loss of $70, you probably should buy the insurance. The worst-case loss, $20,000, is so high that, if the flood occurred, you wouldn't have sufficient resources to repair the basement without the insurance.

3. Choose the most appropriate risk management tool. Once you understand the risks you face, you're ready to formulate an organized plan for managing those risks. Risk management methods include various ways to reduce the frequency and severity of the risk or to pay for the loss if it does occur. The most commonly used methods are risk avoidance, risk reduction, risk transfer, and risk retention; we look at each of these in more detail below. Although risk transfer, through insurance, is probably the first method that comes to mind, it isn't always the most appropriate way to deal with risk. Sometimes, for example, complete insurance is unavailable or it's too expensive to be practical. To organize your thinking about risk management methods, the table in Exhibit 9.3 offers suggestions for methods appropriate for certain combinations of severity and frequency.

Avoid the Risk. You can manage some kinds of risk by simply avoiding the situation that produces it. For example, you can avoid losing your valuables by locking them in a safe deposit box and never using them. You can avoid being in an airplane crash by never flying. To some extent, you can avoid smoking-related health risks by not smoking cigarettes. Although risk avoidance is effective for some risks, it's often impractical or impossible to avoid property and liability risks completely. For example, to avoid being injured in an auto accident, you'd have to walk or bike everywhere. Even then, you could be injured by another driver while you're walking or biking, so you'd need to bike or walk only on bike trails and sidewalks. In short, if you own property and venture beyond your living room, you can expect to be exposed to some unavoidable risks.

EXHIBIT 9-3 **Risk Management Tools by Frequency and Severity**

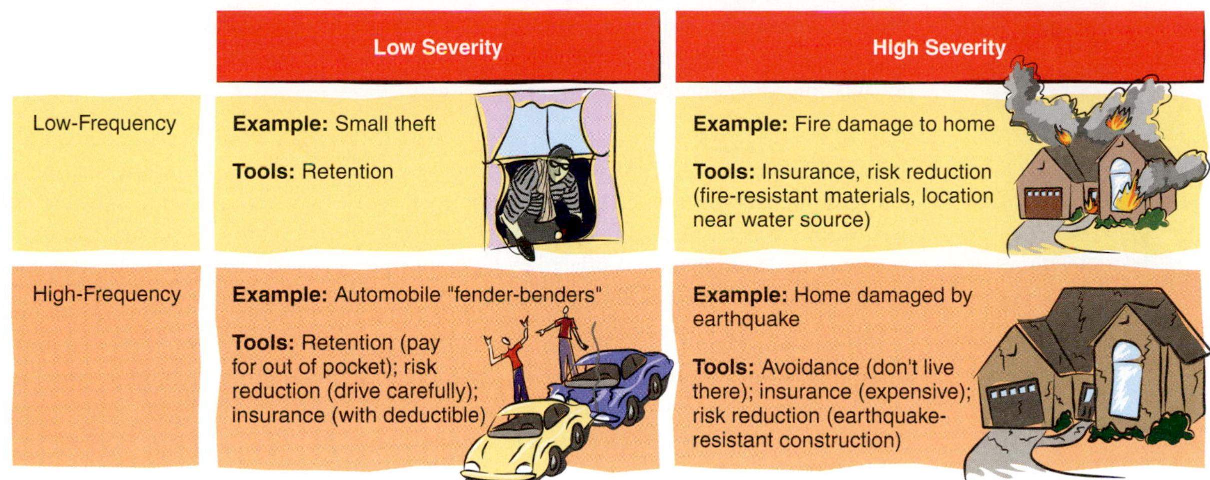

	Low Severity	High Severity
Low-Frequency	**Example:** Small theft **Tools:** Retention	**Example:** Fire damage to home **Tools:** Insurance, risk reduction (fire-resistant materials, location near water source)
High-Frequency	**Example:** Automobile "fender-benders" **Tools:** Retention (pay for out of pocket); risk reduction (drive carefully); insurance (with deductible)	**Example:** Home damaged by earthquake **Tools:** Avoidance (don't live there); insurance (expensive); risk reduction (earthquake-resistant construction)

Reduce the Risk. Even though you can't avoid risk entirely, you can reduce the frequency or severity of your risk exposures by using **loss control** methods. Wearing a seatbelt significantly reduces the severity of injuries sustained in auto accidents. Using fire-resistant materials in the construction of your home can reduce the amount of damage to your home in the event that a fire occurs. Note that these particular examples of loss control don't actually affect the likelihood that risk will occur—only the severity of the loss if it does occur.

loss control

Actions taken to reduce the frequency or severity of expected losses.

In contrast, some risk reduction methods are directed at reducing the frequency of loss. For example, to reduce the frequency of auto accidents, you might plan to drive more defensively, avoid speeding, and own a car with snow tires and antilock brakes. Promptly shoveling your driveway and sidewalks after a snowfall can reduce the frequency with which people will be injured from slipping on your property (and hence your risk of being sued for their injuries). Building a tall fence around your swimming pool can reduce the frequency of accidental drownings. In some cases, a given loss control strategy (like practicing healthy eating habits and exercising regularly) might reduce both the frequency and severity of risk.

Natural disasters often cause damage to many properties in the same geographic region. In 2004, four separate hurricanes hit Florida, leaving many homeless and causing billions of dollars in damage.

Transfer the Risk. The most common method for dealing with pure risks is to shift them to another party—usually an insurance company. As you'll see in the following section, by pooling the risks of many policyholders, insurers are able to spread the risk so that no single individual is faced with a catastrophic loss.

Risk can also be transferred to others by contractual arrangements. If your child plays high-school football, the school is likely to require you to sign a form that releases it from liability for sports injuries. The school is transferring its liability risk to you. Although you could ask everyone who visits your home to sign a release of liability before allowing them on the premises, you probably wouldn't want to do that.

Retain the Risk. As an alternative to insuring, you may simply decide to pay for losses out of pocket, if they occur. This method of risk management, known as **risk retention**, is often referred to as "self-insurance," although in fact it's not insurance at all. Retention is a particularly appropriate risk management method when the risks are very small and predictable and you can budget easily for potential losses. For example, even when you buy an insurance policy, the policy will often require that you retain the risk of small losses through contract terms that require you to pay for part of the losses that occur. You might also choose to retain a risk if you're wealthy enough to cover a loss or if the price of insuring is too expensive. Insurance for risks

risk retention

Risk management method in which a person pays for losses out of pocket instead of purchasing insurance against the risk of those losses.

Should you buy a warranty plan for your cell phone?

with both high frequency and high severity is often quite costly. People who live in floodplains or earthquake-prone areas often find that they cannot obtain coverage for these risks at reasonable prices, for example. Although retention has a place in any insurance plan, many people retain risks not by choice but by accident—they simply fail to recognize the risks and therefore make no conscious decision about how to manage them.

4. Implement your risk management plan. Once you've considered all your options and made your decision on how to manage your risks, you must implement your plan. For auto and homeowner's risks, implementation will nearly always mean buying insurance. You'll need to research types of policies, coverage limits, costs, deductibles, optional additional coverages available, and premiums offered by different insurers in order to select the most appropriate insurance policy. We'll consider these policy features later in the chapter.

5. Periodically reevaluate your risk management plan. Even the best thought out risk management plan must be revisited regularly. Over time, your needs may change, your asset values will likely increase, and policy provisions and premiums offered by your insurer may change. How often should you reevaluate your insurance? You might consider shopping around at your renewal dates, since that's when your insurer will generally notify you of premium increases. If your circumstances change significantly, you should definitely reevaluate your plan at that time. For example, you'll want to review your risk management plan if you buy a new house or car, if your teenaged son gets his driver's license, if you cause a car accident and are notified that your insurance premiums will be increased, or if you become a collector of expensive sports memorabilia.

Learning by Doing 9-1

You've just bought a cell phone for $100. For $25, you can buy an insurance plan that will repair the phone or replace it if it's damaged in the next two years.

1. What risks do you face and what is your potential loss?
2. What are your risk management choices?
3. Should you buy the repair plan?

LEARNING Objective

 Understand how insurance works.

How Insurance Works

Insurance companies are financial institutions that provide a valuable risk-spreading service by pooling premium dollars and using the money to pay losses incurred by policyholders during the policy period. Just how does risk pooling work? In this section, we examine risk pooling and other basic insurance principles.

Risk Pooling and Insurance

law of large numbers

A principle holding that, for large pools of identical risks, the risk that actual losses per person will be greater than predicted decreases as the size of the pool increases.

The concept of risk pooling is based on the **law of large numbers**, which holds that, for large pools of identical risks, the risk that actual losses per person will be greater than predicted decreases as the size of the pool increases. To better understand how an insurance pool works, consider a group of 1,000 homeowners, all in different cities in the United States. Each owns a home worth $150,000. We'll assume that each homeowner has the same risk of having their home destroyed by a fire: 1 in 1,000. On average, then, we can expect that one of these 1,000 homeowners will suffer the devastating loss of a home in the coming year.

Now suppose all the homeowners got together at the beginning of the year, and each contributed an amount of money equal to his or her share of the pool's total expected loss of $150,000 (the value of one home). The cost to each would be only $150 ($150,000/1,000 = $150 per home). Then, at the end of the year, the person who experienced the loss could collect the money from the pool. If, however, two houses happened to burn down that year, the pool would not have enough funds to cover the $300,000 total loss. In that case, we could go back to the pool members and ask each of them to chip in another $150. Do you think everyone would pay up?

Suppose, instead, that the pool is even larger, perhaps 100,000 homeowners or more, as is the case with insurance company risk pools. The average individual share of the cost is still the same, $150. But the larger size of the pool implies a reduced risk of deviations from the expected 100 claims per year. Furthermore, the insurer can charge each policyholder a little more than his or her share of the expected loss, enough to offset the small chance that losses in a given year will be greater than expected.

Insurance Premiums

The amount an insurer charges each policyholder for insurance protection is called a **premium**. In determining what premium to charge a policyholder, insurers estimate the expected loss by classifying policyholders according to their risk characteristics. Thus, for homeowner's insurance, people in rural mountain areas will have a different **risk classification** than those whose homes are situated next to the local fire station. Homes with cedar shake siding will be classified as riskier than those covered in fire-resistant stucco. A riskier classification implies a higher expected loss and therefore normally results in a higher premium.

premium

The price an insurer charges a policyholder for insurance protection.

risk classification

The categorization of policyholders by characteristics that affect their expected losses; insurers use risk classification to price policies fairly.

If insurers can accurately classify policyholders and predict the losses of a pool, they can charge each policyholder a premium that is fairly close to that person's individual expected loss. However, in addition to expected losses, insurers must add on charges for expenses and profit. Some insurers may be able to charge lower premiums than others because they are better at keeping their costs down. In some cases, an insurer's premiums are lower because it has estimated expected loss differently than other insurers.

In actual practice, it isn't always easy for insurers to estimate the average expected risk for a pool of policyholders. There are three types of risks for which insurance is generally in short supply, because the nature of the risk makes it difficult to estimate expected losses, prevents the pooling mechanism from working, or limits how well it works:

1. *Correlated risks.* Risks that affect large numbers of policyholders at once in the same area (homes in floodplains, damage due to war or terrorism). The *News You Can Use,* "Many Insurers Washed Up After Florida Hurricanes," shows the extent to which this problem can be devastating to the insurance industry.
2. *Nonrandom risks.* Risks that are within the control of the policyholder (intentional acts, suicide).
3. *Unpredictable risks.* Risks with potentially unlimited severity, so that it's impossible to estimate the pool's expected loss with any certainty. Several categories of liability risk now fall into this category because of escalating jury verdicts for environmental damage (oil spills, chemical dumping, mold contamination) and certain types of liability.

Most homeowner's and renter's policies limit the amount payable for loss of jewelry from $1,000 to $5,000.

NEWS you can use

Many Insurers Washed Up after Florida Hurricanes

Hurricane Andrew hit the Florida coast on August 24, 1992, and caused $26 billion in insured losses, an amount that far exceeded the previous record loss of $1 million caused by Hurricane Hugo in 1989. The only event that has ever caused more damage was the terrorist attack of September 11, 2001 ($40 billion), but Hurricane Andrew still holds the record for the number of claims resulting from a single event (more than 700,000). The insurance industry was ill prepared for a disaster of this size and scope. The risk had not been factored into rates, and too many insurers had high concentrations of policyholders in coastal areas. In the wake of the hurricane, many insurers faced insolvency, others left the state, and rates increased sharply. In 2004, Florida was bombarded by Hurricanes Charley, Frances, Ivan, and Jeanne, and it is estimated that the combined total damages might rival that of Andrew. It's still too early to predict the impact on insurers in the state.

"The risk had not been factored into rates."

Insurance Policies and Terminology

insurance policy

A contract between an insured and an insurer in which the insured agrees to pay a premium in return for the insurer's promise to pay for certain covered losses during the policy period.

exclusion

A potential loss that is expressly excluded from coverage by an insurance policy.

rider

Addendum to an insurance policy that requires payment of additional premium in return for additional specified insurance coverage.

principle of indemnity

The principle that insurance will only reimburse the policyholder for actual losses.

deductible

The amount of a loss that must be paid by an insured before the insurance company will pay any insurance benefit.

An **insurance policy** is a contract, between you (the insured) and a financial institution (the insurer), in which you promise to pay a certain amount of money per period in return for the insurer's promise to pay for certain covered losses if they occur during the policy period. The policy explains all the rights and responsibilities of the parties to the contract. The law requires that insurance contracts be written clearly and in language that can be understood by people who don't have expertise in law or insurance. Nevertheless, these documents can be relatively complicated and difficult to comprehend. It's important to read your insurance policies and understand your coverage. Many people make the mistake of failing to do so until they want to make a claim, only to find out that their loss isn't covered.

Insurance policies generally include terms that are intended to increase the predictability of the loss to the insurer and reduce premium costs to the insured. These include exclusions and limitations, incentives for hazard and loss reduction, and deductibles. An **exclusion** is a contract clause that specifically identifies losses that aren't covered under the policy at all. For example, your automobile insurance might exclude coverage for hail damage. In addition, limitations may be placed on specific categories of losses, as in the case of a homeowner's insurance policy that covers a maximum of $1,000 for lost or stolen jewelry. For an additional premium amount, most insurers offer supplemental coverage for limited or excluded items in the form of a contract addendum called a **rider**. The rates on this coverage can be substantially more expensive per dollar of coverage than on the rest of the policy. Property and liability policies commonly also include an upper limit on total losses, although you can usually increase the limit by paying a higher premium.

The basic purpose of insurance is to restore you to the financial condition you were in before the loss occurred. The **principle of indemnity**, which underlies insurance law, says that you should never be able to recover more from your insurance than what you've lost. Thus, even if you insure your $100,000 home for $120,000, the most you can recover from your insurance is $100,000. Similarly, if you have health insurance policies with two insurers, you won't be able to collect for the same health expenses from both of them.

Insurers attempt to make premiums more affordable by incorporating elements in the insurance policy that reduce their expected losses. For example, your policy terms will commonly include a **deductible**, which is an amount that you must pay out of pocket before the insurance company is obligated to pay anything. If your deductible is $250 and you have a $1,000 loss, you will pay the first $250, and the insurer will reimburse you for the remaining $750. Some types of insurance (auto and homeowner's insurance) apply the deductible to each individual loss and others (health insurance) require that you pay the deductible only once per year, after which the insurer will compensate you for your losses. Another method of keeping your premium costs down is to impose a limit on the total losses payable under the contract or on certain categories of losses. Homeowner's policies are priced based on the value of the home, since that is the natural limit for the loss of the property. Such policies will also place limits on total personal property losses, certain categories of losses, and liability losses, as will be discussed later in the chapter.

Managing Homeowner's Risk

LEARNING Objective

3 Identify your homeowner's or renter's property and liability risk exposures.

A home is the single largest asset owned by most families. In addition to providing necessary shelter, home ownership has allowed U.S. households to benefit from steadily increasing real estate values over time. Home ownership is not risk-free, however. In addition to the financial risk of fluctuating real estate values (which can provide either loss or gain), homes are exposed to many pure risks. These include the risks of loss or damage (from theft, fire, wind, and rain) as well as the risks of financial losses arising out of legal rules that hold homeowners responsible for injuries to visitors. Insurance can help homeowners with paying the costs of both property risks and liability risks.

What Risks Are Covered by Homeowner's Insurance?

Homeowner's insurance generally protects the homeowner against property and liability risks. Even renters are subject to liability risk and to the risk of damage to or loss of personal property, neither of which is covered by the landlord's insurance policy which insures only the building itself. For that reason, renters often purchase **renter's insurance**, which has coverage and terms that are similar to homeowner's insurance, except that the policies cover a more limited number of risks. In this section, we focus on homeowner's insurance.

Specifically, homeowner's insurance policies are designed to cover losses in one or more of the following risk categories:

1. The risk that the physical building or its contents will be damaged by a covered event or peril, such as fire, rain, wind, hail, or other natural occurrence.
2. The risk that personal property, either in the home or in another location, will be stolen or damaged by others.
3. The risk of liability, or being held legally responsibility for another person's losses.

The first two categories are fairly clear-cut, covering most of the property risk exposures we considered earlier in Exhibit 9-2. In evaluating your exposure to property risks, you should consider the safety of the neighborhood you live in (crime rate, proximity to fire and police protection), your home's safety features (locks, alarm, smoke alarms, sprinklers), and your geographic location (wildfire area, hurricane zone, flood zone). In contrast, understanding your liability risk exposures requires that you have some additional knowledge about the law.

homeowner's insurance

Insurance purchased by a homeowner to cover property and liability losses associated with a home.

renter's insurance

Insurance purchased by a renter to cover personal property and liability losses but not damage to the building itself.

Fact #1

If you suffer a loss of property in your rented apartment due to fire or theft, your landlord's homeowner's insurance will not cover you. The landlord's insurance covers the building and the infrastructure—plumbing and electrical systems, for example—but not the contents of individual units. Of the more than 80 million renters in the United States, it is estimated that two-thirds do not carry renter's insurance, even though this coverage is very affordable.

What Is Liability Risk?

If a person or a person's property is injured on your premises, you may be held responsible for the loss. This usually occurs when the person sues you in a court of law to get you to pay for the injuries or losses. The fact that you are sued, however, doesn't automatically mean you'll be held responsible. Generally, you'll only be held financially responsible when the loss was caused by your **negligence**. This requires that the injured person prove three things:

- You had a duty to that person.
- You didn't fulfill your duty.
- Your failure to fulfill your duty directly caused the other person or the person's property to suffer a loss.

For example, if you're a homeowner, you have a duty to keep your property reasonably safe for people who come onto your property. If you fail to clear your sidewalk of snow and your neighbor slips on an icy spot on the way to your front door, you may be responsible for the resulting medical costs.

In a few rare situations, you may be held to an even higher duty. For example, most states have a special standard called **strict liability** that applies whenever children are injured by an "attractive nuisance" on your property—defined as a dangerous environment that might be attractive to children, such as a swimming pool or construction equipment. Strict liability holds you responsible for a child's injuries in this situation, even if you weren't negligent. Similarly, pet owners are generally held strictly liable for injuries caused by pets that are known to be dangerous. In

negligence

A failure to fulfill a legal duty to another that causes injury to that person or to his or her property.

Fact #2

Strict liability for injuries to children implies that you are responsible even if you were not negligent. So if a child climbs over your six-foot fence without your permission or knowledge, falls into your pool, and is injured or drowns, you will be held financially responsible even though you did your best to prevent the injury from occurring by building the fence.

strict liability

A rule of law that holds a person liable for damages without proof of negligence.

NEWS you can use

Do Dogs Really Get Two Bites?

About 40 percent of U.S. households have at least one dog. Since the mid-1990s, with the growing popularity of aggressive dog breeds such as pit bulls, rottweilers, and wolf hybrids, dog attacks have become the single largest cause of homeowner's insurance litigation. On average, 4.7 million people are bitten by dogs each year, resulting in total annual costs of more than $1 billion (and $300 million in insurance claims paid), according to the Insurance Information Institute.

All states impose strict liability on owners for damages caused by "known dangerous animals" kept on their property, and more than half the states have passed laws that impose criminal penalties as well. Obviously, if you keep a mountain lion for a pet, you'll be responsible for any injuries it causes. But what about Rufus, your family pet, who has never harmed a soul?

"4.7 million people are bitten by dogs each year"

The idea that "dogs get two bites"—that is, that you won't be responsible the first time a pet harms someone—comes from the logic that you couldn't have known a dog was dangerous until after it had bitten someone. Today, though, some insurers, such as Nationwide Mutual Insurance Company, have decided that it's just too risky to let some dogs have their first bite and are excluding coverage for certain breeds, while others are making case-by-case decisions.

Sources: www.insure.com, www.iii.org, www.akc.org, and www.lapuppyclasses.com.

contributory negligence

A defense to a claim of negligence available when the injured party contributed to his or her own injury.

assumption of risk

A defense to a claim of negligence available when the injured party voluntarily took on the risk.

Many homeowner's insurance policies exclude certain dog breeds from policies or deny coverage to dog owners.

the past, dog owners often used the excuse that they didn't *know* their dog was dangerous because the dog had never bitten anyone before, but this won't always get you off the hook today. If you own a dog or plan to buy one in the future, read the *News You Can Use* box, "Do Dogs Really Get Two Bites?" to learn more about your liability for dog bites and how your choice of breed might affect your homeowner's insurance.

In some cases, you may be able to defend yourself against a negligence lawsuit by claiming that one of two legal rules applies: contributory negligence or assumption of risk. **Contributory negligence** is when the injured person actually contributed to his or her own injury. If the person bears some fault for the injury, he or she may not be able to hold you financially responsible. Similarly, if the injured person knew about the risk and voluntarily exposed him- or herself to it, you may be able to use the defense of **assumption of risk** to avoid legal liability.

Consider again the example in which you neglected to shovel your sidewalk after a snowstorm and your neighbor slipped on the ice and was injured. The direct cause of the injury is your negligence in failing to clear the snow. But if your neighbor was running up the sidewalk in high-heeled shoes at the time, you could claim that she contributed to her own injury. And if the ice was clearly visible, you could argue that she had assumed the risk by stepping on the ice—in which case she wouldn't be able to hold you financially responsible. As a homeowner, it's important to understand these rules so that you can protect yourself in advance from potential liability. If, for example, you temporarily have a dangerous condition on your property, such as a pothole or a broken step on your porch, it's a good idea to warn your friends and neighbors or put up a sign.

Learning by Doing 9-2

1. Denise is an 18-year-old college sophomore. She rents an apartment with three other students. She has just completed a course in personal finance and thinks that she and her roommates should purchase renter's insurance. Help her to convince her roommates by identifying some risks that might subject her and her friends to financial losses.

Homeowner's Insurance

Many injuries occur on backyard trampolines.

As we've seen, any homeowner or renter will inevitably be exposed to certain property and liability risks that could result in financial obligations to others. Although you can take certain actions (e.g., installing smoke alarms and clearing snow from your sidewalk) to reduce the potential frequency and severity of losses, you can't eliminate the risks entirely. For this reason, most homeowners and many renters choose to transfer some of the risk by buying insurance.

How do you choose the right insurance policy for you? How much insurance should you buy? How much will it cost? Like many other types of insurance contracts, homeowner's insurance contracts are standardized, making it easier to comparison shop. In this section, we first compare different types of policies and then look at the pricing of homeowner's insurance. We then consider guidelines for making a choice when buying insurance.

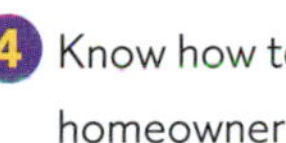

LEARNING Objective

4 Know how to select the right homeowner's or renter's insurance for you.

Homeowner's Coverages

In general, homeowner's insurance provides coverage for both property losses and liability losses, including damage to buildings, costs of additional living expenses while a home is being repaired, loss or damage to personal property, and financial losses due to liability for injuries to others or to their property. The six homeowner's policy forms (commonly labeled HO forms), the type of home they apply to, and what they cover are summarized in Exhibit 9-4. All the forms are divided into two parts: Section I, for property, and Section II, for liability. The coverage under each section is described in more detail below.

Section I Property Coverage. When most people think of homeowner's risks, they tend to focus on the risk of fire, since that is the most widely reported type of injury to homes. However, homes are subject to damage from many other sources as well, and homeowner's insurance provides broad coverage for financial losses from most of these risks.

EXHIBIT 9-4

Types of Homeowner's Policies

Form Type	Coverage[a]	Comments
HO-1 Basic Form	Fire, lightning, windstorm, hail, explosion, riots, damage from aircraft or vehicles, smoke, vandalism, theft, glass breakage, and volcano	No longer sold in most areas.
HO-2 Broad Form	All HO-1 perils, plus falling objects, weight of ice/snow/sleet, discharge of water/steam, pipes bursting from heat/cold, electrical surge damage	No longer sold in most areas.
HO-3 All-Risk Form	All perils except those excluded: flood, earthquake, war, and nuclear accidents	
HO-4 Renter's Contents	All HO-2 perils but only covers contents, not buildings	Landlord's insurance covers the building and liability for landlord's negligence.
HO-6 Condominium	All HO-2 perils but only covers contents; similar to HO-4 for renters	Condominium association carries coverage for common areas and building.
HO-8 Older Home	Covers restoration, but not necessarily with the same quality and detail as the original	Designed for older or historic homes that have high replacement cost relative to market value.

[a]*Note:* All types include coverage for personal liability, medical payments for guests, and additional living expenses during repairs.

Buildings and Structures. The property coverage component of homeowner's insurance applies to financial losses from damage or destruction of your property—most important, your house and any attached structures. Fire, lightning, windstorm, hail, explosions, and vandalism are examples of perils included under all types of policies. Also included is coverage for detached structures on your property and for landscaping, limited to 10 percent of the home's coverage. HO-4 Renter's Contents and HO-6 Condominium are the only forms that do not include this coverage. In most cases, unless you pay an extra premium for replacement-cost insurance, your policy will pay you the depreciated value of what you have lost. In areas of the country where home values are much lower than the cost of building new, this amount may be insufficient to rebuild. The HO-8 Older Home form is recommended if you have a historic home that would require much more expensive renovation to restore to its original value.

Personal Property. Personal property is covered regardless of where it was located at the time it was lost or stolen. Suppose you go to the bookstore at the beginning of the semester and purchase all your textbooks for the semester, spending $500 in total. During the day, your backpack is stolen with all your books in it. Your homeowner's or renter's insurance would cover your loss, subject to the applicable deductible. If your parents still claim you as a dependent, their homeowner's insurance will probably cover the loss, even if you don't live with them. Personal property coverage is limited to 50 percent of the amount of insurance on the house, and specific categories of personal property may have individual limits. Pets are not considered to be personal property.

Living Expenses. If you're forced to leave your home because of an insured loss (such as fire or smoke damage), your policy will cover reasonable living expenses during repairs, up to a limit of 20 percent of the amount of insurance on the home. If you normally receive rental income from your property, the insurance will also cover the lost rent.

Section II Liability Coverage. The United States has experienced an explosion of litigation in recent decades, making it more important than ever to purchase insurance protection to cover potential liability risks. Most homeowner's insurance policies provide $100,000 in basic personal liability coverage. For minor injuries and accidents, policies include no-fault medical coverage in the amount of $1,000, as well as no-fault property coverage of $250. *No-fault coverage*, in this context, means the insurer will pay the loss without requiring that the injured party prove negligence.

To see how the no-fault provision might apply, suppose your friend is visiting and trips on a rock in your driveway, breaking her arm and ripping her suit jacket, resulting in medical costs of $800 and property loss of $50. Your friend will be reimbursed for her expenses without having to file a lawsuit. If your friend's injuries turn out to be more severe, perhaps resulting in the long-term loss of function of her arm, she may decide to sue you, in which case your policy will cover the liability judgment up to the limit of $100,000.

If your negligence causes someone to be severely injured on your property, it wouldn't be unusual for a jury verdict to be well in excess of the $100,000 liability limit. In that case, you would be held personally liable for the remaining amount. For this reason, it's often advisable to purchase an **umbrella policy**, which comes with a limit of $1 million or more, to supplement your basic coverage, particularly if you have significant net worth. Umbrella coverage supplements your other liability coverage and also includes coverage for personal injury claims against you that wouldn't be normally covered under your homeowner's insurance, such as libel, slander, and invasion of privacy.

umbrella policy
A supplemental personal liability insurance policy.

Pricing of Homeowner's Insurance

The price of homeowner's insurance is primarily determined by characteristics of the home being insured—its location, the amount of coverage (which usually depends on replacement cost or market value), the type of structure, and discounts. Insurers may also consider your risk characteristics based on previous loss history and your credit score. We consider each of these factors below. The insurer calculates a base rate per $1,000 of insured property and then applies discounts as appropriate. A separate (and much higher) rate per $1,000 of coverage will be applied

ask the expert How Can I Save Money on Homeowner's Insurance?

Insurance Information Institute

The Insurance Information Institute is a non-profit entity whose mission is to collect information about insurance-related issues and to disseminate it to the public. The organization's website, www.iii.org, includes the following advice to consumers who are interested in saving money on homeowner's insurance:

- Shop around.
- Raise your deductible.
- Buy your home and auto policies from the same insurer.
- Make your home more disaster-resistant.
- Don't confuse what you paid for your house with rebuilding costs.
- Ask about discounts for home security devices.
- Seek out other discounts (such as discounts for senior citizens, upgraded electrical systems, and upgraded plumbing).
- See if you can get group coverage.
- Stay with the same insurer.
- Review policy limits and the value of your possessions annually.
- Look for private insurance if you are in a government plan.
- When you're buying a home, consider the cost of homeowner's insurance given the home's risk characteristics.

Source: Excerpted from Insurance Information Institute, "How Can I Save Money," at http://www.iii.org/individual/homei/hbs/. Used by permission.

if you buy extra coverage for personal property, such as jewelry or artwork. The Insurance Information Institute gives some good advice on how to save money on homeowner's insurance in the accompanying *Ask the Expert* box. Perhaps the best advice is to consider some of the relevant factors *before* purchasing a home. Once you own a home that has high risk factors, you can do little to change them.

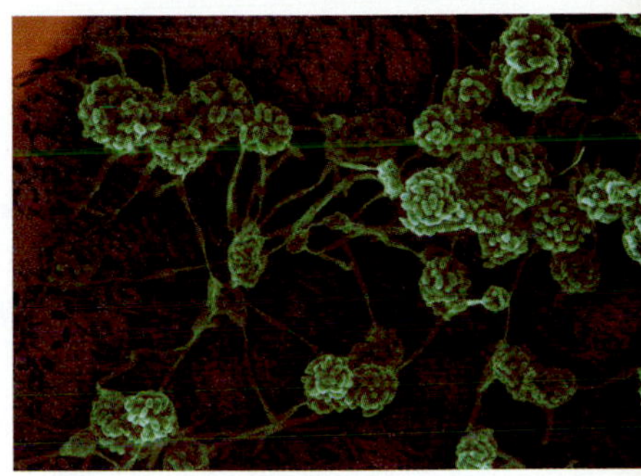

Water-damaged homes are the perfect breeding ground for stachybotrys chartarum, a mold that makes some people sick.

Location. Your risk of property and liability loss has a lot to do with where your property is located. For example, wildfires are more common in the West; wind damage in areas where tornadoes and hurricanes happen; and theft in certain urban areas. And even if you really love the idea of living in a rural mountain cabin, you may not be able to purchase property insurance at a reasonable price; if your house catches fire, it's too far from available water sources and fire protection equipment.

In May 2003, in anticipation of a drought-driven year of high wildfire risk, State Farm Insurance notified many of its rural customers in the western part of the country that their insurance would not be renewed unless they took risk management steps suggested by fire authorities, including the clearing of land within a certain distance of the homes. Homeowners had similar problems in obtaining coverage for beachfront properties in the wake of Hurricane Andrew.

A recent development in homeowner's insurance is mold risk—the risk that mold contamination in a home, usually due to continued moisture and heat conditions, may cause damage to the structure and contents, as well as significant health problems for residents (asthma, migraines, and others). Homes in high-humidity areas (Texas, Florida, California) have cost insurers millions of dollars in claims and litigation costs, resulting in increasing homeowner's premiums in those states. For this reason, more than half of all states have approved revised homeowner's policy forms that exclude coverage for mold.

For more information on mold litigation, check out www.toxlaw.com.

Coverage Purchased. Premiums are based on the **face amount** of coverage you select, which depends on the value of what you're insuring. Since the market value of your home includes both the building and the land (which can't be destroyed), your insurance should be based on the value of the structure alone (either replacement cost or market value, which usually are not equal). Although this can vary by geographic area, a common rule of thumb is that the land value is about one-fifth of the total market value of a home. If you purchase a home for $150,000, you will therefore purchase less than $150,000 in coverage, perhaps $120,000, since you don't need to insure the land value. You shouldn't underinsure your home, however—buying $80,000 in coverage when you should buy $120,000, for example. Most policies include a requirement that the face amount be at least 80 percent of the actual value. If not, the insurer will proportionally reduce your loss reimbursement. For example, if you bought insurance that was two-thirds of the correct amount ($80,000/$120,000) and you incurred fire damage of $60,000 during the policy period, the insurer would only reimburse you for two-thirds of the damage, or $40,000. Your insurance agent can help you to determine the amount of necessary coverage. If

face amount

Value of assets insured under a policy.

you have a mortgage on your property, your lender will require that you carry coverage with a face amount at least equal to the amount of the mortgage.

Recall from our earlier discussion that a deductible is an amount which you must pay before the insurer will pay any losses. The higher the deductible chosen, the lower the premium. So, to keep your premium costs down, you should choose as high a deductible level as you can, retaining the risk of smaller losses that you can afford to budget for. Although the standard deductible is a fairly low $250, your premium will be about 10 percent lower with a $500 deductible and about 30 percent lower with a $1,000 deductible. The reason that the premium drops so dramatically is that a large proportion of claims on homeowner's insurance policies are for fairly small dollar losses. The deductible provision effectively removes these from coverage, so the insurer's estimate of expected losses on your policy is lower.

schedule

A list of otherwise excluded valuables that are to be covered under a homeowner's or renter's policy for an additional premium.

Limitations on Coverage. One of the ways insurers keep homeowner's insurance premiums affordable is to limit coverage for certain items, such as jewelry, collectibles, guns, and antique cars, and to allow individuals to purchase additional coverage for these items as desired. This ensures that people who need the coverage have access to it, but that other policyholders don't have to share in the cost unnecessarily.

Most homeowner's policies provide coverage for jewelry and collectibles (such as artwork, comics, and antiques) up to a specified dollar amount. For jewelry, the limit might be as low as $1,000, which is less than the value of many wedding rings. To get additional insurance for your valuables, you'll pay a dollar amount per $1,000 value, and this rate will be substantially higher than the rate on the rest of the policy. You also will usually be required to make a specific list, or **schedule**, of the insured property; in some cases, you may need to get an appraisal of the property to verify its value.

In deciding whether to buy extra coverage for jewelry or other personal property, you should evaluate the probability of loss and the replacement cost to determine whether the additional cost is justified. For example, suppose it will cost you $50 per year to insure your wedding ring, but you never take it off your finger, so the probability of loss is pretty low. You may decide the insurance isn't worth it. One of the factors to consider is that, in the event of a loss, the value placed on the claim will be the resale value of the item. Sentimental value will not be considered.

Fact #3

In addition to risk factors related to your home and your claims history, homeowner's insurance premiums are also affected by the past loss history of individual insurers. In years following disasters, such as floods, hurricanes, and wildfires, insurers commonly raise premiums across the board to compensate for losses to their policy pool. For example, homeowner's premiums increased an average of 28 percent following expensive natural disasters and rising construction costs in 2003.

Characteristics of the Insured. Your own characteristics can affect your premium. If you and your family are nonsmokers, for example, you may get a lower rate because so many house fires are caused by careless smokers. Your previous loss history is also relevant. When you apply for insurance, your insurer will commonly look up your loss history on a national electronic database for insurance claims, called the Comprehensive Loss Underwriting Exchange (CLUE), which can include all previous claims paid by auto and homeowner's insurers, as well as inquiries to insurers regarding losses that did not result in paid claims. If you have a clean record, the insurer will consider you a better risk and may offer you a lower premium. If you've had a lot of losses in the past, you may have difficulty getting insurance or, at a minimum, will pay a higher rate. In addition, a poor credit score will affect the company's assessment of your risk and result in a higher premium for homeowner's insurance.

The Insurance Information Institute at www.iii.org provides additional information on the use of credit-based insurance scoring under their media section "Hot Topics and Issues." Research suggests that the use of credit score has benefited more people, in the form of lower premiums, than it has harmed.

Discounts. Insurers usually give you discounts on your insurance premium for factors that limit expected claims costs. For example, if your home includes features such as smoke detectors, sprinklers, or fire extinguishers, it will be judged to have a reduced risk of damage from fire. If your home has a security system, you may qualify for a discount, since your risk of theft is lower. Many insurers also give a discount to customers who have more than one type of insurance with the same company.

Characteristics of the Property. Your homeowner's insurance premium will also be affected by characteristics of your property. In addition to discounts discussed in the previous section for risk-reducing features of your home, your insurer will consider factors that might increase their risk. An older home with expensive-to-replace moldings or a home that is in an obvious state of disrepair may result in higher premiums. Homes with pools and wood-burning stoves are considered higher risks as well. When you buy a home, you should ask the current owner for a copy of the CLUE report to see if there have been previous problems with the home.

Learning by Doing 9-3

1. Identify whether each of the following will likely increase or decrease your homeowner's or renter's insurance premium:
   a. You buy a more expensive home.
   b. You acquire a valuable comic book collection.
   c. You move to a high-crime area.
   d. Your home is made from fire-resistant materials.
   e. You have a bad credit history.

Automobile Insurance

LEARNING Objective

5 Identify your automobile insurance coverage requirements, options, and costs.

Unless you're into extreme sports, your riskiest behavior is probably driving an automobile. Although you may be a very good driver, each time you get behind the wheel, you're exposing yourself to others who are driving while talking on cell phones, eating lunch, speeding to make it to the carpool on time, or—worst of all—driving while intoxicated. According to the National Highway Traffic Safety Administration, an organization that tracks automobile accidents and encourages safety testing of vehicles, auto accidents result in approximately 3 million injuries and 42,000 fatalities each year. With more than 200 million cars on the road, that means your risk of an accident resulting in injury is about 1.5 percent.

Managing Automobile Risks

When you're on the road, you risk injury to yourself, your passengers, and your vehicle, as well as injury to others resulting from your negligent driving. Given that you probably don't have the choice of not driving, your risk management plan should include strategies for protecting yourself physically by owning a safe car, avoiding driving when intoxicated, and obeying traffic laws. You should also protect yourself financially by carrying sufficient auto insurance. Indeed, all states have laws requiring car owners to carry at least a minimal amount of auto liability insurance.

For more information on automobile risks and vehicle safety, consult the Insurance Institute for Highway Safety at www.iihs.org and the National Highway Traffic Safety Administration at www.nhtsa.dot.gov.

Most states have **compulsory automobile insurance laws**, which require proof of liability insurance as a prerequisite to car registration, and all states have **financial responsibility laws**, which require drivers who have been in a traffic accident to show proof of insurance or the ability to pay a claim. The requirements vary by state; commonly, insurance must cover (1) $20,000 or $25,000 per person in the accident, (2) $40,000 or $50,000 total for all people in the accident, and (3) $10,000 or $15,000 for all property damage. Accordingly, insurers commonly quote rates by specified amounts of coverage for those three categories, as illustrated in Exhibit 9-5.

compulsory automobile insurance laws

State laws that require proof of liability insurance as a prerequisite to auto registration.

financial responsibility laws

State laws that require proof of ability to cover the cost of injury to persons or property caused by an auto accident.

As shown in Exhibit 9-6, minimum insurance requirements differ significantly across states and, in most cases, are insufficient to cover potential losses for serious traffic injuries. For example, if you cause an accident that totals another person's car, it's likely that the $10,000 minimum coverage applicable in more than half the states will not be enough to cover the loss. In that situation, you'll be personally liable for the difference between the insurance coverage and the actual loss. Thus, in deciding on the amount of coverage you should buy, it's a good idea to consider your potential liability in the event of an accident as well as the household resources that you put at risk if you underinsure.

EXHIBIT 9-5

Automobile Liability Quotations

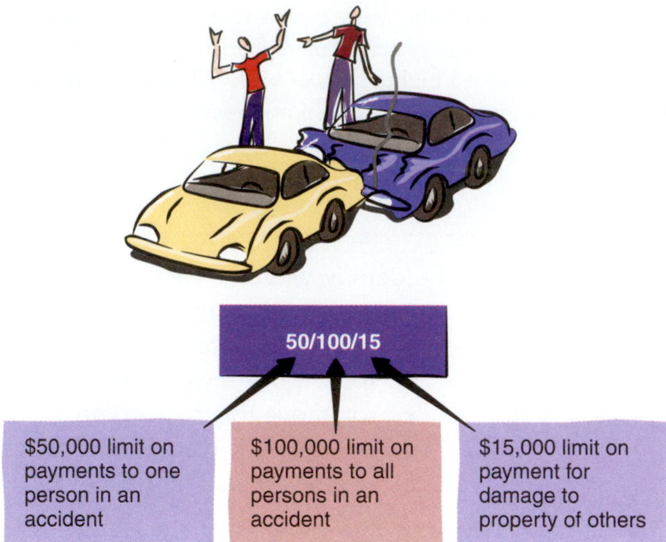

In order to better evaluate your insurance options, you need to understand the types of coverage offered under typical automobile insurance policies, as well as the impact of various factors on your premium costs. In the following sections, we identify the major types of automobile insurance coverage and the factors that affect insurance premium levels.

The Personal Automobile Policy (PAP)

Like homeowner's insurance, automobile insurance includes coverage for both property and liability risks. Each state has a standard automobile insurance contract form—the personal automobile policy (PAP) for individual coverage or the family automobile policy (FAP) for several people in a family who are driving the same car. The standardization of contracts helps make coverage comparable across companies. Exhibit 9-7 shows the components of coverage for these two types of policies under the categories of bodily injury coverage and property damage coverage.

EXHIBIT 9-6

Minimum Auto Liability Limits by State

State	Minimum Liability Limits	State	Minimum Liability Limits	State	Minimum Liability Limits
Alabama	20/40/10	Kentucky[NF]	25/50/10	North Dakota[NF]	25/50/25
Alaska	50/100/25	Louisiana	10/20/10	Ohio	12.5/25/7.5
Arizona	15/30/10	Maine	50/100/25	Oklahoma	10/20/10
Arkansas	25/50/25	Maryland	20/40/15	Oregon	25/50/10
California	15/30/5	Massachusetts[NF]	20/40/5	Pennsylvania[NF]	15/30/5
Colorado	25/50/15	Michigan[NF]	20/40/10	Rhode Island	25/50/25
Connecticut	20/40/10	Minnesota[NF]	30/60/10	South Carolina	15/30/10
Delaware	15/30/10	Mississippi[NC]	10/20/5	South Dakota	25/50/25
D. C. [NF]	25/50/10	Missouri	25/50/10	Tennessee[NC]	25/50/10
Florida[NF]	10/20/10	Montana	25/50/10	Texas	20/40/15
Georgia	25/50/25	Nebraska	25/50/25	Utah[NF]	25/50/15
Hawaii[NF]	20/40/10	Nevada	15/30/10	Vermont	25/50/10
Idaho	25/50/15	New Hampshire[NC]	25/50/25	Virginia[NC]	25/50/20
Illinois	20/40/15	New Jersey[NF]	15/30/5	Washington	25/50/10
Indiana	25/50/10	New Mexico	25/50/10	West Virginia	20/40/10
Iowa	20/40/15	New York[NF]	25/50/10	Wisconsin[NC]	25/50/10
Kansas[NF]	25/50/10	North Carolina	30/60/25	Wyoming	25/50/20

[NF] = State has no fault option.
[NC] = State does not have compulsory insurance.

EXHIBIT 9-7

Auto Insurance Coverage

Bodily injury coverage

Part A: Bodily injury liability
Part B: Medical expenses coverage
Part C: Uninsured motorist protection

Property damage coverage

Part A: Property damage liability coverage
Part D: Collision coverage
Comprehensive physical damage coverage

Bodily Injury. As you can see in the exhibit, bodily injury coverage includes three types of protection:

- Part A protects you from legal liability for auto accidents by covering your financial costs, (including the judgment against you, should you lose in court), your legal defense costs, and court costs. Part A covers liability losses for both bodily injury and damage to other people's property.
- Part B covers medical costs for you and any passengers injured in an accident.
- Part C, which is required in some states, covers injuries you incur in an accident caused by an uninsured motorist. Note that in most states, the costs associated with your personal injuries would normally be the responsibility of the at-fault driver (or that driver's insurer).

Property Damage. Your automobile property risk includes the risk that you will be liable for other people's property losses as well as the risk that your own property will be damaged or stolen. As noted, Part A of the PAP covers your liability for property damage to others. Coverage for loss or damage to your own property is optional under Part D of the PAP. This section includes both **collision coverage**, which insures you against loss or damage to your vehicle if you are in an accident, regardless of who is at fault, and **comprehensive physical damage coverage**, which covers loss or damage to your vehicle from any other peril (such as fire, theft, a falling object, or hitting a deer on the road). If you're in an accident caused by someone else, your collision coverage will still pay you, but your insurer will be entitled to recover the loss from the other driver's insurer.

collision coverage

Insurance that covers loss or damage to your vehicle caused by an automobile accident.

comprehensive physical damage coverage

Insurance that covers loss or damage to your vehicle caused by any peril other than an automobile accident.

Under both collision and comprehensive coverage, the insurer's payment obligation is limited to the actual cash value of the vehicle and is usually subject to a deductible. If the cost of repairing the vehicle exceeds its value, the insurer will pay you the actual cash value and take the vehicle (often referred to as "totaling the car"). For this reason, it's not always a good idea to carry physical damage coverage on old reliable vehicles that have very low market value such that any damage at all would result in the vehicle's being totaled.

Most lenders require property damage insurance coverage as a condition for an auto loan, since they want to be certain that you'll maintain the value of the vehicle, which is collateral for their loan to you. They usually also require that they be named as an insured party on the policy.

Learning by Doing 9-4

1. You rear-end another driver at a stoplight because you were talking on a cell phone and didn't see the light change. Your hefty SUV has about $600 in damage to the front bumper, but the sports car you hit is so seriously damaged that the cost of the repairs ($18,000) exceeds the value of the car ($17,000). In addition, the other driver suffers a neck injury, which may have long-term consequences. You have a PAP with limits of 50/100/15 and a collision deductible of $250. What coverages will apply, and how?

No-Fault Auto Insurance

Suppose you're in an accident that was caused by the negligence of another driver. You sustain significant neck and back injuries, you miss work for several weeks, and your car is totaled. If the insurer for the other driver decides to contest the claim, how long do you think it will take to settle the dispute and get your losses paid? If you have adequate health and disability insurance (or available sick days), your immediate medical costs and lost earnings will be covered, but you may spend years trying to get reimbursed for your other losses as the case moves through the overcrowded court system. For some people, particularly those with the most serious injuries and those without other sources of reimbursement, this can be a significant financial burden.

Beginning in the 1970s, many state legislatures attempted to help auto accident victims receive prompt compensation for their injuries by enacting **no-fault automobile insurance** laws, under which each driver looks to his or her own insurer to pay his or her economic losses, regardless of who was at fault in the accident. The intent of this type of insurance arrangement, commonly called personal injury protection (PIP), is twofold:

no-fault automobile insurance

A type of automobile insurance system in which each insured driver in an accident collects his or her claim from his or her own insurer regardless of who is at fault.

- Prompt (and adequate) compensation of accident victims
- Reduced premiums for state residents as a result of the reduction in litigation costs

Unfortunately, no-fault laws have fallen short of the mark in achieving these objectives. Although allowed economic loss benefits generally include medical expenses and lost wages, subject to a maximum, the adequacy of the statutory benefit limit varies widely across states. Furthermore, health-care costs have been rising at a much faster rate than inflation, which has translated into increasing premiums for the medical cost component of no-fault auto insurance.

NEWS you can use

Shopping for Auto Insurance Can Save You Money

Anna Robinson is a 21-year-old college senior majoring in finance. After getting notice of a premium increase from her auto insurer in May 2003, she decided to shop around before renewing. She requested quotes from six major Colorado insurers, specifying the minimum state insurance requirements with a $500 deductible and giving each insurer the required information on her auto make and model (2000 Honda Civic EX), her perfect driving record, and her good-student status. Here are the quotes she received:

"Prices vary widely for essentially the same product"

Anna's simple survey demonstrates something that has long been true in auto insurance—prices vary widely for essentially the same product. Anna only called well-known companies with a reputation for good service, but a nationwide survey by Progressive Insurance in 2000 found an average price difference of $586 per six months. Most consumers indicated an unwillingness to shop for better rates, although younger people and men were more likely to do so.

Note: Progressive Insurance survey reported in Kathy Chu, "Comparing Rates to Insure Autos Could Cut Bills," *Wall Street Journal*, May 8, 2003.

Insurer	Monthly Premium	Good-Student Discount
American Family Insurance	$114.73	Yes
Country Insurance	$121.00	Yes
Shelter Insurance	$136.90	Yes
AllState Insurance	$153.89	Yes
Progressive Insurance	$235.83	No
SafeCo Insurance	$250.00	No

No-fault has also failed to significantly reduce litigation costs, mainly because state legislatures have left open the opportunity for an injured person to sue for damages in excess of the no-fault limits. In most no-fault states, if the injury exceeds a verbal threshold ("accidents resulting in death or dismemberment" or "serious bodily injury") or a monetary threshold ("economic loss in excess of $2,000," or some other dollar amount), the injured person can go to court to seek compensation for pain and suffering and other unreimbursed losses. Since the largest cost savings under no-fault are achieved when litigation is significantly reduced, the fact that most no-fault states still allow injured parties to collect from their own insurer *and* sue the other driver has limited the usefulness of the no-fault system. The problem, according to many public policy experts, is not in the concept but rather in the implementation. Rising premium levels and public dissatisfaction have led several states to modify their no-fault systems or scrap them altogether. Today, only 12 states and the District of Columbia have no-fault laws in place.

Auto Insurance Premiums

As with other types of insurance, auto insurers charge premiums that are intended to cover their expected losses and expenses and generate a reasonable amount of profit for the company. Expected losses are determined by the company's assessment of each policyholder's risk level, which is determined based on rating factors that can differ substantially from one company to the next. The most common factors include how much you drive, how well you drive, your risk characteristics, where you drive, and the vehicle you drive. Your choice of insurer can also make a difference in the premium you pay.

How Much You Drive. The more you drive your car, the higher your probability of being in an auto accident. If you drive only occasionally, you should pay a lower premium than if you're a salesperson who puts 30,000 miles on the car each year. Although some newer vehicles are being tested with global positioning system (GPS) technology that can report this information to insurers, at present, insurers don't have a perfect method for assessing how many miles you drive per year. For this reason, they use other factors that they know are correlated with miles driven. For example, you probably already know that young female drivers pay lower auto insurance rates than young males. What's less commonly known is that this isn't because women are inherently better drivers—it's because teenage girls drive less, on average, than teenage boys. Since insurers can't accurately measure how much you drive (and people, if asked, would be likely to underreport their actual mileage to save on insurance costs), gender acts as a proxy for miles driven for this age group. For the same reason, most insurers give discounts for multiple cars in the same household, on the principle that you'll be driving each one less than if you only had one car.

Fact #4

It's a misconception that teenage girls get better insurance rates than teenage boys because they're better drivers. It's true that accident rates for young men are much higher, as are accident fatalities—the fatality rate for male drivers age 16 to 19 is about 22 per 100,000 drivers, compared with 11 per 100,000 for women in this age group. It is also the case that alcohol is twice as likely to be a factor in fatal accidents involving male teens. However, the primary reason for lower insurance rates is that boys drive nearly twice as many miles per year as girls their age.

How Well You Drive. If you've had many accidents or traffic tickets, this history will negatively affect your premium. The more serious the violation, the bigger the impact. For example, charges for driving under the influence (DUI) or driving while intoxicated (DWI) are treated very seriously. A second offense in either of these categories will likely result in cancellation of your policy. In general, insurers will consider only your recent driving record (covering the last three years), so you'll eventually be able to enjoy lower premiums if you don't continue to violate the law.

Your Risk Characteristics. Insurers have found that people who are responsible in other areas of life are also better drivers. For years, they've given good-student discounts to students who have a B average or better and to new drivers who successfully complete a driver education course. Married couples often get lower rates than singles. Many insurers give better rates to nonsmokers as well. As in the case of homeowner's insurance, credit reporting information is also a factor in auto insurance rates—the worse your credit rating, the higher your premium.

Where You Drive. Auto insurance rates also depend on your place of residence. If you live in New Jersey and regularly use congested roadways, you'll pay higher rates on average than if you're a rural customer in Wyoming, where there are few other cars on the road at the same

Fact #5

The National Highway Traffic Safety Administration estimates that more than 7,000 people are alive today because of airbags. When cars are equipped with airbags, deaths in frontal crashes are reduced by about 26 percent among drivers using seat belts and 32 percent for those without seatbelts. It is estimated that the combination of an airbag plus a lap-and-shoulder belt reduces the risk of serious head injury by 81 percent, compared with a reduction of 60 percent for belts alone. Only 200 deaths have actually been caused by airbags since their inception, and about half the victims were unbelted children.

time as yours. Drivers in Utah enjoy lower rates because of the low incidence of alcohol and substance abuse in that state.

What Type of Vehicle You Drive. Certain makes and models of cars are more subject to theft than others. In addition, foreign cars and rare collectible cars are more expensive to repair. In these cases, you'll pay a higher premium for your property damage coverage. On the positive side, you may be eligible for discounts if your vehicle has airbags, antilock brakes, or other safety features.

Who Your Insurer Is. Premiums for auto insurance vary widely from insurer to insurer. As described in the accompanying *News You Can Use* box, "Shopping for Auto Insurance Can Save You Money," you may find that some insurers charge double what others charge for the same policy terms and limits. This range exists partly because companies have different costs, but it also results from the fact that these companies operate in a highly competitive market in which consumers are reluctant to switch insurers for small reductions in premiums. New companies entering an area must heavily undercut established firms to build their business. They know they'll lose money in the first few years, but expect that they'll make up the difference in investment returns and be able to charge higher premiums later on without great risk of customer cancellation.

Although such heavy competition might seem to offer you an opportunity to get a good deal on auto insurance, keep in mind that any firm pricing its policies at a loss runs the risk of going bankrupt before it can make it to the profitable years. The company is thus more likely to skimp on service and to deny otherwise payable claims in an effort to cut costs. You should always consider reputation and financial solvency ratings when choosing an insurer. Later in the chapter, we outline the basic steps you should take in shopping for all your property and liability insurance needs.

What to Do If You Have an Auto Accident

Even if you have so far avoided having an auto accident, the odds are that eventually you'll have one. Taking the correct steps can save you trouble and make the process of filing an insurance claim run more smoothly. Immediately following the accident, you should do the following:

- Stop your vehicle and wait at the scene of the accident for a police officer.
- If you or someone else on the scene has a cell phone, call 911 to report the accident and seek medical assistance for anyone who is injured. Otherwise, send someone to the nearest phone to seek help.
- Exchange names, addresses, phone numbers, and insurance information with the other driver or drivers.
- Obtain contact information for any witnesses.
- When police officers arrive, provide information that they request, but do not admit fault.
- Obtain a copy of the police report.

Buying Insurance and Filing Claims

Exhibit 9-8 identifies the steps to follow in buying property and liability insurance. In the earlier sections, we have examined the process for evaluating your property and liability risk exposures and determining needed home and auto coverage. The next step is to actually buy it. Whether

EXHIBIT 9-8

Steps to Buying Property and Liability Insurance

1. Determine how much coverage you need: structure, personal property, potential liability, and household resources at risk.
2. Identify the top insurers and agents in your area.
3. Call them for price quotes on the coverage you need.
4. Choose the best package, considering the discounts offered.
5. Reevaluate at least annually and with changes in property owned, personal risk characteristics, or premium increases by your insurer.

you're purchasing auto, homeowner's, or renter's insurance, this step involves choosing an agent, getting price quotes, and selecting the best policy.

Finding Agents and Insurers

People often buy insurance from insurance agents, who may also be called brokers or producers. An insurance agent can be an **exclusive** or **captive agent**, who works directly for a specific insurer and sells only that insurer's products, or an **independent agent**, who sells insurance products for a number of different insurers. You also have the option of buying insurance directly from the insurance company. In deciding among these options, you should consider the tradeoffs between service and cost, as well as the ability of the agent to offer a greater variety of products to meet your insurance needs. Selling insurance directly to you is cheaper for the company than selling through an agent, who must be paid a commission. But you may find that a commissioned agent will provide you with better, more personalized, service, helping you through the claims process and making sure that you maintain adequate insurance over time. In deciding between insurance agents, you should consider the recommendations of friends, relatives, and colleagues, as well as the agents' experience and certifications.

exclusive or captive agent

An insurance agent who sells products for only one insurer.

independent agent

An insurance agent who sells products for multiple insurers.

To evaluate the quality of insurance companies, consult A. M. Best's *Key Rating Guide on Property and Casualty Insurers*, available on the A. M. Best website at www.ambest.com. A company that consistently has high ratings is unlikely to become insolvent in the near future and so will be around to pay your future claims.

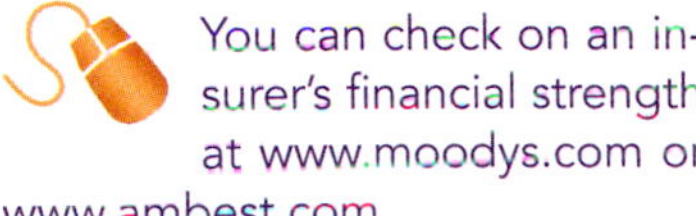

You can check on an insurer's financial strength at www.moodys.com or www.ambest.com.

Getting Price Quotes

One way to get insurance price quotes is to call local agents and insurers. In addition, there are many Internet sources for price quotes on auto and homeowner's insurance. In comparing your alternatives, be sure that the price quotes you receive are all comparable. Consider whether you have provided all the companies with the same information and requested quotes on policies with the same limits and deductibles. You can use the worksheet in your *Personal Financial Planner* to compare quotes on different types of coverage. Once you've collected all your information, you'll need to weigh the price quotes against differences in quality and service.

You can get insurance price quotes on the Web at www.insquote.com, www.insweb.com, and www.quotesmith.com. For insurers that don't use agents, such as Geico, Erie, and USAA, you can also go directly to the insurer's website for a quote.

Worksheet 37: Comparison Shopping for Auto Insurance

Making a Claim on Your Insurance

If you have suffered a loss that you think is covered under your insurance policy, you must decide whether you want to file a claim. Unless it's a very small loss, it's probably worthwhile to do so, but you'll need to consider the impact the claim will have on your future insurance premiums. If you decide to make a claim, you should take the following steps:

- Promptly notify your insurance agent or insurer, and follow the directions he or she provides. This will usually involve filling out required forms, providing a copy of the police report in the case of an accident or theft, and taking steps to minimize further damage or loss.
- Document your losses. Documentation can include photos, receipts for lost or stolen items, a written description of the event, names and addresses of witnesses, and other information that will verify your loss.

- Document the progress of the claim. Keep copies of all records, phone calls, letters, and other materials that you submit to the insurer and anything that supports your claim.
- Refrain from signing anything that limits your ability to receive further payment from the insurer until you're satisfied that the entire claim has been paid. The insurer will commonly designate a person, called a **claims adjuster**, to assess whether the loss is covered under your policy and to assign a dollar amount to the loss. If you disagree with that assessment, you may need to provide independent evidence of the value of your loss (such as a repair estimate from your local auto body shop). It's not uncommon for an insurance adjuster to offer to settle a homeowner's claim fairly promptly following a fire or theft loss by writing a check on the spot. Although it may be tempting to take the money and run, once the excitement of the initial loss event has passed, homeowners often later discover that additional items have been damaged or stolen, so it's advisable to let some time pass before agreeing to a final settlement amount.

claims adjuster

Person designated by the insurer to assess whether a loss is covered by your policy and to assign a dollar value to the loss.

Summary

1 **Apply the risk management process to developing an insurance plan.** The risk management process consists of (1) identifying your risk exposures, (2) evaluating the relative likelihood of losses occurring and the financial impact of loss exposures, (3) selecting the most appropriate method for managing your risk exposures, (4) implementing your risk management plan, and (5) periodically reevaluating your plan. The most common methods for managing risk are avoidance, reduction, transfer, and retention.

2 **Understand how insurance works.** Insurance is a financial product involving your payment of a premium in return for the insurance company's promise to reimburse you for covered losses that occur during the policy period. By selling many policies, an insurer is able to spread the risk of loss across its policyholders. Insurance companies classify policyholders according to their risk characteristics so that each person pays a premium that is related to his or her own expected loss.

3 **Identify your homeowner's or renter's property and liability risk exposures.** If you own or rent a home, you are exposed to both property and liability risks. You bear the risk of loss or damage to your personal property (if you are either a renter or a homeowner) and to your home (if you are a homeowner). Both homeowners and renters are also exposed to the risk that someone who comes onto their property will sue them for injuries to person or property.

4 **Know how to select the right homeowner's or renter's insurance for you.** Homeowner's insurance will reimburse you for financial losses that arise out of covered perils in the policies, such as theft, wind, rain, and fire. There are six standardized homeowner's policies available, and you can elect the amount of coverage based on the value of your home and personal property. You can also purchase supplemental coverage for earthquake, flood, personal property, and liability in excess of the regular policy limits. The major determinants of homeowner's insurance premiums are the characteristics of the home being insured person (location, value, condition), the characteristics of the insured person (past claim history, credit score), and the coverage purchased (limits, deductibles).

5 **Identify your automobile insurance coverage requirements, options, and costs.** Operation of a motor vehicle exposes you to risks of bodily injury and loss of property, as well as liability risk for injuries caused by you to the person and property of others. Most state laws require that you purchase automobile insurance to cover the losses you cause to others, but coverage for damage to your own vehicle is optional. Some states apply a no-fault rule in which each person looks to his or her own insurer for payment of losses. The major determinants of auto premium costs are how much you drive, your driving record, your risk characteristics, your geographic location, and the vehicle being insured.

Key Terms

Key Calculations

Expected loss = Expected frequency × Expected severity

Concept Review Questions

1. What is the difference between pure risk and speculative risk? Give an example of each.
2. What are the steps in the risk management process? How are they similar to the steps in the financial planning process?
3. How does risk management fit into an integrated, comprehensive financial plan?
4. What are some reasons that people don't recognize their own risk exposures?
5. Explain the difference between loss frequency and loss severity.
6. Explain why some losses are not insurable. Give an example of a loss that is difficult to insure.
7. What are the most common methods for managing risks? Give an example of each.
8. For each of the following risks of loss, identify whether each is high or low in frequency and high or low in severity. Then suggest one or more methods for managing the risk.
   - **a.** Ding in your car door
   - **b.** Complete destruction of your home in a fire
   - **c.** Theft of your laptop from your dorm room
9. For each of the following risks, suggest a method for reducing the frequency of loss:
   - **a.** Injury to a person due to slipping on your sidewalk
   - **b.** Hitting a deer while driving at dusk
10. For each of the following, suggest a method for reducing the severity of loss:
    - **a.** Bodily injury in an automobile collision
    - **b.** Fire damage to your home
11. Describe four ways you can reduce the cost of homeowner's insurance.
12. Why do insurers use risk classification in pricing insurance policies?
13. Define the following insurance terms:
    - **a.** Face amount
    - **b.** Exclusion
    - **c.** Deductible
    - **d.** Indemnity
14. What is the difference between homeowner's insurance and renter's insurance?
15. Explain the six types of standardized homeowner's policies.
16. What is the difference between negligence and strict liability? Under what circumstances are homeowners held strictly liable?
17. What are two possible defenses you can use if you are sued for negligence? Give an example of when each might apply.
18. Why do insurers place limits on coverage for certain types of personal property? What are some common items that are subject to limits?
19. How can your credit history affect your insurance premium costs? What is the rationale for insurers' using this as a factor in pricing?
20. Identify whether each of the following is likely to increase or decrease your homeowner's insurance premium, and explain the effect:
    - **a.** You refinish your basement.
    - **b.** You receive an engagement ring from your boyfriend.
    - **c.** You upgrade the plumbing and electrical systems in your home.
    - **d.** You make a large claim on your homeowner's insurance.
21. Explain the difference between compulsory automobile insurance laws and financial responsibility laws.
22. Your automobile insurance limits are 25/50/10. Explain what each of those numbers means.
23. What is the difference between comprehensive coverage and collision coverage?
24. How does no-fault insurance work, and why should it be expected to reduce the costs of automobile insurance?
25. What are the primary determinants of auto insurance premiums?
26. Describe three ways a consumer can reduce his or her auto insurance premiums.
27. What is the purpose of umbrella liability insurance? Who needs it?
28. Describe the steps you should take in filing an insurance claim.
29. What is the difference between an exclusive agent and an independent agent.

Application Problems

1. ***Risk Management Process.*** Zelda is considering the purchase of a BB gun for her son. Apply the steps in the risk management process to this decision.
2. ***Risk Pooling.*** One of your classmates suggests that you can save money on renter's insurance by forming a risk pool. All 100 students in the class agree to contribute money to the pool and agree that anyone who experiences loss or damage to personal property in his or her place of residence can make a claim on the pool's funds over the course of the year.
   - **a.** How would you decide how much money to charge each person in the class?
   - **b.** Is it fair to charge everyone the same amount?
   - **c.** If, at the end of the year, it turned out that the total losses to the group were larger than the amount of money in the pool, what could you do?
   - **d.** What are some potential problems associated with this arrangement?
3. ***Estimating Expected Losses.*** Patrick O'Hara owns a 1999 Honda Civic in great running condition. It is currently worth $4,000. Patrick has just taken a part-time job delivering pizza, and he is concerned about his increased risk of having an accident. He figures that he has a 50 percent probability of having an accident within the next

year. If he does have an accident, he estimates that there is a 25 percent chance it will cause significant damage to his vehicle ($3,000) and a 75 percent change it will cause only minor damage ($500).

   a. What is Patrick's expected frequency of loss?
   b. What is Patrick's expected severity of loss?
   c. What is Patrick's expected total loss?
   d. If Patrick asks your advice on whether to purchase collision coverage with a $500 deductible, what would you suggest, and why?

4. ***Homeowner's Coverage.*** Mindy Stern currently insures her home for 100 percent of its replacement cost with an HO-3 policy, providing her with $200,000 in dwelling coverage under Part A.
   a. What is her maximum coverage for personal property in the home?
   b. What is her maximum coverage for the cost of staying in a motel while her home is being repaired following a loss?
5. ***Effect of Underinsuring.*** When Ernie Franklin originally bought his home for $150,000, he followed the advice of his agent and purchased homeowner's insurance in the amount of $120,000 to cover the value of the dwelling, not including the land. His home value has now gone up to $210,000, but he has not increased the amount of coverage.
   a. If Ernie's home is completely destroyed in a fire, will his loss be completely covered? Explain.
   b. Suppose Ernie had increased dwelling coverage to $160,000. If he bought actual value rather than replacement cost insurance, will his loss be completely covered? Explain.
6. ***Auto Insurance Coverage.*** Bonita Baca has a personal auto policy with coverage of $20,000/$40,000 for bodily injury liability, $15,000 for property damage liability, and $5,000 for medical payments. Bonita has collision coverage with a $250 deductible. How much will Bonita have to pay herself and how much will her insurer pay in each of the following situations:
   a. She runs a red light and causes an auto accident in which three people are injured. Each of them sues her for $20,000 in personal injury and $5,000 for vehicle damage. (There is no injury to Bonita or her car.)
   b. Bonita backs into her garage door, causing $1,000 damage to the garage and $2,000 damage to her car.

Using Web Resources for Financial Planning

1. ***Reduce Your Premiums.*** Go to *www.quicken.com/insurance* and take the "Auto Savings Quiz" and "Homeowners Savings Quiz" to get some tips on how to save on your insurance premiums.
2. ***Find Auto Insurance Ratings.*** Look up your auto insurance company's ratings at *www.ambest.com*. What does a rating of A++ mean?
3. ***Are You Prepared for a Disaster?*** Go to the Yahoo website's insurance section and click on "Family Disaster Supplies Kit Checklist." Recommended first aid, food and water, tools and supplies are provided in a convenient printable list. (*insurance.yahoo.com*).
4. ***Hot Topics in Auto and Homeowners Insurance.*** Go to the Insurance Information Institute website at *www.iii.org* and find out about the latest hot topics in auto and homeowner's insurance. What are the main concerns of regulators today? What impact is this having on insurance prices?

Learning by Doing Solutions

LBD 9-1: 1. Risks: Cell phone gets lost, stolen, dropped, damaged. Potential loss up to $100 for replacement plus time and inconvenience.; 2. Risk reduction, risk transfer; 3. If you estimate that the probability of damage to the phone in the next two years is more than 25 percent, then the $25 cost is worth it.

LBD 9-2: 1. Theft of computer equipment, stereo system, or jewelry from the apartment; damage to personal property due to leaving open a window in a rainstorm; loss of laptop on campus; injury to someone at a party in the apartment.

LBD 9-3: 1a. Increase; b. increase, if scheduled; c. increase; d. decrease; e. increase.

LBD 9-4: 1. Since you were negligent, your PAP Part A will pay for the other driver's medical expenses up to $50,000 and Part C will pay for the other person's car damage up to $15,000. Since your liability for each of these may exceed the limits, you will be responsible for the remainder. PAP Part D will cover your $600 damage less the deductible for a total of $350.

Building Financial Planning Skills Through Case Applications

Case 9-1 The Zumwalts Buy Homeowner's Insurance

Ken and Erin Zumwalt are buying a new home in southern California. The property is in a lovely wooded community outside of San Diego, not far from an area that experienced a serious wildfire the previous year. The home is valued at $400,000, not including the land, and the couple estimates that they have about $100,000 in personal property, including $10,000 in jewelry. The Zumwalts have a net worth, including their home equity, of about $250,000.

a. What type of homeowner's insurance is best for the Zumwalts?
b. What is the minimum amount of homeowner's insurance the Zumwalts should purchase? If their policy requires that the face amount be 90 percent of the actual value and the Zumwalts insure for less than that amount, what financial risk do they face?
c. Should the Zumwalts consider additional coverage for their personal property?
d. Should the Zumwalts consider purchasing an umbrella policy? Why or why not?
e. What other risk management tools should the Zumwalts employ to reduce their risk of losses due to wildfire?

Case 9-2 Actual Cash Value Versus Replacement Cost

Over the holidays, David and Mary Costanza's Christmas tree caught fire, and they sustained significant damage to their home and personal property. They had to clean and repaint their living room and replace the living room carpet and furniture at a cost of $7,000. While the work was being done, the family stayed in a motel for three days at a total cost of $300. The Costanzas had an actual cash value homeowner's insurance policy with a deductible of $250. The insurance company's adjuster came to the Costanzas' home and looked at the damage. He estimated the actual cash value of the furniture, hand-me-downs from Mary's parents, at $750 and of the carpet, which had needed replacing for some time, at $350.

a. How much do you estimate that the insurer will pay the Costanzas?
b. If the Costanzas had purchased replacement cost insurance, how much would they have received from their insurer after the loss?
c. If the Costanzas were concerned about the effect of replacement cost insurance on their premium, what other suggestions could you offer that would help reduce their homeowner's premium cost.

Case 9-3 Limits of Liability

Carrie Richmond is 30 years old and single. She has had some moderate success as a professional photographer and now earns $50,000 before taxes. Carrie has been fairly diligent about establishing a financial plan and working toward achieving her financial goals. Two years ago, she bought a condominium and it has appreciated sufficiently that she has $40,000 in home equity. She also has accumulated $25,000 in savings and paid off her student loan. Recently, Carrie paid off the remaining balance on the car loan for her 2002 vehicle. After looking at Carrie's financial situation, her insurance agent suggested that she consider increasing her automobile coverage. Her current coverage is $25,000 Part A bodily injury liability per person, $50,000 per accident, and $15,000 property damage liability. She also has Part B medical expense coverage of $10,000 per person and uninsured motorist protection of $25,000 per person at $50,000 per accident. Since she previously had a bank loan on the car, she has been carrying property damage insurance on the car.

a. Given the value of Carrie's household assets, what auto insurance liability limits would you recommend? Explain.
b. Under what circumstances will Carrie need uninsured motorist protection? Is she adequately insured for this risk? If not, what limits would you recommend?
c. Assuming that her car is in fairly good condition and is worth $10,000, should she carry property damage insurance and, if so, in what types and amounts?

DEVELOPING PERSONAL FINANCIAL skills for life

Learning about Yourself

9-1. Are You a Risk-Taker?

PFP Worksheet 34
Are You a Risk-Taker?

Individual demand for insurance depends in part on how comfortable you are with risk. For each of the following questions, indicate whether it is true of your behavior or opinion (1) usually, (2) sometimes, or (3) rarely.

_____ **1.** I always obey the speed limit.
_____ **2.** I get a regular annual physical exam every year.
_____ **3.** I brush my teeth and floss every day.
_____ **4.** I never leave my home unlocked when I'm away.
_____ **5.** I always pay my bills on time.
_____ **6.** When I drive in traffic, I make sure that I'm not too close to the car in front of me.
_____ **7.** I don't often pass slow-moving vehicles even if it means I'll be late for work or school.
_____ **8.** I never set off fireworks on the Fourth of July.
_____ **9.** Before I leave my house, I check to be sure that electrical appliances (such as the coffeemaker or iron) are turned off.
_____ **10.** When it snows, I clear my driveway and sidewalks promptly.
_____ **11.** If I had a child, I wouldn't let him or her have a trampoline because it's too dangerous.
_____ **12.** I don't participate in any dangerous sports.

Scoring:
Add up your total points. The higher your score, the more of a risk-taker you are in the nonfinancial aspects of your life. In a later chapter, we'll consider investment risk-taking, and it will be interesting to see if your willingness to take personal risks is similar to your willingness to take financial risks.

Developing Your Skills

9-2. Property and Liability Insurance Inventory

PFP Worksheet 36
Property and Liability
Insurance Inventory

Summarize your current insurance coverage for property and liability risk. Make a plan for any additional coverage you may need or any changes in your current coverage that you should consider. Your *Personal Financial Planner* includes a worksheet to use for this purpose.

9-3. Evaluate Your Auto Risk

PFP Worksheet 37
Comparison Shopping
for Auto Insurance

Based on your driving record, personal characteristics, and type of vehicle, what auto insurance discounts might you be eligible for? Consider checking with your current insurer to see if you are currently receiving any of them.

9-4. Shop for Homeowner's or Renter's Insurance

Contact three or more insurance agents in your area and request a quote for homeowner's or renter's or auto insurance. Use the following worksheet or the one provided in your *Personal Financial Planner* to compare the insurers, agents, and policies.

In comparison shopping for property and liability insurance, it's important to provide the same information to each potential insurer so that your quotes will be comparable

Automobile

Vehicle characteristics (year, make, model) ______________________________

Insured characteristics (age, sex, driving record, full-time or occasional driver)

____

Potenial discounts (good student, driver education) ______________________

Company Name	1.	2.	3.
Agent's Name Address Phone			
Policy term (6 or 12 months)			
Total premium			
Liability coverage Per person Per accident Property			
Deductibles Collision Comprehensive			
Medical payments per person			
Uninsured motorist Per person Per accident			
Other coverage			
Other factors to consider (e.g., multiple policy discounts, insurer reputation)			

THE NAVIGATOR

- ☐ Review Before Studying this Chapter list.
- ☐ Scan Learning Objectives.
- ☐ Take Myth or Fact quiz and find the answers throughout the chapter.
- ☐ Read chapter and answer Learning by Doing exercises.
- ☐ Review Key Terms and Key Calculations.
- ☐ Do end-of-chapter exercises.
- ☐ Take review quiz.
- ☐ Solve end-of-chapter cases.

BEFORE studying this chapter, you should review

- Inflation (Chapter 1).
- Marginal analysis (Chapter 1).
- Tax deductibility and tax deferral (Chapter 4).
- Risk management and insurance fundamentals (Chapter 9).

Analyzing Jobs and Employee Benefits: Health, Disability, and Retirement Plans

CHAPTER 10

Myth or Fact?

Consider each of the following statements and decide whether it is a *myth* or a *fact*. Look for the answers in the *Fact* boxes in the chapter.

	MYTH	FACT
1. On average, total compensation, including the value of employee benefits, is worth about a third more than salary alone.	☐	☐
2. Medical costs have been rising at about the same rate as overall inflation and wages.	☐	☐
3. If I'm injured on the job, my health insurance won't cover the resulting medical costs.	☐	☐
4. If I'm laid off by my employer, I can stay in the health insurance plan as long as I pay for it myself.	☐	☐
5. Contributions to most employer retirement plans are tax-free.	☐	☐

LEARNING objectives

1. Understand and value the components of a compensation package that includes employee benefits.
2. Evaluate your expected health-related expenses and incorporate health insurance funding in your financial plan.
3. Identify the types of health insurance plans and understand their features.
4. Calculate your disability income needs and select appropriate insurance.
5. Incorporate employer-sponsored retirement plans in your financial plan.
6. Compare job offers according to geographic location, salary, and benefits packages.

...applying the planning process

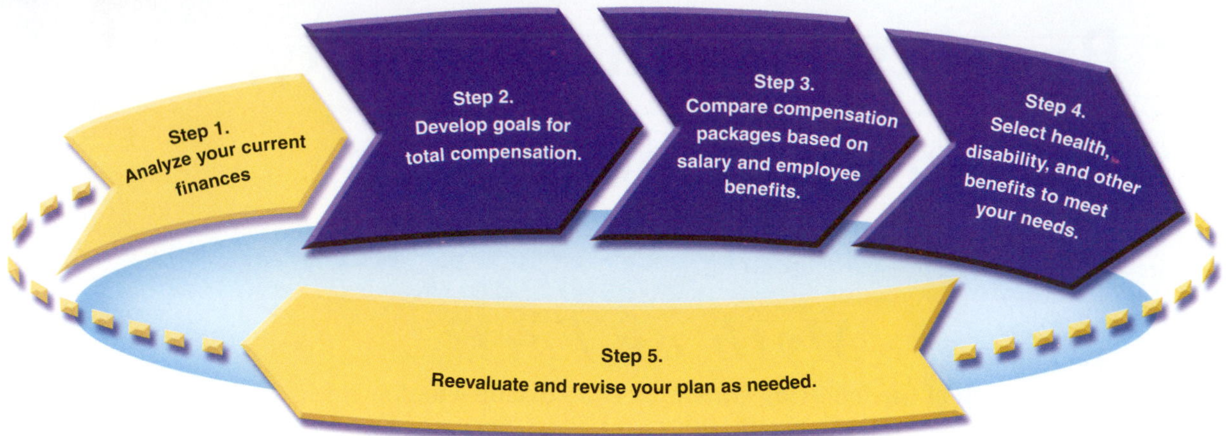

Chapter 3 outlined the steps you should use to identify your career goals and establish a plan to achieve them. Although some people choose to be self-employed, most will at some point work for someone else, whether a small company, a large corporation, non-profit organization, or a government entity. Even though you may have a pretty good idea of what to expect as a starting salary in your chosen profession, it's likely that you haven't given much thought to the other employee benefits that might be offered. These include everything from paid vacations to health insurance and retirement plans. Some employers even pay for membership in a health club or health insurance for your pets! In choosing among prospective job opportunities and employers—whether for your first permanent employment or a job change later in your career—you'll need to understand the various components of compensation and how to determine their monetary value.

As with many of the other financial planning decisions we've discussed, you must first identify your alternatives before you can evaluate them. Since salary and employee benefits can differ radically between otherwise similar employers, you shouldn't take a job offer without carefully considering the value of the benefits being offered. Furthermore, employer-provided benefits may make it easier to achieve your other financial goals and to avoid financial crises caused by health and disability risks.

In this chapter, we begin with the basics: the types of benefits that are typically offered and why you might prefer to receive compensation in the form of noncash benefits. We then examine in detail how to evaluate your needs and choices in several specific areas: health insurance, disability insurance, and retirement plans. Life insurance will be covered in Chapter 16. Finally, we provide some strategies for comparing compensation offers that differ in salary and benefits.

Chapter Preview

Components of Employee Compensation	Health Insurance and Your Financial Plan	Types of Health Insurance	Planning for Disability Income Needs	Employer-Sponsored Retirement Plans	Comparing Compensation Packages
• Tangible Versus Intangible Benefits • How Employee Benefits Vary • Why Benefits Are Preferable to Cash Compensation	• Health Insurance Needs Analysis • Strategies for Controlling Health-care Costs	• Fee-for-Service Plans • Managed-Care Plans • Consumer Choice Plans • Government-Sponsored Plans • Special Circumstances	• What Is Disability? • Disability Income Needs Analysis • Sources of Disability Income	• Tax Advantages of Qualified Plans • Defined-Benefit Versus Defined-Contribution Plans • Features of Defined-Benefit Plans • Features of Defined-Contribution Plans	• Comparing Salary Offers • Comparing Benefit Packages • Developing a Comparison Worksheet

The Components of Employee Compensation

LEARNING objective

1 Understand and value the components of a compensation package that includes employee benefits.

Suppose that after you graduate from college, you receive two interesting job offers, or suppose you already have a job but have an opportunity to move to a job with a different company. Naturally, in addition to considering the nature of the jobs themselves, you'll look at the compensation packages the employers offer. The most obvious component of these packages is, of course, the salary or hourly wage, but many jobs offer much more in the form of employee benefits, sometimes called *fringe benefits.* These may include tangible benefits, such as various types of insurance or retirement contributions, as well as intangible elements, such as flexible hours or a pleasant working environment. You'll need to take into account all the components of an employment opportunity and estimate the value of the total package before making your decision. In this section, we identify the different types of benefits you might expect and explain the advantages of group provision of certain types of benefits.

Tangible Versus Intangible Benefits

Although you'll often find that the differences in wage and salary compensation between similar jobs in a given geographical area are fairly small, the same cannot be said about fringe benefits. Some employers are very generous in what they offer their employees, and others are pretty stingy. What types of benefits are offered depends a lot on the size of the employer and its attitudes about compensation. As noted, the benefits may be tangible or intangible. Tangible benefits may include any or all of the following:

- Wage or salary compensation
- Cash-equivalent benefits, including contributions to retirement plans, health and life insurance, paid vacation, sick leave, personal leave, and education reimbursement
- Noncash benefits, such as the use of a company car, unpaid vacation, sick leave and personal leave, wellness programs, and access to child-care facilities or a health club membership.

Although the focus of this chapter is on tangible benefits that have a financial value to you, your employment choices may also differ in important ways that are not as quantifiable. Intangible benefits, which may still have an actual cost to your employer and a significant value to you, may include any or all of the following:

- Flexible work hours
- Opportunities for training and advancement
- Job location
- Working environment
- Quality and personality of coworkers

How Employee Benefits Vary

Employee benefit packages commonly include vacation and sick days, various types of insurance (health, dental, vision, disability, and life), and retirement plans. Whether your employer will offer any or all of these options depends on the employer's size, the type of employment, and competitive factors. Benefits are sometimes completely paid for by the employer, in which case they're said to be noncontributory. If, instead, you're required to pay some or all of the cost yourself, the benefit plan is called a **contributory plan**. Some employers offer a **cafeteria plan**, in which they provide a sum of money to be used for benefits but allow you to choose the benefits you need from a menu.

contributory plan
An employee benefit plan for which the employee pays some or all of the costs.

cafeteria plan
An employee benefit plan in which the employer provides a sum of money and allows employees to choose the benefits they want from a menu.

EXHIBIT 10–1

Percent of Small and Large Firms Offering Certain Employee Benefits

Type of Benefit Plan	All Employees		Professional, Technical, and Related		Clerical and Sales Employees		Blue Collar and Service Employees	
	Small Firms	Large Firms	Small Firms	Large Firms	Small Firms	Large Firms	Small Firms	Large Firms
Insurance								
Health	64%	76%	76%	79%	59%	78%	56%	74%
Dental	31	59	40	64	35	59	24	56
Vision	12	26	14	28	11	25	12	24
Life	62	87	72	94	68	91	54	81
Disability								
Paid sick leave	50	56	66	73	64	73	35	38
Short-term	29	55	32	54	32	52	25	58
Long-term	22	43	39	62	30	52	10	28
Retirement								
Defined benefit	15	50	12	52	16	49	15	50
Defined contribution	38	57	51	70	46	63	28	46
Paid Time Off								
Holidays	80	89	86	89	91	91	71	88
Vacation	86	95	90	96	95	97	79	94
Personal leave	14	20	21	23	18	33	8	13
Family leave	2	2	3	3	3	3	1	1
Unpaid Time Off								
Family leave	48	93	53	95	52	96	43	91
Other								
Severance pay	15	36	23	48	19	43	9	26
Child care	2	10	4	14	2	10	0	7
Wellness programs	8	36	11	44	9	36	5	32
Fitness center	4	21	6	31	5	19	7	16
Job-related education	38	67	56	81	45	68	27	58
Unrelated education	5	20	6	25	6	18	4	18
Cafeteria Plan	23	52	31	70	29	62	16	36

Source: Information from U.S. Department of Labor, Bureau of Labor Statistics, 2003, Survey of Employee Benefits, and National Compensation Surveys. Small firms are defined as those with 100 or fewer employees.

The U.S. Department of Labor's Bureau of Labor Statistics regularly surveys employers to see what types of benefits they offer employees. The key results of the most recent survey are summarized in Exhibit 10–1. One thing to note is that large employers, on average, offer many more benefits than small employers (defined as employers with fewer than 100 employees). For example, whereas 64 percent of small firms provide health insurance to employees (compared with 76% of large firms), only 38 percent offer reimbursement for job-related education (compared with 67% of large firms). Also, large firms are nearly twice as likely to offer vision, dental, and disability insurance. Although it's not apparent in this table, very small firms (those with fewer than 25 employees) tend to offer even fewer fringe benefits. In addition, professional employees in both small and large firms tend to have more comprehensive benefit packages than clerical and blue collar workers.

Fact #1

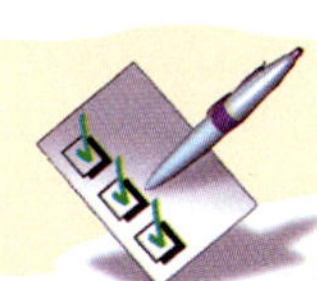

The Department of Labor estimates that, on average, 27.2 percent of all compensation costs in 2002 went to pay for employee benefits, while 72.8 percent went to pay wages and salaries. Another way to think about this statistic is that—assuming you fit the average—if your salary is $30,000, your employer is actually paying $41,209 (= $30,000/72.8%) in total compensation.

The reasons for differences across firms are largely due to costs. Employers incur substantial costs, both to provide the benefits and to administer the plans. Paid leave accounts for 6.6 percent of costs, insurance 6.4 percent, and retirement plans 2.9 percent, on average. This partially explains why small employers offer less generous benefit packages than large employers—it may not be cost-effective for them to do so, since they can't spread the administrative costs across a large group. But even employers that don't provide benefits such as health and retirement plans still incur costs for legally mandated programs. Approximately 8.3 percent of compensation costs go to pay for Social Security, Medicare, unemployment, and workers' compensation insurance.

If benefits cost so much, why do employers provide them at all? Why don't they just give you the extra money and let you buy the benefits on your own or keep the cash? Employers with less generous plans essentially do just that. But some employers recognize that passing on cost and tax savings to their employees can be beneficial to the company as well. Or they may be "doing what's best for you," ensuring that you'll actually have the benefits you need.

Why Benefits Are Preferable to Cash Compensation

Although some employers offer benefits to employees for purely altruistic reasons, in general, competition is the driving force. If a firm is able to provide something that employees value, it will be able to attract the most highly qualified workers and will benefit from reduced turnover and increased employee loyalty, productivity, and job satisfaction. If there are additional advantages of receiving compensation in the form of group benefits, such as tax savings, reduced costs, and better coverage, employees will value the benefits even more.

Let's illustrate the advantages of benefits over cash with the following example. Suppose you're considering two employment opportunities. Company A is offering a salary of $26,000 and fully paid health insurance. Company B is offering a salary of $30,000 and no health insurance. If you take the Company B job, you'll have to purchase individual health insurance on your own. Since both companies are competing in the same market, we'll also assume that the cost to Company A of providing you with health insurance is $4,000 per year, so that the two companies have identical total compensation costs. Which one would you choose? The reasons you might prefer the job with the benefits rather than the extra salary are related to the advantages of group insurance, availability of private market insurance alternatives, and taxes, as discussed below.

Advantages of Group Insurance. **Group insurance** is insurance purchased on a group basis by an employer for the benefit of employees. The primary advantages of group insurance are related to **group underwriting** and cost. Recall from Chapter 9 that insurance companies normally consider your individual risk characteristics before selling you an insurance policy, using a process called *underwriting*. If you have higher risk of auto accidents, you pay a higher rate for your insurance, for example. This is not the case with group insurance. When an insurer insures a group, as in the case of health, disability, or life insurance offered through an employee benefit plan, the individuals in the group are not individually considered for insurability. Since the contract is with the employer rather than the individuals, there is a single application for the entire group, and the insurer's decision is based on the risk of the group as a whole, rather than on characteristics of individual group members. Members of the group are also protected from the risk of policy cancellation due to changes in their individual risk characteristics during the period of employment. So, for example, if you were diagnosed with a chronic illness, such as cancer or multiple sclerosis, you would continue to have insurance coverage, and the insurer couldn't raise your premium (unless it raised the premiums for the entire group).

group insurance
Insurance purchased on a group basis by an employer for the benefit of employees.

group underwriting
Underwriting in which the premium is based on the risk of the group as a whole rather than on characteristics of individual group members.

Group insurance may offer some cost advantages as well. In general, the administration of a group insurance plan is cheaper for an insurer than individual insurance, and these cost savings can be passed on to the employer and employee. The cost savings usually come from reduced expenses, since the insurer deals with only one insured (the employer) instead of many and the employer handles some of the administration, premium collection, and record keeping. The insurer also may have lower risk exposure, since the group will likely include a balanced mix of healthy and unhealthy and young and old individuals.

Let's go back to the example given above, where Company A is paying the entire health insurance premium and Company B isn't. Could you buy the insurance yourself for the $4,000 salary difference if you took the Company B job? If you're young and healthy, it's possible you *could* buy comparable health insurance in the private market for less, but if you're older or in poor health, you might find private market alternatives to be much more expensive than $4,000. Similarly, if your employer offers a contributory plan, you'll pay a portion of the per-person group premium, but you'll be paying the cost of the *average* risk in your group. Again, this may be more or less than what you'd pay in the private market, depending on your age and health.

Limitations of Individual Insurance. In considering private-market individual insurance as an alternative to group insurance, an important question is whether such insurance will always be available to you. Although many insurers sell individual policies, these policies are individually underwritten, and they usually aren't guaranteed to be renewable. Suppose, returning to our example, that you find an insurer willing to provide a comparable individual health insurance policy for $2,500 per year, so you take the $30,000 job with Company B. Setting aside taxes for the moment, let's consider what would happen if your health status changed unexpectedly for the worse—at the policy renewal date your insurance policy could be canceled or your premium could increase dramatically.

Two important features of group insurance are that everyone in the group has access to the insurance regardless of his or her health status and that no member of the group can have his or her insurance canceled. If you're diagnosed with cancer, your individual insurer will cover you to the end of your current contract, but it can elect not to renew for the following year (or to dramatically increase your premium). Even if you then have the option of signing up for your employer's plan, you could find yourself uninsured for several months, because you may have to wait for a specified date to enroll in the plan. These issues are discussed in more detail in a later section, but the important point here is that group insurance protects you from the risk of policy termination and future unavailability of coverage. It also insulates you from premium increases related to changes in your individual risk characteristics. Over your lifetime, you'll find that qualification for group benefits will be essential for continued coverage at reasonable prices.

The Tax Advantages of Employee Benefits. Compared with equivalent cash compensation, employee benefits have some tax advantages. To employers, there's no real tax difference between offering cash compensation and offering employee benefits. Subject to some limitations, employers can deduct both types of compensation as a business expense. However, the tax law *does* allow you to receive certain noncash benefits without reporting the value as taxable income. Similarly, if the plan is contributory, your taxes will be calculated on your income after subtracting the benefit costs. These tax advantages apply to most types of benefits, such as life insurance and contributions to employer-sponsored retirement plans.

Returning to the example above, let's calculate the tax effect of receiving cash versus receiving a fringe benefit. Since the taxes on the first $26,000 of both jobs will be the same, marginal analysis implies that we can ignore this part of the problem. With the job offered by Company A, you won't owe any taxes on the health insurance benefit paid for by your employer, whereas you *will* have to pay tax on the additional $4,000 in cash compensation from Company B. If your marginal tax rate, including all applicable taxes, is 30 percent, that $4,000 will result in only $4,000 × (1 − 0.30) = $2,800 in net income. And if you use the extra $2,800 from Company B to buy individual health insurance, that expense will only be tax-deductible if you itemize deductions and your total medical costs exceed 7.5% of AGI. Note that even though the difference in salary is equivalent to the dollar cost of the benefit—$4,000—the marginal difference between the two jobs is a savings of up to $1,200 in taxes if you take the job offered by Company A.

Even if your employer requires that you completely pay the group benefit costs, you will still save on taxes. For example, suppose you have another employment opportunity with Company C, which offers a starting salary of $30,000 and gives you the opportunity to purchase group health insurance for $4,000 per year out of your own pocket. You'll have the same after-tax income as with Company A. Your taxable income will be reduced by $4,000, again saving you $1,200 in taxes.

Although the examples given in this section relate to health insurance, your employer may offer many types of benefits that will provide you with similar cost and tax advantages. The next sections provide some background that will make it easier for you to understand and value your health, disability, and retirement plan benefits.

Health Insurance and Your Financial Plan

LEARNING objective

 Evaluate your expected health-related expenses and incorporate health insurance funding in your financial plan.

Health insurance is a benefit often found in compensation packages. Whether you participate in an employer plan or purchase individual insurance, however, health insurance is an important component of your financial plan, since illnesses and injuries can place a tremendous financial burden on your family. In this section, we consider how to evaluate your health insurance needs, identify your insurance alternatives, and suggest methods for selecting the most appropriate coverage and minimizing your future out-of-pocket health costs.

Health Insurance Needs Analysis

Health insurance provides protection against unexpected costs due to illness, accident, or disability. This type of insurance works in the same way as property and liability insurance, discussed in Chapter 9. Since a particular individual's health-related expenses are not correlated with those of other individuals (except in rare cases of health epidemics such as meningitis, SARS, and AIDS), insurers can pool these risks and spread the cost over many policyholders. Insurers use statistical data to estimate future costs and charge premiums sufficient to cover their expected losses and expenses.

In Chapter 9, you analyzed the expected frequency and severity of property and liability risks. Similarly, you should begin this component of your financial plan with a realistic estimate of your expected health costs, taking into consideration your family situation and national trends in the costs of medical care.

Fact #2

Over the last two decades, health-care costs have increased at a much faster rate than wages and the prices of other goods and services. For example, despite a low overall inflation rate of 2.2 percent and average wage increases of only 3.1 percent between the spring of 2002 and the spring of 2003, monthly premiums for employer-sponsored health insurance during that time rose 13.9 percent, according to a Kaiser Family Foundation study.

Expected Health Costs. National statistics suggest that more than 40 million people in the United States have no health insurance at all. Although it's true that your risk of experiencing a large health loss is relatively small, particularly if you're currently young and healthy, you don't want to be among those without health insurance. Even regular, predicable medical expenditures, such as annual diagnostic tests, prescription drugs, and office visits for minor illnesses, can rapidly deplete household resources. In Chapter 9, we suggested that the high administrative costs associated with insuring small, predictable losses make it preferable to budget for them rather than insure them, and this is the case in health insurance, too. However, budgeting for more serious health problems is another matter. Specialists commonly charge $250 or more for office visits. Regular ambulance services may cost $1,000 or more, and a helicopter ambulance can run as much as $10,000 for one trip. If you require hospitalization, you can expect to pay several thousand dollars per day—more if you require intensive care.

If you have or plan to have children, you can expect to incur costs every year for illnesses, injuries, and wellness care. Having a new baby can be surprisingly expensive. Not including costs for the obstetrician, anesthesia, and hospitalization for the birth, the first-year costs for recommended office visits and immunizations average $1,200 per child.

For some people, expected health-care costs are higher than average because of a family history of cancer, diabetes, or heart disease. In assessing your potential health-care needs, you should consider your family history, even if you haven't been diagnosed with a particular condition or illness.

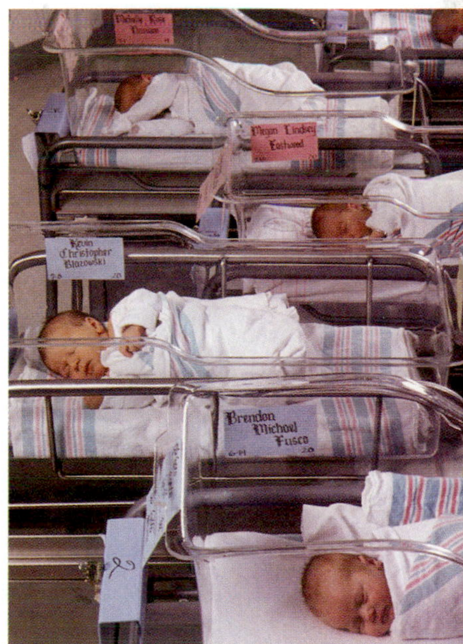

Having a baby can be very expensive if you don't have adequate health insurance.

National Trends in Health Costs. Even if you're relatively healthy, you can expect your medical care and health insurance costs to increase over time. For a variety of reasons, including increased quality of care and escalating prescription drug prices, medical costs and health insurance premiums have increased at an alarming rate over the last two decades, and this trend is expected to continue. As you can see in Exhibit 10–2, wage increases have not kept up with increases in health insurance benefit costs over the last several years.

EXHIBIT 10-2

Increasing Cost of Employer-Sponsored Family Health Insurance Coverage Relative to Wage Growth and Inflation

Sources: Bureau of Labor Statistics and Kaiser Family Foundation Survey of Employer-Sponsored Health Benefits

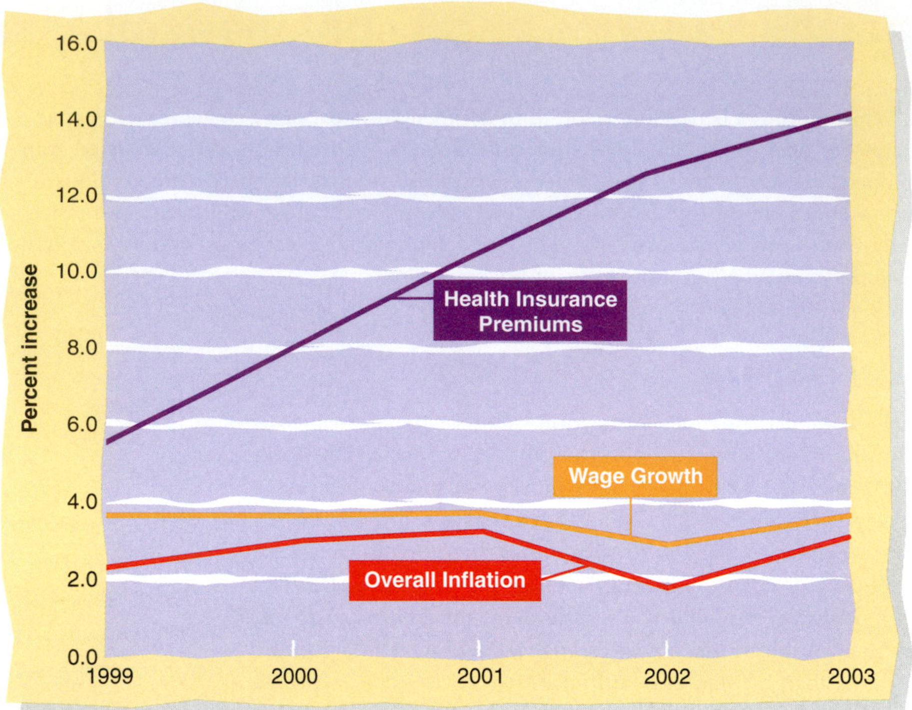

Although health insurance premiums have been rising steadily, the share paid by employers has so far remained relatively stable. Exhibit 10–3 shows the average dollar amounts paid by employers and employees, respectively, for different types of health plans in 2003. As you can see, employers paid most of the cost of single coverage for conventional health plans ($3,195 of the average $3,576 premium, or 89%) but a smaller percentage of the cost of family coverage ($6,426 of the $8,800 average premium, or 73%). The average proportion paid by employers is likely to decline in the near future, particularly as smaller employers are finding it increasingly difficult to absorb the rapidly increasing costs. In addition, you can expect that employers will add cost-saving measures to their plan design, such as larger deductibles and more limitations on prescription drugs.

Strategies for Controlling Health-Care Costs

The price you'll pay for medical services in the future is pretty much out of your control. However, there are some ways that you can reduce your expected future out-of-pocket costs for insurance premiums and other health-care expenses.

1. Invest in your own health. Eat healthy, stay active, and don't smoke. If you're healthy, chances are you'll have reduced health expenditures over your lifetime and lower premiums for health, life, and disability insurance.

2. Choose an employer that offers generous health insurance benefits. The best situation is one in which the employer pays the full cost, even for family coverage. But as we've already seen, even if your employer's plan is contributory, it's preferable to have access to group insurance.

3. Budget for small expenditures. Plans with high deductibles are less expensive than low-deductible plans, and the difference in cost is greater than the difference in deductibles. So if you're paying part or all of the premium, you'll be better off if you opt for the lower-cost, higher-deductible option and pay the deductible out of pocket instead of the extra premium.

flexible spending account (FSA)
An account maintained by an employer in which the pretax earnings of an employee are set aside for qualified medical and child-care expenses.

4. Take advantage of beneficial tax rules. Let the IRS pay part of your health costs. If your employer offers you the opportunity to set up a **flexible spending account (FSA)**, take advantage of it. These arrangements enable you to set aside some of your income *pretax* for the payment of qualified medical and child-care expenses. The funds can be used to cover health

EXHIBIT 10-3 **Average Annual Employer and Employee Share of Health Insurance Costs, Single and Family Coverage, 2003**

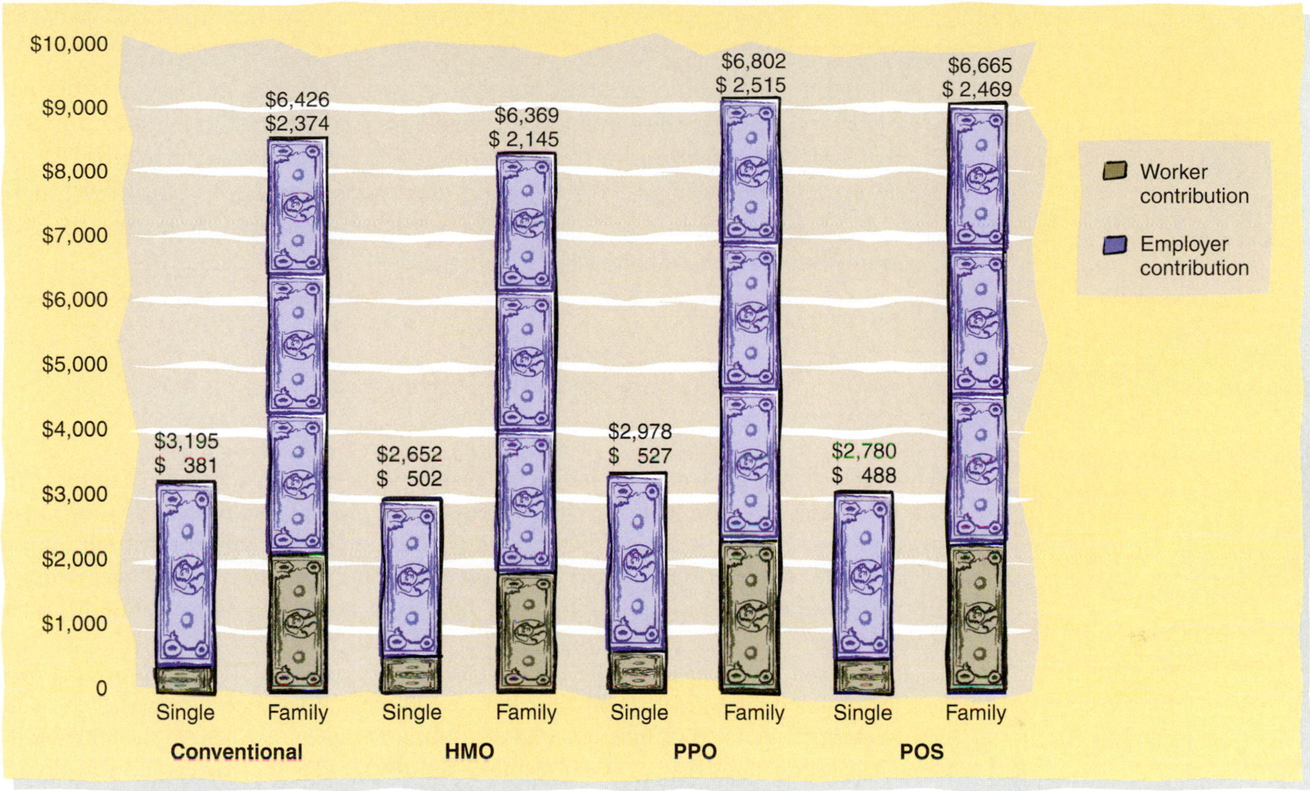

Sources: Kaiser Family Foundation and Health Research and Educational Trust Survey of Employer-Sponsored Health Benefits, 2003 Summary Findings.

insurance deductibles and copayments as well as a wide range of medical, dental, and vision expenses that might not be covered under your health-care plan. Although you're using your own money to pay these expenses, you're paying less than if you'd had to first pay taxes on that income.

As an example of how a flexible spending account works, suppose you have a $600 deductible on your insurance and a marginal tax rate of 40 percent. You would normally have to earn $1,000 to accrue $600 in after-tax income to pay the deductible. By setting up the FSA and paying the deductible out of it, you save $400 in taxes. That amounts to $400 more in your pocket. The downside to this beneficial tax rule is that the IRS doesn't allow you to recover or roll over excess dollars in the account at the end of the year. Therefore, the amount you put into the flexible spending account each year should be based on out-of-pocket expenses that you are fairly certain to incur, such as the cost of new eyeglasses or contacts, orthodonture, plan deductibles, over-the-counter medications, and any other regular expenses not covered by insurance.

Under a new tax rule, you may be able to set up a **health savings account (HSA)** (formerly called a *health reimbursement account* or *medical savings account*), which operates similarly to an FSA in that contributions to the account are made from pretax dollars. The differences are that you can earn interest on the amounts in the account, the annual contribution limit is only $1,000 (whereas FSA limits are set by the employer and commonly allow $3,000 to $5,000 per year for medical), and you can roll over unused amounts from year to year.

health savings account (HSA)

An investment account in which an employer deposits pretax dollars allocated for payment of an employee's health-related expenses.

5. Take advantage of opt-out rules. Some employers allow you to "opt out" of their health plan and either give you the cash instead or allow you to apply it to other benefits. This is a good idea if you have better or cheaper coverage through your spouse's employer.

The conclusion you can draw from all of this is that, in the future, your family's medical costs are going to take a bigger bite out of your budget than they do at present, even if you're covered by a group plan at your place of employment. Your financial plan needs to take this into consideration. You can, however, keep your future costs down by maintaining a healthy life style and being a good consumer of both health care and health insurance. You also should understand your health coverage options and make choices that best meet your needs.

Learning by Doing 10-1

1. Margo is a 30-year-old divorced mother of two. Since her employer offers no employee benefits, she's looking for a new job. What are the most important employee benefits that she should look for in a compensation package?
2. If Margo normally has $5,000 in child-care expenses each year, how much would she save if she could pay for it out of a flexible spending account, assuming her marginal tax rate is 25 percent?

LEARNING objective

3 Identify the types of health insurance plans and understand their features.

fee-for-service plan

A health insurance plan that reimburses the insured for medical expenses incurred or pays the provider directly.

managed-care plan

A health insurance plan that attempts to reduce costs through contractual arrangements with providers and financial incentives for low-cost alternatives.

health maintenance organization (HMO)

A managed-care plan that attempts to control health care costs by encouraging preventive care and limiting participants to providers with whom the plan has contracted.

preferred provider organization (PPO)

A managed-care plan that provides participants with financial incentives to use certain providers.

basic health care insurance

Health insurance that covers hospital, surgical, and physician expenses.

Types of Health Insurance

Many different types of group and individual health insurance plans are available in the marketplace today. You may have several to choose from at your place of employment. If your employer doesn't provide a health insurance benefit, you'll find hundreds of insurers that sell individual policies in the private market. To select the right type of insurance for you and your family, you first need to understand the similarities and differences among the different health insurance arrangements.

All types of health insurance have certain features in common. They all provide a mechanism for paying the medical care provider (doctor, hospital, or laboratory), whether through reimbursement to you for costs incurred or, more commonly, direct payment to the provider. They differ in the limitations they place on membership, the services they cover, and the physicians they include.

In this section, we examine the features of several types of private and government-sponsored plans. Private health plans are usually categorized as either traditional fee-for-service plans or managed-care plans. A **fee-for-service plan**, sometime called an *indemnity plan*, reimburses for the actual medical costs incurred (sometimes subject to a limit). So, for example, if you have an x-ray or blood test, the bill is submitted to the insurer, and it pays the provider or reimburses you if you have paid the cost out of pocket. In contrast, a **managed-care plan** controls your access to or use of medical services in an attempt to reduce plan costs. Two common examples of managed-care plans are a **health maintenance organization (HMO)**, which limits your selection of providers to those under contract with the plan, and a **preferred provider organization (PPO)**, which gives you financial incentives to use specific providers. In 1990, most employment-based plans were fee-for-service plans, but today, the vast majority of employees are covered under managed-care plans, as shown in Exhibit 10–4. Such a large change in only a decade is the result of employers seeking lower-cost alternatives for providing health insurance benefits.

Fee-for-Service Plans

Traditional fee-for-service medical expense coverage is usually divided into two categories: basic health-care and major medical insurance. Another classification is comprehensive medical coverage, which is a special type of major medical. Both basic health-care and major medical insurance can be purchased on either a group basis or an individual basis, although about 90 percent of all medical coverage, including fee-for-service and other plan types, is group insurance.

Basic Health Care Insurance. **Basic health care insurance** benefits include hospital, surgical, and physician expenses. These types of policies usually provide first-dollar coverage—that is, there's no deductible for the policyholder to pay. They may limit the types of expenses they cover, however, and have relatively low maximum dollar limits of protection. For example, a basic health care plan will commonly pay for x-rays and lab tests if they're done in connection with hospitalization, but not if they're done in connection with an outpatient procedure.

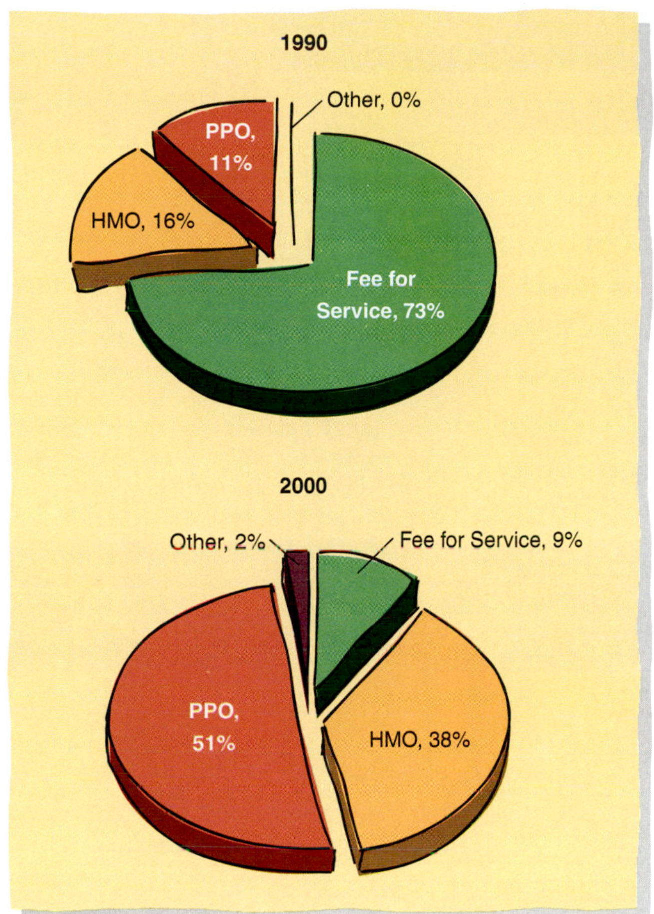

EXHIBIT 10-4

Percentage of Full-Time Employees Participating in Employment-Based Health Plans by Plan Type, 1990 and 2000

Sources: Employee Benefits Research Institute, "Research Highlights: Health Benefits" *EBRI Issue Brief 257*, May 2003.

Major Medical Insurance. **Major medical insurance** adds to the protection offered by basic health insurance by providing coverage for additional expenses and a wider range of medical services. Plans typically have the following features:

- *High maximum limits (such as $1 million).* The **maximum limit** is the total amount of your covered expenses that an insurer will pay over your lifetime.
- *Annual deductibles.* The deductible amount might be as low as $250 per person or as high as $2,000 or more. Plans with deductibles set at very high levels may be called *catastrophic health insurance* plans.
- *Coinsurance provisions.* Under a **coinsurance** arrangement, the insured person pays a percentage of his or her medical costs, often 10 to 30 percent, up to an annual out-of pocket limit, or **stop-loss limit**. After your total covered out-of-pocket costs reach the stop-loss limit, the insurer will cover 100 percent of covered charges. Your required contribution is sometimes called a **copay**.

The objective of deductibles and coinsurance is to deter the overuse of medical services by putting you at some financial risk. While you, of course, would never intentionally break your arm, you might consider going to the doctor for a minor cold if you didn't have to pay any of the cost out of pocket. These provisions also keep down the overall costs of insurance by reducing the number of small claims, which generally involve disproportionately high administrative costs for processing and record keeping—costs that have to be passed on to the policyholders. The *Go Figure!* box, "Deductibles and Coinsurance," provides an explanation of how deductible and coinsurance provisions are applied to figure your out-of-pocket costs.

major medical insurance
Insurance that covers the costs of most medical services prescribed by a doctor, subject to deductibles and coinsurance.

maximum limit
Lifetime maximum paid by the insurer to an insured person.

coinsurance
An arrangement providing for the sharing of medical costs by the insured and the insurer.

stop-loss limit
The maximum out-of-pocket cost to be paid by an insured in a given year, after which the insurer pays 100 percent of covered charges.

copay
Dollar amount of medical costs paid by the insured under a coinsurance provision, after meeting the annual deductible.

GO FIGURE!

Deductibles and Coinsurance

Problem: David's health insurance is a traditional indemnity plan with a $500 annual deductible. He has 90 percent coinsurance for participating providers and 80 percent for nonparticipating providers. On a recent snowboarding trip, David took a bad fall and tore a ligament in his right knee. He needs arthroscopic surgery to repair it and would like to go to a sports medicine specialist. In addition to being more expensive ($5,000 compared to $4,000), the specialist does not participate in his plan. If David hasn't incurred any other health costs this year, how much will his out-of-pocket costs be for a participating provider? for the nonparticipating provider he'd prefer to use? What should he consider in deciding between the two?

Solution: In deciding whether to go to the nonparticipating provider, David will obviously want to consider factors such as the qualifications and experience of the physician and the convenience of the location. If the specialist is located in a ski area, it might be difficult for him to get back for follow-up visits. The table below shows the calculation of David's out-of-pocket costs for each provider:

	David's Out-of-Pocket Costs	
	Participating Provider	Nonparticipating Provider
1. Total charge	$4,000	$5,000
2. Deductible	500	500
3. Remainder after deductible	3,500	4,500
4. Coinsurance	350 (10%)	900 (20%)
5. Total out-of-pocket	$500 + $350 = $850	$500 + $900 = $1,400

Another factor that David should consider is whether his insurance plan incorporates "usual and customary" limits on allowed provider charges for services. In such a case, the amount paid by the insurer will be a percentage of the standard cost for the procedure, rather than the actual specialist's charge. If we assume that $4,000 is the usual and customary charge, David will be left with a much larger portion of the specialist's bill. His plan will subtract the deductible from the usual and customary charge and then pay 80 percent of the remainder. Thus, the provider's insurance reimbursement will be $(4{,}000 - 500) \times 0.8 = \$2{,}800$. This will leave David with a bill of $\$5{,}000 - \$2{,}800 = \$2{,}200$.

Comprehensive Medical Insurance. Comprehensive medical insurance is similar to group major medical except that it usually carries a smaller deductible and covers a broader range of inpatient and outpatient services. The objective is to reduce the financial burden of medical costs for the insured.

Managed-Care Plans

The important thing to remember about managed-care plans is that the overall objective is to keep costs down by providing cost-saving incentives to providers and patients. Many types of managed-care plans are available today. Although the lines separating the different types are blurring, they are still primarily distinguishable by the type of arrangement made with the providers. Two major categories, as mentioned earlier, are health maintenance organizations and preferred provider organizations.

Health Maintenance Organizations. Health maintenance organizations (HMOs) were the original type of managed-care plan. HMOs attempt to control rising health-care costs by providing relatively comprehensive health insurance, encouraging preventive medicine (checkups, diagnostic tests, and immunizations), and giving health-care providers financial incentives to control costs. For example, a doctor who contracts with a plan might be given a fixed fee per participant per year regardless of the number of office visits, tests, and procedures. The HMO physician also commonly serves as a "gatekeeper" to other medical services; in other words, you must get a referral from your regular HMO physician to see a specialist or to be hospitalized. In a *group practice plan*, the doctors are actually employees of the HMO, combining medical care and insurance in one organization. The most common HMO arrangement today is an *individual practice association* made up of independent physicians who have their own practices, which include both fee-for-service patients and HMO participants. The advantage of this type of plan, compared with a group practice HMO, is that you may be able to continue with the same doctor if you switch from a fee-for-service plan to an HMO.

The primary disadvantage of the HMO model of health care is that the patient often has a limited choice of physicians and limited access to specialist care. However, your out-of-pocket costs in an HMO (not including your share of the premium) will generally be lower than in a fee-for-service plan. HMOs normally do not require the payment of a deductible and usually charge only modest copays for office visits ($5 to $15 per visit), although the amounts can vary substantially by plan. HMO medical coverage tends to be very comprehensive, most notably in the area of preventive care, which can result in a huge cost saving for families with children. Whereas fee-for-service arrangements typically only cover medically necessary treatment for illness or injury and often exclude or limit certain types of costs (such as mental health services), the philosophy of HMOs is that early intervention can reduce the likelihood of more serious health-care problems later.

Preferred Provider Organizations. A preferred provider organization (PPO) is a group of medical care providers who contract with the insurer to provide services at a reduced rate. If you have a PPO plan, you can get the benefit of this discount arrangement by using physicians and hospitals that are "preferred providers." Typically, you will still have coverage when you use a health-care provider that doesn't belong to the plan, but you'll pay a larger share of the cost. For example, once you've paid your deductible, the insurer might pay 90 percent of your expenses when you use a participating provider but only 70 percent if you use a nonparticipating provider. Since the providers are usually paid according to the services they provide, this type of plan looks something like a traditional fee-for-service insurance plan. It is also similar to the HMO model, however, in that limitations on choice result in lower costs.

Other Managed-Care Alternatives. A fairly new entrant into the health plan market, a **point of service (POS) plan** is similar to a preferred provider organization in that it allows participants to seek treatment from both participating and nonparticipating providers but requires greater cost-sharing in the latter case. The advantage of a POS plan is that the participating physicians are affiliated with an HMO, so the coverage is more comprehensive than in PPOs or fee-for-service plans and copays are smaller. Another alternative is the **exclusive provider organization (EPO).** An EPO is like a PPO in that it negotiates discounts with certain providers. The difference is that if you don't use an affiliated provider, the plan doesn't pay *any* of your costs. This type of arrangement is sometimes used for prescription drug plans.

point of service (POS) plan

Health-care plan in which participating providers are affiliated with an HMO, but participants can still use nonparticipating providers if they are willing to pay a bigger share of the cost.

exclusive provider organization (EPO)

Health-care plan that only covers medical costs from participating providers.

Consumer Choice Plans

A consumer choice plan attempts to control health costs by giving consumers incentives to control their own costs. In the other health insurance arrangements we've discussed, if you go to the doctor and she tells you that you need a particular procedure or prescribes a certain medicine, you have little incentive to say "Are there any cheaper alternatives?" In fact, if you have full coverage, you may actually have the incentive to buy the *most* expensive health care, to ask for *more* tests, and to generally overutilize medical providers. Consumer choice plans, sometimes called consumer-directed health care, attempt to address this concern by making you more sensitive to the cost of medical care and thus wiser in deciding what care to receive, when, and from whom. The *News You Can Use* box, "Winning by Losing: Insurance Incentives for Weight Loss," provides an example of how consumer choice plans are particularly well-suited to providing consumers with incentives to invest in their own health.

consumer choice plan

A health plan that includes financial incentives for preventive care and cost reduction.

NEWS you can use

Winning by Losing: Insurance Incentives for Weight Loss

Obesity is epidemic in the United States, according to statistics from the U.S. Centers for Disease Control and Prevention. Some 30 percent of American adults are obese, defined as being at least 20 percent over their recommended weight, and extra weight is associated with many chronic health problems, such as heart disease and diabetes. One study reported that $93 billion per year in health-care spending can be attributed to the obese and overweight; and experts predict that poor diet and physical inactivity may soon surpass tobacco as the leading cause of death in the United States.

Tommy Thompson, U.S. Secretary of Health and Human Services, has urged business and insurance companies to help fight the epidemic. Companies can make it easier for workers to exercise every day, Thompson says, and insurers can give discounts to people who improve their health behavior by losing weight and exercising.

Employers are getting the message, motivated at least in part by the prospect of reducing health-related costs. According to one estimate, about 40 percent of employers offer health management benefits. Common programs include educational materials, on-site fitness centers, health screenings, nutrition counseling, and reimbursement for gym memberships.

Although insurers traditionally haven't given incentives for weight control practices, they're also beginning to get into the act. One interesting example is offered by Destiny Health of Oak Brook, Illinois, whose consumer-driven health plans now incorporate incentives for healthy lifestyles. Participants who lose weight can earn points good for such things as health club discounts, frequent flier miles, discounted movie tickets, and vacation packages.

> **"Participants who lose weight can earn frequent flier miles."**

Sources: Associated Press, "Corporations Launch War on Fat," *MSNBC Health*, October 31, 2003 (www.msnbc.msn.com/id/3076957); "HHS Secretary Calls on Corporate, Government Forces to Help Fight Obesity," *Health and Medicine Week*, June 14, 2004, p. 496; Sarah Lueck, "Personal Health (Special Report); Costs; Winning by Losing," *Wall Street Journal*, October 20, 2003; John A. MacDonald, "Extra Pounds Cost Big Dollars for U.S. Government, Businesses," *Knight Ridder/Tribune Business News*, August 17, 2003; United Press International, "HHS Campaign to Combat U.S. Obesity," March 11, 2004.

Here's an example of a consumer choice plan. Suppose your employer offers a major medical plan with a high deductible ($2,000) in combination with a flexible spending account (FSA) or a health savings account (HSA), which were described earlier in the chapter. The employer could give you an additional amount of salary on a pretax basis ($1,000), which you could deposit in the HSA and use to pay part of the deductible or expenses not covered by the plan. Subject to certain IRS limitations, the HSA funds that are not used in a given year can be rolled over to the next year, so you essentially get to keep whatever you don't spend on health care. Since you're now paying out of pocket for many medical costs, you have an incentive to choose lower-cost options for medical care. Theoretically, this should result in reduced total medical costs per person.

workers' compensation insurance
State-run program requiring employers to pay lost wages and medical costs associated with job-related illness or injury.

Medicare
Federal health insurance program for people age 65 and over.

Medicaid
State-run program providing health-care coverage for the poor.

Government-Sponsored Plans

Government sources of health insurance include state **workers' compensation insurance**, which pays lost wages and medical costs associated with job-related illness or injury; the **Medicare** program, which pays some health-care costs for Social Security participants age 65 and over; and state-run **Medicaid** programs, which provide health-care coverage for the poor.

Workers' Compensation. Suppose you're lifting some heavy boxes at work and you strain your back. Who will pay the medical costs? Today, all states have laws that make your employer strictly liable for employment-related injuries or illnesses. Recall from Chapter 9 that strict liability means your employer will be financially responsible for your injury regardless of fault—so you don't have to sue to recover your costs and it won't matter if it was your fault you were injured. In fact, state workers' compensation laws actually limit your right to sue your employer for additional damages, such as pain and suffering. Although state laws differ, all provide for payment of medical expenses, rehabilitation costs, lost wages, and specific lump-sum benefits for death and dismemberment.

The Social Security Medicare Program. Social Security is much more than just a public retirement plan. It also provides disability insurance, income for surviving spouses and children of plan participants, and health insurance. More than 34 million elderly and 6 million disabled individuals are currently enrolled in Medicare, a health insurance program for qualified Social Security participants age 65 and over and anyone who is receiving Social Security disability benefits. While you're employed, a portion of your Social Security payroll tax (2.9% split between you and your employer) goes to Medicare. There is no limit on the amount of income subject to this tax.

Medicare includes two parts: Part A and Part B. Part A is mandatory hospital insurance, including room and board (subject to an annual deductible of $912 and $228 per day coinsurance for days 61–90 and $456 for days 91–50 in 2005), prescription drugs furnished by the hospital, and posthospitalization extended-care services up to 100 days ($114 per day coinsurance after 20 days). Part B is supplemental medical insurance for which you pay a monthly premium ($78.20 in 2005, regardless of age, health status, or gender) to insure the costs of physicians and surgeons, home health services, and other medical costs, such as x-rays, lab tests, medical equipment, and ambulance service. There's also a deductible ($110 in 2005) and a 20 percent coinsurance payment for most services.

As part of the Balanced Budget Act of 1997, Medicare participants are now allowed to opt for a managed-care plan in lieu of the standard Parts A and B. Options for these "Medicare + Choice Plans" include HMOs and PPOs. About 14 percent of Medicare participants are in one of these plans. You can find more information on these options in the booklet *Medicare & You*, published in 2003 by the Centers for Medicare and Medicaid Services.

Fact #3

Medical costs associated with on-the-job injuries are the responsibility of your employer and won't be covered by your health insurance. If you're injured on the job, you should contact your benefits office immediately to see what to do. Federal and state law requires that this contact information be prominently displayed in the workplace. Since workers' compensation plans often include contractual arrangements with certain providers, you may be required to see a particular physician to get your costs fully paid.

More information on Medicare options can be found on the Social Security website, www.ssa.gov. The Medicare handbook is downloadable from www.medicare.gov. Click on "Publications" to view, order, or download information.

Medicare Supplement Insurance. Although the Medicare program provides a valuable source of health insurance to many who would otherwise be uninsurable in the private market, participants are exposed to many gaps in coverage. The coinsurance provisions and deductibles can add up to substantial sums each year, and the plan doesn't currently cover routine checkups, immunizations, vision care, and hearing care. In December 2003, in response to concerns about gaps in retirees' prescription drug coverage, Congress passed the Medicare Prescription Drug, Improvement, and Modernization Act (MPDIMA), which added prescription drug coverage to Medicare, subject to the payment of an additional premium.

To fill in the gaps in Medicare coverage, many private insurers offer one or more Medicare Supplement plans, commonly called **Medigap policies**. In 2004, there were 10 standard plans, labeled A through J, with A offering the least coverage and J offering the most, as outlined in Exhibit 10–5. As the MPDIMA is gradually implemented, the allowed Medigap policies will be revised to incorporate the new provisions of the law. The standardization of Medigap policies is beneficial because it makes it easier to compare policies. Still, there are differences among companies in terms of premiums charged and services provided. The *Medicare Supplement Buyers Guide*, available free of charge from sellers of these products, provides detailed information on the various plan types and coverages. In 2002, the average cost of a group Medigap policy was $2,631 per year, a significant out-of-pocket expense for the typical retiree whose only source of retirement income was Social Security.

Medigap policies

Insurance policies designed to pay deductibles and other costs that are not covered by Medicare.

When it's time for you to retire, it's important that you purchase Medigap within six months of enrolling in Medicare Part B, especially if your health status is poor. After the six-month period has passed, your eligibility for Medigap insurance isn't guaranteed. Medicare Choice Plans don't have the same gaps in coverage as the traditional Medicare program, so you don't need Medigap if you belong to one of these plans. In fact, it's illegal for an insurer to sell you a Medigap policy under those circumstances.

If you're one of the lucky few, you may be eligible for group Medigap coverage through a former employer. Although 37 percent of retirees report that they have health insurance through a former employer, recent government estimates suggest that only 12 percent of all private companies currently offer health benefits to retirees, and these are primarily large firms. Furthermore,

EXHIBIT 10-5 Benefits Provided by Medigap Plans

Basic Benefits in All Plans

Part A: coinsurance amount per day	\$210 per day for days 61–90 \$420 per day for days 91–150 100% of remaining hospital expenses to a maximum of 365 days
Part B: coinsurance amount	20% of covered charges after \$100 deductible
Blood: reasonable cost of first 3 pints per year	

Medigap Plan	A	B	C	D	E	F	G	H	I	J
Basics benefits	✓	✓	✓	✓	✓	✓	✓	✓	✓	✓
Part A deductible (\$840 per year in 2003)		✓	✓	✓	✓	✓	✓	✓	✓	✓
Skilled nursing care coinsurance (\$105 per day for days 21–100)			✓	✓	✓	✓	✓	✓	✓	✓
Expenses incurred in foreign country (80%, \$250 deductible)			✓	✓	✓	✓	✓	✓	✓	✓
Part B deductible (\$100 per year in 2003)			✓			✓				✓
At-home recovery assistance (\$40 per visit to maximum \$1,600 per year				✓			✓		✓	✓
Part B doctors' charges in excess of allowed amount						100%	80%		100%	100%
Prescription drugs (50% after \$250 deductible)								✓	✓	✓
Preventive screening (\$120 per year for physical and tests)					✓			✓		

Source: Vickie L. Bajtelsmit, "The Medicare Prescription Drug, Improvement, and Modernization Act of 2003: What Does It Mean for Your Clients?" Journal of Financial Service Professionals, March 2004. Used by Permission.

this percentage has been declining steadily, and employers have tightened up eligibility requirements (e.g., requiring more years of service) and reduced their subsidy of premium costs.

Medicare is currently in financial difficulty. The aging of the U.S. population and rising health-care costs are putting more and more pressure on the Medicare system. Many are concerned that the new prescription drug benefits will cost much more than previous forecasts suggested. Without major changes, the system can't survive. What does this mean for you? As in other areas of your personal finances, you need to take personal responsibility for ensuring your future welfare. Instead of assuming that the government will take care of your medical costs in retirement, you should consider additional savings targeted to the payment of these future costs. In the *Ask the Expert* box, "How Much Is Needed to Fund Retiree Health Costs?" two economists at the Employee Benefit Research Institute provide some estimates for how much you need to save to fund your retirement health insurance needs under current rules, but you should probably assume that your costs will be even higher.

Medicaid. Whereas Medicare is a federal program, Medicaid is a state-run and federally financed program that provides relatively comprehensive health coverage for more than 28 million individuals with low income and assets. Approximately 3 million people who are over age 65 *and* poor qualify for both programs and may use Medicaid payments to meet Medicare deductibles and co-pays. The use of Medicaid for long-term care costs will be discussed in Chapter 16. States differ in eligibility requirements and coverage provided. Because the programs place low limits on physician charges to control costs, it's sometimes difficult to find participating providers.

Dealing with Special Circumstances

The best-laid plans sometimes go wrong. You had a terrific job with an employer that offered a comprehensive benefit package, but you just got laid off. Thousands of workers have faced this reality in the last several years as employers responded to the demands of a recessionary economy.

ask the expert How Much Is Needed to Fund Retiree Health Costs?

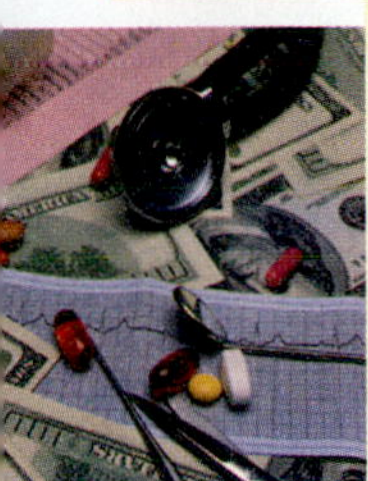

Paul Fronstein and Dallas Salisbury
Employee Benefit Research Institute

How much would you need to have saved by the time you retire to fully fund your expected health costs in retirement, including out-of-pocket expenses and insurance premiums? Paul Fronstein and Dallas Salisbury, of the Employee Benefit Research Institute, recently considered this question and made some forecasts. Assuming reasonable increases in current Medigap and Medicare Part B premiums and out-of-pocket costs, 7 percent health-care cost inflation, and 4 percent return on invested assets, these researchers estimate that a retiree without group coverage in 2003 would need to have saved as much as $354,000 by age 65 to fully fund the expected costs of retiree health care, depending on life expectancy. People with lower life expectancy and those with access to employment-based insurance would require less savings, as shown in the table.

	Amount to Cover 100% of Type J Medigap + Part B Premium + Maximum Out-of-Pocket	
Age at Death	Employment-Based Group Insurance ($)	Individual Medigap Insurance ($)
80	80,000	116,000
85	109,000	164,000
90	141,000	219,000
95	176,000	282,000
100	216,000	354,000

Source: Paul Fronstein and Dallas Salisbury, "Retiree Health Benefits: Savings Necessary to Fund Health Care in Retirement," *EBRI Issue Brief 254*, February 2003.

Or maybe you're recently divorced and are no longer covered under your spouse's employer-sponsored plan. Or you might be a student who has lost dependent status and isn't eligible for coverage under your parents' health plan. Perhaps the most important special circumstance is when you have a serious preexisting condition, such as kidney failure, diabetes, or multiple sclerosis. Here, we examine each of these special circumstances in more detail.

Continuation Coverage under COBRA. The Consolidated Omnibus Reconciliation Act of 1986 (COBRA) is a federal law that applies to all employers with 20 employees or more, with the exception of the federal government and religious institutions. Under this law, if you lose or quit your job, you're eligible to purchase coverage through your previous employer's plan for a period of 18 months (extendable under some circumstances to 36 months). To elect this coverage, you must notify your employer no later than 60 days after your last day of work.

Fact #4

If you're laid off or quit your job, you'll be able to continue in your group health plan if your employer has 20 employees or more. However, you'll have to pay the full premium plus an administrative charge of up to 2 percent. In total, your insurance costs can easily amount to from $4,000 to $8,000 per year for family coverage.

Divorce. A disproportionate percentage of divorced women, whether employed or not, have inadequate health insurance or are uninsured. This is largely because women are more likely to work for employers that offer limited employee benefits. If you were participating in a health plan through your former spouse's employer before the divorce, you can elect to pay for COBRA continuation coverage under his or her plan for up to 36 months after the divorce (unless your former spouse worked for the federal government, a religious institution, or a firm with fewer than 20 employees). In many cases, this coverage is prohibitively expensive, so you may be better off buying individual insurance. Health insurance continuation should be a factor in divorce settlements, at a minimum requiring inclusion of the children under the employed parent's plan and fair division of their uninsured medical costs, deductibles, and copays. Too often, the health insurance effects of divorce don't become apparent until the ink is dry on the divorce decree.

NEWS you can use

Recent Legal Changes That Affect Your Health Coverage

Several new laws affect your health coverage, as described below.

- **The Health Insurance Portability and Accountability Act (HIPAA).** Applies to participants in group health plans and their covered family members. Key provisions of the law limit exclusions for preexisting conditions; make it easier to apply for new coverage upon loss of existing coverage, marriage, or addition of a dependent; prohibit discrimination in enrollment and premiums based on health status; and guarantee availability and renewability of health insurance coverage for small employers.

"Group health plans that pay for mastectomies must also pay for breast reconstruction."

- **Newborns' and Mothers' Health Protection Act.** Requires plans that offer maternity coverage to pay for at least a 48-hour hospital stay following childbirth (96 hours for a caesarian section).
- **Women's Health and Cancer Rights Act**. Requires that plans offering mastectomy coverage also include coverage for breast reconstruction.
- **Mental Health Parity Act.** Requires that annual or lifetime dollar limits on mental health benefits (other than those for substance abuse or chemical dependency) be no lower than the dollar limits for medical and surgical benefits offered by the group health plan.

Loss of Dependent Status. Many students are covered under their parents' health insurance plans. What happens if you lose your dependent status? The good news is that, as a relatively healthy young person, you'll probably be eligible to purchase individual health insurance at favorable rates. If you have a serious health condition that makes it impossible for you to find coverage in the individual market, you have the right under federal law to elect COBRA continuation coverage under a parent's policy for up to 36 months if that parent works for a firm subject to that law. As in the case of continuation after divorce, however, this coverage may be quite expensive. As another option, most educational institutions provide group coverage opportunities for full-time students.

Preexisting Conditions. A preexisting condition is an illness or injury, such as diabetes or heart disease, that significantly increases your expected claims costs under an insurance policy and that began before you were covered under that policy. Historically, insurers didn't cover preexisting conditions for new policyholders for a specific period of time (typically three to six months). However, under the Health Insurance Portability and Accountability Act of 1996 (HIPAA)—discussed in the *News You Can Use* box, "Recent Legal Changes That Affect Your Health Insurance," you can't be subject to a preexisting condition waiting period when you move from one plan to another. You should still look carefully at plan exclusions and limitations, though, since an insurance plan can exclude coverage entirely for certain conditions, as long as the exclusion applies to all participants in the plan. The reason for these limitations and exclusions is obvious—to keep the costs down for the members of the pool.

Additional Types of Insurance

Medical costs associated with dental and eye care are normally excluded from health insurance policies. Your employer may, however, offer dental expense insurance, vision care insurance, or discount programs that will help you to cover these costs.

Dental Expense Insurance. Dental expense insurance, which is primarily available as a group benefit, is very similar to health insurance in that you pay a premium in return for being reimbursed for qualified medical expenses. You'll normally have to pay deductibles and coinsurance as well, and you may be subject to limits on some procedures (such as root canals and crowns) and exclusions of others (such as orthodontic work). Most dental plans provide first-dollar coverage for annual cleanings, x-rays, and check-ups, but they usually require the insured to pay a fairly large proportion of the covered charges, often 50 percent. In addition, they typically place a maximum on the total payable by the insurer under the plan in a given year, sometimes as low as $1,000. Thus, if you're considering paying for a contributory plan, you need to consider whether your out-of-pocket dental expenses for the year will exceed the policy limit less the premium cost. And don't forget human nature—many people miss their regular dental check-ups even when they've paid for dental insurance simply because they hate going to the dentist.

Dental expense insurance may help pay for orthodontics.

Vision Care Insurance. Vision care insurance provides reimbursement or discounts on eye examinations, glasses, and contact lenses. Normally, your regular health insurance will cover care related to diseases of the eye, such as glaucoma or macular degeneration. This implies that vision care insurance policies essentially cover an annual expense that you can easily estimate and budget for. Although nearly every person over the age of 40 requires eye correction of some sort, vision care insurance is often expensive relative to the benefit received. As with dental expense insurance, you should look carefully at what the plan offers before agreeing to pay for it. Particularly in the case of "vision discount plans," which charge a fee in return for special discounts at participating merchant locations, many consumers have found that the discounts are also available to people who don't participate in the plan, so they've paid the premium for nothing.

Learning by Doing 10-2

1. What type of health insurance is each of the following people most likely to have?
   a. Retired person age 70
   b. Child living in a low-income household
   c. Lawyer
   d. Freelance writer

Planning for Disability Income Needs

LEARNING objective

4 Calculate your disability income needs and select appropriate insurance.

Most people underestimate their risk of becoming disabled. The fact is that you have a 33 percent chance of being disabled for at least three months during your working life. In any given period, your risk of disability is much higher than your risk of death. Unless you have sufficient financial resources, the loss of income during a period of disability can be financially devastating. You may be unable to work, but you'll still have to meet the expenses of daily living. Understanding your disability income needs and your sources of disability income insurance are therefore an essential component of your financial plan.

What Is Disability?

In general, a *disability* is an illness or injury that prevents you from earning your regular income or reduces how much you can earn. Insurance policies may apply more restrictive definitions; for example, they may define a disability as the inability to perform the regular requirements of your job or the inability to work at any job for which you are reasonably suited by education and experience.

Disability Income Needs Analysis

If you were disabled tomorrow and were unable to earn your regular income, how much money would you need to meet your basic needs? You should be able to answer this question easily by reviewing the personal cash flow statement you developed in Chapter 2, omitting expenditures for anything that isn't necessary, and subtracting any income you receive from investments.

An extended period of disability can be a financial drain on household resources.

For example, when we considered Cindy and Dave Thompson's household budget in Chapter 3 (Exhibit 3–10), they estimated their total monthly expenses for 2005 at $4,768. In the event that Dave became disabled, however, the family could eliminate discretionary spending on clothing, gifts, entertainment, and charity. They also could temporarily suspend contributions to college and retirement savings. Making these adjustments to their budget leaves approximately $3,200 per month to cover groceries, housing and auto expenses, utilities, and insurance. In the event of a long-term disability, Cindy and Dave could also consider more drastic cost-saving measures such as downsizing their house and cars.

Sources of Disability Income

In the example above, we see that the Thompsons estimate they would need income of at least $3,200 per month if Dave were disabled. Since Cindy left the workforce to care for their new baby, they might be able to at least partially meet their income needs if she returned to work. Other sources of income include government programs, Dave's accumulated paid leave at his place of employment, and disability income insurance. **Disability income insurance**, which replaces lost income during a period of disability, is available from a number of sources including government, employer, and individual insurance.

disability income insurance

Insurance that replaces the policyholder's lost income during a period of disability.

Government-Sponsored Disability Income Protection. Most states require that some type of workers' compensation insurance be carried on all employees, as discussed earlier in this chapter. So if your injury or illness is job-related, you may be eligible for income replacement from that source. However, benefits and waiting periods can vary substantially from state to state, and you can't be sure that the benefits will be sufficient to cover your expenses.

If your injuries are serious enough, you may be eligible for Social Security disability insurance. Under that program, you must be unable to work at *any job* (the most restrictive definition of disability), and you must have been out of work at least five months and expect to remain disabled at least one year. The benefits under Social Security depend on your participation in the Social Security system and your average income over your working career.

Employer-Sponsored Disability Income Protection. Employers may provide disability income protection in several ways, including personal days, paid vacation time, sick leave, and group short- and long-term disability income insurance. If you become ill or are injured and expect to be away from your job for more than a few days, you should consult with your employer's benefits office, since there are often specific requirements regarding qualification and waiting periods for each program. Your employer may require that you exhaust all or a portion of your sick days, personal days, and vacation time before accessing short-term disability insurance, for example.

Some employers provide *short-term disability insurance* for workers with a qualifying disability. This type of insurance pays a portion (commonly 60 or 70%) of your predisability earnings after you've exhausted your sick days and you've been unable to work for a specified waiting period (commonly 15 to 30 days). Although plans differ, these policies commonly replace income for from 6 to 12 months.

Long-term disability income insurance is often an optional contributory benefit under employee benefit plans, but it can also be purchased by individuals directly from an insurer. Even under a group policy, the premiums are usually age-related, so that older employees will pay more per month to participate in the plan. Like short-term disability insurance, long-term disability plans specify the definition of disability that qualifies you for income replacement, the waiting period before you're eligible to receive benefits (often three to six months of continued disability), the percentage of predisability income replacement (usually 60%), and the length of time benefits will be paid. Many such policies pay benefits to age 65 if the policyholder is permanently disabled. As discussed earlier, it's advantageous to purchase group disability insurance, if available, because individual insurance costs will increase and availability will decrease as your age or health condition becomes less favorable.

When you purchase disability insurance through your employer, you're usually given the option of paying for it with either after-tax dollars or pretax dollars. Although it's generally preferable to use pretax dollars for benefits, *you should buy disability insurance on an after-tax basis.* If you pay for the insurance with after-tax income and later are disabled, the income benefit you receive while disabled will be tax-free. In contrast, if you use pretax dollars for the insurance premium, you'll have to pay tax on the income received. As mentioned, most disability policies pay benefits equal to 60 percent of your salary; additional taxation could reduce your income to a degree that it wouldn't cover your needs. For example, if Dave Thompson's pretax monthly income is $5,500, then 60 percent income replacement would give the family $3,300 per month, just enough to cover expected expenses. If the insurance benefit were subject to tax, however, the Thompsons wouldn't have enough income protection.

Individual Disability Insurance. If no employer-sponsored plan is available to you, or if you believe you need additional disability income protection, you can also purchase coverage in the individual market. Difficulties with fraud and abuse in this market in recent years, however, have resulted in a smaller number of insurers and higher premiums.

Although there are many variations on individual disability insurance policies, the best types are those that replace lost income if you're unable to perform the duties of your particular job—often called "own occupation" insurance. For example, a surgeon who has a hand injury could receive income replacement even if he or she could still work in another medical specialty. These policies are usually sold based on a dollar amount of income replacement with limits on what percentage of predisability income will be replaced. For example, you might buy a policy that will pay you $1,000 per month as long as that doesn't exceed 30 percent of your predisability income.

Obviously, the more disability income coverage you purchase, the higher your premium. Other factors that increase the cost of individual disability income insurance are your profession, your age, and your existing health status. Key features to look for in disability income insurance policies include the following:

- *Waiting period.* How long do you have to be disabled before you can begin receiving benefits? This period can be anywhere from 30 days to one year.
- *Benefit duration.* How long can you continue to receive benefits, assuming you continue to meet the definition of disability? A policy may pay benefits for a short time, such as two years, or until age 65, or for life. Generally, all else equal, you want a plan that will cover you for as long as possible. The longer the coverage, however, the more expensive.
- *Income replacement.* How much will the benefit be? Your objective is to meet your expenses, but you need to consider that if your disability continues for a long period of time, these costs may rise with inflation. A cost-of-living increase feature is therefore desirable.
- *Renewability.* If your health deteriorates, can the insurer drop your disability insurance policy? You should look for policies with a guaranteed renewability feature. Some policies also waive your premium if you are disabled.

Employer-Sponsored Retirement Plans

5 Incorporate employer-sponsored retirement plans in your financial plan.

One of your most important employee benefits is the retirement or pension plan. Since the enactment of the Employee Retirement Income Security Act (ERISA) in 1974, the number of employer-sponsored retirement plans has increased steadily, as have pension coverage rates, defined as the percent of people covered by an employer pension or retirement plan. About half of all workers are covered by some type of employer retirement plan. If you define pension coverage to include situations in which at least one spouse has an employer-sponsored plan, then the coverage rate goes up to about 75 percent. Coverage by a pension or retirement plan, however, doesn't imply that the plan will produce *adequate* retirement income. Most large employers offer some sort of retirement plan to their workers, but the terms and conditions can vary substantially, so careful consideration of this element of your benefit package is very important. Although retirement planning will be discussed in more detail in Chapter 15, this section outlines the tax advantages of employment-based retirement plans and the types that are commonly offered.

Tax Advantages of Qualified Plans

tax-qualified retirement plan

A retirement plan that qualifies under federal law for tax deferral; taxes on contributions made to the plan and earnings on plan assets are not due and payable until withdrawal at retirement.

If your employer's plan meets certain requirements, it's said to be a **tax-qualified retirement plan** under ERISA, which entitles the firm and you to the following tax benefits:

- Contributions to the plan are tax-deductible by your employer in the year in which the contributions are made.
- Your own contributions to the plan are made on a pretax basis and not subject to current federal, state, or local income tax.
- Taxes on your contributions to the plan, benefit accruals, and any income or capital gains you earn on your invested dollars are deferred until withdrawal.

As discussed in Chapter 4, tax deferral means that you don't have to pay the taxes until some point in the future. For retirement plans, this is usually at the time the funds are withdrawn during retirement. Although you'll eventually have to pay tax on the withdrawn funds, it may be far in the future, so the present value of the tax payment is less than what you would have had to pay on that income today. Furthermore, you may be subject to a lower marginal tax rate when you receive the funds during retirement.

Fact #5

Contributions to qualified employer retirement plans are tax-deferred, but that's not the same as tax-free. You don't have to pay current income or payroll taxes on the contributions made by your employer or on your own contributions, and you don't have to pay current tax on investment earnings you make on plan assets. But you'll have to pay taxes when you receive a benefit or withdraw the funds at retirement. Allowing tax deferral costs the federal government millions of dollars in lost tax revenue, but that translates into more dollars in the pockets of retirees.

The powerful effect of tax-deferred contributions and earnings is illustrated by the following example: Suppose you have \$100 in pretax income to invest and you put it in a tax-deferred account earning 8 percent per year. After 40 years, your \$100 investment, with compound interest, will have grown to $\$100 \times (1.08)^{40}$, or \$2,172. Compare that to the amount you'd have if your contribution and earnings were not tax-deferred but were instead subject to a marginal tax rate of 25 percent. In that case, you'd have only \$75 to invest after paying 25 percent tax on the \$100 in income. And on each year's interest earnings, you'd have to pay tax of 25 percent, so you'd net only 6 percent per year after taxes ($0.08 \times [1 - 0.25] = 0.06$). The final outcome after 40 years will therefore be $\$75 \times (1.06)^{40} = \$771$, about one-third as much! Of course, you'll eventually owe taxes on the \$2,172 in the first example, so the net difference isn't quite this large—but, even after taxes, you're about twice as well off with the benefit of tax deferral.

Given the tax advantages, you can see why you need to take full advantage of opportunities for tax-deferred investment. If you don't work for an employer that offers a plan, you should consider tax-deferred investment opportunities for private savings, as discussed in Chapter 15.

Defined-Benefit Versus Defined-Contribution Plans

There are generally two approaches to employer retirement plans—the employer can make either a *benefit promise* or a *contribution promise.* We look at the general features of each approach here and then consider both in more detail later in the section.

defined-benefit (DB) plan

A retirement plan in which the employer promises employees a retirement benefit determined by a formula, commonly based on pre-retirement earnings and years of service.

In a **defined-benefit (DB) plan**, sometimes called a pension plan, the company promises that, when you retire, it will pay you a benefit, which will be determined by a particular formula. In the simplest case, the formula is a lump sum. More commonly, formulas are based on a percentage of the salary you're making at the time you retire and number of years you've worked for the firm (commonly called "years of service"). For example, your employer might promise you a retirement benefit equal to 2 percent of your final salary for each year of service. So, if you've worked for the same employer for 25 years, your annual benefit would be half of your final salary ($0.02 \times 25 = 0.50$, or 50%).

Notice that, in a defined-benefit plan, all the financial risk is on your employer. It must invest money today in order to have sufficient funds to pay promised benefits to you in the future. If the stock market slumps immediately before you retire, the employer is still obligated to pay your promised benefit.

DB plans are more common at large industrial firms with unionized workers.

Instead of a defined-benefit plan, your employer might offer a **defined-contribution (DC) plan**. Under a DC plan, the employer promises to make periodic contributions to your retirement account but makes no promise about the benefit that might result from these contributions. The contribution made by the employer is determined by a formula, often related to salary; the average contribution is 3 percent of the employee's salary. Alternatively, the contribution can be a specific dollar amount or shares of employer stock, or it may vary with the profitability of the firm, with larger contributions in good years and smaller or no contributions in bad years. The actual benefit you'll receive at retirement will depend on the accumulated value of the account at the retirement date, which in turn depends on the amount of contributions made and the investment returns over time. Depending on the type of plan, investment decisions might be made by the employer or they might be your responsibility. Either way, the risk of poor investment performance falls on the employee.

defined-contribution (DC) plan

Retirement plan in which the employer promises to make regular contributions to employees' retirement accounts but does not guarantee the benefits that will result.

Recently, some employers have tried to combine the features of these two approaches in what is called a **cash balance plan**. Here, the employer makes a benefit promise (as in a DB plan), but the actual benefit depends in part on the performance of an investment account kept on behalf of the plan participant (as in a DC plan), which again pushes some of the investment risk on the employee.

cash balance plan

A defined-benefit retirement plan that includes an investment component similar to a defined-contribution plan.

Like many other types of employee benefits, a retirement plan may be noncontributory, in which case it is funded entirely by the employer, or contributory, in which case employees are allowed or required to make contributions to the plan as well. In many DC plans, the employer promises to match employee contributions up to a certain percentage of salary. For example, your employer might offer to contribute 50 cents for every dollar contributed by you, up to a maximum of 3 percent of your salary. In that case, if you make no contribution to the plan, the employer will have no obligation to contribute. But if you make contributions equal to 6 percent of your salary, the employer will match your contribution with an additional 3 percent, for a total of 9 percent.

Important Features of Defined-Benefit Plans

If your employer offers a defined-benefit plan, there are several features that you should be aware of and understand. These include benefit formulas, vesting rules, portability, normal retirement age, and any insurance incorporated in the plan.

Benefit Formula. As we've already seen, the benefit formula for a defined-benefit plan is likely to be based on salary and service. The salary used in the formula might be your final salary, your highest salary, or an average of three to five of your highest years' salaries. The percent of salary per year of service may be fixed, or it may increase for longer service periods. For example, you might get 0.5 percent per year for the first 10 years and 1 percent for each additional year. Benefit accruals can even be designed to encourage early retirement by reducing or eliminating the percent of salary after a certain point. For example, the benefit formula might be 2 percent of final salary per year of service up to 35 years of service. In that case, if you work more than 35 years, your benefit percentage will not increase beyond 70 percent. You should also consider whether the plan includes a regular cost of living adjustment (COLA) to the benefit you receive. Although your initial benefit might be plenty to live on, inflation will gradually make it more difficult to make ends meet. Many DB plans don't promise specific COLAs.

Vesting and Portability Rules. Before the passage of ERISA, employees were commonly eligible for benefits under their employer's pension plan only if they stayed with the firm until retirement. Today, **vesting rules** determine the number of years of employment required before an employee has a legal right to accrued retirement benefits. Employees who are *vested* have these rights,

vesting rules

Rules that define employees' rights to accrued retirement plan contributions and benefits.

whereas employees who are fired or leave their jobs without being vested have no right to contributions already made on their behalf and will not receive any retirement benefit from the employer.

How do you become vested? Under ERISA, your employer *must* have a vesting rule that's at least as favorable as one of the following:

- *Five-year cliff vesting.* Under this rule, you have no rights to benefits if you've worked less than five years at the firm. At the five-year mark, you'll be 100 percent vested—fully entitled to the benefits that have accrued in the plan (even though you won't be eligible to receive them until retirement).
- *Three- through seven-year graded vesting.* Under this rule, you'll accrue rights to 20 percent of the accrued benefit for each year of service from three to seven years. For example, if you leave the firm with six years of service, you'll be entitled at retirement to 80 percent of the accrued benefit.

portability

An employee's right to take retirement plan assets from one place of employment to another when the employee changes jobs.

Portability refers to the ability to take plan assets from one employer to another. Very few DB plans are currently portable, but the trend is toward increased portability. When an employer's plan isn't portable, the employer must keep records of the benefits due to vested employees who leave the company before retirement, since these employees have the right to request benefit payments when they do retire. Many defined-benefit plans have large numbers of unclaimed benefits, since individuals commonly forget about small entitlements and fail to file the paperwork necessary to receive the benefit. Contributions that you make yourself are always immediately vested and portable.

Normal Retirement Age. Each plan defines the normal retirement age at which an employee will be entitled to receive full benefits. IRS rules for tax-qualified plans set a minimum normal retirement age of $59\frac{1}{2}$, but the age is higher in many plans. If you take a disbursement from a retirement plan before age $59\frac{1}{2}$, you'll owe a 10 percent penalty to the IRS.

To see if you or a retired family member are entitled to a retirement benefit from a previous employer, you can check http://search.pbgc.gov that lists unclaimed benefits from many employers' defined-benefit plans.

Guaranteed Benefits. What happens if your employer has promised you a retirement benefit but then goes out of business before you retire? The Pension Benefit Guarantee Corporation (PBGC), a quasi-governmental organization established under ERISA, guarantees pension benefits to participants in most private DB plans. Thus, if your employer goes bankrupt, you'll still be entitled to vested benefits at retirement. In plans using salary and service formulas, though, the guaranteed benefit will likely be much less than what you would have received if the plan had not prematurely terminated. This is because the benefit will be calculated based on your salary and service at the time of termination of the plan rather than at the time of your retirement (with no adjustment for wage increases and inflation to the date of retirement).

Disability, Survivors, and Retiree Health Insurance. Many DB plans include elements of insurance. If you become disabled before you're eligible for retirement, you may be entitled to a disability benefit payment, commonly 50 to 70 percent of your retirement benefit. If you die before retirement age, your surviving spouse will probably be eligible to receive a benefit from the plan. Depending on the terms of the plan, he or she might receive a lump sum distribution or a series of payments. Some DB plans, particularly those in the public sector, also include a promise of health insurance for retirees up to age 65 (when they qualify for Medicare), but this benefit is becoming less and less common due to escalating costs.

Learning by Doing 10-3

You're currently 25 years old and you're considering a public-sector job that offers a mandatory DB plan. The plan has a five-year cliff-vesting rule and promises a benefit equal to 1.5 percent of final salary for each year of service up to 30 years.

1. If you quit after three years, what benefit will you be entitled to at retirement, assuming your final salary was $40,000?
2. If you quit after 10 years, what benefit will you be entitled to at retirement, assuming your final salary was $60,000?
3. If you stay with this employer to retirement, what is the maximum you could receive as a retirement benefit, assuming your final salary was $100,000?

Important Features of Defined-Contribution Plans

Although Congress is considering some changes that would greatly simplify the rules for defined-contribution plans, currently there are several types of arrangements, which may be subject to different rules and limits. Next, we look at these types and provide an overview of the differences between them.

Types of DC Plans. The general category of defined-contribution retirement plans includes money-purchase plans and profit-sharing plans. These arrangements differ by the type of contribution promise being made by the employer. In a **money-purchase plan**, the employer promises to contribute a set percentage of salary. For example, your employer might promise to add 3 percent of your salary to a retirement account each year. In a **profit-sharing plan**, the employer's contributions are discretionary but are commonly defined as a percentage of either profits or salary. As with the money-purchase plan, the employer might pay 3 percent per year into your account, but it doesn't *have* to.

Your plan may also be designated as a **cash-or-deferred arrangement (CODA)**. This means that, in addition to your employer's money-purchase or profit-sharing contribution, you can make additional tax-deferred contributions to the account out of your pretax income. The 401(k) plan, named for the section in the IRS code that outlines the rules for CODAs, is by far the best-known type of defined-contribution plan. A 401(k) may be purely a salary deferral plan, with no employer contributions, or the employer may provide a matching contribution to encourage employee participation. The employer contribution may depend on company profits. A 403(b) plan, another type of CODA, sometimes called a tax-sheltered annuity plan (TSA), is similar to a 401(k) plan but is sponsored by a nonprofit organization such as a government entity or religious group.

Stock bonus plans and **employee stock ownership plans (ESOPs)** are special types of profit-sharing plans that invest in employer stock. These types of plans are very popular with larger companies, since they can give participants company stock rather than cash to meet contribution promises.

Investment of Plan Assets. Some DC plans are designed to allow participants to specify how they want their account balances invested—for example, the percentage to be placed in risky versus less risky assets. Others may hire professional investment managers or specify the investment allocation. In either case, DC plan participants face much more uncertainty about retirement income than do defined-benefit plan participants. If your plan allows investment choice, it's important that you take the time to learn about your investment alternatives so you can make informed investment allocation decisions. In the next several chapters, we'll consider these issues in some detail. One of the most common mistakes that individuals make with their retirement funds is to invest too heavily in employer stock when they have other alternatives. The *Money Psychology* box, "Why Do Employees Like Employer Stock?" offers some explanations for these decisions.

Limits on Employee and Employer Contributions. All qualified retirement plans are subject to maximum contribution limits for the employer and the employee. The Economic Growth and Tax Relief Reconciliation Act of 2001 increased the maximum tax-deductible employer contribution to 25 percent of compensation, with a maximum of $40,000 per year. The limits on your own contributions are $14,000 for 2005 and $15,000 in 2006, after which the limit will increase annually with inflation in increments of $500. If you're age 50 or over, a catch-up provision in the law allows you to contribute $18,000 in 2005, and $20,000 per year thereafter. This maximum is applied to the total of all contributions you make to tax-deferred arrangements in a given year, even if the contributions are made to several different plans.

Defined-Contribution Plans for Small Businesses. Several types of retirement plan arrangements are specifically intended to meet the needs of self-employed individuals and small business owners. These include Simplified Employee Pension Plans, Savings Incentive Match Plans for Employees of Small Employers, and Keough plans.

A simplified Employee Pension Plan (SEP) is a type of defined-contribution plan that has simplified administrative rules and doesn't lock the employer into a particular contribution level.

money-purchase plan

A defined-contribution retirement plan to which the employer contributes a set percentage of the employee's salary.

profit-sharing plan

A defined-contribution retirement plan in which employer contributions are discretionary.

cash-or-deferred arrangement (CODA)

A defined-contribution retirement plan in which employees can contribute some of their salary to the plan on a tax-deferred basis.

employee stock ownership plans (ESOPs)

Profit-sharing plans that make contributions to employee accounts in the form of employer stock.

Money Psychology

Why Do Employees Like Employer Stock?

Janice went to work one morning only to find out that she was out of a job. Even more distressing, her retirement nest egg, which had been entirely invested in her employer's stock, was now worthless. Janice's situation isn't unique—employees of Enron Corporation, Rite Aid, Lucent Technologies, Qwest Communications, WorldCom, and other companies have all watched the value of their retirement accounts plunge. The employees who are most badly hurt in these situations are, like Janice, those who have invested exclusively in their employer's stock. Despite the well-known principle that you shouldn't put all your eggs in one basket, the unfortunate truth is that about a third of large-firm retirement plan assets are held in employer stock.

Money psychology offers an explanation for why employees love to invest in company stock even when advised not to. Psychologists have long observed that human beings display a persistent preference for things which are *familiar.* When you're familiar with a company, you incorrectly assume that you have some control over its performance—that it's safer—so you're biased in favor of investing in it. And what company are you most familiar with? The one you work for, of course. Overcoming this inherent bias may be difficult, but you should limit your investment in company stock to no more than 10 to 20 percent of your total retirement account.

The SEP limit is the lesser of $40,000 or 25 percent of compensation. Savings Incentive Match Plans for Employees of Small Employers (SIMPLEs), authorized by the Small Business Protection Act of 1996, are for small employers (up to 100 employees) that don't offer another qualified plan. In a SIMPLE, employees can make contributions of up to $10,000 in 2005 through payroll deductions (plus $2,000 for individuals age 50 or over, increasing to $2,500 in 2006), and employers can make either matching or fixed contributions subject to certain limits. The limits are scheduled to increase with inflation in $500 increments. If you have income from self-employment, you can make tax-deferred contributions to a Keogh plan, also known as an HR-10 plan, even if you're participating in a qualified plan through your primary employer. The limits are the same as for SEPs. This type of plan can be set up to cover partners and employees as well.

Learning by Doing 10-4

1. Retirement plans can be defined-benefit or defined-contribution plans.
   a. Which type places the most risk on the participants?
   b. What kinds of risk?
2. Michael is 25 years old and earns $50,000 per year before taxes.
   a. How much can he contribute to his 401(k) plan in 2005?
   b. How much will that save him in current income taxes if his marginal tax rate is 34 percent?

Comparing Compensation Packages

LEARNING objective

6 Compare job offers according to geographic location, salary, and benefits packages.

With an understanding of some of the elements of employee benefit plans, you're better prepared to compare the compensation packages you may be offered by prospective employers. The world is a smaller place today than it was for previous generations of job seekers. It's not uncommon for college seniors to be considering jobs with vastly different companies in several geographic areas—perhaps including countries other than the United States. Even if you're already employed, it's likely that you'll change jobs, and even careers, several times over your working life. When you're considering these different job opportunities, you'll want to take into account a variety of factors, including the culture of the workplace, opportunities for advancement, and the fit with your interests and abilities. Here, we consider the elements of this decision that relate to financial planning. In this section, you'll learn to compare job offers based on cost-of-living differences and benefits packages.

Comparing Salary Offers

If you've traveled around the country much, you know that the prices of food, clothing, housing, child care, and transportation can vary greatly by geographic area. In general, it's more expensive to live on the East or West Coasts than in the middle of the country, and it's generally more expensive to live in urban areas than in rural areas. Although salaries are a little higher in expensive areas, you'll probably find that they're not *enough* higher—a high salary in New York City will likely result in a lower standard of living than the lower salary in a small Midwest town.

Recall that Danelle Washington, from our continuing case, is a college senior studying to become a high school biology teacher. Let's suppose that she's comparing two teaching positions, one in Boston, Massachusetts, at a starting salary of $35,000 and the other in Tallahassee, Florida, at a salary of $28,000. She knows it will be more expensive to live in Boston and would like to determine whether the salary differential is enough to offset the cost difference. In Chapter 1, you read about how changing prices are measured by the consumer price index (CPI). Although the CPI is based on national trends, regional differences in prices are regularly tracked as well. This is usually reported as a cost-of-living index for each location, which tells you how the cost of goods and services in that geographic area compare to the national average.

Internet sites for cost-of-living information include www.monstermoving.monster.com; www.bankrate.com/brm/movecalc.asp; and www.money.cnn.com/tools/costofliving/costofliving.html.

How do you find cost-of-living indexes for different locations? There are a number of sources for this information, including www.monster.com, a job search website that provides a great deal of valuable information for job seekers. At that website, in addition to cost-of-living information, you can look up job descriptions, average salaries, and benefits packages for comparison.

Suppose Danelle checks the indexes and finds that:

- Tallahassee's costs are 95 percent of the national average.
- Boston's costs are 120 percent of the national average.

She can use the following equation to determine whether the $35,000 salary in Boston will give her purchasing power equivalent to the $28,000 salary in Tallahassee—in other words, to determine the high-cost-area salary (S_H) that will be equivalent to a given low-cost-area salary (S_L):

$$\text{Equivalent high-cost salary } S_H = \frac{\text{Index}_H \times S_L}{\text{Index}_L}$$

where Index_H is the cost-of-living index for the high-cost area and Index_L is the cost-of-living index for the low-cost area. For this example,

$$\text{Equivalent high-cost salary } S_H = \frac{1.2 \times \$28{,}000}{0.95} = \$35{,}368$$

Based on this calculation, the salary offers from these two cities are fairly equivalent in purchasing power; but the Boston salary falls $368 short of giving Danelle the purchasing power of the Tallahassee salary.

Comparing Benefits Packages

The next step in comparing job offers is to evaluate the fringe benefits packages. As we've seen, the benefits offered by employers and the value of these benefits packages vary widely. You can simplify this problem by considering only the benefits that are valuable to you at your current stage in the life cycle. For example, if you're unmarried and have no children, the availability of a child-care facility has no value to you. Exhibit 10–6 identifies the benefits that are likely to be most important for particular life circumstances. Use marginal analysis by focusing on the *differences* between job offers rather than trying to value all the benefits. For

EXHIBIT 10-6

Benefits over the Life Cycle

- **College student**
  - Health insurance—basic coverage
- **Young single or couple, no children**
  - Health insurance—catastrophic coverage
  - Retirement plan
  - Education assistance
  - Parental leave (if children are planned)
- **Married couples and single parents with young children**
  - Health and disability insurance—comprehensive coverage
  - Life insurance
  - Retirement plan
  - Child care assistance
  - Parental leave (if more children are planned)
- **Older single or couple, no children at home**
  - Health insurance—catastrophic coverage, continuation in retirement
  - Disability insurance—income protection
  - Retirement plan
  - Long-term care insurance
- **Older single or couple with aging parents**
  - Health insurance—catastrophic coverage, continuation in retirement
  - Disability insurance—income protection
  - Retirement plan
  - Long-term care insurance
  - Elder care benefits
- **Retired person**
  - Health insurance—prescription drug coverage, Medigap
  - Long-term care insurance

PFP Worksheet 38
Employee Benefits Checklist

example, if two employers offer comparable health insurance, you can ignore this benefit in your decision making. With your focus on the benefits that are most important to you and that differ between job offers, you can start your comparison.

It may be somewhat difficult to get all the information you need for comparison. Many employers, particularly those without large benefits offices, don't provide complete benefits information until you actually accept a job offer. Even those with relatively comprehensive information on their websites may limit access to current employees. If you have a job offer in hand, don't be afraid to call the human resources or benefits office and ask for the information you need. If the person you talk to isn't cooperative, that may be a piece of qualitative information that will be valuable in your employment decision, since it may imply a lack of cooperation with current employees as well. Whether you are examining your current benefits or those offered by a prospective employer, Exhibit 10-7 lists information that you may want to know. This checklist is also available in your *Personal Financial Planner*.

Let's return to Danelle Washington's example to illustrate what kinds of information you'll be collecting about benefits. Suppose she's spoken with both schools' personnel offices and found the following information: The Boston employer provides fully paid health insurance, $20,000

EXHIBIT 10-7

What You Should Know about Your Employee Benefits

Surveys repeatedly demonstrate that many people don't have a good understanding of the provisions of their employer-sponsored benefit package. Whether you're considering a new employment opportunity or simply don't have all the facts about your current benefits, you can use the following checklist to help you ask the right questions:

1. Holidays
   ________ days per year
   ________ paid ________ unpaid
2. Vacation/Personal Leave
   ________ days per year
   ________ paid ________ unpaid
3. Disability Coverage
   ________ sick days per year
   ________ paid ________unpaid
   ________ days short-term disability
   ________ day waiting period ________ % of salary paid
   ________ days long-term disability
   ________ day waiting period ________ % of salary paid
4. Group Health Insurance
   Paid by: ________ Employer ________ Employee ________ Both
   Type: ________ Fee-for-service (like Blue Cross Blue Shield)
   ________ HMO
   ________ PPO or other managed-care plan
   ________ Catastrophic
   ________ Prescription drug plan
5. Employer-Sponsored Retirement Plans
   Type: ________ Defined-benefit
   ________ 401k or other defined-contribution plan
   ________ Employee stock ownership plan
   ________ Profit sharing plan
   ________ Mandatory participation ________ Optional participation
   Contribution by: ________ Employer ________ Employee
6. Life Insurance
   Type: ________ Term (no cash value) ________ Permanent
   Amount: ________________
   Paid by: ________ Employer ________ Employee ________ Both
7. Dental Expense Insurance
   Paid by: ________ Employer ________ Employee ________ Both
8. Other Fringe Benefits

Employer Offers	Employer Pays for
________ Flexible spending account	________
________ Child-care facility	________
________ Vision/hearing	________
________ Other	________

in life insurance, and five personal days with pay and makes an annual contribution equal to 4 percent of salary to a defined-contribution retirement plan. The Tallahassee employer provides fully paid health insurance, no life insurance, and six personal days with pay and contributes 7 percent to a defined-contribution retirement plan. Although Danelle has no dependents and doesn't think she needs life insurance at this point in her life, she is curious about how much this benefit is worth. She therefore calls a local insurance agent and determines that she could purchase $20,000 in life insurance for only $25 per year. She decides to ignore this benefit in her comparison of the two jobs.

Developing a Comparison Worksheet

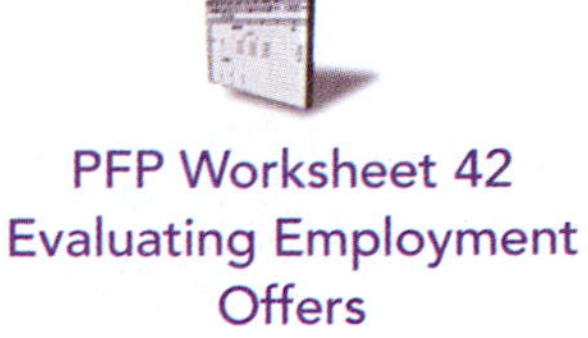

PFP Worksheet 42 Evaluating Employment Offers

After estimating the purchasing power of salary offers and collecting benefits information, the next step is to summarize the differences between your offers. You can use the worksheet in your *Personal Financial Planner* for this purpose or develop one of your own. A sample using Danelle

Washington's case is provided in the *Go Figure!* box, "Comparing Jobs and Benefits." The comparison works best if you use one job as a base and compare all others to that job. For Danelle's example, we'll use the Boston job as the base and compare the Tallahassee job to it using the information given earlier.

We can start with the salaries. The Boston job offers a salary of $35,000 and the Tallahassee job, $28,000. As we determined earlier, though, Danelle would need to make $35,368 in Boston to have as much purchasing power as $28,000 would give her in Tallahassee, so the difference is $368 in favor of Tallahassee. Both jobs offer fully paid health insurance benefits, so there's no difference in that category. To determine the difference between the paid personal days—five for Boston and six for Tallahassee—Danelle first calculates the value of each day's work (in Boston dollars) by dividing the Boston-equivalent salary by the 180 required work days per year required of school teachers. The extra day in Tallahassee is therefore worth $35,368/180 = $196. Finally, the Boston employer will contribute 4 percent of her salary toward a retirement plan, for a dollar value of $1,400 ($35,000 × 0.04 = $1,400), while the Tallahassee employer will contribute 7 percent, for a dollar value of $1,960 ($28,000 × 0.07 = $1,960). Note that, in this comparison, we use the actual dollars contributed rather than the Boston cost-of-living equivalent since this money is being allocated to an investment program rather than to spending on

GO FIGURE!

Comparing Jobs and Benefits

Problem: Danelle Washington is comparing two job offers:

1. Boston: salary, $35,000; cost of living, 120 percent of national average; fully paid health insurance; $20,000 in paid life insurance; five paid personal days; defined-contribution retirement plan contribution equal to 4 percent of salary.
2. Tallahassee: salary, $28,000; cost of living, 95 percent of national average; fully paid health insurance; no life insurance; six paid personal days; defined-contribution retirement plan contribution equal to 7 percent of salary.

Which job is preferable based on salary and benefits?

Solution: Based on the comparison worksheet shown here, Danelle finds that the Tallahassee job, despite its lower salary, is worth $1,124 more per year to her than the higher-salary Boston job.

	Base Case: Boston	Tallahassee	How does Tallahassee differ from Boston?
Salary	$35,000	$28,000 Purchasing power compared to high-cost area = (1.2 × $28,000)/0.95 = $35,368	$35,368 − $35,000 = +$368
Health insurance	Fully paid	Fully paid	0
Life insurance	$20,000 worth	None	0 (She doesn't need life insurance.)
Personal days	5 paid	6 paid	1 extra day is worth $35,368/180 = + $196
Retirement plan	4% contributed: $35,000 × 0.04 = $1,400	7% contributed: $28,000 × 0.07 = $1,960	$1,960 − 1,400) = +$560
Net difference			+$1,124

goods and services. The difference, $560, again favors the Tallahassee job. After considering these differences, Danelle concludes that the Tallahassee job is preferable to the Boston job financially. In terms of purchasing power, she'll be $1,124 per year better off in Tallahassee.

Comparing compensation packages isn't always as straightforward as in the example above. For example, one job might offer a comprehensive health plan and another might offer much less coverage. If you can't purchase the difference in coverage in the private market, you'll need to estimate the additional out-of-pocket health expenses you'll incur if you don't have the additional insurance. Similarly, you may have to compare an employer that offers a defined-benefit retirement plan with one that offers a defined-contribution retirement plan or an employee stock ownership plan. In such cases, you'll need to make judgments about the relative values of various benefit options to you, given your family circumstances and life cycle stage.

Learning by Doing 10-5

1. You're considering two job offers in different areas of the country. Job A offers a salary of $40,000 and Job B a salary of $35,000. If the cost of living in the Job A area is 102 percent of the national average and the cost of living in the Job B area is 88 percent of the national average, which salary offer is better, all else being equal?
2. You're considering two jobs in the same area of the country. The only differences between the job offers are that the Job A salary is $40,000 and the firm will contribute 5 percent of your salary to the retirement plan, whereas the Job B salary is $42,000 and the firm doesn't offer a retirement plan. Which opportunity is better?

Summary

1 **Understand and value the components of a compensation package that includes employee benefits.** Compensation packages may include not only salary but also valuable employee benefits. These benefits may be tangible, such as various types of insurance and retirement contributions, or intangible, such as flexible hours and a pleasant working environment. In choosing among employment opportunities, you should consider the total value of all components of compensation.

2 **Evaluate your expected health-related expenses and incorporate health insurance funding in your financial plan.** Whether you participate in an employer plan or purchase individual insurance, health insurance is an important component of your financial plan, since illnesses and injuries can place a tremendous financial burden on your family. In evaluating your expected health costs, you should consider your life circumstances as well as national trends in health costs. Your plan should include strategies for funding these costs and minimizing future out-of-pocket health costs.

3 **Identify the types of health insurance plans and understand their features.** Health insurance can be obtained on a group basis through an employer or bought individually. Government plans, such as Medicare, Medicaid, and workers' compensation, also cover health costs for those who qualify under the programs. Two major approaches to health insurance are fee-for-service arrangements and managed-care arrangements. Although both types include mechanisms for paying medical service providers, they differ in what services they cover, whether you have a choice of service providers, and how much you'll pay out of pocket. Other types of health insurance that may be available through an employer include dental expense insurance and vision care insurance.

4 **Calculate your disability income needs and select appropriate insurance.** Your financial plan should include strategies for dealing with the financial difficulties you'd face if you became disabled or were unable to earn your regular income due to illness or injury. In calculating your disability income needs, you should consider the minimum amount of income necessary to pay your expenses while disabled. These needs can be met through group or individual disability income insurance. In the case of work-related disability, you might qualify for workers' compensation benefits.

5 **Incorporate employer-sponsored retirement plans in your financial plan.** Subject to certain limits, participants in qualified retirement plans can receive employer contributions and make their own contributions on a pretax basis, and they can earn investment returns on plan assets without owing current taxes. The financial benefits of tax deferral make employer retirement plans an important component of your financial plan. The two general types of retirement plan arrangements are defined-benefit plans, in which the employer promises you a benefit at retirement, usually based on a formula that incorporates salary and years of employment, and defined-contribution plans, in which regular contributions are made to an investment account.

6 **Compare job offers according to geographic location, salary, and benefits packages.** In deciding between job offers, you should develop a comparison worksheet that includes not only the salaries offered, adjusted for cost-of-living differences, but also the value of the benefits provided.

Key Terms

basic health care insurance (314)
cafeteria plan (307)
cash balance plan (327)
cash-or-deferred arrangement (CODA) (329)
coinsurance (315)
consumer choice plan (317)
contributory plan (307)
copay (315)
defined-benefit (DB) plan (326)
defined-contribution (DC) plan (327)
disability income insurance (324)
employee stock ownership plans (ESOPs) (329)
exclusive provider organization (EPO) (317)
fee-for-service plan (314)
flexible spending account (FSA) (312)
group insurance (309)
group underwriting (309)
health maintenance organization (HMO) (314)
health savings account (HSA) (313)
major medical insurance (315)
managed-care plan (314)
maximum limit (315)
Medicaid (318)
Medicare (318)
Medigap policies (319)
money-purchase plan (329)
point-of-service (POS) plan (317)
portability (328)
preferred provider organization (PPO) (314)
profit-sharing plan (329)
stop-loss limit (315)
tax-qualified retirement plan (326)
vesting rules (327)
workers' compensation insurance (318)

Key Calculations

$$\text{Equivalent high-cost salary } S_H = \frac{\text{Index}_H \times S_L}{\text{Index}_L}$$

Concept Review Questions

1. Identify the major components of a compensation package.
2. Explain why it's important to consider all the components of compensation and not just salary.
3. What is the difference between a contributory employee benefit plan and a noncontributory plan? Which would you prefer?
4. Why do large employers generally offer more generous employee benefit plans than small employers?
5. Explain why it's better to receive group insurance through your employer than to receive equivalent cash compensation out of which you must purchase the insurance on your own.
6. Explain the advantages of group insurance.
7. Under what circumstances might you have difficulty obtaining and maintaining health and life insurance in the individual market?
8. Why is health insurance an important component of your financial plan?
9. What is the national trend in health-care costs, and what are some explanations for this trend? How will this trend impact your future health insurance premium costs?
10. Identify several ways you can reduce your expected future out-of-pocket costs for health insurance premiums, deductibles, copays, and taxes.
11. What is a flexible spending account, and how can it help you to save money?
12. What is a health savings account, and how does it differ from a flexible spending account?
13. Define the following: (a) fee-for-service plan; (b) managed-care plan.
14. How do managed-care plans attempt to control costs compared with fee-for-service plans?
15. What are the similarities and differences between a health maintenance organization, a preferred provider organization, and an exclusive provider organization?
16. Describe the two major categories of traditional fee-for-service coverage, and give examples of covered services under each type.
17. What is the purpose of imposing deductibles and coinsurance on health plan participants?
18. Under what circumstances might it be a good idea to purchase catastrophic health insurance only?
19. What is a consumer choice plan, and how does it attempt to control health costs?
20. What are the major government-sponsored sources of health coverage, and under what circumstances might you be eligible for each?
21. If you're injured on the job, what benefits can you expect from your employer's workers' compensation insurance?
22. What types of insurance are provided under the Social Security program, and how is it funded?
23. How comprehensive is Medicare coverage for retirement health needs? What gaps in coverage exist?
24. What types of benefits are offered by Medigap policies, and who should buy this insurance?
25. If you're laid off from work, what are the rules about continuing coverage under your former employer's health plan?
26. What is a preexisting condition, and why might this be an important consideration in your choice of a health plan?
27. What is a disability, and why is it important to plan for disability income protection?
28. How does workers' compensation disability protection differ from Social Security disability protection?
29. What are the key features of disability income insurance? Give an example of each. Why is it important to consider the definition of disability in the policy?
30. What are the tax advantages of a qualified employer-sponsored retirement plan?
31. What is the difference between a defined-benefit plan and a defined-contribution plan? Which one places more risk on the employee? What kind of risk?
32. What is a vesting rule, and what are the minimum allowed vesting schedules?
33. Why is it important for your retirement plan to be portable? If you quit working for an employer that offered a defined-benefit

plan which wasn't portable, will you still be able to receive a retirement benefit from the plan in the future?

34. What is the difference between a money-purchase plan and a profit-sharing plan? Which one is better for employees?
35. Explain why it isn't a good idea to invest all your retirement plan funds in employer stock.
36. What types of retirement plans are specifically designed for small businesses and self-employed individuals?
37. How can you compare salary offers in geographic regions that differ in cost of living? Why is it important to do so?
38. In comparing job offers, what factors should you consider?

Application Problems

1. ***Deductibles and Coinsurance.*** Your health insurance requires the payment of an annual deductible of $500 per person or $1,000 per family. After meeting the deductible, you must pay 20 percent of covered charges until you reach the stop-loss limit of $5,000. If your child requires emergency surgery and the total covered charges are $20,000, all incurred in the same plan year, how much will you end up paying out of pocket?
2. ***Comparing Health Insurance Plans.*** Your employer offers two health plan choices and requires that employees pay part of the premium cost. The fee-for-service option will cost you $100 per month for single coverage, does not cover preventive care, and imposes a $300-per-person annual deductible and 20 percent coinsurance to a stop-loss limit of $2,000. The fee-for-service plan also covers prescription drugs after a copay of $30 per prescription. The managed-care option (an HMO) will cost you $200 per month, covers all medical services (including preventive care and prescription drugs) but requires a $10 copay for each office visit or prescription. For each of the following scenarios, which cover one year, calculate how much your out-of-pocket expense would be under each plan:
   - **a.** You have an annual physical ($200), visit the doctor twice for illness ($50 per visit), and incur prescription drug costs of $500 (10 prescriptions at $50 each).
   - **b.** You have an annual physical, have surgery for a skiing injury ($3,000 covered charges), and incur prescription drug costs of $200 (4 prescriptions at $50 each).
3. ***Defined-Benefit Plans.*** Your employer offers a defined-benefit plan with the following formula: 1 percent of final salary for each of the first 15 years of service, 1.5 percent of final salary for each of the next 15 years of service, and 2 percent of salary for each of the next 20 years of service. The firm has a three- to seven-year vesting schedule.
   - **a.** If you work for the firm for your entire 45-year career and your final salary is $100,000, how much will you receive as a benefit?
   - **b.** If you work for the firm for only five years, how much benefit will you be entitled to receive at retirement, assuming your final salary with the company is $40,000?
4. ***COBRA Coverage.*** You've been laid off by your employer and had been participating in its contributory health-care plan. Your share of the health premiums, $200 per month, was 50 percent of the actual cost to the employer.
   - **a.** Under what circumstances should you consider getting continuation coverage through your employer's plan? How soon do you need to decide?
   - **b.** If your employer adds a 2 percent administrative charge, how much will you have to pay per month for the coverage?
   - **c.** What alternative sources of health coverage do you have? Are they likely to be more or less expensive?
5. ***Comparing Salaries in Different Areas.*** You are offered a job in Urban City that will pay $50,000 per year. You currently have a comparable job with comparable benefits in Rural Town, but it only pays $40,000. If the cost of living for Urban City is 105 percent of the national average and the cost of living in Rural Town is 85 percent of the national average, which job will actually give you more purchasing power?
6. ***Disability Income Needs.*** Allison currently earns $3,000 per month and takes home $2,300. Her monthly expenses total $2,000. Her employer provides 5 sick days and a short-term disability policy that kicks in after 30 days of disability. The policy will pay 60 percent of her gross income for up to 12 months. The disability income payments wouldn't be taxable since she used after-tax dollars to pay the premiums.
   - **a.** If Allison wants to have sufficient liquid assets to cover the short-term needs that aren't met by her employer's plan, how much should she set aside for this purpose?
   - **b.** If Allison is considering purchasing long-term disability insurance to cover a disability that lasts more than 12 months, assuming she wouldn't qualify for Social Security disability, what would the monthly benefit need to be, again assuming she will pay the premiums with after-tax dollars?

Using Web Resources for Financial Planning

1. ***Are There Mandatory Health Benefits in Your State?*** Many state legislatures have passed laws requiring employers to provide minimum benefits in their health plans. Go to the website for the Insurance News Network, *www.insure.com*, and click on "Health Laws" to find out what is mandated in your state.
2. ***What Is Your Probability of Disability?*** Go to *www.northwesternmutual.com* and click on "Learning Center." Use the disability calculator to find the probability that you will be disabled for 90 days or more between now and the time you reach age 65.
3. ***What Social Security Disability Benefit Would You Qualify for?*** Go to the planner section of the Social Security website, *www.ssa.gov/planners/*, and select the Disability Planner.
   - **a.** What is the definition of *disability* under this program?
   - **b.** How much would you qualify for, given your current history of participation in Social Security?
   - **c.** Does Social Security provide adequate disability income protection?

4. ***Evaluate Health Insurers.*** The National Committee for Quality Assurance provides information on all accredited health plans. Go to their website, *www.ncqa.org*, and click on "Health Plan Report Card" to look up your health insurer and see how it compares with others. You can also use information from this website to help you choose between insurance company alternatives.
5. ***Find Out if You or a Family Member Are Entitled to Unclaimed Pension Benefits.*** Go to the website for the Pension Benefit Guarantee Corporation, *www.pbgc.gov*. Click on Pension Search to find the names of people who are entitled to unclaimed PBGC-insured pension benefits from companies that have gone out of business.
6. ***Compare Health Insurance Alternatives.*** At *money.cnn.com/pf/insurance* you can use an interactive worksheet to help you decide between health insurance plan alternatives based on your preferences.

Learning by Doing Solutions

LBD 10–1: 1. Margo should look for an employer that offers sufficient sick leave, vacation time, health insurance, disability insurance, and a retirement plan. A flexible spending account would help her save on child-care costs and out-of-pocket medical expenses, and a dental plan would also be helpful.; 2. $5,000 × 0.25 = $1,250 savings.

LBD 10–2: 1a. Medicare; 1b. May be uninsured or covered by Medicaid; 1c. group health insurance; 1d. individual health insurance.

LBD 10–3: 1. You won't be entitled to any benefit; 2. 10 × 0.015 × $60,000 = $9,000 per year; 3. 30 × 0.015 × $100,000 = $45,000.

LBD 10–4: 1a. DC plan; 1b. risk of outliving their assets, investment risk; 2a. $14,000; 2b. 0.34 × 14,000 = $4,760.

LBD 10–5: 1. Job B is better. The equivalent salary in high-cost area A would have to be (1.02 × $35,000)/0.88 = $40,568; 2. The Job A retirement contribution of 5 percent of salary is exactly equal to the difference in salary, but since the retirement benefit is pretax, it is actually more valuable than the $2,000 in salary.

Building Financial Planning Skills Through Case Applications

Case 10–1 Anna Trebuca Considers a Cafeteria Plan

Anna Trebuca, age 40, has just accepted a job as a legal secretary in a large law office. The law firm has a cafeteria plan and gives each employee $4,000 in pretax dollars to spend on a menu of benefit options. Any dollars that are not spent can be received as cash compensation. Anna has the following options to choose from:

Benefits	Monthly Premiums
Health plan A: Fee-for-service plan including basic and major medical; $250 annual deductible and 20 percent coinsurance; $5,000 stop-loss limit; and $500,000 maximum limit.	Employee only: $150 per month Employee + 1: $200 per month
Health plan B: Preferred provider organization covering most services for in-network providers at 100 percent after a $100 deductible; out-of-network providers require a 25 percent copay.	Employee only: $200 per month Employee + 1: $300 per month
Dental Insurance: Pays 100 percent of checkups and cleaning; 50 percent of additional services to a maximum benefit of $1,000.	Employee only: $40 per month Employee + 1: $60 per month
Long-term disability insurance: Pays 60 percent of predisability income for up to two years if unable to perform the duties of current job; 12-month waiting period.	$15 per month

a. If Anna is single, and childless, and has no other group health insurance available, explain to her why she should participate in one of the health plans, even if she could find individual insurance for a slightly lower premium.

b. What factors should Anna consider in deciding between the fee-for-service and the PPO health insurance plans?

c. Which health plan would result in a lower total out-of-pocket expense for the year if Anna incurred $10,000 in medical expenses for a surgical procedure, assuming she used a participating provider?

d. If Anna is married and her husband's employer provides a health plan at a lower out-of-pocket premium cost, how should Anna take this into consideration in allocating her benefit dollars?

e. Is the dental insurance a good deal if Anna normally incurs very low dental costs each year ($150 for checkup and cleaning)? How much would her dental costs have to total for her to break even on the cost of the dental insurance?

Case 10–2 Juan Morales Analyzes His Disability Risk and Coverage.

Juan Morales is a single father and is worried about what would happen to his family finances if he were to become disabled. Total household expenses are $3,000 per month, although he estimates that, in a pinch, they could be cut to $2,200 per month. Juan currently earns $4,000 per month before taxes at his job as a retail store manager. His employer provides 5 sick days per year, 10 days of paid annual leave, and a short-term disability policy (purchased with after-tax dollars) that, after 30 days of continuous disability, will pay 55 percent of predisability gross income for 12 months. He is wondering whether he should also buy long-term disability income insurance through his employer's group plan that, after 12 months of continuous disability, would pay 60 percent of predisability gross income for up to five years of continued disability.

a. What are Juan's short-term disability income needs?

b. Suppose Juan can't work due to an injury at home. Assuming he hadn't yet used any of his paid leave or sick days when he became injured, how long will he continue to receive income, and how much will he get? If Juan is disabled for 12 months, does he have sufficient disability income protection?

c. Explain why Juan should look carefully at the definition of *disability* in both the short-term and long-term insurance policies.

d. If Juan permanently injures his back and is no longer able to perform the duties of his current job, will he be eligible for Social Security disability income? Why or why not? If he estimates that his Social Security disability benefit would be $500 per month, how should he incorporate this in his long-term disability planning?

Case 10–3 Clare Deluna compares Job Offers

Clare Deluna is in her last semester of school at a major public university, where she is double-majoring in finance and construction management. Her hard work has paid off, and she's faced with deciding between two job offers at civil engineering firms. Matheson, Inc., a Denver-based firm, has offered her a $40,000 starting salary with an expected annual bonus of $5,000. Brandis Construction, a Seattle-based firm, will pay a starting salary of $48,000 but doesn't give annual bonuses. The firms have also provided Clare with some information about their company benefits packages, which include 401(k) retirement plans and health insurance. The major differences between the two benefits packages are: (1) Matheson pays the full cost of employee-only or family health insurance, whereas Brandis pays $200 per month toward the total cost of employee-only health insurance (currently $240 per month for single coverage, $420 for employee + one, and $600 for a family), and (2) Matheson matches employee contributions to the 401(k) in cash up to 3 percent of salary, while Brandis matches employee contributions to the 401(k) in employer stock up to 3 percent of salary.

a. Compare the two salary offers, assuming that the Denver cost of living is 105 percent of the national average and the Seattle cost of living is 110 percent of the national average. How should Clare take the Matheson bonus into account?

b. Are the retirement plan benefits comparable? Why or why not?

c. Develop a comparison worksheet to help Clare decide between these two jobs.

d. How would her decision change if she needed employee + one insurance coverage?

LIFELONG PLANNING CASE

PART II: Michael and Tori Garcia Plan for a Growing Family

Life Circumstances: Both age 30, married eight years, daughter Holly, age 1

Financial Challenges: Growing family, home purchase, new job

When we last saw Michael and Tori Garcia, they had been married three years and were childless. Now, five years have gone by, and their family is growing. Michael recently called you for an appointment to talk about revising their financial plan.

Five years ago, you helped the Garcias develop a plan for increasing their household savings and reducing their debt so that Michael could go to graduate school. This plan was successful, but he ended up staying in his job and attending school part-time instead of quitting to go full-time. Last year was a banner year—Michael received his MBA, and the couple also became the proud parents of a daughter, Holly, who is now one year old.

Recently, Michael and Tori discovered that they're expecting another baby, which prompted them to think about making some changes in their financial plan. Tori has continued to work at the real estate office where she's been an office manager for the last several years, but she's now only working part-time—about 25 hours per week. As a result, the Garcias actually have less gross income than they did five years ago. With a growing family to support, Michael thinks it may be time for him to see if he can leverage his new MBA into a higher-paying job. That could make it easier for them to afford to buy a home (they're currently renting a three-bedroom apartment), and Tori might be able to take more time off from work after the baby is born. The company allowed her to take three months off without pay after Holly was born, but she'd like to take six months this time.

The Garcias have provided you with the following household balance sheet and cash flow information. As you can see, over the past five years, they have paid off both their car loans and a substantial portion of their student loan debt. They recently traded in Michael's old car and bought a new one.

Income and Cash Flow		Selected Expenses	
Tori's income		Rent	$1,200
Gross	$2,500	Credit card payments	150
After-tax	1,970	Car loan payment	300
Michael's income:		Car maintenance and gas	300
Gross	3,800	Student loan payments	170
After-tax	2,975	Health insurance	250
Net monthly cash flow	$−325	Uninsured medical	$150

Assets		Debts	
Checking account	$2,300	Car loan (Michael)	$16,000
Savings account	8,500	Student loan (Michael)	3,500
Home furnishings	20,000	Student loan (Tori)	2,300
Clothing/personal assets	10,000	VISA balance	1,200
Mutual fund (stocks)	18,000	MasterCard balance	2,100
Michael's car	19,000	Dillard's credit card	500
Tori's car	$3,200	Sears credit card	1,200
		Current bills due	$2,000

1. Based on what you know about the Garcias' current life situation and family circumstances, what short-term and long-term personal financial planning goals should they give priority to? Do these priorities seem consistent with their intentions? Is it a problem that the Garcias haven't consulted a financial planner during the last five years? Why or why not?
2. Assume that Michael has decided to take a sales management position with a local company at a salary of $60,000 per year (gross income). In addition to the salary, the company offers the following benefits package:
   - 401(k) retirement plan: Company matches employee contributions to the plan up to 3 percent of salary.
   - Health plan: Company contributes $300 per month to the cost of family coverage. Employee portion of the premium depends on choice between HMO with a $10 copay per office visit ($300 per month) and fee-for-service plan with annual deductible of $500 per person and $1,000 per family ($20 per month).
   - Term life insurance with face value equal to one year's salary.
   - Flexible spending account with up to $5,000 for child care and $5,000 for unreimbursed medical expenses.
   - Company car, including gas, maintenance, and automobile insurance.

a. In what ways will the new job affect the family's finances?
b. Explain how the Garcias should make the decision between the two types of health insurance offered by the new employer.
c. What is the minimum that Michael should contribute to his 401(k) retirement plan? Explain. Is it realistic at this time for him to contribute the maximum allowed by law? Why or why not?
d. What is the value of having the use of a company car? Estimate the monthly savings that will result from such a benefit.
e. The Garcias aren't familiar with flexible spending accounts. Explain to Tori and Michael how this type of arrangement works. Should they take advantage of this benefit? If so, how much should they deposit in the account based on their current spending patterns? How much will they save in taxes by doing so, assuming their marginal tax rate is 25 percent? How might the new baby affect this decision?

3. Michael and Tori would like to investigate their housing options. Based on financial information they've provided, how much do you think they can allocate to a down payment for a home and still have adequate emergency funds? (Don't forget that they should be able to sell one of the cars after Michael starts his new job.)

4. Tori and Michael have checked with local lenders for mortgage rates. Fixed-rate conventional 30-year mortgages are at 8 percent per year. These lenders require that the mortgage debt service cannot exceed 31 percent of gross income and total debt payments cannot exceed 41 percent of gross income.
   a. Based on their current balance sheet and cash flow information and assuming that homeowner's insurance and property taxes will run them $200 per month, what is the maximum mortgage amount the Garcias can qualify for?
   b. What would the mortgage loan be with the monthly payment you estimated in 4a?
   c. Assuming the Garcias want to make a $20,000 down payment, and closing costs are expected to be around $4,000, what effect will this have on the household emergency fund?
   d. Given their financial situation, what home price do you think would be a reasonable maximum for the Garcias to consider? If they purchased a home at this price, what would the monthly mortgage debt service be?
   e. If the Garcias could get an adjustable rate mortgage at a 5 percent rate with a 1 percent annual rate cap and a 5 percent lifetime rate cap, how would this affect their housing decision? Should they consider this option?
   f. If the Garcias buy a home, will they save any money on their taxes? Explain.

DEVELOPING PERSONAL FINANCIAL skills for life

Learning about Yourself

10–1. How Much Do You Know about Your Current Benefits?

Without reviewing any supporting documents, see if you can answer the following questions about the benefits offered by your current employer. After you've answered the questions, check your knowledge by comparing your answers to the actual plan documentation, or consult with a person in the benefits department to obtain that information. If you're not currently employed, consider asking one of your parents or a friend to answer the questions. If you're currently a full-time student, answer the questions related to your life and health insurance coverage.

Benefit Facts	Your Guess	Actual Answer
1. Does your employer offer any opportunities for tax-deferred retirement saving?		
2. Does your employer offer a retirement plan? If so, is it a defined-benefit plan or a defined-contribution plan?		
3. If your employer sponsors a retirement plan, is it contributory or noncontributory?		
4. If you contribute to an employer-sponsored retirement plan, will your employer match your contributions?		
5. Can you receive or pay for health insurance through your employer or school on a pretax basis?		
6. Does your employer or school provide any group life insurance?		
7. Does your employer allow you to set up an account to pay for uninsured health and dependent care expenses pretax?		
8. If you had to miss work for jury duty, would your employer pay you for the time missed?		
9. If you had to miss work for the birth of a child, would you get any paid leave?		
10. How many sick days do you get per year?		
11. How many days of paid vacation and annual leave do you get per year?		
12. Does your employer reimburse for any training and education expenses?		
13. Are you covered by any disability insurance?		
14. Will your employer allow you to set up a flexible spending account or health savings account?		

If you answered most of these questions correctly, then you're better informed than the average employee. Several surveys have shown that employees are not well informed about benefits and often miss out on opportunities for tax-advantaged saving.

Developing Your Skills

10–2. Current Insurance Inventory

Use the worksheet in your *Personal Financial Planner* to inventory your current insurance coverage in the areas of health, life, and disability.

a. What are the gaps in your coverage?
b. List some ways you could improve your coverage in these areas.

PFP Worksheet 39
Health, Life, Disability, and Long-Term Care Insurance Inventory

10–3. Health Insurance Needs Analysis

a. Review your records from last year and make a list of all health-related costs incurred by yourself or your family. Summarize these expenditures and how they were paid for in your *Personal Financial Planner*.

b. Consider the financial impact of a large unexpected health cost ($20,000) on your family resources, given your current financial resources and insurance coverage. Evaluate whether your current health insurance is adequate to meet this type of risk. If it isn't, consider your alternatives for improving this element of your financial plan.

PFP Worksheet 40
Health Insurance Needs Analysis

10–4. Disability Income Needs Analysis

Analyze your disability income needs by completing the worksheet in your *Personal Financial Planner*.

a. How much income would you need during a period of disability to meet your minimum household expenses?

b. What are your current sources of disability income protection?

c. If your current protection is inadequate, make a list of alternatives you should consider for improving this element of your financial plan.

PFP Worksheet 41
Disability Insurance Needs Analysis

THE NAVIGATOR

- ☐ Review Before Studying this Chapter list.
- ☐ Scan Learning Objectives.
- ☐ Take the Myth or Fact quiz and find the answers throughout the chapter.
- ☐ Read chapter and answer Learning by Doing exercises.
- ☐ Review Key Terms and Key Calculations.
- ☐ Do end-of-chapter exercises.
- ☐ Take review quiz on the text website.
- ☐ Solve end-of-chapter cases.

BEFORE studying this chapter, you should review

- Components of a comprehensive financial plan (Chapter 1).
- Present and future value (Chapter 2).
- The benefits of tax deferral of income (Chapter 4).

Fundamental Concepts in Investing

CHAPTER 11

Myth or Fact?

Consider each of the following statements and decide whether it is a *myth* or a *fact*. Look for the answers in the *Fact* boxes in the chapter.

	MYTH	FACT
1. Lending money to a business is riskier than being an owner of the business.	☐	☐
2. As you get older, you should take on more risk in your investment portfolio.	☐	☐
3. It's best to buy shares of stock that pay you a regular dividend.	☐	☐
4. Men generally achieve better investment results than women because they're willing to take more risk.	☐	☐
5. The earlier you start investing, the easier it will be to achieve your financial goals.	☐	☐

LEARNING objectives

1. Develop realistic investment goals that are consistent with your financial plan, risk tolerance, and life stage.
2. Identify your investment alternatives.
3. Understand the risk-return tradeoff.
4. Recognize the importance of asset allocation and diversification of your portfolio.
5. Decide whether you will be an active or passive investor and what your primary investment strategy will be.
6. Invest successfully by incorporating taxes in your investment decisions and using available information resources.

...applying the planning process

Throughout this text, we've emphasized the importance of planning to achieve your goals. Although personal financial planning covers a wide range of topics, investment planning is an especially critical piece of the process. In order to accumulate the funds that will enable you to achieve your future spending goals, you'll need to save and invest on a regular basis throughout your life. This will require that you stick to a budget so you can allocate funds to this endeavor, and it will also require that you make informed investment decisions.

Investing is all about taking advantage of the time value of money. You already understand that, over time, compound interest can help your savings grow. But you've also learned another basic time value principle—the more you can earn on your investments, the more quickly your savings will grow. If you leave all your money in low-interest bank savings accounts, it will take you a lot longer to build your wealth. In the next several chapters, you'll learn about the many investment alternatives that are available to you and how to make informed investment decisions. Today, literally thousands of possible investments compete for your funds, and it's easy to make some bad choices if you don't have the right information or if you listen to the wrong advice. To avoid costly mistakes, you should make sure your personal financial plan includes establishing and implementing a plan for developing investment knowledge and taking an active role in household investment decisions.

In this chapter, we begin our study of investing to meet financial goals. We first examine the process of setting investment goals and then consider some fundamental investment concepts. This chapter will also provide you with a broad overview of the various investment alternatives available today. Chapters 12 through 14 provide more details about each of these investment options.

Chapter Preview

Developing Realistic Investment Goals	Understanding Your Investment Alternatives	The Risk-Return Tradeoff	Diversification and Asset Allocation	Establishing Your Investment Strategy	Key Strategies for Investment Success
• First Things First: Establishing a Firm Foundation • Investing to Meet Your Goals • Estimating Your Target and Investment Contribution • Getting the Money to Invest	• Investing by Lending and by Owning • The Major Asset Classes	• Evaluating Your Risk Tolerance • Factors Affecting Risk Tolerance • Measuring Risk and Return for Individual Securities	• How Diversification Works • The Importance of Asset Allocation	• Active Versus Passive Investing • Passive Investing Strategies	• Take Advantage of Favorable Tax Rules • Take Advantage of Investment Information Resources • Follow Some Simple Rules

Developing Realistic Investment Goals

LEARNING objective

1 Develop realistic investment goals that are consistent with your financial plan, risk tolerance, and life stage.

In investing, as in other areas of your financial plan, you should begin by setting specific goals that are realistic and within your control. Since you're investing to accumulate funds to meet other household objectives, your investment process should begin with a reevaluation of your overall plan. Have you established the necessary foundation elements of your plan, prioritized your financial goals, and developed a budget that will allow you to set aside sufficient funds for investing? If so, you can move ahead in the investment planning process.

First Things First: Establishing a Firm Foundation

Although it might sound like fun to jump right in and start investing, there are a few things you should take care of first. As you learned in Chapter 1, a comprehensive financial plan has many components, some of which have priority over others. Before you begin to develop an investment plan, you should make sure that you have a secure foundation to build on. To see if you're ready for this step, ask yourself the following questions:

- Have I established my financial goals?
- Am I living within my budget and meeting my basic needs?
- Have I reduced my outstanding high-interest credit?
- Do I have an emergency fund in cash or liquid savings accounts?
- Do I have adequate insurance coverage?
- Have I bought a home or established a plan for doing so?

If you can answer "yes" to all these questions, then you're ready to begin your investment planning. That doesn't mean you should immediately call a broker and buy 100 shares of Google stock. Before you take any specific action, you'll need to establish your investment objectives and educate yourself about the investment marketplace and your investment alternatives. The investment planning process is summarized in Exhibit 11-1.

Investing to Meet Your Prioritized Goals

In developing your investment plan, you should ask yourself "Why am I investing?" The answer is probably that you're trying to achieve one or more of the following financial goals identified in Chapter 3:

- Increase current income.
- Take a vacation.
- Make a major purchase, such as a car or home.
- Start a business.
- Save for education costs (for yourself or your children).
- Meet retirement income needs.

If you've prioritized your financial goals, you know which ones you'll focus on first. How much do you need to accumulate to meet these goals? How much time do you have? How much money can you allocate to this part of your financial plan? Since different types of investments yield different average returns over time, the amount you'll need to invest to achieve your goals will depend on your choice of investments. You'll also need to consider the riskiness of different investments relative to your preferences and time horizon. If you're saving for a long-term goal, you might be able to weather some ups and downs in your investments, but if you need the money next year for a particular purpose, you can't afford to take much risk.

EXHIBIT 11-1 **Steps in the Investment Planning Process**

7. Monitor your investment plan.

6. Select investments that are appropriate for you, given your risk tolerance, time horizon, and investment objectives.

5. Learn about your investment alternatives.

4. Evaluate your risk tolerance.

3. Estimate how much you can apply to your investment program both in current lump-sum and regular future payments.

2. Estimate how much you need to accumulate to achieve your goals.

1. Identify your goals.

In setting your investment goals, try to make sure that they're realistic, specific, and measurable. Go back to your prioritized financial goals and, for each goal, identify:

- The purpose of the investment plan
- The amount needed in the future to meet your financial goal
- The amount you can currently allocate to your investment plan
- How much time until you need the money
- How much risk, and what types of risk, you can afford to take

PFP Worksheet 43 Setting Investment Goals

To illustrate this process, let's consider the case of Janine and Mark Gallegos, who have recently married and would like to save $10,000 for a down payment on a house, preferably within the next five years. The *Go Figure!* box, "Developing Your Investment Goals," shows how they can use a worksheet to identify their financial goals and constraints and to estimate the amount they need to allocate to this objective on a regular basis. A blank worksheet is provided in the *Personal Financial Planner* for you to use in developing your own investment goals. In this section, we'll consider some of the steps in more detail.

GO FIGURE!

Developing Your Investment Goals

Financial goal: Accumulate a downpayment for the purchase of a house
Amount needed: $10,000 or more
When needed: Flexible, but prefer within 5 years
Risk tolerance: Low

Use this worksheet to estimate how much you need to allocate to your investment plan:

Value of Initial Investment	
1. Amount to accumulate	$10,000
2. Amount of initial investment (if any)	$600
3. Number of Years (*n*)	5
4. Average after-tax return (*i*)	4%
5. FVIF (*n* years, *i* return) (from Appendix A-1)	1.217
6. Future value of initial investment (=line 2 × line 5)	$730
7. Amount remaining to meet goal (= line 1 − line 6)	$9,270

Regular Investment Payments	Annual	Monthly
7. Amount remaining to meet goal (= line 1 − line 6)	$9,270	$9,270
8. FVIFA (*n* periods, *i* return) (from Appendix A-3)	5.416	66.30
9. Payment necessary to reach goal (= line 7 ÷ line 8)	$1,712	$139.82

Estimating Your Target Accumulation and Regular Investment Contribution

Even if you're investing to meet long-term goals, it's important to have several target figures in mind as you begin your investment program. First, how much will you need to accumulate? Answering this question may be relatively straightforward—for example, if your goal is to buy a new car or to save for a down payment on a home. Figuring out how much you'll need may sometimes be much more complex, however, as when you're estimating your retirement income needs.

Since the down payment is a relatively near-term goal for Janine and Mark, they don't want to take too much risk. Using the worksheet, they estimate that, if they begin with the $600 they currently have in savings and can earn 4 percent after taxes on this investment over the next five years, they'll need to invest an additional $1,712 per year to reach their goal.

This is a good application of the time value of money concepts introduced in Chapter 2. Recall that if you know the present value, you can estimate the future value by using the equation for the future value of a lump sum. In our example, the present value—the amount Janine and Mark have to invest today—is $600, the interest rate they expect to earn is 4 percent, and the time involved is five years. You can solve the problem using a financial calculator or electronic spreadsheet by entering $PV = 600$, $I = 4$, and $N = 5$ and then solving for $FV = \$730$. Alternatively, you can use the future value equation to solve for $FV = \$600 \times (1.04)^5 = \$730$. Whatever method you use, the result should be the same value. This leaves $9,270 ($10,000 − $730 = $9,270) that Janine and Mark must save to meet their goal.

Next, they must estimate the payment necessary to accumulate $9,270 in five years. This is a problem involving the future value of an annuity. With a financial calculator, we can solve the problem by entering $FV = 9{,}270$, $N = 5$, and $I = 4$ and solving for PMT; the answer is $1,711.49 (slightly different from the table solution shown in the box, due to rounding). Janine and Mark will need to save $1,711.49 per year for the next five years, in addition to their current savings, to accumulate $10,000 in five years. If we assume monthly interest compounding, we can enter $FV = 9{,}270$, $N = 5 \times 12 = 60$, and $I = 4/12 = 0.333$ and solve for PMT. We'll find the necessary monthly payment to be $139.82.

If you are solving this problem using an electronic spreadsheet, such as Excel, or a financial calculator, you can easily change the inputs to test out different scenarios for the investment plan. For example, what would happen if Janine and Mark earned a higher rate of return or if

Once you've paid off an installment loan contract, consider allocating the payment amount to your investment plan instead.

they decided to delay buying a home for a longer period of time? Based on what you know about the time value of money, it should be apparent to you that increasing either of these factors would result in a lower required monthly savings amount.

Getting the Money to Invest

The actual process of investing is not especially difficult. The most common stumbling block is not having the necessary funds to invest. An essential element of your financial plan must therefore be to prioritize your spending so that investing for the future receives sufficient attention. You'll probably have to sacrifice current spending to have money available to devote to your investment plan. Depending on where you are in your career and life cycle, you may need to start out small and build your investment program as your income increases. You may not think investing small amounts is worthwhile. But keep in mind what you've learned about the time value of money—when saving for long-term goals, the earlier you start, the less you need to save to achieve a specific goal. Taking the first step is the toughest part—once you get started, you'll find it easier to continue.

Here are a few ideas to help make it less painful to find the money in your budget for investing.

1. Pay yourself first. This is a rule of thumb you encountered in previous chapters and one that is regularly offered by financial advisors. If your budget includes an amount that you've allocated to saving or investing, take it right off the top at the beginning of the month. You can often accomplish this by having the amount automatically withdrawn from your checking account and deposited in your investment account. Most people find that, if they wait until the end of the month to invest what's left over, the funds are no longer there—they were whittled away by small and often unnecessary expenditures.

2. Save your raise. Maybe you truly don't have any excess funds in your budget—all your current income is going to pay for necessaries. But what if you make a deal with yourself that you'll allocate all—or at least a significant portion—of your next raise to your savings and investment plan? This works best if you have a high proportion of fixed expenses in your budget, such as car and loan payments. In that case, when your income goes up, your expenses will not go up proportionally. So if you don't let yourself become accustomed to the extra income but instead immediately set it aside for your investment plan, it won't feel like you're cutting back on immediate consumption.

3. Set aside bonuses, tax refunds, and other lump sums. When the money you're applying to investments has never been part of your regular income, it's even less painful to set it aside. Bonuses and other lump-sum windfalls such as birthday gifts, tax refunds, and inheritances can be immediately applied to your investment plan. And if these lump sums are fairly significant amounts to start with, you'll see that the dollars accumulate more quickly.

4. Continue a payment plan. When you've finished paying off an installment loan, such as a car loan or student loan, consider shifting those dollars immediately to your investment plan. Since you haven't been spending that portion of your income on consumption, you can put it toward this new use without feeling the loss. Your $300 monthly car payment could put you closer to achieving your investment goals by $3,600 per year.

5. Participate in employer-sponsored retirement plans. Your employer may offer you the opportunity to participate in a company-sponsored retirement savings plan. Whether or not your employer also makes contributions to the plan, you should try to contribute regularly. As explained in Chapter 10, these dollars generally are invested on a pretax basis, which means that you'll avoid paying current federal, state, and local income taxes on this money. In addition, the taxes on earnings in your retirement fund will be deferred until you take the money out—and that may be many years in the future. Without the eroding effect of taxes, your investments will be able to grow more quickly.

6. Stop up a cash leak. When you developed your cash budget, you may have identified some regular household expenditures that could be avoided or reduced. If so, you can try to allocate to your new investment plan the amount you would have spent on these items. For example, suppose you decide to "brown bag" your lunch three times a week instead of eating out every day, saving about $15 per week, or $60 per month. If you take that $60 and invest it instead (at the beginning of the month), you'll accumulate $720 plus interest by the end of the year. Other examples of little budget reductions include taking books out of the library instead of buying them and renting DVDs instead of going to the movies. If you have a gas-guzzling car, you might consider taking public transportation or biking to work. If you normally drive 15,000 miles per year and you can cut down your driving by 10 percent, you'll save between $150 and $300 per year, depending on the fuel efficiency of your car and the current price of gasoline. If you replaced your car with a more fuel-efficient one, you could save more than $1,000 in gas costs per year (although you'd also have to take into consideration the effect this might have on your car payments and car insurance premiums).

7. Go on a financial diet once or twice a year. Many people find it easier to tighten their belts in short stretches. Try being a cheapskate for one or two months a year, trimming your budget down to just the necessities and banking the rest.

8. Take a second job. Although you wouldn't want to work two jobs indefinitely, consider taking a second job for one or two months and applying all the additional income to accumulating some investment capital.

Learning by Doing 11-1

1. You estimate you'll need $100,000 to pay for your child's college education 18 years from now. How much do you need to save each year (assume end-of-year payments) if you can earn 2 percent after taxes on your investment?
2. In the preceding problem, how much would you need to save each year if you could earn 6 percent after taxes on your investments?

Understanding Your Investment Alternatives

LEARNING objective

2 Identify your investment alternatives.

When it's time to decide how to invest your money, you'll have many alternatives. Before making any decisions, you'll need to understand the two major ways to invest—by lending and by owning. We present an overview of the advantages and disadvantages of each in this section and identify the major categories of investment alternatives. These investments will be considered in greater detail in later chapters.

Investing by Lending and by Owning

There are generally two ways to invest—you can be either a lender or an owner. When you lend, you're a **debt investor**; and when you own, you're an **equity investor**. In either case, the return on your investment will come from some combination of:

1. Regular cash flow, such as the payment of interest or dividends
2. **Capital gain**, or the growth in the value of your investment over time

The amounts earned and the risks you're exposed to with these two methods of investing differ in important ways.

The Advantages and Disadvantages of Lending. When you lend to others—whether to an individual, government entity, financial institution, or other business—your cash flows will include regular interest payments and the eventual repayment of your original loan. If you sell your debt investment to someone else before the loan is due in full, it's possible that you may realize a capital gain on the investment as well. Such investments are called debt investments, since they represent a debt obligation to the borrower. They also may be referred to as **fixed-income investments**, since the interest cash flows to the lender commonly are a series of equal payments over time. This relative certainty about future cash flows is one of the advantages of debt in-

debt investor

An investor who lends money to an individual, a government entity, a financial institution, or other business.

equity investor

An investor who has an ownership interest in a business.

capital gain

Growth in the value of an investment over time.

fixed-income investments

Debt investments that provide a fixed interest payment to the investor over the term of the investment.

vesting. Of course, the investor still runs the risk that the borrower might get into financial difficulty and fail to pay the interest promised or to repay the original amount borrowed. In the event of financial difficulties, however, the firm's obligation to debt investors is given first priority—the owners will not receive anything unless the debt investors have first been paid what they're owed.

There are many types of lending opportunities, and they differ in terms of risk and return. The relationship between risk and return should be familiar to you from previous chapters. Recall that one of the basic principles of finance is that the lower the risk, the lower the return. Your bank savings account, for example, is a very low-risk, federally insured loan made to your financial institution. The bank, in return for your deposit, promises to pay you regular interest on your savings and to return your funds to you upon request; however, because the risk is so low, the rate of interest the bank pays is very low as well. In contrast, if you lend money to the government or to a business and commit your funds for a long period of time for the loan (often 20 years or more), you're exposed to greater risk and will therefore be paid a higher annual rate on the debt investment.

Although debt investments offer the security of receiving regular cash flows, their rates of return in general tend to be lower than those of some of the other investment alternatives we'll look at later. If you lend to a business, and the business later becomes extremely profitable, you have no right to any of the additional profits, as you would if you were an owner. Since you're a lender, you don't get to share in the company's good fortune except insofar as it reduces the risk that you won't be paid what you're owed.

Fact # 1

It's generally less risky to be a lender than it is to be an owner. If the firm gets into financial difficulties, the lenders are paid first. But there's a cost associated with lower risk—the average return on stocks has averaged between 10 and 12 percent over time, whereas the average return on long-term bonds has averaged only 6 to 8 percent.

The Advantages and Disadvantages of Owning. If you're an entrepreneur at heart, you can invest by owning your own business. This, of course, requires certain skills and a substantial investment of time and money. Alternatively, if you want to share in the profits of a business without having to run the business yourself, you can become a partial owner of a company and allow others to manage it. This type of investment is often referred to as an equity investment and, as an equity investor, you expect to receive a return on your investment in the form of growth in the value of your investment over time and/or regular distribution of business profits.

Your cash flows as an owner are much less certain than your cash flows as a lender. If the company does very well, your income stream may increase over time, but you also run the risk that the company's profits will be less than expected or that the company will experience a loss or go out of business. Whereas the company *is obligated* to make payments to its debt investors, it has no similar obligation to its owners; in a bad year, there may be nothing left to distribute to equity investors.

The Major Asset Classes

asset classes
Broad groups of investments that have certain characteristics in common.

securities
Investments in which the investor contributes a sum of money to a common enterprise with the intention of making a profit through the efforts of others.

stock
Investment security that represents a proportionate ownership interest in a corporation.

Although, as mentioned, there are many investment choices, if you're a novice investor you'll probably want to stick to the basics—stocks, bonds, mutual funds, and perhaps investment real estate. These categories, commonly referred to as **asset classes**, are broad groups of investments that have certain characteristics in common. As you gain experience, you may decide to branch out to more complex investments, but you need to start out simple and add to your knowledge base as you go. Your objective will be to build a diversified *portfolio*, or collection, of investments that fulfills your objectives.

You may see many types of investments referred to as **securities**, defined as investments in which the investor contributes a sum of money to a common enterprise with the intention of earning a profit through the efforts of others. The law requires that companies selling securities meet certain reporting and disclosure requirement which will be discussed in more detail in later chapters. Stocks, bonds, and mutual fund shares are common examples of financial securities, but many other business ventures might qualify. The *News You Can Use* box, "Can a Security Wiggle?" describes one of the more unusual cases.

Common Stock. As mentioned earlier, a share of **stock** in a company represents a share of ownership in a business. If you own a share in a company that has a total of 1 million sharehold-

NEWS you can use

Can a Security Wiggle?

Florida residents John Rowles, Jim Cole, and Wayne Minton decided to supplement their regular nine-to-five income by opening a worm ranch. They paid $50,000 for a franchise from B&B Worm Farms of Oklahoma and invested another $100,000 in start-up costs. In return for the franchise fee, B&B promised to buy all the worms they produced for $7 a pound for sale to chicken farms, dairies, and agricultural facilities that need worms to process compost. At that price, the three friends estimated they'd recoup their initial investment in less than a year. The worms seemed like a no-risk investment.

"The worms seemed like a no-risk investment."

Jim's garage was soon too small for their operation, so they expanded to a greenhouse. Before long, they had more than 200 manure-filled bins and lots of wiggly merchandise. Unfortunately, in March 2003, with more than 11 million worms ready for market, the entrepreneurs found that B&B was being investigated by the Oklahoma Department of Securities for securities law violations—which meant that B&B could no longer buy their worms. The state eventually sued B&B, which had already been prohibited from doing business in Kentucky and Mississippi.

Jim, John, and Wayne eventually found buyers for the worms, so they didn't lose all their money. They also learned some hard lessons about investing. First, there's no such thing as a "no-risk" investment. Second, it isn't a good idea to have everything tied up in a single investment. Finally, always do your homework before investing your cash—a call to the Department of Securities at the outset would have prevented Jim, John, and Wayne from making this mistake.

Sources: "Lots of Wiggle Room," *Tampa Tribune*, January 16, 2003; "Worm Ranch in Sticky Situation," *Tampa Tribune*, April 15, 2003; Paul Monies, "States Sue Worm Buy Back Scam Companies," *The Oklahoman*, April 15, 2003.

ers, your single share means you have a 1/1,000,000 ownership share of the firm. Your share entitles you to vote on major issues, such as election of the board of directors of the company. If the board decides to distribute some of the company's profits to its shareholders in the form of dividends, you're entitled to a proportional share of the dividend distributions.

Although neither form of return is guaranteed, stock investors generally expect to make a return on their investment in the form of **dividends**, which are the periodic distributions of profits to equity investors, and capital gains, the increase in the value of their shares over time. Both of these forms of cash flow are fairly risky. Dividends can only be paid if the company has funds available after paying all its other obligations. Shares of stock have no maturity date, so the firm never has to pay you back the amount you've put into the firm, but you can sell your shares to other investors or pass them on to future generations, assuming the firm is still in existence at that time. Stock investing is covered in more detail in Chapter 12.

dividends

Periodic distributions of profits to equity investors.

Bonds. The most common long-term debt investment is a **bond**. A bond generally has a fixed maturity date (often 20 years or more in the future), at which time the borrower promises to repay the loan in full. In addition, the bondholder is entitled to receive a fixed periodic payment of interest, with payments normally made semiannually, or every six months. Unlike mortgage loans, this type of loan is not amortized, so the regular payments include interest only, and the full amount of principal is due at the end of the term. For example, a corporate bond with a $1,000 face value might promise an $80 interest payment per year, or 8 percent of the face value. The investor would receive half of this interest, or $40, every six months and be repaid the $1,000 in full on the maturity date.

bond

An investment representing a loan to a governmental or business entity, which usually pays a fixed rate of interest for a fixed period of time.

Bonds are commonly issued by federal, state, and local governments and by corporations to finance operations and expansion. Like stock investors, bond investors expect to make a return on their investment from both current income (periodic interest payments) and capital gains (change in value of the bond over time). Although the interest payments are usually fixed for the life of the bond, the bond value is not. Chapter 13 describes the factors that affect bond values.

preferred stock

A type of stock that pays a fixed dividend.

Preferred Stock. In addition to common stock, companies also sometimes issue **preferred stock**. This type of investment has characteristics that make it look like a hybrid of a stock and bond. Like a share of common stock, a share of preferred stock has no maturity date and represents an ownership interest in the firm. Like a bond, a share of preferred stock produces a constant cash flow for the investor, because the dividend is a fixed dollar amount per share per year. Although the constant cash flow makes preferred stock look something like bonds, it's a riskier investment than bonds because it does, in fact, represent an equity interest. In the event of financial difficulties, the company must make its debt payments before paying any dividends to the preferred shareholders; preferred shareholders do, however, have priority over common shareholders. Preferred stock is discussed further in Chapter 13.

mutual fund

A collection of investments, managed by a professional investment firm, in which investors can buy shares.

Mutual Funds. Investors can also invest in stocks, bonds, and other assets by purchasing shares of a **mutual fund** that invests in these assets. The mutual fund takes investors' funds and hires professionals to select and manage a portfolio of investments on behalf of the fund owners. As a mutual fund investor, you're a proportionate owner of the fund assets, and you're therefore entitled to share in the income and the growth of the investment pool. These shares are quite similar to stock investments, but the return and risk of each will depend on the return and risk of the particular assets that each mutual fund invests in. Mutual funds are discussed in Chapter 14.

Real Estate. The advantages of home ownership as an investment were identified in Chapter 8, but you may also want to consider investment real estate. Real estate offers investors the opportunity to receive cash flows from net rental income and capital gains from the growth in the property's value. The large minimum amount of funds required to get started in real estate investing may preclude you from considering this investment alternative until you've built up some wealth. In addition, you'll need to consider the added risk you'll face from having so much of your wealth tied up in an asset that isn't highly liquid. Real estate investing is also considered in more detail in Chapter 14.

derivative securities

Investments that derive their value from some underlying security's changes in price over time.

speculative investments

High-risk investments made in the hope of making a short-term profit.

commodities

Contracts to buy or sell raw materials or agricultural products in the future.

futures contract

A contract to buy or sell financial securities in the future.

option

A contract that gives the holder the right, but not the obligation, to purchase or sell a specified investment at a set price on or before a specified date.

Derivatives. The investment marketplace has expanded in recent years to include a large number of complex and risky securities. Many of these fall into a general category of investments called **derivative securities** because they derive their value from the price movements of some other underlying assets. Common examples of derivatives include commodities, futures, and options. These assets are highly speculative in nature since they are usually purchased in the hope of making a short-term profit based on changes in supply and demand. **Speculative investments** don't usually pay dividends or interest, so you're entirely dependent on the change in value to make a return on your investment. Although it's possible to make a large return on some types of speculative investments, you run the risk of quickly losing everything you've invested. And this is more likely to happen to inexperienced, uninformed investors.

Commodities are contracts to buy or sell raw materials (like oil and precious metals) and agricultural products (such as corn, wheat, and sugar) at some point in the future at a price set at the time the contract is made. A similar type of investment is a **futures contract,** which is a contract to buy or sell a financial security, such as a government bond or stock index, in the future. Since the price and date are set in advance, the buyers and sellers of both commodities and futures contracts are making bets on which way prices will go in the future.

An **option** contract is like a commodities and futures contract except that the buyer is not obligated to go through with the contract to buy or sell in the future—he or she simply has the *option* to do so. A buyer of a *call option* has the right, but not the obligation, to purchase the underlying asset at a set price on or before the call's maturity date. A buyer of a *put option* has the right, but not the obligation, to sell the underlying asset at a set price on or before the put's maturity date. Although these investments may seem a bit less risky than commodities and futures, the buyer of an option has to pay a price up front for that right, so even if prices move in a favorable direction, the cost of the option itself may offset any profit made.

Indexed Securities. An indexed security is an investment whose cash flows mimic the returns and risk of a broad class of securities. For example, if you're interested in investing in stocks, you can buy index shares that will track the performance of the 500 large company stocks in the S&P 500 Index or the 30 industrial stocks in the Dow Jones Industrial Average. There are also indexes based on specific industry sectors, such as energy, technology, and financial services, and indexes based on different classifications of bonds. Index investors receive a return on their investment from some combination of price appreciation and dividends. These securities will be discussed in more detail in later chapters.

The Risk-Return Tradeoff

LEARNING objective

3 Understand the risk-return tradeoff.

As already mentioned, one of the most important concepts in investing is the relationship between risk and return. Almost all investments expose you to some amount of risk. In general, however, riskier investments provide you with higher average rates of return over time. Since there are two sources of return, current cash flow and capital gains, you need to worry about two kinds of risk that may adversely affect your ability to meet your financial goals:

- The risk that you won't receive expected cash flows from the investment
- The risk that the value of your investment will decline over time

Depending on the type of investment you make, you may have more or less exposure to these two types of risk.

Not everyone is comfortable with taking investment risk, and for this reason, it's important that you make sure your investments are consistent with your risk preferences. Your investment risk exposure should not be greater than your desire and ability to bear risk. How do you know whether an investment is too risky for you? First, you need to understand your own risk tolerance. Second, you need to be able to assess the expected returns and risks for each of your investment alternatives so that you can evaluate whether their expected performance is consistent with your risk tolerance.

Evaluating Your Risk Tolerance

You may already have a good feel for how much risk you're willing to take in your investments. Your first reaction might be "None at all!" in which case we would say that you're very risk-averse, which just means that you don't like risk. In finance, we often use a more precise definition of **risk aversion**, defining a risk-averse person as someone who prefers an amount of money that is certain to a gamble that would on average produce the same amount of money. For example, suppose you're offered the following gamble: We'll flip a coin, and if it's heads, you win $100; if it's tails, you get zero. How much would you be willing to pay to play that game? Paying $50 would represent a "fair" gamble—that is, if you could play the game many times, on average you'd break even. Even so, a risk-averse person wouldn't be willing to pay $50 to play, since he or she would rather have the $50 for certain than take the risk. The risk-averse person might, however, be willing to pay $40 or $30 to play. The less you're willing to pay, the more risk-averse you are. In other words, a risk-averse person is only willing to take a gamble if he or she gets something extra for taking the risk. In an investment context, the "something extra" is a higher rate of return on investment.

risk aversion

A tendency to dislike risk and to be unwilling to invest in risky securities unless they earn higher investment returns.

At www.kiplinger.com, click on "Tools," then "Investing," then "Stocks" to take the Risk Tolerance quiz.

Most of us are risk-averse to some extent, but are willing to take on a little risk to get a little more benefit. Furthermore, all of us have a personal preference for just how much extra benefit we require. Investment advisors usually evaluate their clients' risk tolerance before recommending investment strategies, since they have an ethical obligation to recommend investments that are consistent with their clients' preferences and appropriate for their life circumstances. In Chapter 9, you had the opportunity to assess your level of risk aversion in the context of nonfinancial decisions, but your attitudes toward financial risks may be quite different. How would you answer the question used by the Federal Reserve in its triennial Survey of Consumer Finances as reported in the *Money Psychology* box, "Demographic Differences in Stated Risk Aversion." How does your answer compare to the answers given by survey respondents in 2001?

Money Psychology

Demographic Differences in Stated Risk Aversion

The Survey of Consumer Finances, sponsored by the Federal Reserve Board every three years, asks its participants the following question:

Which of the following statements comes closest to the amount of financial risk that you are willing to take when you save or make investments:

a. Take substantial financial risk expecting to earn substantial returns;
b. Take above-average financial risk expecting to earn above-average returns;
c. Take average financial risks expecting to earn average returns;
d. Not willing to take any financial risks.

Data from the most recent survey year reveals some significant differences among demographic groups.

Characteristic	Unwilling to Take Any Financial Risk (%)	Willing to Take Substantial or Above-Average Financial Risk (%)
All households (4,442)	39.8	22.8
Male	31.5	30.3
Female	46.7	16.5
Age 65+	61.2	8.9
Age 30–50	33.1	27.0
Income over $100,000	10.5	44.1
Income under $25,000	66.5	10.3
Net worth over $1 million	7.4	41.6
Net worth under $50,000	54.0	15.9
White	34.9	24.3
Black	51.7	16.2
Hispanic	64.6	16.9

Source: Tabulations of Federal Reserve Board, 2001 Survey of Consumer Finances.

Factors Affecting Risk Tolerance

As the national survey results in the *Money Psychology* box indicate, individuals demonstrate wide variation in the willingness to bear investment risk. Differences in risk tolerance arise from many factors. These include life-cycle stage; demographic factors such as income, net worth, household makeup, and gender; education and investment experience; and confidence about the future.

Life Cycle Effects. Although age is often associated with risk-taking tendencies, it's actually your life-cycle stage that makes the biggest difference. In the early life-cycle stages, you're working on developing a foundation for the future. During this period, you "invest" in your education and career, building your human capital—an asset that will provide returns to you in the form of increased earning potential. The focus on liquidity and safety during this period of your life means that you're less inclined to take substantial risks. During the wealth accumulation stage of the life cycle, individuals who have already established their foundations (insurance and emergency funds) tend to be more willing to take risks in order to accumulate the funds necessary to achieve their future goals. The focus shifts from building human capital to building financial capital. As individuals approach retirement their focus shifts to protecting their principal. They tend to gradually become more risk-averse again, probably because they realize that they have less time to recover from a loss in their investment portfolio. This trend continues through the retirement years.

Demographic Differences. Wealthier people tend to be more willing to take risk. If you have more, it makes sense that you can afford to risk losing some. Income has a similar effect, although stability of income is perhaps even more important than level of income. If you have a secure job—for example, if you're a tenured university professor—you might be more willing to take a little risk in your investments. In contrast, a salesperson with irregular income from commissions might not be able to commit to regular contributions and might be nervous about the possibility of losing money in his or her portfolio.

In general, families with children tend to be less willing to take financial risk. This tendency may be due to their greater need for liquidity (for emergencies) or the cost of raising children, which effectively delays the next stage in the life cycle. Once the foundations for financial security are established, a parent could be more willing to take some investment risk. There is some evidence that women are less inclined to take risk than men, but this difference is less pronounced in younger generations, perhaps because the education and work experience of young men and women are more similar today than was the case in previous generations.

Fact #2

Most investment advisors recommend that individuals reduce their investment risk exposure as they approach retirement. When your investment horizon is shorter, it's more difficult to recover from an unexpected decline in the value. For example, if you had all your retirement wealth in a stock account and the stock market fell by 25 percent just before your anticipated retirement, the decline in the value of your portfolio would result in an equivalent reduction in your expected retirement income. It might even mean you'd have to delay your retirement date.

Education and Experience. The effect of education on risk tolerance is less clear cut than some of the characteristics previously mentioned. Studies have not shown a significant difference between the risk-taking behavior of those with and without a college education, for example. Some evidence exists that specific investment education can impact your financial risk-taking. People who have participated in investor education seminars or taken a class in personal finance are usually more comfortable with taking a little risk in their investment portfolios than those who have not.

Consumer Confidence. Your willingness to take risk is also related to your confidence about the future. Whether you're worrying about the possibility of a future job loss or downturn in the economy, negative prospects for the future will make you less willing to bear risk. Studies have shown that when overall consumer confidence is low, the proportion that households invest in equities is reduced.

Measuring Return and Risk for Individual Securities

The amount of risk that you're willing to take should depend on whether you expect to be adequately rewarded for taking that risk. Even if an investment were truly risk-free, you'd still expect to be compensated for investing your money instead of being able to spend it for current consumption. This minimum return is referred to as the *real risk-free rate*. The additional return you earn from any investment is your compensation for bearing risk. As you get started in developing an investment plan, you'll need to have a working understanding of some of the basic terminology commonly used in describing the return and risk of various securities. It will also be helpful to understand the different components of risk and how they influence the returns on investments.

Fact #3

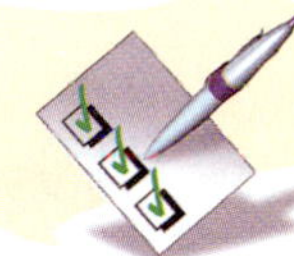

Although many investors prefer to buy stocks that pay regular dividends, that may not be the best approach for achieving long-term investment goals. When you receive a current dividend, you'll owe income taxes on that money if it's in a taxable account, which will reduce your after-tax investment yield.

Rate of Return. Investors expect to make money from current income generated by their investments (such as interest, dividends, or rents) and the gains in the value of their investments over time. These are often referred to collectively as the return on investment and may be expressed as a **rate of return** or **yield** (in percent), or a dollar return over a given period of time. The annual rate of return is calculated as follows:

rate of return or **yield**
The total income earned on an investment over a period of time, including interest or dividends and capital gains, divided by the original amount invested.

$$\begin{aligned}\text{Rate of return} &= \text{Current yield} + \text{Capital gain yield}\\ &= \frac{\text{Current income}}{\text{Beginning price}} + \frac{\text{End price} - \text{Beginning price}}{\text{Beginning price}}\\ &= \frac{\text{Current income} + \text{End price} - \text{Beginning price}}{\text{Beginning price}}\end{aligned}$$

As an example, suppose you buy a share of stock for $20. Over the course of a year, the stock pays you a cash dividend of $1 (which is 5% of your original purchase price), and the stock also increases in value to $22 (a gain of $2, or 10% of the original purchase price). The combined value of the dividend income and the gain in value gives you a $3 return for the year, so you have earned a rate of return or yield of $3/$20 = 15% on the stock investment.

Learning by Doing 11-2

1. You invest $1,000 in Xenon Corporation stock (10 shares at $100 per share) and $1,000 in Xenon Corporation bonds (one bond at $1,000), which pay 8 percent interest. Xenon has a phenomenal year and distributes $5 per share to its shareholders. The stock value also increases to $115 per share. The bond value stays at $1,000. What is your return on investment for each of these investments in that year?
2. The following year, Xenon experiences a loss. It pays no dividends, and its stock price falls from $115 to $105. The bond value stays the same. What is your return on investment for each of these investments in that year?

Risk Premiums. As we've seen, investors require a premium to be willing to bear risk. An easy way to think about the relationship between risk and return is that investors will require a certain amount of return, or a risk premium, for *each type of risk* to which they're exposed. For debt securities, these may include inflation risk, interest-rate risk, reinvestment risk, default risk, liquidity risk, and market risk. Equity investments expose you primarily to inflation risk, reinvestment risk, and market risk. An investment with more of these components of risk will generally provide a greater level of return than one that has very few. This concept is illustrated in Exhibit 11-2 for representative debt securities that differ in risk and return.

inflation risk

The risk that inflation will erode the purchasing power of investment returns.

nominal risk-free rate

The expected return on a short-term risk-free investment such as a Treasury bill, equal to the real risk-free rate plus an inflation risk premium.

Inflation Risk. We noted earlier that, even if an investment were virtually risk-free, you'd require compensation for delaying consumption. With most investments, you'll also be exposed to **inflation risk**—the loss in spending power over the investment period. Thus, the minimum rate of return you'd expect from any investment would include compensation for delaying consumption and for bearing inflation risk. This minimum rate of return is usually called the **nominal risk-free rate**—a rate that is higher during periods of rising inflation than during periods of low inflation. The shortest-term debt security issued by the federal government, a 13-week Treasury bill, is an investment that is expected to earn the nominal risk-free rate since it doesn't

EXHIBIT 11-2

Risk Premiums and Yields for Representative Debt Investments

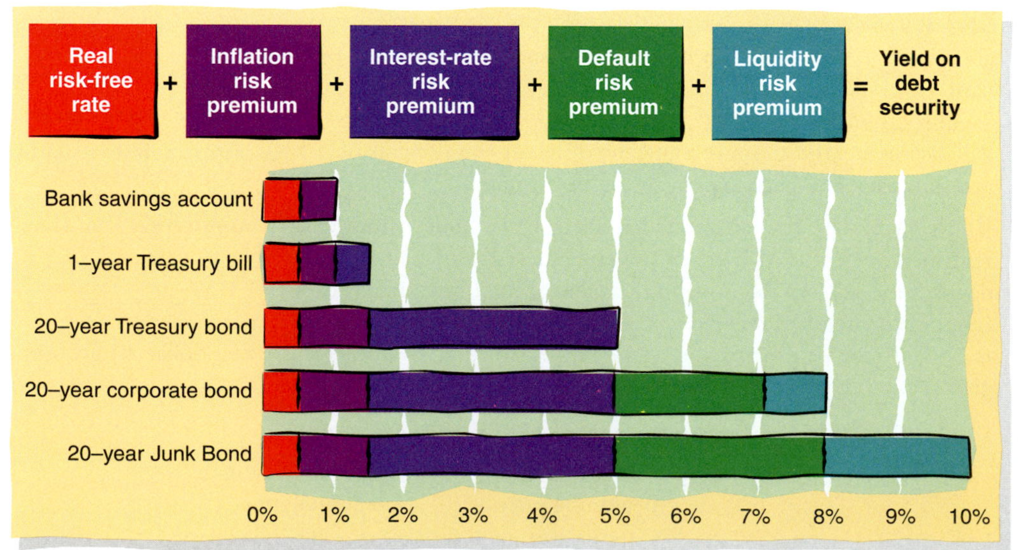

expose you to any of the other types of risk discussed below. Inflation risk normally increases with the term to maturity, so a one-year Treasury bill will have a slightly larger inflation-risk premium than a 13-week Treasury bill.

Interest-Rate Risk. Although interest rates can have an effect on all investments, some types of securities—bonds and preferred stock—are more highly influenced by interest-rate changes. When interest rates go up, the present value of cash flows to be received in the future goes down. This causes prices to fall. When rates go down, prices go up. The longer the term to maturity, the more the price of the security is affected. This is commonly called **interest-rate risk**, although it's sometimes called *maturity risk* or *price risk* because of the strong interrelationship among interest rates, maturities, and prices. Investors expect to be compensated for this risk with an interest-rate risk premium. Short-term securities have a lower interest-rate risk premium—they provide a lower return on investment, all else equal—than longer-term securities.

interest-rate risk
The risk of price changes due to changes in interest rates.

A corollary to interest-rate risk is **reinvestment risk**—the risk that you'll have to reinvest returns at a time when rates of return have fallen. Whereas interest-rate risk is greatest for long-term debt securities, reinvestment risk is highest for short-term debt investments. Suppose, for example, you invest $1,000 in a one-year CD at 6 percent per year, receiving $60 in interest for the year. When the year is up, you find that interest rates have fallen to 4 percent, which means that if you roll over the CD, investing the $1,000 in another one-year CD, the following year's income will be only $40. Any investment that pays you current cash flows, such as interest or dividend payments, exposes you to reinvestment risk since you'll have to invest those cash flows as you receive them regardless of the market conditions at the time.

reinvestment risk
The risk that short-term investments will have to be reinvested at lower rates when they come due.

Default Risk. The risk that you won't receive expected cash flows from an investment is called **default risk**. Although any company can run into financial difficulties, some corporations and government entities are considered more likely to default than others. The issuers of risky bonds must offer investors a higher rate of return to compensate them for default risk. For equity investors—who can't technically be defaulted on, since they haven't been promised any particular return—there's still the risk of business failure. In a bankruptcy proceeding, the value of an equity investment is likely to be zero.

default risk
The risk of not receiving promised cash flows from an investment.

Liquidity Risk. **Liquidity risk** is the risk that you won't be able to convert your investment to cash on short notice without losing value. This risk is lowest for securities that have active markets—lots of buyers and sellers, as is the case for publicly traded stocks and bonds. In contrast, real estate is fairly difficult to sell on short notice since there aren't as many buyers interested in any given property and it takes a while to finalize the transaction. Investors expect to receive a premium when they invest in less liquid assets, but it may be insufficient to offset the cost of not being able to sell something when you need to.

liquidity risk
The risk of not being able to convert an asset to cash without losing value.

Market Risk. In addition to the components of individual risk discussed above, all investments expose you to **market risk**, the risk associated with general market movements and economic conditions. In a recession, when businesses are cutting back on spending and unemployment rates are high, investment values tend to decline, resulting in a "bear market," as illustrated in Exhibit 11-3. When times are good, as in the late 1990s, the result is a "bull market" characterized by increasing asset values fueled by high business profits, low interest rates, and economic growth. Although both debt and equity markets are influenced by market conditions, they don't necessarily move together. You could, for example, simultaneously have a bull stock market and a bear bond market.

market risk
Investment risk associated with general market movements and economic conditions.

Market risk is related not only to economic conditions in the United States but also to global risks. After the events of September 11, 2001, and their well-publicized effect on financial markets around the world, it's easy to see why global and political factors are important to investors. The attack on the World Trade Center, the hub of financial transactions in this country, brought the markets to a complete halt for more than a week. And terrorism is not the only global risk investors are exposed to. Even in calmer political times, exchange rates and the balance of trade can strongly influence the economic environment and the profitability of firms. Investors are also exposed to domestic political risk, such as changes in tax laws, changes in tariffs, and other business legislation that might affect future profits. Furthermore, although investing

EXHIBIT 11-3

Bear and Bull Markets

overseas is easier now than ever before, it's important to remember that many of the legal protections we take for granted in this country (such as information disclosure and standardized accounting practices) are not applicable elsewhere. Investor fraud is commonplace in many areas of the world, so the caution "buyer beware" takes on new meaning in those contexts.

Learning by Doing 11-3

1. Which categories of risk are most important for each of the following types of investment:
   a. Federally insured bank deposit account
   b. Actively traded corporate bond issued by a large, stable company
   c. Actively traded stock issued by a technology company

Diversification and Asset Allocation

LEARNING objective

4 Recognize the importance of asset allocation and diversification of your portfolio.

diversification

An investment strategy that involves spreading money across a range of investments in order to reduce the overall risk of the portfolio.

If you could see the future and know with certainty which of your investments would do best, you could put all your money there and never lose a dime. The *News You Can Use* box, "The Benefit of Perfect Foresight," provides a dramatic illustration of just how valuable a crystal ball could be to an investor. But in reality, no one can accurately predict the ups and downs of specific companies or even of broad asset classes. By spreading your money over a selection of investments and asset classes—that is, by diversifying your investments—you reduce the risk that one bad choice will cause you to lose everything. The principle of **diversification** can be summed up this way: Don't put all your eggs in one basket. In practice, deciding exactly which "baskets" to use and how many "eggs" to put in each is a little more difficult.

How Diversification Works

Suppose you have $10,000 to invest in a portfolio of stocks. At the beginning of the year, you put half the money in Stock A and half in Stock B. Both are expected to earn a return of 10 percent per year, on average. But these are risky investments, so the *actual* return in each year will

NEWS you can use

The Benefit of Perfect Foresight

If you had invested $1 in short-term federal government debt securities (Treasury bills) in 1933 and then reinvested the principal and interest each year, your portfolio would have grown to about $15 by 2004. If the same dollar had instead been invested in the S&P 500 Index, which is comprised of large company stocks, and you'd reinvested all your dividend income each year, you'd have about $3,000 in 2004, more than 200 times as much.

But just suppose you had a crystal ball that could perfectly predict the future. Each year, you'd look ahead to see which investment would earn a higher return in the coming year—the S&P 500 Index or Treasury bills. When you foresaw stocks outperforming Treasury bills, you'd move all your money to stocks for the year, and when you foresaw Treasury bills doing better, you'd move all your money there for the year. With perfect foresight, your single dollar in 1933 would have grown to around $65,000 by 2004, resulting in a portfolio more than 20 times greater than stocks alone and more than 4,000 times your accumulation in Treasury bills alone! Although no one has the ability to perfectly predict the future performance of the market, there are two lessons to take from these results. First, despite its ups and downs, the stock market has produced far greater returns over time than low-risk investments like Treasury bills. Second, even if you can't predict with perfect accuracy, a little knowledge goes a long way. Even if you just avoided the five worst loss years in the stock market, you'd have about $12,500 at the end, more than four times what you'd have if you'd left the money in the stock market for the entire 70 years.

"A little knowledge goes a long way"

not always be 10 percent. Rather, the returns will fluctuate around an average of 10 percent and may even, in some years, be negative. Over a two-year period, the actual annual returns for your investment portfolio, counting dividends and capital gains, are as follows:

	Actual Returns	
	Year 1	Year 2
Stock A	18%	2%
Stock B	4%	16%
Average	11%	9%

As you can see, if you'd put all your money in Stock B, you would have realized a return of only 4 percent on your investment in Year 1. Because Stock A earned 18 percent in Year 1, however, you were able to earn an overall return of 11 percent on your two-stock portfolio. In Year 2, Stock A earned only 2 percent, but Stock B earned 16 percent, so again your average return was near the expected return of 10 percent. Splitting your money between these two stocks reduced the risk that your investment portfolio return would deviate too far from your expected return. You paid a cost for reducing the risk, however; although your returns were higher than if you had happened to have only the poorly performing stock in a given year, they were lower than if you had happened to have only the higher-performing stock.

The principle of diversification is that you shouldn't put all your eggs in one basket.

As you increase the number of investments in your portfolio, the variability of the returns on your portfolio will decline, since the ups and downs of individual investments will cancel each other out. That's because many of the things that affect a given firm's profitability are company-specific. One company has a labor dispute when another introduces a new product. One company is named in a product liability lawsuit when another expands its operations into South America.

Your diversification objective is to have enough investments so that all these kinds of company-specific risks average out, resulting in reduced variability of return for your total portfolio. Exhibit 11-4 graphically illustrates the risk-reducing effect of adding more stocks (or other investments) to your portfolio: The more you have, the lower your risk. Although the graph shows

EXHIBIT 11-4

Risk-Reducing Impact of Diversification

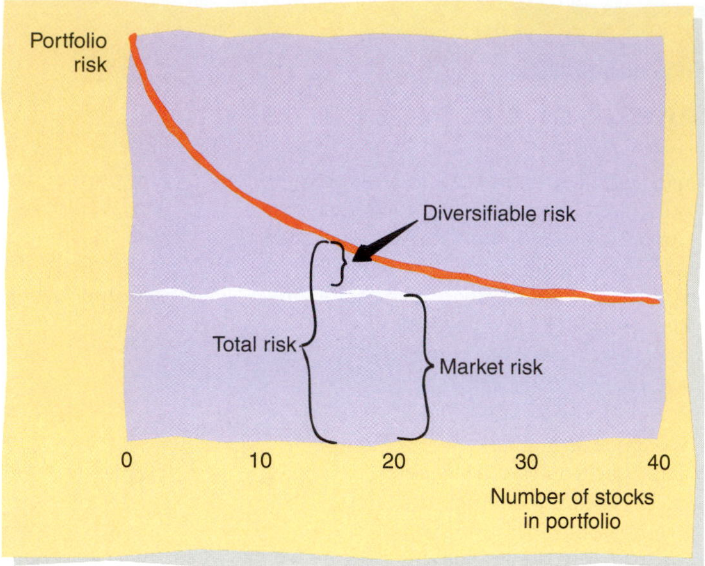

that random asset selection will get rid of most company-specific risk after you have about 40 stocks in your portfolio, there actually isn't a "magic number" of investments that will result in perfect diversification. Diversification depends on many factors—your choice of specific investments, the relationships between the investments you hold in your portfolio, market conditions, and your own risk tolerance, for example. It's also important to understand that, even if your portfolio is well diversified, it still isn't risk-free. After all the company-specific, or diversifiable, risks are canceled out, what will be left is market risk—the risk of portfolio fluctuations caused by common market factors.

What if you're pretty sure that a single investment is going to do so well that you want to put all of your money in it? For example, suppose you work at a terrific company that gives you stock bonuses or contributes stock to your retirement plan. In the past, you've seen the value of that stock rise at a rate faster than the market as a whole. Under those circumstances, is it necessary to diversify? In 2001, thousands of employees of Enron Corporation found out the hard way that being undiversified—in this case, holding nothing but Enron stock in their portfolios—involves a lot of downside risk. When the company went bankrupt after allegations of accounting irregularities, these people not only lost their jobs but also lost most of their nest eggs. Although financial advisors have for years warned individuals about the hazards of being completely undiversified—having all your financial *and* human capital tied to the performance of the same firm—people like to invest in what they understand, or *think* they understand. The company you work for may seem like a good investment, but you need to resist the urge to go overboard. As a general guideline, financial advisors recommend that you invest no more than 10 percent of your total portfolio in any single investment.

The Importance of Asset Allocation

asset allocation
The process of deciding what proportion of a portfolio to invest in each asset class.

Asset allocation is the process of deciding what proportion of your portfolio to invest in each of several broad investment classes—stock, bonds, real estate, cash—as opposed to individual security selection within an asset class. Asset allocation is the method by which you achieve diversification. Most investment professionals say that asset allocation is the most important component of building an investment portfolio. Some academic studies have shown that as much as 90 percent of the overall performance of a long-term portfolio is attributable to the asset allocation mix, as opposed to individual investment selection of assets within each asset class.

Your allocation of funds between broad asset classes should change over your life cycle to be consistent with your investment objectives, family situation, time horizon, and risk tolerance. There's no hard-and-fast rule that applies to everyone, but most people will want to allocate a higher proportion of their portfolios to stocks when they're younger. With a longer time to in-

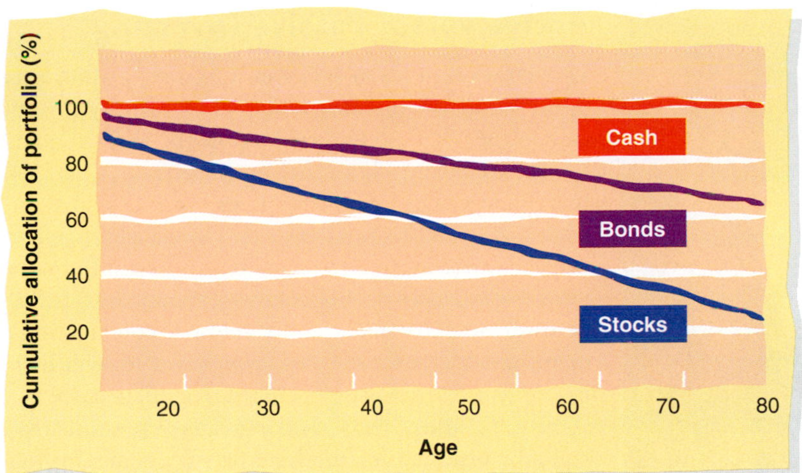

EXHIBIT 11-5

Possible Asset Allocation over the Life Cycle

vest, you can afford to take more risk, and you should have more of your wealth in assets that have the potential for greater returns. As you approach retirement and your investment horizon shortens, it will be advisable to gradually shift your portfolio toward lower-risk asset classes. Your goal at that point will be to maintain the wealth you've already accumulated, so you don't want to take too much risk. When you reach your retirement years, you'll be spending rather than saving, but you'll need to earn enough on your money to offset the eroding effect of inflation. Thus, even in retirement, you'll want to allocate some of your money to stocks. After all, if you retire at 65 and expect to live to be 90, you'll still have a long investment horizon.

Although there's no magic formula for asset allocation over the life cycle, investment advisors commonly provide their clients with rules of thumb for asset allocation decisions. These rules aren't universally accepted and haven't been scientifically validated. But they have the positive effects of discouraging overly conservative investment behavior at young ages and encouraging risk reduction at older ages. For example, an advisor might suggest the following rule: The percent of money you should invest in stocks is 110 minus your age and the rest of your portfolio should be equally allocated to bonds and cash. By that rule, at age 25, you would invest 85 percent in stocks, and at age 65, you would invest only 45 percent in stocks. The remainder of your portfolio would be a combination of bonds and cash. Exhibit 11-5 shows how this allocation might evolve over a typical person's life cycle. Note, however, that a different financial advisor might advise you to allocate based on a different formula—perhaps 100 minus your age.

Learning by Doing 11-4

1. Kenny has $5,000 to invest, and this amount represents his entire net worth. He decides to split his money evenly among five stocks in different industries. Is Kenny diversified? Why or why not?
2. You're currently age 30. Using the allocation rule described above, how much should you be allocating to stocks, bonds, and cash respectively?

Establishing Your Investment Strategy

LEARNING objective

5 Decide whether you will be an active or passive investor and what your primary investment strategy will be.

The next step in the investment planning process is to establish an investment strategy that's appropriate for your risk tolerance, expertise, time, and life-cycle stage. In this section, we explain why it's advisable for you to be a passive investor and describe several passive investment strategies you might employ. In later chapters, we'll talk in greater detail about how to invest in stocks, bonds, and mutual funds, and we'll identify asset-specific investment strategies.

Active Versus Passive Investing

Do you want to be an active or a passive investor over the long term? An **active investor** attempts to identify investments and asset classes that are undervalued in the short run and to make returns by buying those that are underpriced and selling those that are overpriced. In the extreme, an active investor might be what is called a "day trader"—one who makes many trades in a single day, attempting to capitalize on new information or temporary imbalances in supply and demand. In contrast, a **passive investor** attempts to carefully select a combination of investments that will, over the *long term*, result in achieving his or her investment return goals. The objective of an active investor is to "beat the market," or to make greater returns than would normally be expected for the level of risk in the portfolio. Passive investors are happy to do *as well as* the market on average earning a return that is appropriate for the portfolio risk. In general, as you'll soon see, individual investors are well advised to choose one or more of the passive investment strategies described later in this section.

If you want to be an active investor, you'll need to devote a lot of time to tracking your portfolio.

active investor

Investor who actively buys and sells securities, attempting to make short-run gains.

passive investor

Investor who invests to make long-run returns and doesn't actively engage in buying or selling.

Can Active Investors "Beat the Market"?

As you learn more about investing, you may be tempted to capitalize on your newfound knowledge by doing some active investing. Before you do, however, you should carefully consider the evidence regarding the long-run performance of professionally managed funds. Many studies show that portfolios actively managed by professional money managers achieve lower annual returns, on average, than the market as a whole. This implies that investors have paid for the services of these professionals when they would have been better off simply buying shares of an indexed security. But aren't some professional investors more successful than others? The evidence shows otherwise—the managers who achieve the highest returns in a given year are rarely at the top of the list the following year.

Since you're not as experienced or knowledgeable as these professionals, it follows that you probably won't be able to do any better than they do. If this is true, why do so many investors think they can beat the odds? As we've emphasized throughout this text, there are many psychological forces at work, which result in sometimes irrational financial decisions. In the *Money Psychology* box, "Beyond Greed and Fear," author Hersh Shefrin suggests that an inherent feature of human nature—hope—is the driving factor.

Fact #4

Women tend to be more conservative investors than men. However, a recent study examining transactions in a large mutual fund found that the women investors ended up with better overall performance than the men. Although the women did, in fact, make somewhat more conservative investment choices than the men, the men made more trades, apparently "playing" with their money more. The men's higher transaction costs left them with lower overall returns.

Are Markets Efficient?

One of the explanations commonly offered for why investors are unlikely to be able to make short-run returns from active investing is that markets for financial securities are relatively efficient. In all of financial economics, no topic has been the subject of more studies than market efficiency; the originator of the theory, Eugene Fama, received a Nobel prize for his work on this subject. Yet the debate rages on.

Market efficiency means that, at any given time, all publicly available information has already driven security prices to the correct level, given that information. If, as the theory implies, financial assets are always correctly priced, then you can't make any extra profit by buying underpriced securities and selling overpriced securities, the essence of an active investment strategy. Investors under this theory will receive the return that is justified by the risk of the investment but won't be able to get any extra return by incurring additional trading costs or by investing time in research or education. As you might expect, stock analysts and investment managers, who attempt to make a living doing exactly that, are not too keen on this theory.

market efficiency

A theory that suggests prices immediately adjust to reflect all publicly available information.

On a very basic level, market efficiency can be thought of as being related to how *quickly* prices react to news. Since information is so easily available today and there are so many investors in the marketplace, all trying to identify undervalued securities, the window of opportu-

Money Psychology

Beyond Greed and Fear

Hersh Shefrin, a finance professor at Santa Clara University, is the author of *Beyond Greed and Fear* (New York: Oxford University Press, 2002), a fascinating look at how investors' irrationality contributed to the market upswing in the 1990s and to the later bursting of the "market bubble." In the introduction to his book, Shefrin notes that experts have long cited greed and fear as the factors that drive individual investor behavior. He notes, however, that our current knowledge of market psychology extends well beyond greed and fear. Over the last 25 years, psychologists have discovered two important facts. First, the primary emotions that determine risk-taking behavior are not greed and fear but *hope* and fear. Second, although to err is indeed human, financial practitioners of all types, from portfolio managers to corporate executives, make the same mistakes repeatedly. Behavioral finance, as a field of study, is thus concerned with the identification, classification, and prevention of these errors in decision making.

nity for capitalizing on any new information has to be fairly small. If, for example, you hear that a company is coming out with an innovative new product and you believe that this will cause the stock price to go up, you may want to try to buy some shares at the current price and sell them after the price rises with the good news. But everyone else has heard the good news, too, so lots of investors will immediately start buying up as many shares as possible, and the price will rise. By the time you try to buy the shares, the stock price may already be high. The moral of this story is that market efficiency means that it's difficult, though not impossible, to make a profit on any new information. You just have to be at the front of the line.

Today, the efficiency of the market makes it riskier than ever to be an active investor. Prices of actively traded stocks and bonds react to information so quickly that they sometimes even move in advance of the actual public announcement on the strength of expectations. Generally, if you see the information reported in the financial press, it's going to be too late to act on that information to make a short-term profit.

Passive Investing Strategies

Although being a passive investor implies that you're not making regular changes in your portfolio, most passive investors continue to build their portfolios over time. Therefore, they must make regular investment contributions and selections. The most common strategies for doing so include buy-and-hold, dollar cost averaging, and direct investment and reinvestment plans.

Buy-and-Hold. In general, most passive investment strategies by their very nature fall into the category of **buy-and-hold**. When you use a buy-and-hold strategy, you select an asset allocation appropriate for your life stage and risk tolerance and then choose a diversified set of securities within each asset class. After making your investment selections, you hold them for the long term, making changes only as necessary to maintain your asset allocation and to reflect changes in information about the assets in your portfolio. The advantages of a buy-and-hold strategy are that you can capture the long-term gains for each asset class while avoiding most of the transaction costs associated with buying and selling securities. You pay less in brokerage commissions, and you defer the taxes on your gains until you choose to sell.

buy-and-hold

A passive investment strategy in which the investor identifies his or her target asset allocation and then selects appropriate securities to hold for the long run.

Dollar Cost Averaging. Many investment advisors recommend a strategy for passive investors called **dollar cost averaging**. This strategy involves buying in equal dollar amounts at regular intervals rather than making a large purchase at one time. Since most individual investors attempt to make regular contributions to investments from current income, this strategy is a natural fit for their financial plans.

dollar cost averaging

An investment strategy in which you invest in equal dollar amounts at regular intervals regardless of fluctuations in price.

The logic behind dollar cost averaging is that you can't predict whether market prices today are high or low compared with what they'll be later. By spreading your purchases over time, however, you'll average out the ups and downs of purchase prices. When prices are rising, your payment will purchase fewer shares at the higher prices. When prices are falling, you'll be able to buy more shares at lower prices, which means that the average purchase price per share in your portfolio will be lower than the long-term average price for the investment. This idea is illustrated in the *Go Figure!* box, "How Does Dollar Cost Averaging Work?" The example compares your end-of-year investment outcomes under the assumption that you invest a total of $3,600 in a particular stock during the year, either all at once at the beginning of the year (without dollar cost averaging) or $300 per month at the beginning of each month (with dollar cost averaging). In the example, dollar cost averaging results in a slightly higher portfolio value at the end of the year, primarily because you've been able to buy a number of

GO FIGURE!

How Does Dollar Cost Averaging Work?

Problem: You plan to invest $3,600 in a particular stock mutual fund this year. You're trying to decide whether you should buy all the shares at the beginning of the year or buy $300 worth at the beginning of each month. Based on last year's share prices for this mutual fund, which strategy would have resulted in a greater portfolio value?

Solution: To answer this question, you need to calculate the number of shares you would have been able to purchase each month, given the price of the shares at the time. You can set up a table such as the one below to compare the outcomes. In this case, dollar cost averaging would have allowed you to buy more shares (191 instead of 180) because the share price fell below the January 1 level in later months. In some months, your $300 would have resulted in a fractional share, so you ended up investing slightly less than the $3,600 you'd have invested at the beginning. Even so, at the end of the year, you would have had $4,011 compared with $3,780 without dollar cost averaging, a difference of $231. From February to July, you would have paid less than the original $20; in other months, you would have paid more, and the average price paid ended up being $19. Note, however, that this example doesn't take into account any transaction costs you would have incurred or any interest earnings you could have made on the uninvested dollars. If the net difference was less than the $231 benefit from dollar cost averaging, you would still have wound up ahead.

	With Dollar Cost Averaging					Without Dollar Cost Averaging		
Date	Price per Share	Number of Shares Bought	Dollars Invested This Period	Total Shares Held	Market Value of Shares	Dollars Invested This Period	Total Shares Held	Market Value of Shares
January 1	$20	15.00	$300.00	15	$300	$3,600	180	$3,600
February 1	18	16.00	288.00	31	558	0	180	3,240
March 1	16	18.00	288.00	49	784	0	180	2,880
April 1	15	20.00	300.00	69	1,035	0	180	2,700
May 1	16	18.00	288.00	87	1,392	0	180	2,880
June 1	17	17.00	289.00	104	1,768	0	180	3,060
July 1	18	16.00	288.00	120	2,160	0	180	3,240
August 1	20	15.00	300.00	135	2,700	0	180	3,600
September 1	22	13.00	286.00	148	3,256	0	180	3,960
October 1	21	14.00	294.00	162	3,402	0	180	3,780
November 1	20	15.00	300.00	177	3,540	0	180	3,600
December 1	21	14.00	294.00	191	$4,011	0	180	$3,780
Total Invested			**$3,515**			**$3,600**		
Market Value					**$4,011**			**$3,780**
Average Price	**$19**							

shares at lower prices during the first few months when prices were falling. As a result, you end up with more shares than you would have had if you'd invested all your money at the outset. It's important to note however, that dollar cost averaging doesn't always result in higher portfolio values—if the stock price had continually risen over the year, you would have missed out on the gain in value on the shares you could have purchased earlier at the lower price and you'd end up with fewer shares. In addition, the profits you make on smaller transactions may be offset by your transaction costs.

Direct Investment and Dividend Reinvestment Plans. In general, it's beneficial, from a financial planning perspective, to have and stick to a plan for making regular investments. While you can do this in a number of ways, it's best to avoid brokerage commissions on small trades. For this reason, most large corporations have a **direct investment program** whereby you can purchase stock directly from the company without being charged a brokerage commission. For a list of companies that offer these plans, call the Direct Stock Purchase Plan Clearinghouse at (800)774-4117 or check their website, www.enrolldirect.com. Mutual funds also encourage regular contributions and will arrange for automatic monthly transfer of funds from your checking or savings account toward the purchase of mutual fund shares.

direct investment program

Program offered by a publicly traded company to allow investors to automatically purchase shares of the company's stock on a regular basis without incurring a brokerage fee.

If you hold stock in a company or mutual fund that pays regular dividends, you'll probably have the opportunity to reinvest your cash dividends in the stock through a **dividend reinvestment plan (DRIP)**. Such plans automatically take any cash distributions and use them to buy additional shares for you. Suppose, for example, that you're entitled to a $20 dividend distribution on the 100 shares you own of a particular company's stock, which is currently valued at $10 per share. Under a dividend reinvestment plan, you'd receive two additional shares instead of the dividend. If you're interested in knowing which companies offer DRIPs, consult Standard & Poor's *Directory of Dividend Reinvestment Plans.*

dividend reinvestment plan (DRIP)

Program that allows investors to receive dividends in the form of additional shares of stock instead of cash.

Indexing. Indexes were mentioned earlier as an investment alternative. Recall that an index is an investment whose risk and return track those of a broad asset class, such as large-company stocks. You can buy shares of an index security directly, or you can buy a mutual fund trying to mimic that market. For example, a mutual fund that is indexed to the Dow Jones Industrial Average will be invested in shares of all 30 stocks making up that index. Indexing is a good way for passive buy-and-hold investors to achieve their objectives with fairly low expenses. We discuss this investment strategy in more detail in Chapter 14.

Timing. Just because you're a passive investor doesn't mean you should have your blinders on and ignore what's going on around you. Some investors attempt to avoid general downturns and take advantage of general increases in particular markets by strategically reallocating their portfolios, a strategy called **timing**. For example, suppose you thought the stock market was about to take a nose dive. You could pull all your money out of stocks and put it into cash to avoid such losses. This is an example of *market timing*, in which you try to anticipate major moves in certain asset markets. Alternatively, you might try to implement a *business cycle timing* strategy, in which you put more money into your investment portfolio when the economy is expanding and you pull out when the economy is contracting.

timing

Investment strategy in which you attempt to shift your asset allocation to capture upturns and avoid downturns in specific markets.

The problem with timing strategies is that even the experts aren't that good at correctly predicting what the market is going to do. In practice, investors probably get it right less than half the time. In the late 1990s, for example, when the market moved continuously upward, many business cycle timers pulled money out of the stock market too soon and missed out on the strong returns at the end of the decade. Other individual investors waited too long to *start* investing in the stock market in the late 1990s, buying at the high point and shortly thereafter watching their portfolio values decline sharply. As an example, in response to the stock market crash of October 1987, investors sold more than $15 billion in stock mutual funds in 1988, missing out on a 17 percent gain on the S&P 500 Index for the year. Even missing a few of the best days of a bull market can significantly reduce your portfolio's performance. From 1980 to 2002, if you'd missed the top 10 days, you'd have 40 percent less than a simple buy-and-hold strategy. Although some timers have had good success over the long term, you'll probably find that you'll be better off selecting a diversified portfolio and letting it ride.

Key Strategies for Investment Success

LEARNING objective

6 Invest successfully by incorporating taxes in your investment decisions and using available information resources.

In addition to developing your investment goals and understanding your investment alternatives, your investment plan must incorporate taxes and continued information acquisition.

Take Advantage of Favorable Tax Rules

In making any financial decisions, you must take taxes into consideration. Investments, as we've seen, can produce two types of income—current cash flows, such as interest and dividends, and capital gains from selling the investment for a profit. Both of these types of income are potentially taxable, which will reduce your annual returns and the cumulative value of your portfolio.

Income Versus Capital Gains. Current income from investments held in taxable accounts may be taxable as ordinary income. In other words, you'll pay a tax on this income equal to your marginal tax rate. If you're in the 25 percent tax bracket, for example, your interest income of $100 will net you $75 after taxes. In contrast, the tax on capital gains depends in part on how long you hold the investment before selling it. Profits on the sale of investments held for less than one year are also taxed as ordinary income. However, if you hold an investment longer than one year, the gain on the sale is subject to a special lower tax rate—5 percent for taxpayers in the 10 and 15 percent tax brackets and 15 percent for those in higher tax brackets. These rates, under a new tax law, also apply to certain dividend income. Thus, a long-term capital gain of $100 will be subject at most to $15 in taxes.

Another advantage of capital gains over interest and dividend income is that the increase in an asset's value isn't taxed until the asset is sold, so if your investment has grown by $100 in value over the year but you haven't sold it, you won't owe any current tax on the gain. For this reason, while you're in the wealth-building stage of your life cycle, you'll do better to invest in growth assets, which provide a return to investors primarily in the form of increased value, rather than income assets, which pay potentially taxable interest and dividends.

Tax-Exempt and Tax-Deferred Investments. We've just been examining the distinction between income and capital gains taxes for investments on which you must pay taxes—that is, taxable investments. However, some investments are tax-deferred or tax exempt. A *tax-deferred* investment allows you to delay paying taxes on both income and capital gains until the money is withdrawn for a specific allowed purpose, such as paying for college or retirement. Examples of tax-deferred accounts include employer-sponsored retirement plans and traditional individual retirement accounts (IRAs). A *tax-exempt* investment's returns are not subject to certain taxes at all. The U.S. Constitution requires that interest on municipal bonds (debt issued by state and local governments) be exempt from federal income tax, and your interest earnings on these bonds will also be exempt from state income tax if you're a resident of the state that issued the bond. Similarly, interest on federal government debt securities is exempt from state and local income taxes.

As an example of how these differences can affect investment outcomes, consider the case of two investors, Tax-wise Tammy and Careless Carla, both in the 25 percent marginal tax bracket. Each of them decides to invest $3,000 per year, after taxes, for 40 years, until they retire; both choose an investment that earns 6 percent per year before taxes. Tammy invests in a retirement account that allows her to accumulate earnings tax-free (such as a Roth IRA that was explained in Chapter 4), and Carla does not. Tammy will have $464,286 in her account at retirement, and none of it will be subject to taxes. Carla will have to pay taxes on her 6 percent earnings each year, so her after-tax earnings will be only 4.5 percent. The accumulated value in her account will be $321,091, about 30 percent less than Tammy's. Depending on the type of investment, Carla may also end up owing capital gains taxes on increases in the value of her investment as well.

It's safe to conclude that all investors, regardless of tax bracket, should look for tax-preferred ways of saving. The higher your tax bracket, the more you'll benefit from the tax savings. But there are costs as well. Most of these tax-preferred savings vehicles, such as employer retirement plans, college savings plans, and IRAs, place limitations on your ability to use the money. Furthermore, some have income maximums so that the very rich can't take advantage of them. In later chapters, we'll explore these limitations in more detail.

Take Advantage of Investment Information Resources

There are numerous sources of reliable information for investors.

In today's information-overloaded world, there are so many sources of financial information that it's easy to become overwhelmed. However, as an investor, you must take the time to learn about the financial markets and to stay informed. To do this effectively, you need to be selective about what you choose to read. Useful sources of information include company and mutual fund annual reports, various Internet sites, financial periodicals, investment advisors, and investment clubs.

Annual Reports. If you own shares in a publicly traded company or mutual fund or if you're interested in buying shares, it's a good idea to read the annual report of the company or fund. Publicly traded companies are required to report each year on their financial performance for the current year and prior years and to make projections about the company's future. For many firms, these reports are available online, but you can also obtain them by request from the company, in a large library, or through a brokerage firm.

Internet Resources. The Internet is a tremendous resource for investors. Before its inception, much "publicly available" information about companies was actually available only to those who subscribed to expensive data services. In today's Web-based environment, you can easily call up price histories for stocks, read analysts' reports, and track general market movements online. In addition, the major websites include tutorials on a variety of subjects related to personal finance.

To see examples of company annual reports, go to the websites for Intel and Nike. At www.intel.com, click on "Investor Relations." At www.nike.com, click on "About Nike" and then "Investors." Most firms now post their recent financial information in a section of their website designated for investors.

Periodicals. The investment community widely reads the *Wall Street Journal*, which implies that, as an informed investor, you should too. This newspaper and its companion Internet version provide up-to-date and well-written news coverage related to the securities marketplace and to individual securities in the market. Other subscription services, some of which are quite expensive, provide historical data on stocks and bonds, recommend specific investments, or cater to particular kinds of investors. Standard & Poors, Moody's, Value Line, and MorningStar are popular examples.

Brokers and Financial Advisors. Although individual investors certainly can obtain much of the information they need on their own, brokers and financial advisors may be able to add value to the process, particularly for investors who don't have enough time or expertise to stay fully informed. Brokerage firms, for example, often produce regular newsletters for their clients, reporting on interest-rate and market movements as well as other economic and company-specific news. As noted in Chapter 1, financial advisors are compensated in different ways. For investment professionals, these differences in payment arrangements are associated with different levels of service to clients. Such arrangements will be discussed in more detail in the next chapter.

Although there are many Internet resources to choose from, two websites that are particularly informative and easy to use are finance.yahoo.com (Yahoo) and www.kiplinger.com (Kiplinger). For educational resources, go to Smart Money University, university.smartmoney.com. For example, you might try their free tutorial called "Investing 101."

Investment Clubs. Investment clubs are groups of individuals who get together on a regular basis to share information about particular investments and to jointly manage an investment fund. The advantage of an investment club is that you can profit from the knowledge, experience, and time invested by others; the disadvantage is that you may find yourself in a case of "the blind leading the blind." If you're interested in forming an investment club or learning more about them, contact the local chapter of the American Association of Individual Investors.

You can join the American Association of Individual Investors or find information about local chapters at www.aaii.org.

There are literally thousands of small investment clubs like this one. The members regularly get together to make decisions about their investments.

Follow Some Simple Rules

This chapter has laid the groundwork for learning about the specific investments covered in the next three chapters. We conclude with some general rules of thumb that will make you a better investor.

Start Early. The time value of money will benefit you the most if you get started investing as soon as possible. Even if you're a typical college-age student, it's not too early to start thinking about how you'll save for a down payment on a home or developing a plan for retirement saving. Beginning the financial planning process while you're still in school will help you to "hit the ground running" so that you'll be able to achieve your financial goals sooner.

Fact #5

The sooner you start investing, the sooner you'll reach your goals. If you add $2,000 to an investment account earning 8 percent after taxes at the end of each year for just 10 years, starting when you're 21, the account will be worth $428,390 by the time you're 65. If instead you wait until you're 30 to start investing $2,000 each year and you contribute every year for the remaining 35 years until retirement, you'll only have $344,634 by the time you're 65!

Keep Good Records. Record keeping is an aspect of your investment plan that you can't afford to ignore. Not only must you keep records for tax purposes, but you also need to be able to make changes promptly if circumstances require it. Keeping good records doesn't have to be an onerous task. There are many simple ways to track your portfolio, ranging from worksheets that you update periodically to more complex investment-tracking software. As with any system of record keeping, if you start using one when your investment plan is in the early stages, it will be easier to continue it as your finances become more complicated. You can regularly update the value of each of your holdings, the value of your total portfolio, and your return on investment. You might want to try doing this for a play-money portfolio before you start investing in the real world. In the next chapters, we'll explain how to use worksheets in your *Personal Financial Planner* for tracking specific investments.

Do Your Homework. Being an informed investor requires that you carefully consider your investment plan in light of your financial objectives, that you select the right mix of investments for your circumstances, and that you investigate each investment with care.

ask the expert How to Avoid Five Common Pitfalls in Investing

There's nothing like a bear market to test the resolve of buy-and-hold investors. Emotional and psychological factors make it very hard to stick to an investment allocation strategy when your investments are falling in value. Experienced personal financial planners suggest that long-term investors avoid falling into the following pitfalls:

1. *Questioning your decisions.* When the market falls, instinct may tell you to pull out, but doing so will mean that you're selling at a time when prices are low. In the extreme, some investors lose so much confidence in a market downturn that they stop contributing to their investment plans altogether.
2. *Ignoring asset allocation.* When the stock market was booming in the late 1990s, investors tended to ignore the wisdom of spreading their money among different asset classes, concentrating most of their wealth in high-growth stocks. In 2003, when stocks were performing poorly and bonds were performing well, they made the same mistake again, shifting too much into bonds.
3. *Holding on at all costs.* Some investors can't seem to let go, even when they know their investment will never recover. You shouldn't hold on to a loser that no longer fits with your investment plan just to avoid taking the loss.
4. *Failing to rebalance.* If your objective is to have a portfolio with 50 percent invested in stocks and 50 percent in bonds, but the value of your stocks has declined since you bought them, your actual allocation may no longer be 50-50. You should regularly rebalance your portfolio so that it's consistent with your target allocation, risk tolerance, and time horizon.
5. *Trying to recover quickly.* Losses often happen quickly, and it's human nature to want to bounce back fast as well. However, you shouldn't take on extra risk in your portfolio just to try to recover from prior losses more quickly. Such a strategy can backfire and leave you even worse off if the high-risk investments lose money as well.

Source: Rick Sauder, "Looking Past Pitfalls," *Stages: Fidelity Investments' Magazine for Retirement Plan Investors,* Spring 2003, pp. 8–9.

Stick to the Plan. To achieve long-term goals, you have to stick to the plan over the long term. That means weathering the ups and downs in your investments, continuing to curtail current consumption in favor of contributions to your investment program, and taking risk that's appropriate for your family circumstances and life-cycle stage. Sticking to the plan is perhaps the most difficult part of investing. You'll note that several of the traps identified in the *Ask the Expert* box, "How to Avoid Five Common Pitfalls in Investing," are related to the failure to do so.

Learning by Doing 11-5

1. Sally has been investing money in stocks for the last 10 years, but she's not very good at keeping track of her investments. She's now thinking about going back to school to get a graduate degree and needs to liquidate some of her investments. Explain why her lack of careful record keeping could be a problem as she tries to decide what assets to sell.

Summary

1. **Develop realistic investment goals that are consistent with your financial plan, risk tolerance, and life stage.** Investment goals should be realistic, measurable, and consistent with prioritized household financial goals. Your plan should identify the purpose of each component of the investment plan, the amount needed in the future to meet the specific financial goal, the cash flow or assets that will be allocated to achieving this goal, and the risk you can afford to take, given the purpose and investment horizon you've identified.
2. **Identify your investment alternatives.** You have many investment alternatives, including stocks, bonds, mutual funds, real estate, and derivative securities. These asset classes differ in the return you can expect from income and capital gains, as well as in the level of risk they expose you to.
3. **Understand the risk-return tradeoff.** One of the most important concepts in investing is the relationship between risk and return. All investments expose you to some amount of risk, including inflation risk, interest-rate risk, reinvestment risk, default risk, liquidity risk, and market risk. In general, investments that are riskier will earn a greater return over time.
4. **Recognize the importance of asset allocation and diversification of your portfolio.** The principle of diversification holds that investors can reduce investment risk by holding many different investments in their portfolios. Even a well-diversified portfo-

lio, however, is exposed to the market risk associated with general market movements and economic conditions that affect broad groups of securities at the same time. Asset allocation is the process of deciding on the proportion of your portfolio to allocate to different asset classes so as to achieve a desired level of diversification.

5 **Decide whether you will be an active or passive investor and what your primary investment strategy will be.** Before beginning to invest, it's a good idea to develop an investment strategy that's appropriate for your risk tolerance, expertise, time, and life-cycle stage. You'll first decide whether to be an active or a passive investor. Passive investment strategies include buy-and-hold, dollar cost averaging, and direct investment and reinvestment plans. Over the long run, you're likely to best achieve your financial goals through a consistent buy-and-hold strategy in combination with reviewing and changing your asset allocation as necessary over your life cycle.

6 **Invest successfully by incorporating taxes in your investment decisions and using available information resources.** In developing an investment plan, it's important to take taxes into consideration. In taxable accounts, you'll usually pay a lower tax rate on long-term capital gains than on current income. Wherever possible, you should take advantage of tax rules that allow tax-exempt and tax-deferred earnings. Sources of useful information for individual investors include company annual reports, Internet sites, financial periodicals, brokerage firms, and investment clubs.

Key Terms

active investor (364)
asset allocation (362)
asset classes (352)
bond (353)
buy-and-hold (365)
capital gain (351)
commodities (354)
debt investor (351)
default risk (359)
derivative securities (354)
direct investment program (367)
diversification (360)
dividend reinvestment plan (DRIP) (367)
dividends (353)
dollar cost averaging (365)
equity investor (351)
fixed-income investments (351)
futures contract (354)
inflation risk (358)
interest-rate risk (359)
liquidity risk (359)
market efficiency (364)
market risk (359)
mutual fund (354)
nominal risk-free rate (358)
option (354)
passive investor (364)
preferred stock (354)
rate of return (357)
reinvestment risk (359)
risk aversion (355)
securities (352)
speculative investments (354)
stock (352)
timing (367)
yield (357)

Key Calculations

$$\text{Rate of return} = \text{Current yield} + \text{Capital gain yield}$$
$$= \frac{\text{Current income}}{\text{Beginning price}} + \frac{\text{End price} - \text{Beginning price}}{\text{Beginning price}}$$
$$= \frac{\text{Current Income} + \text{End price} - \text{Beginning price}}{\text{Beginning price}}$$

$$\begin{array}{c}\text{Yield on Debt}\\ \text{Security}\end{array} = \text{Real risk-free rate} + \text{Inflation risk premium} + \begin{array}{c}\text{Interest-rate}\\ \text{risk premium}\end{array}$$
$$+ \begin{array}{c}\text{Default risk}\\ \text{premium}\end{array} + \begin{array}{c}\text{Liquidity}\\ \text{risk premium}\end{array}$$

Concept Review Questions

1. What elements of your financial plan should you take care of before you begin to develop a plan for building your wealth? Why is this important?
2. Which time value of money concepts are most useful in determining how much money you need to save now to achieve a future goal?
3. What does it mean to "pay yourself first"? How can this strategy help you to stick to your financial plan? What are some other methods you can use to begin a regular investment plan when you currently don't have excess cash flow to allocate to this purpose?
4. What is the difference between investing by lending and investing by owning? Which method of investing is generally riskier, and why?
5. What are the advantages and disadvantages of debt investing?
6. What are the advantages and disadvantages of equity investing?
7. What is an asset class? Give several examples.
8. Explain the difference between common stock and preferred stock. What cash flows are you entitled to when you invest in common stock? in preferred stock?
9. What is a corporate bond? What cash flows are corporate bond investors entitled to?
10. What is a mutual fund, and why might a passive investor prefer this method of investing?
11. What makes derivative securities riskier than other investments?
12. What is the relationship between the risk and the return of investments?
13. What are the two ways of getting a return on an investment?
14. What does it mean to be risk-averse? Are all investors risk-averse? Why or why not?

15. How risk-averse would you expect each of the following people to be, and why?
    a. Older person
    b. Young parent
    c. Person with high income
16. What are the types of risk for which debt investors expect to receive a risk premium? Give an example of each.
17. For each of the following, indicate what type of risk it relates to:
    a. Interest rates are expected to rise over the next several years.
    b. The prices of goods and services are rising rapidly.
    c. The company's management is indicted for fraud, and the company declares bankruptcy.
    d. The United States declares war on Iraq.
18. What is the difference between dividends and interest?
19. Why is it a good idea to invest in assets that are relatively liquid?
20. Why do many investment advisors recommend stocks for long-run investors?
21. How does the diversification of a portfolio help reduce its risk?
22. Should investors change their asset allocation over the life cycle? Why or why not?
23. Explain the difference between passive and active investing. Why is active investing riskier than passive investing?
24. Explain why market efficiency makes it more difficult to be successful at active investing.
25. Define the following terms and give an example of each:
    a. Buy-and-hold
    b. Dollar cost averaging
    c. DRIP
26. What is the maximum tax rate on a long-term capital gain? How can this tax rule help you to achieve your financial goals faster?
27. What kinds of investment information can you find on the Internet? Do you think that all information you find on the Internet is reliable? Why or why not?
28. What are some reasons for keeping complete and accurate records of your investments?

Application Problems

1. ***Rate of Return.*** You own 100 shares of stock that you bought one year ago when the stock price was $30 per share. During the year, you've received dividends totaling $1 per share, and the stock is now worth $32 per share.
    a. What is your pretax rate of return for the year?
    b. Assume that you sell your shares at the $32 price. If you're in the 25 percent federal income tax bracket and your dividends and capital gains both qualify for taxation at the capital gains tax rate, what is your after-tax rate of return?
2. ***Rate of Return.*** You bought a corporate bond one year ago for $1,000. The bond is still worth $1,000 and you have received interest payments totaling $90 during the year.
    a. What was your pretax rate of return?
    b. If your marginal tax rate is 25 percent, what is your after-tax rate of return?
3. ***Saving for a Goal.*** You want to save up to buy a new car in four years. If you expect to need $6,000 four years from now, and your investment earns 5 percent interest after taxes, how much do you need to contribute at the end of each month to achieve your goal?
4. ***Investment Growth.*** Maria contributes $150 per month to her investment account at the end of each month, earning 4 percent per year after taxes. How much will she have after six years?
5. ***Investment Growth.*** Lavonne received a settlement of $100,000 when she was divorced. Consider each of the following scenarios independently:
    a. She puts all the money in a taxable debt security that earns 5 percent per year before tax and reinvests all the interest. How much will she have after 20 years with annual compounding, assuming that her marginal tax rate is 25 percent?
    b. She puts all the money in a stock mutual fund that earns 10 percent per year before tax and holds it in a tax-deferred account. How much will she have in the account after 20 years, assuming she has not sold any of her shares and that her earnings are entirely capital gains?
6. ***Capital Gains Tax.*** More than a year ago, George purchased 100 shares of Stock A for $5 per share. He sold them during the current tax year for $10 per share. At the same time, he purchased 50 shares of Stock B for $25 per share, and he sold them during the current tax year for $23 per share. Neither stock paid any dividends. How much will he owe in capital gains tax, assuming he is in the highest marginal tax bracket for federal income taxes?
7. ***Components of Risk.*** The nominal risk-free rate is currently 3 percent. You are considering investing in a 20-year corporate bond. The interest-rate risk premium is 2 percent, the default risk premium is 1.5 percent, and the liquidity risk premium is 1 percent. What should your yield on this bond be?
8. ***Asset Allocation.*** Your mother received a $50,000 judgment (after tax) as the outcome of a lawsuit, and she has asked you to recommend an asset allocation strategy for investing it. She is 45 years old, divorced, and in danger of being laid off from her job in the next two years. She has an emergency fund equal to three times her monthly expenses, she doesn't own a home, her credit card debt currently totals $5,000, and she owes $3,500 on a car loan.
    a. Should she invest the entire $50,000?
    b. Should she pay for the services of an investment advisor?
    c. What proportion of the funds, if any, should she invest in stocks? Explain your reasoning.

Using Web Resources for Financial Planning

1. ***Looking Up Company Information.*** Go to Yahoo Finance, *finance.yahoo.com*. Type in the symbol for Microsoft (MSFT). What has happened to Microsoft's stock price over the last 30 days? Does it look like the stock price is generally increasing or decreasing? Read the summary information about the company to see if you can determine the reason for recent price movements. Do you think this is a good company to invest in? Why or why not?
2. ***What's the Latest Financial News?*** Go to *www.kiplinger.com*, the website for *Kiplinger's Personal Finance Magazine*. What are the top news items that relate to personal investing? How could you use this information to help you make current investment choices?

3. ***Find Out How to Set Up a "Play Money" Investment Account.*** There are several sites that allow you to track a portfolio with "play money." Check out your options at *www.fantasystockmarket.com* and *www.stocktrak.com.* Make a chart that compares these investment games, including any fees to set up the account, the range of securities you can experiment with, the types of performance reports generated, ranking against competing players, availability of investment advice, and other features.
4. ***Evaluate Equity Risks.*** RiskGrades Inc. has developed a different method for rating the risks of various investments. Although they are generally interested in selling their services to investors, some of the information on their website is free. Their website *www.riskgrades.com* was ranked as a Forbes Favorite in that magazine's 2004 "Best of the Web" review.
   a. Find the "Risk Map" of the stock market (S&P 500). Which company has the least risk according to RiskGrades?
   b. Take the "Risk Profile Quiz."
5. ***The Fun Side of Investing.*** Motley Fool is an online financial site that has something for everyone. The difference between this website and its competitors is that it tries to approach investing with a sense of humor. Go to the "Fool's School" section of *www.fool.com* and find the "13 Steps to Investing Foolishly." Consider whether this advice is consistent with what you've learned so far about investing.

Learning by Doing Solutions

LBD 11-1: 1. $4,670; 2. $3,236.

LBD 11-2: 1. Stock return = 20% and bond return = 8%; 2. Stock return = −8.7% and bond return = 8%.

LBD 11-3: 1a. inflation; b. inflation, interest rate, default, liquidity; c. inflation, liquidity, market.

LBD 11-4: 1. Kenny isn't really diversified. Although he has invested in five different industries, he still has all his wealth in the stock market. He should first think about asset allocation, perhaps putting a portion of the funds in money market securities or bonds; 2. 80%, 10%, 10%.

LBD 11-5: 1. Sally will need to know which investments have been and will continue to be good performers, what are the tax consequences of each sale, how many shares she has of each, and what their current values are. Her failure to keep good records will make this difficult to determine.

Building Financial Planning Skills Through Case Applications

Case 11–1 Income Versus Growth

Terrie and Jeff Sanders recently sold a vacant lot next to their home and have $35,000 available to invest. They've been married for three years and have two young children. Their combined after-tax income is $45,000 per year, and their net cash flow each month is close to zero. Their home is worth $110,000, and they have a mortgage of $80,000. They have a $4,000 emergency fund. Both Terrie and Jeff contribute to employer-sponsored retirement plans, and they have adequate health and life insurance through employee benefit plans. Their two biggest investment goals are to buy a bigger house and to start a college fund for the kids. Terrie would like to take the $35,000 and invest it in a stock mutual fund, because she's heard that this will give them the biggest return on investment. Jeff thinks they should consider taking care of some of their other needs first and, even if they invest the money, he would like to put some of it in less risky assets. He also wonders whether it would make sense to put some of the funds into their retirement accounts, since they currently aren't contributing the maximum allowed.

a. Based on the information provided, have Terrie and Jeff established all the foundation elements of their financial plan? If not, what do they still need to do?

b. Would you agree with Terrie or Jeff regarding the way the money should be invested? Explain your reasoning.

c. In this case, would it be advisable to invest some of the money in retirement accounts? Why or why not?

d. Jeff suggests to Terrie that they use some of the money to pay $8,000 in credit card debt, on which they pay an average finance charge of 18 percent. Would this be a good use of their money? Explain.

Case 11-2 Benefits of Diversification

Winken, Blinken, and Nod are triplets, but they have very different attitudes toward investing. Five years ago, each began an investment program with $10,000. Winken, a risk-taker, invested the entire amount in a high-growth stock mutual fund. Blinken is extremely conservative and invested his $10,000 in a high-grade, low-risk, corporate bond fund. Nod took a personal finance class in college, so she's invested half her money in the stock fund and half in the bond fund. Taking into account both income and growth, the after-tax annual returns on the funds over the last five years have been as follows:

Year	Stock Fund (%)	Bond Fund (%)
1	5.0	8.0
2	−8.0	10.0
3	18.0	2.0
4	−2.0	7.0
5	25.0	4.0

a. What was the average annual return for each fund and for the 50/50 combination? Which one was riskier? Explain.

b. At the end of the five years, what was the value of each of the triplets' portfolios? Did diversifying across two funds provide any advantages to Nod?

Case 11-3 Life-Cycle Differences

The Herring family recently had dinner at Great-Grandma Anna's house. Present at the gathering were Great-Grandma Anna, age 96, Grandma and Grandpa Herring, both age 70, and their five children, Vickie, Jill, Ron, Ken, and Holly (ages 30 to 50) with respective spouses and the grandchildren ranging in age from 5 to 25. The conversation turned to investment risk, and Anna, who was still sharp as a tack, commented that she would never have put any money in the stock market. "It's like gambling!" she said. "I'm not even sure you can trust the banks to keep your money safe. That's why I always keep some cash in my freezer." Grandma and Grandpa Herring chuckled, since they'd long ago given up on getting Anna to keep all her cash in the bank. Talking more to his kids than to her, Grandpa argued that everyone should invest in the stock market, citing how he'd been able to almost double the value of an inheritance received by Grandma from an elderly aunt several years before. "Why earn 5 percent when you can earn 10?" he asked. "Besides," said Grandpa, "assuming I live to be as old as Great-Grandma Anna, my investment horizon is pretty long, so I can afford to take a little risk." The adult children were amazed to hear their dad talk this way, because they all tended to be a bit more risk-averse in their investing. Not a single one had more than 50 percent of his or her investments in the stock market. But the oldest great-grandchild, Kristopher, said "Way to go, Grandpa! If I had any money, I'd take your advice."

a. Do you think that members of each generation of the Herring family demonstrate typical attitudes toward investment risk for their age and life-cycle stage? Why or why not?

b. If it's true that Great-Grandma Anna has kept a significant amount of her cash savings in her freezer over the years, has she avoided all investment risk? If not, what kind of risk has she been exposed to?

c. Is Grandpa Herring right in saying that everyone should invest in the stock market? If you also knew that both he and his wife had a government pension that would provide them with a reasonable income for life, would this help explain Grandpa's risk attitude? Why or why not?

d. Is it likely that Kristopher would follow through on his stock-investing strategy if he suddenly came into some money? Should he? Why or why not?

DEVELOPING PERSONAL FINANCIAL skills for life

Learning about Yourself

11-1. Assessing Your Risk Tolerance

PFP Worksheet 44
Investment Risk Tolerance

Investment advisors commonly attempt to evaluate their new clients' risk preferences, either through an oral or a written series of questions. How comfortable are you with taking investment risk? To find out, complete the following questionnaire by selecting the answer that best represents your opinion:

1. Three months after you put money into an investment, the price drops by 25 percent. If nothing else has changed about the company, what would you do?
   - **a.** Sell to avoid further worry and try something else.
   - **b.** Do nothing and wait for the price to go back up again.
   - **c.** Buy more, since it's a cheap investment now and you still like the company.
2. Consider the same situation as in question 1, but assume that the investment is part of a portfolio targeted to achieve a short-term objective (three years or less in the future). What would you do?
   - **a.** Sell.
   - **b.** Do nothing.
   - **c.** Buy more.
3. Consider the same situation as in question 1, but assume that the investment is part of a portfolio targeted to achieve a long-term objective (15 years or more in the future). What would you do?
   - **a.** Sell.
   - **b.** Do nothing.
   - **c.** Buy more.
4. You are investing for retirement, which is at least 40 years in the future. What would you rather do?
   - **a.** Invest in a low-risk money market fund. You know that the returns will be low, but you like having virtually no risk of default or of losing any of your accumulated funds.
   - **b.** Invest half in bonds and half in stocks. The bonds will give you the security of having regular cash flows, and the stocks will allow for some growth in the value of your portfolio.
   - **c.** Invest all of your money in aggressive growth (high-risk, high-return) stock funds. Although the value of your portfolio is likely to go up and down over time, these funds will give you the best chance for large gains. Since you have a long time horizon, you can afford to take a few losses now and then.
5. You just won a $10 million lottery. You can either receive an annuity of $400,000 per year for 25 years or a cash lump sum of $4 million. Which would you do?
   - **a.** Take the annuity.
   - **b.** Take the cash, invest it in income-producing securities, and only spend the income.
   - **c.** Take the cash and invest it aggressively.
6. You are presented with a great investment opportunity, but you don't have enough cash, so you'll have to borrow to make the investment. Would you take out a loan?
   - **a.** Definitely not
   - **b.** Maybe
   - **c.** Yes
7. Which of the following best describes your investment attitudes:
   - **a.** I'm uncomfortable with the idea of my portfolio value fluctuating. I'm willing to give up the possibility of higher returns in order to keep my principal intact. I'm satisfied with an investment that stays ahead of inflation.
   - **b.** I expect the value of my investments to fluctuate, but not too much. I could potentially suffer a loss of 3 to 5 percent in a single year, but I'm willing to accept this risk for the opportunity to earn higher returns.
   - **c.** Increasing the value of my portfolio is my goal. I'm willing to risk an occasional drop of 10 percent or more in my investments for the opportunity to achieve superior growth.

Scoring:
Add up the number of a, b, and c answers you gave and score your risk tolerance as follows:

Number of "a" answers	______	× 1 =	______
Number of "b" answers	______	× 2 =	______
Number of "c" answers	______	× 3 =	______
Total score			______

If you scored 7 to 12, you may be a conservative investor.
If you scored 13 to 16, you may be a moderate investor.
If you scored 17 to 21, you may be an aggressive investor.

Developing Your Skills

11-2. Setting Investment Goals

Choose one of your personal financial planning objectives, and develop an investment plan to achieve that goal. You can use the worksheet in your *Personal Financial Planner* to record your plan. Be sure the plan answers the following questions:

a. How much money do you need to accumulate to achieve this goal?
b. What is your time horizon?
c. How much have you already accumulated toward this goal?
d. How much can you afford to allocate to this goal on a regular basis?
e. When do you plan to start?

PFP Worksheet 43
Setting Investment Goals

11-3. Are Risk Preferences Consistent with Behavior?

Ask several friends and family members to provide an assessment of their personal preferences for investment risk-taking. You can use the full risk tolerance questionnaire from this section or simply ask the risk assessment question given in the first *Money Psychology* box in this chapter. After you've recorded their answers, ask them how much of their investment funds they have allocated to stocks, bonds, real estate, and cash.

a. Based on the answers you receive, do you think that their stated risk aversion is consistent with their investment practices?
b. Compare your survey results to general differences in risk aversion suggested in the chapter. Do you see any patterns based on gender, age, life-cycle stage, or income?

THE NAVIGATOR

- ☐ Review Before Studying this Chapter list.
- ☐ Scan Learning Objectives.
- ☐ Take Myth or Fact quiz and find the answers throughout the chapter.
- ☐ Read chapter and answer Learning by Doing exercises.
- ☐ Review the Key Terms and Key Calculations.
- ☐ Do end-of-chapter exercises.
- ☐ Take review quiz on the text website.
- ☐ Solve end-of-chapter cases.

BEFORE studying this chapter, you should review

- The advantages and disadvantages of equity investing (Chapter 11).
- The taxation of dividends and capital gains (Chapter 4).

Investing in Stocks

CHAPTER 12

Myth or Fact?

Consider each of the following statements and decide whether it is a *myth* or a *fact*. Look for the answers in the *Fact* boxes in the chapter.

	MYTH	FACT
1. Stocks will always give you higher returns than bonds.	☐	☐
2. You must have a stockbroker if you want to trade shares on the New York Stock Exchange.	☐	☐
3. People convicted of insider trading never have to go to jail.	☐	☐
4. The best way to evaluate how well your investments are doing is to compare current performance to past years' returns.	☐	☐
5. Investment information obtained from the Internet is generally reliable and accurate.	☐	☐

LEARNING objectives

1. Know the basic terminology used by stock investors.
2. Classify stocks according to their characteristics.
3. Describe how stocks are bought and sold.
4. Understand how the regulation of securities markets is beneficial to investors.
5. Analyze investment alternatives and evaluate portfolio performance.
6. Identify sources of information for stock investors.

...applying the planning process

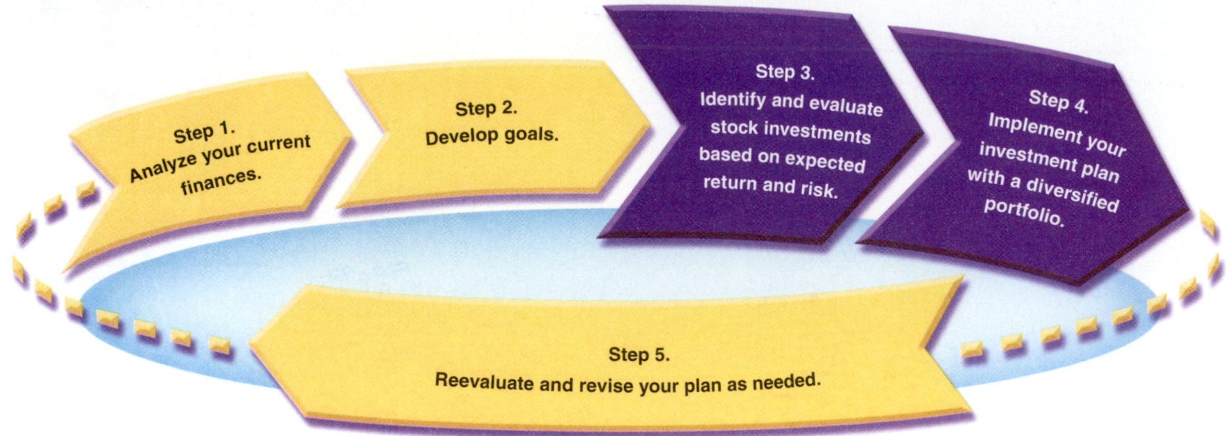

In the preceding chapter, you read about investing to meet your personal financial goals. One investment alternative is stock—ownership shares in individual corporations. If you think you want to incorporate stock investing in your financial plan, the next step is to understand as much as possible about this interesting asset class. Before you can get started actually investing, you'll need to learn the terminology used by stock investors, how to make individual stock selections, and how to buy and sell stock. In this chapter, we'll cover all the basics, beginning with an overview of the advantages and disadvantages of stock investing and an explanation of commonly used terminology.

You already know from Chapter 11 that stocks tend to provide higher returns than other asset classes, but this isn't true of every individual stock, nor is it true in all time periods. Since there are literally thousands of stocks to choose from, you'll need to select carefully. In this chapter, we'll identify where to obtain the information necessary to evaluate the return and risk of investment alternatives so you can be sure they're consistent with your risk preferences and investment objectives.

Once you've decided on your stock investing plan and made individual stock selections, you can implement your plan by actually purchasing the shares. Consistent with the financial planning process, however, you should regularly track the performance of your investment portfolio to see whether it's successfully moving you toward achieving your financial goals. With that in mind, we'll also discuss methods of performance evaluation.

Chapter Preview

Common Stock
- What Is Common Stock, and Why Is It Issued?
- What Are the Stockholders' Rights and Obligations?
- Advantages of Stock Investing
- Disadvantages of Stock Investing
- The Stock Market

Classifications of Common Stock
- Income Versus Growth Stocks
- Blue Chip Stocks
- Cyclical Versus Defensive Stocks
- Industry and Sector Stocks
- Market Capitalization

Buying and Selling Stocks
- Looking Up the Stock Price
- Placing an Order
- Long Versus Short
- Using a Broker

Regulation of the Securities Market
- History of Federal Securities Laws
- Information Disclosure Requirements
- Anti-fraud Provisions
- Other Regulation

Stock Selection and Performance Evaluation
- Measuring Expected Stock Returns
- Measuring Stock Risk
- Valuation Methods
- Evaluating Portfolio Performance Against Stock Indexes

Sources of Information for Stock Investors
- General Economic Conditions
- Company Information
- Industry Information
- Internet Resources
- Self-Help Books

Common Stock

Before you consider investing in common stock, there's a lot you need to know. Many beginning investors make the mistake of jumping in without really understanding what they're buying. If they're lucky, or if the economy happens to be in a growth phase, their investment portfolios might do well. Unfortunately, inexperienced investors have too often lost their life savings by making poorly thought out investment decisions.

You already know from Chapter 11 that when you buy shares of stock, you're actually becoming a part owner of a business. You wouldn't consider buying into a local business, even with your best friend, without checking whether the business is in good financial shape. Is it making a profit? Does the company have good prospects for the future? If you invest in the company, will you make a reasonable return on your investment? Your decision to buy shares of stock isn't really so different, and it deserves just as careful deliberation. To evaluate your stock investment alternatives, you'll first need to understand the terminology used by stock investors and the rights and obligations of corporate stockholders.

LEARNING objective

1 Know the basic terminology used by stock investors.

What Is Common Stock, and Why Is It Issued?

Common stock represents a share of ownership in a **corporation**, a type of business organization that exists as a legal entity separate from its owners, the shareholders. The corporate form of organization enables the company to have many owners with limited rights and obligations, as we'll see later. In contrast, the owners of companies organized as sole proprietorships and partnerships have more extensive rights (such as the ability to directly participate in the management of the business), but they also have greater responsibility (such as personal liability for the debts of the business).

corporation

A form of business organization that exists as a legal entity separate from its owners who have limited liability for corporate losses.

Corporations can be classified as private or public. Private corporations have few shareholders, and their stock isn't usually bought or sold. In this chapter, we're primarily concerned with public corporations, whose stock is traded (bought and sold by individual investors) in the securities market.

When you purchase shares of common stock in a public corporation, you're buying an ownership interest in that company. Each shareholder owns a proportionate share of the firm equal to the number of shares owned divided by the total number of shares the firm has outstanding. A common shareholder's claim on the firm is said to be a **residual claim**. That means they have a right to share in the assets and income of the corporation, but only after other, higher-priority claims (such as interest payments on bonds) are satisfied. If the firm goes bankrupt, each shareholder will be entitled to a proportionate share of whatever is left over after all the firm's creditors are paid back.

residual claim

A common shareholder's right to the firm's assets and income after all the other claimholders are paid.

Why do companies issue stock? Even multibillion-dollar companies such as WalMart and Microsoft began as small private companies with only a few owners. These owners eventually found it necessary to sell shares of stock to the public to get the funds they needed to grow their companies. Even though this means that the original owners have a smaller proportional ownership interest than they did before selling shares, they generally expect their return on investment to increase as a result of the expansion. As a company continues to grow larger over time, it may again need funds, which can come from current earnings, borrowed funds (bonds, as will be discussed in Chapter 13), or the sale of additional shares of stock. Most large publicly traded companies have millions of shares of stock outstanding, so each individual share represents only a very small ownership interest in the firm.

What Are the Stockholders' Rights and Obligations?

Investors who buy company stock are hoping to share in the future income and growth opportunities of that firm. Their investment comes with very few strings. They have limited rights to influence the management of the firm, as well as limited liability for the firm's losses. Stockholders' rights and obligations are discussed below.

Bill Gates owns more than 10 percent of Microsoft stock, making him one of the richest men in the world.

Voting Rights. Each common stockholder has the right to vote for members of the board of directors at an annual election. The board is responsible for selecting the top-level management, or officers, of the firm and for making major policy decisions for the company. The day-to-day operations of a corporation are handled by the officers, led by the chief executive officer (CEO) and sometimes the chief financial officer (CFO). In general, corporations follow a one-vote-per-share system, so if you own 100 shares of a particular firm's stock, you'll be able to cast 100 votes in the annual election. Of course, your 100 votes won't make a huge difference in the outcome of an election if there are 5 million shares outstanding. It's also commonly true that large blocks of shares are held by a few shareholders. Bill Gates, for example, owns more than 10 percent of Microsoft stock (1.1 billion out of a total 10.8 billion shares outstanding in 2004), so his vote will make a big difference. If you can't go to the annual meeting, or don't care to, you're allowed to pass your voting right to someone else through a written agreement called a **proxy**. Generally, the current management team will solicit your proxy before the election; if there are opposing candidates for particular board seats, you may receive a proxy solicitation from them as well.

proxy

A written agreement in which a shareholder gives another person the right to vote in his or her place.

Limited Liability. In Chapter 11, we introduced the concept of **limited liability**, an important right given to stockholders of corporations by state law. Limited liability means that the most you can lose when you own a share of stock is the value of the share itself. Without the limited liability right, no one would be willing to buy shares of stock, since doing so would put their personal assets at risk of being taken to pay for corporate debts in the event of company failure.

limited liability

Statutory right given to corporate shareholders limiting their potential losses to the value of the shares held.

Claim on Income. In return for providing equity capital to the firm, a common shareholder expects to share in the profits of the firm, either through dividends or price appreciation. If the firm's revenues are greater than its expenses, the board of directors can decide to distribute a cash dividend to the shareholders or it can decide instead to reinvest the funds for future growth. Shareholders benefit in either case. As a shareholder, if you receive dividend income, you have the immediate benefit of cash flow to spend or invest. Alternatively, if the firm reinvests the money instead of distributing it to you, the value of your shares should go up to reflect the firm's new investment in earning power and the potential for future dividends. If you choose to sell at that point, you'll realize a capital gain—the difference between the price you sell the share for now and what you paid for it previously.

In some cases, a firm issues a **stock dividend** in place of a cash dividend. Rather than receiving cash, you get additional shares of the firm's stock in proportion to the number of shares you already hold. While a stock dividend doesn't really benefit you currently as much as a cash dividend or capital gain, it has the potential to provide you with benefits in the future. Since all stockholders receive these additional shares, everyone's percentage of ownership remains the same. In fact, the value of each share usually declines after an announcement of a stock dividend to reflect the new value of each share. To see how this makes sense, consider the following example. You and three friends pool your funds to buy an apple pie for $12, each paying $3 for your share. If you cut it in 12 slices, you'll each have 3 slices, but the total value of your share is still $3. Getting a stock dividend is similar to cutting up your pie into smaller slices. You have more slices, but each one is worth less. So if you originally owned 100 shares at $10 per share and the firm gave you 3 shares as a dividend, you'd end up owning 103 shares at $9.70 per share—still a $1,000 ownership interest.

stock dividend

A dividend given to shareholders in the form of shares of stock instead of cash.

Recall that one of the risks of stock ownership is that firms are not *required* to pay dividends to shareholders. Even if a firm has issued dividends in the past, it may choose to reduce or eliminate them in the future. Conversely, firms that never issued dividends in the past may decide to begin doing so. This creates some inherent uncertainty for stockholders, since they never know in advance just how much current income they'll earn on their investment. But in return for bearing this risk, stockholders have the benefit of unlimited opportunity for gain. If the firm does poorly, the stockholders might lose all of their investment, but if it does unusually well, they'll share in the bounty.

Preemptive Rights. When companies sell additional shares of stock, it's like cutting the pie into more slices, so current stockholders risk seeing the value of their shares decline. In some cases, though, shareholders are entitled to maintain their proportionate interest in a company as the number of shares outstanding increases with new issues. This is called a **preemptive right**.

preemptive right

The right of a stockholder to maintain his or her proportionate ownership when the company issues additional shares of stock.

EXHIBIT 12-1

Smaller Slices, Same Pie

For example, suppose you own 100 shares in a company that currently has 1 million shares outstanding. If the company decides to issue another 250,000 shares, and if you have preemptive rights, you'll be able to buy 25 shares of the new issue before it goes on sale to the public in order to maintain your current percentage ownership (100/1,000,000 = 125/1,250,000). In order to take advantage of this right, of course, you must have enough money to be able to buy the shares at that time.

Stock Splits. Corporations sometimes decide to declare a *stock split,* which is similar to a stock dividend in that each shareholder gets a number of new shares in proportion to the number of shares already held. The price of the shares is adjusted so that the total value remains the same. The most frequent type of stock split is a two-for-one split, but three-for-one or three-for-two splits are also relatively common. To use our pie analogy (see Exhibit 12–1), a two-for-one stock split is like taking the 12 pie slices and splitting each in two, for a total of 24 pieces. If you owned three slices before, you now have six, but it's still only one-fourth of the pie. Similarly, if you own a share of stock worth $100 per share and the corporation announces a two-for-one split, you'll instead own two shares valued at $50 per share.

Investors tend to view a stock split as favorable information about the corporation's prospects for future growth, so the stock price often increases a little when a company announces a split. Your $50 shares might soon be worth $51 if the company does well, so the split would result in an increase in wealth for you. Why is a split good news? The logic is that management likes to keep the share price below some maximum value that is perceived as affordable to the company's investors. Announcement of a split is seen as a signal that management expects the stock price to rise above this maximum value. To the extent that this is news to investors, they'll respond by buying the stock and driving up the price. If it has occurred to you that this stock price reaction might create an opportunity to make a quick profit—buying the shares just as the announcement is made and then selling them after the stock price increases in response to the announcement of the split—you're not alone. Many investors attempt to implement this type of active investing strategy. However, market efficiency implies that the price change will occur incredibly fast.

Advantages of Stock Investing

Chapter 11 introduced several of the advantages of investing as an owner rather than a lender. Let's explore these advantages and a few others in a bit more detail.

No Management Responsibility. Stock investing allows you to participate in the profits of a firm without having to contribute anything except money to the venture. While you might be able to earn as much or more by starting your own business and keeping all the profits for yourself, it would require a lot more effort on your part. And, as discussed earlier, your ownership interest as a stockholder has the added advantage of limited liability, so you can never be held personally responsible for losses incurred as a result of poor management.

Higher Long-Run Returns. Investors generally require a higher rate of return to be willing to invest in riskier assets. We know that being an equity investor is riskier than being a debt investor because there's no guarantee of a regular cash flow from the investment. And indeed, examination of historical trends in investment returns shows that, over time, stocks provide greater returns for long-term investors than any other asset class. How much greater? The answer depends on how long you invest and what you invest in. A comparison of returns on several asset classes is given in Exhibit 12–2. This table looks at all the possible holding periods of particular lengths over the last 15 years, so it doesn't necessarily reflect what you would have actually earned if you held the assets from beginning to end. Over this period, the average annual return on a stock portfolio was more than 12 percent per year (a little more with small stocks), whereas the average annual return on five-year Treasury notes was around half that much. You can see that, for longer holding periods, stock investments provide higher average returns and are less likely to result in losses to investors.

Fact #1

Although stocks tend to earn higher long-run returns than other asset classes, they have their ups and downs in the short run. Over the last 19 years, the annual return on a large stock portfolio was lower than the annual return on Treasury bonds, a low-risk investment, in 8 of the 19 years. If we look at monthly returns, we can see even more variation. Over that same period, the monthly return on a large stock portfolio was lower than the monthly return on Treasury bonds in 94 of the 228 months.

To see the impact that higher returns can have on wealth accumulation, let's do a quick time value calculation. Assume that you plan to put $1,000 in an investment account today. What will it be worth in 20 years if you invest in government bonds and earn 6 percent? To find the answer, we solve for the future value of a lump sum using any of the methods from Chapter 2. With the financial calculator, for example, we enter $PV = 1{,}000$, $N = 20$, and $I = 6$, and solve for $FV = \$3{,}207$. The result, $3,207, is the amount you'd have in 20 years if you invested in government bonds. Now, what if instead you invest in stocks and earn 12 percent per year? Using the same method, we can determine that your $1,000 investment will be worth $9,646 at the end of 20 years—almost three times as much. If your $1,000 is held in a taxable account, of course, the after-tax investment returns will be lower for both asset classes.

Liquidity. As you know, a liquid asset is one that can be converted to cash quickly without loss of value. Bad news can cause a stock's value to decline rapidly, so we wouldn't place this asset in the same category as liquid savings and checking accounts. However, if you need access to your cash, you can usually sell shares of stock quickly, easily, and at relatively low cost, which makes stock more liquid than some other investment alternatives, such as municipal bonds and investment real estate.

EXHIBIT 12-2

Holding Period Returns for Various Asset Classes

	13-week T-Bills	5-year T-notes	10-year T-bonds	Large Stocks DJIA	Small Stocks NASDAQ
1-Year holding period					
Average return	4.7	6.3	6.7	12.3	12.8
Minimum	1.0	2.3	3.4	−11.4	−37.9
Maximum	8.6	8.7	9.2	42.7	43.8
5-Year holding period					
Average return	4.9	6.5	6.8	16.1	18.5
Minimum	2.6	4.4	5.0	−0.7	−3.9
Maximum	7.0	8.4	8.6	36.2	58.7
10-Year holding period					
Average return	4.8	6.4	6.7	23.6	29.1
Minimum	3.8	5.2	5.6	15.1	12.8
Maximum	5.7	7.4	7.8	33.8	64.1
15-Year holding period					
Average return	4.9	6.5	6.8	28.8	32.8
Minimum	4.1	5.8	6.2	20.7	19.2
Maximum	5.4	7.0	7.3	46.7	71.3

Low Interest-Rate Sensitivity. Recall from Chapter 11 that the values of debt securities are highly influenced by interest rates, creating interest-rate risk that increases with the term to maturity on the bond. When rates go up, bond prices fall, and vice versa. One of the advantages of stocks in a portfolio is that stock values are less sensitive to interest-rate movements. It's not that interest rates have *no* effect on stock prices. The time value of money still implies that if rates go up, the discounted present value of the future stream of cash flows will go down, so the price might go down to reflect this change. But countervailing effects can make stock prices less sensitive to interest-rate changes than debt securities. If the reason interest rates are increasing is because the economy is in an expansionary period of the business cycle, for example, the cash flows of the firm will be increasing as well, so the value of the firm will not necessarily decline.

Diversifiable Risk. One of the fundamental principles of investing is that you can lower your risk, as measured by variability of returns, by having a variety of investments in your portfolio. Diversification was introduced in Chapter 11 in conjunction with the concept of asset allocation, since holding several different asset classes has a diversifying effect on your portfolio. But diversification can reduce risk *within* asset classes as well, as long as you select individual investments that aren't too similar. If you hold a portfolio of many different stocks, some of them will do well when others are doing poorly. Holding a number of stocks will therefore allow you to cancel out much of the company-specific variability in returns. What you'll be left with is the risk that can't be diversified away—market risk, which comes from factors common to all stocks.

Disadvantages of Stock Investing

Although stock investing clearly offers some advantages for long-run investors, it may not be for everyone. Investing in stock exposes you to substantial risk. Depending on your personal risk preferences, personal financial goals, and investment time horizon, you may not be willing or able to bear this level of risk in your portfolio.

Risk. An old saying warns, "If you can't take the heat, get out of the kitchen." Stock investors must be prepared to "take the heat" in the form of ups and downs in stock prices. However, not all stocks expose you to the same types or the same degree of risk. Consider, for example, the monthly stock price histories for Dell Inc. (DELL) and Anheuser-Busch Companies, Inc. (BUD) from May 1998 to May 2004, as shown in Exhibit 12–3. Although the stock prices of both firms had many ups and downs over that period, you can see a strong upward trend for

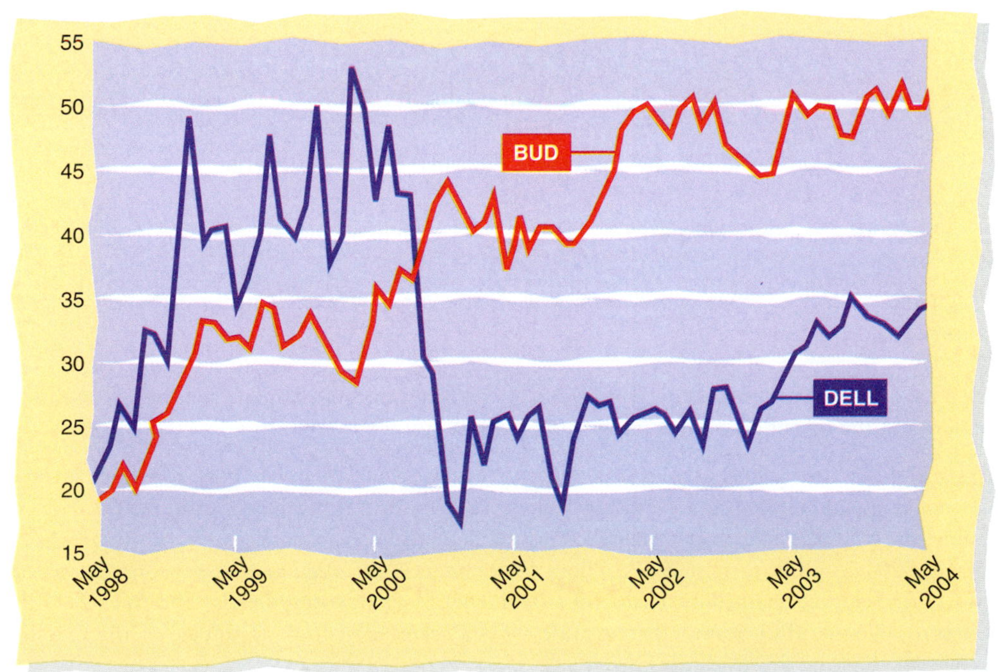

EXHIBIT 12-3

Monthly Prices for Anheuser-Busch Companies Inc. (BUD) and Dell Inc. (DELL), May 1998–May 2004

BUD. In contrast, DELL experienced a big drop with the "technology bust" that began in late 1999, followed by an upward trend. The variability shown in this graph is typical of most companies' stock, since stock prices react to company-specific events as well as industry, national, and global market conditions. If you had held both BUD and DELL in your portfolio, DELL's price declines would have been at least partially offset by BUD's price increases. You can't always offset individual company risk completely, however; bad news affecting the economy in general can affect even a diversified portfolio. If you look closely at the graph, you'll see that BUD's price declined in many of the same months as DELL's; the decline just wasn't quite as dramatic.

Learning by Doing 12-1

1. Most stocks experienced a price decline during the recession that began in 1999. What are some explanations you might offer for BUD's generally positive performance during this recessionary period, as illustrated in Exhibit 12–3?
2. How did the stock prices for BUD and DELL react to the September 11, 2001, terrorist attack on the World Trade Center? How can you explain the difference between these reactions?
3. From the graph, can you identify when the economy began to turn the corner to economic recovery?

No Control. We've already seen that, as a stock investor—particularly in a large, publicly held corporation—you have little power to influence the actions of management. And management can do many things that cause your share value to decline. Top managers can make business decisions that increase the risk of the company or reduce the firm's competitive advantage. Their financial decisions may dilute your ownership interest if they issue more shares or your residual interest if they take on more debt. In the extreme, they may make self-interested decisions that line their own pockets at your expense. Even if you know what they're doing and object to it, you have little recourse, since your limited voting rights make it almost impossible to effect any managerial change. For this reason, it's commonly said that stockholders "vote with their feet." In other words, if you don't like what management is doing, you'll get out by selling your shares. Unfortunately, by the time you know what's wrong, market efficiency implies that the value of the stock will probably already reflect the bad news, so you're likely to lose money.

The Stock Market

Stocks are bought and sold in the stock market. This market has two parts:

primary market
The market in which securities are sold by corporations to the public for the first time.

secondary market
The market in which previously issued securities are traded between investors.

initial public offering (IPO)
A company's first stock offering to the public.

- The **primary market**, where stocks are sold to the public by the issuing corporation for the *first time.*
- The **secondary market**, where stocks that have already been issued are traded *between investors.*

Even though most individual investors' transactions occur in the secondary market, it's useful to understand the role of both these parts of the market.

Primary Versus Secondary Market. When a company issues stock for the first time, we say it's "going public," and the stock issue is called an **initial public offering (IPO)**. For example, the company that started the Google search engine announced its intentions to go public during 2004 in order to raise $2.7 billion. Cofounders Larry Page and Sergey Brin as well as CEO Eric Schmidt retained ownership of a significant block of voting shares. The *News You Can Use* box, "Google IPO Scam," demonstrates how a scam artist took advantage of the investor frenzy surrounding this stock offering.

NEWS you can use

Google IPO Scam

If something looks too good to be true, it probably is. Several unsuspecting investors learned this the hard way. In late 2003, Shamoon Rafiq, age 30, sold nearly $3 million in bogus "pre-IPO" Google stock. He falsely represented that he was able to obtain pre-IPO shares because he was a college buddy of the Google founders and a partner in an investment firm handling the IPO. In fact, the IPO date had not even been set, and Rafiq had no connection with the firm. In 2004, he pleaded guilty in federal court to wire fraud and will serve 51 to 63 months in jail.

"unsuspecting investors bought nearly $3 million in bogus Google stock"

The IPO process is usually handled by one or more investment banking firms (the Google IPO had more than 25), such as Merrill Lynch or Goldman Sachs, which *underwrite* the issue. Underwriting involves helping the firm determine a price for the new issue, facilitating the paperwork, and managing the selling process. Sometimes, it's difficult to determine exactly how much a new company is worth, particularly if it's expected to grow quickly after the infusion of cash from the sale of stock. The underwriter may guarantee a minimum price to the issuing firm or it may buy the entire issue itself and then resell it to the public. In an innovative departure from the usual process, Google decided to set its IPO stock price through an auction in which interested investors placed bids, naming the number of shares they were willing to buy and the price they were willing to pay.

New stock issues are advertised in the financial press in a format called a **tombstone ad**, such as the one shown in Exhibit 12–4. If you see a tombstone in the *Wall Street Journal* and would like to know more about the new issue, you can ask the company for a **prospectus**, a document that includes all the important information about the company and its stock.

tombstone ad

A formal advertisement of a stock issue in the financial press.

prospectus

A document that gives financial information about a stock issue and the issuing company to potential investors.

New Issue *May 19, 2004*

$73,312,500

Animas
CORPORATION

Initial Public Offering

4,887,500 Shares - Price $15.00 Per Share
NASDAQ Symbol: PUMP

Joint Book-Running Managers

Piper Jaffray JPMorgan

Thomas Weisel Partners LLC

This announcement is neither an offer to sell nor a solicitation of offers to buy any of these securities. The offering is made only by the Prospectus. Copies of the Prospectus may be obtained from the undersigned or others as may legally offer these securities in compliance with the securities laws of the respective states.

EXHIBIT 12-4

Tombstone Advertisement

This tombstone advertisement announcing the initial public offering for Animas Corporation appeared in the *Wall Street Journal* on May 19, 2004.

The New York Stock Exchange is the oldest and largest securities exchange.

Although you may someday have an opportunity to purchase shares directly from a company through an initial public offering, it's more likely that your transactions will be with other investors in the secondary market. The existence of an active secondary market makes stocks more attractive to investors because it reduces liquidity risk. Billions of shares change hands on any given day, so you can almost always find willing buyers and sellers to deal with. In other words, if you have money tied up in stock and you need the cash for something else, you can easily call your broker and sell some of your shares. Note that trades in the secondary market don't result in any cash flows to the corporation whose stock is being bought or sold. A corporation only acquires cash for shares when it sells them for the first time in the primary market.

Securities Exchanges. Trading among investors can be accomplished through an organized **securities exchange**, which is an actual physical location where trades are implemented, or through an electronic marketplace referred to as the **over-the-counter (OTC) market**. The oldest, largest, and best-known securities exchange is the New York Stock Exchange (NYSE), where approximately 2,800 stocks valued at nearly $18 trillion are traded. With more than 1.5 billion shares traded per day, this exchange accounts for 80 to 90 percent of all trades made on organized exchanges. Other exchanges include the American Stock Exchange (AMEX, the second largest exchange), the Pacific Stock Exchange, and the Philadelphia Stock Exchange. A particular stock can be traded on more than one exchange.

Each exchange has its own rules governing how a stock can qualify to be a **listed security**, or one that is offered for sale on the exchange. A listed firm may be delisted if it falls below the minimums. For example, the NYSE has relatively stringent standards for listing, including the following:

- At least 2,200 shareholders with an average monthly trading volume of 100,000 shares, or 500 shareholders with an average monthly trading volume of 1 million shares, or 2,000 shareholders holding at least 100 shares each
- At least 1,100,000 shares outstanding
- At least $100,000,000 market value of shares
- At least $10 million in pretax earnings over the last three years and $2 million in each of the last two years

securities exchange

A physical location at which securities are traded; the largest is the New York Stock Exchange.

over-the-counter (OTC) market

An electronic network for trading securities through securities dealers.

To make trades at securities exchanges such as the NYSE, you must have a **seat on the exchange**. There are a limited number of seats on any given exchange, and most of them are owned by brokerage firms (some of these firms own several seats on a given exchange). For this reason, individual investors must use the services of a brokerage firm to execute trades on securities exchanges.

Fact #2

Not just any investor can buy and sell securities on an organized exchange. You have to own a seat on the exchange to trade there; to own a seat, you have to buy it. The price of a seat fluctuates over time with supply and demand. At the end of the 1990s, the price for an NYSE seat was over $2 million—more than five times the price of a seat following the stock market crash in 1987.

Exhibit 12–5 illustrates a typical stock transaction on an organized exchange. First, the buyer places an offer to purchase the stock with a broker whose employing firm is a member of the exchange; similarly, the seller indicates to his or her broker a desire to sell a number of shares. To implement the buyer's request, the brokerage firm contacts its representative at the securities exchange to relay the price offer, or **bid price** and the seller's broker relays the sale offer, or **ask price**, through their respective representatives at the exchange. Both brokerage representatives then go to the **specialist** for that stock at a physical location on the floor of the exchange called the *specialist's post*. The specialist is the person at the exchange who is responsible for matching up the buy and sell orders for a particular stock. Based on the bid and ask information received from many buyers and sellers, the specialist is able to match up buyers and sellers fairly. If there are too many buyers relative to sellers, or vice versa, the specialist will actually sell or buy the shares as necessary to meet the market's demand. For this reason, specialists are sometimes referred to as *market makers*. Once the match is made, the brokerage firms relay the information back to the buyer and seller of the shares. Transfer of money and shares is then accomplished through accounts at the respective brokerage firms.

listed security

A security that is approved to be bought or sold on a particular exchange.

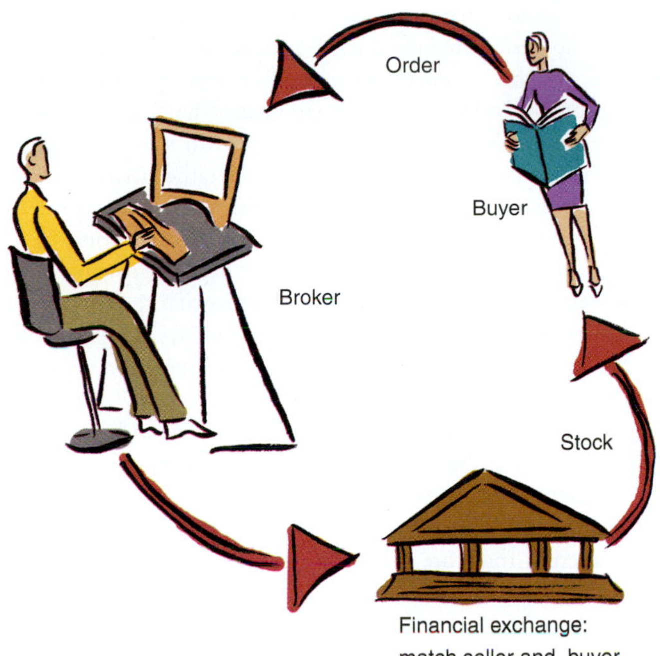

EXHIBIT 12-5

Sample Stock Transaction

seat on the exchange

Membership in an organized securities exchange, which allows the holder to transact business there.

bid price

The stock price offered by a potential buyer.

ask price

The stock price requested by a potential seller.

specialist

A person responsible for matching a particular stock's buy and sell orders at a specific securities exchange.

NASDAQ

National Association of Securities Dealers Automated Quotation System, an electronic reporting system for more frequently traded OTC stocks.

In contrast to the organized securities exchanges, the over-the-counter market is not a formal exchange and doesn't have a physical location. Instead, it's a network of securities dealers communicating electronically to quote the prices (bid and ask) at which they're willing to buy or sell securities. About 35,000 companies have stocks that are traded over the counter, in many cases because the companies are too small, or the stocks are traded too infrequently, to qualify for listing on a securities exchange. About 3,300 of the most frequently traded OTC stocks participate in an electronic reporting system called the **NASDAQ**, which stands for National Association of Securities Dealers Automated Quotation System. If you want to buy a stock that's listed on the NASDAQ, your broker can post your bid on the system, where a NASDAQ dealer will match you up with a seller. Generally, the small size and lower liquidity of stocks traded exclusively over the counter make them riskier investments than stocks listed on organized exchanges.

Classifications of Common Stock

LEARNING objective

 Classify stocks according to their characteristics.

Common stock is usually classified according to broad, and sometimes overlapping, categories related to cash flow, risk, and line of business. Although these classifications have no official status, understanding the common "lingo" used by investment professionals will help you to better communicate with financial advisors and comprehend what you read in the financial press. An important cautionary note is that the companies within each of these classifications differ widely from one another, so it's always important to analyze the individual companies independently rather than to rely solely on their classifications to make judgments about their suitability for your portfolio. We look at some of the more common groupings in this section.

Income Versus Growth Stocks

As previously discussed, investors usually expect to receive some combination of current cash flow and price appreciation in return for providing capital to a firm. Stocks are often classified based on whether the company tends to reward its investors primarily with current income or with capital gains. An **income stock** is one that pays investors a regular dividend rather than concentrating on reinvestment of profits. Because these stocks pay most of their profits in dividends instead of reinvesting for future growth, there is usually less capital appreciation. The relative

income stock

Stock that compensates investors primarily through the regular payment of dividends.

certainty of a dividend cash flow stream makes these stocks attractive to more conservative stock investors and to those who desire a regular income stream, such as retirees.

growth stock

Stock that compensates investors primarily through increases in value of the shares over time.

A **growth stock** is one that compensates investors primarily through increases in the value of the shares over time. Stocks issued by younger companies that are experiencing high growth in earnings and assets are more likely to be classified as growth stocks. During this high-growth phase, firms tend to reinvest profits to meet capital needs rather than distribute profits as dividends. Many of these types of stocks trade in the OTC market. Obviously, the attraction of growth stocks to investors is the opportunity to share in the future profits of these companies as investments in growth eventually pay off. As you might expect, growth companies also expose investors to greater uncertainty, since there are no guarantees that today's reinvestment will translate into tomorrow's growth in value. Younger investors who have long investment time horizons are more likely to focus on growth investments, while investors who want investment income and stability are less inclined to invest in these companies.

Some growth stocks are highly risky—their prices fluctuate widely, and they have very uncertain future prospects. During the 1990s, many Internet companies issued stock despite the fact that they had failed to show a profit. In spite of the uncertainty, investors flocked to buy these stocks, and a few of the companies succeeded. However, for every success story, such as eBay.com and Amazon.com, there are a dozen failures—companies whose anticipated future profits never materialized or were overestimated.

Blue Chip Stocks

blue chip stock

A stock that is issued by a large, stable, mature company.

A **blue chip stock** is one issued by a large, stable, mature company. These firms' earnings and growth tend to track the growth in the overall market. As consistent performers, they're considered less risky than growth stocks; however, they don't offer opportunities for unexpectedly high earnings. They are the "slow and steady" performers, often leaders in their industry, and they commonly pay dividends in addition to offering the opportunity for some growth in value over time. Examples include Anheuser-Busch, Procter & Gamble, and Coca-Cola.

Cyclical Versus Defensive Stocks

cyclical stock

A stock exhibiting above-average sensitivity to the business cycle.

A **cyclical stock** exhibits above-average sensitivity to the business cycle—that is, it tends to perform well during strong economic climates and poorly in downturns. Cyclical companies include firms that produce consumer durable goods and luxury items—cars, appliances, furniture, and sporting equipment—since purchases of such goods can nearly always be put off when money is tight. Companies connected to the home-building industry (such as Home Depot) and companies that provide services or goods to other businesses (such as transportation and technology firms) are also cyclical, because during recessions, construction and investment projects tend to be put on hold.

defensive stock

Stock that is relatively insensitive to the business cycle.

The opposite of a cyclical stock is a **defensive stock**—one that is less sensitive to market ups and downs and therefore can help stabilize your portfolio during market downturns. Stocks that are related to food and beverages (Anheuser-Busch and Coca-Cola), pharmaceuticals (Pfizer), and utilities (Duke Energy) are examples, since their products are in demand regardless of economic conditions.

Industry and Sector Stocks

Stocks are also often categorized by the industry or sector of the issuing companies. Classifications and representative companies include the following:

- Airline: United Airlines
- Automobile: Ford Motor Company
- Banking: BankAmerica
- Chemicals: Dow Chemical
- Financial Services: Merrill Lynch
- Food and Beverage: Coca-Cola

- Industrial Goods and Services: General Electric
- Media: Disney
- Retail: Home Depot
- Technology: Intel

In the 1990s, the hot sector for investment was technology, but after September 11, 2001, industries related to military spending (commonly called defense stocks, not to be confused with the defensive stocks discussed earlier) became more popular investments.

Market Capitalization

Market capitalization is the total value of a company's shares at its current market price. It is calculated as

Market capitalization = Current market price × Number of shares outstanding

On the basis of capitalization, companies are classified as large-cap, mid-cap, or small-cap. Some investors also refer to subsets of the largest and smallest groups. Here, we consider the general parameters for these classifications, but these definitions aren't engraved in stone—investors tend to include companies in these groups based on not only market capitalization but also revenues, growth potential, and past history.

Large-cap companies have market capitalization of $5 billion or more (although some investors and reporting services classify companies as large-cap with as little as $3 billion). These are the largest firms in the country. They typically have been in existence for many years, and their stock tends to experience less price fluctuation than the stock of mid-cap and small-cap companies. Consequently, their stock is perceived as being less risky and may be preferred by more conservative stock investors. Examples include McDonald's, with market capitalization of $33 billion, and Disney, with market capitalization of $48 billion. **Mid-cap** companies have $1 billion to $3 billion in market capitalization—they're still large but not giants. A **small-cap** company generally has market capitalization of less than $1 billion and annual revenues of less than $250 million. Although that may not seem very small to you, these firms are small *relative to* many others and generally are young, growing companies. Small-caps rarely pay dividends (since they reinvest their profits to promote growth), but have historically seen larger investment returns than other asset classifications over time. However, small-cap stock prices tend to be more sensitive to market movements, which means that their investors will experience larger losses in economic downturns. This effect is even more pronounced for the micro-caps—those with less than $100 million in capitalization.

market capitalization
The total outstanding value of a company's stock at current market prices; calculated as the current stock price times the number of shares outstanding.

large-cap
Market capitalization in excess of $5 billion.

mid-cap
Market capitalization of $1 billion to $3 billion.

small-cap
Market capitalization of less than $1 billion.

Learning by Doing 12-2

1. For each of the following stocks, identify the appropriate classifications:

Company	Market Capitalization	Classifications
a. Microsoft Corporation	$283.1 billion	________
b. JetBlue Airways	$2.95 billion	________
c. Longs Drug Stores	$801 million	________
d. Trump Hotel & Casino Resort	$59 million	________

Buying and Selling Stocks

Buying stock isn't like making the consumer purchases we've discussed in previous chapters—you can't just go out and buy stocks directly from other investors. Transactions in the secondary market require the services of a licensed broker as a middleman. In this section, we'll walk through the process you'd follow if you wanted to buy some shares of a particular company. We'll discuss

LEARNING objective

3 Describe how stocks are bought and sold.

how you might decide what shares to buy a bit later in the chapter. For the example, let's assume that you'd like to buy 100 shares of Dell Inc. In order to implement this transaction, you'll need to find out what the current price is and place a specific order with a broker.

Looking Up a Stock Price

To determine how much you'll pay for the shares, you must first look up the current price. There are numerous sources of information on stock prices. In addition to several websites that give price quotes, the *Wall Street Journal* and other financial newspapers report stock prices. Exhibit 12–6 shows an example of the way information is reported in the stock section of the *Wall Street Journal*. Stocks traded on the NYSE, the American Stock Exchange, and the NASDAQ are listed alphabetically in separate sections.

The highlighted section of the exhibit shows the information reported for Dell Inc. (a NASDAQ-listed stock) on July 16, 2004. Every publicly traded stock has a *ticker symbol*, which is a universally accepted shorthand reference for the company. In the *Wall Street Journal*, the ticker symbol—DELL in our example—is given in boldface type. The annual dividend is reported in the column immediately after the company name; in this case, we see that DELL shareholders didn't receive a dividend. If you look at the next-to-last column, you'll observe that the **close price** reported for the stock was $34.87. This is the price the stock sold for in the last transaction on July 15, 2004, the previous trading day. The other reported information is defined in the exhibit for your reference.

close price

The last price at which a stock sold at the close of the previous business day.

EXHIBIT 12-6

How to Read Stock Market Quotations in the *Wall Street Journal*

YTD	52 week				Yield		VOL		NET
% CHG	HI	LOW	STOCK (SYM)	DIV	%	PE	100s	CLOSE	CHG
−15.7	11.50	5.98	Datastream **DSTM**		...	26	z44284	6.62	0.01
193.3	26.24	6.46	DawsnGeo **DWSN**		...	73	1562	22	0.03
11.4	27.01	17.58	DebShop **DEBS**	.50a	2.1	24	z5592	23.97	−0.28
31.4	31.07	6.50	DeckrsOutdr **DECK**		...	30	4717	26.93	−1.07
−5.1	13.80	2.45	deCodeGntcs **DCGN**		...	dd	1709	7.77	0.14
−9.4	11.36	8.25	DcomaInt **DECA**	.28g	...	...	22	9.33	0.14
2.6	37.18	30.70	Dell **DELL**		...	33	139777	34.87	0.03
147.1	15.93	4.31	DeltaPet **DPTR**		...	cc	3185	15	−0.20
28.5	16.72	5.36	Dendreon **DNDN**		...	dd	3718	10.36	−0.32
2.5	19.77	12.12	DendriteInt **DRTE**		...	30	2762	16.09	0.03
14.5	52.84	41	DENTSPLY **XRAY**	.21	.4	19	2520	51.72	−0.22
−34.4	8.97	4.67	DepoMed **DEPO**		...	dd	z53127	4.65	−0.08
−12.0	30.60	19.30	Deswell **DSWL**	1.18e	5.2	14	z8197	22.89	−0.34
−26.0	6.28	1.75	DialgSemi ADS **DLGS**		...	...	7	3.22	0.02
−20.9	12	3.90	DiamondClstr **DTPI**		...	dd	z63918	8.07	−0.12
−10.2	49.45	25.71	DigeneCp **DIGE**		...	cc	1600	36.01	0.63
12.1	12.33	5.36	DIGI Intl **DGII**		...	35	1691	10.76	0.78

Columns	Explanation
YTD % CHG	The percentage change in price since the beginning of the calendar year, adjusted for stock splits and dividends that exceed 10% of the stock price. Dell's price has increased 4%.
52 WEEK HI LO	The high and low stock prices over the course of the last year. Dell's price has ranged from $29.23 to $37.18 over the last 52 weeks.
DIV	The annual dollar dividend per share. Dell doesn't pay a dividend so there is no entry in this column.
%	Dividend percent yield, which equals the dividend divided by the close price. Since Dell pays no dividend, this isn't applicable.
PE	The price-to-earnings ratio is 33, which is the current price per share divided by earnings per share. Note that although EPS isn't reported, you can calculate it by dividing the price by the PE.
VOL 100s	The number of shares traded, reported in round lots of 100. For Dell Inc., the reported volume of 157382 means that 15.7 million shares traded that day.
NET CHG	Dell's price changed by 0.03% since the previous day.

Source: WALL STREET JOURNAL. Copyright 2004 by DOW JONES & CO INC. Permission granted via Copyright Clearance Center.

Checking the financial press, such as the *Wall Street Journal*, is an easy way to loosely keep track of stock values. For more current price information, you can check one of the financial websites on the Internet or call your broker.

finance.yahoo.com allows you to enter a stock ticker symbol to look up the price history and other information on the stock. If you aren't sure of the ticker symbol, the site allows you to look it up.

Placing an Order

Suppose you think the reported $34.87 price for Dell stock makes it a good investment for you. You decide to place an order for 100 shares. Regardless of the type of brokerage firm you use, there are three types of orders you can make: a market order, a limit order, and a stop order. Orders are normally made in a **round lot**, or a unit of 100 shares. If you want to buy fewer than 100 shares (an *odd lot*), you may have to pay an extra fee.

round lot

A group of 100 shares of stock; stock is normally traded in round lots.

When you make a **market order**, you ask the broker to execute your trade at whatever the market price is at the time your trade is actually finalized. You say, "Buy 100 shares of Dell at market." The broker will have quoted you the most recent price, but the price may change before you get your shares, even if the broker acts quickly. This may result in a more favorable price, or it may mean you end up paying more for your shares than you had intended. For example, if the price has fallen to $34.00 by the time your trade is executed, you'll pay that price per share (plus the commission to the broker).

market order

An offer to buy stock at the market price.

But what if the stock price is creeping upward and you're worried that it might increase beyond what you can afford or beyond what you think the stock is worth? For example, suppose you don't want to pay more than $36 per share for the Dell stock. In that case, you can give a **limit order** to the broker, in which you say, "Buy 100 shares of Dell stock for me as long as the price is no more than $36." You can also give a limit order to sell, which will specify the minimum price that you're willing to accept from a potential buyer. If the current price is too high (or too low in the case of a sell order) to execute the order, the limit order will remain in effect until you cancel it, so you might get the shares you want a few days or weeks later. If you don't want to leave your order open, you can place a time limit on it, the most common being a *day order*, in which your order expires at the close of trading for the day. An order can also be *fill-or-kill*, which means that it's canceled if not immediately filled.

limit order

A request to buy stock at any price up to a given maximum or to sell stock at any price above a given minimum.

The third type of order is a **stop order**, which is commonly used to minimize losses or protect gains on a particular stock. For example, suppose you buy the Dell stock at $35 and it subsequently goes up to $38 per share. You can sell it and take the profit of $3 per share, or you can hold on to it in the hope that the price will increase even more. If you hold on to it, though, you don't want to take the chance of losing all the profit you've gained on paper if it were to subsequently decline in value. To protect against that possibility, you can place a stop order with your broker that says, "Sell all my Dell shares if the price drops to $36.50." If the price begins to fall, this order will be executed, and you'll have locked in $1.50 profit per share.

stop order

An order to buy or sell stock holdings when the market price reaches a certain level.

Now suppose instead that your Dell stock has dropped from its original $35 purchase price to $33 per share. You may not want to sell it now and take the $2 loss—perhaps you think there's a chance it will recover in value. But you also may not want to lose much more money. In this case, you can place a stop order instructing the broker to sell your shares if the price falls below, say, $30 per share. This type of stop order is often called a *stop-loss order*, for obvious reasons. If the order results in a sale at $30 per share, you'll have lost $5 on your original $35 investment, or about 14 percent, but you'll have cut off the risk of further losses if the stock price continues its downward slide. With 20-20 hindsight, many investors regret their failure to use stop-loss orders during market declines.

Long Versus Short

As a long-term investor, you'll primarily be a buyer of stocks rather than a seller. When you're a buyer and hold stock in your portfolio, you're said to be *long* in stock. You'll make money when the stock price goes up and lose money when the stock price goes down. Your objective is to *buy low and sell high*, in that order.

You'll sometimes hear investors talk about making money on their investments by **selling short**. This happens when they issue a sell order to their broker but don't actually have the stock to sell; instead, they borrow it from their broker's account. They're betting that the price of the stock will go down so that they can replace the stock later at a lower price and make a profit on

selling short

A strategy in which an investor borrows stock from a broker, sells the stock, and later buys stock on the market to replace the borrowed stock.

Stock is usually sold in round lots of 100 shares.

stockbroker

A licensed professional who buys and sells securities on behalf of clients.

the difference. A short seller's objective is therefore to *sell high and buy low,* in that order. Although short sellers can sometimes be quite successful, earning a return without putting up much cash of their own, the key factor is that they're counting on being right about the direction the price will move. What happens if the stock price goes up instead of down? They end up paying whatever the current market price is for the stock as well as repaying the broker for any missed dividends.

Learning by Doing 12-3

1. Use the excerpt from the *Wall Street Journal* given in Exhibit 12–6 to find the following information about Deb Shops, Inc., a clothing retailer:
   - a. Ticker symbol
   - b. Annual dividend
   - c. Close price
   - d. 52-week high

Using a Broker

full-service brokers

Brokers that offer a full range of services to clients.

discount brokers

Brokers that facilitate transactions but usually do not offer investment advice or research services to clients.

brokerage account

An investor's account at a brokerage firm, from which the investor pays for purchases and into which the firm deposits proceeds from sales.

buying on margin

Using borrowed funds from your broker to make a trade.

Since you can't directly buy and sell securities yourself, you must hire someone to help you execute your trades. A **stockbroker** is a licensed professional who facilitates securities transactions for clients. Generally, a stockbroker works for a particular brokerage firm, such as Merrill Lynch or Raymond James Financial, and the firm will be a member of one or more organized exchanges. Next, we look at the types of brokers and how they interact with you to buy and sell securities.

Full-Service Versus Discount Brokerage Firms. Brokers, and the brokerage firms they work for, are categorized based on the level of service that they provide to their clients. All brokers, of course, trade on their clients' behalf. In addition, **full-service brokers** provide such services as account management, investment research, recommendations on specific securities and asset allocation, and loans. **Discount brokers**, which include a wide range of financial service firms and online brokerage sites, are generally much less expensive than full-service brokers but are likely to offer fewer services. Some discount brokers primarily take orders over the phone, while others operate online. As time goes on, competition in the brokerage marketplace is blurring the lines between broker types—full-service brokers are providing low-cost trading services to their clients, and discount brokers are offering investment research services. The end result is good news for small investors, who now have more access to information and incur lower costs for trading than they did a decade ago.

Brokerage Accounts. When you do business with a brokerage firm, you'll be required to open a **brokerage account** and keep a minimum amount there, in either cash or securities. Your funds may be insured against brokerage firm failure by the Security Investor Protection Corporation (SIPC), as discussed in the following section. Although your account records will include the specific shares you own, the actual documents that evidence your ownership interest—your stock certificates—are held in the name of the brokerage firm and maintained at its office. This simplifies transactions, since the individual companies don't have to update their ownership records every time the shares change hands.

Most brokers offer three types of accounts: cash accounts, margin accounts, and discretionary accounts. If you have a *cash account,* you're required to make payment in full within three days of a buy order. Since three days isn't enough time to mail in a check, you'll need to have an electronic transfer system between your bank and your brokerage account.

Brokers spend a lot of time on the phone taking and implementing customer orders.

If you have sufficient funds in your brokerage account, your broker can execute buy orders using those funds. But what if you don't have sufficient funds? If you have a *margin account,* you can buy more stock than you have the funds for, borrowing the rest from the brokerage firm. This is called **buying on margin**. Although margin trading allows you to buy more stock than you could if you used only your own money, it's also riskier, since you have to earn enough on the stock to pay back the loan with interest. The advantage is that, if the stock goes up in value, you don't have to share the gain with the brokerage firm—you only owe the amount of the loan plus interest. This means that your return on investment is higher than it would have been if you had put up all the money for the stock. If you buy $2,000 in stock, paying only half of the amount with your own money and borrowing the rest, a $200 gain represents a 20 percent return on your investment of $1,000, whereas it would only be a 10 percent return if you'd had to invest the full $2,000.

The Federal Reserve requires that the margin—the equity in the account divided by the stock value—be at least 50 percent. To guard against the possibility that the value of the stock is less than the loan amount, brokers also set a maintenance margin (such as 30 percent). Thus, if stock prices fall sufficiently you may get a **margin call** from your broker requesting that you deposit additional funds into your account so that you can meet the maintenance margin limit. For example, if you buy $5,000 in shares using $2,500 of your own money and $2,500 borrowed from the brokerage firm, you have a 50 percent margin. If the share prices fall, so that the shares in your account are only worth $3,500, your margin is now (3,500 − 2,500)/3,500 = 28.6 percent, which is less than the 30 percent minimum. You'll need to pay back at least $50 to meet the required minimum.

margin call

A request from a brokerage firm that the holder of a margin account add money to the account to maintain the required minimum.

The last type of brokerage account is a *discretionary account* in which you delegate the decision-making authority for buying and selling to the broker. Since the broker makes more money by making more trades, you run the risk that the broker might make lots of trades just to get the commissions. There are ethical restrictions on **churning**, or excessive trading, in discretionary accounts, but how much is too much is subject to disagreement.

churning

Excessive trading in a discretionary account.

Transaction Costs. In return for their services, brokers charge a commission fee—either a dollar amount per transaction or a decreasing percentage based on the size of the trade. As mentioned, shares usually trade in round lots of 100 shares, so an order for an odd lot, which has less than 100 shares, may require the payment of an additional fee. Brokers' fees cover their costs of handling transactions and general overhead expenses, and they can differ substantially from firm to firm. Full-service brokerage firms charge higher commissions than discount brokers, and fees also vary among firms. You might pay as little as $5 per trade with an online broker or many times more for a full-service broker. The results of a recent survey of brokers are summarized in Exhibit 12–7.

EXHIBIT 12-7

Survey of Brokers' Fees

	Minimum Investment ($)	Trading Cost ($)	Phone Wait Time (seconds)
Premium Discount Brokers			
American Express	2,000	19.95	252
Charles Schwab	10,000	32.95	55
Fidelity	2,500	32.95	148
H&R Block	2,500	29.95	110
JB Oxford	2,000	14.50	58
Quick & Reilly	None	23.95	100
Strong	2,500	24.95	97
T. Rowe Price	2,500	19.95	148
USAA	2,000	24.95	35
Vanguard	3,000	25.00	158
Basic Discount Brokers			
Ameritrade	2,000	10.99	125
Banc of America	None	24.95	161
Bidwell	None	12.75	16
BrownCo	15,000	5.00	47
Cititrade	2,000	24.95	85
E*Trade	1,000	22.99	622
Firsttrade	None	6.95	22
Harrisdirect	None	20.00	59
Merill Lynch Direct	2,000	29.95	143
Muriel Siebert	None	14.95	38
Scottrade	500	7.00	5
TD Waterhouse	None	12.95	141
Wells Fargo	1,000	24.95	38

Note: Trade costs are for 1,000 shares, with fees; phone wait time is for customer service. You can access the full survey results, which include rankings of each broker based on quality of service, commissions and fees, and research tools, at www.smartmoney.com. Information from 2003 Broker Survey, SmartMoney.com.

Money Psychology

Which Household Decision Makers Use Financial Advisors?

Based on a survey funded by the TIAA-CREF Institute, the authors of a recent article find that women's involvement in household financial decisions increases when they contribute a larger proportion of total household income. The study also finds that the use of financial advisors by households depends in part on whether the primary decision maker in the household is a man or woman. Only 55 percent of married households in which the man is the primary decision maker have consulted a financial advisor, compared with 65 percent for households in which the woman is the primary decision maker and 69 percent for households in which the couple jointly makes financial decisions. This finding is consistent with research on gender differences in decision-making styles and with common wisdom that suggests women are more comfortable with asking directions.

Source: Alexandra Bernasek and Vickie L. Bajtelsmit, "Predictors of Women's Involvement in Household Financial Decision-making," *Financial Counseling and Planning* (2002) pp. 1–9.

Selecting a Broker. Because of the high variability in brokers' fees, it's important to investigate as many options as possible before choosing a broker. In making your choice, you should first determine whether you can benefit from the extras offered by a full-service broker. If you don't plan to make use of the investment advice offered by these firms and will not be trading frequently, you'll probably be better off selecting one of the lower-cost discount brokers. You should also be aware that you may not need the extra services offered by a full-service firm if you're obtaining similar services elsewhere, as when you're paying for the services of a financial planner. Survey evidence reported in the *Money Psychology* box, "Which Household Decision Makers Use Financial Advisors?" suggests that women are more likely to ask for help. In any event, your choice of broker should be based on your individual needs. Some specifics that you may want to investigate before making your decision include the following:

Go to www.smartmoney.com and click on "Stocks" to find the results of their broker surveys, including ratings based on quality of service, commissions and fees, research tools, and phone waiting time.

- Is the account insured by the SIPC?
- Does the brokerage firm have a useful website, and, if trades are to be executed on the site, can it provide evidence of past reliability during high-traffic trading periods?
- What is the commission structure?
- Will the broker pay you interest on any uninvested cash in your account? If so, at what rate?
- What services does the broker provide in addition to executing trades?

Online Investing. A growing percentage of individual investors are choosing the convenience and reduced transaction costs associated with online investing. Online brokers offer investor education, banking and financial services, quick transactions, access to extensive investment databases, and portfolio management tools. Before you start investing in this way, a few cautions are in order. First, you should only use a reputable online broker. Second, don't let the ease of trading lure you into being a **day trader**—someone who buys and sells during the day to make a quick profit—since that type of active trading is highly risky and thus unlikely to be consistent with your financial planning objectives.

day trader
An active investor who buys and sells many times during the day to make quick profits.

Learning by Doing 12-4

1. You can attempt to make investment gains by either buying stocks you think will increase in value or selling short stocks you think will decrease in value. In either case, you take the risk that the price will go in an unfavorable direction. Explain why selling short is an inherently riskier investment strategy.
2. You have a margin account with a minimum maintenance margin of 30 percent. You buy 100 shares of stock at $20 per share using only $1,200 of your own money. If the stock price fell to $15, would you get a margin call?

Regulation of the Securities Market

LEARNING objective

4 Understand how the regulation of securities markets is beneficial to investors.

The U.S. securities market is heavily regulated by the federal government, and as an individual investor, you reap many benefits from this regulation. As we've seen in other areas of personal finance, government regulations are designed to ensure that you have access to accurate information and to protect you from the fraudulent actions of others. To better understand the motivation for and importance of U.S. regulation of the securities market, you need to know a little bit about history. In this section, we provide some historical context for current securities law and summarize the most important elements of federal securities regulation.

History of Federal Securities Laws

In the early part of the last century, our securities market was very different than it is today. Investor fraud was commonplace, and a "buyer beware" environment prevailed. It was very difficult for stockholders to obtain financial information about potential investments or even about the companies whose stock they held. The worst economic downturn in U.S. history, now called the Great Depression, was precipitated by widespread mistrust of financial markets combined with an unusually large number of bank failures in the 1920s and with the 1929 stock market crash. In the early 1930s, faced with thousands of business failures, double-digit unemployment rates, and other related problems, Congress was motivated to enact far-reaching legislation in many areas, including banking and securities regulation. The overriding objective of the federal securities laws was investor protection, since it was generally believed that restoring investor confidence was a prerequisite for the nation's economic recovery.

Information Disclosure Requirements

Two acts passed by Congress in the 1930s, the Securities Act of 1933 and the Securities Exchange Act of 1934, are still in place today and form the foundation for federal securities regulation. In addition, each state has its own securities laws (commonly called *blue sky laws* in reference to the objective of giving investors a clear view of company finances). Because of the overlap in legal rules, state securities regulators don't usually deal with securities and trading issues, but instead focus on state licensing and registration of brokers and brokerage firms and on prevention and prosecution of other types of investment fraud.

Today, all traded securities must be registered with the Securities and Exchange Commission (SEC), an independent agency of the federal government charged with enforcement of the securities laws and broad oversight of the securities market, OTC trading, brokers, and dealers. Issuers of new securities are required to fully disclose all relevant information to prospective investors and to make periodic, detailed financial reports on their performance to the SEC, in a report commonly referred to as the "10-K," and to their stockholders, in an annual report. By requiring full information disclosure, this regulatory requirement helps to level the playing field for small investors and makes it easier to compare companies based on financial performance.

To see what corporate insiders are doing, you can go to moneycentral.msn.com and click on "Investing," then "Stocks," then "Insider Trading." Enter the symbol of the company you're interested in and you can see all the recent insider trades.

Antifraud Provisions

In addition to requiring information disclosure, federal law protects investors by prohibiting fraud and misrepresentation in the sale of securities. Although the broad language of the law encompasses most types of misrepresentation, there are specific rules aimed at preventing price manipulation through **insider trading**. Insider trading is an illegal act in which corporate "insiders"—those who are privy to information about the company that isn't available to the general public—buy or sell company stock based on their inside information. Although the definition of insider obviously includes the officers and directors of a company, a recent Supreme Court case broadens the definition to include anyone who knowingly uses nonpublic information to deceive other investors. To make it easier to track these transactions, officers, directors, and major stockholders are required to report all transactions in their company's stock to the SEC. The Insider Trading and Securities Fraud Enforcement Act of 1988 increased the penalties for securities fraud.

insider trading

Trading based on company information not available to the public, illegal under federal law.

Despite the legal consequences for insider trading, including penalties and jail time, there is evidence that such activities persist. As described in the *News You Can Use* box, "What Event Studies Tell Us about Insider Trading," stock prices often seem to react in advance of the release of public information. These price movements suggest that insiders sometimes leak the information, perhaps to family and friends. Furthermore, examination of the profits made by insiders on their reported trades compared with the profits made by other investors in the same stocks tends to indicate that these trades are motivated by better-than-average knowledge of the firm's future prospects.

Other Regulation

Several additional statutes have expanded protections for investors. The Maloney Act of 1938 requires securities trade associations to register with the SEC. The act also authorized the forma-

NEWS you can use

What Event Studies Tell Us about Insider Trading

An event study is a way of looking at market efficiency by measuring how quickly new information affects stock prices, but it can also tell us whether there are leaks of inside information in advance of public announcements that are expected to affect stock prices. When a company makes an important announcement, such as a change in dividend policy, a new product introduction, or a merger with another company, when do you think the stock price will react? If no one knew about the change before the announcement except company insiders (and we know they aren't allowed to trade on that information), then all the price reaction should come *after* the announcement. Interestingly, though, many studies have indicated that prices show some upward movement prior to the announcement of good news (as shown in the hypothetical graph below) and downward movement prior to the announcement of bad news. This can only happen if the news is anticipated by investors (even though not yet officially announced), or it may be that the information has been leaked.

> "prices show some upward movement prior to the announcement of good news"

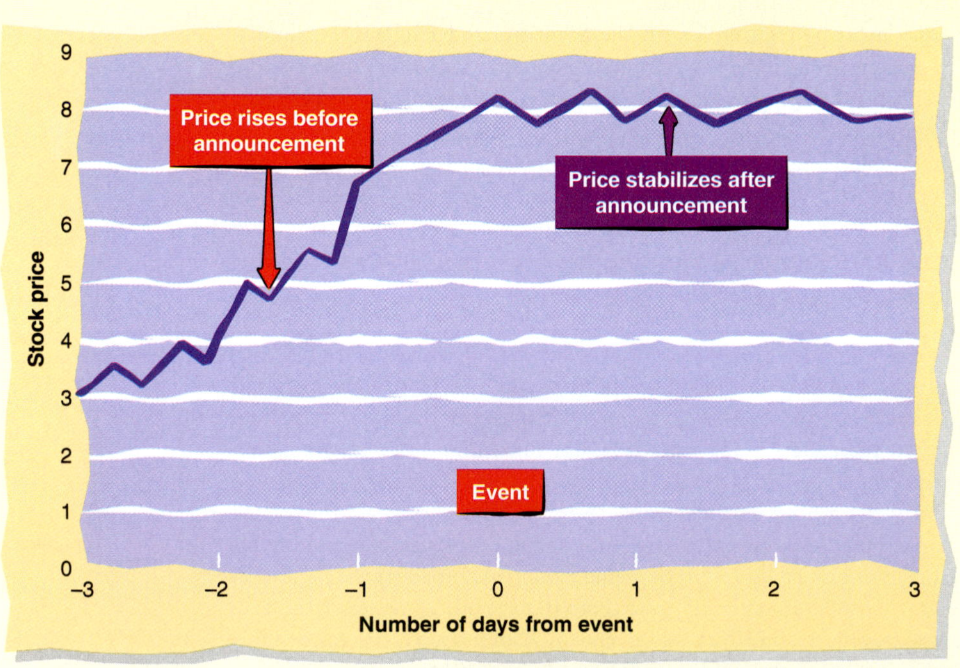

tion of the National Association of Securities Dealers (NASD). This organization tests and licenses securities dealers and enforces a code of ethics.

The Investment Company Act of 1940 and the Investment Advisors Act of 1940 extended SEC registration and disclosure rules to mutual funds and mutual fund advisors. To protect investors' accounts from losses when their brokers experience financial difficulties, the Securities Investor Protection Act of 1970 created the Security Investor Protection Corporation (SIPC), to which most brokers belong. If your account is insured by the SIPC, you're protected against losses of up to $500,000 in securities (of which $100,000 can be cash). This protection doesn't extend to investment losses on the account that occur while the broker's finances are being straightened out, however. The insurance promises that the securities in investors' accounts will be returned to them but makes no guarantees about the securities' value. So, for example, if you had 100 shares of stock valued at $75 per share and they had fallen in value to $50 per share by the time they were returned to you, you'd be stuck with the $25 per share loss.

Fact #3

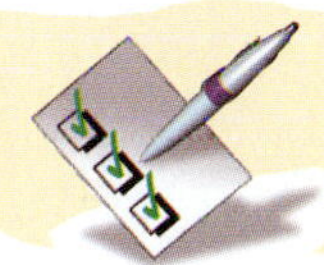

If you do the crime, be prepared to do the time. A person convicted of insider trading must pay back any profits and will likely spend some time in jail as well. Recent sentences have been from two to six years.

After the stock market crash in 1987, the securities industry made some changes to its system of self-regulation to protect against extreme market volatility. The stock market now has in place a set of **circuit breaker rules** that kick in when the market experiences a large drop. The idea is that a temporary halt in trading will allow investors to obtain the information they need to determine whether the price movements are justified. In effect, the rules are an attempt to slow the mass panic that appears to capture the market during large downward movements. The current circuit breaker rules are as follows (based on Eastern Standard Time):

circuit breaker rules

Securities industry rules that act to temporarily halt trading in the event of an unusually large drop in the market.

If the Dow declines	By	Trading is halted for
10%	2 P.M.	1 hour
10%	2 P.M.–2:30 P.M.	½ hour
10%	after 2:30 P.M.	no effect
20%	1 P.M.	2 hours
20%	1 P.M.-2 P.M.	1 hour
20%	after 2 P.M.	rest of the day
30%	any time	rest of the day

The longest period of market closure was seen during the week following the September 11, 2001, terrorist attack on the World Trade Center. The circuit breakers led to market closure that morning and the market didn't reopen until the following Monday, September 17. Price declines were initially moderate, but continued downward through September 21, with the S&P 500, Dow, and NASDAQ indexes losing from 12 to 16 percent from the day preceding the closure.

Stock Selection and Performance Evaluation

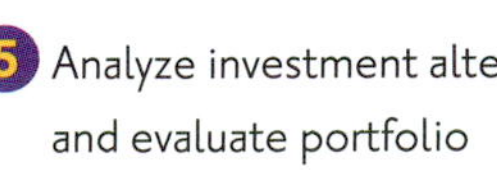

Selection of individual stocks for your investment portfolio should be based on your evaluation of expected returns as well as an assessment of how much risk the investment will add to your portfolio. In this section, we introduce several return and risk measures and explain how to evaluate an investment's performance by comparing it with benchmark indexes.

Measuring Expected Stock Returns

In addition to looking at historical rates of return on particular investments, investors commonly use the earnings per share and the price-to-earnings ratios to help them estimate future rates of return. In this section, we'll explain how each of these measures is used to evaluate stock investments.

Chapter 11 defined the annual rate of return on an investment as the current yield plus the capital gains yield. For stock investors, the current yield is usually called the *dividend yield*, since the current income to a stock investor is the annual dividend payment. The two components of a stock's rate of return, **dividend yield** and **capital gains yield**, are therefore defined as follows:

dividend yield

Component of stock investor's total return equal to the ratio of annual dividends to the market price of a stock.

capital gains yield

Component of stock investor's total return equal to the ratio of the annual change in price to the market price of a stock.

$$\text{Dividend yield} = \frac{\text{Annual dividend}}{\text{Market price of stock}}$$

$$\text{Capital gains yield} = \frac{\text{Annual change in price}}{\text{Market price of stock}}$$

As an example, suppose you're considering the purchase of stock with a market price of $50 per share. If the stock pays an annual dividend of $1 per share, you'll earn a dividend yield of $1/$50 = 0.02, or 2 percent. Your total annual return on the stock will be the 2 percent dividend yield plus the expected capital gains yield. If, historically, the stock has increased in value an average of 10 percent per year, you might expect the price to rise to $55 by the end of the year. In this case, you'd earn a total rate of return of 12 percent on your stock investment for the year—2 percent in dividend yield and 10 percent in capital gains yield. Normally, the price that you'll use for the denominator of this equation will be the price you paid (or expect to pay) for the shares.

Investors usually estimate future dividends based on dividends paid in the previous year, but it can be much more difficult to estimate expected capital gains. For this reason, investors sometimes use various ratios that have been found to be good indicators of future performance. Perhaps the "most-watched" ratio is the company's **earnings per share (EPS)**, which is measured as follows:

earnings per share (EPS)

A measure of company profitability equal to annual earnings divided by the number of shares outstanding.

$$\text{Earnings per share (EPS)} = \frac{\text{After-tax net income}}{\text{Number of shares outstanding}}$$

Since stock investors own a proportionate share of the company, they have an interest in a proportionate share of the firm's annual after-tax net income, commonly called "earnings." The company can use those dollars to pay dividends, or it can reinvest them to grow the firm. Either way, stockholders stand to benefit if earnings go up. When a company reports better than expected earnings, its stock price tends to go up, since investors see that as a good sign for the future, but when earnings fall or are lower than expected, the stock price tends to fall as well.

The EPS ratio provides a rough measure of profitability and can be compared over time for a particular firm. However, it's not very useful as a decision-making tool, since there isn't a universally accepted "good" or "bad" value (as long as EPS is positive). Consider two similar companies that both had earnings per share equal to $2 last year. You can't conclude that they'd be equally profitable to you as an investor, since that would depend in part on what you'd have to pay to get this level of earnings. If one company's stock is half as expensive as the other's, you'd have to conclude that the lower-priced share was giving you a better relative level of earnings. Generally, differences in company size, industry, and share price all make it difficult to directly compare companies based on EPS.

You can sometimes use EPS to compare companies if you consider it relative to some other variable. For example, you can use the **price-to-earnings (P/E) ratio**, which measures the relation of share price to earnings per share. The P/E ratio is calculated as follows:

price-to-earnings (P/E) ratio

Measure of a company's future earnings potential calculated as market price divided by earnings per share.

$$\text{Price-to-earnings (P/E) ratio} = \frac{\text{Stock price}}{\text{Earnings per share}}$$

The P/E ratio is seen as a measure of future earnings potential. Thus, a high P/E ratio is generally considered a positive indicator of the firm's potential for future growth. The implication is that investors perceive the firm as being "worth" the extra price. However, a high P/E ratio can also be an indication that a stock is currently overpriced. Although P/E ratios differ over time and across industries, the average for large company stocks is usually between 15 and 25, whereas P/E ratios for high growth stocks can be much higher.

As an example of how P/E ratios can differ across industries, let's consider the ratios for Anheuser-Busch (BUD) and Dell Inc. (DELL). Anheuser-Busch is in the food and beverage industry, and Dell is a computer manufacturer and retailer. On July 16, 2004, the following price and P/E information appeared in the *Wall Street Journal*:

Firm	Price	P/E
Dell Inc. (DELL)	$34.87	33
Anheuser-Busch (BUD)	$53.92	20

The P/E ratios for these two firms show that investors are willing to pay a much higher multiple of earnings per share for Dell stock (33) than for Anheuser-Busch stock (20). We can interpret this difference to mean that investors are much more optimistic about Dell's prospects for growth. That should make sense to you, since, as you might expect, beer sales tend to be fairly stable over time, whereas Dell is a relatively young company in a high-growth industry.

Does this mean you should buy Dell stock? Not necessarily. As a technology stock, Dell may be much riskier. We'll evaluate the risk of the two companies relative to their returns in the next section. In addition, you should compare the P/Es of individual stocks to the average for its industry. Some studies have shown that stocks with very high P/E ratios, relative to the industry average, tend to have lower returns in the following year. Similarly, companies with low P/E ratios relative to their industry average tend to outperform the average in the following year. A possible explanation for these findings is that so many investors buy the stocks of the "good" companies that their stock prices are driven up to levels that make them no longer a good buy.

Measuring Stock Risk

By its nature, all stock is risky. When you buy stock, you get no guarantee that you'll receive any cash flow, and you're not entitled to the return of your investment capital from the company in the future. In addition, the actual return on your investment will vary over time and with economic conditions.

We saw in earlier chapters that risk is the probability of experiencing an outcome different from what you expected. Accordingly, we usually measure the risk of securities based on the variability of past stock returns. Although, on average, you can expect to receive a higher average rate of return for bearing additional risk, in the short run you'll undoubtedly experience ups and downs in your portfolio value.

Quantifying the Risk-Return Relationship. In Chapter 11, we noted that investors require higher rates of return for riskier investments. Exhibit 12–8 illustrates this relationship graphically for several investment classes. Although, in practice, the relationship between risk and return will not be a perfect continuum like that illustrated in the exhibit, over the long term, you'll find that this theoretical relationship holds true. Treasury bills expose you to very little risk—if you hold them to maturity (which is no more than one year), you'll receive the yield you expected when you bought the securities—about 1.5 percent in 2004. The primary risk you face is that your purchasing power may be affected if inflation changes drastically in the short time you hold the T-bills. Bonds, which we'll consider in more detail in Chapter 13, generally fall on the lower portion of the graph, because the risk of investing in bonds (with the exception of junk bonds, which are issued by less creditworthy companies) is relatively low. Stocks pose more risk, and derivatives still more.

Remember that the measure of investment risk is the variability of the returns you can expect from the investment—the more variable the returns, the higher the risk. Let's consider an example to illustrate the variability of returns. We've already looked at a monthly price history for Dell and Anheuser-Busch in Exhibit 12–3. Now let's consider how periodic changes in price translated into returns for investors over a longer time period. Exhibit 12–9 shows the *annual* returns for Dell and Anheuser-Busch stock over 15 years, from May 1990 to May 2004. As a reference point, the graph also includes the returns for the Dow Jones Industrial Average (DJIA), a large-stock index, for comparison. Although the market clearly experienced some ups and downs during that period of time, you can see that Dell's returns were much more variable

EXHIBIT 12-8

The Risk-Return Relationship

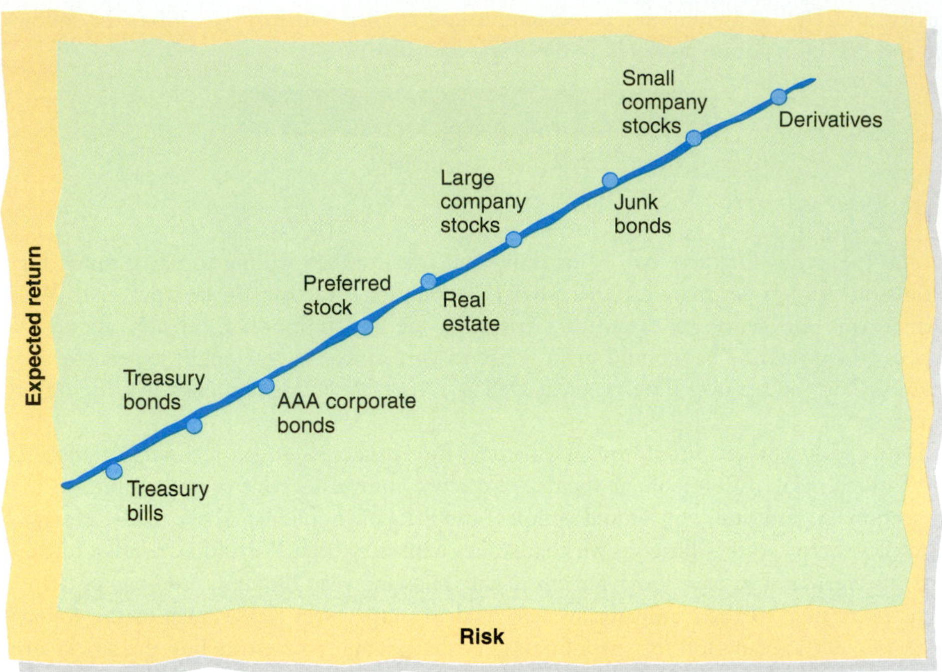

than those of Anheuser-Busch or the DJIA—illustrated by the larger range of positive and negative returns.

How can you incorporate investment risk in your investment decision process? Investors use different measures for risk, but here we'll focus on some of the easiest to understand and apply. These include the range of returns (difference from highest to lowest) and the probability of experiencing a loss (number of periods in which the stock declined in value out of the total number of periods). We can summarize this information for DELL, BUD, and the DJIA (May 1990–May 2004) as follows:

	DELL	BUD	DJIA
Average annual return	67.4%	24.0%	10.5%
Highest annual return	306.4	68.4	29.9
Lowest annual return	−43.5	3.0	−10.8
Range (highest–lowest)	349.9	63.4	40.7
Year with losses/total	2/15	0	2/15

Based on this data, we can see that Dell's stockholders enjoyed much higher average returns over the 15-year period, but also were exposed to much more variation in returns. In one year, Dell's stock value actually fell by 43.5 percent. BUD's average returns were still fairly high (24%), more than double the average for the market (10.5%), but the range of returns for BUD was double that of the market average.

In comparing the risk of different investments, you can also use a math statistic called the *standard deviation* to measure variability. Although we won't go into the mathematical calculation here, standard deviation is a more precise measurement of the variability of a series of numbers around the average value of the series. The more variation around the average, the higher the standard deviation and the higher the risk. The standard deviation of annual returns for this period is 90.1 percent for Dell and 18.3 percent for Anheuser-Busch. For the same period, the DJIA standard deviation was 12.0 percent. As you can see, this measure of risk is telling a similar story as our other measures. BUD is less risky than Dell, and the market index is less risky than BUD.

It's not surprising that the DJIA standard deviation has the lowest risk of the three. The variability of the market as a whole is usually lower than that of individual stocks because of the diversification effect discussed in Chapter 11. When stocks are put together in a portfolio (and the DJIA includes 30 stocks), some of the individual company risks are canceled out. Therefore, if you're a diversified investor, you're not primarily interested in how variable a particular stock is by itself; rather, you want to know how it will affect the variability, or risk, of your overall portfolio. This requires that you have a way of measuring the market risk of individual securities—the components of risk that can't be diversified away.

Measuring Market Risk. A measure commonly used to estimate the risk of stock investments held in a diversified portfolio is the **beta**. A stock's beta measures its degree of market risk, or how much it tends to move with the overall market. Since we've already seen that Dell's stock returns seemed to be much riskier than the market as a whole, its beta should help us to more precisely quantify that relationship.

beta

A measure of the market, or nondiversifiable, risk of a stock.

A beta equal to 1 means that the stock has about the same degree of risk as the overall market (and should therefore give you about the same percent of return if held in a diversified portfolio). A beta less than 1 means the stock is less risky than average and will give you proportionally lower return, and a beta greater than 1 means the stock is riskier than average and will give you proportionally more return. Although stocks rarely have negative betas (which would imply that they would have negative returns when the market had positive returns), there are occasional examples where this happens.

Most financial services firms, brokers, and investment advisors will provide you with an estimate of the beta for particular stocks. For example, the beta reported for Dell Inc. stock on finance.yahoo.com in July 2004 was 1.7. This figure suggests that if the overall stock market goes up, Dell's stock will go up proportionally more, and if the stock market goes down, Dell's stock will decline by a greater percentage. Most technology and Internet companies have high betas—the type of business they're in has higher market risk since sales tend to slump in recessions and surge forward during recovery periods. Investors expect to receive a much higher return to compensate them for this higher risk.

Let's see how you could apply this to selecting stocks for your portfolio. Suppose you're a bit conservative and don't want your portfolio to be highly sensitive to general market movements. You can use screening tools on various websites to identify low-beta stocks

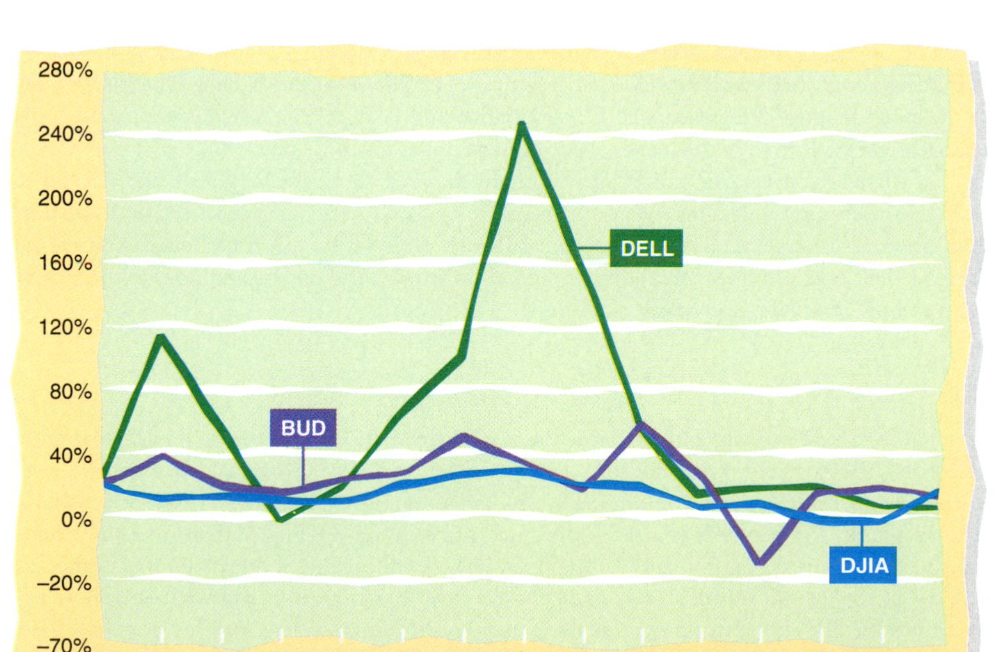

EXHIBIT 12-9

Annual Returns for Anheuser-Busch, Dell, and DJIA, May 1990 to May 2004

You can find the beta for any publicly traded stock at www.moneycentral.msn.com (click on Research, then Company Report) or finance.yahoo.com (click on Company, then Key Statistics).

(i.e., stocks with betas of less than 1) in each of several industries; these stocks will make up your portfolio. The beta for the portfolio will be the average of the betas for the stocks you select, weighted according to the proportions of the stocks held in the portfolio. Note that you can use this concept to offset the risk of a single investment as well. If you've bought a relatively risky stock like Dell, you can balance that with a stock with low market risk like Anheuser-Busch.

Learning by Doing 12-5

	Seesaw Incorporated	SlowMo Corporation
Beta	2.2	0.75
Last year's return	2%	12%
Average 5-year return	25%	8%
P/E ratio	45	12

1. Which stock is riskier?
2. Which one is probably a growth stock? Does that mean it will give you a higher return?
3. What can you tell from the P/E ratios?

The Time Diversification Debate. In the mid-1990s, Jeremy Siegal, a professor of finance at the Wharton School of Business at the University of Pennsylvania, wrote a book called *Stocks for the Long Run* based on the results of a research project examining long-run risk and return on various investments. In it, Dr. Siegal reached a controversial conclusion: For long holding periods, well-diversified portfolios of stocks are actually *less risky* than T-bills or corporate bonds. How could that be? The answer lies in a controversial concept called *time diversification.* This viewpoint argues that the average risk of stock investing declines as the time horizon gets longer, since ups and downs cancel each other out, much as asset diversification acts to the benefit of diversified investors. This argument is the basis for the commonly held viewpoint that long-run investors should be in stocks.

The opposing viewpoint is that investors are not just looking for low variability of return but are also concerned with downside risk, or the probability of losing money. The longer you're in the stock market, the greater the risk of experiencing a large loss. So while your average risk may decrease with time in the market, your average dollar loss does not.

So what's an investor to do? While we might disagree about the degree of risk, it's still the case that stocks provide higher average long-run returns, and thus greater wealth accumulation, than other asset classes. Thus, it is beneficial for investors with long time horizons to allocate some of their portfolio to stocks, but they should do so with the understanding that this exposes them to higher average risk as well.

Valuation Methods

So far in this section, we've looked at some ways in which you might select particular stocks based on their expected return and risk. In some cases, you may also want to estimate what the price of a stock *should be*, so you can make a judgment about whether the current price is favorable or not. If, for example, you think the stock price should be higher than it is now, then it may be a good investment for you. If you buy it when it's cheap and it quickly moves to the "correct" price, you could realize an *excess return*—a return that is greater than what you should get based on the risk alone. Investment analysts, large portfolio managers, and investment advisors spend a lot of time trying to find undervalued stocks for this reason. Two methods used for this purpose are fundamental analysis and the discounted dividend model.

Fundamental Analysis. Fundamental analysis involves comprehensive analysis of factors, many of which we've already discussed, that are expected to influence stock price. The primary objective is to determine whether the stock price is likely to increase in the future based on company factors, industry factors, and economic conditions. Company factors that might be considered include the potential for future earnings growth, dividend payouts, the financial strength of the company, market risk, and the quality of management. Industry factors include the potential for growth and whether it's a cyclical business. General economic conditions, such as interest rates, inflation, productivity, unemployment, and foreign exchange rates may also be considered. With so many factors to consider, fundamental analysis is more an art than a science, but the more you're involved in investing, the better you'll be at recognizing how these factors can be expected to affect stock prices.

The Discounted Dividend Model. In contrast to fundamental analysis, which considers many factors in estimating the value of stocks, the discounted dividend model focuses on expected cash flows to investors (which, of course may be influenced by some of the fundamentals as well). This model is an application of the time value of money tools introduced in Chapter 2. If investors are interested in buying stocks in order to get future cash flows in the form of dividends, then it follows that the value of a share of stock should be equal to the present value of the future cash flows—in this case, dividends—to be received. Since we don't know exactly how much those future dividends will be, the model assumes that dividends will grow at a constant rate, based on past growth rates of dividends. Discounting each of the dividends by the rate you could earn on alternative investments (your opportunity cost, or discount rate), you get the present value of future dividends, which (theoretically) should be equal to the stock price.

According to the discounted dividend model, then if you know the dividend D, the growth rate of dividends g, and the discount rate r, you can calculate the value of the stock with the following equation:

$$\text{Value} = \frac{D \times (1 + g)}{r - g}$$

The equation is fairly simple to apply. Suppose you know that Anheuser-Busch paid a dividend of 88 cents per share last year; based on past dividend increases, you expect the dividend to grow by 10 percent every year (the growth rate g). Suppose, too, that you require a 13 percent rate of return for stocks of this risk level (your discount rate r). The value of this stock should therefore be

$$\text{Value} = \frac{0.88 \times 1.10}{0.13 - 0.10} = \$32.27 \text{ per share}$$

As we saw earlier, the actual price of Anheuser-Busch stock in July 2004 was much higher than estimated here, so the model would say you shouldn't buy this stock. Relative to the cash flows being received by Anheuser-Busch investors, the price is quite high.

The problem with the discounted dividend model is that it makes some very strong assumptions that often don't hold true in practice. For one thing, dividends rarely grow at a constant rate, and some companies (Dell, for instance) don't even pay dividends. Furthermore, the riskiness of the company might not be constant over time, so your required return, or discount rate, might change. Nevertheless, this model, with modifications, is widely used by professionals to estimate value. As a result, stock prices usually go up when companies announce an increase in dividends, particularly if it seems to indicate that dividends will be increasing at a faster rate in the future.

Evaluating Portfolio Performance Against Stock Indexes

A **stock market index** tracks the performance of a particular group of stocks. This is useful as a way of gauging general market conditions and is also commonly used to evaluate the performance of specific stocks and portfolios. Some portfolio managers specifically identify a certain index as their *benchmark*, which means that their goal is to perform at least as well as the group of stocks in the index while maintaining a similar level of risk.

stock market index

An indicator that shows the average price movements of a particular group of stocks representing the market or some market segment.

Although the first stock index originated in1884, as discussed in the *News You Can Use* box, "How the Dow Jones Average Began," the indexes we commonly use today didn't appear until many years later. We look at the most popular indexes here and suggest how you can use them to evaluate the performance of your stock portfolio.

NEWS you can use

How the Dow Jones Average Began

The "Dow" in Dow Jones Industrial Average comes from Charles Henry Dow, newsman, market analyst, and cofounder (in 1882) of Dow Jones & Company, the publisher of the *Wall Street Journal* and *Barron's*. Like other market analysts since the earliest days of stock and bond trading, Dow attempted to discern underlying trends in each day's price fluctuations. Dow began computing the average price of a representative group of stocks as a tool to help analyze these movements. His first stock average included only 11 stocks and appeared on July 3, 1884, in the *Customers' Afternoon Letter*, a two-page financial news bulletin. Nine of the stocks in this index were railroad issues, reflecting the economic importance of railroads at that time. Dow's first industrial stock average, including 12 stocks, appeared on May 26, 1896, which makes it the oldest continuous price index of the U.S. stock market. The roster was increased to 20 representative stocks in 1916 and then to 30 on October 1, 1928. Of the original 12 stocks, only General Electric remains in the average.

"The Dow is the oldest continuous price index of the U.S. stock market"

For more information about specific stock indexes, go to the Dow Jones website at www.dowjones.com or the NYSE website at www.nyse.com.

The Dow Jones Industrial Average (DJIA). When you hear in the news that "the market" has gone up or down, the newscaster is usually referring to the Dow Jones Industrial Average (DJIA), commonly referred to as the Dow. The Dow, which includes 30 blue chip stocks considered representative of the overall U.S. stock market, is the most widely watched and reported index in use today. Given the large number of stocks in the marketplace, it might seem that too much emphasis is placed on this index of only 30. But the fact is that these 30 companies (listed in Exhibit 12–10) are so large and have so many investors that they represent a significant percentage of the value of the broader market. You can see in Exhibit 12–11, which shows historical returns on three popular indexes, that the returns tend to move together even though the S&P 500 and the NASDAQ (described below) include many more stocks than the Dow. Over the 19-year period depicted in the graph, the average return on the Dow was 12.3 percent, whereas the S&P averaged 10.7 percent, and the NASDAQ averaged 12.8 percent. (Note, though, that this similarity doesn't mean these indexes are interchangeable, since differences in the way they are calculated could make one or another preferable for a specific purpose.)

Originally, the value of the Dow was determined by adding up the share prices of the stocks in the index (which is called *price weighting*, since stocks with higher prices have more effect on the value of the index). Now, however, the value is calculated by summing the share prices of the Dow stocks and then dividing by a factor that takes into account stock splits, spin-offs, and dividends. This adjustment is necessary so that the Dow can be compared over time. Because of the adjustment, the Dow is not actually an "average," in spite of its name.

Fact #4

In evaluating your portfolio's performance, it doesn't make sense to just look at your own past returns as a benchmark. A diversified stock portfolio should be compared to a diversified index that includes stocks with similar risk and return characteristics. Even if your portfolio returns were lower than you'd hoped based on your past experience, you can still pat yourself on the back if you've beaten the market index for the period.

S&P 500 Index. Standard & Poor's, an investment advisory service, offers several indexes. The most popular is the S&P 500 Index, which tracks the performance of 500 large companies, most of them traded on the NYSE. Since this index represents a broader cross-section of American industry than the DJIA, the S&P 500 is probably a better indicator of market performance. The S&P 500 is the benchmark most commonly used by mutual funds and money managers to assess performance.

In contrast to the price weighting of the DJIA, the S&P 500 index is value-weighted. This means that companies with higher market capitalization have a greater impact on the index than those with lower capitalization. The rationale for this method of calculation is that it better reflects the influence of large companies on the market as a whole.

EXHIBIT 12-10

The Stocks of the Dow

The Dow Jones Industrial Average, as of May 2004, included the following 30 stocks:	
AIG	Intel Corp.
Alcoa Inc.	J.P. Morgan
American Express	Johnson & Johnson
Boeing	McDonald's
Caterpillar	Merck & Co.
Citigroup Inc.	Microsoft Corp.
Coca-Cola Inc.	Minnesota Mining
Dupont Co.	Pfizer
Exxon Mobil Corp.	Philip Morris
General Electric Co.	Procter & Gamble
General Motors Corp.	SBC Communications Inc.
Home Depot Inc.	United Technologies Corp.
Honeywell International Inc.	Verizon
Hewlett-Packard Co.	Wal-Mart Stores Inc.
IBM	Walt Disney

Other Stock Market Indexes. Both the Dow and the S&P 500 measure the performance of large-cap stocks. If your portfolio includes smaller companies or is weighted more heavily toward a certain sector (technology or financial services, perhaps), you may want to compare its performance to some other subsection of the market. Both Standard & Poor's and Dow Jones offer indexes that track other groups of stocks, including those in particular industry sectors, such as financial services and technology, and those of companies in different-size groups, such as small-cap and mid-cap companies. In addition, the NYSE Composite Index and the AMEX index track price movements for the groups of stocks that trade on their respective exchanges. The NASDAQ Composite Index tracks the over-the-counter market, which includes more small-company stocks. Another broad market indicator, the Wilshire 5000 Index, includes around 6,500 of the most actively traded stocks.

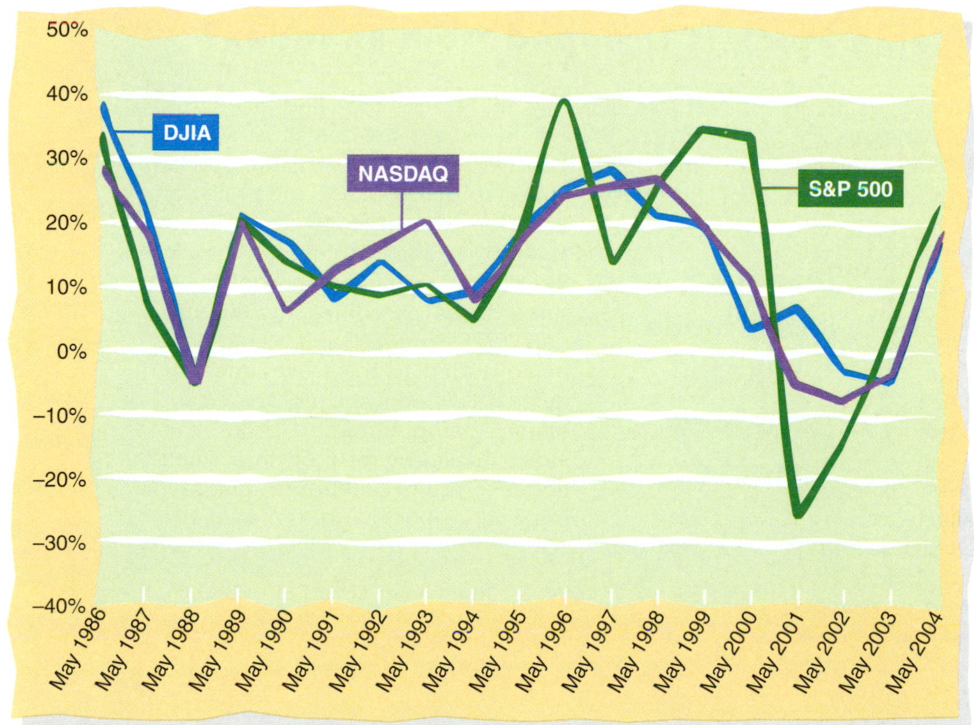

EXHIBIT 12-11

Annual Returns on Popular Indexes, May 1986 to May 2004

PFP Worksheet 46
Stock Tracker

Tracking Your Portfolio Performance. Although you should always be looking out for future investments, it's important to keep track of those you already have. Keeping good records of your stock purchases and sales and tracking performance relative to your objectives should become business as usual for you. Although you can buy financial investing software to help you in your record keeping, a simple Excel spreadsheet or a handwritten log will suffice. The important thing is to be consistent. You can use the worksheet in your *Personal Financial Planner* to get started.

In order to assess how well you've done, you need to have something to compare your results against. An index that has risk and return characteristics similar to those of your portfolio is an obvious choice. If you use an investment advisor or brokerage firm, that individual or firm will provide you with a regular report that summarizes your short-run and long-run performance compared with a benchmark. If you're investing on your own, you should select your own benchmark and regularly evaluate your performance relative to that index.

Indexing. In Chapter 11, we mentioned an investment strategy called indexing. Although this chapter has focused on the selection of a portfolio of individual stocks, it's worth noting here that if your objective is to closely mimic the performance of an index, you'll save on transaction costs by simply buying an index security or shares in an indexed mutual fund, as will be discussed in Chapter 14. You can also achieve this outcome, however, by buying shares of all the stocks in a particular index (in the same proportions as in the index). If you wanted to track the DJIA, for instance, you could simply buy an equal number of shares of all 30 stocks that are in the index. Many investors and mutual funds do exactly that. Occasionally, the stocks in the index are changed to better reflect the overall market. As a result, investors have to do a little shuffling of their portfolios, which can influence the prices of the stocks added and dropped, as discussed in the *News You Can Use* box, "What Happens When a Stock Is Dropped from an Index?"

NEWS you can use

What Happens When a Stock Is Dropped from an Index?

The stocks included in the major indexes are in hot demand by investors and fund managers who are attempting to achieve returns that are in line with those indexes. But the stocks in the index don't remain constant over time. In 1997, the DJIA dropped four stocks (Chevron, Union Carbide, Sears, and Goodyear) and added four stocks (Home Depot, Intel, Microsoft, and SBC Communications). More recently, in April 2004, AT&T, Eastman Kodak, and International Paper were dropped in favor of AIG, Pfizer, and Verizon. These changes were motivated by the desire to better reflect the technology and financial services sectors in the average.

What impact does being added or dropped from an index have on an individual stock? Managers of index funds sell the dropped stocks and buy the stocks that had been added. We would expect the forces of supply and demand to cause the prices of the stocks that were dumped to go down and the prices of the added stocks to go up. A recent study by finance professors Patricia Ryan and Richard Johnson measured these outcomes for the period 1929 to 1999 and found that being added to the Dow Jones Industrial Average had no significant effect. Being dropped from the index, however, resulted in a small negative return within the first day, but a large positive return over the next two years.

"Managers of index funds sell the dropped stocks"

Source: Patricia A. Ryan and Richard D. Johnson, "Changes in the DJIA: An Examination of Market Reaction, Risk, and Long-term Wealth Effects 1929 to 1999," Colorado State University Working Paper 2004.

Sources of Information for Stock Investors

LEARNING objective

 Identify sources of information for stock investors.

A wealth of information is available to investors today. In fact, some may feel that the sheer volume of information is a bit overwhelming. Smart investors need to figure out how to make sense of what's available and how to keep their knowledge up-to-date. The information that is most useful to stock investors falls into the categories discussed below.

General Economic Conditions

Being an informed investor means that you can't keep your head in the sand. You need to keep up with national news related to the economy, monetary policy, and tax policy—anything that can affect the value of your investments. The best source for this type of information is the financial press. You should get in the habit of regularly reading the *Wall Street Journal* or browsing through financial magazines such as *Fortune*, *Money*, *Forbes*, *Barrons's*, and *Kiplinger's Personal Finance*. Other alternatives include various financial websites we've previously mentioned.

Company Information

Before you invest in a company, you should understand what it does and why it's likely to make money for you. Even if your stockbroker recommends a particular stock, you should do some research on your own to be sure you agree. As you attempt to learn about a stock, keep in mind the factors that are indicators of future increases in value—the potential to grow, financial stability, good management, and the ability to stay ahead of the competition. Sources for this type of information include the company's website, its annual report, the prospectus for any new stock issue, the 10-K report filed with the SEC, and investment reports by rating agencies, industry groups, and stock analysts. Your broker may provide you with some of this material, or you can pay for an information service. Most public and university libraries subscribe to Value Line, a company that regularly summarizes company fundamentals and analysts' opinions.

Fact #5

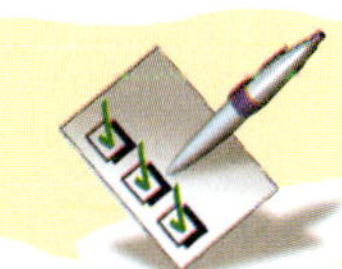

The anonymity of the Internet makes it easy for scam artists to perpetrate frauds on unsuspecting investors. A few years ago, for example, a savvy teenager attracted a huge following of interested investors when he began posting investment tips on his website (and of course didn't reveal his age). Convinced that he was an experienced stock expert, people bought any stock he recommended. By quickly selling his own holdings after the buying surge caused a price increase, he was able to make a tidy profit. Since his stock tips were entirely made up, what he was doing was a form of investment fraud, and he was eventually caught. The moral of this story is that you can't trust everything that you read on the Internet. Anyone can have a website, so you should stick to the sites sponsored by known companies and government entities to be sure that what you're reading is actually based on sound research.

Industry Information

As you evaluate specific companies, keep an eye on how different industries are faring in current economic conditions. What are the top industries, based on performance? Which ones are expected to do well in the next part of the economic cycle? The *Value Line Investment Survey*, available in most libraries, will give you an overview of industry trends in addition to the company data mentioned above. Standard and Poor's also publishes periodic industry surveys. If you regularly read the financial press for economic trends, you'll find industry analysis there as well—the annual industry performance evaluation that appears in *Forbes* is an example. Full-service brokerage firms often provide their clients with in-depth research on specific industries or sectors.

Companies' 10-K reports are available on the SEC website at www.sec.gov.

Internet Resources

As mentioned, there are many useful financial websites on the Internet. These websites often provide general investor and financial planning education, but many include a host of useful data and tools for stock investors. On the major sites, such as www.kiplinger.com, finance.yahoo.com, and

ask the expert Avoiding Irrational Exuberance

Robert Shiller
Stanley B. Resor, Professor of Economics, Yale University

In the late 1990s, Federal Reserve Chairman Alan Greenspan suggested that "irrational exuberance" on the part of market participants was partly responsible for run-up in stock prices that eventually resulted in a stock market crash. Robert Shiller, Stanley B. Resor Professor of Economics at Yale University and author of *Irrational Exuberance* and *The New Financial Order: Risk in the 21st Century*, is a renowned expert on the topic of investor behavior. In response to questions by *TIAA-CREF Participant* magazine in August 2003, excerpted below, Dr. Shiller provides some suggestions for how investors can make more rational investment decisions.

What are some of the steps investors can take to avoid the tendency toward irrational or illogical behavior?

Dr. Shiller: One, make it a personal rule to talk with others—or at least your spouse—before making any important investment decision. Two, consult with a personal financial advisor. Three, make it a point from time to time to read magazines or columns on personal finance, or tune in to financial advice shows, even if investing is not a congenial topic for you; don't leave it all to your advisor. Four, make it a personal rule to diversify broadly across all asset classes. Five, reflect on the fact that you, as a member of the human race, are vulnerable to psychological issues such as attention anomalies and overconfidence.

When making investment decisions, what facts or issues should people focus on?

Dr. Shiller: History is not a reliable guide to the future, so one should avoid the classic investor error of chasing past returns by investing heavily in assets that have shown a high return in the past. One should try to understand the actual situation today and not blindly assume that some aspect of the past much talked about will repeat itself. For example, people today still are very much influenced by the constantly repeated fact that the stock market has performed well for over a century. But, going forward, the thing we call the stock market includes different companies and different world environments. One must think about what stocks essentially are: vehicles designed to concentrate the risks of whatever corporate enterprise they are applied to for investors who can bear risks and do not require insurance or guarantees. Moreover, one must reflect on the price one is paying for the shares, compared with some measures of fundamental value. Be aware that investments can sometimes go through bubbles. One must resist being influenced by them, and, at the very least, don't let bubble enthusiasms deflect you from a broad diversification strategy.

Source: "Better Financial Decisions: An Interview with Robert Shiller," originally published in *Participant* (August 2003), a magazine published by TIAA-CREF. Reprinted by permission.

www.moneycentral.msn.com, you can access stock price histories, find investment research and relevant articles, screen stocks based on your criteria, track your investment portfolio, and use financial calculators.

Self-Help Books

The SEC Office of Internet Enforcement offers tips on how to avoid Internet investing scams at www.sec.gov/investor/pubs/cyberfraud.htm.

At your local bookstore or Internet book distributor, you'll find literally hundreds of self-help resources for investors. As with Web resources, some trade books are based on sound research and experience, and some are not. To narrow your reading material choices, look for reputable reviews in the financial press and examine closely the credentials of the authors. In the *Ask the Expert* box, "Avoiding Irrational Exuberance," we highlight some tips offered by a highly reputable source, Yale economist Robert Shiller, an investor psychology expert and the author of two investments books that should be on your reading list.

Summary

1 **Know the basic terminology used by stock investors.** Common stock represents a share of ownership in a corporation. Shareholders have a right to share in the assets and income of the corporation, but only after other claims have been satisfied. In return for bearing equity risk, shareholders have some voting rights, but they enjoy limited liability and do not participate in the management of the firm. Initial public offerings are made in the primary market, whereas transactions between investors take place in the secondary market, which includes organized securities exchanges and the over-the-counter market.

2 **Classify stocks according to their characteristics.** Common stock investments are usually classified according to broad categories related to cash flow, size, risk, and line of business. For example, a stock may be classified by its industry group (technology or retail), market capitalization (large-cap, mid-cap, or small-cap), method of compensating investors (income or growth), or sensi-

tivity to the business cycle (cyclical or defensive), or it may be classified as a blue chip stock.

3 **Describe how stocks are bought and sold.** Buying or selling stocks in the secondary market requires the services of a brokerage firm, for which you'll usually pay a commission. Full-service brokers charge higher fees than discount brokers. After you've determined what you want to buy and what price you're willing to pay, you can place your order with a broker, who will implement the transaction at the exchange or through a dealer in the over-the-counter market.

4 **Understand how the regulation of securities markets is beneficial to investors.** The securities market in the United States is highly regulated. The existing laws protect investors by requiring extensive information disclosure, prohibiting fraud in securities transactions, and providing for the licensing of investment professionals and insurance for brokerage accounts.

5 **Analyze investment alternatives and evaluate portfolio performance.** Selection of individual stocks for your portfolio requires that you estimate expected return and risk to be sure that the investment is consistent with your investment objectives and risk tolerance. When you take greater risk, you expect to earn a higher return in the long run, but your returns may be much more variable in the short run. Stock investors should keep good records for tax purposes so that they can track their portfolio returns. Stock indexes, such as the Dow Jones Industrial Average and the S&P 500 Index, can be used as benchmarks for portfolio performance.

6 **Identify sources of information for stock investors.** The financial press and financial websites are readily available and reliable sources for information about general economic conditions, as well as industry and individual company information. More detailed company information can be obtained from corporate annual reports, 10-K filings, and investment services.

Key Terms

ask price (389)
beta (403)
bid price (389)
blue chip stock (390)
brokerage account (394)
buying on margin (394)
capital gains yield (400)
churning (395)
circuit breaker rules (399)
close price (392)
corporation (381)
cyclical stock (390)
day trader (396)
defensive stock (390)
discount brokers (394)
dividend yield (400)
earnings per share (EPS) (400)
full-service brokers (394)
growth stock (390)
income stock (389)
initial public offering (IPO) (386)
insider trading (397)
large-cap (391)
limit order (393)
limited liability (382)
listed security (388)
margin call (395)
market capitalization (391)
market order (393)
mid-cap (391)
NASDAQ (389)
over-the-counter (OTC) market (388)
preemptive right (382)
price-to-earnings (P/E) ratio (400)
primary market (386)
prospectus (387)
proxy (382)
residual claim (381)
round lot (393)
seat on the exchange (389)
secondary market (386)
securities exchange (388)
selling short (393)
small-cap (391)
specialist (389)
stockbroker (394)
stock dividend (382)
stock market index (405)
stop order (393)
tombstone ad (387)

Key Calculations

Market capitalization = Current market price × Number of shares outstanding.

$$\text{Dividend yield} = \frac{\text{Annual dividend}}{\text{Market price of stock}}$$

$$\text{Capital gains yield} = \frac{\text{Annual change in price}}{\text{Market price of stock}}$$

$$\text{Discounted Dividend Model:} = \frac{D \times (1 + g)}{r - g}$$

$$\text{Earnings per share (EPS)} = \frac{\text{After-tax net income}}{\text{Number of shares outstanding}}$$

$$\text{Price-to-earnings ratio (P/E)} = \frac{\text{Price per share}}{\text{Earnings per share}}$$

Concept Review Questions

1. What is common stock, and why do corporations issue it?
2. What kind of ownership interest do common stockholders have? What rights does a stockholder have?
3. Explain the difference between a stock dividend and a cash dividend. Which type is preferable?
4. What is a stock split, and why would a company take this action?
5. Summarize the advantages and disadvantages of common stock investing.
6. What is the difference between market risk and company-specific risk? Which type should diversified investors be more concerned with?
7. What is the difference between the primary market and the secondary market? Which one are you more likely to transact business in?
8. What is an initial public offering?
9. How do organized exchanges differ from the over-the-counter market? How do the firms that trade in these markets differ?
10. Identify the major U.S. securities exchanges.
11. Identify the steps you would take to make a stock purchase.
12. What is the difference between a bid and an ask price?
13. Define the following pairs of terms:
    a. Income versus growth
    b. Cyclical versus defensive
    c. Large-cap versus small-cap
14. What is a blue chip stock, and why is it considered to be less risky than other classifications of stock?
15. Under what circumstances would you want to make a limit order? a stop order?
16. Under what circumstances will selling short generate a capital gain for an investor? In what ways is short selling a riskier strategy than taking a long position in a stock?
17. What is the difference between a full-service brokerage firm and a discount brokerage firm? Which one would you be more inclined to use, and why?
18. How can a margin account benefit a stock investor? What are the minimum margin requirements? Is a margin investor exposed to any additional risk? Explain.
19. Why is the securities market so heavily regulated? Has this always been the case?
20. What are the two primary areas of securities market regulation, and how does each of these help to level the playing field for individual investors?
21. Why is it illegal for insiders to trade on nonpublic information? When this happens, who is hurt? What are the penalties for those who are caught trading on insider information?
22. How does a circuit breaker work?
23. What are the components of stock return on investment, and how are they calculated?
24. Identify three ways of estimating expected return for individual stocks.
25. If a stock has a high P/E ratio, what does that tell you about the market's expectations for this company?
26. What is market risk, and how is it usually measured?
27. What is meant by time diversification? Does everyone agree on this issue? What is the opposing viewpoint?
28. What factors are considered in fundamental analysis? Will all investors who use this method come to the same conclusion about the value of a particular stock? Why or why not?
29. What is the basic premise of the discounted dividend model? What types of companies might this valuation method be best used for? Which types would it be less applicable to?
30. How can market averages and indexes be used in the investment process? Describe the most commonly used stock indexes.

Application Problems

1. ***Risk and Return.*** You are considering three potential stock investments. Stock L is a blue chip stock issued by a company with $8 billion in market capitalization. Its dividend yield has been about 6 percent per year for several years, but its price hasn't appreciated much. It has a P/E ratio of 8. Stock M has a $1 billion market cap, pays a very small dividend, and has seen an average annual price appreciation of 15 percent over the last several years. Its P/E ratio is 14. Stock S has a $500 million market cap and pays no dividend. Although it has yet to show a profit since it went public three years ago, its price has increased 25 percent per year in each of the last two years.
    a. Classify each of the companies according to market capitalization.
    b. Classify each of the companies as income or growth, if applicable.
    c. If you're an aggressive stock investor, which stock would be most appropriate for you and why?
    d. If you're a conservative stock investor, which stock would be most appropriate for you and why?
    e. If you have a five-year time horizon for achieving your investment objectives, would any of these investments be appropriate? Explain.
2. ***Classify Stocks.*** For each of the following companies, identify what classifications might apply to its stock. If you don't have sufficient information about the company, check the company website for more details. (Ticker symbols appear in parentheses.)
    a. KMart (KMRT)
    b. Intel (INTC)
    c. General Motors (GM)
    d. Level 3 Communications (LVLT)
3. ***Stock Split.*** You bought 150 shares of ABC Corporation stock at $70 per share. When the stock price rose to $90 per share, the company management announced a three-for-one stock split.
    a. How many shares will you now own?
    b. What will the price per share be immediately after the split?
    c. If investors view the split as positive information, what do you expect will happen to the value of your shares?
4. ***Margin.*** Marian is buying $3,000 in stock and holding it for one year. Ignoring transaction costs, what will her return on investment be in each of the following scenarios:
    a. She pays $50 per share in cash, receives no dividend, and sells the shares for $55 per share one year later.
    b. She pays $50 per share, with 45 percent margin, and sells the shares for $55 per share one year later.

5. ***Types of Orders.*** The current price of a stock is $25 per share. You place a buy order for 100 shares with a discount broker who charges $20 per transaction. By the time the order can be implemented, the price has risen to $25.50. How much will you pay per share, including any commission charge, if your order was:
   a. A market order
   b. A limit order at $25.75
   c. A limit order at $25.25
6. ***Ratios.*** A stock is currently selling for $30, an increase of $3 for the year, and there are 1 million shares outstanding. The company recently reported after-tax net income of $2 million. The dividend per share is $1.
   a. What is the company's earnings per share?
   b. What is its P/E ratio?
   c. What is the dividend yield to investors over the last year?
   d. If you bought the stock one year ago, what was your total rate of return for the year?
7. ***Market Risk.*** You have the following information about several potential stock investments:

Company	Beta
Vixen Inc.	2.5
Denicorp	1.2
Ferengi Oil	0.8
Luke Enterprises	0.5
S&P 500	1.0

   a. Which of these stocks has the most market risk, and which has the least?
   b. If the S&P 500 increased by 10 percent, what change would you expect for Vixen Inc.?
   c. If the S&P 500 decreased by 10 percent, what change would you expect for Luke Enterprises?
   d. If you held equal proportions of your portfolio in each of the stocks, what would the beta of your portfolio be?
8. ***Dividends.*** You own 400 shares of a blue chip company's stock, which currently is worth $65 per share. The company pays a quarterly dividend of $0.90 for a total of $3.60 per year.
   a. How much will your dividend check be this quarter?
   b. What tax rate will be applicable to this dividend if the stock is held in a taxable account and you're in the 15 percent federal income tax bracket?
   c. What is the dividend yield on this stock (pretax)?
9. ***Locking in Profits.*** Ariel bought 100 shares of Puck Stores stock for $20 per share one year ago. She placed a limit order before the market opened to sell her stock at a price of $26 per share. The stock price at the market open was $25.50; it hit a high of $27 at around noon but was back down to $25.50 by the close.
   a. If the stock paid no dividends and her trading costs were $35 per transaction, what was Ariel's return on investment?
   b. If she had placed a market order instead, how much would she have sold her shares for and what would her return on investment be?

Using Web Resources for Financial Planning

1. ***Stock Screening.*** You can find out more about companies and their stock on the Money Central website, *www.moneycentral.msn.* Enter a company's ticker symbol and then try the following:
   a. Click on Snapshot for recent price information and a chart of historical prices.
   b. Click on Financial Results to find company's earnings information, growth rates, and financial ratios.
   c. Click on Company Report to find the company's beta.
2. ***Set Up a Play Money Stock Portfolio.*** Give yourself some play money and try your hand at stock investing at finance.yahoo.com.
   a. Decide on how you will diversify your stock portfolio across different classifications as discussed in this chapter (e.g., by industry, capitialization, risk). Start your account by selecting at least 10 stocks.
   b. Track your portfolio over several weeks. Compare your performance to that of a benchmark index over the same time period.
3. ***Find Out about Online Trading.*** Go to the website for E*Trade, one of the largest online brokerage firms, at *www.etrade.com.* Browse the site to find the answers to the following questions:
   a. What services does E*Trade offer to investors?
   b. What types of investor education can be obtained through E*Trade?
   c. What is the minimum amount required to open an account?
   d. What types of investments can be purchased through E*Trade?
   e. What other financial services does E*Trade offer?
4. ***Learn How to Read a Company Financial Report.*** Select a company that you would like to know more about and find its annual report on the Internet. Most large companies post these in the investor sections of their websites. Then go to the IBM investor website, *www.ibm.com/investor/financialguide*, and read the *Guide to Financials.* This report will explain how to get the most out of a company's annual report. Answer the following:
   a. What aspects of recent performance are highlighted in the report?
   b. Does the chief executive officer (CEO) make any unusual or interesting points in his or her letter to the shareholders? Does the letter hint at any negative news about the company's future performance?
   c. How did the company's financial performance compare to the previous year's performance?
5. ***Visit the New York Stock Exchange.*** Go to the New York Stock Exchange website at *www.nyse.com* . Click on "About the NYSE" to see its organization and "The Trading Floor" to learn about its operations.

Learning by Doing Solutions

LBD 12–1: 1. The demand for Anheuser-Busch's products may not be very sensitive to economic ups and downs.; 2. Dell's stock dropped dramatically over the last half of 2001, but Anheuser-Busch's fell only a little. Both were back up to their pre-September 11 levels by early 2002. The reason these stocks reacted differently to the terrorist attacks is probably because investors believed that the technology sector would be more adversely affected; 3. Although the Anheuser-Busch stock price showed an upward trend throughout the period, both companies showed steady price increases beginning in early 2003.

LBD 12–2: 1a. Microsoft: large-cap, technology, cyclical; b. JetBlue Airways: mid-cap, airline, cyclical; c. Longs Drug Stores: small-cap, retail, defensive; d. small- or micro-cap, hotel.

LBD 12–3: 1a. DEBS; b. 0.50 per share; c. $23.97, d. $27.01.

LBD 12–4: 1. First, you're betting against the general long-run upward trend in stock prices. Second, in the event that you're wrong, you must still make good on the transaction. If you're long and the price falls, you can simply hold on to your investment in the hope that it will recover, whereas losses on a short position must be realized; 2. You've borrowed $2,000 − $1,200 = $800 from the broker. If the stock price fell to $15, your margin would be (1,500 − 800)/1,500 = $46.7 percent so you wouldn't get a margin call.

LBD 12–5: 1. Seesaw is riskier. Its beta is significantly greater than 1; indicating high market risk, whereas Slowmo's beta is less than 1; 2a. Based on its past returns, Seesaw is probably a growth stock. b. The fact that it's a growth stock doesn't mean you'll always get higher returns with Seesaw. Over the long term, it has outperformed Slowmo, but in the past year, it did not; 3. Slowmo's P/E (12) is much lower than Seesaw's (45), indicating that the market doesn't think its prospects for growth are as good. Seesaw's high P/E may imply that it's overvalued at its current price.

Building Financial Planning Skills Through Case Applications

Case 12–1 Jeff Goldberg Considers Stock Investing

A recent college graduate, Jeff Goldberg, is currently working as an office supply store manager. He wants to save money for a down payment on a home in a few years, and he's heard that stock investing will help him build his investment faster. Jeff can invest about $3,000 at the end of each of the next three years, and he thinks he'll need to save $15,000 to $20,000 for the down payment. Jeff will hold this money in a taxable account, and his marginal tax rate is 15 percent.

a. If Jeff puts the money in a CD earning 5 percent per year, how much will he have after five years?

b. An investment advisor has suggested that Jeff can earn at least 10 percent per year in stocks. If he earns 10 percent, how much will he have after five years?

c. Would you advise Jeff to invest in stocks, given his investment objective and time horizon? Why or why not?

d. If he does decide to invest in stocks, what types of stocks would you recommend? Explain.

Case 12–2 The Morinis Evaluate Their Stock Portfolio Performance

One year ago, Joe and Marissa Morini made several large-cap stock investments. Their purchases included the following:

100 shares of Stock A at $26 (annual dividend $0.16)
100 shares of Stock B at $35 (annual dividend $0.60)
100 shares of Stock C at $40 (annual dividend $0.50)
100 shares of Stock D at $15 (no dividend)

The current stock prices are as follows: Stock A, $29; Stock B, $33; Stock C, $41; and Stock D, $18.

PFP Worksheet 46 Stock Tracker

a. Set up a portfolio-tracking worksheet for the Morinis. You can develop your own or use the one in your *Personal Financial Planner*.

b. Assuming that they used no margin and paid $25 per transaction, what was the total start-up cost for their investment portfolio?

c. What is the current value of the Morinis' portfolio?

d. Calculate the dividend yield and capital gains yield for each of these stocks, ignoring transaction costs.

e. Calculate the annual return on investment for the Morinis' investment portfolio.

f. Based on their stock selections, what index or market average would you recommend they use as a benchmark for their portfolio? Assuming that the market average return for the same period was 12 percent, how well did the Morinis do?

g. If the Morinis would like to add to their current stock portfolio, in what ways could they improve their diversification?

DEVELOPING PERSONAL FINANCIAL skills for life

Learning about Yourself

12–1. Attitudes Toward Stock Investing

Even though investment advisors commonly recommend that their clients invest at least some of their portfolio in equities, not everyone feels comfortable with the risk of stock investing. This assessment will help you determine whether you're psychologically ready to think about investing in stocks.

For each of the following statements, indicate the degree to which it is consistent with your viewpoint as follows: 5 = strongly agree; 4 = agree; 3 = neutral; 2 = disagree; 1 = strongly disagree.

1. I think that stock investing is a lot like casino gambling, since you risk losing all your money.
2. I'm not comfortable with making investments in risky assets like stocks that have a good chance of actually declining in value.
3. If any of my investments were losing money, I would have trouble sleeping at night.
4. I'd rather not invest in stocks because I don't have enough time to do the research it would require.
5. Although I know that stocks might give me a better return over the long term, I'm satisfied with obtaining a lower return if my investment is less risky.
6. I don't trust the managers of corporations to act in the best interest of their stockholders.
7. If I were to invest in stocks, I'd only consider those that paid generous dividends and have fairly stable prices.

Scoring:
Add up your total score. The higher your score, the less likely you are to consider stock investing at this point in your life. Keep in mind, however, that your attitudes are likely to change with your income and wealth. If you're currently a full-time student, you probably can't afford to risk what little you own.

Developing Your Skills

12–2. Matching Your Investments to Your Goals

As we've emphasized, your choice of investments should take into consideration your investment horizon. Since stock investing exposes you to greater short-term risk, it won't be an appropriate choice for many of your short- and intermediate-term financial goals. In Chapter 3, you developed a list of personal financial goals. For each of the goals you listed, explain why stock investing is or is not an appropriate strategy to use for achieving it. You can use the worksheet in your *Personal Financial Planner* for this purpose. If you haven't yet established any personal financial goals, you can complete the worksheet for the following hypothetical goals:

PFP Worksheet 45 Matching Goals and Investments

a. Save to go to graduate school in five years.
b. Build a college fund for your two-year-old daughter.
c. Fund your retirement in 40 years.
d. Establish an emergency fund.

12–3. Index Benchmarks

Using an Internet resource or a financial newspaper like the *Wall Street Journal*, look up the current value and the 52-week high and low for each of the following market indexes:

a. Dow Jones Industrial Average
b. S&P 500
c. NYSE Composite
d. NASDAQ Composite

THE NAVIGATOR

- ☐ Review Before Studying this Chapter list.
- ☐ Scan Learning Objectives.
- ☐ Take Myth or Fact quiz and find the answers throughout the chapter.
- ☐ Read chapter and answer Learning by Doing exercises.
- ☐ Review Key Terms and Key Calculations.
- ☐ Do end-of-chapter exercises.
- ☐ Take review quiz on the text website.
- ☐ Solve end-of-chapter cases.

[BEFORE] studying this chapter, you should review

- Time value of money calculations (Chapter 2).
- Calculation of annual percentage increase (Chapter 1).
- The differences between debt and equity investing (Chapter 11).
- The risk-return tradeoff (Chapter 11).

Investing in Bonds and Preferred Stocks

CHAPTER 13

Myth or Fact?

Consider each of the following statements and decide whether it is a *myth* or a *fact*. Look for the answers in the *Fact* boxes in the chapter.

	MYTH	FACT
1. Young people should never invest in bonds because the returns are too low.	☐	☐
2. Treasury bonds are issued by the U.S. government to finance the federal deficit.	☐	☐
3. Some state governments are raising money by selling bonds that will be paid back from legal settlements with tobacco companies.	☐	☐
4. Although you don't get as high a rate of return on bonds, at least you can't lose the principal you've invested.	☐	☐
5. When the stock market is down, people tend to move their money to fixed-income securities.	☐	☐

LEARNING objectives

1. Know the basic terminology used by bond investors.
2. Classify bonds according to their characteristics.
3. Analyze bond investment alternatives and evaluate performance.
4. Explain how the features of preferred stocks are similar to those of both common stocks and bonds.
5. Identify sources of information for investors in bonds and preferred stocks.

...applying the planning process

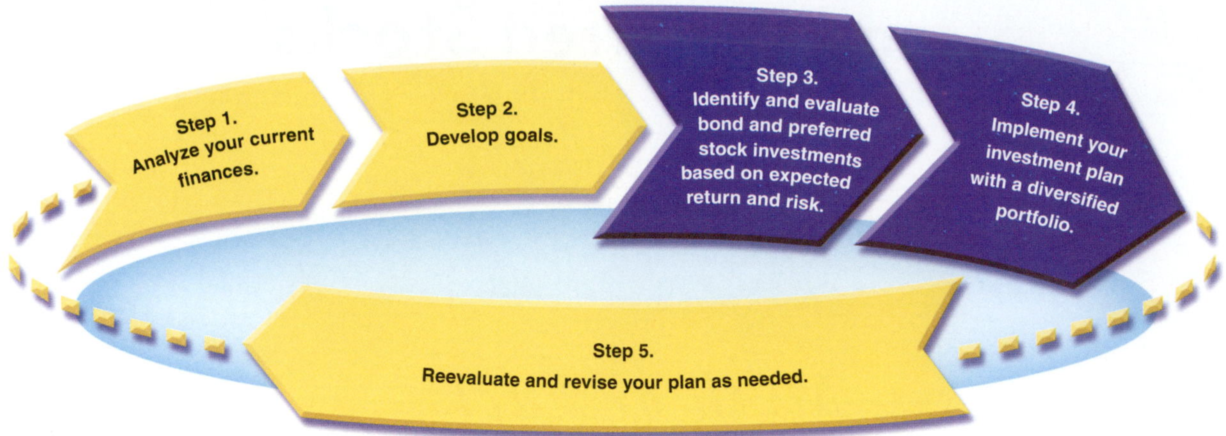

Chapters 11 and 12 emphasized the relationship between risk and return and suggested that you diversify across asset classes and consider investing at least some of your portfolio in stocks if your risk preferences and investment time horizon permit. Most investors should also have some of their portfolio invested in fixed-income securities such as bonds and shares of preferred stock. These asset classes will increase the diversification of your portfolio and are generally less risky than common stock. For some investors—retirees in particular—the fixed payment stream that bonds and preferred stock offer may be desirable as a means of meeting income needs.

You may find that bonds are somewhat easier to understand than stocks, since estimating the present value of a fixed set of cash flows using time value of money principles is a fairly straightforward task. At least for bonds issued by creditworthy entities, the uncertainty surrounding these cash flows is generally minimal and predictable.

In this chapter, you'll learn the terminology used by bond investors, the various types of bonds and their respective returns and risks, and the process of buying and selling bonds. We'll also look more carefully at preferred stock, which is like a cross between bonds and common stock. Since most government entities and corporations have fixed-income securities outstanding, you have many to choose from, so it's useful to know how to look up current prices and where to obtain the information necessary to choose among your alternatives. The chapter concludes with this information.

Chapter Preview

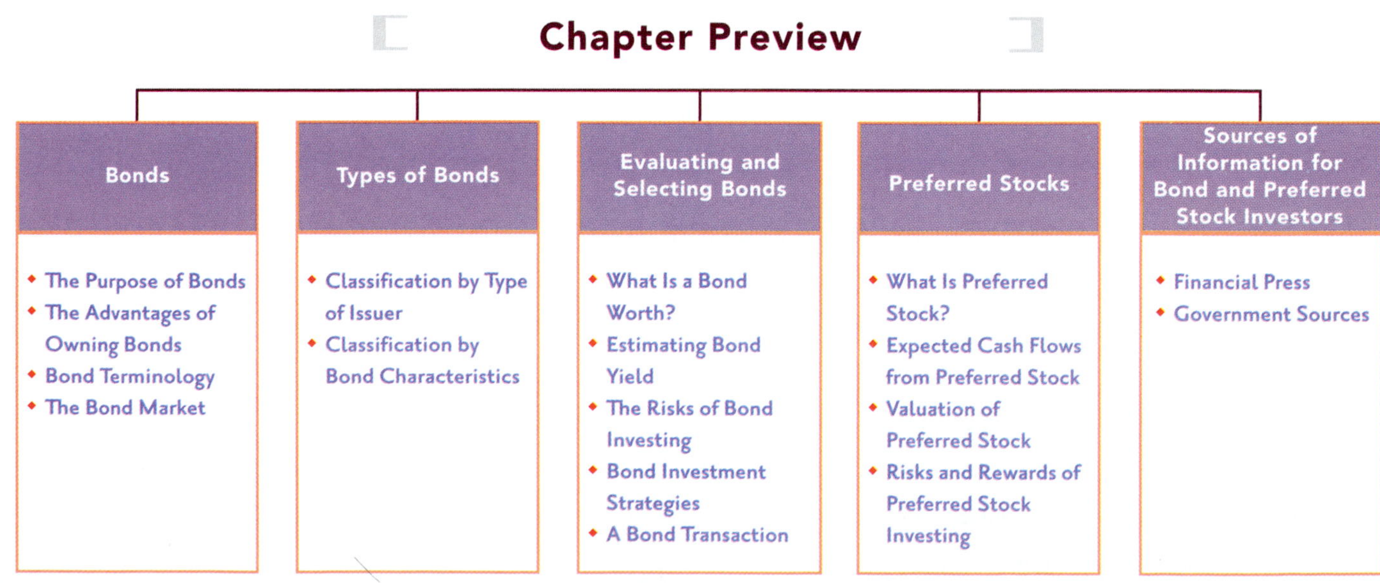

Bonds

LEARNING objective

 Know the basic terminology used by bond investors.

Chapter 11 introduced the choice between investing as a lender and as an owner. When you buy stock in a company, you're an owner; when you buy bonds, you're a lender. A bond is a type of financial security that represents your long-term loan of money to a company or governmental entity and gives you the right to receive interest payments and to have your loan repaid in the future. To understand whether bonds fit in your investment plan, you need to know more about the cash flows, risks, and tax implications of investing in bonds. In this section, we begin by considering why bonds are issued in the first place, since the motivations of the issuers have an impact on the returns to investors and the differences in risk between bonds and stocks. Then we focus on the basic terminology used by bond investors.

The Purpose of Bonds

In general, an organization seeks outside investors when it doesn't have enough current cash flow to support its needs. A business firm may need cash because it's growing rapidly or its revenue is insufficient to cover its costs. Similarly, a government entity—federal, state, city, or municipal—may need money to pay for a large construction project or to cover budgeted costs that exceed tax revenues collected. Borrowing money to spread the cost of a large expenditure over time is sometimes a good financial strategy, whereas using long-term borrowing to fund budget shortfalls will most likely cause future financial difficulties. Therefore, businesses and government entities almost always use long-term bond issues to fund projects that they expect to have a long-term payoff. If they need funds for only a short time, they're likely to issue short-term debt or take out a short-term bank loan instead.

You may wonder why organizations choose to borrow instead of selling stock. With government entities, of course, there isn't really a choice; these organizations don't have the option of selling shares to the public. Other than raising taxes, federal, state, and local authorities have no alternative but to borrow the money. Since businesses do have an alternative, you might ask why they would ever issue bonds instead of stock, given that bondholders expect to receive regular payments of interest and to be paid back when their bonds mature, whereas stockholders aren't entitled to dividends or repayment of their principal. The reasons are related to cost, taxes, control, and the benefits of financial leverage.

Cost. Debt is cheaper than equity. Although stockholders aren't entitled to a regular dividend, they still expect the firm's management to create value for them in the form of increased share price. Since they bear more risk than bondholders, equity investors expect to earn a higher rate of return. This puts greater pressure on management to generate profits and increase the value of the firm. In contrast, the company can afford to pay the bond interest even if it's only moderately profitable.

Another cost-related factor is the expense associated with the actual issuance of the bonds. Bonds are issued in significantly higher denominations (usually $1,000 each) than common and preferred stock, and they're often sold to a small number of large investors in the primary market. This makes a bond issue less costly to the firm (in advertising, legal, and accounting expenses) per dollar of capital raised than selling common stock to a large number of equity investors.

Taxes. Another reason that companies like to issue bonds stems from the tax treatment of the cash flows they pay to bond and stock investors. Interest payments are tax-deductible to the firm, and dividend payments are not. Therefore, the after-tax cost of bond interest payments, particularly for highly creditworthy companies, is fairly low. If, for example, the company issues bonds that require 8 percent annual interest payments and the firm's marginal tax rate is 40 percent, then the after-tax cost is only $0.08 \times (1 - 0.40) = 0.048$, or 4.8 percent. Since equity costs are not tax-deductible to the firm, it bears the full cost.

Control. When a company sells additional shares of stock, the percentage ownership of existing shareholders is reduced. If current owners have any influence over management (as when a small group of shareholders owns a large block of shares), these owners may be able to convince management not to dilute their ownership share. Issuing debt allows the company to raise the necessary funds for expansion without forcing current owners to give up any of their control.

Leverage. Stockholders also benefit from the effects of financial leverage associated with using borrowed funds. Debt improves the returns to existing shareholders. That is, if a company can borrow money at a low rate and earn a higher rate of return, the profit accrues to the residual owners—the shareholders. So as long as debt is relatively cheap, then, it benefits the owners. Chapter 8 introduced the benefits that leverage can have on your personal finances. If you buy a home and finance 80 percent of the cost with a home mortgage, the increase in the value of your home over time accrues entirely to you—you don't have to share the capital gain with the mortgage lender. This substantially increases your return on the small investment of your down payment. The same is true for business firms, although they generally are not as highly leveraged as homeowners. On average, firms finance less than one-third of their assets with debt.

The Advantages of Owning Bonds

Even if it makes sense for corporations and government entities to sell bonds, there wouldn't be a market for these securities unless investors were willing to buy them. As we've seen, bonds generally provide a lower rate of return to investors over time than stocks. Despite this, fixed-income securities make up a substantial proportion of individual investors' portfolios. There are five primary reasons individual investors buy bonds:

- They want to diversify their portfolios.
- They need a regular source of predictable income.
- They hope to profit from future increases in the value of their bonds.
- They want to lower their risk.
- They want to match the term of their investment to their investment time horizon.

Diversification. As you know, you can dampen the effect of a downturn in the market for one asset class by having at least some of your portfolio in another asset class. Thus, in a stock market downturn, your bond income can help to offset your stock losses.

Predictable Source of Income. Some investors hold bonds because they need or want a steady stream of income. When you retire, for example, you could purchase long-term bonds and live off the interest. The interest payments are usually a fixed amount for the life of the bond, so you'll know with certainty how much income you'll be receiving.

Fact #1

Although the returns on bonds are lower than the returns on stock, financial advisors usually recommend that you have at least some of your portfolio in this asset class, even if you're young. The benefits of diversification outweigh the reduction in your portfolio return.

Profit on Price Changes. We saw in Chapter 11 that bond prices go up and down over time in response to changes in market interest rates—when interest rates go up, bond prices go down, and vice versa. If you're a buy-and-hold investor, this won't matter to you, since you'll be holding the bond to maturity and you know you'll receive the face value at that time. If you need to sell a bond before its maturity date, however, you may find that the market price is more (or less) than what you paid for it, resulting in a capital gain (or a capital loss). Active bond investors attempt to buy bonds in anticipation of interest rate declines, hoping to make gains on future increases in price. Alternatively, when they think rates will be rising, they might sell bonds short in anticipation of price declines. In order for these investment strategies to work, an investor's return must be enough to offset his or her trading costs; and of course, the investor must be able to correctly anticipate market interest rate changes in advance of the rest of the market. As we've discussed, market efficiency implies that this isn't as easy as it sounds.

Lower Risk. If you've assessed your risk tolerance and find that you prefer to bear less risk, even though it may mean receiving a lower return, you may prefer bond investing to stock investing. When you buy a bond from a creditworthy company, you know that you'll most likely receive your promised interest payments and that your principal will be repaid at maturity. For many investors, this level of certainty is more important than the uncertain possibility of greater returns from a risky stock.

Matching Time Horizon. Since bonds have a fixed maturity date, some investors like them because they can match the time horizon of their investment with their future needs for the funds. Similarly, the fixed period of interest payments may be consistent with an investor's income needs. For example, a retired couple might buy 20-year bonds so that they will have 20 years of interest income during their retirement period.

Bond Terminology

As in other areas of investing, you'll need to master a few specific terms to understand bonds and bond investing. In discussing bond terminology, we'll refer to the advertisement for a new bond issue that's shown in Exhibit 13–1. In this advertisement, Cavalier Corporation is telling potential investors that it's interested in raising $10 million by selling bonds to the public. The firm may need this money to finance an anticipated expansion or to purchase needed assets. In return for lending Cavalier the money, investors will be paid 7.2 percent interest per year through 2024.

Prospectus. As with new stock issues, a bond issuer must provide all prospective investors with the pertinent information about the company and the security in a document called a *prospectus.* If you were interested in a particular company's bonds, you'd probably want to know, for example, what the company's primary business is, how the funds raised by the bond issue will be used, the financial strength of the issuer, and how the company plans to make good on its promises to pay interest and to repay the principal at maturity. To learn more about the Cavalier bond issue, you could contact the management firm identified in the advertisement, and it would send you the required information.

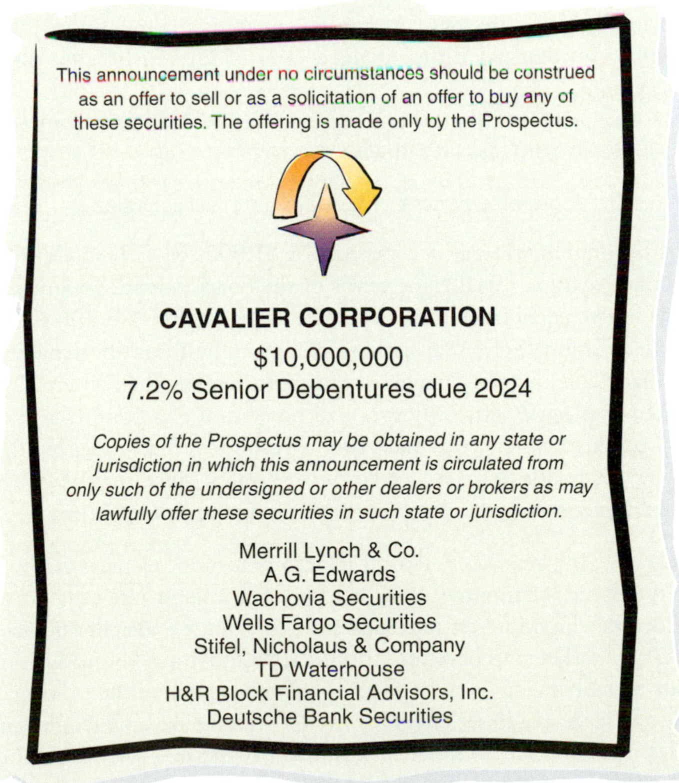

EXHIBIT 13-1

Advertisement for New Bond Issue by Cavalier Corporation

indenture
A legal document that details the rights and obligations of the bondholders and bond issuer.

trustee
The legal representative for the owners of a bond issue.

face value
The dollar amount the bondholder will receive at the bond's maturity date.

Indenture. The contract between a bondholder and the issuer of the bond is a legal document called an **indenture**. The indenture specifies all the important terms of the bond agreement, including the rights and obligations of the bondholders and the issuer. A **trustee**, usually a bank trust department, is assigned to keep an eye on the company, making sure that the bondholders' rights are protected. If, for example, the trustee finds that the company has violated a promise specified in the indenture, it can bring a legal action on behalf of all the bondholders to force the company to remedy the situation.

Face Value. The **face value** or *par value* of a bond is the amount that will be repaid to the bondholder when the bond *matures*, or comes due. Corporate bonds are usually issued with a face value of $1,000, but the face value can be larger. If we assume that the Cavalier Corporation bonds have a face value of $1,000, and the company initially sells each bond for a price equal to the face value, it will need to sell 10,000 bonds to raise the $10 million it requires.

Unlike car loans and mortgages, bonds are not amortized. That means the issuer does not pay back any of the principal of the loan until the end, often 20 years or more from the date of issue. Over that period, the bonds will likely be traded in the secondary securities market, just as common stocks are. No matter what happens to the price of the bonds in the secondary market, however, the face value will remain at $1,000; whoever owns the bond on the maturity date will receive that amount.

maturity date
The date on which a bond comes due and the bond issuer must pay the face value to the bondholder.

Maturity Date. The **maturity date**, as just noted, is the date on which the bond comes due—when the issuer must repay the loan in full. Most corporate bonds are issued for 20- to 30-year terms. The maturity date for the Cavalier Corporation bonds is 2024. Since the bonds are being issued in 2004, they have a 20-year maturity. Government bonds also can have long terms but are issued for shorter periods as well, in which case they are usually called notes instead of bonds.

coupon rate
The annual rate of interest on a bond, quoted as a percent of the face value.

Coupon Rate and Payment. The **coupon rate** on a bond is the fixed rate of interest that the issuer will pay the holder of its bonds each year; it is quoted as a percentage of the face value. The Cavalier Corporation is offering to pay 7.2 percent on its bonds. The coupon rate is determined when the bond is issued based on prevailing market rates for similar bonds. Thus, when market interest rates are relatively low, bonds will be issued with lower rates than when market rates are high. At any given time, a company may have several outstanding issues of bonds that pay different fixed rates of interest because they were issued at different points in time.

coupon payment
The annual dollar interest payment on a bond, equal to the coupon rate times the face value, usually paid to investors in two equal installments.

Knowing the face value and the coupon rate, we can calculate the **coupon payment**—the dollar payment of interest per year—as follows:

$$\text{Coupon payment} = \text{Coupon rate} \times \text{Face value}$$

Thus, Cavalier Corporation will pay 7.2 percent of $1,000, or $72, interest per year on each bond until the bonds mature. Usually, the terms of the bond indenture require that the interest payment be made in two equal installments over the year—in this case, $36 every 6 months.

The term *coupon* originates from an earlier time, when bond certificates actually had tear-off coupons on the back and investors mailed them in to request their interest payments. These bonds were called *bearer bonds*, since whoever had possession of a bond (the "bearer") could request the coupon payment when it was due. Although some of these older bonds are still in existence, buyers of newer bonds don't even receive certificates, since their contact information is kept electronically. Nevertheless, the "coupon" terminology continues in use.

call provision
A contract term that allows a bond issuer to buy back a bond issue before the maturity date.

Call Provisions. In some cases, a bond issuer might want to repay the loan early. For example, suppose the issuer is currently paying a high fixed interest rate on a bond issue (because the bond was issued in a high-interest-rate environment), but the current rate on similar bonds is much lower (because market rates have since declined). Clearly, the company could save costs on interest payments by refinancing—just as when homeowners reduce their mortgage payments by refinancing their mortgage at a lower rate. However, a bond issuer can't require an investor to sell back a bond unless the bond indenture includes a **call provision**—a contractual term that allows early repayment, often at a slight premium over the face value.

Because callable bonds are better for the company, most corporate bonds have call provisions, although some may include restrictions on the company's right to call—for example, specifying that a call can take place no sooner than five years after initial issuance. The call provisions also specify the price that the company will pay the investor to call the bond—an amount greater than the face value.

Generally, investors aren't very happy when a company exercises its call rights—it usually means they'll no longer be earning a rate of interest higher than the going rate. Suppose, for example, that you're a retiree on a fixed income. You have some bonds that are paying you 12 percent interest per year, or $120 each. Since the time you bought the bonds, interest rates on similar securities have fallen to around 9 percent. If your bonds are called because of the drop in interest rates, you'll be able to reinvest the money in new bonds, but the coupon rate on the new bonds will reflect the lower interest rate—and so will your income. Instead of $120 per bond, you'll only be earning $90 per bond, a reduction of 25 percent in income.

Sinking Funds. When the Cavalier bonds come due in 2024, the company will be obliged to repay the $10 million it borrowed from the bondholders. Although the company may be able to issue new bonds at that time to pay off the old ones, it's hard to tell right now if it will be in good enough financial shape to be able to do so. Since it's unlikely that a firm will have enough to pay the bondholders back out of its annual cash flow in the year of maturity, many bond indentures include provisions that require the company to establish a **sinking fund**, a pool of funds set aside to pay future bond obligations. The company regularly adds money to the fund and may use the fund not only to pay the bonds' face value when they come due or are called but also to regularly buy back bonds in the secondary market, so that fewer bonds will be outstanding when the issue reaches maturity. The existence of a sinking fund reduces the risk of future defaults for investors.

sinking fund

A fund accumulated to pay an amount due at a specific time in the future, such as when a bond issue comes due.

Convertibility. Some bond issues include a special provision that allows the bondholders to convert the bonds to shares of common stock in the future. The contract will say how many shares a bondholder can get for each bond. For example, suppose you hold one of the Cavalier bonds, with a face value of $1,000, and the bond is convertible to 50 shares of Cavalier stock. If Cavalier stock is currently valued at $10, you wouldn't want to convert at the moment, since you'd give up a $1,000 bond for only $500 in stock. But if the stock price later rises to more than $20, you might want to convert. Since convertibility is an attractive feature, a convertible bond will usually pay a coupon rate that's one to two percentage points lower than a comparable non-convertible bond. This reduced income potential is somewhat offset by the greater potential for capital gains—when the stock price rises, the market value of the convertible bond will also rise.

The Bond Market

The bond market is very similar to the stock market, which was discussed in Chapter 12. As with stocks and other securities, new bond issues require registration with the Securities and Exchange Commission. The issuers originally sell their bonds in the primary market, and then investors trade their bonds in the secondary market, both at organized exchanges and, more commonly, over the counter through bond dealers. The biggest difference between the stock and bond markets has to do with volume—the number of trades per day. Other than Treasury securities, which have a fairly active market, bonds tend to be buy-and-hold investments, so trading can be quite "thin." This means that bond investors are exposed to greater liquidity risk than stock investors, since they may not be able to find a buyer or seller to trade with at a particular time.

Learning by Doing 13-1

1. The coupon rate on a corporate bond issue is 8.5 percent. If you own one bond with a face value of $1,000, how much interest will you receive every six months from this investment?
2. Suppose Cavalier Corporation has a sinking fund arrangement for paying back its bond issue. It exercises its call rights and pays bondholders out of the sinking fund. Explain how this is both good and bad for investors.

Types of Bonds

LEARNING objective

2 Classify bonds according to their characteristics.

Bonds are commonly classified according to the type of issuer and by certain characteristics of the bonds, such as collateral for the loan, if any, and risk. Some of these topics were briefly introduced in Chapter 11. Here, we examine your options for bond investing in more detail.

Classification by Type of Issuer

Bonds are issued by corporations and various government entities. Since these issuers have different prospects for the future and different sources of cash flow, their bond issues are distinctly different in risk characteristics.

Corporate Bonds. Corporate bonds are long-term, interest-bearing debt securities issued by a corporation to help finance its long-term assets or operations. They are usually issued in denominations of $1,000 and promise semiannual interest payments based on a fixed rate. Terms to maturity can vary from 5 to 30 years or more, with the most common maturities being 20 and 25 years. With so many corporations in existence, there are many corporate bonds to choose from, and these bonds can differ substantially in cash flows and risks. Bonds may also incorporate special features or contract terms that make them more or less valuable. For example, a corporate bond may include a call provision or convertibility feature. Although most bonds have fixed coupon rates, you'll sometimes see bonds with variable rates.

Fact #2

The federal government auctions Treasury bonds four times a year, in the first weeks of February, May, August, and November. The borrowed funds are used to supplement federal budget spending when tax revenues are insufficient. In recent years, the total amount of federal debt outstanding has been increasing rapidly, reaching $3.7 trillion in early 2004, and is expected to climb even further. Eventually, this debt will have to be repaid by future generations of taxpayers.

U.S. Treasury Bonds. The U.S. government regularly issues debt with various terms to maturity. We've previously considered Treasury bills, which have maturities of one year or less. Although T-bills may be an appropriate choice for funds you've allocated to short-term objectives, such as an emergency fund or money market account, the rate of return is too low to be an option for your intermediate- and long-term investment plan. In this section, therefore, we consider only Treasury notes and bonds. If the term is 10 years or less, the security is called a *Treasury note*; if the term is more than 10 years, it's a *Treasury bond*. Other than maturity, the only real difference between the two types of securities is that some older Treasury bonds are callable (at par value) during the last five years before maturity. More recent issues don't have a call provision.

The primary reason for the issuance of Treasury securities is that the federal government rarely, if ever, stays within its budget. When spending exceeds taxes collected, the government borrows the rest by issuing Treasuries. Individual investors can buy federal government debt issues directly from any Federal Reserve Bank, without paying a broker commission, in units of $1,000 each. We usually consider Treasury issues to be default-risk-free, since the federal government has the power to raise taxes to pay its obligations in the future. Some investors may also find Treasuries attractive because the interest paid on them, while federally taxable, is exempt from state and local income taxes. Because of the minimal risk and the tax benefits, the yield on this type of debt investment is lower than that on corporate bonds with similar maturities.

Budget surpluses in the 1990s led many to think that the federal government would issue far less debt in the future and perhaps even reduce the outstanding debt by using surpluses to pay down existing debt levels. However, the combined impact of the terrorist attacks of September 11, 2001, the costs of the war in Iraq, and tax cuts implemented by the Bush administration contributed to significant budget deficits, which required the issuance of more rather than less federal debt and resulted in an increase in the total federal debt.

For more information about buying Treasury issues, check the U.S. Treasury website at www.publicdebt.treas.gov.

Corporations often issue bonds to finance expansion and building projects.

Agency Issues. An **agency issue** is a bond issued by a federal agency, such as the Government National Mortgage Association (Ginnie Mae), the Federal National Mortgage Association (Fannie Mae), the Federal Home Loan Mortgage Corporation (Freddie Mac), or the Student Loan Marketing Association (Sallie Mae). These bond issues are generally backed by pools of mortgages or, in the case of Sallie Mae, by pools of student loans.

agency issue

Bond issued by a federal agency.

Each agency specializes in a particular segment of the market, buying particular types of loans from banks and savings institutions. It finances the cost of buying the loans by borrowing the money from bond investors, as illustrated in Exhibit 13–2. The agency can afford to make the interest payments to bond investors because it receives regular payments of interest and principal from the individuals who are making payments on their home mortgages or other loans.

Agency bonds are issued in large denominations (a minimum of $25,000) and bought primarily by large institutional investors, such as pension funds and insurance companies. Because of the large size of the required investment, most individual investors who are interested in this type of bond invest indirectly by purchasing shares in mutual funds that invest in agency bonds, an option we'll discuss in more detail in Chapter 14.

Although agency issues are considered virtually risk-free, they are not U.S. government obligations and thus have slightly higher risk than Treasury securities. As a result, they pay higher rates of interest as well. Maturities average around 15 years but can be as long as 40 years.

Municipal Bonds. A **municipal bond** is a long-term debt security issued by a state or local government entity. The money raised from a municipal bond offering might be earmarked to pay for airport construction, public schools, parks, infrastructure improvements (such as roads and bridges), or ongoing government expenditures. One of the most important features of municipal bond investments is that interest payments are exempt from federal income tax. If the investor lives in the state of issuance, they are usually exempt from state and local taxation as well.

municipal bond

Long-term debt security issued by a state or local government entity.

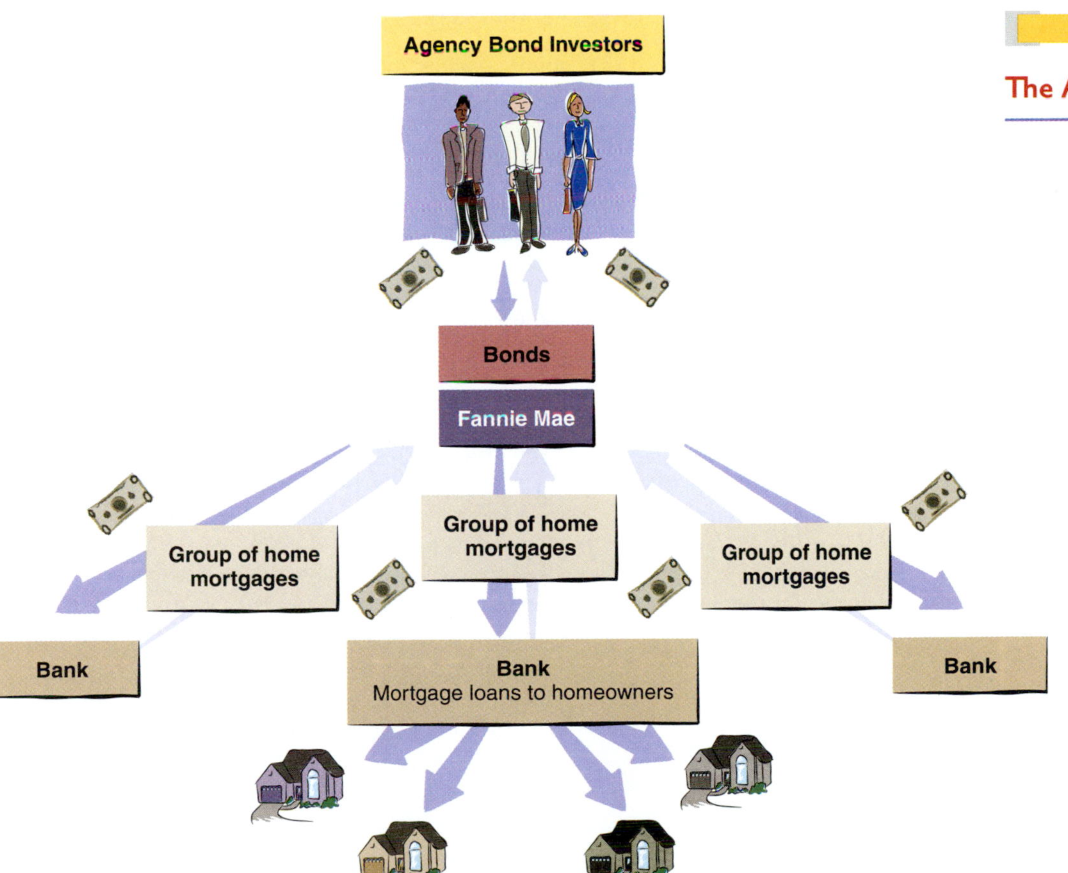

EXHIBIT 13-2

The Agency Bond Process

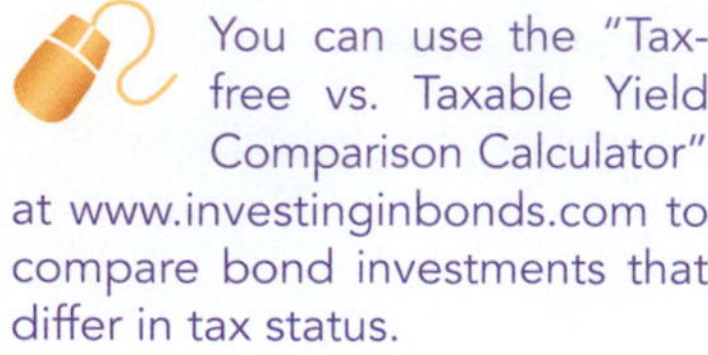
You can use the "Tax-free vs. Taxable Yield Comparison Calculator" at www.investinginbonds.com to compare bond investments that differ in tax status.

general obligation bond

Municipal bond that will be repaid from the operating cash flows of the issuing entity; backed only by the full faith and credit of the issuer.

revenue bond

Municipal bond that will be repaid from income generated by the project financed by the bond issue.

However, capital gains earned on the sale of a municipal bond are still subject to tax. The *Go Figure!* box, "Calculating After-Tax Yields on Different Types of Bonds," considers the financial impact of the differential tax treatment of federal, municipal, and corporate bond interest.

A "muni"—as a municipal bond is called for short—can be either a general obligation bond or revenue bond. If it's a **general obligation bond**, the interest and principal payments will come from the normal operating cash flows of the issuing entity, and the security for the bond is just the "full faith and credit" of that entity. Normally, general obligation bonds can only be issued by states, cities, and other entities that have taxing authority (the power to assess taxes on property, sales, or income). In contrast, a **revenue bond** will be repaid from the income generated by the project it is issued to finance. For example, for a bond issued to fund the building of a bridge, interest and principal repayments could be made from future tolls charged for the use of the bridge. In some cases, after the bond issue is repaid, the government may decide to keep the tolls in place to pay for ongoing repairs.

Municipal bonds can sometimes be fairly risky investments. State and local governments with serious budget problems may find it difficult to make good on their obligations. Sometimes, the projects financed by revenue bonds are subject to construction delays or fail to generate as much revenue as expected. The construction of the Denver International Airport, for example, was partially financed by a municipal bond issue. As the airport neared completion, problems associated with its state-of-the-art baggage-handling system caused bond-rating agencies to sharply downgrade the bonds to reflect a higher risk of default. Since the bonds had been paying a rate of interest appropriate for a lower rate of risk, the increased risk caused the bond prices to fall dramatically in the secondary market.

GO FIGURE!

Calculating After-Tax Yields on Different Types of Bonds

Problem: Katerina wants to buy bonds but isn't sure which type will give her the best after-tax income. She'll be holding the bonds in a taxable account, and her marginal tax rate is 15 percent (10% federal and 5% state). She has the following two choices:

Type of Bond	Term to Maturity	Current Price	Coupon
AAA-rated corporate bond	20 years	\$786.45	Coupon rate = 5% Semiannual coupon = \$50/2
AAA-rated municipal bond (issued by her state)	20 years	\$1,000.00	Coupon rate = 5% Semiannual coupon = \$50/2

Solution: The first step is to calculate the before-tax yield to maturity for these bonds. Katerina applies time value of money principles to solve for the yield. For the corporate bond, she enters in her financial calculator $N = 20 \times 2 = 40$, $PV = -786.45$, $PMT = 25$, and $FV = 1{,}000$ and then solves for the semiannual yield, $I = 3.5$. She multiplies by 2 to get the before-tax annual yield of 7 percent. For the municipal bond, she enters $N = 40$, $PV = -1{,}000$, $PMT = 25$, and $FV = 1{,}000$, and solves for the semiannual yield $I = 2.5$. So, the before-tax yield is $2.5 \times 2 = 5.0\%$.

Next, Katerina calculates her after-tax yield to maturity for each investment as follows:

$$\text{After-tax interest yield} = \text{Before-tax interest yield} \times (1 - T)$$

where T = applicable marginal tax rate.

- *Corporate bond.* Since the bond is fully taxable, her after-tax yield is $7.0\% \times (1 - 0.85) = 5.95\%$.
- *Municipal bond.* Because municipal bond interest income is exempt from federal and state tax (for state residents), Katerina won't have to pay any tax, so her after-tax yield will be the same as her before-tax yield: 5%.

Katerina finds that, because she has a fairly low marginal tax rate, the bonds that offer tax-exempt interest are not as beneficial for her. She decides to invest in the corporate bond.

Default rates have generally been higher on revenue bonds than general obligation bonds. To reduce this risk, investors can purchase insured municipal bonds, but these bonds pay a lower rate of interest to balance the cost of the insurance and the reduced risk of default. Remember the general rule—lower risk, lower return. Like corporate bonds, municipal bonds may also have call provisions, but most are protected from early calls for the first five to ten years. Such call provisions still increase the reinvestment risk associated with these bonds.

Major municipal projects, such as the Denver International Airport, are often financed with bond issues.

Classification by Bond Characteristics

In addition to the major classifications based on type of issuer, bonds are sometimes classified into categories based on differences in specific characteristics that affect their return and risk.

Secured Versus Unsecured Bonds. Most corporate and government bonds are **debentures**, which is a legal term for unsecured bonds. When a bond issue is unsecured, the promise of payment of interest and principal in the future is backed only by the creditworthiness of the company or governmental body, which will presumably rely on regular cash flows to make the payments. In contrast, some bonds are secured. With a **secured bond**, the issuer has pledged specific assets or future cash flows as collateral. In the event of nonpayment, the bondholders, through their trustee, have the right to take the pledged assets in payment of the debt.

Although the existence of collateral for the loan can reduce the risk of default to bondholders, the amount of risk reduction (and consequent reduction in yield) depends on the value of the security and its resulting cash flows. For example, we've already seen that municipal bonds might be secured by future revenue from a particular project. If the project fails to generate the expected net revenue (either through insufficient gross revenue or greater-than-expected costs), then the bondholders are still exposed to default risk. Suppose, for example, that a city uses a bond issue to build a public aquarium, but it turns out that the planners had overestimated the number of annual visitors to the aquarium and underestimated the costs of running it. As a result, the city is losing money on the project and decides to close it down. The bond investors, unless they were insured, will be out of luck.

Examples of secured bonds include mortgage bonds, which are backed by real estate (much the same as a home mortgage), and equipment bonds, which are backed by valuable equipment or vehicles. In a recent innovation discussed in the *News You Can Use* box, "Investing in Your Favorite Rock Star," the assets backing the bond are future royalties from CD sales.

To find out more about how changes in default risk can impact your bond investments, read "What You Should Know about Bond Rating Changes" at www.investinginbonds.com.

debenture

Unsecured bonds.

secured bond

Bond for which interest and principal payments are backed by assets or future cash flows pledged as collateral.

NEWS you can use

Investing in Your Favorite Rock Star

A recent novelty in the bond market is the creation of bonds secured by the future royalties to be received from a musician's work. Holders of copyrights to songs and lyrics are normally entitled to be paid a royalty whenever those songs are played, the words are used by another, or the music is published in any venue. By contractual arrangement, this future stream of cash flows can be shared by a combination of parties, including the songwriter, the musician, the publisher, and the manager.

"the more popular an artist's music, the higher the demand for the bonds"

In the late 1990s, David Bowie issued $55 million in Bowie Bonds™—10-year notes paying 7.9 percent annual interest. The issue, backed by Bowie's future royalties, was designed to enable Bowie to get immediate compensation for his albums. This was followed quickly by issues from several other singers and songwriters, including Iron Maiden and James Brown. There isn't a large volume of trading in these securities, which increases their liquidity risk premium. Another factor to consider is that investors may buy these bonds for reasons other than simply investment return. As you might expect, the more popular an artist's music, the higher the demand for the bonds. This causes the price to be bid up, which tends to result in a lower yield to investors.

floating-rate bonds

Bonds whose interest payments are adjusted periodically according to current market interest rates.

indexed bond

Bond whose interest payments are adjusted periodically according to a market index.

Treasury Inflation Protected Securities (TIPs)

Federal government bonds that are adjusted for inflation.

zero-coupon bond

A bond that doesn't make interest payments but instead is discounted at the time of sale.

Coupon Arrangements. Bonds are also classified according to how interest is calculated and paid to investors. Although the most common arrangement is for bond coupon payments to be fixed until maturity and paid in semiannual installments, variations on this arrangement can be found. For example, with **floating-rate bonds**, interest payments are tied to current market interest rates and adjusted periodically, similar to an adjustable-rate mortgage. The issuer of floating-rate bonds gains the advantage of keeping the interest it pays on the bonds close to the market rate of interest. If rates go down, investors will get a lower coupon rate, but they also avoid the problems associated with having their bonds called.

A variation on the floating-rate bond is the **indexed bond**. Here, the interest rate is tied not to another interest rate but to a general price index or the price of a commodity or other market index. **Treasury Inflation Protected Securities (TIPs)**, discussed in the *Ask the Expert* box, "Here's an Investment TIP," protect investors from inflation by adjusting the face value of the bond.

A **zero-coupon bond** makes no coupon payments but instead is discounted at the time of sale. Thus, the price you pay for a zero-coupon bond with a face value of $1,000 will always be less than the $1,000 to be received at the maturity date. Your entire yield comes from the capital gain, the face value less the price you pay for the bond. The price is the discounted present value of the face value. Zero-coupon bonds are issued by both corporations and governments, with the U.S. Treasury being the primary issuer.

If you aren't interested in current income but have a specific investment goal in mind, such as paying for your child's education 18 years from now, it might appear that a zero-coupon bond would be an attractive investment. The major problem with these bonds, however, lies in their current federal income tax treatment. Even though you don't receive interest in the form of regular payments, the IRS considers the annual appreciation in the value of the bond to be "undistributed interest" and requires that you recognize it as taxable income each year.

To see how this would work, suppose you bought a 20-year zero-coupon bond, with a face value of $1,000, one year ago for $240. Today, it has 19 years to maturity, and its value is $258. The $18 increase in value will be taxable as interest income to you, even though you haven't actually received it. For this reason, these bonds are best held in tax-deferred accounts or by minor children who are subject to low tax rates.

Another disadvantage of zero-coupon bonds is that, since their only cash flow is the $1,000 to be received many years in the future, they expose investors to greater interest-rate risk than coupon bonds. Although an increase in interest rates will cause all bond prices to decline, the prices of zero-coupon bonds tend to experience larger declines as a percentage of value. Zeros also expose you to inflation risk if actual inflation turns out to be greater than what was expected at the time of issue. Nevertheless, zero-coupon bonds are very popular with buy-and-hold investors who plan to hold the bonds to maturity so they aren't concerned with interim swings in value.

Fact #3

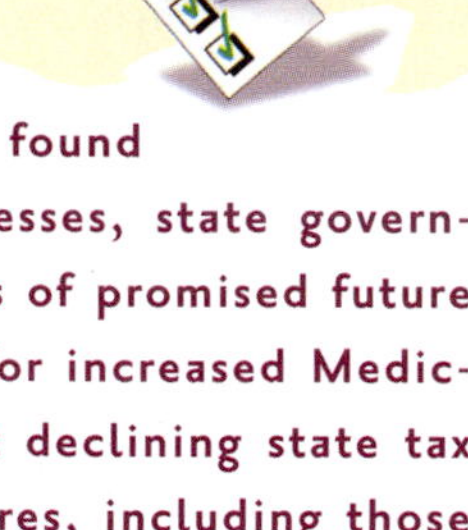

When tobacco companies were found liable for cigarette-related illnesses, state governments were the happy recipients of promised future payments to compensate them for increased Medicaid expenditures. To help offset declining state tax revenues, several state legislatures, including those in California and Colorado, proposed bond issues secured by the future tobacco settlement payments. If these bond issues are approved, they might solve short-term cash shortfalls for the states, but future generations of state taxpayers will have to foot the bill for the tobacco-related Medicaid costs, since the payments from Big Tobacco will be going to pay back the bondholders instead of into the state treasury.

Risk. Since default risk is so important to bond investors, bonds are often classified according to risk. Several rating agencies, including Moody's, Standard & Poor's, Duff & Phelps, and Fitch Investors Service, regularly evaluate large corporate and municipal bond issues and provide ratings based on risk. The two most popular rating systems—Moody's and Standard & Poor's—are described in Exhibit 13–3. Bonds rated Baa and above under the Moody's system and BBB and above in Standard & Poor's are called **investment-grade bonds**, whereas those with lower ratings are called **speculative-grade bonds**, or **junk bonds**. Since higher risk usually translates into higher returns, these bonds are also sometimes referred to as *high-yield bonds.* Certain financial institutions, such as pension funds and insurance companies, are heavily invested in bonds, but they're often required to hold only investment-grade bonds. For this reason, if a bond issue is downgraded to speculative grade, the value is likely to fall substantially as these investors sell their holdings to meet their investment requirements.

investment-grade bonds

Medium- and high-grade bonds with low risk of default on interest or principal.

speculative-grade bonds or **junk bonds**

Bonds with a high risk of default.

ask the expert Here's an Investment TIP

Dr. Zvi Bodie
Professor of Finance, Boston University
Author, Worry-Free Investing: A Safe Approach to Achieving Your Lifetime Financial Goals

If you want to earn a truly risk-free return, it's not enough to buy safe U.S. Treasury bonds or FDIC-insured CDs. You need an investment that also protects you against the risk of inflation. Zvi Bodie, the author of *Worry-Free Investing* (Prentice Hall, 2003), suggests that you consider buying U.S. government bonds that are linked to the CPI. These come in two forms: Series I savings bonds (I bonds for short) and Treasury Inflation Protected Securities (TIPS for short). These inflation-indexed bonds, which the Treasury started issung in 1997, guarantee a real rate of return. In the case of I bonds, the interest credited to your account consists of a stated real rate that remains fixed for 30 years plus the actual rate of inflation. No taxes are paid on the interest earned until the bonds are cashed in by the holder. In the case of TIPS, the face value of the bonds is adjusted for inflation, and the coupon payments and principal repayment are based on this inflation-adjusted value. For example, if your TIPS bonds offer a real 2.5 percent coupon rate, and inflation turns out to be 3 percent, the face value of the bond will increase with the inflation rate to $1,030, and your coupon payment will be 2.5 percent of the new $1,030 face value. If you're relying on the income from your bond portfolio to pay your regular expenses, the inflation adjustment will cause the cash flow from the bond to increase with the cost of goods so you never lose purchasing power. Unlike I bonds, the interest on TIPS is taxable on an annual basis unless held in a tax-advantaged account such as an IRA.

Until the 1980s, there were no new issues of junk bonds—the low-grade bonds outstanding were simply former stars that had seen better times. These "fallen angels" had low ratings but had not actually produced many serious defaults, an observation that gave Michael Milken, a trader with the investment firm Drexel Burnham Lambert, the idea to create a market for new issues of low-grade bonds. By matching medium-risk companies with investors who were interested in higher yields than they could get in the existing bond market, and by promising to buy back the bonds if investors wanted to sell them (essentially serving as an artificial secondary market), Drexel started a junk bond craze. Unfortunately, an increasing default rate, rising interest rates, and Milken's indictment on securities fraud charges caused junk bond investors to become nervous in the late 1980s. Drexel eventually declared bankruptcy in 1990 when it was unable to make good on its promise to buy back all

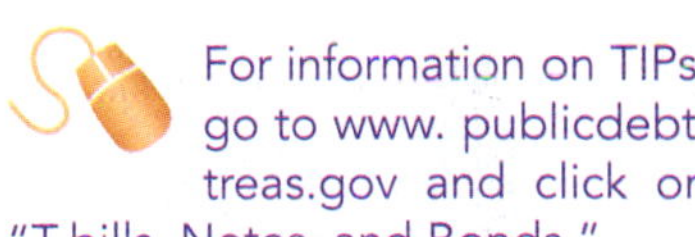
For information on TIPs, go to www. publicdebt. treas.gov and click on "T-bills, Notes, and Bonds."

EXHIBIT 13-3

Bond Ratings and Their Meaning

The ratings presented here are the primary ratings, but finer gradations are sometimes given by the suffixes 1, 2, 3 (Moody's) or + and – (Standard & Poor's).

General Rating	Moody's	Standard & Poor's	Explanation
Very high quality	Aaa Aa	AAA AA	High-grade bonds. Extremely strong or very strong capacity to pay interest and principal. Companies that have been profitable over the years and are unlikely to default.
High quality	A Baa	A BBB	Medium-grade bonds. Strong or adequate capacity to pay but can be susceptible to adverse economic conditions or changing circumstances.
Speculative	Ba B	BB	Low-grade bonds. Capacity to pay interest and repay principal is speculative. It may still have some good elements, but there is great uncertainty about the company's exposure to adverse conditions.
Very poor quality	Caa C	CCC D	These bonds pose the highest risk, and some may already be in default. C-rated bonds are income bonds that are no longer paying interest, and D-rated bonds are in default on interest and/or principal. There is little chance of recovery.

Michael Milken, the infamous junk bond trader, ended up in jail on charges of securities fraud.

the junk bonds that bondholders wanted to sell. Although this was a temporary setback in the development of the high-yield bond market, it wasn't the end of it. By the late 1990s, a true secondary market was in place. Nevertheless, these bonds are still substantially riskier than bonds issued by low-risk companies, not only because of the difference in default risk, but also because of liquidity. Junk bonds are much less actively traded and tend to be more sensitive to economic conditions.

Catastrophe Bonds. An interesting innovation in the bond market—although not a recommended choice for individual investors—is the catastrophe bond. These bonds, which are usually issued by insurance companies, give investors the opportunity to bet against the occurrence of a disaster, or catastrophe. The bonds pay interest and principal at a favorable rate as specified in the indenture *unless* a catastrophe of a certain size—measured by the issuing insurance company's losses in a given year or from a single event, such as a hurricane or earthquake—occurs. Depending on the terms of the bond, the investors might lose interest only or principal and interest. As a funding source for insurers, these bonds make sense, since the insurers can raise funds without obligating themselves to making costly interest payments in high-loss years. The bonds pay higher yields to compensate for the risk of losing future cash flows and for the low level of liquidity in the market, but are generally only appropriate for institutional investors who can better diversify this risk.

Learning by Doing 13-2

1. Indicate appropriate classifications for each of the following bonds:
   a. Bond issued by the state of Texas to finance construction of an interstate highway, with payments to be made from tolls
   b. Bond issued by a fairly young, high-growth technology company that pays interest at five percentage points over the 10-year Treasury bond yield

Evaluating and Selecting Bonds

LEARNING objective

3 Analyze bond investment alternatives and evaluate performance.

Now that you have a better idea of what your bond investment alternatives are, you're ready to think about selecting appropriate bonds for your portfolio. As noted, you'll probably do better to think of bonds as a buy-and-hold investment designed to provide diversification to your portfolio and a predictable rate of return. Nevertheless, as with all investments, you still need to keep track of the value of your holdings and consider buying additional bonds or selling those you currently own when it's advantageous to do so. This requires that you know how bonds are valued, what types of risks they expose you to, and how to access the information you need.

What Is a Bond Worth?

Before investing in bonds, you need to have a working understanding of the determinants of bond value. As already mentioned earlier in this chapter, the value of a bond (or, for that matter, any investment) is the discounted present value of the cash flows you'll receive. If you hold the bond to maturity, these are:

1. The fixed semiannual coupon interest payments
2. The repayment of the face value at the fixed maturity date

Using time value of money principles, we can calculate the value of a bond by breaking the problem into two parts: The coupon payments are an annuity, and the repayment of the face value at the end is a lump sum. You can therefore calculate the present value of the bond as

$$\begin{aligned}\text{Value of bond} &= \text{Present value of semiannual coupon interest payments}\\ &\quad + \text{Present value of repayment of face value at maturity}\\ &= \left(\frac{\text{Annual coupon payment}}{2} \times \text{PVIFA}_{i,n}\right) + \left(\text{Face value} \times \text{PVIF}_{i,n}\right)\end{aligned}$$

Recall from Chapter 2 that, since we have *semiannual* coupon interest payments, the number of periods n is the number of years times 2, and the interest rate i is the annual rate divided by 2. As in the case of stock valuation, the rate you should use in this calculation is the rate you could earn on alternative investments of similar risk (your opportunity cost or discount rate).

Let's consider an example to illustrate how you can use this formula. Suppose that a semiannual coupon bond has a face value of $1,000, a coupon rate of 8 percent, and 10 years to maturity. If similar bonds would currently provide you with an annual return of 6 percent, then the discount rate is 6 percent. Using the present value factor tables in the appendix (Exhibits A–2 and A–4), we can calculate the value of this bond as follows:

$$\begin{aligned}\text{Value of bond} &= (\$80/2 \times \text{PVIFA}_{3\%,20}) + (\$1{,}000 \times \text{PVIF}_{3\%,20}) \\ &= (\$40 \times 14.877) + (\$1{,}000 \times 0.554) \\ &= \$595.08 + \$554.00 = \$1{,}149.08\end{aligned}$$

Alternatively, you can use a financial calculator to solve this problem by entering the variables you know and solving for the one you don't know. With a calculator, you don't have to break up the problem into the annuity and lump-sum components but can solve both parts simultaneously. Enter: $N = 20$, $I = 6/2 = 3$, $PMT = (8\% \times 1{,}000)/2 = 40$, and $FV = 1{,}000$ and solve for PV. You should get an answer of $1,148.77 (slightly different due to the rounding of the table factors).

Estimating Bond Yield

Theoretically, the bond's present value is what an investor should be willing to pay for the bond. In practice, though, individual investors don't get to name their own price—they'll pay whatever the going rate is plus a mark-up for the dealer. So, it's actually more useful to think about evaluating bonds in terms of their expected **yield**, or return on investment. As you know, the return on a bond investment has two components—the return on investment that comes from receiving regular payments of interest, often called the *coupon yield* or *current yield*, and the capital gain (or loss) on the difference between the price you pay for the bond and the amount you get for it at maturity (or upon sale to another investor). This component is normally called the *capital gains yield*. You may recall from Chapter 12 that a stock investor's yield similarly comes from current yield (or dividend yield) and capital gains yield. If you buy a bond and plan to hold it to maturity, both of these components of yield are known with certainty at the outset, subject only to the risk of default by the issuer. In this section, we'll explain how to calculate the two components of yield and the total yield to maturity.

yield

Annual return on investment, including current yield and capital gains yield.

Current Yield.

The *current yield* is the component of total yield that is attributable to regular interest payments. It is usually stated as a percentage equal to the annual dollar amount of interest divided by the current price of the bond. Note that this rate is not the same as the coupon rate unless the bond is selling for the par value of $1,000, since the coupon rate is a percentage of the face value, whereas the current yield is a percentage of the current price.

To illustrate the calculation of current yield, let's suppose that a particular semiannual coupon bond is priced at $932 and has a face value of $1,000. The coupon rate is 7 percent, and there are 15 years to maturity. The current yield for the bond is calculated as follows:

$$\text{Current yield} = \frac{\text{Coupon}}{\text{Current price}} = \frac{\$70}{\$932} = 0.0751 \quad \text{or} \quad 7.51\%$$

Notice that in this case the current yield, 7.51 percent, is greater than the coupon rate, which is 7 percent. This situation occurs whenever market rates of interest rise so that the yield on similar securities is greater than the coupon rate. If a bond currently is selling for a premium (for more than its face value), then the current yield is less than the coupon rate.

Capital Gains Yield.

The second component of bond yield is the *capital gains yield*, or the percentage gain or loss in value over a particular period, such as a year. If you know the beginning and ending value, the capital gain or loss over that period can be calculated as follows:

$$\text{Capital gains yield} = \frac{\text{Ending price} - \text{Beginning price}}{\text{Beginning price}}$$

Returning to the example above, suppose you bought the bond for \$932 and sold it one year later for \$951. Your capital gains yield would be

$$\text{Capital gains yield} = \frac{\$951 - \$932}{\$932} = 0.0204 \quad \text{or} \quad 2.04\%$$

holding-period return

Return on investment over a particular period of time.

In this example, your total annual yield for the investment, including both the current yield (7.51%) and capital gains yield (2.04%), is 9.55 percent. This is known as a **holding-period return**, or the return on your original investment, given the cash flows that you receive during the holding period. Combining the equations for current and capital gains yield, we can calculate the holding-period return as follows:

$$\text{Holding-period return} = \frac{\text{Annual interest received} + \text{Ending price} - \text{Beginning price}}{\text{Beginning price}}$$

yield to maturity

Annualized return on a bond, if it is held to maturity and all interest payments are reinvested at the same rate.

Yield to Maturity. Long-term investors more often evaluate their bond investments using **yield to maturity (YTM)**, which is the annualized yield you get if you hold a bond to maturity, receive all promised cash flows from the date of purchase, and reinvest annual payments at the same rate. In the simplest case, where you pay exactly the face value for a bond, the yield to maturity will be the same as the coupon rate. Since there is no difference between the \$1,000 you pay at the beginning and the \$1,000 you receive at the end, your only income is the annual interest received. Therefore, your total yield is the current yield. However, if you don't pay face value for the bond, the yield to maturity will include any change in price (which can be a loss or gain) between the time you buy the bond and the maturity date. Thus, your yield to maturity will be the coupon yield plus the annualized capital gains yield. You can approximate the yield to maturity using the following equation:

$$\text{Approximate YTM} \approx \frac{\text{Annual coupon payment} + \dfrac{\text{Face value} - \text{Price}}{\text{Years to maturity}}}{\dfrac{\text{Face value} + \text{Price}}{2}}$$

For the example above, the approximate yield to maturity at the time you bought the bond for \$932 would be calculated as follows:

$$\text{Approximate YTM} \approx \frac{70 + \dfrac{1{,}000 - 932}{15}}{\dfrac{1{,}000 + 932}{2}} = \frac{70 + 4.53}{966} = 0.0772 \quad \text{or} \quad 7.72\%$$

Alternatively, you can use a financial calculator to determine the yield to maturity more precisely. As with the time value calculations in Chapter 2, we simply enter the information we know about the bond and solve for what we don't know, using the time value keys. In this case, we enter: N = number of semiannual payments = 2 × 15 = 30, PV = price paid for the bond = −932, PMT = semiannual coupon payment = (7% × 1,000)/2 = 35, and FV = 1,000 and solve for the semiannual yield I = 3.89. Multiplying by 2 gives the annual yield to maturity of 7.78%, just a little more than the value we obtained using the approximation formula.

This means that, if you invest in this bond at its current price and hold it to maturity, you'll earn an average annualized return of 7.78 percent on your \$932 investment. Recall that 70/932, or 7.51 percent, is the bond's current yield; thus, the remaining 0.37 percent is annual capital gains yield. Notice that most of your return is in the form of income; in contrast, with a common stock investment, you'd expect to get most of your return in the form of a capital gain since dividend yields tend to be relatively small.

To find the latest average yields on bond indexes, go to the Dow Jones Indexes website at averages.dowjones.com and click on "Corporate Bond."

Historical Yields on Bonds. What yield to maturity should you expect to earn on bond investments over time? Despite the general misconception that bonds are safe, their yields aren't constant. Yields tend to track fairly closely with market interest rates, which vary over time with general economic conditions. Exhibit 13–4 shows the average yields on Aaa corporate bonds compared with Treasury bond and bill yields over the last decade. The differences in yield between bond investment alternatives and over time are driven by what investors require from issuers to compensate them for risk, as discussed in the next section.

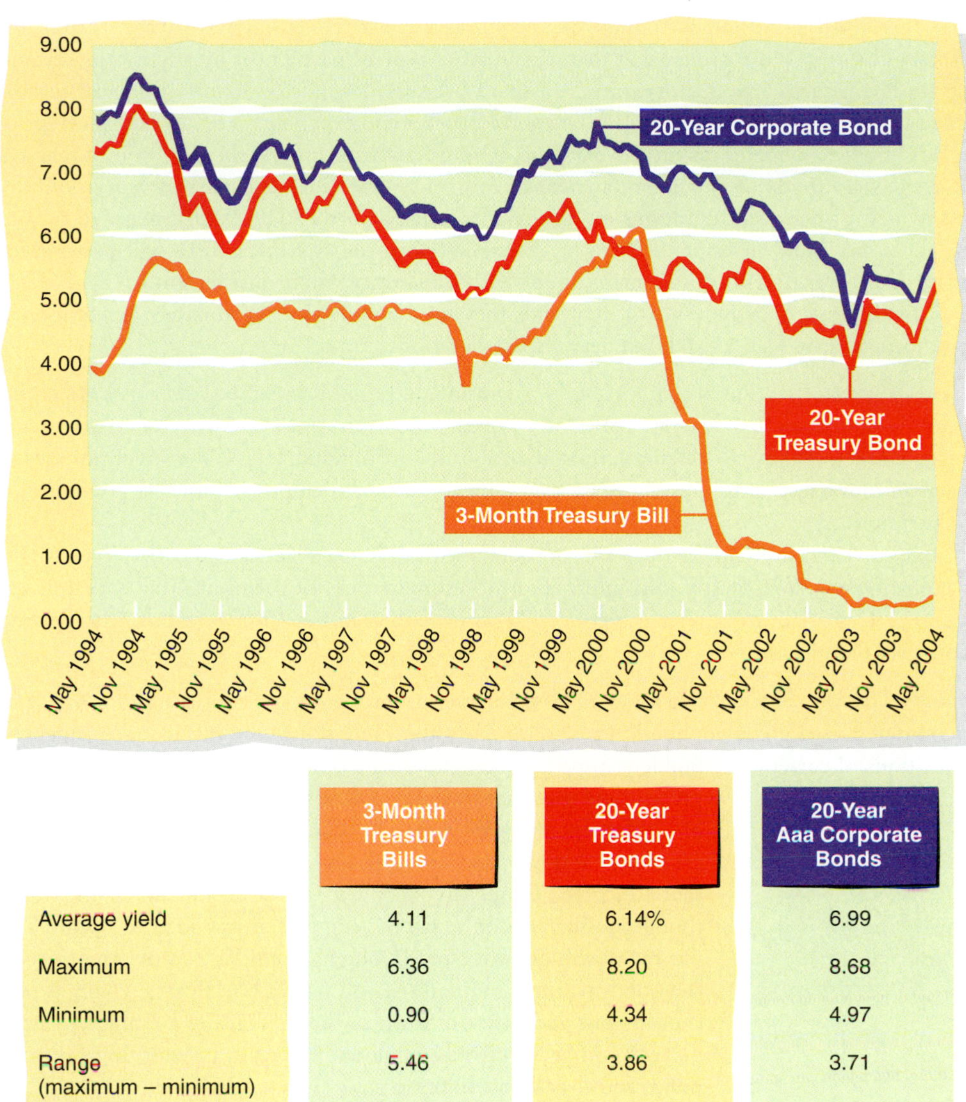

EXHIBIT 13-4

Yields on Debt Securities over Time

	3-Month Treasury Bills	20-Year Treasury Bonds	20-Year Aaa Corporate Bonds
Average yield	4.11	6.14%	6.99
Maximum	6.36	8.20	8.68
Minimum	0.90	4.34	4.97
Range (maximum – minimum)	5.46	3.86	3.71

The Risks of Bond Investing

The value of a bond, as we've seen, is the present discounted value of the cash flows an investor expects to receive. Since bonds offer cash flows that are known in advance, the bond values are affected by fewer factors than are stock values, and the risks are more easily identified. If you buy a bond and hold it to maturity, you *will* realize the yield to maturity that you expected at the outset of your investment as long as the issuer makes payments as promised. Therefore, in evaluating the risks of bond investment alternatives, you should be concerned with primarily two types of risk: default risk and the risk that the yield to maturity will turn out to be insufficient relative to other investments of comparable risk. Over a 20- or 30-year holding period, the risk premiums for default, inflation, interest rate, liquidity, and maturity risk, which were introduced in Chapter 11, can change quite dramatically.

What if you don't hold the bond to maturity? Unfortunately, if you need to sell some or all of your bond holdings, you face the risk of having a capital loss—the value of your bonds may now be less than what you paid for them. You may also face liquidity risk if the bonds you hold don't have an active secondary market. We've already seen that when interest rates rise, the value of bonds declines, and when interest rates fall, the value of bonds rises. Thus, the risk of declines in portfolio value is directly related to the variability of market interest rates and the sensitivity of particular bonds' prices to interest rate movements. The various risk factors and their impact on bond values are discussed below.

Default Risk. Although a bond issuer promises to make regular interest payments to its investors and to repay the principal at maturity, neither type of payment is by any means certain. The confidence that investors have in the issuer's promise depends on its past financial performance and its prospects for the future. The bond issuer could experience a temporary shortage of cash and miss a payment; or in the worst case, it could go bankrupt. At the time you purchase a bond, the yield to maturity will be sufficient to compensate you for the issuer's *current* risk of default, which is measured by various rating agencies, as described earlier. With respect to default risk, therefore, bond investors need to be concerned with the risk that a firm will become *less* creditworthy over time. If this happens, their yield to maturity will be insufficient to compensate them for this risk, and the value of the bonds they hold will decline. Fortunately, reductions in credit ratings, as well as actual bond defaults, are fairly uncommon.

Liquidity Risk. Recall that a security is considered liquid if it can be sold on short notice without a significant loss of value. For bonds, liquidity depends on the existence of an active secondary market. Although Treasury bonds involve little or no liquidity risk, the small number of traders in municipal and some corporate issues may make it difficult to sell those types of bonds on short notice.

Exhibit 13–5 summarizes the yields on bonds with different risk characteristics at a particular point in time. You can use this information to estimate the risk premiums that investors expect to receive for bearing certain types of risk as explained in the *Go Figure!* box, "Estimating Bond Risk Premiums."

Interest Rate Risk. We know that when interest rates go up, bond prices go down, and when interest rates go down, bond prices go up. To better understand why this is so, consider the motivations of current bondholders. Suppose you're holding a bond that pays a coupon rate of 7 percent and interest rates rise so a new issue from another company of similar risk will pay 9 percent. You may decide to sell the 7 percent bond and buy the 9 percent bond so that you can get more interest income. Other investors will likely decide the same thing, though, so many people will be selling their low-interest bonds, and not many will be interested in buying them; as a result, the price of the bonds will fall. Similarly, if you have a bond that's paying 9 percent interest and rates go down so that new issues are only paying 7 percent, other investors will look jealously at your high-interest bond, and they'll be willing to pay a higher price for it.

Just how much difference does a change in interest rates make? Exhibit 13–6 shows bond prices for several combinations of coupon rate, term to maturity, and investor required return. Consider the bond (circled in the table) that has a 7 percent semiannual coupon rate and 10 years to maturity. If the current required rate of return on a bond of this type is 7 percent, then the price will be equal to the par value of $1,000. The columns to the left and right of the circled value show what would happen to the price of this bond if the market required rate of return immediately decreased or increased by two percentage points. If rates decline by two percentage points, to 5 percent, the value of the bond will increase to $1,156, a 15.6 percent increase. But if rates increase to 9 percent, the value of the bond will decrease to $870, a 13 percent decrease.

Fact #4

Even though bonds are called fixed-income securities, their prices definitely aren't fixed. As interest rates go up and down, the prices of bonds go in the opposite direction. From mid- to late 2004, as the Federal Reserve acted to increase short-term interest rates, the values of individual bonds and bond mutual fund shares fell. For bond investors who think they're in a "safe" investment, it's often a surprise when they see that their bonds are worth less than what they paid for them.

EXHIBIT 13-5

Yields on Bonds with Different Risk Characteristics, June 2, 2004

Time to Maturity	U.S. Treasuries	Corporate Bonds		Municipal Bonds	
		AAA	A	AAA	A
2 Years	2.63	2.78	3.04	1.86	1.99
5 Years	3.89	4.03	4.36	2.96	3.09
10 Years	4.73	5.26	5.39	3.78	4.12
20 Years	5.42*	5.87	6.17	4.61	4.87

*This is the yield reported for 30-year Treasury bonds.
Source: bonds.yahoo.com/rates/html

GO FIGURE!

Estimating Bond Risk Premiums

Problem: In May 2004, Kevin Reed decided to invest in bonds. In deciding what type to buy, he first wanted to determine how much more he'd be able to earn if he were willing to take greater default and maturity risk.

Solution: You can estimate how much default risk and maturity risk are worth by considering the differences in yields on various debt securities at a given point in time. By finding two bonds that differ only in one risk characteristic, you can determine how much investors think the extra risk is worth. Accordingly, Kevin considers the average yield information for various debt securities as reported in Exhibit 13–5. In June 2004, he finds that 20-year Treasury bonds are yielding about 0.69 percentage points more than 10-year Treasuries (5.42% compared with 4.73%)—this is an estimate of the maturity risk premium. He also notes that the difference in yield for 10-year and 20-year AAA corporates is about the same (0.61). The difference in yield between 5-year and 20-year Treasuries maturities is 1.53 percentage points.

The difference in yield between 20-year Treasury bonds, which are free of default risk, and 20-year corporate bonds issued by the most creditworthy firms (those with AAA rating) is 0.45 percent, so this is the minimum default risk premium. If Kevin buys a slightly lower grade bond (A rating), he'll earn another 0.75 percent more in yield than he would with the 20-year Treasuries.

Inflation Risk. Expectations about inflation affect bond prices in a way connected to interest rate risk, since expected inflation is incorporated in the market rate of interest at any given time as a component of the nominal risk-free rate. Thus, when investors think that inflation is going to rise in the future, they'll require higher yields on all securities to compensate for this risk. As a result, market rates will rise, and when rates go up, bond prices go down.

Maturity Risk. Recall from Chapter 11 that the prices of securities with longer maturities are more sensitive to interest rate changes than the prices of those with shorter maturities. This can be beneficial to buy-and-hold investors, who earn a risk premium for taking the risk of buying longer-term securities but who aren't actually worried about intermediate fluctuations in value. But let's look at how maturity risk can affect the value of your portfolio if you needed to sell bonds before they've matured.

Again using Exhibit 13–6, compare the circled 10-year bond to a bond with the same coupon rate and only one year to maturity (in the first highlighted row). If market rates fell by two percentage points, to 5 percent, the value of the one-year bond would climb to $1,019, an increase of 1.9 percent; if market rates rose by two percentage points, the value of the bond

EXHIBIT 13-6

Sensitivity of Bond Prices to Interest Rates

Years to Maturity	Annual Coupon	Required Return		
		5%	7%	9%
1	$50	$1,000	$981	$963
1	$70	$1,019	$1,000	$981
1	$90	$1,039	$1,019	$1,000
5	$50	$1,000	$917	$842
5	$70	$1,088	$1,000	$921
5	$90	$1,175	$1,083	$1,000
10	$50	$1,000	$858	$740
10	$70	$1,156	$1,000	$870
10	$90	$1,312	$1,142	$1,000
20	$50	$1,000	$786	$632
20	$70	$1,251	$1,000	$816
20	$90	$1,502	$1,214	$1,000

would fall to $981, a 1.9 percent decrease. As we've already determined, the 10-year bond would increase in value by 15.6 percent in response to a two percentage point decline in interest rates and would decrease in value by 13 percent in response to a two percentage point increase in interest rates—a much larger change than for the one-year bond. Therefore, the longer the average maturity of the bonds in your portfolio, the more your portfolio will decline in value for a given increase in interest rates. If you needed to sell bonds in a hurry, you'd likely have to take a capital loss to do so.

We can also see from the exhibit that the amount of the coupon also makes a difference in the bond's maturity risk, or price sensitivity to interest rates. For any given maturity, the price of the bond with the lowest coupon experiences the largest price decline with an increase in rates. Comparing 10 year bonds, where we saw a 13 percent decline for the 7 percent coupon bond when rates rose from 7 to 9 percent, the 5 percent coupon bond would have lost 13.8 percent in value [($740 − $858)/$858 = −0.138 or −13.8 percent]. The smaller the coupon, the bigger this effect, so zero coupon bonds can be expected to have the greatest maturity risk—their prices will exhibit the largest changes in response to increases or decreases in market rates.

Maturity risk factors can be summarized as follows:

1. The longer the time to maturity, the greater the percentage change in bond value for a given change in required return.
2. The smaller the coupon rate, the greater the percentage change in bond value for a given change in required return.

Bond Risk in a Diversified Portfolio. Although both bonds and stocks are affected by market interest rates, their price changes are not perfectly correlated. Thus, holding both bonds and stocks in a diversified investment portfolio can reduce the risk of the portfolio. Over the last 10 years, an investor who maintained a 50-50 allocation between bonds and stocks would have had lower returns during the stock market run-up in the 1990s than an all-equity investor but would have softened the blow of the market downturn, since the interest rate declines during the 2001 to 2003 period caused bond prices to rise. The net result on the portfolio would have been slightly lower average return and significantly lower risk.

Learning by Doing 13-3

1. For each of the following pairs, indicate which will be more sensitive to changes in interest rates:
   a. A 5 percent coupon bond with 20 years to maturity or a 7 percent coupon bond with 20 years to maturity
   b. A 7 percent coupon bond with 5 years to maturity or a 7 percent coupon bond with 20 years to maturity
2. What will happen to the price of a bond if the issuer is downgraded from an AAA rating to an AA rating?

Bond Investment Strategies

As discussed in Chapter 11, your investment plan should include determining your investment strategies as well as regularly reevaluating your portfolio and your progress toward achieving your goals. As we've emphasized, you can be an active or a passive investor, but the risks associated with active investing, along with the time and energy required, may not make it a practical option. Most of the investment strategies discussed in previous chapters can be applied to bond investing as well—for example, diversification, buy-and-hold, dollar cost averaging, and timing. In addition, laddering and maturity matching are strategies that are unique to fixed-income securities.

Diversification. Holding a portion of your portfolio in bonds is itself a form of diversification, as we've seen. But within this asset class, it's a good idea to diversify by holding bonds from a number of issuers with differing risk characteristics. For example, you wouldn't want all of your bonds to be from issuers in the same industry, since an economic downturn in that industry might affect the default risk of all your bonds at the same time. You can diversify your bond holdings across type of issuer, industry, maturity, risk, and other characteristics. However, the large price you pay per bond makes it a bit costly to hold many different bonds.

Buy-and-Hold. If you buy and hold bonds, you'll earn the yield to maturity that you calculated at purchase, and you'll avoid paying trading costs beyond the initial commission for the purchase. Since bond risk actually declines as the term to maturity shortens, your portfolio will have lower risk if you follow this strategy than it would if you were buying and selling frequently.

Dollar Cost Averaging. Recall from Chapter 11 that dollar cost averaging requires that you make regular purchases over time rather than buying in a single larger increment. Although you might still apply this principle to bond investing through mutual funds, as discussed in the next chapter, it isn't usually recommended for direct bond investment unless you can make sizable purchases on a regular basis. This is because the transaction costs are high relative to the yield on the investments.

Laddering. Laddering is a type of buy-and-hold bond investing strategy in which you purchase a collection of bonds with different maturities spread out over your investment horizon. If, for example, you have a 10-year investment horizon, you could buy bonds that mature in 1, 2, 3, 4, 5, 6, 7, 8, 9, and 10 years. As each bond matures, you'll use the money to buy a bond that matures in 10 years (so that you'll always have one bond from each maturity in the portfolio). The advantage of this strategy is that it balances the risk and return elements in the portfolio, because the bonds with shorter terms to maturity will not be as sensitive to interest rate changes, while the bonds with longer terms to maturity will give slightly higher yields.

Maturity Matching. Maturity matching is similar in concept to laddering, but it requires that you purchase assets which have cash flows that coincide with the period in which you need the funds. Thus, if your time horizon is 10 years from now, you'll purchase only bonds with 10 years to maturity. Zero-coupon bonds are often used for this purpose since they don't pay any interest in the interim and you'll receive the full principal at maturity. Alternatively, you might buy bonds that will make interest payments for the period when you'll need the funds—let's say 20-year coupon bonds that will make interest payments over the expected 20-year period of your retirement.

Fact #5

Changing your asset allocation in response to what's happening at the moment is "timing" at its worst and generally results in below-average portfolio performance. Unfortunately, many individual investors display this type of knee-jerk reaction in what's sometimes called the "flight to quality." When the stock market goes down, for example, they pull their money out and put it in fixed-income securities. When the stock market goes up, they move more money into stocks. The end result is that they're always buying high and selling low—the opposite of what they need to do to profit on price changes. Timing only works if you can make the appropriate move before the beneficial price change occurs.

Timing. Although we previously discussed timing as an active investment strategy, you can also time purchases of assets you plan to buy for the long term. You can apply some of what you know about interest rates and their effect on bond prices and yields to time your selection of bonds for your buy-and-hold portfolio. For example, if rates are currently fairly low relative to historical averages, you may not want to buy long-term bonds, since you'll be locking in a low yield to maturity. You could, instead, buy relatively short-maturity bonds in anticipation of future rate increases. When your bonds mature, if rates have since risen, you'll be able to purchase bonds with longer maturities at lower prices and lock in a more favorable yield.

A Bond Transaction

Now that we've examined expected bond yield and risk and reviewed some investment strategies, let's walk through the process of actually buying a bond. Individual investors buy bonds in the same ways they buy stock—usually through a broker. If you use a full-service brokerage firm, the broker will provide you with advice and information about prices and yields. In return for this, though, you'll pay a higher commission. If you already know what you want to buy, you'll save money by using a discount broker or buying online. In this section, we'll assume you've decided to invest in Ford Motor Credit bonds. First, we'll see how you can look up the price of these bonds in the paper, and then we'll walk through the transaction.

Most bonds are bought and sold through broker-dealers instead of at securities exchanges.

Internet sources for bond information include www.moodys.com, www.standardpoor.com, www.investinginbonds.com, www.bondsonline.com, finance.yahoo.com, and www.morningstar.com.

Reading Bond Quotations. The *Wall Street Journal* regularly reports prices and yields for Treasury issues and some municipal and corporate bonds. Exhibit 13–7 provides an example of how the information on corporate bonds was reported in the July 16, 2004, issue of the *Journal* (with information from the close of the previous day). It includes the coupon rate, maturity date, prices, and yields for transactions of $1 million or more for the forty most actively traded corporate bonds (in order from highest to lowest volume of trading).

Let's look more closely at the highlighted Ford Motor Credit bond. Note that the bond reported for Ford pays a 7.45 percent coupon rate per year, or $74.50, which is 7.45 percent of the face value of $1,000. Although the exhibit doesn't say so, these bonds pay their coupons semiannually, so you'd receive $37.25 every six months if you owned one of these bonds. The bond will mature on July 16, 2031, which tells us that the coupon payments are made on January 16 and July 16 of each year and the last coupon will be paid on July 16, 2031, 27 years from the date of the newspaper report, at which time the investors will also receive their $1,000 par value.

The "Last Price" column reports the price as a percent of the face value. The Ford bond is priced at 95.455 percent of the face value, so it is selling for $954.55 per bond. The "Last Yield" is the yield to maturity assuming you bought the bond for the current price, but not including the interest that accrues between coupon payment dates. You can use your financial calculator to arrive at this answer as follows: Enter $PV = -954.55$, $FV = 1{,}000$, $PMT = 37.25$, $N = 27 \times 2 = 54$ and solve for I, the semiannual yield, which is 3.929 percent. Multiplying this result by 2 gives you the annual yield, 7.858 percent which is reported in the "Last Yield" column. The difference between the yield on this bond and a Treasury security of comparable term to maturity

EXHIBIT 13-7

***Wall Street Journal*, Corporate Bonds, July 16, 2004**

Corporate Bonds

Thursday, July 15, 2004

Forty most active fixed-coupon corporate bonds

COMPANY (TICKER)	COUPON	MATURITY	LAST PRICE	LAST YIELD	*EST SPREAD	UST†	EST $ VOL (000'S)
Electronic Data Systems (EDS)	6.000	Aug 01, 2013	96.095	7.090	261	10	234,039
Merrill Lynch (MER)	5.450	Jul 15, 2014	99.818	5.474	99	10	212,310
GlaxoSmithKline Capital Inc (GSK)	4.375	Apr 15, 2014	94.777	5.060	57	10	132,428
Ford Motor Credit (F)	7.375	Oct 28, 2009	107.396	5.727	204	5	132,149
Sprint Capital (FON)	6.900	May 01, 2019	102.363	6.645	216	10	114,510
Ford Motor Credit (F)	7.450	Jul 16, 2031	95.455	7.858	264	30	113,856
AT&T Corp (T)	6.000	Mar 15, 2009	96.750	6.824	314	5	101,999
General Motors Acceptance (GM)	8.000	Nov 01, 2031	102.995	7.733	252	30	93,336
General Motors (GM)	8.375	Jul 15, 2033	105.504	7.889	268	30	86,314
Citizens Communications (CZN)	9.250	May 15, 2011	109.125	7.511	303	10	85,160
Altria Group (MO)	7.000	Nov 04, 2013	103.264	6.524	204	10	81,121
Morgan Stanley (MWD)	4.750	Apr 01, 2014	93.697	5.600	112	10	78,494
Ford Motor Credit (F)	7.000	Oct 01, 2013	102.015	6.701	222	10	77,398
Credit Suisse First Boston (USA (CRDSUI)	5.125	Jan 15, 2014	98.082	5.386	90	10	74.104
Merrill Lynch (MER)	3.700	Apr 21, 2008	99.094	3.961	27	5	72.780
Harrah's Operating (HET)	8.000	Feb 01, 2011	112.191	5.735	125	10	71.456
HSBC Bank USA (HSBC)	4.625	Apr 01, 2014	94.707	5.330	85	10	69,535
National Rural Utilites Cooperative Finance (NRUC)	7.250	Mar 01, 2012	114.422	4.952	46	10	66,555
General Motors Acceptance (GM)	4.150	Feb 07,2005	100.985	2.327	n.a.	n.a.	64,543
Schering-Plough (SGP)	6.500	Dec 01, 2033	102.680	6.536	132	30	63,987
Ford Motor Credit (F)	5.800	Jan 12, 2009	101.809	5.340	166	5	62,863
General Motors Acceptance (GM)	6.750	Jan 15, 2006	104.941	3.315	71	2	62,189
Wyeth (WYE)	5.500	Feb 01, 2014	96.971	5.920	144	10	60,892
Sprint Capital (FON)	8.375	Mar 15, 2012	116.157	5.735	125	10	56,676
Tyco International Group SA (TYC)	6.375	Oct 15, 2011	107.437	5.130	65	10	55,849
UFJ Finance Aruba AEC (UFJ)	6.750	Jul 15, 2013	107.300	5.700	121	10	55,629
International Business Machines (IBM)	6.220	Aug 01, 2027	102.183	6.043	82	30	55,003
General Electric Capital (GE)	2.850	Jan 30, 2006	100.225	2.698	9	2	54,472
Verizon Global Funding (VZ)	4.375	Jun 01, 2013	92.943	5.386	90	10	53,886
General Motors Acceptance (GM)	6.875	Sep 15, 2011	102.649	6.405	192	10	52,583
International Business Machines (IBM)	4.750	Nov 29, 2012	98.706	4.940	46	10	52,048
Ford Motor Credit (F)	5.625	Oct 01, 2008	101.877	5.120	143	5	51,908
Kellogg (K)	6.600	Apr 01, 2011	110.383	4.769	27	10	51,667
Vodafone Group PLC (VOD)	7.625	Feb 15, 2005	103.210	2.031	n.a.	n.a.	51,628
Time Warner (TWX)	7.700	May 01, 2032	110.625	6.839	162	30	49,421
J.P. Morgan Chase (JPM)	5.900	Nov 15, 2011	104.796	5.105	62	10	49,266
Merrill Lynch (MER)	4.125	Jan 15, 2009	99.536	4.240	56	5	48,758
Target (TGT)	7.500	Feb 15, 2005	103.111	1.975	n.a.	n.a.	48,721
SBC Communications (SBC)	5.875	Aug 15, 2012	103.695	5.305	82	10	47,238
Time Warner (TWX)	6.875	May 01, 2012	109.100	5.424	94	10	46,120
Tyco International Group SA (TYC)	6.375	Feb 15, 2006	105.116	3.011	41	2	44.310

Volume represents total volume for each issue; price/yield data are for trades of $1 million and greater. *Estimated spreads, in basis points (100 basis points is one percentage point), over the 2, 3, 5, 10 or 30-year hot run Treasury note/bond. 2-year: 2.750 06/06; 3-year: 3.125 05/07; 5-year: 3.625 07/09; 10-year: 4.750 05/14; 30-year: 5.375 02/31. †Comparable U.S. Treasury issue.

Source: Wall Street Journal. Copyright 2004 by Dow Jones & Co Inc. Permission granted via Copyright Clearance Center.

(the number of years given in the UST column)—an amount called the *estimated spread*—is given in the column labeled "Est Spread." The unit in which the estimated spread is given is the *basis point*, which is 1/100 percent, so the estimated spread of 264 means that the Ford bond will give you an estimated 2.64 percentage points more yield than the 30-year Treasury security. The last column, labeled "Est $ Vol (000's)," gives the total value of bonds that traded on that day, which in this case was $113,856,000.

The Brokered Deal. In Chapter 12, we discussed how you might implement a purchase of stock. The process is similar for buying a bond. As noted, you can find out the price at which the bond traded on the previous day. Your broker will quote you a higher price that includes trading costs. The price will also be adjusted to reflect any portion of the next coupon payment that should accrue to the person selling the bond. For example, if you buy a bond three months from the date of the semiannual coupon, you'll have to give the seller half of the interest for that period, and the price you're quoted will reflect this. Your broker will implement the trade at an organized exchange if the bond you want is traded in that way. Most bonds, however, are traded by bond dealers, so your broker will actually contact a dealer and buy your bond through that firm. You'll pay a commission to your broker and the dealer will make a profit called a mark-up. For a $1,000 bond, you can expect your transactions costs to be anywhere from $25 to $60, the equivalent of almost a full year's interest payment.

Learning by Doing 13-4

1. You have a three-year-old child, and you'd like to fund the costs of his college education. Explain how you could use zero-coupon bonds to implement a maturity matching strategy to meet this objective.
2. Use Exhibit 13–7 to find the coupon rate, maturity date, price, and last yield for a bond issued by IBM.

Preferred Stocks

LEARNING objective

4 Explain how the features of preferred stock are similar to those of both stocks and bonds.

In addition to common stocks and bonds, you may want to consider investing in preferred stock. As noted in Chapter 11, this type of security offers the advantage of paying regular, fixed dividends that take precedence over dividends to common shareholders. In this section, we review the most important features of preferred stock.

What Is Preferred Stock?

Preferred stock shares have similarities to both common stock and bonds. Like both bonds and common stock, preferred stock is issued by companies as a means of raising capital to fund ongoing operations or expansion. Like bonds, most preferred stock pays a fixed cash flow to investors. Like common stock, though, preferred stock has no set maturity date, and the company never has to repay the original investment amount. Exhibit 13–8 shows the differences in cash flow streams that might be realized by a bond investor, a preferred stock investor, and a common stock investor, if we assume an initial investment of $1,000 in each case. At this point, the actual dollar amounts of the cash flows are not important. Instead, focus on the timing and certainty of the cash flows. Note that the bond's cash flow stream has a specific end date, whereas the cash flows of the two types of stock extend to infinity (or at least, as long as the company is in existence). Note also that the owners of the bond and the preferred stock know what the amount of their cash flow will be with certainty (if we assume that the issuer doesn't miss any payments or default), whereas the owners of common stock don't know what the dividends will be in the future. Like bonds, the current price of a share of preferred stock may be higher or lower than its par value and will depend on the dividend rate relative to market rates at the time. When rates on similar risk investments are higher than the dividend rate, the price will be lower than the par, and vice versa.

EXHIBIT 13-8

Comparison of Annual Cash Flows for Bonds, Preferred Stock, and Common Stock

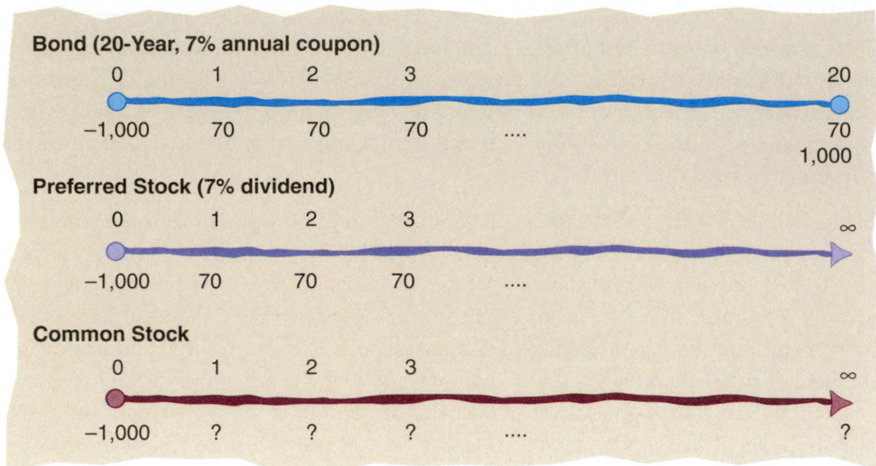

Expected Cash Flows from Preferred Stocks

To understand preferred stocks well enough to decide whether they're suitable for your investment plan, you'll need to understand more about the cash flows associated with this type of security. As with other investments, your cash flows from a share of preferred stock will be some combination of income and a capital gain (or loss) upon sale of the stock. By design, preferred stock is primarily an income investment, although its price is highly sensitive to interest rate movements in the same way as a bond's price.

Preferred stock usually pays a quarterly dividend based on a fixed percentage of its par value. **Par value** is the term used for an arbitrary initial value assigned to the preferred stock shares at issuance, usually a round number like \$25, \$50, or \$100. For example, if a company has issued shares of preferred stock with a \$100 par value and a 10 percent dividend rate, each stockholder will receive a dividend equal to 10 percent of \$100, or \$10, per year, which will be paid out in installments of \$2.50 per quarter per share. Since the shares have no maturity date, this payment stream is perpetual, continuing for as long as the company is in existence. Unlike the face value of a bond, the par value of preferred stock is never owed to the investors.

par value

An arbitrary initial value assigned to shares of preferred stock at issuance and used to calculate the dividend payment.

Contract Terms That Affect Preferred Stock Cash Flows

What we've just described is the "plain vanilla" type of preferred stock arrangement. However, many contract variations are used by issuing firms to make their preferred stock more attractive to investors. Some firms have many issues of preferred stock that differ in their contract terms and promised dividend rates. Several variations are discussed below.

Cumulative Dividends. What happens if a company doesn't have enough cash to pay the dividend on its preferred stock in a given year? Unlike the case with bonds, the failure to pay under these circumstances doesn't put the company in default. Preferred shareholders have a little more protection from this downside risk if they hold **cumulative preferred stock.** With a cumulative feature, the company accumulates an obligation to its preferred stock investors that must be paid in subsequent years before any dividends can be paid to common shareholders. For noncumulative preferred stock, the missed dividends are lost and never need to be repaid.

cumulative preferred stock

Preferred stock that gives holders the right to receive past unpaid dividends before any dividends can be paid to common stockholders.

Call Provisions. Suppose a company issues preferred stock during a period when interest rates are relatively high, so the dividend rate is also high. When rates fall, the company must continue paying what amounts to a high cost of capital, even though they might be able to get better rates on alternative financing. In order to reduce this risk, many issuers of preferred stock retain the right to *call*, or repurchase, the stock from investors. If market rates fall, a company can exercise its call rights and retire older preferred stock that carries a high dividend rate. It can then issue new preferred stock with a lower rate. Generally, a call provision makes the stock less attractive to investors, who would rather keep the high-dividend stock in their portfolios than be forced to sell it back to the company. Thus, callable preferred stock pays a higher dividend rate than comparable noncallable preferred stock.

Fixed Versus Adjustable Dividends. Preferred dividends are normally fixed-rate payments. As noted, if market rates on comparable investments fall, the company may be required to call the issue in order to keep its costs down. This can be a fairly expensive and time-consuming process. In a relatively new variation, some companies are now issuing **adjustable-rate preferred stock**, which pays a dividend that is tied to a market interest rate. As an investor, you may not be happy to find that the rate on your stock has gone down, but at least you'll avoid the necessity of reinvesting the money due to the exercise of the call provision. And when rates go up, the dividend will rise as well.

adjustable-rate preferred stock

Preferred stock that pays a dividend tied to a market interest rate.

Participation. Although preferred stockholders have an advantage over common stockholders in that they have a promised dividend rate, they normally don't have the right to vote at the corporation's annual meetings, and they have no right to the residual profits of the firm beyond what they earn in dividends. However, some companies issue *participating preferred stock*, which allows preferred stock investors to share with common stockholders in the profits that are left over after the normal preferred and common stock dividends have been paid. This feature is relatively rare.

Convertibility. Preferred stock sometimes has a convertibility feature. As with convertible bonds, this means that you can convert your preferred shares to common stock under certain conditions. The number of shares for which each preferred share can be exchanged is determined by contractual agreement. This feature is beneficial to investors in that it gives them the option of participating in the future growth of the company if it becomes favorable to do so. The associated cost is that the dividend rate for convertible preferred stock is lower than that for preferred stock which isn't convertible.

If you own convertible preferred stock, the decision of whether to convert or not will depend on the current market prices of the preferred and the common stock in conjunction with the conversion ratio (the number of shares of common you get for each share of preferred). Suppose, for example, that each of your preferred shares is convertible to four shares of common (conversion ratio = 4). Assume also that the current market price of common stock, which pays no dividend, is \$22 and that the market price of the preferred, which pays an annual dividend of \$8, is \$95. If you convert, you'll receive 4 × \$22 = \$88 worth of common stock and lose the \$8 dividend for the year, so it wouldn't be to your advantage to do so. If the market value of the common stock goes up sufficiently, it may be beneficial to consider converting at a later date. In making this decision, you'll of course have to compare the expected future cash flows and risks for each of these investments.

Valuation of Preferred Stock

As you know, the value of any asset can be thought of as the present discounted value of the cash flows it will generate. Since the cash flows of preferred stock are known with a fair degree of certainty, then we just need to know how to calculate the present value. The difficulty in applying the time value of money here is that, rather than a straight annuity, preferred stock dividends are a **perpetuity**—a constant cash flow that continues into infinity. Fortunately, there's a simple formula for the present value of a perpetuity:

perpetuity

A constant cash flow stream that continues into infinity.

$$\text{Present value of a perpetuity} = \frac{\text{Constant cash flow}}{i}$$

where i is the investors' required rate of return, or discount rate. Using this formula, we calculate the value of a share of preferred stock as

$$\text{Value of preferred stock} = \frac{\text{Dividend}}{i} = \frac{\text{Par value} \times \text{Dividend rate}}{i}$$

Suppose, for example, that the stock pays a \$10 dividend and the required rate of return is 8 percent. Then the value of the share would be \$10/0.08 = \$125. To convince yourself that this shortcut equation makes sense, redo this calculation as a normal present value of an annuity problem, but assume a very large number of periods, such as 100. For example using a financial calculator, you could enter $PMT = 10$, $N = 100$, and $I = 8$ and solve for $PV = \$124.94$. Even though 100 isn't infinity, you can see that, for this purpose, it's close enough.

Let's consider what happens to the value if interest rates go up. If rate increases caused preferred stock investors to require a 9 percent return, the value of the share would fall to \$10/0.09 = \$111. The dollar amount of the dividend is constant over time, so the only thing that causes the value of the stock to change is the discount rate used. As we've seen, investors' discount rates depend on the return they need to compensate them for the risk of the investment. As overall interest rates go up and down with general economic conditions, and as inflation expectations change, the required returns of investors will also go up and down, and preferred stock values will move in the opposite direction, just as bond values do.

Since prices are generally driven by the market, it's not usually necessary to calculate the value of preferred stock—you can just look up the market price you'll have to pay. Instead, investors usually evaluate preferred stock based on the expected yield. Since the yield for a buy-and-hold investor comes entirely from the dividend cash flows, the appropriate yield to consider is the dividend yield, calculated as follows:

$$\text{Dividend yield} = \frac{\text{Annual dividend}}{\text{Price}}$$

If you observe that the price of an issue of preferred is \$125, and you know that the dividend is \$10 per year, then your dividend yield is \$10/\$125 = 0.08 or 8%.

Risks and Rewards of Preferred Stock Investing

The primary attraction of preferred stock is its steady dividend stream, which provides a yield that is usually greater than the pretax yield on long-term bonds of similar risk. These dividends are taxable income to the investor and are not deductible by the issuer. A special tax rule allows corporations that hold the stock of other corporations to exclude 70 percent of the dividends from taxable income. Although this is good for corporate investors, it's a disadvantage to individual investors, since these tax-advantaged investors are willing to pay more for the stock and therefore drive up the price.

The most important risks faced by preferred stock investors are interest rate risk, call risk, and default risk. Much like bond values, preferred stock values are extremely dependent on market rates of interest. For example, if a company issues 10 percent preferred stock with a \$100 face value when market rates on comparable risk securities are also at 10 percent, the value of the stock will be equal to its face value of \$100 (since \$10/0.1 = \$100). But if market interest rates go up so that the required rate of return on this preferred stock increases to 11 percent, the value of the stock will fall to \$91 (\$10/0.11 = \$91). What if interest rates decline? We might expect that falling rates would benefit the investor through increased prices and above-market yield. However, in the case of callable preferred shares, the issuing corporation is likely to exercise its call rights and retire the stock. Thus, the investor gets the worst of both worlds—the price declines when rates rise, and stock is called when rates fall.

Default risk depends on the issuing firm's business risk. Riskier companies on average pay higher dividend rates than less risky companies. In the event the issuing company experiences a cash shortfall, preferred stock investors, particularly holders of cumulative preferred stock, are in a better position than common stock investors. Although bondholders still get paid first, preferred shareholders must be paid their dividends before the company can declare a dividend for the common shareholders—making this type of investment generally less risky than common stock and more risky than bonds. As with bonds, rating agencies such as Moody's and Standard and Poor's regularly provide ratings of credit risk for issues of preferred stock.

Learning by Doing 13-5

1. You own 100 shares of preferred stock that has a \$100 par value and pays an 8 percent dividend each year. Your share is currently worth \$95. Based on this information, is the required rate of return on comparable risk preferred stock more or less than your 8 percent dividend rate? (No calculation is necessary.)
2. You own 100 shares of preferred stock that has a \$50 par value and pays a 10 percent dividend each year.
   a. What is the amount of the annual dividend?
   b. If the current price is \$50, what is the rate that investors currently require on preferred stock of this risk level?

Sources of Information for Bond and Preferred Stock Investors

LEARNING objective

5 Identify sources of information for investors in bonds and preferred stocks.

As with other areas of investing, bond investors need to be knowledgeable about the companies they invest in, the industries or business sectors they operate in, as well as general economic conditions. Most of the information resources identified in Chapters 11 and 12 will also be useful to you as a bond investor. For example, you'll want to keep track of economic conditions, and particularly interest rate movements, by regularly reading the financial press and checking investment websites such as finance.yahoo.com, www.fool.com, and www.moneycentral.com. Specific company information can be found at the company's website, in its annual reports, and in the financial press.

Since most bond investors follow a buy-and-hold strategy and many bonds aren't traded on exchanges, it's more difficult to get current pricing information for bonds than for stocks, and there aren't as many sources for free investment advice as there are for stock investors. If you're interested in Treasury bonds, the federal government is a valuable source of information. Research from the Federal Reserve (www.federalreserve.gov) is free to the public. You can find out more about municipal bonds in your state by contacting your state and local governments directly.

Summary

1. **Know the basic terminology used by bond investors.** A bond is a debt security issued by a corporation or a government entity to finance its operations and growth. Bond investors usually receive fixed semiannual interest payments, called coupon payments, and are repaid the face value at the maturity of the bond. Some bonds also include other features that affect their value, including call provisions, sinking funds, and convertibility.
2. **Classify bonds according to their characteristics.** Bonds are commonly classified according to the type of issuer and by certain characteristics of the bonds. Issuers include corporations and various government entities, including the U.S. government, federal agencies, states, cities, and municipal authorities. Bonds are also classified as secured or unsecured, by coupon arrangement, and by the risk level of the issuer.
3. **Analyze bond investment alternatives and evaluate performance.** Bond value is determined by the present value of the future expected cash flows, which include the interest payments to be received and the repayment of face value at maturity. Investors commonly evaluate bond issues based on expected yield to maturity, which is the coupon yield plus the capital gains yield. Bondholders are exposed to various degrees of default risk, liquidity risk, interest rate risk, inflation risk, and maturity risk, depending on the characteristics of the bonds held in their portfolio. Bond investment strategies include diversification, buy-and-hold, dollar cost averaging, timing, laddering, and maturity matching.
4. **Explain how the features of preferred stock are similar to those of both common stocks and bonds.** Preferred stock shares have similarities to both common stock and bonds. Like both bonds and common stock, preferred stock is issued by companies as a means of raising capital to fund ongoing operations or expansion. Like bonds, most preferred stock pays a fixed cash flow to investors. Like common stock, though, preferred stock has no set maturity date, and the company never has to repay the original investment amount.
5. **Identify sources of information for investors in bonds and preferred stocks.** Bond investors need to be knowledgable about bond issuers, including the industries or business sectors in which they operate, as well as general economic conditions. Most of the information resources identified in Chapters 11 and 12 will also be useful to you as a bond investor. For example, you'll want to keep track of economic conditions, and particularly interest rate movements, by regularly reading the financial press and checking investment websites.

Key Terms

adjustable-rate preferred stock (441)
agency issue (425)
call provision (422)
coupon payment (422)
coupon rate (422)
cumulative preferred stock (440)
debentures (427)
face value (422)
floating-rate bonds (428)
general obligation bond (426)
holding-period return (432)
indenture (422)
indexed bond (428)
investment-grade bonds (428)
junk bonds (428)
maturity date (422)
municipal bond (425)
par value (440)

perpetuity (441)
revenue bond (426)
secured bond (427)
sinking fund (423)
speculative-grade bonds (428)
Treasury Inflation Protected Securities (428)
trustee (422)
yield (431)
yield to maturity (YTM) (432)
zero-coupon bond (428)

Key Calculations

$$\text{Value of preferred stock} = \frac{\text{Dividend}}{i} = \frac{\text{Par value} \times \text{Dividend rate}}{i}$$

$$\text{Preferred stock dividend yield} = \frac{\text{Annual dividend}}{\text{Price}}$$

$$\text{Annual coupon payment} = \text{Coupon rate} \times \text{Face value}$$

$$\begin{aligned}\text{Value of bond} &= \text{Present value of semiannual coupon interest payments} \\ &\quad + \text{Present value of repayment of face value at maturity} \\ &= \left(\frac{\text{Annual coupon payment}}{2} \times \text{PVIFA}_{i,n}\right) + \left(\text{Face value} \times \text{PVIF}_{i,n}\right)\end{aligned}$$

$$\text{Approximate YTM} \approx \frac{\text{Annual coupon payment} + \dfrac{\text{Face value} - \text{Price}}{\text{Years to maturity}}}{\dfrac{\text{Face value} + \text{Price}}{2}}$$

$$\text{After-tax interest yield} = \text{Before-tax interest yield} \times (1 - \text{T})$$

Concept Review Questions

1. What are the primary reasons that corporations and government entities issue bonds instead of stock?
2. Why is debt financing cheaper than equity financing for a firm?
3. What are the main advantages of owning bonds?
4. Why are bond investments less risky than stock investments?
5. Define the following bond terminology:
   a. Face value
   b. Prospectus
   c. Indenture
   d. Coupon rate
   e. Coupon payment
   f. Trustee
   g. Maturity date
6. Why is a bond with a call provision less attractive to an investor than one without a call provision? What effect will this have on the yield for a callable bond?
7. What is a sinking fund, and how does it reduce the risk to bond investors?
8. Under what circumstances would you want to have a bond with a convertibility feature? What effect will that feature have on bond yield? Explain.
9. What are the primary types of bond issuers? How do these bond classifications differ in risk and tax status?
10. What are the two types of municipal bonds? Which has a greater risk of default? Why?
11. What is a secured bond? What types of security are most common?
12. Most bonds pay fixed-rate semiannual coupons. What other types of coupon arrangements are possible?
13. What is a zero-coupon bond? In what ways is it riskier than a coupon bond? How are zero-coupon bond investors taxed?
14. What is a junk bond? In what ways is a junk bond riskier than an investment-grade bond?
15. What are the usual cash flows expected by bond investors?
16. How are bonds valued? Why is it easier to determine a value for a bond than for a share of common stock?
17. Why do bond investors normally focus more on yield than on value in making their investment decisions?
18. What are the two components of bond yield? Which one is usually more important to investors in fixed-coupon bonds?
19. What is the relationship between market interest rates and bond prices?
20. What is the difference between holding-period return and yield to maturity?
21. Why does a buy-and-hold bond investment strategy make more sense than an active investing strategy for most individual investors?
22. When you invest in bonds, what are the primary risks you're exposed to? Is the answer to this question different for buy-and-hold investors than for active investors?
23. For each of the following pairs, indicate which has greater interest-rate risk, all else being equal:
    a. Long-maturity bond versus short-maturity bond
    b. Coupon bond versus zero-coupon bond
24. Describe several ways in which you can diversify a bond portfolio.
25. What is meant by "laddering"? What advantages does this investment strategy offer for bond investors?
26. What is maturity matching? Give an example of a situation in which this investment strategy would make sense.
27. What is preferred stock, and how does its risk differ from common stock and bonds?
28. What cash flows does a preferred stock investor expect to receive?
29. If a firm gets into financial trouble and can't make good on all its obligations, what rights does a preferred stockholder have compared with the rights of bondholders and common stockholders?
30. How is preferred stock valued? What is the primary determinant of value?

31. How are dividends on preferred stock calculated?
32. What are cumulative dividends, and how does this feature reduce the risk to preferred stock investors? What effect will it have on yield?
33. What is convertible preferred stock? Under what circumstances would a preferred stock investor prefer this type of stock?
34. What are the primary risk exposures for preferred stock investors? How does this differ from the risk exposures for investors in common stock?

Application Problems

1. ***Reading Bond Quotations.*** Using the excerpt from the *Wall Street Journal* in Exhibit 13–7 and assuming that today is July 15, 2004, find the following information for the bonds of Time Warner:
   a. Coupon rate
   b. Years to maturity
   c. Last yield
   d. Price
2. ***Bond Coupon Payments.*** Ford Motor Company has a semiannual fixed-rate coupon bond outstanding that pays a coupon rate of 7.45 percent. Assuming that the face value of the bond is $1,000, how much will each bondholder receive every six months?
3. ***Current Yield.*** You look up the price of a company's semiannual coupon bonds and find they have three issues outstanding. Each has a face value of $1,000. Given the following information, calculate the current yield for each bond:
   a. 20 years to maturity, 5.6 percent coupon, price = $850
   b. 15 years to maturity, 6 percent coupon, price = $1,000
   c. 10 years to maturity, 6.28 percent coupon, price = $1,100
   d. Given that these bonds are all issued by the same company, how can you explain the differences in current yield?
4. ***Approximate Yield to Maturity.*** You buy a semiannual fixed-rate coupon bond that has a face value of $1,000 and 10 years to maturity.
   a. The current market price is $910, and the coupon rate is 8 percent. Use the formula given in the chapter to calculate the approximate yield to maturity.
   b. What would the approximate yield to maturity be if the current price is $1,080.
   c. Use a financial calculator to solve for a more precise yield to maturity for these bonds, assuming the price is $910.
5. ***Effect of Interest Rates on Bond Price.*** For the bond in Problem 4, assume that market rates of interest increase by one percentage point and the rate of return required by bond investors increases accordingly and is now 10.4%.
   a. What effect does an increase in interest rate have on the bond?
   b. Calculate the new price, assuming there are still 10 years to maturity.
   c. By what percentage has the bond's price changed from its original $910 value?
   d. If the bond had 15 years to maturity, would there be a bigger or smaller change in price? Calculate the new price and percent change.
6. ***Maturity Risk.*** You are deciding between two semiannual coupon bonds. Both are issued by the same highly rated company, offer a coupon rate of 6 percent and have a face value of $1,000. Bond A has 10 years to maturity (current price $928.94), and Bond B has 20 years to maturity (current price $802.07).
   a. If both bonds are issued by the same company and pay the same coupon rate, why is one cheaper than the other?
   b. Calculate the approximate yield to maturity for each bond (or the exact yield using a financial calculator).
   c. Now assume that one year later, the yields on comparable investments have risen to 8% and 9% respectively. Calculate the new price for each of these bonds.
   d. Which bond had a larger percentage decrease in value?
7. ***After-Tax Interest Income.*** Simone owns 10 bonds from the same bond issuer. Each has a $1,000 face value and a 9 percent coupon rate. If Simone has a marginal tax rate of 25 percent, what is her annual after-tax interest income from these bonds?
8. ***After-Tax Yield.*** For each of the following, calculate the after-tax yield, assuming that the marginal federal income tax rate is 25 percent and the marginal state tax rate is 5 percent:
   a. Corporate bond held in taxable account, 8 percent before-tax yield
   b. Municipal bond (issued in the purchaser's state of residence) held in taxable account, 7 percent before-tax yield
   c. U.S. Treasury bond held in taxable account, 5 percent before-tax yield
9. ***Holding Period Return.*** One year ago, you bought one semiannual 8 percent coupon bond for $850. You sell it today for $900.
   a. Calculate your current yield.
   b. Calculate your capital gains yield for the year.
   c. Calculate your holding period return.
   d. Provide a plausible explanation for why the price of the bond increased during the year.
   e. Compute the holding period return, assuming that the bond's price fell from $900 to $850 during this year. What do you expect caused the decline in value?
10. ***Preferred Stock Dividends.*** A company's preferred stock has a par value of $25 and dividend rate of 7.5 percent. How much will be paid per share each year?
11. ***Value of Preferred Stock.*** A company is planning to sell preferred stock with a par value of $100 and dividend rate of 7 percent. If shares of preferred stock of other companies with similar risk characteristics are currently yielding 8 percent per year, what will investors be willing to pay for these shares?
12. ***Interest Rates and Preferred Stock Price.*** You are considering the purchase of shares of preferred stock with a par value of $110 and dividend rate of 8.2 percent.
   a. If the market price of the stock is currently $95, what is the yield?
   b. If market interest rates increase so that investors in these securities now require one percentage point more in yield, how will this affect the price of the stock?
13. ***Zero-Coupon Bonds.*** Bonnie wants to buy zero-coupon bonds as a means of saving for retirement. She finds that the current price

of a zero-coupon bond with a face value of $1,000 and 30 years to maturity is $231.40.

a. If she buys this bond and holds it to maturity, what annual yield to maturity will she earn before taxes?
b. Explain why it is advisable that Bonnie hold these bonds in a tax-deferred or tax-exempt retirement account.

14. ***Tax-Equivalent Yield.*** Lenore is subject to a 30 percent marginal tax rate, and she has purchased 6.5 percent municipal bonds which are exempt from federal and state taxes. What yield would she have to earn before tax on a taxable investment to obtain an after-tax interest yield equivalent to what she is earning on the municipals?
15. ***Bond Conversion.*** Kareem inherited 20 corporate convertible bonds that have a 5 percent coupon rate. Each has a face value of $1,000 and is convertible to 27 shares of the same firm's common stock. If the current market price of the company's stock is $30, should Kareem consider converting? If not, at what stock price would conversion be attractive?

Using Web Resources for Financial Planning

1. ***Investor Checklist.*** Go to *www.investinginbonds.com*, a website sponsored by the Bond Market Association, and click on "Investor's Checklist" for questions to consider in bond investing. Answer these questions to determine whether bond investing is appropriate for you, given your risk tolerance, investment objectives, and time horizon.
2. ***How Large Is the Federal Debt?*** Go to another Bond Market Association website at *www.bondmarkets.com* and click on "Research" to find the total value of U.S. Treasury Securities outstanding.
   a. How much has the federal debt increased since 2000 (in dollars)?
   b. What is the percentage increase since 2000?
3. ***Find Out How to Handle Accrued Interest.*** As explained in the chapter, when you buy a bond, a portion of the next coupon payment may accrue to the seller. Go to *www.bondsonline.com* and click on "Bond Basics" and then "Buying, Selling and Trading Bonds" to find the tutorial titled "Handling Accrued Interest When Bonds Are Traded." Use this to solve the following problem: You are buying a $1,000 bond that pays a semiannual 7 percent coupon on June 15 and December 15 of each year. You buy the bond on August 15. How much accrued interest will the bond seller be entitled to?
4. ***Find Bond Dealers.*** If you want to find banks and mutual funds that are members of the Bond Market Association, go to *www.investinginbonds.com* and click on "Bond Dealers." Locate one that has an office in your town.
5. ***Find Bond Ratings.*** Go to *www.standardandpoors.com/ratings* and look up the current rating of General Motors and Ford Motor bonds. Based on the ratings, which company's bonds would you expect to provide a greater yield to maturity?

Learning by Doing Solutions

LBD 13–1: 1. 8.5% × $1,000 = $85, so you'll receive $85/2 or $42.50 per six-month period; 2. The sinking fund is good because it lowers the risk that Cavalier will default on the bonds. The call is bad because you may be forced to sell back your bonds when you might not want to do so.

LBD 13–2: 1a. Municipal, secured, revenue; b. Corporate, unsecured, junk or high-yield, indexed.

LBD 13–3: 1a. Lower coupon, higher maturity risk; b. Longer time, higher price risk; 2. Decrease.

LBD 13–4: 1. You could buy zero-coupon bonds that will mature when your child is expected to go to college. You may want to hold them in a tax-deferred account or in your child's name in order to minimize the taxes you pay; 2. On July 15, 2004, one of the bond issues reported for IBM had a coupon rate of 4.75 percent and a maturity date of November 29, 2012. The price on that date was $987.06, and the bond's yield was 4.94 percent. The other issue reported had a coupon rate of 6.22 percent, matured in August 1, 2027, had a price of $1021.83 and a yield of 6.043 percent.

LBD 13–5: 1. The price is less than the par value, so the market rate is greater than the dividend rate; 2a. 10% × 50 = 5; b. The price equals the par value, so the market rate is equal to the dividend rate.

Building Financial Planning Skills Through Case Applications

Case 13–1 Ernie and Belinda Maxwell Evaluate Their Investment Plan

Ernie and Belinda Maxwell often tell people that they're "68 years young." They have an active lifestyle, playing golf, regularly volunteering at church, and traveling around the country in their RV to visit their three children and five grandchildren. But as they approach their 50th wedding anniversary, the couple admit that they're beginning to worry about their finances. When Ernie first retired in the mid-1990s, his retirement fund accumulation of over $1 million had seemed more than sufficient to support their lifestyle.

Their house was paid off, and their children were grown. After investing all the retirement money in corporate bonds with a laddered maturity structure of 20 years (since they didn't want to risk it in the stock market), they were happy to find that their nest egg produced income of about $80,000 a year before taxes. Ten years later, the Maxwells (who are in the 25% tax bracket) are finding that it's harder to live on that amount of income each year. They've gradually been selling bonds, so they now have less to invest. Their retirement fund currently represents about $850,000 in face value and is generating only $60,000 in before-tax income. And as they've reinvested money from maturing bonds, Ernie and Belinda have been dismayed to find that market yields have fallen since they originally retired to the present level of 5.5 percent for 20-year corporate bonds. The Maxwells, who are in excellent health, expect to live into their 90s based on their family histories, and looking forward to this, they're worried about outliving their money.

a. What was the average coupon rate on original bonds in their portfolio? If market rates rise, will their income rise accordingly? Why or why not?
b. What is the average coupon rate on their current $850,000 (in face value) retirement fund?
c. Why have the average coupon rates fallen over the past ten years?
d. Are the Maxwells correct to worry about outliving their assets? Explain.
e. Is their present asset allocation (100% corporate bonds) appropriate for their life-cycle stage and risk preferences? Why or why not?
f. Over the late 1990s, what did the Maxwells give up when they chose a fixed-income investment strategy? If they continue to buy and hold bonds, is their investment strategy fairly low-risk? What risk exposures do they still face?

Case 13–2 Great Uncle Clyde Leaves Mike a Bundle

Mike Hettwer was pleased to find that his Great Uncle Clyde, who lived to the ripe old age of 87, had remembered all his nieces and nephews in his will. Instead of leaving them with cash, however, Clyde's will said that he wanted them all to get a taste of investing. Clyde's bequest to Mike was a portfolio of bonds issued by different corporations, with a total face value of $60,000. Mike is 25 years old and earns $40,000 per year. His marginal tax rate is 15 percent, and he has no other investments at the moment. Mike asked you for advice on his investments, and you requested that he look up some information on them first. He has summarized the information as follows:

Issuing Company	No. of Bonds	Moody's Rating	Term to Maturity	Coupon Rate	Yield	Price
Bond 1	10	Aaa	25	5.3	6.0	910.00
Bond 2	10	Aaa	13	6.7	5.2	1,140.46
Bond 3	10	Ba	20	7.5	7.5	1,000.00
Bond 4	10	Ba	10	8.2	7.0	1,085.27
Bond 5	10	B	17	9.0	8.5	1,044.54
Bond 6	10	B	5	7.8	8.0	991.89

a. Based on the information on this table, estimate the market value of Mike's portfolio.
b. Mike is pretty excited to find out how high the average yield on these investments is. Do you agree that these are good investments for him? Explain.
c. Mike asks you why the two bonds with Aaa ratings don't have the same yield. Explain.
d. Is the difference in yield between the Aaa-rated bonds and the other bonds reasonable?
e. How diversified is Mike's portfolio based on default risk? Assuming he decides to stay invested in bonds, should he consider any changes in asset allocation?
f. Mike is wondering whether it would make sense to sell some or all of these bonds and invest in stocks instead. What would you recommend?

DEVELOPING PERSONAL FINANCIAL skills for life

Learning about Yourself

13–1. Attitudes Toward Bond Investing

Does bond investing fit with your risk attitudes and personality? Take the following assessment to find out more. For each of the following statements, indicate the degree to which it is consistent with your viewpoint as follows: 5 = strongly agree; 4 = agree; 3 = neutral; 2 = disagree; 1 = strongly disagree.

1. At this stage in my life, I need to focus on building my wealth.
2. No matter what I decide to invest in, I plan to be an active trader.
3. It's okay if an investment exposes me to the risk of losing money, as long as the returns are high.
4. I would be embarrassed to tell my friends that I'm investing in bonds—they're more appropriate for old people.
5. I don't like the idea of investing in something that is so dependent on what the government decides to do with interest rates.
6. I don't need an investment that will give me a regular income.
7. I want to be able to average a return of at least 10 percent on my investments.
8. I don't have very much money available to invest at the moment.

Scoring:

Add up your total score. The higher the score, the less likely you are to consider bond investing at this stage in your life. You should consider your answers to this assessment in conjunction with those from the Chapter 12 assessment. It may be that you're not ready for bond investing because you have insufficient funds, or it may be that you consider both stocks and bonds to be too risky because you still need to build the safety layer of your financial plan and can't afford to take the risk of losing principal. In any case, you should revisit the answers to both these assessments as your income and wealth change over your life cycle.

Developing Your Skills

13–2. Matching Your Investments to Your Goals

In Chapter 12, you considered whether stock investing was an appropriate strategy for achieving each of your personal financial goals. Revisit this question, again using the worksheet in your *Personal Financial Planner*, and determine whether bond investing would be a more appropriate strategy for achieving any of your goals. In completing the worksheet, be sure to include consideration of the type of bond you might select, including issuer, tax status, and time to maturity.

PFP Worksheet 45
Matching Goals
and Investments

13–3. Keeping Tabs on Interest Rates

The key variable in bond portfolio yield and performance is market interest rates. Go to finance.yahoo.com and click on "Market Indices" to find the recent history of yields on Treasury bonds.

a. Look at the graph of the last year's Treasury bond rates. What trend do you observe?
b. Based on the recent history, what do you expect rates to do in the next year?
c. Search the website for news stories or analysts' opinions on interest rate expectations. Are they consistent with your opinion? Why or why not?

13–4. Tracking Bond Values

PFP Worksheet 47
Bond Tracker

Select several bonds that you think you'd like to invest in. If possible, select bonds that differ in maturity, type of issuer, coupon rate, and credit risk. Use the worksheet in your *Personal Financial Planner* to track their values for a period of time.

a. In this chapter, we presented several rules of thumb regarding the effect of interest rate changes on prices. See if you can find support for the differences in interest rate sensitivity based on maturity, default risk, and coupon rate.
b. Based on the yields of the bonds you've selected, can you estimate default risk premiums and maturity risk premiums?

13–5. Preferred Stock versus Bonds

Select a company that has both preferred stock and bonds outstanding by consulting the "Preferred Stock Listings" and "Corporate Bonds" sections of the *Wall Street Journal* (or another reputable source).

a. Summarize the data reported on each type of security.
b. Calculate the approximate yield to maturity for the bond issue and compare it to the yield reported for the preferred stock. How can you explain the difference?
c. If the company has more than one bond issue outstanding, how can you explain the difference in yield on each?
d. If the company has more than one preferred stock issue outstanding, how can you explain the difference in yield on each?

THE NAVIGATOR

- ☐ Review Before Studying this Chapter list.
- ☐ Scan Learning Objectives.
- ☐ Take Myth or Fact quiz and find the answers throughout the chapter.
- ☐ Read chapter and answer Learning by Doing exercises.
- ☐ Review Key Terms and Key Calculations.
- ☐ Do end-of-chapter exercises.
- ☐ Take review quiz on the text website.
- ☐ Solve end-of-chapter cases.

BEFORE studying this chapter, you should review

- Investing fundamentals (Chapter 11).
- Secondary mortgage market (Chapter 8).
- Costs and benefits of home ownership (Chapter 8).

CHAPTER 14

Mutual Funds, Investment Real Estate, and Other Investment Alternatives

Myth or Fact?

Consider each of the following statements and decide whether it is a *myth* or a *fact*. Look for the answers in the *Fact* boxes in the chapter.

	MYTH	FACT
1. Selecting stocks by shooting a dart at the stock page of the *Wall Street Journal* has sometimes produced more profitable portfolios than those selected by professional money managers.	☐	☐
2. Although you can expect to get a lower annual return in a bond mutual fund than in a stock fund, you can't actually lose money.	☐	☐
3. Investors who split their money among several mutual funds are better diversified than investors who only have shares in one or two funds.	☐	☐
4. A sure way to make money in real estate is to buy a "fixer upper" house, remodel it, and sell it for a profit.	☐	☐
5. Buying collectibles such as comic books and dolls rarely provides a competitive investment return.	☐	☐

LEARNING objectives

1. Describe the benefits and costs of investing in mutual funds.
2. Classify mutual funds by their investment objectives and portfolio composition.
3. Establish strategies for selecting among mutual funds and evaluating fund performance.
4. Identify the advantages and disadvantages of direct and indirect real estate investments.
5. Explain why investments in precious metals, gems, collectibles, and derivatives are speculative.

...applying the planning process

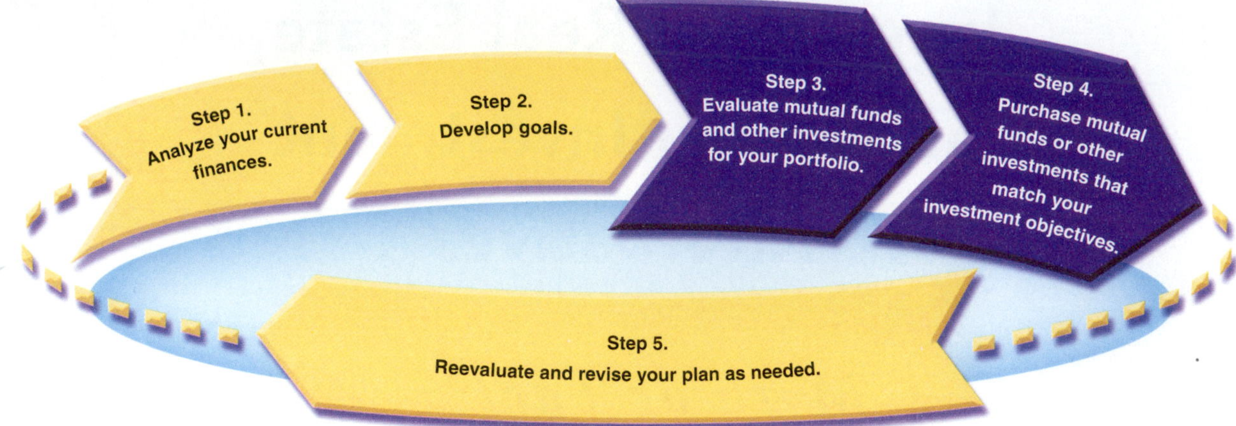

In the last three chapters, you've read about the basics of investing and how to evaluate stock and bond investment alternatives for your portfolio. Although developing a portfolio of individual stocks and bonds may sound like fun, it's not a realistic alternative for everybody. If you don't have much money to invest right now, you probably won't be able to achieve enough diversification in your portfolio, at least in the beginning, and the trading costs will be too high relative to your returns. In addition, many people are too busy with work, school, family, or all three, to take the time to make informed stock and bond investment decisions. These reasons provide an explanation for why more than half of all U.S. households own mutual funds.

In this chapter, you'll learn how mutual funds can enable you to participate in the stock and bond markets while achieving better overall diversification with lower transactions costs. We begin by looking at what types of funds are available and how to evaluate and select funds for your portfolio. We also examine several other investment alternatives, including investment real estate and a variety of more speculative investments. Despite the varying subject matter, the principles are the same as those we've considered in the last three chapters—you still must consider your goals and use what you know about investing to make decisions that will help you meet those goals.

Chapter Preview

What Is a Mutual Fund?

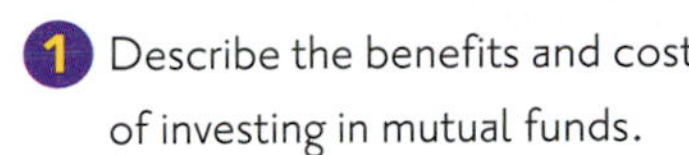

1 Describe the benefits and costs of investing in mutual funds.

A **mutual fund** is technically an open-end investment company, as described in more detail below, but the term is often applied more broadly to any arrangement in which investors' funds are pooled and used to purchase securities. Although the mechanism can differ across funds, the cash flows generated by the securities in the pool are later distributed to the investors. Investors who purchase shares in mutual funds are like other corporate shareholders—they have no say in the day-to-day decisions about buying and selling securities for the pool, but they have an equity interest in the pool of assets and a residual claim on the profits of the pool. We first take a closer look at the net asset value, a measure of a mutual fund investor's ownership interest. Next, we review the growing popularity of mutual funds, the various types of investment companies, and the advantages and costs associated with mutual fund investing.

mutual fund
An open-end investment company that uses its investors' funds to purchase stocks, bonds, or other financial assets.

What Does a Mutual Fund Investor Actually Own?

One measure of the value of an investor's claim on mutual fund assets is called the **net asset value.** This is calculated as assets minus liabilities, per share:

$$\text{Net asset value} = \frac{\text{Market value of assets} - \text{Market value of liabilities}}{\text{Number of shares}}$$

net asset value
The market value of a mutual fund's assets less the market value of its liabilities, per share.

For example, suppose you own one share of a mutual fund that has 5 million shares outstanding. The fund portfolio is currently worth \$100 million, and its liabilities include \$2 million owed to investment advisors and \$1 million in rent, wages, and other expenses. Your net asset value is therefore

$$\text{Net asset value} = \frac{\$100{,}000{,}000 - \$3{,}000{,}000}{5{,}000{,}000} = \frac{\$97{,}000{,}000}{5{,}000{,}000} = \$19.40 \text{ per share}$$

If the securities that are held in a mutual fund increase in value, the net asset value of the shares of the mutual fund should also increase in value, even though these increases are technically unrealized capital gains. The objective of fund managers is therefore to invest in assets that will continue to grow in value over time. This is an important point to keep in mind as you learn more about this type of investment—mutual fund values will tend to track the performance of the assets they invest in. So if the stock market is down, stock mutual fund values will decline as well, since the assets they have invested in will have lower market values.

Learning by Doing 14-1

1. Use the following information from the January 1, 2005, balance sheet for the Balanced Growth and Income mutual fund sponsored by Frontier Investment Company to calculate the net asset value:

Assets	\$150 million
Liabilities	\$10 million
Shares	12.3 million

2. If the value of the assets in Frontier's portfolio increased in value during 2005, what would happen to the net asset value?

The Increasing Popularity of Mutual Funds

Mutual fund investing by individuals has dramatically increased over the last two decades. As detailed in Exhibit 14-1, less than 6 percent of households owned mutual fund shares in 1980 compared with nearly 50 percent in 2003—more than 50 million households. Although some of this growth has been attributable to an increase in defined contribution employment retirement plans, which invest primarily in mutual funds on behalf of employees, the bull market of the 1990s had an effect as well. The lure of double-digit increases in portfolio value was hard to resist, and the number of individual investors more than doubled during that decade. Over the last three decades, probably in response to investor demand, the number of mutual fund investment alternatives available to individuals has risen significantly as well. Exhibit 14-2 shows recent

EXHIBIT 14-1

Percent and Number of U.S. Households Owning Open-End Mutual Funds, 1980 to 2003

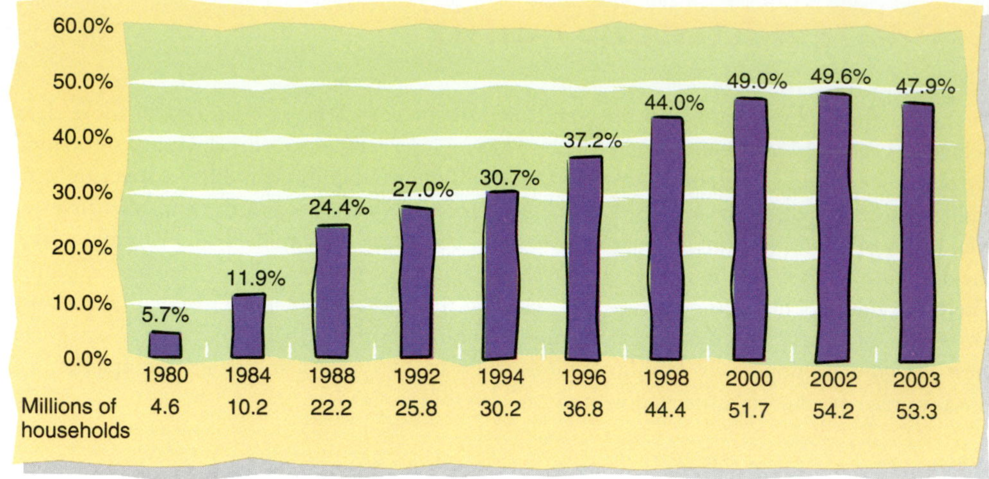

Source: Data from *2004 Mutual Fund Fact Book*, Washington, D.C.: Investment Company Institute, (2004), p. 80; www.ici.org.

EXHIBIT 14-2

Growth of Open-End Mutual Funds, 1970 to 2003

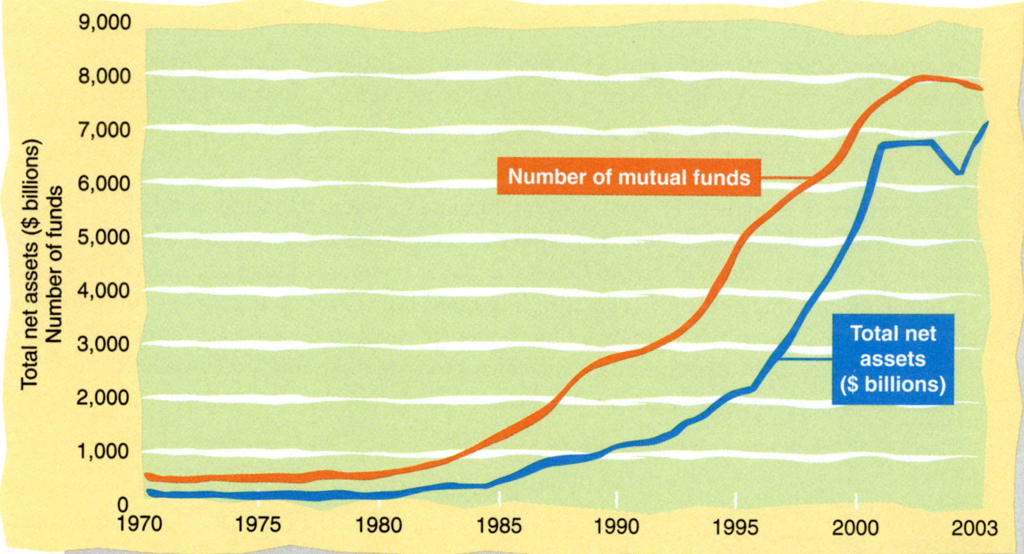

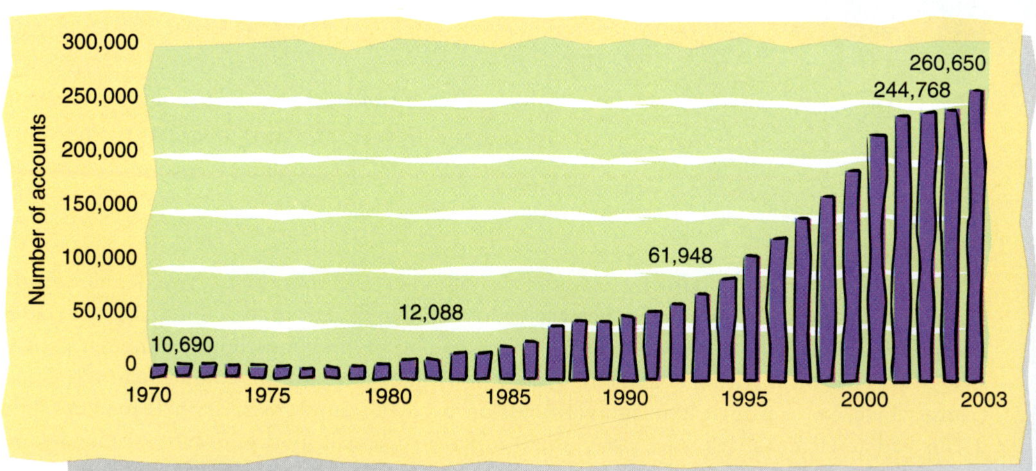

Source: Data from *2004 Mutual Fund Fact Book*, Washington, D.C.: Investment Company Institute, (2004), Table 1, p. 105; www.ici.org.

growth in the number of mutual funds, the value of the funds, and the number of accounts. Although there were only 1,000 U.S. mutual funds in existence 20 years ago, today investors have more than 8,000 to choose from.

Types of Investment Companies

As mentioned, a mutual fund is technically a type of **investment company,** usually a corporation but sometimes a partnership or trust. Investment companies are financial intermediaries that provide the service of pooling small dollar amounts from many investors and investing those funds in a wide variety of assets. Each investor buys shares in the company, and the company uses the dollars to make investments on behalf of the investment pool. Until the enactment of comprehensive securities laws in the 1930s, investors had little confidence in this type of investment. Today, however, these investment shares are considered securities under the legal definition of the word and are therefore entitled to all the protections afforded to other financial assets. That means the investment company must provide all potential investors with disclosure information, much like the information you'd get for a stock or bond investment, and it must make regular reports to the Securities and Exchange Commission, which regulates them. Since fund investors depend on the managers to make decisions that are in their best interests, actions that are in conflict with this fiduciary duty such as those discussed in the *News You Can Use* box, "Mutual Fund Scandals Prompt SEC to Act," tend to create negative publicity for the entire industry.

investment company

A financial intermediary that invests its funds in securities or other assets.

NEWS you can use

Mutual Fund Scandals Prompt SEC to Act

New York Attorney General Eliot Spitzer is credited with uncovering a host of trading abuses in the mutual fund industry in 2003. His investigation found that several fund companies, including Janus and Bank of America, were engaging in market timing and late trading. *Market timing* refers to the frequent buying and selling of mutual fund shares to exploit price discrepancies in securities held by the fund. Using this strategy, some fund managers were making big profits at the same time their shareholders were losing money. For example, investors in the PBHG Growth Fund lost 65 percent from March 2000 through November 2001 (an annualized loss of 45%), while the fund manager, Gary Pilgrim, earned a positive 49 percent per year, $3.9 million in total, on his own stake in the company. How could this happen? Pilgrim owned his stake through an investment in a hedge fund (an unregulated investment pool) called Appalachian Trail. Appalachian bought and sold PBHG Growth a total of 240 times during the short period in question, making its profit by betting that the value of the fund would decline. This, of course, creates a conflict of interest for the fund manager, who has a fiduciary obligation to the shareholders, who only gain if the fund increases in value.

"Several fund companies were engaging in market timing and late trading"

Late trading refers to buying or selling mutual fund shares after financial markets have closed but getting that day's closing price. In June 2004, the SEC filed fraud charges based on late trading against Geek Securities, which had accepted trades from customers after the market closed at 4 P.M. but used a time stamp that showed the orders had been received before the close. Spitzer has compared this strategy to betting on a race after the horses have crossed the finish line.

As a result of the mutual fund scandals, several big-name fund companies and executives agreed to settlements worth hundreds of millions of dollars to resolve improper trading cases. In June 2004, the SEC passed a regulatory change that requires the chairman of a board of directors of a fund to be independent of the company (or companies) managing the fund. Previously, most chairs had close ties with the parent investment company.

Sources: Allen Sloan, "The Mutual Fund Scandal: Unfair Fight," *Newsweek*, December 8, 2003; Associated Press, "SEC Accuses Florida Firm of Mutual Fund Abuses," June 7, 2004; Associated Press, "Mutual Funds Should Aid Investors," June 15, 2004.

Although different types of investment companies are often lumped together in a discussion of mutual funds, the Investment Company Act of 1940 identifies several distinct types that provide pooling opportunities for individual investors. These include open-end funds, closed-end funds, unit investment trusts, and real estate investment trusts.

open-end fund

An investment company that sells its shares directly to investors and buys them back on request.

Open-End Funds.

When people talk about mutual fund investing, they're generally referring to buying and selling shares of open-end investment companies, or open-end mutual funds. By far the most common type of investment company, an **open-end fund** is different from the other types discussed in this section in that: (1) it is required to buy back shares at any time an investor wants to sell, and (2) it continuously offers new shares for sale to the public. The price for purchases and sales is usually the net asset value plus trading costs, which will be explained in a later section. The issuing company provides the only market for the shares, since they aren't traded in the secondary market between investors. The investment company is free to issue new shares at any time to raise additional funds for investment and to meet investor demand for the shares. Open-end funds can be very large, with many billions of dollars under management.

closed-end fund

An investment company that has a fixed number of shares, which are traded in the secondary market.

Closed-End Funds.

A **closed-end fund** is an investment company that issues a fixed number of shares that trade on a stock exchange or in the over-the-counter market. The process of issuing shares is very similar to that discussed in Chapter 12 for stocks. The initial public offering of shares is sold directly to investors, after which the shares trade between investors in the secondary market. Closed-end funds hire professional managers to invest the funds in a diversified set of assets that are intended to meet stated investment objectives.

For more information on closed-end funds, exchange-traded funds, and unit investment trusts, visit the Investment Company Institute website at www.ici.org.

Closed-end funds trade primarily on the major stock exchanges, such as the New York Stock Exchange, the American Stock Exchange, and the NASDAQ. You can find a listing of funds, along with their dividends, close prices, and net change in value from the previous day's trading, in the *Wall Street Journal* under the heading "Closed-End Funds." The market values of shares traded on the secondary market fluctuate with supply and demand and may be greater or less than the value of the assets held in the fund. Although closed-end funds make up only a small proportion of the total number of mutual funds in existence (around 600 in the United States, compared with 8,000 open-end funds), they are growing in popularity—the number of closed-end funds increased more than 20 percent from 2000 to 2003.

exchange-traded fund (ETF)

An investment company with professionally, but not actively, managed assets, often intended to track a market index, and shares that trade in the secondary market.

Exchange-Traded Funds.

An **exchange-traded fund (ETF)** combines some of the characteristics of open-end and closed-end funds. It is technically an open-end fund, since the company is free to issue new shares or redeem old shares to increase or decrease the number of shares outstanding. But like a closed-end fund, an ETF is traded on an organized exchange, and share prices are determined by market forces. Investors buy ETF shares through a broker just as they would purchase common stock shares of any publicly traded firm.

Although the number of ETFs is still small relative to other types of investment companies, as you can see in Exhibit 14-3, their size and popularity are growing rapidly. This is largely because many are designed to be index funds, investing in a set of securities that mimic the performance of a particular market index such as the S&P 500 with low expenses (since they aren't actively managed). In addition, most have fairly low minimum investment amounts. For these reasons, since

EXHIBIT 14-3

Number and Size of Different Types of Investment Companies

	Open-End Funds		Closed-End Funds		Exchange-Traded Funds	
	Number of Funds	Assets ($million)	Number of Funds	Assets ($millions)	Number of Funds	Assets ($millions)
1996	6,248	3,525,800	498	146,991	19	2,411
1997	6,684	4,468,200	488	151,845	19	6,707
1998	7,314	5,525,210	193	155,814	29	15,568
1999	7,791	6,846,340	512	147,016	30	33,873
2000	8,155	6,964,670	482	143,134	80	65,585
2001	8,305	6,974,950	493	141,251	102	82,993
2002	8,244	6,390,360	545	158,805	113	102,143
2003	8,126	7,414,080	586	213,973	119	150,983

Source: Data from 2004 Mutual Fund Fact Book, Washington, D.C.: Investment Company Institute (2004), Table 5, p. 105; Table 41, p. 145; Table 43, p. 147; www.ici.org.

their inception, the financial press has been strongly advising this type of fund for individual investors seeking diversification and low costs. Investors who buy shares in an ETF based on the S&P 500 (called a "Spider") will see an increase in the value of their shares when the S&P 500 increases in value. Similarly, investors in "Diamonds," ETFs based on the Dow Jones Industrial Average, will benefit when the Dow goes up. Fortunately, these gains don't have to be recognized for tax purposes until the shares are sold at some point in the future.

Unit Investment Trusts. Another type of investment company is a **unit investment trust (UIT),** which buys and holds a fixed portfolio of securities for a period of time that's determined by the life of the investments in the trust (usually, fixed-maturity debt securities). Since there isn't any change in the portfolio over the period of investment, this type of fund is essentially unmanaged. The manager of the pool, called the trustee, initially purchases the pool of investments and deposits them in a trust. Owners are issued redeemable trust certificates, which entitle them to proportionate shares of any income and principal payments received by the trust and a distribution of their proportionate share of the proceeds at the termination of the trust.

unit investment trust (UIT)

An investment company that buys and holds a fixed portfolio of securities for a period of time determined by the life of the investments in the trust.

The investors in a unit investment trust generally pay a premium over what it costs the trustee to purchase the underlying assets, providing the equivalent of a commission to the trustee for the service of pooling the funds and distributing the income and principal. Since the funds are unmanaged, the fee should be lower than that for a comparable managed fund, but it still can be as high as 3 to 5 percent. Why would an investor by willing to incur such a high cost? The answer lies in the type of securities that make up unit investment trusts. About 90 percent of these assets are fixed-income securities, primarily municipal bonds. Each trust specializes in a certain type of security, so one might hold only municipal bonds and another only high-yield corporate bonds. The high cost of individual bonds (usually $1,000 minimum) makes it otherwise difficult for individual investors to include these investment classes in their portfolios. The availability of unit investment trust shares means that small investors can still participate in a relatively diversified pool of specialized debt securities. Although there isn't an active secondary market for the trust certificates, the trustee will usually buy them back on request.

A unit investment trust continues in existence only as long as assets remain in the trust. Thus, a trust invested in short-term securities might exist for only a few months, whereas a trust holding municipal bonds might have a life of 20 years or more depending on the maturities of the bonds held.

Real Estate Investment Trusts. A **real estate investment trust (REIT)** is a special type of closed-end investment company that invests in real estate and mortgages. By law, a REIT must have a buy-and-hold investment strategy, a professional manager (the trustee), and at least 100 shareholders. The trustee initially issues shares of stock and then uses the funds to invest in a portfolio of assets according to the terms of the trust, much as in a unit investment trust. The difference is that the REIT doesn't have a limited lifespan, since most real estate investments don't have fixed maturities.

real estate investment trust (REIT)

A closed-end fund that invests primarily in real estate or mortgages.

REITs offer individual investors the opportunity to diversify their investment portfolios into real estate. Many investors wouldn't otherwise have access to this investment class because of the high initial investment required and the liquidity risk involved. In many respects, REITs look like stock investments and closed-end mutual funds, trading on national exchanges and distributing profits to the investors through dividends. They aren't as liquid as stocks, however, and they must distribute most of their income each year to investors, resulting in higher tax obligations for investors. Even though recent tax law changes reduced the tax rate on most corporate dividends, REIT dividend distributions are still generally taxable as ordinary income.

REITs are usually distinguished by the types of real estate investments they make. Equity REITs, which make up about 90 percent of the market, specialize in making direct investments in rental and commercial properties, such as office buildings and shopping centers. Mortgage REITs focus on mortgage investments such as residential and construction loans.

During the stock market downturn from 2000 to 2002, if you had been invested primarily in stock mutual funds, as so many investors were, you would have lost at least one-third of your wealth. If instead you had some, or all, of your portfolio in REITs, you would have fared substantially better. In fact, REITs were the only bright spot on the equity investment landscape. Although the S&P 500 fell 40.1 percent from December 1999 to December 2002, equity REIT values increased 48.3 percent during that same period. The fact that REIT returns are not highly correlated with overall stock market returns makes them valuable for diversifying your portfolio.

The Advantages of Mutual Fund Investing

Mutual funds have some advantages that make them preferable to investments in stocks, bonds, and other financial assets, from the point of view of individual investors. The advantages include increased diversification, reduced transaction costs, professional money management, and greater liquidity. Although these points apply to most types of investment companies, we focus more specifically on open-end funds in several of the examples since they represent such a large share of the total number of funds.

Diversification. Suppose you have $200 per month to invest. If you buy stocks or bonds directly, it will be difficult for you to buy more than one company's securities at a time, and you might even have to save up for several months before you can make certain investments such as bonds (which often cost around $1,000 each). Furthermore, if one of the companies you've invested in goes downhill, a big chunk of your investment portfolio will go downhill with it. Now, consider instead what will happen if you split the $200 and invest half in a diversified stock mutual fund and half in a diversified bond mutual fund. You'll not only be able to allocate your money between two asset classes, but you'll also become an owner (although admittedly a small one) of a diverse pool of investments in each asset class. If a single company's stock or bond price declines in value, it should have only a minimal impact on your portfolio.

Mutual funds are broadly invested in the financial markets, as you can see in Exhibit 14-4, which shows the overall distribution of open-end mutual fund assets across different asset classes.

EXHIBIT 14-4

Open-End Mutual Fund Portfolio Asset Allocation, 1993 and 2003

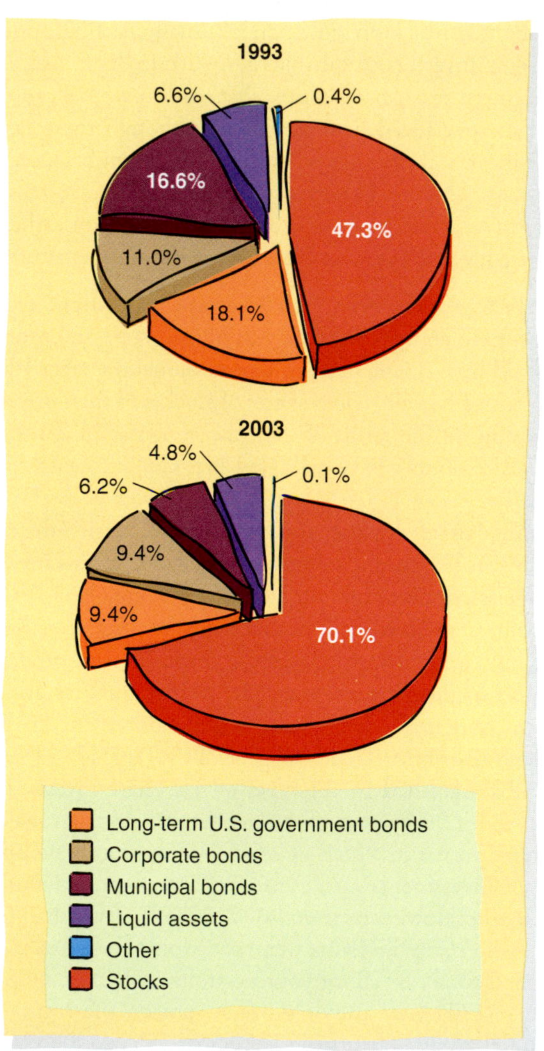

Source: Data from *2004 Mutual Fund Fact Book*, Washington, D.C.: Investment Company Institute (2004), Table 23, p. 127; www.ici.org.

An interesting thing to note is that the percentage in stocks has increased so much, from less than half of all mutual fund assets in 1993 to more than two-thirds in 2003.

Although Exhibit 14-4 tells us about diversification in the aggregate, it doesn't tell us anything about the diversification within each fund. To determine the asset allocation of a particular fund, you have to look at its annual report, which lists all the fund's holdings as of the end of the reporting period. As we'll see, mutual funds normally specialize in one or a few asset classes, so they don't individually have the kind of asset allocation shown in the exhibit.

As an example, let's take a look at the distribution of fund assets for the Quaker Mid-cap Value A fund in June 2004 as shown in Exhibit 14-5. This fund has 94.8 percent of its assets in stocks and the remainder primarily in cash. Although it's classified as a mid-cap fund, the allocation by market cap indicates that the fund still holds some large- and small-cap stocks. With more than $6 billion invested in more than 12 industry segments, this fund has far more business sector diversification than most small investors could hope to achieve by buying stocks individually. Its largest allocations are in industrial materials (25.97%), business services (16.14%), and financial services (13.63%). Many mutual funds are invested in thousands of different securities, and their quarterly investor reports, that list the exact holdings, are dozens of pages long.

Fact #1

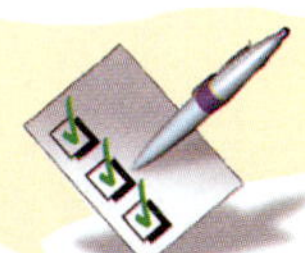

Professional money management doesn't necessarily produce better returns than random selection. The results of several years of contests in which the skills of several investment professionals were pitted against stock picks made by throwing a dart at the stock page showed the experts' stock picks outperforming the dartboard about 60 percent of the time, but barely edging out the Dow Jones Industrial Average. Since the pros tended to pick riskier stocks, on average, than either the darts or the index, it's really hard to argue that they won the contest.

Transaction Costs. If you trade individual stocks, you must pay brokerage fees. Although these costs can be relatively low, you still must recoup them before you start to earn a profit on your investments. Since mutual funds make large-volume trades, their costs per trade are likely to be substantially lower than yours as an individual. Of course, you may also pay fees to invest in some mutual funds, as discussed later in this chapter. Another cost savings to consider is the time you would spend making decisions for an investment portfolio made up of individual stocks and bonds. Investment companies will provide reports to help you keep track of your investments with them, including your capital gains distributions, dividends, purchases, and sales.

Professional Money Management. One reason investors like mutual funds is that the individual investment selection decision is taken out of their hands. The investment company

EXHIBIT 14-5

Asset Allocation in a Mutual Fund Portfolio, June 2004

Fund name: Quaker Mid-cap Value A

Market capitalization: $6.69 billion

Allocation of Portfolio by Sector		**Allocation of Portfolio by Market Cap**	
Information sector		Giant	1.23%
Software	0.05%	Large	18.33
Hardware	7.23	Medium	70.38
Media	0.08	Small	10.06
Telecommunications	2.28	Micro	0.00
Total	9.64%	Total	100.00%
Service sector		**Allocation of Portfolio by Asset Class**	
Health care	2.68%	Cash	4.1%
Consumer services	7.70	Stocks	94.8
Business services	16.14	Bonds	0.0
Financial services	13.63	Other	1.1
Total	40.15%	Total	100.0%
Manufacturing sector		**Allocation of Portfolio by Country**	
Consumer goods	8.26%	United States	91.3%
Industrial materials	25.97	Foreign	8.7
Energy	8.34	Total	100.0%
Utilities	7.64		
Total	50.21%		

hires professionals whose job it is to manage the funds, generally making use of the most current data and analysis tools available. Many of the largest companies (not including those that simply buy and hold) have full-time staffs of security analysts. Of course, even the experts aren't always right, so professional management is no guarantee of performance, but you can probably assume that the professional money manager knows more than you do and that his or her overall objective is the same as yours—to increase the value of your investment.

Liquidity. Recall that liquidity is the ability to convert an asset to cash without loss of value. Under this definition, we'd have to conclude that mutual funds are *somewhat* liquid. If you need access to your money, it's fairly easy to sell your mutual fund shares if you own a closed-end fund, but the price will depend on market supply and demand forces. If you own shares in an open-end fund, you can nearly always sell them back to the investment company, but the price you get will depend on the value of the total portfolio at the time you sell. In either case, you may have to pay a transaction fee, as discussed later in the chapter.

Although the shares of a mutual fund may not be quite as liquid as some of the stocks and bonds the fund invests in, they can be far more liquid than other investments you might make. Municipal bonds and real estate, for example, have fairly low liquidity, so holding shares in a mutual fund that invests in these assets provides you with much more liquidity than you'd have if you invested in the assets directly.

Dividend Reinvestment. Most mutual funds allow you to automatically reinvest dividends and capital gain distributions, similar to the dividend reinvestment plans for stocks discussed in Chapter 11. Instead of receiving immediate cash flow, you use your dividends and distributions to buy additional shares in the mutual fund. Since the majority of mutual fund investors are still in the wealth accumulation phase and therefore don't need the current cash flow, this is a very desirable feature.

Beneficiary Designation. When you open a mutual fund account, you can usually designate where you want the funds to go when you die. This is an advantage because it will allow your heirs to avoid the costs and hassles of probate, which are discussed in further detail in Chapter 17.

Withdrawal Options. Although you initially invest in a mutual fund to save for a future goal, the time will come when you want to start converting the shares to cash. Mutual funds provide several options for this process. You can receive a set amount per month, redeem a certain number of shares per month, take only the current income (distributions of dividends and capital gains), or make a lump sum withdrawal of all or part of the account. For funds designated as tax-qualified retirement accounts, specific limitations apply to when you can begin withdrawing the money, as will be discussed in the following chapter.

The Costs of Mutual Fund Investing

The benefits offered by mutual funds—such as liquidity, professional management, and diversification—don't come free. Fund investors can therefore expect to pay a variety of fees and expenses. The fund is required to disclose its fees and expenses in a standardized fee table at the front of its prospectus, a document which must be provided to investors. The fee table must break out the fees and expenses shareholders can expect to pay so that they can easily compare the costs of different funds. We can divide these costs into those paid directly by shareholders and those paid for out of fund assets.

Shareholder Fees. Fees paid directly by shareholders may include one or more of the following:

- A one-time sales charge, commonly known as a "load," to compensate a financial professional for arranging the transaction.
- A redemption fee to cover the costs, other than sales costs, of the investor's sale of shares back to the company.
- An exchange fee when an investor transfers money from one fund to another within the same fund family.
- An annual account maintenance fee charged to cover the costs of providing services to investors who maintain small accounts.

Fund Expenses. In addition to the charges paid directly by investors, funds incur expenses that are deducted directly from the funds' assets before earnings are distributed. These expenses impose an indirect cost on investors, since they reduce the investors' returns. They may include some combination of the following:

- An annual management fee charged by the fund's investment advisor for managing the portfolio.
- Annual distribution fees, commonly known as 12b-1 fees, to compensate sales professionals for marketing and advertising fund shares. These fees are increasingly being used to compensate professional advisers for services provided to fund shareholders at the time of purchase, but are limited to a maximum of 1 percent of fund assets per year.
- Other operational expenses, such as the costs of maintaining computerized customer account services, maintaining a website, record keeping, printing, and mailing.

You can find out more about the types and amounts of fees for various funds at several investment websites, including www.morningstar.com (Morningstar Mutual Funds, Inc.), www.brill.com (Brills Mutual Funds Interactive), and www.mfea.com (Mutual Fund Investors Center).

Comparing Costs. As mentioned, the prospectus for each fund must include a standardized fee table so that investors can compare the costs of investing in different funds. In addition, there are many other resources that can help you to make direct comparisons of expenses. The *Wall Street Journal* daily mutual fund quotations include an indicator for each type of fee, although the actual amount isn't reported. Many websites also make this information available. In comparing the costs of different funds, it's useful to understand the differences between load and no-load funds and how to interpret the expense ratio.

Load Versus No-Load. As noted above, mutual fund purchasers may pay a commission or sales charge, called the load. Mutual funds are thus classified as either load, if they charge a fee, or no-load, if they don't. Most open-end mutual funds assess a **front-end load** at the time of purchase. The load can be as high as 8.5 percent of the purchase price of the shares; however, the average is around 5 percent, and some loads are as low as 2 percent. Some load funds charge a **back-end load,** officially known as a *contingent deferred sales charge,* if you sell your shares back to the fund within a certain period after your purchase. These fees often become smaller over time and are intended to encourage investors to hold on to their shares. For example, you might have a charge of 6 percent if you sell the first year, 5 percent the second year, and so on.

front-end load

A commission or sales charge paid by mutual fund investors at the time they purchase shares.

back-end load

A charge paid by mutual fund investors at the time they sell shares.

A fund that carries a front-end load has the effect of reducing the amount of your investment. For example, if you have $1,000 to invest and the fund has a 5 percent load, or $50, you'll be paying $1,000 but only getting $950 worth of shares. As with other types of transaction costs, you'll need to earn a rate of return on your investment that's sufficient to offset the costs and also compensate you for the risk that you bear. In other words, if you receive a dividend distribution this year in the amount of $50, you won't really have earned a positive return on your investment—you'll only be back to the $1,000 you started with. Since front-end loads are only charged at the time of purchase, a buy-and-hold investor is less affected by them. Over a 10- or 20-year holding period, a one-time $50 sales charge is relatively insignificant. But if you're an active investor, it isn't a good idea to buy load funds.

A **no-load fund** charges no commission at the time of purchase or at the time of sale. Although this is obviously going to save you money, you need to look carefully at what you're giving up by purchasing a no-load fund and at the fund's other expenses and charges to see if it is really a better deal than a low-load fund (a load of up to 3% is considered low). Instead of charging investors at the time of purchase or sale, no-load funds tend to have higher management expenses. Whereas load funds generally provide investors with professional advice from brokers and financial planners (who receive a portion of the load charge), a no-load fund will either have to skimp on this service or charge you for it in a different way, often through 12b-1 fees. In order to be designated as no-load, however, a fund can't impose a 12b-1 charge of more than 0.25 percent.

no-load fund

A mutual fund that doesn't charge a front-end or back-end load.

Expense Ratios. Management expenses, as mentioned, include trading costs and operating expenses, as well as the costs of professional investment management, security analysis, and legal and accounting services. Even though all funds charge their investors for providing these services, some are much more efficient in managing costs than others and pass this savings on to investors. For this reason, it's important to take expenses into account when evaluating potential

expense ratio

The ratio of annual mutual fund expense charges to fund assets.

mutual fund purchases. A fund's **expense ratio** is measured by the expenses per dollar of assets under management, as follows:

$$\text{Expense ratio} = \frac{\text{Total expenses}}{\text{Total assets in fund}}$$

All else equal, the lower this ratio, the better. The expense ratio must be disclosed in the fund's prospectus; it's usually between 0.5 and 1.25 percent but can be as high as 2 percent. Since many of the fund's operating costs are related to trading, you can expect the expense ratio for an index fund that does very little trading to be much lower than that of an actively managed fund which frequently buys and sells securities within the portfolio. Some funds with higher expense ratios give investors better returns, so you need to consider this variable in light of all the information you have about a fund. If the expenses are paying for better analysis, security selection, investor advisory services, website tools, or other things of value to you, it might be worth paying the cost.

Mutual Fund Classes by Fee Structure. Just as a corporation can sell different types of stock (e.g., common and preferred), a mutual fund can offer a menu of share classes that differ in load and expenses. For example, Class A shares usually have front-end loads of 4 to 5 percent; Class B shares carry a back-end load and impose a 12b-1 fee; and Class C has no back-end load but charges a higher 12b-1 fee. Some funds also have a Class D, which carries a front-end load and a smaller 12b-1 fee. If you like a particular mutual fund but aren't sure which class of shares to purchase, the most important consideration is your time horizon. Front-end loads are a one-time charge, whereas management fees and 12b-1 fees are incurred on an annual basis. Therefore, if you plan to hold the mutual fund for a long time, the front-end load may be the best option, since you'll incur it only once. Back-end loads are also less important if you plan to hold the mutual fund beyond the point at which it disappears. A 5 percent load on Class A shares may seem like a lot, but you'll pay up to 1 percent per year in 12b-1 fees every year if you buy Class C shares instead.

Learning by Doing 14-2

1. Suppose you're considering a fund that offers the following classes of shares:
   Class A: front-end load, 5 percent
   Class B: back-end load, 5 percent (reduced 1% per year); 12b-1 fee, 0.5 percent
   Under what circumstances would the Class B shares be preferable to the Class A?

Mutual Fund Investment Classifications

LEARNING objective

2 Classify mutual funds by their investment objectives and portfolio composition.

Mutual funds are usually classified based on investment objectives and portfolio composition. As the number of mutual funds continues to rise, each fund has more incentive to try to distinguish itself from its competitors, creating so much diversity that it isn't always easy to categorize funds. The classifications suggested in this section aren't uniformly applied, but will familiarize you with some of the terms commonly used to describe mutual funds. As an alternative, the classification system used by the Investment Company Institute, an industry trade group, is provided in Exhibit 14-6. In general, you'll find that the most important distinctions among funds are the type of investment (equity versus debt), the source of expected return (income versus capital gain), and the tax status.

Classification by Investment Objective

Each mutual fund has a specific investment policy, which is described in the fund's prospectus. For example, money market mutual funds, which were discussed in Chapter 5, consider the preservation of capital to be an important investment objective. To achieve this objective, the fund managers must invest in short-term, low-risk debt securities. Investors know this in ad-

Category	Subcategories Within General Category
Equity funds	*Capital appreciation funds* seek capital appreciation and don't focus on dividends. *Total return funds* seek a combination of current income and capital appreciation. *World equity funds* invest in the stocks of foreign companies.
Taxable bond funds	*Corporate bond funds* seek current income by investing in high-quality debt securities issued by U.S. companies. *High-yield funds* invest two-thirds or more of their portfolios in lower-rated U.S. corporate bonds (rated Baa or lower by Moody's and BBB or lower by Standard and Poor's). *Government bond funds* invest in U.S. government bonds of varying maturities and seek high current income. *Strategic income funds* invest in U.S. fixed-income securities to provide a high level of current income. *World bond funds* seek the highest level of current income available by investing in debt securities offered by foreign companies and governments.
Hybrid funds	*Hybrid funds* invest in a mix of equity and fixed-income securities.
Tax-exempt bond funds	*National municipal bond funds* seek high current income free of federal tax by investing in the bonds of various municipal issuers in the United States. *State municipal bond bonds* seek high after-tax income for residents of particular states by investing in municipal bonds issued by a particular state.
Money market funds	*Taxable money market funds* seek the highest level of income consistent with the preservation of capital by investing in high-grade money market securities with average maturities of 90 days or less. *Tax-exempt money market funds* seek the highest level of income, free from federal and sometimes state and local income taxes, consistent with the preservation of capital by investing in municipal securities with average maturities of 90 days or less.

EXHIBIT 14-6

Mutual Fund Classification System Used by the Investment Company Institute

vance and therefore have specific expectations about the performance of the fund based on its objectives. The most common general investment policy categories are capital appreciation (growth), income, and preservation of capital, but the objectives of a given fund may include more than one of these.

Growth. The primary objective of a **growth fund** is capital appreciation. Managers attempt to select assets for the portfolio that will experience above-average growth in value over time. Since growing companies tend to be riskier than stable companies, growth mutual funds are more appropriate for investors who are willing to bear a little more risk to achieve a higher long-run return. Growth funds are often placed in subcategories depending on the level and type of risk represented by the investment portfolio. For example, an aggressive growth fund invests only in risky companies that pay no dividends, whereas a moderate growth fund, while still focused on capital appreciation, might invest in larger companies that pay stable dividends but have the potential for good appreciation in value. Aggressive growth funds, as you'd expect, are much riskier and expose you to greater potential losses in the event of a market downturn.

growth fund

A mutual fund that focuses on capital appreciation.

Income Funds. In contrast to growth funds, an **income fund** holds stock and bond investments that provide high current income, either in dividends or interest. These funds tend to be viewed as less risky than growth funds, since the investor is realizing immediate gains rather than taking the risk of waiting for future gains. As with growth funds, there are various subcategories within this group, most commonly based on the source of the income (e.g., interest versus dividends) and the risk level (e.g., high-quality debt versus junk bonds).

income fund

A mutual fund that focuses on providing stable dividend and interest income.

Growth and Income. Some funds try to straddle the fence, providing reasonable income to investors while still investing in companies that have good potential for growth in value. Primarily invested in growth-oriented blue chip stocks, these funds have generated respectable returns over time and have been more stable than the market as a whole.

balanced fund

A mutual fund invested in both stocks and bonds.

Balanced Funds. A **balanced fund,** sometimes called a hybrid fund, provides investors with the opportunity to benefit from investments in both stocks and bonds. Because they are better diversified than funds that are entirely invested in stocks, and because they tend to focus on high-grade securities, balanced funds tend to have stable returns over time. These funds are similar to income funds but focus more on reducing investment risk.

value fund

A mutual fund that invests in companies perceived to be undervalued by the market.

Value Funds. A **value fund** manager attempts to invest in companies that are currently undervalued by the market—companies with good fundamentals whose stock prices are low relative to the companies' perceived potential. Of course, there are always many other investors seeking these same undiscovered gems, so the risk of being wrong is fairly high. Value stock funds tend to be invested in companies with relatively low P/E ratios and good growth potential, so they are a little less risky than growth funds but still offer fairly good returns.

life-cycle fund

A mutual fund that designs its asset allocation to meet the needs of individuals in a particular life stage.

Life-Cycle Funds. A **life-cycle fund** attempts to capture the asset allocation needs of individual investors at particular points in their life cycle. Thus, a fund designed for individuals under age 40 might be invested primarily in growth stocks, whereas a fund designed for a retiree would be more heavily allocated to fixed-income securities. These funds usually allow investors to move their invested dollars to a new life-cycle fund as they reach different points in the life cycle at no cost. Given the financial planning emphasis on changing needs over the life cycle, the idea behind the design of these funds is sound. There's still some disagreement as to what the ideal portfolio composition ought to be for each life stage, however. And since these funds are relatively new in concept, they don't yet have particularly long track records.

Fact #2

As many investors have discovered, investing in a bond fund doesn't protect you from loss of principal. When interest rates go down, the value of bond fund shares goes up, and vice versa. In addition, the income from bond funds tends to fluctuate with interest rates. When rates are falling, high-coupon bonds held in the portfolio may be called, and the fund will have to replace them with new bonds that have lower coupon rates.

Classification by Portfolio Composition

In addition to being classified by investment objective, funds are also commonly separated based on portfolio composition. This can occur through some combination of asset class, industry representation, and index benchmark.

Asset Class. Mutual funds commonly confine their investments to certain asset classes, such as stocks versus bonds, although as we've seen, some funds hold both stocks and bonds. Within each broad asset class, funds may be further classified according to such features as size of company (large-cap, mid-cap, or small-cap) or type of asset (long-term Treasury bonds, high-grade corporate bonds, or municipal bonds). When you invest in a mutual fund that is concentrated in a particular asset class, the performance of your fund is likely to mimic the overall performance of that asset class. Your share values will respond to economic conditions in much the same way as do investments in individual stocks and bonds.

sector fund

A mutual fund that invests primarily in securities from a particular industry or sector.

Industry or Sector. A **sector fund** specializes in particular industries or business sectors. Common examples include technology, financial services, telecommunications, health care, and utilities. These funds tend to focus on growth rather than income, and they enable investors to allocate more of their money to the sector believed to offer the most attractive returns. Since this strategy results in less diversification, sector funds tend to be riskier over time than those that cover more industry groups. For example, during the stock market run-up of the late 1990s, technology stocks were the stars—but they also took the biggest hit in the later market downturn.

international fund

A mutual fund that invests primarily in securities from countries other than the United States.

global fund

A mutual fund that invests in U.S. and foreign securities.

Geographical Location. When the U.S. stock market is down, investors can benefit from global diversification. An **international fund** invests exclusively in securities from other countries. Some funds include securities from a particular region, such as Latin America or Asia; others, commonly referred to as *country funds,* specialize in securities from a particular country. In contrast, a **global fund** attempts to diversify globally, investing in U.S. as well as foreign securities.

Index Funds. Many funds try to mimic the performance of a particular index, such as the S&P 500 index, but without necessarily buying every stock that is included in the index. With other types of funds, a fund manager's performance is judged at the end of a period, compared to the benchmark index's performance to see whether the manager's efforts produced the desired outcome. Many academic studies have shown that it's difficult for an actively managed fund to beat its benchmark index. As an alternative, index funds attempt to buy and hold a selection of stocks that can mimic the market more exactly and at lower cost. If the index fund is targeting the Dow Jones Industrial Average or the S&P 500, for example, it will usually buy *all* the stocks in that index in about the same proportions and will therefore be able to track the index almost exactly. For indexes that include a much larger number of stocks—such as the New York Stock Exchange Index, with more than 3,000 different stocks—the index fund might try to buy a smaller selection of representative stocks. Since index funds buy and hold, trading costs are minimal.

Socially Responsible Funds. If the "bottom line" is not your primary focus, you might be interested in a **socially responsible fund.** The manager of this type of fund is charged with selecting stocks issued by companies that meet some predefined standards for moral and ethical behavior. Although the objectives of various funds differ, common issues that are considered are a company's policies toward employees and the environment. Socially responsible funds also commonly avoid securities of companies that are involved in "sin industries" such as tobacco, alcohol, and gambling. The *Money Psychology* box, "What Does It Cost to Feel Good?" suggests that investors pay a price for being socially responsible, since the performance of these funds, on average, has lagged behind that of funds that aren't as restrictive.

socially responsible fund

A mutual fund that limits its holdings to securities issued by companies that meet certain ethical and moral standards.

Learning by Doing 14-3

1. Considering your own life-cycle stage and risk preferences, which type of mutual fund do you think would best match your needs?
2. Suppose you want to split your money between stocks and bonds. You could choose a fund that has a specific asset mix, or you could buy a stock fund and a bond fund to achieve the same type of diversification. What would be some of the advantages and disadvantages of each strategy?

Money Psychology

What Does It Cost to Feel Good?

Some investors screen their investments based on criteria related to social responsibility. They get a certain amount of satisfaction from integrating their values, ethics, and societal concerns with their investment decisions. In her senior honors thesis, Jennifer Gagnon asked the question "How much is it worth to feel good?" She compared the risk and return on several Lipper funds classified as socially responsible investors (SRI) to those on similar non-SRI funds for the period 1999 to 2003. SRI funds buy the securities of corporations with reputations for good employee relations, strong records of community involvement, excellent environmental impact policies and practices, respect for human rights around the world, and safe products. They avoid companies related to tobacco, alcohol, gambling, firearms, and nuclear power.

The reality is that it costs more to be socially responsible and customers aren't always willing to pay a higher price for goods produced by socially responsible companies. Therefore, it's not surprising that investors in SRI mutual funds often earn a lower return than those in non-SRI funds. However, Jennifer finds that the cost of "feeling good" isn't that large, and it differs by the type of fund and holding period, as summarized in the table below. Based on this analysis, you would have earned almost 4 percent less per year investing in a mixed-capitalization SRI fund (which invests in companies in different capitalization categories), but in small-caps, you'd have been 0.5 percent better off over the five-year period.

Annualized Cost of Being Socially Responsible

	1-Year	2-Year	5-Year
Large-cap	1.48%	−0.23%	0.87%
Mixed-cap	5.90%	2.52%	3.68%
Small-cap	4.84%	3.12%	−0.51%

Note: A negative value on the table means that the SRI fund earned more, on an annualized basis, than the non-SRI fund for that same period.

Source: Jennifer Gagnon, "What Is the Cost of Being Socially Responsible?", senior honors thesis, Colorado State University, April 2004.

Selecting and Evaluating Mutual Funds

LEARNING objective

3 Establish strategies for selecting among mutual funds and evaluating fund performance.

Assuming you've decided to buy one or more mutual funds, now comes the step that requires some homework on your part. With so many to choose from, how do you pick the ones that are best for you? The answer is to return to the decision-making process we've used throughout this text. You need to consider your goals, evaluate your alternatives, and select the investment alternatives that best meet your needs. An outline of the steps to take is provided in Exhibit 14-7.

To illustrate this process, let's return to the Thompson family continuing case. Cindy and Dave Thompson, age 32, want to start contributing to a retirement savings account for Cindy in 2005, and they plan to invest $3,300 the first year. We'll walk through the process they might apply in deciding how to invest this money.

Matching Fund Classification with Investment Objective

The first step in the mutual fund decision process is to identify your investment objective, which includes a number of factors:

- The outcome you'd like to achieve
- The time horizon you have for achieving it
- The amount of risk you're willing to take
- Minimizing taxes owed

We know that the Thompsons' primary objective for this investment is to build retirement wealth. Since Cindy is only 32 years old, she has a long time horizon, at least 30 years, within which to achieve this objective. The Thompsons are prepared to take some risk for greater return, and they want to keep their current tax cash outflows to a minimum.

Having determined their investment objective, we next identify fund classifications that would be appropriate for their objectives. They should, at a minimum, determine whether they'll invest in debt versus equity, income versus growth, and taxable versus tax-exempt funds.

Not surprisingly, given their time horizon and wealth-building objectives, the Thompsons want to concentrate more on growth than income. Receipt of current income would just require that they reinvest the money, and they can afford to take a little more risk with such a long time horizon. Most financial planners recommend that investors with long time horizons allocate more of their portfolio to equity securities, since that asset class has historically generated greater returns over time. The Thompsons decide to target a large-cap growth fund initially. As Cindy's investment portfolio grows, she'll probably spread her money among several stock funds and, as she nears retirement and her objectives turn more toward preservation of capital, she can gradually shift her investments to a less risky asset allocation.

Another aspect of fund classification selection is the tax status, but since this is a retirement account, the Thompsons plan to set it up as an individual retirement account (IRA). The choice between traditional and Roth IRAs will be discussed in Chapter 15, but in either case, no current taxes will be due on the income and capital gains earned by the fund. If the Thompsons were saving for a goal other than retirement, they would have to pay taxes on distributions from the fund. In that case, they might want to avoid income funds and those that trade frequently to capture capital gains, since these investment activities will generate a bigger current tax liability.

With respect to taxes, it's important to remember that tax consequences are often factored into the prices of investments. For example, the current yield on a tax-exempt security (tax-free interest income divided by the price) will often be comparable to the after-tax current yield for a taxable security (after-tax interest income divided by the price) with similar risk characteristics. To see why this is so, consider what would happen if you had two similar bonds paying the same amount of interest each year, one with taxable income and one tax-exempt. If the tax-exempt bond was priced the same as the taxable bond, people who invested in the tax-exempt bond would realize a greater after-tax return. Clearly, all investors would want to buy that bond, and they wouldn't want to buy the taxable bond. With higher demand in the market for the tax-exempt bond, the price would rise, and the return would go down, since the same amount of interest divided by a higher price gives you a smaller yield. The opposite would happen to the taxable bond—its price would fall until the after-tax returns on the two securities were equal.

What does this mean for investors? If your tax situation is different from the average investor's, certain securities may be a better or worse "deal" for you than they are for others. For example, if you're investing through a tax-deferred or tax-exempt retirement account, you don't want to be investing in tax-exempt bonds. They offer you no tax savings and have higher relative prices that reflect the average investor's tax savings, not yours. An example from the opposite point of view involves the tax effects of investing in a very actively managed mutual fund, which generates a lot of capital gains income that is taxable to investors. If you're investing through an IRA, you don't need to worry about this, since you won't have to pay the tax. In addition, the fund might be advantageously priced, reflecting the taxes that must be paid by other investors.

The final decision Cindy and Dave need to make before narrowing their mutual fund choices is whether they're willing to pay a load. They know that some funds charge high fees and that these expenses can erode their long-run returns. They definitely want to consider the historical expense ratios on the funds they're evaluating. Since they don't plan to withdraw the money until far in the future, they're willing to bear a small front-end load but would like to minimize the management expenses and 12b-1 fees each year.

Identifying Fund Alternatives

Cindy and Dave have narrowed their choices to large-cap growth funds and are ready to identify particular funds that meet their objectives. Although in many cases, the name of a fund gives a hint as to its investment objectives—such as "Value Fund" or "Life Cycle A"—this isn't always the case, so you need to do your homework to be sure that you've identified all likely prospects. The Thompsons do this by using a financial website's fund screener to identify the best performers in the large-cap growth classification over the last few years. Since they're interested in funds with low expenses, they also screen on this criterion. Let's assume their screens result in a list of 20 mutual funds.

You can screen mutual funds on the Morningstar Mutual Funds website (www.morningstar.com), which provides extensive information about funds, including style, performance, and ratings.

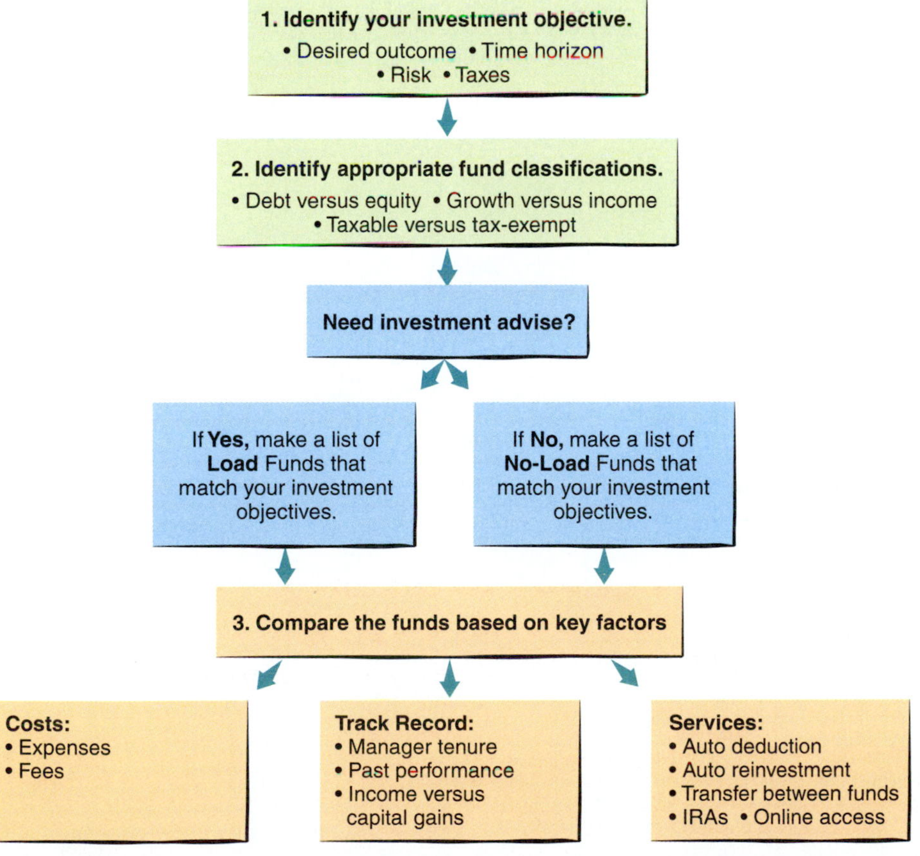

EXHIBIT 14-7

Deciding on a Mutual Fund

Comparing Funds Based on Key Factors

Now that the Thompsons have identified their alternatives, they can narrow their selection based on the criteria that are most important to them. These criteria can include ratings, expenses, net asset value, manager tenure, and services provided by the company. Morningstar and other mutual fund services firms provide information on the names and job histories of fund managers, as well as analysis of previous performance. Why is the fund manager important? Suppose you're considering a fund that has had a fairly good track record but now has a new manager. The past performance was attributable—at least in part—to the skill of the previous fund manager, so the future performance could be totally different. Although a fund is supposed to stick with its investment objectives, some managers are better at that task than others, and how the objectives are interpreted may vary among managers as well.

fund family

An arrangement in which a single company operates several separately managed mutual funds with different investment objectives.

Another factor to consider is whether the fund is part of a **fund family,** an arrangement in which a single company, such as Fidelity or Vanguard, operates several separately managed mutual funds with different investment objectives. There are some advantages to choosing a fund that is part of a fund family. Firms that offer families of funds will allow you to transfer money between funds within a family at little or no cost, which makes it easy to make changes in asset allocation. So if Cindy decides in the future that she'd like to invest some of

EXHIBIT 14-8

The Thompsons Select a Mutual Fund

1. Investment objective: Retirement fund
2. Appropriate type of fund: Equity, growth, taxable, no load

	Mutual Fund Alternatives		
	A	B	C
Company name	Excel Growth	ABC Fund	Future Progress
Fund objective	Growth	Growth	Growth
Price per share	$45	$32	$29
Net asset value	$40	$35	$28
Minimum initial purchase	$1,000	$2,000	$1,500
Minimum additional purchase	$500	$100	$200
Past performance			
1-year	15%	13%	17%
3-year	8%	7%	4%
5-year	6%	6%	8%
Expenses	2%	1.5%	1%
Front-end loan			
Back-end loan	√	√	
12b-1 fee	0.5%	1.0%	0.5%
Fund manager tenure	3 years	2 years	10 years
Services			
Auto deduction	√	√	√
Auto reinvestment	√	√	√
Transfer between funds	√	√	√
IRAs	√	√	√
Online access	√	√	√
Ratings (Morningstar)	5-star	5-star	5-star

her portfolio in a different type of fund, she can easily switch. All life-cycle funds belong to fund families, since the assumption is that you would shift to a different life-cycle fund as your life progresses.

PFP Worksheet 48 Evaluating Mutual Fund Alternatives

Based on their criteria, the Thompsons narrow their selection to three funds. In making this type of comparison, it's helpful to organize the key information for each fund you're considering. Exhibit 14-8 provides an example of Cindy and Dave's analysis. A blank worksheet is provided in your *Personal Financial Planner*.

Cindy ultimately decides to invest in the Future Progress mutual fund. She bases this decision on its low expenses, the long tenure of its manager, and its short- and long-run performance.

How Many Funds?

Now that the Thompsons have made their decision, let's take a minute to consider the issue of how many funds you should invest in. A common misconception of mutual fund investors is that having a lot of funds necessarily reduces their risk. It's true that having more funds from different fund families reduces the risks related to investment company failure or wrongdoing. It doesn't reduce market risk, though, unless you invest in funds that include different asset classes and different securities within those asset classes. Many funds are highly invested in the same stocks—large-cap funds will be heavily invested in companies that make up the Dow Jones Industrial Average and the S&P 500, for example. If Cindy and Dave had decided to split their money among several large-cap funds that track the same index, and the stock market experienced a significant decline, all their mutual funds would likely lose value as well, and they'd have incurred higher expenses than if they had only bought shares in one stock fund.

But suppose you want to diversify your mutual fund holdings. After all, diversification is an often-recommended investment strategy. Instead of investing in a number of similar funds, you should buy shares in funds that focus on different areas. For example, you might invest in a large-cap fund, a small-cap fund, an international fund, an investment-grade bond fund, and a REIT.

Fact #3

Although more tends to be better when you're investing in individual stocks and bonds, that isn't necessarily the case when you're investing in mutual funds. Splitting your money among several funds with similar investment objectives doesn't provide much diversification benefit and tends to increase your transactions costs. That's because funds with similar objectives tend to be invested in the same companies' stocks and bonds, so their performance is likely to be highly correlated.

The Mutual Fund Transaction

Once you've decided what mutual fund or funds you want to buy, you must actually make the purchase. We consider that process next.

What Is the Current Price? You can find the current price of the mutual funds you're considering in the financial newspapers and on many of the financial websites we've already discussed. For open-end funds, the *Wall Street Journal* reports the net asset value as of the previous day, the daily change in value, and the year-to-date return. Closed-end fund information includes the exchange on which the fund trades, the net asset value, the market price as of the market close on the previous day, the percentage difference between the market price and the net asset value, and the 52-week return based on market price plus dividends. Examples are provided in Exhibit 14-9.

Making the Purchase. There are several ways to purchase shares of a mutual fund, and many people are surprised to find that they don't necessarily have to use a broker. Since brokers receive commissions for the sale, many investment companies keep their costs down by marketing their funds directly. They advertise through the mail, by phone, in print media, and on the Internet. You can contact these companies directly by phone to set up an account and purchase shares.

About half of all funds are sold through brokers, and in many cases shares of funds are available through "financial supermarkets." In these arrangements, a supermarket firm such as Fidelity Networks or Charles Schwab & Co. allows investors access to a large number of funds from different fund families under its umbrella. The greatest advantage of this type of arrangement for investors is that they can purchase from several fund families, switch money among them easily, and

EXHIBIT 14-9

Examples of *Wall Street Journal* Mutual Fund Quotations

MUTUAL FUNDS

FUND	NAV	NET CHG	YTD %RET	3-YR %RET
A				
AAL Mutual A				
Balanced p	11.58	−0.08	−0.8	0.2
Bond p	9.94	−0.04	−1.4	5.1
Cgrowth p	29.26	−0.27	−0.1	−4.1
Equinc p	12.75	−0.14	1.8	−2.5
HiYBdA	6.41	−0.01	−1.6	7.1
Intl p	8.74	−0.19	−0.5	−3.2
MidCap p	14.12	−0.19	1.7	0.0
MuniBd	11.12	−0.02	−1.9	4.6
SmCap	16.33	−0.25	2.6	6.1
AAL Mutual Inst				
Balance	11.58	−0.08	−0.6	0.6
AARP Invst				
Balanced	16.86	−0.11	1.1	−0.8
CapGr	41.54	−0.30	2.1	−6.0
GNMA	14.80	−0.07	−1.1	4.1
Global	22.51	−0.57	−3.2	−1.2
GroINc	20.49	−0.19	1.7	−2.0
Income	12.54	−0.05	−1.1	4.5
MgdMuni	8.99	−0.01	−2.0	5.0
ShtTmBd	10.30	−0.03	−0.6	3.3

CLOSED-END FUNDS

STOCK (SYM)	DIV	LAST	NET CHG
NYSE			
ACM OppFd **AOF**	0.72	7.75	−0.11
ACM IncFD **ACG**	0.81	7.68	−0.15
ACM MgdDir **ADF**	0.81	7.72	0.06
ACM MgdInco **AMF**	0.42	1.03	−0.09
ACM MuniSec **AMU**	0.87	11.15	−0.05
ASA **ASA**	0.60a	34.33	−0.82
AbrdnGlobIncFd **FCO**	0.72	11.93	0.03
AdamsExp **ADX**	0.78e	12.42	−0.14
AdvntClymrFd **FCO**	2.06a	24.34	−0.04

Source: Wall Street Journal. Copyright 2004 by Dow Jones & Co Inc. Permission granted via Copyright Clearance Center. June 15, 2004, pp. C8, D8.

still receive a consolidated financial report from the supermarket company. In addition, many of these funds can be purchased without paying a sales commission because the supermarkets have made deals with the mutual fund companies to split the management fee. Not all funds sold in this way are offered on a no-fee basis, however, and some have relatively high fees.

After Congress passed the Financial Services Modernization Act in 1999, banks and insurance companies obtained the right to create and market mutual funds. Today, most large financial institutions also have mutual fund holding companies, essentially corporations owned by the parent bank or insurer. Since the funds offered by these firms are still relatively young, it will be several years before they have track records sufficient to allow us to compare them with some of the more experienced funds and fund managers. However, many of these companies (e.g., State Farm and AIG) are extremely large and have extensive investment experience, so it's possible that the competition they provide to existing firms will benefit investors in the form of lower costs and better performance.

Cindy and Dave Thompson decide to buy their shares directly from the investment company that sponsors the fund. Since this company is part of a large and well-respected fund family, they don't feel that they need to go through a fund supermarket to have access to other investment alternatives.

PFP Worksheet 49
Mutual Fund Tracker

Visit IndexFunds.com, at www.indexfunds.com, to find index performance information. Morningstar Mutual Funds, at www.morningstar.com, will provide you with a comparison of your fund's performance to the S&P 500.

Tracking Your Portfolio

You've made the mutual fund purchase, but your job isn't done. Now, you'll need to keep track of your portfolio and continue to make additional contributions to your investment fund. Cindy and Dave Thompson will probably want to set up a mutual fund account with an automatic deposit arrangement. They should also regularly review the performance of the fund relative to its investment objective and the index that it tracks. An easy way to do that is to look at the Lipper Indexes reported daily in the *Wall Street Journal,* as shown in Exhibit 14-10. These indexes show the daily, weekly, and year-to-date performance of funds with specific objectives. A worksheet for tracking your mutual funds is provided in your *Personal Financial Planner.*

EXHIBIT 14-10

Lipper Indexes as Reported in the *Wall Street Journal*, June 15, 2004

Lipper Indexes

STOCK-FUND INDEXES	PRELIM CLOSE	PERCENT CHANGE FROM PREVIOUS CLOSE	WEEK AGO	DEC 31
Large-Cap Growth	2990.28	−0.98	−0.28	+0.43
Large-Cap Core	2199.49	−0.95	+0.18	+0.79
Large-Cap Value	9552.33	−1.02	+0.18	+1.67
Multi-Cap Growth	2588.28	−1.32	−0.76	+1.39
Multi-Cap Core	6870.83	−1.13	−0.28	+1.62
Multi-Cap Value	4092.70	−1.02	+0.03	+2.00
Mid-Cap Growth	631.39	−1.40	−0.87	+1.71
Mid-Cap Core	635.75	−1.26	−0.61	+2.01
Mid-Cap Value	966.79	−1.20	−0.32	+3.84
Small-Cap Growth	511.82	−1.65	−1.71	−1.54
Small-Cap Core	382.98	−1.40	−0.73	+2.59
Small-Cap Value	609.56	−1.59	−0.62	+2.19
Equity Income Fd	4113.40	−1.00	+0.03	+1.46
Science and Tech Fd	612.27	−2.19	−1.55	−3.66
International Fund	764.57	−2.12	−1.07	+0.76
Balanced Fund	4933.94	−0.81	−0.12	+0.52
Bond-Fund Indexes				
Short Inv Grade	252.10	−0.19	−0.24	−0.42
Intmdt Inv Grade	296.23	−0.39	−0.41	−1.31
US Government	390.49	−0.40	−0.46	−1.58
GNMA	426.82	−0.43	−0.49	−1.25
Corp A-Rated Debt	1054.23	−0.37	−0.38	−1.29

Indexes are based on the largest funds within the same investment objective and do not include multiple share classes of similar funds.

Source: Lipper, Inc. Published in the Wall Street Journal. Copyright 2004 by Dow Jones & Co Inc. Permission granted via Copyright Clearance Center. p. C2

Real Estate Investment

LEARNING objective

4 Identify the advantages and disadvantages of direct and indirect real estate investments.

Real estate can add value to your investment portfolio, increase your diversification, and provide less volatile returns over time. However, it's an investment class that requires a substantial amount of hands-on management and expertise, including legal knowledge, so it isn't for everyone. In this section, we'll consider your real estate investment alternatives, including your primary residence, investment properties, and indirect methods of participating in this market.

Your Home as an Investment

In Chapter 8, you read about selecting and purchasing a home. Since housing is a basic need, we didn't approach buying a home as an investment decision in that chapter. Even if your home increases in value over time, the reality is that you can't easily access the returns from that investment without incurring substantial costs. If you sell the house, you'll have to buy another and incur the costs of the search and the move. If you access the built-up equity in the house by taking a home equity loan, you incur the costs of repayment and potential damage to your credit. Therefore, it's probably better to think of your home separately from your investment portfolio.

Even though we're not considering your home primarily as an investment asset, it clearly has investment characteristics that are beneficial to you. For example, during 2001 and 2002, when stock portfolios declined an average of 43 percent, home values in the United States increased 17.4 percent. For homeowners, increasing home equity served to reduce the impact of the market decline on aggregate household wealth. However, real estate has not always been a haven, and even when home values in general are increasing, they may not be increasing in every market. In both of the last two recessions, several areas of the country saw substantial devaluation of home prices.

A local recession can cause sharp declines in real estate values as many people try to sell their homes at the same time.

Another concern is that the recent increase in real estate values, which some have termed a "housing bubble," has been attributed to factors that may not be sustainable. First, baby boomers

To find out more about housing price increases, check the Conventional Mortgage Home Price Index, offered on the website for secondary mortgage market giant Freddie Mac, at www.freddiemac.com/finance/cmhpi. There you'll find a measure of housing price inflation for the overall United States, each state, and most large metropolitan areas.

are in their peak earning years and have generally invested in larger and larger homes as their incomes have increased. This could be a problem for the real estate market if the "bubble" bursts as boomers downsize their homes in the next several decades. The baby boomers make up a larger group than the generations that followed them—the so-called generations X and Y. If lots of people are selling homes and there aren't as many people to buy them, home values could drop steeply. Two other factors that have contributed to strong housing values are the generally low level of mortgage interest rates over the last decade and the high volatility of returns on other investment assets. Real estate is a tangible asset that most people understand and feel comfortable with.

We've seen in earlier chapters that home equity represents a large percentage of household wealth in America—probably too large a percentage from the standpoint of a diversified portfolio. However, if you think that your household portfolio could benefit from additional investment in real estate, there are several alternatives for achieving this diversification. You can make a direct investment or one of several types of indirect investments, as discussed in the next sections.

Direct Versus Indirect Real Estate Investment

Real estate investments can be either direct or indirect. An investor who has made a *direct real estate investment* holds title to the actual property. By this definition, your home is a direct investment, but you can also invest directly in a second home, a rental apartment, vacant land, or commercial property. In contrast, you make an *indirect real estate investment* when you invest through a trustee or company that holds the title to the real estate. Earlier in the chapter, you saw an example of an indirect real estate investment—a real estate investment trust. Recall that a REIT investor buys a share in a trust and the trust manager uses the money to buy investment real estate. Mortgage-backed securities are another example of an indirect investment in real estate.

Advantages of Direct Real Estate Investment

Your choices for direct real estate investment include many types of income-generating properties, as well as vacant land or a second home. An income property is one that will generate cash flows to you as the owner, usually in the form of rental income. As with other types of investments, investors in real estate generally expect to benefit from some combination of price appreciation and cash flow. Although non-income-generating real estate might still be expected to increase in value over time, it won't provide the positive cash flow benefits you'd get with a rental property (and you'll still have cash outflows for taxes and maintenance), so we concentrate our discussion below on income properties.

After-Tax Cash Flows. When you make an investment in an income property, you hope it will produce a positive cash flow for you, either currently or in the future. You'll collect rents from your tenants, and you'll have to pay the expenses of the property from those dollars. These expenses are similar to those you incur as a homeowner—property taxes, repair and maintenance costs, insurance, and the debt service on the mortgage, if any. Since the mortgage costs are usually fixed for the life of the loan, your property may begin with negative operating income but will eventually produce a positive cash flow as you raise the rent over time.

Your cash flow may also benefit from certain favorable tax rules that apply to rental properties. When you invest in rental property, you're allowed under tax laws to take a deduction against your net operating income for depreciation. Effectively, the IRS is allowing you to spread the cost of your initial investment in the home (not the land) over $27\frac{1}{2}$ years ($39\frac{1}{2}$ years for commercial properties). If you purchase a residential rental property that includes a home worth \$100,000, you'll be able to deduct 100,000/27.5 = \$3,636 per year from your rental income.

Other allowed deductions include interest expense (not including any payment of principal on the loan), property taxes, insurance, utilities, and expenses for repairs and maintenance—basically any reasonable expenses that you incur in the management of the property. The net effect of all this is that many properties generate positive net cash flow to the investors but have *negative taxable income.* When you have negative taxable income (a tax loss) from an investment real estate property that you actively manage, you're allowed to deduct the losses against other taxable income up to a maximum of \$25,000 per year, as long as your adjusted gross income (AGI) is less than \$100,000. The allowed maximum loss deduction is phased out for AGIs between $100,000 and $150,000. If we assume that you meet the income limitation, the cash flow benefit of the tax deduction is the amount of the loss times your marginal tax rate.

If you have a vacation home, you're allowed to rent it out up to 14 days per year without reporting the income. But if you go over the 14 days, the IRS considers the vacation home an investment property, and you must report the income.

Price Appreciation and Leverage. As with any investment, you expect that the value of your direct real estate investment will increase over time. On average, the price of real estate has increased at a faster rate than the prices of other goods, making it a good hedge against inflation. However, the appreciation of any individual property depends primarily on its location, which will determine its resale value and potential rental income, if it's an income property. Therefore, your purchase decision must be made in light of surrounding real estate and, if applicable, the expected rental demand for the property in the future.

As has been noted elsewhere in this text, investors can benefit from the use of leverage—using borrowed funds to make an investment purchase that will earn more than the cost of financing. If you borrow the money to purchase investment real estate, your actual return on investment will be higher than if you pay cash, since the increase in value relative to the equity you have in the property will be higher. To see how this works, consider an investment in a rental property that costs $100,000. You borrow $75,000 and put up $25,000 of your own money. If the property increases in value the first year by 5 percent, to $105,000, the value of your equity investment has increased from $25,000 to $30,000, or 20 percent. Note, however, that this isn't your true return on investment, since it doesn't take into account the interest you had to pay or your current yield from the net rental income. The *Go Figure!* box, "Calculating Return on Investment for Income Properties," explains how you can calculate your total yield on this type of investment more precisely.

Fact #4

Many young investors have found that they can leverage their time and effort into increased property values through "sweat equity"—buying a "fixer-upper" property that's in disrepair, remodeling it, and selling it. Since most home buyers don't want the hassle of remodeling, the prices of these properties are often discounted more than the cost of the repairs. There are many examples of people who have made a fortune on fixer-uppers—but there are also plenty who haven't done so well. An important thing to remember is that remodeling can take a lot of time, and your time has value. The gains you make on the investment might be offset by the personal costs.

GO FIGURE!

Calculating Return on Investment for Income Properties

Direct investment in income real estate produces both current income and capital gains over time. The difference between this type of investment and others we've previously considered is that real estate investors are often highly leveraged, and this improves their return on investment, or total yield.

Problem: You have bought a condominium for $100,000, borrowing $75,000 of the cost and paying the rest from your own funds. The loan is interest-only at a rate of 8 percent. (This is like a bond—you pay interest on the total principal amount, which is due in full at the maturity of the loan.) You rent the property for $600 per month and incur no additional expenses the first year. In one year, the condo increases 5 percent in value to $105,000. What is your total return on investment?

Solution: To calculate your return on investment for an income property, use the following equation:

$$\text{Real estate return on investment} = \frac{\text{Increase in value} + \text{Net rental income} - \text{Interest paid}}{\text{Beginning investment}}$$

Here, net rental income is your annual rental income less any expenses for maintenance and repairs, and interest paid is the annual total interest you've paid on your mortgage loan. Note that this equation is almost the same as the equation for total yield we've used elsewhere. The differences are that you must deduct your continuing expenses and you're dividing by your equity investment rather than the initial price of the property. For the problem above, we therefore calculate as follows:

Return on investment

$$= \frac{\$5{,}000 + (\$600 \times 12) - (0.08 \times \$75{,}000)}{\$25{,}000}$$

$$= \frac{\$6{,}200}{\$25{,}000} = 0.248, \text{ or } 24.8\%$$

Disadvantages of Direct Real Estate Investment

Direct real estate investments can earn high returns, but as you know, investments that earn higher returns usually do so because of their greater level of risk. Thus, you shouldn't be surprised to learn that direct real estate investment involves several disadvantages and that some of these disadvantages are related to risk.

Large Initial Investment. To invest in real estate, you have to have a substantial amount of money up front to cover the down payment (typically, 20 to 30% for investment properties) and closing costs.

Lack of Liquidity. Whereas stocks, bonds, and mutual funds can be traded fairly easily, there isn't an active secondary market where you can sell your direct real estate investments. In any given area, only a limited number of potential buyers exist, particularly for more expensive properties, and it typically takes three to six months to find a buyer and close the deal. Even if you do find a buyer, it will be difficult to say whether you've gotten a fair price for the property. The real estate market isn't as efficient as the stock or bond markets, where thousands of investors influence the market price of a given security. When only one or two people are interested in your property, you're likely to get a lower price than you'd like.

Reduced Diversification. Since real estate investments tend to require a large chunk of your money, you'll inevitably be less diversified when you have part of your portfolio in real estate. Given that you probably already have a home in the same geographic area, you're already exposed to the risks associated with local economic conditions. What if the major employer in your town suddenly decides to close its plant? Your home value will undoubtedly decrease as the workers pull up roots to move elsewhere, reducing the demand for housing in the area. At the same time, the value of your investment property will also decline, causing a double hit on your net worth.

If you make real estate investments in several geographic areas, you'll increase your diversification within this asset class, but your portfolio will still be overly exposed to risks that are peculiar to the real estate market. If it turns out that the retirement of the baby boomers causes a real estate crash, for example, all geographic markets in the U.S. will be hard-hit.

Transaction Costs. Relative to other types of investments, real estate has very high transaction costs. Buyers incur substantial closing costs, as discussed in Chapter 8. When you sell a property, in addition to other closing costs, you can usually expect to pay a commission of 6 to 7 percent on developed property and 10 percent on vacant land. Mortgage interest rates for investment properties also tend to be higher than those for owner-occupied properties and lenders require lower loan-to-value ratios.

limited partnership

A partnership in which limited partners provide investment funds, have limited liability, and participate in profits but a general partner manages the investment.

Hassles. If you own rental real estate, you must be prepared to deal with the day-to-day management of the property. This can include everything from legal liability for injuries to people on your property to eviction of problem tenants. Although you can pay a real estate management company to do some of this for you, the costs of such services are usually fairly high—often one month's rent per year.

Even with the disadvantages, the returns generated by many direct real estate investments are a strong lure. If you think you'd like to try your hand at real estate investing, consider the advice offered by a real estate specialist in the *Ask the Expert* box, "How Do I Get Started Investing in Real Estate?"

Limited partnerships often invest in shopping malls and strip centers.

Indirect Real Estate Investment

You can get some of the benefits of real estate investment without incurring the costs and risks of direct investment by making indirect investments through limited partnerships, real estate investment trusts, and mortgage-backed securities.

Limited Partnership. In a **limited partnership,** several investors (the limited partners) put up the money to buy a property, such as a shopping mall or apartment complex, and a general partner manages the investment. The limited partners are so called because they have limited liability—the most they can lose is their original investment, much like a corporate stockholder. At the same time, they have no right or obligation to participate in the management of the prop-

ask the expert How Do I Get Started Investing in Real Estate?

Dr. Karen Lahey
Charles Herberich, Professor of Real Estate, University of Akron

1. **Acquire the necessary skills.** As with other types of investing, real estate requires fairly specialized knowledge of valuation principles and law. In addition, if you manage your own properties, you need to know how to run a small business, supervise remodeling, and deal with tenants. You can learn these skills by taking appropriate college-level courses or through continuing education programs. It may also be helpful to seek employment with an established firm to learn more about what's involved, for example, with a property manager, real estate broker, real estate lawyer, or mortgage company.
2. **Do your research.** The value of any asset is determined by the present value of the future cash flows to the investor. For income real estate property, your cash flows (net rental income) will be affected by the economic conditions in the area. You will need to do a little research to find out what the supply and demand conditions are, investigate rent levels, and consider new construction projects that will impact the market.
3. **Accumulate the necessary capital.** Before you invest in real estate, you need to have saved enough to make a downpayment, pay closing costs, and cover any initial repair and maintenance expenses. The downpayment required for an investment property is usually substantially greater than for owner-occupied properties.
4. **Be prepared to invest a lot of time.** Direct real estate is usually a hands-on type of investment. Do you have the time to manage your properties (show them to prospective tenants, negotiate contracts, collect rents, and deal with repairs and maintenance)?

erty. In return for their invested dollars, they receive a proportional distribution of the net cash flows generated by the investment. These cash flows may be similar to those of a direct real estate investment; however, the tax benefits are not as good, since real estate investors must *actively* manage their investments to be able to take deductions for tax losses.

Real Estate Investment Trusts. Real estate investment trusts, or REITs, which were introduced earlier in this chapter, are probably the most attractive of indirect real estate investment alternatives. However, like other mutual funds, REITs can be very different from one another, so you need to do your homework to find out who is managing a particular fund and how well it has performed over the years. If you're interested in investing in REITs, you can get more information from the National Association of Real Estate Investment Trusts, an industry trade group.

Find out more about REIT investing from the National Association of Real Estate Investment Trusts at www.nareit.com.

Mortgage-Backed Securities. Another way to invest indirectly in the real estate market is by purchasing securities that are backed by pools of mortgages. For example, the Government National Mortgage Association (GNMA), or "Ginnie Mae," which is one of the federal agencies discussed in Chapter 11, buys federally insured mortgages and then sells shares in the pool. For example, the agency might have a pool of 1,000 mortgages for a total value of $100 million. If each share in the pool costs $1,000 and each shareholder owns one share, then each shareholder owns 1/100,000 of the pool and will receive that proportion of net cash flows from interest and principal repayments. In actuality, the shares in the pool cost more than $1,000, but individual investors can participate in this market by purchasing shares of mutual funds that invest in the certificates. Funds may also invest in securities offered by other government agencies, such as Fannie Mae and Freddie Mac. Note that although the funds are indirectly related to real estate, their performance is highly dependent on market interest rates, and so they are more closely related to the bond market than the real estate market.

Other Investment Alternatives

LEARNING objective

5 Explain why investment in precious metals, gems, collectibles, and derivatives are speculative.

We won't spend much time talking about the investment alternatives in this section, since you shouldn't even consider them if you're a novice investor. Investments such as precious metals, gems, collectibles and art, and derivative securities don't fit in most people's financial plans because they're too speculative. Whereas investment is the process of building wealth to achieve your financial goals, speculation exposes you to the risk of losing *all* your money. Even though higher risk implies the potential for higher returns, you don't want to take that kind of risk with your nest egg. If you're already so wealthy that you have extra money to play with, you might consider some speculative investments, but generally even then such investments should make up no more than 5 percent of your portfolio.

Precious Metals and Gems

Investments in precious metals such as gold, silver, and platinum or in precious stones such as diamonds, sapphires, and rubies can be made directly or indirectly. These investments require high up-front costs and provide no regular cash flow, so their returns are unlikely to exceed those of other investment alternatives.

Although it might seem like your personal jewelry collection is an investment when you consider how much you paid for each piece, the resale market for jewelry is relatively inefficient, so in most cases you probably won't be able to recoup what you paid. Furthermore, the potential for fraud is fairly high, since most buyers can't tell a diamond from a cubic zirconium. For this reason, "buyer beware" is a warning that you should take to heart in this market.

Investments in gold and other precious metals are often marketed as good ways to achieve diversification, since gold values tend to increase during times of political uncertainty and inflation and decrease when economic conditions are more stable. In general, however, the average returns on these investments are so low that they drag down overall portfolio returns in good times.

If you want to invest directly in gold or other metals, you can buy coins or bars from dealers or banks, paying a commission of at least 2 percent. When you sell the gold, you'll have to pay another commission fee. Direct investment in metals also means that you'll have to pay for a safe place to store it—it's not a good idea to have gold bars sitting around the house, and your homeowner's insurance will not cover them if they're lost or stolen. Alternatively, you can participate in precious metals by purchasing shares of gold or silver mutual funds or stock in mining companies. However, keep in mind that the performance of these investments may not perfectly track the value of the underlying metals.

Fact #5

An investor bought a 1960s Chanel woman's suit at an auction in 1993 for $805 and sold it in 1999 for $3,220, an increase of 300 percent, or 20 percent per year. But for every success story, there are a thousand collectors who have boxes full of comic books, Barbie dolls, and Beanie Babies that aren't worth any more than what they paid for them. In general, collectible investing is an investment strategy that's unlikely to give you a competitive return on your investment relative to the risks it exposes you to. However, if you choose to collect something that provides other benefits, such as visual enjoyment, collecting still may be worthwhile.

Collectibles and Art

Do you have a collection of rare comic books or perhaps some original pieces of art? Some people invest in rare coins, vintage cars, or antique quilts. These types of investments serve a dual purpose—you get enjoyment out of them today (think of it as a dividend that isn't taxed), and they may have value in the future. Like gold and gems, these collectibles don't generate any form of regular cash flow (unless you can charge people to come see them), so you're relying totally on their appreciation in value over time; this value depends on supply and demand, as well as collector fads. In addition, investors who must go through dealers, as is often the case with art and antiquities, pay very high transaction costs.

How much are your Beanie Baby investments worth today?

Although historically, the resale market for collectibles was small, making them a fairly risky investment, the advent of the Internet has changed the collectible marketplace for the better. If you have a rare Spiderman #1 in mint condition or an original 1950s Barbie still in its original packaging, the odds are good that you can find an investor out there who will buy it from you. But what it's worth will now be driven by a more efficient market, and there might be several other 1950s Barbies that are in better condition than yours. Although you can buy or sell just about anything on eBay and other auction sites, the Internet is still best suited for small items that don't require close examination to determine their value.

In deciding whether to invest in collectibles, you should consider the risk and return factors we've previously identified. And don't forget to take the time value of money into consideration when you evaluate your return on investment. If you bought a collectible Barbie in 1980 for $100 and it's worth $200 in 2005, you've doubled your initial investment, but your annualized return is much lower. After all, you've held the investment for 25 years. As we've seen before, you can calculate the average change in value, which is equivalent in this case to your annualized return on investment, using the following formula:

$$\text{Average annual return on investment} = \left(\frac{\text{Current price}}{\text{Purchase price}}\right)^{1/n} - 1$$

where n is the number of years you've held the investment.

Alternatively, you can use your financial calculator to find the annual return, entering $PV =$ purchase price, $FV =$ current market value, $N =$ number of years held, and solving for I. (Don't forget to enter the present value as a negative number, since it's an outflow to you.). Using this method, we find that the Barbie "investment" earned an average annual return of less than 3 percent, about as much as the inflation rate over that time period. If you had put the same $100 in a 25 year bond in 1980, your return would have been at least double that amount.

Financial Derivatives

You may recall from Chapter 11 that there's a whole class of widely traded securities called *derivatives,* so named because they derive their value from some underlying asset. The best known of these are futures and options. A *futures contract* is one in which you promise to buy or sell the underlying security at some point in the future at a price that is determined today. The underlying security might be a commodity, such as a bushel of corn, or a financial security, such as a Treasury bill. An *options contract* is similar except that it gives you the *right* to buy or sell in the future at a specified price but doesn't require you to go through with the purchase or sale. These rights expire on a future date specified in the option contract. A *call option* is the right to buy something in the future, and a *put option* is the right to sell something in the future.

The advantage of these investments is that you can participate in the price movements of the underlying security without buying the security itself. For example, suppose that, for $2 per share, you can buy a call option that gives you the right to buy a particular stock for $100 per share. You're hoping the stock price will rise as much as possible over $102 (the price of the share plus the cost of the option) before the expiration of the option. Let's say that the price goes up to $103. You can then exercise the option to buy at $100 and immediately sell at the market price of $103, making $1 per share. Your return on investment is 50 percent, because you've made a profit of $1 on an investment of $2, which is what you paid for the option. If, instead, you had bought the actual stock for $97 and the price rose to $103, your return on investment would have been only $6/$97 = 0.062, or 6.2 percent.

As you can see, when the price movement goes in your favor, you may realize a much greater return by investing in options than by investing in the underlying security itself, because the amount you have to spend up front is low relative to the cost of the underlying asset. However, the risk you take for this extra return is substantial. You actually risk losing your entire investment. In our example, if the stock price had stayed at $97, you wouldn't have exercised the option, so you would have paid $2 and gotten nothing (a loss of 100% of your investment). If instead you'd bought the underlying stock, you'd still own the $97 share, and it might increase in value in the future.

You should be able to see that futures and options are complex financial investments that require in-depth understanding of the markets and the products. Investors who get into this market without the appropriate expertise can lose a lot of money—and even supposed experts have lost billions of dollars (of other people's money for the most part). In most of these cases, the losses occurred because the investors didn't fully understand what they were doing and became greedy after a few lucky investments. In other cases, additional investments were made to cover up losses made on earlier investments, and the problems snowballed.

The risk of art investments may be offset by personal enjoyment of the artwork itself.

Although trading in futures and options is often speculative, these securities can also be used to *reduce* risk in your underlying portfolio. If you invest in a derivative contract that will increase in value when something else in your portfolio decreases in value, you are said to be *hedging*. This is an investment strategy that reduces the overall risks of your portfolio by protecting you from big swings in value. For example, many farmers in the United States hedge their crop price risks by selling futures contracts to lock in the price they will get for their crops at harvest time. For these investors, the futures contract is not speculative because they are promising to sell something they actually have. For nonfarmer investors, however, selling a futures contract is just a way of speculating on the price of corn.

If the concept of derivative investing doesn't seem crystal clear to you after reading this brief introduction, don't be surprised. Derivatives are complex and risky securities that take many years to truly understand.

Should You Consider Alternative Investments?

Before deciding to get into riskier investments as a means of making bigger profits, take a close look at your financial plan. Have you met all your security needs? Have you accumulated sufficient wealth toward your larger financial goals? Have you adequately diversified your portfolio into the other asset classes? What are the opportunity costs of making an investment in this area—the costs of liquidating other investments, the possibility of reduced diversification, the tax consequences? Do you have the time to educate yourself about these investments? And most important, can you afford to lose the money?

Learning by Doing 14-4

1. Vincent Van Gogh's painting "Sunflowers" was sold at auction in 1987 for $36 million. It had sold in 1889 (98 years earlier) for $125. If your great-grandfather had purchased the painting in 1889 and you had sold it in 1987, what annual rate of return would your family have made on that investment?

Summary

1 **Describe the benefits and costs of investing in mutual funds.** A mutual fund is a type of investment company. Open-end and closed-end investment companies sell shares to investors and use the funds to purchase portfolios of securities. The investors have an equity interest in the pool of assets and share in the cash flows generated by and capital appreciation of the fund's assets. The advantages of investing in this type of asset include increased diversification, reduced transaction costs, professional money management, and greater liquidity. The costs include fees, or loads, paid to purchase or sell the shares and regular fund expenses, including management fees and 12b-1 fees.

2 **Classify mutual funds by their investment objectives and portfolio composition.** Mutual funds are commonly classified according to investment objectives and portfolio composition. Common investment objectives include capital appreciation, income, or preservation of capital. Classification by portfolio composition is usually based on some combination of asset class, industry representation, or index benchmark.

3 **Establish strategies for selecting among different mutual funds and evaluating fund performance.** The process of mutual fund investing is to screen mutual fund alternatives to identify those with investment objectives that are a good match with your time horizon, wealth-building objectives, and tax preferences. Criteria for evaluating particular funds include ratings, expenses, net asset value, manager tenure, and services provided by the company.

4 **Identify the advantages and disadvantages of direct and indirect real estate investments.** You can invest in real estate either directly, by purchasing and managing the property yourself, or indirectly, by owning an interest in a partnership or investment company that invests in the real estate. Real estate investing can provide a regular source of cash flow, potential tax deductions, price appreciation, and leverage benefits. The disadvantages are the usually large up-front costs, low liquidity, high transaction costs, and reduced diversification.

5 **Explain why investments in precious metals, gems, collectibles, and derivatives are speculative.** Investments such as metals, gems, collectibles, and art require high up-front costs, provide no regular cash flow, and incur storage costs. Derivative investments, while they may have smaller costs up-front, expose you to the risk of losing your entire investment. All of these alternative investments are considered riskier than other investment alternatives and are deemed speculative.

Key Terms

back-end load (461)
balanced fund (464)
closed-end fund (456)
exchange-traded fund (ETF) (456)
expense ratio (462)
front-end load (461)
fund family (468)
global fund (464)
growth fund (463)
income fund (463)
international fund (464)
investment company (455)
life-cycle fund (464)
limited partnership (474)
mutual fund (453)
net asset value (453)
no-load fund (461)
open-end fund (456)
real estate investment trust (REIT) (457)
sector fund (464)
socially responsible fund (465)
unit investment trust (UIT) (457)
value fund (464)

Key Calculations

$$\text{Net asset value} = \frac{\text{Market value of assets} - \text{Market value of liabilities}}{\text{Shares outstanding}}$$

$$\text{Expense ratio} = \frac{\text{Total expenses}}{\text{Total assets in fund}}$$

$$\text{Average annual return on investment} = \left(\frac{\text{Current price}}{\text{Purchase price}}\right)^{1/n} - 1$$

$$\text{Real estate return on investment} = \frac{\text{Increase in value} + \text{Net rental income} - \text{Interest paid}}{\text{Beginning investment}}$$

Concept Review Questions

1. What is a mutual fund?
2. How is net asset value calculated? Is this the same thing as share price? Why or why not?
3. Discuss the growth of mutual funds over the last two decades. What factors have contributed to this trend?
4. Identify and describe the four types of investment companies. Which type is usually called a "mutual fund"?
5. Under what circumstances would an exchange-traded fund be a good investment choice? Why?
6. What is a real estate investment trust? What types of assets does an REIT invest in?
7. Identify the main advantages of mutual fund investing for individual investors.
8. In what ways can a mutual fund provide better diversification of your portfolio than you can get by investing in individual stocks and bonds?
9. Identify the major categories of expenses paid by shareholders in mutual funds. Why are some funds so much more expensive than others?
10. What is the difference between a front-end load and back-end load?
11. What is a no-load fund? Is it necessarily less expensive for investors than a load fund? Why or why not?
12. What types of expenses are paid for by 12b-1 fees? What is the maximum on this type of charge?
13. What is an expense ratio? How should it be used in comparing funds?
14. In what ways are mutual funds commonly classified?
15. Explain the difference between the following mutual fund classifications:
    a. Growth versus value
    b. Large-cap versus small-cap
    c. Equity versus debt
16. What is a life-cycle fund, and why is this type of fund useful from a financial planning perspective?
17. What is a sector fund? Why might an investor be interested in investing in this type of fund?
18. What is a socially responsible fund? What activities might disqualify a company for purchase by one of these funds?
19. Describe the process to use in selecting mutual funds for your portfolio.
20. What are some of the factors you should consider in matching your investment objectives to particular mutual fund alternatives?
21. In screening for funds that meet your needs, what factors should you consider?
22. In what ways is your home an investment? How does this affect your household's level of diversification?
23. What is the difference between direct and indirect real estate investment?
24. What are the advantages of direct real estate investment? Give three examples of this type of investment.
25. What are the disadvantages of direct real estate investment?
26. Identify several examples of indirect real estate investment.
27. Explain why investments in precious metals, gems, collectibles, and derivatives are speculative.

Application Problems

1. ***Net Asset Value.*** The ABC Small-Cap Fund, a closed-end fund, has total assets of $240 million, total liabilities of $10 million, and 15 million shares outstanding.
   a. Calculate the net asset value.
   b. If the current share price is $17, is this a good deal? Explain your reasoning.
2. ***Net Asset Value.*** The Verity Large-Cap Value Fund has total assets of $50 million, total liabilities of $500,000, and 5 million shares outstanding.
   a. Calculate the net asset value.
   b. If you bought the shares one year ago and, at that time, the net asset value was $8 per share, what was the annual increase in NAV?
3. ***Expense Ratio.*** Cruella owns shares in a fund that has a net asset value of $40 per share. The expenses are $1 per share. What is the expense ratio?
4. ***Front-End Load.*** You are buying 50 shares of the Xavier Fund that is priced at $35 per share. The sales charge is 4 percent.
   a. How much commission will you pay?
   b. What will your total investment per share in Xavier be after the purchase?
5. ***12b-1 Fees.*** You have $10,000 invested in a no-load fund that charges a 0.5 percent 12b-1 fee. The net asset value of the fund is $100 million.
   a. How much will you pay directly?
   b. How much will the net asset value of the fund be affected by this fee? Will this affect the value of your shares?
6. ***Back-End Load.*** You purchased $3,500 worth of shares in a mutual fund that does not charge a front-end load. However, there is a contingent deferred sales charge of 5 percent if you sell in the first year, decreasing one percentage point per year. You sell $1,000 worth of shares in the third year. How much will your back-end load be?
7. ***Matching Investment Objectives with Funds.*** For each of the following investors, suggest some mutual fund classifications consistent with the stated investment objective and time horizon, and explain your reasoning.
   a. A 20-year-old woman saving money for a down payment on a home
   b. A 60-year-old retired couple looking for a regular source of income
   c. A 30-year-old couple saving for their 5-year-old child's college education
8. ***One-Year Returns.*** You bought 60 shares of a mutual fund one year ago for $50 per share. The front-end load is 5 percent. The fund paid $1.50 per share in dividends during the year.
   a. As of today, the fund's net asset value increased 12 percent. What is the percent return for the year?
   b. Assume that the fund's net asset value fell 15 percent instead. What is the percent return for the year?
9. ***Return on Investment.*** You own 100 shares in a mutual fund that you purchased two years ago for $31 per share. The shares currently are worth $36 each, and the fund has paid you a dividend of $2 per year.
   a. What is your 2-year holding period return?
   b. What is your annual return on investment?
10. ***Return on Investment Real Estate.*** You purchase a rental property for $180,000 in 2005. The net rental income is $12,000 per year.
   a. If you paid cash for the property (no mortgage), what is your return on investment if the value of the property increases to $190,000 by the end of the first year?
   b. If you borrowed 50 percent of the purchase price from a local bank to finance the purchase, paying 6 percent, interest-only, what is your return on investment?
   c. What expenses will you probably incur if you choose to sell the property for $190,000 and how will this affect your actual return on investment?
11. ***Return on Collectible Investment.*** You bought an original painting at an art auction 10 years ago for $1,000. You have been offered a price of $2,500 for it today. If you sell for that price, what was your annual return on investment?

Using Web Resources for Financial Planning

1. ***Mutual Fund Research.*** Several financial websites provide screening and research tools to help you select and evaluate mutual funds. For example, at *moneycentral.msn.com,* you can click on "Investing" and select "Funds." On the Fund Research page, you can enter the ticker symbol for any mutual fund to access a variety of information on that fund. You can also search by certain fund classifications to find the top funds in each category. To try this out, look up the following funds:
   - Quaker Mid-Cap Value A (QMCVX), a mid-cap value fund
   - Dreyfus Premier Enterprise A (DPMGX), a small-cap growth fund
   - Fidelity Advisor High Inc Advant A (FAHSX), a high-yield bond fund

   Create a table that summarizes:
   a. Ratings for risk and return
   b. Expense ratio
   c. Load
   d. Net asset value
   e. Close price
2. ***Compare Similar Funds.*** Select a class of mutual funds that interests you (e.g., large-cap value or mid-cap income). Use the fund screener at *biz.yahoo.com/funds* or another financial site to find the top funds in your chosen category. (Note that the Fund Research main page at *moneycentral.msn.com* provides a listing of top funds for a different category each day.) Answer the following questions:
   a. What were the top performers in the last year?
   b. What criteria is this assessment based on?
   c. Are there any other criteria you should consider?
3. ***Find a Prospectus.*** You can download the prospectus for any U.S. mutual fund at *biz.yahoo.com/funds.* Select a fund based on your research in item 2 and download the prospectus. Answer the following:
   a. What is the fund objective?
   b. What fees and expenses do investors in the fund incur?
4. ***Estimate Mutual Fund Costs.*** Select a mutual fund that you currently own or are considering purchasing, or use one of the funds you researched in items 2 and 3 above. At the SEC website,

www.sec.gov, click on "Calculators" under Investor Information and use the Mutual Fund Cost Calculator to see what impact the fees and expenses will have on your returns.

5. ***Debunk the Real Estate Gurus.*** Investment real estate is probably the area of personal finance that can boast the most self-proclaimed experts. There are literally hundreds of books and articles on "How I Made a Million in Real Estate." For a candid critique of the most popular real estate "gurus," go to *www.johntreed.com* and click on "Real Estate Investment" and then "Real Estate Guru Ratings." Summarize the main criticisms offered by John Reed.

Learning by Doing Solutions

LBD 14-1: 1. NAV = (150 − 10)/12.3 = $11.38 per share; 2. NAV would increase.

LBD 14-2: 1. It depends on your investment time horizon. If you plan to hold the shares at least two years, the total costs will be about the same—for the A, 5 percent; and for the B, 4 percent back load plus two years of 0.5 percent 12b-1 fees. After five years, the back-end load will be gone, but you'll continue to pay the 0.5 percent 12b-1 fees each year, which can add up.

LBD 14-3: 1. Answers will differ; 2. If you have enough money to invest, it's probably better to buy a high-quality fund in each investment classification. This will guarantee that you get the asset allocation mix you desire (since the hybrid fund's managers will have a lot of leeway in the actual allocation of the fund) and will provide better diversification against the risk of problems with the particular fund.

LBD 14-4: 1. $(36{,}000{,}000/125)^{1/98} - 1 = 13.7\%$. Using a financial calculator; enter $PV = -125$, $N = 98$; $FV = 36{,}000{,}000$, and solve for $I = 13.7\%$.

Building Financial Planning Skills Through Case Applications

Case 14-1 Elena Musinski Evaluates Mutual Fund Options

Elena Musinski is divorced and has two daughters, ages five and six. Her ex-husband is paying $100 per child per week in child support in accordance with a court order. Since the kids are in school full-time, Elena has returned to work as a high-school math teacher and earns sufficient income to support the family. She's decided to put the child support money in a college fund for the girls. For the last year, she's been depositing the money in a savings account earning only 1 percent annual interest, and she's accumulated $10,600. She realizes that she needs to invest this money to earn a better return.

a. What is Elena's specific investment goal?

b. What types of mutual funds might be appropriate to meet this goal? Explain.

c. Should Elena consider tax-exempt investments? Explain.

d. Assuming that her ex-husband will continue to pay the same amount of child support until each of the children reaches the age of 18, calculate how much she will be able to accumulate under three scenarios: (1) She earns 1 percent on the funds after taxes, (2) she earns 4 percent on the funds after taxes, and (3) she earns 6 percent on the funds after taxes. For ease of computation, you can assume end-of-year child support payments of $5,200 per year for each child.

e. Assuming that tuition costs increase 5 percent per year, how much will $2,000 of tuition today cost in 15 years?

Case 14-2 Gabe and Della Lopez Are Disappointed in Their Bond Fund

In June 2003, Gabe Lopez made the big decision to retire at the age of 60 from his 35-year career as manager of the auto parts department at a large dealership. He and his wife Della, also 60, decided that she would continue to work until she could qualify for Social Security benefits. Gabe took the money from his 401(k) retirement plan ($600,000) and bought shares in a long-term, AAA-rated, corporate bond fund, since he wanted to be conservative with their retirement nest egg. Recent stock market declines had reinforced his belief that stocks were too risky. In June 2003, 20-year AAA corporate bonds yielded about 5.0 percent. The Lopezes own their home free and clear, so they figured that the income from their bond fund, combined with Della's income, would be plenty to live on. The first year, Gabe's mutual funds generated $30,000 in income before taxes. Although this was about half what he had earned at his job, he was pleased to find that they didn't have to dip into the principal to support their lifestyle.

As rates on AAA corporate bonds rose over the course of 2004 to about 6 percent by June 2004, Gabe was alarmed to see that the value of his bond mutual fund shares declined to $533,000. He and Della were confused—they thought that bonds were safe investments. They wonder if they should switch to a different type of investment.

a. Is the asset allocation chosen by the Lopezes appropriate for their life situation and risk tolerance? Explain.

b. Explain why the value of their bond mutual fund has declined.

c. Would you expect that the annual income generated by the Lopezes' bond fund will also decline? Why or why not?

d. Would it be a good idea for the couple to move their money to a different type of investment? Why or why not? If you think they should, what would you recommend they invest in?

e. Do you think that a financial planner would have recommended that the Lopezes put 100 percent of their money in bond mutual funds in June 2003? Why or why not?

Case 14-3 Christine McClatchey Considers a Real Estate Investment

Christine McClatchey is a single lawyer, age 30. Her income is substantially more than her expenses, and she has saved up enough to begin an investment plan. Although she has considered investing in stocks, she doesn't feel that she has the expertise or time to make well-informed decisions. She has a 401(k) plan with her employer in which she has accumulated $50,000 in a diversified mutual fund. She thinks she'd like to leverage her knowledge of the legal aspects of real estate by using her savings to invest in some rental property.

Chris has found a small house that has two apartments in it, located near the local university campus. She estimates that she'll need to invest about $10,000 to recarpet, paint, and do a few repairs before she can rent the apartments. Her rental income will be $15,000 per year. The purchase price of the property is $145,000. She has $42,000 to cover the $3,000 closing costs, the remodeling, and a 20 percent down payment. She'll finance the rest with an 8 percent mortgage.

a. How much will her mortgage payment be, assuming a fixed-rate mortgage with monthly payments for 30 years, not including property taxes and insurance?

b. Assuming she incurs $2,500 in expenses per year, calculate her before-tax net cash flow for the first year, after financing costs.

c. If the property increases in value to $160,000 in one year, what is the dollar amount of her unrealized capital gain? Don't forget to take into account the additional investment she has made in the property.

d. At the end of one year, assuming the apartments were rented for the full 12 months, what will her before-tax total return on investment be after interest costs (which total $9,250 for the year)?

e. Is this investment more or less risky for Chris than stocks and bonds? Explain.

f. Given her life situation, is Chris sufficiently diversified?

DEVELOPING PERSONAL FINANCIAL skills for life

Learning about Yourself

14-1. Is Socially Responsible Investing for You?

As mentioned in the chapter, socially responsible investment funds limit their investments to securities issued by companies that meet certain screens. Check each of the following statements that you agree with to see whether this type of investing is consistent with your values and ideals:

_____ **1.** I would prefer to invest in a company with lower earnings than to invest in a firm that makes business decisions I consider unethical.

_____ **2.** I would never want to invest in a company that employs children in Third World countries.

_____ **3.** I would never want to invest in a company that sells or manufactures firearms.

_____ **4.** I would never want to invest in a company that sells or manufactures alcoholic beverages.

_____ **5.** I would never want to invest in a company that sells or manufactures tobacco products.

_____ **6.** I would never want to invest in a company involved in the casino or gambling industry.

_____ **7.** I would never want to invest in a company that does business with oppressive foreign regimes.

_____ **8.** I will only invest in companies that treat their employees fairly.

_____ **9.** I will only invest in companies that don't use animals for testing.

_____ **10.** I will only invest in companies that make regular charitable donations.

Scoring:
If you've checked three or more, then socially responsible investing may be something you'd like to consider for your portfolio. Since the return differential between these funds and comparable risk funds is relatively small, the benefit of feeling good (ethically and morally) about your investments may outweigh the slight reduction in investment returns.

Developing Your Skills

14-2. Matching Investment Goals to Mutual Funds

Your investment goals will differ with age, family circumstances, and life situation. Use the worksheet in your *Personal Financial Planner* to decide on mutual funds that are appropriate for you today.

a. Considering where you are currently, what is your most important investment goal?
b. What type of mutual fund is most appropriate to meet your investment needs? (You can identify more than one type if appropriate.)
c. Identify several funds of this type and make a chart that compares their key features.
d. Based on your research, which mutual fund or funds would you choose?

PFP Worksheet 48
Evaluating Mutual Fund Alternatives

14-3. Asset Allocation

Many studies have shown that asset allocation is the most critical determinant of long-term portfolio performance.

a. Make a table that summarizes your household's current percentage allocation to each of the following asset classes: cash, stock, bonds, real estate, other.
b. Evaluate whether this allocation is appropriate for your current age and life-cycle stage. If not, what changes do you plan to make?
c. Fast-forward 10 years. At this point in your life, what would be an appropriate asset allocation for your portfolio? Explain.

14-4. Tracking Mutual Fund Investments

Select two or more mutual funds and record their performance over a period of time using the worksheet in your *Personal Financial Planner*. Compare the funds' performance to an appropriate benchmark.

PFP Worksheet 49
Mutual Fund Tracker

THE NAVIGATOR

- ☐ Review Before Studying this Chapter list.
- ☐ Scan Learning Objectives.
- ☐ Take Myth or Fact quiz and find the answers throughout the chapter.
- ☐ Read chapter and answer Learning by Doing exercises.
- ☐ Review Key Terms and Key Calculations.
- ☐ Do end-of-chapter exercises.
- ☐ Take review quiz on the text website.
- ☐ Solve end-of-chapter cases.

[BEFORE] studying this chapter, you should review

- Impact of inflation (Chapter 1).
- Traditional versus Roth IRAs (Chapter 4).
- Tax advantages of qualified retirement plans (Chapter 10).
- Defined contribution plans versus defined benefit plans (Chapter 10).

Saving for Distant Goals: Retirement and Education Funding

CHAPTER 15

Myth or Fact?

Consider each of the following statements and decide whether it is a *myth* or a *fact*. Look for the answers in the *Fact* boxes in the chapter.

	MYTH	FACT
1. In retirement, your expenses will only be about 70 percent of your pre-retirement expenses.	☐	☐
2. Most people under 30 don't think that Social Security will be around when they retire.	☐	☐
3. Double-income couples with no children are in much better shape for retirement than couples with children.	☐	☐
4. Most people are confident they'll be able to save enough to retire comfortably.	☐	☐
5. College education costs have generally risen faster than family income and inflation, making college less and less affordable for low-income families.	☐	☐

LEARNING objectives

1. Estimate your retirement income needs.
2. Evaluate your future benefits from employer-sponsored retirement plans and Social Security.
3. Determine your retirement wealth goal and monthly savings target.
4. Describe your alternatives for personal retirement saving.
5. Understand your options for retirement income payouts.
6. Develop a plan for funding your children's education, taking tax rules into account.

...applying the planning process

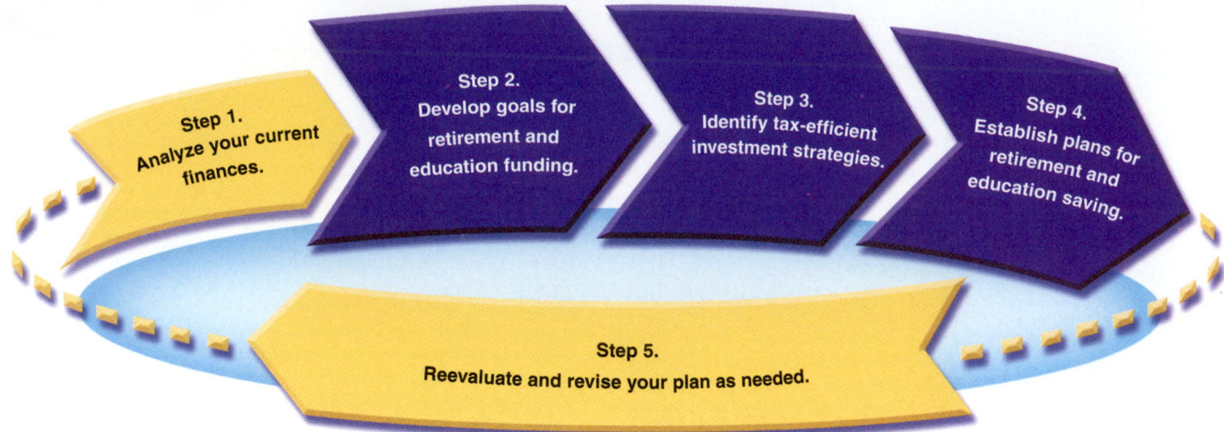

Successful planning for distant goals requires that you apply many concepts we've emphasized throughout this text. Establishing realistic goals, estimating their costs, and evaluating the most appropriate ways to achieve them are essential elements of this process. In this chapter, we apply the steps in the planning process to developing a plan for two important future goals: funding your own retirement and funding your children's college education. As you know, the earlier you begin your planning, the more successful you'll be at meeting your long-term objectives, and the easier it will be for you to weather the unknowns you'll face in the future.

You'll begin the planning process by reviewing the goals you established in Chapter 3. Your objectives concerning retirement may have been fairly vague—"live comfortably in retirement" or "retire at age 55," for example. If you planned to send one or more children to college, perhaps you included "Send my kids to college" on your list. In order to set up a plan to meet your goals, you'll need to get a lot more specific about just what you really want and need. This chapter explains how to estimate more accurately your retirement income and college funding needs so that you can apply the time value of money concepts to determine how much to save on a regular basis. Although we deal with these two topics in separate parts of the chapter—first focusing on retirement and then on the college funding decision—it will quickly become apparent that these two planning areas are integrally related. If you don't develop and implement a plan for each one early in your adult life, you'll likely find that, instead of socking money away for retirement during your peak earning years, you'll be paying it out to institutions of higher education.

Chapter Preview

Estimating Your Retirement Income Needs
- What Are Your Retirement Goals?
- What Will Your Expenses Be in Retirement?
- Adjusting for Inflation
- Adjusting for Income Taxes

Sources of Retirement Income: The Three-Legged Stool
- Estimating Your Benefits from Employer-Sponsored Plans
- Estimating Your Social Security Benefits

Establishing a Monthly Savings Target
- Retirement Income Shortfall
- Total Retirement Wealth Needed
- Monthly Savings Target
- The Importance of Starting Early

Personal Retirement Savings Options
- Individual Retirement Accounts (IRAS)
- Investing in Taxable Accounts
- Asset Allocation in Retirement Accounts

Preparing for Retirement Payouts
- Distributions from Retirement Accounts
- Tapping Your Home Equity
- What Happens If You Don't Have Enough Money to Retire?

Education Funding
- How Much Will You Need?
- Monthly Savings Target
- Tax Programs to Help You Save for Education Expenses

Estimating Retirement Income Needs

LEARNING objective

1 Estimate your retirement income needs.

For most college students, retirement probably seems pretty far in the future. After all, how can you think about retirement when you haven't even started your career? But most of us find that the time goes by all too fast. And unlike many of the personal financial goals we've considered thus far, this one is going to eventually cost you a *lot* of money, probably more than a million dollars. Consequently, it's that much more important for you to begin planning for retirement at as early an age as possible. If you do so, you'll be able to save a smaller proportion of your current income, and you'll be more likely to meet your retirement objectives.

As with other goals we've considered, you'll have to identify your needs, which in this case will require that you estimate how much retirement income your investments will need to generate. You'll first need to settle on some retirement goals, such as when you'll retire and how much income you'll need at that time. From this, you'll subtract any income you expect to receive from other sources to arrive at the income shortfall your investment program will have to generate. These steps are discussed in more detail in the following sections.

What Are Your Retirement Goals?

One person's ideal retirement isn't the same as another's, which implies that the cost of paying for retirement isn't the same for everyone. And, of course, since you have to save for this future expense now, you'll have to make a tradeoff between current and future consumption. So if you're willing to accept a lower standard of living in retirement, you can spend more today. But if you want to retire young, travel, golf, and spoil your grandchildren, you'll probably need to sacrifice some current spending to achieve your retirement goals.

When do you plan to retire? Obviously, the younger you retire, the longer your retirement period and the shorter the time you have to accumulate the wealth necessary to support yourself during your retirement. When surveyed, most people say they want to retire "early," which usually means in their mid- to late 50s. This is extremely optimistic, and many people have to revise their expectations as they approach their target retirement age. Although the average age of retirement has declined slightly over time, particularly for men, the most common retirement age is still age 65. As the age for normal Social Security retirement is gradually being increased to 67, as explained later in the chapter, it's likely that more people will delay retirement to that age. Nevertheless, it's not a bad idea to have an optimistic target date if this means you'll be more aggressive about saving toward that goal today.

To help you formulate some specific retirement objectives, take a look at the list provided in Exhibit 15-1. For each item, indicate whether it's very important to you, somewhat important, or not important at all. If you have any additional goals, add them to the list. Keep in mind that your goals and priorities will likely change between now and your retirement date, so this is a step in the process that will need to be revisited. For your convenience, the worksheet is also included in your *Personal Financial Planner.*

PFP Worksheet 50
Retirement Goals

Unless you're independently wealthy or expect to receive a large inheritance prior to retirement, you're not likely to reach the goals you've identified in Exhibit 15-1 unless you take steps today to accumulate sufficient wealth in time for retirement. Unfortunately, most households have unrealistic expectations about the retirement they can afford, given their current savings patterns. According to one study, the baby boom generation is saving at only one-third the rate necessary to meet its retirement goals. Unless they increase their savings rate substantially, they'll find themselves delaying their retirement date, relying on their children, or having a much lower standard of living in retirement. The *Money Psychology* box, "Why Don't People Plan Better for Retirement?" summarizes some of the psychological biases you may have to overcome to do a good job of retirement planning.

Do you want to have enough money in retirement to visit your grandchildren frequently, perhaps even taking them on vacations with you?

Once you've established some goals for the kind of retirement you'd like to have, the next step is to estimate how much it will cost you. This isn't a particularly easy task, since there are so many factors to consider. As a result, many people simply omit this step in their retirement planning. That's a mistake, though, and is likely to lead to poor planning and insufficient saving. If you don't know how much you'll need, how will you know if you're saving enough to get there?

Exhibit 15-2 is a worksheet you can use for this part of the retirement planning process. The worksheet outlines the steps to follow—estimating your future expenses and subtracting

EXHIBIT 15-1

Developing and Prioritizing Retirement Goals

Directions: For each of the following retirement goals, indicate its importance to you by checking the appropriate box.

Retirement Goal	Very Important	Somewhat Important	Not at All Important
Economic security			
Maintain standard of living	☐	☐	☐
Improve standard of living	☐	☐	☐
Financial independence	☐	☐	☐
Afford to keep home	☐	☐	☐
Family			
Bequests to heirs	☐	☐	☐
College costs	☐	☐	☐
Support children or parents	☐	☐	☐
Continue family business	☐	☐	☐
Medical			
Cover health-care costs	☐	☐	☐
Extras			
Better/more vacations	☐	☐	☐
Increased hobby costs	☐	☐	☐
Contributions to charity	☐	☐	☐
Other			
____________________			
____________________			

Money Psychology

Why Don't People Plan Better for Retirement?

Why do so many people fail to prepare adequately for retirement? As in many areas of personal finance, much of the answer boils down to psychological factors. Although it's unlikely that you'll be able to avoid all the psychological biases identified here, recognizing them is half the battle.

- *Myopia.* More than ever, our society embraces a "live for today" ethos. Myopia, or near-sightedness, is the term used by economists to describe this phenomenon. Households are constantly bombarded with advertising that reinforces natural tendencies for current spending and immediate gratification, which makes it more difficult to allocate funds for far-distant goals such as retirement.
- *Inflation illusion.* Most people don't understand inflation. As a result, they underestimate the amount of money they'll need to fund an inflation-adjusted income in retirement.
- *Focus on averages.* People tend to focus on averages rather than looking at the full range of possible outcomes. This mistake can create a number of difficulties, particularly in estimating life expectancy and investment returns. Based on average life expectancy, you probably understand that you'll live into your mid-80s. But if you use this age to estimate how much you need to save for retirement, you have a 50 percent chance of saving too little. As medical treatments continue to extend life, it will become increasingly common for people to live to 100 years of age, approximately doubling the average retirement period. We're guilty of the same bias in estimating investment returns, often using a long-run average return in forecasting instead of recognizing the variability to which we're exposed.
- *It Won't Happen to Me.* A common psychological bias is the tendency to think that bad things happen to everyone else but you. Despite the high rates of divorce, widowhood, and disability, most people don't have a plan for how they'll deal with these issues if they come up. These events produce income shocks that inevitably affect the ability to accumulate funds for retirement.

EXHIBIT 15-2

Retirement Planning Worksheet

Step 1 Estimate before-tax income needs.
a. Enter current household expenses. ______
b. Adjust for changes in expenses in retirement.
Possible reductions: Employment expenses
Retirement savings
Housing expenses
Total reductions ______
Possible increases: Health care/insurance
Leisure activities
Gifts/donations
Total increases ______
c. Adjusted expenses in current dollars (1a. − 1b. + 1c.) ______
d. Adjust for inflation to future dollars:
(i = expected inflation; n = years to retirement)
After-tax income needs =
Adjusted expenses in current dollars × $(1 + i)^n$ = ______

e. Calculate before-tax total income needs:

$$\text{Before-tax } \$ = \frac{\text{After-tax } \$}{(1 - \text{Average tax rate})} = \_\_\_\_\_\_$$

Step 2. Estimate annual retirement income from defined benefit retirement plan(s).
Use most recent statement from your pension sponsor
or estimate based on known benefit formula.
Plan 1______
Plan 2______
Total income in future dollars from defined benefit plans = ______

Step 3. Estimate annual retirement income from Social Security.
Use calculator at www.ssa.gov or Exhibit 15-4 to estimate
in future dollars. ______

Step 4. Calculate retirement income shortfall. (1e − 2 − 3) = ______

Step 5. Estimate total retirement wealth needed.
a. Retirement wealth factor: ______
(from Exhibit 15-6, assuming ______ years in retirement and
______% average investment return)
b. Retirement income shortfall × Retirement wealth factor = ______

Step 6. Estimate retirement savings goals.
a. Value of current retirement savings accounts. ______
b. Future value of current accounts (6a × $FVIF_{i,n}$) [Exhibit A-1] = ______
c. Retirement savings goal (5b − 6b) = ______

Step 7. Estimate monthly savings required to meet savings goals.
(Use time value of money calculation for payment) ______

PFP Worksheet 51
Retirement Planning

Most financial websites include a retirement planning worksheet that will help you estimate how much you need to save for retirement. At www.troweprice.com, under "Individual Investors," click on "Investment Planning & Tools" and then "Tools and Calculators." At www.smartmoney.com, click on "Personal Finance" and then "Retirement."

your expected income from employer-sponsored retirement plans and Social Security to arrive at your expected retirement income shortfall. Based on the expected shortfall, you can estimate how much wealth you'll need to accumulate by the date of retirement and how much you'll need to save each month to meet that goal. The following sections walk you through the steps in this process.

What Will Your Expenses Be in Retirement?

The two methods most commonly used for estimating retirement income needs are the replacement ratio method and the adjusted expense method. The **replacement ratio method** assumes that your retirement expenses will be some fixed proportion of your preretirement expenses, such as 70 or 80 percent. For example, suppose you've estimated that your current household expenses are $40,000 per year. If you assume that your expenses after retirement will be 80 percent of current expenses, the replacement ratio method will yield an estimate of $32,000 in today's dollars. Although this method is relatively commonly applied, the problem is, you have no guarantee that your expenses will be lower in retirement.

replacement ratio method

A method for estimating after-tax retirement income needs in current dollars by multiplying current expenses by a factor of 70 to 80 percent.

adjusted expense method

A method for estimating after-tax retirement income needs in current dollars by adjusting current expenses for changes expected in retirement.

The **adjusted expense method** for estimating retirement income will take a little more time but will result in a more accurate forecast. This method is the one applied in Step 1 of the retirement planning worksheet in Exhibit 15-2. Here, you take your current expenses by category and adjust each one based on your estimates of expenses in retirement. For example, if you expect to have a larger mortgage payment in the future (e.g., with the purchase of a larger home), or if you have arranged to have your mortgage paid in full by the time you retire, you'll adjust the mortgage expense amount accordingly. If you'll need to pay for your own health insurance after you leave your current employer (highly likely, given current trends), you'll add the additional insurance premium cost. You should use the goals that you developed earlier to help you identify the necessary adjustments. Keep in mind that you're doing this estimate in today's dollars, so if it would cost you $5,000 a year for golf club membership today, that's the figure you'll use on the worksheet.

Fact #1

There's no scientific evidence that expenses in retirement are 70 percent of preretirement expenses. Although nobody is sure where this rule of thumb originated, it's been repeated often enough that many people take it as truth rather than doing the calculations themselves. Today, retirees don't want to simply stay at home and putter in their gardens. They plan to take expensive vacations, join a golf club, and entertain more than they did during their years in the workforce. The popularity of the bumper sticker "We're spending our children's inheritance" says it all.

Adjusting for Inflation

Once you've estimated your expenses in current dollars by either of the methods above, you need to adjust this amount for inflation between now and retirement to arrive at total income needs in your first year of retirement. To do this, you'll use the time value of money calculation for the future value of a lump sum. The present value is your annual expenses in today's dollars, and you'll solve for the future value—what your expenses will be when you retire n years in the future compounded at the estimated rate of inflation. Although inflation has been lower in recent years, the long-run average is between 3 and 4 percent, so a compounding rate of 3 to 4 percent is a reasonable estimate to use.

Recall that the future value equation is

$$FV = PV \times (1 + i)^n$$

At www.fool.com, the Motley Fool website, you can use one of the "Foolish Calculators" to estimate your postretirement expenses. After you enter the required information, the calculator will give you an estimate of your expenses in future dollars.

In this case, as noted, PV is your estimated retirement expenses in current dollars, n is the number of years from now to your anticipated retirement, and i is the estimated rate of inflation. Let's assume that you've estimated your retirement expenses at $32,000 in today's dollars, that you expect to retire in 40 years, and that you expect inflation will average 4 percent over that time period. Substituting these values in the equation, we see that your income requirement for the first year of retirement will be $\$32{,}000 \times (1.04)^{40} = \$153,633$. Alternatively, you can arrive at the same answer by using the appropriate future value factor from Exhibit A-1 ($\$32{,}000 \times 4.801 = \$153,632$, the slight difference being due to rounding) or by solving the problem on your financial calculator (input PV = 32,000, $N = 40$, and $I = 4$ and solve for FV = $153, 633). Although $153,633 may seem like a lot of money, keep in mind that it will be equivalent in spending power to $32,000 today.

How much difference will it make if inflation over the next 40 years is more or less than what you've estimated? The short answer is—*a lot.* If, for example, inflation averages only 3 percent, the future value of your expenses is $104, 385, about one-third less than your estimate. If inflation averages 5 percent, your expenses will be $225,280, about 50 percent more. It should be clear why it's so important to take inflation into account.

Adjusting for Income Taxes

Some or all of your income in retirement may be subject to federal and state income taxation. Of course, we can't predict how the tax code may change in the future. Nevertheless, you need to consider the effect of taxes as best you can. Since the expenses you've estimated in the previous section will primarily be paid from after-tax dollars, you need to determine the before-tax income that will be necessary to meet these expenses. This is easily calculated using an equation you've seen before:

$$\text{After-tax amount} = \text{Before-tax amount} \times (1 - t)$$

where t is the expected average tax rate. When you solve for the before-tax amount, the equation becomes

$$\text{Before-tax amount} = \frac{\text{After-tax amount}}{1 - t}$$

If you need $153,633 in after-tax dollars to meet your first year's retirement expenses, and you estimate that you'll pay 25 percent in taxes, then you'll need $153,633/(1 − 0.25) = $204,844 in before-tax income.

Learning by Doing 15-1

1. You estimate your current expenses at $30,000 and expect 3 percent inflation from now until retirement. Use an 80 percent replacement ratio to estimate your pretax retirement income needs in your first year of retirement, assuming that you're currently 22 years old and will retire at age 67.
2. Use the same facts as above, but assume you're currently age 42.
3. Using the same facts as in item 1, estimate your pretax retirement income needs in current dollars using the adjusted expense method. Assume that your reduced household expenses for employment costs and mortgage payments will save you $15,000 per year in current dollars and that your additional costs for insurance and vacations will be $10,000.

Sources of Retirement Income: The Three-Legged Stool

LEARNING objective

2 Evaluate your future benefits from employer-sponsored retirement plans and Social Security.

Once you have an estimate of your retirement income needs, the next step is to consider the various ways you can meet those needs. The "three-legged stool of retirement income" is a metaphor originated in the Congressional discussions that led up to the passage of the act that created Social Security many decades ago. The fact that it's often mentioned in government policy discussions today demonstrates its continued relevance. Each individual's retirement income security can be visualized as a three-legged stool, with the three "legs" being:

- Social Security
- Employer-sponsored retirement plans
- Private savings

For retirement planning, this is a particularly apt analogy: Like a three-legged stool, your retirement plan can be expected to topple over if one of the legs is too short, as shown in Exhibit 15-3.

Unfortunately, most retirees today rely too much on Social Security, making the stool a bit lop-sided. Many of them (24% of retirees in 2002) find it necessary to continue to work in retirement to supplement their income or to have access to affordable health benefits (so we could say that their stool has to have an extra leg to support their retirement). Not counting employment income, the Social Security Administration estimates that 25 percent of aggregate retirement income comes from earnings on assets, 22 percent from government and private pensions, and 53 percent from Social Security benefits. More than two-thirds of all retirees get at least half their income from Social Security, and 31 percent rely on it to provide more than 90 percent of their total income.

Today's workers, who will be tomorrow's retirees, face many challenges in balancing the three legs of the stool, including higher levels of household debt, uncertainty about the future of Social Security, and increased investment risk in employer retirement plans. For women, this problem is exacerbated by persistent differences in labor market experience that make it more difficult for them to prepare for retirement, as explained in the *News You Can Use* box, "Why Do Women Have Lower Retirement Income Than Men?"

EXHIBIT 15-3

Three-Legged Stool of Retirement Income

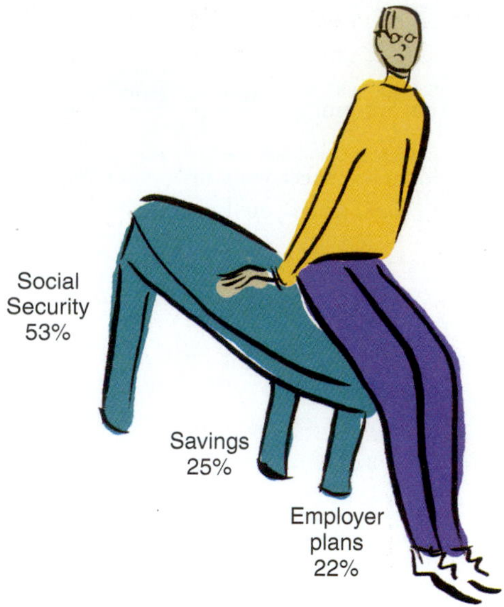

The point of all this is to emphasize the importance, in your own planning, of making decisions today that will maximize your access to multiple sources of income in retirement. As discussed in Chapter 10, you may want to seek employment with a firm that sponsors a generous retirement plan for its employees. This, combined with Social Security benefits, will reduce the amount of income shortfall that you'll have to finance from your investments or from continued employment after retirement. In the next two sections, we'll consider your potential income from employment–based retirement plans and public pension benefits.

Estimating Your Benefits from Employer-Sponsored Plans

Chapter 10 discussed the various types of tax-qualified retirement plans. For each type, plan sponsors are required to report certain information to participants at least annually. These reports give the current value of each investment account and an estimate of the benefit that's likely to result from the plan under current assumptions. If you're eligible for an employer-sponsored retirement plan, you can use this information to complete Step 2 of the retirement planning worksheet in Exhibit 15-2.

NEWS you can use

Why Do Women Have Lower Retirement Income Than Men?

A disproportionate percentage of elderly women are poor. While this is nothing new—Congress used this statistic in justifying the creation of Social Security many decades ago—the persistence of this gender-based retirement income gap is of concern to public policy makers. A recent research report sponsored by the American Association of Retired Persons found that much of the retirement income gender gap is caused by differences in labor market experiences. Women continue to earn less than men during their working years, and they have shorter working careers, both factors leading to reduced Social Security benefits. In addition, there is evidence of occupational segregation—women are more likely to work in firms and industries that don't have employer-sponsored retirement plans. These factors combine to make it more difficult for women to adequately prepare for retirement.

> **"Women continue to earn less than men."**

Note: To read the entire report, see Olivia S, Mitchell, Phillip B. Levine, and John W. Phillips, "The Impact of Pay Inequality, Occupational Segregation, and Lifetime Work Experience on the Retirement Income of Women and Minorities," AARP Public Policy Institute #9910, September 1999.

Retirement Income from Defined Benefit Plans. As you may recall from Chapter 10, your future benefit from a defined benefit plan is usually based on a formula that takes into account the number of years you've worked for the employer and how much you earn. For example, an employer might use the following formula: 2 percent of final salary for each year of service up to a maximum of 80 percent. If you work for this employer for 35 years, you'll receive a benefit equal to 70 percent of your salary at retirement. If you have a generous defined benefit plan that also adjusts benefits for inflation during retirement, your risk of outliving your assets will be significantly reduced. In the extreme, you may find that the benefits you receive over your lifetime far exceed the amounts contributed to the plan, as in the example discussed in the *News You Can Use* box, "How Anna Swanson Got Her Money's Worth."

Many production workers in the manufacturing sector have generous defined benefit pension plans that will protect them from outliving their assets.

Even though your employer provides a benefit estimate, you'll need to adjust the amount given, since it will be based on your *current* salary and years of employment (rather than your projected final salary and years of employment at retirement) and there's no guarantee that you'll continue to work for the same employer. For this reason, a more precise estimate of your expected income shortfall requires that you take the time to project your future salary and apply the appropriate percentage. For example, suppose your current salary is \$40,000 and you'll retire in 20 years, at which time you will have 35 years of service. When we apply the future value equation as before, if your salary increases at a rate of 4 percent, your salary at retirement will be $\$40,000 \times (1.04)^{20} = \$87,645$. Using this salary amount, you can then estimate your projected pension benefit utilizing the applicable benefit formula as above.

If you expect to receive income from more than one employer-sponsored defined benefit plan, you should estimate each income amount separately and input the total in Step 2. Note, however, that, if you have a vested benefit from a previous employer's plan that uses salary in its formula, the benefit amount will be calculated based on your final salary with *that firm*, not on your earnings when you actually retire.

Income from Defined Contribution Plans. If you work for an employer that sponsors a 401(k) or other type of retirement savings program, contributions to your account can be expected to continue, and even to increase, until you retire. When you retire, you'll probably convert this fund to an income stream, either by purchasing an annuity, or by spending the investment earnings and principal during retirement. Unlike a defined benefit plan, the amount of income this fund will generate for you in retirement is fairly uncertain since it depends on

NEWS you can use

How Anna Swanson Got Her Money's Worth

Anna Swanson was born in 1902 in Sweden but, faced with few prospects at home, left her family and friends behind in 1920 to make a new life for herself in the United States. Ultimately, she married and settled in Northern Virginia, where she went to work for the U.S. Census Bureau in 1935. Like many others in her generation, she worked for the same employer until she retired. As a federal civil servant with only a high-school education, Anna was never paid a stellar salary. In fact, her gross income at the time she retired at age 58 was only \$7,000 (the equivalent of about \$25,000 in 2004), and her first-year pension benefit was only \$3,500. The benefits, however, automatically increased with inflation every year, so by the time Anna died in 1999, she was receiving approximately \$8,000 per year. Anna enjoyed good enough health to live independently until the year before she died at age 97, and she loved to tell her family and friends what a wonderful deal she'd gotten from the federal government. She worked for only 25 years and received a pension for nearly 40. She certainly got her money's worth! This true story illustrates an important concept about retirement planning—you need a plan that will last your *whole life*, no matter how long that might turn out to be. Without the life annuity from her defined benefit pension, Anna would have ended up like so many older women—dependent on financial support from family or public assistance.

"She worked for 25 years and received a pension for nearly 40."

how much is contributed each year and the rate of return on invested assets for many years into the future. Although you will receive an annual report from the plan each year that tells you how much you have saved so far and an estimate of the income your account is expected to generate in retirement, instead of entering an income amount for this fund, we'll treat this as we do in Step 5 for other investment plans you may have in place.

Once you've arrived at the total estimated annual retirement income that will be generated from employer defined benefit retirement plans, enter the total annual amount in the space provided for Step 2 on the retirement planning worksheet.

Estimating Your Social Security Benefits

We've already discussed some aspects of Social Security, but it's worthwhile reviewing a few key features of this program so that you'll better understand how to estimate your future benefits. We'll also examine the financial problems the program is expected to experience in the near future and whether you should expect these problems to affect your benefits at retirement.

What Is Social Security and How Is It Funded?

As you may recall from previous chapters, Social Security is a defined benefit program administered by the U.S. Social Security Administration (SSA). In addition to the health, disability, and survivor benefits identified earlier, the program is intended to provide at least subsistence-level retirement income to program participants, who include nearly all workers in the United States. About 40 million people currently receive retirement benefits from the program.

Social Security is funded by a payroll tax called FICA, authorized by the Federal Insurance Contributions Act. The tax burden is shared by employers and employees (5.3% each on the first $87,900 of income per year in 2004, a maximum that increases annually with inflation). An additional shared tax of 1.8 percent (0.9% each) goes to the disability program (also subject to the income limitation), and 2.9 percent (1.45% each) goes to the Medicare program (but is assessed on total income). Self-employed people pay both portions of all three of these tax components, for a total of 15.3 percent. Social Security is referred to as a "pay-as-you-go" system, since the money received from current workers is used to pay benefits to current beneficiaries. As the number of workers per retiree has decreased over the years (from 42 in 1945 to fewer than 4 today), the payroll tax has gradually increased to keep the system in balance.

Who Is Eligible to Receive Social Security Benefits?

You can be eligible to receive Social Security benefits either based on your own earnings history or based on your spouse's. To be eligible based on your own earnings, you must be "fully insured."

Fully Insured Status. To be fully insured, you must have participated in the system, paying FICA payroll taxes on your earnings, for a total of 40 three-month periods (quarters) totaling 10 years and earned at least a specified minimum dollar amount in each of those quarters. Fully insured participants who retire at the normal retirement age are entitled to benefits as defined by law. The normal retirement age, originally age 65, has been changed, as shown in Exhibit 15-4, and the normal retirement age for anyone born in 1960 or later is now age 67. Participants can also opt for "early retirement" at age 62, in which case they receive a reduced benefit to account for the reduced years of payroll tax contributions and increased years of expected benefit receipt. Even though the early retirement reduction is fairly substantial—$6\frac{2}{3}$ percent for each year prior to the normal retirement age—many people opt for early receipt of benefits.

EXHIBIT 15-4

Social Security Normal Retirement Age

Year of Birth	Retirement Age	Year of Birth	Retirement Age
Before 1938	65 years	1955	66 years, 2 months
1938	65 years, 2 months	1956	66 years, 4 months
1939	65 years, 4 months	1957	66 years, 6 months
1940	65 years, 6 months	1958	66 years, 8 months
1941	65 years, 8 months	1959	66 years, 10 months
1942	65 years, 10 months	1960–present	67 years
1943–1954	66 years		

Spousal Benefits. Another way you can qualify for Social Security benefits is to have a spouse who is fully insured. Because Social Security was designed in an era when single-earner households were the norm rather than the exception, Congress included some protections for women in the program. In today's era of equal opportunity, these protections might seem unnecessary, but they have significantly reduced the poverty rate for elderly women. Consider an example: Barbara and Dave are 65 years old. Barbara didn't work outside the home until her last child left for college. At that time, she was 57 years old, so she's only contributed to Social Security for seven years—not enough time to achieve fully insured status. Barbara's husband Dave, however, is eligible for a monthly benefit of $1,600. Under the current system, Barbara is eligible for a spousal benefit equal to 50 percent of her husband's benefit. Furthermore, even if Barbara did qualify on her own earnings history, the law would allow her to receive a benefit based on either her own earnings or 50 percent of her husband's benefit, whichever was greater. And if Dave dies before her, she'll receive a survivor benefit equal to 100 percent of Dave's benefit. Divorcees who haven't remarried are eligible for Social Security benefits equal to 50 percent of their ex-husbands' benefits as long as the marriage lasted at least 10 years. Conceivably, the same man could have been married four times, each for 10 years, and all four of his ex-wives could receive benefits at retirement equal to 50 percent of his benefit, as long as they hadn't remarried.

Social Security survivor benefits help elderly widows remain independent in retirement.

How Much Will I Get from Social Security?

Social Security benefits are based on a multistep calculation. The SSA first calculates your **average indexed monthly earnings (AIME),** using your top 35 years of earnings (up to the taxable maximum for each year), adjusted for inflation to current-year dollars. If you've worked for less than 35 years, you'll have some zeros averaged in. The AIME is then used in a formula to calculate your **primary insurance amount (PIA)**, the monthly benefit you'd be entitled to if you retired at the normal retirement age. Although the dollar amounts in the formula are adjusted annually for inflation, you can get the idea by looking at the formula for 2004

$$\text{PIA} = [0.09 \times (\text{first } \$606 \text{ of AIME})] + [0.32 \times (\text{AIME up to } \$3{,}653 - \$606)] + [0.15 \times (\text{AIME} - \$3{,}653)]$$

average indexed monthly earnings (AIME)

The average of a person's 35 highest years of monthly earnings, adjusted for inflation, used in computing that individual's Social Security benefit.

primary insurance amount (PIA)

The Social Security benefit payable to a program participant who retires at the normal retirement age.

This formula is designed to have a redistributive effect by replacing a larger percentage of preretirement income for low-income retirees than for average- and high-income retirees. A low-income person (AIME = $1,000) retiring in 2004 would have been eligible for a monthly benefit of $671.48, an amount that would have replaced about two-thirds of his or her preretirement income:

$$\begin{aligned}\text{PIA} &= (0.9 \times \$606) + [0.32 \times (\$1{,}000 - \$606)]\\ &= \$545.40 + \$126.08\\ &= \$671.48\end{aligned}$$

At the other end of the spectrum, a person who consistently earned at least as much as the income maximum ($87,900/12 = $7,325 per month) would have been eligible for the maximum benefit under the program that year, $2,071.24, which would have replaced less than one-third of his or her preretirement income:

$$\begin{aligned}\text{PIA} &= (0.9 \times \$606) + [0.32 \times (\$3{,}653 - \$606)] + [0.15 \times (\$7{,}325 - \$3{,}653)]\\ &= \$545.40 + \$975.04 + \$550.80\\ &= \$2{,}071.24\end{aligned}$$

On average, Social Security beneficiaries receive a retirement benefit of $900 ($1,500 for a couple) per month. The benefit amount is annually adjusted for inflation, a feature that ensures that a retiree's purchasing power will not decline over time.

To complete Step 3 of the Retirement Planning Worksheet in Exhibit 15-2, you can use the retirement calculator on the SSA webpage (www.ssa.gov) to estimate your benefit in future dollars. Alternatively, Exhibit 15-5 provides benefit estimates for a range of age and salary combinations, assuming average wage increases over your lifetime and retirement at the normal retirement age. For example, if you're currently 25 and have a salary of $30,000, you can estimate that your annual Social Security benefit at age 67 (your normal retirement age) will be $62,772 in future dollars. This is the amount you'll enter in Step 3 of the worksheet.

EXHIBIT 15-5

Annual Social Security Retirement Benefit Estimates

2004 Income	Age in 2004						
	25	30	35	40	45	50	55
$20,000	48,444	39,960	32,904	26,928	21,876	17,064	13,620
$25,000	55,608	45,864	37,764	30,876	25,044	19,476	15,504
$30,000	62,772	51,780	42,624	34,836	28,224	21,900	17,388
$35,000	69,936	57,684	47,484	38,784	31,392	24,312	19,272
$40,000	77,100	63,588	52,344	42,732	34,560	26,736	21,156
$45,000	84,252	69,504	57,204	46,680	37,740	29,148	23,040
$50,000	88,332	72,852	60,048	49,308	40,296	31,560	24,924
$55,000	91,692	75,624	62,328	51,156	41,784	32,940	26,592
$60,000	95,040	78,396	64,608	53,016	43,272	34,080	27,468
$65,000	98,400	81,168	66,888	54,864	44,760	35,208	28,356
$70,000	101,760	83,940	69,156	56,724	46,248	36,348	29,232
Maximum	113,100	93,276	77,064	63,648	52,512	42,024	34,404

Values in future dollars obtained from Social Security Administration Quick Benefit Calculator at http://www.ssa.gov, assuming average wage increases over the worklife and retirement at the normal retirement age.

Will Social Security Be Around When I Retire? Your eligibility for Social Security benefits makes a big difference in the amount of income shortfall you'll need to fund, so the question of whether the program will still be around when you retire is an important one. Chances are good that it will be, but there's a strong possibility that it won't be quite as generous as it is today. You need to understand a little about how the financing works to see why this is the case.

Financing of the System. As mentioned, Social Security is a pay-as-you-go system—current payroll taxes are used to fund current benefit payments. When payroll taxes collected exceed the total being paid out in benefits to current retirees, as has been the case for the last several years, the Social Security Administration invests the extra money in special-issue Treasury bonds. The accumulated value of these bonds is called the Social Security trust fund. You know enough about government bonds to understand that what this really means is that the federal government has borrowed the money from Social Security in return for an IOU that will eventually have to be repaid.

Causes of Projected Insolvency. Until the members of the baby boom generation reached their peak earnings years, the Social Security trust fund was really just a short-term parking place for funds, as Congress tweaked the benefit formula and payroll tax percentage to ensure that the money coming in was just enough to cover the benefits to be paid. However, tax inflows currently are much larger than benefit payments, so the fund is growing steadily, accumulating the extra funds that will be necessary to pay benefits to future retirees. Despite this, current forecasts by the Social Security Administration predict that the retirement of the baby boomers will place a corresponding drain on program funds. Under current projections, tax inflows will start to lag benefit outflows in 2018, and the trust fund will be depleted (meaning all the bonds will have been cashed in) by 2044. And this doesn't even take into account the fact that the federal government is somehow going to have to come up with the funds to make good on its pile of IOUs to the Social Security trust fund.

This potentially negative outcome is due to several factors. One is simply that people are living longer and so are collecting benefits over longer periods. Another, as already suggested, is that the baby boom generation is larger than the generations that preceded and followed it. This means that as baby boomers retire, more and more retirees will be receiving benefits, and there'll be fewer workers paying taxes to cover those benefits. In another 20 years, when the bulk of the baby boomers have retired, there'll be only two workers paying into the system for every retiree receiving benefits. It doesn't take a math genius to figure out that this won't work! Congress has aggravated the problem by responding to voters who want benefits and eligibility requirements to be more generous, rather than less. For example, even though the average number of years that retirees collect benefits has more than doubled since the program's inception, the normal retirement age remained at 65 until recently and is scheduled to increase only to 67.

Prospects for Reform. It has become apparent that some type of Social Security reform is necessary, and various proposals have been discussed. When the stock market was booming, many thought a defined contribution approach was the way to go. In this type of plan, a portion of each worker's payroll tax would be deposited in an investment account, and his or her benefits would depend on the growth in value of this account over time (much like a 401(k) plan sponsored by an employer). While it's possible that this type of plan might find support in Congress in the near future, there will be several problems with its implementation. First, older participants don't have the time to accumulate enough in an investment account to replace their current benefit promise, so they'll have to continue under the old program rules. Increasing federal budget deficits make it unlikely that the government will be able to help fund the transition period, so the younger participants' payroll taxes will have to be sufficient to cover the projected benefit obligations under the revised benefit and insurance formulas, their own account contributions, and the "grandfathered" retirees under the old system. Last but not least, recent market volatility raises concerns about the increased risk an individual account approach would place on plan participants.

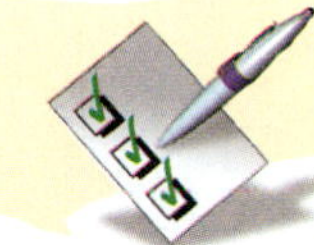

Public opinion polls show that the members of generations X and Y are skeptical about their prospects of receiving Social Security benefits. In fact, the percentage of those polled who believed that aliens had landed on earth was larger than the percentage who believed Social Security would be around when they retired.

Instead of introducing a major reform of Social Security, it's much more likely that politicians will choose to take small steps—perhaps raising the normal retirement age a little more, tweaking the PIA formula, or limiting benefits for the wealthy. In striving not to alienate older voters who are counting on the current system to remain unchanged, politicians are more likely to dodge the bullet, leaving the problems for future generations to face. In light of this, as you consider your personal retirement plan, you should probably be conservative about your estimated Social Security benefit so that you don't underestimate your retirement income shortfall.

Learning by Doing 15-2

1. Mark is a 30-year-old professional who earns $50,000 per year. Assuming that he'll retire at the normal Social Security retirement age for his birth date (67), use Exhibit 15-5 to estimate his first-year Social Security benefit in future dollars.
2. Marissa worked as a homemaker until she was 50. Since then, she has worked part-time as a retail clerk, and she is now ready to retire at age 65. Her husband's Social Security AIME is $3,000, and hers is only $500. Will she be able to qualify for benefits based on her husband's earnings history?

Establishing a Monthly Savings Target

LEARNING objective

3 Determine your retirement wealth goal and monthly savings target.

So far we've evaluated two of the legs of the three-legged stool of retirement—income from employment-based pensions and income from Social Security. In this section, we'll turn our attention to the third leg—your personal savings and investments. We'll first estimate your retirement income shortfall and then use this to estimate the total wealth you'll need to accumulate by the time you retire. From this, we'll subtract any other funds you can apply to this goal and then estimate the monthly savings necessary to accumulate the remainder.

Retirement Income Shortfall

Let's return to the retirement planning worksheet to determine your retirement income shortfall—the amount of retirement income you'll need to generate from your investments. In Step 4, we determine the shortfall by subtracting the total amount of your annual employment-based retirement benefits and Social Security benefits from your after-tax retirement income needs, as follows:

Retirement income shortfall = Total before-tax income needs − Projected income from employer retirement plans − Projected Social Security benefit

The retirement income shortfall estimated in Step 4 is actually the amount you'll need in your first year of retirement. You'll need an amount of income in each subsequent year that provides you with equivalent purchasing power.

Total Retirement Wealth Needed

You can use time value of money tools to estimate your total retirement wealth needed—the amount of accumulated savings necessary at retirement to provide you with the income shortfall you estimated in Step 4. This may seem like a fairly straightforward present value of an annuity problem, but it is actually a bit more complicated, for two reasons:

1. The number of years you'll live in retirement is uncertain.
2. The amount of income you'll need in retirement will increase each year with inflation and as your needs change.

If you simply calculate the present value of an annuity equal to the first year's shortfall, you'll underestimate how much money you'll need to live on, since the purchasing power of this amount will gradually decline over your retirement years. Similarly, if you use the average expected life span to estimate the number of years you'll receive that annuity, you have a 50 percent chance of outliving your assets. If you use your lump sum at retirement to purchase a 20-year annuity, but the 20th year arrives and you're still living, you won't have anything left to live on.

There are two approaches you can use to estimate your total retirement wealth needed, and both are summarized in the *Go Figure!* box, "Estimating Total Retirement Wealth Needed." In the first approach, you can set your goal to be sufficient for you to use the interest earnings alone, preserving the principal. If you need $60,000 per year and can earn 10 percent on your investments after taxes while in retirement, for example, you'll require $600,000 in savings. The advantages of this approach are that you won't outlive your assets and, upon your death, you'll have an estate to pass on to your heirs. The disadvantage is that your savings will produce less current income than if you were willing to deplete the principal over time.

inflation-adjusted annuity

A series of payments at equal intervals that increase with inflation.

The second approach uses the time value of money to estimate the present value of an **inflation-adjusted annuity.** In other words, you make the assumption that the income shortfall you've estimated in Step 4 of the retirement planning worksheet will need to increase at the rate of inflation each year. Since you're calculating an annuity, you'll end up spending both principal and interest over time. As with other time value problems, there's a formula you can use to calculate the present value of an inflation-adjusted annuity. As a shortcut, you can estimate the total retirement wealth you will need by multiplying the income shortfall by the appropriate factor from Exhibit 15-6,

EXHIBIT 15-6

Retirement Wealth Factors for Estimating Retirement Savings Goal

To calculate the total retirement wealth you will need, multiply your retirement income shortfall by the retirement wealth factor in the table, given your estimated years in retirement and expected annual investment return. This table assumes 4% inflation in retirement.

	Retirement Wealth Factor				
	Investment Return During Retirement				
Years in Retirement	5%	6%	7%	8%	10%
5	4.6721	4.5423	4.4181	4.2992	4.0759
10	9.1258	8.6720	8.2506	7.8590	7.1550
15	13.3715	12.4265	11.5752	10.8067	9.4811
20	17.4189	15.8399	14.4591	13.2475	11.2384
25	21.2771	18.9432	16.9607	15.2685	12.5659
30	24.9551	21.7646	19.1308	16.9420	13.5688
35	28.4612	24.3297	21.0133	18.3277	14.3264
40	31.8036	26.6617	22.6462	19.4751	14.8987

GO FIGURE!

Estimating Total Retirement Wealth Needed

Problem: After estimating your future income from employment retirement plans and Social Security, your retirement income shortfall is \$50,000 per year (in future dollars). You think you can earn an 8 percent return on your invested assets (r%) during retirement, and you expect inflation to average 4 percent during retirement. How much money do you need to have at retirement to fund your estimated income needs if (1) you plan to live on investment income alone, or (2) you plan to use both investment income and principal?

Solution:

1. *If you plan to live on investment returns alone:* If you want to live on investment income alone, you can use the following equation to estimate the amount of wealth you need:

$$\text{Wealth necessary to generate constant income} = \frac{\text{Income}}{r\%}$$

You therefore need to accumulate wealth of \$50,000/0.08 = \$625,000. Note, however, that this will produce a constant income stream of \$50,000. Because the amount won't increase with inflation, you may have to dip into your principal in later years. When you die, you'll be able to leave the remaining principal to your heirs.

2. *If you plan to use both the investment earnings and the principal to fund your income needs:* The total retirement wealth you'll need, the present value of an inflation-adjusted annuity, can be calculated as follows:

Total retirement wealth needed

$$= \frac{\text{First-year income}}{(r - i)} * \left[1 - \left(\frac{1+i}{1+r}\right)^y\right]$$

where

y = Number of years in retirement

r = Average annual investment return

i = Average inflation rate

Example: Using the same example as above, if you estimate that you will live 25 years in retirement, then

Total retirement wealth needed

$$= \frac{50{,}000}{(0.08 - 0.04)} \times \left[1 - \left(\frac{1.04}{1.08}\right)^{25}\right]$$

$$= \$1{,}250{,}000 \times (1 - 0.3893)$$

$$= \$763{,}425 \text{ (if you don't round until the end)}$$

You can also estimate this value by multiplying the first-year retirement income shortfall by the appropriate value from Exhibit 15-6, given your number of years in retirement and your expected investment return. If you expect to earn 8 percent on your investment and live 25 years in retirement, then multiply \$50,000 × 15.2685 = \$763,425; this is the same answer you got using the equation. Note, however, that this table assumes inflation of 4 percent, so if you expect a different inflation rate, you must use the formula above.

given your expected return on invested assets and the number of years you expect to live in retirement. This table assumes inflation will be 4 percent per year during your retirement period, so if you think it will be more or less, you may prefer to use the formula approach.

Monthly Savings Target

You now have an estimate of the total funds you'll need to have saved by the time you retire. You may have already begun saving toward this goal or you may have an employer-sponsored savings program that will provide a sum of money for you at retirement. In Step 6, you should estimate the values of these funds in future dollars and subtract those amounts from the total retirement wealth needed to arrive at a retirement savings goal. For example, if you currently have \$10,000 in a savings account earning 5 percent per year and will retire in 30 years, you can estimate that it will be worth \$10,000 × $(1.05)^{30}$ = \$43,219 when you retire, if we assume you make no future contributions to the account. In the *Ask the Expert* box, "Top Tips for Retirement Saving," a retirement expert offers some suggestions for maximizing the future value of your employer-sponsored retirement plan assets.

Given your retirement savings goal, you can estimate the monthly savings required to achieve that goal. Step 7 on the worksheet is a relatively straightforward application of the time value of money. You're calculating the payment that will be sufficient to fund a specific future value.

ask the expert Top Tips for Retirement Saving

Jack VanDerhei
Director, Employee Benefit Research Institute Fellows Program, Washington, D.C.

Jack VanDerhei is a professor at Temple University and the Director of the Research Fellows Program at the Employee Benefit Research Institute, a Washington, D.C. public policy group. He offers the following tips for saving through employer-sponsored retirement plans:

1. *Maximize your employer match.* Many employers base the amount they put into your defined contribution account on the amount that you contribute yourself, up to some limit. A dollar for dollar match is the equivalent of getting 100 percent return on your investment the first year.
2. *Maximize your pretax contributions.* Try to contribute the maximum allowed to your tax-deferred accounts. If you can't afford to do that now, keep increasing the amount of your contribution each year until you reach this goal. If you don't have an employer plan, be sure to start an IRA and contribute the maximum each year. If you're over 50, take advantage of the catch-up provisions that allow you to make larger annual contributions to your retirement accounts.
3. *Don't borrow against your retirement plan assets.* When you borrow against your retirement plan, you're reducing the principal on which you're earning investment returns.
4. *Start early.* The sooner you start investing for retirement, the more quickly you'll accumulate wealth, and the earlier you'll be able to retire.

As an example, suppose you've determined that you need to have $500,000 saved (*FV*) by the time you retire 40 years from now (*N*), and you think you can earn 8 percent per year, or 0.67 percent per month (8%/12), on your investments (*I*). Using your financial calculator, you'll enter $FV = \$500,000$, $I = 8/12$, and $N = 40 \times 12 = 480$ and solve for $PMT = \$143.23$. This is the amount you need to save each month until retirement to accumulate $500,000 by the time you retire. Note that, if you don't have a financial calculator, you can arrive at the same answer using the annuity formula and substituting the appropriate periodic interest rate and number of periods. Recall that this formula is

$$FV = PMT \times \frac{(1 + i)^n - 1}{i}$$

So in the example above, we can use the appropriate periodic interest rate (0.08/12) and number of periods (480) to calculate

$$\$500{,}000 = PMT \times \frac{(1 + .08/12)^{480} - 1}{.08/12}$$

$$= \text{PMT} \times 3{,}491$$

$$\text{PMT} = \frac{\$500{,}000}{3{,}491} = \$143.23$$

Fact #3

An increasingly large demographic group is made up of couples with "double income, no kids"—the DINKs. Even though parents may look enviously at their DINK neighbors, the DINKs' apparent prosperity doesn't mean that they've used their extra money to save for retirement. After controlling for other differences, such as age and education, studies have found that DINKs actually have less wealth than comparable households with children. But the DIPPIEs (double income, plural pensions) tend to be better prepared for retirement than either parents or DINKs.

The Importance of Starting Early. You may calculate the monthly savings required to meet your goal and find that you can't afford to save that much right now. You can still reach your retirement savings goal by saving less now and more later. However, as we've seen before, the power of compound interest will be greatest for your earliest contributions. To illustrate this effect, consider the impact of getting a late start on your investments. Suppose that, in the example above, you wait 10 years before starting to save for retirement ($N = 360$ instead of 480). To accumulate the same $500,000, you'll need to save $335.49 per month for 30 years—more than twice as much per month. But if you manage to save only $50 per month for the first 10 years, you can reach your $500,000 goal with an investment of only $268.37 per month for the last 30 years. Clearly, early contributions make the most difference in the end.

Earnings on Investment Make a Big Difference. Another reminder: Along with an early start, the rate of return on your investments makes a big difference in your accumulated wealth. In the example above, you saw that a monthly amount of $143.23 invested at 8 percent would result in a retirement nest egg of $500,000 in 40 years. What if you could earn 10 percent? At the same level of monthly contribution, you'd end up with $905,798. Alternatively, you could get to your $500,000 goal by investing only $79.06 per month at 10 percent. In contrast, if you invested more conservatively, earning only 6 percent, you'd have to make substantially larger monthly contributions to reach your retirement wealth goal.

Learning by Doing 15-3

1. Use Exhibit 15-6 to estimate your retirement wealth goal under the following assumptions: Your estimated retirement income shortfall is $18,753.49, you expect to live 40 years in retirement, you earn 6 percent on your investments during retirement, and you need your retirement income to increase 4 percent per year during retirement to offset inflation.
2. Assuming that your retirement wealth goal is $500,000 and that you'll earn 6 percent on your investments for the next 40 years, until you retire, what annual contribution do you need to make to your retirement fund?

Personal Retirement Saving Options

LEARNING objective

4 Describe your alternatives for personal retirement saving.

Now that you know how much you have to save, you'll need to decide what form your personal retirement savings will take. Possibilities include investments in taxable and tax-deferred accounts, investments in income-producing real estate, and home equity. We've already discussed the mechanics of real estate investing in Chapters 8 (home) and 14 (investment real estate), so we'll focus on retirement savings accounts here.

Congress has established several programs designed to encourage increased personal retirement saving. These programs generally provide tax incentives to low- and middle-income individuals and small business owners who make contributions to certain types of retirement plans. Individual retirement accounts (IRAs) were defined and briefly discussed in Chapter 4. In this section, we'll review the differences between the types of IRAs, explain the rules for using them, and cover the tax advantages they offer to individual savers in more detail.

IRS Publication 590 explains the tax regulations that affect IRAs. You can read the publication online at www.irs.gov or order it by calling 1-800-829-3676.

Individual Retirement Accounts

Since the early 1980s, individuals have had the opportunity to make tax-deferred contributions to individual retirement accounts (IRAs), which can be easily set up through financial institutions. The Tax Reform Act of 1986, the Tax Relief Act of 1997, and the Economic Growth and Tax Relief Reconciliation Act of 2001 together define the types of individual retirement accounts that are available, the tax preferences involved, and the contribution limits. The two main types of savings vehicles are the traditional IRA, sometimes called the deductible IRA, and the newer Roth IRA.

Traditional IRAs. Traditional IRAs are subject to rules that are very similar to those governing employer-sponsored defined contribution plans. Your contributions are tax deductible in the year in which you make them if you're not an active participant in an employer-sponsored retirement plan. If you participate in an employer-sponsored plan, the deductibility of IRA contributions depends on your adjusted gross income. For each of the tax years shown below, your IRA contribution will be fully deductible if your income is less than the lower number in the salary range given or partially deductible if your income is within the range given. If your income is greater than the highest end of the range, you won't be able to deduct your IRA contribution at all. So, for example, if you're married and file a joint return, you'll be able to fully deduct an IRA contribution made in 2005 if your joint adjusted gross income is less than $70,000.

	Individual	Married and Filing Jointly
	Adjusted Gross Income	Adjusted Gross Income
2004	$45,000–$55,000	$65,000–$75,000
2005	$50,000–$60,000	$70,000–$80,000
2006	$50,000–$60,000	$75,000–$85,000
2007	$50,000–$60,000	$80,000–$90,000

Even when the contribution is not deductible, the earnings are tax-deferred until withdrawal, at which time they're taxed as ordinary income. If you withdraw funds before you reach age $59\frac{1}{2}$, however, the withdrawal is subject to a 10 percent penalty unless you use the funds to pay for qualified educational expenses, medical expenses, or a first-time home purchase.

The maximum allowable annual IRA contribution per person is the person's adjusted gross income or the limit on the schedule below, whichever is smaller. Recent tax law changes include gradual increases in the deductible amount, as well as catch-up provisions for taxpayers age 50 and over, as indicated:

	General Limit	Age 50 and Over
2004	$3,000	$3,500
2005	$4,000	$4,500
2006	$4,000	$5,000
2007	$4,000	$5,000
2008	$5,000	$6,000

Beyond 2008, the limit will be adjusted annually for inflation in increments of $500.

Roth IRAs. The Roth IRA takes a different approach, requiring that contributions be made with after-tax dollars but allowing investments to accumulate tax-free with no tax due on withdrawal, as long as the taxpayer has reached age $59\frac{1}{2}$ or is using the proceeds for qualified educational, medical, or first-time home purchase expenses. The contribution limits for the Roth IRA are the same as for the traditional IRA, but the income limits are higher, making this an option for middle-income households. Full contributions can be made by singles with an adjusted gross income of no more than $95,000 and married joint filers with an adjusted gross income of no more than $150,000. Above that income level, the contribution is phased out up to the income limits of $110,000 for singles and $160,000 for joint filers.

To encourage retirement saving by low-income families, a tax credit will be allowed through 2006 for up to 50 percent of contributions to IRAs and employer plans, depending on income, with a maximum credit of $2,000. For example, a qualifying taxpayer could make a $1,000 contribution to an IRA in 2005, and he or she would get a $500 reduction in taxes owed for the year. In effect, that individual only has to pay $500 to accumulate $1,000 in his or her account.

Investing in Taxable Accounts

IRAs offer some tax advantages, but in return for these advantages you give up some financial flexibility, since your retirement assets are not very liquid—although you can cash them out before retirement in an emergency, you will pay a premium for doing so. Suppose, for example, that you're subject to a 20 percent marginal tax rate and you have a financial emergency that requires withdrawal of $10,000 from a deductible IRA account. In the year of withdrawal, you'll pay $3,000 to the government—$2,000 goes to taxes and $1,000 is the 10 percent penalty for withdrawing before age $59\frac{1}{2}$. This represents a substantial drain on your retirement funds. For some individuals, IRAs provide the discipline they need to leave their money alone for a long period of time. For others, it may be advisable to put some of their investment funds in taxable accounts.

Asset Allocation in Retirement Accounts

In addition to deciding on the type of account you'll use for your savings, you'll need to make decisions about what to invest in. Your options are many. You can put your retirement funds in everything from CDs to stock mutual funds. You can have them professionally managed or you can manage them yourself. Although we've covered the investment decision process in other chapters, it's worthwhile to repeat a few fundamentals here that have direct application to asset allocation decisions for your retirement accounts.

1. *Take your time horizon into account.* If retirement is a long time from now, you can probably afford to take a little more risk to get a little more return.
2. *Don't forget about taxes.* If you're holding your funds in a taxable account, it may be worthwhile to consider investments that are exempt from certain taxes (such as federal or municipal bonds). It's not a good idea to hold tax-exempt investments in an IRA since the higher price you pay for these bonds will not be offset by any tax savings. You can also use a taxable account for investments that grow in value over time but don't produce current income (such as growth stocks) since you won't have to pay tax on the increase in value until you sell. However, the same isn't true of stock mutual funds (even if they're growth funds), since the investors normally receive distributions of capital gains and income each year that would be taxable. In general, you should avoid holding investments that generate a lot of currently taxable income (such as corporate bonds) in a taxable account, but they might be a good choice for an IRA.
3. *Diversify.* This recommendation should go without saying by this time. In addition to being diversified across your entire household portfolio, it's important to be diversified within your retirement portfolio. As we've mentioned, many individuals who had allocated their IRAs and employer-sponsored investment accounts primarily to high-risk stocks in the 1990s (and accumulated substantial wealth as a result) were dismayed to see their portfolio values plummet when the market turned. Those in their 40s still have time to recover, but older investors will find themselves retiring a little later than they'd hoped.

Preparing for Retirement Payouts

At this point, you probably aren't ready to think about the decumulation stage of your life—when you'll be spending your wealth instead of saving. Nevertheless, our discussion of retirement planning wouldn't be complete without a few words of advice on this component of your plan. A little advance planning can save you money in the long run.

objective

5 Understand your options for retirement income payouts.

Distributions from Retirement Accounts

In general, distributions from employer plans will be taxable when they're received, whereas you may have other sources of cash flow, such as Roth IRAs, that you can access without owing any taxes. Since it's always better to pay taxes later rather than sooner, your financial plan for receipt of retirement income should include strategies for delaying the receipt of cash flows that will trigger taxation. If you have other sources of income, you can wait to claim defined benefit annuities to which you're entitled for a few years, and you can take defined contribution plan assets and deposit them in an IRA (commonly called a "rollover") to delay paying the taxes due. You'll eventually have to pay the tax, of course. Tax rules require that you begin taking payouts from both employer plans and IRAs by April 1 of the year after you reach age $70\frac{1}{2}$.

When you retire under an employer plan, you may receive a lump sum, an annuity, or some combination of the two, depending on the plan terms and your own choices. A lump sum payout means that you'll need to manage the funds yourself, but it also gives you more flexibility. An annuity will provide you with monthly or annual payments, which can be helpful in budgeting.

annuity for a specific term

An annuity that provides a stream of equal payments for a specific period of time.

In some cases, you may be able to choose between an annuity for a specific term, a single life annuity, or a joint and survivor annuity. An **annuity for a specific term** will provide a stream of equal payments for a certain number of years, often 10, 15, or 20 years. These payments will likely be larger than life annuity payments, but you'll be exposed to a significant risk of income shortfall if you live longer than the term of the annuity. If you die before the end of the term, your beneficiaries are usually entitled to receive the remaining payments. A **single life annuity** promises to pay you an amount per year until you die, whereas a **joint and survivor annuity** pays an amount per year to you and your spouse until the last one dies. Some joint and survivor annuities allow the option of a reduced annuity after the first spouse dies in return for a greater annuity while both spouses are living. Obviously, the same amount of wealth will produce a lower benefit in the case of joint and survivor annuities, but such an arrangement protects the last spouse to die. It is unfortunately all too common an occurrence for an elderly woman to become impoverished as a result of her husband's final illness.

single life annuity

An annuity that provides a stream of equal payments until death.

joint and survivor annuity

An annuity that provides a stream of equal payments until the death of the second spouse.

Tapping Your Home Equity

If you've paid off your mortgage or you have substantial home equity at retirement, another option for generating tax-free retirement income is to use some of your equity. While in years past this might have required that you sell the home, today it's relatively easy to get a home equity loan or a home equity line of credit. These will require that you make payments, but you may be able to spread out the payments for a fairly long time. The interest you pay is tax-deductible, and you'll still benefit from any increase in the value of your property while you continue to own it.

Another alternative you might consider is a reverse annuity mortgage, discussed in Chapter 8. You may recall that in this type of arrangement, you trade your home equity for an income stream, and you're allowed to remain in the home for the period of the annuity, which may be a period of years or for life, after which the lender assumes ownership of the home. Given average home values, a reverse annuity mortgage may not provide a big enough income stream to risk losing your equity if you die prematurely. If your home is worth $150,000 and you buy a 20-year annuity, for example, you'll get around $12,000 per year.

Fact #4

The Retirement Confidence Survey, sponsored by the Employee Benefit Research Institute, shows that only one-fourth of American workers are very confident about having enough money to live comfortably throughout their retirement years. Only one-third say they've ever tried to calculate how much money they need to save for retirement, and 38 percent have saved less than $25,000 so far.

What Happens If You Don't Have Enough Money to Retire?

You may find that your ideal retirement age arrives but you can't afford to retire. Whether this is due to children's college costs, bad investments, divorce, health issues, or some other cause, the end result is still unpleasant. To meet your income needs, you may need to consider some of the following options:

Many retired people find it necessary to supplement their retirement income by working part-time.

- *Reduce expenses.* Downsizing housing, cars, vacations, and other expenses will make it possible to live on a more modest income.
- *Continue to work.* If your health permits, delaying retirement will allow you to continue your retirement savings program and will reduce the number of years of retirement income that your nest egg must support. Working after you've begun to collect Social Security may result in reduced benefits, however.
- *Increase savings.* If you still have a few years to go before retirement, you can attempt to increase your savings rate. Taking an extra job and allocating all of that income to retirement saving may be an option.
- *Rely on family.* In earlier times, families were often called on to support their parents and grandparents. Although this is less common today, it still occurs. Family members may simply provide financial support, or older family members may actually move in with younger ones to stretch retirement savings.
- *Rely on public assistance.* Many elderly people live below the poverty level and qualify for public assistance, such as food stamps.

Hopefully, none of these outcomes will apply to you. If you start planning for retirement now, establish goals, and work toward meeting those goals, you'll have a better chance of funding a comfortable retirement.

Learning by Doing 15-4

1. Your friend Ravi is considering putting money in either a traditional IRA or a Roth IRA. Explain to him the tax consequences of his decision.
2. You participate in a defined contribution plan at work and earn $40,000. Your wife works part-time and earns $3,000 per year. Can you and your spouse each contribute to an IRA in 2005 if you file joint taxes?

Funding Your Children's Education

LEARNING objective

6 Develop a plan for funding your children's education, taking tax rules into account.

Like retirement funding, education funding takes advance planning. Fortunately, college funding isn't as costly as retirement, but the costs are still substantial, and you generally won't have as long to save (18 years if you start when your child is born). The education funding problem is remarkably similar to that of retirement funding, so the methodology for estimating the monthly savings amount you'll need is the same. You'll first estimate how much you'll need and then calculate the monthly contribution you should make to meet your savings goal.

How Much Will You Need?

The average cost of one year of undergraduate education (tuition, room, board, and books) at a public in-state university in 2005 is estimated to be $13,500. Private universities are expected to average $34,000. Exhibit 15-7 provides estimated future costs for the next 18 years under various assumptions concerning annual increases in costs (from 4 to 8%). Since state university budgets have taken big hits in recent years, resulting in double-digit tuition increases, total expenses for children who are nearing college age today are likely to be on the high end of this table.

Fact #5

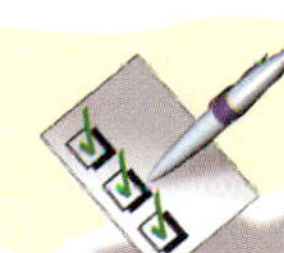

State legislators, faced with tax shortfalls, have slashed public university budgets in the last few years. The impact on university tuition across the country has been dramatic. According to the College Board, which tracks college costs, the average increase in tuition and fees at 4-year state institutions for the 2003 to 2004 school year was 14.1 percent, many times the average rates of inflation and wage growth. The increase in two-year public institution tuition and fees was 13.8 percent. For low- and moderate-income families, a college education is becoming relatively more expensive.

Recall that Cindy and Dave Thompson in our continuing case have a 14-year-old son Kyle from Cindy's previous marriage and are expecting a new baby. In Chapter 3, the Thompsons decided that one of their personal financial goals was to establish college funds for both children. We'll illustrate the education funding decision using Kyle Thompson as an example.

Consulting Exhibit 15-7 and assuming 6 percent college cost increases, Cindy and Dave find that the cost of one year at a four-year public university will be approximately $17,000 four years from now. Exhibit 15-8 shows the calculation they make to estimate the amount they need to save. A blank version of this worksheet is included in your *Personal Financial Planner*.

PFP Worksheet 52 Education Funding

To estimate the costs for four years, we'll use the simplifying assumption that the Thompsons' college investment account will be able to earn the same rate of return as the rate of inflation they'll experience for the four years Kyle is in school. Whenever you're calculating the present value of a series of cash flows that are increasing at the same rate as the rate you're discounting at, the present value of the series of cash flows is simply the initial value times the number of periods. If your investment earnings are greater than the increase in college costs, this method will overestimate how much you need (and lower investment earnings means you'd need to save more).

EXHIBIT 15-7 **Future Cost of One Year of College (Tuition, Room, Board, and Books)**

Child's Age Today	Public In- State School			Public Out-of-State School			Private University		
	Annual College Cost Inflation			Annual College Cost Inflation			Annual College Cost Inflation		
	4%	6%	8%	4%	6%	8%	4%	6%	8%
18	$13,500	$13,500	$13,500	$19,500	$19,500	$19,500	$34,000	$34,000	$34,000
17	14,040	14,310	14,580	20,280	20,670	21,060	35,360	36,040	36,720
16	14,602	15,169	15,746	21,091	21,910	22,745	36,774	38,202	39,658
15	15,186	16,079	17,006	21,935	23,225	24,564	38,245	40,495	42,830
14	15,793	17,043	18,367	22,812	24,618	26,530	39,775	42,924	46,257
13	16,425	18,066	19,836	23,725	26,095	28,652	41,366	45,500	49,957
12	17,082	19,150	21,423	24,674	27,661	30,944	43,021	48,230	53,954
11	17,765	20,299	23,137	25,661	29,321	33,420	44,742	51,123	58,270
10	18,476	21,517	24,988	26,687	31,080	36,093	46,531	54,191	62,932
9	19,215	22,808	26,987	27,755	32,945	38,981	48,393	57,442	67,966
8	19,983	24,176	29,145	28,865	34,922	42,099	50,328	60,889	73,403
7	20,783	25,627	31,477	30,019	37,017	45,467	52,341	64,542	79,276
6	21,614	27,165	33,995	31,220	39,238	49,104	54,435	68,415	85,618
5	22,478	28,795	36,715	32,469	41,592	53,033	56,612	72,520	92,467
4	23,378	30,522	39,652	33,768	44,088	57,275	58,877	76,871	99,865
3	24,313	32,354	42,824	35,118	46,733	61,857	61,232	81,483	107,854
2	25,285	34,295	46,250	36,523	49,537	66,806	63,681	86,372	116,482
1	26,297	36,352	49,950	37,984	52,509	72,150	66,229	91,554	125,801
0	27,349	38,534	53,946	39,503	55,660	77,922	68,878	97,048	135,865

Author's calculation of 2005 base case estimated by applying expected cost increases to 2003–2004 tuition, room, and board costs reported at www.collegeboard.com and adding expected costs for textbooks and other expenses.

Multiplying the $17,000 first-year cost by 4 gives a total of $68,000 for the four years of college. Under the terms of Cindy's divorce, Kyle's biological father has agreed to split the cost of their son's college education, and the Thompsons also assume that Kyle will pay for some of his own costs and qualify for grants or scholarships. They therefore estimate that they'll need to save $19,000 by the time Kyle goes to college.

Monthly Savings Target

College education costs are expected to continue to escalate, particularly at state institutions.

Once the Thompsons know how much they want to accumulate in total, they can use the time value of money to estimate the monthly savings amount required. This is the same calculation we used to determine monthly retirement savings. Using a financial calculator, they enter the target college funding goal ($FV =$ $19,000), the number of months until Kyle goes to college ($N = 4 \times 12 = 48$), and the monthly interest rate they expect to earn on their investments ($I = 6/12$) and solve for *PMT*. The result is $351.22. Exhibit 15-8 also shows how you can get the same answer using the formula approach to solve for the payment.

Based on this calculation, Cindy and Dave need to save $351 per month in order to have sufficient funds available to pay their share of Kyle's education expenses in four years. We know from our previous examination of this family's financial situation that they probably won't be able to meet this objective immediately. Cindy's decision to quit work will make it difficult for the family to save much for the next few years. However, since the Thompsons have cut their budget to be able to live on Dave's income, they'll be able to apply some of Cindy's income to paying Kyle's college costs once she returns to the workforce.

Tax Programs to Help You Save for Education Expenses

As with retirement, there are state and federal programs that include tax incentives designed to encourage saving for educational expenses. These incentives fall into the general categories of tax-preferred savings plans and tax credits.

EXHIBIT 15-8

Education Funding Worksheet

		Kyle Thompson's Example
Step 1. Estimate total college costs.		
Use Exhibit 15-7 to estimate the annual		
costs for one year of college.	17,000	
Total costs = Annual cost × 4	× 4 =	68,000
Step 2. Subtract other sources of funding.		
Grants and scholarships	10,000	
Child's own savings or employment income	10,000	
Support from other family	29,000	
Future value of current savings	0	
Total from other sources		49,000
Step 3. College fund needed (Step 1 − Step 2).		19,000
Step 4. Calculate monthly savings needed.		
FV = College fund needed (Step 3)	19,000	
N = Number of periods to save	= 4 × 12	
I = After-tax return per period	= 6/12	
Solve for PMT.		$351.22

Alternative Step 4 using the formula for future value of an annuity:

$$\$19{,}000 = \text{Payment} \times \text{FVIFA}_{i\%,n} = \text{Payment} \times \frac{(1+i)^n - 1}{i}$$

$$\$19{,}000 = \text{Payment} \times \frac{[1 + (0.06/12)]^{48} - 1}{0.06/12}$$

$$\text{Payment} = \frac{\$19{,}000}{54.098} = \$351.22$$

Tax-Preferred Savings Plans. Both the federal government and state governments offer methods for tax-preferred education saving. Three of the most important of these are summarized in Exhibit 15-9. For example, the federal government has authorized **Coverdell Education Savings Accounts**, previously called Education IRAs. The tax treatment of these accounts is similar to that of Roth IRAs—contributions are made with after-tax dollars, but interest earnings aren't taxed, and no taxes are due when the funds are withdrawn. You can contribute up to $2,000 per year per child to a Coverdell.

As an alternative, you can participate in a **Section 529 plan** offered by one of the states. This can be either a prepaid tuition plan or savings plan. Both types of plans require after-tax contributions, although some states allow state residents to deduct the contribution from income in calculating *state* taxes owed.

The prepaid tuition plans enable you to pay in advance for college costs at state universities either by paying a lump sum or making a series of payments. The amount you pay is based on assumed future increases in tuition. For example, your state's plan might allow you to effectively buy your child's tuition at today's price. The plan then invests those dollars so that the value of the tuition promise you bought will be able to increase with the tuition inflation rate. Theoretically, by the time your child goes to school, it will be worth one year's tuition at the

Coverdell Education Savings Accounts

Education savings arrangement which allows after-tax contributions of $2,000 per year per child and tax-free withdrawals.

Section 529 plans

State-sponsored programs that provide tax benefits for college saving.

EXHIBIT 15-9

Key Features of College Savings Plan Programs

	Section 529 Prepaid Tuition Plan	Section 529 Savings Plan	Coverdell Education Savings Account
Available from	States	States	Financial institutions
Contribution limit	Depends on plan and age of student; up to $11,000 per per year free of gift tax.	Depends on plan; up to $11,000 per year free of gift tax.	$2,000 per child per year; no contribution in same year as 529 saving plan
Taxation of contributions	May be exempt from state income tax.	May be exempt from state income tax.	Taxable
Income limits	Most plans have none.	Most plans have none.	AGI maximum: $95,000 for singles, $220,000 for married couple filing jointly
Tax benefits	No tax on growth or withdrawals	No tax on growth or withdrawals	No tax on growth or withdrawals
Qualified expenses	Most allow use for all higher education: tuition, fees, room, board, and books. A few limit to tuition and fees.	All higher education costs: tuition, fees, room, board, and books	All education costs, including elementary, secondary, and higher education: tuition, fees, room, board, and books
Transferability	Depends on plan.	Can transfer to different 529 plan.	Can transfer to different fund or to 529 plan.
Effect on eligibility for tax credits	Can still take the credit if withdrawal used for different expenses.	Can still take the credit if withdrawal used for different expenses.	Can still take the credit if withdrawal used for different expenses.
Effect on eligibility for financial aid	Considered asset of the student so will reduce eligibility.	Considered asset of the contributor so may reduce eligibility to some extent.	Considered asset of the student so will reduce eligibility.
Account control	Contributor	Contributor	Student at age 18
How long to use funds?	Depends on plan.	Depends on plan.	Age 30.
Investment	By plan administrators	Choice of mutual funds	By account owner
Assignability	Can assign to an immediate family member.	Can assign to an immediate family member.	Can assign to an immediate family member.
Penalty for nonqualified withdrawal	Income tax plus 10% penalty	Income tax plus 10% penalty	Income tax plus 10% penalty

then applicable price. Originally, the amount was guaranteed, but greater-than-expected tuition increases in the last few years have forced many of these plans to limit their guarantees to some maximum annual increase per year (e.g., up to 5% per year). When your child reaches college age, you can request reimbursement from the prepaid tuition plan for qualified education expenses (which include room, board, tuition, and books), and you won't owe any taxes on the amount received. Although rules may vary from state to state, most plans are open to residents of any state, and many now allow the transfer of tuition credits to institutions outside of the state. So if your child decides that she doesn't want to go to "State U," you can apply the funds to the costs of an out-of-state or private university. Of course, the amount you've invested to fund in-state tuition will probably fund only a small portion of the costs at an out-of-state or private institution.

In contrast to Section 529 prepaid tuition plans, Section 529 savings plans are more similar to IRAs—you choose how much to invest, and you may be able to allocate your money to investment vehicles that differ in risk and return. The amount you accumulate in your account will depend on how your investments do over time. As with the tuition plans, you can apply the money to any qualified education expenses.

Some of the important questions you should consider before deciding on college funding options include limits on contributions to the various types of plans, transferability of accounts, and the effect on your child's eligibility for financial aid. Some of the account choices described above will technically be considered an asset of your child, which means that contributions to the account will be treated as gifts that are subject to gift tax if they exceed $11,000 per year (as you'll see in Chapter 17). Since the accumulated funds belong to your child, he or she is less likely to qualify for financial aid. Finally, you need to think about what will happen if your child decides not to go to college. With Coverdell accounts, your child has control over the account when he or she reaches age 18, whereas Section 529 plans leave control with the contributor.

Tax Credits for Education. There are two tax credits that you might be able to use to help defray education expenses. The **Hope Scholarship tax credit** can be claimed on your federal income taxes for up to $1,500 per year of eligible college expenses (100% of the first $1,000 of expenses and 50% of the next $1,000) during your child's first two years of college. The **Lifetime Learning tax credit** allows you to claim 20 percent of the first $5,000 of college expenses up to a maximum of $1,000 for every eligible dependent who has incurred these expenses during the year. As long as the two credits are not used to cover the same expenses, you can take both the Hope Scholarship credit and Lifetime Learning credit for the same student. Both tax credits are subject to income limitations.

Hope Scholarship tax credit

A tax credit of up to $1,500 per year for eligible expenses incurred during the first two years of college.

Lifetime Learning tax credit

A tax credit of 20 percent of the first $5,000 of college expenses up to a maximum of $1,000 for every eligible dependent who has incurred these expenses during the year.

Learning by Doing 15-5

1. Your child is currently 8 years old. You anticipate that she'll go to an in-state public university. Use Exhibit 15-7 to estimate how much this education is likely to cost, assuming tuition inflation averages 6 percent per year for the next 10 years.
2. You estimate that you'll need $100,000 in 18 years to pay for your new baby's college education. If you can earn 8 percent on a tax-deferred investment, how much should you save each year?
3. Your child's first-year college expenses were $20,000. You paid for the tuition expenses, $6,000, with a withdrawal from your Section 529 Prepaid Tuition Plan. Are you eligible for any tax credits for the other $14,000 you paid?

Summary

1. **Estimate your retirement income needs.** The retirement planning process requires that you first develop goals for retirement and estimate your postretirement expenses. Two methods for estimating expenses are the replacement ratio method, in which you apply a fixed ratio to your current expenses, and the adjusted expense method, in which you attempt to more accurately forecast the changes in expenditure patterns you can expect in retirement.
2. **Evaluate your future benefits from employer-sponsored retirement plans and Social Security.** The next step in retirement planning is to use your expected future expenses to estimate how much pretax income you'll need. From this, you'll subtract any income you expect to receive from other sources, such as employer-sponsored retirement plans and Social Security benefits, to arrive at your retirement income shortfall.
3. **Determine your retirement wealth goal and monthly savings target.** You can use your estimated retirement income shortfall to determine how much wealth you need to accumulate by the time you retire. This amount is the present value of an inflation-adjusted annuity, with the initial payment being your first year's retirement income. You'll need to make assumptions about how long you'll live in retirement, how much your investments will earn, and what the rate of inflation will be. From the total retirement wealth you need, you'll subtract the estimated future value of any current savings you have to arrive at your retirement savings goal. From this, you can calculate the necessary monthly contribution to your savings. The longer you have to save and the greater your return on investment, the less you'll need to save each month.

4 **Describe your alternatives for personal retirement saving.** Individual retirement accounts (IRAs) offer the opportunity to save for retirement on a tax-preferred basis. Traditional deductible IRAs allow you to make contributions with after-tax dollars and to defer payment of taxes until withdrawal after retirement. Roth IRAs require that contributions be made with after-tax dollars, but you won't owe any tax on withdrawal. Both types impose penalties for withdrawal prior to age $59\frac{1}{2}$ unless the funds are used to pay for certain qualified expenses. For financial flexibility, you may want to invest some of your retirement savings in taxable accounts.

5 **Understand your options for retirement income payouts.** When you have accumulated funds in a retirement account, you may be able to receive the payout at retirement as a lump sum or an annuity. Types of annuities include the annuity for a specific term, single life annuity, and joint and survivor annuity. If you've accumulated substantial home equity, you can access it to pay for postretirement expenses with a variety of types of mortgages.

6 **Develop a plan for funding your children's education, taking tax rules into account.** The college funding process involves estimating that total amount you need to save and calculating the monthly savings necessary to meet your goal. The federal government and most state governments authorize a variety of college saving programs that have tax advantages. In addition, the federal government allows some taxpayers to take tax credits for education expenses.

Key Terms

adjusted expense method (490)
annuity for a specific term (503)
average indexed monthly earnings (AIME) (495)
Coverdell Education Savings Account (507)
Hope Scholarship tax credit (509)
inflation-adjusted annuity (498)
joint and survivor annuity (504)
Lifetime Learning tax credit (509)
primary insurance amount (PIA) (495)
replacement ratio method (489)
Section 529 plan (507)
single life annuity (504)

Key Calculations

$$\text{Wealth necessary to generate constant income} = \frac{\text{Income}}{r\%}$$

$$\text{Present value of an inflation-adjusted annuity} = \frac{PMT}{(r-i)} * \left[1 - \left(\frac{1+i}{1+r}\right)^y\right]$$

where

PMT = Payment in first year
y = Term of annuity
r = Average annual investment return
i = Average inflation rate

$$\text{Future value} = \text{Payment} \times \frac{(1+i)^n - 1}{i}$$

Concept Review Questions

1. List and briefly explain the steps in the retirement planning process.
2. What happens if you don't save enough for retirement?
3. Explain why it's important to estimate how much you need to save for retirement.
4. Identify and explain the two methods for estimating your postretirement expenses.
5. In what ways should you take inflation into account in your retirement planning?
6. In what ways should you take income taxes into account in your retirement planning?
7. What is meant by the "three-legged stool of retirement income"? Do most retirees receive income from all three sources? Why or why not? Are there any other sources of income in retirement?
8. How should you estimate your retirement income shortfall?
9. How can you estimate how much income you'll receive from an employer-sponsored defined benefit plan?
10. How can you estimate how much income you'll receive from an employer-sponsored defined contribution plan?
11. How is Social Security funded? What is the current payroll tax rate?
12. What is required to qualify for receipt of Social Security benefits?

13. How are Social Security benefits determined?
14. What is the normal retirement age under Social Security? At what age is early retirement allowed, and what effect will it have on benefits?
15. How does Social Security protect nonworking spouses?
16. Is Social Security regressive or progressive? Explain. Are millionaires entitled to receive benefits?
17. What financial problems are projected for the Social Security system, and what are the causes of these problems?
18. What Social Security reforms are we likely to see in the next few decades? Explain.
19. Describe the steps you should take to estimate the amount of money you need to invest each month in order to meet your retirement income shortfall.
20. Why is it important to assume that you'll need your retirement income to be an inflation-adjusted annuity?
21. Why are so many people at risk of outliving their assets?
22. Explain the similarities and differences between a traditional deductible IRA and a Roth IRA.
23. What is the penalty for withdrawing your money from a tax-deferred retirement account prior to age $59\frac{1}{2}$? Are there any exceptions to this rule?
24. Use an example to illustrate how investing in a tax-deferred account can give you a better outcome than investing in a taxable account.
25. Comment on the following statement: "Once I retire, I won't have to worry about my investments anymore."
26. What options are there for receipt of benefits in retirement?
27. Why is it important for married couples to opt for a joint and survivor annuity? What do they give up by doing so?
28. How can home equity be used to support your retirement?
29. What are the pros and cons of reverse annuity mortgages?
30. If you reach retirement age and don't have sufficient savings to support your income needs, what are your options?
31. Describe the process you should use in planning for funding your children's education. How is this similar to the retirement planning process?
32. What federal programs allow parents to save for college on a tax-deferred basis?
33. What state programs allow parents to save for college on a tax-deferred basis?
34. What is the difference between the two types of Section 529 plans?
35. Describe the tax credits that are allowed for expenditures on education.

Application Problems

1. ***Monthly Savings Required.*** You are currently 37 years old, and you plan to retire in 30 years. You've estimated that you need to accumulate $1 million by the time you retire in order to fund your retirement income shortfall.
   a. If you invest your funds to earn 8 percent per year, how much do you need to save each month?
   b. If you can earn 10 percent, how much do you need to save each month?
2. ***Inflation-Adjusted Retirement Income.*** Based on your estimates, you'll need $40,000 per year to cover your expenses after you retire this month. You expect your expenses to increase with inflation at 4 percent per year, and you hope to live 30 years after retiring. How much retirement wealth do you need to have now if you'll invest your funds to earn 5 percent per year?
3. ***Effect of Employer Match.*** Fred has just started a new job. His employer requires that he contribute 2 percent of his salary to a qualified retirement plan and will match any additional contributions up to 3 percent. Fred's salary isn't very high ($28,000), so he's thinking about just contributing the 2 percent minimum.
   a. How much does he need to contribute to get the maximum from his employer?
   b. Calculate the future value of Fred's first-year contribution, assuming that he contributes only the 2 percent and that his account earns 10 percent per year until retirement in 40 years.
   c. Redo the calculation, assuming that Fred contributes enough to get the full employer match and the funds earn 10 percent per year until retirement. Calculate separately the future values of Fred's own contributions and his employer's contributions.
   d. Based on your answer to the two previous questions, what is the cost of losing the employer match?
4. ***Income Generated by an Investment Account.*** Loveta has saved $250,000 by the date of her retirement, and she earns 5 percent per year on her investments.
   a. How much annual cash flow will this investment generate, assuming that Loveta doesn't want to touch the principal?
   b. How much annual cash flow will this investment generate, assuming that Loveta wants to withdraw equal annual payments over the next 20 years?
5. ***The Effect of Early Investing.*** Tom decides to get an early start on retirement and, beginning at age 22, he invests $3,000 per year in a Roth IRA for 10 years in a row. At that point, he stops contributing to the account but leaves the money invested until age 65 (a period of 33 years). Harry doesn't start investing until he's 32 but from then on invests $3,000 in a Roth IRA each year for 33 years until retirement at age 65. If both men earn 10 percent per year on their investments, compounded annually, which one has more in the account at the end? How much more?
6. ***Future Cost of Education.*** Assume that the first-year cost of attending college for four years is currently $15,000 and these costs are increasing at a rate of 5 percent per year.
   a. What is the amount needed now to fund four years of college, assuming that your invested funds earn 5 percent per year after taxes.
   b. What will be needed in six years to fund a four-year college education?
7. ***College Funding.*** You've estimated that you'll need to have saved $90,000 to fund your child's future college education in 12 years. How much do you need to save each month to reach this goal if you expect to earn 6 percent per year?
8. ***Effect of Early Withdrawal from IRA.*** Rich was laid off three months ago and has exhausted his emergency funds. His new job doesn't pay enough to cover his expenses, so he's had to withdraw $15,000 from his IRA. If his marginal tax rate is 20 percent, how much of this money will he actually have available to use?

Using Web Resources for Financial Planning

1. **Take a Retirement IQ Test.** Go to *moneycentral.msn.com* and click on "Planning" and then "Retirement" to find a retirement IQ test. If you've studied this chapter, you'll probably know most of the answers.
2. **What Should You Do to Prepare for Retirement?** The Department of Labor, in conjunction with the Department of the Treasury and more than 100 private- and public-sector partners, launched the Retirement Savings Education Campaign in July 1995. This consortium formed the American Savings Education Council (ASEC), which now has more than 200 institutional partners and focuses on raising public awareness about what's necessary to ensure financial security for all Americans. Go to *www.asec.org* and click on "Savings Tools" to find the "Top Ten Ways to Beat the Clock and Prepare for Retirement." Summarize the points made in that article.
3. **What Should Women Do to Ensure a Secure Retirement?** The Women's Institute for a Secure Retirement (WISER), at *www.wiser.org,* offers educational materials that are directed to the special needs of women. Visit their website to find numerous resources and links that are designed to help women better understand the challenges they face in planning for retirement and direct them where to go for assistance. Based on the information you find, do you think that women face different challenges in saving for retirement than men do?
4. **Find Out More about Reverse Annuity Mortgages.** Go to the website for the American Association of Retired Persons at *www.aarp.org.* Click on "Money and Work" and then "Reverse Mortgages" to read about reverse annuity mortgages. Based on what you read here, would you recommend this type of arrangement to an elderly relative?

Learning by Doing Solutions

LBD 15-1: 1. $30,000 × 0.8 = $24,000 in current dollars. Pretax income needs at retirement = $24,000 × $(1.03)^{45}$ = $90,758; 2. $24,000 × $(1.03)^{25}$ = $50,251; 3. $30,000 − $15,000 + $10,000 = $25,000 in current dollars.

LBD 15-2: 1. $72,852; 2. She is eligible to receive a benefit equal to 50 percent of her husband's benefit.

LBD 15-3: 1. 26.6617 × $18,753.49 = $500,000; 2. $3,230.77 per year.

LBD 15-4: 1. Roth contributions are made with after-tax dollars, but no tax is due on withdrawal at retirement; traditional IRA contributions are deductible in the year made, but withdrawals are taxable; 2. Yes. Even though you have a DC plan, your joint income is less than the $70,000 limit for traditional IRAs and less than the $150,000 limit for Roth IRAs. You can contribute $4,000 in 2005, and your wife can contribute $3,000.

LBD 15-5: 1. $24,176 x 4 = $96,704; 2. Enter $FV = 100{,}000$, $N = 18$, $I = 8$ and solve for $PMT = \$2{,}670.21$; 3. Yes, you can take the Hope credit for $1,500 and the Lifetime Learning credit for $1,000.

Building Financial Planning Skills Through Case Applications

Case 15-1 Choice of Annuities

Henry decided to take early retirement at age 55 to care for his wife, who was in poor health. Since he was certain he'd outlive his wife, he convinced her that they should take the pension annuity payout as a single life annuity for his lifetime instead of a joint and survivor annuity. The difference in the monthly payment was substantial—he'd get $2,500 per month instead of only $1,700 with the joint and survivor annuity. To save money, Henry also reduced the amount of his life insurance policy. When he was 57, Henry had a heart attack while jogging his daily five-mile run and died.

a. What benefit will Henry's wife be eligible for under Henry's pension?
b. Were the assumptions that led to Henry's pension annuity decision reasonable?
c. If Henry's widow is also 57 years old, can she qualify for Social Security benefits?
d. If she has no other sources of income, what are her options?

Case 15-2 An Older Widow Plans for Retirement

Margaret Bradford is 64 years old and has been widowed for 12 years. She was married to her second husband Charles for 15 years. Since they hadn't expected him to die so young, they hadn't gotten around to doing much retirement planning before his death. She did receive a life insurance settlement of $100,000, which she used to pay the uninsured medical expenses from Charles' illness and to repay the remaining balance on her home mortgage.

Charles' pension plan gave her a lump sum benefit of $250,000, which she rolled into an IRA invested in government bonds. It's been earning an average of 4 percent per year and is now worth $400,000. After her second husband's death, Margaret took a job as an office manager in a law office, where she earns $30,000 per year, and she's been contributing to a 401(k) plan in which she's accumulated $115,000. Margaret would like to retire when she turns 65 next year. She knows she'll qualify for Social Security benefits based on her deceased husband's earnings history, and her home is worth $200,000.

a. If Margaret had invested the IRA a little less conservatively and earned 6 percent instead of 4 percent per year for the last 12 years, how much would her account be worth today?

b. Margaret's annual expenses are currently $18,000 per year. Use the replacement ratio method to estimate her postretirement expenses beginning one year from now, assuming that inflation is 4 percent.

c. Estimate the Social Security benefit Margaret will receive using the benefit calculator at the www.ssa.gov website or use the PIA equation provided in this chapter. Assume that Charles was fully insured and had average indexed monthly earnings equal to $2,917 per month ($35,000 per year) in today's dollars.

d. If Margaret continues to earn 4 percent on her invested assets throughout retirement, can she afford to retire? Does she face any risk of outliving her assets? Explain.

Case 15-3 Getting a Late Start on College Planning

Rosanne and Benjamin Carter married young and had three children by the time they were 25. They had trouble making ends meet until Rosanne returned to work when Kaitlyn, their youngest, was in school full-time. Rosanne currently earns $25,000 per year after taxes, and the couple estimates that they can allocate a substantial portion of her income to the kids' college fund. The Carters are now 31 years old, and their children are 10, 7, and 6. They want to begin a savings program to help them pay for their kids' college education at an in-state public university.

a. Assume that education costs will increase at a rate of 4 percent per year. Set up a table that shows the Carters' total expected education costs per year beginning when their eldest starts college at age 18.

b. If the Carters' children can contribute one-fourth of the costs and they qualify for student loans and financial aid to cover another one-fourth of the costs, how much will the family need to save for each of the children? (Estimate each separately.)

c. Is it realistic for the Carters to think they'll be able to afford to send their three children to college if they can earn 6 percent on their investments after taxes? Why or why not?

d. Should the Carters consider setting up 529 plans for each of the college funds? What are the pros and cons of doing this?

e. Assuming that current tax laws remain in place, what effect will the family's education expenses have on their taxes?

f. If the Carters haven't yet thought about retirement planning, what effect will education funding have on their ability to adequately fund their retirement? Will it be possible for them to work toward both long-term goals simultaneously?

Case 15-4 Defined Benefit Versus Defined Contribution Plans

Ernie Chu, currently age 27, has just taken a job as an instructor at a large public university. His starting salary is $50,000, and he has been told that salary increases have averaged 4 percent per year. After looking at the benefits package, he learns that the state recently changed its retirement plan from a defined benefit plan, which paid retirees up to 70 percent of final salary with cost-of-living adjustments, to a defined contribution plan. Participants contribute 8 percent of their salary to the plan, and the state contributes another 9 percent, all of which can be invested in a variety of mutual funds. He also finds that his employer is exempt from Social Security, so he won't have to pay the retirement portion of the payroll tax.

a. Assume that Ernie works for a total of 40 years. How much is his salary at years 10, 20, 30, and 40, respectively, if salaries continue to grow at 4 percent per year?

b. If he had been able to participate in the defined benefit plan and was eligible to receive the maximum benefit, how much would it be?

c. Assume that Ernie and his employer contribute a combined 17 percent of his salary each year until he retires. What is his first-year contribution? How much will he have in his retirement account in 40 years, assuming his investments earn an average rate of 4 percent per year? If the rate that a cash flow (CF) increases each year is equal to the rate of return on the invested assets (i), the future value can be calculated as

$$FV = n \times CF \times (1 + i)^n.$$

d. Assuming that Ernie will live for 25 years in retirement and continues to earn 4 percent on his investments, what constant level of income would this amount of retirement wealth provide him? What if he wants his income to increase with inflation?

e. Based on this analysis, is Ernie better off with the defined contribution plan? Why or why not? What risk does he face now that he wouldn't have faced with the defined benefit plan?

LIFELONG PLANNING CASE

Part III Michael and Tori Garcia Invest for the Future

Life Circumstances: Both age 35, married 13 years, daughter Holly, age 6 and son Michael Jr., age 4.

Financial Challenges: Investing for retirement and children's education

Michael and Tori Garcia's family has experienced many changes in the last five years. They've been in their new home for almost 5 years. Michael has been promoted twice by his employer and now grosses $90,000 per year. Tori took a year off from work when Michael Jr. was born, but is now a licensed real estate agent. So far, she's only been selling houses part-time, netting $30,000 per year after expenses, but she plans to double her efforts once Michael Jr. is in full-time preschool this year.

As their income has increased, the Garcias have been pretty conscientious about saving. Both Michael and Tori's retirement accounts have done fairly well. They also set up savings accounts for each of the kids. But they aren't sure that they are saving enough for some of their larger goals, the kids' college funds and their own retirement. They have come to you for help in developing an investment plan. Their current assets and debts are summarized below.

Assets		Debts	
Checking account	$3,000	MasterCard	$ 500
Savings account	7,000	Home mortgage	90,000
Home furnishings	25,000	Current bills due	$1,600
Clothing/personal assets	15,000		
Mutual fund (stocks)	15,000		
Tori's car	10,000		
College savings	8,000		
Value of home	130,000		
Michael's 401k	40,000		
Tori's 401k	$33,000		

1. What are Tori and Michael's investment goals? Explain to them the process they should take to estimate how much they should be saving on a monthly basis to meet these goals.
2. The Garcias' monthly expenses currently total $6,500. They would like to be able to afford about the same lifestyle in retirement as they have today. However, they know they'll have to pay for their total health insurance costs at that time and they won't have to pay the expenses

associated with their children. They estimate that health insurance will cost them $700 per month and they'll save about $1,300 per month in other expenses (in current-year dollars). Use this information to help them estimate their annual before tax expected expenses at the start of retirement (in 32 years). Assume that inflation between now and then will average 4 percent per year and that their tax rate is 25 percent.

3. Currently, Michael has about $40,000 in his employment-based retirement 401(k) account. According to his most recent statement, if he continues with his retirement plan contributions until retirement, his monthly benefit will be $11,200. Tori has $33,000 in her 401(k). She plans to continue to invest, and her monthly benefit in 32 years will be $4,600. The couple has $15,000 in a stock mutual fund (taxable). Based on Michael's most recent Social Security statement, his earnings averaged $50,000 per year.
   a. Estimate the annual retirement expenses that will be covered by Michael and Tori's 401(k) plans.
   b. Estimate Michael's annual social security benefit payment at age 67. Tori will receive a spouse benefit equal to one-half of her husband's.
   c. How much is their annual retirement income shortfall?
   d. The Garcias think they can earn 10 percent on their investments through retirement, and they want to have retirement income that increases with inflation (estimated at 4 percent). How much do they need to have saved by the time they both retire at age 67? They expect to live to age 90.
   e. How much do they need to save each month between now and retirement (32 years from now) in order to have enough to meet their retirement income goals? Assume that their stock mutual fund of $15,000 will earn 10 percent per year. To simplify this calculation, you can use annual computations and divide the result by 12. This will overstate the monthly amount, but it is a reasonable estimate.

PFP Worksheet 51
Retirement Planning

4. Make a recommendation about asset allocation for this account and explain your reasoning. Is there any other information you should get from the Garcias before making this recommendation?
5. The Garcias have accumulated $8,000 in an account that they've earmarked for their children's college expenses. They know that this isn't nearly enough, but aren't sure how to figure out how much they need. The money is in a taxable savings account that's only earning 2 percent per year, so they also are wondering about whether to set up a 529 savings plan and invest in mutual funds.
   a. They expect their children will attend an in-state public university. Holly and Michael Jr. will be expected to save enough to cover 10 percent of their total costs and to qualify for scholarships that will reduce their total costs by 5 percent. What amount of money do Tori and Michael need to have accumulated by the time each child turns 18? (Estimate each separately.)
   b. Assume the Garcias plan to invest their current $8,000 savings and also make regular monthly payments to achieve the college funding goal. How much do they need to invest each month, assuming they can earn 10 percent on their tax-deferred investment account?
6. Given the Garcias' time horizon for their college fund goal, what types of investments would be most appropriate? Explain.
7. Combine the new monthly investments you computed for the Garcias' retirement needs and those for their two children's college fund. Their current net cash flow is $1,055 per month. Will they be able to fund these new investments? Why or why not?
8. Is an annual return estimate of 10 percent reasonable? What would happen if the return was less than 10 percent, for instance 8 percent? Is the annual return estimate important to these investment decisions?

DEVELOPING PERSONAL FINANCIAL skills for life

Learning about Yourself

15-1. How Confident Are You About Retirement?

For each of the following statements related to retirement planning issues, decide whether you are very confident (VC), confident (C), somewhat confident (SC), or not too confident (NC):

______ **1.** I will have enough money/income to live comfortably throughout my retirement years.

______ **2.** I will have enough money/income to take care of basic expenses during retirement.

______ **3.** I will do a good job of managing my money in retirement so I won't outlive my savings.

______ **4.** I will do a good job of preparing for retirement.

______ **5.** I will have enough money to take care of my medical expenses in retirement.

______ **6.** I will have enough money to pay for long-term care expenses in retirement.

These questions are the same ones that are asked as part of the annual Retirement Confidence Survey, which is cosponsored by the American Savings Education Council, an educational consortium, and the Employee Benefit Research Institute, a nonpartisan public policy research organization. You can compare you answers to those of the nationally representative sample for the most recent wave of the survey at www.ebri.org/rcs.

Developing Your Skills

15-2. Determine Your Retirement Goals

PFP Worksheet 50 Retirement Goals

a. Use the worksheet in your *Personal Financial Planner* to summarize your retirement goals.
b. If you were retired today, would your expenses be more or less than your actual expenses today? In what areas do you expect to spend more, and in what areas do you expect to spend less?
c. Given your answer to the previous question, would the replacement ratio approach make sense for estimating your retirement expenses?
d. How do you expect these goals might change as you near retirement?

15-3. Retirement Planning

Using the worksheet in your *Personal Financial Planner,* complete the following steps to determine how much you need to save each month to meet your retirement goals. Use your own financial information or, alternatively, estimate the worksheet as if you are currently 25 years old, earn a $30,000 salary, and have expenses of $20,000 per year.

a. Use the replacement ratio and adjusted expense methods to estimate your postretirement expenses in current dollars.
b. Calculate the future value of postretirement expenses.
c. Estimate your future benefit from Social Security.
d. Assuming you don't have an employer retirement plan, estimate your retirement income shortfall.
e. How much wealth will you need to accumulate between now and when you retire at age 67?
f. What monthly savings amount will allow you to meet this goal?

15-4. Education Funding

Assume that you've just found out you and your spouse are expecting a baby girl. You'd like to set up a college fund for her as soon as possible.

a. Estimate the total cost of sending your daughter to an in-state public university in future dollars. How much more would it cost to send her to a private university?

b. Assuming you plan to send your daughter to the in-state alternative and that she'll cover half her total costs with scholarships, grants, and employment income, use the worksheet in your *Personal Financial Planner* to estimate the amount you should save each month between now and when she starts college in 18 years.

PFP Worksheet 52
Education Funding

THE NAVIGATOR

- ☐ Review Before Studying this Chapter list.
- ☐ Scan Learning Objectives.
- ☐ Take the Myth or Fact quiz and find the answers throughout the chapter.
- ☐ Read chapter and answer Learning by Doing exercises.
- ☐ Review Key Terms and Key Calculations.
- ☐ Do end-of-chapter exercises.
- ☐ Take review quiz on the text website.
- ☐ Solve end-of-chapter cases.

BEFORE studying this chapter, you should review

- The fundamentals of risk management and insurance (Chapter 9).
- Medicare and Medicaid insurance programs (Chapter 10).

Life Insurance and Long-Term Care Planning

CHAPTER 16

Myth or Fact?

Consider each of the following statements and decide whether it is a *myth* or a *fact*. Look for the answers in the *Fact* boxes in the chapter.

	MYTH	FACT
1. Children born today are likely to live much longer than their parents or grandparents.	☐	☐
2. Most households have enough life insurance to meet their needs.	☐	☐
3. If you're a smoker, you can expect to pay more for life insurance, but drinking alcohol won't raise your premiums.	☐	☐
4. Once people buy life insurance, they usually keep the policies rather than letting them lapse.	☐	☐
5. Most nursing care for the elderly is provided by family members.	☐	☐

LEARNING Objectives

1. Assess your life insurance needs.
2. Evaluate insurers and policy types to determine which will best meet your needs.
3. Understand the terms and conditions in life insurance policies.
4. Recognize the costs associated with long-term care.
5. Identify and evaluate long-term care insurance alternatives.

...applying the planning process

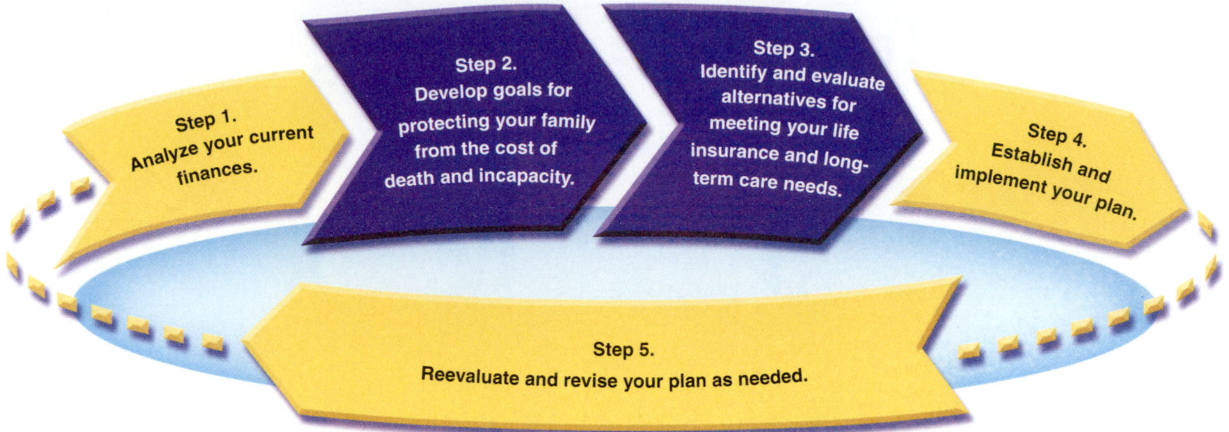

The last two chapters in this text deal with issues related to protecting your loved ones and dependents. In Chapter 9, you learned about how property and liability insurance can protect you and your family from the financial burdens associated with property and liability risk. In this chapter, we'll apply many of the same concepts to decisions related to managing mortality and incapacity risks; and in Chapter 17, we'll look at how to pass your estate to your heirs without paying too much in taxes. Although it's not always easy to contemplate these issues, the reality is that everyone eventually dies and many people experience periods of incapacity before their death. Since funerals and nursing home care are quite expensive, the failure to plan for these eventualities will place a significant financial strain on your family.

Illness and death are both difficult topics to talk about; if you're relatively young, you may not see the immediate relevance. For this reason, we begin the chapter with an assessment of your life insurance needs. What are your risk exposures, and what resources do you currently have in place to meet the needs created by those exposures? How might your needs change over the life cycle? Although your current needs may be low if you're unmarried and childless, you may be surprised at how great your needs can become during the child-rearing years.

As with other components of the financial planning process, once you've identified your needs, you'll need to evaluate alternative methods of meeting those needs. We'll consider the types of life insurance that are available, as well as combinations of insurance and investment plans you should consider. The chapter concludes with a related topic—how to plan for the costs of incapacity in old age. We'll consider the possible financial impact of both your own and your parents' long-term care needs and how you can use insurance to help meet nursing home expenses.

Chapter Preview

Life Insurance and Your Financial Plan
- How Does Life Insurance Work?
- How Is Life Insurance Different?
- Assessing the Financial Consequences of Dying

Selecting a Life Insurer and Type of Policy
- Choosing an Insurer
- Choosing an Agent
- Choosing the Type of Policy
- Term Life Insurance
- Permanent Life Insurance
- Buy Term and Invest the Difference?

Reading Your Policy
- Policy Declarations
- Key Provisions in a Life Insurance Policy

Planning for Long-Term Care Costs
- How Much Will Long-Term Care Cost?
- Sources of Funds for Long-Term Care

Long-Term Care Insurance
- When Is the Best Time to Buy Long-Term Care Insurance?
- Features to Look for in Long-Term Care Insurance
- Talking with Your Parents about Long-Term Care Insurance
- Selecting a Nursing Home Facility

Life Insurance and Your Financial Plan

LEARNING objective

1 Assess your life insurance needs.

A wise person once said that the only things we can be sure of are death and taxes. Even though few would disagree with this statement, many people fail to adequately prepare for their deaths. In this section, we'll first look at some general characteristics of life insurance and mortality risk. Then we'll consider whether you should include life insurance in your financial plan and, if so, how much you need to buy.

How Does Life Insurance Work?

Chapter 9 explained the principles of property and liability insurance. Life insurance basically works in the same way. In fact, it's even simpler, since only one event—a death—can trigger a claim on the policy, whereas many different events can lead to a property or liability insurance claim. Since people die with a certain degree of predictability and each person's death is, in general, independent of the deaths of others, mortality is a type of pure risk for which the pooling mechanism is particularly well suited.

Like other insurance products, life insurance is based on the concept of risk pooling. You pay a premium, which is small relative to the size of your potential loss, and if the bad outcome occurs (you die), your beneficiaries are paid a sum of money, which they can use to offset any losses incurred as a result of your death. Unlike property insurance, where the insurance benefit is designed to pay you back for a specific dollar loss, life insurance is designed to replace the income you would have earned if you hadn't died prematurely. This is similar in concept to disability insurance, which we considered in Chapter 10, except in that case, the policy usually was designed to pay out the lost income in installments, whereas it's more common to get the life insurance benefit in a single lump sum.

Since the risk of dying is related to your health and family history, you'll also find that the information required by an insurer to underwrite your policy (decide on whether to insure you and how much to charge) is similar to what you have to provide when you apply for individual health and disability insurance. For example, you'll commonly be asked about your individual and family health history and, for larger amounts of insurance, you'll usually have to undergo a medical exam and blood test. Obviously, if you have a terminal illness, such as AIDS, an insurer isn't going to be willing to sell you a life insurance policy.

How Is Life Insurance Different?

Although life insurance is similar in principle to other kinds of insurance, it's different in an essential respect. Unlike the insurable risks discussed in Chapters 9 and 10, your death will occur with 100 percent certainty. The only question is *when*. Although advances in medical science have nearly doubled the average human life span in a little more than a century, and some believe that still more advances are to come, the human body has a natural limit. The very certainty of the insured event makes life insurance inherently different from the property, liability, and health insurance policies we've previously considered. In addition, life insurance policies tend to be longer-term in nature than other policies. These differences give rise to differences in how premiums are determined and in the role of the insurer's investments.

Determinants of Premiums. As with other types of insurance, the premium you're charged for life insurance is directly related to the insurer's estimate of your risk—in this case, your risk of dying during the policy period. As you get older, the cost of insuring your death risk will increase. In addition to the expected loss, life insurance premiums include additional amounts to cover the insurer's expenses (such as commissions to agents and claims handling) and its profit to shareholders. They also add a little extra, commonly called the *risk charge*, to account for the chance that their estimate of your mortality risk is inaccurate. These extra charges differ widely among insurers. As you might expect, larger insurers can often provide better rates than small insurers because they can spread these expense, profit, and risk charges across a larger group of policyholders. Some insurers may also spend more money and time deciding whether to insure you (e.g., requiring more extensive medical tests) in an attempt to limit their pool of policyholders to those with lower-than-average risk of dying during the policy period.

The Investment Component. You also learned in Chapter 9 that insurers take the premium dollars they receive and invest the money to earn a return that can help to reduce premiums to their policyholders. An important difference between life insurers and property insurers is that the average term of a life insurance policy is much longer—about half of all policies sold today are long-term policies. That means life insurers are receiving extra premium dollars today that will have to be available to pay death claims many years in the future. Because of the long-term nature of their liability, they can invest in long-term securities without worrying about having access to sufficient funds to pay claims. The life insurer's investment experience is therefore very important to its long-term financial performance—insurers with better investment experience can charge lower premiums and capture larger market shares.

The Benefits of Life Insurance. Although we'll discuss many of these issues in more detail later in the chapter, it's worthwhile to outline here some of the reasons that life insurance is uniquely suited to meeting certain personal financial goals. In addition to providing a sizable amount of protection at a relatively low cost, the proceeds are free from the claims of creditors and tax authorities.

Large Amount of Coverage. Life insurance allows you to buy a fairly large amount of protection for a relatively small annual cost. Your greatest need for protection is likely to be at the time in your life when you're still in the wealth accumulation phase. For a young family, household resources are unlikely to be sufficient to meet the financial costs of an untimely death. But for a few dollars a month, the family can buy insurance to cover these costs.

Protection from Creditors. In the event of your death, the proceeds of your life insurance policy are not subject to the claims of your creditors, whereas your other financial assets are. Thus, you can be sure that the funds will be available to meet the financial needs of your survivors.

Tax Savings. The proceeds of a life insurance policy are not subject to income tax. If your policy includes an investment component, the increase in the value of that investment is income-tax-free as well. And as we'll discuss in Chapter 17, with some minimal planning you can also ensure that your estate will pay no gift and estate taxation on life insurance benefits.

Assessing the Financial Consequences of Dying

Whether you live a long life or die prematurely, there will be costs associated with your death. At a minimum, the funeral costs will have to be paid. More important, your survivors will suffer if they relied on you for financial support. Life insurance will pay your beneficiaries a sum of money after you die to help meet the costs of your death. Before you buy life insurance, though, you must first carefully evaluate their *needs,* just as you've done with the other financial products discussed in this text. This isn't particularly easy, since it requires that you look seriously at your own mortality, or probability of dying, and think about the negative outcomes that might result from your death.

Buying life insurance can give you the peace of mind that comes with knowing your family will be financially secure even if you die.

Here, we'll get the most unpleasant part out of the way first by thinking about your mortality risk. Then we'll consider how your life circumstances, income, and wealth may affect this element of your financial plan. Finally, we'll provide a method for estimating the potential financial impact of your death, so that you can better quantify your family's needs for protection.

What Are the Odds? Our previous discussion of risk management began with an estimate of expected loss based on frequency and severity. The same principles apply to managing your mortality risk. What are the odds of dying in the next year, or 10 years, or 20 years? In other words, what is your *mortality risk*? In the life insurance business, a person's risk of dying is estimated by the use of standardized mortality tables. These tables, based on many years of statistical data on millions of lives, provide yearly probabilities of dying and surviving based on current age. Women tend to live longer than men, on average, so there are separate tables for each gender. It's also common for life insurers to use different tables for smokers and nonsmokers. The standard tables are updated every 20 or 25 years to account for changes in mortality risks resulting from factors such as better health care and nutrition. Exhibit 16-1 reproduces a portion of the most recent update, the 2001 CSO Standard Mortality Table (which replaced a 1980 version previously in effect).

You can see in the mortality table that only 1 of every 1,000 20-year-old males will die before he reaches his 21st birthday, representing a 1/1,000 chance of dying in that year. This may

EXHIBIT 16-1

National Association of Insurance Commissioners 2001 Standard CSO Mortality Table

	Male			Female		
Age	Deaths per 1,000	Life Expectancy	Prob. Live to Age	Deaths per 1,000	Life Expectancy	Prob. Live to Age
Newborn	1.0	76.6	0.9990	0.5	80.8	0.9995
1	0.6	75.7	0.9984	0.4	79.9	0.9991
2	0.4	74.7	0.9980	0.3	78.9	0.9988
3	0.3	73.8	0.9977	0.2	77.9	0.9986
4	0.2	72.8	0.9975	0.2	76.9	0.9984
5	0.2	71.8	0.9973	0.2	76.0	0.9982
6	0.2	70.8	0.9971	0.2	75.0	0.9980
7	0.2	69.8	0.9969	0.2	74.0	0.9978
8	0.2	68.8	0.9967	0.2	73.0	0.9976
9	0.2	67.9	0.9965	0.2	72.0	0.9974
10	0.2	66.9	0.9963	0.2	71.0	0.9972
11	0.3	65.9	0.9960	0.2	70.0	0.9970
12	0.3	64.9	0.9957	0.3	69.1	0.9967
13	0.4	63.9	0.9953	0.3	68.1	0.9964
14	0.5	63.0	0.9948	0.3	67.1	0.9961
15	0.6	62.0	0.9942	0.4	66.1	0.9957
16	0.7	61.0	0.9935	0.4	65.1	0.9953
17	0.9	60.1	0.9926	0.4	64.2	0.9949
18	0.9	59.1	0.9917	0.4	63.2	0.9945
19	1.0	58.2	0.9907	0.5	62.2	0.9940
20	1.0	57.2	0.9897	0.5	61.3	0.9935
21	1.0	56.3	0.9888	0.5	60.3	0.9930
22	1.0	55.3	0.9878	0.5	59.3	0.9925
23	1.0	54.4	0.9868	0.5	58.3	0.9920
24	1.1	53.5	0.9857	0.5	57.4	0.9915
25	1.1	52.5	0.9846	0.5	56.4	0.9910
26	1.1	51.6	0.9835	0.6	55.4	0.9904
27	1.2	50.6	0.9824	0.6	54.5	0.9898
28	1.2	49.7	0.9812	0.6	53.5	0.9893
29	1.2	48.7	0.9800	0.7	52.5	0.9886
30	1.1	47.8	0.9789	0.7	51.6	0.9879
31	1.1	46.8	0.9778	0.7	50.6	0.9872
32	1.1	45.9	0.9768	0.8	49.6	0.9864
33	1.2	45.0	0.9756	0.8	58.7	0.9856
34	1.2	44.0	0.9744	0.9	47.7	0.9847
35	1.2	43.1	0.9733	1.0	46.8	0.9837
36	1.3	42.1	0.9720	1.0	45.8	0.9827
37	1.3	41.2	0.9707	1.1	44.8	0.9817
38	1.4	40.2	0.9694	1.2	43.9	0.9805
39	1.5	39.3	0.9679	1.2	42.9	0.9793
40	1.7	38.3	0.9663	1.3	42.0	0.9780
50	3.8	29.2	0.9397	3.1	32.7	0.9578
60	9.9	20.6	0.8787	8.0	24.1	0.9063
70	25.8	13.3	0.7335	17.8	16.4	0.7974
80	70.1	7.5	0.4571	43.9	9.9	0.5866
90	187.7	3.8	0.1166	121.9	5.3	0.2503
100	363.2	2.1	0.0050	275.7	2.6	0.0261

sound like pretty good odds—the chances of dying in any given year are in fact fairly low through your 40s or 50s—but keep in mind that the table gives *annual* probabilities. The third column in the exhibit shows the cumulative probability of surviving to a particular age. For the 20-year-old male, it's about 99 percent. With each successive year, the risk of dying increases, and the cumulative probability of surviving to that age gets smaller. About 94 percent of men born the same year as you (your birth cohort) will still be alive at age 50, but by the time you reach 70, more than one-fourth of your birth cohort will have died, and only 45 percent will survive to age 80. For women, the odds of surviving are better at all ages.

Fact #1

The average life expectancy of a child born in 2001 is 77.2 years (74.4 for men and 79.8 for women). This represents a gain of 6.4 years from the previous generation—a child born from 1959 to 1961 had a life expectancy of 70.8 (66.6 for men and 73.2 for women). The life expectancy of a child born from 1929 to 1931 was only 59.2 (57.5 for men and 60.9 for women). The 18-year increase in life expectancy over the last two generations is primarily attributable to the availability of antibiotics and vaccines for many previously fatal illnesses and infections.

Another interesting piece of information included in this table is an estimate of your life expectancy. You should note that, as you survive to each successive year, your life expectancy, measured as expected age at death, actually increases. For example, a 20-year-old male has a life expectancy of 57.2 years, so he's expected to live to be 20 + 57.2 = 77.2. This is older than his life expectancy at birth, which was 76.6. If he lives to be 40, he can expect to live to be 78.3 years old on average, and so on.

So what does this table tell you? First, it demonstrates that mortality is a very real risk. In any year of your life, you could die. Second, you have a pretty good chance of living to be *very old*. In the previous chapter, we pointed out that it's dangerous to assume you'll only live the average life expectancy for your age cohort. Although not shown here, the new mortality tables give life expectancies through age 120, where the previous one stopped at 99. If you live to be 100, you'll probably live to be 102. (Although not everyone wants to live *that* long, the *News You Can Use* box "Live Long and Prosper" offers some suggestions for getting to the upper end of the longevity distribution.) The lesson overall is that you need to invest for longevity but plan for mortality.

Why Buy Life Insurance? Let's say you accept that you're going to die someday. If it happened tomorrow, is there anyone who would experience financial distress as a result? What about your spouse, children, or parents? Would your dog end up in the pound with no one to take care of him? The process of determining the potential financial impact of your death on

NEWS you can use

Live Long and Prosper

Although you can't prevent your eventual death, you can take steps to stall it. Gerontologists—scientists who study issues related to aging—have found that people who live longer than average have many of the following characteristics in common:

- They don't smoke. Nonsmokers live an average of 10 years longer than smokers. If you quit smoking early enough, your life expectancy will return to "normal."
- They take care of their physical health. Exercising regularly and eating a healthy diet have been linked to longevity.
- They are happy. Research shows that people with positive outlooks live longer than pessimists.
- They have long-term marriages. One research study found that married men lived longer than singles (although it doesn't appear that being married lengthens a woman's life).
- They drink only in moderation. Substance abuse of any type reduces life expectancy.

"People with positive outlooks live longer."

others is called *needs analysis*. In most cases, your needs will be motivated by your desire to replace your income, preserve household wealth, provide for your family's future monetary needs, or cover business losses.

Replacing Your Income and Services. If you're providing necessary income or services to the household, your death will result in a loss to your survivors. This may seem obvious when you're considering insurance for the major breadwinner of the household, but consider too that a stay-at-home mom's housekeeping, child-care, and transportation services can be very costly to replace.

Preserving Household Wealth. If you die prematurely, your dependents may need to sell the house or spend household resources to meet their living expenses. Life insurance can provide the necessary funds to keep the household running so that your dependents won't have to resort to selling the house and the car.

Providing for Future Family Needs. Even if your survivors would be able to make ends meet financially without you, life insurance can provide them with greater financial security and can fund the extras they might otherwise be unaffordable—for example, allowing your spouse to work part-time until the children are grown or paying for your children to attend a more expensive college.

Covering Business Losses. If you're a partner or key person in a business venture, your death might cause significant hardship to your surviving business partners, who will be faced with the cost of finding a replacement for you. Of course, money can't replace things such as creativity and vision. As a result, even when there's insurance in place, the loss of a talented CEO can sometimes result in significant stock price declines for the company involved. (If no one likes the CEO, the reverse may be true.) Life insurance that names the company as the beneficiary can, however, offset some of the losses and provide the cash necessary to help the business continue operating. In some cases, family-owned businesses buy life insurance in an amount sufficient to cover estate taxes that would be payable at the death of the last surviving parent. As we'll see in Chapter 17, this may not be necessary in the future due to changes in the estate tax system.

Factors Affecting Your Life Insurance Needs. Not everyone needs life insurance. And those who do require it don't all need to carry the same amount of coverage. If your death wouldn't impose financial costs on anyone, then none of the motivations above apply to your situation. For example, if you have no one relying on your income or services (no "significant other," no children, no pets, no business obligations), then the only financial cost of your death will be your funeral costs. If you have sufficient assets to cover this cost, then you probably don't need life insurance. You may still *want* to buy it so that you can provide a financial benefit to someone, but you don't *need* to buy it. Over your lifetime, however, your needs for life insurance may change with your changing circumstances. Some of the factors that will influence your life insurance needs over the life cycle include the following:

- *The number and age of your dependents.* The more dependents you have and the younger they are, the more life insurance you'll need.
- *Your age and life-cycle stage.* You'll need more life insurance during the child-rearing years and less once your children are independent.
- *Your spouse's earning capacity.* If your spouse can't work or earns a lot less than you, you may need more life insurance.
- *Financial wealth and obligations.* The lower your wealth and the higher your financial obligations, the more life insurance you'll need.
- *Your health.* If you have signification health problems, you may need more life insurance, since your risk of dying prematurely is higher than average.
- *Your dependents' health.* If your spouse or children have health problems, your death might make it difficult for them to maintain health insurance and to meet medical costs, so you may need more life insurance.

Approaches to Life Insurance Needs Analysis.

In the event of your death, your existing wealth can obviously be a source of support for your survivors. But since you've already earmarked this wealth for specific purposes (such as a college fund for your children or retirement income for you and your spouse), you'll usually purchase life insurance to provide whatever else might be needed. In this section, we discuss two approaches commonly used to estimate life insurance needs. Note that although the simpler approach—the income-multiple method—is quicker, it's much less likely to accurately identify your needs. The more sophisticated financial needs approach will take more time, but is more likely to result in your purchase of an appropriate amount of life insurance.

income-multiple method

A method for estimating life insurance needs as a multiple of income.

Income-Multiple Method. The simplest approach, and one that is often used as a shortcut to life insurance needs analysis, is the **income-multiple method**. With this method, you simply multiply your income by a factor of 5 to 10. If you have income of $40,000, for example, you need between $200,000 and $400,000 in life insurance, according to this approach. The idea is that the life insurance should be sufficient to replace your income for a period of time.

The problems with this approach are many. One is the assumption that "one size fits all." As with other financial rules of thumb (like the 70% replacement ratio for retirement expenses mentioned in Chapter 15), there's no scientific evidence that this is the "right" amount of insurance to carry. Some people need far more, and others don't need any at all. Another problem is that there's usually no good explanation for why you should be on the high end or the low end of the multiple. Furthermore, the multiplier method doesn't take into consideration the resources you already have to meet your financial needs. Finally, when you consider the time value of money, you can probably see that a straight multiple might not be the best approach to replacing your annual income. Since the income is effectively an inflation-adjusted annuity, it would be more appropriate to estimate the present value of that cash flow stream.

Despite its disadvantages, the income multiple approach does have the advantage of simplicity, and since most people don't even have the minimum amount of insurance recommended by this approach, it serves the purpose of identifying a shortfall.

Fact #2

Only 69 percent of families have any life insurance protection, and most of them have too little. The average face amount of policies purchased in 2002 was $119,000, and the average total life insurance per insured household is about $200,000. Men are much more likely to carry life insurance than women.

financial needs method

A method for estimating life insurance needs based on expected capital and income replacement needs.

Financial Needs Method. A more accurate method of determining your life insurance needs is to carefully estimate the funds your family will need after your death. In general, if you use the **financial needs method**, you'll estimate separately your capital needs (sums earmarked for paying off debts or funding future needs like education) and income replacement needs. You'll then calculate the lump sum amount required to fund the income needs and add it to the capital needs to arrive at a total. From this total, you'll subtract any financial resources you have in place to meet the capital needs

Your financial needs will generally fall into the following categories:

- Costs of death
- Lump sum needs for dependents' education costs, spouse's retirement plan, and debt repayment
- Household maintenance expenses

An Example: The Thompsons.

To illustrate life insurance needs analysis, let's work through an example in which we estimate the life insurance needs of the Thompson family using the financial needs method. In Chapter 3, one of the Thompsons' personal financial goals was to purchase adequate life insurance for both Dave and Cindy. At that time, Dave had $50,000 in life insurance and Cindy had none. We'll assume that they're evaluating this component of their financial plan shortly after the birth of their new baby Julia. Cindy has quit her job and plans to stay home for the next several years until Julia goes to kindergarten.

Since Dave is currently the sole provider for the household, he'll obviously need to carry more life insurance than his wife. However, Cindy's death would result in additional household

PFP Worksheet 53
Life Insurance
Needs Analysis

expenses for such things as child care and household maintenance. A needs analysis for Dave and Cindy Thompson appears in Exhibit 16-2. This worksheet, which is also available in your *Personal Financial Planner*, is organized in sections for the different categories of expenses a household might incur in the event of premature death. Some of the costs on this worksheet, particularly the costs at death, are one-time expenses; others are lump-sum capital needs, such as the cost of paying off household debts and setting up an emergency fund. In contrast, some of the costs involve ongoing, long-term cash flow needs, such as continuing household expenses; for those, we'll need to estimate the annual costs and then apply time value principles to determine the present value of the future cash flows. Next, we'll consider various approaches to estimating each type of cost.

Costs at Death. When a family member dies, the survivors generally incur a number of one-time costs, including medical costs, funeral costs, and legal costs for settling the estate (discussed in Chapter 17). Out-of-pocket medical expenses depend to a large extent on the cause of death and whether the deceased person had comprehensive health coverage. Funeral expenses vary based on wealth and tastes, but the average is around $10,000. The Thompsons estimate that their uninsured medical costs would be $1,000 and that it would cost $5,000 to settle the estate. They also include $500 to cover the cost of family counseling for the survivors.

Lump Sum Needs. Many families include in their life insurance needs analysis sufficient funds to establish an emergency fund, settle large household debts, and fund the future education needs of their children (and sometimes grandchildren) or retirement fund needs for a surviving spouse. Although the family may have a plan in place for financing those needs, the loss of a primary earner often makes continued debt repayment or investment contributions more difficult. Dave, for example, includes enough in his needs analysis to repay the mortgage on the Thompsons' house and their outstanding car loan. In addition, he plans to purchase enough life insurance to pay for his children's college fund and Cindy's retirement account. Note, however, that none of these amounts is included in the estimate of Cindy's life insurance needs, since Dave's continued income would be sufficient to make the ongoing payments.

Household Maintenance. The most important category addressed in the needs analysis is the cost of maintaining the household. This step of the calculation estimates the net effect on household cash flows by summing the lost income and the cost of services provided by the person who died and then adjusting for the reduction in household expenses (one less person in the household) and expected Social Security survivor benefits. The remainder is the expected annual income shortfall.

If Dave were to die, the family would lose his income, but Social Security survivor benefits would replace almost half, and the household's expenses would also be lower by an estimated $13,200 (25% of total expenses). The reduction in expenses that would occur in the event of Cindy's death would be somewhat less since she doesn't currently have any work-related expenses. Social Security, in addition to being a retirement program, provides survivor benefits. As with retirement benefits discussed in Chapter 15, your survivors' eligibility for full benefits depends on whether you're considered fully insured under the programs—forty quarters of covered employment prior to your death or $1\frac{1}{2}$ years of covered employment in the last three years. Although the program may change in the future, benefits are currently payable for each child under 18 and for a nonworking surviving spouse who stays home with children, up to a family maximum. Since the Thompsons' oldest child, Kyle, is a teenager, the benefits will drop significantly in a few years. But by then, the couple estimates that Cindy will likely be able to return to work. Benefits payable to the surviving spouse are phased out beginning at a fairly low earnings level if the spouse is employed (which is why the Thompsons estimate no benefits from Social Security would be payable if Cindy were to die). Using the benefit calculator on the Social Security website, Dave estimates that the family will be eligible to receive the maximum family benefit, which translates to approximately $26,000 per year in 2004. Exhibit 16-3 summarizes the approximate annual survivor benefits payable if a fully insured worker died in 2004 and had steady earnings.

Based on these estimates, Cindy would experience an annual household income shortfall of $13,600 if Dave were to die. Unlike the lump sum needs discussed above, the income shortfall

EXHIBIT 16-2

Dave and Cindy Thompson's Life Insurance Needs Analysis

		Dave	Cindy
A. Costs at Death			
1. Uninsured medical expenses (deductible and copay)		$ 1,000	$ 1,000
2. Funeral expense (average $10,000, but less for cremation)		10,000	10,000
3. Settlement of estate (estimate 4% of assets)		5,000	5,000
4. State inheritance taxes (if any)			
5. Counseling costs for adjustment to loss		500	500
Total costs at death	1 + 2 + 3 + 4 + 5	$ 16,500	$ 16,500
B. Lump Sums			
6. Outstanding debts			
a. Mortage		100,000	
b. Car loan(s)		10,000	
c. Credit cards and other loans			
d. Total outstanding debt to repay	6a + 6b + 6c	110,000	0
7. Education costs for children or spouse (see Chapter 15)		120,000	60,000
8. Spouse retirement fund		100,000	
9. Household emergency fund Monthly household expenses × 3		10,000	10,000
Total lump sum needs	6d + 7 + 8 + 9	$340,000	$ 70,000
C. Cost of Household Maintenance			
10. Decreased annual after-tax income		52,800	
11. Annual cost of lost support services (child/elder care, housekeeping)			13,000
12. Reduction in family expenses due to death (estimate 20–25%)		13,200	10,000
13. Annual Social Security survivor benefits		26,000	
14. Net income shortfall	10 + 11 − 12 − 13	13,600	3,000
Total household maintenance fund needs			
Line 14 × Number of years to replace	10 YEARS	136,000	30,000
15. **Total fund needed (sum shaded cells)**		$492,500	$116,500
Available Resources			
16. Total savings and investments		5,000	5,000
17. Group life insurance		50,000	
18. Social Security lump sum benefit			
19. **Total resources to meet needs**	**16 + 17 + 18**	$ 55,000	$ 5,000
Total life insurance needs	line 15 − line 19	$437,500	$111,500

EXHIBIT 16-3

Social Security Survivor Benefits

Worker Age at Death and Family Status	Deceased Worker's Earnings				
	$25,000	$35,000	$45,000	$60,000	$100,000
30					
Child under 18 or spouse w/child	$8,700	$10,896	$13,104	$15,024	$18,324
Retired spouse	11,592	14,532	17,472	20,040	24,432
Family maximum	20,112	26,724	30,660	35,076	42,768
45					
Child under 18 or spouse w/child	8,412	10,500	12,588	14,712	17,976
Retired spouse	11,220	14,004	16,788	19,620	23,976
Family maximum	19,080	26,016	29,748	34,344	41,964
40					
Child under 18 or spouse w/child	8,160	10,152	12,144	14,424	17,760
Retired spouse	10,884	13,548	16,200	19,236	23,676
Family maximum	18,180	25,404	28,956	33,684	41,448
50					
Child under 18 or spouse w/child	7,716	9,528	11,340	13,932	17,100
Retired spouse	10,296	12,708	15,120	18,576	22,800
Family maximum	16,572	23,136	27,516	32,520	39,912
60					
Child under 18 or spouse w/child	7,332	8,988	10,644	13,128	16,392
Retired spouse	9,768	11,976	14,184	17,496	21,852
Family maximum	$15,144	$21,156	$26,268	$30,708	$38,256

Source: Computed by author using Quick Calculator at the Social Security Administration website, www.ssa.gov.

will presumably continue over a period of years. Household expenses are likely to rise with inflation each year, but it's also true that the survivor will be able to invest the proceeds of the life insurance policy to earn at least the rate of inflation. The two effects cancel each other out, which allows us to vastly simplify this calculation and simply multiply the total annual income shortfall by the number of years the cash flow will be needed. This multiplier should take into account the number of years the family will have dependent children in the home and also the time until the surviving spouse could earn sufficient replacement income. She estimates that within 10 years, she would be able to earn enough to offset this income shortfall, so her projection needs for this category are 10 × $13,600 = $136,000.

After summing all the categories of financial need, the Thompsons are surprised to see just how underinsured they are; they never dreamed that their combined life insurance needs would add up to more than $600,000. The Thompsons' household financial resources at the moment are very limited, but they decide that they need to look into increasing Dave's life insurance coverage to about $400,000 and buying $100,000 of coverage for Cindy. Of course, it will be necessary for them to reevaluate their life insurance needs as their family circumstances change.

Changing Needs over the Life Cycle. Like the Thompsons, you'll find that your life insurance needs will change as you move through the stages of the life cycle. As a young single with no dependents, you only need to fund your funeral costs and repay your debt. Once you marry, your life insurance needs will be greater, especially if you're the primary breadwinner; as you have children, your needs will increase even more. During these early years, you probably won't have built up much wealth, so you'll need to rely on insurance to meet the needs of your family in case of your death. In middle age, your needs will begin to decline, since your financial wealth is likely to be growing and your children are becoming independent. For most retirees, life insurance is no longer a necessity, but we'll see in Chapter 17 that it can be an effective estate planning tool.

Learning by Doing 16-1

1. Elaine has just graduated from college, is single, and has no dependents except for her chocolate lab Rufus. She's accepted a job with a starting salary of $40,000, and she has $10,000 in student loan debt. Her employer doesn't provide any group life insurance. Does Elaine need any life insurance? Why or why not? If so, how much would you recommend?
2. Carrie and Brad are a young couple with no children or pets. Both are attorneys who make more than $100,000 per year. Because they're relatively frugal, they have only a small mortgage on their jointly owned condo, and they have no outstanding debt. With their high net cash flow and some wise investment decisions, they've accumulated a sizable net worth, and both have good retirement plans with their employers. Does either of them need life insurance? Why or why not? If so, how much would you recommend?

Selecting a Life Insurer and Type of Policy

LEARNING objective

2 Evaluate insurers and policy types to determine which will best meet your needs.

Once you've determined your need for life insurance, the next steps are to consider which financial institution to do business with and what type of policy will best meet your needs. Since some insurers specialize in certain types of insurance policies, you will probably need to decide on the type of policy first. However, people who don't know much about life insurance usually decide on the insurer first and then rely on their agent to help them decide between policy types. Exhibit 16-4 summarizes the primary features of the different types of policies discussed in this section.

EXHIBIT 16-4 Comparison of Features of Common Types of Life Insurance Policies

Type of Policy	Premium Level	Period of Policy	Death Benefit	Cash Buildup	Choice of Investments	Proof of Insurability
Term Insurance						
Regular term	Increase w/age	Usually 1 year	Constant	No	No	Required
Increasing term	Increase w/age	1–10 years	Increase w/age	No	No	Required
Decreasing term	Constant	1–10 years	Decrease w/age	No	No	Required
Level term	Constant	5–10 years	Constant	No	No	Rules differ
Renewable term	Increase w/age	5–20 years	Constant	No	No	Required at beginning only
Permanent Insurance						
Whole life insurance	Constant	10+ years	Increase w/cash buildup*	Yes	No	Required at beginning only
Universal life insurance	Flexible	10+ years	Increase w/cash buildup*	Yes	No	Required at beginning only
Variable life insurance	Constant	10+ years	Increase w/cash buildup*	Yes	Yes	Required at beginning only
Variable universal life	Flexible	10+ years	Increase w/cash buildup*	Yes	Yes	Required at beginning only
Single-premium life	One-time payment	Whole life	Increase w/cash buildup*	Yes	No	Required at beginning only

*Death benefit is constant but total paid to survivors may be greater if cash value exceeds death benefit promise.

Choosing the Type of Policy

Although insurers are constantly trying to meet the needs of customers by creating "new and improved" life insurance policies, there are really just two basic types—term (or temporary) and permanent (or long-term) life insurance. There are many variations on each general type, which can make the selection and comparison process somewhat confusing. But if you understand the fundamental differences, you'll be headed in the right direction. Here we'll examine important features of the two basic types of insurance—term and permanent.

Term Life Insurance

Term life insurance provides protection for a specific period of time, such as one year or five years, and has no investment component. You pay an annual premium, sometimes in monthly installments; if you die during the contract period, your beneficiary will receive the **face value** of the policy. If you don't die, then the contract concludes at the end of the period. The primary determinant of the price of term insurance is your probability of dying during the contract period. This probability increases with age and health problems. Thus, the annual premium is fairly low when you're young and healthy and increases with your age, as illustrated in Exhibit 16-5. For example, a one-year policy for a 25-year-old woman usually costs less than $100 per year for $100,000 in face value, whereas she might pay $500 per year at age 50 for the same level of protection.

term life insurance

A type of life insurance that provides death protection for a specified term, often one year, and no cash value.

face value

The dollar value of protection payable to beneficiaries under the terms of a life insurance policy.

Term life insurance allows you to buy a fairly large amount of protection for a relatively modest premium—a real advantage when your financial needs are large relative to your household resources. When you get older, you can decrease your level of coverage as your household wealth grows and your dependents' needs are reduced.

There are two primary problems with term insurance. First, the premiums rise sharply as you get older; beyond a certain age limit, often 65, you'll find that insurers are reluctant to sell term insurance to you at all. Second, in the absence of specific provisions in your insurance contract, your term life insurance will lapse at the end of the term of coverage, and you may have to go through the complete application process all over, including any required medical examination. If your health circumstances make you no longer eligible for the insurance, you might lose coverage just when your family needs it most. To address these problems, insurers make various features available in term insurance policies. Although they may cause your premiums to be higher, you should seriously consider features such as guaranteed renewability and convertibility when you purchase term insurance.

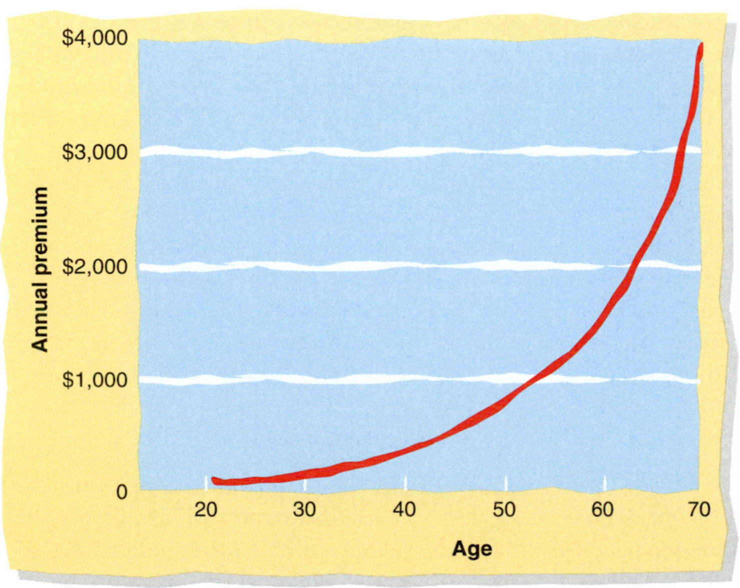

EXHIBIT 16-5

Cost of $10,000 Face Value Yearly Renewable Term Life Insurance

guaranteed renewability

A feature of term life insurance giving the insured person the right to renew the policy without additional proof of insurability.

Renewability. **Guaranteed renewability** is the right to renew the contract without additional proof of insurability, such as a medical exam. In renewable policies of this type, the face value usually remains the same over time, but the premium increases periodically. At each renewal date, the premium for the policy is adjusted upward to reflect the additional mortality risk for your age cohort. The policy may be renewable annually, adjusted each year according to a predetermined schedule, or it may be renewable at longer intervals, such as every five or ten years. When the premium stays the same for more than one year, the rate at the beginning of the term is higher than the rate on an annually renewable policy, since the insurer is spreading your mortality risk over a longer period. Note that renewability has limits. Although there are now some exceptions, in general you can only renew term insurance until you're 65 or 70. Even when it's possible to renew beyond these ages, the premium rates are prohibitively expensive.

convertible

A type of term life insurance policy which allows the insured person to convert the term insurance policy to a permanent life insurance policy without additional proof of insurability.

Convertibility. In some cases, a term policy may be **convertible**, giving you the right to convert to permanent life insurance without additional proof of insurability. As you'll see in the following discussion, permanent life insurance is much more expensive than term. The benefit of the convertibility feature is that it allows you to effectively lock in a premium rate based on a younger age while obtaining a larger amount of protection than you could afford to buy in the form of permanent insurance. If you decide to exercise this type of option, you'll usually have to come up with the back premiums for the permanent coverage. Although this might not seem to be worthwhile, it's actually less expensive than the alternative—being subject to an annual premium rate for permanent insurance based on your current age.

decreasing term life insurance

A type of term life insurance featuring a level premium and decreasing protection.

Decreasing Protection. With **decreasing term life insurance**, the amount of your premium remains the same from year to year, but that premium purchases smaller amounts of coverage each year. Effectively, you're paying an age-related price per $1,000 of coverage, as you would under a standard term policy, but you're reducing the face value of the policy to keep the premium the same. This type of arrangement may make sense if you expect your life insurance needs to decline over time as your household wealth is increasing and your children are growing up and leaving home. It's doubtful, however, that the declines in coverage will exactly match your changing insurance needs.

Permanent Life Insurance

permanent life insurance

A type of life insurance that provides both death protection and a savings vehicle.

cash value

The value of the investment component of a permanent life insurance policy.

Permanent life insurance provides an investment component along with its protection component. It's called permanent because, unlike term insurance, it doesn't need to be renewed—it's intended to be in place for your entire lifetime. The idea is to allow policyholders to stay insured for their lifetimes while paying a guaranteed, level premium. In the beginning, the premium is higher than that for term insurance of comparable coverage, and the insurer invests the difference. As the policyholder grows older and mortality risk increases, the premium stays the same because the accumulated savings in the policy offset the additional risk. Because of the accumulation of savings, permanent life insurance is also commonly referred to as *cash value life insurance.* The buildup of extra funds in the policy that will eventually be used to offset the increased costs of providing death protection at older ages is known as the **cash value**.

The primary advantages of permanent insurance are that the accumulated investment returns are not taxable and provide a mechanism for forced saving. However, it's important to carefully consider alternative investment options before deciding to buy permanent life insurance, since the rates of return on many policies are not competitive with other alternatives and the expenses charged to your account may exceed those of comparable-risk mutual funds.

The primary categories of permanent life insurance are whole life insurance, universal life insurance, and variable life insurance. All are similar in that the policies are long-term in nature and don't require renewal. The differences primarily relate to how premiums are determined and whether you can select how your cash value is to be invested.

whole life insurance

Permanent life insurance that provides death protection for the policyholder's whole life and includes a savings component.

ordinary life insurance

Whole life insurance with premiums payable to the time of death.

limited payment life insurance

Whole life insurance that is paid up after a specified period.

Whole Life Insurance. **Whole life insurance** provides death protection for a person's entire life. If the premiums are also payable over the insured's whole life, the policy is an **ordinary life insurance** policy; if the premiums are paid only for a specified period of time, after which the policy is paid up, the policy is a **limited payment life insurance** policy. Although it's common for people to purchase limited payment life insurance that will be paid up at the time of retirement, typically age 65 or 70, these policies have a wide variety of payment options. You can even purchase **single-premium whole life insurance** with a one-time premium payment. Whatever the type of premium payment arrangement, your beneficiaries will be paid the face amount of the policy, regardless of when you die.

single-premium whole life insurance

Whole life insurance that is paid up with a one-time payment.

As an example of how whole life insurance works, suppose you purchase a $100,000 whole life policy with a level premium of $1,000 per year, payable for your whole life. If you could have bought term insurance for only $100, then we may assume that the insurer can provide you with death protection for that amount of money. In other words, $100 will be sufficient to pay your share of the death claims for its pool of insured persons. This implies that the remaining $900 can be invested to help cover your death protection costs in the future, when it will be more expensive to do so (because you'll be older). In the early years of the policy, as is illustrated in Exhibit 16-6, the insurer is providing death protection that is nearly equal to the face value of the policy. You haven't paid very much into the policy, so if you die, the insurer will be footing almost the entire bill. Over time, however, a larger share of the death protection is coming from the policy's cash value reserves, which implies that less protection is being provided by the insurer. Although you usually won't be credited with any cash value for the first few years as the insurer recoups its issuance costs (commissions to agents, processing of your application), you'll eventually accumulate a cash reserve in the policy. This will be used to cover your mortality costs in later years, when they're greater than the $1,000 premium amount. In addition, you can generally borrow against the cash value at favorable interest rates, subject to a reduction in the death benefit to repay any unpaid loan balance at the time of your death. With a limited payment life policy, you'll no longer pay a premium after a certain point, but your cash value will continue to earn investment returns, effectively increasing the amount that will be payable to your beneficiaries upon your death.

The concept of bundling death protection with an investment product makes sense only if it offers you a cost-effective way of achieving both objectives. Traditional whole life insurance is often criticized for the relatively noncompetitive rates of return that have been credited to policyholders, particularly during periods when the stock and bond markets have done well. For example, if the policy was priced assuming a 4 percent return on investment, but the insurer actually earned 12 percent, the policyholder didn't get to share in the good fortune—the insurer just made a larger profit. In the early 1980s when the inflation and investment returns were very high, the end result was that the investment component of whole life policies didn't even earn enough to offset inflation.

Another problem with traditional whole life insurance contracts is that they are relatively inflexible regarding premium payments. A policyholder who runs into financial difficulties and misses a payment or two can have his or her policy canceled even when there's substantial built-up cash value.

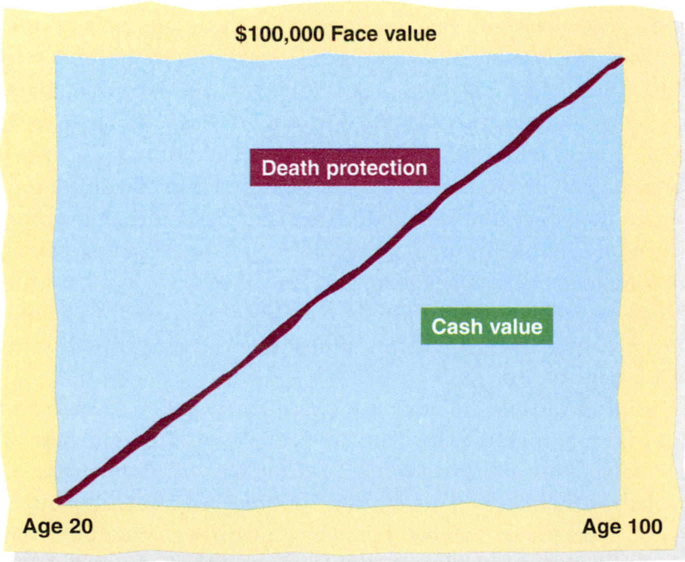

EXHIBIT 16-6

Death Protection and Cash Value Components of Ordinary Life Insurance Issued to 20-Year-Old Male

universal life insurance

A type of permanent life insurance that allows policyholders to benefit from the investment experience of the insurer and provides a flexible premium option.

Universal Life Insurance. **Universal life insurance** is a type of permanent insurance that attempts to address the shortcomings of whole life insurance mentioned above. Universal policies promise death protection and a savings component, as whole life policies do, but if the insurance company earns greater-than-expected returns on its investment portfolio, the policyholder shares in some of that benefit, usually through a reduction in the next year's premium owed. Universal life also includes a flexible premium option—a policyholder with sufficient cash reserves can choose not to pay the premiums, using accumulated cash value to meet mortality costs for the period, or to take some of the funds out of the policy entirely. On the one hand, this flexibility is a benefit; for example, a policyholder won't have to let the policy lapse if she experiences some financial difficulties. On the other hand, it tends to undermine the savings element of the policy—if you don't put the money in and keep it there, you can't accumulate any savings.

current assumption whole life insurance

A type of permanent life insurance with premiums that depend on the insurer's actual mortality, expense, and investment experience.

Current Assumption Whole Life. Another variation on the whole life concept is **current assumption whole life insurance**, which has some similarities to universal life. This type of policy incorporates a variable premium design in which the premium for each period is recalculated based on the mortality, expense, and investment experience of the insurer, subject to a guaranteed maximum. In theory, this could result in lower premiums over time if the insurer does a good job of underwriting and investing, but it could also result in sharply increased premiums in the event of an economic downturn that seriously reduces investment returns.

variable life insurance

Permanent life insurance that has a fixed premium and allows policyholders to choose from different investment alternatives.

variable-universal life insurance

Permanent life insurance that involves a flexible premium feature and allows policyholders to choose from different investment alternatives.

Variable Life Insurance. The most popular types of permanent life insurance in recent years have been **variable life insurance** and **variable-universal life insurance**. Both of these products allow policyholders to direct the investment component of their policies, usually into managed accounts with different risk characteristics, such as a growth stock account, income stock account, high-grade bond account, or government bond account. In this type of arrangement, the insurer provides professional management of the accounts, and the policyholder selects from among several options, much like the choices in employer-sponsored retirement funds. The pricing of the policy takes investment returns into account, so if you assume a little more risk, you may be able to benefit in the form of lower premiums and quicker buildup of cash value. Policyholders are generally allowed to transfer money between investment options subject to some timing restrictions. Variable universal life also includes the flexible premium features of universal life.

Although most variable policies have a stated minimum death benefit, the expectation is that the cash value accumulation resulting from the performance of the selected investments will end up being higher than the stated death benefit amount. For example, the policy premium for a $100,000 policy might be determined assuming a 3 percent return on investment, but if you actually earn 8 percent, the cash value will increase beyond what is required to fund your $100,000 policy. If you were to die, your beneficiaries would receive the face value plus the extra accumulation. You'll generally get no guarantees regarding the interest rate or cash value for these policies, however. Since policyholders are exposed to risks of loss as well as possibilities for gain, the Securities and Exchange Commission has determined that these products are investment securities and must follow all the registration and disclosure rules applicable to securities.

If you maintain a variable life policy for a long time, its features may make it desirable as a combination protection and investment vehicle. Since the buildup of cash value is tax deferred as long as you maintain the policy and is received by your beneficiaries upon your death tax-free, your after-tax return on investment (or, more precisely, your beneficiary's return on investment) is higher than for a comparable taxable investment. Early withdrawals are not subject to the IRS penalties imposed on retirement account withdrawals, but if you cash in your policy, you'll usually be subject to a penalty (surrender charges imposed by the insurer) and income tax liability on the excess of cash value over premiums paid.

The real downside of variable life insurance is risk. Even though all investments expose you to risk, it may not be appropriate to mix the protection-motivated purchase of life insurance with the wealth-building motivation of investing. During the 1990s, when the stock market was climbing spectacularly, insurers found it difficult to entice customers to buy minimal-return whole life insurance, but sales of variable products went through the roof. Many of those investors found out the hard way that their cash values could actually go to zero.

Buy Term and Invest the Difference?

In deciding whether to buy term insurance (death protection only) or permanent insurance (death protection plus a savings vehicle), it's a good idea to compare the permanent insurance alternative with a "buy term and invest the difference" strategy. Premiums for permanent insurance are many times those for term insurance, which can make permanent insurance a prohibitively expensive choice for low- or average-income families. In contrast, term insurance is quite inexpensive if you're young and healthy. Thus, instead of paying high premiums for permanent insurance, you might consider buying decreasing term and investing the premium difference in a mutual fund. As the face value of the term insurance declines over time, the value of your investment portfolio will increase, so you can maintain relatively constant total protection plus wealth accumulation. Whether this is a good strategy depends on several factors:

- Will you stick with your investment plan? A buy term and invest the difference strategy can only work if you really do invest the difference. If you find other things to spend the money on, or if you dip into the investment portfolio on occasion, you'll end up with insufficient protection for your survivors.
- Can you earn more on your investments than the insurer can? Although life insurers are generally experts at investing, it's not very difficult to find mutual fund alternatives with comparable investment performance.
- Is it cheaper to buy term and invest the difference? Whether you buy insurance with an investment component or you buy mutual funds on your own, you'll be exposed to some combination of commissions and management fees as explained in Chapter 14. In deciding between these alternatives, you need to compare these costs.

Fact #3

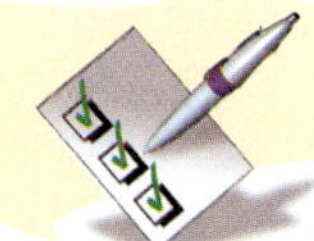

Everyone knows that, on average, smokers have shorter life expectancies than nonsmokers. Therefore, it's no surprise to find that smokers pay higher life insurance premiums. The consequences of alcohol abuse can be just as serious and may also disqualify you from paying standard rates. The Society of Actuaries estimates that excessive alcohol consumption can take an average of 10 to 15 years off your life, increasing your risk of heart disease, cancer, accidents, and suicide. The red flags for insurers are a history of drunk driving or blood tests indicating elevated liver enzymes.

Choosing an Insurer

Life insurers are among the largest financial institutions in the world, but they're not all the same. Insurers differ in the products they offer, their financial arrangements with the agents who sell their products, how they underwrite and price their policies, and their financial solvency. Furthermore, as mentioned in Chapter 5, recent financial deregulation has made it possible for financial institutions to offer products that were previously only available through specialized firms. Thus, you may even find that your bank sells some types of life insurance.

Financial Strength. In choosing an insurer, you should keep in mind that, unlike property and liability insurance contracts, which rarely extend beyond one year, life insurance is often a long-term arrangement and it involves potentially large sums of money. You don't want to take the chance that a company might not be around to pay your beneficiaries after you die or that it doesn't have sufficient funds to pay them the promised benefit. For these reasons, the purchase of life insurance is a financial decision that requires some homework. Luckily, state regulators are also extremely concerned about the safety and soundness of financial institutions, so many information resources are available, including rating agencies such as Best's, Standard & Poor's, Moody's, and Weiss Ratings. Exhibit 16-7 provides a list of U.S. life insurers that were rated AAA (the highest rating) based on their financial strength by Standard & Poor's in 2004. Of course, the fact that a company is rated AAA now doesn't mean it will always be highly rated. Furthermore, you may also want to consider life insurers rated AA or A, but you can still use this list as a starting point.

You can find ratings for insurance companies at www.insure.com, www.ambest.com (A.M. Best Company), www.moodys.com (Moody's Investors Services), www.standardpoors.com (Standard & Poor's Corporation), and www.weissratings.com (Weiss Ratings, Inc.).

Stock Versus Mutual. Another distinction among life insurers is their form of organization. A life insurer can be either a stock company or mutual company. As you know, a stock company is owned by the stockholders, who expect to make a profit on their equity investments. In

EXHIBIT 16-7

Individual Life Insurers Rated AAA by Standard & Poor's, 2004

Name of Company	U.S. Market Share Ranking
AIG Annuity Insurance Co.	390
AIG Life Insurance Co.	85
AIG Life Insurance Co. of PR	316
AIG SunAmerica Life Assurance Co.	169
American General Life & Accident Insurance Co.	46
American General Life Insurance Co.	71
American International Co. of New York	262
American Life Insurance Co. (DE)	23
CM Life Insurance Co.	42
Columbus Life Insurance Co.	133
First Sunamerica Life Insurance Co.	298
Integrity Life Insurance Co.	341
Jefferson-Pilot Financial Insurance Co.	21
Jefferson-Pilot LifeAmerica	236
Jefferson-Pilot Life Insurance Co.	61
Massachusetts Mutual Life Insurance Co.	10
MML Bay State Life Insurance Co.	113
National Integrity Life Insurance Co.	444
Northwestern Mutual Life Insurance Co.	1
SunAmerica Life Insurance Co.	254
Teachers Insurance Assoc. of America	63
TIAA-CREF Life Insurance Co.	281
United States Life Insurance Co. of the City of New York	70
USAA Life Insurance Co.	20
USAA Life Insurance Co. of New York	229
Variable Annuity Life Insurance Co.	719
Western & Southern Life Insurance Co.	125
Western-Southern Life Assurance Co.	94

Source: Summarized from data collected at www.insure.com

contrast, a mutual insurance company is owned by its policyholders. Policies issued by a mutual company are called **participating policies,** since they pay a dividend at the end of the year to compensate the policyholder-owners for their equity interest in the firm. Quoted premiums for participating policies are usually higher than those for nonparticipating policies issued by stock companies, but the difference is made up through the dividend. Since dividends aren't guaranteed, the actual net premium you end up paying each year will vary based on the financial performance of the mutual company. In some cases, stock companies may offer participating policies as well.

participating policies

Life insurance policies issued by mutual insurers that pay dividends to policyholders.

Choosing an Agent

Depending on the insurance companies you decide to get quotes from, you may need to select an agent. As discussed in Chapter 9, insurance products are sold through many distribution channels. You may be able to buy a policy directly from a company, through a captive agent, or through an independent agent. A captive agent is an agent who only sells insurance for a single company, whereas an independent agent can sell insurance for many different insurers. Although it's often a little less expensive to buy from companies that sell directly to you—on the Internet or through direct mail, for example—you can't expect to get much personalized service unless you work with an agent. In general, the more complex the product, the better it is to deal with a well-informed agent who can explain the intricacies of various policies. An independent agent will have a wider selection of products from which you can choose. In selecting an agent, you should consider his or her education, experience, reputation, responsiveness to your needs, and ethics.

Education. An agent who has appropriate education, professional credentials, and certifications is more likely to understand the products he or she is selling. Continuing education is also important, since that shows the agent makes an effort to keep current in his or her area of specialty.

Experience. In general, the more years an agent has been in the business, the more likely he or she will be able to understand and evaluate your needs.

Reputation. Ask your friends and colleagues for recommendations. Have they been satisfied with the professionalism and service provided by a particular life insurance agent? Are there certain local agents they'd recommend you avoid? You can also ask for recommendations from other professionals whom you trust—your lawyer, your financial planner, or your banker, for instance.

Responsiveness. A good agent should provide you with the information necessary to make appropriate decisions. This should include a realistic analysis of your insurance needs, informative answers to your questions, and clear explanations of product details. Keep in mind that you're embarking on what may be a long-term relationship, so you need to feel comfortable sharing your personal and financial information with an agent.

Ethical Behavior. Since insurance agents primarily work on commission, they may have incentives that aren't compatible with your best interests. Although most agents attempt to be professional and ethical in their sales practices, some may not. In addition to high-pressure sales tactics, practices that may be deemed unethical (and in some states, illegal) include: (1) using unrealistically high rates of interest in illustrating the expected premiums and cash value of a policy; (2) encouraging you to replace an existing cash-value policy with a new one; (3) promising that cash-value buildup will cause your premiums to "vanish" within a few years; and (4) suggesting that you should borrow from a whole life policy to buy a variable annuity product.

You should look for agents who will provide you with the service you need, such as coming to your home to get your signature on required documents.

Learning by Doing 16-2

1. Marian, age 45, estimates that she needs to buy $300,000 in life insurance to protect her dependent children from suffering adverse financial consequences in the event of her death. As a single parent, she's on a pretty tight budget. Will term or permanent insurance be more appropriate to meet her needs right now? Explain.
2. Richard, age 35, is married and childless. His wife also is fully employed. He would like to have $100,000 in life insurance coverage and is interested in a policy that will also give him some investment earnings. Should he consider term insurance?

Reading Your Policy

LEARNING objective

3 Understand the terms and conditions in life insurance policies.

Your life insurance policy is a legal contract and, as an informed consumer, you need to be aware of the terms to which you're agreeing. Although some policies are relatively straightforward and easy to understand, others involve more complex rights and obligations. Furthermore, you generally have no right to negotiate for different contract language that might be more favorable to you. Luckily, there are some protections for policyholders. State insurance laws generally require that insurance contracts be written in clear and unambiguous language that can be easily understood by consumers; in the event of a dispute over the meaning, any ambiguities in the contract will be interpreted in the light most favorable to you. Unlike homeowner's insurance, there are no standard forms in life insurance. However, if you understand the common features and clauses discussed below, you should be able to interpret your policy effectively.

Policy Declarations

All life insurance policies have a policy declarations page, which includes basic information about the policy such as the following:

- The name of the insurance company
- The name of the insured and policyholder
- The face amount of the policy
- The policy issue date
- The type of insurance and key features
- The period of time that the policyholder has to back out of the contract, often called the "free look period"
- The insurer's promise to pay

Although the placement of the information may differ from policy to policy, the items included are fairly consistent.

Key Provisions in a Life Insurance Policy

By state law, a life insurance policy may be required to include certain provisions, such as the grace period, the ability to borrow against any accumulated cash value, and a time limitation on the insurer's ability to get out of the contract. Many other provisions are optional. A policy may thus include one or more of the provisions discussed below.

Grace Period. Insurance premiums are due on a particular date, and if you don't pay a premium on time, your policy lapses. For example, if you have an annually renewable policy, the premium for the next year's coverage will normally be due on the anniversary of the date your policy originally went into effect. Insurers are required to give you a grace period for payment of the premium, usually one month for fixed-premium policies and two months for flexible-premium policies. Generally, insurers don't charge interest on overdue payments. If you haven't paid by the last day of the grace period, some insurers will still allow you to reinstate your policy, but they aren't required to do so. If your policy lapses, you'll have to provide additional proof of insurability, which could be a problem if your health status has changed since your first application; you may also be subject to higher rates.

Fact #4

Many people have good intentions about including life insurance in their financial plans, but they fail to stick to their decisions. The lapse rates on new policies are relatively high—about 15 percent of permanent life insurance policies are dropped in the first two years, compared to a 6 percent overall lapse rate.

Policy Loans. If you have a cash value policy, you're allowed to borrow from your accumulated funds without terminating the policy. Outstanding loans accrue interest, usually at an attractively low rate, and there's no set schedule for repayment. In the event of death, the death benefit will be reduced by any outstanding amounts due. Therefore, you should only take out a policy loan if you've carefully considered your other borrowing options and your family's need for protection.

incontestable clause

An insurance contract clause stating that the insurer cannot contest a claim for misrepresentation after a policy has been in force for a specified period of time.

Incontestable Clause. Under general contract law, a contract is voidable by one of the parties if that party entered into it as a result of misrepresentations made by the other party. Suppose you have a serious medical condition but, when asked about your medical history, you fail to disclose this information on your life insurance application. If the policy is issued and you subsequently die, the insurer has the right to refuse to pay the benefit to your survivors on the grounds that the policy was void due to your misrepresentation. Since this has the effect of leaving your beneficiaries without protection, states have generally limited insurers' right to contest the claim, or refuse payment, on these grounds to a specific period of time from the policy's issue date, often one or two years. The rationale for this **incontestable clause** is that, without such a limitation, insurers might be tempted to do very limited underwriting investigations, collect premiums for years, and then refuse to pay when the policyholder dies. By making the policy incontestable after a certain amount of time has passed, insurers are given incentives for more careful up-front underwriting.

Policyholder Dividends. As mentioned previously, policies issued by mutual companies are participating policies, which means that the policyholders are entitled to dividend distributions, much like stockholder dividends. The IRS treats these dividends as a return of premium, so they aren't taxable to the policyholder. Participating policies must include a clause that describes how and when dividends will be paid—usually on the policy anniversary and conditional on the policyholder's timely payment of premiums. These dividends are not guaranteed up front but depend on the insurer's financial performance.

Although it's common to apply the dividend to reduce future premiums, policyholders may be given several options for receipt of dividends. In some cases, you can opt to take the dividend as cash, put it in an interest-bearing account, or use it to purchase small amounts of additional paid-up insurance or one-year term insurance.

Entire Contract Clause. Most policies include an entire contract clause which explicitly states that the written contract is the entire agreement between the insurer and the insured. This rule applies whether or not your policy explicitly states it, however, and is designed to prevent the insurer from imposing its own interpretation or changing the agreement in some way without your knowledge after the contract has been issued.

Nonforfeiture. As we've seen, when you buy permanent insurance with level premiums, the premiums in the early years are greater than the mortality expense for the insurer, and the extra amount is used to build up a cash reserve that will cover the greater mortality expenses in the later years. Nonforfeiture laws require that, if your contract lapses before maturity but after some minimum amount of time, such as three years, the insurer must refund a fair amount of the cash reserve. You have the option of receiving it (1) in cash; (2) as a paid-up policy in whatever amount the cash value is sufficient to purchase; (3) as a term life policy with the same face value as the lapsed policy but for a period the cash value is sufficient to purchase, given your current age; or (4) as an annuity for retirement income. Many people find the latter alternative useful in financial planning, since they can purchase appropriate protection during their child-rearing years and later convert the accumulated cash value to a cash flow stream to be received in retirement.

Reinstatement. In some cases, you may be entitled under the terms of your policy to reinstate a policy that has lapsed. For example, suppose you purchased a whole life policy in 1995, and by January 2005, it had a cash value of $20,000. You're laid off from work and can't afford to make the required premium payment for 2005. Although you might decide to surrender the policy at that time for its cash value, under some circumstances it might be preferable to reinstate the policy once your financial situation allows it. If your policy permits reinstatement, you'll normally have to provide proof of insurability (commonly, a blood test and physical examination) and pay any missed premiums with interest.

Beneficiaries. You'll be required to designate a primary beneficiary for your life insurance policy—the person, persons, estate, or business entity to receive the proceeds of the policy upon your death. You normally should also name a contingent beneficiary in case the primary beneficiary doesn't outlive you. In naming your beneficiaries, you should be as specific as possible in order to avoid problems in identifying the recipients at a later date. It's also a good idea to review your policies regularly to ensure that you always have at least one living beneficiary and that you've included everyone you intended. For example, if your policy names "my sons James and Robert," but you now have a third child, Jessica, your sons will be entitled to 50 percent each and Jessica will be entitled to nothing upon your death.

Suicide Clause. If the insured person commits suicide, his or her beneficiaries may still be entitled to payment under the policy. This will depend on the terms of the *suicide clause*, which allows the insurer to deny coverage if the insured commits suicide and the policy has been in force less than a specified period of time, usually two years. In a particularly sad case several years ago, a businessman, who was in significant debt and could see no other solution to his problems, purchased a large amount of insurance on his life, naming his wife as beneficiary. The policy included a one-year suicide clause, so he waited until the one-year anniversary and shot himself in his office. Unfortunately, he was mistaken about the effective date of the policy (which was one day after he made his application) and committed suicide one day too early.

waiver of premium

An insurance option that allows the insured to waive premium payments under certain conditions, such as permanent disability.

accelerated benefits

An option under which a terminally ill policyholder can receive a portion of his or her life insurance proceeds before death.

accidental death benefit

A life insurance contract provision by which the benefit is doubled for accidental death.

Waiver of Premium. Many insurers offer a relatively expensive option called **waiver of premium**. A policyholder who has purchased this option is allowed under some limited circumstances, usually permanent disability, to keep the policy in force without further payment of premium.

Accelerated (or Living) Benefits. Many life insurance policies now offer an **accelerated benefits** option under which terminally ill policyholders can receive a portion of their life insurance proceeds before their death. More than half the states have adopted a model regulation governing this type of benefit. The regulation lists the conditions that will trigger the benefit, including AIDS, acute heart disease, permanent brain damage from stroke, and kidney failure. This option may be an automatic feature of a policy, or it may require an additional premium. Although you might envision using your life insurance under these circumstances for the trip to Europe you never got to take while you were healthy, in most cases the insurance proceeds are used to help pay for medical treatments and hospice care. Another way to access the value of your life insurance in advance of your death, if allowed in your state, is to sell the policy to someone else, as described in the *News You Can Use* box "The Ethics of Viatical Settlements."

Accidental Death Benefit. Your life insurance policy may include a rider or amendment that doubles the face value payable under the policy if your death is caused by an accident instead of natural causes. For this reason, the **accidental death benefit** is sometimes referred to as the "double indemnity" clause. Since the percentage of deaths that occur from accidents is fairly small, this is an inexpensive benefit to provide. However, individuals tend to overestimate the probability of accidental death for reasons discussed in the *Money Psychology* box "What's the Risk of an Airplane Crash?" and thus tend to overestimate the value of this benefit.

Guaranteed Purchase Option. Although you may not need much life insurance right now, you'll probably want to increase your coverage over time as your family circumstances change. You can always simply buy additional policies in the future to meet your growing needs, but you run the risk that you may become uninsurable in the future. Diagnosis with a serious illness or development of a disability might make it impossible to find insurance or might make the insurance prohibitively expensive. A guaranteed purchase option gives you the right to pur-

NEWS you can use

The Ethics of Viatical Settlements

Did you know that you could actually buy an interest in someone else's life insurance policy? Under a viatical settlement agreement, an investor purchases the policy from its owner and becomes the beneficiary of the policy. The original owner is usually paid from 50 to 80 percent of the death benefit, depending on life expectancy and other factors (cash value, quality of the insurer, and premiums necessary to keep the policy in force) and gives up all rights to the policy. The new owner pays the premiums and receives the death benefit when the original owner dies. Viatical investors commonly pool their funds and purchase a large number of policies, thereby spreading their risk. Whereas insurers make more money on life policies if their insureds *stay alive*, a viatical investor only makes money *when people die*. For this reason, some policymakers have argued that we shouldn't allow this type of financial arrangement at all.

"A viatical investor makes money when people die."

Why would an insured person want to sell his or her policy to you? About 90 percent of viatical settlements cover victims of AIDS—people who have relatively short life expectancies and face large uninsured medical or hospice expenses. In some cases, a person might want to pay for an experimental life-extending treatment that isn't covered by insurance.

Money Psychology

What's the Risk of an Airplane Crash?

Studies show that many people misestimate their risk exposures. People often don't recognize that a risk exists until it's pointed out to them. Conversely, people may perceive some risks to be much greater than they are. This is particularly true for events that are fairly rare but receive extensive media coverage when they do occur. Insurers often take advantage of this psychological bias by selling insurance policies or adding contract features that cover risks involving very small expected losses. For example, at many airports, kiosks offer traveler's life insurance to people about to take airplane trips. This insurance costs only a few dollars and will pay your beneficiaries in the event that you're killed in a plane crash. Because people overestimate the risk of airplane fatalities (which is actually a fraction of the risk of being in an auto accident), this insurance is very popular—and also very profitable for insurance companies. Traveler's insurance is also a common "freebie" advertised by credit card companies.

chase additional amounts of insurance in the future without proof of insurability and without "restarting the clock" on the suicide and incontestable clauses. (Many group life insurance plans offered by employers also include this feature, allowing you to increase your insurance by from $10,000 to $25,000 per year as long as you have continuous coverage.)

Settlement Options. Settlement options are choices regarding how the beneficiaries are to receive the proceeds of the policy. You can make this choice, or you can leave it to the beneficiaries to decide after your death. Suppose you have a term life insurance policy with a face amount of $200,000 with your wife as the sole beneficiary. Your wife's choices for receipt of the funds after your death may include some or all of the following:

- *Lump sum of $200,000.* Your wife can receive the entire benefit as a lump sum. She can invest this money or purchase an annuity with it (without being limited to choices offered by your insurer). If she could earn 5 percent after taxes on the lump sum, she could spend $10,000 per year without touching the principal.
- *Periodic interest only.* Your wife can leave the money with the insurer, who will pay her the interest on the accumulated value. When she dies, the funds will become part of her estate.
- *Income for a period of time.* If your wife needs more money than interest alone can provide, she can receive the funds from your insurer as a series of payments for a period of time. The payments can be calculated as an annuity that will completely deplete the principal over a period of time. This will produce higher payments than the interest-only option because the payments will likely include principal. It is possible, however, that your wife will outlive the payment stream.
- *Income of a specific amount.* Your wife can elect to receive a fixed amount per year until the principal and interest are exhausted.
- *Income for life.* If your wife wants to be sure she doesn't outlive her income stream, she can elect to receive a life annuity. The amount of income payable will depend on her life expectancy, but the risk of outliving her assets will be borne by the insurer.

Learning by Doing 16-3

1. All else equal, which of the following clauses or terms, if included in your policy, would be likely to increase the cost of coverage compared with a policy that doesn't include it?
   a. Convertibility
   b. Waiver of premium
   c. Guaranteed renewability

Planning for Long-Term Care Costs

LEARNING objective

4 Recognize the costs associated with long-term care.

So far in this chapter, we've focused on planning for the costs that would be incurred by your family in the event of your death. Another related risk that many people fail to plan for is the risk of being incapacitated in old age. The aging of the population in the United States has given rise to an increase in the number of people who require nursing home care. This risk is not limited to the elderly, but it's clearly age-related. Although only 4 percent of people aged 65 and older reside in a nursing home at any given point in time, 43 percent of those who reach 65 (33% of men and 52% of women) will eventually require institutionalization. This was not always the case. In earlier generations, the elderly and infirm often relied on home care provided within an extended family. It's still true that the elderly are more likely to be cared for by a family member, usually female, but the demand for alternative caregiving sources is increasing. This is primarily the result of a dramatic change in the structure of households—more single parents, more working women, fewer children, and families more geographically dispersed.

Fact #5

Although about half of all women and a third of all men will eventually require nursing home care, their care will initially be provided by family. Whereas about 9 million Americans are currently in long-term care, the National Alliance for Caregiving estimates that about 35 million individuals in the United States (17% of the adult population) are providing unpaid care to a person age 50 or older (with the average age being 75). About 61 percent of caregivers are women. The typical caregiver is a 46-year-old, college-educated woman who is providing at least 20 hours of care per week to her mother.

The risk of incapacity, like the risk of death, is difficult to talk about and deal with. The specter of being unable to take care of oneself is not pleasant and, as with other financial decisions we'd rather avoid, many people ignore this component of their plan. A survey by the National Council on Aging shows that 67 percent of Americans believe that the cost of long-term care is the greatest threat to their standard of living, but only 35 percent have done any planning for it. As you think about planning for incapacity, it's important to remember that you're not really planning for yourself but for those who will be burdened in the event that you're someday incapacitated. Having a plan in place will not help your family deal with the personal cost of your incapacity, but it will at least lessen the financial cost.

How Much Will Long-Term Care Cost?

Most people first confront nursing home expenses when an older relative—perhaps a parent or a grandparent—can no longer live alone. Often, the first step is to have them move in with another family member. Perhaps the family will need to hire a medical professional to provide home health and personal care at a cost of $5,000 to $15,000 per year. Eventually, escalating medical needs or mental incapacity will force the family to consider a nursing home facility. The shock of finding out what these facilities cost can be tremendous. The average ranges from $50,000 to $60,000 per year; however, costs vary widely among regions. In Louisiana, for example, the average annual cost of a nursing home is $35,900 per year, whereas Alaskan residents pay an average of $166,700, according to the 2003 survey results reported in Exhibit 16-8. Other factors that affect costs include the level of medical care required (intensive nursing care is obviously more expensive than limited assistance) and how long the person will be in the facility (the average stay is 2.3 years).

long-term care

Medical and personal care for persons with an extended illness or disability that is not provided in a hospital.

Long-term care (**LTC**) is a term that is broadly used to describe all supportive medical, personal, and social services needed by people who are unable to meet their basic living needs for an extended period of time because of accident, illness, or frailty. LTC involves receiving the assistance of another person to perform the essential activities of daily living (dressing, bathing, eating, and household chores) and may be performed at home (by paid caregivers, such as home health aides, or by informal unpaid caregivers, such as family members or friends) or in a nursing home.

The length of time that a person requires long-term care obviously depends on the person's health and age at the time of illness or incapacity. On average, we can expect to live into our 70s or 80s, but many people live much longer. Today, many nursing home residents are victims of Alzheimer's disease, a brain disorder that results in significant mental incapacity. A patient who enters a nursing facility at age 70 with Alzheimer's, but who is otherwise in good health, might survive for another 20 years, at a cost of more than $1,000,000. Currently, about $100 billion per year is spent on nursing home care and another $30 billion on home health care, the total representing more than one-tenth of all health-care costs in the United States.

EXHIBIT 16-8

The Average Annual Cost of Nursing Home Care by State, 2003

State	Average Cost	State	Average Cost	State	Average Cost
Alabama	$46,600	Kentucky	$51,100	North Dakota	$71,300
Alaska	166,700	Louisiana	35,900	Ohio	55,900
Arizona	58,600	Maine	72,800	Oklahoma	40,700
Arkansas	39,300	Maryland	64,300	Oregon	52,600
California	59,900	Massachusetts	87,500	Pennsylvania	66,100
Colorado	52,500	Michigan	62,000	Rhode Island	69,300
Connecticut	97,400	Minnesota	56,700	South Carolina	46,800
Delaware	59,100	Mississippi	43,800	South Dakota	43,400
D.C.	82,800	Missouri	42,100	Tennessee	45,800
Florida	60,400	Montana	46,400	Texas	43,200
Georgia	43,200	Nebraska	49,400	Utah	47,900
Hawaii	84,700	Nevada	55,100	Vermont	68,200
Idaho	54,000	New Hampshire	72,500	Virginia	50,200
Illinois	54,100	New Jersey	80,100	Washington	62,700
Indiana	54,700	New Mexico	53,200	West Virginia	50,900
Iowa	42,000	New York	92,100	Wisconsin	56,200
Kansas	$41,100	North Carolina	$50,300	Wyoming	$51,400

Source: Reprinted from 2003 "GE Financial Nursing Home Cost of Care Survey" commissioned by GE Financial Long Term Care Division and performed by Evans Research Associates. Used by permission of Genworth Financial (formerly GE Financial).

Selecting a Nursing Home Facility

Many families find themselves in the unfortunate position of having to make the decision to put a relative in a nursing home. Perhaps, for example, your mother has been living with your family for a few years, but she's become a danger to herself or others. Or perhaps there are medication issues that you can't deal with at home. To add to the stress level, your parent may be openly resistant to moving to a long-term care facility. And don't be surprised if you find yourself someday having to make difficult decisions related to aging parents at the same time you're dealing with the complexities of getting your children through their teen years.

Fortunately, many sources of information are available to help you assess the quality, price, and appropriateness of various facilities. Based on your physician's recommendation, you'll need to first determine what level of care will be required. Many facilities offer graduated care options that will allow you to opt for lower levels of care (at lower prices, but still expensive) at first and gradually increase the level of care (and the annual price) as the need arises. Once you've narrowed your selection based on availability, services provided, location, and quality, you should visit each of the remaining facilities in person.

The website for Medicare and Medicaid Services, www.medicare.gov, includes data on about 17,000 Medicare-certified nursing homes. At the home page, click on "Nursing Home Compare" to access information on quality and staffing.

Sources of Funds for Long-Term Care

How can the average family afford the expected future costs of long-term care? Instead of waiting for the need to arise, good financial planning requires that you consider this risk and put in place a plan for how your family will finance the cost. Some options to consider include household and community resources, Medicare, Medicaid, and long-term care insurance.

Household Resources. If you're wealthy, you may be able to fund all your long-term care needs from your household resources. One of the problems associated with this strategy is that the nursing home expenses of the "first to care" in a married couple may exhaust household resources, leaving the survivor with inadequate wealth to finance retirement. Some experts have suggested that the large percentage of elderly widows living at or below the poverty level is at least partially attributable to this problem.

Home health care is a less expensive alternative to nursing home care, but most health insurance policies do not provide coverage for these services.

Community Resources. Since the most expensive long-term care is institutional care, it makes sense to try to maximize home health-care options before resorting to nursing home care. Community resources can help an infirm person—particularly one who needs a relatively low level of care—to remain at home or in a relative's home for a longer time. Services that may be available in your community include Meals on Wheels, which delivers regular meals to elderly people; household chore services; visitation programs; and caregiver respite services. For more information about these services, you can call the Eldercare Locator at 1-800-677-1116 to locate your local Office on Aging. Many religious institutions offer services for elderly members as well.

Resource information for home health care options is available at www.aoa.dhhs.gov (Administration on Aging) and www.nlm.nhh.gov/medlineplus/homecareservices (National Library of Medicine and National Institute of Health).

Medicare. If you're over 65, Medicare Part A will provide benefits for skilled nursing care following a hospital stay of at least three days. The nursing home coverage is limited to 100 days. Medicare will also cover the full cost of home visits by nurses and related medical expenses. No coverage is available for assistance in the activities of daily living, however.

Medicaid. People who are indigent or have exhausted all or most of their financial assets may be eligible for Medicaid coverage of nursing home expenses. As described in Chapter 10, Medicaid is a federally authorized and state-administered health insurance program for the poor. In the past, examples of Medicaid fraud arose in which relatively wealthy individuals attempted to qualify for Medicaid coverage of nursing home care by transferring all their assets to their children. Today, new rules make this unethical practice more difficult and impose sanctions on those who attempt it.

Your Life Insurance Policy. Most long-term care insurance is purchased in the form of stand-alone policies, which we'll consider in the next section of this chapter. However, many insurers are now offering acceleration and extension riders on life and disability income policies to provide benefits for long-term care. We previously discussed acceleration clauses as a way for people who are seriously ill to access the cash value of their life insurance policies before they die. This type of provision may also allow a policyholder to take an advance on his or her life insurance to pay for long-term care. The limit on the advance is the amount of the death benefit. An extension benefit increases the limit beyond the amount of the death benefit. In either case, though, the amount that can be withdrawn each month may be insufficient to cover actual costs.

Other Insurance Options. In addition to the methods just discussed, you should at least consider the purchase of long-term care insurance. As the U.S. population has aged, more and more alternatives have become available.

Long-Term Care Insurance

LEARNING objective

5 Identify and evaluate long-term care insurance alternatives.

long-term care insurance

An insurance policy designed to pay health-care expenses associated with incapacity, such as nursing home costs.

Perhaps the hottest new financial product, **long-term care (LTC) insurance** is designed to pay health care expenses associated with incapacity. Because there are many possible terms and conditions, and because premiums—even for the same level of coverage—can vary dramatically across insurers and in different states, it pays to shop around and carefully evaluate what each policy covers. Obviously, the LTC policies that provide the greatest amount of coverage will cost more. Your age and health will also affect your premium costs and may even prevent you from being able to find coverage. As with other types of insurance, you'll need to consider the financial soundness of the company as well. In this section, we identify when you should buy LTC insurance and what features you should consider in your policy selection.

When Is the Best Time to Buy Long-Term Care Insurance?

Unfortunately, there's no magic answer to the question of when to buy LTC insurance. As with other types of long-term insurance policies, premiums may be fixed for a period of years. This implies that you'll pay a smaller annual amount if you buy the policy at a younger age (since the insurer figures you'll be paying the premium for years to come). The quoted premiums can rise dramatically with age. But since you'll pay premiums until you go into long-term care, which may be never, your lifetime cost for the insurance may end up being much higher if you purchase the insurance at too early an age. For example, a healthy 50-year-old male might be able to get a policy that pays $100 per day for nursing home care at a cost of around $1,000 per year, whereas that same policy will cost $2,000 per year by the time he is 60. If he waits until age 60, though, he'll have saved about $10,000 in premium costs. The odds of a man requiring nursing home care between the ages of 50 and 60 are fairly low, particularly if he's married and can therefore rely on home caregiving as a first resort. Although it may seem that he should delay the purchase of LTC as long as possible, the risk he runs is that he'll be incapacitated in the meantime and thus be unable to obtain coverage when he reaches age 60.

Some professionals have argued that, because LTC insurance is a product that is relatively new, uncertainty about future claims costs and a low level of competition have resulted in mispricing. However, there is some disagreement as to whether the policies have been too cheap or too expensive. Insurers generally raised premium rates in 2003, and some even increased premium rates for policyholders who thought they had bought fixed premium policies (but hadn't read the fine print). As more insurers enter the market and actuaries get more comfortable with estimating long-term care costs, some experts believe that prices will fall. This rationale would argue in favor of putting off the purchase of LTC insurance for a few more years, if you're still under the age of 60 and healthy. However, the American Health Care Association—a federation of 50 state health organizations representing assisted living facilities, nursing facilities, long-term care facilities, and other care providers—recommend that you buy the insurance between ages 50 and 55 to obtain the optimal price.

In rare circumstances, you might want to consider buying LTC at an earlier age. For example, if your employer offers an attractively priced group plan, you might want to take advantage of the opportunity to buy the insurance with pretax dollars. Under the provisions of the Health Insurance Portability and Accountability Act, you may also be able to get a tax deduction for premiums you pay for individual long-term care insurance, as discussed in the *Ask the Expert* box, "Tax Considerations in Long-Term Care."

Features to Look for in Long-Term Care Insurance

If you decide to buy long-term care insurance, you'll want to consider the following features.

Benefit Amount. Unlike the typical indemnity type of health insurance policy, which reimburses you for specific expenses, LTC insurance generally will pay you a set amount of money per day of qualified care. This may have little to do with the actual cost of the care that you receive. You should select a benefit amount that corresponds to the average cost of care in the area where you live, less an amount that you can afford to pay out of pocket.

Inflation Protection. Since the cost of care is likely to increase over time, your policy should include an inflation protection provision that increases the daily benefit each year. This can be an expensive addition to the policy but is very important if you buy the insurance at a young age. Remem-

ask the expert — Tax Considerations in Long-Term Care

Robert N. Bua
Author, The Inside Guide to America's Nursing Homes (Warner Book, Inc, 1998)

Both old and new laws offer deductions and incentives related to nursing home care and services. With these laws, Congress has attempted to encourage Americans to rely on themselves rather than Medicare and Medicaid to (1) pay for nursing home services and/or (2) buy long-term care insurance to pay for or help pay for such services. Author Robert Bua's book identifies and discusses the following tax incentives and provisions.

Deductions for Health-Care Costs
The Health Insurance Portability and Accountability Act of 1996 (HIPAA) states that the cost of qualified long-term care services, including home care services, can be deducted as a medical expense. These costs are deductible to the extent that, when combined with the taxpayer's medical expenses, they exceed 7.5 percent of adjusted gross income.

Deductions for Long-Term Care Insurance Premiums
HIPAA also provides that premiums paid for a LTC insurance policy can be deducted, with certain limitations, as a medical expense. In addition, benefits received from long-term care insurance policies are not treated as taxable income up to a certain limit.

Penalty-Free 401(k) Withdrawals to Pay for LTC Insurance
Americans can withdraw money from a 401(k) plan or IRA before they reach age $59\frac{1}{2}$ without incurring the usual 10 percent penalty for early withdrawal if the funds are used to purchase long-term care coverage. They will, however, have to pay any income taxes owed. Funds can also be used to pay for other medical expenses and prescription drug costs.

Dependency Exemption
For tax purposes, you may be able to claim a dependency exemption for an elderly parent cared for in your home.

ber that $100 will not buy as much in the future as it does today. Be aware, though, that having a benefit that increases with inflation doesn't necessarily mean the policy will keep up with LTC costs. Like other medical costs, the costs of nursing home care have been increasing at an alarming rate. Between June 2002 and June 2003, when the CPI rose by 2.1 percent, the average cost of in-home care rose 3 percent and the average cost of a private room in a nursing home rose 8 percent.

Benefit Period. You can buy LTC insurance that will provide lifetime benefits, or you can choose a shorter period of coverage. Recognizing that the average nursing home stay is less than three years and 75 percent of admissions are for less than one year, you might consider purchasing a policy that has a three-year benefit period. The risk you run is that you might require care for a much longer period, but the cost of the shorter-term policy can be as much as 30 percent less than that for a lifetime benefit policy.

To learn more about LTC insurance and the options that are available to you, go to www.acli.com, the website of the American Council of Life Insurers. Click on "Consumers," then "Long-Term Care" to find information on this topic as well as their brochure "What Long-Term Care Insurance Can Do for You."

Waiting Period. Like disability insurance, LTC insurance typically includes a waiting period of 30, 60, or 100 days. The waiting period is the number of days you'll need to receive (and pay for) care before the insurance begins to pay for it. You can significantly reduce your premium if you take a longer waiting period. Because some coverage is available from Medicare for the first 100 days, this is a popular waiting period selection.

Services Covered. You should select a policy that will cover the services which you expect to need. You can select a policy that covers nursing home care only or one that also pays for home health care providers such as in-home therapists and nurses. Some policies provide benefits for in-home care provided by family members as well, which can be important if providing care results in lost income to the caregiver.

Talking with Your Parents about Long-Term Care Insurance

Many students of personal financial planning are far too young to be thinking about buying LTC insurance. The importance of this topic for you right now is to alert you to issues you'll be facing with your parents in the coming years. If you're currently 20 to 30 years old and your parents are 40 to 60 years old, it's not too early to start talking with them about their plans concerning long-term care. You might even consider broaching the subject by mentioning what you've learned in this course. Although most people find it difficult to talk about these issues, they generally feel better once they've done so. It's even possible that your parents have wanted to talk with you about their plans but didn't know how to start the dialogue. In addition to asking your parents about their LTC plans, you might also expand the conversation to include questions about their plans for retirement, life insurance, and estate planning (covered in Chapter 17).

Learning by Doing 16-4

1. Under what circumstances might it be advisable to buy long-term care insurance for your parents, spending money out of your own pocket?
2. If you have limited wealth and no dependents, would it ever make sense to buy long-term care insurance for yourself?
3. Why do you think women are more likely to eventually require nursing home care?

Summary

1 Assess your life insurance needs. Adequate life insurance protection is an important component of most financial plans, since it provides a relatively inexpensive way of protecting your loved ones from the financial consequences of your death. Although it's simple to apply an income multiple to determine how much you need, it's better to assess your life insurance needs by estimating the financial costs that will actually arise upon your death, balanced against existing household resources. The financial needs method takes into consideration the costs of death; any lump sums needed to fund future expenses such as dependent education costs, retirement funds, and debt repayment; and the future cost of household maintenance.

2 Evaluate insurers and policy types to determine which will best meet your needs. The two major categories of policies are term life insurance and permanent life insurance. Term policies provide death protection only and are usually short-term. The premiums usually increase with the policyholder's age. Permanent insurance is a long-term contract that includes an investment component. Excess premium dollars in the early years are invested on the policyholder's behalf to help cover the increased cost of death protection in the later years. There are many variations on both of these types of policies. In selecting a life insurer, you should pay careful attention to financial strength. If you decide to buy through an agent, you should consider educational credentials, experience, reputation, and responsiveness to your needs, and you should avoid agents who engage in unethical sales practices.

3 **Understand the terms and conditions in life insurance policies.** An insurance policy includes many important terms and clauses that you should understand. These include provisions for payment of premiums, receipt of benefits, policy loans, designation of beneficiaries, and accidental death, among others.

4 **Recognize the costs associated with long-term care.** Many people eventually require nursing home care or home health care in old age, and these services can be very expensive. You should therefore have a plan for how these costs will be paid for, whether out of existing household resources, public programs, or long-term care insurance.

5 **Identify and evaluate long-term care insurance alternatives.** Long-term care insurance is a product that reimburses the insured for qualified health expenses, usually at a daily rate, associated with incapacity. You should understand the key contract features of these policies and have a plan for when to purchase such insurance.

Key Terms

accelerated benefits (540)
accidental death benefit (540)
cash value (532)
convertible (532)
current assumption whole life insurance (534)
decreasing term life insurance (532)
face value (531)
financial needs method (526)
guaranteed renewability (532)
income-multiple method (526)
incontestable clause (538)
limited payment life insurance (532)
long-term care (542)
long-term care insurance (544)
ordinary life insurance (532)
participating policies (536)
permanent life insurance (532)
single-premium whole life insurance (533)
term life insurance (531)
universal life insurance (534)
variable life insurance (534)
variable-universal life insurance (534)
waiver of premium (540)
whole life insurance (532)

Concept Review Questions

1. How does life insurance differ from property insurance discussed in Chapter 9 in each of the following areas:
   a. Predictability of loss
   b. Term of contract
   c. Factors that will result in an increase in premium
2. Explain why life insurance is an important component of financial planning.
3. Does everyone need life insurance coverage? Why or why not?
4. What categories of financial costs might be incurred by a family with dependent children upon the death of the primary earner?
5. What are the two approaches to estimating how much life insurance is needed? Is one preferable to the other? Explain.
6. How do life insurers assess your probability of dying within the policy period? Explain why this estimate is likely to be very accurate on average for a large pool of policyholders.
7. Explain how each of the following factors might affect the amount of life insurance you need:
   a. The number of children you have
   b. The age of your children
   c. Your age and life expectancy
   d. Your spouse's earning capacity
   e. Your financial wealth
   f. Your outstanding debt
   g. Your health
8. How can life insurance be used to help your survivors accomplish household financial goals in the event of your death? For what types of goals would this be best suited?
9. If you are a stay-at-home parent and don't contribute any earnings to the household budget, why might you still need to have some amount of life insurance?
10. How can you assess the financial strength of life insurers?
11. What factors are important in choosing a life insurance agent?
12. How are life insurance agents compensated, and what impact does this have on policy premiums?
13. Give three examples of life insurance sales practices that are unethical.
14. What are the two main categories of life insurance? Explain their primary differences.
15. Why are premiums for permanent insurance so much more expensive per dollar of coverage than premiums for term life insurance?
16. Define the following terms:
    a. Guaranteed renewability
    b. Convertibility
    c. Grace period
    d. Incontestable clause
    e. Participating
    f. Nonforfeiture
    g. Waiver of premium
    h. Accelerated benefits
17. What is decreasing term insurance, and why might you want to purchase this type of policy?
18. What are the three main types of permanent insurance? Explain their similarities and differences.
19. In what ways is the cash value of permanent life insurance similar to a savings plan? In what ways is it different?
20. What are the common criticisms of whole life insurance, and how does universal life insurance address these issues?
21. Why did variable life insurance become so popular in the 1990s?
22. Compare the purchase of permanent insurance to a "buy term and invest the difference" strategy based on risk, tax consequences, and flexibility.
23. What are the possible choices given to beneficiaries for receipt of the proceeds of a life insurance policy?
24. What is long-term care, and why do so many people fail to plan adequately for this cost?
25. If you or a member of your family requires in-home health care or nursing home care, what are your options for funding this expense?
26. What is long-term care insurance? Is it a product that everyone should buy? Why or why not?
27. Why is it probably not cost-effective to buy long-term care insurance at an early age?
28. What features are important to consider in evaluating alternative long-term care insurance products?

Application Problems

1. ***Life Expectancy.*** John (age 60) plans to attend his high school reunion soon. His class size was 200 (50% men and 50% women). Use Exhibit 16-1 to answer the following questions.
   a. How many of his high school classmates should he expect to still be alive for the reunion.
   b. Ten years from now, how many will still be alive?
   c. How many will die over the next 20 years?
2. ***Life Expectancy.*** Cathy (age 50) is working on her financial plan. Mary, her mother, is age 80. Use Exhibit 16-1 to answer the following questions.
   a. How old will Cathy be when she dies if she has an average life expectancy?
   b. How many more years does Mary expect to live if she has an average life expectancy?
   c. Which of them, at present, is expected to live to the oldest age? Does this surprise you?
3. ***Life Insurance Needs Analysis.*** Your current income is $50,000 and your wife's income is $35,000. If your financial planner recommends an income multiplier of 4, how much life insurance should you each have?
4. ***Life Insurance Needs Analysis.*** Kate is a single parent and earns $40,000 per year. Household expenses are $28,000 per year. If she were to die, she estimates that the costs of her death would total $10,000. She has not participated in Social Security long enough to be fully insured. She would also want her life insurance to provide an education fund for her twin children who are age 10 and a lump sum to provide for their continued care, which she estimates will cost $15,000 per year until they are 18.
   a. Would an income multiple approach result in Kate's purchase of sufficient life insurance? Why or why not?
   b. Using a financial needs approach, how much life insurance would you recommend she buy?
   c. If Kate was fully insured under Social Security and her children would be eligible for total annual benefits of $10,000, how much difference would this make in her life insurance needs?
5. ***Life Insurance Policy Terms.*** For each of the following, indicate whether this variation on the standard term life policy will result in an initial premium that is higher or lower, or the same:
   a. Decreasing term
   b. Guaranteed renewability
   c. Increasing term
   d. Convertibility
6. ***Life Insurance Policy Terms.*** For each of the following, indicate whether this variation on ordinary life policy will result in an initial premium that is higher or lower, or the same:
   a. Limited payment
   b. Variable life in which you select a stock investment account for the investment component
   c. Increasing premium over time
   d. Decreasing face value over time
7. ***Comparing Life Insurance.*** You have been quoted a premium of $120 per year for $100,000 in term life insurance, with a premium that is fixed for five years, and $1,120 per year for a permanent policy with an equivalent face value.
   a. If you bought the term insurance and invested the difference, how much would you have to invest? Would this amount stay constant over time? Explain.
   b. If you invested the difference between the two premium amounts at the beginning of every year for the next five years, and earned 6 percent after taxes, how much would you accumulate after five years?
   c. In order to decide whether it would be better for you to buy term and invest the difference, what else would you need to know about the term policy?
8. ***Nursing Home Costs.*** Use Exhibit 16-8 to answer the following questions:
   a. Are you surprised to see such a wide difference in nursing home costs between the states? What are some possible explanations for these differences?
   b. Your father lives in Georgia. You expect that he will need to move to a nursing home in five years. How much will one year cost if Georgia's nursing home care costs grow at 6 percent per year?
   c. Your mother-in-law lives in Colorado. You expect that she will need to move to a nursing home in three years. How much will it cost if Colorado's nursing home care costs grow at 6 percent per year?
9. ***Nursing Home Costs.*** Your grandmother needs to go into a nursing home. She currently lives in Illinois and you live in Arizona. You're deciding whether it will be worthwhile financially to move her out to Arizona. A facility in Illinois will cost you $55,000 per year and in Arizona it will cost $60,000 per year. You estimate it will cost you $7,000 to make the move and $3,000 per year to travel back and forth to visit each year.
   a. What is the annual difference in cost between these two strategies the first year?
   b. If you estimate she'll stay in the facility for five years and the cost difference between the two facilities will stay constant over time, which is the better choice? What if she only stays in the facility for three years?
10. ***Costs of Household Maintenance.*** Your after-tax income is $50,000. Your spouse is also employed full-time. Your family's annual expenses are $60,000. Your average indexed earnings for Social Security computations are $45,000. You are 40 years old. If you died today, what would be the cost of household maintenance under the following circumstances?
    a. Family expenses drop by 20 percent.
    b. Family expenses drop by 25 percent.

Using Web Resources for Financial Planning

1. ***How Much Life Insurance Do You Need?*** Most financial websites include calculators that will help you assess your life insurance needs. At the website for insurance giant Northwestern Mutual, *www.northwesternmutual.com*, click on "Life Insurance" and use the calculator provided for this purpose. Use the calculator to estimate your life insurance needs. Does this calculator use an income multiple approach or a needs approach? Then go to the Motley Fool website at *www.fool.com* and click on "Personal Finance," next "Life," then "How Much?" to see another insurance needs calculator. Compare the answers you arrived at with the two calculators.

2. ***Compare Policies Using a Cost Index.*** The National Association of Insurance Commissioners has approved two standardized methods for comparing the costs of different life insurance policies. Find out how these are calculated and how to access the values for particular policies by going to the USAA Educational Foundation's website at *www.usaaedfoundation.org* and clicking on "Insurance" and then "Comparing Life Insurance Policies."
3. ***Find Out More about the Financial Health of Life Insurers.*** Look up three of the insurers listed in Exhibit 16-7 at *www.insure.com*. Find the following information for each of the three companies:
   a. Standard & Poor's rating
   b. Fitch rating
   c. Allocation of business by type of insurance
   d. Whether the company is licensed to do business in your state of residence
4. ***Find Out More about Social Security Survivor Benefits.*** Go to the Social Security website at *www.ssa.gov* and click on "Survivor Benefits." If you're married or have children, enter your own financial information to see what benefit you or your children could be entitled to collect. If not, enter hypothetical information based on what you think your financial circumstances will be ten years from now.
5. ***Find Out How to Select a Long-Term Care Policy.*** Visit several financial websites (such as *www.fool.com*, *www.insweb.com*, *www.insure.com*, and *www.kiplingers.com*) and search for any discussion or articles related to selecting a long-term care policy. Summarize the most common suggestions. Based on what you've read, at what age do you think you should begin looking for this type of insurance?

Learning by Doing Solutions

LBD 16-1: 1. Elaine may want to carry sufficient insurance to repay her outstanding debts and her funeral expenses. She may also want to add enough to pay for Rufus' support if she dies before he does; 2. They probably don't need life insurance.

LBD 16-2: 1. She won't be able to afford the premium for that amount of permanent coverage, so term will be a better choice; 2. No. He should consider products that include death protection and a savings element. Alternatively, he could buy term and invest the difference in a mutual fund.

LBD 16-3: All these terms may increase the cost of coverage.

LBD 16-4: 1. You might want to buy it for your parents if you expect to be the primary caregiver and provider of financial support in the event of incapacity; 2. No. Medicaid will cover your costs; 3. Women tend to provide home health care for their husbands. Since they tend to live longer, there's no one to provide this type of care for them.

Building Financial Planning Skills Through Case Applications

Case 16-1 Vanna and Patrick O'Hara Evaluate Their Life Insurance Need

Vanna and Patrick O'Hara, ages 30 and 40, respectively, are considering the purchase of additional life insurance. They're both employed full-time, and they have two children who are 7-year-old twins. Vanna's after-tax income is $30,000 and Pat's is $50,000. Currently, Vanna has a $30,000 term life insurance policy paid for by her employer, and Pat has a $75,000 individual term life insurance policy. The O'Haras would like to have enough life insurance on each of them so that, in the event of either's death, it would cover the lost cash flow to the household, help pay off some household debts, and fund their children's college costs. They have estimated these costs as follows:

College fund for children	$130,000
Pay off existing mortgage on home	150,000
Pay off credit cards	10,000
Costs at death	15,000

In addition, they estimate that their household expenses of $60,000 will be about 10 percent less if either one of them dies. If Vanna were to die, the cost of replacing her services to the household would be $10,000 per year for the next 11 years. If Pat were to die, this annual cost would be $5,000. They don't anticipate that either of them would qualify for a Social Security benefit due to continued employment, but the children would be eligible for combined benefits of $2,000 a month until they reached the age of 18. The O'Haras currently have about $50,000 in home equity and another $35,000 in savings.

a. What would be the financial consequences for the O'Haras' children in the event of a tragic car accident in which both parents were killed?
b. Using the income multiple method, what is the minimum amount of life insurance that each should have?
c. Apply the financial needs method to determining how much life insurance Vanna and Pat should individually have.
d. What type of insurance policy would you recommend for each? Explain your reasoning.
e. If they choose to buy term insurance, what risks do they face? Are there any contract terms they should look for to reduce this risk?

Case 16-2 Kurt Nelson Considers Buying Long-Term Care Insurance

Kurt Nelson is 63 years old and has been retired for several years. Two years ago, his wife of 40 years passed away after two years of battling cancer. During her entire illness, Kurt provided the in-home care she required. Shortly thereafter, his mother became incapacitated and moved in with him. He hired a nurse to come in for a couple of hours each day to cook dinner and help with his mother's personal needs, but otherwise he took care of her himself. His mother died six months ago.

Kurt has five surviving adult children and ten grandchildren, all of whom are financially secure. He would like to leave the bulk of his estate to his family but is worried that, should he require long-term care, the costs would rapidly deplete his hard-earned capital. He also wants to ensure that his beloved dog Zubi will be well-cared for if he's incapacitated or dies. Zubi isn't particularly good with children and is accustomed to a lot of personal attention. He knows that none of his children would be willing to take the dog, so he wants to set up a fund for this purpose. He estimates that he could hire someone to perform this service for $5,000 per year. Kurt is considering the purchase of additional life insurance as well as long-term care insurance. At his age, he finds that both will be relatively expensive despite the fact that he's in good health. He estimates his net worth at $500,000 and that his investments earn an average of 4 percent per year. He has a defined benefit pension that provides $32,000 in after-tax annual income. He started receiving Social Security benefits at age 62 and his current benefit is $18,000. His annual expenses, excluding those related to Zubi, are $40,000.

a. What is Kurt's current after-tax cash flow?
b. If Kurt required extended long-term care for three years beginning this year, would his current income and assets be enough to pay for it, assuming the annual cost is $60,000 per year? If he goes into long-term care, he estimates that his annual expenses would drop to $20,000, including those for Zubi.
c. What would his situation be if he didn't need long-term care until he reached the age of 88 (25 years from now)? Assume that long-term care costs grow at 8 percent per year. To answer this, you'll need to calculate the future cost of long-term care and the future value of his net worth.
d. Does Kurt need life insurance? Explain your reasoning.
e. Assume that long-term care premiums are $6,000 for the first 10 years, $12,000 for the next 10 years, and $24,000 for the next 10 years. If Kurt expects to enter a long-term care facility at age 73 (10 years from now) for one year, would he be better off investing the money or buying the long-term care insurance? What impact does the number of years of required long-term care have on his decision?
f. Should Kurt consider buying a life insurance policy with a long-term care acceleration rider instead? Explain your reasoning.

DEVELOPING PERSONAL FINANCIAL skills for life

Learning about Yourself

16-1. Confronting Mortality

For each of the following statements, indicate the degree to which it is consistent with your viewpoint as follows: 5 = strongly agree; 4 = agree; 3 = neutral; 2 = disagree; 1 = strongly disagree.

_____ **1.** I tend to avoid discussing unpleasant subjects.

_____ **2.** I don't like to think about what would happen to my family if I were to die.

_____ **3.** I'm too young to die.

_____ **4.** I've never experienced the death of a close relative or friend.

_____ **5.** My family doesn't talk about money matters.

_____ **6.** My parents have never discussed their life insurance decisions with me.

_____ **7.** No one would be financially impacted by my premature death.

_____ **8.** I should take better care of my health and exercise more.

_____ **9.** At this point in my life, I'm pretty self-centered.

_____ **10.** I never visit sick people in the hospital because it's too depressing.

Scoring:

This assessment is about how comfortable you are with your own mortality. People who accept their own risk of dying are more likely to be able to deal with the financial preparations for their death, such as buying life insurance, writing a will, and estate planning. If your total score is between 35 and 50, this is an indication that you're not very comfortable with these issues and are less likely to have taken appropriate actions. If your score is between 10 and 20, you may have had a little more experience with the deaths of others and will therefore be more likely to plan.

Developing Your Skills

16-2. Assess Your Life Insurance Needs

Use the worksheet in your *Personal Financial Planner* to assess your own needs for life insurance at this point in your life. Then redo the worksheet using hypothetical information for your household 10 years from now.

PFP Worksheet 53
Life Insurance
Needs Analysis

16-3. Shop for Term Insurance

Identify five insurers based on their product offerings and financial strength. Obtain price quotes for a term insurance policy with a face value of $100,000 from all the insurers, either on their websites or by calling an agent. If you're a smoker, be sure to let them know this so that they can underwrite your policy appropriately.

16-4. Talk with Your Family about Long-Term Care

Ask a parent or another member of your family about his or her plan for long-term care. (This exercise will be more effective if you can ask someone who is over 50 years old, since people of that age are more likely to have considered the problem.) Has this person purchased insurance or does he or she plan to do so in the future? Has he or she had any experience with Medicare and/or Medicaid coverage, either personally or with an older relative? What is the person's opinion about the ethics of wealth reduction strategies used by some families to enable their family members to qualify for Medicaid? If the person hasn't considered these issues, what would you recommend that he or she do at this time?

THE NAVIGATOR

- ☐ Review Before Studying this Chapter list.
- ☐ Scan Learning Objectives.
- ☐ Take the Myth or Fact quiz and find the answers throughout the chapter.
- ☐ Read chapter and answer Learning by Doing exercises.
- ☐ Review Key Terms and Key Calculations.
- ☐ Do end-of-chapter exercises.
- ☐ Take review quiz on the text website.
- ☐ Solve end-of-chapter cases.

BEFORE *studying this chapter, you should review*

- Personal financial statements (Chapter 2).
- Tax planning fundamentals (Chapter 4).

Estate Planning

CHAPTER 17

Myth or Fact?

Consider each of the following statements and decide whether it is a *myth* or a *fact*. Look for the answers in the *Fact* boxes in the chapter.

	MYTH	FACT
1. You don't really need an estate plan unless you're wealthy.	☐	☐
2. Although many people don't have an estate plan in place, most adults at least have a will.	☐	☐
3. If you and your spouse die without a will, your family will get to decide who will be the guardian of your children.	☐	☐
4. Federal estate taxes have been eliminated by recent legislation.	☐	☐
5. Large charitable contributions are subject to a gift tax.	☐	☐

LEARNING objectives

1. Understand the process of estate planning.
2. Identify the key elements of an estate plan.
3. Understand why your heirs will benefit if you have a valid will and well-organized legal and financial records.
4. Estimate the size of your estate and the taxes that would be owed upon your death.
5. Know how to use trusts, gifts, and charitable contributions to minimize estate taxes.

...applying the planning process

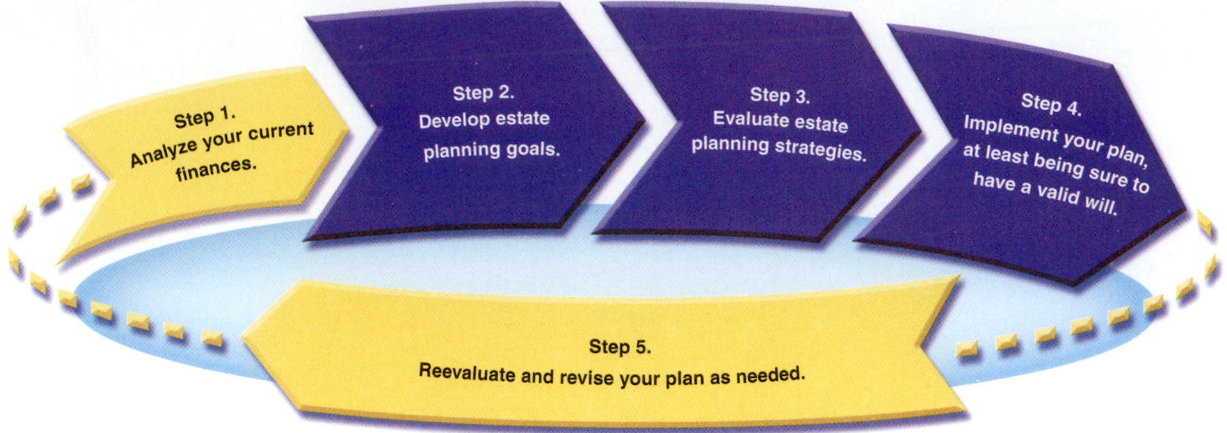

This chapter is all about death and taxes—preparing for the first and avoiding the second. It's never easy to think about the prospect of your own death or that of a loved one, but the reality is that it's inevitable. Like the matters discussed in the previous chapter, these issues may be difficult to discuss with your family. But the failure to plan for what will happen upon your death can result in significant additional hardship for your survivors, both personal and financial. If you're currently at a stage in your life when you have no dependents or wealth, the topics in this chapter will have greater relevance to you if you apply them to your parents' situation instead of your own. What would happen to you or your younger siblings if your parents were to die unexpectedly without any advance planning for distribution of their assets or custody of their children? Would you be able to finish college? Who would take responsibility for household financial decisions? Whether you consider these issues as they apply to your parents or in the context of your own estate plan, this chapter will provide you with a roadmap for getting started by helping you to understand the process and the legal rules that can affect your plan. We'll begin by providing an overview of the estate-planning process, and then identify the key components of an estate plan. We then explain why everyone should have a will and how to make sure that it will be legally valid. Although current legislation has scheduled the estate tax for repeal in the future, this change won't be completely implemented for several years, so the last section of this chapter explains the current system of taxation and what you might expect in the future.

Chapter Preview

What Is Estate Planning?

LEARNING objective

 Understand the process of estate planning.

In recent chapters, we've focused primarily on accumulating wealth to meet household financial goals. The objective of estate planning is to distribute that wealth according to your wishes after your death and to plan for the care of your dependents. In this context, your **estate** is your net worth at death—all your assets less all your debts, just as we defined net worth in Chapter 2. Although federal estate taxes are gradually being phased out, the long-term status of this tax is uncertain, and current law still imposes a hefty tax on larger estates. Thus, one of the additional objectives of estate planning is to avoid paying excessive estate taxes. In this section, we'll provide an overview of estate planning and why it should be a component of your financial plan.

estate

A person's net worth at death.

estate planning

The development of a plan for what will happen to your wealth and dependents when you die.

The Estate-Planning Process

Estate planning is the process of developing a plan for what will happen to your wealth and your dependents when you die. This involves both financial and legal considerations and in most cases will require the advice of a professional, such as an estate lawyer or a financial professional with specific knowledge and skills in this area. Nevertheless, you'll save both time and money if you've done some of the work before you seek professional guidance. Thus, the purpose of this chapter is not to give you everything there is to know about estate planning, but rather to provide you with an understanding of the fundamental concepts so that you can begin making some important decisions about your estate plan.

Fact #1

Even if you're not wealthy, you should have an estate plan if you want to: (1) make sure your assets go where you intend for them to go after you die; (2) have a say in who becomes your children's guardian; (3) reduce the chance of family discord over the distribution of your assets; (4) minimize the costs of settling your estate.

Like other elements of financial planning, the estate-planning process requires that you first evaluate your financial situation. If you've been applying the exercises in this book to your own personal finances all along, this should be relatively easy. By estimating the value of your estate, you can determine whether additional tax planning will be necessary to reduce your potential tax liability. If you have children, you'll also need to plan for what will happen to them after you die. You'll have to make a will, and you may also want to consider several other legal documents discussed in this chapter to ensure that your wishes are carried out upon your death.

Who Needs an Estate Plan?

Because everyone will eventually die, everyone should have an estate plan. However, because people's needs—and their estates—differ, some estate plans are necessarily more complex than others. If you're a typical college student with no dependents and negative net worth, your plan will be simple. Your biggest problems might be: Do you want your roommate to have your CD collection if you die unexpectedly? Who would take care of your cat? (See the *News You Can Use* box, "The Bird Lives On.") Do you want to be cremated? What kinds of life-extending measures do you want doctors to take if you're physically or mentally disabled in the future? If, on the other hand, you are relatively wealthy, have dependent children, or own property in multiple states, your plan will be more complicated. More important, the consequences of failing to plan could be much more serious.

The legal process of settling your estate—paying your debts and distributing your assets according to your wishes—is called **probate**. This process is supervised by a local court, which will appoint someone to administer the distribution of assets. Since only certain assets have to be distributed through this process, one of the objectives of your estate plan will be to arrange for as much of your wealth as possible to avoid the probate process. If you die without a valid will or if your family can't locate necessary documents, the probate process can take a long time—many months, and sometimes years. In some cases, your survivors may experience financial hardship if they don't have access to necessary funds during the probate process.

probate

The legal process of settling an estate.

NEWS you can use

The Bird Lives On

Although it's obvious that you need to think about your human dependents in estate planning, many people fail to consider what will happen to their pets. Fido and Fluffy might have several good years left, but if you don't provide for the costs of their care, your heirs may be inclined to give them away or have them put to sleep. Large birds, such as parrots and macaws, have life spans comparable to those of humans and sometimes live to be 100 years old. Since these birds are highly intelligent, their owners are often concerned about the emotional trauma that would result from change of ownership. Bird enthusiasts often caution new owners about the long-term nature of the relationship and suggest that provisions for the bird be made in an owner's will.

> large birds "sometimes live to be 100 years old. . ."

This little baby, like many large birds, could live to be 100 years old, so your will should provide for the costs of his care after you die.

The Consequences of Failure to Plan

Most people in the United States don't have adequate estate plans. More than half don't even have valid wills. If you die without an estate plan or a will, the value of your estate may be unnecessarily eroded by the following costs:

- Federal estate taxes (top marginal rate 47% in 2005, depending on size of estate)
- State inheritance taxes (0–10%, depending on the state you live in)
- Probate costs (2–5%)

In addition, your heirs may experience the following personal costs:

- Delays in settlement of the estate
- Distress over having to make difficult health-care decisions on your behalf
- Distress over having to make funeral arrangements without knowing your wishes
- Disagreements among family members regarding distribution of your personal effects
- Potential financial hardship for your spouse or children if the state's distribution of your assets leaves them with insufficient financial resources
- Personal upset for your dependent children if they don't like the state-appointed guardian

Estate Planning over the Life Cycle

Like other parts of your financial plan, your estate plan must change as your life situation changes. Suppose you consult an estate-planning attorney and set up a plan that meets your needs today. Many people make the mistake of assuming that once they've established a plan, they're set for life, but such is not the case. Remember Cindy and Dave Thompson, our continuing-case family? In the process of getting their financial plan in order, they consulted an estate-planning attorney and discovered the following problems:

- Both Cindy and Dave have wills, but they didn't write new wills after they were married. Under Cindy's old will, her ex-husband is her primary beneficiary. Dave's old will leaves everything to his brother Tom. The provisions in Cindy's will favoring her ex-husband, by law, will have been automatically revoked, or canceled, but that's not true of the provisions in Dave's will favoring his brother. Due to Cindy and Dave's marriage, the legal status of both old wills is questionable, but clearly they're inconsistent with Cindy and Dave's intentions.

- Although Cindy's old will includes a provision for guardianship of her son from her previous marriage, the named guardian is her ex-husband's mother, who is now deceased. Neither Cindy's will nor Dave's provides for additional children, so even if their wills were found to be valid, their new daughter Julia would not be entitled to anything should they both die before executing new wills.

Needless to say, the Thompsons' attorney has advised them to write new wills promptly.

Over your life cycle, you'll need to revisit your estate plan whenever you have a major change in circumstances. At a minimum, such changes include divorce, remarriage, birth or adoption of a child, death of anyone named in your will, change of state of residence, change of job, acquisition of new assets, or change in dependent status of your children. Optimally, you should reconsider your estate plan regularly—perhaps as often as annually when you reevaluate your financial plan.

Although your plan will be fairly simple when you're young, it should grow in complexity with the complexity of your family circumstances and finances. Through your 40s and 50s, your primary estate-planning concerns will be the protection of your spouse and children, but as you age, it will probably shift to providing for your spouse's retirement and passing your wealth to your grandchildren or your favorite charities.

Tax Planning

As noted earlier, much of this chapter is concerned with tax planning. Since estate taxes, or "death taxes" as they are often called, can take a large bite out of your wealth, the impact of careful tax planning can be quite significant. It is worthwhile to recall that the objective of *tax avoidance* is not the same as *tax evasion*. As we discussed in Chapter 4, good financial planning requires that you take advantage of rules and regulations which allow you to *legally* reduce or avoid the taxes you pay. If you fail to do so, it's like giving away your hard-earned money to the government.

LEARNING objective

2 Identify the key elements of an estate plan.

Key Components of an Estate Plan

Although estate plans can be very different from one another, most share certain key components. These may include a will, a living will, a letter of last instruction, and any trust instruments deemed necessary. We look at each of these components next.

will

A legal document that transfers property upon the death of the property owner.

heir

Person or entity designated to receive something from your estate after your death.

Will

The most important component of your estate plan is your will. A **will** is a legal document that specifies how you want your property to be distributed upon your death. A person or entity designated to receive something from your estate after your death is called your **heir**. The will can also specify who will have responsibility for the care of your surviving minor children and other dependents. (In this context, *minor* children are those under the age of 18.) Different types of wills and the legal requirements for a valid will are discussed in the next section.

Whether you have a will or not, state law will require that your assets be distributed after your death. If you die **intestate**—without a valid will—there are rules in every state as to how your property will be distributed. Although the manner of distribution differs among states, these rules will not necessarily divide up your assets in the way you would have chosen had you drafted a will yourself. In addition, you will have no say in determining who becomes the guardian for your children. In most states, for example, your spouse usually gets no more than half your assets, with the other half going to surviving children or

Fact #2

Estate planning is the most neglected component of financial plans. Estate-planning professionals estimate that as many as 70 percent of American adults do not even have a valid will in place.

intestate

Without a valid will.

escheat

The legal process by which the state government acquires the estate of a person who dies without a will and has no living relatives.

your parents. If you have no children, your spouse will likely have to share the wealth with other relatives, which might leave him or her in financial difficulty. If you die without a will and have no living relatives, all your assets will become the property of the state government through a legal rule called **escheat**.

Living Will or Durable Power of Attorney

living will

A legal document that specifies a person's preferences as to medical care in the event that he or she becomes unable to make decisions because of illness or disability.

You may also want to have a **living will**. Whereas wills have been around for thousands of years, living wills are a by-product of modern medical care. In this document, you specify what kind of medical care you want to receive if you become unable to make decisions for yourself due to terminal illness, or physical or mental disability. This document can greatly ease the burden your family will have to bear if you become incapacitated. You've probably heard on the news about families who have kept their loved ones alive for years without much hope of improvement in condition, as illustrated in the story in the *News You Can Use* box, "Life or Something Like It: The Case of Terry Schiavo." If you don't decide in advance how you want to deal with situations of this kind, your family may be unable or unwilling to make the tough decisions for you, instead bearing a significant and continuing financial and emotional burden themselves.

Go to www.estateplanningattys.com and click on "Free Legal Forms" to download a sample living will. For $5, you can order a copy of "The Five Wishes," a more comprehensive living will document, at www.agingwithdignity.org.

The most difficult part of drafting a living will is deciding what limitations to place on the level of extreme medical care you're willing to receive. For example, you can be fairly vague and specify just that no "heroic measures" be taken to keep you alive by artificial means. In that case, it will be up to your family to decide exactly what constitutes a heroic measure (respirator, kidney dialysis, feeding tubes?), and they may disagree with each other on this point. Or you might limit the living will's applicability to situations in which your brain function is severely reduced to the extent that you have no reasonable chance of living a productive life. Although greater specificity can be helpful to the members of your family who will be called on to make the difficult decisions, you'll need to be general enough to cover all the possible circumstances that might arise. You wouldn't necessarily want your living will to prevent you from benefiting from advances in medical knowledge or improved chances of survival as time goes on.

durable power of attorney

A legal document in which a person designates another to make decisions on his or her behalf in the event of incapacity.

The format of living wills can vary greatly depending on your preferences, and many lawyers will draft one along with your regular will at no additional charge. Most states have a particular legal form that they recognize for this purpose, but other forms will be acceptable if they include the necessary elements. An example of a living will is provided in Exhibit 17-1.

A **durable power of attorney** is similar to a living will but should be used in conjunction with one. In it, you designate a person to make decisions on your behalf in case you are temporarily or permanently unable to do so. You can give very explicit instructions to the designee

NEWS you can use

Life or Something Like It: The Case of Terry Schiavo

Imagine that you suffer a heart attack and the loss of oxygen to your brain leaves you in what your doctors term a "persistent and irreversible vegetative state." With no hope of recovery, your husband wants to move on with his life. But your parents have taken legal action to prevent him from ordering your feeding tubes removed. This is what happened to Terry Schiavo of Tampa, Florida. In 2003, after 13 years on life support, her husband Michael convinced a court to allow him to remove the tubes that were keeping Terry alive. Six days later, the state legislature passed a controversial bill ("Terry's Law") that gave Governor Jeb Bush the right to order reinstatement of the feeding tube. A circuit court judge later struck down the bill as an unconstitutional invasion of privacy. Although Michael Schiavo and two other relatives testified that Terry wouldn't have wanted this type of medical intervention, she didn't have a living will. If you don't want this to happen to you, you should write down specific instructions concerning the circumstances and conditions under which you want heroic measures taken to keep you alive.

"she didn't have a living will. . ."

EXHIBIT 17-1

Sample Living Will

Living Will

To my family, my physicians, my attorney, my minister, and any person or institution responsible for my health and welfare, I make this declaration while I am of sound mind and after full reflection.

This statement is intended to apprise you of my wishes in the event that I can no longer make medical decisions on my own behalf.

If I should ever become in a terminal state and there is no reasonable expectation of my recovery, I direct that I be allowed to die a natural death and that my life not be prolonged by extraordinary measures. I do, however, ask that medication be mercifully administered to me to alleviate suffering even though this may shorten my remaining life.

I direct that, in the event of a terminal diagnosis, the physicians supervising my care discontinue feeding and hydration, should the continuation of feeding and hydration be judged to result in unduly prolonging my life.

I hereby authorize my family to effectuate my transfer from any hospital or other health care facility in which I may be receiving care should that facility decline or refuse to carry out the instructions in this document.

I hereby release any and all hospitals, physicians, and others for myself and for my estate from any liability for complying with this instrument.

Signed ______________________ Date__________
Address______________________________
Social Security Number______________________
Witness______________________ Date__________
Copies of this request have been given to my physician and attorney.

about what you want, or you can give the designee broad powers to make decisions as he or she sees fit. In addition, a durable power of attorney can be designed to cover health-care decisions only (in which case it may be called a *health-care power of attorney*), or it can be broader, enabling the holder to make both financial and legal decisions.

Letter of Last Instruction

Although not a legal document, the **letter of last instruction** serves the purpose of helping your survivors through the process of your death. You could use this document to communicate your personal wishes regarding funeral arrangements, to identify people who should be notified of your death, and to list important information, such as bank accounts and pin numbers, contact information for insurance companies and brokerage firms, and safe deposit box locations and numbers. Although specific bequests must be in your will to be legally binding, you can also use a letter of last instructions to give your survivors advice about how to distribute some of your minor personal property (your favorite CDs, your old football jersey, family items that have sentimental but not financial value). The letter of last instruction should be copied and distributed to several people (including your attorney) to ensure that it is found in the event of your death.

letter of last instruction

A nonbinding document that provides helpful information to survivors after the writer's death.

trust

A legal entity that holds and manages assets on behalf of someone else.

Trusts

For many estate plans, it's desirable to set up legal arrangements called trusts. A **trust** is a legal entity that holds and manages assets on behalf of someone else. Trusts are commonly used in estate planning for a variety of purposes, as will be discussed later.

Wills and Other Important Documents

LEARNING objective

3 Understand why your heirs will benefit if you have a valid will and well-organized legal and financial records.

The failure to have a valid will can easily result in your assets being distributed contrary to your wishes. So why do so few people have valid wills? Many assume that their property will pass to their spouses or that they don't have enough assets to worry about having a will. What they may

Once you've prepared a will, you'll gain the peace of mind that comes with knowing that you've made things easier for your family.

not realize is that the failure to have a will is sure to complicate the settlement process and create added hardship for their survivors. This section focuses on how you can ensure that your estate goes where you want it to go. Along with a valid will, your decisions regarding legal ownership of certain assets are important elements of this process.

Preparing a Valid Will

A will enables the person writing it, the **testator**, to direct the disposition of his or her assets to specific **beneficiaries**, those who will receive the assets. Wills can be very simple or very complicated but must satisfy certain legal requirements to be valid. If your will is declared to be invalid, the property will be distributed as if you had died intestate, so it is generally worthwhile to hire a lawyer to draft or at least review your will for legality. The cost of having a simple will drawn up may be as little as $200 but can be much higher for more complex estates. Exhibit 17-2 summarizes the minimum requirements for a valid will in most states, and Exhibit 17-3 provides a sample will for Cindy Thompson to illustrate the common clauses and sections found in most wills.

testator

The writer of a will.

beneficiaries

The individuals or entities receiving a distribution under the terms of a will.

capacity

The mental competence to make a will, including understanding the nature and content of the document and not acting under threat or coercion from anyone.

Capacity to Make the Will.

Even if all the other requirements are met, a will can be declared invalid if the testator did not have the legal **capacity** to make the will. For this reason, many wills begin with the language "I, [testator name], being of sound mind and body. . . ." In this context, "of sound mind" addresses the requirement of legal capacity. The testator is considered to be of sound mind if he or she understands the nature and content of the document, is mentally capable of making decisions regarding the distribution of his or her assets, and is not acting under threat or coercion from anyone. Capacity is a requirement for making any legally binding contract, but in the case of a will, it is particularly important, since the elderly are often unwitting victims of greedy relatives and scam artists.

Common Elements of a Will.

As illustrated in the sample document in Exhibit 17-3, a will usually includes clauses or sections for the introduction, payment of debts and taxes, distribution of assets, appointment of executor, appointment of guardians and trustees, and execution. These elements are described in more detail below.

Introduction. Wills usually begin with a set of introductory declarations in which the testator identifies him- or herself and the state of residency, and states that the will replaces all previous wills that he or she may have written. Since you may revise your will several times over the years, it's important to date it and to identify each new one as your last will. To ensure that a previous version of your will is not inadvertently identified, you should notify your attorney and your relatives when you write a new will. It's also a good idea (although not necessary for legal validity) to destroy any old ones.

Payment of Debts and Taxes. This clause instructs the estate to pay your debts and expenses, including funeral expenses, medical expenses, and any taxes due. Since creditors are generally protected by other laws, the important component of this clause is the instruction to pay taxes. In the absence of such a clause, most states have laws that will allocate the taxes among the beneficiaries based on their shares of the estate. Thus, if you want to be sure that Aunt Grace gets $10,000 from your estate, you need to include a clause that directs payment of taxes *before* distribution of specific bequests to ensure that her $10,000 isn't reduced by a share of the estate tax.

EXHIBIT 17-2

Requirements for a Valid Will

In order to be valid in most states, your will must meet the following criteria:

1. You must be of legal age (usually 18).
2. You must have the mental capacity to make a will:
   a. You must understand the nature and extent of your assets.
   b. You must understand whom you intend your assets to be distributed to.
   c. You must understand how you are distributing your assets.
3. You must intend for the document to be your will.
4. The will must be in writing and, with some limited exceptions, typed or printed.
5. The will must be dated.
6. The will must be signed in the presence of two witnesses who are not your relatives or named beneficiaries in the will.
7. The will must name an executor.

EXHIBIT 17-3

Sample Last Will and Testament

Last Will and Testament

Article 1 Introduction
I, Cindy Thompson, Marlboro, New Jersey, being of sound mind and body, declare this to be my last will and I revoke all wills and codicils made prior to this will. My husband is David Thompson, also of Marlboro, New Jersey.

Article 2 Payment of Debts and Expenses
I direct my Executor to pay my medical expenses, funeral expenses, debts, and the costs of settling my estate.

Article 3 Distribution of Assets
I give to the Boy Scouts of America the sum of $20,000. All the rest of my estate, real and personal, I give to my beloved husband David Thompson. If my husband dies before me, I give my estate to be shared equally by my children Kyle and Julia Thompson, also of Marlboro, New Jersey.

Article 4 Appointment of Executor and Guardian
I hereby nominate my beloved husband David Thompson to be the Executor of this Will. If he is unable to serve, then I nominate my sister Teri Bradley of Colts Neck, New Jersey. If my husband dies before me, then I appoint my sister Teri Bradley of Colts Neck, New Jersey as Guardian of the person and property of my children Kyle and Julia Thompson until they each reach the age of 18. If she is unable to serve as Guardian, then I appoint my brother Kenneth Chandler of Somers Point, New Jersey.

Article 5 Power of Executor
The Executor of this Will has the power to receive payments, buy or sell assets, and pay debts owed and taxes owed on behalf of my estate.

Article 6 Payment of Taxes
I direct my Executor to pay all estate, inheritance, or other similar taxes imposed by the government.

Article 7 Execution
IN WITNESS THEREOF, I hereby sign and declare this to be my Last Will and Testament, which consists of two pages, each of which I have initialed, this the 15th day of January, 2005.

______________________	______________________
Cindy Thompson	Date

Article 8 Witness Clause
The above-named person signed in our presence and in our opinion is mentally competent.

______________________	______________________	____________
Witness 1 Name	Address	Date
______________________	______________________	____________
Witness 2 Name	Address	Date

Distribution of Assets. The distribution of assets is usually the primary purpose of a will. You can distribute your assets very simply, or you can provide a lot of detailed instructions. A very simple will might give the entire estate to the named beneficiaries, such as spouse or children, without any specific bequests. Other wills direct that specific personal effects be given to named beneficiaries before the distribution of the remainder of the estate. If you have a long list of specific items to be distributed, you may want to include this list with your letter of last instruction instead of in the will itself. That way, you can make changes as necessary over time without having to draw up a new will. After specific gifts have been distributed, the remainder of the estate, called the *residual estate*, will go to the residual beneficiaries as named in the will.

Appointment of Executor or Executrix. In your will, you'll need to name the person who will handle the settlement of your estate, called the **executor** (executrix if female) or, in some cases, the *personal representative*. This person has the legal and ethical obligation of making sure that your assets are distributed as you have directed and that taxes are paid according to the law. If your estate is complex, you should consider naming a lawyer or bank trust department instead of a family member to fill this role. You should also be realistic about the other time commit-

executor

A person designated to carry out the provisions of a will.

ments of any person you're considering naming as your executor and whether the person lives close enough to handle the details of financial transactions related to settlement of the estate. In addition to naming your executor, your will can provide for the executor to be compensated for his or her services and expenses incurred in settling the estate. This compensation is commonly a small percentage of the total value of the estate.

Appointment of Guardian. If you have minor children, your will should identify the person or persons who will take care of them and who will manage their inheritance (the trustee) until they reach the age you have designated in your will. If your child's other parent is living, you'll probably designate him or her as the primary guardian and trustee. However, it's important to designate a secondary guardian and trustee in the unfortunate event that both of you die at the same time. The guardian and the trustee do not have to be the same person.

What if you have one or more children who are over the age of 18, the age of majority in most states? At the age of majority, a child legally becomes an adult and can manage his or her own affairs and may even act as a guardian for younger siblings. Nevertheless, your will can specify that your children will receive their inheritance at a later age if you prefer. Some wealthy parents, fearing that the promise of a future inheritance will adversely affect their children's incentives for achievement, have established wills that provide for guardianship and financial support until a specific age, after which the entire residual is given to charity. Others require satisfaction of specific goals, such as graduation from college, as conditions of inheritance.

Fact #3

If you die without a will, and your spouse is also deceased, the decision on who will be appointed as your children's guardian will be made by the state. Although your family will have input in the process, the outcome may not be consistent with your preferences.

Execution. A will is not valid until *executed*, a legal term for the process of signing and witnessing a document to make it legally valid. To be properly executed, a will must be in writing and signed by the testator in the presence of at least two witnesses, who also must sign the will in each other's presence. In general, witnesses should be people who are not named in the will as beneficiaries. To avoid having to locate the witnesses later for verification, most states will accept the execution of the will if the witnesses sign a statement, in the presence of a notary public, declaring that they observed the testator sign the will while of sound mind and under no undue influence. (Standard will forms usually have a statement of this sort printed in the place where witnesses are supposed to sign.) Even though it's unlikely the witnesses will have to come forward later, it's still a good idea to include contact information for them, just in case.

The purpose of the witnesses' signatures is to verify that the testator had the capacity to make the will—was of sound mind and was not acting under coercion. Most challenges to wills are made by family members who question whether this was in fact the case. Some famous examples have resulted in lengthy legal battles, such as that resulting from the decision of Howard Hughes, the eccentric multibillionaire, to leave his large estate to a very young female companion. You may also have read the John Grisham novel *The Testament*, in which a wealthy man with money-grubbing relatives executes a holographic will (just before killing himself) whereby he cancels his previous will and names a formerly secret illegitimate daughter as his sole heir. The family sought to have the will declared invalid because it was handwritten and had no witness signatures. A *holographic will*—one that is completely handwritten and signed by the maker—doesn't have to be witnessed if it can be shown that the person actually wrote it and if it meets the other requirements for a valid will. The holographic will is a very limited exception to the general requirements, summarized in Exhibit 17-2, that wills be typed and witnessed. All this leads to a simple rule of thumb: If you want to make absolutely sure your will is valid, have it witnessed by people who can validate that you wrote it with full mental capacity.

Should a Lawyer Draft Your Will? Although many websites, software packages, and self-help books suggest a "do it yourself" approach to writing a will, this is clearly an area where you don't want to be "penny wise and dollar foolish." It would be a shame for your will to be invalidated based on a legal technicality. Therefore, no matter how small your estate is, you'd be well advised to get professional help in drafting your will. This is particularly important if you have children for whom you need to appoint a legal guardian or establish a trust. To minimize the cost, assemble all the necessary information before meeting with the lawyer. Think through the important issues, such as whom to appoint as executor and guardian. You might even prepare a rough draft. Most lawyers will charge a flat price for preparing a simple will.

What if you truly can't afford the expense at the moment? Since it's clearly better to have a will than not to have one, you can at least draw up and properly execute a simple will on your own. At the same time, though, you should add getting a legal review of your will to your short-term financial planning "to do" list.

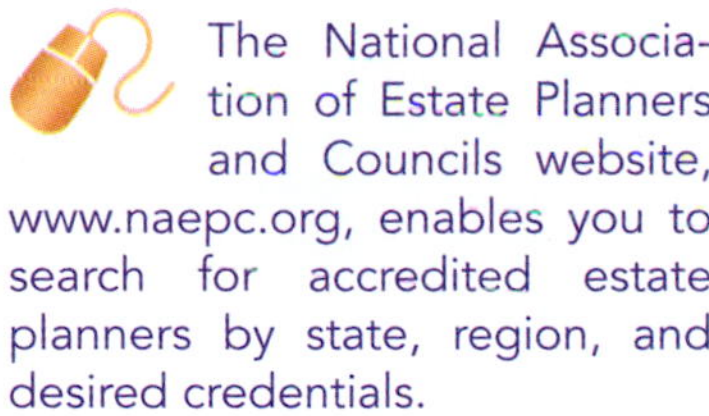

The National Association of Estate Planners and Councils website, www.naepc.org, enables you to search for accredited estate planners by state, region, and desired credentials.

Making Changes to Your Will. You can change or revoke your will at any time, as long as you still have the mental capacity to execute a new will. As mentioned before, you should review your will periodically as your circumstances change to make sure that it still accurately reflects your intentions. You may want to add or subtract beneficiaries, make additional charitable bequests, or name a different executor or guardian. For example, suppose that six years ago you wrote a will identifying your unmarried sister as the guardian of your three children. Since then, she has married and has had three children of her own. Although she might be a wonderful mother, having six children to raise might be too great a burden. Instead, you could now name your unmarried brother as the guardian (subject to his agreement, of course).

To make small changes to your will, you can write a **codicil**, a short (usually single-page) document that reaffirms your original will except for a small provision that is being changed. A codicil can be used to change a named guardian or trustee, for example, or to add a new baby to your list of heirs. Since the codicil is a legal document, it should be drawn up, executed, and witnessed in the same way as a will. For larger changes, rather than adding a codicil to your will, you should make a new will and revoke the old one.

codicil

A legal amendment to a will.

Passing Property Outside of a Will

Any wealth transferred by will is part of your estate and must go through probate—which, depending on the complexity of your estate, can be a lengthy process. Any assets of which you are the sole owner must go through probate. It follows, then, that you can keep property out of probate by using a different mode of ownership. You can accomplish this by holding assets jointly with your heirs and by naming specific beneficiaries for life insurance and retirement accounts.

Ownership of Assets. Assets can be owned in various ways. When two people own property in a **joint tenancy with right of survivorship**, the ownership of the property automatically passes to the surviving owner upon the death of the other without going through probate. The property will also be free of claims from creditors, other heirs, or executors. Joint ownership of this type is not divided—all the owners share ownership of the entire property. Thus, if you and your brother own your parents' former home as joint tenants, you don't own the other half of the property, and you therefore can't leave your interest in the property to your wife or children. Total ownership of the property will automatically pass to your brother upon your death. In some states, a special form of ownership, called *tenancy by the entirety*, applies to married couples and is essentially the same as joint tenancy with right of survivorship.

joint tenancy with right of survivorship

A form of property ownership in which, after the death of one owner, the property passes to the surviving owner without going through probate.

Joint ownership involves both advantages and disadvantages. The primary advantage, as suggested, is that the survivor gets immediate ownership of the property without going through probate. Consider, for example, what would happen if household checking and savings accounts were not owned jointly—the surviving spouse might not have access to the necessary funds to pay household expenses during the process of probate. Joint ownership is also easy and inexpensive to set up.

The disadvantages of joint ownership with right of survivorship as an estate-planning tool are as follows:

- You lose some control over the property during your lifetime. While living, joint tenants have to agree on all decisions regarding the property, much as in a partnership. If you have a falling out with the other joint tenant, this could spell disaster.

- You lose complete control over what happens to the property after you die. The property will eventually pass according to the will of the last to survive. Suppose you're married and both you and your wife have adult children from previous marriages. If you own a home together as joint tenants and you die first, your wife will then own the home. Upon her death, her estate will pass according to her own will, and your children might end up with nothing.
- The transfer may result in greater tax liability. Although the transfer to a spouse initially bypasses the estate tax, as we'll discuss later in the chapter, it may result in higher taxes when he or she dies, since the estate might then be large enough to trigger the tax.
- You lose the ability to have the property pass to a trust. If the property is owned in joint tenancy, it is no longer yours to dispose of according to any other terms of your will.

Despite these disadvantages, joint tenancy with right of survivorship is the most common form of joint ownership, particularly for married couples. The flexibility it offers to the surviving spouse in the form of immediate access and control of the assets is deemed to outweigh the disadvantages.

An alternative to joint tenancy with right of survivorship is a type of ownership called **tenancy in common**. Here, each tenant retains the right to transfer his or her ownership interest independently. Your portion of the property will be included in your estate and passed by the terms of your will.

tenancy in common

A type of ownership in which each person owns his or her share independently and retains the right to transfer that share by sale or will.

Finally, some states have a form of property ownership for married couples called **community property**. In these states, it is assumed that any property acquired during the marriage is owned jointly by both spouses. One spouse's share of the property can be willed to someone other than the surviving spouse, however, as in a tenancy in common.

community property

A property law in some states by which any property acquired during a marriage is considered to be jointly owned by both spouses.

Retirement Assets. When you die, your retirement accounts—such as funds held in IRAs and 401(k) plans—will pass to the person you've named as the beneficiary. As mentioned in previous chapters, one of the great tax advantages of employer retirement accounts and IRAs is that they allow investments to grow tax-deferred or, in the case of Roth IRAs, tax-exempt. If your spouse will not have immediate need for your retirement assets, you might consider naming a younger child as the beneficiary of your retirement account in order to allow the funds to maintain their tax advantages for a longer period of time, as suggested in the *Ask the Expert* box, "Choosing a Pension Beneficiary."

ask the expert — Choosing a Pension Beneficiary

Margaret A. Malaspina, *Author, Cracking Your Retirement Nest Egg (Without Scrambling Your Finances), Bloomberg Press (2003).*

Many people don't realize that the choice of beneficiaries for their qualified retirement plans can make an important difference. Several rules of thumb will help you decide whom to name as your plan beneficiary:

1. Spouses can roll over the entire inherited retirement plan into another qualified plan or IRA, whereas other beneficiaries cannot.
2. Required withdrawals from the retirement account will be spread over a longer time if you name a younger beneficiary. This allows the assets to grow tax-deferred for a longer period.
3. Leaving a Roth IRA to your youngest beneficiary will maximize its tax benefits.
4. You should always have at least one contingent beneficiary in case your primary beneficiary dies before you.
5. Don't forget to change your beneficiary designation when you experience major life changes, such as divorce, remarriage, or the birth of a child. It would be a shame for your retirement fund to go to your ex-spouse instead of your new one.

EXHIBIT 17-4

Estate-Planning Checklist

Use the following checklist to help you organize your personal and financial information for estate-planning purposes. Your list should include location of the relevant documents and any necessary contact information. Copies of the list and the individual documents should be given to someone you trust for safekeeping.

- Wills (including living will and letter of last instruction)
- Trust documents
- Powers of attorney (durable power of attorney or health-care power of attorney)
- Tax returns (federal and state income tax, gift tax, estate tax)
- Personal legal records (Social Security number, prenuptial agreements, birth certificate, marriage certificate, divorce decree, court judgments, military records)
- Bank account information (account numbers, address and phone of financial institutions)
- Investment information (brokerage accounts, mutual funds, CDs, annuities, stock and bond certificates)
- Debt information (loans and credit cards)
- Business interests (partnership and buy-sell agreements, sole proprietorships)
- Retirement accounts (IRAs, 401(k), Keogh and similar retirement investment accounts, annuities, pension plans, Social Security records)
- Insurance (life insurance and other types of policies)
- Real estate and personal property (deeds, mortgages, title insurance, rental properties, timeshares, leases, vehicle titles)

Organizing Financial and Legal Documents

If you've ever suffered the death of a loved one and had to subsequently handle any of that person's affairs, you'll recognize how helpful it is for everyone to have his or her financial and legal documents organized, accessible, and easy to understand. Unfortunately, this is the exception rather than the rule. In most families, one person takes responsibility for the bill paying and record keeping, and it's often the case that their spouse doesn't have a clue where anything is. Since the survivor is also grieving for the loss of his or her spouse, dealing with unfamiliar household finances adds an unnecessary burden.

An important component of estate planning is the organization of your legal and financial records so the right people—spouse, trustee, trusted family member, lawyer, or estate planner—can easily find them. Not only will this make it more likely that the bills will be paid and that the most recent version of your will is the one that will be opened, but it's also simply a kind thing to do for your survivors. If you take the time while you're living to organize your financial affairs, your family will have one less source of stress to deal with in their time of grief.

It makes sense to keep one copy of each important document with your estate attorney or planner and one copy at home in a fireproof file. Don't put wills, living trusts, or powers of attorney in a safe-deposit box, since these are often sealed at death (although it's okay to keep a copy there). If critical information is stored on your computer, make a disk copy and a paper copy. A checklist of records that you should have readily available is provided in Exhibit 17-4 and in your *Personal Financial Planner*. In addition to your will, your executor is going to need to have access to nearly every legal document related to your financial and personal life. In Chapter 3, we suggested that organizing all this information is an important component of your personal financial plan. In fact, you might note that the checklist here is remarkably similar to the one we provided earlier.

PFP Worksheet 54
Estate-Planning Checklist

Learning by Doing 17-1

1. Eva is about to take a trip away from her family, and she's concerned that she doesn't have a will. Since she left the task of writing one to the last minute, she doesn't have time to consult an attorney. So she decides to write up a simple will on her own and take care of the details when she returns from her trip. After writing her will and signing it, Eva gets two of her neighbors to witness it. Her will is as follows:

I, Eva Malone, being of sound mind, declare this to be my last will.
I give all that I have to my beloved husband James Malone.
I nominate my daughter Katie Malone to be the Executrix of my estate, since she is the only one in the family with any sense.

____
Eva Malone

Do you think Eva's will is valid? Why or why not?

Estate and Gift Taxes

LEARNING objective

4 Estimate the size of your estate and the taxes that would be owed upon your death.

If you have a large estate that you'd like to pass to your heirs, you can do so either while you are living, through gifts, or after you die, through bequests in your will. In either case, the money may be subject to taxes. Since gifts and bequests are alternative ways to accomplish the same end—passing your wealth to the next generation—estate tax and gift tax laws work together, so we'll discuss them both in this section. We'll first look at how gift and estate taxes are currently calculated and then discuss ways that you can minimize the amount paid by those who receive inheritance or gifts from you.

Federal Gift Taxes

Under federal law, you may be subject to a tax on gifts you make during your lifetime if they exceed certain limits. Currently, you and your spouse can each give up to $11,000 per person per year tax-free to as many people as you like. This limit is scheduled to increase annually for inflation in increments of $1,000 (which means it will likely stay at $11,000 through at least 2005). If you give more than the allowed annual amount to anyone, you'll have to file a gift tax return (IRS Form 709), and the excess amount will be applied to reduce the amount of your estate that is exempt from the estate tax, as discussed below. Effectively, this means your estate will have a lower estate tax exclusion (reduced by the amount of taxable gifts at the time of your death). The lifetime limit on tax-free gifts is currently $1,000,000.

Fact #4

Although the estate tax is scheduled for a slow death, implemented through declining tax rates and increasing exemptions phased in through 2010, it is scheduled to come back to life in 2011. Congress will have to pass new legislation to make the estate tax repeal permanent.

There are two important exceptions to the limits on gifts. First, there is no limit on how much you can give your spouse. Second, there is no limit on gifts for the payment of medical expenses or certain educational costs, provided that you make the payments directly to the service provider or educational institution. This means that your rich great uncle can pay the bill for your college tuition and fee expenses directly to the school without exceeding the gifting limit.

Like federal income taxes, estate and gift taxes have increasing marginal tax rates, going from 37 percent for the lowest bracket up to the maximum tax rates, which are shown in Exhibit 17-5. The rate schedule is the same for both gifts and estates that exceed the exclusion amounts shown in Exhibit 17-6. Under the Economic Growth and Tax Relief Reconciliation Act of 2001, the maximum rate will be gradually reduced over the next few years until the estate tax is eliminated altogether in 2010. At that point, the gift tax maximum rate will be equal to the individual income tax maximum rate (35%), with the first $1,000,000 exempt from tax, as before. In 2011, however—unless the estate tax repeal is made permanent by Congress in the meantime—the tax rates and exemption amounts will revert to prereform levels, as indicated in the two graphs.

EXHIBIT 17-5

Maximum Estate Tax Rates Under the Economic Growth and Tax Relief Reconciliation Act of 2001 and After the Sunset Provisions

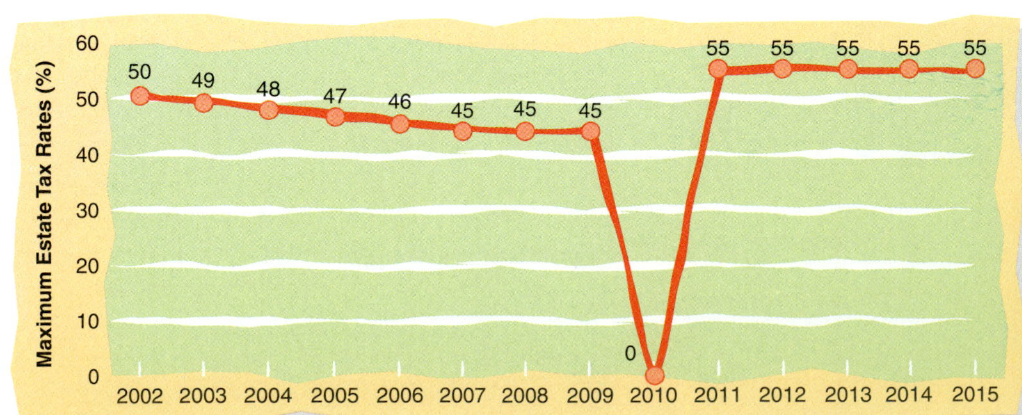

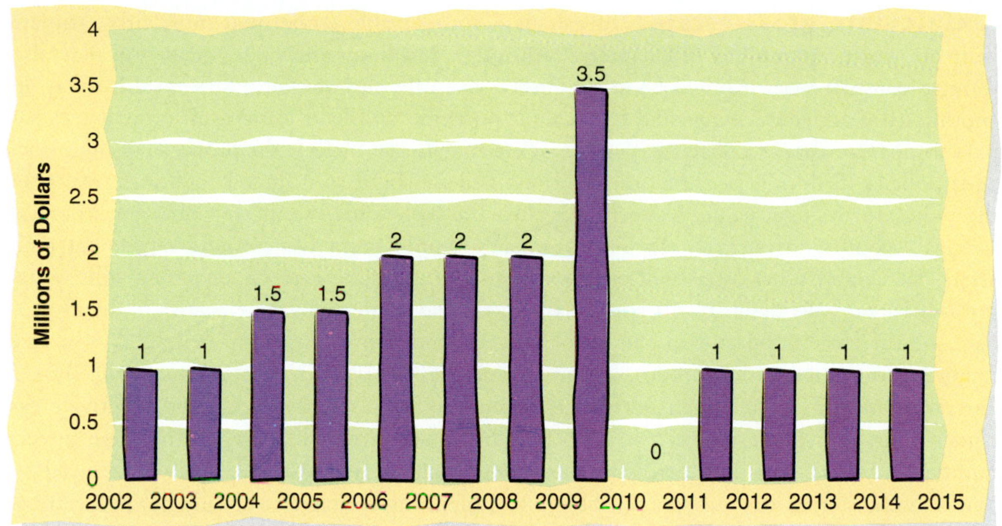

EXHIBIT 17-6

Estate Tax Unified Credit Exemption Under the Economic Growth and Tax Relief Reconciliation Act of 2001 and After the Sunset Provisions

Federal Estate Taxes

If you don't give your wealth away while you're living, you can give it away at your death. Under current law, the amount of your estate that exceeds the allowed exclusions in Exhibit 17-6 may still be subject to a pretty hefty tax rate (47% on estates of over $1.5 million in 2005). As discussed above, the estate tax is due to be repealed in 2010 but will be reinstated in 2011 (with a maximum tax rate of 55%) unless Congress passes further legislation to make it permanent.

An important feature of estate tax law for married couples is that the surviving spouse can inherit the entire estate without paying any tax, regardless of the size of the estate. Therefore, the primary purpose of estate tax planning is actually to minimize the taxes payable by your surviving spouse's estate (or your estate if you leave your wealth to someone other than your spouse).

You can use the worksheet in Exhibit 17-7, which is also available in your *Personal Financial Planner*, to estimate the amount of your estate that could be subject to estate tax at your death. Each of the steps is discussed in more detail below.

PFP Worksheet 55
Estate Tax Calculation

EXHIBIT 17-7

Calculation of Taxable Estate

1. Calculate gross estate:		
Net worth (Note: include only proportional interest of property held as joint tenant)		______
Less assets excluded		
Life insurance held in irrevocable trust	______	
Other irrevocable trust assests	______	
Assets transferred through family limited partnership	______	
Gross estate		______
2. Calculate adjusted gross estate:		
Estate expenses		
Funeral expense	______	
Executor's fee	______	
Legal fees	______	
Court fees	______	
Estate administration fees	______	
Total estate expenses	______	
Adjusted gross estate = Gross estate − estate expenses		______
3. Calculate taxable estate:		
Amount to spouse	______	
Amount to charity	______	
Total unlimited deductions	______	
Taxable estate = adjusted gross estate − unlimited deductions		______
4. Unified exemption ($1.5 million in 2005)	______	
Amount subject to tax = Taxable estate − Exemption		______

1. Calculate gross estate. To calculate your taxable estate, you must first estimate your net worth, as you did in Chapter 2. Although you know the value today, you may also want to consider what it might be in the future. Even if you have fairly little wealth today, in another 10 years your savings and investment portfolio will have grown substantially, and it pays to plan for that contingency. Your gross estate will also include the proceeds of life insurance policies if, during your lifetime, you retained the right to change beneficiaries, turn in the policy for its cash value, or borrow against the cash value. Similarly, your checking and savings accounts, investment accounts, annuities, employment pension and retirement plan assets, IRAs, and other assets will be part of your gross estate even though they will bypass probate if you have designated a beneficiary to receive them upon your death. To avoid probate, it's therefore important to name a beneficiary and also a contingent beneficiary (in case the beneficiary dies before you do). In completing the first step on the worksheet, you should enter your net worth and then subtract the value of any assets that you have effectively excluded from your estate. You can remove them from your gross estate by placing them in certain types of trusts, as will be discussed later in the chapter. Since no estate tax will be owed on amounts transferred to your spouse, these estate planning strategies will only be important if you list someone other than your spouse as the beneficiary on your life insurance policy or retirement account.

2. Calculate adjusted gross estate. Your gross estate is reduced by funeral costs and settlement expenses to arrive at your adjusted gross estate.

3. Calculate taxable estate. To calculate your taxable estate, you'll start with your adjusted gross estate, subtract marital and charitable bequests, and add any taxable gifts. As discussed above, your spouse can inherit an unlimited estate without being subject to federal estate tax; the deduction for charitable giving is also unlimited. In this step of the calculation, you may also need to make adjustments for gifts made during your lifetime that exceeded the allowed exclusion, as discussed above. Thus, if you gave more than $11,000 per year to someone or if you've exceeded the $1,000,000 lifetime exclusion, you'd add the excess to your taxable estate. Finally, you'll need to subtract the applicable exemption amount from Exhibit 17-6. The amount you end up with—the remainder of your estate—will likely be subject to estate taxation if the total exceeds the allowed exemption amount for that year. Although prior law allowed a tax credit for state estate taxes paid, this credit is repealed as of 2005.

Fact #5

If in your will you leave everything you own to your favorite charity, neither your family nor the tax authorities will be particularly happy. Charitable gifts are 100 percent exempt from estate and gift tax.

Let's look at an example of this process. Suppose you plan to leave your entire estate to your adult daughter. You have a life insurance policy that will provide her a benefit of $250,000 and your net worth is $1,200,000, $1 million of which is your 401(k) retirement plan. Assume also that you haven't made any taxable gifts and you aren't leaving anything to charity. You anticipate that the expenses of settling your estate will be $10,000. If you died in 2005, your adjusted gross estate would be calculated as follows:

Net worth	$1,200,000
Life insurance	250,000
Gross estate	$1,450,000
Expense of death	−10,000
Adjusted gross estate	$1,440,000

Since the exemption amount for 2005 to 2010 is greater than $1,440,000, your estate will not owe any taxes, and your daughter will be able to receive the entire amount tax-free. If you were to die in 2011 or later, however, the exemption amount will revert to $1 million, so $440,000 of your estate will be subject to tax. You can avoid this problem by gifting the life insurance to an irrevocable trust with your daughter as beneficiary, thereby excluding that asset from your estate.

Can You Count on the Death Tax to Stay Dead?

As indicated above, the federal estate tax is scheduled to be completely repealed by 2010 under the provisions of the Economic Growth and Tax Relief Reconciliation Act of 2001. What will happen to estate and gift taxation after 2010? Despite politicians' assertions that the "death tax" is dead, certain realities may make it necessary to reinstate the tax or make its terms less generous. For one thing, federal budget shortfalls have been growing quickly in recent years, and this trend is expected to continue. Furthermore, soon after 2010, the retirement of the baby boom generation is expected to cause Social Security outflows to exceed inflows, as discussed in Chapter 15. Due to the high degree of uncertainty about the future of the estate tax, you should plan for the worst case—that the tax will be reinstated in 2011 and that this might affect your estate.

As illustrated by the calculation of taxable estate, there are a number of ways to reduce your potential tax liability. In the next section, we look at ways you can legally reduce your taxable estate and thus minimize taxes that might be payable in the future. Even if the estate tax stays "dead," it won't hurt you to implement these strategies, since doing so isn't terribly costly and will have little impact on your current financial situation.

State Death Taxes

Almost half of U.S. states impose some type of tax on property received from someone who has died. Federal estate tax law currently gives you a credit against taxes owed for the amount of state death taxes you pay, but this credit provision is repealed for future years. States calculate their taxes in different ways. Some apply a flat percentage of the value of the property transferred (usually with exemptions for marital and charitable transfers), and others simply charge an amount equal to the state death tax credit under federal law. The effect of the latter has been to simply shift money from the federal to the state government since the same taxes would have been owed to the federal government if the state had not imposed its death tax. Many states will have to revise their current estate tax laws if they want to continue to receive revenue from this source.

Learning by Doing 17-2

1. Your adjusted gross estate is worth $5 million. If you leave everything to your husband, will any estate taxes be payable at your death in 2006?
2. If you leave all your wealth to your children at your death in 2007, how large can your estate be without being subject to federal estate taxes?

Reducing Taxes Through Trusts and Gifts

LEARNING objective

5 Know how to use trusts, gifts, and charitable contributions to minimize estate taxes.

The larger your taxable estate, the greater the likelihood that your heirs or your spouse's heirs may be subject to estate taxation. There are two general ways to reduce the size of your taxable estate. You can move money or assets to legal vehicles called trusts, or you can give away your assets, either as gifts before your death or through charitable bequests in your will. In this section, we'll discuss these strategies in more detail.

grantor A person or entity who legally passes ownership to another person or entity.

trustee A person or entity who manages assets on behalf of another.

When Are Trusts Useful?

As mentioned earlier, a trust is a legal entity that holds and manages assets on behalf of someone else. The **grantor**, the person putting the assets in the trust, transfers the assets to the trust, which is managed by a **trustee** for the benefit of the beneficiary of the trust. Trustee services are

You can set up trusts for your children and grandchildren to reduce the impact of gift and estate taxes on future generations.

commonly provided by banks, financial institutions, and law firms. Trusts are used in estate planning for several purposes:

- To bypass probate, providing your heirs with immediate access to the property upon your death
- To remove property from the taxable estate thereby minimizing taxes owed
- To ensure that the estate achieves certain purposes after the grantor's death, such as providing income to surviving dependents

If this all sounds very technical, it's because it *is*. Since trusts are fairly sophisticated legal arrangements, before attempting to implement one, you should seek out the advice of an experienced estate-planning lawyer. He or she will provide advice as to what type of trust will best meet your needs and will draft the appropriate legal documents.

Types of Trusts

The type of trust that will best meet your needs depends on your objectives. Here, we briefly review some of the important distinctions among the various types of trusts and how they can help you meet one or more of the objectives in the previous section.

irrevocable trust
A trust that the grantor cannot revoke; it is not subject to probate or estate taxes.

revocable trust
A trust whose terms the grantor can change during his or her lifetime; it bypasses probate but is still subject to estate taxes.

living trust
A trust established during the grantor's lifetime.

testamentary trust
A trust established by the terms of a will.

pourover will
A will that leaves a person's remaining assets to a trust.

Revocable Versus Irrevocable Trusts. If your primary purpose is to reduce estate taxes, then you'll need to set up an **irrevocable trust**, which means that you can't change the terms of the trust once it is established. Irrevocable trusts bypass probate and are not subject to federal or state estate taxes. If, instead, you create a **revocable trust**, you retain the right to change the terms of the trust during your lifetime. In that case, the trust will still bypass probate but will be subject to any applicable state and federal estate taxes.

Living Versus Testamentary Trusts. You can set up a trust that takes effect now or one that will not come into being until the occurrence of some future event, such as your death. A **living trust**, or *inter vivos trust*, is one that is established while you are alive. In contrast, a **testamentary trust** is one that is established through the terms of a will.

Common Types of Living Trusts. Although living trusts can be revocable or irrevocable, a fairly common practice is to set up a revocable living trust that becomes irrevocable upon your death or incompetence. You place your assets in the trust, but you can still use them, receive income from them, or sell them while you're alive. If you can no longer manage them, either because of death or incompetence, the trustee will take over. This type of arrangement will not reduce estate taxes, but it does bypass probate so that your assets are immediately transferred to your beneficiaries after your death. Since you can give directions to the trustee regarding distribution of the trust assets, a living trust is similar in effect to a will. In addition to the living trust, you may want a **pourover will**, a legal document simply stating that any of your assets which have not been specifically transferred to a trust by the time of your death are "poured over" into one or more trusts at that time.

If any of the following circumstances apply to you, you should consider establishing a revocable living trust:

- You own property in more than one state. By holding the property in a trust, you avoid the costs and aggravation of multiple probate proceedings.
- You want the terms of your will to be private. Once a will is probated, it is a public record, whereas a trust document is not.
- You would like to receive income from your assets but do not want to manage them. A trustee can be given the responsibility of managing all your assets for your benefit during your lifetime.
- You are concerned about what will happen to your assets should you become incompetent.

Two specific types of living trusts are life insurance trusts and qualified personal residence trusts. You'd form an irrevocable **life insurance trust** for the purpose of keeping life insurance proceeds out of your estate. The insurance policy names the trust as beneficiary, and the trustee is given instructions on how to distribute the proceeds. This type of trust is particularly useful for life insurance policies that name a beneficiary who is not the spouse of the deceased. For many heirs, the proceeds of a life insurance policy can be the single largest component of the total estate. Note that the payment of premiums is considered a gift for tax purposes under this arrangement, so the allowable annual tax-free gift limits ($11,000 per person per year in 2004) apply.

life insurance trust

A type of living trust designed to remove the proceeds of a life insurance policy from your estate.

Another type of living trust is the **qualified personal residence trust**, which removes one or more personal residences from your estate. If you retain the right to live in the residence, the residence will pass to the person designated in the trust without going through the probate process. However, your estate will still include the value of the residence for the purposes of calculating estate taxes.

qualified personal residence trust

A type of living trust designed to remove a personal residence from your estate for probate purposes.

Common Types of Testamentary Trusts. Unlike a living trust, a testamentary trust is created by your will and goes into effect after your death. These trusts are commonly used to avoid estate taxes and to provide asset management for children or grandchildren who are too young or too irresponsible to manage the estate proceeds themselves. The most important types of trust in this category are the standard family trust and the qualified terminable interest property (Q-TIP) trust.

The **standard family trust** goes by many names, including *credit shelter trust, residuary trust, A-B trust, unified credit trust,* and *exemption equivalent trust.* The purpose of this type of trust is to allow you to transfer your entire estate to your spouse and then to his or her heirs (your children) upon his or her death without any estate taxes being paid. In the absence of such a trust, you could transfer everything to your spouse free of tax in your will, but your spouse's heirs might later owe taxes when the estate passes to them.

standard family trust

A trust for married couples designed to avoid estate taxes on the estate of the surviving spouse.

Suppose you're concerned that your spouse will remarry and the assets will never reach your children. In that case, you can set up a **qualified terminable interest property (Q-TIP) trust.** A Q-TIP trust is much like a standard family trust except that the grantor retains control over the ultimate beneficiaries of the estate. Instead of being transferred by your spouse's will, the trust automatically transfers to your children (or other designated beneficiary) upon your spouse's death.

qualified terminable interest property (Q-TIP) trust

A trust for married couples in which the grantor retains control over the ultimate beneficiaries of the estate.

Prior to the new estate tax reductions, estate planners would commonly recommend that wealthier clients establish trusts for children (or other family members) and fund them with the maximum amount allowed under estate tax exemption rules, with the remainder going to the surviving spouse. Let's look at how this type of arrangement might benefit your heirs. Suppose that you and your spouse have an estate valued at $4 million. You die first, in 2005, and leave your half of the estate to your wife, tax-free because of the unlimited marital deduction. It's possible, of course, that your wife will live long enough to deplete the estate, but suppose instead that she dies a year after your death, and the $4 million estate is still intact. The 2006 exemption amount under the Economic Growth and Tax Relief Reconciliation Act is $2 million, so your estate will be subject to estate taxes on the other $2 million (the maximum rate, 46% in 2006). If, instead, your will had designated a Q-TIP trust to receive your $2 million estate, to be used by your wife during her lifetime with the remainder going to your children when she died, then no estate tax would be due upon her death, since the trust assets would not be included in your wife's estate. This simple strategy would save your heirs several hundred thousand dollars.

Charitable Trusts. Trusts can also be established for the benefit of charitable institutions. As we've discussed, your will can transfer wealth to charities free of estate tax, so the purpose of this type of trust is not to avoid estate taxes. Instead, the objective of a charitable trust is to allow a charity to benefit from your assets during your lifetime while allowing you to retain either the use of or the income from an asset and to take an income tax deduction for the charitable donation. A **charitable remainder trust** allows you to give away an asset but retain the cash flow generated by that asset during your lifetime. Upon your death, the charity is the beneficiary of the trust assets. In contrast, a **charitable lead (or income) trust** provides income to the charity during your lifetime or for a period of years, after which the property goes to a beneficiary of your designation. If you set up this type of trust, you get an immediate income tax deduction for the present value of the expected future income to be received by the charity.

charitable remainder trust

A trust that enables the grantor to give an asset to a charity but retain the cash flow generated by that asset during his or her lifetime.

charitable lead (or income) trust

A trust that enables the grantor to give income to a charity during his or her lifetime or for a period of years but transfer the asset upon his or her death to a chosen beneficiary.

Gifting Alternatives

In making gifts, it's important to consider the tax consequences. If charitable giving is one of your estate planning objectives, you should make the gifts in a way that will take advantage of income tax rules as well. Charitable gifts will never be subject to estate taxation and, while you're alive, are deductible from your current income in calculating your federal income tax liability. You can also reduce the taxes payable upon your death by gifting your tax-deferred retirement plan assets to a charity. Since the contributions to these accounts were made with pre-tax dollars, the assets will be subject to income tax when distributed (while you're alive or after you die). However, these taxes can be avoided if you specifically designate in your will that qualified retirement account assets will go to a charity. These organizations are tax-exempt, so you'll be effectively giving the charity the full amount of your account whereas anyone else you gave it to would only receive the net after taxes.

You can also reduce the estate taxes that will be payable upon your death by giving away some of your assets while you are alive. As previously discussed, gifts that you make to individuals during your lifetime are subject to annual and lifetime limits. Exceeding these limits may result in greater estate taxes being owed upon your death. However, since you can give the allowed annual amount to any number of people, individuals with sizable estates should seriously consider gifting during their lifetime. Not only will they have the immediate gratification of seeing the results of their gifts, whether to charity or individuals, but they will also reduce the likelihood that their estates will be eroded by taxes when they die.

Learning by Doing 17-3

1. You'd like to leave all your wealth to your grandchildren when you die, but you want to be sure that you and your wife will have enough to live on in the meantime. What type of trust could you use to accomplish this?
2. You have a portfolio of bonds that generate substantial income every year. You've heard that your alma mater is having some current cash flow problems. How can you help out your alma mater but still leave all your assets to your children when you die? Does this strategy offer any current tax advantages to you?

Summary

1 **Understand the process of estate planning.** Estate planning is the process of developing a plan for what will happen to your wealth and dependents when you die. The estate-planning process requires that you evaluate your financial situation to determine your needs, establish strategies that will accomplish your objectives, and regularly reevaluate your plan as your life situation changes. These steps may require the assistance of an estate-planning attorney or other professional.

2 **Identify the key elements of an estate plan.** Estate plans may include a will, a living will, a durable power of attorney, a letter of last instruction, and various trusts.

3 **Understand why your heirs will benefit if you have a valid will and well-organized legal and financial records.** Having a valid will in place reduces family stress at the time of your death, ensures that your assets are distributed according to your wishes, and allows you to be the one to determine the guardianship of your children. Your family will also benefit if you have your financial and personal records well organized and accessible, since that will allow the settlement of your estate to occur with a minimum of difficulty.

4 **Estimate the size of your estate and the taxes that would be owed upon your death.** Your gross estate is your net worth plus the value of certain life insurance and retirement plan assets. To determine the taxable amount of an estate, the gross estate is reduced by the costs of administering the estate and the unlimited marital and charitable deductions. Under current law, the estate is then allowed to exempt a certain amount of wealth, and the estate tax is applied to the remainder before distribution to heirs. The estate tax is gradually being phased out and will be repealed as of 2010; however, a "sunset" provision will reinstate the tax in 2011 unless further legislation is passed by Congress.

5 **Know how to use trusts, gifts, and charitable contributions to minimize estate taxes.** You can reduce the size of your taxable estate by making gifts during your lifetime or by transferring some of your assets to trusts. Gifts are tax-free as long as they don't exceed allowable annual and lifetime limits. In addition, you can transfer an unlimited amount of wealth to charity through your will without it being subject to estate or gift tax.

Key Terms

beneficiaries (560)
capacity (560)
charitable lead (or income) trust (571)
charitable remainder trust (571)
codicil (563)
community property (564)
durable power of attorney (558)
escheat (558)
estate (555)
estate planning (555)
executor or executrix (561)
grantor (569)
heir (557)
intestate (557)
irrevocable trust (570)
joint tenancy with right of survivorship (563)
letter of last instructions (559)
life insurance trust (571)
living trust (570)
living will (558)
pourover will (570)
probate (555)
qualified personal residence trust (571)
qualified terminable interest property (Q-TIP) trust (571)
revocable trust (570)
standard family trust (571)
tenancy in common (564)
testamentary trust (570)
testator (560)
trust (559)
trustee (569)
will (557)

Concept Review Questions

1. What is an estate plan, and why is it important for everyone to include one in his or her personal financial plan?
2. What are some of the adverse consequences that can result from the failure to do any estate planning?
3. How might your estate plan be expected to change over your life cycle?
4. Identify and explain the key components of an estate plan.
5. What does it mean to "die intestate"? What happens to your estate under those circumstances?
6. What is a living will, and what are the advantages of having one?
7. What types of information would you probably want to include in a letter of last instructions? If this is not a legally binding document, why should you bother to draft one?
8. What are the requirements for a valid will? What elements are commonly included in a will?
9. Why do so many people not have valid wills?
10. Why must there be witnesses to your will?
11. Aside from passing property by will, what other methods can be used to transfer property at death?
12. What changes are currently being made to federal estate taxes? Are these changes permanent?
13. How are estate and gift taxes related to each other? How do the changes in federal estate taxes affect the gift tax?
14. What are the current limits on tax-free gifts?
15. Does a wife ever have to pay estate tax on an inheritance from her husband? Why or why not?
16. What are the two primary ways of reducing the size of your taxable estate? Why would you want to do this?
17. What is a trust, and what are the purposes of such an arrangement in the context of estate planning?
18. Describe two types of living trusts, and explain when each of them might be appropriate for an estate plan.
19. Describe two types of testamentary trusts, and explain when each of them might be appropriate for an estate plan.
20. Describe two types of charitable trusts, and explain when each of them might be appropriate for an estate plan.

Application Problems

1. ***Estate Planning over the Life Cycle.*** For each of the following, identify estate-planning goals that would be appropriate considering life-cycle stage and family circumstances:
   a. Single college student, age 20, negative net worth
   b. Married couple, age 30, two dependent children, $150,000 net worth
   c. Retired couple with independent adult children, $1 million net worth
   d. Retired widower with dependent children, $5 million net worth
2. ***Estate-Planning Tools.*** For each of the following estate-planning goals, indicate what type of estate-planning tool or strategy could be used to help accomplish the goal:
   a. Ensure that your daughter ends up with the family china (instead of your sister, who lives closer and will likely come to help clean out your belongings after you die)
   b. Ensure that you aren't kept alive by artificial means when there's no chance of your recovery from a terminal illness or mental incompetence
   c. Provide for your children's college education after you die
   d. Make sure your children don't have to pay estate taxes
3. ***Type of Trust.*** For each of the following situations, identify what type of trust would be appropriate, if any:
   a. You want to leave your estate to your wife but at the same time ensure that, upon her death, your children will inherit what's left.
   b. You want to keep your life insurance proceeds out of your taxable estate, and your daughter is the named beneficiary.
   c. You want to be able to live in your home until you die and have it pass automatically to your children without becoming part of your estate.

d. You want to give income from your investment account to a charity while you are living and have the account pass to your heirs when you die.

PFP Worksheet 55
Estate Tax Calculation

4. ***Calculating Taxable Estate.*** Ryan Stern died in 2005 and left an estate valued at $2,000,000 after the payment of his debts. His will gave $50,000 to the Humane Society, $100,000 to the University of Missouri, $150,000 to the Boy Scouts of America, and the remainder to his sister Mindy. The expenses of settling the estate were $10,000 for the funeral, $5,000 to his brother as executor, and $3,000 to accountants and lawyers.
   a. Use the worksheet in your *Personal Financial Planner* to calculate the gross estate, adjusted gross estate, and taxable estate.
   b. What is the applicable exemption for 2005?
   c. What amount of Ryan Stern's estate will be taxable, and what is the maximum tax rate?

Using Web Resources for Financial Planning

1. ***Try Out an Estate Tax Calculator.*** To see how various aspects of your estate will affect your tax obligations in the future, go to *www.willsandprobate.com* and click on the "Estate Tax Calculator." If you don't have much wealth now, you can enter hypothetical information. For example, suppose you carry $500,000 in life insurance, your retirement plan assets total $750,000, you have $400,000 in other assets, and you owe $200,000 in debts. What estate tax would be owed on your death?
2. ***Write Your Living Will.*** The Partnership for Caring, together with other organizations, has formed the Last Acts Partnership, which is intended to help people plan for their deaths. At the organization's website, *www.partnershipforcaring.org* you can download free living will and medical power of attorney sample documents. You can also find suggestions for talking about these issues with your family by clicking on "Talking" to find the booklet "Talking About Your Choices."
3. ***Look Up the Wills of Famous People.*** Since probated wills are public documents, you can find the wills of the rich and famous online. At *www.courttv.com/people/wills*, find out to whom Jerry Garcia (lead singer and guitarist for the Grateful Dead) left his guitars. Other legends included on the site are Elvis Presley, John Lennon, and Marilyn Monroe.
4. ***Prepare for Your Visit to an Estate-Planning Lawyer.*** In order to help you with your estate plan, a lawyer will need a lot of financial information about you. At *www.estateplanningattys.com*, you can print out an "Estate Planning Questionnaire." This fairly lengthy document will ask you for all the information an estate-planning professional will need.

Learning by Doing Solutions

LBD 17-1: 1. Eva's will doesn't meet the requirements for a valid will because she didn't date it and she didn't sign it in front of witnesses.

LBD 17-2: 1. No estate taxes are due since a wife can leave as much as she wants to her husband; 2. The 2007 exemption is $2,000,000. An amount above this exemption will be subject to estate tax.

LBD 17-3: 1. Establish a Q-TIP trust to allow you and your spouse to utilize the assets and income while you're alive. When you both die, the trust's remaining assets will go to the beneficiaries, your grandchildren; 2. Use a charitable income trust. The charity will receive the trust's income during your lifetime. When you die, your beneficiaries will receive the trust's assets. You'll get a current tax deduction for the present value of the income stream.

Building Financial Planning Skills Through Case Applications

Case 17-1 Mina Bhatti Needs a Will

Mina Bhatti is a successful entrepreneur. She started a small bakery when she graduated from college and has turned it into a multi-million-dollar business. Mina is divorced and has had sole custody of her daughter Naitra, age 10, since her ex-husband left them six years ago. He provides no financial support for Naitra. Mina has spent a great deal of time running her business—so much that she has sometimes neglected her financial plan. Recently, though, she consulted a financial planner, who was adamant that she immediately take care of a few very important elements of her financial plan. First and foremost, he wants her to make a will right away. Mina and her ex-husband had made wills many years ago, but they predated Naitra's birth. In her old will, Mina left all her wealth to her husband. Mina's current assets are as follows:

Equity in family home	\$100,000
Business assets	\$250,000
Retirement account	\$200,000
Other investments	\$50,000
Total net worth	\$600,000

In the event of her death, Mina would want her sister Janna to be Naitra's guardian. Janna is aware of Mina's wish and has agreed to act in this capacity. Mina's brother Sanjay was named as the executor in her prior will and will probably be willing to continue in that role.

1. Does Mina need a will? What would happen if she died today (before drafting a new will)?
2. What features should Mina incorporate in her will?
3. Does she need to include a trust in her will? Why or why not?
4. If Mina names Janna as Naitra's guardian but Janna dies before she does, who will end up being guardian?
5. What duties will Sanjay have to perform as executor of the estate?

Case 17-2 A Plan to Minimize Estate Taxes

Crystal and Richard Ball are wealthy retirees who have an estate worth \$15 million. They have four adult children, ages 32 to 40, who are financially secure professionals, but their youngest child, Ricky, age 26, is a struggling rock musician. Since Richard always wished he had pursued a music career, Crystal and Richard have been providing continued support for their youngest in the hope that he might realize his dream. His siblings have not always been supportive of their parents on this issue, thinking that Ricky should "get a real job." Crystal's will currently leaves everything to Richard, and names their five children as equal contingent beneficiaries. Richard's will similarly leaves everything to Crystal. The Balls have recently consulted an estate-planning attorney and would like to put in place an estate plan that will minimize the estate taxes which might be payable upon their deaths and also achieve some other goals:

- Provide continued support for Ricky, as long as he is actively pursuing his music career
- Leave a modest inheritance (\$100,000) to each of their ten grandchildren, currently ages 2 to 11, to be received when they each reach the age of 30
- Provide for the income needs of the spouse who outlives the other
- Leave the remainder of their estate to the National Endowment for the Arts

1. Do Crystal and Richard need to write new wills to accomplish their objectives? Explain.
2. If they have done no additional estate planning and each carries a \$200,000 face value life insurance policy on the other, will any estate taxes be payable when one of them dies?
3. If the Balls simply rewrote their wills designating their grandchildren as the beneficiaries, would any estate tax be payable when either one of them died?
4. What types of trusts, if any, would you recommend they establish to meet their objectives?
5. What might be the Balls' motivation for not giving their grandchildren any inheritance until they reach the age of 30?
6. To minimize the family strife that might occur later, would you recommend that they discuss their estate plan with their children now? Why or why not?

LIFELONG PLANNING CASE

Part IV: Michael and Tori Garcia Deal with Aging Parents

Life Circumstances: Both age 40, married 18 years, daughter Holly age 11 and son Michael Jr. age 9.

Financial Challenges: Tori's parents are no longer able to care for themselves. The family must turn their attention to estate planning and long-term care.

Michael and Tori Garcia are doing well financially. The time they have invested in financial planning over the last fifteen years has had a beneficial impact. They have managed to keep their credit usage to a minimum, and they've increased their savings for education and for their children's education. With both children in school full-time, Tori has been able to focus more on her career as a real estate agent and her earnings have increased substantially.

The financial challenge faced by the Garcias at this point in their life is related not to their own finances, but to their parents'. Tori's mother and father, Juan and Maria Salvador, are ages 70 and 60, respectively, and live about four hours from the Garcias. Tori's other siblings live in other states. Juan was diagnosed with early-onset Alzheimer's disease a few years ago, and his condition has gradually deteriorated. Maria has thus far been able to care for her husband at home but unfortunately, she recently fell and broke her hip. Tori is currently taking care of her father and her parents' 10-year-old dog while her mother is in the hospital. Because of the distance, she is staying at her parents' home and has had to refer some of her real estate clients to other agents in her office. Michael has made arrangements to leave work early each day so that he can be home for the children after school. Maria's doctors have indicated that she will need to have nursing home or in-home care for a few weeks while she recuperates. It is doubtful that she will be able to continue taking care of Juan at home (even though she wants to), so Tori and Michael are trying to determine what their next steps should be. They have collected the following information about Tori's parents' finances:

Assets and Debts	
Bank accounts	$5,000
CDs (2 year maturity)	15,000
Value of home	250,000
Mortgage balance	30,000
Automobile	10,000
Camper	8,000
Investments	25,000
Juan's whole life insurance	50,000

Income (monthly)	
Social Security-Juan	$2,000
Investment income	400

Expenses (monthly)	
Health and medigap insurances	$700
Household expenses	800
Prescription drugs	300
Mortgage (5 years to go)	650

1. Make a list of each of the planning areas that must be addressed by the family in the near future. Would you recommend the Garcias consult with one or more planning professionals and, if so, which type(s) would be most appropriate?
2. Do the Salvadors have sufficient life insurance? In answering this, assume that their $50,000 face value policy has been paid-up since Juan turned age 65 and that the current cash value is $62,000. Maria does not have a life insurance policy. Do you think they would be eligible to purchase additional insurance, assuming they could afford the premium amount? Why or why not?
3. The Salvadors have never purchased long-term care insurance, and Maria's health insurance is basic plus major medical with a $1,000 deductible. Her husband is eligible for Medicare and pays for a medigap policy and a prescription drug discount card.
   a. If Maria must stay in a long-term care facility for 60 days, will her insurance pay for any of this expense? Will any public health care program help to cover her costs? Why ot why not?
   b. If Juan must be moved to a nursing home, will any of his insurance pay for it? For how long? How will he pay for it after that?
   c. Why do you suppose that the Salvadors never purchased long-term care insurance? Would it be possible to purchase it now? Why or why not? Could Tori purchase the insurance on behalf of one or both of her parents? Why might she want to do this?
4. Assume that the Salvadors have not done any estate planning to date.
   a. Identify some reasons why they may have neglected this component of their financial plan.
   b. Assuming that Tori can convince her mother to face these problems now, what are the most critical areas that need to be addressed?
   c. If both the Salvadors were to die in 2005, would there be any estate taxes due? Explain.
   d. If one of them died, would the surviving spouse experience any financial hardship? Explain.
   e. What could be done now to minimize future financial costs?
5. Tori and Michael are worried that both parents may need to be in an assisted-living environment before long. For the moment, they think that the best solution is to have Tori's mother move in with them and place her father in a nearby nursing home. The current cost for this type of custodial care is $3,000 per month, but is expected to rise at a rate of 5% per year and could also be higher if he becomes ill and requires a higher level of care.
   a. Assuming that her father lives to the average life expectancy, how long can they expect him to require long-term care?
   b. Will the Salvadors' assets be sufficient to cover this cost?
   c. Assuming that Maria doesn't require long-term care until after her husband dies, how much of their joint wealth will be left to cover her future costs?
   d. If their joint assets are depleted, how will Maria be able to afford long-term care?
6. In evaluating her parents' financial situation, Tori also discovers that her parents don't have valid wills. Why is this potentially a serious problem for them at this point in their lives? What would you suggest they do?
7. Should the Salvadors consider any of the following for their estate plan at this time? Why or why not?
   a. Gifting
   b. Trusts
   c. Living wills
8. Michael and Tori now realize that there can be serious consequences from the failure to plan. Michael would like to talk with his own parents about this subject. How would you suggest he bring it up, and what should he ask them?

DEVELOPING PERSONAL FINANCIAL skills for life

Learning about Yourself

17-1. The Top Ten Excuses for Not Having a Will

If you're like most people, you don't have a valid will. You probably aren't worried about estate taxes at this stage in your life, but after reading this chapter, you know more about how your family could be hurt if you die without a will. Why do so many people put off writing their wills? Consider the following excuses for not having a will and see how many apply to you:

_____ **1.** I'm young, so I don't need to worry about dying yet.
_____ **2.** I have very little in assets, so I don't need a will.
_____ **3.** Once I'm dead, I don't care who gets my stuff.
_____ **4.** Writing a will has been on my "to do" list for a while now.
_____ **5.** I'm always so busy that I just don't have the time to get my will done.
_____ **6.** I don't have enough money to pay a lawyer to draw up a will for me.
_____ **7.** It's too depressing to think about.
_____ **8.** It's pretty unlikely that both my spouse and I would die at the same time.
_____ **9.** I've given instructions to someone I trust about how to divide up my assets.
_____ **10** I don't even know where to start.

Developing Your Skills

17-2. Estate Planning Now and Later

1. Make a list of estate-planning objectives, given your current life-cycle stage and family situation.
2. Pretend that it's now 20 years in the future. Redo the list for the life-cycle stage and anticipated family situation that will be applicable at that time.

17-3. Making (or Revising) Your Will

If you don't currently have a will, use this exercise to write a first draft to present to a lawyer for finalizing. If you already have a will in place, use the exercise to review its terms and update it as necessary. To help you formulate the contents of your will, answer the following questions:

1. To whom do you want to leave your assets in the event of your death? Do you have any special items that you would like to give to certain people?
2. If you have children, whom would you like to be their guardian after your (and their other parent's) death? How will you provide (financially) for your children's care and education?
3. If you have pets, how will they be taken care of after you die?
4. Do you have adequate life insurance? Have you named a beneficiary and contingent beneficiary?
5. Have you named a beneficiary for your pension or retirement plan?

17-4. Write a Living Will

Use the sample living will provided in the chapter (or look at samples online) to think through your personal preferences for medical care in the event of terminal illness. Draft a living will that will help your family to make decisions on your behalf in those circumstances.

17-5. Estimate Your Estate Taxes

PFP Worksheet 55
Estate Tax Calculation

Use the worksheet in your *Personal Financial Planner* to estimate your taxable estate. Do the calculation for your current financial circumstances and also for your finances ten years from now. Note that this will require you to estimate the future value of real estate and other investment accounts as well as the amount of life insurance you expect to have in force at that time in your life.

Time Value of Money Calculations

Exhibit A-1 Future Value of a Lump Sum ($FVIF_{i\%,n}$)

$$FV = PV \times (1 + i)^n$$
$$= PV \times FVIF_{i,n}$$

Exhibit A-2 Present Value of a Lump Sum ($PVIF_{i\%,n}$)

$$PV = FV \times \left(\frac{1}{1 + i}\right)^n$$
$$= FV \times PVIF_{i,n}$$

Exhibit A-3 Future Value of an Annuity ($FVIFA_{i\%,n}$)

$$FVA = PMT \times \frac{(1 + i)^n - 1}{i}$$
$$= PMT \times FVIFA_{i,n}$$

Exhibit A-4 Present Value of an Annuity ($PVIFA_{i\%,n}$)

$$PVA = PMT \times \frac{1 - \left(\frac{1}{1 + i}\right)^n}{i}$$
$$= PMT \times PVIFA_{i,n}$$

Exhibit A-5 Monthly Payment Factors for Amortized Loans

$$PMT = \frac{\text{Loan Amount}}{1{,}000} \times \text{Payment factor}_{i,n}$$

Exhibit A-6 Present Value of Monthly Payments (Mortgage $\text{factor}_{i\%,n}$)

$$\text{Maximum mortgage amount} = \text{Affordable mortgage payment} \times \text{Mortgage factor}_{i,n}$$

Exhibit A-1 Future Value of a Lump Sum of $1 Compounded for a Given Number of Periods

Period	1%	2%	3%	4%	5%	6%	7%	8%	9%	10%	11%
1	1.010	1.020	1.030	1.040	1.050	1.060	1.070	1.080	1.090	1.100	1.110
2	1.020	1.040	1.061	1.082	1.103	1.124	1.145	1.166	1.188	1.210	1.232
3	1.030	1.061	1.093	1.125	1.158	1.191	1.225	1.260	1.295	1.331	1.368
4	1.041	1.082	1.126	1.170	1.216	1.262	1.311	1.360	1.412	1.464	1.518
5	1.051	1.104	1.159	1.217	1.276	1.338	1.403	1.469	1.539	1.611	1.685
6	1.062	1.126	1.194	1.265	1.340	1.419	1.501	1.587	1.677	1.772	1.870
7	1.072	1.149	1.230	1.316	1.407	1.504	1.606	1.714	1.828	1.949	2.076
8	1.083	1.172	1.267	1.369	1.477	1.594	1.718	1.851	1.993	2.144	2.305
9	1.094	1.195	1.305	1.423	1.551	1.689	1.838	1.999	2.172	2.358	2.558
10	1.105	1.219	1.344	1.480	1.629	1.791	1.967	2.159	2.367	2.594	2.839
11	1.116	1.243	1.384	1.539	1.710	1.898	2.105	2.332	2.580	2.853	3.152
12	1.127	1.268	1.426	1.601	1.796	2.012	2.252	2.518	2.813	3.138	3.498
13	1.138	1.294	1.469	1.665	1.886	2.133	2.410	2.720	3.066	3.452	3.883
14	1.149	1.319	1.513	1.732	1.980	2.261	2.579	2.937	3.342	3.797	4.310
15	1.161	1.346	1.558	1.801	2.079	2.397	2.759	3.172	3.642	4.177	4.785
16	1.173	1.373	1.605	1.873	2.183	2.540	2.952	3.426	3.970	4.595	5.311
17	1.184	1.400	1.653	1.948	2.292	2.693	3.159	3.700	4.328	5.054	5.895
18	1.196	1.428	1.702	2.026	2.407	2.854	3.380	3.996	4.717	5.560	6.544
19	1.208	1.457	1.754	2.107	2.527	3.026	3.617	4.316	5.142	6.116	7.263
20	1.220	1.486	1.806	2.191	2.653	3.207	3.870	4.661	5.604	6.727	8.062
25	1.282	1.641	2.094	2.666	3.386	4.292	5.427	6.848	8.623	10.835	13.585
30	1.348	1.811	2.427	3.243	4.322	5.743	7.612	10.063	13.268	17.449	22.892
35	1.417	2.000	2.814	3.946	5.516	7.686	10.677	14.785	20.414	28.102	38.575
40	1.489	2.208	3.262	4.801	7.040	10.286	14.974	21.725	31.409	45.259	65.001
45	1.565	2.438	3.782	5.841	8.985	13.765	21.002	31.920	48.327	72.890	109.530
50	1.645	2.692	4.384	7.107	11.467	18.420	29.457	46.902	74.358	117.391	184.565

Period	12%	13%	14%	15%	16%	17%	18%	19%	20%	25%	30%
1	1.120	1.130	1.140	1.150	1.160	1.170	1.180	1.190	1.200	1.250	1.300
2	1.254	1.277	1.300	1.323	1.346	1.369	1.392	1.416	1.440	1.563	1.690
3	1.405	1.443	1.482	1.521	1.561	1.602	1.643	1.685	1.728	1.953	2.197
4	1.574	1.630	1.689	1.749	1.811	1.874	1.939	2.005	2.074	2.441	2.856
5	1.762	1.842	1.925	2.011	2.100	2.192	2.288	2.386	2.488	3.052	3.713
6	1.974	2.082	2.195	2.313	2.436	2.565	2.700	2.840	2.986	3.815	4.827
7	2.211	2.353	2.502	2.660	2.826	3.001	3.185	3.379	3.583	4.768	6.275
8	2.476	2.658	2.853	3.059	3.278	3.511	3.759	4.021	4.300	5.960	8.157
9	2.773	3.004	3.252	3.518	3.803	4.108	4.435	4.785	5.160	7.451	10.604
10	3.106	3.395	3.707	4.046	4.411	4.807	5.234	5.695	6.192	9.313	13.786
11	3.479	3.836	4.226	4.652	5.117	5.624	6.176	6.777	7.430	11.642	17.922
12	3.896	4.335	4.818	5.350	5.936	6.580	7.288	8.064	8.916	14.552	23.298
13	4.363	4.898	5.492	6.153	6.886	7.699	8.599	9.596	10.699	18.190	30.288
14	4.887	5.535	6.261	7.076	7.988	9.007	10.147	11.420	12.839	22.737	39.374
15	5.474	6.254	7.138	8.137	9.266	10.539	11.974	13.590	15.407	28.422	51.186
16	6.130	7.067	8.137	9.358	10.748	12.330	14.129	16.172	18.488	35.527	66.542
17	6.866	7.986	9.276	10.761	12.468	14.426	16.672	19.244	22.186	44.409	86.504
18	7.690	9.024	10.575	12.375	14.463	16.879	19.673	22.901	26.623	55.511	112.455
19	8.613	10.197	12.056	14.232	16.777	19.748	23.214	27.252	31.948	69.389	146.192
20	9.646	11.523	13.743	16.367	19.461	23.106	27.393	32.429	38.338	86.736	190.050
25	17.000	21.231	26.462	32.919	40.874	50.658	62.669	77.388	95.396	264.698	705.641
30	29.960	39.116	50.950	66.212	85.850	111.065	143.371	184.675	237.376	807.794	2,619.996
35	52.800	72.069	98.100	133.176	180.314	243.503	327.997	440.701	590.668	2,465.190	9,727.860
40	93.051	132.782	188.884	267.864	378.721	533.869	750.378	1,051.668	1,469.772	7,523.164	36,118.865
45	163.988	244.641	363.679	538.769	795.444	1,170.479	1,716.684	2,509.651	3,657.262	22,958.874	134,106.817
50	289.002	450.736	700.233	1,083.657	1,670.704	2,566.215	3,927.357	5,988.914	9,100.438	70,064.923	497,929.223

Exhibit A-2 Present Value of a Lump Sum of $1 to Be Received at the End of a Given Number of Periods

Periods	1%	2%	3%	4%	5%	6%	7%	8%	9%	10%	11%
1	0.990	0.980	0.971	0.962	0.952	0.943	0.935	0.926	0.917	0.909	0.901
2	0.980	0.961	0.943	0.925	0.907	0.890	0.873	0.857	0.842	0.826	0.812
3	0.971	0.942	0.915	0.889	0.864	0.840	0.816	0.794	0.772	0.751	0.731
4	0.961	0.924	0.888	0.855	0.823	0.792	0.763	0.735	0.708	0.683	0.659
5	0.951	0.906	0.863	0.822	0.784	0.747	0.713	0.681	0.650	0.621	0.593
6	0.942	0.888	0.837	0.790	0.746	0.705	0.666	0.630	0.596	0.564	0.535
7	0.933	0.871	0.813	0.760	0.711	0.665	0.623	0.583	0.547	0.513	0.482
8	0.923	0.853	0.789	0.731	0.677	0.627	0.582	0.540	0.502	0.467	0.434
9	0.914	0.837	0.766	0.703	0.645	0.592	0.544	0.500	0.460	0.424	0.391
10	0.905	0.820	0.744	0.676	0.614	0.558	0.508	0.463	0.422	0.386	0.352
11	0.896	0.804	0.722	0.650	0.585	0.527	0.475	0.429	0.388	0.350	0.317
12	0.887	0.788	0.701	0.625	0.557	0.497	0.444	0.397	0.356	0.319	0.286
13	0.879	0.773	0.681	0.601	0.530	0.469	0.415	0.368	0.326	0.290	0.258
14	0.870	0.758	0.661	0.577	0.505	0.442	0.388	0.340	0.299	0.263	0.232
15	0.861	0.743	0.642	0.555	0.481	0.417	0.362	0.315	0.275	0.239	0.209
16	0.853	0.728	0.623	0.534	0.458	0.394	0.339	0.292	0.252	0.218	0.188
17	0.844	0.714	0.605	0.513	0.436	0.371	0.317	0.270	0.231	0.198	0.170
18	0.836	0.700	0.587	0.494	0.416	0.350	0.296	0.250	0.212	0.180	0.153
19	0.828	0.686	0.570	0.475	0.396	0.331	0.277	0.232	0.194	0.164	0.138
20	0.820	0.673	0.554	0.456	0.377	0.312	0.258	0.215	0.178	0.149	0.124
25	0.780	0.610	0.478	0.375	0.295	0.233	0.184	0.146	0.116	0.092	0.074
30	0.742	0.552	0.412	0.308	0.231	0.174	0.131	0.099	0.075	0.057	0.044
35	0.706	0.500	0.355	0.253	0.181	0.130	0.094	0.068	0.049	0.036	0.026
40	0.672	0.453	0.307	0.208	0.142	0.097	0.067	0.046	0.032	0.022	0.015
45	0.639	0.410	0.264	0.171	0.111	0.073	0.048	0.031	0.021	0.014	0.009
50	0.608	0.372	0.228	0.141	0.087	0.054	0.034	0.021	0.013	0.009	0.005

Periods	12%	13%	14%	15%	16%	17%	18%	19%	20%	25%	30%
1	0.893	0.885	0.877	0.870	0.862	0.855	0.847	0.840	0.833	0.800	0.769
2	0.797	0.783	0.769	0.756	0.743	0.731	0.718	0.706	0.694	0.640	0.592
3	0.712	0.693	0.675	0.658	0.641	0.624	0.609	0.593	0.579	0.512	0.455
4	0.636	0.613	0.592	0.572	0.552	0.534	0.516	0.499	0.482	0.410	0.350
5	0.567	0.543	0.519	0.497	0.476	0.456	0.437	0.419	0.402	0.328	0.269
6	0.507	0.480	0.456	0.432	0.410	0.390	0.370	0.352	0.335	0.262	0.207
7	0.452	0.425	0.400	0.376	0.354	0.333	0.314	0.296	0.279	0.210	0.159
8	0.404	0.376	0.315	0.327	0.305	0.285	0.266	0.249	0.233	0.168	0.123
9	0.361	0.333	0.308	0.284	0.263	0.243	0.225	0.209	0.194	0.134	0.094
10	0.322	0.295	0.270	0.247	0.227	0.208	0.191	0.176	0.162	0.107	0.073
11	0.287	0.261	0.237	0.215	0.195	0.178	0.162	0.148	0.135	0.086	0.056
12	0.257	0.231	0.208	0.187	0.168	0.152	0.137	0.124	0.112	0.069	0.043
13	0.229	0.204	0.182	0.163	0.145	0.130	0.116	0.104	0.093	0.055	0.033
14	0.205	0.181	0.160	0.141	0.125	0.111	0.099	0.088	0.078	0.044	0.025
15	0.183	0.160	0.140	0.123	0.108	0.095	0.084	0.074	0.065	0.035	0.020
16	0.163	0.141	0.123	0.107	0.093	0.081	0.071	0.062	0.054	0.028	0.015
17	0.146	0.125	0.108	0.093	0.080	0.069	0.060	0.052	0.045	0.023	0.012
18	0.130	0.111	0.095	0.081	0.069	0.059	0.051	0.044	0.038	0.018	0.009
19	0.116	0.098	0.083	0.070	0.060	0.051	0.043	0.037	0.031	0.014	0.007
20	0.104	0.087	0.073	0.061	0.051	0.043	0.037	0.031	0.026	0.012	0.005
25	0.059	0.047	0.038	0.030	0.024	0.020	0.016	0.013	0.010	0.004	0.001
30	0.033	0.026	0.020	0.015	0.012	0.009	0.007	0.005	0.004	0.001	0.0004
35	0.019	0.014	0.010	0.008	0.006	0.004	0.003	0.002	0.002	0.0004	0.0001
40	0.011	0.008	0.005	0.004	0.003	0.002	0.001	0.001	0.0007	0.0001	0.00003
45	0.006	0.004	0.003	0.002	0.001	0.001	0.001	0.0004	0.0003	0.00004	0.00001
50	0.003	0.002	0.001	0.001	0.001	0.0004	0.0003	0.0002	0.0001	0.00001	0.000002

Exhibit A-3 Future Value of a Given Number of $1 End-of-Period Payments

Periods	1%	2%	3%	4%	5%	6%	7%	8%	9%	10%	11%
1	1.000	1.000	1.000	1.000	1.000	1.000	1.000	1.000	1.000	1.000	1.000
2	2.010	2.020	2.030	2.040	2.050	2.060	2.070	2.080	2.090	2.100	2.110
3	3.030	3.060	3.091	3.122	3.153	3.184	3.215	3.246	3.278	3.310	3.342
4	4.060	4.122	4.184	4.246	4.310	4.375	4.440	4.506	4.573	4.641	4.710
5	5.101	5.204	5.309	5.416	5.526	5.637	5.751	5.867	5.985	6.105	6.228
6	6.152	6.308	6.468	6.633	6.802	6.975	7.153	7.336	7.523	7.716	7.913
7	7.214	7.434	7.662	7.898	8.142	8.394	8.654	8.923	9.200	9.487	9.783
8	8.286	8.583	8.892	9.214	9.549	9.897	10.260	10.637	11.028	11.436	11.859
9	9.369	9.755	10.159	10.583	11.027	11.491	11.978	12.488	13.021	13.579	14.164
10	10.462	10.950	11.464	12.006	12.578	13.181	13.816	14.487	15.193	15.937	16.722
11	11.567	12.169	12.808	13.486	14.207	14.972	15.784	16.645	17.560	18.531	19.561
12	12.683	13.412	14.192	15.026	15.917	16.870	17.888	18.977	20.141	21.384	22.713
13	13.809	14.680	15.618	16.627	17.713	18.882	20.141	21.495	22.953	24.523	26.212
14	14.947	15.974	17.086	18.292	19.599	21.015	22.550	24.215	26.019	27.975	30.095
15	16.097	17.293	18.599	20.024	21.579	23.276	25.129	27.152	29.361	31.772	34.405
16	17.258	18.639	20.157	21.825	23.657	25.673	27.888	30.324	33.003	35.950	39.190
17	18.430	20.012	21.762	23.698	25.840	28.213	30.840	33.750	36.974	40.545	44.501
18	19.615	21.412	23.414	25.645	28.132	30.906	33.999	37.450	41.301	45.599	50.396
19	20.811	22.841	25.117	27.671	30.539	33.760	37.379	41.446	46.018	51.159	56.939
20	22.019	24.297	26.870	29.778	33.066	36.786	40.995	45.762	51.160	57.275	64.203
25	28.243	32.030	36.459	41.646	47.727	54.865	63.249	73.106	84.701	98.347	114.413
30	34.785	40.568	47.575	56.085	66.439	79.058	94.461	113.283	136.308	164.494	199.021
35	41.660	49.994	60.462	73.652	90.320	111.435	138.237	172.317	215.711	271.024	341.590
40	48.886	60.402	75.401	95.026	120.800	154.762	199.635	259.057	337.882	442.593	581.826
45	56.481	71.893	92.720	121.029	159.700	212.744	285.749	386.506	525.859	718.905	986.639
50	64.463	84.579	112.797	152.667	209.348	290.336	406.529	573.770	815.084	1,163.909	1,668.771

Periods	12%	13%	14%	15%	16%	17%	18%	19%	20%	25%	30%
1	1.000	1.000	1.000	1.000	1.000	1.000	1.000	1.000	1.000	1.000	1.000
2	2.210	2.130	2.140	2.150	2.160	2.170	2.180	2.190	2.200	2.250	2.300
3	3.374	3.407	3.440	3.473	3.506	3.539	3.572	3.606	3.640	3.813	3.990
4	4.779	4.850	4.921	4.993	5.066	5.141	5.215	5.291	5.368	5.766	6.187
5	6.353	6.480	6.610	6.742	6.877	7.014	7.154	7.297	7.442	8.207	9.043
6	8.115	8.323	8.536	8.754	8.977	9.207	9.442	9.683	9.930	11.259	12.756
7	10.089	10.405	10.730	11.067	11.414	11.772	12.142	12.523	12.916	15.073	17.583
8	12.300	12.757	13.233	13.727	14.240	14.773	15.327	15.902	16.499	19.842	23.858
9	14.776	15.416	16.085	16.786	17.519	18.285	19.086	19.923	20.799	25.802	32.015
10	17.549	18.420	19.337	20.304	21.321	22.393	23.521	24.709	25.959	33.253	42.619
11	20.655	21.814	23.045	24.349	25.733	27.200	28.755	30.404	32.150	42.566	56.405
12	24.133	25.650	27.271	29.002	30.850	32.824	34.931	37.180	39.581	54.208	74.327
13	28.029	29.985	32.089	34.352	36.786	39.404	42.219	45.244	48.497	68.760	97.625
14	32.393	34.883	37.581	40.505	43.672	47.103	50.818	54.841	59.196	86.949	127.913
15	37.280	40.417	43.842	47.580	51.660	56.110	60.965	66.261	72.035	109.687	167.286
16	42.753	46.672	50.980	55.717	60.925	66.649	72.939	79.850	87.442	138.109	218.472
17	48.884	53.739	59.118	65.075	71.673	78.979	87.068	96.022	105.931	173.636	285.014
18	55.750	61.725	68.394	75.836	84.141	93.406	103.740	115.266	128.117	218.045	371.518
19	63.440	70.749	78.969	88.212	98.603	110.285	123.414	138.166	154.740	273.556	483.973
20	72.052	80.947	91.025	102.444	115.380	130.033	146.628	165.418	186.688	342.945	630.165
25	133.334	155.620	181.871	212.793	249.214	292.105	342.603	402.042	471.981	1,054.791	2,348.803
30	241.333	293.199	356.787	434.745	530.312	647.439	790.948	966.712	1,181.882	3,227.174	8,729.985
35	431.663	546.681	693.573	881.170	1,120.713	1,426.491	1,816.652	2,314.214	2,948.341	9,856.761	32,422.868
40	767.091	1,013.704	1,342.025	1,779.090	2,360.757	3,134.522	4,163.213	5,529.829	7,343.858	30,088.655	120,392.883
45	1,358.230	1,874.165	2,590.565	3,585.128	4,965.274	6,879.291	9,531.577	13,203.424	18,281.310	91,831.496	447,019.389
50	2,400.018	3,459.507	4,994.521	7,217.716	10,435.649	15,089.502	21,813.094	31,515.336	45,497.191	280,255.693	1,659,760.743

Exhibit A-4 Present Value of a Given Number of $1 End-of-Period Payments

Periods	1%	2%	3%	4%	5%	6%	7%	8%	9%	10%	11%
1	0.990	0.980	0.971	0.962	0.952	0.943	0.935	0.926	0.917	0.909	0.901
2	1.970	1.942	1.913	1.886	1.859	1.833	1.808	1.783	1.759	1.736	1.713
3	2.941	2.884	2.829	2.775	2.723	2.673	2.624	2.577	2.531	2.487	2.444
4	3.902	3.808	3.717	3.630	3.546	3.465	3.387	3.312	3.240	3.170	3.102
5	4.853	4.713	4.580	4.452	4.329	4.212	4.100	3.993	3.890	3.791	3.696
6	5.795	5.601	5.417	5.242	5.076	4.917	4.767	4.623	4.486	4.355	4.231
7	6.728	6.472	6.230	6.002	5.786	5.582	5.389	5.206	5.033	4.868	4.712
8	7.652	7.325	7.020	6.733	6.463	6.210	5.971	5.747	5.535	5.335	5.146
9	8.566	8.162	7.786	7.435	7.108	6.802	6.515	6.247	5.995	5.759	5.537
10	9.471	8.983	8.530	8.111	7.722	7.360	7.024	6.710	6.418	6.145	5.889
11	10.368	9.787	9.253	8.760	8.306	7.887	7.499	7.139	6.805	6.495	6.207
12	11.255	10.575	9.954	9.385	8.863	8.384	7.943	7.536	7.161	6.814	6.492
13	12.134	11.348	10.635	9.986	9.394	8.853	8.358	7.904	7.487	7.103	6.750
14	13.004	12.106	11.296	10.563	9.899	9.295	8.745	8.244	7.786	7.367	6.982
15	13.865	12.849	11.938	11.118	10.380	9.712	9.108	8.559	8.061	7.606	7.191
16	14.718	13.578	12.561	11.652	10.838	10.106	9.447	8.851	8.313	7.824	7.379
17	15.562	14.292	13.166	12.166	11.274	10.477	9.763	9.122	8.544	8.022	7.549
18	16.398	14.992	13.754	12.659	11.690	10.828	10.059	9.372	8.756	8.201	7.702
19	17.226	15.678	14.324	13.134	12.085	11.158	10.336	9.604	8.950	8.365	7.839
20	18.046	16.351	14.877	13.590	12.462	11.470	10.594	9.818	9.129	8.514	7.963
25	22.023	19.523	17.413	15.622	14.094	12.783	11.654	10.675	9.823	9.077	8.422
30	25.808	22.396	19.600	17.292	15.372	13.765	12.409	11.258	10.274	9.427	8.694
35	29.409	24.999	21.487	18.665	16.374	14.498	12.948	11.655	10.567	9.644	8.855
40	32.835	27.355	23.115	19.793	17.159	15.046	13.332	11.925	10.757	9.779	8.951
45	36.095	29.490	24.519	20.720	17.774	15.456	13.606	12.108	10.881	9.863	9.008
50	39.196	31.424	25.730	21.482	18.256	15.762	13.801	12.233	10.962	9.915	9.042

Periods	12%	13%	14%	15%	16%	17%	18%	19%	20%	25%	30%
1	0.893	0.885	0.877	0.870	0.862	0.855	0.847	0.840	0.833	0.800	0.769
2	1.690	1.668	1.647	1.626	1.605	1.585	1.566	1.547	1.528	1.440	1.361
3	2.402	2.361	2.322	2.283	2.246	2.210	2.174	2.140	2.106	1.952	1.816
4	3.037	2.974	2.914	2.855	2.798	2.743	2.690	2.639	2.589	2.362	2.166
5	3.605	3.517	3.433	3.352	3.274	3.199	3.127	3.058	2.991	2.689	2.436
6	4.111	3.998	3.889	3.784	3.685	3.589	3.498	3.410	3.326	2.951	2.643
7	4.564	4.423	4.288	4.160	4.039	3.922	3.812	3.706	3.605	3.161	2.802
8	4.968	4.799	4.639	4.487	4.344	4.207	4.078	3.954	3.837	3.329	2.925
9	5.328	5.132	4.946	4.772	4.607	4.451	4.303	4.163	4.031	3.463	3.019
10	5.650	5.426	5.216	5.019	4.833	4.659	4.494	4.339	4.192	3.571	3.092
11	5.938	5.687	5.453	5.234	5.029	4.836	4.656	4.486	4.327	3.656	3.147
12	6.194	5.918	5.660	5.421	5.197	4.988	4.793	4.611	4.439	3.725	3.190
13	6.424	6.122	5.842	5.583	5.342	5.118	4.910	4.715	4.533	3.780	3.223
14	6.628	6.302	6.002	5.724	5.468	5.229	5.008	4.802	4.611	3.824	3.249
15	6.811	6.462	6.142	5.847	5.575	5.324	5.092	4.876	4.675	3.859	3.268
16	6.974	6.604	6.265	5.954	5.668	5.405	5.162	4.938	4.730	3.887	3.283
17	7.120	6.729	6.373	6.047	5.749	5.475	5.222	4.990	4.775	3.910	3.295
18	7.250	6.840	6.467	6.128	5.818	5.534	5.273	5.033	4.812	3.928	3.304
19	7.366	6.938	6.550	6.198	5.877	5.584	5.316	5.070	4.843	3.942	3.311
20	7.469	7.025	6.623	6.259	5.929	5.628	5.353	5.101	4.870	3.954	3.316
25	7.843	7.330	6.873	6.464	6.097	5.766	5.467	5.195	4.948	3.985	3.329
30	8.055	7.496	7.003	6.566	6.177	5.829	5.517	5.235	4.979	3.995	3.332
35	8.176	7.586	7.070	6.617	6.215	5.858	5.539	5.251	4.992	3.998	3.333
40	8.244	7.634	7.105	6.642	6.233	5.871	5.548	5.258	4.997	3.999	3.333
45	8.283	7.661	7.123	6.654	6.242	5.877	5.552	5.261	4.999	4.000	3.333
50	8.304	7.675	7.133	6.661	6.246	5.880	5.554	5.262	4.999	4.000	3.333

Exhibit A-5 End-of-Month Payment Required for a $1,000 Amortized Loan for a Given Number of Months

YEARS	1	2	3	4	5	6	10	15	20	25	30
MONTHS	12	24	36	48	60	72	120	180	240	300	360
4%	85.150	43.425	29.524	22.579	18.417	15.645	10.125	7.397	6.060	5.278	4.774
4.50%	85.379	43.648	29.747	22.803	18.643	15.874	10.364	7.650	6.326	5.558	5.067
5.00%	85.607	43.871	29.971	23.029	18.871	16.105	10.607	7.908	6.600	5.846	5.368
5.50%	85.837	44.096	30.196	23.256	19.101	16.338	10.853	8.171	6.879	6.141	5.678
6.00%	86.066	44.321	30.422	23.485	19.333	16.573	11.102	8.439	7.164	6.443	5.996
6.50%	86.296	44.546	30.649	23.715	19.566	16.810	11.355	8.711	7.456	6.752	6.321
7.00%	86.527	44.773	30.877	23.946	19.801	17.049	11.611	8.988	7.753	7.068	6.653
7.50%	86.757	45.000	31.106	24.179	20.038	17.290	11.870	9.270	8.056	7.390	6.992
8.00%	86.988	45.227	31.336	24.413	20.276	17.533	12.133	9.557	8.364	7.718	7.338
8.50%	87.220	45.456	31.568	24.648	20.517	17.778	12.399	9.847	8.678	8.052	7.689
9.00%	87.451	45.685	31.800	24.885	20.758	18.026	12.668	10.143	8.997	8.392	8.046
9.50%	87.684	45.914	32.033	25.123	21.002	18.275	12.940	10.442	9.321	8.737	8.409
10.00%	87.916	46.145	32.267	25.363	21.247	18.526	13.215	10.746	9.650	9.087	8.776
10.50%	88.149	46.376	32.502	25.603	21.494	18.779	13.493	11.054	9.984	9.442	9.147
11.00%	88.382	46.608	32.739	25.846	21.742	19.034	13.775	11.366	10.322	9.801	9.523
11.50%	88.615	46.840	32.976	26.089	21.993	19.291	14.060	11.682	10.664	10.165	9.903
12.00%	88.849	47.073	33.214	26.334	22.244	19.550	14.347	12.002	11.011	10.532	10.286
14.00%	89.787	48.013	34.178	27.326	23.268	20.606	15.527	13.317	12.435	12.038	11.849
16.00%	90.731	48.963	35.157	28.340	24.318	21.692	16.751	14.687	13.913	13.589	13.448
18.00%	91.680	49.924	36.152	29.375	25.393	22.808	18.019	16.104	15.433	15.174	15.071
20.00%	92.635	50.896	37.164	30.430	26.494	23.953	19.326	17.563	16.988	16.785	16.710
22.00%	93.594	51.878	38.190	31.506	27.619	25.126	20.670	19.058	18.571	18.412	18.360
24.00%	94.560	52.871	39.233	32.602	28.768	26.327	22.048	20.583	20.174	20.053	20.016

Exhibit A-6 Present Value of a Given Number of $1 End-of-Month Payments

	Number of Monthly Payments			
Annual Rate	120	180	240	360
4.0%	98.770	135.192	165.022	209.461
4.5%	96.489	130.720	158.065	197.361
5.0%	94.281	126.455	151.525	186.282
5.5%	92.144	122.387	145.373	176.122
6.0%	90.073	118.504	139.581	166.792
6.5%	88.068	114.796	134.125	158.211
7.0%	86.126	111.256	128.983	150.308
7.5%	84.245	107.873	124.132	143.018
8.0%	82.421	104.641	119.554	136.283
8.5%	80.654	101.550	115.231	130.054
9.0%	78.942	98.593	111.145	124.282
9.5%	77.281	95.765	107.281	118.927
10.0%	75.671	93.057	103.625	113.951
10.5%	74.110	90.465	100.162	109.321
11.0%	72.595	87.982	96.882	105.006
11.5%	71.126	85.603	93.771	100.980
12.0%	69.701	83.322	90.819	97.218
12.5%	68.317	81.134	88.017	93.698

GLOSSARY

A

Accelerated benefits. An option under which a terminally ill policyholder can receive a portion of his or her life insurance proceeds before death.

Acceleration clause. A loan term that requires immediate repayment of the total amount due on an installment loan that is in default.

Accidental death benefit. A life insurance contract provision by which the benefit is doubled for accidental death.

Active investor. Investor who actively buys and sells securities, attempting to make short-run gains.

Adjustable-rate mortgage (ARM). Mortgage loan with an interest rate that, by contract, varies over time with market conditions.

Adjustable-rate preferred stock. Preferred stock that pays a dividend tied to a market interest rate.

Adjusted expense method. A method for estimating after-tax retirement income needs in current dollars by adjusting current expenses for changes expected in retirement.

Adjusted gross income (AGI). Earned income and unearned income minus certain allowed adjustments to income.

Agency issue. Bond issued by a federal agency.

Agent. A person who is acting on behalf of another through a contractual agreement.

Alternative minimum tax. Federal income tax calculations designed to ensure that people who receive certain tax breaks pay their fair share of taxes.

Amortization. The process of calculating equal payments on a loan that include principal repayment and interest on the declining balance.

Annual compounding. Compounding in which interest is calculated at the end of each year.

Annual percentage rate (APR). Standardized annual cost of credit, including all mandatory fees paid by the borrower, expressed as a percentage rate.

Annual percentage yield (APY). The amount of interest paid each year, given as a percentage of the investment; the APY makes it possible to compare interest rates across accounts with different compounding periods.

Annuity. A series of equal payments made at regular intervals for a period of time.

Annuity due. An annuity with beginning-of-period payments.

Annuity for a specific term. An annuity that provides a stream of equal payments for a specific period of time.

Ask price. The stock price requested by a potential seller.

Assessment ratio. Proportion of market value used to calculate assessed value of real estate on which the property tax rate will be assessed.

Asset allocation. The process of deciding what proportion of a portfolio to invest in each asset class.

Asset classes. Broad groups of investments that have certain characteristics in common.

Assets. Everything you own, including liquid assets, real and personal property, and investments.

Assumption of risk. A defense to a claim of negligence available when the injured party voluntarily took on the risk.

Attitudes. Opinions and psychological differences between people.

Audit. Process by which the IRS more carefully examines particular tax returns for errors and omissions.

Automated teller machine (ATM). Computer terminal used to complete certain financial transactions, including obtaining account balances, making deposits and withdrawals.

Average daily balance. The average of the balances owed on each day of the credit card billing cycle.

Average indexed monthly earnings (AIME). The average of a person's 35 highest years of monthly earnings, adjusted for inflation, used in computing that individual's Social Security benefit.

Average tax rate. The proportion of a taxpayer's total taxable income that goes to paying taxes.

B

Back-end load. A charge paid by mutual fund investors at the time they sell shares.

Balanced fund. A mutual fund invested in both stocks and bonds.

Balloon loan. A loan for which the regular installment payments are relatively low because they are calculated using a longer amortization period, but a single large payment is required after a shorter period of time to repay the balance in full.

Bank credit card. Credit card issued by a depository institution.

Bankruptcy. The legal right under the U.S. Bankruptcy Act of 1978 to be relieved of certain debts and obligations by a court of law.

Basic health care insurance. Health insurance that covers hospital, surgical, and physician expenses.

Beneficiaries. The individuals or entities receiving a distribution under the terms of a will.

Beta. A measure of the market, or nondiversifiable, risk of a stock.

Bid price. The stock price offered by a potential buyer.

Billing date. The last day of a billing cycle; credit card transactions made after that date appear on the next month's bill.

Bi-weekly mortgage. An arrangement in which mortgage payments are made every two weeks in an amount equal to half of the required monthly payment, resulting in an extra month's payment over the course of a year.

Blue chip stock. A stock that is issued by a large, stable, mature company.

Bond. An investment representing a loan to a governmental or business entity, which usually pays a fixed rate of interest for a fixed period of time.

Brokerage account. An investor's account at a brokerage firm, from which the investor pays for purchases and into which the firm deposits proceeds from sales.

Brokerage firm. A nondepository financial institution that helps its customers to buy and sell financial securities.

Budget. A plan for spending and saving.

Buy-and-hold. A passive investment strategy in which the investor identifies his or her target asset allocation and then selects appropriate securities to hold for the long run.

Buyer broker. A real estate broker who works exclusively for the buyer and owes no legal duty to the seller.

Buying on margin. Using borrowed funds from your broker to make a trade.

C

Cafeteria plan. An employee benefit plan in which the employer provides a sum of money and allows employees to choose the benefits they want from a menu.

Call provision. A contract term that allows a bond issuer to buy back a bond issue before the maturity date.

Capacity. The mental competence to make a will, including understanding the nature and content of the document and not acting under threat or coercion from anyone.

Capital gain. (1) Profit on the sale of an investment; subject to a lower tax rate if the investment has been held for more than one year. (2) Growth in the value of an investment over time.

Capital gains yield. Component of stock investor's total return equal to the ratio of the annual change in price to the market price of a stock.

Captive agent. An insurance agent who sells products for only one insurer.

Cash advance. A cash loan from credit card account.

Cash balance plan. A defined-benefit retirement plan that includes an investment component similar to a defined-contribution plan.

Cash management. Management of cash payments and liquid investments.

Cash-or-deferred arrangement (CODA). A defined-contribution retirement plan in which employees can contribute some of their salary to the plan on a tax-deferred basis.

Cash reserve. Liquid assets held to meet emergency cash needs.

Cash surrender value or **cash value.** The amount the insurer will pay to the policy owner if a cash-value insurance policy is canceled.

Certificate of deposit (CD). An account that pays a fixed rate of interest on funds left on deposit for a stated period of time.

Charitable lead (or income) trust. A trust that enables the grantor to give income to a charity during his or her lifetime or for a period of years, but to transfer the asset upon his or her death to a chosen beneficiary.

Charitable remainder trust. A trust that enables the grantor to give an asset to a charity but retain the cash flow generated by that asset during his or her lifetime.

Churning. Excessive trading in a discretionary account.

Circuit breaker rules. Securities industry rules that act to temporarily halt trading in the event of an unusually large drop in the market.

Claims adjuster. Person designated by the insurer to assess whether a loss is covered by your policy and to assign a dollar value to the loss.

Closed-end credit. Loans for a specific purpose paid back in a specified period of time, usually with monthly payments.

Closed-end fund. An investment company that has a fixed number of shares, which are traded in the secondary market.

Closed-end lease. Lease in which the lessor bears the risk that the value of the car at the end of the term is less than originally estimated.

Close price. The last price at which a stock sold at the close of the previous business day.

Closing. Meeting at which participants sign the required paperwork to finalize a home purchase and mortgage agreement.

Closing costs. Transaction costs paid at the closing of a home purchase.

Codicil. A legal amendment to a will.

Coinsurance. An arrangement providing for the sharing of medical costs by the insured and the insurer.

Collateral. Valuable assets or real property that can be taken by the lender in the event of a loan default.

Collision coverage. Insurance that covers loss or damage to your vehicle caused by an automobile accident.

Commercial bank. A depository institution offering a wide variety of cash management services to business and individual customers.

Commission. Percentage of sales price paid to broker(s) who assist in the sale of a home or in other financial transactions.

Commodities. Contracts to buy or sell raw materials or agricultural products in the future.

Community property. A property law in some states by which any property acquired during a marriage is considered to be jointly owned by both spouses.

Compounding. The process by which interest is paid on both the original investment and interest already earned.

Comprehensive physical damage coverage. Insurance that covers loss or damage to your vehicle caused by any peril other than an automobile accident.

Compulsory automobile insurance laws. State laws that require proof of liability insurance as a prerequisite to auto registration.

Consumer choice plan. A health plan that includes financial incentives for preventive care and cost reduction.

Consumer credit. Credit used for personal needs other than home purchases.

Consumer finance company. A nondepository institution that makes loans to riskier consumers.

Consumer price index (CPI). A measure of the price of a representative basket of household goods and services in the U.S. market.

Contributory negligence. A defense to a claim of negligence available when the injured party contributed to his or her injury.

Contributory plan. An employee benefit plan for which the employee pays some or all of the costs.

Convenience check. A check supplied by a credit card lender for the purpose of making a cash advance.

Conventional mortgage. A fixed-rate, fixed-term, fixed-payment mortgage loan.

Convertible. A type of term life insurance policy that allows the insured person to convert the term insurance policy to a permanent life insurance policy without additional proof of insurability.

Copay. Dollar amount of medical costs paid by the insured under a coinsurance provision, after meeting the annual deductible.

Corporation. A form of business organization that exists as a legal entity separate from its owners who have limited liability for corporate losses.

Cosigner. A person who agrees to take responsibility for repayment of a loan if the primary borrower defaults.

Coupon payment. The annual dollar interest payment on a bond, equal to the coupon rate times the face value, usually paid to investors in two equal installments.

Coupon rate. The annual rate of interest on a bond, quoted as a percent of the face value.

Coverage. Insurance that covers loss or damage to your vehicle caused by any peril other than an automobile accident.

Coverdell Education Savings Accounts. Education saving arrangement that allows after-tax contributions of $2,000 per year per child and tax-free withdrawals.

Cover letter. A letter of introduction sent with a résumé to prospective employers.

Credit. Arrangement to receive cash, goods, or services now and pay later.

Credit bureaus. Companies that collect credit information on individuals and provide reports to interested lenders.

Credit card. A plastic card printed with an account number and identifying the holder as a participant in a revolving credit agreement with a lender.

Credit limit or **credit line.** Preapproved maximum amount of borrowing for open-end credit account.

Credit union. A non-profit depository institution owned by its depositors.

Cumulative preferred stock. Preferred stock that gives holders the right to receive past unpaid dividends before any dividends can be paid to common stockholders.

Current assumption whole life insurance. A type of permanent life insurance with premiums that depend on the insurer's actual mortality, expense, and investment experience.

Cyclical stock. A stock exhibiting above-average sensitivity to the business cycle.

D

Day trader. An active investor who buys and sells many times during the day to make quick profits.

Dealer's invoice price. The price that a dealer pays to purchase a new vehicle from the manufacturer.

Debenture. Unsecured bonds.

Debit card. A plastic card that effects immediate electronic withdrawal of funds from a bank account.

Debt investor. An investor who lends money to a individual, government entity, financial institution, or other business.

Debt payment ratio. Financial ratio that measures percentage of disposable income required to make debt payments.

Debt ratio. Total debt divided by total assets.

Debts. Everything you owe to others, including unpaid bills, credit card balances, car loans, student loans, and mortgages.

Decreasing term life insurance. A type of term life insurance featuring a level premium and decreasing protection.

Deductible. The amount of a loss that must be paid by an insured before the insurance company will pay any insurance benefit.

Default. Failure to meet the terms of a loan agreement, as when payments are not made in a timely fashion.

Default risk. The risk of not receiving promised cash flows from an investment.

Defensive stock. Stock that is relatively insensitive to the business cycle.

Defined-benefit (DB) plan. A retirement plan in which the employer promises employees a retirement benefit determined by a formula, commonly based on preretirement earnings and years of service.

Defined-contribution (DC) plan. Retirement plan in which the employer promises to make regular contributions to employees' retirement accounts but does not guarantee the benefits that will result.

Demand deposits. Deposit accounts, such as checking accounts, from which money can be withdrawn with little or no notice to the financial institution.

Dependent. Member of a household who receives at least half of his or her support from the head of the household.

Depository institutions. Financial institutions that obtain funds from customer deposits.

Depreciation. The decline in value of an asset over time due to wear and tear, obsolescence, and competitive factors.

Derivative securities. Investments that derive their value from some underlying security's changes in price over time.

Direct investment program. Program offered by a publicly traded company to allow investors to automatically purchase shares of the company's stock on a regular basis without incurring a brokerage fee.

Disability income insurance. Insurance that replaces the policyholder's lost income during a period of disability.

Discount bonds. Bonds that sell for less than their face value.

Discount broker. A broker that facilitates transactions but usually does not offer investment advice or research services to clients.

Discounting. The process of calculating the present value of a lump sum or a series of payments to be received in the future.

Discount points. Interest paid up front to a lender in return for a reduction in annual rate on a mortgage.

Diversification. An investment strategy that involves spreading money across a range of investments in order to reduce the overall risk of the portfolio.

Dividend reinvestment plan (DRIP). Program that allows investors to receive dividends in the form of additional shares of stock instead of cash.

Dividends. Periodic distributions of profits to equity investors.

Dividend yield. Component of stock investor's total return equal to the ratio of annual dividends to the market price of a stock.

Dollar cost averaging. An investment strategy in which you invest in equal dollar amounts at regular intervals regardless of fluctuations in price.

Down payment. The amount of the purchase price that a buyer pays in cash.

Due date. The date by which payment must be received by the lender if the holder is to avoid late penalties and, in some cases, interest on new transactions.

Durable power of attorney. A legal document in which a person designates another to make decisions on his or her behalf in the event of incapacity.

E

Earned income. Income from salaries, wages, tips, bonuses, commissions, and other sources.

Earnings per share (EPS). A measure of company profitability equal to annual earnings divided by the number of shares outstanding.

Economic cycle. A pattern of ups and downs in the level of economic activity.

Electronic cash. Money in digitized format.

Employee stock ownership plans (ESOPs). Profit-sharing plans that make contributions to employee accounts in the form of employer stock.

Equity investor. An investor who has an ownership interest in a business.

Escheat. The legal process by which the state government acquires the estate of a person who dies without a will and has no living relatives.

Escrow account. A reserve account held by the mortgage lender in which it collects a monthly prepayment of property taxes and insurance and then pays these bills as they come due.

Estate. A person's net worth at death.

Estate planning. The development of a plan for what will happen to your wealth and dependents when you die.

Exchange-traded fund (ETF). An investment company with professionally, but not actively, managed assets, often intended to track a market index, and shares that trade in the secondary market.

Exclusion. A potential loss that is expressly excluded from coverage by an insurance policy.

Exclusive agent. An insurance agent who sells products for only one insurer.

Exclusive provider organization (EPO). Health-care plan that only covers medical costs from participating providers.

Executor. A person designated to carry out the provisions of a will.

Exemption. Dollar amount per household member that is subtracted from adjusted gross income in calculating taxable income.

Expansion. A phase in the economic cycle characterized by increased business investment and increasing employment opportunities.

Expense ratio. The ratio of annual mutual fund expense charges to fund assets.

Express warranty. Written or oral promise by seller.

Extended warranty. Service contract agreement that, for a set price, extends an original warranty or adds services or coverage.

F

Face amount. Value of assets insured under a policy.

Face value. (1) The dollar amount the bondholder will receive at the bond's maturity date. (2) The dollar value of protection payable to beneficiaries under the terms of a life insurance policy.

Federal Deposit Insurance Corporation (FDIC). A government-sponsored agency that insures customer accounts in banks and savings institutions.

Federal funds rate. The rate that banks charge each other for short-term loans.

Federal Reserve. The central bank in the United States, which controls the money supply.

Fee-for-service plan. A health insurance plan that reimburses the insured for medical expenses incurred or pays the provider directly.

FICA tax. A payroll tax levied on earned income by the U.S. government to fund Social Security and Medicare.

Filing status. Household type for tax filing purposes.

Finance charge. The dollar amount of periodic interest charged by the lender on a credit account.

Financial needs method. A method for estimating life insurance needs based on expected capital and income replacement needs.

Financial responsibility laws. State laws that require proof of ability to cover the cost of injury to persons or property caused by an auto accident.

Fixed expenses. Expenses that are a constant dollar amount each period.

Fixed-income investments. Debt investments that provide a fixed interest payment to the investor over the term of the investment.

Fixed-rate loan. Loan for which the rate of interest remains the same throughout the term of the loan.

Flat tax. A single tax rate imposed on every dollar of income for every taxpayer.

Flexible spending account (FSA). An account maintained by an employer in which pretax earnings of an employee are set aside for qualified medical and child-care expenses.

Floating-rate bonds. Bonds whose interest payments are adjusted periodically according to current market interest rates.

Frequency of loss. The probability that a loss will occur.

Front-end load. A commission or sales charge paid by mutual fund investors at the time they purchase shares.

Full-service broker. A broker that offers a full range of services to clients.

Fund family. An arrangement in which a single company operates several separately managed mutual funds with different investment objectives.

Futures contract. A contract to buy or sell financial securities in the future.

Future value (FV). The value a given amount will grow to in the future if invested today at a given rate of interest.

Future value of an annuity (FVA). The amount to which a regular series of payments will grow, with compounding, if invested at a given rate of interest for a particular period of time.

G

General obligation bond. Municipal bond that will be repaid from the operating cash flows of the issuing entity; backed only by the full faith and credit of the issuer.

Global fund. A mutual fund that invests in U.S. and foreign securities.

Good faith estimate. An estimate of loan costs provided by the lender to the borrower.

Grace period. The time before interest begins to accrue on new credit card transactions.

Graduated payment mortgage. Mortgage that allows for gradually increasing payments over the life of the loan, resulting in negative amortization during the early years.

Grantor. A person or entity who legally passes ownership to another person or entity.

Gross income. Income from all sources, including earned income, investment income, alimony, unemployment compensation, and retirement benefits.

Group insurance. Insurance purchased on a group basis by an employer for the benefit of employees.

Group underwriting. Underwriting in which the premium is based on the risk of the group as a whole rather than on characteristics of individual group members.

Growing equity mortgage. A mortgage whose payments increase over time, with the increase applied to reduce the balance owed on the loan.

Growth fund. A mutual fund that focuses on capital appreciation.

Growth stock. Stock that compensates investors primarily through increases in value of the shares over time.

Guaranteed renewability. A feature of term life insurance giving the insured person the right to renew the policy without additional proof of insurability.

H

Health maintenance organization (HMO). A managed-care plan that attempts to control health-care costs by encouraging preventive care and limiting participants to providers with whom the plan has contracted.

Health savings account (HSA). An investment account in which an employer deposits pretax dollars allocated for payment of an employee's health-related expenses.

Heir. Person or entity designated to receive something from your estate after your death.

Holding-period return. Return on investment over a particular period of time.

Home equity. The market value of a home minus the remaining mortgage balance.

Homeowner's insurance. Insurance purchased by a homeowner to cover property and liability losses associated with a home.

Hope Scholarship tax credit. A tax credit of up to $1,500 per year for eligible expenses incurred during the first two years of college.

Human capital. The present value of your future earnings, based on skills, abilities, and education.

I

Implied warranty. Legal obligation that product for sale be suitable for intended use.

Income fund. A mutual fund that focuses on providing stable dividend and interest income.

Income-multiple method. A method for estimating life insurance needs as a multiple of income.

Income stock. Stock that compensates investors primarily through the regular payment of dividends.

Incontestable clause. An insurance contract clause stating that the insurer cannot contest a claim for misrepresentation after a policy has been in force for a specified period of time.

Indenture. A legal document that details the rights and obligations of the bondholders and the bond issuer.

Independent agent. An insurance agent who sells products for multiple insurers.

Indexed bonds. Bonds whose interest payments are adjusted periodically according to a market index.

Individual retirement account (IRA). Tax preferred method of saving for retirement. See *Traditional IRA* and *Roth IRA.*

Inflation. Change in the prices of goods and services over time.

Inflation-adjusted annuity. A series of payments at equal intervals that increase with inflation.

Inflation risk. The risk that inflation will erode the purchasing power of investment returns.

Informational interview. An interview requested by a job seeker for the purpose of learning more about a potential career or job.

Initial public offering (IPO). A company's first stock offering to the public.

Insider trading. Trading based on company information not available to the public, illegal under federal law.

Insolvency. The inability to pay debts as they come due.

Installment loan. A loan that requires repayment in equal periodic installments that include both interest and principal.

Insurance policy. A contract between an insured and an insurer in which the insured agrees to pay a premium in return for the insurer's promise to pay for certain covered losses during the policy period.

Interest rate. Cost of borrowed money or return on invested money.

Interest-rate caps. Caps on annual and lifetime increases in an ARM interest rate.

Interest-rate risk. The risk of price changes due to changes in interest rates.

Internal Revenue Code. A compilation of all statutes, regulations, and court decisions relating to U.S. income tax.

Internal Revenue Service (IRS). The U.S. government agency responsible for collecting federal income taxes and enforcing tax laws and regulations.

International fund. A mutual fund that invests primarily in securities from countries other than the United States.

Intestate. Without a valid will.

Investment company. A financial intermediary that invests its funds in securities or other assets.

Investment-grade bonds. Medium-grade and high-grade bonds with low risk of default on interest or principal.

Irrevocable trust. A trust that the grantor cannot revoke; it is not subject to probate or estate taxes.

IRS e-file. A system allowing electronic filing of federal tax returns.

Itemized deductions. An alternative to the standard deduction in which the taxpayer reports and deducts actual expenses in certain allowed categories to arrive at taxable income.

J

Joint and survivor annuity. An annuity that provides a stream of equal payments until the death of the second spouse.

Joint tenancy with right of survivorship. A form of property ownership in which, after the death of one owner, the property passes to the surviving owner without going through probate.

Junk bonds. Speculative-grade bonds with a high risk of default.

L

Large-cap. Market capitalization in excess of $5 billion.

Late payment penalty. Penalty fee charged to an account for making a payment after the due date.

Law of large numbers. A principle holding that, for large pools of identical risks, the risk that actual losses per person will be greater than predicted decreases as the size of the pool increases.

Lemon laws. State laws that protect consumers against chronically defective vehicles.

Lender buy-down mortgage. Mortgage that imposes a schedule of increasing interest rates over the life of the loan, resulting in gradually increasing payments.

Lessee. A person who pays money for the privilege of using someone else's vehicle or real property for a period of time.

Lessor. An owner of an asset, commonly a vehicle or real property, who charges money for the use of that asset for a period of time.

Letter of last instruction. A nonbinding document that provides helpful information to survivors after the writer's death.

Liability risk. The risk that you will be held financially responsible for losses to another person or that person's property.

Lien. Public notice of a right to real property.

Life-cycle fund. A mutual fund that designs its asset allocation to meet the needs of individuals in a particular life stage.

Life insurance company. A nondepository financial institution that obtains funds from premiums paid for life insurance, invests in stocks and bonds, and makes mortgage loans.

Life insurance trust. A type of living trust designed to remove the proceeds of a life insurance policy from your estate.

Lifetime Learning tax credit. A tax credit of 20 percent of the first $5,000 of college expenses up to a maximum of $1,000 for every eligible dependent who has incurred these expenses during the year.

Limited liability. Statutory right given to corporate shareholders limiting their potential losses to the value of the shares held.

Limited partnership. A partnership in which limited partners provide investment funds, have limited liability, and participate in profits but a general partner manages the investment.

Limited payment life insurance. Whole life insurance that is paid up after a specified period.

Limited warranty. Less than full promise to repair or replace, often covering parts and labor for specifically identified types of problems.

Limit order. A request to buy stock at any price up to a given maximum or to sell stock at any price above a given minimum.

Liquid assets. Cash and near-cash assets that can be easily converted to cash without loss of value.

Liquidity ratio. Financial ratio that measures ability to pay household expenses out of liquid assets in the absence of regular income.

Liquidity risk. The risk of not being able to convert an asset to cash without losing value.

Listed security. A security that is approved to be bought or sold on a particular exchange.

Living trust. A trust established during the grantor's lifetime.

Living will. A legal document that specifies a person's preferences as to medical care in the event that he or she becomes unable to make decisions because of illness or disability.

Lockbox. A fireproof safe that may be kept in the home.

Lock-in. Agreement with a lender that guarantees a particular mortgage interest rate at closing.

Long-term care. Medical and personal care for persons with an extended illness or disability that is not provided in a hospital.

Long-term care insurance. An insurance policy designed to pay health-care expenses associated with incapacity, such as nursing home costs.

Loss control. Actions taken to reduce the frequency or severity of expected losses.

Luxuries. Things that you want but can live without.

M

Major medical insurance. Insurance that covers the costs of most medical services prescribed by a doctor, subject to deductibles and coinsurance.

Managed-care plan. A health insurance plan that attempts to reduce costs through contractual arrangements with providers and financial incentives for low-cost alternatives.

Marginal reasoning. Analysis that considers the increased benefit that would result from a particular decision.

Marginal tax effect. The change in taxes owed as a result of a financial decision.

Marginal tax rate. Tax rate imposed on the taxpayer's next dollar of income.

Margin call. A request from a brokerage firm that the holder of a margin account add money to the account to maintain the required minimum.

Market capitalization. The total outstanding value of a company's stock at current market prices; calculated as the current stock price times the number of shares outstanding.

Market efficiency. A theory that suggests prices immediately adjust to reflect all publicly available information.

Market order. An offer to buy stock at the market price.

Market risk. Investment risk associated with general market movements and economic conditions.

Market value. The price that something can be sold for today.

Maturity date. (1) For a CD, the date on which the depositor can withdraw the invested amount and receive the stated interest. (2) For a closed-end loan, the date on which the last payment is due. (3) For a bond, the date on which the bond issuer must pay the face value to the bondholder.

Maximum limit. Lifetime maximum paid by the insurer to an insured person.

Medicaid. State-run program providing health care for the poor.

Medicare. Federal health insurance program for people age 65 and over.

Medigap policies. Insurance policy designed to pay deductibles and other costs that are not covered by Medicare.

Mid-cap. Market capitalization of \$1 to \$3 billion.

Minimum payment. Minimum amount that must be paid by the due date to maintain good credit standing and avoid late payment penalties on a credit card.

Money market account. A savings account that pays interest which fluctuates with market rates on money market securities.

Money market mutual fund. A mutual fund that holds a portfolio of short-term, low-risk securities issued by the federal government, its agencies, and large corporations and pays investors a rate of return that fluctuates with the interest earned on the portfolio.

Money-purchase plan. A defined-contribution retirement plan to which the employer contributes a set percentage of the employee's salary.

Mortgage. A long-term amortized loan that is secured by real property.

Mortgage debt service. Total dollar amount of monthly mortgage principal, interest, property taxes, and homeowner's insurance.

Mortgage debt service ratio. Percentage of gross income used for mortgage debt service.

Mortgage insurance premium (MIP). Insurance charged to a mortgage borrower to protect the lender against the risk of borrower default.

Municipal bond. Long-term debt security issued by a state or local government entity.

Mutual fund. (1) A nondepository financial institution, technically an open-end investment company, that sells shares to investors and uses investors' funds to purchase stocks, bonds, or other financial assets. (2) A collection of investments, managed by a professional investment firm, in which investors can buy shares.

Mutual savings institution. A savings institution owned by its depositors.

N

NASDAQ. National Association of Securities Dealers Automated Quotation System, an electronic reporting system for more frequently traded OTC stocks.

Necessities. Things needed for basic living, such as food, clothing, and shelter.

Negative amortization. Addition to loan balance that occurs when the monthly payment is insufficient to cover the monthly interest cost.

Negligence. A failure to fulfill a legal duty to another that causes injury to that person or to his or her property.

Negotiated order of withdrawal (NOW) account. A type of checking account that pays interest.

Net asset value. The market value of a mutual fund's assets less the market value of its liabilities per share.

Networking. The process of developing contacts with people who might be helpful in your career.

Net worth. The amount of wealth you would have left after paying all your outstanding debts.

No-fault automobile insurance. A type of automobile insurance system in which each insured driver in an accident collects his or her claim from his or her own insurer regardless of who is at fault.

No-load fund. A mutual fund that doesn't charge a front-end or back-end load.

Nominal risk-free rate. The expected return on a short-term risk-free investment such as a Treasury bill, equal to the real risk-free rate plus an inflation risk premium.

O

Open-end credit or **revolving credit.** Preapproved continuous loan that can cover many purchases and usually requires monthly partial payments.

Open-end fund. An investment company that sells its shares directly to investors and buys them back on request.

Open-end lease. Lease in which the lessee is responsible for the additional depreciation at the end of the lease term if the value of the car is less than originally estimated.

Opportunity cost. What you have to give up in order to take a particular action.

Option. A contract that gives the holder the right, but not the obligation, to purchase or sell a specified investment at a set price on or before a specified date.

Ordinary annuity. An annuity with end-of-period payments.

Ordinary life insurance. Whole life insurance with premiums payable to the time of death.

Overdraft protection. An arrangement by which a financial institution places funds into a depositor's checking account to cover overdrafts.

Overlimit charge. Penalty fee charged to a credit card account holder for exceeding the credit limit.

Over-the-counter (OTC) market. An electronic network for trading securities through securities dealers.

P

Participating policies. Life insurance policies issued by mutual insurers that pay dividends to policyholders.

Par value. (1) The dollar amount the bondholder will receive at the bond's maturity date. (2) An arbitrary initial value assigned to shares of preferred stock at issuance and used to calculate the dividend payment.

Passive investor. Investor who invests to make long-run returns and doesn't actively engage in buying or selling.

Payroll withholding. Money regularly withheld from employees' pay by employers for payment of the employees' taxes.

Periodic rate. The nominal rate divided by the number of billing or compounding periods per year.

Permanent life insurance. A type of life insurance that provides both death protection and a savings vehicle.

Perpetuity. A constant cash flow stream that continues into infinity.

Personal balance sheet. A financial statement that details the value of what you own and what you owe to others to arrive at an estimate of your net worth at a given point in time.

Personal cash flow statement. A summary of income and expenditures over a period of time, such as a month or year.

Personal finance. The study of individual and household financial decisions.

Personal financial planning. Developing and implementing an integrated, comprehensive plan to meet financial goals and prepare for financial emergencies.

Personal financial statements. Reports that summarize personal financial information.

Point of service (POS) plan. Health-care plan in which participating providers are affiliated with an HMO, but participants can still use nonparticipating providers if they are will to pay a bigger share of the cost.

Portability. An employee's right to take retirement plan assets from one place of employment to another when the employee changes jobs.

Pourover will. A will that leaves a person's remaining assets to a trust.

Preemptive right. The right of a stockholder to maintain his or her proportionate ownership when the company issues additional shares of stock.

Preferred provider organization (PPO). A managed-care plan that provides participants with financial incentives to use certain providers.

Preferred stock. A type of stock that pays a fixed dividend.

Premium. The price an insurer charges a policyholder for insurance protection.

Prenuptial agreement. A written contract in advance of a marriage that specifies how the assets will be distributed in the event of a divorce.

Prepayment penalty. A fee charged to the borrower when a loan balance is repaid before the end of the loan term.

Present value (PV). The amount of money that would have to be invested today to grow to a given future value over a specified period at a specified interest rate.

Present value of an annuity. The lump-sum amount that must be deposited today to provide for equal periodic payments for a given number of periods in the future.

Price to earnings (P/E) ratio. Measure of a company's future earnings potential calculated as market price divided by earnings per share.

Primary insurance amount (PIA). The Social Security benefit payable to a program participant who retires at the normal retirement age.

Primary market. The market in which securities are sold by corporations to the public for the first time.

Primary mortgage market. Market in which lenders originate mortgage loans with borrowers.

Principal. (1) A person who has delegated responsibility to an agent and to whom the agent has a duty. (2) The original amount borrowed or invested.

Principle of indemnity. The principle that insurance will only reimburse the policyholder for actual losses.

Probate. The legal process of settling an estate.

Profit-sharing plan. A defined-contribution retirement plan in which employer contributions are discretionary.

Progressive tax. A tax that requires higher-income taxpayers to pay proportionately more in taxes, through either higher tax rates or other rules.

Promissory note. Legal contract that specifies the terms and conditions of the borrower's agreement to repay a sum of money.

Property tax rate. Local tax assessed on real estate proportional to value.

Prospectus. A document that gives financial information about a stock issue and the issuing company to potential investors.

Proxy. A written agreement in which a shareholder gives another person the right to vote in his or her place.

Pure risk. Exposure to risk of loss.

Q

Qualified personal residence trust. A type of living trust designed to remove a personal residence from your estate for probate purposes.

Qualified terminable interest property (Q-TIP) trust. A trust for married couples in which the grantor retains control over the ultimate beneficiaries of the estate.

R

Rate of return. The total income earned on an investment over a period of time, including interest or dividends and capital gains, divided by the original amount invested.

Real estate broker. Professional who helps homeowners find buyers for their homes and assists in the purchase transaction, in return for a fee.

Real estate investment trust (REIT). A closed-end fund that invests primarily in real estate or mortgages.

Recession. A phase in the economic cycle characterized by reduced business investment and increasing unemployment.

Reconciling a budget. Adjusting income, expenses, and saving so that you don't spend more than you earn.

Refinancing. Obtaining a new mortgage to pay off a previous, usually higher-rate mortgage.

Regressive tax. A tax that places a disproportionate financial burden on low-income taxpayers.

Regular checking account. Checking account that does not pay interest and requires the payment of a monthly service charge unless a minimum balance is maintained in the account.

Reinvestment risk. The risk that short-term investments will have to be reinvested at lower rates when they come due.

Renter's insurance. Insurance purchased by a renter to cover personal property and liability losses but not damage to the building itself.

Replacement ratio method. A method for estimating after-tax retirement income needs in current dollars by multiplying current expenses by a factor of 70 to 80 percent.

Residual claim. A common shareholder's right to the firm's assets and income after all the other claimholders are paid.

Résumé. A written summary of a person's education, experience, and other qualifications.

Retail credit card. Credit card that can only be used at the sponsoring retailer's outlets.

Revenue bond. Municipal bond that will be repaid from income generated by the project financed by the bond issue.

Reverse annuity mortgage. An arrangement in which the homeowner sells equity in a home in return for a stream of income but retains the use of the home.

Revocable trust. A trust whose terms the grantor can change during his or her lifetime; it bypasses probate but is still subject to estate taxes.

Revolving credit or **open-ended credit.** Preapproved continuous loan that can cover many purchases and usually requires monthly partial payments.

Rider. Addendum to an insurance policy that requires payment of additional premium in return for additional specified insurance coverage.

Risk. Uncertainty with regard to potential loss.

Risk aversion. A tendency to dislike risk and to be unwilling to invest in risky securities unless they earn higher investment returns.

Risk classification. The categorization of policyholders by characteristics that affect their expected losses; insurers use risk classification to price policies fairly.

Risk retention. Risk management method in which a person pays for losses out of pocket instead of purchasing insurance against the risk of those losses.

Roth IRA. Individual retirement account to which contributions are made with after-tax dollars, but investment earnings and withdrawals at retirement are tax-free.

Round lot. A group of 100 shares of stock; stock is normally traded in round lots.

Rule of 72. Method of calculating the time for a sum of money to double by dividing 72 by the rate of interest earned on the funds.

Rule of 78's. A mathematical formula used to calculate the amount of interest remaining to be paid on an add-on installment loan.

S

Safe deposit box. A secure private storage area maintained at a remote location, often a financial institution's place of business.

Sales finance company. A nondepository institution that makes consumer loans to buyers of products offered through its parent company.

Savings and loan association (S&L). A depository institution that receives funds primarily from household deposits and uses most of its funds to make home mortgage loans.

Savings ratio. Financial ratio that measures the percentage of after-tax income going to savings.

Schedule. A list of otherwise excluded valuables that are to be covered under a homeowner's or renter's insurance policy for an additional premium.

Seat on the exchange. Membership in an organized securities exchange, which allows the holder to transact business there.

Secondary market. The market in which previously issued securities are traded between investors.

Secondary mortgage market. Market in which lenders sell mortgages after initial origination.

Section 529 Plans. State-sponsored programs that provide tax benefits for college saving.

Sector fund. A mutual fund that invests primarily in securities from a particular industry or sector.

Secured bond. Bond for which interest and principal payments are backed by assets or future cash flows pledged as collateral.

Secured loan. A loan that includes a pledge of collateral.

Securities. Investments in which the investor contributes a sum of money to a common enterprise with the intention of making a profit through the efforts of others.

Securities exchange. A physical location at which securities are traded; the largest is the New York Stock Exchange.

Security deposit. Dollar amount required at the beginning of a lease to cover the costs of any damage to the property over the lease term.

Selling short. A strategy in which an investor borrows stock from a broker, sells the stock, and later buys stock on the market to replace the borrowed stock.

Sensitivity analysis. Estimation of the change in outcome that results from a change in assumptions.

Severity of loss. The dollar value of a loss.

Shared appreciation mortgage. Mortgage that gives the lender a right to a proportion of the increase in the value of the home in return for a lower rate of interest.

Single life annuity. An annuity that provides a stream of equal payments until death.

Single-payment loan. A loan that requires the repayment of interest and principal in a single payment at a specified date in the future.

Single-premium whole life insurance. Whole life insurance that is paid up with a one-time payment.

Sinking fund. A fund accumulated to pay an amount due at a specific time in the future, such as when a bond issue comes due.

Small-cap. Market capitalization of less than $1 billion.

Smart card. Card that stores identification and electronic cash in a computer chip.

Socially responsible fund. A mutual fund that limits its holdings to securities issued by companies that meet certain ethical and moral standards.

Specialist. A person responsible for matching a particular stock's buy and sell orders at a specific securities exchange.

Speculative-grade bonds. Bonds with a high risk of default.

Speculative investments. High-risk investments made in the hope of making a short-term profit.

Speculative risk. Exposure to risk of loss or gain.

Standard deduction. Dollar amount based on filing status that is subtracted from adjusted gross income in calculating taxable income.

Standard family trust. A trust for married couples designed to avoid estate taxes on the estate of the surviving spouse.

Sticker price. The manufacturer's suggested retail price (MSRP) for a new vehicle, including manufacturer-installed accessories and options.

Stock. Investment security that represents a proportionate ownership interest in a corporation.

Stockbroker. A licensed professional who buys and sells securities on behalf of clients.

Stock dividend. A dividend given to shareholders in the form of shares of stock instead of cash.

Stock-held savings institution. A savings institution owned by stockholders.

Stock market index. An indicator that shows the average price movements of a particular group of stocks representing the market or some market segment.

Stop-loss limit. The maximum out-of-pocket cost to be paid by an insured in a given year, after which the insurer pays 100 percent of covered charges.

Stop order. An order to buy or sell stock holdings when the market price reaches a certain level.

Stop payment order. An order by which a financial institution promises not to honor a check that a depositor has written.

Strict liability. A rule of law that holds a person liable for damages without proof of negligence.

Speculative risk. Exposure to risk of loss or gain.

T

Tax avoidance. Strategic use of knowledge of tax rules to avoid overpayment of taxes.

Tax bracket. The range of income to which a particular marginal tax rate applies.

Tax credit. A reduction applied directly to taxes owed rather than to income subject to taxes.

Tax evasion. Deliberate nonpayment of taxes legally owed.

Taxable income. The amount of income that is subject to taxes under the law.

Tax-qualified retirement plan. A retirement plan that qualifies under federal law for tax deferral; taxes on contributions made to the plan and earnings on plan assets are not due and payable until withdrawal at retirement.

Teaser rate. Short-term below-market interest rate intended to encourage new customers to apply for a credit card.

Tenancy in common. A type of ownership in which each person owns his or her share independently and retains the right to transfer that share by sale or will.

Term life insurance. A type of life insurance that provides death protection for a specified term, often one year, and no cash value.

Testamentary trust. A trust established by the terms of a will.

Testator. The writer of a will.

Time deposit account. A savings account from which the depositor may not withdraw money, without penalty, until after a certain amount of time has passed.

Time value of money. The principle that money received today is worth more than money to be received in the future because of the power of compounding.

Timing. Investment strategy in which you attempt to shift your asset allocation to capture upturns and avoid downturns in specific markets.

Tombstone ad. A formal advertisement of a stock issue in the financial press.

Total income. Gross income less certain exclusions allowed by the IRS.

Traditional IRA. Individual retirement account that allows the holder to subtract current contributions from taxable income and to defer income tax until withdrawal at retirement.

Transaction date. The date on which you make a credit card purchase.

Travel and entertainment (T&E) card. Credit card that requires payment of the full balance each billing cycle.

Treasury Inflation Protected Securities (TIPs). Federal government bonds that are adjusted for inflation.

Trust. A legal entity that holds and manages assets on behalf of someone else.

Trustee. (1) The legal representative for the owners of a bond issue. (2) A person or entity who manages assets on behalf of another.

U

Umbrella policy. An insurance company that provides supplemental personal liability coverage with high limits.

Unearned income. Income from investments, interest, dividends, capital gains, net business income, rents, and royalties.

Unit investment trust (UIT). An investment company that buys and holds a fixed portfolio of securities for a period of time determined by the life of the investments in the trust.

Universal life insurance. A type of permanent life insurance that allows policyholders to benefit from the investment experience of the insurer and provides a flexible premium option.

U.S. savings bonds. Bonds issued by the U.S. Treasury that pay interest which fluctuates with current Treasury security rates and are exempt from state and local taxes.

V

Value fund. A mutual fund that invests in companies perceived to be undervalued by the market.

Values. Fundamental beliefs about what is important in life.

Variable expenses. Expenses that vary in amount from period to period.

Variable-rate loan. Loan for which the rate of interest varies periodically with a changing market rate, such as the prime rate.

Variable life insurance. Permanent life insurance that has a fixed premium and allows policyholders to choose from different investment alternatives.

Variable universal life insurance. Permanent life insurance that allows policyholders to choose from different investment alternatives and incorporates flexible premiums.

Vesting rules. Rules that define employees' rights to accrued retirement plan contributions and benefits.

W

Waiver of premium. An insurance option that allows the insured to waive premium payments under certain conditions, such as the diagnosis of a permanent disability.

Warranty. A promise or guaranty made by the manufacturer or seller of a product, which may include repair or replacement of defective or damaged merchandise.

Whole life insurance. Permanent life insurance that provides death protection for the policyholder's whole life and includes a savings component.

Will. A legal document that transfers property upon the death of the property owner.

Wire transfer. Electronic transmittal of cash from an account in another location; requires payment of a fee.

Workers' compensation insurance. State-run program requiring employers to pay lost wages and medical costs associated with job-related illness or injury.

Y

Yield. The total income earned on an investment over a period of time, including interest or dividends and capital gains, divided by the original amount invested.

Yield to maturity. Annualized return on a bond, if it is held to maturity and all interest payments are reinvested at the same rate.

Z

Zero-coupon bond. A bond that doesn't make interest payments but instead is discounted at the time of sale.

Index

A

B

J

S

Y

Z

Photo Credits

Chapter 1

Page xxxvi: David Sacks/Taxi/Getty Images. Page 6 (top): Kwame Zikomo/SUPERSTOCK. Page 7: Ronnie Kaufman/Corbis Images. Page 10 (left): Bettmann/Corbis Images. Page 10 (right): Gene Blevins/LA Daily News/Corbis Images. Page 16: PhotoDisc, Inc./Getty Images. Page 21: Courtesy CFP, Canada.

Chapter 2

Page 28: John Burcham/Image State. Page 31: David Young-Wolff/PhotoEdit. Page 33: Digital Vision/Getty Images. Page 51: Ariel Skelley/Corbis Images. Page 55: Deborah Davis/PhotoEdit.

Chapter 3

Page 66: John Burcham/Image State. Page 69: Comstock Images/Allsport/Getty Images. Page 70: Alamy Images. Page 77: Kathy McLaughlin/The Image Works. Page 79: Alamy Images. Page 80: Image State. Page 81: Ron and Caryl Krannich, "America's Top Internet Job Site, 2e," www.impactpublications.com. Page 82: Courtesy Bill Shuster.

Chapter 4

Page 98: The Image Bank/Getty Images. Page 101: Dick Blume/The Image Works. Page 111: Royalty-Free/Corbis Images. Page 113: Alamy Images. Page 125: Image State. Page 127: Alamy Images. Page 133: PhotoDisc, Inc./Getty Images.

Chapter 5

Page 136: Mecky/Photonica. Page 140: Chip Henderson/Index Stock. Page 146: Courtesy John Olienyk. Page 150: Clayton Sharrard/PhotoEdit. Page 158: Dion Ogust/The Image Works. Page 164: ©AP/Wide World Photos.

Chapter 6

Page 170: Patrick Clark/Photonica. Page 176: Courtesy Pat Prill. Page 178: David Young Wolff/PhotoEdit. Page 183: Myrleen Ferguson Cate/PhotoEdit. Page 192 (left): Jan Cook/Taxi/Getty Images. Page 192 (right): Comstock Images/Getty Images.

Chapter 7

Page 198: Johner/Photonica. Page 202: Getty Images News and Sport Services. Page 203: Brownie Harris/Corbis Images. Page 206: Rick Gomez/Corbis Images. Page 223: Pahl, Greg, "The Unofficial Guide to Beating Debt," 2000. New York: John Wiley & Sons, Inc. Page 225: Digital Vision/Getty Images.

Chapter 8

Page 234: Johner/Photonica. Page 241: Gary Conner/PhotoEdit. Page 242: Insurance Institute for Highway Safety. Page 247: PhotoDisc, Inc./Getty Images. Page 249: Getty Images. Page 266: David Young-Wolff/PhotoEdit.

Chapter 9

Page 274: Johner/Photonica. Page 281: Getty Images News and Sport Services. Page 282: Digital Vision. Page 283: Bluestone Productions/SUPERSTOCK. Page 286: The Image Bank/Getty Images. Page 287: Brand X Pictures/Alamy Images. Page 289 (top): Courtesy Insurance Information Institute. Page 289 (bottom): SciMAT/Photo Researchers.

Chapter 10

Page 304: Photolibrary.com/Photonica. Page 311: John Griffin/The Image Works. Page 321: Corbis Digital Stock. Page 323: Arlene Sandler/SUPERSTOCK. Page 324: David Young-Wolff/PhotoEdit. Page 327: R. Ian Loyd/Masterfile. Page 331: Digital Vision/Getty Images. Page 340: PhotoDisc, Inc./Getty Images.

Chapter 11

Page 344: Sharon Green/Image State. Page 350: Bob Abraham/Corbis Images. Page 361: Sonda Dawes/The Image Works. Page 364: David Young-Wolff/PhotoEdit. Page 369: Spencer Grant/PhotoEdit. Page 370: Spencer Grant/PhotoEdit. Page 371: Corbis Digital Stock.

Chapter 12

Page 378: Rob Casey/Image State. Page 382: Reuters/Corbis Images. Page 388: Reuters/Corbis Images. Page 393: The Stock Solution/Image State. Page 394: Najlah Feanney/Corbis Images. Page 410: Michael Marsland, Yale University Photographer, Office of Public Affairs.

Chapter 13

Page 416: Jake Wyman/Photonica. Page 424: Jeff Greenberg/The Image Works. Page 427: Chris Rogers/Corbis Images. Page 429: Courtesy Zvi Bodie. Page 430: Reuters/Corbis Images. Page 437: Mark Peterson/Corbis Images.

Chapter 14

Page 450: Stuart Westmorland/Corbis Images. Page 468: Alamy Images. Page 471: David Young-Wolff/PhotoEdit. Page 474: Amy Etra/PhotoEdit. Page 475: Courtesy Karen Lahey. Page 476: Syracuse Newspapers/The Image Works. Page 478: Van Gogh "Sunflowers," 1888. Scala/Art Resource, NY.

Chapter 15

Page 484: Aaron Windsor/Photonica. Page 487: Myrleen Ferguson Cate/PhotoEdit. Page 493: Danny Lehman/Corbis Images. Page 495: Karen Preuss/The Image Works. Page 500: Vickie Bajtelsmit. Page 504: Michael Prince/Corbis Images. Page 506: Michael Siluk/The Image Works. Page 514: PhotoDisc, Inc./Getty Images.

Chapter 16

Page 518: Michael Powers/Image State. Page 522: Greg Friedler/SUPERSTOCK. Page 526: Alamy Images. Page 537: Don Smetzer/Stone/Getty Images. Page 543: Rob Lewine/Corbis Images. Page 545: PhotoDisc, Inc./Getty Images.

Chapter 17

Page 552: Johner/Photonica. Page 556 (top): Alamy Images. Page 556 (bottom): Alamy Images. Page 560: PhotoDisc, Inc./Getty Images. Page 564: ©Don Morris Design. Courtesy Bloomberg Press. Page 570: PhotoDisc, Inc./Getty Images. Page 576: PhotoDisc, Inc./Getty Images.

Personal Financial Planner Worksheets